CONTEMPORARY Black Biography

ISSN-1058-1316

CONTEMPORARY

Profiles from the International Black Community

Volume 128

GALE
CENGAGE Learning

Farmington Hills, Mich • San Francisco • New York • Waterville, Maine
Meriden, Conn • Mason, Ohio • Chicago

GALE
CENGAGE Learning™

Contemporary Black Biography, Volume 128

Kepos Media, Inc.: Deborah A. Ring, Derek Jacques, and Paula Kepos, editors

Project Editor: Margaret Mazurkiewicz

Image Research and Acquisitions: Amanda L. Kopczynski, Ashley Maynard

Editorial Support Services: Nataliya Mikheyeva

Manufacturing: Dorothy Maki, Rita Wimberley

Composition and Prepress: Mary Beth Trimper, Gary Leach

Imaging: John Watkins

For product information and technology assistance, contact us at **Gale Customer Support, 1-800-877-4253.** For permission to use material from this text or product, submit all requests online at **www.cengage.com/permissions.** Further permissions questions can be emailed to **permissionrequest@cengage.com**

While every effort has been made to ensure the reliability of the information presented in this publication, Gale, a part of Cengage Learning, does not guarantee the accuracy of the data contained herein. Gale accepts no payment for listing; and inclusion in the publication of any organization, agency, institution, publication, service, or individual does not imply endorsement of the editors or publisher. Errors brought to the attention of the publisher and verified to the satisfaction of the publisher will be corrected in future editions.

EDITORIAL DATA PRIVACY POLICY. Does this publication contain information about you as an individual? If so, for more information about our editorial data privacy policies, please see our Privacy Statement at www.gale.cengage.com.

Gale
27500 Drake Rd.
Farmington Hills, MI, 48331-3535

ISBN-13: 978-1-4103-1197-9

ISSN 1058-1316

This title is also available as an e-book.
ISBN 13: 978-1-4103-1208-2
Contact your Gale sales representative for ordering information.

Printed in Mexico
1 2 3 4 5 6 7 19 18 17 16 15

Advisory Board

Contents

Introduction ix

Cumulative Nationality Index 171

Cumulative Occupation Index 195

Cumulative Subject Index 227

Cumulative Name Index 279

Jacob Anderson 1
    British actor and musician who appeared on HBO's Game of Thrones

Kenny Barron 3
    Jazz pianist who played with Dizzy Gillespie, Stan Getz

Willie T. Barrow 6
    Unsung hero of the civil rights movement in Chicago

Anthony Batts 10
    Baltimore police commissioner fired in the aftermath of 2015 riots

Big Freedia 14
    New Orleans hip-hop artist known as the "Queen of Bounce"

Todd Bowles 17
    Head coach of the New York Jets

Anthony Braxton 20
    Groundbreaking jazz composer and musician

W. Herbert Brewster 25
    Memphis pastor who composed gospel hits

Jamal Bryant..27
    Minister and community leader in Baltimore

Muhammadu Buhari 30
    Former military ruler elected president of Nigeria in 2015

Lorenzo Cain 33
    MVP center fielder for the Kansas City Royals

Ben Carson..36
    World-renowned neurosurgeon turned presidential candidate

The Chantels 40
    Influential female vocal group of the 1950s and 1960s

Sonny Clark 43
    Jazz pianist who succumbed to addiction

Freddy Cole 46
    Singer known for his sophisticated jazz vocals

Chad L. Coleman...49
    Character actor who appeared on The Wire, Walking Dead

Vince Coleman 52
    Base-stealing phenom for the St. Louis Cardinals in the 1980s

Honi Coles 55
    Tap dancer famous for the "fastest feet in show business"

Sonny Criss 58
    Pioneering jazz saxophonist

Edwidge Danticat..60
    Award-winning Haitian-American author

Michael Eric Dyson..65
    Influential scholar who studies race, culture, and social injustice

The Falcons 69
    R&B group that launched Wilson Pickett's career

Andrew Gillum 71
    Young mayor of Tallahassee, Florida

Wardell Gray..74
    Jazz saxophonist who played swing, bebop

Brittney Griner...77
    Dominant female professional basketball player

Darryl Hill 81
    Player who broke the color barrier in Southern college football

Marc Lamont Hill...84
    Academic who studies the intersection of hip-hop and education

Helen Humes 87
    Versatile singer of jazz, blues, and R&B

Ben E. King..90
  Legendary R&B singer
Don King...93
  Flamboyant boxing promoter
Kenny Lattimore...98
  Smooth, soulful R&B singer
Little Eva..101
  *Pop singer who had a hit in 1962 with "The
  Loco-Motion"*
Anthony Mason...103
  NBA forward known for his bruising style
Audra McDonald..106
  Tony Award–winning Broadway actress
Juanita Jackson Mitchell..111
  *Civil rights activist and first black woman to practice
  law in Maryland*
Marilyn Mosby...114
  *Baltimore state's attorney prosecuting police officers
  accused of brutality*
William C. Nell..117
  *Abolitionist who penned history of black soldiers of the
  American Revolution*
Trevor Noah..120
  *South African comedian chosen as new host of The
  Daily Show*
Anthony Overton..123
  Businessman who led first black-owned conglomerate
Carl Perkins..126
  Brilliant jazz pianist whose career was cut short
Stephanie Rawlings-Blake..129
  Embattled mayor of Baltimore, Maryland
Lance Reddick...132
  *Character actor best known for his roles on police
  dramas*

RZA...135
  Popular hip-hop artist
Percy Sledge 139
  *R&B singer who had an enduring hit with "When a Man
  Loves a Woman"*
Peter Spencer..142
  *Church leader who founded the Union Church of
  Africans*
Bryan Stevenson 144
  Tireless human rights lawyer
Bermane Stiverne 147
  *First Haitian-born boxer to become heavyweight
  champion*
Bryant Terry 150
  Food justice activist and "eco-chef"
Nat Towles 153
  *New Orleans bandleader who led popular swing
  ensemble*
Treacherous Three 155
  Pioneering rap trio of the 1980s
Ollie Tyler...157
  Louisiana educator elected mayor of Shreveport
Andrew Wiggins...160
  NBA Rookie of the Year in 2014–15
Gerald Wiggins 163
  *Jazz pianist who accompanied Lena Horne, Louis
  Armstrong*
Bernie Williams 165
  *Five-time All-Star center fielder for the New York
  Yankees*
Goodwill Zwelithini 168
  Eighth Zulu monarch in South Africa

Introduction

Contemporary Black Biography provides informative biographical profiles of the important and influential persons of African heritage who form the international black community: men and women who have changed today's world and are shaping tomorrow's. *Contemporary Black Biography* covers persons of various nationalities in a wide variety of fields, including architecture, art, business, dance, education, fashion, film, industry, journalism, law, literature, medicine, music, politics and government, publishing, religion, science and technology, social issues, sports, television, theater, and others. In addition to in-depth coverage of names found in today's headlines, *Contemporary Black Biography* provides coverage of selected individuals from earlier in this century whose influence continues to impact on contemporary life. *Contemporary Black Biography* also provides coverage of important and influential persons who are not yet household names and are therefore likely to be ignored by other biographical reference series. Each volume also includes listee updates on names previously appearing in *CBB* .

Designed for Quick Research and Interesting Reading

- **Attractive page design** incorporates textual subheads, making it easy to find the information you're looking for.
- **Easy-to-locate data sections** provide quick access to vital personal statistics, career information, major awards, and mailing addresses, when available.
- **Informative biographical essays** trace the subject's personal and professional life with the kind of in-depth analysis you need.
- **To further enhance your appreciation** of the subject, most entries include photographic portraits.
- **Sources for additional information** direct the user to selected books, magazines, and newspapers where more information on the individuals can be obtained.

Helpful Indexes Make It Easy to Find the Information You Need

Contemporary Black Biography includes cumulative Nationality, Occupation, Subject, and Name indexes that make it easy to locate entries in a variety of useful ways.

Available in Electronic Formats

Diskette/Magnetic Tape. Contemporary Black Biography is available for licensing on magnetic tape or diskette in a fielded format. Either the complete database or a custom selection of entries may be ordered. The database is available for internal data processing and nonpublishing purposes only. For more information, call (800) 877-GALE.

On-line. Contemporary Black Biography is available online through Mead Data Central's NEXIS Service in the NEXIS, PEOPLE and SPORTS Libraries in the GALBIO file and Gale's Biography Resource Center.

Disclaimer

Contemporary Black Biography uses and lists websites as sources and these websites may become obsolete.

We Welcome Your Suggestions

The editors welcome your comments and suggestions for enhancing and improving *Contemporary Black Biography*. If you would like to suggest persons for inclusion in the series, please submit these names to the editors. Mail comments or suggestions to:

The Editor

Contemporary Black Biography

Gale, Cengage Learning

27500 Drake Rd.

Farmington Hills, MI 48331-3535

Phone: (800) 347-4253

Jacob Anderson

1990—

Actor, musician

Anderson, Jacob, photograph. Karwai Tang/WireImage/Getty Images.

Jacob Anderson, also known by the stage name Raleigh Ritchie, is a British actor and musician who is most recognized for his role as the warrior Grey Worm on the hit HBO series *Game of Thrones.* Anderson snagged his first major acting role when he was 18, in Noel Clarke's British crime drama *Adulthood* (2008). Within a few years his career was on the upswing, and in 2012 he landed a recurring role on Showtime's popular series *Episodes.* The following year Anderson joined the *Game of Thrones* cast while also appearing in the BBC America series *Broadchurch.* By 2013 Anderson's music career also had begun to take off. He signed that year with Columbia Records, calling himself Raleigh Ritchie, and within a year he had released two EPs while preparing his full-length debut album.

Anderson was born in London in 1990 and grew up in Bristol in southwest England. As a child he struggled to fit in with his peers, and his primary school years were plagued by bullying. His alienation continued into adolescence, although the bullying lessened as he mastered the art of blending in. Reflecting on those years in an interview with Michael Hann of the London

Guardian, Anderson shared, "I worried about people not liking me. The fact that I was into things that other people weren't. I worried a lot about that. I worried about whether I'd be able to do the things I wanted."

He made his first screen appearance in the short film *Pool Shark* when he was 13 years old. The role required little acting, however—in the eight-minute film, he played one of 11 swimmers. Encouraged by his drama teacher, Anderson began auditioning for television roles, and he landed his first episode when he was 16, appearing on the BBC series *Doctors.* The next year he moved to London to pursue his career, although he hoped to make it as a musician, not an actor. As he shared with Alistair Foster of the *London Evening Standard* in 2014, "Acting was the happiest accident I could hope to have had. My drama teacher at school encouraged me to audition for a TV show … and it just spiralled out of control from there. I really love it, but music is what I've been doing since I was at school and I never really stopped."

Despite this conviction, he initially had little success on the London music scene. Acting roles continued to

At a Glance . . .

Born Jacob Anderson on June 18, 1990, in London, United Kingdom.

Career: Television and film actor, 2003—; recording artist (as Raleigh Ritchie), 2013—.

Addresses: *Talent agent*—Independent Talent Group, 40 Whittfield St., London W1T 2RH. *Web*—http://www.raleighritchie.com. *Twitter*—@raleighritchie.

come his way, though. In 2008, in addition to a handful of episodes and two made-for-television movies, he landed his first feature film role in Noel Clarke's *Adulthood,* in which he played a teenage hit man. Anderson also contributed to the film's soundtrack, appearing alongside hip-hop artist Plan B on the single "I Need Love."

That track failed to kick-start Anderson's singing career, however, and 2009 was a rough year for the young performer. He earned only one acting credit that year, a role in the British ITV network's *Gunrush,* which was panned by critics. The time marked a low point in Anderson's life. At 19, he was struggling both professional and personally. Concerned, his parents intervened, and Anderson soon found himself in therapy. He turned more seriously to music, not just as a potential career but also as a way to work out his personal concerns.

In 2010 Anderson appeared in one television movie and two feature films, including Clarke's crime thriller *4.3.2.1.* Although none of his projects from that year received glowing reviews, the work was enough to get Anderson back on his feet. In 2011 he landed several parts, including three episodes of the popular ITV miniseries *Injustice.* The following year, his acting career got a boost when he landed his first recurring television role on Showtime's *Episodes.* Playing the part of Kevin, Anderson appeared in eight episodes of the show, a comedy series about an intelligent British television show that is dumbed down when an American version is filmed.

Episodes marked a turning point in Anderson's career. In 2013 he landed recurring roles in two popular British series, the crime drama *Broadchurch* with David Tennant and a comedy, *The Mimic.* That same year he also was cast in the popular HBO series *Game of Thrones* as Grey Worm, the commander of an elite group of warriors. The good fortune carried over to his music career as well. That year he signed with Columbia Records and released his debut EP, *The Middle Child,* under the name Raleigh Ritchie (a moniker

based on two characters from the 2001 Wes Anderson film *The Royal Tenenbaums*). The album's sound, according to Hann of the *Guardian,* was "the very model of a modern British fusion menu: a bit of soul, a bit of R&B, a bit of hip-hop, a bit of pop, a bit of alternative."

In January of 2014, Columbia released Anderson's second EP, *Black and Blue,* and uploaded a YouTube video of the four-track's first single, "Stronger Than Ever." Within a week the video had received more than 1.2 million views, and several months later, the single made the Hot 40 U.K. chart, debuting at number 39 and peaking at number 24. In June of the following year, Anderson released the single "Never Say Die" online for free download. His debut album remained forthcoming.

Selected works

Television

West 10 LDN (television movie), BBC Three, 2008.
The Things I Haven't Told You (television movie), BBC Three, 2008.
Gunrush (television movie), ITV, 2009.
Royal Wedding (television movie), BBC, 2010.
Injustice (miniseries), ITV, 2011.
Episodes, Showtime, 2012.
Broadchurch, BBC America, 2013.
The Mimic, BBC, 2013–14.
Game of Thrones, HBO, 2013–15.

Films

Pool Shark (short), Army and Eye Films, 2003.
Adulthood, Cipher Films, 2008.
Chatroom, Ruby Film, 2010.
4.3.2.1., Unstoppable Entertainment, 2010.
Demons Never Die, S.Kids, 2011.
The Swarm (short), Stray Bea, 2011.
Comedown, Serotonin Films, 2012.

Albums

The Middle Child (EP), Columbia Records, 2013.
Black and Blue (EP) (includes "Stronger Than Ever"), Columbia Records, 2014.

Sources

Periodicals

Complex (UK), June 2, 2015.
Daily Mirror, June 20, 2008; March 27, 2014.
Guardian (London), August 29, 2009; May 4, 2015,.
Independent (London), February 17, 2015.
London Evening Standard, July 16, 2014.
TMRW, February 7, 2014.

—Candice Mancini

Kenny Barron

1943—

Jazz pianist, music educator

Barron, Kenny, photograph. Alfaguarilla/Shutterstock.com.

Pianist and music educator Kenny Barron has been earning the acclaim and affection of audiences around the globe for more than 50 years. A jazz virtuoso known for his light touch and for his immense abilities as a composer and arranger, he has collaborated with dozens of the genre's leading figures, including trumpeter Dizzy Gillespie and saxophonist Stan Getz. Barron has also established an enviable reputation for the quality of his own albums and for his work as a faculty member at Rutgers University and other institutions. Honored with a Jazz Masters Fellowship from the National Endowment for the Arts in 2010, Barron was described by *Jazz Weekly,* in a comment quoted on his website (KennyBarron.com), as "the most lyrical piano player of our time."

Barron was born on June 9, 1943, in Philadelphia, long a hotbed of jazz talent. His study of the piano began with lessons around the age of six. By his own account, classical music failed to move him, and it was not until he heard a delivery man play some blues chords that he began to take a real interest in his instrument. With the encouragement of his older brother Bill, a saxophonist, Barron made rapid prog-

ress, and by the middle of high school he had forged ties with a number of players around the city, including famed drummer Philly Joe Jones. Barron's first major gig as a professional came in 1961, when he joined his brother in a group led by trumpeter Mel Melvin. Several months later Barron moved to New York City, where he found work with saxophonist James Moody. That gig, in turn, led to a long engagement with Gillespie, who hired him solely on the basis of Moody's recommendation.

Barron's five-year stint (1962–67) with Gillespie proved to be a pivotal period in his career. Under Gillespie's direction he toured widely, contributed to influential albums such as *Jambo Caribe* (1965), and "developed an appreciation," according to his website, "for Latin and Caribbean rhythms." Barron's enthusiasm for those sounds continued to grow over the remainder of the decade, as he moved on to work with stars such as trumpeter Freddie Hubbard and drummer Buddy Rich, both of whom shared his interest in conga drums and other elements of Cuban and Caribbean music.

Meanwhile, the jazz world was changing rapidly. As audiences turned to newer styles, including the often

At a Glance . . .

Born on June 9, 1943, in Philadelphia, PA. *Education:* Empire State College, BA, music, 1970s.

Career: Jazz pianist, early 1960s—; Rutgers University and other institutions, faculty member, 1970s–2010s(?).

Awards: Jazz Masters Fellowship, National Endowment for the Arts, 2010.

Addresses: *Agent*—Karen Kennedy, 24/Seven Artist Development, 6 Richmond St., Newark, NJ 07103. *Web*— http://kennybarron.com.

harsh sounds of "free jazz" and jazz-rock "fusion," musicians with a more melodic approach, Barron among them, had to adapt to changing tastes. He did so, in part, by joining in the early 1970s an ensemble led by Yusef Lateef, a multi-instrumentalist with a unique, genre-stretching approach. While Lateef regularly incorporated elements of free jazz and fusion, his work remained accessible even to casual fans, thanks in part to his ongoing focus on melody. That eclectic approach deeply influenced Barron, as did Lateef's emphasis on improvisational technique and music education. With Lateef's encouragement, Barron returned to school during this period, earning a bachelor's degree in music from Empire State College.

By this time Barron's recording career was progressing steadily. In addition to helping Lateef complete a string of well-received albums, including *The Gentle Giant* (1972) and *Hush 'n' Thunder* (1973), Barron completed several as a leader, the best known of which were *Sunset to Dawn* (1973) and *Peruvian Blue* (1974). Evident throughout all of those recordings were Barron's composing and arranging skills. His talents in those areas were apparent as early as 1960, when he composed one track and arranged another for Lateef's album *The Centaur and the Phoenix*. He did similar work on Gillespie's *Jambo Caribe*, to which he contributed two tracks, and on his own debut as a leader, *You Had Better Listen* (1967). The latter album, a joint project with trumpeter Jimmy Owens, showcased Barron's ability to use rhythm and minor-key chord progressions to convey a broad range of emotion.

After leaving Lateef about 1976 Barron focused on a variety of projects, including long and productive engagements with bassists Ron Carter and Buster Williams. The latter musician helped Barron launch a quartet called Sphere in the early 1980s; rounding out the group were drummer Ben Riley and saxophonist Charlie Rouse. Dedicated to reviving and reimagining the music of legendary pianist Thelonious Monk,

Sphere released several well-received albums before Rouse's death in 1988; a decade later the group reunited, this time with saxophonist Gary Bartz. In the interim Barron strengthened his ties with Getz, whom he had been backing off and on since about 1986. His partnership with Getz was typical of the many transient but resilient relationships that together have earned him an immense number of recording credits. Highlights of this period include *People Time* (1992), a Grammy-nominated live recording of duets with Getz, and several albums that Barron made as a leader, including *Invitation* (1990); *Wanton Spirit* (1995), completed with bassist Charlie Haden and drummer Roy Haynes; *Canta Brazil* (2002); and *The Traveler* (2008).

A champion of music education since his days with Lateef, Barron has taught at a number of institutions over the years, including the Juilliard School, the Manhattan School of Music, and Rutgers, where he remained on the faculty for more than 25 years (roughly 1973–2000). A number of his students have gone on to distinguished careers, among them saxophonist David Sánchez.

More than half a century after his debut as a professional, Barron remained a prominent and highly active figure on the international jazz scene. In 2015 he maintained an ambitious touring schedule, with gigs from Sweden to San Francisco to Singapore. Joining him for many of those engagements was the bassist Dave Holland, with whom he completed an album called *The Art of Conversation* in 2014.

Selected discography

(Composer and arranger) Yusef Lateef, *The Centaur and the Phoenix,* Riverside, 1960.
Dizzy Gillespie, *Jambo Caribe,* Verve, 1965.
(With Jimmy Owens) *You Had Better Listen,* Atlantic, 1967.
Freddie Hubbard, *High Blues Pressure,* Atlantic, 1968.
Yusef Lateef, *The Gentle Giant,* Atlantic, 1972.
Yusef Lateef, *Hush 'n' Thunder,* Atlantic, 1973.
Sunset to Dawn, Muse, 1973.
Peruvian Blue, Muse, 1974.
Ron Carter, *Patrão,* Milestone, 1981.
Sphere, *Four in One,* Elektra, 1982.
Sphere, *Flight Path,* Elektra, 1983.
Invitation, Criss Cross, 1990.
(With Stan Getz) *People Time,* Verve, 1992.
(With Charlie Haden and Roy Haynes) *Wanton Spirit,* Verve, 1995.
Canta Brazil, Sunnyside, 2002.
The Traveler, EmArcy, 20008.
(With Dave Holland) *The Art of Conversation,* Impulse!, 2014.

Sources

Online

arwulf, arwulf, "Kenny Barron: Artist Biography," All Music.com, http://www.allmusic.com/artist/kenny-barron-mn0000081181/biography (accessed July 18, 2015).

"Kenny Barron: Bio," National Endowment for the Arts, http://arts.gov/honors/jazz/kenny-barron (accessed July 17, 2015).

"Kenny Barron," http://kennybarron.com/cms/wp-content/uploads/2014/02/biography.pdf (accessed July 17, 2015).

Verney, Victor, "Kenny Barron: A Musical Autobiography," All About Jazz, January 30, 2007, http://www.allaboutjazz.com/kenny-barron-a-musical-autobiography-kenny-barron-by-victor-verney.php?&pg=2 (accessed July 17, 2015).

—R. Anthony Kugler

Willie T. Barrow

1924–2015

Minister, activist

Barrow, Willie T., photograph. Tannen Maury/AFP/Getty Images.

The Reverend Willie T. Barrow was one of the unsung heroes of the civil rights movement in the United States. As a minister and antipoverty activist in Chicago, Barrow spent decades working with the Reverend Jesse Jackson and Operation PUSH. Her expertise was in negotiating with mainstream companies to promote fair hiring and employment opportunity practices for African Americans. Among her fellow activists, Barrow was known as the "Little Warrior," a sobriquet that referred to both her tenacity and her diminutive stature at just four feet, 11 inches. "Don't be confused. I cover every inch of the ground I stand upon," Barrow once told a college commencement audience at Chicago's Adler School of Professional Psychology. "I speak as a voice of authority. I am a living testimony to what the spirit and power of connected men and women who are committed to challenging unjust, unfair systems can accomplish."

Worked as a Minister and Activist

Barrow was born in 1924 in Burton, Texas, where her father owned a plot of land that he farmed to support his family. He was also a minister in the Church of God, a religious group based in Anderson, Indiana. Barrow followed him into the church ministry during her late teens. By that time she had already broken a barrier that discriminated against African-American children in her town. As Karen Grigsby Bates of National Public Radio reported following Barrow's death in 2015, 12-year-old Willie Taplin knew that the school bus that passed her every day was nowhere near full. White children rode while black children walked, even though they attended the same school. One day, with her black classmates following behind her, she boarded the bus and confronted the driver. Barrow recounted the incident: "I said, 'We all alike—we've all got butts, and all we got to do is just sit down on the seat. And you got plenty of room—so why you want me to get off, just cause I'm black? Nooo, we got to change that.'" With no court order, no petition, and no further incident, Barrow and her black peers rode the bus to school from then on.

After graduating high school, Barrow moved to Portland, Oregon, to enroll at the School of Theology at Warner Pacific College, which was affiliated with the

At a Glance . . .

Born Willie Beatrice Taplin on December 7, 1924, in Burton, TX; died on March 12, 2015, in Chicago, IL; daughter of Nelson Taplin (a farmer and minister) and Octava Taplin; married Clyde Raymond Barrow (a welder and union official), 1945(?); children: Patricia Carey (adopted); Keith Errol Barrow. *Politics:* Democrat. *Religion:* Christian. *Education:* Attended Warner Pacific School of Theology, Moody Bible Institute, and Central Conservatory of Music; University of Monrovia, Liberia, DDiv.

Career: Ordained minister in the Church of God in Anderson, IN; founded Church of God congregation in Portland, OR, 1942(?); Langley Avenue Church of God, youth minister, after 1945; Vernon Park Church of God, associate minister, 1950s–2015; Southern Christian Leadership Conference, field organizer, late 1950s, and special projects director, Operation Breadbasket, 1960s; Operation PUSH, national vice president, 1976(?), executive director, 1984–89, vice chair, chief consultant, and board chair emerita.

Memberships: Coalition of Black Trade Unionists; Coalition of Labor Union Women; League of Black Women; National Association for the Advancement of Colored People; National Urban League.

Awards: Woman of the Year, City of Chicago, 1969; Image Award, League of Black Women, 1972; Special Human Services Award, National Conference of Black Lawyers, 1982; Dr. Martin Luther King Jr. Award, Student Bar Association of Howard University, 1982; Excellence and Social Responsibility Award, National Council for Black Studies, 1982; Black Heritage Award, Mahogany Scholarship Heritage Foundation, 2006; Bill Berry Award, Chicago Urban League, 2012; Champion of Freedom Award, City of Chicago, 2014.

Church of God. While living in Portland, she established the city's first African-American Church of God congregation, one of the first in the denomination. She also worked as a welder to pay her tuition and living expenses. It was while working that job that she met her future husband, Clyde Barrow, a native of Belize.

The Barrows settled in Chicago during the mid-1940s, and she enrolled at the Moody Bible Institute. She later earned a doctorate of divinity degree from the University of Monrovia in the West African nation of Liberia. In Chicago, Barrow became active in the National Urban League, an early and influential civil rights group, while she worked as the youth pastor at the Langley Avenue Church of God. During the late 1950s she started her ministerial career at the Vernon Park Church of God on South Stony Island Avenue, where she would remain until the end of her life.

Barrow's activism led her to the Southern Christian Leadership Conference (SCLC), the groundbreaking civil rights group whose first president was the Reverend Martin Luther King Jr. Barrow became a field organizer for the SCLC in Chicago, and in that capacity she marshaled supporters of the movement to take part in protest actions in the South. She also arranged bus caravans for the 1963 March on Washington and the 1965 march from Selma to Montgomery, Alabama. The SCLC had also created Operation Breadbasket in 1962 to alleviate economic discrimination in Northern cities through boycotts and other means. Its Chicago branch gained traction during the mid-1960s, when the Reverend Jesse Jackson, a young associate of King's, displayed his dynamic leadership skills by persuading African Americans in Chicago to boycott the A&P grocery chain.

At the time, A&P had almost single-handedly created the modern American supermarket and dominated the grocery sector in several U.S. states, with 40 of stores in Chicago alone. Because none of the A&P stores in Chicago employed African-American workers, Jackson decided to target the chain. Barrow played an instrumental role in negotiations between the grocery chain and Operation Breadbasket, and the company finally agreed to build stores in black neighborhoods, hire blacks and promote them to store managers, and contract with black businesses and suppliers.

Led Operation PUSH

Over the next few years, Barrow would turn up frequently in the pages of *Jet, Ebony,* and other publications aimed at African-American readers. Operation Breadbasket formally broke with the SCLC in 1971, with Jackson establishing Operation PUSH, or People United to Save Humanity. The acronym was later changed to People United to Serve Humanity.

As one of the organization's key early leaders, Barrow became a national vice president during the mid-1970s. She succeeded Jackson as executive director when he made a bid for the Democratic presidential nomination in 1984. As executive director of Operation PUSH, she continued to lead national boycotts against companies both large and small. For example, a 1985 protest against WBBM-TV, Chicago's CBS affiliate, led to the hiring of African-American anchor Lester Holt, who would go on to a distinguished career with NBC. Operation PUSH also instigated a boycott

against Revlon for comments that one executive made about hair care product companies that targeted African-American consumers.

Barrow stepped down as executive director of Operation PUSH in 1989, but she remained on the board as vice chair, chief consultant, and, later, board chair emerita. She was still active in the ministry of the Vernon Park Church of God in late 2004, when 800 guests helped her celebrate her 80th birthday at a Chicago hotel. "Every TV station and newspaper was there," she told James Mitchell of *Jet.* "For awhile I thought it was my funeral," she joked, but added that she was thrilled to "see, feel and smell my flowers while I am alive. I call it a big thank you party. People came up to me and said, 'We wanted to find a way to thank you because you have really given us service.'"

Despite declining health in her later years, Barrow never retired and remained devoted to the pursuit of social justice through the work of the Rainbow/PUSH Coalition, leading demonstrations on Saturdays and mentoring more than 100 people in the Chicago area. One of them was Barack Obama, a young lawyer who in 2008 would become the first African-American president of the United States. Following her death, President Obama called her "a constant inspiration, a lifelong mentor, and a very dear friend." He added, "I was proud to count myself among the more than 100 men and women she called her 'Godchildren.'" Barrow also privately helped dozens of Chicago students get to—and through—college by paying for their tuition and helping them get scholarships, and she was instrumental in raising funds for after-school programs as well as for an assisted living center for seniors in the underserved area of Chicago's South Side.

Lost Son to AIDS

Barrow was widowed in 1998. A few years later, she published the book *How to Get Married and Stay Married* (2004), which was based on the tenets of relationship wisdom she had dispensed to *Jet* in November of 1997. "When choosing marriage, one should think in terms of choosing a partner first: then lover," she asserted. "Suppose your love life ended on a dead-end street? You can still survive as partners in a ship of things: home, children, grandchildren, business, church, work, companionship."

Her own 53-year-marriage weathered one particularly difficult period: the death of their son from AIDS in 1983. Keith Barrow had gained fame in his 20s as an R&B singer-songwriter, and the combination of his talent and good looks led to a deal with Columbia Records. He had a hit during the summer of 1978 with the single "You Know You Want to Be Loved," an opulently arranged slow-dance song that peaked at number 26 on the Billboard R&B chart. She spoke of his death from AIDS five years later, in April of 1988,

when she told *Jet,* "I never put him aside" when she learned about his sexual orientation. "I brought him closer to me, because I felt that if there was a problem he didn't need to be pushed aside."

Barrow and her husband also cared for Keith at home during the last four months of his life. She told *Jet* that discrimination against those who were HIV-positive or afflicted with AIDS was misplaced. "I didn't experience fear, but love," she said. "I experienced a lot of hope and faith. He was not only our son, he was our friend. Keith never gave up. So I never gave up."

Saw Election of First Black President

Barrow's earliest presidential campaign work was as a leader in Jesse Jackson's 1984 and 1988 unsuccessful campaigns for the Democratic nomination. Bates characterized her as "a supporter, organizer and strategist who would not allow herself to be muscled aside by the mostly-male entourage" of the Jackson campaign staff. She was a "superdelegate" at the Democratic National Convention in 2008, when Barack Obama was nominated as the Democratic candidate for the presidency, and she was with President Obama in Chicago on the night of his reelection on November 6, 2012.

Chicago's gun violence troubled Barrow greatly during the early 2000s. Concerned that young people seemed increasingly unaware of the civil rights era figures who had fought, sacrificed, and died to achieve legal standing and political opportunity for African Americans, Barrow was outspoken about the need to engage a new generation in pursuit of social justice. In 2012 she told the *Chicago Sun-Times,* "If these youth don't know whose shoulders they stand on, they'll take us back to slavery. And I believe that's why the Lord is still keeping me here." In the wake of the 2013 U.S. Supreme Court decision that invalidated a portion of the Voting Rights Act of 1965, Barrow spoke out against a flurry of new voter identification laws that passed in multiple states, all of which appeared to disproportionately affect low-income, urban, young adult, and minority voters. She also called on Congress to update and reauthorize the Voting Rights Act, which remained in limbo months after her death.

Barrow died at her home in Chicago on March 12, 2015, at age 90, following a hospitalization for a blood clot. The *Chicago Tribune*'s Lolly Bowean quoted Chicago mayor Rahm Emmanuel, who noted, "Rev. Barrow spent her life on the front lines in the fight for justice." Jackson told Eddie Arruza and Kristen Thometz of WTTW-TV, "She had no fear of unpopular causes. She always had time for those people with their backs against the wall." More than two decades before her death, Barrow told *Chicago Tonight*'s John Callaway, "I never plan to retire. I plan to keep on working until God calls me." She added, "I want a long funeral when I die 'cause I lived a long life."

Selected writings

How to Get Married and Stay Married, Cool Springs Publishing, 2004.

Sources

Periodicals

Associated Press, December 21, 1988.
Baltimore Afro-American, June 24, 1986, p. 10.
Chicago Sun-Times, March 20, 2015.
Chicago Tribune, July 11, 1998; March 12, 2015; March 19, 2015.
Jet, July 14, 1979, pp. 6–7; April 18, 1988, pp. 24–25; January 8, 1990, pp. 30–31; November 17, 1997, p. 34; January 10, 2005, p. 59.
New York Times, October 7, 1987; March 14, 2015.

Online

Arruza, Eddie, and Kristen Thometz, "Remembering Rev. Willie Barrow," *Chicago Tonight,* March 12, 2015, http://chicagotonight.wttw.com/2015/03/12/remembering-rev-willie-barrow (accessed June 11, 2015).
Bates, Karen Grigsby, "Reverend Willie T. Barrow, A 'Little Warrior' for Civil Rights, Dies," National Public Radio, March 14, 2015, http://www.npr.org/sections/codeswitch/2015/03/14/392858516/reverend-willie-t-barrow-a-little-warrior-for-civil-rights-dies (accessed June 11, 2015).
Obama, Barack, "Statement by the President on the Passing of Reverend Willie T. Barrow," March 12, 2015, https://www.whitehouse.gov/the-press-office/2015/03/12/statement-president-passing-reverend-willie-t-barrow (accessed June 11, 2015).
Saunders, Lonna, "Civil Rights Icon Rev. Barrow Looks Back," Huffington Post, May 25, 2011, http://www.huffingtonpost.com/lonna-saunders/civil-rights-icon-rev-wil_b_795328.html (accessed June 11, 2015).
"Willie T. Barrow," National Visionary Leadership Project, http://www.visionaryproject.org/barrowwillie/ (accessed June 4, 2010).

Other

Barrow, Willie T., commencement address at the Adler School of Professional Psychology, Chicago, October 28, 2007.

—Pamela Willwerth Aue

Anthony Batts

1960—

Police officer, administrator

Batts, Anthony, photograph. Andrew Burton/Getty Images News/ Getty Images.

Anthony Batts is a lifelong law enforcement officer who received nationwide scrutiny for his handling of violent civil unrest in Baltimore following the death of Freddie Gray, an African-American man who sustained fatal injuries while he was in police custody in April of 2015. Chosen as police commissioner in Baltimore in 2012, Batts was fired three years later in the wake of rioting and looting throughout the city.

Since beginning his career in the 1980s, Batts has espoused the principles of community policing, which seeks to reduce urban crime by building productive relationships between law enforcement agencies and the neighborhoods they serve. He has also cultivated a reputation as a reform-focused leader capable of rooting out departmental corruption. Supporters describe Batts as charismatic and attentive; some critics, however, have chosen less flattering terms, such as arrogant or dismissive. In an interview with the *Baltimore Sun* in 2012, Doris Topsy-Elvord, former vice mayor of Long Beach, California, where Batts began his career as a police officer, predicted that he would be a leader who is "going to do what's best for the city. And he'll tell you what's best."

Aimed for a Career in Law

Batts was born in Washington, DC, in 1960 and moved with his parents to California when he was five years old. His parents separated within the next year, and he grew up in South Central Los Angeles, raised by his mother, who worked hard to provide as many opportunities as possible for Batts and his sister. Their neighborhood was rough, and Batts was frequently admonished by his mother to stay out of the alleys, where he might get into trouble.

Recalling his rejection of that edict, Batts has often told audiences and interviewers about the day he saw the body of a young black woman as he cut through an alley on his way to school. He had disobeyed his mother, so he kept the discovery to himself, but then he felt doubly traumatized by the incident. Sometime later, without revealing his alley encounter, Batts asked his mother whether anyone in authority cared at all about the lives of people who looked like them. In an interview with *Oakland North* in 2011, Batts shared his mother's answer: "There may not be much you can

do about this now, but you can do different things about it in the future."

With his mother's encouragement, Batts joined the Los Angeles Police Department Explorer Scouts as a teenager and took advantage of an opportunity to attend a high school outside his neighborhood. He dreamed of going to law school and working as an attorney. Batts began his college education at Santa Monica College and, while there, enrolled in the Santa Monica police cadet program. Although he was not planning on a career in law enforcement, he thought the experience would look good on a law school application. Before long he realized that in order to support himself and pay for his education, he would need a full-time job, and his education and experience more than qualified him for police work. In 1982 he applied for a position with the Long Beach Police Department. As he worked his way through the ranks, he continued his academic career, eventually earning a bachelor's degree in law enforcement, a master's degree in business, and a doctorate in public administration.

Became Long Beach's Youngest Commander

In 1991 Batts became commander of the East Patrol Division of the Long Beach Police Department. At age 31, he was the force's youngest commander in the department's history. Eight years later he was named deputy chief of investigations, and in October of 2002

he became the city's chief of police. He would remain in Long Beach until 2009. During his tenure as the city's top cop, homicides fell by 45 percent, and overall crime went down 15 percent. People in the community saw Batts as accessible and concerned, and he worked to develop lines of communication within the police force as well between the rank and file and the leadership. At the same time, he set increasingly high standards for his officers. Writing in the *Baltimore Sun* in 2012, Justin Fenton described Batts as "a stickler for accountability" during this period. Robert Luna, who served as chief of staff for Batts, told Fenton, "If somebody was shot, he wants to know about it and wants to make sure his command is aware of it."

In 2009, after 27 years in Long Beach, Batts was hired as chief of police for the troubled Oakland Police Department. Batts explained to Fenton that although he had decided that it was time to leave Long Beach, he had not applied for the Oakland job but had been approached by a recruiter. According to Batts, he initially turned down the invitation. He changed his mind in the aftermath of a tragedy for the Oakland Police Department, when four officers were gunned down in the line of duty on the same day. Batts visited Oakland, met with residents, and attended funerals for the officers. Mayor Ron Dellums, pleased at Batts's change of heart, told Fenton, "What I felt I was doing when I employed him was to say to ... the community, 'Here is a guy who looks like you, that you can both respect and trust and have confidence in.' He delivered on that."

When he arrived in Oakland, Batts had a force of 800 officers and support from the city's administration. Within a year, though, Dellums, a hands-off mayor, had been replaced with Jean Quan, who insisted on significantly more oversight of police department operations. Under Quan's administration, Oakland's police force was reduced to 640 officers. Batts had to contend not only with diminishing resources but also with increasing restrictions on his ability to make strategic and tactical decisions. Fenton reported that in November of 2011, Batts wrote an open letter of resignation to the citizens of Oakland in which he asserted, "I found myself with limited control, but full accountability." Some of Batts's critics accused him of not having been fully committed to the department or the city. Dan Siegel, an advisor to Mayor Quan, described Batts to Fenton as "kind of an absent police chief." He added, "A lot of people were very enthusiastic about him. But at the level of actually running the department, nothing happened on his watch."

Chosen as Baltimore's Top Cop

When Batts resigned from the top job in Oakland, he considered himself retired. In a 2015 interview with C-SPAN's Brian Lamb, Batts reminisced about the first months, sharing, "I went out and bought a Harley motorcycle and grew a beard and grew my hair ... and

went riding up and down the coast." He also arranged to teach a course at Harvard University in the fall of 2012 and set up a consulting firm to maintain his professional connections in law enforcement. Then he was contacted by a recruiter on behalf of the city of Baltimore, one of the most crime-ridden cities in the country. Bypassing internal candidates, Baltimore mayor Stephanie Rawlings-Blake identified Batts as her choice of a commissioner whose mission would be to reduce Baltimore's high rate of violence and reform a police department that was infamous for corruption, excessive force lawsuits, and a lack of respect for, or from, the community. After he accepted the job, Batts told Fenton, "To be perfectly honest.... I miss the uniform, I miss the camaraderie, I miss the job." He added, "It feels extremely good to be back in it."

The events that would catapult Batts into the national spotlight began in the morning of April 12, 2015, when a bystander's cell phone video captured the arrest of Freddie Gray, a 25-year-old African-American man who had run from four bicycle patrol officers. During his arrest Gray requested an inhaler because he had difficulty breathing. The video shows officers picking him up, hands cuffed behind his back, and placing him on the floor in the back of a police van that had been called to the scene. Batts later confirmed that officers had not followed the department's policy of restraining Gray with a seat belt. By the time Gray arrived at a police station, approximately 45 minutes after his arrest, he was nonresponsive. He remained in a coma at the Shock Trauma Center at the University of Maryland with a spinal cord injury until he died a week later. His spine had been nearly severed. Many of Gray's friends and family members, along with outside observers, asserted that he had been subjected to a "rough ride"—a well-known tactic of deliberately trying to cause discomfort to an individual placed under arrest—at the hands of Baltimore police officers. In late June, autopsy findings released without authorization confirmed that Gray had died of an injury similar to what might result from a head-first dive into shallow water.

Protests began on April 18. Following Gray's death the next day, crowds grew in size and intensity. NBC News reported that Batts lauded the protesters for remaining peaceful, saying, "They're sharing their concerns, and I hear them and I understand." However, the Maryland State Police were soon called in by Governor Larry Hogan as tensions rose and crowds swelled. On April 25 a dozen people were arrested for hostile actions, including throwing rocks at police, smashing windows, and looting a local 7-Eleven. The streets of Baltimore erupted in violence on April 27 following Gray's funeral. Police were targeted with rocks, bricks, and cinder blocks. Cars were set on fire, and many businesses, including a CVS drugstore, were looted and burned. The Maryland National Guard was sent in under a state of emergency declared by the governor.

Criticized for Handling of Baltimore Riots

Both Batts and Rawlings-Blake were criticized for following a "stand-down" policy that allowed unruly protesters to vandalize local businesses. Several more days and nights of unrest ensued, despite city-wide curfews from 10:00 p.m. to 5:00 a.m. Meanwhile, protests against the use of excessive police force spread to other cities in response to Gray's death—the latest in a growing list of African-American deaths at the hands of uniformed police officers, most of whom were white.

Maryland state's attorney Marilyn Mosby announced on May 1 that six Baltimore police officers would be charged with offenses including assault, misconduct in office, manslaughter, and second-degree murder. Batts told CNN later that week that this had come as a surprise; he had not known until 10 minutes before the press conference that any of his officers would be charged in Gray's death. He admitted to CNN that the department had not been adequately prepared for the violent protests. Foreshadowing what was to come, Batts also told CNN that he had concerns about morale among the city's officers.

Conflict inside the department and crime on the streets escalated in May of 2015, as police officers appeared to deliberately slow down patrols and arrests. Jamelle Bouie of Slate reported that arrests dropped 43 percent between April and May, while crimes skyrocketed: "Less policing has meant more crime, especially in the violent neighborhoods of East and West Baltimore.... Shootings are up, as are assaults and other violent crimes." Bouie recounted public comments by Batts about the wariness of his officers: "[T]hey've said ... to me, 'If I ... make a stop for a reasonable suspicion that leads to probably cause but I make a mistake on it, will I be arrested?'"

In June of 2015, nearly three years after he had arrived in Baltimore with a mission to improve relations between the community and its police force and to eliminate corruption and mistrust within the ranks, Batts acknowledged that there was still much to accomplish on both counts. Predicting that many of his officers "will be unhappy reading these words," Batts detailed, in an op-ed published in the *Baltimore Sun,* some of the steps taken since his arrival in 2012, noting that many obstacles remained. He called out departmental critics, noting that those "who have profited, either materially or through position, will continue to fight against the reforms we are enacting." He concluded, "Reform is not easy. It comes with a cost. It is a cost we should be willing to pay for the future of our city."

Less than a month later, Batts was fired by Mayor Rawlings-Blake, an action that came as the city's religious leaders and the police union had begun calling for Batts to resign. Explaining her decision, Rawlings-

Blake cited the dramatic increase in Baltimore's murders during May, June, and the first week of July. She denied that Batts's firing was a response to calls for his resignation, yet she acknowledged, according to the *Washington Post,* "It is clear that the focus has been too much on the leadership of the department and not enough on the crime fight."

Sources

Periodicals

Baltimore Business Journal, June 10, 2015.
Baltimore Sun, September 22, 2012; June 19, 2015; June 21, 2015.
City Paper (Baltimore, MD), June 9, 2015.
Oakland (CA) North, November 7, 2011.
Washington Post, June 24, 2015; July 8, 2015.

Online

Bouie, Jamelle, "Criminal Neglect," Slate, June 18, 2015, http://www.slate.com/articles/news_and _politics/politics/2015/06/baltimore_police_are _virtually_on_strike_the_city_deserves_something _better.html (accessed June 21, 2015).

Bradner, Eric, "'We Are Part of the Problem,' Baltimore Police Commissioner Says," CNN.com, May 5, 2015, http://www.cnn.com/2015/05/05/politics/ anthony-batts-baltimore-police-riots-problem/ (accessed June 11, 2015).

Lamb, Brian, "Q & A with Anthony Batts," C-SPAN, January 20, 2015, http://www.c-span.org/video/ ?323886-1/qa-anthony-batts (accessed June 11, 2015).

Ortiz, Erik, "Freddie Gray: from Baltimore Arrest to Protests, a Timeline of the Case," NBC News, May 1, 2015, http://www.nbcnews.com/storyline/balti more-unrest/timeline-freddie-gray-case-arrest-pro tests-n351156 (accessed June 21, 2015).

Yocuboski, Phil, "72 Forced Separations during Commissioner Anthony Batts' Tenure," WBAL-TV, June 3, 2015, http://www.wbaltv.com/news/72-forced -separations-during-commissioner-anthony-batts-te nure/33375726 (accessed June 11, 2015).

—Pamela Willwerth Aue

Big Freedia

1981(?)—

Hip-hop artist, reality television star, author

Big Freedia, photograph. lev radin/Shutterstock.com.

Rapper Big Freedia is the self-proclaimed "Queen of Bounce," the most visible ambassador for the energetic, booty-shaking brand of hip-hop known as bounce that originated in the clubs of New Orleans. Since 2010, when Big Freedia first gained attention outside of New Orleans, the rapper has become ubiquitous, with appearances on late-night television and at music festivals around the country; a Guinness World Record for leading the most people twerking, set in 2013 in New York City; an album, *Free to Be,* released in 2014; a reality television series, *Big Freedia: Queen of Bounce,* that was in its third season in 2015; and a memoir, *Big Freedia: God Save the Queen Diva!,* published in the summer of 2015. Big Freedia (pronounced FREE-da) is the stage name of Freddie Ross, an openly gay, gender-nonconforming performer. Standing six feet, three inches tall, Freedia is a man but dresses as a woman on stage. Most fans refer to Freedia as "she," but the rapper answers to pronouns of both genders and is unconcerned with such labels. "People get confused by if am 'he' or 'she,'" Freedia said in an interview with the *Los Angeles Times.* "I am me."

Big Freedia was born Freddie Ross in New Orleans and raised there by his mother, a hairdresser, and stepfather, a truck driver. Drawn to music at a young age, he learned to play the piano and sang in the choir. Later, at Walter L. Cohen High School, he was the choir director and began writing his own music. He first identified as gay when he was 12 or 13 years old. Ross began his performing career in the late 1990s as a backup singer and dancer for Katey Red, a drag queen who performed bounce music in New Orleans clubs. Ross soon adopted the stage name Big Freedia, calling himself "Big Freedia Queen Diva," and released his first single, "An Ha, Oh Yeah," in 1999. Freedia's first full-length album, *Dancehall Queen Diva,* followed in 2003.

Bounce music originated in New Orleans as a local variety of hip-hop in the early 1990s, an outgrowth of the city's housing projects. Influenced as much by the chants of the local Mardi Gras Indians and the second-line brass bands that are a staple of New Orleans jazz as by hip-hop, bounce is marked by its fast tempo, heavy bass, and call-and-response vocals. Most bounce tracks are based on a small handful of samples, most notably, "Drag Rap," a 1986 track by a New York–based group

called the Showboys. The sound of bounce is meant to evoke a party, and it is best heard live, as it depends on heavy audience participation. Bounce music is overtly sexual and meant for dancing: the term "bounce" also refers to a style of provocative booty-shaking that later would be called twerking.

Early on, most bounce artists were straight, but beginning in the late 1990s, artists such as Red and Freedia helped usher in a new generation of openly gay, gender-nonconforming artists, giving rise to a subgenre that some have derisively termed "sissy bounce." Big Freedia rejects such distinctions. "All Bounce is Bounce," according to Freedia's website. "There's no need to separate it out. All types of people—gay, straight, rich, poor, black, white come to my shows." Indeed, inclusion is Freedia's mantra and the hallmark of his shows. "When you come to a Big Freedia show, it's a big party," he explained in an interview with the *Los Angeles Times.* "There's no color, no size, no judging. It's just a big open party for everybody to come and let their hair down and just enjoy bounce music."

After Hurricane Katrina devastated New Orleans in 2005, Freedia and other bounce performers temporarily relocated to Texas and introduced the genre there. Freedia moved back to New Orleans at the first opportunity and performed 6 to 10 shows a week as the city began to rebuild. "Freedia was one of the first artists to come back after the storm and start working," New Orleans music journalist Alison Fensterstock told the *New York Times* for a 2010 article on bounce music, "and she worked really, really hard.... If you lived here, it became impossible not to know who she was."

In 2010 Big Freedia released a second album, *Big Freedia Hitz Vol. 1,* and embarked on a busy tour schedule. That fall Big Freedia made his first national television appearance on *Last Call with Carson Daly,* and suddenly he was a sensation. In 2011 he was named best emerging artist and best hip-hop/rap artist at the Best of the Beat Awards and received a nomination for outstanding music artist at the GLAAD (Gay and Lesbian Alliance Against Defamation) Media

Awards. That same year he appeared on two episodes of the HBO series *Treme,* set in New Orleans, and in 2012 he performed at the South by Southwest festival in Austin, Texas.

By 2013 Big Freedia seemed to be everywhere. That year the first season of the rapper's reality television series, *Big Freedia: Queen of Bounce,* aired on the Fuse network, chronicling his rise to stardom and life in New Orleans. Later that year Big Freedia led a crowd of more than 350 dancers in New York City, which set a Guinness World Record for the largest number of people twerking simultaneously. The following year Big Freedia released his first "official" album, *Free to Be,* on his own label Queen Diva Music. The album rose to number 48 on the Billboard Top R&B/Hip-Hop Albums chart and number 28 on the Heatseekers Albums list. The rapper's memoir, *Big Freedia: God Save the Queen Diva!,* was published in July of 2015.

Selected works

Albums

Dancehall Queen Diva, 2003.
Big Freedia Hitz Vol. 1, 2010 (re-released by Scion A/V, 2011).
Just Be Free, Queen Diva Music, 2014.

Television

Big Freedia: Queen of Bounce, Fuse TV, 2013—.

Books

(With Nicole Balin) *Big Freedia: God Save the Queen Diva!,* Gallery, 2015.

Sources

Books

Los Angeles Times, March 4, 2015.
New York Times, July 22, 2010.
Times-Picayune (New Orleans, LA), October 7, 2010; February 24, 2015.
Washington Post, April 4, 2012; June 12, 2014.

Online

"Big Freedia Lays Out the Basics of Bounce," *All Things Considered,* National Public Radio, January 27, 2013, http://www.npr.org/2013/01/27/170 276604/big-freedia-lays-out-the-basics-of-bounce (accessed June 30, 2015).
Edwards, Florence, "Big Freedia Dishes on Marriage, Her Sexuality and Her New Memoir," Huffington Post, March 30, 2015, http://www.huffingtonpost. com/florence-edwards/big-freedia-dishes-on-mar_b _6958334.html (accessed June 29, 2015).
Newman, Jason, "Queen of Bounce Big Freedia

'Explodes' on New Song," RollingStone.com, April 24, 2014, http://www.rollingstone.com/music/news/queen-of-bounce-big-freedia-explodes-on-new-song-premiere-20140424 (accessed June 30, 2015).

Thomas, Ann Marshall, "My New Orleans: 20 Ques-tions with Big Freedia," GoNOLA.com, July 16, 2014, http://gonola.com/2014/07/16/my-new-orleans-20-questions-with-big-freedia.html (accessed June 29, 2015).

—Deborah A. Ring

Todd Bowles

1963—

Professional football player, coach

Bowles, Todd, photograph. Tibrina Hobson/WireImage/Getty Images.

Todd Bowles is head coach of the New York Jets. A former standout defensive back at Temple University, Bowles played for eight seasons in the National Football League (NFL), primarily with the Washington Redskins. The high point of his professional career came in 1987, when he was the starting free safety during Washington's successful Super Bowl run. After retiring from the game in 1994, Bowles embarked on a career in coaching. A defensive specialist known for his calm demeanor and meticulous attention to detail, Bowles worked as a secondary coach for several NFL franchises before becoming defensive coordinator for the Arizona Cardinals in 2013. In two years in Arizona, Bowles helped transform the Cardinals into one of the stoutest defenses in the league. The unit made its most impressive effort in 2014, when it allowed only 18.7 points per game, the fifth-best average in the NFL. Bowles's success made him a prime candidate for a number of head coaching vacancies, and he was hired by the Jets shortly after the conclusion of the 2014 regular season.

Exhibited Leadership Skills at Young Age

Bowles was born on November 18, 1963, in Elizabeth, New Jersey, the youngest child of Joan Bowles, a librarian and school worker. Bowles first discovered his passion for sports while growing up in the Pioneer Homes projects, where he felt pushed to excel by other young athletes in the neighborhood. "For me, you have some streetball legends that live there," Bowles recalled to Steve Serby in the New York Post in 2015. "So you learn how to play in the streets, as opposed to going away for camps. If you got any kind of skill set, it's gonna test you every day so it gets better, but there were a lot of people down there that did a lot of things to help me get to where I am." Bowles eventually continued his athletic career at Elizabeth High School, where he starred as both a free safety and defensive back for the Minutemen. He also earned praise for his maturity and leadership during those years. "Todd had special gifts," his coach, Don Somma, later told Hank

At a Glance . . .

Born Todd Robert Bowles on November 18, 1963, in Elizabeth, NJ; son of Joan Bowles; married Jill Jenkins, 2000 (divorced, 2008); married Taneka, 2012; children: Todd Jr., Troy, Tyson, Sydni. *Education:* Attended Temple University, 1981–86.

Career: Washington Redskins, defensive back and free safety, 1986–90, 1992–93; San Francisco 49ers, free safety, 1991; Green Bay Packers, player personnel staff, 1995–96; Morehouse College, defensive coordinator, 1997; Grambling State University, defensive coordinator, 1998–99; New York Jets, secondary coach, 2000; Cleveland Browns, secondary coach, 2001–04; Dallas Cowboys, secondary coach, 2005–07; Miami Dolphins, assistant head coach and secondary coach, 2008–10, interim head coach, 2011; Philadelphia Eagles, secondary coach and interim defensive coordinator, 2012; Arizona Cardinals, defensive coordinator, 2013–14; New York Jets, head coach, 2015—.

Awards: First-Team All-East, 1984; inducted into Temple University Athletics Hall of Fame, 2001.

Addresses: *Office*—c/o New York Jets, 1 Jets Dr., Florham Park, NJ 07932.

Gola in the *New York Daily News.* "Todd was just one of many who believed in what we were doing. He was a leader."

Bowles continued his football career at Temple University, where he anchored the defensive backfield. While at Temple he played under head coach Bruce Arians, who would later become head coach of the Arizona Cardinals. Over the course of his collegiate career, Bowles accumulated 245 tackles and seven interceptions. He gave his best performance during his junior season, when he collected 86 tackles and four sacks en route to earning First-Team All-East honors. However, he suffered a setback the following year, when his playing time was cut short because of a severe wrist injury. When he was unable to complete his strength tests at the 1986 NFL Scouting Combine, it became uncertain whether Bowles would ever receive the chance to compete at the professional level. Although he went unselected during the 1986 draft, he eventually earned tryout opportunities with a number of NFL clubs, finally earning a spot with Washington. Bowles appeared in 15 games during his rookie campaign, including two starts, and finished the year with two interceptions. During the strike-shortened 1987 sea-

son, he started 12 games as a free safety, intercepting four passes and recovering a fumble. Bowles also started all three postseason games that year, including the team's 42–10 victory over the Denver Broncos in Super Bowl XXII.

Between 1988 and 1990, Bowles started every game as a free safety for the Redskins. In 1991 he joined the San Francisco 49ers and then returned to Washington in 1992. Following the 1993 season, Bowles retired from football. He returned to the NFL in 1995, joining the player personnel department of the Green Bay Packers. Two years later Bowles accepted a job as defensive coordinator at Morehouse College. At Morehouse he worked under head coach Doug Williams, the former Redskins quarterback who had led Bowles and his teammates to victory in Super Bowl XXII. A year later, Bowles followed Williams to Grambling State University, a historically black institution in Grambling, Louisiana, where he remained for the next two seasons. While at Grambling he met coaching legend Eddie Robinson Sr., who had retired in 1997 with the most coaching wins in the history of college football. "Eddie had just retired, but he came back. He would sit out on the stoop and he would just tell stories," Bowles told Marcus Hayes in the *Philadelphia Daily News* in 2012. "You would sit there in amazement. He'd been through eras of football."

Built a Strong Coaching Resume in NFL

In 2000 Bowles returned to the NFL to become secondary coach with the New York Jets. In New York he worked under general manager and former coach Bill Parcells, who provided him with vital encouragement during the early phase of his coaching career. "From the time I got to the Jets, he told me I'd be a head coach in this league and he taught me accordingly," Bowles recalled to McClatchy-Tribune News Service's Nicholas J. Cotsonika in 2009. "I mean, he kept me by his side. He taught me step-by-step the structure of how to put a team in place and keep a team in place and not be a one-hit wonder." After one season with the Jets, Bowles was named secondary coach of the Cleveland Browns, where he remained for the next three years. In 2005 he rejoined Parcells on the coaching staff of the Dallas Cowboys. In 2008 Bowles followed Parcells to the Miami Dolphins, where he served as assistant head coach under Tony Sparano while continuing to oversee the secondary unit. After Sparano was fired with three games remaining in the 2011 season, Bowles was promoted to interim head coach, compiling a record of 2–1.

In 2012 Bowles accepted a position as secondary coach with the Philadelphia Eagles. He helped improve the team's pass defense almost immediately, due primarily to his painstaking approach to game preparation. One of Bowles's most effective innovations in-

volved the use of video montages to help teach his players to identify certain tendencies of opposing teams. These videos, which Bowles dubbed "cut-ups," proved popular with members of Philadelphia's defensive backfield. "He makes it so easy for you," Eagles cornerback Brandon Boykin told Jeff McLane in the *Philadelphia Inquirer* in 2012. "He tells you what to expect, what not to expect, and what this person's strengths and weaknesses are." To veteran safety Nate Allen, Bowles's unique approach was transformative. "He's made a huge difference," Allen told McLane, "not even just with the secondary, but with the entire defense."

As Bowles's reputation spread, he began earning consideration for more high-profile coaching jobs. In 2013 he left Philadelphia to become defensive coordinator with the Arizona Cardinals, where he worked under Arians, his former coach at Temple. During his first season with the Cardinals, Bowles presided over a defense that allowed an average of 20.2 points per game, which was the seventh-best average in the NFL. Arizona's defensive unit was more impressive the following year, allowing only 18.7 points per contest despite losing linebacker Daryl Washington, who had led the team in tackles the previous year, to a season-long suspension. At season's end, Bowles was being discussed for a number of head coaching jobs, notably, in New York, Atlanta, and Chicago.

In the end, Bowles signed a four-year, $16 million deal to take over the Jets. His understated demeanor marked a stark departure from former head coach Rex Ryan, whose brash, outspoken personality had shaped the team's character for the previous six seasons. From the beginning, Bowles made it clear that the team would adopt a different philosophy going forward. "We have to teach them our culture," Bowles told Rich Cimini in January of 2015, shortly after taking over the team. "Not that the other culture was bad, but it didn't win. Our culture will be to try to instill different things in them from a winning organization's point of view to make us go forward and make the playoffs." With the Jets hoping to earn its first Super Bowl berth since 1969, Bowles's approach offered a glimmer of hope for a fan base that had become desperate for a title.

Sources

Periodicals

Chicago Tribune, January 5, 2015.
McClatchy-Tribune News Service, January 14, 2009.
Morning Call (Allentown, PA), October 23, 2012, p. C1.
New York Daily News, January 14, 2015.
New York Post, January 25, 2015.
Orlando Sentinel, December 13, 2011, p. C3.
Palm Beach Post, December 15, 2011, p. C1.
Philadelphia Daily News, February 9, 2012, p. 54.
Philadelphia Inquirer, October 8, 2012; October 16, 2012; January 18, 2013.
Wall Street Journal, June 11, 2015.

Online

Cimini, Rich, "Bowles Wants to Change Jets' Culture," ESPN.com, January 22, 2015, http://espn.go.com /new-york/nfl/story/_/id/12205472/todd-bowles -new-york-jets-says-working-getting-own-rings (accessed June 23, 2015).
"Todd Bowles," Pro-Football-Reference.com, http:// www.pro-football-reference.com/players/B/BowlTo 20.htm (accessed June 23, 2015).
Wesseling, Chris, "New York Jets Announce Todd Bowles as Head Coach," NFL.com, January 13, 2015, http://www.nfl.com/news/story/0ap30000 00458689/article/new-york-jets-announce-todd -bowles-as-head-coach (accessed June 23, 2015).

—Stephen Meyer

Anthony Braxton

1945—

Musician, composer, educator

Braxton, Anthony, photograph. Peter Van Breukelen/Redferns/ Getty Images.

Multi-instrumentalist and composer Anthony Braxton is a major figure in modern music history, an artist so innovative that biographer Mike Heffley declared that his body of work "is to 'jazz,' 'Western art music,' and 'African-American composer's tradition' what Einstein was to physics, Picasso to Impressionism, Dylan to folk music." Braxton came of age on the South Side of Chicago during the early 1960s, when the free jazz movement associated with alto saxophonist Ornette Coleman was taking hold. He embraced the new music, with its disregard for the conventions of tempo, consonance, tonality, and structure, and embarked on a career of musical experimentation known as much for its theoretical grounding as for its imaginative mixing of the visceral components of jazz with classical and concert styles.

Braxton's music is nearly impossible to categorize, and he has always been at odds with jazz purists. Although he flirted with commercial success during the 1970s and even signed a contract with the major label Arista, Braxton's densely intellectual approach ultimately prevented mainstream acceptance. He has maintained a relatively small but devoted following and counts among his disciples talented young jazz musicians such as Nat Baldwin, Taylor Ho Bynum, Kyle Brenders, Mary Halvorson, and James Fei. Given Braxton's prickly relationship with the jazz establishment, no one was more surprised than he to learn that he had been named a 2014 recipient of the nation's highest honor in the field, the National Endowment for the Arts (NEA) Jazz Masters Fellowship.

A virtuoso alto saxophonist, Braxton plays nearly all of the instruments in the saxophone, clarinet, and flute families as well as the piano and percussion. His music is highly cerebral, an improvisational aesthetic born of the Afrocentric cultural and political ethos of the 1960s, the democratic spirt of jazz, and the iconoclasm and religious mysticism that defined the 20th-century art music of German composer and theoretician Karlheinz Stockhausen and his American counterpart John Cage. Braxton developed a radical system of composition that he called "sonic geometry," codified by a complicated notational vocabulary of his own invention that relies on mathematical symbols and equations, computer language, and visual designations, including flowcharts, line drawings, hieroglyphic images, and other graphic and symbolic

At a Glance . . .

Born on June 4, 1945, in Chicago, IL; son of Clarence Dunbar Braxton (a railroad worker) and Julia Samuels Braxton; married Nickie Singer, 1975; children: Terri, Tyondai, Keayr, Donari. *Military service:* U.S. Army, 1963–66.

Career: Performing artist, 1963 ; recording artist, 1967—; music educator, 1985–2013.

Memberships: Association for the Advancement of Creative Musicians, member, 1966–69; Tri-Centric Foundation, founder, 1994—.

Awards: Guggenheim Fellowship, John Simon Guggenheim Memorial Foundation, 1981; MacArthur Foundation Fellowship, 1994; Doris Duke Performing Artist Award, Jazz, Doris Duke Charitable Foundation, 2013; Jazz Masters Fellowship, National Endowment for the Arts, 2014.

Addresses: *Web*—http://tricentricfoundation.org.

elements, some of which are used as the titles for his pieces. An exceedingly prolific artist, Braxton has recorded more than 200 albums and written hundreds of pieces, from solos and duets to multi-orchestral compositions and operas. He is also the author of *Tri-Axium Writings* (1985) and *Composition Notes* (1988), self-published books in which he explains his influences and theories.

Inspired by the Jazz Renaissance

Born in Chicago on June 4, 1945, Braxton grew up in the South Side neighborhood of Washington Park. His parents, Clarence Dunbar Braxton and Julia Samuels Braxton, split up when Anthony was very young. His mother remarried, and Anthony and his brothers, Lafayette and Clarence Jr., became part of a blended family that included their stepfather, Lawrence Fouché, and stepbrothers Donald and Gregory. Washington Park was one of several poor black neighborhoods on the city's South Side that was experiencing a rise in crime and gang activity, a trend influenced by job shortages, employment discrimination, and inadequate housing. At the same time, the South Side was home to a burgeoning cultural scene that yielded many new styles of music. Braxton's family was better off than many others, and he enjoyed a relatively peaceful childhood sheltered from the streets. He became a fan of rhythm and blues, rock and roll, and doo-wop, and

when he was around 11 or 12 years old, he discovered the music of jazz pianist Ahmad Jamal.

During his first year at Chicago Vocational High School, Braxton's father bought him an alto saxophone. He began taking lessons at the Chicago School of Music with Jack Gell. Braxton also took an interest in science, the visual arts, literature, and mechanics, and he was the champion of the chess club. For the most part, Braxton kept to himself. He practiced his horn several hours a day and ventured out to nightclubs to hear the jazz revolution firsthand.

In 1963 Braxton enrolled at Wilson Junior College. He spent only a semester there but formed lasting friendships with several jazz musicians, notably, alto saxophonist Roscoe Mitchell and drummer Jack De-Johnette. To make money for further schooling, Braxton enlisted in the U.S. Army. He completed his basic training at Fort Knox, Kentucky, and then was stationed with the Fifth Army Band in Highland Park, north of downtown Chicago. Braxton continued his lessons with Gell until 1965, when the army transferred him to Seoul, South Korea.

Joined the AACM

After he got out of the service, Braxton enrolled as a part-time music student at Roosevelt College. The emphasis at Roosevelt on European tradition, to the exclusion of jazz, popular, and world music, soured Braxton on a university musical education. At Mitchell's urging, Braxton turned his attention to the Association for the Advancement of Creative Musicians (AACM), a cooperative of black artists formed in 1965 by members of Chicago's jazz community. The AACM promoted innovation and experimentation, sponsored concerts and events, and provided free music education for inner-city youth. In an interview with the NEA's Jo Reed in 2014, Braxton fondly recalled his time with the AACM: "This was 1966. Up until 1966 I had always found myself the odd guy out. And so the Association for the Advancement of Creative Musicians was—a group of—spiritualists who were trying to search for what is the meaning of music. What is music all about anyway? Is it just about writin' a song and making $800 billion? Why do we love music so much? And it was one of the best things that had ever happened to me to discover this group of—incredible musicians. No one worked. Very little work. Nobody had any money. We all come from poverty. And no one would give an inch with respect to their aesthetics and their music."

Playing with the AACM bands, Braxton developed collaborations that led to his first recordings. In 1967 Braxton formed a trio called the Creative Construction Company with violinist Leroy Jenkins and trumpeter Leo Smith, both of whom were featured, along with pianist Muhal Richard Abrams, on Braxton's debut as a leader, *Three Compositions of New Jazz* (1968). The

album challenged mainstream convention, dispensing with the rhythm section and traditional harmony and melody, and the record sleeve provided the scores in curious graphics that resembled algebraic formulas. This release was followed by *For Alto* (1969), which was historically significant as the first-ever recording for solo alto, unaccompanied by other instrumentation. In an article for the website All About Jazz in 2000, Derek Taylor reaffirmed the status of *For Alto* as a precedent-setting event in the timeline of free jazz: "Over three decades after its original release it still has the capacity to dumbfound and astound.... This is a recording and artistic statement that completely changed the rules. Braxton's gall seemed audacious to some, but revolutionary to far more and the hindsight of history has proven this latter camp correct. His opened the gates for solo improvisatory expression for all players up to the challenge to pass through and in the intervening years many of the giants of improvised music have followed suit. Joe McPhee, Evan Parker, Peter Brötzmann, so many others; all have raised their reeds to their lips on record in the absence of others with only their thoughts and facility to guide them."

In 1969 Braxton moved to Paris with the Creative Construction Company. The group was not successful, and Braxton returned to the United States, where he lived in New York at the SoHo home of Ornette Coleman. Concert gigs were few and far between, so Braxton resorted to hustling chess in Washington Square Park to make ends meet. Introduced to keyboardist Chick Corea by DeJohnette, Braxton joined with Corea, bassist Dave Holland, and percussionist Barry Altschul in the short-lived but influential group Circle. After the group dissolved, Braxton began leading his own bands. Holland and Altschul remained with him as part of a quartet that variously included brass players Kenny Wheeler, George Lewis, and Ray Anderson. The core members of the group, along with reedist and flutist Sam Rivers, released the seminal 1973 recording *Conference of the Birds,* which was regarded as a landmark of free jazz. Braxton made his way back to Paris for a time, where he created some of his early piano music and recorded several albums on French labels.

Signed with Arista

Braxton's star was on the rise, especially with the delayed success of *For Alto.* In 1974 Clive Davis of Arista Records signed Braxton to a recording contract. Braxton's earliest releases for Arista, including *New York, Fall 1974* (1974) and *Five Pieces* (1975), were designed for entry into the commercial market and highlighted his most accessible material. The strategy worked. Braxton, who up to this time had only enjoyed popularity in France, now came to the attention of American audiences. Critics gushed over him, adorning him with labels such as "high priest of jazz" and "jazz messiah." His mainstream reputation was sealed by a 1977 profile in *Newsweek* magazine in which

Hubert Saal called him "the most innovative force in the world of jazz."

By the late 1970s Arista agreed to devote its major-label resources to recordings of Braxton's concert music. With the release of *For Trio* (1977) and *For Four Orchestras* (1978), many critics who had once applauded Braxton now balked at his rebellion and defected to the camp of purists, claiming that Braxton was not truly a jazz musician. The timing of these more idiosyncratic releases was inopportune, coinciding with the beginning of a resurgence of interest in traditional jazz. Braxton had in fact recorded much of the standard jazz repertoire, or at least his spin on it, and he frequently cited Thelonious Monk, Paul Desmond, and Charlie Parker as influences. However, it was his unyielding eclecticism and nonjazz sources, including classical music and parade marches, that offended the orthodox jazz watchdogs. Braxton's subsequent Arista recordings attracted scarce attention, and the label dropped him in 1982.

After his departure from Arista, Braxton continued to produce music at a dizzying pace, mostly on small independent labels. The evolution of his music during the 1980s and 1990s is perhaps best witnessed in his classic quartet with pianist Marilyn Crispell, drummer Gerry Hemingway, and bassist Mark Dresser. Braxton introduced the notion of multiple logic structures, a collage-like aesthetic that invited the performers to play their parts simultaneously, individually, or in any combination. Other memorable collaborations during this period include his duo with bebop pioneer Max Roach and his trio with bassist Adelhard Roidinger and drummer Tony Oxley. Braxton's work increasingly took on visual, theatrical, and narrative elements, as in his planned 12-opera cycle *Trillium.* As always, he composed for a wide variety of instrumentation, including solo saxophone, string quartets, tuba ensembles, big bands, multiple orchestras, and piano.

Founded Tri-Centric Foundation

Married in 1975, Braxton lived with his wife and children in New Haven, Connecticut, until 1985, when he was hired to teach at Mills College in Oakland, California. Five years later, Braxton was named to the faculty at Wesleyan, and the family returned to Connecticut. In 1994 Braxton was awarded a MacArthur Foundation Fellowship—the prestigious "genius" grant—which allowed him to finance his Tri-Centric Foundation, an arts cooperative modeled on the AACM that was devoted to the preservation and production of Braxton's work. After a period of dormancy, the Tri-Centric Foundation was revived in 2010.

The Tri-Centric Foundation has benefited greatly from the contributions of Braxton's students at Wesleyan, who have played a major role in staging his various

musical, multimedia, and interdisciplinary compositions. Braxton explained in a 2007 interview with the website Tomajazz, "Part of the value of Academia has been the possibility to find young people who are interested in my work and to teach them what it is, and, in this way it is possible to evolve the system. I can't evolve the system if I just bring in jazz musicians, or if I just bring in classical musicians who would play the notated material, but not understand how to use the improvised material, or who can play the notated material and the improvised material, but not understand how to integrate it into the plane of signals.... I need people who are doing homework, who can execute very difficult notated music, or who can function with no notated music, or who can play from graphic scores, or gesture scores ... I need people who are not limited to one idiom."

Braxton's recent work has included several large-scale projects dauntingly complex in approach and scale and divided into various families of composition strategy: Ghost Trance Music, Diamond Curtain Wall Music, Falling River Music, Echo Echo Mirror House Music, and Pine Top Aerial Music. These systems of composition expand on previous areas of exploration such as graphical scores and abstract visuals and introduce new elements, including interactive electronics. Taken together, they represent for Braxton a type of social organism of spatial dimension. He even refers to some of his compositions as city-states, villages, or towns. "The essential characteristic of the model I'm trying to build involves everything happening at the same time," Braxton told Kevin Whitehead of the online music publication *Wondering Sound* in 2014. "The compositions can be put together in different orders: They're a giant erector set that can be used in different kinds of ways, to suit the needs of the creative improviser or composer."

In April of 2013 Braxton received the lucrative Doris Duke Performing Artist Award. He left Wesleyan in December of that year and has since devoted most of his time to finishing the *Trillium* operas. The *Trillium* complex is intended to articulate the philosophical ideas contained in the *Tri-Axium Writings* and is so named because it represents the three aspects of his life's work: music (sound logic) systems, thought (philosophical) systems, and ritual and ceremonial (belief) systems. The operas are inspired by the totality of Richard Wagner's *Ring* cycle. "The difference being," Braxton explained to Whitehead, "I've tried to fashion my model more on the I Ching rather than, say, organized religion." Braxton has completed five of the 12 operas—*A, M, R, E,* and *J*—and is currently at work on *Trillium X.* He envisions the completed version as a set of 36 one-act works interconnected by 12 recurring character archetypes that represent the main components of his logic system.

Selected works

Books

Tri-Axium Writings, Synthesis Music, 1985.
Composition Notes, Synthesis Music, 1988.

Albums

Three Compositions of New Jazz, Delmark, 1968.
For Alto, Delmark, 1969.
Town Hall, 3D Japan, 1972.
Conference of the Birds, ECM, 1973.
New York, Fall 1974, Arista, 1974.
Five Pieces, Arista, 1975.
Duets 1976, Arista, 1976.
For Trio, Arista, 1977.
For Four Orchestras, Arista, 1978.
NW5-9M4: For Trio, Arista, 1978.
Open Aspects (Duo), Hat Hut, 1982.
Six Monk's Compositions, Black Saint, 1987.
Wesleyan (12 Alto Solos), hatART, 1992.
Composition No. 174: For Ten Percussionists, Slide Projections, Constructed Environment, Leo, 1994.
Piano Quartet, Yoshi's 1994, Music & Arts, 1996.
Trillium R: Composition 162—An Opera in Four Acts, Braxtonhouse, 1999.
Triotone, Leo, 2004.
Beyond Quantum, Tzadik, 2008.
Trillium E, New Braxton House, 2011.
12 Duets, New Braxton House, 2014.
Trio (New Haven) 2013, New Braxton House, 2014.

Sources

Books

Broomer, Stuart, *Time and Anthony Braxton,* Mercury Press, 2009.
Ford, Alun, *Anthony Braxton: Creative Music Continuums,* Stride Publications, 1997.
Heffley, Mike, *The Music of Anthony Braxton,* Greenwood Press, 1996.
Lock, Graham, *Blutopia: Visions of the Future and Revisions of the Past in the Work of Sun Ra, Duke Ellington, and Anthony Braxton,* Duke University Press, 1999.
———, *Forces in Motion: The Music and Thoughts of Anthony Braxton,* Da Capo Press,1988.
Radano, Ronald Michael, *New Musical Figurations: Anthony Braxton's Cultural Critique,* University of Chicago Press, 1993.

Periodicals

Atlantic, February, 2000.
Chicago Reader, November 27, 2008.
Down Beat, April, 1994.
JazzTimes, May 2007.

Newsweek, August 8, 1977.
New York Times, October 4, 2011.
Telegraph (London), January 21, 2015.

Online

"Anthony Braxton," AllMusic.com, http://www.allmusic.com/artist/anthony-braxton-mn0000924030 (accessed June 17, 2015).

De Urbina, Fernando Ortiz, Diego Sánchez Cascado, and José Francisco Tapiz, "Tomajazz Interviews Anthony Braxton," Tomajazz, 2007, http://www.tomajazz.com/perfiles/braxton_2007_eng.htm (accessed June 18, 2015).

Heffley, Michael, "Anthony Braxton: The Third Millennial Interview," 2001, http://www.academia.edu/2314587/Anthony_Braxton_The_Third_Millennial_Interview (accessed June 17, 2015).

Mandel, Howard, "A Grand Musical Thinker, Inviting 'Friendly Experiencers'," National Public Radio, October 15, 2011, http://www.npr.org/2011/10/15/141365450/a-grand-musical-thinker-inviting-friendly-experiencers (accessed June 17, 2015).

Reed, Jo, "Interview with Anthony Braxton," National Endowment for the Arts, 2014, http://arts.gov/audio/anthony-braxton (accessed June 17, 2015).

Taylor, Derek, "Anthony Braxton: *For Alto,*" All About Jazz, September 1, 2000, http://www.allaboutjazz.com/for-alto-anthony-braxton-delmark-records-review-by-derek-taylor.php (accessed June 18, 2015).

Whitehead, Kevin, "Anthony Braxton: Jazz Outcast," *Wondering Sound,* March 26, 2014, http://www.wonderingsound.com/feature/anthony-braxton-interview/ (accessed June 17, 2015).

—Janet Mullane

W. Herbert Brewster

1897(?)–1987

Minister, composer, broadcaster, gospel vocalist

A towering figure in gospel music for more than half a century, the Reverend W. Herbert Brewster played a crucial role in the growth and development of that genre. The longtime pastor of East Trigg Avenue Baptist Church, a Memphis landmark famous for its music and for its racially integrated membership, Brewster wrote more than 200 compositions, including familiar favorites such as Mahalia Jackson's "Move On Up a Little Higher" (1947), widely believed to be the first gospel song to sell more than a million copies. Best remembered for his ability to impart important theological teachings through memorable melodies, powerful rhythms, and simple but uplifting lyrics, Brewster was a mentor to many leading gospel performers, led several groups of his own, hosted two widely heard radio programs, and helped lead his city through the turbulence of the civil rights era. In a piece published in conjunction with his posthumous induction into the Memphis Music Hall of Fame in 2013, writer William Ellis called Brewster "one of the most prolific and popular religious composers of the 20th century."

The son of sharecroppers and the grandson of former slaves, William Herbert Brewster was born on a farm just outside Somerville, Tennessee, a small town not far from Memphis. As he told interviewer Charles V. Crawford of Memphis State University in 1983, the year of his birth was always a mystery to him; official records at the time were inconsistent, and his family could tell him only that he was born in either 1897 or 1899. Over time he came to prefer the earlier date, a choice that was heeded by news organizations such as the *New York Times,* which described him as 90 years old at the time of his death in 1987.

Music and church were central to Brewster's life from an early age. His father was a skilled singer who taught his children and many of his fellow parishioners how to read music. Brewster's grandparents played an important role in his musical training as well; in his later years he frequently recalled the influence of the hymns, spirituals, and work songs they taught him. A strong student, he attended classes at the Howe Institute, a pioneering African-American institution in Memphis, before enrolling at Roger Williams University in Nashville, where he earned an undergraduate degree in 1922. After graduation he returned to Memphis, where he focused on a variety of educational efforts, including opening his own theological institute, before assuming the leadership of East Trigg Avenue Baptist Church in 1930. He retained that post for the next 57 years.

Although he had begun to write his own lyrics as early as age 10, it was not until he was well established at East Trigg that Brewster began to compose for publication. One of his first hits was a song called "I'm Leaning and Depending on the Lord." Published in 1939, it proved popular with audiences and performers alike. The enthusiasm of gospel performers for the son helped spread Brewster's message beyond Memphis. Although he recorded only rarely, groups named in his honor and based at East Trigg sold thousands of copies of his songs, thanks in part to the participation of church member Queen C. Anderson, a major performer in her own right.

Even more successful was Mahalia Jackson, who was instrumental in bringing Brewster's music to the attention of audiences outside the South. A resident of Chicago, Jackson had a warm and versatile voice that was well suited to the wide-ranging melodies of compositions such as "Move On Up a Little Higher." The release of her rendition of that song in the fall of 1947 was an important moment in the history of gospel. An enduring, widely covered hit, it helped solidify Jackson's reputation as the "Queen of Gospel Music" and Brewster's status as one of the genre's foremost composers. Two years later his prominence was underscored when the Ward Singers released "Surely God Is Able," an iconic hit and a classic example of the up-tempo, percussion-heavy style known as "shouting." Throughout his career Brewster excelled at shout songs, which were closely related to the field songs he had learned from his grandparents.

As a leader of the African-American community in Memphis, then one of the most segregated cities in the country, Brewster played a significant role in the civil rights movement of the 1950s and 1960s. "He was a real pioneer in race relations," Samuel Turner, Brewster's successor at East Trigg, told Ellis. "Back when you didn't have whites and blacks socially mixing, he had as many whites in attendance as blacks—that was unheard of in Memphis!" Among the whites who came to hear Brewster preach and sing was rock legend Elvis Presley, whose vocal style owed a great deal to black gospel. The interracial harmony evident at East Trigg was also apparent in Brewster's weekly radio shows, which involved frequent interaction with a racially mixed studio audience. Broadcast by two of the region's most powerful stations, Brewster's *Gospel Treasure Hour* and *Camp Meeting of the Air* programs reached listeners across the South.

Although the pace of his output varied over time, Brewster continued to write music until the end of his career. Although he is most famous for his work from the mid-1940s to the early 1960s, a period that coincides with the so-called golden age of gospel music, his later efforts also drew considerable attention across the gospel spectrum, from local choirs to nationally known performers.

Brewster remained at East Trigg until June of 1987, when health problems forced his retirement. Several months later, in October of that year, he died of a heart attack at a Memphis hospital, leaving behind a daughter, several siblings, a grandchild, and a great-grandchild; a son and his wife Julianna predeceased him. In the years since his passing Brewster's reputation has continued to grow, and he remained a familiar figure to gospel fans around the world and a widely beloved figure in Memphis, where an elementary school was named in his honor in 2006.

Selected works

(Composer) "I'm Leaning and Depending on the Lord," 1939.
(Composer) Mahalia Jackson, "Move On Up a Little Higher," 1947.
(Composer) Ward Singers, "Surely God Is Able," 1949.

Sources

Periodicals

New York Times, October 18, 1987.

Online

"Church Facts," East Trigg Avenue Baptist Church, http://www.easttrigg.com/easttrigg_files/Page346.htm (accessed July 11, 2015).

Crawford, Charles V., "The Robert R. Church Family: Interview with Reverend W. Herbert Brewster, July 6, 1983," Memphis State University, https://archive.org/stream/robertrchurchfa00craw#page/n5/mode/2up (accessed July 12, 2015).

Ellis, William, "Rev. Herbert Brewster," Memphis Music Hall of Fame, http://memphismusichalloffame.com/inductee/herbertbrewster/ (accessed July 12, 2015).

—R. Anthony Kugler

Jamal Bryant

1971—

Pastor, activist

Bryant, Jamal, photograph. Ira Bostic/Shutterstock.com.

Jamal Bryant is an African-American pastor and the founder of a Baltimore-based megachurch affiliated with the African Methodist Episcopal (AME) denomination. Known for his penchant for custom-tailored suits and for his Bentley automobile, Bryant promulgates his "prosperity gospel" ministry through social media, syndicated television broadcasts, and international speaking engagements. His headquarters is a 10,000-member urban congregation called the Empowerment Temple whose attendees are attracted by Bryant's hip-hop-accented messages of social redemption and spiritual and economic reward. In 2014 and 2015, Bryant became increasingly visible for his participation in the #BlackLivesMatter movement in the United States. He was one of several religious leaders arrested during protests in Ferguson, Missouri, following the August of 2014 shooting of Michael Brown by a white police officer. A year later Bryant delivered the eulogy at the funeral of Freddie Gray, a 25-year-old African-American man whose death while he was in police custody in April of 2015 sparked protests that turned into widespread rioting on the streets of Baltimore, Maryland.

Promoted Spirituality, Sexuality, and Second Chances

Bryant was born in 1971 in Baltimore. His father and grandfather were both preachers and, later, bishops at Baltimore's Bethel AME Church. His mother was an ordained pastor and missionary as well. As an adolescent, Bryant was determined to forge his own path, not following his elders into church leadership. His father told *Baltimore Sun* writer Joe Burris, "One high school teacher captured the essence of Jamal: He was someone who hadn't decided whether he wanted to be the next Dr. Martin Luther King or the next Eddie Murphy." Frequently in trouble for a variety of classroom infractions, Bryant was dropped from a gifted and talented program after the 11th grade. Soon afterward the family moved to Liberia when the elder Bryant was appointed as an AME bishop. Jamal Bryant remembered this time as a wake-up call. He told Burris, "I met people who had to pay for their education," continuing, "People there couldn't understand why I failed an education that I got for free."

At a Glance . . .

Born Jamal Harrison Bryant on May 21, 1971, in Baltimore, MD; son of John Richard Bryant and Cecilia Williams-Bryant (both pastors); married Gizelle Graves, 2002 (divorced); children: Topaz (with Crystal Madison), Naomi (with Michelle Wedderburn) Grace, Angel, Adore (with Gizelle Bryant). *Religion:* Christian. *Education:* Morehouse College, BA, political science, international studies, 1994; Duke University, MDiv, 1997; Graduate Theological Foundation, DMin, 2005.

Career: National Association for the Advancement of Colored People (NAACP), national youth and college director, 1995–2000; Bethel African Methodist Episcopal Church, Baltimore, assistant pastor, 1997–2000; Empowerment Temple, Baltimore, founder and pastor, 2000—.

Memberships: Kappa Alpha Psi Fraternity.

Addresses: *Home*—Baltimore, MD. *Office*—Empowerment Temple, 4217-4221 Primrose Ave., Baltimore, MD 21215. *Web*—http://www.jamalbryant.org.

Back in the United States, Bryant earned his GED and enrolled at Morehouse College, graduating in 1994 with a degree in political science and international studies. From 1995 to 2000, he served as the national youth and college outreach director for the National Association for the Advancement of Colored People (NAACP), which had experienced a steep decline in membership among young adults. Bryant's charisma helped the organization add more than 100 college chapters in one year alone during his tenure. Speaking at a rally in Brooklyn, New York, in 1997, Bryant challenged attendees to channel their anger about social injustice into action by joining the NAACP, telling them, "We must stop the violence but not just with guns, not just with knives. You have to stop the violence in your own mind.... We have got to love ourselves and we have got to get involved."

In 1997 Bryant became assistant pastor at the church of his youth, Bethel AME in Baltimore. Despite his earlier resistance to working in the ministry, he now felt driven not only to become a pastor but also to lead a congregation of his own. Starting with a dozen friends who met in his home, Bryant set out a vision for the Empowerment Temple, which held its first service in a nightclub on Easter Sunday in April of 2000. The congregation numbered fewer than 50 people at the time. Nine months later, the church had grown mod-

estly, but it was nowhere near the megachurch that it would soon become.

Bryant actively promoted his new church through fliers, billboards, and personal invitations. Early in 2001 he announced an upcoming sermon titled "Foreplay: Sexual Healing for Spiritual Wholeness." He later published a book of the same title. His focus was on how Christianity teaches abstinence while refusing to openly talk about sex. In 2006 Michael Britton, a board member at Empowerment Temple, told Burris of the *Baltimore Sun*, "It was nontraditional in every aspect," adding, "It reached many people, and it changed the dynamics of the church." After several moves during the next three years, the congregation converted a Northwest Baltimore skating rink into a 2,500-seat worship center.

By 2007 Bryant's burgeoning Empowerment Temple ministry claimed as many as 12,000 parishioners. Services were held three times every Sunday. More than 150,000 global "Internet partners" watched live-streamed services or subscribed to daily "empowering" text and voice messages. Bryant, who was known to enjoy a well-heeled lifestyle, had been married since 2002 and had three daughters with his wife, Gizelle, as well as a daughter born in 1998. In 2007 Bryant was forced to acknowledge that he was the father of yet another daughter, who was then seven years old, when child support litigation news became public. Rumors swirled that Bryant had been involved in more recent extramarital affairs, and in 2008 Bryant and his wife separated and filed for divorce, which was finalized a year or two later. In 2013 Bryant recalled this chapter of his life in an interview with journalist and commentator Roland Martin, noting that as his congregation dwindled from thousands to hundreds, he became depressed, lost weight, and began therapy. He asserted, "Slowly, but surely, God [began] to rebuild it: new families, new groups, an absolutely different congregation ... God has been faithful even when I was unfaithful." During these years Bryant continued to expand his ministry's media offerings through books, online video resources, and social media platforms.

Protested Police Brutality against African Americans

As his ministry began to flourish once again, Bryant took a more prominent role in political and civic life, both in Baltimore and elsewhere. In 2014 and 2015, Bryant frequently joined other civic and religious leaders in marching against police brutality as part of what had become known as the #BlackLivesMatter movement, a response to several high-profile deaths of young African-American men at the hands of white police offers across the United States. In October of 2014, two months after Michael Brown was shot in Ferguson, Missouri, 100 clergy men and women from

around the country led a protest in Ferguson. Bryant was one of several religious leaders arrested during that action. He told CBS Baltimore that renewed attention to social justice issues in the aftermath of Brown's death was essential, observing, "I think it's peeling off the Band-Aid." He continued, "All of America is bleeding and it has to be addressed."

Just six months later the spotlight turned to Baltimore, where in April of 2015, 25-year-old Freddie Gray sustained fatal spinal cord injuries during his less than 45 minutes in police custody. Bryant organized local protests and prayer vigils. He also took action to help quell the widespread looting and violence that followed Gray's funeral, at which Bryant delivered the eulogy. Days after the Maryland National Guard was called in to patrol the city, Bryant appeared on NBC's *Today* show to discuss the situation. "Violence and justice never go together in the same sentence," he said, while acknowledging that Baltimore's minority community had reached a breaking point. In late April he told Danielle C. Belton of the website The Root, "People are looking at it just from the last 11 days and don't realize that Baltimoreans have been under suppressed rage for years." He added, "I gotta change my city."

In June of 2015 Bryant and other city pastors announced the creation of several programs and initiatives to improve recreation, health, and safety for children and teens in Baltimore's most economically challenged neighborhoods. The Empowerment Temple congregation agreed to turn an unused building into the Freddie Gray Children's Empowerment Center, a youth-focused resource offering free summer camps, breakfast and lunch daily, and year-round recreational and education enrichment activities. Businesses and individuals recruited by a fire dispatcher had raised more than $30,000 to refurbish West Baltimore's Martin Luther King Jr. Recreation Center. Together with other community organizers, the coalition of pastors also planned to host several supervised midnight basketball tournaments and promised that on weekend nights, between 8:00 p.m. and 1:00 a.m., Baltimore's most crime-ridden neighborhood streets would be patrolled, not by security personnel but by clergy and other community leaders, to build trust and stability. Bryant explained to the *Baltimore Sun,* "We're endeavoring to ... be a lamplight example of what can be done when the community comes together."

Selected works

Books

Foreplay: Sexual Healing for Spiritual Wholeness, GreenPope Press, 2002.
Finding Yourself in Scripture, Words2Empower Publishers, 2009.
World War Me, Empowerment Publishing Group, 2010.
World War Me II, Destiny Image, 2011.
The Big Idea: When God Impregnates Your Imagination, Life to Legacy, 2014.

Television

Got Power?, syndication.

Sources

Periodicals

Baltimore Sun, April 8, 1997; February 16, 2008; August 6, 2008; May 26, 2015; June 2, 2015.
Black Collegian, October 1997.
Ebony, September 2007.

Online

Belton, Danielle C., "Is the Rev. Jamal Bryant the Man to Save Baltimore?," The Root, April 29, 2015, http://www.theroot.com/articles/culture/2015/04/is_the_rev_jamal_bryant_the_man_to_save_baltimore.html (accessed June 11, 2015).
"Drama in the Church: Temptation Ended His Marriage, Nearly Destroyed the Ministry of Pastor Jamal Bryant," Roland Martin Reports, May 19, 2013, http://rolandmartinreports.com/blog/2013/05/drama-in-the-church-temptation-ended-the-marriage-nearly-destroyed-the-ministry-of-pastor-jamal-bryant-video/ (accessed June 11, 2015).
Empowerment Temple, http://www.empowermenttemple.org/ (accessed June 11, 2015).
Kim, Eun Kyung, "Baltimore Pastor Who Eulogized Freddie Gray: 'Violence and Justice Never Go Together,'" Today.com, April 28, 2015, http://www.today.com/news/baltimore-protests-pastor-who-eulogized-freddie-gray-says-violence-justice-t17856 (accessed June 11, 2015).
"Two Baltimore Reverends among 50 Arrested at Ferguson, Mo. Protests," CBS Baltimore, October 14, 2014, http://baltimore.cbslocal.com/2014/10/14/two-baltimoreans-among-those-arrested-in-ferguson-monday/ (accessed June 23, 2015).

—Pamela Willwerth Aue

Muhammadu Buhari

1942—

Military officer, head of state

Buhari, Muhammadu, photograph. Pius Utomi Ekpei/AFP/Getty Images.

Muhammadu Buhari was elected president of Nigeria on March 31, 2015, and sworn in nearly two months later in what marked the first peaceful transfer of power in that African nation since the end of British colonial rule in 1960. This was not Buhari's first stint as Nigeria's head of state; in December of 1983 he seized power in a military coup, but his rule ended less than two years later when he, too, was overthrown. Following Buhari's electoral victory, the *Economist* called him "the least bad presidential candidate" on the ballot, but added, "there is reason to hope that he has learnt from past mistakes."

Buhari was born in Daura, in the northern state of Katsina, in 1942, during the era of British colonialism in Nigeria. He was the youngest of more than 20 children born to his father, who died when Buhari was four years old. Buhari graduated from secondary school during the first year of Nigerian independence. He joined the Nigerian Army and almost immediately began additional military training and education. During the following two decades, he advanced through the ranks, ultimately becoming a major general. He attended military training programs in Nigeria, the

United Kingdom, India, and the United States. In 1971 he married and, with his first wife, had five children. Buhari divorced her in 1988, remarried the next year, and had five more children.

His first governmental leadership role came in 1975 when, following a military coup by Murtala Mohammed that ousted Yakubu Gowon, Buhari was appointed governor of the North-Eastern State. This administrative region of Nigeria was much later reorganized into six states: Adamawa, Bauchi, Borno, Gombe, Taraba, and Yobe. In March of 1976, following the assassination of Murtala Mohammed, Buhari was named federal minister of petroleum and natural resources, a position he held until June of 1978. In September of 1979 Buhari returned to his regular army duties.

On December 31, 1983, Buhari participated in another military coup, this one aimed at ridding Nigeria of the elected civilian government of Shehu Shagari. Buhari assumed the top command of the country. He was known for imposing strict discipline on employees, the news media, and other segments of society. Buhari claimed that his zero-tolerance stance on matters of

At a Glance . . .

Born Muhammadu Buhari on December 17, 1942, in Daura, Katsina State, Nigeria; son of Hardo Adamu and Zulaihat Musa; married Safinatu Yusuf in 1971 (divorced, 1988; deceased, 2006); married Aisha Halilu, December 1989; children: Zulaihat (deceased), Fatima, Musa (deceased), Hadiza, Safinatu (first marriage); Aisha, Halima, Yusuf, Zarah, Amina (second marriage). *Military service:* Nigerian Army, 1961–85. *Politics:* All Nigeria People's Party; Congress for Progressive Change; All Progressives Congress. *Religion:* Muslim. *Education:* Katsina Provincial Secondary School (now Government College Katsina), 1956–61; Military Training College, Kaduna, 1961–62; Mons Officer Cadet School, England, 1962–63; Army Mechanical Transport School, United Kingdom, 1964; Defence Services Staff College, Wellington, India, 1973; United States Army War College, 1979–80.

Career: Nigerian Army, 1961–85, achieved rank of major general; governor of North-Eastern State, August 1975–March 1976; federal minister of petroleum and natural resources, March 1976–June 1978; head of state, December 1983–August 1985; Petroleum Trust Fund, chairman, 1995–99; overthrown and imprisoned in Benin City, 1985–88; elected president, 2015—.

Addresses: *Web*—https://www.facebook.com/MuhammaduBuhari.

corruption, as well as over infractions such as tardiness, was necessary to improve Nigerian society; critics accused him of trying to silence dissent and punish dissenters. Human rights observers noted Buhari's increasingly oppressive rule with alarm. Eventually, even Nigeria's military leadership rejected him. Buhari was detained in August of 1985 when Major General Ibrahim Babangida became the military head of state.

Buhari remained under detention until late in 1988. In 1995 he was tapped to become chairman of the Petroleum Trust Fund, where he remained until 1999. Critics raised questions about money missing from the fund during his oversight, yet no official investigation was ever undertaken and no evidence of wrongdoing on Buhari's part ever came to light.

Buhari first ran for the presidency in 2003 as a candidate for the All Nigeria People's Party (ANPP). He was unsuccessful in his effort to oust the incumbent, Olusegun Obasanjo of the People's Democratic Party

(PDP). Four years later Buhari once again represented the ANPP. Again he lost to the PDP candidate, this time to Umaru Musa Yar'Adua.

In 2011 Buhari ran as the candidate of the Congress for Progressive Change, which he cofounded. His opponent was PDP candidate Goodluck Jonathan, who had become president after the death of Yar'Adua the previous year. The incumbent prevailed. During the next four years, however, falling oil prices rocked Nigeria's economy, and terrorist assaults by the Islamic militant group Boko Haram eroded national security. As Jonathan's first elected term as president came to an end, voters perceived that he had not adequately responded to these challenges, so he was vulnerable as a candidate, despite Nigeria's history of reelecting the incumbent president.

In 2014 Buhari made it clear that he intended to try once again to win the presidency through a democratic election. Aligned with the All Progressives Congress this time, Buhari selected a Christian pastor, Yemi Osinbajo, as his running mate. This move was intended to reassure Nigerians that Buhari, a Muslim from the north, would not discriminate against Christians in the southern part of the country. During the campaigns, Jonathan tried to have Buhari disqualified over a question having to do with his education, but the attempt failed.

Terrorist violence and unrest caused the election to be postponed for several weeks, but on March 31, 2015, Buhari finally made history by defeating incumbent president Goodluck Jonathan. Voters had lost confidence in Jonathan due in part to his handling of terrorist incursions by Boko Haram, the most infamous of which was the kidnapping of more than 275 school girls in Chibok in April 2014. Beset by an economy reeling from low global oil prices and fearful of Boko Haram's potential to inflict further harm on their country, Nigerian voters decided to take their chances with Buhari. The election was also noteworthy as the first democratic succession of power from one party to another in Nigeria since the end of British colonial rule in 1960. Buhari was sworn in as president on May 29, 2015.

Sources

Books

"Buhari, Muhammadu," in *An African Biographical Dictionary,* Grey House, 2006, pp. 94–95.

Periodicals

Christian Century, April 29, 2015, p. 15.
Economist, April 4, 2015, p. 12.
International Business Times, June 12, 2015.
New African, February 2015, p. 16.
New York Times, April 2, 2015.

Online

Culliane, Susannah, and Stephanie Busari, "Who is Nigeria's Muhammadu Buhari?" CNN.com, March 31, 2015, http://www.cnn.com/2015/03/31/afri ca/nigeria-muhammadu-buhari/ (accessed June 12, 2015).

Muhammed, Garba, "Suicide Bombs in Nigeria's Kaduna Kill 82, Ex-leader Buhari Targeted," Reuters (UK), July 23, 2014, http://uk.reuters.com/article/ 2014/07/23/uk-nigeria-violence-idUKKBN0FS1 9N20140723 (accessed June 12, 2015).

"Nigeria's Muhammadu Buhari in Profile," BBC News, http://www.bbc.com/news/world-africa-12890807 March 31, 2015, (accessed June 12, 2015).

"Things You Never Knew about Aisha Buhari," naij - archives, March 23, 2015, http://www.nairaland .com/2213626/things-never-knew-aisha-buhari (accessed August 3, 2015)

—Pamela Willwerth Aue

Lorenzo Cain

1986—

Professional baseball player

Cain, Lorenzo, photograph. Hannah Foslien/Getty Images.

Lorenzo Cain is a standout center fielder with the Kansas City Royals. Despite having never played organized baseball until his sophomore year in high school, Cain has developed into one of the best defensive outfielders in the game, known for his combination of elite speed and exceptional instincts. At the same time, he has proven himself a reliable contributor on offense, batting .282 with 73 stolen bases over his first six major league seasons. Cain first rose to national prominence during the 2014 postseason, when his combination of stellar fielding and timely offense helped lead Kansas City to its first World Series berth in nearly 30 years. In addition to his abilities on the field, Cain brings a strong leadership presence to the Royals clubhouse, energizing his teammates with the enthusiasm with which he approaches the game. "You're talking about a guy who loves life," teammate Eric Hosmer told Andy McCullough of the *Kansas City Star* in 2014. "Enjoys every minute of it."

Discovered Baseball in High School

Lorenzo Cain followed an improbable path to baseball stardom. He was born on April 13, 1986, in Valdosta, Georgia, and raised in Madison County, Florida. His father died when he was four years old, leaving his mother, Patricia, to raise Cain and his brother by herself. During his childhood, Cain devoted much of his free time to helping his mother run the household, leaving him few opportunities to compete in athletics. He eventually developed an interest in basketball and tried out for the Madison County High School team as a freshman. After failing to make the roster, however, Cain looked for another outlet for his athletic ability. Prohibited from playing football by his mother, he decided to try baseball, even though he had barely played the sport as a child.

Although he had never played organized baseball, Cain earned a chance to compete during his sophomore year, when the school's junior varsity squad found itself one player short of a full roster. His lack of experience was evident from the beginning. Upon taking the field for the first time, Cain wore a glove on his throwing hand, and he had no idea how to grip a baseball bat properly. Cain also demonstrated little understanding of the rules of the sport, running the bases on fly balls

At a Glance . . .

Born Lorenzo Lamar Cain on April 13, 1986, in Valdosta, GA; son of Patricia Cain; married Jenny, 2013; children: Cameron. *Education:* Attended Tallahassee Community College, 2004–05.

Career: Milwaukee Brewers, center fielder, 2010; Kansas City Royals, center fielder, 2011—.

Awards: Most Valuable Player, American League Championship Series, 2014.

Addresses: *Home*—Norman, OK. *Office*—c/o Kansas City Royals, 1 Royal Way, Kansas City, MO 64129.

and standing still on grounders to the infield. "I don't even think he had *seen* a baseball game," his first coach, Barney Myers, later told McCullough. "Much less played in one."

Despite these miscues, Cain showed signs of natural talent during those early practices. In particular, his ability to anticipate where to run to catch a fly ball, almost from the moment the ball left the hitter's bat, showed that he had rare instincts for the defensive aspects of the game. More importantly, the young outfielder's dedication to improvement set him apart from other young players. From the beginning, he pleaded with Myers to hit fly balls to him after practice, long after his teammates had gone home. At the same time, he showed a comparable dedication for improving his offense, spending his school lunch hours taking swings in the batting cage. Before long, Cain proved himself a capable hitter, demonstrating a power and plate discipline that was unique for a player with so little experience.

By his junior season, Cain had earned a spot on the varsity baseball team, although he saw little playing time that year. His potential became evident when he was a senior, as his combination of defensive prowess, athletic ability, and talent for hitting began to attract the attention of professional scouts. In 2004, during the spring of his senior year, Cain was surprised to receive a phone call from a scout for the Milwaukee Brewers, who informed the young outfielder that the club had chosen him in the 17th round of the Major League Baseball amateur draft. At first Cain did not grasp the magnitude of having been drafted by a professional baseball team. "I just went back to playing video games," Cain recalled to McCullough. "I didn't think anything about it. The next thing I know, it was all in the paper. I was like, 'Oh, this is a big deal.'"

Worked His Way to the Majors

Even with this rare opportunity, Cain was initially reluctant to leave home, opting to spend a year playing at Tallahassee Community College before joining Milwaukee's farm affiliate in Arizona. He made his minor league debut in 2005, appearing in 50 games for the organization's rookie team, batting .356 with 12 stolen bases. His first full season came a year later, when he hit .307 and stole 34 bases in 132 games with the franchise's Single-A squad in West Virginia. Over the next four years, Cain slowly worked his way through the Milwaukee farm system, putting in time with the club's Single-A+, Double-A, and Triple-A affiliates, while also participating in the organization's Arizona Fall League. He finally earned his first promotion to the big leagues in 2010, when he appeared in 43 games for the Brewers, batting .306 with a home run and 17 runs batted in (RBIs).

Although Cain's initial major league performance showed promise, he was not a part of Milwaukee's long-term plans, and in December 2010 he was traded to the Kansas City Royals as part of a six-player deal. The change temporarily derailed his ascent to the big leagues, and he spent nearly the entire 2011 season playing in the minors before finally joining the major league squad in 2012. During this period, Cain's progress was also delayed by injuries, caused primarily by his unorthodox running style. After being limited to only 176 games in 2012 and 2013, Cain began working with a track coach at Kansas City Kansas Community College in the off-season, with the aim of correcting his stride. He also devoted time after games and practice to working with the team's training staff, intent on remaining healthy enough to endure the rigors of a full major league schedule.

Cain's breakout season came in 2014, when he played a career-high 133 games for the Royals, batting .301 with five home runs, 53 RBIs, and 28 stolen bases, while also establishing himself as the anchor of the team's outfield defense. He elevated his performance during the 2014 playoffs, notably during the American League Championship Series against the Baltimore Orioles, when he batted .533 while making a number of game-saving plays in center field. Cain's play in Kansas City's four-game sweep of Baltimore earned him series most valuable player honors.

Cain produced another strong performance during the team's World Series matchup against the San Francisco Giants, when he batted .308 with two doubles and four RBIs. Although the Royals ultimately fell in seven games, Cain's sudden rise to stardom gave the team reason for optimism heading into the future. He continued to impress during the early phase of the 2015 season, batting .294 over the team's first 61 games, as the Royals took over first place in the American League Central Division. More than anything, the star outfielder's will to win was a key

component in the team's continued success. "It's a long season," Cain told the *Topeka Capital Journal* in April of 2015. "There's going to be ups and downs, bumps and bruises. But to a man, we all want to get back to the playoffs. That's where we all want to be."

Sources

Periodicals

Baltimore Sun, October 12, 2014, p. D5.
McClatchy-Tribune Business News, June 27, 2010.
Topeka (KS) Capital Journal, April 21, 2015, p. B1.
Washington Post, October 30, 2014.

Online

"Lorenzo Cain," Baseball-Reference.com, http://www.baseball-reference.com/players/c/cainlo01.shtml (accessed June 23, 2015).

McCullough, Andy, "A Late Bloomer, Royals Outfielder Lorenzo Cain Making Up for Lost Time," KansasCity.com, May 23, 2014, http://www.kansascity.com/sports/mlb/kansas-city-royals/article402287/A-late-bloomer-Royals-outfielder-Lorenzo-Cain-making-up-for-lost-time.html (accessed June 23, 2015).

Schoenfield, David, "Lorenzo Cain Catching Everything in Center," ESPN.com, October 5, 2014, http://espn.go.com/blog/sweetspot/post/_/id/52293/lorenzo-cain-catching-everything-in-center (accessed June 23, 2015).

White, Paul, and Rachel Axon, "Lorenzo Cain's Road from 'Terrible' to the World Series," USAToday.com, October 21, 2014, http://www.usatoday.com/story/sports/mlb/2014/10/20/lorenzo-cain-late-bloomer-kansas-city-royals-world-series/17640339/ (accessed June 23, 2015).

—Stephen Meyer

Ben Carson

1951—

Neurosurgeon, researcher, educator, author, politician

Carson, Ben, photograph. Andrew Burton/Getty Images News/ Getty Images.

Dr. Benjamin Carson is a world-renowned neurosurgeon and former director of pediatric neurosurgery at Johns Hopkins Hospital in Baltimore, Maryland. Described as "one of the acknowledged miracle workers of modern medicine" by Christopher Phillips of *Reader's Digest,* Carson received recognition throughout the medical community for his skill in performing complex and delicate neurosurgical procedures, primarily on children. Among his accomplishments are a number of successful hemispherectomies, a complicated surgical process in which a portion of the brain of a critically ill seizure victim or other neurologically diseased patient is removed to restore normal function. Carson performed his most famous operation—one that gained him international acclaim—in 1987, when he separated a pair of Siamese twins who had been joined at the back of their heads. In the landmark operation, which lasted 22 hours, Carson led a surgical team consisting of 70 doctors, nurses, and technicians.

Carson is also an accomplished author, publishing several best-selling nonfiction books on such subjects as individual achievement and the American political sys-

tem. After retiring from Johns Hopkins in 2013, Carson embarked on a career in politics, sparking controversy for his outspoken criticism of President Barack Obama, as well as for his staunchly conservative views on social issues such as same-sex marriage.

Carson's rise to the top of his field began in the rough inner-city neighborhoods of Detroit, Michigan. Raised by his divorced mother, Carson was a failing student with a penchant for fighting until the age of 10, when his mother imposed a reading program— two books weekly—on him and strictly limited his television viewing. Carson soon became an avid reader and his grades improved, putting him near the top of his class. In high school he continued to excel, so much so that he received offers from several Ivy League universities. Carson attended Yale University on a scholarship and went on to study medicine at the University of Michigan, where his initial plan was to become a psychotherapist. During his first year of medical school, however, he discovered neurosurgery. "I loved dissecting things," Carson told *Ebony.* "And I always felt that I was very good with my hands. Neurosurgery was a natural for me."

Performed Complex, High-Risk Surgical Procedures

Carson did both his internship in general surgery and his residency in neurosurgery at Baltimore's Johns Hopkins Hospital, which is considered one of the nation's elite medical centers. He became the hospital's first-ever black neurosurgical resident. In 1983 he moved with his wife to Perth, Australia, where he was senior neurosurgical resident at the Sir Charles Gairdner Hospital, one of Australia's leading centers for brain surgery. Because of the lack of neurosurgeons in Australia and Carson's advancing medical skills, he obtained much valuable work experience during his year at the hospital. "I was operating so much," he told *Ebony*, "I was able to concentrate several years of experience into one year." He returned to Johns Hopkins in 1984 and quickly became one of the hospital's leading surgeons. Within a year he was promoted to director of pediatric neurosurgery and, at age 34, was one of the youngest directors of a surgical division in the United States.

Carson rapidly gained a reputation within the medical community as a skilled surgeon who was especially adept at performing operations that typically carried high mortality rates. Such is the case with hemispherectomies and the separation of craniopagus conjoined twins—Siamese twins who are joined together at the head—a procedure that usually results in the loss of one twin. The twins whom Carson operated on in 1987 were joined through a common blood vessel at the back of their heads. He devised a plan to separate the twins by completely shutting down their blood flow, severing the common vessel, and then restoring their individual circulatory systems. Even though the entire procedure lasted 22 hours, Carson and another surgeon had only one hour to conduct the actual surgery and restoration. Carson commented to *Ebony* on the success of the operation, "Not only was it exciting to be part of a history-making event, but the significant fact is that we put together an incredibly complex scene with a team of incredibly competent people who submerged their egos and pulled off what was perhaps the most complex surgical feat in the history of mankind." Since 1987 Carson has participated in four other twin separation surgeries, including a rare attempt to separate adult conjoined twins in 2003.

Besides his duties as director of pediatric neurosurgery at Johns Hopkins Hospital, Carson was also a professor at the hospital's medical school on subjects including neurosurgery, plastic surgery, oncology, and pediatrics. His neurosurgery practice saw him completing between 400 and 500 operations per year, including a famous case in 1999 in which he performed a hemispherectomy on a 15-year-old girl. The radical procedure, which involves the removal of half the brain, is used on children in cases of severe seizure disorder and other diseases that affect one side of the brain, such as Rasmussen's syndrome. Carson developed techniques that have dramatically improved the success of this procedure, saving and improving the lives of many children. In 2001 he worked on treatments for a type of cancer that attacks the brain stem. According to *Time*, "The tumor's location makes surgery difficult and prospects for survival bleak. But those are exactly the kinds of odds that Carson has faced before and beaten."

Became a Best-Selling Author

As his fame grew, Carson realized that his rags-to-riches life story could serve as an inspiration to young people. In 1990 he decided to share this story with the public by writing the memoir *Gifted Hands,* in which he detailed how he rose from poverty in Detroit's inner city to become one of the world's preeminent neurosurgeons. The book became a best seller and won Blackbook Publishing's Humanitarian Award in 1991.

Carson followed his memoir with the self-help book *Think Big: Unleashing Your Potential for Excellence* in 1992. The book outlines Carson's personal steps for success, with a focus on the importance of education, religion, and positive thinking. Subsequent writings have followed *Think Big*'s pattern of pairing experiences from the surgeon's life with inspirational philosophies or life strategies. In 1999 he published his third book, *The Big Picture: Getting a Perspective on What's Really Important in Life,* and in 2008 he released *Take the Risk: Learning to Identify, Choose, and Live with Acceptable Risk.*

The proceeds from all of his books go to the Carson Scholars Fund, which Carson and his wife, Lacena, established in 1994, with a personal commitment to donate $500,000. As Carson told the *Saturday Evening Post,* "[Education] was probably the single most important factor that distinguished me from others who grew up in the same environment. Fortunately, I recognized early on the difference education makes in our society." He was dismayed that schools routinely award athletes with trophies and rallies but typically ignore academic prowess. "I find that in a lot of schools, kids think it's not cool to be smart," he told *Time.* He hoped to change that with the scholarship fund, which awards students in grades 4 through 12 who not only achieve good grades but also demonstrate a commitment to their community. The first recipient went on to the Massachusetts Institute of Technology and maintained a perfect grade-point average there. As of 2009, the Carson Scholars Fund had chapters in 8 states, was active in 18 others, and was working toward its declared goal of granting a scholarship in each of the 50 states.

Celebrated for His Achievements

Carson has been showered with awards for his achievements in both medicine and philanthropy. He has been awarded more than 40 honorary doctorates from universities throughout the world and received recognitions, including the Certificate of Honor for Outstanding Achievement in the Field of Medicine from the National Medical Fellowship (1988), the American Black Achievement Award from Ebony & Johnson Publications (1988), Clinical Practitioner of the Year from the National Medical Association (1988), and memberships in the Alpha Omega Alpha Medical Honor Society since 1991 and in the Horatio Alger Association of Distinguished Americans since 1994. Additionally, in 2000 the Library of Congress, in celebration of its bicentennial, declared Carson a "Living Legend"; in 2001 *Time* declared him one of the top 20 doctors and scientists in the United States; in 2004 he was asked to join the President's Council on Bioethics; in 2008 a new pediatric neurosurgery professorship at Johns Hopkins Medical School was endowed in his honor; and later that year he was awarded the Presidential Medal of Freedom, the highest civilian honor given by the U.S. government.

Increasing Carson's exposure to a mass audience, in 2009 *Gifted Hands* was adapted as a television movie, starring Academy Award winner Cuba Gooding Jr. The film received mixed reviews, with some critics faulting its conventional structure and lack of suspense. However, most critics went out of their way to praise the lead performances by Gooding and Kimberly Elise, in the role of Carson's mother, Sonya. In the *Hollywood Reporter,* Ray Richmond noted that Gooding's portrayal of Carson "does him more than proud with a portrayal at once sensitively wrought and quietly moving."

Despite these accolades and his growing public profile, Carson remained modest about his individual achievements. A devout Seventh-day Adventist, he views his medical accomplishments in terms of his religious faith. "God created the body," he told *Ebony.* "He knows more about it than anybody else and can heal virtually every problem. It's only a matter of whether we're willing to let Him work through us." In an article that Carson wrote for *Ebony,* he cited his mother's influence as crucial to his success. He singled out her philosophy of "no excuses for anything" and "if anybody can do something, you can do it better."

Embarked on Political Career

In 2012 Carson and his wife coauthored *America the Beautiful: Rediscovering What Made This Nation Great.* A celebration of what Carson views as traditional American values, the work also offered a stern warning, asserting that expanded government power and a steadily growing welfare system are imperiling the nation's economic and cultural future. The publication of *America the Beautiful* excited the country's political conservatives while offering an in-depth look into Carson's ideological views.

Carson continued to garner notice for his conservative beliefs in February of 2013, when he was invited to serve as the keynote speaker at the National Prayer Breakfast in Washington, DC. With President Barack Obama seated nearby, Carson launched into a scathing attack of Obama's tenure in office, condemning the president's tax policies while equating the Patient Protection and Affordable Care Act of 2010 with

"slavery." Despite its controversial tone, Carson's speech energized conservative voters across the country. Shortly after his remarks, a political action group formed the National Draft Ben Carson for President Committee in the hope of persuading the surgeon to run for the nation's highest office in 2016.

After retiring from Johns Hopkins in July of 2013, Carson began to seek ways to increase his public profile. A week after leaving the medical profession, the former surgeon began writing a weekly political column for the *Washington Times*. In 2014 he published a new book, *One Nation: What We Can Do to Save America's Future,* in which he expanded on his conservative ideals. As he embarked on a book tour, he began visiting with political constituencies in electoral districts throughout the country in an effort to gauge support for a potential presidential run. Although Carson's harsh criticism of the president alienated many African-American voters, his views on such issues as same-sex marriage, taxation, and health care found widespread support among conservative groups. In March of 2015, he filed paperwork with the Federal Election Committee for his presidential run. Although registered as an independent, Carson announced that he would seek the Republican nomination in 2016. Meanwhile, by May of 2015 the Draft Ben Carson for President Committee had raised $16 million to support his campaign. As a world-famous surgeon who attributed his success to both hard work and religious faith, it seemed that Carson's background could prove to be his most powerful asset as he moved forward with his political career.

Selected writings

(With Cecil Murphey) *Gifted Hands,* Zondervan/ HarperCollins, 1990.

(With Cecil Murphey) *Think Big: Unleashing Your Potential for Excellence,* Zondervan/HarperCollins, 1992.

(With Gregg Lewis) *The Big Picture: Getting a Perspective on What's Really Important in Life,* Zondervan/HarperCollins, 1999.

(With Gregg Lewis) *Take the Risk: Learning to Identify, Choose, and Live with Acceptable Risk,* Zondervan, 2008.

(With Candy Carson) *America the Beautiful: Rediscovering What Made This Nation Great,* Zondervan, 2012.

(With Candy Carson) *One Vote: Make Your Voice Heard,* Tyndale, 2014.

(With Candy Carson) *One Nation: What We Can Do to Save America's Future,* Sentinel, 2014.

(With Gregg Lewis and Deborah Shaw Lewis) *You Have a Brain: A Teen's Guide to Think Big,* Zondervan, 2015.

Sources

Periodicals

Baltimore Sun, March 17, 2013, p. A1.
Black Enterprise, October 1988.
Chicago Tribune, March 24, 2013.
Ebony, January 1988; May 1990.
Hollywood Reporter, February 5, 2009.
Jet, September 28, 1987; August 2, 1999, p. 38.
Nation's Cities Weekly, December 17, 2001, p. 49.
People Weekly, June 21, 1999, p. 137.
PR Newswire, April 3, 2000.
Reader's Digest, April 1990.
Saturday Evening Post, July 1999, p. 50.
Time, August 20, 2001, p. 34.
Washington Post, August 29, 2014; May 2, 2015.

Online

Carson Scholars Fund, http://carsonscholars.org (accessed June 22, 2015).

"Hopkins Surgeon Ben Carson Receives Medal of Freedom," Johns Hopkins Children's Center, June 20, 2008, http://www.hopkinschildrens.org/news Detail.aspx?id=4946 (accessed June 22, 2015).

—Gloria Lam, Candace LaBalle, Derek Jacques, and Stephen Meyer

The Chantels

Female vocal group

The Chantels were one of the first important female vocal groups of the late 1950s, scoring a string of hits between 1957 and 1960, including "Maybe," the group's best-selling single. Following a series of unsuccessful recordings thereafter, the original group broke up in 1960. A few years later they regrouped with a new lead singer and a different record label, but they fared little better, recording their last single to reach the charts in 1963. Nevertheless, over the next five decades, the Chantels continued to perform and record with a rotating lineup on various record labels, putting out a new album, *Eternally,* in 2010.

The Chantels, photograph. Gilles Petard/Redferns/Getty Images.

Recorded Biggest Hit as Teenagers

The group formed when Arlene Smith, Lois Harris, Sonia Goring, Rene Minus, and Jackie Landry began singing together as elementary school students at St. Anthony of Padua School in the Bronx, New York. Calling themselves the Chantels, they performed in the school's gymnasium after home basketball games and at talent shows held at local public schools. In 1957 the girls, who were then between 14 and 17, approached Richard Barrett, who was the lead singer of a doo-wop group called the Valentines and a producer for George Goldner's End Records. They chose Barrett because he

had been actively involved in building the careers of other young doo-wop acts, including 13-year-old Frankie Lymon, who had a hit in 1956 with "Why Do Fools Fall in Love?"

After hearing the Chantels sing "The Plea," Barrett arranged for them to audition for Goldner, who immediately ushered them into the recording studio. The group recorded their first single, with "The Plea" on the B-side and a new song, "He's Gone," on the A-side. Confident in the results, Barrett convinced the renowned New York disc jockey Jocko to bring the Chantels on stage at the Apollo Theater in Harlem for an unbilled performance of "He's Gone." The group was a hit, and "He's Gone" climbed to number 71 on the Billboard Hot 100 singles chart.

The group's next single, "Maybe," featuring Barrett on the piano, was recorded in an acoustic-friendly church in Midtown Manhattan. An instant success, the song reached number two on the R&B chart and spent 18 weeks at number 15 on the Billboard Hot 100. The single was, in fact, more successful than the charts suggested, as other small record labels sold pirated copies of the song. In all, it has been estimated that more than a million copies were sold. Although "Maybe" was written by the 16-year-old Smith (who

also contributed lead vocals), the song was originally credited to Goldner.

Dropped by Their Record Label

"Maybe" proved to be the Chantels' most famous song, both for its musical prowess and for its impact on girl groups that followed. In 2011 *Rolling Stone* ranked "Maybe" at number 199 on its list of the "500 Greatest Songs of All Time." As Dave Thompson of AllMusic.com recalled, "'Maybe' was, arguably, the first true glimmering of the girl group sound … With its entire lyric focused around Smith's ability to draw the title alone out of virtual verse-length, the song itself is built firmly in the tradition of the doo wop street singers then taking the charts by storm."

The Chantels were primarily influenced by the sounds they had grown up with, especially gospel and classical music. The new sound of rock and roll also made an impact, however, and in an interview with music writer Tony Fletcher, Smith noted the musical influences of the Drifters, Joni James, Johnnie Ray, Peggy Lee, and the Harptones. Upon hearing the Harptones for the first time, Smith told Fletcher, "I never heard harmony like that, never heard a voice like that."

Following the success of "Maybe," Barrett quit the Valentines to focus on producing. The Chantels returned to the studio and in 1958 released "Every Night (I Pray)," which peaked at number 39 on the pop chart and number 16 on the R&B list. That year the Chantels became the first female R&B group to release an EP, the four-song *I Love You So*. The title song hit number 42 on the Hot 100 and number 14 on the R&B singles chart. End Records followed up with a second Chantels EP, *C'est Si Bon*, that same year, a risky move for a young group with only a handful of songs. The gamble did not pay off, and the second EP was considered a failure. The following year, the Chantels made just recording, and by 1960 the group was no longer listed with End Records. Harris, recalling reports that they had been dropped from the label, shared in a 2014 interview with the blog *Musicguy247*, "They did not drop us. They told us that they were bankrupt and they in fact stole a lot of our money."

Regrouped with New Lead Singer

Assuming that their time together was up, the group members made alternative plans. Landry secured a job at a bank, and Harris began planning her wedding. Smith, still in school (along with Minus and Goring), resumed solo performing. Within a year, however, Barrett was back in touch, asking the Chantels to regroup and record a new song, "Look in My Eyes." Harris, recently married, did not return to the Chantels, while Smith was contractually obligated to her solo career, having signed with Big Top records.

Minus, Landry, and Goring jumped at the opportunity, and Barrett introduced them to vocalist Annette Smith (unrelated to Arlene Smith), who became the new lead. Signing with Carlton Records, the quartet recorded "Look in My Eyes," along with the aptly titled "Glad to Be Back" for the B-side. When "Look in My Eyes" climbed to number 19 on the Billboard Hot 100, it seemed as if more success would follow. Within a year, however, both Landry and Annette Smith left to have babies, halting the group's momentum. Yvonne Fair and Sandra Dawn (as lead vocalist) were brought in to keep the quartet intact, but a couple of less successful recordings prompted their label to drop them.

With Barrett, the Chantels signed with Ludix in 1963 and recorded the single "Eternally," which peaked at number 77 on the Billboard Hot 100, their last song to reach the charts. Ludix dropped the Chantels after one more recording in 1963, and in 1965, the group made one more recording for TCF/Arrawak before they were dropped again. Despite their few recordings during these years, the Chantels embarked on a busy touring schedule, performing at clubs and college fraternity houses on the East coast and in Canada. During this time Landry and Annette Smith performed intermittently, and another singer, Helen Leibowitz, filled in from time to time. Limiting their number to five, the availability of all members meant that one had to sit

out. The result was a roster of five that changed regularly. By this point, however, the group was traveling with their own band, the Brooklyn-based Dayton Selby Trio, which provided a sense of cohesion.

Split with Barrett

By 1965 disagreements between Barrett and the Chantels had resulted in a split, and the Chantels became self-managed for the first time. At this point, Minus was singing lead, and Leibowitz had become a regular member. Following their unsuccessful record with TCF/Arrawak, the Chantels signed with Verve, recording two singles for the label in 1966. After those records flopped, the group disbanded in 1967. Arlene Smith, meanwhile, continued to perform and record as a soloist.

In 1970 RCA orchestrated a reunion of the Chantels, and all of the original members, including Arlene Smith, signed on to record "Love Makes All the Difference in the World/I'm Gonna Win Him Back." Despite the hype created by RCA, the record fell short, and Smith once again returned to her solo career. The other members remained together, enlisting Christine Iron to take Smith's place, and for two years they played the New York club scene before calling it quits once again. More than two decades later, the original members were back on stage, inspired by their 1995 induction into the United in Group Harmony Hall of Fame. A Rhythm and Blues Foundation Pioneer Award in 1996 continued the momentum for all but Arlene Smith, who departed once again. In 1997 she was replaced by Ami Ortiz. When Landry died of breast cancer that year, the group did not replace her and became a quartet.

In 2002 the Chantels received inductions into the Bronx, New York Walk of Fame and the Vocal Group Hall of Fame. In 2004 they were presented with a Pioneer Image Award from the Atlanta Doo-Wop Association, and in 2007 they earned a star on Wildwood, New Jersey's Pacific Avenue of the Stars. As a quartet, Ortiz, Goring, Harris, and Minus continue to perform across the United States. In 2010 they released a new album, *Eternally.*

Selected discography

Singles

"He's Gone/The Plea," 1957.
"Maybe/Come My Little Baby," 1957.
"Every Night/Whoever You Are," 1958.
"I Love You So/How Could You Call It Off," 1958.
"Sure of Love/Prayee," 1958.
"Congratulations/If You Try," 1958.
"I Can't Take It/Never Let Go," 1958.
"Goodbye to Love/I'm Confessing," 1959.
"Whoever You Are/how Could You Call It Off," 1960.

"Look in My Eyes/Glad to Be Back," 1961.
"Well I Told You/Still," 1961.
"Summertime/Here It Comes Again," 1962.
"Eternally/Swamp Water," 1963.
"That's Why You're Happy/Some Tears Fall Dry," 1963.
"Take Me As I Am/There's No Forgetting You," 1965.
"You're Welcome to My Heart/Soul of a Soldier," 1966.
"It's Just Me/Indian Giver," 1966.
"Love Makes All the Difference in the World/I'm Gonna Win Him Back," 1970.

Albums

I Love You So (EP) (includes "I Love You So"), End, 1958.
C'est Si Bon (EP), End, 1958.
We Are the Chantels, End, 1958.
The Chantels, End, 1958.
There's Our Song Again, End, 1961.
The Chantels on Tour, Carlton, 1958.
The Chantels Sing Their Favorites, Forum, 1964.
Arlene Smith and The Chantels, Murray Hill, 1987.
Eternally, Chantel Records, 2010.

Sources

Books

Clemente, John, *Girl Groups: Fabulous Females Who Rocked the World,* Krause, 2000.
Fletcher, Tony, *All Hopped Up and Ready to Go: Music from the Streets of New York 1927–77,* W. W. Norton, 2009.

Periodicals

Rolling Stone, April 7, 2011.

Online

The Chantels, http://www.thechantels.com/ (accessed June 16, 2015).
"The Chantels," Vocal Group Hall of Fame, http://www.vocalgroup.org/inductees/the_chantels.html (accessed June 16, 2015).
James, Gary, "Interview with Arlene Smith of the Chantels," Classic Bands, http://www.classicbands.com/ChantelsInterview.html (accessed June 16, 2015).
Thompson, Dave, "Maybe," AllMusic.com, http://www.allmusic.com/song/maybe-mt0007747018 (accessed June 16, 2015).
Von Bernewitz, Robert, "The Chantels—An Interview with Lois Harris from the Pioneering Girl Group," *Musicguy247* (blog), May 2014, http://musicguy247.typepad.com/my-blog/2014/05/the-chantels-an-interview-with-lois-harris-from-the-pioneering-girl-group.html (accessed June 16, 2015).

—Candice Mancini

Sonny Clark

1931–1963

Jazz pianist

Clark, Sonny, photograph. Michael Ochs Archives/Getty Images.

Although his music career lasted scarcely more than a decade, jazz pianist Sonny Clark left a significant body of work and a lasting impression on all who heard him. Largely self-taught, Clark backed dozens of leading figures, including vocalist Dinah Washington and saxophonists Jackie McLean, Sonny Rollins, and Dexter Gordon. He is best remembered, however, for the long string of albums that he completed as a bandleader, the last of which was released just months before his death in 1963 at age 31. A favorite of his peers, who appreciated both his skills at the keyboard and his engaging personality, Clark had "an intricate and hard-swinging harmonic sensibility," noted Thom Jurek of AllMusic.com, "that was full of nuance and detail."

The son of a coal miner who had moved north from his native Georgia, Conrad Yeatis Clark was born on July 21, 1931, in Herminie, a small but ethnically diverse town in western Pennsylvania. Known as "Sonny" from an early age, he moved to nearby Pittsburgh at age 12. The youngest of eight children, he began his study of the piano with the encouragement of an older brother. His skills developed quickly, and he was playing for pocket change even before he relocated to

Pittsburgh. He remained in that city until about 1951, when he moved to California and launched his career in earnest.

On the West Coast, Clark found a vibrant and close-knit jazz scene and a "cool," relatively relaxed style of play. His partners during this period included clarinetist Buddy DeFranco, with whom he toured widely, and Howard Rumsey, a bassist based in Southern California. Clark's reputation there grew steadily, and he had no shortage of work; as he told critic Leonard Feather in liner notes posted on Eric B. Olsen's Hard Bop Homepage, "I could have stayed as long as I liked." By his own account, however, Clark missed his family in and around Pittsburgh, and in 1957 he became an accompanist for Washington, largely because she was based on the East Coast.

It was also around this time that Clark began a long and successful collaboration with Blue Note Records. Although he had done some work at recording studios on the West Coast, backing DeFranco and others, it was not until his debut with Blue Note that he began to draw the attention of record buyers around the nation. His first album for that label, *Dial "S" for Sonny* (1957),

At a Glance . . .

Born Conrad Yeatis Clark on July 21, 1931, in Herminie, PA; died on January 13, 1963, in New York, NY; son of a coal miner.

Career: Jazz pianist, 1950s–63.

was an unqualified success, charming critics and casual fans alike with its bright tones and complex rhythms. Completed with the help of an excellent backing group that included saxophonist Hank Mobley, trombonist Curtis Fuller, and trumpeter Art Farmer, it was soon followed by *Sonny's Crib* (1957), an album prized by many jazz aficionados for its memorable exchanges between Clark and saxophone legend John Coltrane, and *Cool Struttin'* (1958), a work that Jurek described as "Clark's classic." Anchored by its brilliant title track, one of the pianist's own compositions, *Cool Struttin'* "has earned nearly a cult status among hardcore jazz followers," noted Jim Merod of the website The Stereo Times.

Although Clark's subsequent recordings were not quite as popular as that masterpiece, virtually all won strong reviews. Typical of his work in this period was *Leapin' and Lopin'* (1961), which several critics ranked on a par with *Cool Struttin'*. Its champions over the years have included C. Andrew Hovan of the website All About Jazz, who has described it as a "ringer," adding, "In terms of musicianship, variety, memorable originals, and pacing, it's an album th[at] is simply hard to surpass."

In addition to his own recordings, Clark continued to find the time to back other artists, both on tour and in the studio. Over the course of just two years in the early 1960s, for example, he made important contributions to a host of albums, including McLean's *Jackie's Bag* (1960) and *A Fickle Sonance* (1961); guitarist Grant Green's *Nigeria* and *Oleo* (both of which were recorded 1962 but not released until 1980); Rollins's *Sonny's Time* (1962); and Gordon's *Go* (1962). Of these, *Jackie's Bag* and *Go* drew particularly wide praise. Often regarded as exemplars of hard bop, the swinging, blues-tinged sound that dominated jazz at the time, they solidified Clark's growing reputation for sensitive, understated accompaniment. His skills as a composer, meanwhile, came to the fore on McLean's *A Fickle Sonance,* which featured two of his pieces ("Five Will Get You Ten" and "Sundu").

Amid this success, however, there were indications of trouble in Clark's personal life. Like many working musicians he spent much of his time in nightclubs, where long hours, professional pressures, and the ready availability of drugs and alcohol proved a dangerous combination. Clark became addicted to heroin, the

effects of which he managed to hide for a time from all but his closest colleagues. By the end of 1962, however, it was clear that he had a serious problem. Just weeks later, on January 13, 1963, he died of a heart attack in New York City. Although a variety of health problems likely contributed to his death, his addiction is considered to have been the precipitating factor.

In the decades since his passing there have been a number of efforts to keep Clark's memory and music alive. Much of his work has been remastered and rereleased, and several musicians have performed in his honor. In the mid-1980s, for example, the composer and multi-instrumentalist John Zorn cofounded the Sonny Clark Memorial Quartet, which recorded an album called *Voodoo,* whose title track was a new rendition of a piece that Clark had written for *Leapin' and Lopin'*. As of 2015 the best known of these tributes remained "NYC's No Lark," a composition written soon after Clark's death by his friend and fellow pianist Bill Evans. That piece, whose title is an anagram of "Sonny Clark," was featured on Evans's highly regarded album *Conversations With Myself* (1963); it has since become a familiar standard to jazz fans around the world.

Selected discography

Dial "S" for Sonny, Blue Note, 1957.
Sonny's Crib, Blue Note, 1957.
Cool Struttin' (includes "Cool Struttin'"), Blue Note, 1958.
Jackie McLean, *Jackie's Bag,* Blue Note, 1960.
Jackie McLean, *A Fickle Sonance* (includes "Five Will Get You Ten" and "Sundu"), Blue Note, 1961.
Leapin' and Lopin' (includes "Voodoo"), Blue Note, 1961.
Grant Green, *Nigeria,* Blue Note, 1962 (released 1980).
Grant Green, *Oleo,* Blue Note, 1962 (released 1980).
Sonny Rollins, *Sonny's Time,* Jazzland, 1962.
Dexter Gordon, *Go,* Blue Note, 1962.

Sources

Online

Hovan, C. Andrew, "New Blue Note RVGs: Three Tenors, a Bone, and Sonny," All About Jazz, March 19, 2009, http://www.allaboutjazz.com/new-blue-note-rvgs-three-tenors-a-bone-and-sonny-by-c-andrew-hovan.php (accessed June 25, 2015).
Jurek, Thom, "Sonny Clark: Artist Biography," AllMusic.com, http://www.allmusic.com/artist/sonny-clark-mn0000036934/biography (accessed June 9, 2015).
Merod, Jim, "John Hicks and Gust Tsilis at the Atheneum, La Jolla, California," Stereo Times, September 10, 2002, http://www.stereotimes.com/mr091002.shtml (accessed June 25, 2015).
Olsen, Eric B., and Leonard Feather, "Sonny Clark,"

Hard Bop Homepage, http://hardbop.tripod.com/clark.html (accessed June 9, 2015).

"Sonny Clark," All About Jazz, http://musicians.all about jazz.com/sonnyclark (accessed June 9, 2015).

Stephenson, Sam, "Sonny Clark," TheParisReview .org, January 13, 2011, http://www.theparisreview .org/blog/2011/01/13/sonny-clark/ (accessed June 9, 2015).

—R. Anthony Kugler

Freddy Cole

1931—

Jazz vocalist

Cole, Freddy, photograph. Josh Sisk/For The Washington Post/Getty Images.

Although he has never been as familiar to the general public as his older brother Nat King Cole, Freddy Cole enjoys an enviable reputation among fans of soulful, sophisticated jazz. A vocalist like his legendary sibling, he has been entertaining audiences for more than 60 years, touring the globe and releasing a long string of well-received albums. Rigorously trained in a variety of musical styles, he has been described by the *New York Times,* in a comment quoted on his website (FreddyCole Music.com), as "the most maturely expressive male jazz singer of his generation, if not the best alive."

The fifth child of minister Edward Cole and his wife Paulina, Lionel Frederick Cole was born in Chicago on October 15, 1931. More than a decade younger than his brother Nat, he was strongly influenced by that prodigy's musical interests and by his mother's enthusiasm for the piano. His own lessons on the piano began no later than age five or six. Throughout his youth, Cole noted on his website, "Music was all around." Initially, however, it was not clear that he would follow Nat into the world of jazz clubs and recording studios, as his primary interest was athletics, not music. A football star in high school, he might well

have played professionally had an injury not brought his gridiron career to a sudden end. In the wake of that setback he focused on singing, honing his technique in small clubs near his home and in classes at Chicago's Roosevelt Institute. Soon thereafter he moved to New York City for further studies at the Juilliard School, one of the most distinguished conservatories in the country. After earning an undergraduate degree there he completed his education with a master's degree in 1956 from one of Juilliard's few rivals, the New England Conservatory of Music in Boston.

His career by that point was developing rapidly. His first single, a song called "The Joke's On Me," appeared on a small Chicago label, Topper Records, in 1952. Although its sales were modest, in part because of limitations in Topper's marketing and distribution efforts, it drew the attention of several other labels. Over the remainder of the decade, Cole recorded steadily, completing singles designed to showcase his broad vocal range and "swinging" sense of rhythm. Although his vocals bore some superficial resemblance to his brother's, there were a number of significant and readily apparent differences as well. Grittier and

earthier than Nat's smooth baritone, Freddy's voice lent itself particularly well to heartfelt ballads such as "Whispering Grass," a modest hit for him in 1953.

In addition to his recording gigs, Cole also found time for live performance, primarily in New York. As he worked to establish a place for himself in that city's competitive jazz scene, he made a conscious effort to study the techniques of his fellow musicians, particularly the instrumentalists who backed him. "During his formative years in New York," noted Joan Merrill of National Public Radio (NPR), "Freddy listened closely to the way horn players formed phrases in their solos and cultivated a spare, swinging style that would become his signature." His partners during this period included saxophonists Earl Bostic and Benny Golson, both of whom were known for blending jazz with the blues and R&B. Cole's openness to those genres was particularly evident on *Waiter, Ask the Man to Play the Blues,* one of his first full-length recordings. Released in 1964 by Dot Records and completed with the help of a top-notch band that included bassist Milt Hinton, it featured an engaging mix of standards and originals. Thom Jurek of AllMusic.com expressed the critical consensus when he described the album as "a stellar example of vocal jazz and blues with Cole's considerable gifts on full display."

Cole's fan base, meanwhile, was growing steadily, particularly in Europe and South America. A pivotal moment came in 1978, when he completed an album called *One More Love Song.* Released by Decca and several other European labels, it enjoyed strong sales, particularly in Brazil. "Because his intimate singing style resembled that of many Brazilian balladeers," noted Merrill of NPR, "the Brazilians embraced him like one of their own." Overseas audiences also appreciated Cole's ability to sing in other languages, a skill that he honed on his frequent tours abroad.

His fame in the United States, however, remained relatively modest. Although American critics and jazz aficionados shared the enthusiasm of their counterparts overseas, many casual fans were only dimly aware of his talents. That situation began to change in the mid-1990s, when he signed new contracts with major labels such as Muse, which released his 1995 album *This Is The Life,* and Fantasy, for which he made a number of prominent recordings. A highlight of his work during this decade was *Le Grand Freddy,* issued by Fantasy in 1999. A tribute to the composer Michel Legrand, it featured no fewer than 11 of Legrand's songs, from standards such as "The Windmills of Your Mind" and "How Do You Keep the Music Playing" to lesser-known pieces such as "Make the World Your Own."

From Fantasy Cole moved on to Telarc Records, which in 2000 issued *Merry Go Round,* the best-known album of his late career. The record showcased Cole's ability to inject new life into beloved but well-worn standards such as "Smoke Gets in Your Eyes." Other well-received albums in the 2000s and 2010s included *Because of You* (2006) and *Talk to Me* (2011), both of which appeared on HighNote Records.

A longtime resident of Atlanta, Cole has received a steady stream of accolades over the years, including induction into the Georgia Music Hall of Fame in 2007 and an honorary doctorate from the New England Conservatory of Music in 2012. Still active in his mid-80s, he maintained an ambitious touring schedule, appearing at more than two dozen venues across the United States in 2014. Joining him for many of those gigs were guitarist Randy Napoleon, drummer Quentin Baxter, and bassist Elias Bailey.

Selected discography

Singles

"The Joke's On Me," 1952.
"Whispering Grass," 1953.

Albums

Waiter, Ask the Man to Play the Blues, Dot, 1964.
One More Love Song, Decca, 1978.
This Is the Life, Muse, 1995.
Love Makes the Changes, Fantasy, 1998.
Le Grand Freddy (includes "The Windmills of Your Mind," "How Do You Keep the Music Playing," and "Make the World Your Own"), Fantasy, 1999.
Merry Go Round (includes "Smoke Gets in Your Eyes"), Telarc, 2000.

Because of You, HighNote, 2006.
Talk to Me, HighNote, 2011.

Sources

Online

"About Freddy Cole," FreddyColeMusic.com, 2015, http://freddycolemusic.com/about-freddy-cole/ (accessed July 16, 2015).

"Freddy Cole: 'I'm Not My Brother, I'm Me,'" IRock Jazz.com, May 2, 2014, http://irockjazz.com/2014 /05/freddy-cole-im-not-my-brother-im-me/ (accessed July 16, 2015).

Henderson, Alex, "Freddy Cole: Artist Biography," AllMusic.com, http://www.allmusic.com/artist/fred dy-cole-mn0000155901/biography (accessed July 16, 2015).

Jurek, Thom, *"Waiter, Ask the Man to Play the Blues*: Review," AllMusic.com, http://www.allmusic.com/ album/waiter-ask-the-man-to-play-the-blues- mw0000213134 (accessed July 17, 2015).

Merrill, Joan, *"Jazz Profiles* from NPR: Freddy Cole," National Public Radio, http://www.npr.org/pro grams/jazzprofiles/archive/cole_f.html (accessed July 16, 2015).

—R. Anthony Kugler

Chad L. Coleman

1960(?)—

Actor

Coleman, Chad L., photograph. Mike Pont/Getty Images Entertainment/Getty Images.

Veteran character actor Chad L. Coleman is best known for his role on the HBO series *The Wire,* the gritty crime drama set in Baltimore, on which he played Dennis "Cutty" Wise, a former drug-dealing street tough readjusting to life on the outside after a decade behind bars. After that popular show ended, Coleman went on to appear on the AMC series *The Walking Dead* as Tyreese, the hammer-wielding leader of a group of survivors of a zombie apocalypse.

Born in Richmond, Virginia, Coleman was not yet a year old when he and his two brothers and two sisters were abandoned by their parents in their apartment in a housing project in the city's East End. When his older brother Donald tried to cook an egg for his siblings, he set the apartment on fire. In the aftermath of the incident, the authorities took charge of the five siblings, and eventually an older couple, George and Lottie Byrd, took them in as foster children. Coleman credited the Byrds with saving his life and setting him on the right path. Eventually the Byrds left the area and Coleman chose to stay behind, living in Richmond with his maternal grandmother when he was a teenager. Years later, after he was a grown man, Coleman's mother sought him out and asked for his forgiveness, which he gave. It was a lesson in redemption that he later would put to use in his acting work.

The theater bug bit Coleman while he was a student at Richmond's Armstrong-Kennedy High School, where he was involved in an after-school program called the All City Theatrical Troupe, run by a veteran drama teacher, Robert Pemberton. Pemberton was an exacting mentor who both demanded and inspired excellence from his students. One day Coleman was working on a monologue from the Lorraine Hansberry play *A Raisin in the Sun.* Pemberton teacher jabbed a finger at Coleman, telling him that he needed to find the motivation inside himself to bring the words to life. The next time Coleman delivered Hansberry's lines with an authenticity and intensity that he did not know he had. It was, he said in a 2013 interview with *Richmond Magazine,* "an out-of-body experience"—one that sold him on acting.

After graduating high school in 1984, Coleman went on to Virginia Commonwealth University on a full

At a Glance . . .

Born in Richmond, VA; raised by foster parents George and Lottie Byrd; married Sally Stewart, 1999 (separated); two children: Sacha, Caleb. *Military service:* U.S. Army, 1985–89. *Religion:* Christian. *Education:* Attended Virginia Commonwealth University.

Career: Television and film actor, 1992—.

Addresses: *Talent agent*—TalentWorks, 3500 W. Olive Ave., Suite 1400, Burbank, CA 91505. *Twitter*—@ChadLColeman.

scholarship, but the school's theater program seemed like a step backward after his studies with Pemberton. Coleman dropped out after only a year and joined the army. During his time in the service, he trained in video production, but when he was discharged in 1989, he could not find work as a cameraman. He decided to move to New York City and look for any job he could find in the performing arts. He worked for a Broadway ticket service for a time, which allowed him to get into shows for free, and later took a job as a technical assistant on the hit television series *The Cosby Show.* During that time Coleman got to know Malcolm-Jamal Warner, the actor who played Cosby's fictional son. That acquaintance led to a role on an episode of *Here and Now,* Warner's *Cosby* spinoff that aired in the fall of 1992. Several other one-off television roles followed In 1997 Coleman won a part in a touring production of *Othello* that starred Patrick Stewart in the title role opposite a black cast.

In time Coleman began to land meatier roles. He played the male lead in the short television movie *The Gilded Six Bits* (2001), based on a short story by Zora Neale Hurston, and portrayed O. J. Simpson in the TNT television movie *Monday Night Mayhem* (2002). Coleman's big break came in 2004, when he read for and won the part of Cutty Wise on *The Wire,* a drama widely regarded as one of the most compelling and innovative in television history. After appearing in several episodes of the show's third season, Coleman joined the regular cast for the fourth season. On the show, Cutty, paroled after serving 14 years in prison, is enticed back into the drug world but finds that he no longer has what it takes to be an enforcer. Instead, he goes straight and opens a boxing gym.

Coleman won critical praise for his performance, but after *The Wire* ended in 2008, he was once again a character actor hustling for work. He made his Broadway debut in 2009 as Herald Loomis in a revival of August Wilson's play *Joe Turner's Come and Gone.* Coleman returned to television for a three-episode stint on *It's Always Sunny in Philadelphia* and was cast in the regular role of a divorced father in the Fox sitcom *I Hate My Teenage Daughter.* The actor Seth Rogen, a fan of *The Wire,* cast Coleman in his 2011 super-hero comedy *The Green Hornet* (2011). The actor had a small part in another highly successful Hollywood comedy, *Horrible Bosses* (2011), and provided the voice of "Coach" for the video game *Left 4 Dead 2.*

In 2012 the comic book writer Robert Kirkman, creator of the AMC series *The Walking Dead,* offered Coleman the part of Tyreese, a former professional football player who leads a group of survivors of a zombie apocalypse. As on *The Wire,* Coleman was promoted from a recurring to a regular cast member as the show began its fourth season in 2013. *The Walking Dead* won the highest audience ratings of any series in cable television history. Coleman acknowledged his remarkable luck in being part of not one but two successful and pathbreaking programs. This time around, he vowed to stay focused and not to put his ego in front of him. "My appreciation is greater," he told *Richmond,* "because I completely understand the value of the experience I'm having as opposed to what can it get me, what's next."

Making constructive contributions to society is central to Coleman's Christian faith. He regularly talks and connects with teenagers, especially those who have been in foster care. He is involved with the Make a Film Foundation, an organization that helps terminally ill children express themselves through video. He also serves as spokesman for Camp Diva, a Richmond-based nonprofit dedicated to the empowerment of teenage girls, and its annual "Date With Dad" event. For several years Coleman helped produce a documentary film about an ex-convict who was the inspiration for the character of Cutty. In December of 2014 he returned to Richmond as grand marshal of the city's annual Dominion Christmas Parade.

Late in 2014 the Syfy network announced that Coleman would join the cast of the upcoming series *The Expanse,* which was set to premiere in December of 2015.

Selected works

Films

Carlito's Way: Rise to Power, Universal Pictures, 2005.
The Green Hornet, Columbia Pictures, 2011.
Horrible Bosses, Warner Bros., 2011.

Television

The Gilded Six Bits (television movie), Showtime, 2001.

Monday Night Mayhem (television movie), TNT, 2002.

The Wire, HBO, 2004–08.

Wifey (television movie), BET, 2007.

I Hate My Teenage Daughter, Fox, 2010–12.

The Walking Dead, AMC, 2012–15.

The Expanse, Syfy, 2015.

Sources

Periodicals

New York Times, January 13, 2008.

Richmond Free Press, December 12, 2014.

Richmond Magazine, February 27, 2013.

Style Weekly, February 12, 2013.

Variety, November 20, 2014.

—Roger K. Smith

Vince Coleman

1961—

Professional baseball player, coach

Coleman, Vince, photograph. Amanda Edwards/Getty Images Entertainment/Getty Images.

Dubbed "Vincent Van Go" and the "Man of Steal" by sportswriters and teammates for his incredible base-stealing ability, outfielder Vince Coleman tallied more than 750 stolen bases during his 13-year Major League Baseball career, from 1985 and 1997. During his first year with the St. Louis Cardinals, Coleman set a major league record for stolen bases by a rookie (110) while earning National League Rookie of the Year honors, and he is the only player to have stolen 100 bases in his first three major league seasons. Between September of 1988 and July of 1989 alone, Coleman stole 50 consecutive bases without once being put out. He stole bases with such stealth that he was successful 81 percent of the time over his career. To this day, Coleman ranks sixth of all time in career stolen bases and holds the record for three of the top six stolen base totals in a season.

Despite his exceptional base-stealing ability, Coleman ranked as only an average player overall. "In most aspects of the game," Chris Jaffe of the website Hardball Times noted, Coleman "wasn't anything special." He played left field, "not a sign of the best fielding acumen," and he could "hit a little, but not much more than a little," according to Jaffe. "But in one aspect of the game Coleman was great; he could run. Lord, could he ever run." The peak of Coleman's career came early, when he played for the Cardinals for five seasons, and thereafter he bounced from team to team. Coleman retired from the game in 1997 but returned to the majors 15 years later as a base-running coach, teaching his signature skill to a new generation of big leaguers.

Vincent Maurice Coleman was born in 1961 in Jacksonville, Florida. He was a natural athlete. At Florida A&M University, Coleman was already demonstrating his prowess at stealing bases, making 65 of 69 attempts in 1981, when he set the school's all-time record for stolen bases in a season. Baseball was not his only sport at Florida A&M: Coleman also was a kicker and punter for the football team. He was twice named to the all-conference team, and in a 1979 game against the highly ranked University of Miami, Coleman kicked the game-winning field goal. The National Football League showed real interest in him.

Coleman decided to pursue a career in professional baseball instead, and he was drafted in the 10th round

At a Glance . . .

Born Vincent Maurice Coleman on September 22, 1961, in Jacksonville, FL. *Education:* Attended Florida A&M University.

Career: St. Louis Cardinals, outfielder, 1985–90; New York Mets, outfielder, 1991–93; Kansas City Royals, outfielder, 1994–95; Seattle Mariners, outfielder, 1995; Cincinnati Reds, outfielder, 1996; Detroit Tigers, outfielder, 1997; Houston Astros, base-running instructor, 2013–15; Chicago White Sox, base-running instructor, 2015—.

Awards: National League Rookie of Year, 1985; Major League Baseball All-Star selection, 1988, 1989; National League stolen base champion, 1985-90.

Addresses: *Office*—Chicago White Sox, 33 E. 35th St., Chicago, IL 60616.

of the 1982 Major League Baseball amateur draft by the St. Louis Cardinals. He spent two seasons in the minor leagues, racking up hundreds of stolen bases. During his first season in the majors, 1985, he set a rookie record for stolen bases in a single season with 110—a number that still ranks as the third-highest total in major league history—and earned Rookie of the Year honors.

He helped take the Cardinals to the playoffs that year, but just before game 4 of the National League Championship Series against the Los Angeles Dodgers, Coleman suffered a bizarre injury. On October 13, 1985, Coleman was doing pregame drills with the Dodgers. It was raining lightly in St. Louis, and the ground crew had turned on the automated tarp to protect the field. Coleman had his back to the machine, and before anyone realized what was happening, the tarp rolled over his left leg as he was stretching. Coleman was briefly trapped under the tarp, and it took several players to lift it off him. The damage was done, however: he suffered bruising on his left leg and a chipped bone in his knee. The injuries sidelined Coleman and ended his rookie season. Although the Cardinals managed to the National League pennant without their star base stealer, they lost to the Kansas City Royals in the World Series.

Coleman remained with the Cardinals through the 1990 season and then, as a free agent, went to the New York Mets, signing a four-year, $12 million contract. His star would never shine as brightly as it had in St. Louis, though. Injuries and suspensions took their toll on Coleman, keeping him out of 215 games over

three seasons. His base-stealing prowess also began to decline. Then, in 1992, Coleman, along with two other Mets players, was the subject of a rape investigation involving a 31-year-old Florida woman. Although no charges ever were brought, the allegation besmirched Coleman's reputation.

There also were rumors of bad relations between Coleman and the Mets coaches and management, and a physical confrontation with a manager in 1992 led to his suspension for the rest of the season. "Coleman was … a difficult-to-figure character in the dugout and clubhouse," wrote Joe Sexton in the *New York Times.* "He annoyed teammates with his laughing during and after losses. He infuriated coaches with his refusal to look for signs or interpret them correctly on the base paths. He repeatedly made questionable strategic decisions in trying to steal bases, and he was no better than a mediocre defensive player."

Coleman's career with the Mets came to an end when he was found guilty of throwing a firecracker into a crowd of fans in the parking lot at Dodger Stadium, injuring three people, including one child. He was sentenced to 200 hours of community service, although he continue to deny any wrongdoing. In August of 1993, the Mets ownership announced that Coleman would be leaving the team at the end of the season. He was traded to the Kansas City Royals, where he managed 76 steals in 179 games in 1994. The next year he was traded again, this time to the Seattle Mariners, where he lasted one season before going to the Cincinnati Reds, where he also stayed for one season, putting in a mediocre performance. Coleman played his last season in the majors with the Detroit Tigers in 1997, seeing limited playing time and managing only a few stolen bases. Although Coleman tried to make a comeback with the Cardinals in 1998, he was sent down to the minors. In May of 1998, Coleman decided to call it quits, and he retired from baseball.

After 15 years out of baseball, Coleman returned to the game in 2013 as a base-running instructor for the Houston Astros, teaching young players the skill he knew best. "Everyone can't be fast, but it takes a knowledge of what you look for," Coleman explained to Brian McTaggart of MLB.com. "It takes exceptional knowledge, exceptional studying of the craft. You can't be intimidated or have fear. You have to have confidence, which is a key component to being successful."

In 2015 Coleman joined the Chicago White Sox in a similar capacity. "It's an opportunity of a lifetime and I know that with my work ethic and my personality we're going to get a lot accomplished this year," Coleman said in an interview with CSN Chicago. "I'm just so happy to be covering the baserunning and the outfield since I have a Ph.D. in that. I'm going to try to show 'em all I can."

Sources

Books

Rains, Rob, and Keith Schildroth, *St. Louis Cardinals: Where Have You Gone? Vince Coleman, Ernie Broglio, John Tudor, and Other Cardinal Greats,* Sports Publishing, 2005.

Periodicals

New York Times, July 26, 1993; August 27, 1993.

Online

Godar, Ben, "Vince Coleman: The One-Tool Player," SB Nation, June 26, 2014, http://www.vivaelbirdos.com/2014/6/26/5818542/vince-coleman-the-one-tool-player (accessed June 6, 2015).

Hayes, Dan, "Doctor in the House: Vince Coleman Educates White Sox," CSN Chicago, February 26, 2015, http://www.csnchicago.com/white-sox/doctor-house-vince-coleman-educates-white-sox (accessed June 6, 2015).

Jaffe, Chris, "10,000 Days since Vince Coleman and the Tarp," Hardball Times, February 28, 2013, http://www.hardballtimes.com/tht-live/10000-days-since-vince-coleman-and-the-tarp/ (accessed June 6, 2015).

McTaggart, Brian, "Coleman Instills Basestealing Attitude to Astros," MLB.com, http://m.mlb.com/news/article/41942164/vince-coleman-instills-basestealing-attitude-to-astros (accessed June 6, 2015).

"Vince Coleman," Baseball-Reference.com, http://www.baseball-reference.com/players/c/colemvi01.shtml (accessed June 6, 2015).

"Vince Coleman Off and Running as White Sox Instructor," USAToday.com, February 28, 2015, http://www.usatoday.com/story/sports/mlb/2015/02/28/vince-coleman-off-and-running-as-white-sox-instructor/24193741/ (accessed June 6, 2015).

—J. Sydney Jones

Honi Coles

1911–1992

Actor, tap dancer, dance teacher

Tap dancer Honi Coles was said to have the "fastest feet in show business," earning a reputation for his intricate, high-speed footwork and for his graceful, polished style. During the 1940s Coles and his long-time partner Charles "Cholly" Atkins performed with the biggest swing bands of the era, including those led by Cab Calloway, Louis Armstrong, and Count Basie, before forming their own popular tap act in the second half of the decade. Coles and Atkins were among the last of the so-called class acts, performing precisely choreographed tap numbers while outfitted in impeccably tailored suits. As the popularity of tap dancing waned during the 1950s, Coles and Atkins split. By the 1970s, when tap returned to Broadway, Coles was at the forefront of a tap revival, appearing at festivals across the country and teaching tap to a new generation of dancers. In 1983 Coles, then in his 70s, capped his career with a Tony Award for his performance in the Broadway musical *My One and Only*.

Developed Impressive Tap Technique

Coles was born on April 2, 1911, in Philadelphia, the son of George and Isabel Coles. When he was a boy, his older sister gave him the nickname "Honey," and it stuck. Later Coles would change the spelling to "Honi." Entirely self-taught, he learned to dance on the streets of Philadelphia during the 1920s, a time when "hoofers," as tap dancers were then known, performed on nearly every corner, challenging one another to "cut-ting" contests. Coles also watched tap dancers such as John Bubbles, Eddie Rector, and Bill "Bojangles" Robinson perform at local theaters and then practiced the moves he saw on his way home.

In 1931 he teamed with brothers George and Danny Miller to form an act called the Three Millers, performing at local clubs and talent shows. They made their New York City debut in 1931 at the Lafayette Theater in Harlem, but soon after that, the Miller brothers replaced Coles with another dancer. He returned to Philadelphia determined to improve his technique, practicing for up to eight hours a day in a rented room. "[O]ne year later, I came out of that room with the fastest feet in show business," he told the *Philadelphia Inquirer* in 1986.

Coles returned to New York City in 1932 with a new technique, performing smooth, close-to-the-floor steps and creating long lines of rapid-fire taps without a break. At the Hoofers Club, a New York hangout for some of the best jazz and tap performers of the period, Coles was regarded as one of the most graceful dancers of his day. He signed with an agent who booked him at the Apollo Theater and the Harlem Opera House. "[E]very dancer in New York came to catch me," he told the *Philadelphia Inquirer*. "I was doing stuff that was unbelievable—everything uptempo, double-timing, triple-timing, quadruple-timing." From 1936 to 1939 he performed with the Lucky Seven Trio, dancing atop huge cubes made to look like dice and going through as many as 10 costume changes in a night.

At a Glance . . .

Born Charles Coles on April 2, 1911, in Philadelphia, PA; died on November 12, 1992, in New York, NY; son of George and Isabel Coles; married Marion Edwards (a dancer), 1944; children: Isabelle Coles-Dubar, one son. *Military service*: U.S. Army, 1943–45.

Career: Performed with the Three Millers, 1931, Lucky Seven Trio, 1936–39, Coles and Atkins, 1945–60; Apollo Theater, stage manager, 1960–76; dance faculty at Yale, Cornell, Duke, and George Washington universities, 1970s–92.

Memberships: Negro Actors Guild.

Awards: Tony Award, Best Featured Actor in a Musical, Drama Desk Award, Outstanding Featured Actor in a Musical, and Fred Astaire Award, 1983, all for *My One and Only*; Dance Magazine Award, 1985; Award of Honor for Arts and Culture, New York City, 1986; Capezio Dance Award for Lifetime Achievement, 1988; National Medal of Arts, 1991; inducted into Tap Dance Hall of Fame, 2003.

Performed "Class Act"

Tap dancers often performed with the big bands of the era, and by 1940 Coles had hooked up with Cab Calloway's band. While performing with Calloway, he met fellow tapper Charles "Cholly" Atkins. Both men joined the U.S. Army in 1943, briefly interrupting their careers. When they returned home in 1945, they formed a tap act called Coles and Atkins. Initially the pair intended to perform their act only until they had enough money to open a dance studio, but they were such a hit that they abandoned their plans for the studio. Over the next four years, Coles and Atkins performed on Broadway and at theaters across the United States, and they danced with Calloway's band as well as others led by Louis Armstrong, Count Basie, Lionel Hampton, and Billy Eckstine. In 1948 they made a successful tour of England.

Coles and Atkins performed what was known as a "class act," wearing smartly tailored suits and dancing in a precise, elegant style. Their 12-minute routine—much longer than most tap acts of the time—began with a fast-paced song-and-dance number, then transitioned into a soft-shoe, and finished with a "tap challenge" in which each dancer showed off his signature style. In his solos, Coles performed quick and rhythmi-

cally complex tap sequences, appearing light and elegant from the waist up while his feet tapped at a rapid-fire pace. Coles looked so graceful that Lena Horne once said that he made "butterflies look clumsy," according to the *New York Times*. In 1949 Coles and Atkins were cast in the Broadway musical *Gentlemen Prefer Blondes*, performing their own choreography in a show-stopping number called "Mamie Is Mimi." They spent two years on Broadway at the Ziegfeld Theatre and another on tour with the show.

By the early 1950s, however, jobs for tap dancers were drying up. The big band era was coming to a close, giving way to new styles of jazz such as bebop. Around the same time, Agnes de Mille introduced modern dance to Broadway, and shows began to integrate choreography into the musical plot rather than having stand-alone tap numbers. In 1954 Coles and a partner finally opened a dance studio on 52nd Street in New York City, but interest in tap dancing was declining. Coles and Atkins broke up their act in 1960. Atkins went on to become a choreographer for Motown acts, while Coles took a job as a stage manager at the Apollo Theater, where he worked for the next 16 years. During those years he also served as president of the Negro Actors Guild and continued his association with the Copasetics, a tapping fraternity that he had helped found in 1949. Coles and other veteran members of the group performed together in 1962 at the Newport Jazz Festival.

Contributed to Tap Revival

Tap experienced a resurgence of popularity in the 1970s following the hit Broadway musical *No, No, Nanette*, which featured several tap routines. Coles was at the forefront of the tap revival. In the 1970s he began a long-lived collaboration with dancer Brenda Bufalino, with whom he toured the United States and Europe. Bufalino featured Coles and other members of the Copesetics in her 1975 documentary *Great Feats of Feet*. Coles returned to Broadway in 1976 in the musical revue *Bubblin' Brown Sugar*. Thereafter he performed as a soloist, appearing at Carnegie Hall and Town Hall. In 1978 he received a standing ovation for his performance with the Joffrey Ballet's production of De Mille's *Conversations on the Dance*. The following year Coles appeared in two major stage shows, *Steps in Time* at the Brooklyn Academy of Music and *Black Broadway, 1900–1945* at Avery Fisher Hall.

In 1983, at age 72, Coles originated the role of Mr. Magix in the Tommy Tune musical *My One and Only*, for which Coles won the Tony Award, Drama Desk Award, and Fred Astaire Award for best featured actor in a musical. He also sang and danced on the big screen, appearing in *Rocky II* (1979), *The Cotton Club* (1984), and *Dirty Dancing* (1987).

Throughout his late career Coles was a fixture at tap festivals across the United States, and he taught dance

and dance history at Yale, Cornell, Duke, and George Washington universities. Coles received numerous accolades for his contributions to dance and to American arts. He received the Dance Magazine Award in 1985 and the Capezio Award for Lifetime Achievement in 1988. In 1991 President George H. W. Bush presented Coles with the National Medal of Arts. Coles died at age 81 at his home in New York City on November 12, 1992. That year he was honored by Tommy Tune in his musical revue *Tommy Tune Tonite!,* which featured Coles's choreography and was dedicated to the veteran tapper. In 2003 Coles was posthumously inducted into the Tap Hall of Fame.

Selected works

Theater

Gentlemen Prefer Blondes, Ziegfeld Theatre, New York, 1949–51.

Bubbling Brown Sugar, ANTA Playhouse, New York, 1976–77.

My One and Only, St. James Theatre, New York, 1983–85.

Films

Basin Street Revue, Studio Films, 1956.
Rocky II, United Artists, 1979.

The Cotton Club, Orion Pictures, 1984.
Dirty Dancing, Vestron Pictures, 1987.

Sources

Books

Frank, Rusty E., *Tap! The Greatest Tap Dance Stars and Their Stories, 1900–1955,* William Morrow, 1990.

Periodicals

New York Times, July 17, 1984; November 13, 1992.
Philadelphia Inquirer, March 26, 1986.

Online

Charles 'Honi' Coles," Tap Dance Hall of Fame, http://www.atdf.org/awards/honi.html (accessed June 28, 2015).

"Honi Coles … The Class Act," YouTube, https://www.youtube.com/watch?v=jHD78dZIDoE (accessed June 28, 2015).

West, Jenai Cutcher, "Charles 'Honi' Coles (1911–1992)," Dance Heritage Coalition, http://www.danceheritage.org/treasures/coles_essay_west.pdf (accessed June 28, 2015).

—Deborah A. Ring

Sonny Criss

1927–1977

Jazz saxophonist

Although he never became as familiar to the public as some of his peers, saxophonist Sonny Criss had an impressive impact on the growth and development of jazz. A fierce individualist whose relative indifference to the commercial aspects of music undoubtedly cost him a measure of fame, he was described by critic Bob Porter as "one of the great underground musicians of all time." Highly esteemed by his colleagues and by jazz aficionados around the world, Criss is remembered especially for a brilliant piece called "West Coast Blues" (1956) and for the long string of fine albums that he completed for a variety of labels between the mid-1950s and mid-1970s. His death at age 50 prompted a new appreciation for his many contributions to jazz music. "He was pioneering and when you're pioneering, it's kind of more difficult to get recognition," fellow saxophonist Big Jay McNeely said, in a comment quoted by critic Steven A. Cerra. "You have to suffer when you're a pioneer. So that's what happened, really, I think, with Sonny. He was just early."

William "Sonny" Criss was born on October 23, 1927, in Memphis. Drawn to the saxophone at an early age, he was already a skilled player by the time he relocated with his family to Los Angeles about 1942. That move proved a pivotal moment in his musical development, as it brought him into the midst of Southern California's vibrant jazz scene. Along Central Avenue, a major thoroughfare in Los Angeles and the center of the region's African-American community, Criss found a number of jazz clubs, many of them receptive to bebop, a highly improvisational style that was then in its early stages. Older saxophonists in the area, notably Charlie

Parker and Dexter Gordon, were laying the foundations for bebop's growth, and under their influence Criss developed a rich tone that was well suited to the new style. Club owners soon recognized his talents, and by the time he graduated high school he was performing up and down Central Avenue.

A major break came in 1947, when Criss joined a touring group led by singer Billy Eckstine. Although Eckstine was not known for bebop, his ability to spot young talent was famous, and his imprimatur gave a significant boost to Criss's career. After leaving Eckstine's group about 1948, Criss worked for impresarios Norman Granz, whose primary project was a touring exhibition called Jazz at the Philharmonic, and Howard Rumsey, who led the house band at the Lighthouse, a popular club in a Los Angeles suburb. Those gigs occupied him until the early 1950s, when he took a number of short-term gigs and then joined drummer Buddy Rich for what proved to be an extended engagement (1955–58).

Criss's recording career, meanwhile, was developing significantly, albeit at an uneven pace. Although he had made a few recordings as early as the mid-1940s, it was not until 1956 that he completed his full-length debut as a leader. That album, Jazz—U.S.A., was a breakthrough effort, selling well across the country despite relatively little promotion; Thom Jurek of All-Music.com described it as "one of the true underground classics" of its time. Crucial to its success was the track "West Coast Blues," a haunting ballad that Criss had composed himself.

At a Glance . . .

Born William Criss on October 23, 1927, in Memphis, TN; died on November 19, 1977, in Los Angeles, CA; son of Lucy Criss.

Career: Jazz saxophonist, 1940s–77.

The months that followed were a particularly significant period in his development. Although Imperial Records, the label behind *Jazz—U.S.A.,* quickly brought him back into the studio to complete some follow-ups, it failed once more to provide much promotional support, and Criss had to rely on word of mouth to get his work into the hands of jazz fans. That pattern was repeated with several other labels. By all accounts an introverted man, he rarely asserted himself in negotiating with record executives. As a result he tended to be overlooked in the allocation of promotional resources, and his status as an underground musician grew ever stronger. Although he remained unknown even to many jazz aficionados, those who were aware of his talents often became fervent supporters, eagerly awaiting albums such as *Sonny Criss Plays Cole Porter* (1956) and *Go Man!* (1956), both Imperial issues. Soon after their release he moved on to Peacock Records, for which he completed *At the Crossroads* (1959), and then to a succession of other labels, including Prestige Records, for which he recorded extensively in the mid-1960s.

Typical of Criss's albums during this period was *This Is Criss!,* released by Prestige in 1966. A mix of standards and originals, it featured fine contributions by bassist Paul Chambers, pianist Walter Davis, and drummer Alan Dawson. In a clear indication of the status he enjoyed among his peers, Criss was able throughout his career to attract first-rate artists for his backing band. This was true even during relatively slow periods such as the mid- to late 1960s, when the melodic style that was his specialty was yielding to the harsher sounds of free jazz. On 1968's *Sonny's Dream (Birth of the New Cool),* for example, he was backed by a large group that included luminaries such as pianist Tommy Flanagan, arranger Horace Tapscott, and fellow saxophonist Teddy Edwards.

A frequent traveler to Europe, where he found an enthusiastic reception, Criss enjoyed a surge of publicity in the mid-1970s, thanks in part to new deals with several record labels and to a number of well-received concerts, many of them overseas. Beneath that veneer of good fortune, however, he was facing a profound personal crisis. The depth of his struggles did not become clear to his friends and colleagues until November 19, 1977, when Criss took his own life in Los Angeles. His mother later revealed that he had been suffering from stomach cancer, an illness that he had concealed from his peers. "Criss rarely complained about whatever troubles he faced, medical or otherwise," critic Ted Gioia noted. "Just as rarely did he dwell on his achievements or his hopes for the future. He let his music speak for him."

Selected discography

Jazz—U.S.A. (includes "West Coast Blues"), Imperial, 1956.
Sonny Criss Plays Cole Porter, Imperial, 1956.
Go Man!, Imperial, 1956.
At the Crossroads, Peacock, 1959.
This Is Criss!, Prestige, 1966.
Sonny's Dream (Birth of the New Cool), Prestige, 1968.
Crisscraft, Muse, 1975.

Sources

Online

Cerra, Steven A., "Sonny Criss: An Overlooked Giant," *Jazz Profiles* (blog), May 21, 2012, http://jazzprofiles.blogspot.com/2012/05/sonny-criss-overlooked-giant.html (accessed July 4, 2015).
Jurek, Thom, "Sonny Criss: Artist Biography," All Music.com, http://www.allmusic.com/artist/sonny-criss-mn0000755431/biography (accessed July 4, 2015).
Olsen, Eric B., Bob Porter, and Ted Gioia, "Sonny Criss," Hard Bop Homepage, http://www.members.tripod.com/~hardbop/criss.html (accessed July 4, 2015).
"Sonny Criss," Discogs.com, http://www.discogs.com/artist/319761-Sonny-Criss (accessed July 4, 2015).

—R. Anthony Kugler

Edwidge Danticat

1969—

Author

Danticat, Edwidge, photograph. Amanda Edwards/Getty Images Entertainment/Getty Images.

Edwidge Danticat is one of a small number of contemporary authors of Haitian heritage writing in English. Born in Haiti, she moved to the United States when she was 12 years old and grew up in Brooklyn, New York, where she learned English as her third language, after French and Haitian Creole. English eventually would become the language of her literary expression. In 1994, at age 25, Danticat published her debut novel, *Breath, Eyes, Memory,* to wide acclaim. In her fiction, including the short story collection *Krik? Krak!* (1995) and the novels *The Farming of Bones* (1998), *The Dew Breaker* (2004), and *Claire of the Sea Light* (2013), as well as in autobiographical works such as *Brother, I'm Dying* (2007), Danticat writes unflinchingly of the lives and losses of Haitians both at home—where poverty, political repression, and fear have been everyday experiences for decades—and as transplants to America. Danticat's writing has earned her an American Book Award, a National Book Critics Circle Award, and a prestigious MacArthur "Genius Grant." An advocate for issues affecting Haitians on the island and in the diaspora, Danticat is often regarded as a

spokesperson for her people, a role that she accepts with reservations. "I think I have been assigned that role, but I don't really see myself as the voice for the Haitian-American experience," she told the *New York Times* in 1995. "There are many. I'm just one."

Immigrated to America from Haiti

Danticat (pronounced dahn-tee-CAH) was born in Léogâne, a rural area of Haiti west of the capital of Port-au-Prince, in 1969, during brutal dictatorship of Francois "Papa Doc" Duvalier. When Danticat was two years old, her father immigrated to New York City to find a better life for the family; two years later her mother followed, leaving Danticat and her younger brother in the care of an uncle. Although her parents promised to send for her and her brother when they were settled in America, it would be many years before that happened, and Danticat did not know whether she would ever see her parents again. "At the airport my uncle had to peel me off my mother's body," she recalled in a 2004 profile in

the London *Guardian.* "The hardest part was not knowing if it would be for days or years."

Danticat was raised by her uncle and his wife in a large household filled with extended family members. From the elder members of the family, she learned the Haitian tradition of storytelling. "My best writing teachers were my aunts and uncles, who were all storytellers," Danticat recalled in an interview with the *Wild River Review* at the 2011 Langston Hughes Festival. "Storytelling and oral tradition, was, when I was growing up, a strong part of how things were passed on. That's what made me want to tell stories. It was a kind of gift. A moment where children and adults could interact in a free way."

When she was 12 years old, her parents sent for her and her brother to join them. Arriving in New York, Danticat met her two younger brothers, who had been born in the intervening years. Her parents and her new siblings were strangers to her. "I didn't know these people," she told the *Miami Herald* in 1995. "I felt like I was adopted." The transition was difficult, too, because Danticat knew only a few words of English. She

worked hard to learn the language, studying the classics. The first complete book that she read in English was Maya Angelou's *I Know Why the Caged Bird Sings.* At school she was teased for her Haitian Creole accent, prompting her to rarely speak above a whisper. The 1980s, when Danticat was coming of age, was a time when Haitians were vilified, as Haitian refugees in makeshift boats washed up on Florida beaches, and Haitian immigrants were classified as being at high risk of having AIDS. "It was very hard," Danticat recalled in a 1995 interview with the *New York Times.* "'Haitian' was like a curse. People were calling you, 'Frenchy, go back to the banana boat,' and a lot of the kids would lie about where they came from. They would say anything but Haitian."

Danticat found solace in writing. English became her primary language at school and, eventually, the language in which she would write. In high school she joined a teen magazine called *New Youth Connections,* and it was there that she found her voice, publishing her first article at age 14. Although she longed to write, her parents did not view that as a respectable career, and they urge her to become a doctor. As a compromise she settled on nursing, attending Clara Barton High School in the Bronx and volunteering at Kings County Hospital after school. The experience ultimately dissuaded her from becoming a nurse. Instead she enrolled at Barnard College in New York City and majored in French literature, finishing her undergraduate degree in 1990.

Published Debut Novel at 25

After college Danticat won a scholarship to attend Brown University in Providence, Rhode Island, and enrolled in the graduate writing program. There she was in class with two future Pulitzer Prize winners, playwrights Paula Vogel and Nilo Cruz, and joined a writing workshop taught by the novelist Robert Coover. Her master's thesis, *Breath, Eyes, Memory,* became her debut novel, published in 1994 when Danticat was just 25 years old.

The novel was among the first to chronicle the Haitian-American experience, focusing on three generations of Haitian women: a Haitian grandmother; her daughter, who is raped by a member of the brutal Haitian secret police, the Tonton Macoutes, and becomes pregnant; and the granddaughter, Sophie, who is the product of that rape. Brought up by her grandmother in Haiti, Sophie is forced at age 12 to leave her homeland to join her mother in New York. Sophie's mother carries on the tradition of "testing," probing her young daughter's body to be sure that she is a virgin. Danticat's willingness to tackle controversial subject matter earned her comparisons to African-American author Alice Walker. Some Haitians, however, objected to the novel, criticizing Danticat for speaking openly about the practice of testing and for portraying Haitian culture in a negative light. Nevertheless, *Breath, Eyes,*

Memory was praised by critics. Danticat received a Literary Award for fiction from the Black Caucus of the American Library Association, and the *New York Times* declared her one of 30 artists under age 30 who were "likely to change the culture for the next 30 years."

As Danticat was enjoying her first flush of literary success, political events in Haiti were making headlines, causing reverberations in her own life. The Duvalier regime had spiraled to an end in 1986, and four years later, Roman Catholic priest Jean-Bertrand Aristide had become the nation's first freely elected leader. In 1991 Aristide was ousted in a military coup, forcing him to flee the country. The international community responded by imposing a trade embargo, which deeply hurt the already impoverished Haitian people, and a United Nations peacekeeping force was deployed to maintain order. Many Haitians fled to Florida on makeshift boats; those intercepted were put into refugee camps in which conditions were abysmal. Aristide was restored to the presidency in 1994.

After receiving her master's degree, Danticat took a job in the New York office of filmmaker Jonathan Demme; in that capacity she worked as an associate producer on *Courage and Pain,* a documentary about survivors of torture in Haiti. In an interview with Ingrid Sturgis that appeared in *Emerge* magazine, Danticat spoke of the outlaw status of writers in Haiti's dictatorial past. "In our world, if you are a writer, you are a politician, and we know what happens to politicians. They end up in a prison dungeon, where their bodies are covered in scalding tar before they're forced to eat their own waste." With Demme she traveled back to Haiti in 1994 for the first time since leaving 13 years earlier and viewed the ceremony marking Aristide's official return to power.

Won American Book Award

Danticat followed up with a collection of short stories, *Krik? Krak!,* published by Soho Press in 1995. The volume takes its title from Danticat's Creole language: "Krik?" one inquires to another at the onset of a folk tale, roughly meaning "I have a story—would you like to hear it?" and "Krak!" comes the reply, the equivalent of "Yes, go ahead!"

In nine interrelated stories, Danticat used her own family's experiences as the basis for the lives of the characters. Much of the action takes place in the capital city of Port-au-Prince and the rural Ville Rose, where women must sometimes walk two miles each morning for the day's water. The story "1937" follows the travails of a woman who is imprisoned and tortured for witchcraft. Another takes place on one of the infamous doomed boats heading for Florida. "Children of the Sea" recounts a journey through letters written by a pair of lovers who never receive the other's missives.

Through the letters, Danticat's story provides insight into the difficulties of life in Haiti and why so many risked their lives to escape.

"The best of these stories," wrote Robert Houston in the *New York Times Book Review,* "humanize, particularize, [and] give poignancy to the lives of people we may have come to think of as faceless emblems of misery, poverty, and brutality." Joanne Omang in the *Washington Post* asserted that Danticat "has woven the sad with the funny, the unspeakable with the glorious, [and] the wild horror [with the] deep love that is Haiti today." Reviewing *Krik? Krak!* for the *Seattle Times,* Michael Upchurch found that "Danticat's often-sobering subjects are leavened by the bracing elegance of her prose and by her fondness for riddle." *Krik? Krak!* was nominated for the National Book Award in 1995.

Danticat published her second novel, *The Farming of Bones,* in 1998. The work tells the story of Amabelle Desir, a Haitian housemaid working in the Dominican Republic, against the historical background of an infamous 1937 massacre of Haitian migrant workers directed by Dominican dictator Rafael Trujillo Molina. Writing in the *New York Times,* Michael Upchurch stated that Danticat "evokes the shock with which a small personal world is disrupted by military mayhem…. Danticat knows the value of understatement in bringing nightmarish scenes to life, and a spare, searing poetry infuses many of the book's best passages." *The Farming of Bones* won the American Book Award that year.

Wrote of Painful Haitian History

In her next work, *The Dew Breaker,* published in 2004, Danticat used a more experimental form, crafting a series of interconnected tales—at once a novel and a short story collection—tracing back to Baby Doc Duvalier's brutal Tonton Macoutes. The reader gradually discovers that the characters in the stories are both victims and perpetrators, all haunted in different ways by the events that occurred during this bloody period in Haitian history. Writing in the *New York Times,* Michiko Kakutani described *The Dew Breaker* as "Ms. Danticat's most persuasive, organic performance yet." Widely acclaimed, *The Dew Breaker* was awarded the Story Prize, a $20,000 award for the best short story collection of the year, and the Anisfield-Wolf Book Award. The book also was a PEN/Faulkner Award finalist.

That same year Danticat's uncle, Joseph Dantica, became a victim of the political unrest in Haiti and the official indifference of the U.S. government. In the aftermath of military intervention by United Nations troops and Haitian police against armed gangs and political factions in his Port-au-Prince neighborhood, Dantica, then 81 years old, was threatened with death

by gang members who claimed that 15 of their friends had been killed by military snipers shooting from the roof of his church and that he would have to pay for their funerals or be killed. Dantica escaped by hiding under a neighbor's bed for three days and eventually fled to the United States on a valid visa. Upon his arrival, he explained that he would be killed if he returned and applied for temporary asylum. Plagued by heart problems and high blood pressure, Dantica collapsed during his interview and began vomiting; the medic on duty announced that he was "faking" illness. Arrested and held in detention, Dantica was denied access to his medication and died while in custody.

Three years later Danticat published *Brother, I'm Dying,* a memoir centered on her father and uncle. As in her other works, Danticat depicted the intersection of private lives with Haiti's tragic history, portraying two brothers on opposite side of the immigration divide: Mira, the hardworking immigrant who sacrificed everything to secure a better future for his children, and Joseph, who remained in Haiti as long as possible—despite his family's pleas for him to emigrate—seeking to serve his congregation and community. *Brother, I'm Dying* was awarded the National Book Critics Circle Award for autobiography and was nominated for a National Book Award.

Responded to 2010 Earthquake in Haiti

In 2009 Danticat was awarded a prestigious MacArthur Foundation Fellowship, known as the "Genius Grant," which comes with a $500,000, no-strings-attached stipend. In announcing Danticat's selection, the MacArthur Foundation described Danticat as "a novelist whose moving and insightful depictions of Haiti's complex history are enriching our understanding of the Haitian immigrant experience," noting that the author "provides a nuanced portrait of the intersection between nation and diaspora, home and exile, and reminds us of the power of human resistance."

The following January a 7.0-magnitude earthquake struck Haiti, destroying homes and buildings and killing more than 100,000 people. After several days Danticat learned that her cousin Maxo had been killed, crushed beneath the four-story home where his family lived. Once again Danticat turned to writing to cope with her loss, penning a poignant essay for the *New Yorker* just a few weeks later. In September of that year, she published a picture book for children, *Eight Days: A Story of Haiti,* about a boy who is buried under debris during the earthquake and eventually rescued after eight days. The book was inspired by Danticat's five-year-old daughter, who struggled to understand the disaster and whether their relatives in Haiti were safe. "I wrote this story to try to explain to her what had happened," Danticat told National Public Radio, "but also to find a kind of hopeful moment in it

so it wasn't, at least to a child, all devastation." Danticat also narrated a documentary about the earthquake, *Nou Bouke (We're Tired),* that aired on PBS in 2011 on the anniversary of the tragedy.

Danticat also published a nonfiction work, *Create Dangerously: The Immigrant Artist at Work,* in 2010. In it, Danticat explores the lives and works of Haitian immigrants artists who inspired her own writing. *Create Dangerously* was chosen as one of the best books of the year by the *Miami Herald* and was a *New York Times Book Review* Editor's Choice. The following year it won the OCM Bocas Prize for Caribbean Literature in the nonfiction category.

Returned to Fiction

In 2013 Danticat published her first work of adult fiction in nearly a decade, *Claire of the Sea Light.* Similar in structure to *The Dew Breaker,* the book is a collection of intertwined stories, telling a story from a diversity of perspectives and eventually circling back on itself. The Claire of the title is a seven-year-old girl whose mother died giving birth to her. On her birthday—a day that begins with a freak wave coming from the ocean and devouring a local fisherman—Claire disappears suddenly, just as her father is deciding to give her up to be raised by a local woman who lost her own child. The stories of Claire, her parents, and the other residents of Ville Rose are told through flashbacks and overlapping anecdotes, until Claire finally reappears in the last pages of the book. Reviewing *Claire of the Sea Light* in the *New York Times,* Deborah Sontag noted that "Danticat's work, lightly peppered with Creole, studded with observations familiar to those who know Haiti, opens itself to a broader readership through her deft intertwining of the specific and the universal." In the *Washington Post,* Ron Charles praised Danticat's delicate, ethereal narrative, noting that "in her rich new novel ... Danticat continues, as she always has, to speak in a captivating whisper. While disasters threaten to reduce the Haitian people to an undifferentiated mass of misery, her work pushes back, clearing space for individuals, restoring the variegated colors of humanity that storms and death ... would wash away." In 2014 Danticat was short-listed for the Andrew Carnegie Medal for Excellence in Fiction for *Claire of the Sea Light.*

In addition to her adult fiction, Danticat has written several young adult novels, including *Behind the Mountains* (2002) and *Anacaona: Golden Flower, Haiti, 1490.* Another novel for young readers, *Untwine,* was slated for publication in 2015. She also had edited a number of anthologies of Haitian literature, including *Butterfly's Way* (2003) and *Haiti Noir* (2011). Another picture book for children, *Mama's Nightmare,* was forthcoming in 2015.

Danticat lives in Miami with her husband, Faidherbe "Fedo" Boyer, and their two daughters. She was a

visiting professor of creative writing at New York University in 1996–97 and at the University of Miami in 2000 and 2008.

Selected works

Fiction

Breath, Eyes, Memory, Soho Press, 1994.
Krik? Krak!, Soho Press, 1995.
The Farming of Bones, Soho Press, 1998.
The Dew Breaker, Alfred A. Knopf, 2004.
Claire of the Sea Light, Alfred A. Knopf, 2013.

Nonfiction

After the Dance: A Walk Through Carnival in Jacmel, Haiti, Crown, 2002.
Brother, I'm Dying, Alfred A. Knopf, 2007.
Create Dangerously: The Immigrant Artist at Work, Princeton University Press, 2010.

Young adult fiction

Behind the Mountains, Scholastic, 2002.
Anacaona: Golden Flower, Haiti, 1490, Scholastic, 2005.

Picture books

Eight Days: A Story of Haiti, Orchard Books, 2010.

Sources

Periodicals

Brown Alumni Magazine, January/February 2011.
Emerge, April 1995, p. 58.
Guardian (London), November 19, 2004.
Islands, May/June 1995.
Miami Herald, April 19, 1995.
New York, November 20, 1995.
Newsday, March 30, 1995; May 16, 1995.
New Yorker, February 1, 2010.

New York Times, January 26, 1995; October 23, 1995; September 27, 1998; March 10, 2004; September 9, 2007; August 30, 2013.
New York Times Book Review, April 23, 1995, p. 22.
New York Times Magazine, November 20, 1994.
Philadelphia Inquirer, November 17, 1994.
Progressive, January 1997.
Seattle Times, April 30, 1995.
USA Today, October 20, 1995; November 9, 1995, p. D6.
Village Voice, September 4, 2007.
Washington Post, May 14, 1995; October 14, 2007; August 27, 2013.

Online

"Children's Book Finds Hope in Haiti's Rubble," *Morning Edition,* National Public Radio, September 9, 2010, http://www.npr.org/2010/09/09/129729646/childrens-book-finds-hope-in-haitis-rubble (accessed June 29, 2015).
"Edwidge Danticat," MacArthur Foundation, http://www.macfound.org/fellows/49/ (accessed June 29, 2015).
"Edwidge Danticat," Voices from the Gaps, University of Minnesota, http://conservancy.umn.edu/bitstream/handle/11299/166140/Danticat%2c%20Edwidge.pdf?sequence=1&isAllowed=y (accessed June 29, 2015).
"Haitian Youth Illuminated in 'Sea Light,'" *Weekend Edition,* National Public Radio, August 25, 2013, http://www.npr.org/2013/08/25/214857669/haitian-youth-illuminated-in-sea-light (accessed June 29, 2015).
Nagy, Kimberly, and Lauren McConnell, "Interview: Create Dangerously: A Conversation with Edwidge Danticat," Wild River Review, January 2012, http://www.wildriverreview.com/Literature/Interview/Edwidge-Danticat/Create-Dangerously/Nagy/McConnell/January-2012 (accessed June 29, 2015).

—Carol Brennan, Paula Kepos,
and Deborah A. Ring

Michael Eric Dyson

1958—

Professor, political analyst, author

Dyson, Michael Eric, photograph. Debby Wong/Shutterstock.com.

Michael Eric Dyson is a long-time professor, scholar, and author who addresses issues of race and culture in diverse publications such as the *New York Times* and *Rolling Stone*. He has published 18 books, including the well-received *Making Malcolm: The Myth and Meaning of Malcolm X* (1995) and *I May Not Get There with You: The True Martin Luther King, Jr.* (2000). He has also appeared on many popular talk shows, served as a political analyst for MSNBC, taught academic courses on gangsta rap and hip-hop music, and even testified before congressional subcommittees on issues of concern to black Americans.

Born in October of 1958 in Detroit, Michigan, Dyson grew up in a comfortable middle-class family. His father was an autoworker and his mother was a paraprofessional in the city schools. In a piece published in *Details* magazine, Dyson suggested that, in large part because of his age, he was somewhat isolated from the bitter civil rights struggles that occurred during the 1960s. "I was nine years old when Martin Luther King, Jr. died," he said. "I had never heard of him before then. I remember a newscaster interrupted the regular programming and broke the news. My father, sitting in his chair, went *hmph*. A *hmph* that said both 'I can't believe it' and 'How predictable.' That was my initiation into the world of white and black."

Dyson developed his oratorical skills early on by delivering speeches to the members of his Baptist church. When Dyson was a teenager, a well-meaning neighbor gave him a full set of the Harvard Classics. This standard literature of mostly white European authors may not sound like preferred reading for a black teenager, but Dyson devoured the whole set and eventually earned a scholarship to a well-known and respected boarding school in Michigan. Everything seemed to be falling into place for Dyson, but all that changed when he arrived at boarding school at age 16.

Young Spirit Tainted by Racism

At school Dyson discovered that he had been living a life of segregation. All of the schools and clubs he had ever belonged to had been made up of African Americans, and he had had very little contact with people of other ethnic backgrounds, especially those with white skin. It wasn't long before Dyson began feeling uncomfortable around his classmates, who treated him poorly,

At a Glance . . .

Born on October 23, 1958, in Detroit, MI; son of Everett (an autoworker) and Addie (a public school aide); married Marcia Louise, June 24, 1992; children: Michael Jr., Maisha. *Politics:* Democrat. *Religion:* Baptist. *Education:* Carson-Newman College, BA, 1982; Princeton University, MA, 1992, PhD, 1993.

Career: Preacher and minister, various Baptist churches; Chicago Theological Seminary, instructor, assistant professor, 1989–92; Brown University, assistant professor, 1993–95; University of North Carolina at Chapel Hill, 1995–97; Columbia University, visiting distinguished professor, 1997–99; DePaul University, Ida B. Wells-Barnett University Professor, 1999–2002; University of Pennsylvania, Avalon Foundation Professor, 2002—07; Georgetown University, University Professor of Sociology, 2007—.

Memberships: Democratic Socialist Society of America.

Awards: National Magazine Award, National Association of Black Journalists, 1992; NAACP Image Award, Outstanding Literary Work, Non-Fiction, for *Why I Love Black Women*, 2004; NAACP Image Award, Outstanding Literary Work, Non-Fiction, for *Is Bill Cosby Right? Or Has the Black Middle Class Lost Its Mind?*, 2006; American Book Award, 2007, for *Come Hell or High Water: Hurricane Katrina and the Color of Disaster*.

Addresses: *Home*—Washington, DC. *Web*—http://www.michaelericdyson.com. *Twitter*—@MichaelEDyson.

often wrecked his dorm room and possessions, and used racial slurs when referring to him. According to Dyson in an America's Intelligence Wire article, "It was very jarring to me, like a sense of Hitchcockian Vertigo." Dyson lashed out against other students in particular and the boarding school in general, and not long after he was expelled.

Dyson returned to public high school and graduated in 1976, but by that time he had become a father-to-be and was living on welfare. His responsibilities to his unborn child led him to accept a series of jobs in maintenance and auto sales, but he lost his employment just weeks before his son's birth. At that point, Dyson was known on the streets as a hustler and gang member, and it seemed as if this lifestyle was going to continue for quite some time.

Throughout his troubled youth, Dyson continued to attend his Baptist church, where he slowly rediscovered his love of oratory. With the assistance of his church pastor, Dyson studied and became a Baptist minister at age 21. According to Dyson in America's Intelligence Wire, his quest for education came about because "I needed to have a better future for my son." He traveled south to Tennessee's Knoxville College to attend divinity school, and later transferred to Carson-Newman College in Jefferson City, Tennessee, where he earned a bachelor's degree with high honors in 1982.

Wrote about Popular Culture

After college, Dyson honed another of his talents when he took up employment as a freelance journalist. This was intended to improve his writing as well as to raise money to help his younger brother, who had gone to prison during the early 1980s for second-degree murder. He worked for numerous magazines and newspapers, his specialty being African-American popular culture and music. Three years later he began his career in academia by accepting a graduate fellowship at Princeton University. While he was completing his master's and doctoral degrees, he also taught at Princeton, Hartford Seminary, and Chicago Theological Seminary. He earned his doctorate in 1993.

Although many scholars distance themselves from popular culture, Dyson chose to focus on topics of interest to mainstream readers. He became a regular contributor of record reviews to *Rolling Stone*, a popular columnist for the *Nation*, and reviewed books and films for newspapers. His first book-length collection of essays, *Reflecting Black: African-American Cultural Criticism* (1993), was a collection of his articles, including pieces on racism in the seminary, filmmaker Spike Lee, entertainer Michael Jackson, sports star Michael Jordan, and black religious leaders Martin Luther King Jr. and Malcolm X. By addressing himself to some of pop culture's icons, Dyson noted that he was attempting to resist "the labored seductions of all narrow views of black life, whether they be racist, essentialist, or otherwise uncritically disposed toward African American culture."

Dyson embarked on his book *Making Malcolm: The Myth and Meaning of Malcolm X* after a confrontation with some of his black male students at Brown University, where he taught during the early 1990s. The students objected to the presence of whites in Dyson's class on the radical Muslim leader, claiming that the whites "discuss things they don't know about," especially Malcolm X's life and philosophy. In response, Dyson decided to write a "comprehensive and critical examination of what [Malcolm X] said and did, so that his life and thought will be useful to future

generations of peoples in struggle around the globe," according to the book's introduction.

Making Malcolm was published in 1995, and the target audience was hardly just a group of ivory tower academicians. *Los Angeles Times Book Review* critic Natasha Tarpley declared that in *Making Malcolm*, Dyson exhibits "great respect, sensitivity and love—a balance Malcolm himself mastered." The critic added: "Dyson assesses Malcolm's role in the resurgent black nationalism(s) of this generation's young black artists and students ... [and] criticizes this generation for failing to learn Malcolm's greatest lesson, that of self-criticism; for seeing only the parts of Malcolm, of ourselves, of our struggle that we want to see."

Explored Gangsta Rap in Academia

In the wake of the reception for *Making Malcolm,* Dyson addressed another issue in the black community: the cultural significance of gangsta rap. Dyson began writing articles on artists such as NWA, Ice Cube, and his personal favorite, Tupac Shakur. Slowly, he gained a reputation as an authority on rap music, even being asked to testify about it before a congressional subcommittee and, according to the *New Yorker,* being lauded by Chuck D of Public Enemy as a "bad brother."

Dyson furthered his study into the world of rap with his third book, *Between God and Gangsta Rap: Bearing Witness to Black Culture,* in 1996. The purpose of the book, according to Dyson in the *Wichita Eagle,* was to put gangsta rap in its cultural and social perspective. "Gangsta rap often reaches higher than its ugliest, lowest common denominator," he noted, adding that "misogyny, violence, materialism and sexual transgression are not its exclusive domain. At its best, this music draws attention to complex dimensions of ghetto life ignored by most Americans.... Indeed, gangsta rap's in-your-face style may do more to force America to confront crucial social problems than a million sermons or political speeches."

Dyson also took gangsta rap into the classroom. He first tested the waters at the University of North Carolina at Chapel Hill, where he was a professor of communication studies and the head of the Institute for African-American research. The class was an overwhelming success, and students fought to get in every semester between 1995 and 1997, before Dyson left North Carolina to become a distinguished visiting professor at Columbia University.

Rose through Academic and Literary Worlds

During the late 1990s Dyson began work on a book that examined the public and private life of Martin Luther King Jr. To have time to write his new book, he left Columbia University in 1999 to take on a post as the first Ida B. Wells-Barnett University professor at DePaul University in Chicago. With a lighter class load at DePaul, he was able to delve into King's works, personal letters, and correspondence. The book, *I May Not Get There with You: The True Martin Luther King, Jr.* (2000), "offers critical insights into the literal and symbolic meanings of the life of [that] Southern preacher, civil rights leader, and public intellectual," according to an article in the *Western Journal of Black Studies.*

In 2001 Dyson published a book on the life of rapper Tupac Shakur, *Holler If You Hear Me: Searching for Tupac Shakur.* Instead of using the traditional biographical format to explore Shakur's life, Dyson employed a series of essays on topics such as family relations, street violence, education, and religion to explore the world that Shakur created through his lyrics and public image.

In 2002 Dyson accepted a position as an Avalon Foundation professor in the humanities and African-American studies at the University of Pennsylvania, where he refined and focused his teachings on gangsta rap and moved into hip-hop music as well. Nearly 10 years later, Dyson would focus an entire college course at Georgetown University on the hip-hop artist Jay-Z.

Over the course of the next 10 years, Tyson continued to publish new books, sometimes at the rate of two per year and often picking up accolades as he went. His 2003 book *Why I Love Black Women,* which extolls the virtues of African-American women, won an NAACP Image Award for Outstanding Literary Work. *Is Bill Cosby Right? Or Has the Black Middle Class Lost Its Mind?* (2005) also won an NAACP Image Award for Outstanding Literary Work. His book *Come Hell or High Water: Hurricane Katrina and the Color of Disaster,* published in 2006, received the American Book Award.

Dyson's success has led to increased visibility. After years of prolific writing, he began hosting his own radio show. Called *The Michael Eric Dyson Show,* it aired on Morgan State University's radio station in Baltimore from 2009 to 2011. He also serves as a political analyst for the news show MSNBC, where, according to *The Progressive,* "Dyson is part of an effort that is changing the look and feel of cable news. The network leads the cable news market among African-American viewership ... [and Dyson] pronounces scathing, even devastating critiques that arouse smiles in his viewing audience."

Now a professor of sociology at Georgetown University, Dyson has spent more than two decades positioning himself as a fearless public intellectual willing to delve deeply into issues of race, culture, and social injustice. "Dyson is among America's most influential

thinkers," David A. Love wrote for the *Progressive* in 2014. "He is a community scholar whose work seamlessly traverses the contours of the civil rights movement and the hip-hop and millennial generations."

Selected writings

Reflecting Black: African-American Cultural Criticism, University of Minnesota Press, 1993.
Making Malcolm: The Myth and Meaning of Malcolm X, Oxford University Press, 1995.
Between God and Gangsta Rap: Bearing Witness to Black Culture, Oxford University Press, 1996.
Race Rules: Navigating the Color Line, Addison-Wesley, 1996.
I May Not Get There with You: The True Martin Luther King, Jr., Free Press, 2000.
Holler If You Hear Me: Searching for Tupac Shakur, Basic Civitas Books, 2001.
Open Mike: Reflections on Philosophy, Race, Sex, Culture, and Religion, Basic Civitas Books, 2002.
Why I Love Black Women, Basic Civitas Books, 2003.
Mercy, Mercy Me: The Art, Loves, and Demons of Marvin Gaye, New York: Basic Civitas Books, 2004.
The Michael Eric Dyson Reader, Basic Civitas Books, 2004.
Is Bill Cosby Right? Or Has the Black Middle Class Lost Its Mind?, Basic Civitas Books, 2005.
Pride: The Seven Deadly Sins, Oxford University Press, 2006.
Come Hell or High Water: Hurricane Katrina and the Color of Disaster, Basic Civitas Books, 2006.
Debating Race: With Michael Eric Dyson, Basic Civitas Books, 2007.
Know What I Mean? Reflections on Hip Hop, Basic Civitas Books, 2007.
April 4, 1968: Martin Luther King Jr.'s Death and How it Changed America, Basic Civitas Books, 2008.
Can You Hear Me Now? The Inspiration, Wisdom, and Insight of Michael Eric Dyson, Basic Civitas Books, 2009.
(Editor) *Born to Use Mics: Reading Nas's Illmatic,* Basic Civitas Books, 2010.

Sources

Periodicals

American Vision, August 1999, p. 8.
America's Intelligence Wire, January 29, 2002.
Atlantic Monthly, March 1995, pp. 53–70.
Black Issues Book Review, January/February 2003, pp. 52–53.
Details, October 1995, pp. 162–167, 189.
Jet, June 17, 2002, pp. 22–23.
Journal of American Ethnic History, Fall 1998, pp. 103–108.
Los Angeles Times Book Review, March 26, 1995, p. 4.
New Republic, October 22, 2001, pp. 30–37.
New Yorker, January 9, 1995, pp. 73–80.
Philadelphia Inquirer, April 12, 1995, pp. 1F, 5F.
Progressive, October 2014, pp. 34–38.
Washington Post, October 12, 1993, p. 3C.
Washington Post Book World, December 18, 1994, p. 11.
Western Journal of Black Studies, Winter 2001, pp. 240–244.
Wichita (KS) Eagle, July 2, 1995, p. 19A.

Online

"Professor Michael Eric Dyson Defends His Jay-Z Course at Georgetown University," Vibe.com, November 4, 2011, http://www.vibe.com/2011/11/professor-michael-eric-dyson-defends-his-jay-z-course-georgetown-university/ (accessed June 3, 2015).

—Mark Kram, Ralph G. Zerbonia, and Kay Eastman

The Falcons

R&B vocal group

One of the dozens of excellent R&B groups to emerge during the 1950s, a decade regarded as a high point in the history of that genre, the Falcons have never been as well known to the general public as some of their peers. Among fans of "oldies," however, there is general agreement that they deserve broader recognition. Originally an interracial group, one of the first in the country, the Falcons are best remembered for one of the first soul records, 1959's "You're So Fine," and for the song that launched the career of R&B legend Wilson Pickett, 1962's "I Found a Love." Although the group faded soon after the latter single was released, Pickett and several of his band mates went on to distinguished solo careers that owed a great deal to the experience they had gained as members.

The Falcons began in the mid-1950s in Detroit, Michigan, long a hub for music and music education. Its strength in those areas deepened considerably over the first half of the 20th century, as waves of African-American migration from the rural South filled the city with the strains of gospel, traditional blues, and the faster-paced "jump blues," which gave birth to R&B. Although R&B groups were common in cities across the country by the early 1950s, Detroit was quickly recognized as a capital of the new style. Many of the ensembles there specialized in doo-wop, an R&B variant that depended on close vocal harmonies. Because it required very little in the way of instrumentation or formal instruction, doo-wop was a popular choice among young singers who were eager to break into the music business, and the streets and schoolyards of Detroit were filled with competing groups. Among them were the Falcons.

Like many ensembles, the Falcons experienced a number of personnel changes over the years. At the group's core, however, were Eddie Floyd and Willie Schofield, who began singing with Tom Shetler, Bob Manardo, and Arnett Robinson about 1955. Shetler and Manardo were white, a fact that drew considerable attention at the time, as interracial groups were virtually unknown at the time. Both men were soon drafted into the military, however, and with their departure, the ensemble became exclusively African American. Robinson left around the same time. Floyd and Schofield remained, recruiting Joe Stubbs, Mack Rice, and guitarist Lance Finnie. A rapport with the new members was quickly established, and within months the five had built an enthusiastic following in the Detroit area.

The Falcons also began to devote a considerable portion of their time to recording, working closely with Floyd's uncle Robert West, a local producer who owned several small labels. Although they had completed a few singles for Mercury Records when Shetler, Manardo, and Robinson were still involved, it was not until they signed with West's labels that they began to record extensively. None of their singles had more than local success, however, until "You're So Fine," recorded in January of 1959 and released soon thereafter.

A marked departure from the doo-wop style that had long been their primary focus, "You're So Fine" borrowed heavily from the "testifying" style of leading preachers and gospel artists. That influence gave it an emotional power that doo-wop often lacked, and audiences responded accordingly; a major hit, particularly in Detroit and other Northern cities, "You're So Fine" peaked at number two on the R&B list and number 17 on the pop chart. While the Falcons certainly were not the first act to blend gospel and R&B, they were unquestionably one of the first to have a national hit with that mix, which came to be known as soul.

At a Glance . . .

Members included Eddie Floyd; Willie Schofield; Tom Shetler; Bob Manardo; Arnett Robinson; Joe Stubbs; Mack Rice; Lance Finnie; Wilson Pickett.

Buoyed by that success, the group returned quickly to the recording studio, completing a string of singles in quick succession. Two of these—"Just For Your Love" (1959) and "The Teacher" (1960)—were considerable hits, reaching number 26 and number 18, respectively, on the R&B list. Soon after the latter single's release, the group's primary lead, Stubbs, was replaced by Pickett, an Alabama native with a strong background in gospel and the blues. Although his tenure with the Falcons was short, Pickett had a major influence on the group's sound, primarily by strengthening the gospel influence first evident on "You're So Fine." The result of that shift was the brilliant track "I Found a Love," recorded in January of 1962. Described by Bill Dahl of AllMusic.com as a "gospel-fired ballad," it proved an early landmark in the history of soul music, peaking at number six on the R&B chart and prompting a host of imitations.

Amid that success, however, there were signs of internal tension. The popularity of "I Found a Love" upset the group's interpersonal dynamics. Pickett, the newcomer, was now the center of attention, while the solid contributions of the group's veterans were frequently overlooked. The tension that resulted—and the many solo offers that Pickett had begun to receive from producers—led finally to his departure in the first weeks of 1963. Several efforts to regroup followed, but they were unsuccessful, and by the end of the year the Falcons, with their momentum gone, were essentially defunct. Most of the members went on to pursue solo careers. Floyd was particularly successful, repeatedly breaking the top 20 on the R&B list with enduring, well-crafted songs like "Knock on Wood," which peaked at number one in 1966.

In the decades since their demise, there have been a number of efforts to raise awareness of the Falcons'

contributions. Those efforts have been complicated by the popularity of the group's name. Several other R&B ensembles have called themselves the Falcons, and the resulting confusion has stymied even music professionals. Undoubtedly the most prominent of these namesakes, as of 2015, was a group known originally as the Fabulous Playboys. Their reincarnation as the Falcons in 1963 was the work of West, who hoped thereby to capitalize on the popularity of the group that had just disbanded. Although the "new" Falcons toured for more than a decade and had some modest success on the charts, they were not, by most estimates, the equal of the originals.

Since the 1980s there have been periodic attempts to resurrect the Falcons for occasional concerts. The most successful of those efforts occurred around 1982, when all five members of the classic lineup—Floyd, Schofield, Rice, Stubbs, and Finnie—reunited briefly.

Selected discography

"You're So Fine," 1959.
"Just for Your Love," 1959.
"The Teacher," 1960.
"I Found a Love," 1962.

Sources

Periodicals

Blues & Soul, July 27, 2011.

Online

Dahl, Bill, "The Falcons: Artist Biography," AllMusic .com, http://www.allmusic.com/artist/the-falcons -mn0000761002/biography (accessed July 9, 2015).

"The Falcons," SoulWalking.co.uk, http://www.soul walking.co.uk/Falcons.html (accessed July 9, 2015).

Goldberg, Marv, "The Falcons," UncaMarvy.com, 2009, http://www.uncamarvy.com/Falcons/fal cons.html (accessed July 9, 2015).

—R. Anthony Kugler

Andrew Gillum

1979—

Politician

Andrew Gillum made a precocious start in politics at age 23, when he became the youngest person ever elected as a city commissioner in Tallahassee, Florida. Still a student at Florida A&M University when he began his career, Gillum was already deeply involved in campus politics as well as state and national political issues. That year he was named an "Emerging Leader" by the Congressional Black Caucus Foundation. A naturally gifted speaker, Gillum was regarded as a rising star in Florida politics and within the Democratic Party. After serving for nearly a decade on the Tallahassee City Commission, Gillum was elected mayor of that city in 2014.

Gillum was born in Miami, Florida, in 1979, the son of a construction worker and a school bus driver. The fifth of seven children in the Gillum household, he learned the value of hard work and study early on. The family relocated to Gainesville when Gillum was a boy. He finished high school there in 1998 and was named one of that city's "Persons of the Year" by the local newspaper, the *Gainesville Sun,* for his contributions to the community.

At Florida A&M University in Tallahassee, where he studied political science, Gillum immediately became

Gillum, Andrew, photograph. Michael Strider/Getty Images Entertainment/Getty Images.

involved in student government, serving as president of the Senate and then as president of the Student Government Association from 2001 to 2002. Gillum was the first student ever appointed to the university's Board of Trustees and was selected to serve on a number of search committees and advisory boards while he was still a student.

Gillum also became involved in politics on a broader scale, voicing concerns following the 2000 presidential election in Florida, when thousands of voters—many of them African Americans—were purged from the voting rolls after they were falsely identified as felons. In an interview with Bill Moyers of PBS, Gillum commented on the questionable purge of voters: "It was an old Southern tactic at disenfranchising African Americans.... It was one of those tools that should've been gotten rid of, and to believe that in today's day and age that the state would be so careless in the way that it executes this purge, I mean, it's gross. It's gross." Gillum was also responsible for organizing a protest march on Tallahassee following Florida governor Jeb Bush's executive order abolishing affirmative action in both university admissions and state contracting.

At a Glance . . .

Born Andrew D. Gillum on July 26, 1979, in Miami, FL; son of Charles (a construction worker) and Frances (a school bus driver) Gillum; married R. Jai Howard, May 24, 2009; children: Jackson, Caroline. *Politics:* Democrat. *Religion:* African Methodist Episcopal. *Education:* Florida A&M University, BA, political science, 2003.

Career: People For the American Way Foundation, Florida field organizer, 2002, "Arrive with Five" program director, 2003, national deputy director, Young People For, 2004, Young Elected Officials Network, founder, 2006, director of youth leadership programs; Florida Democratic Party, interim deputy political director, 2003; Tallahassee City Commission, 2003–12; City of Tallahassee, FL, mayor, 2014—.

Memberships: Alpha Zeta Chapter of Sigma Pi Phi Fraternity; Florida A&M University National Alumni Association; New World Foundation, board of directors; Opportunity to Learn Action Fund, board of directors, Schott Foundation for Public Education, board of directors.

Awards: Named to "Persons of the Year" list, *Gainesville Sun,*1998; Top Student Leader, 2001, Center for Policy Alternatives; Emerging Leader Award, 2003, Congressional Black Caucus Foundation.

Addresses: *Home*—Tallahassee, FL. *Office*—Mayor's Office, City Hall, 300 S. Adams St., Tallahassee FL 32301. *Web*—http://www.andrewgillum.com.

Gillum made history in his adopted city in 2003 by becoming its youngest elected city commissioner, elected to a one-year term. He immediately set to work trying to close the digital divide in Tallahassee with his Digital Harmony Initiative, which aimed to create a partnership between business and educational leaders to provide, for a period of three years, new computers, Internet access, and free educational software to incoming sixth-graders at a struggling middle school. Gillum was also instrumental in transforming an unused city recreation center into a teen center. In 2004 Gillum was elected to a full four-year term on the Tallahassee City Commission with 72 percent of the vote; he was reelected in 2008, when he ran unopposed, and in 2012, when he received 72 percent of the vote.

During his tenure on the City Commission, Gillum worked on a number of other community initiatives, including several dealing with housing, such as the Landlord Tenant Mediation Program and the Code Enforcement Amnesty program, in which homeowners were granted an amnesty period to bring their properties up to building code standards. Gillum also was instrumental in the creation of the Silver Lake Neighborhood Park and in efforts to stimulate the local economy by offering commercial utility deposit rebates. In 2009 he married R. Jai Howard, whom he had met at Florida A&M.

Gillum demonstrated that he had higher ambitions than city commissioner when, in 2010, he made a bid to become leader of the Florida Democratic Party. Although he ultimately withdrew, his ambition for higher office remained. In 2013 when Tallahassee mayor John R. Marks III declared that he would not run for a fourth term, Gillum declared his candidacy for the office. Just as his campaign was getting under way, Gillum became the proud father of fraternal twins, Jackson and Caroline.

During his campaign Gillum ran on the motto "Tallahassee, we're just getting started," according to TaMaryn Waters writing in the *Tallahassee Democrat* in 2014. He pledged to support local schools, bring more start-up companies to Tallahassee, and strengthen relations between Florida State and Florida A&M universities and Tallahassee Community College, among other issues. On August 26, 2014, Gillum swept the Democratic mayoral primary, winning 76 percent of the vote in a three-way race. Waters quoted Gillum's speech to supporters following this primary victory: "What people can expect from me is a person who will be a consensus builder, a person who will work very hard to bring different sides of our community together, a person who will listen and a person who will take action to address issues that are confronting our community."

Gillum was slated for a run-off against write-in candidate Evin Matthews in the November general election, but when Matthews withdrew from the race a day after the primary, Gillum was named mayor-elect. He was sworn into office as mayor of Florida's capital city on November 21. Gillum lost no time in proposing a number of initiatives that would define his administration. He focused on families with his Family First Agenda and on economic opportunity with his Opportunity Agenda. He also targeted the development of youth leaders in the community through the Tallahassee Mayoral Program and launched the 1,000 Mentors program to provide students mentors who could guide them in achieving their true potential.

Gillum made national news in 2015 when, following the overturning of Florida's ban on same-sex marriage by the U.S. Supreme Court, a number of counties in conservative North Florida indicated that their clerks

would refuse to issue licenses or perform marriages for gay and lesbian couples. The Tallahassee mayor extended an invitation to the "loving couples" of those counties, according to Marc Caputo in the *Miami Herald,* to come to the state capital to be married. "I hope that this issue reminds us that love is never wrong, and that equality must continue to be a part of the progress we work to drive in our community, our state, and in our country," Gillum added. Caputo noted of Gillum's support of gay rights, "The historic decision gave him a chance to shine politically. And he did."

Sources

Periodicals

Jet, July, 2003, p. 31.
Miami New Times, November 23, 2010.
Tallahassee (FL) Democrat, August 27, 2014.
Tallahassee (FL) Magazine, May/June 2015.

Online

Alcock, Andy, "Update: Withdrawal Makes Gillum Mayor-Elect, Focus Shifts to Governing," WCTV, August 27, 2014, http://www.wctv.tv/home/head lines/Gillum-Captures-Tallahassee-Mayoral-Primary -Richardson-Elected-New-Commissioner-27282 04 91.html (accessed June 7, 2015).

"Andrew Gillum Kicks Off 1,000 Mentors Initiative," Volunteer Florida, http://www.volunteerflorida.org/ 1000-mentors-initiative/ (accessed June 7, 2015).

Caputo, Marc A. "Tallahassee Mayor Andrew Gillum to North Fla. Gay Couples: Get Married Here," *Naked Politics* (*Miami Herald* blog), January 6, 2015, http://miamiherald.typepad.com/nakedpolitics/ 2015/01/tallahassee-mayor-andrew-gillum-to-north -fla-gay-couples-get-married-here.html (accessed June 7, 2015).

"Mayor Andrew Gillum," City of Tallahassee, Florida, http://www.talgov.com/mayor/commission-offi cials-gillum.aspx (accessed June 7, 2015).

Moyers, Bill, *Now,* PBS, July 30, 2004, http://www .pbs.org/now/printable/transcript331_full_print .html (accessed June 10, 2015).

"Tallahassee, Fla. Mayor Andrew D. Gillum: YEO Network Executive Director," YEO Network, http:// yeonetwork.org/about-us/yeo-network-team/ (accessed June 7, 2015).

—J. Sydney Jones

Wardell Gray

1921–1955

Jazz saxophonist

Gray, Wardell, photograph. Ray Whitten Photography/Michael Ochs Archives/Getty Images.

More than half a century after his death, saxophonist Wardell Gray remains a revered figure among jazz fans and professional musicians. A versatile and expressive stylist who moved easily between fast-paced swing and introspective bebop, he played with a host of leading figures, including fellow saxophonists Charlie Parker and Dexter Gordon, bandleaders Earl "Fatha" Hines and Benny Goodman, and vocalist Billie Holiday. While he made a number of well-received recordings as a leader, Gray is best remembered for his backup work for other artists and for his kindly and thoughtful demeanor. Pianist Hampton Hawes described him, in a comment quoted by Tom Reney of New England Public Radio, as one of the "keepers of the flame, the ones the younger players held in esteem for their ideas and experience and consistency."

Born in Oklahoma City on February 13, 1921, Carl Wardell Gray moved with his family to Detroit, Michigan, at the age of about eight. Known at the time as a hub of cutting-edge music, Detroit supported a wide array of performers, from street-corner blues vocalists to gospel choirs to swing bands and classical orchestras. Gray's exposure to all of those styles was considerable, particularly after he entered Cass Technical High School, a landmark institution known for the quality of its music programs. He began his musical studies playing the clarinet, noted critic Stuart A. Varden, but switched to the saxophone after hearing a recording by Lester "Prez" Young, whose exuberant, swinging style would have a major influence on his own.

Like many of his fellow musicians, Gray began his career with local gigs when he was still a teenager. The experience that he gained working with regional bandleaders such as Benny Carew helped him draw the attention of Hines, a nationally known star who hired him on a trip through Detroit in 1943. Gray remained with Hines for roughly two years, touring widely, and then moved on to join orchestras led by Billy Eckstine and Benny Carter. About 1946, while working for Carter, he traveled to Los Angeles, where Parker, Gordon, and others were focusing on bebop, which was soon to overtake swing as the dominant sound in jazz. Drawn by the new sound, Gray remained in Southern California for several years. Among his closest collaborators there was Gordon, whom he often faced in friendly competition, trading solos with him on stage and in the recording studio.

At a Glance . . .

Born Carl Wardell Gray on February 13, 1921, in Oklahoma City, OK; died on May 25, 1955, in Las Vegas, NV; son of Eugene Gray and Carrie Maddison Gray; married Jeanne Goings (divorced); married Jeri Walker (divorced); married Dorothy A. Duvall; children: daughter Anita, stepdaughter Paula.

Career: Jazz saxophonist, 1930s–55.

One of those so-called saxophone battles resulted in *The Chase* (1947), a popular and influential recording for which he and Gordon received equal billing. Gray also worked closely with Parker, backing him on a famous piece called "Relaxing at Camarillo" (1947), which is recognized as one of the cornerstones of bebop.

The months that followed were among the most active of Gray's career, thanks in part to an extended gig with Goodman, a swing icon who was beginning to experiment a bit with bebop himself. That engagement brought Gray back East, where he remained for a time after leaving Goodman in the fall of 1949. In both New York City and Chicago, he found ample opportunities. In addition to backup work for stars such as Holiday and another orchestra engagement, this one with Count Basie, he toured and recorded with several small groups of his own.

Gray played a significant role in bringing the bebop techniques developed in Southern California's many jazz clubs to the attention of the public in other areas of the country. In a pointed allusion to this role, one of his bands during this period was named the Los Angeles All Stars. Its members included Hawes, trumpeter Art Farmer, bassist Harper Cosby, drummer Larance Marable, and conga player Robert Collier. Together they helped him complete an album—also called *Los Angeles All Stars*—for New York's Prestige Records in 1953. Featuring new and distinctive renditions of standards such as "Lover Man," it was one of Gray's most ambitious works as a leader since *The Chase*.

An avid reader who frequently carried books to his gigs, Gray avoided for many years the substance abuse that derailed the careers of many of his peers. In the nightclubs that constituted his primary workplace, however, drugs and alcohol were ubiquitous, and by the time he returned to California about 1951, there were indications that he was flirting with addiction himself. As most of those signs were visible only to his band mates and close friends, he retained his reputation among club owners and producers, and he continued to work steadily, typically in California but sometimes farther afield.

In the spring of 1955 he was hired to appear in Las Vegas at the opening of the Moulin Rouge, the city's first racially integrated casino. A routine gig, it tragically proved to be his last. On May 25, 1955, he failed to appear as scheduled, and concerns for his health and safety grew. Those fears were confirmed the following day when he was found dead on a roadside outside the city. The local coroner subsequently determined that Gray had been brought there after suffering severe injuries to his brain and spinal cord in another location.

The precise circumstances of Gray's death have been the subject of considerable controversy for decades. Although it is widely believed that he fell to his death after a drug overdose, it has been suggested repeatedly that he was murdered. His demise has inspired at least one murder mystery (Bill Moody's *Death of a Tenor Man*) and intense speculation regarding possible motives and perpetrators. In any event, his loss was keenly felt throughout the jazz world. In the decades since there have been a number of efforts to keep his legacy alive, including a memorial album (1955's *Wardell Gray Memorial: Volume One*), other reissues of his recordings, and a biographical documentary, *Forgotten Tenor*, completed by director Abraham Ravett in 1994 after five years of work. A faculty member at Hampshire College, Ravett described the project as "a meditation on time, memory, and the evolving histories of American Black classical music."

Selected discography

Singles

Charlie Parker, "Relaxing at Camarillo," 1947.

Albums

One for Prez, Sunset, 1946.
(With Dexter Gordon) *The Chase,* Dial, 1947.
Los Angeles All Stars (includes "Lover Man"), Prestige, 1953.
Wardell Gray Memorial: Volume One, Prestige, 1955.

Sources

Online

Olsen, Eric B., and Ira Gitler, "Wardell Gray," Hard Bop Homepage, http://hardbop.tripod.com/wgray.html (accessed June 30, 2015).

Ravett, Abraham, *Forgotten Tenor,* Hampshire College, http://faculty.hampshire.edu/aravett/films/forgotten_tenor.html (accessed July 1, 2015).

Reney, Tom, "Wardell Gray," New England Public Radio, February 14, 2014, http://nepr.net/music/2014/02/14/wardell-gray/ (accessed June 30, 2015).

Varden, Stuart A., "Biography of Wardell Gray,"

WardellGray.org, http://wardellgray.org/biography.
html (accessed June 30, 2015).

Yanow, Scott, "Wardell Gary: Artist Biography," All Music.com, http://www.allmusic.com/artist/wardell
-gray-mn0000235881/biography (accessed June
30, 2015).

—R. Anthony Kugler

Brittney Griner

1990—

Professional basketball player

Described by ESPN's Kate Fagan as "a gift from the basketball gods," Brittney Griner is among the world's most famous female basketball players. Standing six feet, eight inches, with a wingspan of 88 inches and an amazing athleticism to match her height advantage, Griner is a phenomenon never before seen in the women's game. The most dominant force in the history of women's college basketball, the three-time All-American center for Baylor University swept all of the major national awards in her junior and senior years—the Wade Trophy,

Griner, Brittney, photograph. Phil Stafford/Shutterstock.com.

the Naismith Trophy, the John R. Wooden Award, and Associated Press honors—and led the Lady Bears to the National Collegiate Athletic Association (NCAA) Division I championship in 2012. Chosen by the Phoenix Mercury as the top pick in the Women's National Basketball Association (WNBA) draft in April of 2013, Griner reenergized the franchise with her fabulous blocks and dunks and was the key element in its road to a title win in 2014.

While making headlines for her abilities on the court, Griner also turned heads for her unprecedented step of coming out before the start of her rookie year in the WNBA. The first openly gay athlete signed by Nike to an endorsement deal, Griner frankly discusses her sexuality in interviews, and it is the subject of her 2014 autobiography, *In My Skin: My Life On and Off the Basketball Court*. Her candor has shaken up old-school gender stereotypes and made it easier for her to comfortably inhabit her own body. Griner says she has also come to terms with the many painful episodes of bullying she endured as a teenager, when she was often taunted for being manly. On May 8, 2015, Griner married fellow WNBA player Glory Johnson, a two-time All-Star forward with the Tulsa Shock.

Lashed Out against Taunts

Griner was born in October of 1990 in Houston, Texas. Her father, Raymond, was a police officer, and her mother, Sandra, stayed home to take care of Brittney and her older sister, Pier. She wrote in her autobiography that she grew up in a nice house in a good suburb with loving parents. She described herself as a "rough-and-tumble" kid who liked to push her mother's buttons to see what she could get away with while her father, a former marine and a strict discipli-

At a Glance . . .

Born on October 18, 1990, in Houston, TX; daughter of Raymond Griner (a police officer) and Sandra Griner (a homemaker); married Glory Johnson (a professional basketball player), May 8, 2015. *Education:* Baylor University, BA, general studies, 2013.

Career: USA Basketball Women's National Team, 2011—; Phoenix Mercury, 2013—; Beijing Great Wall (Women's Chinese Basketball Association), 2014.

Memberships: It Gets Better Project, 2013—.

Awards: National Freshman of the Year, U.S. Basketball Writers Association, 2009–10; Big 12 Freshman of the Year, 2010; Wade Trophy, Best Player, National Collegiate Athletic Association (NCAA) Women's Division I, State Farm/Women's Basketball Coaches Association (WBCA), 2011–12, 2012–13; NCAA Division I Defensive Player of the Year, WBCA, 2011, 2012, 2013; Big 12 Player of the Year, 2011, 2012, 2013; Most Outstanding Player, NCAA Women's Basketball Tournament, 2012; Naismith Trophy, Women's College Player of the Year, 2012, 2013; John R. Wooden Award, National Player of the Year, 2012, 2013; Associated Press Player of the Year, 2012, 2013; Women's National Basketball Association (WNBA) All-Star selection, 2013, 2014; WNBA Defensive Player of the Year, 2014; All-Star Game Most Valuable Player, Women's Chinese Basketball Association, 2014; Visibility Award, Human Rights Campaign, 2015.

Addresses: *Agent*—Lindsay Kagawa Colas, VP/Action Sports & Olympians, Wasserman Media Group, 10960 Wilshire Blvd., Suite 2200, Los Angeles, CA 90024. *Web*—http://brittneygriner.com. *Twitter*—@brittneygriner.

narian, was at work. As a young girl, Griner avoided dresses and dolls, preferring to spend her time with her teenage stepbrother, DeCarlo, a mechanic who took her for rides on his motorcycle.

In middle school, when other kids started to tease her for being different, Griner developed a protective shell. She got into fights with classmates who snickered at her tall, thin body, and she started mouthing off to her teachers. When she was in the sixth grade, her father sent her for a stint in reform school.

By the time she was in the seventh grade, Griner had found a refuge in sports. She played volleyball and soccer in middle school, but it was not until her freshman year at Nimitz High School that she began playing basketball. She was an immediate local sensation, and by her junior year she had captured the national spotlight as well. A 2007 YouTube video showing her dunking went viral, and she was named to various All-State and All-American teams. During her senior year her team got its first playoff berth in school history, and she set national single-game records of 25 blocks and seven dunks. She was named High School Player of the Year by the Women's Basketball Coaches Association, Rivals.com, *USA Today,* and *Parade Magazine.* In addition, she was selected as the Gatorade Texas High School Player of the Year and Texas Miss Basketball by the Texas Association of Basketball Coaches.

Starred at Baylor University

Griner verbally committed to Baylor at the end of her junior year, in part because the Waco, Texas, campus was close to home. During her freshman year there, she established a string of school, conference, and national records for dunks, points, blocked shots, and rebounds. She was selected National Freshman of the Year by the U.S. Basketball Writers Association, and she claimed five Big 12 Conference honors: Freshman of the Year, Co-Defensive Player of the Year, All-Big 12 First Team, All-Defensive Team, and All-Freshman Team. Griner's accomplishments were temporarily overshadowed at a March 4, 2010, game against Texas Tech, during which tensions elevated to the point that Griner punched one of her opponents in the face, breaking her nose. Kim Mulkey, the coach of the Lady Bears, announced the following day that Griner would be suspended for one game in addition to the one-game suspension required by NCAA rules.

During her sophomore year Griner scored her 1,000th point, including a career high of 40 points against Green Bay in the Sweet Sixteen of the NCAA Tournament. Baylor lost to Texas A&M University in the Elite Eight round that year, but the Lady Bears took the title the following year with an 80–61 win over the University of Notre Dame sealed by Griner's 26 points, 13 rebounds, and five blocks. That season the Lady Bears became the first NCAA team, men's or women's, to win 40 games. Griner made history as the first Division I player to tally 2,000 career points and 500 blocks.

With ESPN's television coverage of the 2012 NCAA women's tournament built around Griner, there was widespread speculation that she would forgo her senior season and jump to the pros. However, as the tournament came to a close, Griner told reporters that she remained committed to Baylor and to finishing her education. Griner also received a great deal of unwanted attention for her unusual appearance and abilities. News outlets and social media sites were abuzz

with talk of her low voice, flat chest, and size 17 shoes. Rumors swirled that she was really a man or perhaps transgender. There were even reports that she had removed herself from consideration for a spot on the 2012 U.S. Olympic team because she was afraid of genetic testing. As Fagan noted, "When people called Shaq a freak of nature, it was a compliment; when directed at Griner, the term often carries a cruel edge, punctuated with the refrain of 'She's a dude!'"

Returning to Baylor for her last year, Griner led the team to a 34–2 record. In a February 18, 2013, game against the University of Connecticut, Griner scored her 3,000th career point. On Senior Night at the Ferrell Center in Waco—her final regular-season game—Griner electrified a record crowd with her first 50-point game, a 90–68 win over Kansas State University. In one of the biggest upsets in women's tournament history, the University of Louisville stunned Baylor during the regional semifinals, denying them a chance at back-to-back title wins.

Came Out Publicly as Gay

In interviews with *Sports Illustrated* and *USA Today* following the April 15, 2013, WNBA draft, Griner publicly acknowledged that she is gay. She discussed coming out to her parents and the pain of being a closeted player at Baylor, a Baptist-affiliated school with an official policy against homosexuality. Griner elaborated in her autobiography, stating that Coach Mulkey had told her to keep her homosexuality private because it would tarnish the program's image and hurt recruiting. However, Griner also praised Mulkey for defending her against the relentless taunting she was subjected to at games and on Twitter and other social media sites.

Griner made a dazzling debut with the Phoenix Mercury, delivering two dunks, 17 points, and eight rebounds in a game against the Chicago Sky on May 27, 2013. An injury to her knee in June left her sidelined for several games and also caused her to miss the WNBA All-Star Game late in July. The team lost to the Minnesota Lynx in the Western Conference finals. Griner spent the off-season playing for Beijing in the Women's Chinese Basketball Association. She improved in almost every major category her second season with Phoenix. She was honored as Defensive Player of the Year after setting a single-season record of 129 blocked shots. Due to an eye injury sustained during game 2 of the WNBA Finals, Griner was forced to sit out the Mercury's game 3 title clincher against the Sky.

After coming out, Griner became a powerful voice for the lesbian, gay, bisexual, and transgender (LGBT) community. She relished her new role as an inspiration to teens facing harassment. She recorded a video for the It Gets Better Project, a worldwide movement that offers a message of hope to LGBT youth, and she regularly responded to tweets from young people seeking advice on coming out and bullying. She told Michelle Garcia of the *Advocate* that she wrote her autobiography for the "younger kids and teens that are going through the same things that I went through, coming out, and kind of finding themselves. I wanted to write my memoir so I could show them I was there, I made it through, even when I was at my lowest moments.... When I was growing up I really didn't have a role model in sports who came out early in their career—to give me hope." Griner also became something of a lesbian fashion icon. She embraced her lanky frame and large hands and feet, and she liked to show off her unique sense of style—tattoos, bow ties, argyle socks, Chuck Taylors, and menswear vests, pants, and jackets.

Sanctioned by WNBA for Domestic Violence

On April 22, 2015, just a little over a week after she accepted the Visibility Award from the Human Rights Campaign, a civil rights organization devoted to achieving equality for LGBT Americans, Griner and her then fiancée, Glory Johnson, were arrested on charges of domestic violence. According to the incident report, the two got into an argument in their new home in Goodyear, Arizona, that escalated into a physical brawl. Neither of the women needed medical attention or wanted to prosecute the other. Griner pleaded guilty to a misdemeanor charge of disorderly conduct and entered into a diversion program, whereby she agreed to 26 weeks of domestic violence counseling in exchange for the charges being dismissed. Johnson pleaded not guilty.

With partner abuse becoming an hot-button in men's professional sports, the WNBA decided to take a tough stance by handing down seven-game suspensions without pay to both players. A number of Griner's and Johnson's teammates believed the suspensions were excessive, amounting to about 20 percent of the 34-game season, and urged them to appeal. In a phone interview with Phil Thompson in the *Chicago Tribune,* WNBA president Laurel Richie discounted the possibility of leniency: "The issue of domestic violence is one that we as a league take very, very seriously. And the process and investigation was thorough and thoughtful and deliberate. I am completely comfortable with where we ended up and quite firm in where we ended up."

Johnson and Griner went ahead with their wedding plans and were married at a Phoenix resort on May 8. However, 28 days later, on June 5, Griner filed for an annulment. According to Cliff Brunt for the Huffington Post, Griner explained in a public statement, "In the week prior to the wedding, I attempted to postpone the wedding several times until I completed counseling, but

I still went through with it. I now realize that was a mistake." Griner continued to train with the American national team and hoped to compete for the United States at the 2016 Olympics in Rio de Janeiro, Brazil.

Selected writings

(With Sue Hovey) *In My Skin: My Life On and Off the Basketball Court,* It Books/Harper Collins, 2014.

Sources

Periodicals

Advocate, July 29, 2014.
Atlantic, March 26, 2013.
Chicago Tribune, May 29, 2015.
Elle, November 4, 2013.
ESPN The Magazine, May 29, 2013.
New York Times, April 23, 2015; May 11, 2015.
People, May 9, 2015.
Seattle Times, May 15, 2015.
Sports Illustrated, May 18, 2013.

Online

"Brittney Griner," Baylor Athletics, http://www.baylorbears.com/sports/w-baskbl/mtt/griner_brittney00.html (accessed May 31, 2015).
"Brittney Griner: High School Girl Dunker," YouTube, 2007, https://www.youtube.com/watch?v=tuDfRzY2Vqw (accessed May 31, 2015).
"Brittney Griner: It Gets Better," It Gets Better Project, http://www.itgetsbetter.org/video/entry/10164/ (accessed June 1, 2015).
"Brittney Griner," USA Basketball, May 25, 2015, http://www.usab.com/basketball/players/womens/g/griner-brittney.aspx (accessed May 31, 2015).
Brunt, Cliff, "WNBA's Griner Files to Annul Marriage to Fellow WNBA Player," Huffington Post, June 6, 2015, *Huffington Post,* June 5, 2015 (accessed August 5, 2015).
Fagan, Kate, "Held Up in Customs," ESPN.com, October 14, 2014, http://espn.go.com/womens-college-basketball/story/_/id/10787294/wnba-star-brittney-griner-adjusts-life-china-espn-magazine (accessed June 1, 2015).
———, "What Griner Says about Us," ESPN.com, May 28, 2013, http://espn.go.com/womens-college-basketball/tournament/2013/story/_/id/9065613/2013-ncaa-women-tournament-brittney-griner-backlash-not-us (accessed June 1, 2015).
Fedotin, Jeff, "Griner Named Nation's No. 1 Player," Rivals.com, February 26, 2009, https://www.rivals.com/content.asp?cid=916007 (accessed June 1, 2015).
Phoenix Mercury, http://mercury.wnba.com/?sess=1e5426a3aa4f1a54791ae6b267f1973d (accessed June 1, 2015).

—Janet Mullane

Darryl Hill

1943—

Entrepreneur, nonprofit executive

Darryl Hill was a trailblazer in college football during the 1960s, becoming the first African American to play football at the U.S. Naval Academy in 1961 and then the first black player in the Atlantic Coast Conference—or any other Southern athletic conference—when he suited up for the University of Maryland team in 1963. He was the only black player for the Terrapins until his senior year. During his college football career, Hill endured racist taunts from fans, and his coach received death threats, requiring the protection of the National Guard. Following a brief stint with the New York Jets after college, Hill launched a successful business career that took him around the world, working in industries as varied as green energy, road construction, and forestry, before he returned to his alma mater to serve as director of major gifts in 2003. After retiring from that position in 2009, Hill embarked on another career in the nonprofit sector, establishing the Kids Play USA Foundation, an organization that aims to increase access to organized sports among disadvantaged youth.

Broke Color Barrier in College Football

Darryl Andrew Hill was born in Washington, DC, in 1943. His family belonged to the District of Columbia's black elite class. His grandparents had been entrepreneurs. Hill's father, Kermit, owned and operated one of the country's largest black-owned commercial trucking firms of the time, Hill's Transfer Company; his mother, Palestine, was a teacher of Latin and Romance languages in the Washington public schools. In 1954,

following the U.S. Supreme Court's landmark decision in *Brown v. Board of Education* deemed school segregation unconstitutional, she was one of the first black teachers offered a job in a formerly all-white school.

After a short time at a public elementary school, Hill enrolled at Holy Name, a private Catholic school in Washington. By the time he completed primary school, public schools had been desegregated, and Hill attended Gonzaga College High School, where he played football; he was the first African American on the team. Hill helped lead Gonzaga to the 1959 city championship, and upon his graduation in 1960, he earned a football scholarship to Xavier University in Cincinnati, Ohio. After one year at Xavier, he transferred to the U.S. Naval Academy in Annapolis, Maryland, where, as starting half back, he became the first African American to play on the navy's freshman team. With no interest in pursuing a military career but keen to continue playing football, Hill transferred to the University of Maryland in 1962. With the Terrapins he was a pioneer once again, the first African American to play college football in a Southern athletic conference.

Hill endured harsh treatment during his college football career. The University of Maryland's Board of Trustees initially protested Hill's participation, arguing that it was wrong to place a black football player on the team. When he entered the field at the start of away games, he was typically met with booing, a sentiment that was extended to his family in the stands. At his first game at the University of South Carolina, opposing players at first refused to play a team with a black player, and a

At a Glance . . .

Born Darryl Andre Hill on October 21, 1943, in Washington, DC; son of Kermit Hill (a business owner) and Palestine Smith Hill (a schoolteacher); children: Tami, Patrick, Maia. *Education:* Attended Xavier University, 1960–61, U.S. Naval Academy, 1961–62; University of Maryland, BS, economics, 1965; Southern Illinois University, MS, urban planning, 1976.

Career: Restaurateur, 1977–91; Polaris Energy Corporation, Panama, founder, 1982; Northstar International Corporation, founder and chief executive officer, 1991—; University of Maryland, Department of Intercollegiate Athletics, director of major gifts, 2003–09; University of the District of Columbia, professor of entrepreneurship, 2010—; Testudo Film Partners, LLC, president, 2010—; NeXecelerator, chief executive officer, 2012–14; TW Capital, 2015—.

Memberships: 100 Black Men; Terrapin Club; Kids Play USA Foundation, chairman, 2011—; Maryland State Athletic Hall of Fame, board of directors, 2012—.

Awards: Inducted into Gonzaga High School Hall of Fame, 2000; inducted into University of Maryland Athletic Hall of Fame, 2008.

Addresses: *Home*—Columbia, MD. *Office*—Kids Play USA, 1108 Harding Rd., Laurel, MD 20723. *Web*—http://kidsplayusafoundation.org. *Twitter*@Kidsplay usaorg.

riot nearly ensued. At South Carolina's Clemson University, Hill's family was denied entry. Before a 1963 home game against North Carolina State University, an anonymous caller threatened to shoot Hill from the roof of a nearby hall if he entered the playing field. Although the threat was never carried out, the experience understandably left Hill upset. As he shared with Jeremy Hottle of the University of Maryland student newspaper the *Diamondback*, when the Terps scored their first points and the traditional cannon fired, Hill dove for cover. "My teammates—of course, they weren't aware of what happened—were rolling on the ground, laughing. I didn't think it was so funny."

Despite the rampant racism, Hill had advocates in his corner. His teammates refused to stay in hotels that barred black people. As noted by Hottle, University of Maryland president Wilson Elkins told trustees who opposed Hill's participation, "That's not your call—it's

mine. You see me next year at contract negotiations." Hill's mother gained entry to one game at Clemson University, in 1963, when Clemson's president, Robert C. Edwards, invited her to sit with his family. From the president's box that day, Palestine Hill watched her son set a Maryland record by catching 10 passes. At North Carolina's Wake Forest University, while fans relentlessly taunted Hill with racist comments, opposing running back Brian Piccolo (subject of the television movie *Brian's Song*) put an arm around him and apologized for the fans' behavior.

Hill's participation helped spark change, and within a decade, black players were found on college teams throughout the South, including Clemson. For that reason, Hill has often been compared to Jackie Robinson, the first African American to play in baseball's major leagues. Despite his impact and all that he endured, Hill those years with modesty. "If I hadn't done it somebody would have," he told Mark Newgent of the *Baltimore Sun*. "The only thing I think that I probably feel fairly well about is that if I had faltered or failed in some way or something that gone awry or I had quit in the middle of it, it may have delayed the process."

Became a Successful Entrepreneur

Hill finished his junior season with 43 catches, missing the school record by five. A broken foot sidelined him for most his senior year, and after graduating with an economics degree, he had only a brief preseason stint with the New York Jets before retiring from football. Putting his degree to use, in 1977 he opened the first black-owned fine-dining restaurant in the United States, W. H. Bone and Company in Washington, DC. He followed this with two more Southern-style fine-dining restaurants: The Savoy, also in DC, and Wildwood in Atlanta, Georgia. Having developed an interest in green energy, Hill founded and managed Polaris Energy Corporation in Panama in 1982. The following decade, he extended himself further abroad by founding Sibercor International (later renamed Northstar International Corporation), an international business development and financial services firm. For that company, Hill operated businesses in diverse industries across the globe, including forestry in Siberia, Russia, and Brazil; packaging in China; and road building in Nigeria.

In 2003 Hill returned to the University of Maryland, where he served as director of major gifts in the Department of Intercollegiate Athletics. He left the job in 2009, although he was not yet ready to retire. In addition to becoming a professor of entrepreneurship at the University of the District of Columbia, Hill launched Testudo Film Partners, LLC, which was created to coproduce *Illegal Contact,* a feature film about his college football experience. The film's concept is based on a play written by University of Maryland

English professor Michael Olmert, called *Moving the Chains: The Darryl Hill Story*. The play was coproduced by Washington's Theatre J and Lincoln Theatre in March of 2011.

In 2008 Hill was inducted into the University of Maryland Athletic Hall of Fame, both for his football skills and for breaking the color barrier in the Atlantic Coast Conference. Speaking of the latter achievement in a 2011 interview with WAMU 88.5's Rebecca Sheir, Hill identified two of his proudest moments. Of the first, he recalled, "At the end of the [1962] season, I walked off the field at Clemson University, and I was being interviewed in the locker room and the sportscaster said, well, ladies and gentlemen, segregation in college sports died today. And that was poignant." The other moment occurred several years later. As Hill reflected, "Clemson winds up winning the national championship and I just recall when they flashed a picture of the starting lineup, that almost every single player, including the quarterback, was black."

In 2011 Hill established Kids Play USA, a nonprofit organization focused on providing equal opportunities for children to play organized sports regardless of their economic background. The organization's tagline is "No kid shall be left on the sidelines."

Sources

Periodicals

Baltimore Sun, January 30, 2014.

Diamondback (University of Maryland student newspaper), October 23, 2012.
Palm Beach (FL) Post, October 25, 2006.
Washington Post, December 18, 2008.
Washington Times, September 9, 2013.

Online

"Backstage at the Lincoln: 'Moving the Chains: The Darryl Hill Story,'" University of Maryland, Department of English, http://www.english.umd.edu/events/2410 (accessed June 15, 2015).
"Darryl Hill," The History Makers, http://www.thehistorymakers.com/biography/darryl-hill-38 (accessed June 15, 2015).
Ramsburg, Ray, "February 12: 'Changing the Face of College Sports,'" Rotary Club of Frederick (MD), http://www.frederickrotaryclub.org/blog/february-12-changing-the-face-of-college-sports (accessed June 15, 2015).
Sheir, Rebecca, "Darryl Hill Interview," WAMU 88.5, April 22, 2011, http://wamu.org/programs/metro_connection/11/04/22/moving_the_chains_the_darryl_hill_story_transcript (accessed June 15, 2015).
Zirin, Dave, "Darryl Hill: From Maryland to Siberia, and Back," Pro Player Insiders, November 11, 2011, http://proplayerinsiders.com/nfl-player-team-news-features/darryl-hill-from-maryland-to-siberia-and-back/ (accessed June 15, 2015).

—Candice Mancini

Marc Lamont Hill

1978—

Professor, author, media commentator, activist

Hill, Marc Lamont, photograph. John Medina/WireImage/Getty Images.

Marc Lamont Hill is a self-described "hip-hop genera-tion intellectual." A professor of African-American studies and a specialist in contempo-rary education, he has taught a wide range of classes, from literacy workshops for high school dropouts to advanced seminars in pedagogical theory. Hill is best known, however, for his books and for his work as a public affairs commentator, particularly for television networks and web-sites. *Ebony* magazine has named him both a "Leader of the Future" (2005) and one of the most influential African Americans in the country (2011).

Hill was born on December 17, 1978, in Philadelphia, where he was raised. In a 2012 interview with *Ebony*'s Dream Hampton, Hill recalled his early interest in reading and his family's support of his academic pur-suits. A strong student in high school, he won admis-sion to Atlanta's Morehouse College, one of the most prominent African-American institutions in the coun-try. By his own account, however, his coursework there failed to engage him. After dropping out in his fresh-man year, he was persuaded by a number of men-tors—or "elders," as he described them to Hamp-ton—to reconsider that decision, and he soon resumed his education at Temple Uni-versity in Philadelphia, where he received a bachelor's de-gree in education in 2000. He then moved across town to begin graduate studies at the University of Pennsylvania. He completed his doctoral de-gree in 2005 after writing a dissertation in a growing field, the anthropology and ethnog-raphy of education. His work focused, in particular, on the many ways that rap and hip-hop have shaped the class-room experiences of urban high school students.

Hill's dissertation drew the at-tention of Temple, his undergraduate alma mater, which hired him in 2005 as an assistant professor in the Departments of Education and American Studies. Four years later he moved to New York City to become an associate professor of English education and African-American studies at Columbia University's Teachers College, one of the nation's leading centers of education research. He remained at Columbia until 2014, when he was named Distinguished Professor of African American Studies at Morehouse.

His career as an author, meanwhile, was developing steadily. His first major publication was a book that he coedited with Lalitha Vasudevan; titled *Media, Learn-*

At a Glance . . .

Born on December 17, 1978, in Philadelphia, PA. *Education:* Temple University, BS, education, 2000; University of Pennsylvania, PhD, education, 2005.

Career: Media commentator, 2000s—; Temple University, assistant professor of urban education and American studies, 2005–09; author and editor, 2007—; Columbia University, associate professor of English education and African-American studies, 2009–14; Morehouse College, Distinguished Professor of African American Studies, 2014—.

Memberships: My5th, founding board member; American Civil Liberties Union.

Awards: Named one of "30 Leaders of the Future," *Ebony,* 2005; named one of the "Power 100," *Ebony,* 2011.

Addresses: *Office*—African American Studies Program, Morehouse College, 830 Westview Dr. SW, Atlanta, GA 30314. *Web*—http://www.marclamonthill.com/.

commentator on contemporary politics, urban culture, and the law. In the mid-2000s he appeared on the Fox News Channel, a prominent cable television network with a reputation for social and political conservatism. On Fox programs such as *The O'Reilly Factor* and *Hannity,* Hill often found himself in impromptu debates with other guests or with the shows' hosts. His viewpoint in these discussions was generally liberal. A supporter of Barack Obama, he nevertheless criticized the U.S. president sharply on several occasions, most notably for he what he viewed as Obama's failure to pursue nonmilitary solutions to the conflicts in Afghanistan and Iraq.

Hill's tenure at Fox ended abruptly in October of 2009. He shifted quickly to other venues, many of them online. Active on Twitter, YouTube, and other social media sites, he also wrote regularly for more traditional outlets such as Metro Newspapers, a chain of alternative weeklies; hosted a talk show (*BET Live*) for Black Entertainment Television; appeared as a political commentator for CNN; and served the news site Huffington Post in a variety of capacities, including blogger and video host.

Hill's full schedule has not kept him from activism and volunteer work. Since his days at the University of Pennsylvania, he has been involved in a number of nonprofit outreach efforts, many of which have focused on literacy and dropout prevention. As early as 2001 he had designed and implemented a program that relied on hip-hop to reach at-risk students and improve their school performance. Those efforts later became the basis for his dissertation.

Not all of his outreach activities have been confined to the classroom, however. In the mid-2000s Hill was a cofounder of My5th, an organization aimed at increasing young people's awareness of their legal rights, particularly the Fifth Amendment's guarantee of due process. Closely related to that work was his involvement in several initiatives of the American Civil Liberties Union, including its campaigns to reform the nation's drug policies and end the death penalty. Hill has often expressed unease about the government's drug enforcement efforts, arguing that they inflict a heavy and disproportionate toll on the nation's minorities, especially African-American youth.

In 2015 Hill was at work on two new books, tentatively titled *10 Right Wing Myths about Education* and *Written by Himself: Race, Masculinity, and the Politics of Literacy.*

ing, and Sites of Possibility, it appeared in 2007. Two years later he published though Teachers College Press an ambitious, wide-ranging volume called *Beats, Rhymes, and Classroom Life: Hip-Hop Pedagogy and the Politics of Identity.* One of the first in-depth studies of hip-hop's influence on education, it was described by author and educator Michael Eric Dyson, in a comment quoted on Amazon.com, as the work of "one of the most gifted young interpreters of hip-hop culture and educational experience in the nation." Gloria Ladson-Billings of the University of Wisconsin echoed that assessment in the volume's foreword. "This is a book that helps us see the power and potential of pedagogy," she noted, adding, "It is not merely what Hill decides to teach that matters. It is also how he teaches it that connects with the students."

In 2011 Third World Press released Hill's *The Classroom and the Cell: Conversations on Black Life in America,* a volume that he cowrote with the noted prisoner and activist Mumia Abu-Jamal. Two years later Teachers College Press released *Schooling Hip-Hop: Expanding Hip-Hop Based Education across the Curriculum,* a volume that he coedited with Emery Petchauer.

Amid the demands of his teaching and research careers, Hill also found time to establish himself as a

Selected writings

(Editor, with Lalitha Vasudevan) *Media, Learning, and Sites of Possibility,* Peter Lang, 2007.
Beats, Rhymes, and Classroom Life: Hip-Hop Pedagogy and the Politics of Identity, Teachers College Press, 2009.

(With Mumia Abu-Jamal) *The Classroom and the Cell: Conversations on Black Life in America,* Third World Press, 2011.

(Editor, with Emery Petchauer) *Schooling Hip-Hop: Expanding Hip-Hop Based Education across the Curriculum,* Teachers College Press, 2013.

Sources

Online

"*Beats, Rhymes, and Classroom Life: Hip-Hop Pedagogy and the Politics of Identity,*" Amazon.com, http://www.amazon.com/dp/0807749605/ref =rdr_ext_tmb (accessed July 19, 2015).

Durham, Elise, "Marc Lamont Hill Joining the Faculty at Morehouse College," Morehouse College, July 23, 2014, http://www.morehouse.edu/newscenter/ marc-lamont-hill-joining-the-faculty-at-morehouse -college/ (accessed July 19, 2015).

Hampton, Dream, "College Dropout to PhD: The Bold & Beautiful Marc Lamont Hill," Ebony.com, January 7, 2012, http://www.ebony.com/news-views/col lege-dropout-to-phd-the-bold—beautiful-marc-lam ont-hill#.Vauh0vlVikr (accessed July 19, 2015).

Krakauer, Steve, "Liberal Analyst Marc Lamont Hill Fired from Fox News," Mediaite.com, October 16, 2009, http://www.mediaite.com/tv/confirmed -marc-lamont-hill-fired-from-fox-news/ (accessed July 19, 2015).

Marc Lamont Hill, http://www.marclamonthill.com/ about (accessed July 19, 2015).

"Marc Lamont Hill," Huffington Post, http://www .huffingtonpost.com/marc-lamont-hill/ (accessed July 19, 2015).

—R. Anthony Kugler

Helen Humes

1913–1981

Blues, jazz, and R&B vocalist

A versatile vocalist with impressive credentials and an engaging stage presence, Helen Humes handled a variety of styles with ease, from traditional blues to swing jazz to up-tempo R&B. Over the course of a career that spanned more than half a century, she worked closely with some of the biggest names in popular music, including bandleader Count Basie and fellow vocalist Dinah Washington. Although she is best remembered for the hits she recorded at the peak of her career in the 1940s and 1950s, Humes's later work drew high praise as well; a writer for the website All About Jazz, for example, pronounced "her late-period recordings … among the best she ever made."

Humes, Helen, photograph. GAB Archive/Redferns/Getty Images.

her focus was squarely on singing. Humes made her professional debut as early as 1927, when she traveled to St. Louis, Missouri, with her mother, a teacher, to record some blues songs for Okeh Records. Throughout her career, she told interviewer Mary Bobo, her parents were very supportive of her music, escorting her to gigs and recording sessions and even bringing refreshments for her backing bands. Their enthusiasm was particularly crucial at this early stage, as she worked to establish herself in a crowded and competitive field.

The daughter of one of the first African-American lawyers in Kentucky, Humes was born June 23, 1913, in Louisville. In a 1979 interview she recalled her childhood as a happy one, noting in particular her closeness to her parents and her involvement in her church, where she received her earliest musical training singing in the Sunday school choir. She learned to play a variety of instruments as well, including the piano and the organ, but the depth of her vocal talent soon became apparent, and by the time she was a teenager,

After St. Louis, Humes moved to New York City, where she found work with a variety of ensembles, most of them specializing in swing, the fast-paced jazz that dominated the airwaves at the time. A major break came about 1937, when she toured and recorded with the bandleader Harry James. That gig, in turn, led to an extended engagement with Count Basie, with whom she made a number of popular recordings, including "Blame It on My Last Affair" (1939) and "Between the Devil and the Deep Blue Sea" (1939). Typically recorded on short notice, Basie's singles sometimes suffered from hurried arrangements, mediocre lyrics, and other flaws. Known for her professionalism even

early in her career, Humes handled those weaknesses with aplomb, masking even the most serious issues with what Scott Yanow of AllMusic.com described as her "faultless jazz phrasing."

Humes's work with Basie was instrumental in establishing her reputation at the national level. After leaving his group about 1942, she made her way to Los Angeles, which remained her base for most of her career. Her move there coincided with a shift in focus: in place of the light swing for which Basie was famous, she now concentrated on up-tempo R&B. Los Angeles was a hub for that rapidly developing style, and in clubs along Central Avenue, then the center of African-American life in the city, she found an enthusiastic reception. Throughout this period Humes recorded steadily, scoring a major hit in 1945 with a single called "Be-Baba-Leba"; her own composition, it reached number three on the R&B chart. That was followed five years later by what became her signature song, "Million Dollar Secret," described by Yanow as "a classic."

The next decade or so was the most varied and active period of Humes's career. A headline performer at the festivals and revues that were a prominent feature of R&B's early development, she shared the stage in the 1950s with stars such as Washington, crooner Nat King Cole, and the Ravens, a pioneering vocal group. She also continued to record regularly, completing tracks in a variety of styles for Discovery, Decca, Contemporary, and other labels. Among the best known of her releases during this period were the albums that she completed for California-based Contemporary, particularly *Helen Humes* (1960) and *Songs I Love to Sing!* (1961). In keeping with that label's focus on small-group jazz, these recordings featured a classic sound that was considerably more intimate than the rollicking R&B that dominated Humes's live performances. *Songs I Love to Sing!* included a new and definitive version of "Million Dollar Secret," which had become an R&B standard.

The music world, meanwhile, was changing rapidly. By the early 1960s, it was increasingly clear that rapid shifts in public taste, reflected in the explosive growth of rock and roll, were damaging the market for the earlier styles that were her specialty. She responded to the resulting decline in her bookings by moving in

1964 to Australia, where she remained a star attraction. Roughly three years later, however, she returned to the United States to care for her mother, whose health had declined precipitously. That decision silenced her until 1973, when she made a dramatic and well-received comeback, appearing with her old employer Basie at the Newport Jazz Festival in Rhode Island.

Humes's performance at Newport revitalized her career, and for the rest of her life she was active professionally, touring widely and releasing a string of well-received albums. These included *On the Sunny Side of the Street* (1975), notable for its stirring title track, and *Helen Humes and the Muse All Stars* (1980), which she completed for Muse Records with the help of an excellent backing group that included saxophonist and vocalist Eddie "Cleanhead" Vinson and pianist Gerald Wiggins. Soon after the latter album's release, however, her health declined, and on September 13, 1981, she died of cancer in Santa Monica, California, at age 68. In the years since her passing, her reputation has continued to grow, thanks in part to new compilations and reissues of albums such as *Songs I Love to Sing!,* which was remastered and rereleased by Fantasy Records in 1984 and 1988.

Selected discography

Singles

Count Basie, "Blame It on My Last Affair," 1939.
Count Basie, "Between the Devil and the Deep Blue Sea," 1939.
"Be-Baba-Leba," 1945.
"Million Dollar Secret," 1950.

Albums

Helen Humes, Contemporary, 1960.
Songs I Love to Sing! (includes "Million Dollar Secret"), Contemporary, 1961.
On the Sunny Side of the Street (includes "On the Sunny Side of the Street"), Black Lion, 1975.
Helen Humes and the Muse All Stars, Muse, 1980.

Sources

Online

Bobo, Mary, "Helen Humes: Interviewed by Mary Bobo," University of Louisville, June 12, 1979, http://digital.library.louisville.edu/cdm/ref/collection/afamoh/id/108 (accessed July 13, 2015).
"Helen Humes," All About Jazz, http://musicians.allaboutjazz.com/helenhumes (accessed July 13, 2015).
Marion, JC, "Helen Humes," JammUpp, No. 7, 1999, http://home.earthlink.net/~jaymar41/HHumes.html (accessed July 13, 2015).
Yanow, Scott, "Helen Humes: Artist Biography," All

Music.com, http://www.allmusic.com/artist/helen-humes-mn0000671800/biography (accessed July 13, 2015).

—R. Anthony Kugler

Ben E. King

1938–2015

Singer, songwriter

King, Ben E., photograph. Randy Miramontez/Shutterstock.com.

Ben E. King cowrote and sang "Stand By Me," a song that helped define soul music in the early 1960s. The earnest conviction of King's delivery and the power of his smooth baritone voice turned his recording into an enduring classic. But "Stand By Me" was hardly King's only hit record. He began as a doo-wop singer and rang up a flurry of hits as lead singer of The Drifters, becoming a soloist after he left that group in 1960. With a sound rooted in gospel music and a dramatic, elegant crooning style, King's voice helped rhythm and blues cross over into the mainstream and paved the way for the overwhelming success of the Motown sound.

Sang Lead Vocals for the Drifters

The singer was born Benjamin Earl Nelson on September 28, 1938, in Henderson, North Carolina, and spent his earliest years there, first singing in a church choir alongside his mother and other relatives. In 1947 his family moved north to New York City and settled in Harlem, where his father opened a luncheonette. While attending James Fenimore Cooper Junior High School, King and three friends formed a doo-wop quartet called the Four B's. King's future wife, Betty, was the sister of two of the group's members, twins Billy and Bobby Davis. The Four B's sang on street corners and sometimes performed at amateur night competitions at Harlem's Apollo Theater. The local exposure earned King an invitation to join another popular vocal group, the Moonglows, who had a recording contract with Chess Records. The teenage singer felt that he was not ready for the limelight, however, and opted to continue working in his family's restaurant.

King sometimes sang on the job, and his infectious voice caught the ear of Lover Patterson, who lived across the street from the eatery. Patterson, a band manager who was always on the lookout for local talent, talked King into taking a baritone spot with the Five Crowns. The quintet recorded one single for songwriters Doc Pomus and Mort Shuman, whose R&B Records label failed to get off the ground. One evening in the spring of 1958, the Five Crowns had a gig at the Apollo Theater as one of the opening acts for the Drifters. Unbeknownst to them, the Drifters' manager, George Treadwell, was on the verge of firing all of his singers. Treadwell approached Patterson about

bringing in the Five Crowns to become the new Drifters and fulfill the group's concert obligations. Patterson and four of the five vocalists, including King, agreed.

The singers endured several awkward engagements, performing Drifters material before audiences realized the singers were stand-ins. In March of 1959 the group went into the studio to record for Atlantic Records, with the talented team of Jerry Leiber and Mike Stoller as producers. King substituted for the group's lead singer, Charlie Thomas, on "There Goes My Baby," a tune he had cowritten. The result sounded starkly different, not only from the previous Drifters sound but from any prior R&B recording. The song was standard doo-wop material, but Leiber and Stoller gave it a lush orchestration with strings and Latin percussion, and King delivered an impassioned performance. The single shot to number two on *Billboard* magazine's pop chart, eclipsing the Drifters' previous hits and becoming their best-selling single. The group quickly followed up, with King now firmly established as lead vocalist. "This Magic Moment" and "I Count the Tears" were written for the group by Pomus and Shuman, as was the sentimental "Save the Last Dance for Me," which reached number one on both the pop and R&B charts.

Recorded Two Hits in One Day

Despite this success, the 21-year-old King still considered his singing a sideline rather than a career. He and his bandmates were earning only $125 a week, according to the terms of the contract they had signed with Treadwell, and they received no royalties for their hit records. By May of 1960, the singers recognized they were being swindled and approached Treadwell to negotiate new terms. As King later told the story, he agreed to serve as the group's spokesman, but when

they met with the manager in his office, Treadwell cut him loose. The other members lost their nerve and decided to stay on.

King credited Patterson with believing in him and keeping him in the music business at this critical point when he thought he was finished. Patterson arranged for King to go into the studio in October of 1960 to record as a solo artist for Leiber and Stoller, along with producer Phil Spector. Most of that day's work was devoted to "Spanish Harlem," an unusual Leiber-Stoller composition with a Latin beat. The producers devised a sinuous hook played on the marimba. They instructed King to sing the poetic lyrics with a gospel intonation and recorded him with a distinct echo that added to the track's exotic feel. In a public television interview late in his life, reflecting on the recording of "Spanish Harlem," King recalled that Leiber and Stoller had asked him to think of the hymn "Nearer My God to Thee." They "taught me that it's not what you're singing, it's how you're feeling when you're singing it," he said. "And I've always, I don't care what studio I'm in, I don't care what producers [are] producing it, and I don't care what song it is, because they taught me those things I feel so protected wherever I go as far as music."

With a little studio time left in the session, Leiber asked whether King had another song he wanted to record. The singer mentioned a song that he had cowritten and meant for the Drifters. In fact, even after being fired from the group, King had brought the song to Treadwell, who had told him the group did not need it. The song was "Stand By Me," inspired by a spiritual that King had heard performed by Sam Cooke. The producers came up with an arrangement on the spot, later adding a soaring orchestral break.

In a single day's work, Ben E. King made his career. When that day ended, though, he had no idea what was in store for him; he thought he was heading back to his job at his father's restaurant. Leiber and Stoller spoke with Atlantic Records executives Jerry Wexler and Ahmet Ertegun, who agreed to release both tracks as solo vocals, the first ones under the name Ben E. King (after a favorite uncle of the singer's named James King). "Spanish Harlem" was released in March of 1961 and made the top 10 on the pop chart. "Stand By Me," which came out three months later, made it to the top five and reached number one on the R&B chart. Although the chord structure of "Stand By Me" was exactly the same as that of "There Goes My Baby," "This Magic Moment," and countless other doo-wop ditties, the song transmitted the timeworn 1-6-4-5 sequence with such simple grace that it became the prototype of for the "fifties progression"; musicians often refer to this sequence as the "Stand By Me" changes. According to the music licensing group BMI, "Stand By Me" ranks number four on the list of most-performed popular songs of the 20th century, with approximately seven million performances.

Revived His Career after Hollywood Film

With two solo hits in his repertoire, King devoted himself to his show business career. He headlined at concert halls across the country, performed on radio and television, and recorded several albums for Atlantic. Two of his most successful singles were "Don't Play That Song" (1962) and "I (Who Have Nothing)" (1963), which later was a hit for the British pop singer Tom Jones. King's appeal declined as the 1960s wore on, however. In 1969 he left Atlantic, recording a couple of unsuccessful albums for other labels. Ertegun re-signed King in 1975 after hearing his act at a Miami nightclub, and that year King had another top-five hit, a disco piece called "Supernatural Thing (Part I)." He enjoyed a bounce when Aretha Franklin released her dynamic cover of "Spanish Harlem" in 1971 and when John Lennon put out his version of "Stand By Me" in 1975. In 1977 King teamed with the popular funk group Average White Band on the album *Benny and Us.* His Atlantic albums from the late 1970s and early 1980s, including *Let Me Live in Your Life* (1978) and *Street Tough* (1981), were moderately successful with R&B listeners but failed to cross over to the pop charts.

In 1986 Hollywood director Rob Reiner released the nostalgic coming-of-age film *Stand By Me,* named for King's song and featuring his recording over the closing credits and on the soundtrack album. Suddenly, King's throaty rendition was getting airplay again, and a re-release of the single went to the top 10. Around the same time, the song also was heard in a commercial for Levi's jeans. That was enough to revive the singer's career and send him back to the performing circuit. He continued touring and occasionally recording for another quarter century. Highlights from the autumn of his career include the jazzy album *Shades of Blue* (1999) and an album of pop ballads, *Heart and Soul* (2010). King participated in recovery efforts after the Japanese earthquake and tsunami of 2011, recording a benefit cover of the Japanese song "Sukiyaki." King also created an educational and civic charity, the Stand By Me Foundation.

In March of 2015, the Library of Congress announced that it would induct King's original rendition of "Stand By Me" into its national registry of historically significant recordings. "It was King's incandescent vocal," the library said in its statement, "that made it a classic." The 76-year-old songwriter said that the moment was one of the greatest of his life. Only a month later, on April 30, King passed away near his New Jersey home after a brief illness.

Selected discography

Spanish Harlem (includes "Spanish Harlem"), Atlantic, 1961.
Ben E. King Sings for Soulful Lovers, Atlantic, 1962.
Don't Play That Song! (includes "Stand By Me" and "Don't Play That Song"), Atlantic, 1962.
Young Boy Blues (includes "I [Who Have Nothing]"), Atco, 1964.
Seven Letters, Atlantic, 1965.
What Is Soul?, WEA Japan, 1967.
Rough Edges, Maxwell, 1970.
The Beginning of It All, Mandala, 1971.
Supernatural (includes "Supernatural Thing [Part I]"), Atlantic, 1975.
Ben E. King Story, Atlantic, 1975.
I Had a Love, Atlantic, 1976.
(With the Average White Band) *Benny and Us,* Rhino, 1977.
Let Me Live in Your Life, Atlantic, 1978.
Music Trance, Atlantic, 1980.
Street Tough, Atlantic, 1981.
Save the Last Dance For Me, EMI, 1988.
Shades of Blue, Half Note, 1999.
I've Been Around, True Life, 2006.
Heart and Soul, Canam, 2010.

Sources

Books

Bogdanov, Vladimir, Chris Woodstra, and Stephen Thomas Erlewine, eds., *All Music Guide to Soul: The Definitive Guide to R&B and Soul,* Backbeat Books, 2003.

Periodicals

New York Times, May 2, 2015.

Online

Axelrod, Jim, "Ben E. King: Library of Congress Honor is 'Greatest Moment of My Life,'" CBS News, March 25, 2015, http://www.cbsnews.com/news/ben-e-king-library-of-congress-stand-by-me-national-registry/ (accessed June 12, 2015).
Griggs, Brandon, "'Stand By Me' Singer Ben E. King Dies," CNN.com, May 1, 2015, http://edition.cnn.com/2015/05/01/entertainment/ben-e-king-singer-obit-feat/index.html (accessed June 12, 2015).
"Interview With Ben E. King [Part 2 of 3]," WGBH Media Library and Archives, http://openvault.wgbh.org/catalog/76c35a-interview-with-ben-e-king-part-2-of-3 (accessed May 26, 2015).
McCormick, Neil, "Ben E. King: 'Feeling Bristled through Every Note,'" Telegraph.co.uk, May 1, 2015, http://www.telegraph.co.uk/culture/music/11577271/Ben-E-King-best-songs.html (accessed June 12, 2015).

—Roger K. Smith

Don King

1931—

Boxing promoter

King, Don, photograph. JStone/Shutterstock.com.

World-famous boxing promoter Don King is one of the most recognizable faces in American culture. King has been in the public eye since the 1970s, when he orchestrated the legendary "Rumble in the Jungle" in Zaire between heavyweights Muhammad Ali and George Foreman. King's flamboyant persona, electroshock hair, and knack for wheeling and dealing were the perfect match for boxing, a sport synonymous with hype, showmanship, and anything-goes antics. As boxing's major power broker in his heyday—the 1970s, 1980s, and 1990s—King controlled a number of luminaries, including Ali, Foreman, Joe Frazier, Sugar Ray Leonard, Evander Holyfield, Roberto Durán, Mike Tyson, Larry Holmes, and Julio Cesar Chavez. The gregarious impresario became fabulously wealthy as the head of Don King Productions, but controversy was never far away. Many fighters sued King, claiming that he had defrauded them of millions of dollars, and King also faced allegations of insurance fraud, tax evasion, and fight fixing.

King celebrated his 83rd birthday on August 20, 2014. He had not sat atop boxing's throne since the late 1990s, when his decade-long association with Tyson came to an end. However, sportswriters who had declared him a relic had to eat their words when King's Haitian heavyweight, Bermane Stiverne, upset Mexican-American fighter Chris Arreola on April 27, 2014, to claim the World Boxing Council title. The fight may have been King's last hurrah—Stiverne failed to defend his title, losing to Deontay Wilder on January 17, 2015—but it brought him back into the spotlight at his bombastic, over-the-top best. "Tell the people that at this time, in this place, let the word go forth that the heavyweight business is back in business again," King told reporters afterward. Kevin Iole of Yahoo! Sports observed, "The 82-year-old promoter, who made his name by promoting heavyweight champions from Muhammad Ali to George Foreman to Mike Tyson, looked like he'd never missed a beat. He was shouting a slew of catch phrases and generally confusing just about everyone who was listening, but he got more than his share of laughs and took a few digs at fellow promoter Dan Goossen."

Established Numbers Operation

King was born in Cleveland, Ohio, in 1931. When he

of paper with a lucky number on it into each bag of peanuts. Those bags became popular among local gamblers, and the King boys thus became acquainted with some of the city's prominent numbers racketeers.

As a high school student, King became involved in Golden Gloves boxing. It soon became clear that he was more talented as a hustler than as a fighter. After being knocked cold in one of his first bouts, he decided to forget about boxing as a career. Meanwhile, King had gone to work as a numbers runner for one of Cleveland's illegal lottery operators. He was accepted to Kent State University after graduating high school, and he worked for the numbers boss all summer to raise money for tuition. Before he had saved enough for college, however, King misplaced a winning betting slip and had to pay the money out of his own pocket. Instead of going off to college, King stayed in Cleveland and began a numbers business on his own. Although he spent a year taking classes at Case Western Reserve University in Cleveland, he had more or less decided that college was an unnecessary sidetrack. By the time he was 20, King was a successful, yet illicit, businessman and was married to Luvenia Mitchell.

King spent the next decade developing his illegal gambling operation. By the time he was 30, he was running one of Cleveland's biggest numbers games. He was making serious money, and he became a flamboyant figure in the town with his flashy clothes and cars. He was also making enemies. In 1954 King killed Hillary Brown, who was allegedly trying to rob one of his numbers stations. King successfully claimed self-defense in the killing. A few years later, the front of King's house was blown up by the gangster Alex "Shondor" Birns, to whom King had refused to pay protection money. Shortly before King was to testify against Birns on extortion charges, King was shot in the back of the head with a 12-gauge shotgun. Amazingly, he was not seriously injured in the attack.

Meanwhile, King's business continued to flourish. During the late 1950s he bought into a popular Cleveland supper club. It was there that he met Cassius Clay, a young Olympic boxing champion, in 1960. King and Clay became friends, and King began following Clay all over the country to attend his fights. By this time, King's first marriage had fallen apart, and he was now married to Henrietta King, the ex-wife of one of his business associates. Aside from occasional trouble with the Internal Revenue Service, King was riding high through the first half of the 1960s.

Imprisoned for Manslaughter

King's life took a dramatic turn in 1966. That year he got into an argument with an employee, Sam Garrett, who owed him $600. Although accounts of the event vary, the fight became physical, and somehow in the course of the scuffle Garrett's head hit the pavement.

was 10 years old, his father, Clarence King, a steelworker, was killed in an explosion at the mill, leaving Don and his six siblings in the care of their mother, Hattie King. Hattie used the insurance money from her husband's death to relocate the family to a nearby middle-class neighborhood. To support the family, Hattie baked pies and roasted peanuts, which her sons would sell throughout the neighborhood. As a promotional gimmick, Don and his brothers would insert a slip

He eventually died from the injuries. Some witnesses indicated that King had beaten the smaller, sickly Garrett mercilessly, while King claimed that Garrett had attacked him and he was merely defending himself. King was convicted of manslaughter and sent to the Marion Correctional Institution in Ohio.

King used his time in prison to give himself the education that he had earlier chosen to bypass. For four years he immersed himself in classic literature and philosophy. When he was released on parole in 1971, King was, as he told Hunter Davies in an interview, "armed and dangerous. Armed with wisdom and knowledge." King was eventually granted a full pardon by Ohio governor James A. Rhodes in 1983.

Determined to leave the numbers game behind him, King began looking for legitimate business opportunities after his release from prison. Around this time he adopted his trademark hair style, a gravity-defying affair, every strand standing straight up, that he has repeatedly maintained happened by itself as a "sign from God." It did not take King long to settle on boxing as his new racket. His initial stint as a boxing promoter was innocent enough. In 1972 he organized a benefit to help keep Cleveland's only black hospital, Forest City Hospital, from shutting down. For the benefit's main attraction, he was able to lure Muhammad Ali (formerly known as Cassius Clay) into fighting a 10-round exhibition against four different opponents. The event raised over $80,000 for the hospital. It also convinced King that there was money to be made as a boxing promoter and manager.

Made It Big with Ali

King's big breakthrough as a promoter came in 1974, when he was one of the main architects, along with the closed-circuit television company Video Techniques, of the famous "Rumble in the Jungle" heavyweight title fight between Ali and Foreman in Kinshasa, Zaire. With only a very limited background in boxing promotion, King used his natural salesmanship to talk the government of Zaire into putting up more than $10 million in financial backing for the event. The fight was a huge financial success, and it vaulted King to the top of the heap among boxing promoters.

King followed up "Rumble in the Jungle" with "Thrilla in Manila" in 1975 between Ali and Joe Frazier, which was considered by many to be one of the greatest heavyweight bouts of all time. King promoted several more of Ali's championship fights, cementing his position as the sports leading matchmaker. Although Ali eventually defected to the camp of King's archrival, Bob Arum of Top Rank, another closed-circuit firm, many more top-ranked boxers were waiting in line to sign up with King. Larry Holmes, who dominated the heavyweight division in the post-Ali years, was one of them. Several boxers expressed a preference for doing

business with a fellow African American, and King, the only top-line black promoter in the business, was more than happy to exploit that preference.

Even as a "legitimate" business person, King was unable to avoid scandal and controversy. In 1977 a series of fights set up by King with the ABC television network were canceled when the Federal Bureau of Investigation (FBI) produced evidence that King had doctored some of the fighters' records. During the early 1980s he again received the FBI's attention as part of a large-scale investigation of the entire boxing industry. Although all sorts of shady practices were uncovered, no charges against King came out of that investigation. In 1984 King and his secretary, Constance Harper, were indicted on tax evasion charges. Amazingly, the jury acquitted King and convicted Harper. King thanked members of the jury by supplying them with first-class plane tickets and ringside seats for heavyweight fights. That same year King tried his hand at a different branch of the entertainment industry when he promoted the Jacksons' (Michael and brothers) Victory Tour. As with his boxing events, the tour brought in mind-boggling sums of money.

Throughout the rest of the 1980s King continued to dominate his end of boxing, with the only real competition coming from Arum. Among the heavyweight champions with whom he had exclusive promotional contracts during this period were Michael Dokes, Mike Weaver, Tim Witherspoon, James "Bonecrusher" Smith, and Trevor Berbick. In many top matches, both combatants had business relationships with King. Some fighters claimed that they were coerced into signing with King, and many of those deals included managerial contracts with King's son Carl that gave him as much as half of the purse for each fight. During the late 1980s Tyson ushered in a new era of heavyweight dominance and moneymaking for King.

Accused of Exploitation

The role that race played in King's success was, like almost everything else in his life, controversial. At times he waxed utterly patriotic about his success. Only in America could a poor kid from the ghetto rise to such heights of fame and fortune. Just as often, however, King loudly denounced the racism that permeated every facet of life in the United States. Although he was active in and frequently recognized by organizations such as the National Association for the Advancement of Colored People (NAACP), the United Negro College Fund, and Operation PUSH, many of the boxers he promoted felt he used his blackness as just another tool of exploitation. King defended himself in an interview with Kimi Zabihyan of Vibe in September of 1996: "They can say whatever they want, but the fighters were getting slave wages until I came on the scene. I revolutionized the pay scale and the sport of boxing. I took the blacks and the Latinos and made sure they got paid. The irony is that they're trying to make me sound

like the robber of the fighters when I was getting the box office for them.... I never got a fighter because I'm black. Every fighter, including Mike Tyson, came to me after they've been screwed by the other promoters."

During the early 1990s King was confronted with a series of challenges. More and more boxers went public with claims that King had cheated them. Holmes was widely quoted as saying that King "looks black, lives white, and thinks green." Witherspoon sued King and came away with a sizable settlement. Tyson, King's biggest meal ticket, lost the championship to the virtually unknown Buster Douglas and then went to prison for rape. King's ongoing business relationship with the cable-television giant HBO went sour. In 1992 King's former accountant came forward with evidence of an insurance scam, for which King was subsequently indicted. Jack Newfield's scathing biography, *Only in America: The Life and Crimes of Don King,* was published in 1995. In it, Newfield portrayed King as a ruthless charlatan, albeit a brilliant one, whose exploits in the world of boxing were no more legitimate than those of his earlier life in the Cleveland underworld. "Don King is a hip exploiter, an intelligent flash peddler," Newfield wrote. "He knows which fighters to steal, how to exploit anyone's vice, vanity, or insecurity and make a profit for himself."

Somehow, King managed to emerge from it all relatively unscathed, living up to his reputation as the "Teflon Don." Tyson was released from prison and began earning big money once again for both himself and King. Spurned by HBO, King turned to rival Showtime, with whom he formed the joint-venture KingVision to air Tyson's fights on pay-per-view. King's trial for wire fraud in connection with the alleged insurance scam was declared a mistrial in 1995, and although prosecutors planned to retry the case, King considered himself vindicated.

Lost Step with the Times

King's influence began to wane during the first decade of the 21st century, in part because of his advancing years but more so because the world of boxing was changing around him. The sport lost spectators in the United States due to several factors, including the proliferation of governing bodies and the hollowing out of so-called world titles, increased competition from mixed martial arts leagues, and the persistent dominance of east European fighters. Then, too, boxer-turned-promoter Oscar De La Hoya took a sizable chunk out of a territory that once belonged almost exclusively to King and Arum. Although Arum managed to remain competitive with De La Hoya and his Golden Boy Promotions, despite his virtual monopoly on the pay-per-view business, King fell out of step with the times. As Bernard Fernandez observed in TheSweetScience.com in 2015, "The tried-and-true tricks King used to telling effect in the past—opening up a satchel of money, dumping it on a table, and

telling a fighter raised in poverty that he had to sign multiple blank contracts with King if he wanted to leave with the booty, and maybe the keys to a new car—aren't the guaranteed deal-closers that they once were. Nor is the race card King has been known to play with black fighters who were schmoozed into feeling more comfortable with one of their own."

King's reputation as a huckster could not, of course, be discredited in his marginalization. In 1998 Tyson brought a lawsuit against King, claiming that King stole $100 million from him. Tyson dropped the suit in 2004 in exchange for $14 million, almost all of which went to pay off his creditors. Still, the fallout from the Tyson lawsuit was considerable. Many of King's top prospects had abandoned him for promoters—most notably De La Hoya—who claimed to run their businesses on transparency.

King's image was further tarnished by a damning ESPN SportsCentury documentary that aired in 2001. In 2005 King filed a $2.5 billion defamation lawsuit against ESPN and its parent company, Walt Disney, alleging the program savagely portrayed him as a snake oil salesman and greedy con. During the press conference that announced the lawsuit, King expressed his frustration with the media's demonizing of him: "I just felt that this was the straw that broke the camel's back and I can't take it anymore, and I'm going to fight back. I seek justice." He eventually lost the lawsuit when Judge Robert A. Rosenberg ruled that King's lawyers had not sufficiently proven that ESPN had acted with malice or that the statements made in the documentary were "subjectively incorrect."

Authored a Mixed Legacy

King suffered a terrible setback in 2010, when Henrietta, his wife of 51 years, died. In an interview with *USA Today*'s Bob Velin, King said that, while he would likely never recover from the loss of his beloved spouse, her memory would remain with him forever: "The spirit of her, the great rock she was for me, my confidante, friend, lover, mother, all these things she was and continues to be right there beside me in spirit. She motivates me to keep going, not feel sorry for myself." The couple had three children: Eric, Debbie, and Carl.

In the opinion of many people, King was a scoundrel and a cheat. In an essay for Grantland, Jay Caspian Kang discussed King's image issues: "King speaks of himself as a transformative figure, someone who through sheer intellect, hard work, and determination overcame racism, both overt and institutional, and brought millions of dollars and international adulation to the young black men he promoted. All of this is undeniably true. But Don King's PR problem is that we don't see him as a civil-rights pioneer. We see him as a gangster—and as a gangster, he must adhere to the strict ethics of a gangster movie. He stole, without a hint of mercy or contrition, from his own people."

Mired in controversy after controversy, King cannot be regarded as a great role model for the African-American community. Still, he has been a generous contributor to various charities and humanitarian causes, and some boxing insiders have defended his business tactics, claiming he was merely capitalizing on the sport's unstructured environment. Whatever view one takes of King, the story of his transformation from a Cleveland street thug to the most prominent promoter in the history of boxing is nothing short of remarkable. There is no question that King contributed something of value to boxing in at least two ways. He dramatically increased the purses fighters take away, and he brought his own brand of showmanship and charisma to a sport that has always depended on such hype for its following. The recipient of countless accolades, King made history in 1997 as the first promoter inducted into the International Boxing Hall of Fame.

Sources

Books

Davies, Hunter, *Hunting People: Thirty Years of Interviews with the Famous,* Mainstream Publishing, 1994.

Newfield, Jack, *Only in America: The Life and Crimes of Don King,* William Morrow, 1995.

Periodicals

Las Vegas Review-Journal, January 17, 2015.

Los Angeles Times, March 27, 2014.

USA Today, January 26, 2011.

Vibe, September, 1996, pp. 148–151.

Online

Christ, Scott, "Don King's Last Stand: Once the Ruler of Boxing, Aging Promoter Now Barely Hangs On in Changing Sport," SB Nation/Bad Left Hook, April 9, 2013, http://www.badlefthook.com/2013/4/9/4205302/don-king-last-stand-once-ruler-boxing-aging-promoter-barely-hangs-on (accessed June 4, 2015).

Davies, Gareth A., "Don King Back with a Bang as Bermane Stiverne Beats Chris Arreola to Claim WBC Heavyweight Title," *Telegraph* (London), May 12, 2014, http://www.telegraph.co.uk/sport/othersports/boxing/10824180/Don-King-back-with-a-bang-as-Bermane-Stiverne-beats-Chris-Arreola-to-claim-WBC-heavyweight-title.html (accessed June 5, 2015).

Fernandez, Bernard, "The Last Roar of the Lion in Winter?" The Sweet Science, January 17, 2015, http://www.thesweetscience.com/news/articles-frontpage/20134-don-king-the-last-roar-of-the-lion-in-winter (accessed June 5, 2015).

Iole, Kevin, "Don King Is Back, Whether Boxing Likes It or Not," Yahoo! Sports, May 11, 2014, http://sports.yahoo.com/news/don-king-is-back—whether-you-like-it-or-not-050052215-boxing.html (accessed June 4, 2015).

Iron Mike Gallego [Daniel Roberts], "Still King," Sports on Earth, May 14, 2014, http://www.sportsonearth.com/article/75341572/don-king-boxing-icon-muhammad-ali-mike-tyson-bermane-stiverne (accessed June 5, 2015).

Kang, Jay Caspian, "The End and Don King: The Crumbling of an American Icon," Grantland, April 4, 2013, http://grantland.com/features/don-king-faces-end-career/ (accessed June 5, 2015).

Lidz, Franz, "'Golden Boy' Oscar De La Hoya vs. the Boxing Establishment," *Upstart Business Journal,* November 19, 2008, http://upstart.bizjournals.com/culture-lifestyle/culture-inc/sports/2008/11/19/De-La-Hoya-vs-Boxing-Establishment.html?page=all (accessed June 5, 2015).

McCormick, Eliott, "The Making of Machiavelli," The Fight City, October 29, 2014, http://www.thefightcity.com/don-king-making-machiavelli/ (accessed June 5, 2015).

"Promoter Takes Issue with SportsCentury Piece," ESPN.com, January 13, 2005, http://sports.espn.go.com/sports/boxing/news/story?id=1965165 (accessed June 5, 2015).

—Robert R. Jacobson and Janet Mullane

Kenny Lattimore

1970—

R&B vocalist

Lattimore, Kenny, photograph. Photo Works/Shutterstock.com.

With a smooth, soulful tenor reminiscent of the stars of the 1960s, vocalist Kenny Lattimore has spent more than 20 years at the forefront of R&B. Although he is best known for his brilliant self-titled debut in 1996, his later albums have earned strong reviews as well. The winner of a 1997 NAACP Image Award as that year's best new artist, he typically takes a hands-on approach in the recording studio, handling many aspects of production himself.

Kenneth Lee Lattimore was born April 10, 1970, in Washington, DC. The son of Sonya Ryan, a counselor at Washington's Howard University, he grew up in a household filled with gospel music and classic R&B. Drawn as a child to the work of iconic vocalists such as Marvin Gaye and Stevie Wonder, he was soon honing his skills at talent shows and local events. Lattimore had other interests as well, however, and until the end of his teens, there were few signs that he would pursue music as a career. After high school he enrolled at Howard, where he intended to focus on urban planning and architecture. His plans changed, however, when a vocal group that he had joined, Maniquin, began drawing the attention of record executives and the public. By the late 1980s the ensemble had earned a

contract with Epic Records and seemed poised for stardom. A period of intensive touring and studio work followed, and Lattimore's studies were interrupted. The album that resulted was a disappointment, however, and the group parted ways soon thereafter. Firmly ensconced in the music business by that point, Lattimore focused on establishing himself as a solo artist.

By his own account, the next few years were not easy. As he worked to establish himself in a notoriously competitive field, money was tight, and after relocating to New York City in 1993, he lived for a time on credit cards. That risky move eventually paid off, however, as the contacts he made in New York helped him get a demo tape into the hands of executives at Columbia Records. A recording contract followed, and in 1996 *Kenny Lattimore* was released to the public.

An engaging mix of tempos and emotions, Lattimore's debut established his reputation, selling well enough across the country to be certified gold by the Recording Industry Association of America. It also broke the top 20 on *Billboard*'s R&B albums chart, peaking at number 19; on the magazine's Heatseekers chart, a

At a Glance . . .

Born Kenneth Lee Lattimore on April 10, 1970, in Washington, DC; son of Sonya Ryan (a counselor); married Chanté Moore (divorced, 2011); children: one son. *Education:* Attended Howard University, late 1980s.

Career: R&B vocalist, late 1980s—.

Awards: NAACP Image Award, Best New Artist, 1997.

Addresses: *Management*—Benjamin Peterson, Primary Wave, 116 East 16th St., 9th Floor, New York, NY 10003. *Web*—http://KennyLattimore.com.

ranking of new artists, it did even better, taking the top spot. Driving that success were three singles, one of which, "For You," broke the top 10 on the R&B chart, reaching number six, and the top 40 on the pop list, where it hit number 33; it has subsequently become a staple at weddings. The track "Never Too Busy" did nearly as well, peaking at number 19 on the R&B list, while the third single, "Just What It Takes," was a more modest hit, breaking the top 60.

Lattimore quickly returned to the studio to begin work on a follow-up. The resulting album, *From the Soul of Man,* was released by Columbia in 1998. Although it failed to spark the kind of publicity its predecessor had generated, it won positive reviews from critics such as AllMusic.com's Michael Gallucci, who hailed it as "a real treat" and "truly a spirited affair." An unusually lengthy compilation, the album featured no fewer than 15 songs, the majority of which Lattimore wrote or cowrote. Among his compositions were the tracks "Days Like This" and "If I Lose My Woman," both of which were modest hits on the R&B chart. In general, however, audiences seemed to shun the singles in favor of the full-length recording, which actually surpassed *Kenny Lattimore*'s performance on the R&B albums list, peaking at number 15.

After two strong albums, Lattimore, like many of his peers, found it difficult to maintain his momentum. His third recording, released on Arista Records in 2001, was a critical and commercial disappointment. Titled *Weekend,* it spawned only one modest hit, the title track. Its troubles were likely compounded by its release date, which came just weeks after the September 11 terrorist attacks. Lattimore interpreted the setback as a sign that he needed to revamp his approach. For his next album he moved in a new direction, completing a series of romantic duets with his wife Chanté Moore. Released by Arista in 2003, *Things That Lovers Do* revitalized his career, reaching number three on the

R&B albums chart and winning him a host of new fans. Its success led directly to another collaboration with Moore, this one an ambitious and innovative double-length recording called *Uncovered/Covered.* Released by La Face Records in 2006, it was roughly divided between romantic soul and contemporary gospel. It did well among fans of both genres, peaking at number 10 on the R&B chart and number two on the gospel list.

In the months that followed, Lattimore changed direction again, shifting back to the solo R&B he had neglected since *Weekend* five years earlier. With his next recordings, 2008's *Timeless* and 2012's *Back to Cool,* he attempted to reconnect with his core fans, offering them an updated version of the sounds that had catapulted him to stardom in the mid-1990s. *Timeless* was the more successful of the two, peaking at number six on the R&B chart. *Back to Cool* had its fans as well, however, many of whom responded in particular to the track "Find a Way," Lattimore's first single to reach the R&B list in several years. It was a moderate hit, just breaking the top 60.

Back to Cool appeared at a time of considerable upheaval in Lattimore's personal life. Following a very public divorce from Moore in 2011, he struggled to regain his footing professionally. Longtime fans were surprised and delighted when he returned to form in 2015 with *Anatomy of a Love Song.* Widely regarded as one of the most accomplished comebacks in R&B in at least a decade, it was essentially an expanded version of *Back to Cool,* as a number of tracks, including "Find a Way," appeared on both albums. Unlike its predecessor, however, *Anatomy* was well distributed and enjoyed considerable airplay. In a 2015 interview with Elle Breezy of the website SingersRoom.com, Lattimore expressed his pride in the album and his ongoing determination to fulfill the ambitious role he had set for himself as a steward of classic R&B. Asked by Breezy what he would like his legacy to be, he replied, "That I sang to the hearts of women and to the minds of men, and that I always encouraged them in love. That's my musical legacy and purpose. If I can do that, and help somebody by encouraging them in love, then I've done what I was supposed to do musically."

Selected discography

Singles

"Never Too Busy," 1996.
"Just What It Takes," 1996.
"For You," 1997.
"Days Like This," 1998.
"If I Lose My Woman," 1999.
"Weekend," 2001.
"Find a Way," 2012.

Albums

Kenny Lattimore (includes "Never Too Busy," "Just What It Takes," and "For You"), Columbia, 1996.

From the Soul of Man (includes "Days Like This" and "If I Lose My Woman"), Columbia, 1998.
Weekend (includes "Weekend"), Arista, 2001.
(With Chanté Moore) *Things That Lovers Do,* Arista, 2003.
(With Chanté Moore) *Uncovered/Covered,* La Face, 2006.
Timeless, Verve, 2008.
Back to Cool (includes "Find a Way"), Sincere Soul, 2012.
Anatomy of a Love Song (includes "Find a Way"), Sincere Soul, 2015.

Sources

Online

"Biography," KennyLattimore.com, http://www.kennylattimore.com/bio/ (accessed July 19, 2015).
Breezy, Elle, "Kenny Lattimore Talks 'The Anatomy of a Love Song,' Mentoring the Youth, Ex-Wife, His Perfect Woman, More," SingersRoom.com, April 14, 2015, http://singersroom.com/content/2015-04-14/EXCLUSIVE-Kenny-Lattimore-Talks-The-Anatomy-of-A-Love-Song-Mentoring-The-Youth-Ex-Wife-His-Perfect-Woman-More/ (accessed July 19, 2015).
Erlewine, Stephen Thomas, "Kenny Lattimore: Artist Biography," AllMusic.com, http://www.allmusic.com/artist/kenny-lattimore-mn0000082149/biography (accessed July 19, 2015).
Gallucci, Michael, "*From the Soul of Man:* Review," AllMusic.com, http://www.allmusic.com/album/from-the-soul-of-man-mw0000035066 (accessed July 20, 2015).
Rizik, Chris, "Kenny Lattimore: Artist Biography," SoulTracks.com, http://www.soultracks.com/kenny_lattimore.htm (accessed July 29, 2015).

—R. Anthony Kugler

Little Eva

1943–2003

R&B and pop vocalist

Little Eva, photograph. Michael Ochs Archives/Getty Images.

An immensely gifted vocalist whose fame was brilliant but fleeting, Little Eva was one of the biggest pop stars in the country durin the early 1960s. Remembered for her number-one hit "The Loco-Motion" (frequently but less accurately titled "The Locomotion," 1962), an iconic and influential dance number, she bridged the worlds of R&B and pop with dexterity. The material she was given for follow-ups, however, failed to reflect rapid changes in musical tastes, and she had only minor hits for the remainder of her career. In the late 1980s, after nearly two decades out of the industry, Little Eva began touring and recording again. By all accounts a pragmatic and levelheaded person, she was philosophical about her brief brush with fame. "'The Loco-motion,'" she once said, in a comment quoted by the London *Telegraph,* "is a great song, but it ain't no 'Amazing Grace.'"

Eva Narcissus Boyd, known from an early age as "Little Eva" to distinguish her from an aunt of the same name, was born on June 29, 1943, in Belhaven, a small town in eastern North Carolina. One of more than 10 children born to David and Laura Boyd, she learned to sing in church. Her vocal talents were evident at a young age, and by the time she was a teenager, she had already gained singing experience as a member of her family's gospel group, the Boyd Five. Throughout this period she was also drawn to the rock, pop, and R&B that she heard on the radio. Her interest in those genres deepened considerably in the summer of 1959, when she traveled north to see a brother in New York City.

That visit proved to be a pivotal moment in her life, as it gave her what writers Mick Patrick and Malcolm Baumgart described as "a taste for life in the big city." In 1960 she dropped out of high school and returned to New York, where she supported herself with housekeeping and babysitting jobs. Among her first employers there were Carole King and Gerry Goffin, a married couple and songwriting team. It was largely through King and Goffin that she was able to attract the attention of Don Kirchner, a producer who would have a profound impact on her career. Her break came in the spring of 1962, when Kirchner asked King and Goffin to write a dance number for Dee Dee Sharp, a well-established singer. The result was "The Loco-Motion," whose lyrics Little Eva helped inspire with the dance moves she practiced while caring for the couple's toddler. Her attachment to the new song was such that King and

---

At a Glance . . .

Born Eva Narcissus Boyd on June 29, 1943, in Belhaven, NC; died on April 10, 2003, in Kinston, NC; daughter of David and Laura Boyd; married James Harris, 1962 (died, 1983); children: five.

Career: R&B and pop vocalist, 1960s–2003.

Goffin asked her to record a demo version for Kirchner, who was so impressed with her rendition that he formed a new label, Dimension Records, to handle its marketing and distribution.

Released as a single in June of 1962, "The Loco-Motion" was a sensation, rising to the top of both the R&B and the pop charts and sparking a ubiquitous but short-lived dance craze. Still in her late teens, Little Eva burst onto the national scene with an appearance on ABC's *American Bandstand* and a concert at New York's Apollo Theater. Dimension, meanwhile, rushed a full album (1962's *LLLLLoco-Motion*) into production and released the Little Eva's second single, "Keep Your Hands Off My Baby" (1962). Although it failed to match the success of its predecessor, it was a hit nonetheless, rising to number six on the R&B list and to number 12 on the pop chart. Subsequent releases were disappointing, however, with only one, 1963's "Let's Turkey Trot" (number 16 on the R&B chart, number 20 on the pop list), breaking the top 20 on either chart. While there were likely a variety of reasons for that shift, a major factor was undoubtedly the failure to provide her with a broad range of material. Although most of her later releases were novelty dance numbers like "The Loco-Motion," it was increasingly clear by the middle of the decade that the public's enthusiasm for dance fads had faded.

Little Eva responded to the decline in her fortunes by focusing on backup work for other artists. That kept her busy until the early 1970s, when a temporary estrangement from her husband and a steady decline in work opportunities prompted a move back to rural North Carolina. For nearly two decades she lived there in obscurity, taking whatever work she could find to support her family. As most of the profits from her hits had gone to her label, not to her, she had scant savings, and for many years she lived in poverty. Around 1988, however, her circumstances began to improve, thanks in large part to a remake of "The Loco-Motion" by the Australian pop star Kylie Minogue.

Minogue's version was not the first high-profile remake of Little Eva's signature hit; on the contrary, a rendition by the rock band Grand Funk Railroad had gone all the way to number one on the pop list in 1974, with little benefit to her. By the late 1980s, however, she had been out of the public eye for so long that her life was a mystery to many fans. When Minogue's cover brought her back into the spotlight, a string of interviews and "where is she now" stories followed. That publicity enabled her to return to the music industry. She began by recording a gospel album, appropriately titled *Back On Track,* for the Malibu label in 1989. Three years later she joined rock legend Little Richard on a tour of the United Kingdom. She continued to tour periodically for roughly another decade, entertaining relatively small but enthusiastic crowds on the oldies circuit. Health problems then forced her retirement.

Diagnosed in the early 2000s with cervical cancer, Little Eva died of that ailment on April 10, 2003, in Kinston, North Carolina, a small town not far from Belhaven. In 2008 a volunteer effort resulted in the placement of a new marker at her grave, located in a historic but dilapidated cemetery in her hometown. Inscribed on the stone, according to a local television station, was a drawing of a locomotive and the phrase "Singing With the Angels."

Selected discography

Singles

"The Loco-Motion," 1962.
"Keep Your Hands Off My Baby," 1962.
"Let's Turkey Trot," 1963.

Albums

LLLLLoco-Motion (includes "The Loco-Motion"), Dimension, 1962.
Back on Track, Malibu, 1989.

Sources

Online

"Little Eva," SoulWalking.co.uk, http://www.soulwalking.co.uk/Little%20Eva.html (accessed July 7, 2015).
"Little Eva," Telegraph.co.uk, April 14, 2003, http://www.telegraph.co.uk/news/obituaries/1427452/Little-Eva.html (accessed July 7, 2015).
"New Gravestone Unveiled for 'Loco-Motion' Singer," WRAL.com, November 9, 2008, http://www.wral.com/news/local/story/3926740/ (accessed July 8, 2015).
Patrick, Mick, and Malcolm Baumgart, "Little Eva (1943–2003)," Spectropop.com, http://www.spectropop.com/remembers/LEobit.htm (accessed July 7, 2015).
Unterberger, Richie, "Little Eva: Artist Biography," AllMusic.com, http://www.allmusic.com/artist/little-eva-mn0000839369/biography (accessed July 7, 2015).

—R. Anthony Kugler

Anthony Mason

1966–2015

Professional basketball player

Former National Basketball Association (NBA) forward Anthony Mason was among the most formidable low-post defenders and rebounders of his era. At six feet, seven inches tall and 250 pounds, Mason was a powerful presence beneath the rim, capable of containing much larger opponents with his combination of raw strength, keen ball-stopping instincts, and physical tenacity. At the same time, Mason had a deft touch on the offensive end, averaging 10.9 points per game while shooting nearly 51 percent for his career. Mason remains best known as a member of the New York Knicks during the 1990s, and his competitiveness and ruthless style of play were instrumental in shaping the team's identity. "We were a hard-nosed, no-nonsense team," Derek Harper, Mason's teammate during those years, recalled to the *New York Post* in 2015. "Our toughness came through guys like Mase. He was the mainstay of what we were, the epitome of hard work." Paul Silas, a former NBA All-Star who coached Mason in Charlotte, echoed Harper's sentiments. "Mase was tough," Silas told the *Post.* "He didn't give up anything. He wanted to play." Mason's contributions off the bench proved vital to New York's success during those years while earning the forward Sixth Man of the Year honors for the 1994–95 season.

Learned Perseverance as a Child

Anthony Mason was born on December 14, 1966, in Miami, Florida, and raised in the borough of Queens, New York. The hard-nosed work ethic that would define his NBA career was shaped by his early life struggles. He was raised by a single mother, a seamstress who worked two jobs in order to support her son while also taking on additional sewing work from her neighbors. "My whole life has been hard," Mason told the South Florida *Sun-Sentinel* in 2001. "It seems like everyone in my family had to do double what everyone else had to do to keep pace. That's where I get that persona that I'm not going to take any bull. I'm not going to let anybody walk over me or take something from me." Despite these difficult beginnings, Mason managed to avoid trouble during his childhood, impressing adults with his kindness and generosity. "Anthony was the sweetest child any person could have," his mother, Mary Mason, recalled to the *Sun-Sentinel.* "He's always trying to help someone. Every stray dog and cat he'd come across he was trying to bring it home. He was always trying to make an impact, please people."

Although Mason demonstrated exceptional athletic ability at a young age, he did not begin playing basketball until his junior year at Springfield Gardens High School. His head coach, Ken Fiedler, proved a valuable mentor to the young player and was instrumental in teaching him how to become an elite player. During his senior year, he received a scholarship offer to play at Tennessee State University. Mason thrived at the collegiate level, averaging 18.7 points and 8.1 rebounds in four years at Tennessee State. His best performance came during the 1987–88 season, when he led the Ohio Valley Conference with 28 points per contest. For his career, he scored 2,075 points, the fifth-highest total in school history.

At a Glance . . .

Born Anthony George Douglas Mason on December 14, 1966, in Miami, FL; died on February 28, 2015, in New York, NY; son of Mary Mason; children: Anthony, Jr., Antoine, Armon. *Education:* Tennessee State University, BS, criminal justice, 1988.

Career: Efes Pilsen, Turkish League, 1988–89; New Jersey Nets, forward, 1989–90; Denver Nuggets, forward, 1990–91; Tulsa Fast Breakers, Continental Basketball Association, 1990–91; Long Island Surf, United States Basketball League, 1991; New York Knicks, forward, 1991–96; Charlotte Hornets, forward, 1996–98, 1999–2000; Miami Heat, forward, 2000–2001; Milwaukee Bucks, forward and center, 2001–03; Hotaling Group, insurance agent, 2011–15.

Awards: Sixth Man of the Year, 1995; National Basketball Association All-Star selection, 2001.

Even though Mason was selected by the Portland Trail Blazers in the third round of the 1988 NBA draft, he ultimately decided to launch his professional career abroad. He played one season with Efes Pilsen of the Turkish League before returning to the United States in 1989 to sign with the New Jersey Nets. Mason played sparingly for the Nets, appearing in only 21 games before being released in October 1990. He subsequently played for a period with the Tulsa Fast Breakers of the Continental Basketball Association before signing two 10-day contracts with the Denver Nuggets. Following the 1990–91 NBA season, Mason joined the Long Island Surf of the United States Basketball League. It was while playing for Long Island that he attracted the attention of Pat Riley, who had recently been named head coach of the New York Knicks. Impressed by Mason's work ethic and toughness, Riley promptly offered the power forward a contract.

Proved Himself a Valuable NBA Player

Mason quickly established himself as a vital role player with the Knicks. In 1991–92, he averaged 26.8 minutes per game off the bench, scoring seven points and grabbing seven rebounds per contest. A year later Mason's playing time increased, as he logged 30.6 minutes per game as a reserve. Soon Mason's toughness and aggressiveness came to define New York's physical brand of play, as the Knicks emerged as one of the most formidable teams in the Eastern Conference. In 1994–95, Mason was an integral part of the club's postseason run, helping lead the Knicks to hard-fought playoff victories over the Chicago Bulls and Indiana Pacers. In the NBA Finals matchup against the Houston Rockets, Mason averaged 8.6 points and 6.9 rebounds per game, while also playing tough defense against Houston center Hakeem Olajuwon. The Knicks ultimately lost the series, however, falling to the Rockets in seven games.

Mason spent two more seasons in New York. In 1994–95 his contributions as a reserve earned him the NBA Sixth Man of the Year Award. A year later, Mason earned a place in the starting lineup, leading the league by averaging 42.2 minutes per game. Throughout this time, Mason also earned fame for his innovative hairstyles, often appearing on the court with words such as "Mase" or "Knicks" shaved into the side of his head. His tenure in New York came to an end in July 1996, when he was traded to the Charlotte Hornets. Mason quickly established himself as a veteran leader with his new team, setting career-high totals in both points (16.2) and rebounds (11.4) per game during the 1996–97 season while averaging a league-best 43.1 minutes per contest. He produced similar numbers a year later, scoring 12.8 points and collecting 10.2 rebounds per game. Even in the midst of this success, Mason encountered serious legal troubles during his time in Charlotte. In February of 1998 he was arrested after being accused of statutory rape during a charity basketball event in the Jamaica neighborhood of New York City. He ultimately pleaded guilty to the charge of endangering the welfare of a child and was sentenced to 200 hours of community service.

Despite his legendary durability and toughness, Mason was forced to miss the entire 1998–99 season after he suffered a ruptured bicep. After one more year in Charlotte, the power forward was traded to the Miami Heat prior to the 2000–2001 season. Reunited with former Knicks coach Pat Riley, Mason excelled during his one season in Miami, averaging 16.1 points per game en route to earning the first All-Star selection of his career. He later played two seasons with the Milwaukee Bucks before retiring from basketball in 2003.

After leaving the game, Mason worked for a brief period as an insurance agent with the Hotaling Group. He struggled with health issues during his later years, however, and in early 2015 he was hospitalized after suffering a massive heart attack. He died weeks later, on February 28, 2015. In a statement issued following his death, NBA commissioner Adam Silver spoke of Mason's lasting contributions to the league. "Anthony Mason exemplified perseverance for all players fighting for their chance in the NBA," the statement read. "With a gritty style of play and a distinctive skill set, he blossomed from a third-round draft pick into a Sixth Man Award winner, All-NBA selection and, at age 34, an All-Star. NBA fans and players around the league admired his tenacity on defense and playmaking on offense."

Sources

Periodicals

Newsday, February 26, 2000, p. A8.
New York Amsterdam News, March 12, 1994, p. 48.
New York Post, March 1, 2015, p. 112.
New York Times, March 1, 2015.
Sun-Sentinel (South Florida), February 9, 2001, p. 1C; April 15, 2001, p. 10C.
USA Today, February 10, 2000, p. 11C.
Washington Post, February 12, 2015.

Online

"Anthony Mason," Basketball-Reference.com, http://www.basketball-reference.com/players/m/masonan01.html (accessed June 24, 2015).

"Anthony Mason Dead: 5 Fast Facts You Need to Know," Heavy.com, February 28, 2015, http://heavy.com/sports/2015/02/anthony-mason-dead-cause-of-death-weight-heart-attack-family-wife-sons/ (accessed June 24, 2015).

"NBA Statement Regarding the Passing of Anthony Mason," NBA on Twitter, February 28, 2015, https://twitter.com/NBA/status/571709553206800385/photo/1 (accessed June 24, 2015).

Silverman, Robert, "R.I.P. Anthony Mason, Soul of the '90s," The Daily Beast, February 28, 2015, http://www.thedailybeast.com/articles/2015/02/28/r-i-p-anthony-mason-soul-of-the-90s.html (accessed June 24, 2015).

—Stephen Meyer

Audra McDonald

1970—

Actress, singer

McDonald, Audra, photograph. s_bukley/Shutterstock.com.

Audra McDonald is an artist so gifted and versatile that her career can only be defined in terms of superlatives. An icon of the American theater, McDonald made Broadway history in 2014, when she won a record-breaking sixth Tony Award for her portrayal of singer Billie Holiday in *Lady Day at Emerson's Bar and Grill.* With the win, McDonald surpassed theater giants Angela Lansbury and Julie Harris, with five Tony Awards each, and became the first performer to take home awards in all four acting categories. The accomplishment is all the more remarkable given that McDonald has appeared in just 10 Broadway productions since her debut in *The Secret Garden* in 1991. McDonald received her other Tony Awards for her work on *Carousel* (1994), *The Master Class* (1995–96), *Ragtime* (1998), *A Raisin in the Sun* (2004), and *The Gershwins' Porgy and Bess* (2012).

A classically trained singer with a luminous soprano whom *New York Times* music critic Stephen Holden labeled "a defining voice of our time," McDonald is equally at home on Broadway and on the opera stage, and she is as fluent with favorite show tunes and pop standards as she is with contemporary material. She has released five solo albums, appeared on various cast, compilation, and tribute recordings, and sung with virtually every major American orchestra. She has also had several roles in film and television, including television adaptations of *Annie* (1999), *Wit* (2001), *A Raisin in the Sun* (2008), and *The Sound of Music* (2013), and six years starring as Dr. Naomi Bennet on the hit ABC series *Private Practice.* McDonald is a multiple recipient of all the other major theater awards—the Drama Desk Award, the Outer Critics Circle Award, and the Drama League Award—and a two-time Grammy Award winner for the recording of the Kurt Weill opera *Rise and Fall of the City of Mahagonny* (2007).

Enrolled at Juilliard

McDonald was born in Berlin, Germany, on July 3, 1970, while her father, Stanley McDonald, was stationed there with the U.S. Army. In 1972 the family, which by then included Audra's younger sister, Alison, settled in Fresno, California. Audra's mother, Anna Kathryn McDonald, was an administrator at California

At a Glance . . .

Born on July 3, 1970, in Berlin, Germany; daughter of Stanley McDonald Jr. and Anna Kathryn McDonald (both school administrators and musicians); married Peter Donovan (a bassist), 2000 (divorced, 2009); married Will Swenson (an actor), 2012; children: Zoe Madeline (with Donovan). *Education:* Juilliard School of Music, BA, 1993.

Career: Made Broadway debut, 1991; screen actress, 1996—; solo recording artist, 1998—.

Memberships: Covenant House International, board of directors; Broadway Impact, advisory board; Freedom to Marry.

Awards: Tony Award, Best Featured Actress in a Musical, Drama Desk Award, Outer Critics Circle Award, and Theatre World Award, 1994, for *Carousel*; Tony Award, Best Featured Actress in a Play, and Ovation Award, 1996, for *The Master Class*; Tony Award, Best Featured Actress in a Musical, 1998, for *Ragtime*; Tony Award, Best Featured Actress in a Play, Drama Desk Award, and Outer Critics Circle Award, 2004, for *A Raisin in the Sun*; Drama Desk Award and Outer Critics Circle Award, 2007, for *110 in the Shade*; Grammy Award, Best Classical Album, Best Opera Recording, 2008, for *Rise and Fall of the City of Mahagonny*; Tony Award, Best Leading Actress in a Musical, Drama Desk Award, and Outer Critics Circle Award, 2012, for *The Gershwins' Porgy and Bess*; Tony Award, Best Leading Actress in a Play, Drama Desk Award, and Outer Critics Circle Award, 2014, for *Lady Day at Emerson's Bar and Grill*.

Addresses: *Management*—IMG Artists, Pleiades House, 7 West 54th St., New York, NY 10019. *Web*—http://audramcdonald.net/. *Twitter*—@AudraEqualityMc.

Polytechnic State University in San Luis Obispo, and her father was a high school principal. Her parents were both trained musicians, and her aunts toured with a gospel singing group. In an interview with Barry Singer in the *New York Times* in 1998, McDonald joked that if she had not shown musical ability as a child, "I probably would have been sent back."

McDonald's professional career began at age nine, when she participated in shows at Roger Rocka's Music Hall, a Fresno dinner theater that showcased young performers. As a teenager, she appeared in Music Hall productions of *Hello, Dolly!, A Chorus Line,* and *Grease,* and she had the lead role of Dorothy in *The Wiz.* "I remember putting on the cassette of *Funny Girl* and acting out all of the parts in the living room when I came home from school," McDonald told Kipp Cheng of *American Theatre* in 1998. "I've always wanted to be on Broadway."

After high school at the Roosevelt School of the Performing Arts in Fresno, McDonald enrolled at the prestigious Juilliard School of Music in Manhattan. At Juilliard, McDonald focused her studies on voice and did not take any classes in the school's highly regarded drama division. As her career started to take off, McDonald was especially pleased when her acting was praised, particularly her sense of comedy, because of her lack of formal training. "Comedy is difficult for me. I'm good at suffering and dying.... I haven't done much comedy professionally, and I've never really had acting lessons," McDonald told Glenn Collins in the *New York Times* in 1994.

Debuted on Broadway

Broadway was always McDonald's first love, and she was unhappy at the classically oriented Juilliard. "It wasn't me," McDonald said of Juilliard to Singer. "I had danced around the room singing to Barbra Streisand. That's what I wanted to do." McDonald became so severely depressed she attempted suicide. With the help of a therapist at Juilliard, McDonald checked herself into a mental health hospital. Released after a month, McDonald decided to take a break from her studies. She landed a part on Broadway in the chorus of *The Secret Garden,* a musical version of the beloved children's story by Frances Hodgson Burnett. McDonald then toured with the national company of *The Secret Garden.* She eventually went back to Juilliard and finished a bachelor's degree in 1993.

McDonald auditioned several times before being cast in a much-ballyhooed production of *Carousel* at Lincoln Center in 1994. The project was a restaging of a highly praised production of the classic Rodgers and Hammerstein musical done at London's National Theatre in 1992. Reviews in New York were mostly favorable, and McDonald was singled out as one of the stellar performers. For example, David Richards in the *New York Times* described McDonald as "the real find of this production." Stefan Kanfer in the *New Leader,* among the minority of critics who did not like the overall production, had only good words for McDonald, saying that she "possesses great warmth and purity of tone. She also reveals a comic gift."

The character of Carrie Pipperidge, a mill worker in a 19th-century Maine town, is not a specifically African-American part, and there was some criticism of the

nontraditional casting of McDonald and of opera star Shirley Verrett in the role of town matriarch Nettie Fowler. "Is this a color-blind New England town? ... Or are we not supposed to notice hue and ethnicity? In that case, why was the multiracial policy given cease-less self-congratulatory publicity in London and New York?" wrote Kanfer. McDonald dismissed the race issue. "It's a universal story, with universal music and lyrics.... If these people are concentrating on the fact that I'm black ... well, there's nothing I can do about that," she told Collins.

Racked up Tony Wins

For her work in *Carousel,* McDonald won a Tony Award for best featured actress in a musical as well as Drama Desk, Outer Critics Circle, and Theatre World awards. She picked up her second Tony Award, this time for best featured actress in a play, for *The Master Class,* Terrence McNally's fictionalized version of the series of master classes for aspiring opera singers conducted by legendary opera star Maria Callas at Juilliard. In the Broadway production, which opened in November of 1995, Callas was portrayed by Zoe Caldwell and McDonald played Sharon, a talented, attractive student mercilessly bullied by the great diva. McDonald was hesitant to try out for the part of Sharon, which required an impressive delivery of a demanding aria from Giuseppe Verdi's *Macbeth.* She was so frightened of the aria—a piece so challenging that even Callas herself sang it only a few times during her career—that she canceled her first audition. A week later McDonald's agent called to say the part was still open and suggested she make another attempt. She did, and despite her lack of confidence, she came through with flying colors. "She has got it all. She has such natural ability, she doesn't even realize it," *Master Class* director Leonard Foglia said of McDonald to Susan King in the *Los Angeles Times.*

The most valuable aspect of *Master Class* for McDonald was working with Caldwell, one of the theater's most admired actresses. "She is just it for me," McDonald told Cheng. "She's such a force of nature, on and offstage. She is like my touchstone. A ruby-red gem I touch and I get my energy. I learned so much from Zoe."

McDonald won her third Tony for *Ragtime.* Among the most highly touted productions to come to Broadway during the 1990s, *Ragtime* is a musical version of E. L. Doctorow's best-selling 1975 novel about New York at the turn of the century. The sprawling plot concerns three sets of characters: a prosperous white family living in pleasantly suburban New Rochelle, black musicians in Harlem creating the new musical style called "ragtime," and Jewish immigrants strug-gling in poverty on the teeming Lower East Side. McDonald's character, Sarah, a young black washer-woman who abandons her illegitimate child, is the thread that weaves the different characters together. To

the disappointment of many theatergoers, McDonald's part, although important plot-wise, was relatively small (she dies during the first act and comes back only as a ghost figure in the finale). She did get a powerful solo number, "Your Daddy's Son," and shared the duet "Wheels of a Dream" with the lead male character, ragtime pianist Coalhouse Walker Jr., played by Brian Stokes Mitchell.

Produced by the Canadian company Livent, Inc., *Ragtime* came to New York in January of 1998, after playing for a year in Toronto. An album of songs from the musical was made by the Toronto cast (including McDonald) even before the show had been seen by an American audience. This unusual situation allowed *Ragtime* to open on Broadway as a known quantity and a proven success that could survive in regional productions even if it failed in New York. Happily, the musical was a smash hit. Michael Tueth of *America* wrote that "*Ragtime: The Musical* creates a kaleido-scope whose brilliant colors glitter against a constantly threatening darkness," adding that the cast offered "some of the finest voices in American musical theater today," including the "operatic richness of Audra Mc-Donald." John Lahr in the *New Yorker* called McDon-ald "outstanding" and praised *Ragtime* as "a kind of theatrical watershed: an awesome pyrotechnical dis-play of theatrical craft and showmanship ... a big, brave passionate gamble, not just with cash but with content, and it brings the American musical back to its roots as populist commercial entertainment." Written by com-poser Stephen Flaherty and lyricist Lynn Ahrens, with a book by Terrence McNally, *Ragtime* won Tony Awards for best score and best book but lost in the best musical category to the Disney-produced spectacle *The Lion King.*

Attracted a Television Audience

McDonald's first lead role on Broadway was in *Marie Christine* (1999), a musical/opera hybrid written ex-pressly for her by Michael John LaChiusa, one of several young theater composers who penned the songs for her first solo album *Way Back to Paradise* (1998). The story takes place at the turn of the 20th century, with McDonald playing a Creole version of Medea who kills her brother and her children over her obsession with a white man. McDonald followed up with Lady Percy in *Henry IV* (2003), her first major Shakespeare role, before turning in her fourth Tony Award–winning performance in the Broadway revival of *A Raisin in the Sun,* Lorraine Hansberry's land-mark 1959 drama about African-American life on the cusp of the civil rights era. *A Raisin in the Sun* tells the story of the Youngers, a South Side Chicago family torn in several directions by the question of how best to use the $10,000 they receive from the deceased Mr. Younger's insurance policy. Elyse Sommer reviewed the production for the online theater magazine *Curtain Up,* noting, "Audra McDonald, who has been conserv-ing her gorgeous soprano and honing her straight

acting skills, is a seething cauldron of feelings as Walter Lee's loving and oppressed wife Ruth."

McDonald made her return to the musical with *110 in the Shade* (2007), the story of a lovelorn young woman during 1930s Texas who becomes smitten by a charismatic con man who promises to bring rain to her family's drought-stricken cattle ranch. The show ran a modest 330 performances, prompting *New York Times* critic Ben Brantley to observe of McDonald, "She's an overwhelming presence in an underwhelming show." Brantley went on to gush about McDonald's talents as a singing actress: "For what Ms. McDonald makes of Lizzie Curry, an unmarried woman in a household of manly men, is a dazzling case for the musical as a dramatic form that plumbs hearts and minds. She so blurs the lines between spoken and musical expression that one seems like a natural extension of the other."

110 in the Shade opened just two weeks after the tragic death of McDonald's father, an experienced pilot who was killed when the experimental gyroplane he was flying crashed due to mechanical failure. Still grief stricken when the show closed, McDonald hoped the move to Los Angeles for *Private Practice* would give her a fresh start. No newcomer to television, McDonald had already appeared as a series regular in the short-lived dramas *Mister Sterling* (2003) and *The Bedford Diaries* (2006), and she had received an Emmy nomination for the role of nurse Susie Monahan in the Mike Nichols-directed HBO movie *Wit,* which starred Emma Thompson as an English professor forced to reexamine her life when she is diagnosed with terminal cancer.

Enjoyed Triumphant Return to Broadway

After five seasons on *Private Practice,* McDonald returned to the New York theater world with *Porgy and Bess,* George and Ira Gershwin's opera about the poor black residents of Catfish Row, a fictional Charleston, South Carolina, fishing village. Already Broadway royalty, McDonald took home her fifth Tony Award for her performance in the lead role of Bess, a drug- and alcohol-addicted floozy relieved from her desperation, if only temporarily, by the kindness of the crippled beggar Porgy. Next came McDonald's remarkable performance channeling the tragic last days of jazz great Billie Holiday in *Lady Day at Emerson's Bar and Grill.* "From the moment McDonald takes the microphone, a metamorphosis more striking than any in Ovid occurs," Charles McNulty wrote in the *Los Angeles Times.* "Gone is the shimmering operatic prowess that powered through 'Summertime' in *The Gershwins' Porgy and Bess....* In its place are Holiday's distinctive jazz timing and idiosyncratic phrasing, qualities as singular as fingerprints." Accepting her record-breaking sixth Tony Award for the role, this time for

best leading actress in a play, McDonald tearfully thanked her parents "for disobeying the doctors' orders and not medicating their hyperactive girl and finding out what she was into instead, and pushing her into the theater."

Lady Day closed in October of 2014. Two months later McDonald kicked off a concert tour to promote *Go Back Home* (2013), her first solo album in seven years. Like her previous album *How Glory Goes* (2000), *Go Back Home* mixes theater standards with pieces written by a new generation of composers, including Adam Guettel and Adam Gwon. *Happy Songs* (2002) featured a variety of tunes from the 1920s to the 1940s, while *Build a Bridge* (2006) was a crossover attempt designed for greater mainstream acceptance, with tracks by contemporary pop artists such as Burt Bacharach, John Mayer, Rufus Wainwright, Randy Newman, and Elvis Costello. Named *Musical America*'s Musician of the Year for 2013, McDonald joined an elite group of previous winners, including Leonard Bernstein, Beverly Sills, Yo-Yo Ma, and Leontyne Price.

McDonald is also familiar to audiences as a headliner and, since 2012, host of the Public Broadcasting Service performing arts series *Live from Lincoln Center.* Other prestigious venues include Carnegie Hall, the White House, the Kennedy Center, and London's Royal Albert Hall. In addition, McDonald has appeared in bit parts and supporting roles in various films, among them *It Runs in the Family* (2003), starring three generations of the Douglas acting clan (Kirk, Michael, and Cameron), and *Rampart* (2011), with Woody Harrelson. In *Ricki and the Flash* (2015), which stars Meryl Streep as an aging rocker who attempts to reunite with her family, McDonald is married to Streep's ex-husband, played by Kevin Kline. A filmed version of *Lady Day* is headed to HBO, with a tentative air date sometime during the fall of 2015, and McDonald forms part of the star-studded cast of the upcoming live-action adaptation of the Disney fairy tale *Beauty and the Beast.* The cast includes Kline, Emma Thompson, Ewan McGregor, and Emma Watson. McDonald's next theater project—scheduled to open in April of 2016—is a show that explores the backstory of the 1921 jazz musical revue *Shuffle Along,* a surprise hit written and performed entirely by African Americans.

McDonald and her first husband, bassist Peter Donovan, divorced in 2009. They are the parents of Zoe Madeline, born in 2001 and named after McDonald's friends Zoe Caldwell and the late Madeline Kahn. In 2012 McDonald married actor and director Will Swenson. The two make their home in New York and often appear in regional theater together. They are both ardent proponents of marriage equality and in 2012 they received the Parents, Families and Friends of Lesbians and Gays Straight for Equality in Entertainment Award. A dog lover, McDonald shared the stage

in *Lady Day* with a rescued Chihuahua that was cast in the role of Holiday's beloved canine companion, Pepe. McDonald's other causes include Covenant House International, a child care agency for homeless and runaway youth. In 2015 McDonald was named to *Time* magazine's annual roster of the 100 Most Influential People in the World.

Selected works

Theater

The Secret Garden, 1991–93.
Carousel, 1994–95.
The Master Class, 1995–97.
Ragtime, 1998–2000.
Marie Christine, 1999–2000.
Henry IV, 2003–04.
A Raisin in the Sun, 2004.
110 in the Shade, 2007.
The Rise and Fall of the City of Mahagonny, 2007.
Twelfth Night, 2009.
The Gershwins' Porgy and Bess, 2012.
Lady Day at Emerson's Bar and Grill, 2014.

Albums

Way Back to Paradise, Nonesuch, 1998.
How Glory Goes, Nonesuch, 2000.
Happy Songs, Nonesuch, 2002.
Build a Bridge, Nonesuch, 2006.
Go Back Home, Nonesuch, 2013.

Television

Annie (television movie), ABC, 1999.
Having Our Say: The Delaney Sisters' First 100 Years (television movie), CBS, 1999.
Wit (television movie), HBO, 2001.
Mister Sterling, NBC, 2003.
Stephen Sondheim's Passion, PBS, 2005.
The Bedford Diaries, WB, 2006.
A Raisin in the Sun (television movie), ABC, 2008.
Private Practice, ABC, 2007–13.
Audra McDonald in Concert: Go Back Home, PBS, 2013.

The Sound of Music Live!, NBC, 2013.

Films

Seven Servants, Das Werk, 1996.
The Object of My Affection, Twentieth Century Fox, 1998.
Cradle Will Rock, Cradle Productions, 1999.
It Runs in the Family, Buena Vista, 2003.
The Best Thief in the World, Process Productions, 2004.
She Got Problems, Champipple, 2009.
Rampart, Lightstream Pictures, 2011.
Ricki and the Flash, TriStar, 2015.

Sources

Periodicals

America, March 28, 1998.
American Theatre, July/August, 1998.
Los Angeles Times, June 20, 1995; April 13, 2014.
New Leader, April 11, 1994.
New Yorker, February 2, 1998.
New York Times, March 25, 1994; May 15, 1994; August 30, 1998; May 10, 2007; May 10, 2013.

Online

"Audra McDonald," Internet Broadway Database, http://ibdb.com/person.php?id=52250 (accessed June 14, 2015).
"Audra McDonald," Internet Movie Database, http://www.imdb.com/name/nm0567653/ (accessed June 14, 2015).
"Audra McDonald," Playbill Vault, http://www.playbillvault.com/Person/Detail/103974/Audra-McDonald (accessed June 14, 2015).
"Audra McDonald," YouTube, https://www.youtube.com/channel/UCYUL40_lyKpMj3taErPvbHw (accessed June 14, 2015).
Sommer, Elyse, "Review of *A Raisin in the Sun,*" *Curtain Up,* 2004, http://www.curtainup.com/raisininthesunny.html (accessed June 14, 2015).

—Mary Kalfatovic, Sara Pendergast, and Janet Mullane

Juanita Jackson Mitchell

1913–1992

Lawyer, civil rights activist

Juanita Jackson Mitchell had already made many contributions as a civil rights activist before beginning her second career as a lawyer in 1950. The first black woman to practice law in the state of Maryland, Mitchell used her position within the legal system to better the lives of fellow African Americans. She was instrumental in the integration of Maryland's public schools and parks, and she helped force businesses, schools, and colleges in the state to hire more black workers. Throughout her career, both as a civil rights activist and as a lawyer, Mitchell worked to increase voter registration; her campaigns led to tens of thousands of citizens registering to vote.

She was born Juanita Jackson on January 1, 1913, in Hot Springs, Arkansas, one of three daughters of Keiffer and Lillie Jackson. Keiffer Jackson was a light-skinned African American; he easily could have passed for white, but he was proud of his African-American heritage. Keiffer traveled throughout the South showing films in church basements—the only way that many African Americans could see films at the time. He met his wife Lillie, then a schoolteacher, in Baltimore, Maryland, proposing to her after only three trips to Baltimore. After their marriage in 1910, the Jacksons continued showing films throughout the segregated South. The three Jackson girls were born during this time. As the girls got older, they helped their father at work, performing songs or poetry as he changed film reels.

Mitchell became aware of racism at an early age. After her family settled in Baltimore, she watched as white girls attended the high school across the street from her home, but she learned that she would not be allowed to attend the same school. As early as age six, she questioned why she was not allowed to go to schools that received new materials rather than handed-down textbooks. She excelled academically, scoring well enough to skip a grade, and graduated high school at age 14. As a high school student, she challenged the segregation laws that were enforced by stores in downtown Baltimore. She and her friends would wrap their heads in turbans and speak French as shopped. The store owners, thinking the girls were foreigners or the daughters of visiting diplomats rather than local blacks, would allow them to shop.

Denied admission to the University of Maryland because of her race, Mitchell attended Morgan State College before transferring to the University of Pennsylvania. She was surprised at how easily the white students at the University of Pennsylvania accepted black students as their peers, and she enjoyed access to museums and restaurants that had been denied her in Baltimore. She completed her bachelor's degree in education in 1931 and returned to the University of Pennsylvania to earn her master's degree in sociology in 1935.

In 1931, while living in Baltimore, Mitchell and her sister Virginia, with support from their mother and newspaper publisher Dr. Carl Murphy, cofounded the City-Wide Young People's Forum. Lillie Jackson formed an adult advisory council to address problems of race, particularly the denial of service to African

At a Glance . . .

Born Juanita Jackson on January 1, 1913, in Hot Springs, AR; died on July 7, 1992, in Baltimore, MD; daughter of Keiffer Jackson and Lillie May Carroll Jackson (a civil rights activist); married Clarence M. Mitchell Jr., September 7, 1938 (died, 1984); children: Clarence III, Keiffer, Michael, George. *Religion:* African Methodist Episcopal. *Education:* Attended Morgan State College; University of Pennsylvania, BA, 1931, MA, 1935; University of Maryland, JD, 1950.

Career: Worked in NAACP national office, 1935–38; operated legal practice, beginning 1950; worked with husband and son at firm Mitchell, Mitchell, and Mitchell.

Awards: Andrew White Award for Distinguished Public Service, Loyola College of Maryland, 1971; Baltimore's Best Award, 1985; inducted into Maryland Women's Hall of Fame, 1987.

Americans in local stores, and the Young People's Forum attracted college-age people, inviting them to tackle the same problems. Together, in 1933, the groups launched a campaign called "Buy Where You Can Work" that encouraged blacks to shop only at stores that offered employment to black residents. Demonstrators marched in front of stores that employed only white sales clerks. Before long, the owners changed their policies and began hiring black clerks as well. The Young People's Forum also challenged the employment rules of libraries, welfare agencies, and schools; in 1934, a Baltimore library began offering a training program for African Americans, and five black social workers were hired by the Baltimore Relief Commission. It would be many more years before Baltimore schools began hiring black teachers.

Mitchell soon became involved with the struggling Baltimore chapter of the National Association for the Advancement of Colored People (NAACP); her mother became head of the organization in 1935, increasing its membership from only a small group to more than 1,700 in her first year of leadership. Mitchell joined the national NAACP staff in 1935. She resigned just three years later when she married fellow civil rights activist Clarence M. Mitchell Jr. After living in the Midwest for a time, the family settled in Baltimore, where they raised four sons. Although she had given up her employment, Mitchell continued to be involved in civil rights activities. In 1942 she organized a march of 2,000 people in the Maryland capital of Annapolis to encourage an increase in the number of blacks on the

police force and an investigation into police brutality. The march resulted in the formation of the Governor's Interracial Commission. That same year Mitchell launched her first voter registration campaign, registering 11,000 new voters. She continued to run voter registration drives throughout the 1940s, 1950s, and 1960s.

Seeing the crucial role of legal challenges in effecting change, Mitchell decided to pursue a law degree. With the help of her mother and the NAACP, she was admitted to the University of Maryland's School of Law in spite of her race. She graduated in 1950, and although she was denied access to the study courses for the bar examination that were available to white students, she passed the Maryland bar and became the first black woman to practice law in the state. As a lawyer, Mitchell won major desegregation suits against schools and restaurants, beginning with a case in 1950 that ended segregation at state beaches and pools. Mitchell and Thurgood Marshall, who later would become the first black U.S. Supreme Court justice, were among the lawyers who filed suit against the Mergenthaler School of Printing, which denied admission to black students. The suit was a precursor to the landmark *Brown v. Board of Education* (1954) ruling, which held that segregated schools were unconstitutional. In her legal work Mitchell continued to fight for equal access to education, recreation areas such as state parks, and restaurants.

Mitchell was appointed to White House conferences by Presidents Franklin D. Roosevelt, John F. Kennedy, and Lyndon B. Johnson. Eleanor Roosevelt was often a guest in her home. Into her 70s, Mitchell continued to work toward equality in Baltimore, organizing the "Stop the Killing Campaign" in response to the murders of several black teenagers in Baltimore during the 1980s. Widowed in 1984, Mitchell took out loans against her home to cover her sons' legal fees; unable to repay the money, she was supported by local black community leaders, who raised funds to save her home, with additional money earmarked to turn the house into a museum after her death.

Mitchell's sons followed their parents in the fight for equal rights; both Michael Mitchell and Clarence Mitchell III became state senators. In 1985 Mitchell suffered a stroke; four years later she fell down a set of stairs and was left a quadriplegic. She suffered another stroke in 1992 and subsequently died of heart failure on July 7 of that year in Baltimore at age 79.

Sources

Periodicals

Baltimore Sun, July 8, 1992; July 13, 1992.
New York Times, July 9, 1992.

Online

"Juanita Jackson Mitchell," Maryland Women's Hall of Fame, http://msa.maryland.gov/msa/educ/exhib its/womenshall/html/mitchell.html (accessed June 15, 2015).

Kennedy, Kirin, "Women of NAACP Youth and College: Juanita Jackson Mitchell," NAACP.org, March 29, 2011, http://www.naacp.org/blog/entry/wo men-of-naacp-youth-and-college-juanita-jackson -mitchell/ (accessed June 16, 2015).

"Mitchell, Juanita Jackson (1913–1992)," BlackPast .org, http://www.blackpast.org/aah/mitchell-jua nita-jackson-mitchell-1913-1992 (accessed June 16, 2015).

—Alana Joli Abbott

Marilyn Mosby

1980—

Attorney

Marilyn Mosby is the Democratic state's attorney for Baltimore City, Maryland, and the youngest chief prosecutor of any major American urban center. Mosby rose to national prominence in April of 2015, when she announced her decision to prosecute six Baltimore police officers in connection with the death of Freddie Gray, an African-American man who died from injuries suffered while riding in the back of a police van. Gray's death sparked days of protests and civil unrest, in Baltimore and across the country, as demonstrators decried the prevalence of police brutality aimed at African Americans. Although Mosby had been in office for only four months, her swift decision to press charges against the officers involved, in the face of intense media scrutiny, earned her widespread praise within the Democratic Party and among African-American civic leaders. At the same time, Mosby's actions provoked harsh criticism from conservatives, as well as from representatives of the Baltimore police force, who charged that her actions were politically motivated.

Developed Passion for Justice in Childhood

Mosby was born Marilyn James on January 22, 1980, in Boston, Massachusetts, and grew up in the city's predominantly African-American neighborhood of Dorchester. She was descended from a long line of Boston police officers. Her grandfather was one of the first African-American police officers in the state. Her parents, Alan James and Linda Thompson, were also members of the city police force, as were several of her uncles; indeed, Mosby's family home in Dorchester was dubbed the "police house" by neighbors. Her father left the family when Mosby was young, and she was raised primarily by her mother and her grandfather, whom she later described as the principal father figure during her early years. A talented student, Mosby read voraciously as a child, devouring books on African-American history that she received from her mother.

A defining moment in Mosby's life came in 1994, when she witnessed the shooting death of her 17-year-old cousin, Diron Spencer, during a robbery outside her home. The tragic loss of her cousin, who was on the verge of attending college, inspired Mosby to dedicate her life to combatting crime. In high school, Mosby participated in the city's public school desegregation program, receiving her education in the Boston suburb of Dover. While attending Dover-Sherborn High School, Mosby worked as an editor for the student newspaper and participated in student government. After graduating high school in 1998, she enrolled at Tuskegee University, a historically black college in Alabama; she was the first member of her family to attend college. While at Tuskegee she met Nick Mosby, a Baltimore native, whom she would marry in 2004.

While attending Tuskegee, Mosby made her first television appearance when she was the plaintiff on an episode of the reality courtroom program *Judge Judy*. Her appearance on the show stemmed from an incident involving one of Mosby's neighbors, who had vandalized her apartment while she was out of town.

At a Glance . . .

Born Marilyn James on January 22, 1980, in Boston, MA; daughter of Alan C. James and Linda Thompson (both police officers); married Nick Mosby (a Baltimore city councilman), 2004; children: Nylyn, Aniyah. *Politics:* Democrat. *Education:* Tuskegee University, BA, political science, government, 2002; Boston College Law School, JD, 2005.

Career: Baltimore City State's Attorney's Office, clerk, 2005–06, assistant state's attorney, 2006–11, state's attorney, 2015—; Liberty Mutual Insurance, field counsel, 2011–14.

Addresses: *Office*—c/o Office of the State's Attorney for Baltimore City, 9th Floor, 120 E Baltimore St., Baltimore, MD 21202.

Mosby initially filed a complaint with the police, and later she attempted to bring the crime to the attention of the district attorney. After failing to receive an adequate response from the authorities, she decided to try arguing her case on television. In the episode, which aired in 2000, Mosby provided a vivid description of the destruction caused by the perpetrator, which included damage to the front door, the apartment walls, and the bathroom. Mosby's argument proved persuasive to Judge Judy, who awarded her $1,731.90 in damages.

Joined State's Attorney's Office in Baltimore

At Tuskegee Mosby studied government and political science, earning her bachelor's degree in 2002. She subsequently returned home with the aim of attending Boston College Law School. Although her application was originally turned down by the program, she wrote a series of letters and e-mails to the school and eventually earned admission. Upon completing her juris doctor degree in 2005, Mosby joined the Baltimore City State's Attorney's Office as a clerk. A year later, she was promoted to the position of assistant state's attorney. Over the next five years, Mosby worked in the general trial division, prosecuting felony cases throughout the state. In 2011 Mosby temporarily left public service to accept a job with Liberty Mutual Insurance, where she worked as a field counsel.

Mosby's expertise in investigating insurance fraud attracted the notice of Douglas F. Gansler, who served as Maryland attorney general between 2007 and 2015. Impressed by her credentials, Gansler offered Mosby a

position in his office, where she would specialize in prosecuting insurance fraud cases. Mosby declined the offer, opting instead to launch a bid to become the state's attorney for Baltimore City. She announced her candidacy in 2014, presenting a challenge to incumbent state's attorney Greg Bernstein for the Democratic nomination. In her campaign platform, Mosby pledged to prosecute violent crime cases more aggressively while also bringing a greater degree of transparency to the State's Attorney's Office, notably, in cases involving alleged abuses by the police. At the same time, Mosby outlined a plan to establish crime prevention initiatives, including a program designed to help young addicts avoid prosecution for drug offenses.

Mosby's tough stance on crime earned her the support of many city residents, particularly in low-income African-American neighborhoods that had become overrun by violence. Mosby's candidacy also received the endorsement of the local police union, in spite of her determination to bring officers charged in incidents of police brutality to justice. Indeed, throughout the campaign Mosby reiterated her strong support for the city police department, a position rooted in her personal experience. "It is my genuine belief despite what we might all want to think, what we might want to believe, the police officers in this city are doing their jobs," Michael Daly of the Daily Beast website quoted Mosby as stating when she first announced her run for office. "I repeat, the police officers in Baltimore city are doing their jobs and taking bad guys off the street."

Faced Major Challenge upon Taking Office

Despite being outspent by her opponent, Mosby defeated Bernstein in the June of 2014 primary, winning the nomination by a margin of 54 percent to 46 percent. That November she was elected as the new state's attorney, handily defeating the Republican nominee. From the beginning, Mosby made the investigation and prosecution of police corruption one of the top priorities of her department. "I know that the majority of police officers are really hard-working officers who are risking their lives day in and day out, but those really bad ones who go rogue do a disservice to the officers who are risking their lives and taking time away from their families," she told *Baltimore Magazine* in January of 2015. "You have to apply justice fairly and equally, with or without a badge, and that's what I intend to do."

Mosby confronted her first significant test the following April, after Freddie Gray, an African-American Baltimore resident who had been arrested on weapons charges, died of injuries sustained during his incarceration. As the ensuing investigation revealed, following his arrest Gray was shackled and placed into the back of a police van, where he suffered severe spinal injuries while being driven to jail. Gray was subsequently admit-

ted to the hospital, where he died on April 19. His death sparked widespread protests throughout Baltimore, which eventually devolved into looting and violence. On May 1, 2015, Mosby announced that the city would file murder charges against the six arresting officers involved in Gray's arrest. In her press conference, Mosby addressed the protesters directly. "To the people of Baltimore and the demonstrators across America. I heard your call for 'no justice, no peace,'" Mosby declared in a televised speech delivered from the steps of Baltimore's War Memorial Building. "Your peace is sincerely needed as I work to deliver justice on behalf of this young man."

At the same time, Mosby took pains to assuage the concerns of the city police force, many of whom felt her decision to file charges, rather than bring the case before a grand jury, was hasty and ill advised. "To the rank-and-file officers of the Baltimore city police department, please know that these accusations of these six officers are not an indictment on the entire force," Mosby announced. "I come from five generations of law enforcement," she added. "I can tell you that the actions of these officers will not and should not in any way damage important working relationships between police and prosecutors." For a number of politicians and members of the legal profession, Mosby's personal background made her ideally suited to the Freddie Gray case. "She has a natural affinity for police officers and law enforcement types, and at the same time, she is aware of the incredible number of complaints against the Baltimore City police department," Baltimore defense attorney Richard Woods told Elizabeth Chuck of NBC News. "It was important to have somebody who was willing to look at it from both sides, and Marilyn Mosby fit the bill."

From the perspective of the Baltimore Police Department, however, Mosby's involvement in the case posed certain problems. Police union leader Gene Ryan publicly called for Mosby to appoint an independent prosecutor, citing several conflicts of interest that he believed would hinder the state's attorney's ability to pursue the case fairly. Chief among the complaints against Mosby was the fact that she had received a campaign donation from William H. Murphy Jr., the attorney representing Gray's family. These charges of potential bias were echoed in conservative media outlets, notably Fox News, where anchor Megyn Kelly called for Mosby's disbarment. On May 8, 2015, the police officers under investigation filed a motion to dismiss against Mosby, alleging that the prosecution was motivated by political factors.

Despite these criticisms, Mosby remained steadfast in her decision to pursue the case. On June 22 the six officers formally pleaded not guilty to the charges; their trial was scheduled to begin in October of 2015. Two days later, an autopsy report revealed that Gray had died from a "high-energy injury," likely caused by a sudden slowing or stopping of the van in which he was being transported. Although the outcome of the case was a long way from being decided, Mosby's prosecution of the six officers was sure to attract widespread media attention, both in the United States and across the world, in the coming months.

Sources

Periodicals

Baltimore Magazine, January 2015.
Baltimore Sun, May 2, 2015, p. A1; May 27, 2015.
Christian Science Monitor, May 3, 2015; May 9, 2015.
Examiner (Washington, DC), May 28, 2015.
Guardian (London), May 1, 2015,
New York Amsterdam News, May 7, 2015, p. 12.
Wall Street Journal, April 30, 2015.
Washington Post, May 1, 2015.

Online

Capeheart, Jonathan, "Marilyn Mosby's Amazing Press Conference," *PostPartisan* (Washington Post blog), May 1, 2015, http://www.washingtonpost.com/blogs/post-partisan/wp/2015/05/01/marilyn-mosbys-amazing-press-conference/ (accessed June 25, 2015).

Chuck, Elizabeth, "Meet Marilyn Mosby, the Woman Overseeing the Freddie Gray Investigation," NBC News, April 30, 2015, http://www.nbcnews.com/storyline/baltimore-unrest/meet-marilyn-mosby-woman-overseeing-freddie-gray-investigation-n351046 (accessed June 24, 2015).

Daly, Michael, "The Woman Who Could Save Baltimore," The Daily Beast, May 1, 2015, http://www.thedailybeast.com/articles/2015/04/30/can-this-prosecutor-save-baltimore.html (accessed June 24, 2015).

Martinez, Michael, "Report: Autopsy Shows Freddie Gray Suffered 'High-Energy Injury,'" CNN.com, June 24, 2015, http://www.cnn.com/2015/06/23/us/baltimore-freddie-gray-death-officers-indicted-pleas/ (accessed June 25, 2015).

—Stephen Meyer

William C. Nell

1816–1874

Abolitionist, author, historian, postal worker

An important black abolitionist whose work has often been overshadowed by that of his white mentor, William Lloyd Garrison, and his sometime associate, the antislavery orator Frederick Douglass, William C. Nell worked tirelessly to end racial segregation in schools, on public transit, and in other public places in Massachusetts during the mid-19th century. During this time Nell made a living as a printer and copyist and later became the first African-American federal employee when he was employed as a postal clerk in Boston. He remains best known, however, for his history of notable African Americans during the Revolutionary War, *The Colored Patriots of the American Revolution*. Published in 1855, Nell's 400-page tome, which remains in print to this day, was the first history of black Americans based on both written and oral sources and penned by an African-American author.

A native of the Beacon Hill neighborhood of Boston, William Cooper Nell was born on December 20, 1816. He excelled academically, graduating with honors from a segregated school located in the basement of the African Baptist Church. At age 13, Nell received an award from the mayor of Boston. However, unlike the white students who were honored with the same award, who were given a medal and invited to attend a dinner at Faneuil Hall, Nell and his peers from the African school received only an autobiography of Benjamin Franklin and were not invited to attend. Nell found work as a waiter's helper so that he could attend the dinner. The experience was a formative one for him, prompting him to work for the rest of his life to end segregation in schools.

Another early experience fostered Nell's appreciation for the men and women who served during wartime to protect their country. He wrote in his introduction to *The Colored Patriots of the American Revolution* that as a boy, he had enjoyed visiting the Eastern Wing of the State House in Boston. There, an inscription on a stone reads, "Americans, while from this eminence scenes of luxuriant fertility, of flourishing commerce, and the abodes of social happiness, meet your view, forget not those who by their exertions have secured you these blessings." His appreciation for those who had fought on behalf of the United States, particularly black soldiers and militia members, led him to write his history, which he hoped would "deepen in the heart and conscience of this nation the sense of justice, that will ere long manifest itself in deeds worthy a people who, 'free themselves,' should be 'foremost to make free.'"

After finishing school, Nell became active in integrated organizations that worked to achieve rights and equality for African Americans. He had long read the antislavery newspaper the *Liberator,* published by Garrison, and Garrison took him on first as an errand runner and later as a printer's assistant. Nell assisted Garrison, one of the most outspoken abolitionists of the day, in his attempts to end slavery in the South and to keep it from spreading to the Western territories.

In 1840 Nell began his campaign to end segregated public schooling. He began with petitions, signed by more than 2,000 members of the black community, demanding integration. When that tactic failed, he

At a Glance . . .

Born William Cooper Nell on December 20, 1816, in Boston, MA; died on May 25, 1874, in Boston, MA; son of William Guion (a sailor and tailor) and Louisa Nell; married, 1869; two children.

Career: Printer's apprentice, the *Liberator,* Boston, MA, 1840s; American Anti-Slavery Society, office manager, 1840–43; printer, *North Star,* Rochester, NY, 1847–51; assistant to Frederick Douglass, 1851; Office of William L. Bowditch, clerk and law reader; U.S. Postal Department, Boston, MA, clerk, 1861–74.

Memberships: Adelphic Union Library Association; American Anti-Slavery Society; Black Convention Movement; Black National Council; Boston Minor's Exhibition Society; Boston Mutual Lyceum; Histrionic Club; Juvenile Garrison Independent Society (secretary, 1832); New England Freedom Association (founding member); Young Men's Literary Society.

pursued legal means, and in 1849, two lawyers—one of whom had been the first African American to pass the bar in Massachusetts—filed suit. When that suit failed in the Massachusetts Supreme Judicial Court, Nell returned to organizing petitions, this time at the state level. As a result of his efforts, the state legislature acted to end segregated education in Massachusetts in 1855. It was the only state to enact such a law before the Civil War.

In addition to his work to end school segregation, Nell championed integration on public transit, in theaters, and in other public spaces. Although he tended to be conservative in his position on how best to end slavery—some of his contemporaries called for violent rebellion in the slave states or emigration to other countries—Nell worked with the Underground Railroad and opposed the Fugitive Slave Act of 1850. In response to that act's passage, he began to petition for a monument in honor of Crispus Attucks, the first black martyr of the Revolutionary War. (A monument to Attucks was finally erected on the Boston Common in 1888.)

It was in tandem with his work on the monument that Nell began writing his history of black soldiers. Initially composed as a 23-page pamphlet titled *The Services of Colored Americans in the Wars of 1776 and 1812,* the project soon grew into a second edition and, finally, a full history. During the years when he was working on the history, tensions were developing within the abolitionist community. Garrison and Doug-

lass, who had worked together in the American Anti-Slavery Society, differed in their opinions on some matters—such as whether it was right to buy slaves in order to free them—as well as on their strategies for recruiting more people to their cause. Douglass was personally frustrated by his role as an example of a freed slave; white members of the American Anti-Slavery Society sometimes encouraged him to speak less eloquently so that audiences would believe that he really had been a slave. Nell worked closely with Douglass for several years in Rochester, New York, where he was a printer for Douglass's paper *North Star,* and he served as Douglass's assistant in 1851. But when Douglass decided to formally split from Garrison and the American Anti-Slavery Society, Nell returned to Garrison's camp.

Despite their disagreements, Douglass, Garrison, and Nell remained more conservative than activists such as Henry Highland Garnet, who pushed for a more radical rebellion, separate black territories in the United States, or emigration to Liberia, Mexico, or the West Indies. Nell also disagreed with Garrison's antipolitical stance, and he ran for the Massachusetts legislature, unsuccessfully, in 1850. He worked to recruit blacks for military service in the Union Army during the Civil War.

In 1861 Nell was hired by Boston postmaster John Gorham Palfrey to become a postal clerk. At the time it was legally forbidden for a black man to hold such a job, but Palfrey ignored the law, and Nell became the first black federal employee, holding the position until his death. Nell married in 1869 and had two children, but he died five years later on May 25, 1874, at age 57. A monument was placed on his grave in Forest Hills Cemetery in Boston on September 18, 1989.

Selected writings

The Services of Colored Americans in the Wars of 1776 and 1812 (pamphlet), 1851, 2nd ed., 1852.
The Colored Patriots of the American Revolution, 1855.

Sources

Online

McDaniel, W. Caleb, "The Lives of Frederick Douglass," Rice University, January 9, 2013, http://wcm1.web.rice.edu/lives-of-frederick-douglass.html (accessed June 18, 2015).
Nell, William Cooper, *The Colored Patriots of the American Revolution* (electronic ed.), Documenting the American South, University of North Carolina at Chapel Hill, http://docsouth.unc.edu/neh/nell/nell.html (accessed August 3, 2015).
"Nell, William C., Residence," National Historic Land-

marks Program, http://tps.cr.nps.gov/nhl/detail
.cfm?ResourceId=1678&ResourceType=Building
(accessed June 18, 2015).

Ruffin, Herbert G., II, "Nell, William C. (1816–1874),"
BlackPast.org, http://www.blackpast.org/aah/nell
-william-c-1816-1874 (accessed June 18, 2015).

"William C. Nell, Pioneering Black Historian," African
American Registry, http://aaregistry.org/historic
_events/view/william-c-nell-pioneering-black-
historian (accessed June 18, 2015).

—Alana Joli Abbott

Trevor Noah

1984—

Comedian, television host

On March 30, 2015, the Comedy Central network revealed the name of the next host of *The Daily Show,* its flagship program. Jon Stewart, who had transformed the faux news broadcast into a satirical staple in the media diet of political liberals, was stepping aside after 16 years in the anchor's chair. His surprise replacement was a name virtually unfamiliar to most U.S. viewers, Trevor Noah. The 31-year-old comedian, scheduled to take over as host of *The Daily Show* in the fall of 2015, had risen to fame in his native South Africa by incisively extracting humor from the country's tense political culture and fearlessly addressing the complexities of race, including his own mixed race—or, in South African parlance, "colored"—background.

Noah, Trevor, photograph. Electrolysis/Shutterstock.com.

Noah was born in Johannesburg on February 20, 1984. As he put it in his stand-up routine, he was "born a crime," the product of an interracial marriage banned under apartheid laws. When he walked on the streets of his home township of Soweto with his mother, Nombuyiselo Noah, she insisted that the pair keep their distance if they saw a police officer—making him feel, he later joked, "like a bag of weed." If his father, a white man of Swiss and German heritage, was with him, they would walk on opposite sides of the street. Noah shuttled between his mother's home in Soweto and his father's apartment in Johannesburg, where his mother could only enter by pretending that she was the housekeeper. Finally, the authorities found out and arrested Nombuyiselo Noah on charges of immorality. After her release from prison, she raised Noah without his father, who returned to Europe.

Other fabrications were necessary to account for Noah's light complexion to his neighbors in Soweto. He told them that he was an albino—but not to worry, he was the sort of albino who could be outdoors without getting sunburned. His friends called him "the daywalker." Later, he would take that nickname as the title of his first one-man show. These early experiences as a social outsider became the fundamental material of Noah's comedy in the postapartheid era. A self-described "cultural chameleon," he developed the ability to view the nation's racial divides and related social conflicts from multiple perspectives, critiquing the assumptions of all parties. Supplementing his shrewd skills of observation were his uncanny ability to do impersonations and his knack for learning languages—he speaks seven of them.

At a Glance . . .

Born on February 20, 1984, in Johannesburg, South Africa; son of Nombuyiselo Noah.

Career: Television actor and host, 2002—; stand-up comedian, 2007—; host of *The Daily Show,* Comedy Central, 2015—.

Awards: Comic of the Year, South African Savanna Comics' Choice Awards, 2012

Addresses: *Agent*—Levity Entertainment Group, 6701 Center Dr. West, 11th Floor, Los Angeles, CA 90045. *Web*—http://www.trevornoah.com. *Twitter*—@Trevor noah.

Noah recognized a yen for performing during his teenage years. In 2002 he began playing a recurring role in *Isidingo,* a television soap opera. He became a radio host for a youth-oriented Johannesburg station, calling his program *Noah's Ark.* For several years he was a roving television host, serving as emcee on educational, sports, and reality television programs that aired on the state-run South African Broadcasting Corporation (SABC). He also appeared as a contestant on an SABC dance competition series in 2008. Only after he had acquired a few years of experience in the entertainment industry, around 2007, did Noah begin to think of himself as a comic. Stand-up comedy was practically unheard of among South African blacks. For example, Noah had seen Eddie Murphy in movies, but he never imagined that would break into show business doing stand-up.

It was a bold move for Noah to begin performing routines in Johannesburg's comedy clubs, not just because of his race but also because he wanted to talk about race. From the start, his routines focused on the thorniest issues in South African politics and the news, but his approach and demeanor were light, upbeat, and decidedly nonideological. He joked about President Jacob Zuma and his multiple wives and mistresses. He poked fun at the 91-year-old Nelson Mandela. He joked about the Olympic athlete Oscar Pistorius and his murder trial. He worked with great diligence to hone his act, taking any opportunity to practice in front of an audience. His admirers and fellow comics credit him with helping South Africans of all races learn to laugh together and at themselves. "We have a lot of stories to share," Noah said in a 2015 interview with CNN's Jessica Ellis and Teo Kermeliotis. "We have a lot to learn about each other because we were separated for so long, so now we're trying to understand who we are and who everyone around us is as well."

Noah toured South Africa as an opening act for the Canadian comedy star Russell Peters. In 2009 he performed his first full show as a headliner, *The Daywalker,* which was also released on DVD. (David Paul Meyer's 2011 documentary film about Noah, *You Laugh but It's True,* recounts the days leading up to the Johannesburg debut of *The Daywalker.*) His success as a comedian only enhanced his stature as an emcee. In 2009 Noah hosted both the South African Film and Television Awards and the South African Music Awards. He premiered the television talk show *Tonight with Trevor Noah* on the M-Net channel in August of 2010. Around that time, the South African telecommunication provider Cell C unveiled a marketing campaign that featured Noah, who had previously derided the company's service in his routines. The company published an open letter apologizing to him, and he subsequently appeared in ads as Cell C's "customer experience officer"—another sort of CEO.

Noah toured in the United States in 2011 and eventually settled in Los Angeles. He was living there in July of 2012 when he was named Comic of the Year at the South African Savanna Comics' Choice Awards. Six months earlier, in January, he had given a stellar performance on *The Tonight Show with Jay Leno,* the first South African comic ever to appear on the legendary program during its half-century on the air. However, Noah wanted it understood that he did not see himself as a South African comic, but merely as a comic who happens to be from South Africa. Part of his motivation for moving to North America was to prove that his appeal was not limited to his home environment. In 2012 at the Edinburgh Fringe Festival, the world's largest arts festival, he was introduced by the popular British comedian Eddie Izzard before wowing crowds with his one-man show *The Racist,* which was later developed into the television special *Trevor Noah: That's Racist.*

In December of 2014 Noah became an on-air correspondent for *The Daily Show.* He had appeared in only three segments when he was tapped to succeed Stewart as host. Television critics that said the African transplant would bring a fresh and worldly perspective to the Comedy Central franchise, but some wondered whether Noah would be able to replicate Stewart's astute understanding of U.S. political culture. It seemed clear that Noah's cool, unflappable bearing would provide a sharp contrast to the edgy, excitable persona of his predecessor. Stewart himself strongly endorsed Noah, intimating that he would stay on as a producer and occasional contributor. South Africans reacted to the announcement of Noah's big break with a burst of pride. Loyiso Gola, another South African comic, told Stephanie Findlay in the *Toronto Star,* "Trevor Noah hosting *The Daily Show* is like the moon landing. South African standup comedy has changed forever."

Selected works

Films

Trevor Noah: The Daywalker, Mannequin Pictures, 2009.
Trevor Noah: Crazy Normal, Day 1 Films, 2011.
You Laugh but It's True, Day 1 Films, 2011.
Trevor Noah: That's Racist, Day 1 Films, 2012.
Trevor Noah: It's My Culture, Day 1 Films, 2013.

Television

Trevor Noah: African American, Showtime, 2013.

Sources

Periodicals

Daily Maverick, August 6, 2010.

Newsweek, June 18, 2012.
New York Daily News, March 30, 2015.
New York Times, March 31 2015; April 2, 2015.
Times Live (South Africa), July 11, 2012.
Toronto Star, March 31, 2015.

Online

Ellis, Jessica, and Teo Kermeliotis, "Why Mixed-Race Comic Was 'Born a Crime,'" CNN.com, March 30, 2015, http://www.cnn.com/2013/02/13/showbiz/trevor-noah-comedy (accessed June 11, 2015).

"Translating South African Jokes for a U.S. Audience," National Public Radio, July 5, 2012, http://www.npr.org/2012/07/03/156212890/translating-south-african-jokes-for-a-u-s-audience (accessed June 11, 2015).

—Roger K. Smith

Anthony Overton

1865–1946

Lawyer, entrepreneur

According to the Harvard Business School, Chicago's Overton Great Bee Victory Douglass Syndicate was the first major conglomerate to be led and owned by an African American. That man, Anthony Overton, was a lawyer and entrepreneur who managed not only a multimillion-dollar cosmetics company but also, over the course of his long career, a magazine, a newspaper, a bank, and a life insurance company. Overton purchased real estate in Chicago and rented space to other African-American businesses. Despite the pressures of the Great Depression, which hit at the peak of Overton's career, both Overton and his cosmetics company, Overton Hygienic Manufacturing Company, survived the downturn. Overton remained in control of his company until his death in 1946.

In addition to being a businessman, Overton was also a social activist, focusing his attention on promoting the importance of blacks owning their own businesses. He sided with Booker T. Washington in believing that economic success for African Americans was the key to equality. Although he frequently criticized Washington's opponent W. E. B. Du Bois, who took a more radical approach to achieving equality, after the Chicago race riot of 1919, Overton became an outspoken supporter of activist organizations such as the National Association for the Advancement of Colored People (NAACP).

Born in 1865 in Monroe, Louisiana, Overton was either born into slavery (which was abolished later that same year) or the son of newly freed slaves. After studying at public schools in Louisiana, he moved to

Kansas. Overton enrolled at Washburn College in Topeka and then at the University of Kansas, earning a bachelor of laws degree in 1888. That same year he married Clara M. Gregg, with whom he would have four children. Overton was admitted to the Kansas bar in 1889. He established his own legal practice, but he was soon recruited to serve on the bench of the Municipal Court of Shawnee County, Kansas. Although he was successful in his profession, he found his legal career unsatisfying, and other ventures soon beckoned.

In 1892 Overton moved his family to Oklahoma City, Oklahoma, where he bought a general store. There he also dabbled in politics, winning election as Kingfisher County treasurer. In his political position, he met many entrepreneurs and businessmen, and he began to make plans to go into business himself. In 1898 he moved to Kansas City, Missouri, and used his savings of $1,960 to found the Overton Hygienic Manufacturing Company. He had developed his own recipe for baking powder, and it became the company's first product; later he expanded into cosmetics and hair products. Although the business lost money early on, Overton's charisma helped sell his product. He also used the technique of employing homemakers as his sales force. Sales eventually began to increase, and he had recovered his losses by the time the disastrous floods of 1903 hit Kansas City. His offices, factory, and warehouse were all destroyed, and the company quietly went bankrupt.

Overton did not give up, however, and soon found the resources to rebuild. Over the next eight years, his sales

At a Glance . . .

Born on March 21, 1865, in Monroe, LA; died on July 3, 1946, in Chicago, IL; son of Anthony Overton and Martha DeBerry Overton; married Clara M. Gregg, June 14, 1888; children: Everett Van, Mabel Helena (Fowler), Eva (Lewis), and Frances Madison (Hill). *Education:* Attended Washburn College; University of Kansas, LLB, 1888.

Career: Practiced law in Kansas, 1889; appointed to Municipal Court, Shawnee County, KS, 1890–91; owned general store in Oklahoma City, OK, from 1892; ran successfully for treasurer, Kingfisher County, OK, 1892; Overton Hygienic Manufacturing Company, Kansas City, MO (and later Chicago, IL), founder, 1898–1946; *Half-Century Magazine,* publisher, 1916–26; Douglass National Bank of Chicago, president, 1922–32; Victory Life Insurance Company, founder, 1923–33; *Chicago Bee,* publisher, 1920s–40s.

Memberships: Alpha Phi Alpha Fraternity; Appomattox Club of Chicago; Chicago Urban League; Order of Knights of Pythias; Sigma Pi Phi Fraternity; Young Men's Christian Association.

Awards: Spingarn Medal, NAACP, 1927; Harmon Business Award, Harmon Foundation, 1928.

force grew to almost 500 people, he had a line of about 50 products, and his cosmetics were being sold abroad, in Egypt, Liberia, and Japan. Overton's products catered exclusively to African-American women; unlike some other companies targeting that audience, Overton refused to sell products such as skin bleach because of his pride in his black heritage. In 1911 Overton moved his family and company to industrial Chicago, where business boomed. The company had made $117,000 by mid-1912, and Overton was able to hire five full-time African-American employees to market his products. By 1915 he had 32 full-time employees, 62 products, and holding capital of $268,000. Eager to share his success, Overton published a book, *Successful Salesmanship,* in 1915. His company continued to grow, grossing $1 million annually by 1920.

Encouraged by the success of his cosmetics company, in 1916 Overton looked to fill another need of the African-American community by founding *Half-Century,* a magazine geared toward middle-class black housewives. Articles included news and items of cultural interest; after the race riot of 1919, Overton used *Half-Century* as a vehicle to speak out against violence and to encourage support for the NAACP. *Half-Century* remained in print for a decade before Overton ceased publication. Thereafter he founded the *Chicago Bee,* a newspaper serving Chicago's predominantly black South Side.

To show that Overton believed his own philosophy about the viability of a successful African American economy, he hired architect Z. Erol Smith to design two buildings: the Overton Hygienic Building in 1922 and the Chicago Bee Building in 1926. In the Overton building, he leased space to other African-American businesses, including Walter T. Bailey, Chicago's first African-American architect, and the Theater Owners Booking Association, an African-American talent agency. He also used some of the space for a new project: the Douglass National Bank, which he co-founded in 1922. Douglass was one of the first African-American-owned banks in Illinois and the only one to have a national charter.

The bank was a success, and Overton expanded his enterprise by founding the Victory Life Insurance Company a year later. Overton hoped that the insurance company would help provide for widows and orphans in the African-American community. Two prominent African Americans from New York, Dr. P. M. H. Savory and Dr. C. B. Powell, invested in the firm and opened offices in New York, making it the first Illinois company to operate in New York in more than 20 years. The insurance company also had offices in Kentucky, Maryland, Missouri, New Jersey, Ohio, Texas, West Virginia, and Washington, DC.

The stock market crash of 1929 had a severe impact on Overton's businesses. Douglass National Bank managed to stay open until 1932, when it paid out deposits at 38 percent, a higher rate than any bank in the United States. Powell and Savory took over the Victory Life Insurance Company. Overton sold the Overton Hygienic Building and moved his cosmetics company to the Chicago Bee Building. Despite these losses, Overton had been prudent with his resources, and he lived well until his death in Chicago in 1946. He was succeeded by his son and then his grandson as the owner of the Overton Hygienic Manufacturing Company.

Sources

Books

Sullivan, Otha Richard, *African American Millionaires,* John Wiley, 2005.

Periodicals

Chicago Tribune, September 10, 1999.

Online

"Anthony Overton," Black History Now, July 13, 2014, http://blackhistorynow.com/anthony-overton/ (accessed June 19, 2015).

"Anthony Overton: Hygienic Manufacturing Company, 1898–1946," Harvard Business School, http://www.hbs.edu/leadership/database/leaders/anthony_overton.html (accessed June 19, 2015).

Cross, V. M., "Anthony Overton: A Black Manufacturer, Banker, Lawyer and Publisher," *Black History Heroes* (blog), February 2010, http://www.blackhistoryheroes.com/2010/02/anthony-overton-black-manufacturer.html (accessed June 19, 2015).

"Riots to Renaissance: Overton's Beauty Products," WTTW Public Television, http://www.wttw.com/main.taf?p=76,4,2,1&content=overton-beauty-products (accessed June 19, 2015).

—Alana Joli Abbott

Carl Perkins

1928–1958

Jazz pianist

The brief life of jazz pianist Carl Perkins contained adversity and triumph in roughly equal measure. A victim of both polio and substance abuse, he nevertheless managed to build a brilliant career for himself over the course of the 1950s, a decade often regarded as a golden age of jazz. Highly regarded by his peers, he backed leading figures such as saxophonists Dexter Gordon and Harold Land, composed a beloved standard ("Grooveyard"), and released a widely acclaimed album, *Introducing … Carl Perkins* (1956). That release, the only major recording he was able to complete as a leader before his death from drugs and alcohol in 1958, has been described by Dean Rudland of Ace Records as "a wonderful window into what could have been."

Not to be confused with the rock guitarist of the same name, Carl Perkins was born in Indianapolis, Indiana, on August 16, 1928. His early life was shaped by his battle with polio, a debilitating illness that permanently impaired his ability to move his left hand. Despite that handicap he made rapid progress on the piano, particularly after developing a distinctive technique that involved holding his left forearm parallel to the keyboard. Unorthodox though it was, that position allowed him to overcome the limitations imposed by his illness and to refine his own approach to various left-hand tasks, particularly rhythmic timekeeping. His focus there paid off; as bassist Leroy Vinnegar once said of him, in a comment quoted by Samuel Chell of the website All About Jazz, "His time was perfect."

Indianapolis was home in the 1940s to a sizable jazz community, and Perkins played there regularly with several peers who later joined him in the professional ranks; among them was Vinnegar, who had known him since early childhood. A full-time musician by the mid-1940s, when he was still in his late teens, Perkins gained considerable experience with touring bandleaders such as Tiny Bradshaw, whose orchestra played the fast-paced style known as swing. Like many of his peers, however, Perkins was increasingly drawn to bebop, an improvisational and introspective style that was typically played by small groups, not orchestras.

Then in its infancy, bebop was growing rapidly, particularly in Los Angeles, where a relatively small number of musicians were building a framework for the new sound. Perkins joined them about 1946. That move proved a pivotal moment in his nascent career, in part because it brought him to the attention of clubs along Central Avenue, the hub of African-American life in the city. Live work in those venues sustained him until 1949, when he made his recording debut, completing several singles for Savoy Records, including "Smoke Gets in Your Eyes" and "The Rosary." Although these had only modest success commercially, they solidified his growing reputation among producers and record executives, and for the remainder of his life he was able to balance his live gigs with regular work as a studio musician, helping other artists finish their albums. One of his first major credits in this area came in 1952,

At a Glance . . .

Born on August 16, 1928, in Indianapolis, IN; died on March 17, 1958, in Los Angeles, CA.

Career: Jazz pianist, 1940s–58.

when Perkins backed saxophonist Illinois Jacquet on the latter's well-known album *Collates*. Three years later he joined Gordon for *Dexter Blows Hot and Cool,* whose release marked an important moment in bebop's growth.

Dexter Blows Hot and Cool was released by Dootone Records, a Los Angeles label whose founder, Dootsie Williams, was one of the first African-American record executives in the country. Williams proved an important mentor to Perkins, providing him with studio work and making the arrangements for his full-length debut as a leader. The culmination of the latter effort was *Introducing ... Carl Perkins,* which Dootone released in 1956. Anchored by standards such as "The Lady Is a Tramp" and "You Don't Know What Love Is." Perkins's debut also included several originals that showcased his talents as a composer. Notable among these was "Carl's Blues," often regarded as one of the album's strongest tracks, thanks in part to dynamic contributions by Vinnegar and drummer Larance Marable.

Introducing ... Carl Perkins immediately won strong reviews, and the months following its release were unquestionably a critical and commercial peak for him. Critic Noal Cohen argued that Perkins's "best work is concentrated in 1957, a very good year for recorded jazz in general." His partners during this period included guitarist Jim Hall and saxophonist Art Pepper, both prominent members of the Los Angeles jazz scene. At this stage of his career, however, his most significant collaborator was probably bassist Curtis Counce, another stalwart of West Coast jazz. As a member of Counce's quintet, Perkins made crucial contributions to a number of influential recordings, including *You Get More Bounce with Curtis Counce!* (1957), a touchstone of its era. "Counce insisted," noted Chell of All About Jazz, "that the totally unique sound of the group owed more to Perkins than anyone else." Its other members included Land, whose version of Perkins's "Grooveyard" on an album called *Harold in the Land of Jazz* (1958) did much to make that memorable track a standard.

Amid this success, however, there were signs of trouble. At some point in his rise to fame Perkins fell victim to drugs and alcohol. Although he managed for the most part to keep his addictions from interfering with his professional life, the dangers involved grew steadily more severe. Fears for his health were tragically justified on March 17, 1958, when he died in Los Angeles of an addiction-related ailment. Although the circumstances of his death have been the subject of some controversy over the years, there is no doubt that his passing represented a severe loss for jazz and for music in general.

Among the clearest indications of Perkins's lasting influence is the frequency with which his work has been remastered and re-released in the years since his death. *Introducing ... Carl Perkins,* for example, was first reissued as early as the mid-1970s; a deluxe version appeared on Ace Records' Boplicity label in 2013. His work with the Counce quintet has also been re-released, most notably via the group's *Complete Studio Recordings,* issued by Gambit Records in 2007.

Selected discography

Singles

"Smoke Gets in Your Eyes," 1949.
"The Rosary," 1949.

Albums

Illinois Jacquet, *Collates,* Mercury, 1952.
Introducing ... Carl Perkins (includes "The Lady Is a Tramp," "You Don't Know What Love Is," and "Carl's Blues"), Dootone, 1956.
Art Pepper, *The Art of Pepper, Volume Three,* Blue Note, 1957.
Jim Hall, *Jazz Guitar,* Pacific, 1957.
Curtis Counce, *You Get More Bounce with Curtis Counce!* (also known as *Counceltation*), Contemporary, 1957.
Harold Land, *Harold in the Land of Jazz* (includes "Grooveyard"), Contemporary, 1958.

Sources

Online

Chell, Samuel, "Curtis Counce/Jack Sheldon/Harold Land/Carl Perkins/Frank Butler Quintet: *Complete Studio Recordings,*" All About Jazz, June 11, 2007, http://www.allaboutjazz.com/curtis-counce-jack-sheldon-harold-land-carl-perkins-frank-butler-quintet-complete-studio-recordings-by-samuel-chell.php (accessed June 27, 2015).
Cohen, Noal, "The Carl Perkins Discography," Attic Toys.com, http://www.attictoys.com/CarlPerkins/ (accessed June 27, 2015).
Rudland, Dean, "*Introducing ... Carl Perkins,*" Ace Records, http://acerecords.co.uk/introducingcarl-perkins (accessed June 27, 2015).

Yanow, Scott, "Carl Perkins: Artist Biography," AllMu sic.com, http://www.allmusic.com/artist/carl-per kins-mn0000102781 (accessed June 27, 2015).

—R. Anthony Kugler

Stephanie Rawlings-Blake

1970—

Politician

Rawlings-Blake, Stephanie, photograph. Paul Morigi/Getty Images Entertainment/Getty Images.

Stephanie Rawlings-Blake is the mayor of Baltimore, Maryland. She first stepped into the role in 2010 when her predecessor, Sheila Dixon, was forced to resign in the wake of a financial scandal; Rawlings-Blake was subsequently reelected in 2011. She is the second woman to lead the Maryland city of 620,000 people and the fourth black mayor of Baltimore, a city with a rich African-American history and a demonstrated preference for electing Democratic candidates. Rawlings-Blake spent several years on the Baltimore City Council while working in the public defender's office. "I was often surprised when one of my clients had finished high school because most hadn't," she told Eric Siegel in the *Baltimore Sun,* speaking of her former career as a public defender. "The majority of my clients were dependent on illegal drugs; very few of them had steady employment. That basically sums the significant problems of the city." Rawlings-Blake rose to national attention in April of 2015, after African-American Baltimore resident Freddie Gray suffered fatal injuries while being transported to jail in the back of a police van. Rawlings-Blake's handling of the ensuing controversy, which provoked widespread rioting throughout the city, made her the target of intense criticism while putting her political future in jeopardy.

Born into a Political Family

Rawlings-Blake was born in Baltimore in 1970 and grew up in the Northwestern district, which was evolving from a largely Jewish enclave to an African-American residential area during her youth. Her mother, Nina, was one of the first black women to earn a degree from the medical school of the University of Maryland and had a thriving pediatric practice by the time Rawlings-Blake was born; the family included Lisa, Rawlings-Blake's older sister, and Wendall, a younger brother. Their father was Howard "Pete" Rawlings, a well-known figure in Baltimore politics who in 1979 was elected to the Maryland House of Delegates and remained in office until his death 24 years later. Her father would eventually chair the appropriations committee in the state legislature and served as a mentor to an up-and-coming generation of younger

African-American political leaders, including former schoolteacher Sheila Dixon.

Rawlings-Blake graduated from Western High School, an all-girls public school in Baltimore, and entered Oberlin College in Ohio, where she earned a political science degree in 1992. Among her classmates at Oberlin was Adrian Fenty, the future mayor of Washington, DC. Rawlings-Blake went on to law school at the University of Maryland, graduating in 1995. That same year, she stood for and won a seat on the Baltimore City Council from District 5 in the Northwestern district, becoming the youngest person ever elected to the municipal body in the city's history. She practiced law at the same time, working first for the Legal Aid Bureau and then in the Baltimore Office of the Public Defender representing indigent clients in court. In 1999 her colleagues on the council elected her to serve as vice president.

Until 2003 Baltimore voters chose their city council representatives from six districts, each of which was served by three members. When the districts were redrawn in 2004, the electoral reform package reduced the number of council members, and the districts became single-member precincts. Rawlings-Blake faced a tougher challenge to secure her third four-year term, facing off against attorney Melvin Bilal, a black Muslim Republican who claimed that Rawlings-Blake had been ineffectual during her two terms in office.

Rawlings-Blake countered by noting the Home Depot store and drug treatment center she had brought to District 5 and a new "stop receipt" measure she had championed, which compelled Baltimore police to issue a receipt to any person stopped, which would help the city and state compile racial profiling statistics to avoid potential scrutiny by the U.S. Department of Justice. Rawlings-Blake beat Bilal in the 2004 race for the redrawn District 6, her new home base.

Rawlings-Blake was said to have been instrumental in securing her father's endorsement of Martin O'Malley, a council colleague who entered the 1999 mayoral race. The white Democrat succeeded Kurt Schmoke, Baltimore's first black mayor, in that contest and then went on to win the Maryland gubernatorial election in 2006. Because O'Malley still held the mayor's office, council president Sheila Dixon succeeded O'Malley as mayor upon his resignation in January of 2007. At that point Rawlings-Blake succeeded Dixon as the new council president. Dixon ran for mayor in November of 2007 and won, while Rawlings-Blake campaigned for citywide office for the first time in her bid to remain city council president, which she also won.

Became Mayor of Baltimore

Married and the mother of a young daughter, Rawlings-Blake left her job in the public defender's office in late 2006 in advance of succeeding Dixon as council president. Few foresaw Dixon's downfall, which came a little over a year after she became the first woman ever elected by Baltimore voters to serve as mayor. Dixon was accused of using gift cards ostensibly donated by retail chains to help the city's poorest, and she also faced perjury and misconduct charges tied to the scandal. She agreed to resign as part of a plea agreement, thus avoiding a trial and the loss of her city pension.

As city council president, Rawlings-Blake once again succeeded Dixon on the job. She was sworn in as the 49th mayor of Baltimore on February 4, 2010. Initially, there were rumblings that Governor O'Malley might appoint a new mayor, even a Republican, but to reject the rules of the Baltimore City Charter would have incited a contentious political conflagration. "Ironically, all of this anxiety about the racial complexion of the city's leadership has deflected attention from what is perhaps the more interesting and certainly historic feature of Baltimore politics," wrote Sherrilyn A. Ifill on the website The Root in late 2009. "It is the only major city in the U.S. in which all of the major citywide elected positions—mayor, city council president, district attorney and comptroller—are held by black women."

In her first week in office, Rawlings-Blake faced two significant snowstorms that brought the city to a standstill. In her first year in office, she negotiated a tricky

budget battle to resolve a $121 million deficit. While her father had passed away in 2003, Rawlings-Blake's retired physician mother remained a part of her daily life, helping care for her young daughter, who was born just after the city council primary races that year. "I could not do what I do as mayor without my mom," she told Julie Scharper in the *Baltimore Sun*. "She taught me by example how to be a strong person without apologizing for living your own life."

Faced Criticism after Riots

In 2011 Rawlings-Blake ran for reelection. She won a new term handily, claiming 87 percent of the vote. A year later, the city voted to move the next mayoral election to 2016, in order to have it coincide with the presidential election, giving Rawlings-Blake a five-year term. Despite her landslide victory, Rawlings-Blake struggled during her second full year in office. In March of 2012, she came under criticism from city educators when she announced a plan to cut funding for after-school programs, despite having promised during her campaign that she would double the budget for such programs. Over the course of the year, Rawlings-Blake also contended with recurring problems with the city's infrastructure, as a series of water main breaks in high-density areas caused major traffic disruptions throughout the city. At the same time, the city was forced to implement steep increases to water rates in order to cover costs of repairs, frustrating many city residents.

In the midst of these issues, Rawlings-Blake's political profile continued to grow. In January of 2013, she was appointed secretary of the Democratic National Committee, becoming one of the party's leading spokespersons on policy questions. Over the course of the year, Rawlings-Blake made numerous appearances on political television programs, while also traveling to Democratic events throughout the country. Rawlings-Blake's rise to prominence had many political observers speculating that the party might be positioning her for a larger role on the national stage. "Everyone in the political community has noticed that she's been chosen for a higher profile, and presumably she's being groomed for higher office," Larry Sabato, director of the Center for Politics at the University of Virginia, told the *Baltimore Sun* in January of 2014.

In April of 2015, however, Rawlings-Blake's political career was nearly derailed in the wake of the Freddie Gray incident. On April 25, after protests over Gray's death turned violent, Rawlings-Blake came under intense criticism for remarks she delivered at a press conference. In her comments on the unfolding riots, Rawlings-Blake told a reporter that the city had decided not to intervene. "We also gave those who wish to destroy space to do that as well," Michael Daly of the website The Daily Beast quoted Rawlings-Blake as saying. Some African-American leaders, notably Al Sharpton, defended the mayor's comments, asserting that decades of systemic racism and police brutality ultimately bore responsibility for the unrest. After 235 buildings were damaged during days of looting and vandalism, however, Rawlings-Blake's inability to respond to the crisis in a more forceful manner had many wondering whether her political future could survive the crisis. Indeed, in July of 2015 former mayor Sheila Dixon declared her intention to challenge Rawlings-Blake in the 2016 Democratic mayoral primary. Two months later Rawlings-Blake announced that she would not, in fact, run for reelection, saying that she preferred to focus "on the city's future, not my own." Whether she would seek another elective office in the future remained uncertain.

Sources

Periodicals

Baltimore Sun, January 21, 2007; December 3, 2009; May 8, 2010; January 25, 2011; March 30, 2012; December 30, 2012; January 20, 2014; April 23, 2015; May 1, 2015; May 8, 2015; May 29, 2015.
New York Times, September 12, 2015.

Online

Daly, Michael, "Baltimore Mayor Gave Permission to Riot," The Daily Beast, April 28, 2015, http://www.thedailybeast.com/articles/2015/04/28/baltimore-mayor-s-tone-deaf-handling-of-city-s-riot-crisis.html (accessed July 3, 2015).
Ifill, Sherrilyn A., "Baltimore's (Political) Race Men," The Root, October 19, 2009, http://www.theroot.com/views/baltimores-political-race-men (accessed June 22, 2015).
"Stephanie Rawlings-Blake," City of Baltimore, Maryland, http://mayor.baltimorecity.gov/biography (accessed July 3, 2015).

—Carol Brennan and Stephen Meyer

Lance Reddick

1962—

Actor

Character actor Lance Reddick is best known for his role as the steely, intense Lieutenant Cedric Daniels on the critically acclaimed HBO series *The Wire,* appearing on all five seasons of the show from 2002 to 2008. A latecomer to acting in his 30s, Reddick had his breakout role on the HBO prison drama *Oz* in 2000 before landing the career-making part of Lieutenant Daniels on *The Wire.* After that successful series ended, Reddick went on to play roles in two J. J. Abrams series, *Lost* and *Fringe.* Reddick took on another police role in the Amazon series *Bosch,* which premiered online in 2015. The actor also has appeared in a number of Hollywood films, including *Won't Back Down* (2012), *White House Down* (2013), and *John Wick* (2014). Trained as a classical musician before he turned to acting, Reddick released his debut album featuring his own jazz compositions, *Contemplations & Remembrances,* in 2007.

Reddick was born and raised in Baltimore, where his mother taught music in the public schools and his father was an English and social studies teacher who later became a lawyer. Reddick was drawn to music as a boy, learning to play the piano at age seven and

Reddick, Lance, photograph. s_bukley/Shutterstock.com.

singing in the choir at his Episcopal elementary school. He attended the Friends School of Baltimore, a Quaker high school, and studied music at the prestigious Peabody Conservatory at Johns Hopkins University in junior high and high school. Determined to become a musician, Reddick enrolled at the Eastman School of Music in Rochester, New York, initially studying classical composition. By his last year there, however, his plans shifted. "I realized I was in denial and I really wanted to be a rock star," he recalled in an interview with the *Washington Post* in 2013.

He dropped out of school, married, and moved to Boston to pursue a career as a pop singer. Two years later his daughter was born. With a family to provide for, Reddick juggled four different jobs, working as a singing waiter, posing as an artist's model, and delivering newspapers and pizzas. His music career was going nowhere, so Reddick began acting on a whim. "I really started acting because I was floundering and I thought it would help my music career, and it took over my life," he told the *Boston Herald* in 2009. He began landing roles in local theater productions, and at age 29 he decided to apply to the Yale School of Drama. To his

surprise he was accepted, and he completed his degree in 1994.

After finishing acting school, Reddick moved his family to New York City. He scored his first job as an understudy to Jeffrey Wright in Tony Kushner's Tony Award–winning play *Angels in America*. Within a few years he was landing small roles on television, appearing in episodes of *New York Undercover*, *The Nanny*, and *The West Wing* and in made-for-television movies such as *What the Deaf Man Heard* (1997) and *The Fixer* (1998). In 1999 Reddick had a chance to audition for David Simon's miniseries *The Corner*, the precursor to *The Wire*. "I poured myself into it," he told the London *Guardian* in 2010. "And then it was a snowball effect." Reddick played the crack addict Marvin in *The Corner*, which premiered on HBO in 2000, and that same year won his breakout role in the critically acclaimed HBO drama series *Oz*, set in a fictional maximum-security prison. Reddick played the part of Detective John Basil, a cop who goes undercover at the prison as Jamaican drug dealer Desmond Mobay. Already a cult hit, *Oz* was in its fourth season when Reddick joined the cast—although the actor had never actually seen an episode and knew the series only by its excellent reputation.

Reddick appeared in three episodes on the detective series *Falcone* and then had a short-lived recurring role as a medical examiner on *Law & Order: Special Victims Unit*. His next major television role came in 2002 when he was cast as Lieutenant Cedric Daniels in HBO's *The Wire*. He had initially auditioned for two other roles on the series, as homicide detective William "Bunk" Moreland (eventually played by Wendell Pierce) and as drug addict and police informant Reginald "Bubbles" Cousins (played by Andre Royo). *The Wire* was praised by critics for its realistic portrayal of life on the streets of Baltimore. Playing the psychologically complex character of Lieutenant Daniels, a high-ranking police officer with a law degree, gave Reddick

plenty of room to flex his acting skills. "He was a real challenge," Reddick told the *Los Angeles Times* in 2009. "I kept him tight—he was very self-contained and analytical, but he also had a lot of rage." Although *The Wire* was a critical success, regarded by many reviewers as one of the best shows on television, it never had a large audience and won no major awards. Reddick attributed that fact to a "perception that it was a black show," he told the *Los Angeles Times*. "It wasn't funny or melodramatic. It didn't fit the mold."

Following *The Wire*, which ended in 2008 after five seasons, Reddick appeared on the ABC series *Lost* as the enigmatic Matthew Abbadon. His role on that show was short-lived, however, as he was soon cast in the Fox science fiction series *Fringe* as Special Agent Phillip Broyles, another cop role. Reddick appeared in all five seasons from 2008 to 2013. Meanwhile, he began to land small roles on the big screen, appearing in Lee Daniels's film *Tennessee* (2008) with Mariah Carey, *Jonah Hex* (2010) with Josh Brolin, *Won't Back Down* (2012) with Oscar winner Viola Davis, and *White House Down* (2013) with Jamie Foxx.

In 2014 Reddick had short recurring roles on the FX series *American Horror Story* and the CBS drama *Intelligence*, and he voiced the character of Commander Zavala in the video game *Destiny*. The following year Reddick appeared as Deputy Chief Irvin Irving on the Amazon-produced police procedural series *Bosch*, based on the novels of Michael Connelly. The show premiered on Amazon Prime in February of 2015 and the next month was renewed for a second season.

Although Reddick has devoted his career to acting, music still remains an important part of his life. In 2007 he released his debut album, *Contemplations & Remembrances*, a collection of jazz vocals for which he wrote the music and lyrics.

Selected works

Television

What the Deaf Man Heard (television movie), CBS, 1997.
The Fixer (television movie), Showtime, 1998.
The Corner (miniseries), HBO, 2000.
Oz, HBO, 2000–2001.
Keep the Faith, Baby (television movie), Showtime, 2002.
The Wire, HBO, 2002–08.
Lost, ABC, 2008–09.
Fringe, Fox, 2008–13.
American Horror Story, FX, 2014.

Intelligence, CBS, 2014.
Bosch, Amazon, 2015.

Films

Great Expectations, Twentieth Century Fox, 1998.
The Siege, Twentieth Century Fox, 1998.
I Dreamed of Africa, Columbia Pictures, 2000.
Don't Say a Word, Twentieth Century Fox, 2001.
Tennessee, Lee Daniels Entertainment, 2008.
The Way of War, First Look International, 2009.
Jonah Hex, Warner Bros., 2010.
Won't Back Down, Twentieth Century Fox, 2012.
White House Down, Columbia Pictures, 2013.
Oldboy, Good Universe, 2013.
Search Party, Universal Pictures, 2014.
The Guest, ArtAffects Entertainment, 2014.
John Wick, Thunder Road Pictures, 2014.

Albums

Contemplations & Remembrances, Christai Productions, 2007.

Sources

Periodicals

Boston Herald, February 25, 2009.
Guardian (London), June 7, 2010.
Los Angeles Times, February 25, 2009.
Washington Post, June 18, 2013.

Online

Hazell, Ricardo, "Lance Reddick ('The Wire') Talks of Jazz Offering, Veteran Actors Says Music was Always His First Love," December 5, 2010, http://www.philasun.com/entertainment/lance-reddick-the-wire-talks-of-jazz-offering-veteran-actor-says-music-was-always-his-first-love/ (accessed June 28, 2015).

Lance Reddick, http://lancereddick.com/ (accessed June 28, 2015).

Murphy, Joel, "One on One with Lance Reddick," October 2005, http://www.hobotrashcan.com/2005/10/25/one-on-one-with-lance-reddick-2/ (accessed August 3, 2015).

—Deborah A. Ring

RZA

1969—

Hip-hop musician, producer, filmmaker, actor

RZA, photograph. Joe Seer/Shutterstock.com.

Hip-hop artist RZA (or The RZA) banded together with a group of childhood pals and cousins to form the Wu-Tang Clan, a top-selling rap act of the 1990s and one of the most influential bands in the history of hip-hop. RZA and several other members of the group went on to equally profitable solo careers while occasionally reuniting for new Wu-Tang Clan projects. An astute negotiator and a disciple of the Shaolin kung fu martial art and its philosophy, the musician and producer played a key role in the creation of a multifaceted Wu-Tang media empire. He has since become an author, actor, filmmaker, and acclaimed composer of film scores.

RZA was born Robert Fitzgerald Diggs on July 5, 1969, in Brooklyn, New York, the fourth of 11 children. His parents separated while he was young, and for a time he lived with an aunt and uncle in North Carolina, but most of his childhood was spent in housing projects in the Brownsville section of Brooklyn and then on Staten Island. Three cultural influences marked his childhood in important ways. The first was hip-hop music, which he heard for the first time at a block party around the age of eight and inspired him to become a rapper. Next came martial arts movies from Asia. He went with his older brothers and cousins to the rundown theaters in Times Square to see kung fu triple features, and later, when VCRs became more affordable, they began collecting tapes of their favorite action films. He and his friends even reimagined their impoverished, drug-infested urban world as the mythical kingdoms of the martial arts universe. The third formative influence was the Nation of Gods and Earths, also known as the Five Percenters, a Nation of Islam offshoot. References to the spiritual "science" of the Five Percent Nation, such as the Supreme Alphabet and Supreme Mathematics, are plentiful in the Wu-Tang Clan's lyrics.

Formed Clan with Cousins, Friends

RZA began making his first recordings during the late 1980s with a four-track recorder that he and some friends bought together. He started a band with two of his cousins, Gary Grice (who called himself GZA) and Russell Jones (known as Ol' Dirty Bastard). They called themselves Force of the Imperial Master, then All in Together Now Crew. This group formed the core that

At a Glance . . .

Born Robert Fitzgerald Diggs on July 5, 1969, in New York, NY; four children.

Career: Solo recording artist, 1991—; cofounder and member of Wu-Tang Clan, 1992—.

Addresses: *Web*—http://wutang-corp.com. *Twitter*—@ RZA.

became the Wu-Tang Clan. They made a demo tape but did not manage to snag a record deal. Instead, the cousins pursued independent solo contracts. RZA signed with Tommy Boy Records under the name Prince Rakeem, and in 1991 he released the EP *Ooh I Love You Rakeem*.

In 1990 RZA relocated with his mother and younger siblings to Steubenville, Ohio, near the Pennsylvania border. On many weekends he visited his father, who ran a convenience store in Pittsburgh. During this phase of his life, RZA became involved in drug dealing. He was arrested in 1991 on a charge of attempted murder. He claimed that he had fired in self-defense, and the case went to trial in 1992. The jury voted for acquittal, and RZA walked away a free man. Grateful for his second chance, he approached Clifford Smith (known as Method Man), a friend from the Staten Island projects. "I went to Method Man," RZA recalled in an interview with Jon Pareles in the *New York Times* in 1998, "and I said: 'Are you with me? I'm ready to do this. I want to get off these streets. If we don't get out of here, we're going to be dead.'" Four months after the trial ended, RZA formed the company Wu-Tang Productions, which was named after the Chinese region associated with his heroes of martial arts, the disciplined Shaolin fighting monks.

The Wu-Tang Clan included RZA, GZA, Ol' Dirty Bastard, Method Man, and four other musicians from Staten Island: Inspectah Deck (Jason Hunter), Raekwon (Corey Woods), U-God (Lamont Hawkins), and Ghostface Killah (Dennis Coles). Masta Killa (Elgin Turner) was the last to join the group and did not appear on its first single, "Protect Ya Neck." They approached Tommy Boy Records, which briefly considered signing the group but instead chose a trio of white rappers from Long Island called House of Pain.

Executed Five-Year Plan for Stardom

"Protect Ya Neck" was released as an underground single in early 1993 and was soon picked up by RCA Records. By the time the group signed its major-label deal, RZA had worked out an elaborate five-year plan. Like a martial arts guru, he asked Clan members for absolute loyalty and five years of their lives. With the input of their individual talents, he promised to make them the biggest hip-hop act of the 1990s. He read business books, studied the record industry's trade journals, and devised a strategy to conquer the charts. The Wu-Tang Clan would sign to one label, while its individual members would be free to cut solo deals with other labels. RZA would be the producer for all of the releases. Using different labels, RZA correctly discerned, would mean that the several companies would deploy different marketing strategies for each act, ensuring maximum promotion for the group and its members.

The group's debut record, *Enter the Wu-Tang (36 Chambers),* was released in November of 1993. The title was adapted from the well-known kung fu movie *The 36th Chamber of Shaolin.* Critics gave the album accolades for its dark, hazy backing sounds and dense lyrics that shifted seamlessly from ghetto vignettes into flights of Eastern spiritualism. The album peaked at number eight on the U.S. R&B/Hip-Hop chart. Its second single, "C.R.E.A.M." (Cash Rules Everything Around Me), hit number one on the U.S. Hot Dance Music chart. The album would later appear on lists of the most influential records of the decade.

As promised, RZA went back into the studio to produce a string of solo records for the Wu-Tang Clan artists, nearly all of which reached high chart positions during the mid-1990s. To hip-hop listeners, RZA's productions became easily identifiable. They "created an ominous, bombed-out urban sound, with rough-cut rhythms and elegiac, hovering strings," wrote Pareles. "The music was simultaneously raw, ferocious and mournful, full of tension and bleak memories." Capitalizing on the group's success, the Wu-Tang parent company also branched out into other, similarly profitable projects, with a Wu clothing line, comic book series, and video game. RZA also teamed with three other rappers outside of the Wu-Tang Clan to form Gravediggaz, who released the widely acclaimed debut *6 Feet Deep* during the summer of 1994.

The Wu-Tang Clan's second release, *Wu-Tang Forever,* was a stunning double album that debuted at number one on the Billboard 200 albums chart during the summer of 1997 and was nominated for a Grammy Award for best rap album. With that triumph, RZA proclaimed a promise fulfilled. The creative output of the past five years had brought an unimaginable sum pouring into his bank account; he estimated his earnings at $25 million in 1997 alone. At that point, RZA began to relax and indulge himself a bit, releasing control over some of the group's myriad projects. In 1999 he visited China to scale the peaks of the actual Wu-Tang Mountains, home to numerous monasteries.

The Wu-Tang Clan's fortunes appeared to have reached their own peak. With most of its members now engaged in solo recording careers, the band was experiencing overexposure and a consequent decline in popularity.

Broke into Film Scores and Acting

RZA put out his own first solo record, *Bobby Digital in Stereo,* in 1998. To accompany the release, he made a short film starring himself as the eponymous superhero (a play on his birth name, Robert Diggs) and financed its $800,000 production cost out of his own pocket. The experience whetted his appetite for more film work. Screenwriter and director Jim Jarmusch invited him to compose the score for Jarmusch's 1999 film *Ghost Dog: The Way of the Samurai.* RZA's work with Jarmusch led him into a collaboration with *Pulp Fiction* director Quentin Tarantino, another martial arts cinema buff. RZA composed the soundtrack for Tarantino's 2003 movie *Kill Bill: Vol. 1,* which was nominated in the best film music category of the British Academy of Film and Television Arts Awards.

RZA scored a critical success in 2003 with his solo album *The Birth of a Prince.* In the same year came a compilation album of his efforts as a producer, *The World According to RZA.* During the summer of 2004, all nine Wu-Tang Clan members reunited for their first live concerts in five years. One of these performances, at the first Rock the Bells festival in California, was released as the album *Disciples of the 36 Chambers: Vol. 1.* That fall, Ol' Dirty Bastard died suddenly, just two days before his 36th birthday. A toxic combination of prescription painkillers and cocaine was the cause of death. In 2005 RZA published his first book, *The Wu-Tang Manual* (with Chris Norris), which was an introduction to the group's philosophy and diverse influences. A follow-up work, *The Tao of Wu* (2009; also with Norris), delved more deeply into RZA's own life story.

During the early 2000s RZA moved to Los Angeles and deepened his involvement in movies. Besides his film composing work, he began accumulating credits as an actor. He had a cameo in Jarmusch's *Ghost Dog* and, alongside his cousin GZA, appeared opposite Bill Murray in a comic segment of the Jarmusch pastiche *Coffee and Cigarettes* (2003). He played supporting roles in the Clive Owen–Jennifer Aniston thriller *Derailed* (2005) and Denzel Washington's *American Gangster* (2007). He also played the character Samurai Apocalypse in several episodes of the cable television series *Californication* (2012).

Directed, Starred in Major Hollywood Release

However, RZA's new ambition was to direct a major action picture. Besides the *Bobby Digital* film, he had financed and directed the martial arts film *Wu-Tang vs. the Golden Phoenix,* which was never released. Through his collaboration with Tarantino, he had met Eli Roth, director of the successful horror film *Hostel* (2005). Over the course of several years, Roth helped RZA develop his screenplay for *The Man with the Iron Fists,* which the rapper envisioned as a tribute to the kung fu genre. In 2010 Universal Pictures gave the project a green light and a $20 million budget. RZA spent months in China scouting locations and shot the film in 2011, casting himself in the lead role of the blacksmith and emancipated slave. The filmmaker reduced his rough cut from over three hours to 96 minutes before its release in November of 2012. It opened to mixed reviews, and its box office performance was mediocre, although it did manage to earn back its production cost. RZA promoted the film through a U.S. concert tour with the Wu-Tang Clan as headliners. The film's soundtrack album, which RZA produced, served as the debut release of Soul Temple Records, his own independent label.

In 2011 rumors began circulating about a new Wu-Tang Clan studio album, the first since *8 Diagrams* (2007). RZA reopened the Wu-Mansion, his former residence in New Jersey, and updated its studio facilities to serve the group. The band's ringleader told the press he intended to unveil the new album at the group's 20th anniversary in 2013, as a kind of coda to the Clan's achievements. However, strains within the group were evidenced by a public spat between RZA and Raekwon, whom RZA accused of not participating in the recordings. The original release date was pushed back, although the single "Family Reunion" came out in June of 2013 through the Soul Temple website. After the Wu-Tang Clan signed a distribution deal with Warner Brothers Records, *A Better Tomorrow* finally dropped in December of 2014. Reviews were thoughtful but only mildly enthusiastic; several found the album's sound overproduced.

In March of 2015, at the cutting-edge New York Museum of Modern Art PS1, a "listening session" was held for a 13-minute excerpt from the unreleased Wu-Tang Clan double album *Once Upon a Time in Shaolin.* It would, perhaps, be the album's only public airing. In a unique twist on the concept of "limited edition," only one copy of *Once Upon a Time in Shaolin* was to be pressed and sold at auction. RZA told the press the record had already received private bids up to $5 million. The band forbade any commercial sales of the album's contents for 88 years, although the purchaser would be allowed to release the music for free. Also in 2015 came the straight-to-DVD release of *The Man with the Iron Fists 2,* coscripted and starring RZA but not directed by him. Meanwhile, RZA was shooting *Coco,* a musical starring the rapper Azealia Banks.

Selected works

Albums

With Wu-Tang Clan

Enter the Wu-Tang (36 Chambers) (includes "Protect Ya Neck" and "C.R.E.A.M."), Loud, 1993.
Wu-Tang Forever, Relativity, 1997.
The W, Columbia, 2000.
Iron Flag, Loud, 2001.
8 Diagrams, Motown, 2007.
A Better Tomorrow, Warner Bros., 2014.

With Gravediggaz

6 Feet Deep, Gee Street, 1994.
The Pick, the Sickle and the Shovel, Gee Street, 1997.

Solo albums

(As Prince Rakeem) Ooh I Love You Rakeem (EP), Tommy Boy, 1991.
Bobby Digital in Stereo, Gee Street, 1998.
Digital Bullet, Koch, 2001.
The Birth of a Prince, Sanctuary, 2003.
Digi Snacks, Koch, 2008.

Books

(With Chris Norris) *The Wu-Tang Manual,* Riverhead Books, 2005.

(With Chris Norris) *The Tao of Wu,* Riverhead Books, 2009.

Films

Ghost Dog: The Way of the Samurai, Pandora Filmproduktion, 1999.
Coffee and Cigarettes, Asmik Ace Entertainment, 2003.
Derailed, Di Bonaventura Pictures, 2005.
American Gangster, Universal Pictures, 2007.
The Man with the Iron Fists, Arcade Pictures, 2012.
The Man with the Iron Fists 2, Arcade Pictures, 2015.

Television

Californication, Showtime, 2012.

Sources

Periodicals

Billboard, November 25, 1995.
Independent (London), April 24, 2008.
Los Angeles Times, October 3, 2014.
New Yorker, December 8, 2014.
New York Times, November 5, 1998; October 17, 2012.
Pittsburgh City Paper, April 10, 2013.
Rolling Stone, March 3, 2015.

—Carol Brennan and Roger K. Smith

Percy Sledge

1940–2015

Singer, songwriter

Sledge, Percy, photograph. Jim Spellman/WireImage/Getty Images.

Singer Percy Sledge has the distinction of having made the first Southern soul record to become a number-one hit on the pop charts. The song "When a Man Loves a Woman" carried Sledge to stardom in 1966 and became his bread and butter for the rest of his career. His aching, gospel-infused tenor voice helped establish soul as a mainstream commercial music genre during the 1960s. Sledge released nearly a dozen albums, and several of his other songs became minor hits, including "Cover Me," "It Tears Me Up," "Warm and Tender Love," "Take Time to Know Her," and "I'll Be Your Everything." Nevertheless, his name is permanently associated with his one transcendent standard. The song has been covered by dozens of artists, and his own indelible rendition continues to get steady radio airplay half a century after its recording.

Gave Away Credit for Hit Song

Sledge was born on November 25, 1940 (some sources say 1941), in Leighton, Alabama, a poor farming town in the northwestern corner of the state, near Muscle Shoals. One of five children, he was six years old when his father died. He grew up working outdoors, farming with his family and picking cotton, and sang in his church choir and in the cotton fields. Sledge was raised on a steady diet of country singers such as Hank Williams and Marty Robbins, whose brand of heartbreak would influence his own soulful style. "The only radio station we got was country music," Sledge said in an interview with Robert Hilburn in the *Los Angeles Times* in 1998. "That's all I knew. We didn't hear rock 'n' roll but for about 15 minutes real late at night."

In high school Sledge was part of a vocal quintet called the Belltones. He was also a talented quarterback on the football team and an all-around infielder in baseball, his preferred sport. He considered playing professional ball, alongside equally ambitious dreams of becoming a doctor. However, he married early, and with children on the way, more practical paths beckoned. He took a job as a hospital orderly in the nearby town of Sheffield. Later on he worked at a chemical plant. He also continued singing with an R&B combo called the Esquires, featuring bassist Calvin Lewis and keyboard

At a Glance . . .

Born on November 25, 1940, in Leighton, AL; died on April 14, 2015, in Baton Rouge, LA; married Rosa Sledge, 1980; 12 children.

Career: Singer and songwriter, 1966–2014.

Awards: Career Achievement Award, Rhythm and Blues Foundation, 1989; inducted into Rock and Roll Hall of Fame, 2005; inducted into Alabama Hall of Fame, 2010.

player Andrew Wright. The band played on weekends, often on college campuses around the Deep South.

A former patient at the county hospital who had heard Sledge singing encouraged him to get in touch with Quin Ivy, a local disc jockey who owned a record store in Sheffield. Sledge showed up at the record shop, did some impromptu singing for the proprietor, and was invited to cut a record in Ivy's new music studio. The song he selected was one he had had in his head for years, a tune he used to hum in the cotton fields. Recently, he had put lyrics to it, thinking about an old girlfriend who left him. Revising the words, he changed the title from "Why Did You Leave Me" to "When a Man Loves a Woman." His bandmates Lewis and Wright helped him work out the chord sequence for the melody, and, in turn, he generously allowed them to take songwriting credit for the number. "Worst decision I ever made," Sledge told Simon Redley in *Blues and Soul* magazine in 2011 about surrendering all royalties to his career-making composition, a mistake that cost him millions of dollars. "But I am not at all bitter.... The way I feel, it was God's will for me to give it to them. But if I had my time again, I wouldn't do it. Because of my children."

Made Concert Film in South Africa

When Jerry Wexler, the head of Atlantic Records, heard about Sledge's sensational performance on the single, he signed the singer right away. "When a Man Loves a Woman" soared to the top of the pop charts during the spring of 1966, becoming the prototype for what became known as the "Muscle Shoals sound," which was associated with soul musicians such as Arthur Alexander, Wilson Pickett, and the Staple Singers. The single was also an international hit, reaching the top five in England during a peak moment of the "British invasion." That year Sledge recorded his debut album, named after its most popular track. A follow-up single, "Warm and Tender Love," made it into the top 20 on the Billboard Hot 100 and anchored the album *Warm and Tender Soul* (1966).

"Warm" and "tender" were fitting words to describe Sledge's voice and his appeal. He specialized in sentimental ballads about lost love such as "It Tears Me Up" (1966). He had modest hits with cover versions of the Elvis Presley classics "Love Me Tender" (1967) and "Just Out of Reach (Of My Two Empty Arms)" (1967). Another tune in the same vein, "Take Time to Know Her" (1968), became the second most successful of his career. It reached number 11 on the pop chart and number six on the R&B chart and became the title song of his fourth album for Atlantic.

Sledge began touring in the United States as well as internationally and proved to be a popular headline act. He made his first visit to South Africa in 1970. He decided to tour the country and make a concert film there, even though a number of other performers had announced a boycott over South Africa's apartheid policies. By the early 1970s Sledge's record sales had declined, and Atlantic let him go in 1973. He turned up the following year on Capricorn Records with "I'll Be Your Everything," a single that reached the top 20 on the R&B chart. In 1979 he revealed another dimension of his musicality on the album *Percy Sledge Sings Country.*

Returned to the Spotlight

Sledge never recaptured the level of popular success he reached with his very first hit, but he was nevertheless able to cull together a career of live concert appearances and greatest hits albums that satisfied his fans' desire to walk down memory lane. He sang "When a Man Loves a Woman" thousands of times before audiences and, so he claimed, never tired of it. The song remained in the popular consciousness. His recording was used in the 1983 movie *The Big Chill,* whose popular soundtrack album was a collection of Motown and soul oldies. Oliver Stone used it a few years later in his Oscar-winning Vietnam War film *Platoon* (1987). Levi's used the song that year in a jeans commercial, prompting its rerelease in England, where it went to number two on the U.K. singles chart—a higher peak than two decades earlier.

In January of 1989 Sledge performed at the inaugural ceremonies for incoming President George H. W. Bush, at the invitation of Bush's close aide Lee Atwater. Later that year the Rhythm and Blues Foundation presented Sledge with its first Career Achievement Award for his lifelong contributions to the genre. In 1992 the balladeer Michael Bolton had a number-one hit and won a Grammy Award for his cover of Sledge's signature tune. Criticized in the press for failing to mention Sledge's name in his acceptance speech, the singer made sure to praise the soul star enthusiastically in follow-up interviews. Hollywood shined the spotlight on Sledge's song one more time in 1994 with the film *When a Man Loves a Woman,* starring Meg Ryan and Andy Garcia.

With new career momentum, Sledge signed a new recording contract and released *Blue Night* (1994), his first album in 15 years. The album featured 1960s soul tunes and had guest appearances by musicians including Bobby Womack, Barry and Robin Gibb of the Bee Gees, and former Rolling Stones guitarist Mick Taylor. The album was nominated for a Grammy for best contemporary blues album. A European tour to promote Sledge's comeback album was scratched when the singer was charged with tax evasion for failing to report more than $250,000 in income over a three-year period. Sledge pled guilty and was sentenced to six months in a halfway house and five years' probation. He expressed gratitude to the judge for declining to issue a prison sentence.

By the end of the 1990s Sledge was still going strong, averaging more than 100 concerts a year around the world. In 1996 he moved to Baton Rouge, Louisiana, where he lived with his second wife, Rosa. He was inducted into the Rock and Roll Hall of Fame in 2005, a year after releasing the album *Shining through the Rain*. A major retrospective of his work for Atlantic was released in 2010. His last record, *The Gospel of Percy Sledge,* was released in 2013. Sledge died on April 14, 2015, after surviving surgery for liver cancer the prior year.

Selected discography

When a Man Loves a Woman (includes "When a Man Loves a Woman"), Atlantic, 1966.

Warm and Tender Soul (includes "Warm and Tender Love," "It Tears Me Up," and "Love Me Tender"), Atlantic, 1966.

The Percy Sledge Way (includes "Just Out of Reach [Of My Two Empty Arms]"), Rhino, 1967.

Take Time to Know Her (includes "Take Time to Know Her" and "Cover Me"), Collectables, 1968.

My Special Prayer, Atlantic, 1969.

Percy Sledge in South Africa, Atlantic, 1970.

I'll Be Your Everything (includes "I'll Be Your Everything"), Capricorn, 1974.

Percy Sledge Sings Country, 1979.

Blue Night, Virgin, 1994.

Shining through the Rain, Varèse Sarabande, 2004.

The Gospel of Percy Sledge, Elevate Entertainment, 2013.

Sources

Periodicals

Associated Press, April 14, 2015.

Blues & Soul, October/November 2011.

Daily Maverick (South Africa), April 16, 2015.

Los Angeles Times, February 13, 1998.

New York Times, April 14, 2015.

Online

"Percy Sledge Biography," Rock and Roll Hall of Fame, https://rockhall.com/inductees/percy-sledge/bio/ (accessed June 23, 2015).

Pratt, Ed, "Percy Sledge in 1992 Interview," TheAdvocate.com (Baton Rouge, LA), http://theadvocate.com/news/12106895-125/percy-sledge-in-1992-interview (accessed June 23, 2015).

—Brenna Sanchez and Roger K. Smith

Peter Spencer

1782(?)–1843

Church leader, educator

Peter Spencer was a pioneering Methodist leader and educator. He remains best known as the founder of the Union Church of Africans, widely considered to be the first religious denomination in the United States to be organized entirely by African Americans. Over the course of his career, Spencer played a prominent role in all aspects of church life, presiding over marriages and organizing spiritual gatherings while also helping establish new congregations in various communities throughout the Mid-Atlantic region. The church leader's intelligence, strong character, and generosity toward other members of his congregation earned him the nickname "Father Spencer." In addition to his activities on behalf of the church, Spencer achieved renown as an educator, providing instruction to his parishioners and founding a number of African-American schools. Spencer's church was also instrumental in helping African Americans from the South obtain their freedom, collaborating with the Underground Railroad in providing shelter and material support to runaway slaves.

The exact date of Spencer's birth remains uncertain. Most modern sources indicate that he was born in 1782, although some earlier commentators—notably the Reverend Daniel James Russell in his *History of the African Union Methodist Protestant Church* (1920)—provide a birth year of 1779. Born into slavery, Spencer spent his early years on a plantation in Kent County, Maryland. Following the death of his master, Spencer was granted his freedom while he was still in his teens. He moved north to Delaware and settled in Wilmington. Known for his keen intellect,

Spencer actively pursued his education in Wilmington, receiving instruction from a group of local Quakers. He soon learned how to read and write, and he devoted his free time to studying law. He also established a trade during these years, earning his living as a mechanic.

A devout Christian, Spencer became involved in the Asbury Methodist Episcopal Church shortly after his arrival in Wilmington. He soon became disillusioned with the church's treatment of its African-American parishioners, however, as he realized that white worshippers were given preferential treatment within the congregation. For instance, African-American churchgoers were segregated from their white counterparts, forced to sit in a gallery apart from the main body of the church. African Americans also faced discrimination during the service itself, receiving communion only after the white members of the congregation had finished. Over time, white parishioners also imposed restrictions on how African Americans were allowed to worship, even attempting to prevent them from organizing their own meetings in the church.

In the face of this pervasive discrimination, Spencer decided that he and his fellow African-American parishioners would be better served by establishing their own church. In 1805, he and 42 other African-American Methodists left the Asbury Church in order to worship freely. They conducted their first service outdoors and soon began worshipping at a private house. They eventually acquired a parcel of land, where they built a church. Even after they began conducting their own services separately from the white congregation,

Spencer and the other African-American Methodists remained affiliated with the Asbury Church for the next several years. Tensions lingered between the two groups, however, as Asbury Church authorities attempted to exert greater control over the business affairs of the African-American church. Finally, in December of 1812 Spencer and the other African-American worshippers were threatened with expulsion from the church if they continued to resist its authority.

In response to this ultimatum, Spencer and his congregation broke definitively from the Asbury Church, abandoning their new church building in order to establish an independent congregation. By mid-1813 they had acquired another building lot in Wilmington and conducted their first free service on June 1 of that year. On September 8, 1813, Spencer registered the new church with the state of Delaware under the name Ezion African Union Church; the congregation was later renamed the Union Church of Africans. A year later Spencer organized the inaugural Big Quarterly, an annual spiritual revival aimed at establishing ties among African-American Methodists from across the region. Held on the last Sunday of August, the conference soon became known as the August Quarterly. Spencer made the annual meeting into a safe haven for runaway slaves, who were given shelter and transported to the Wilmington station of the Underground Railroad.

As the Union Church of Africans grew, the idea of a larger union of African-American Methodists began to emerge. In April of 1816 Spencer and several other prominent African-American Methodist leaders from the Mid-Atlantic region organized a conference to discuss bringing their various congregations together into a single denomination. Among the participants was Richard Allen, who in 1794 helped found the Bethel Church in Philadelphia, considered to be the first African-American house of worship in the United States. Another representative to the conference, Daniel Coker, later helped the American Colonization Society launch the first Methodist mission in Sierra Leone, Africa. Although the meeting represented a landmark event in the history of the African-American church, Spencer had misgivings about the proposed union, largely due to doctrinal differences with Allen. In the end, Allen, Coker, and other leaders established the African Methodist Episcopal Church, while Spencer decided to maintain his church's autonomy.

Over the next two decades, Spencer dedicated his energy to expanding the Union Church of Africans into other communities, eventually founding a total of 31 individual churches, many of which also had schools. In 1822 he also published *The African Union Hymn Book,* an important early example of church music expressly published for an African-American congregation. Although Spencer's role in the formation and growth of the Union Church of Africans is well documented, little information concerning his later personal life has survived. It is known that he married a woman named Anne and helped raise her two daughters from a previous marriage.

Peter Spencer died on July 25, 1843, in Wilmington. By 1850 a significant rupture occurred within the Union Church, weakening the congregation. Following the Civil War, Spencer's Union Church of Africans joined the First Colored Methodist Protestant Church to form a new entity, the African Union First Colored Methodist Protestant Church. While Spencer fell into relative obscurity in the decades after his death, he became the subject of renewed scholarly interest in the late-20th century. In 1987, Lewis V. Baldwin published *The Mark of a Man: Peter Spencer and the African Union Methodist Tradition: The Man, the Movement, the Message, and the Legacy,* one of the first important studies dedicated to Spencer's life and work. Meanwhile, in the 21st century the Big Quarterly continued to take place each year in Wilmington, making it the oldest African-American folk festival in the United States.

Sources

Online

"History: Union American Methodist Episcopal," St. Mark and St. Luke AE Churches, http://www.smuame.org/_mgxroot/page_10754.html (accessed June 29, 2015).

"Peter Spencer (1782–1843)," August Quarterly, http://www.augustquarterly.org/peterspencer.html (accessed June 29, 2015).

"Peter Spencer Churches and African Union Methodism," Delaware Historical Society, http://dehistory.org/peter-spencer-churches (accessed June 29, 2015).

Russell, Daniel James, "History of the African Union Methodist Episcopal Church" (electronic ed.), Documenting the American South, University of North Carolina at Chapel Hill, http://docsouth.unc.edu/church/russell/russell.html (accessed June 29, 2015).

—Stephen Meyer

Bryan Stevenson

1959—

Lawyer, educator, activist

Called "America's Nelson Mandela," Bryan Stevenson is a talented and tireless defender of the poorest and most vulnerable people in the U.S. criminal justice system, especially African Americans, minors, and the mentally disabled. Stevenson's nonprofit legal organization, the Equal Justice Initiative, founded in 1989, has prevented the deaths of 115 male prisoners and persuaded the U.S. Supreme Court to end life sentences without parole for minors as young as 13. Stevenson is also the author of *Just Mercy: A Story of Justice and Redemption* (2014), which Tim Adams of the London *Guardian* called a "powerful, profoundly affecting memoir" documenting "the policy of mass incarceration, the barely credible inhumanity that has seen young boys kept in solitary confinement for years and decades, and the evidence of institutional racism at the heart of the American justice system."

Stevenson was born in Milton, Delaware, a poor and racially segregated town where he came of age during the 1960s. In an interview with Alex Carp in *Guernica Magazine* in 2014, Stevenson said, "More personally, I grew up in the rural South, in a community where black children couldn't go to the public schools. My parents bore the burden of segregation, with all of that humiliation, with all of that stigma. And I saw that play out in their lives. My dad couldn't go to high school because there was no black high school in our county." Even following the U.S. Supreme Court's 1954 ruling in *Brown v. Board of Education,* which desegregated America's public schools, deeply rooted prejudice and discrimination led to segregated activities at school and in the community. For example, Stevenson could not play on the monkey bars when white children were on them, and he and his family entered through the back door when going to doctor's appointments.

The matriarch of Stevenson's family was his maternal grandmother, Victoria Golden. Her parents had been slaves in Virginia. Golden had grown up with the threat of lynchings before moving north to Philadelphia, Pennsylvania, as part of the Great Migration of blacks out of the South. Stevenson told Adams that his grandmother's stories, the things she had heard from her own father about slavery, left a lasting impression on him, making slavery seem like something close to him and his family and convincing him, from an early age, of the importance and power of law.

"I talk about my grandmother a lot," he told Adams, "because she's an amazing person—not in some dramatic, distinct, unique way, but anybody who is the daughter of enslaved people and who has found a way to be hopeful and create love and value justice and seek peace is a remarkable person. And my parents, who grew up in terror and dealt with segregation and humiliation, nonetheless taught us to be hopeful and open and loving and not hateful toward anyone." Stevenson's mother, a product of the less racially oppressive culture she knew growing up in Philadelphia, also impressed on Stevenson the importance of fighting back against discrimination.

Found His Calling in Law

At Cape Henlopen High School, Stevenson was an

At a Glance . . .

Born Bryan Allen Stevenson on November 14, 1959, in Milton, DE; son of Howard Carlton (a factory worker) and Alice Gertrude (a clerk). *Politics:* Democrat. *Education:* Eastern University, BA, political science, philosophy, 1981; Harvard Law School, JD, 1985; Harvard University, John F. Kennedy School of Government, MPP, 1985.

Career: Alabama Capital Representation Resource Center, executive director, 1989–95; Southern Center for Human Rights, attorney; Equal Justice Initiative, founder and executive director, 1989—; New York University School of Law, assistant professor and associate professor of clinical law, 1998–2002, professor of clinical law, 2003—.

Awards: Reebok Human Rights Award, 1989; National Medal of Liberty, American Civil Liberties Union, 1991; MacArthur Foundation Fellowship, 1995; Wisdom Award for Public Service, American Bar Association; Public Interest Lawyer of the Year, National Association of Public Interest Lawyers, 1996; Citizen Activist Award, Gleitsman Foundation, 2000; Olof Palme Prize, 2000; Award for Courageous Advocacy, American College of Trial Lawyers, 2004; Lawyer for the People Award, National Lawyers Guild, 2004; Distinguished Teaching Award, New York University, 2006; Katharine and George Alexander Law Prize, Santa Clara University School of Law, 2008; Gruber Prize, Gruber Foundation, 2009; Lannan Grant, Lannan Foundation, 2015.

Addresses: *Home*—Montgomery, AL, and New York, NY. *Office*—New York University School of Law, 245 Sullivan St., Suite 628, New York, NY 10012. *Web*—http://bryanstevenson.com.

excellent student and a budding orator, winning several public speaking contests while also serving as president of the student body. He attended Prospect African Methodist Episcopal Church, where he played the piano for the church choir. The church's tradition of parishioners publicly confessing their sins also contributed to Stevenson's future role as a so-called death penalty lawyer. He began seeing people as distinct from their sins, or as more human than even their worst sin would suggest.

Stevenson enrolled at Eastern University, a Christian school in Philadelphia, where majored in political science and philosophy and directed the campus gospel choir. A top student, Stevenson next headed to Harvard University to pursue a law degree and a master's degree in public policy. At Harvard, Stevenson told Paul Barrett in *NYU Law Magazine*, "I stopped almost immediately trying to fit in. I thought about it more like a cultural anthropologist." Although Stevenson felt as if he did not fit in at Harvard, he soon found the right place for himself within the legal world.

In January of 1983 Stevenson traveled to Atlanta, Georgia, for a month-long internship with the Southern Center for Human Rights, a legal and nonprofit advocacy organization working throughout the Southeastern United States. Stevenson began work writing appeals for several death row clients and never looked back. After graduation, he continued to work for the Southern Center for Human Rights, where the organization's founder, Stephen Bright, sent him to defend death row inmates in Alabama. During this same time, Stevenson was sitting inside his car outside of his own apartment when a SWAT unit pulled up, pointed a gun at him, and yelled, "Move and I'll blow your head off!" In an interview with National Public Radio's *Fresh Air* more than 30 years later, Stevenson recalled how the incident had "reinforced what I had known all along, which is that we have a criminal justice system that treats you better if you're rich and guilty than if you're poor and innocent."

Started the Equal Justice Initiative

After several years working in Alabama, Stevenson started his own small legal office in Montgomery, Alabama, in 1989. With one assistant, he founded the Equal Justice Initiative (EJI), a nonprofit that focused on social justice and human rights within the context of America's criminal justice system. The EJI gave free legal services to clients who were the victims of racial bias or poor representation. It was a lean living—the nonprofit relied entirely on contributions—and the kind of crushing work that even the most dedicated lawyers did not often do long term.

However, Stevenson was known for his remarkable record of endurance in the field. Barrett described him as "single and famously ascetic" and cited his ability to virtually work around the clock, not just on his EJI cases but also as a professor of clinical law at New York University. As of 2015, Stevenson had argued five cases before the U.S. Supreme Court and had taken on countless cases of those who had been wrongly accused, tried, and convicted.

One of Stevenson's most well-known cases was that of Walter McMillian, a black man on death row in Ala-

bama who was convicted of killing 18-year-old Ronda Morrison in 1986. During the trial, six black witnesses told a jury of 11 whites and one black they had seen McMillian at a church fish fry at the time of the murder, and yet three other witnesses testified against McMillian. Stevenson took up the case during the early 1990s, finding tapes that proved the police had coerced the three witnesses to falsely testify against McMillian, who had been having an affair with a white woman at the time of Morrison's murder. Stevenson managed to get McMillian exonerated in 1993, after the key witnesses admitted they had been coerced into testifying against McMillian.

Stevenson later told *Fresh Air,* "This is one of the few cases I've worked on where I got bomb threats and death threats because we were fighting to free this man who was so clearly innocent. It reveals this disconnect that I'm so concerned about when I think about our criminal justice system." He added, "It took us six years to get a court to ultimately overturn the conviction. I think it speaks to this resistance we have in this country to confronting our errors, to confronting our mistakes."

Extended His Impact beyond the Courtroom

In 2012 Stevenson gave the TED talk "We Need to Talk about Injustice," in which he outlined his conviction that the United States has never dealt with the trauma and legacy of slavery and that the current criminal justice system is dogged not only by this refusal to recognize the consequences of slavery but also by an increasingly punitive and privatized system wherein corporations are reaping profit from the criminalized lives of blacks and other vulnerable people. A deeply compelling speaker, Stevenson received two standing ovations.

Stevenson's EJI has also branched out from legal defense, hoping to shape the public's understanding of slavery, race, and poverty. In Montgomery, Alabama, where there are no fewer than 59 public markers commemorating the Confederacy, Stevenson sought to erect markers that addressed Montgomery's once-burgeoning slave trade. After resistance, the city permitted him and his colleagues to erect three markers that pertain to Montgomery's history of slave trading. In the future he hopes to take the effort to other cities.

Perhaps as another extension of his desire to educate, Stevenson published the memoir *Just Mercy: A Story of Justice and Redemption* in 2014. He told Adams, "I wrote the book because I am persuaded that if most people in America saw what I see on a regular basis they would not be able to reconcile themselves with these realities." He continued, "But our instinct is to deny. We have the highest rate of incarceration of any country in the world, and yet we don't feel bad about it. I think we sometimes seem to feel that we give up too much power if we even recognise that we have made, and continue to make, colossal mistakes in this area."

Stevenson is the recipient of many honorary degrees and awards, including the Olof Palme Prize, the Gruber Prize, and a Lannan Grant. In a testament to his indefatigable dedication to social justice, his prize money flows directly back to EJI. "Fifty years ago the people doing what I do would have said 'my head is bloody but not bowed,'" Stevenson told Adams. "I don't have to say that. I don't think I can afford to be less courageous than they were."

Selected writings

Just Mercy: A Story of Justice and Redemption, Spiegel & Grau, 2014.

Sources

Periodicals

Guardian (London), February 1, 2015; February 6, 2015.
NYU Law Magazine, 2007.

Online

"Bryan A. Stevenson," New York University School of Law, 2015, https://its.law.nyu.edu/facultyprofiles/profile.cfm?section=bio&personID=20315 (accessed June 10, 2015).
Carp, Alex, "Walking with the Wind," *Guernica Magazine,* March 17, 2014, https://www.guernicamag.com/interviews/walking-with-the-wind/ (accessed June 14, 2015).
"One Lawyer's Fight for Young Blacks and 'Just Mercy,'" *Fresh Air,* National Public Radio, October 20, 2014, http://www.npr.org/2014/10/20/356964925/one-lawyers-fight-for-young-blacks-and-just-mercy (accessed June 14, 2015).

—Kay Eastman

Bermane Stiverne

1978—

Professional boxer

Stiverne, Bermane, photograph. Ethan Miller/Getty Images Sport/ Getty Images.

Bermane Stiverne is a Haitian-Canadian boxer who competes in the heavyweight class. He achieved worldwide recognition in May of 2014 when he defeated Chris Arreola to take the World Boxing Council (WBC) crown. With the victory, Stiverne became the first Haitian-born heavyweight champion in history. Over the course of his 10-year career, he has compiled a record of 24 wins, 2 losses, and 1 draw, with 21 knockouts. At six feet, two inches tall and approximately 240 pounds, Stiverne is a formidable presence in the ring, relying on raw strength and devastating punches to wear down his opponents. At the same time, Stiverne possesses a quickness belied by his massive frame, with an ability to withstand opposing attacks with well-timed counterpunches. Despite his fearsomeness as a fighter, Stiverne is known for his taciturn, unassuming demeanor outside the ring, qualities that have led him to attract less public notice than most other top heavyweight boxers. "We'll be out at dinner and we pretty much won't talk," Don House, Stiverne's trainer, told Kevin Iole of Yahoo! Sports in January of 2015. "Bermane is just one of those quiet guys."

Rose up the Amateur Ranks

Bermane Stiverne was born on November 1, 1978, in La Plaine, Haiti, the youngest boy in a family of 14 children. At age 10, Stiverne immigrated with his mother, Rose Mary, and his sisters to Miami, Florida, where they lived with relatives. Throughout his childhood he divided his time between Miami and Montreal, Canada, and eventually obtained Canadian citizenship. Stiverne originally trained to become a kickboxer before launching his amateur boxing career in 1999. He quickly proved himself a natural talent in the ring, winning the Quebec Golden Gloves heavyweight championship in only his first year of competition; it would be the first of Stiverne's six-straight Golden Gloves titles.

In 2003 Stiverne earned a spot on the Canadian national boxing team. A year later he launched a bid to compete for Canada at the 2004 Summer Olympics in Athens, Greece, taking bronze in the super heavyweight class at the first International Boxing Association Olympic qualifying competition in Tijuana,

At a Glance . . .

Born Bermane Stiverne on November 1, 1978, in La Plaine, Haiti; son of Rose Mary.

Career: Professional boxer, heavyweight class, 2005—.

Awards: World Boxing Council heavyweight champion, 2014–15.

Addresses: *Home*—Las Vegas, NV. *Office*—c/o Eye of the Tiger Management, Montreal, Canada.

Mexico. He ultimately fell short of his goal, however, when he was defeated in his opening bout at the second America's Olympic Qualifier in Rio de Janeiro, Brazil. Stiverne earned some measure of redemption at the Tammer Tournament in Tampere, Finland, later that year when he defeated British fighter David Price with a third-round technical knockout to win gold in the super heavyweight class.

After his victory in the Tammer Tournament, Stiverne announced his decision to begin fighting professionally. In July of 2005 the heavyweight dominated in his professional debut, a bout in North Charleston, South Carolina, by scoring a first-round technical knockout over opponent Roy Matthews. Stiverne enjoyed similar success two months later in Morgantown, West Virginia, earning a technical knockout over Benny Bland a little more than a minute into the fight. In the months that followed, Stiverne continued to move up the heavyweight ranks. By January of 2006, he had compiled a record of 5–0, scoring technical knockouts in the first round of each of his bouts. Stiverne scored his first full knockout in October of 2006 during a bout in Rosemont, Illinois, dropping opponent Charles Brown to the mat in the second round of their six-round matchup.

Stiverne remained dominant through the first half of 2007, scoring knockout victories in four consecutive fights to begin the year. His first professional loss came in July of 2007 when he suffered a technical knockout against Demetrice King at the Harbor Yard Arena in Bridgeport, Connecticut. Stiverne rebounded that October, defeating Edward Gutierrez with a first-round technical knockout at New York City's Madison Square Garden. After handily beating Jimmy Haynes in St. Louis in March of 2008, Stiverne began training for a matchup against Brad Gregory at Uniprix Stadium in Montreal, which would take place in July of 2008; it would mark the first time the boxer fought in his adopted city. Stiverne did not disappoint his hometown fans, destroying Gregory with a first-round technical knockout. He continued to build on his impressive resume in December of 2008 when he knocked out

Lyle McDowell in the first round of a bout in Zurich, Switzerland.

Stiverne fought three times in 2009. In February he won a unanimous eight-round decision against Robert Hawkins in Sunrise, Florida. Two months later, Stiverne fought Charles Davis to a draw, the first tie of his career. After defeating Jerry Butler in Las Vegas in October of 2009, Stiverne took a long hiatus from competition. He returned to the ring in November of 2010, knocking out Ramon Hayes in the first round of a bout in Montreal. Two months later, in January of 2011, Stiverne earned his first opportunity to fight for a championship when he matched up against Kertson Manswell in a bout in Pontiac, Michigan. With his first-round technical knockout, Stiverne claimed several vacated titles, including the WBC international heavyweight title and the United States National Boxing Championship heavyweight title.

Earned First Heavyweight Title Bid

Despite these accolades, Stiverne had yet to fight for a world heavyweight championship. Indeed, Stiverne's inability to attain the highest rank in his sport led many boxing observers to wonder if he had the ability to win boxing's biggest prize. Among his critics was Don House, Stiverne's trainer during the early stage of his career, who felt Stiverne lacked the passion necessary to become world heavyweight champion. "He started off good, but somewhere along the line, he started to get complacent," House recalled to Iole in January of 2015. It was Stiverne's lack of passion that ultimately led House to quit as his trainer. "I finally had to leave him for a while," House told Iole. "Mike Tyson had the speed, the power and the aggression. Bermane had the speed and the power, but he didn't have the aggression like [Mike] Tyson."

House ultimately rejoined Stiverne's corner in 2011. In June of that year, the fighter scored a technical knockout in the 10th round of a 12-round bout against Ray Austin. The victory gave Stiverne a claim to the vacant WBC silver heavyweight title while putting him on the path to earn a heavyweight title bid. His next major victory came in April of 2013 when he defended his silver heavyweight crown by winning a unanimous decision over contender Chris Arreola. A year later Stiverne finally earned his first chance at the WBC world heavyweight title, which had recently been vacated by Ukrainian boxer Vitali Klitschko. In a rematch against Arreola that took place in May of 2014, Stiverne won decisively, scoring a sixth-round technical knockout to win his first major world championship.

Stiverne's status as WBC heavyweight champion proved short-lived. In his first title defense, a bout against American fighter Deontay Wilder in January of 2015, Stiverne was defeated in a unanimous decision.

Following the fight, Stiverne was hospitalized for two days, as he struggled with extreme dehydration. He was later diagnosed with rhabdomyolysis, a disorder that causes muscle fiber to break down and enter the bloodstream, leading to fatigue. In a press conference following his release, Stiverne apologized for his performance against Wilder. "To my fans, I apologize for not being able to perform like Bermane usually does," Dan Rafael of ESPN quoted Stiverne as telling the media. "I know that people who really know me, know how I fight. My last fight with Chris Arreola, I gave you a good show. It is unfortunate that I couldn't do what I wanted to do with my fight with Deontay Wilder." During the press conference, Stiverne also pledged to return to the ring, with the aim of one day regaining his title. "Hopefully, somewhere in the future we will meet again," he added. "I am back on my feet 100 percent right now. I just need a couple of weeks or a month of rest to be back where I left off."

Sources

Periodicals

Daily Breeze (Torrance, CA), May 9, 2014; May 11, 2014; December 26, 2014.

Los Angeles Times, January 21, 2015.

Sunday Times (London), January 11, 2015, p. 3.

Telegraph, May 12, 2014.

Toronto Sun, May 15, 2014.

Tuscaloosa (AL) News, January 10, 2015.

Washington Post, January 18, 2015.

Online

Ambrose, Dan, "Bermane Stiverne to Fight in July," Boxing News 24, March 25, 2015, http://www.boxingnews24.com/2015/03/bermane-stiverne-to-fight-in-july/ (accessed June 25, 2015).

"Bermane Stiverne," BoxRec.com, http://boxrec.com/boxer/324806 (accessed June 25, 2015).

Iole, Kevin, "Former WBC Heavyweight Champion Diagnosed with Rhabdomyolysis," Yahoo! Sports, January 19, 2015, http://sports.yahoo.com/blogs/boxing/former-heavyweight-champion-diagnosed-with-rhabdomyolysis-024914236.html (accessed June 25, 2015).

———, "Why Heavyweight Champ Bermane Stiverne Is Still Trying to Make His Name," Yahoo! Sports, January 16, 2015, http://sports.yahoo.com/news/why-heavyweight-champ-bermane-stiverne-is-still-trying-to-make-his-name-200843366.html (accessed June 25, 2015).

Rafael, Dan, "Bermane Stiverne out of Hospital," ESPN.com, January 20, 2015, http://espn.go.com/boxing/story/_/id/12195616/bermane-stiverne-released-las-vegas-hospital (accessed June 25, 2015).

"Stiverne: I Represent the Country I Was Born in Haiti, and Then Quebec, but I Also Love the United States," FightNews.com, January 12, 2015, http://www.fightnews.com/Boxing/stiverne-represent-country-born-haiti-quebec-also-love-united-states-276004 (accessed June 25, 2015).

—Stephen Meyer

Bryant Terry

1976—

Chef, food justice activist, cookbook author

Bryant Terry is a self-described "eco-chef" and food justice activist who is committed to fostering the development of local, sustainable urban food systems and encouraging organic food production. A key part of that commitment for Terry is educating people, particularly poor African Americans in urban neighborhoods, about how to make healthy food choices, how to cook nutritious dishes for themselves, and, more broadly, how to influence food policy at the local and national levels. A vegetarian since he was a teenager, Terry now follows a vegan diet, consuming no animal products of any kind, and he is an advocate for plant-based eating. He is the author of four cookbooks that explore the intersection of vegan cooking and African-American culture, providing recipes for dishes that are inspired not only by traditional soul food but also by the diverse culinary traditions of the African diaspora. Terry has won praise for his efforts to promote healthy cooking and sustainable agriculture and as an advocate for "food justice"—the belief that healthy and affordable foods should be available to all people, regardless of their race, class, or income. In 2015 the James Beard Foundation recognized Terry's work in this area with its prestigious Leadership Award.

Became a Vegetarian as a Teenager

Terry was born and raised in Memphis, Tennessee, where his mother was a nurse and his father worked as an environmental protection specialist at the U.S. Army's Redstone Arsenal in Huntsville, Alabama. Ter-

ry's family owned farms in rural Mississippi, and he often spent his free time there, bringing home fresh produce. Even in the city, his family always had a garden. He learned his first lessons about gardening from his paternal grandfather, who had his own urban farm in his backyard. "[H]e had this huge TV satellite dish in the middle of the rows of mustard greens and collards and corn and different summer squashes and tomatoes," Bryant recalled in an interview with Meredith May in the *San Francisco Chronicle* in 2014. "He shared with my parents and all of Dad's siblings and gave his surplus to neighbors and folks at church. It was a thriving local food system."

Terry adopted a plant-based diet as a teenager, after he heard the song "Beef" by Boogie Down Productions, which exposed the horrors of factory farming. "That was the thing that catalyzed me to change my own habits, attitudes and politics around food. I knew nothing about factory farming. I was appalled by the fact that animals are treated so horribly and this is what people eat," he explained to Alexandra Phanor-Faury in an April of 2015 interview for *Ebony* magazine.

Although he had always loved to cook, Terry did not think of becoming a chef until much later, when he was in graduate school. After completing his undergraduate degree at Xavier University of Louisiana in New Orleans in 1997, he went on to pursue a master's degree in history at New York University. While he was living in New York, Terry saw firsthand neighborhoods where people had little access to healthy foods. Riding the subway to class each day, Terry was struck by the

number of young people he saw having junk food and soda for breakfast. "They had few resources of healthy, fresh and affordable food," Terry explained to Linnea Covington on the website Food Republic. "I realized we had to talk about the lack of healthy food having the effect on the mind, body and spirit, particularly in regards to people of color living throughout the United States." Terry decided that he could make a difference by teaching people how to cook.

Advocated for a Sustainable Food System

After finishing his master's degree in 2000, Terry enrolled in the chef's training program at the Natural Gourmet Institute for Health and Culinary Arts. He completed the program in 2002, a year after he founded b-healthy (an acronym for Build Healthy Eating and Lifestyles to Help Youth), a five-year initiative aimed at educating low-income youth in New York City about healthy cooking and nutrition and empowering young people to work toward a more just and sustainable food system.

In 2003 Terry met cookbook author Anna Lappé, and three years later the two published *Grub: Ideas for an Urban Organic Kitchen,* in which they outline their argument for supporting local, sustainable agriculture and provide a collection of seasonally inspired dishes. In 2007 Terry appeared on the Sundance Channel series *Big Ideas for a Small Planet* and hosted the 13-episode PBS series *The Endless Feast.*

From 2008 to 2010 Terry was a fellow of the Food and Society Policy Fellows Program, a national initiative of the W. K. Kellogg Foundation that addresses the need of consumers and community leaders to understand issues related to food production in America. With the Kellogg Foundation's support, Terry established the Southern Organic Kitchen Project, which aimed to educate African Americans living in the South about the connection between diet and health, to empower them to make smart choices about healthy foods and local food sources, and to show participants how they can influence local and national food policy. The project targeted a population of poor African Americans, who experience higher rates of obesity, heart disease, and diabetes.

Explored Vegan Diet in Cookbooks

Terry has long advocated a plant-based diet, believing that it is a healthy, sustainable, and environmentally responsible choice. After first becoming a vegetarian as a teenager, Terry eventually adopted a vegan diet, in which no animal products of any kind are consumed, including meat, eggs, dairy, and even honey produced by bees. Terry eschews the label "vegan," however, because of its negative connotations. "I think a lot of people, when they talk about vegan diets the focus is on what's not being eaten," he said in a 2012 interview with National Public Radio (NPR). "I'm more focused on … the diverse varieties of fruits and vegetables and legumes." Rather than being bland and boring, Terry argues, vegan dishes can be hearty and full of flavor, and for that reason, he prefers to describe his style of cooking and eating as "ingredient-driven local, seasonal, soulful food," he told NPR. For Terry, food choices reflect not only what we want to put into our bodies but also our values about how food is produced and the effects of food production. "I want to encourage people to really consider their values—what type of food system do they want to see; how do they want animals to be treated; how do they want the local economy to develop," he explained to NPR.

Terry has written three cookbooks that explore the intersection of vegan cooking and African-American culture. In 2009 he published *Vegan Soul Kitchen: Fresh, Healthy, and Creative African-American Cuisine.* Although soul food and vegan cooking may initially seem to be opposed, given that many traditional soul food dishes rely on pork and fat, Terry

argues that is not the case, and in *Vegan Soul Kitchen* he aims to return soul food to its healthy roots. "If we move past the stereotypes of African American cuisine, the foundations are really healthful foods: nutrient-dense greens like mustards and turnips and kale and collards and dandelions, and butter beans and sugar snap peas and pole beans and black-eyed peas and sweet potatoes," he explained to Joe Yonan in the *Washington Post* in 2014. Terry followed up with two more vegan cookbooks, *The Inspired Vegan: Seasonal Ingredients, Creative Recipes, Mouthwatering Menus* in 2012 and *Afro-Vegan: Farm-Fresh African, Caribbean and Southern Flavors Remixed* in 2014. In the latter book, Terry draws on the diversity of food traditions of the African diaspora, and each recipe is accompanied by a suggested soundtrack. *Afro-Vegan* was named one of the best books of the year and nominated for an NAACP Image Award in the outstanding literary work category.

Terry has received numerous accolades for his work. In 2012 he was among 80 chosen by U.S. Secretary of State Hillary Rodham Clinton to participate in the American Chef Corps, a culinary and cultural exchange program. In 2014 Terry was named artist in residence at San Francisco's Grace Cathedral, and the following year he was chosen as chef in residence of the Museum of the African Diaspora. In 2015 Terry received the James Beard Foundation's Leadership Award "for his efforts to raise awareness of food-justice issues and to empower youth to be active in creating a healthy, just, and sustainable food system."

Selected works

Books

(With Anna Lappé) *Grub: Ideas for an Urban Organic Kitchen,* Tarcher/Penguin, 2006.

Vegan Soul Kitchen: Fresh, Healthy, and Creative African-American Cuisine, Da Capo Press, 2009.

The Inspired Vegan: Seasonal Ingredients, Creative Recipes, Mouthwatering Menus, Da Capo Press, 2012.

Afro-Vegan: Farm-Fresh African, Caribbean and Southern Flavors Remixed, Ten Speed Press, 2014.

Television

The Endless Feast, PBS, 2007.

Sources

Periodicals

San Francisco Chronicle, June 3, 2014.
Washington Post, May 5, 2014.

Online

Andrews, Avital, "9 Chefs Who Are Changing the World," Sierra Club, March/April 2015, http://www.sierraclub.org/sierra/2015-2-march-april/taste-test/9-chefs-who-are-changing-world (accessed June 21, 2015)

Butler, Grant, "Chef Bryant Terry Trumpets the Plant-Based Roots of Soulful Food," OregonLive.com, June 15, 2010, http://www.oregonlive.com/food day/index.ssf/2010/06/the_plant-based_roots_of_soulf.html (accessed June 21, 2015).

Covington, Linnea, "Bryant Terry, Bringing Good Food Politics to Oakland," Food Republic, November 18, 2014, http://www.foodrepublic.com/2014/11/18/bryant-terry-bringing-good-food-politics-to-oakland/ (accessed June 16, 2015).

Internicola, Dorene, "For Afro-Vegan Chef Bryant Terry Recipes Are Political," Reuters, August 12, 2014, http://www.reuters.com/article/2014/08/12/us-food-chefs-terry-idUSKBN0GC0NM20140 812 (accessed June 21, 2015).

"The James Beard Foundation Announces Fifth Annual Leadership Award Recipients," James Beard Foundation, June 9, 2015, http://www.jamesbeard.org/sites/default/files/pressreleases/2015%20 Leadership%20Awards%20Release%20FINAL.pdf (accessed June 21, 2015).

Phanor-Faury, Alexandra, "Vegetarianism: A Black Choice," Ebony.com, April 8, 2015, http://www.ebony.com/life/vegetarianism-a-black-choice-333 #axzz3dGEtjXll (accessed June 16, 2015).

"Tamari Greens, Miso Yams: Chef Gives Vegans Multicultural Flavor," National Public Radio, December 28, 2012, http://www.npr.org/2012/12/28/167 528801/tamari-greens-miso-yams-chef-gives-ve gans-multicultural-flavor (accessed June 21, 2015).

"U.S. Department of State to Launch Diplomatic Culinary Partnership," U.S. Department of State, September 5, 2012, http://www.state.gov/r/pa/prs/ps/2012/09/197375.htm (accessed June 21, 2015).

Walker, Judy, "Food Activist Bryant Terry Returns to New Orleans as Part of the Tennessee Williams Festival," NOLA.com, March 24, 2015, http://www.nola.com/food/index.ssf/2015/03/food_ac tivist_bryant_terry_is.html (accessed June 16, 2015).

—Deborah A. Ring

Nat Towles

1905–1963

Jazz bandleader, bassist, music educator

Our knowledge of the early days of jazz depends to a large extent on historic recordings. Musicians who never entered the recording studio, therefore, are frequently underappreciated, although their skills are often well attested in other ways. Such is the case with bassist, bandleader, and music educator Nat Towles, whose fame largely coincided with the popularity of swing, the fast-paced style that dominated jazz between the 1920s and the mid-1940s. Esteemed by his peers both for his musicianship and for his ability to spot talent, he led a series of orchestras over the course of his career; the most prominent of these, historian Nathan W. Pearson noted, "was widely regarded as among the hottest [groups] of the late 1930s." Gunther Schuller, one of the most prominent critics in jazz, endorsed that judgment, writing, "The Towles orchestra by all evidence, limited and circumstantial although it is, must have been in many respects the equal of any orchestra of that time."

Towles was born on August 10, 1905, in New Orleans, generally considered the birthplace of jazz. Music was part of his life from a very early age. His father, known variously as Phil or Charlie Towles, was a professional bassist who worked regularly with many of the city's leading ensembles. Nat's own involvement with music began with the guitar and the violin, not the bass; according to Eugene Chadbourne of AllMusic.com, he avoided his father's instrument for a time because of its unwieldy size. After changing his mind on that issue, however, he made rapid progress. An experienced performer by his mid-teens, he worked with a variety of ensembles in and around New Orleans before launch-ing his own group, the Creole Harmony Kings, about 1923.

The Kings' reputation grew quickly, and after establishing themselves in Louisiana, they began touring farther afield, often traveling west across Texas and north to Oklahoma for gigs. In doing so they joined a growing number of so-called territory bands—traveling ensembles that toured across the West and Midwest, typically stopping in small towns for one or two shows before moving on to the next engagement. Although these gigs were not well paid or well publicized, they served an important function, as the communities involved often lacked much in the way of music or recreation. Territory bands also provided young and relatively inexperienced musicians with an opportunity to prove themselves. Towles's groups were particularly well known in that regard; in the words of Chadbourne, "His bandstands were proving and training grounds for many players who went on to make names for themselves."

The Creole Harmony Kings stayed together for roughly four years. Towles then took a brief break from band-leading, working primarily as a freelance bassist until about 1930, when he moved to central Mississippi and launched a new group. Although he managed to keep that ensemble going for several years, the deepening of the Great Depression made it difficult to earn a living on the road. Around 1934 he began to supplement his touring income by teaching, primarily at Wiley College, a predominately African-American institution in Texas. His duties there included oversight of the school's band,

At a Glance . . .

Born on August 10, 1905, in New Orleans, LA; died January 1963 in Berkeley, CA; son of Phil Towles (also known as Charlie Towles, a bassist).

Career: Independent musician, 1920s–63; Wiley College, faculty member, 1930s.

a highly regarded ensemble that came to be a fertile recruiting ground for his professional groups.

Economic conditions, meanwhile, were slowly improving, and within a year or two Towles was able to focus once again on touring. By the end of 1936 he had formed what proved to be his most famous band and moved north to Omaha, Nebraska, home to a sizable African-American community and to a small but vibrant jazz scene. As the house band at the Dreamland Ballroom, a focal point of black life in the city, his orchestra had the opportunity to work with some of the biggest names in jazz. Those gigs played a crucial role in raising the profile of his musicians, among them saxophonist Jimmy Heath, who went on to stardom himself the following decade.

Known to his musicians as a gifted but tough-minded leader, Towles managed his career in singular style. Unlike a great number of his peers on the territory circuit, for example, he showed little inclination to move to the East Coast, where there were more opportunities for orchestras, particularly in the area of recording. Although several members of his ensemble did complete a few tracks together in 1940, they were led in the studio by one of his rivals, Horace Henderson; Towles himself is not known to have made any significant recordings. Schuller has suggested that his reluctance to relocate to New York City or another site with ample recording facilities may have stemmed in part from a fear that other, better-financed bandleaders in the area might recruit his musicians. It is clear, in any event, that his preference for the Midwest was not set in stone; during World War II, for example, he and his band appeared at least once at New York's Apollo Theater, the most prominent African-American venue in the country.

The jazz world, meanwhile, was entering a period of rapid change, as saxophonist Charlie Parker and other innovators introduced bebop, a highly improvisational style typically played by small groups, not orchestras. By the second half of the 1940s, the new style was rapidly overtaking swing, and bandleaders such as Towles found it increasingly difficult to secure gigs. Although he endured that situation for some time, leading his own groups well into the 1950s, the music that had been his specialty for decades was increasingly regarded as dated. In the wake of that shift he began to focus on other opportunities, and by 1960 he had left the field almost entirely, turning instead to the management of a bar that he had opened in California. His life there was a quiet one, and the fatal heart attack he suffered in the city of Berkeley in January of 1963 was not widely publicized. In the decades since, however, interest in his life and work has grown, thanks both to the work of writers such as Pearson and Schuller and to a growing enthusiasm for swing and other forms of early jazz.

Sources

Books

Love, Preston, *A Thousand Honey Creeks Later: My Life in Music from Basie to Motown—and Beyond,* Wesleyan University Press, 1997.

Pearson, Nathan W., *Goin' to Kansas City,* University of Illinois Press, 1988.

Schuller, Gunther, *The Swing Era: the Development of Jazz, 1930–1945,* Oxford University Press, 1989.

Online

Chadbourne, Eugene, "Nat Towles: Artist Biography," AllMusic.com, http://www.allmusic.com/artist/nat-towles-mn0001411137/biography (accessed July 10, 2015).

—R. Anthony Kugler

Treacherous Three

Rap music pioneers

The members of Treacherous Three were among the pioneers of rap music. They were one of the first rap groups to record for a major label in the early 1980s, when they released a string of singles on Enjoy and Sugar Hill, two of the first rap labels. Their 1980 single "The New Rap Language" was a landmark, featuring an intricate, fast-paced style of rhyming known as "speed rap." Although the group was short-lived, disbanding by the mid-1980s, Treacherous Three had an important influence on rappers who followed them, including LL Cool J and Big Daddy Kane.

The group formed in Harlem in the late 1970s, when friends Kool Moe Dee (Mohandas Dewese), L.A. Sunshine (Lamar Hill), and Special K (Kevin Keaton), joined by DJ Easy Lee (Theodore Moy'e), came together to form Treacherous Three. Soon after they began performing together, another friend, Spoonie Gee, introduced them to his uncle, producer Bobby Robinson of Enjoy Records. In 1980 Treacherous Three recorded their first single "The New Rap Language," which became the B-side to Spoonie G's now-classic "Love Rap." "The New Rap Language" showcased Kool Moe Dee's signature style of speed rapping. Treacherous Three followed up with two more singles for Enjoy, "Body Rock," which was the first rap song to incorporate rock by using guitars, and "At the Party."

In 1981 Treacherous Three followed Enjoy label mates Grandmaster Flash and the Furious Five to Sugar Hill Records, which had released the Sugarhill Gang's landmark single "Rapper's Delight" two years earlier, helping popularize the nascent rap genre among a mainstream audience. For Sugar Hill, Treacherous Three recorded a handful of singles over the next few years, including "Whip It," which featured singer Phillippe Wynne of the Spinners, and "Feel the Heart

Beat." The group became known for their lyrical dexterity, precipitating a number of "rap battles" in which MCs challenged one another to come up with faster, more inventive raps. In one legendary battle at the Harlem World in 1981, Kool Moe Dee deftly put down "Busy Bee" Starski with an impressive freestyle rap; Kool Moe Dee would go down as one of the greatest rappers of all time.

A Treacherous Three live jam with Funky Four Plus One appeared on the album *Live Convention '81*. In 1984 the group made a cameo appearance in the film *Beat Street,* in which they performed "Xmas Rap" with Doug E. Fresh. In the same year, Kool Moe Dee and Special K briefly cohosted the television show *Graffiti Rock*. By this time, however, the group's popularity was declining as they were eclipsed by harder-sounding acts such as Run-D.M.C. By the middle of the decade, Treacherous Three had disbanded.

Kool Moe Dee embarked on a solo career, releasing his debut album, *How Ya Like Me Now,* in 1986. The album went platinum, selling a million copies, and three years later he was the first rapper ever to perform at the Grammy Awards ceremonies. Special K released one solo single in 1987, "Special K Is Good," and DJ Easy Lee went on to become a producer. After the group's demise, L.A. Sunshine went through a period of addiction and depression before finding a second career mentoring youth in Harlem. He published an autobiography, *L.A. Sunshine: A True Story, the Real Accounts,* in 2011.

Treacherous Three reunited in 1993 to record their only full-length album, *Old School Flava*. Released the next year by Wrap Records, the album featured the original members of the group, with guest appearances

At a Glance . . .

Members included Kool Moe Dee, born Mohandas Dewese on August 8, 1963(?), in New York, NY; L.A. Sunshine, born Lamar Hill; DJ Easy Lee, born Theodore Moy'e; and Special K, born Kevin Keaton.

Career: Recorded for Enjoy Records, 1980, and Sugar Hill Records, 1981–85.

by fellow old-school rappers such as Doug E. Fresh, Big Daddy Kane, Chuck D of Public Enemy, Grandmaster Caz, and Melle Mel. In 2014 Spoonie Gee and Treacherous Three were inducted into the Hip Hop Hall of Fame.

Selected works

Singles

"The New Rap Language," Enjoy, 1980.
"Body Rock," Enjoy, 1980.
"At the Party," Enjoy, 1980.
"Feel the Heart Beat," Sugar Hill, 1981.
"Whip It," Sugar Hill, 1982.
"Xmas Rap," Sugar Hill, 1984.

Albums

Old School Flava, Wrap Records, 1994.

Sources

Books

Hess, Mickey, ed., *Hip-Hop in America: A Regional Guide*, vol. 1, *East Coast and West Coast*, Greenwood Press, 2010.

Periodicals

New York Times, December 5, 2013.

Online

Bush, John, "Treacherous Three: Artist Biography," AllMusic.com, http://www.allmusic.com/artist/treacherous-three-mn0000624518/biography (accessed June 26, 2015).

—Deborah A. Ring

Ollie Tyler

1945—

Educator, politician

Ollie Tyler is a pioneering educator and politician. She first rose to national prominence in December of 2014 when she was elected mayor of Shreveport, Louisiana. With her victory, Tyler became the first African-American woman to hold Shreveport's highest office. Prior to entering politics, Tyler had already garnered praise throughout the state of Louisiana for her service as an educator. For more than four decades, Tyler worked as a teacher and an administrator in public school systems throughout Louisiana. She originally launched her education career as a high school mathematics teacher before eventually becoming a middle school principal. In 1994 she became the first African-American woman to be named superintendent of the Caddo Parish Public School System, and she later became acting superintendent of education for the state of Louisiana. Over the course of her career, Tyler also served on a number of influential state education committees, and in 2004 she was a member of newly elected governor Kathleen Blanco's Education Transition Team.

She was born Ollie Spearman on January 6, 1945, in Blanchard, Louisiana, one of nine children of Leroy and Ida Haley Spearman. Raised on a dairy farm, Tyler spent much of her childhood working to help support her family, picking cotton and performing household chores. During these years, she also proved herself an exceptional student, earning As in all her subjects and graduating as valedictorian of her class at Herndon High School. She subsequently received a National Merit Scholarship to attend Grambling State College, a historically black institution, where she earned a bach-

elor's degree sometime around 1967. About the time she completed her undergraduate education, Tyler married Clyde Harris, whom she had dated since high school. The couple's son, Tony, was born in 1968.

However, Tyler's marriage to Harris soon ended in tragedy. Over the next year, she was physically abused by her husband and would often hide in her house in order to conceal her bruises from friends and family members. At one point, Harris smashed his wife's head into a parked car, causing permanent damage to her eye. Eventually, Tyler began lodging formal complaints with the police; her pleas went unheeded as local law enforcement officials declined to press charges against her husband. As the instances of domestic violence continued, Tyler purchased a handgun at a pawn shop to protect herself.

Tyler's ordeal finally reached a breaking point in August of 1968 when she shot and killed Harris during a dispute at the home of her parents. The actual details surrounding the fatal incident have remained unclear for decades. According to Tyler's original account, she shot Harris in the chest before turning the gun on herself, intent on ending her life. Her younger brother intervened, however, and Tyler ended up shooting herself in the leg. In another attempt to commit suicide, she later jumped out of her father's car as she was being driven to the hospital, but she survived her injuries. After her release from the hospital, Tyler was arrested. Although some reports indicate that she was initially accused of murder, no evidence of formal charges has survived, and she was never indicted. In the

At a Glance . . .

Born Ollie Spearman on January 6, 1945, in Blanchard, LA; daughter of Leroy (a dairy farmer) and Ida Haley Spearman; married Clyde Harris, 1967; married James C. Tyler (a minister), 1972; children: Tony, Wanda. *Religion:* Baptist. *Politics:* Democrat. *Education:* Grambling State College (later Grambling State University), BS, 1967(?); Louisiana State University, MA, education, 1970s(?).

Career: Eden Gardens High School, mathematics teacher, 1969–70; Youree Drive Junior High School, teacher and principal, 1970–94; Caddo Parish Director of Middle Schools, 1994–2000, superintendent, 2003–07; New Orleans Public Schools, deputy superintendent and chief academic officer, 2000–2003; State of Louisiana, deputy superintendent of education, 2007–11, acting superintendent of education, 2011–12; City of Shreveport, LA, mayor, 2014—.

Memberships: Governor's Education Transition Team, 2004; Deputies Leadership Commission's Executive Committee for State Deputy Superintendents, 2008–11; Governor's Louisiana Women's Policy and Research Commission, 2008–12.

Awards: Louisiana Association of School Executives Educator of Distinction Award, 1999; Louisiana Superintendent of the Year, 2007; Athena Award, 2007.

Addresses: *Office*—c/o Mayor's Office, 505 Travis St., Shreveport, LA 71101.

end, the police ruled Harris's killing an "accidental and justifiable homicide," and Tyler was released from custody.

After surviving this trauma, Tyler soon embarked on her career in education. In 1969 she found her first teaching job, becoming a math instructor at Eden Gardens High School in Shreveport. Around this time she also pursued her graduate education at Louisiana State University in Baton Rouge, where she eventually earned her master's degree in education. In 1970 as Louisiana schools underwent systematic integration, she began teaching math at Youree Drive Junior High School (later Middle School) in Shreveport, becoming the first African-American instructor to join the school's faculty. A year later she married Reverend James C. Tyler, a minister at the Upper Zion Baptist Church. The couple would remain married until Reverend Tyler's death in 1990.

Although she endured racial discrimination during her first years at Youree Drive, Tyler gradually rose to a position of authority at the school. For a period she served as head of the Mathematics and Science Department, and in 1990 she became the first African-American principal in the school's history. In 1994 Tyler became director of middle schools for Caddo Parish, where she remained for the next six years. During this period, Tyler launched a number of groundbreaking educational initiatives, including summer programs aimed at helping district students meet standardized testing goals. Her work with the Caddo Parish middle schools soon earned her statewide recognition, and in 1999 she was given an Educator of Distinction Award by the Louisiana Association of School Executives.

In 2000 Tyler left Caddo Parish to become deputy superintendent and chief academic officer for the New Orleans public school system. For the next three years, she oversaw a number of new programs aimed at improving education standards in the district. Among her notable initiatives included an alliance with local colleges and universities to help train teachers at some of the city's struggling schools. After three years in New Orleans, Tyler returned to Shreveport to become superintendent of the Caddo Parish school system. In 2004 she served on the Education Transition Team of newly elected Louisiana governor Kathleen Blanco. During her tenure as Caddo Parish superintendent, Tyler's accomplishments earned her a number of important distinctions. In 2007 she was named public school Superintendent of the Year for the state of Louisiana. That same year she received the Athena Award in recognition of her leadership and commitment to improving the lives of people in her district.

In 2007 Tyler was appointed deputy superintendent of education for Louisiana. Four years later she became acting superintendent of education. She retired in 2012. In 2014 she launched her first bid for public office, running for mayor of Shreveport as a Democrat. Her campaign pledges included plans for reducing poverty, improving infrastructure, and implementing economic initiatives aimed at attracting new businesses to the city. Late in the campaign, Tyler's candidacy was nearly derailed after news stories about the death of her first husband surfaced in the local media. Although the reemergence of this tragic incident threatened to tarnish her reputation, Tyler remained focused on winning the election. "I'm not going to and I haven't let this stop me from serving for 46 years," she told the *Shreveport Times* in October of 2014, "and I'm not going to let it stop me now." On December 6, 2014, Tyler won the mayoral seat with 63 percent of the vote. As she entered her 70th year, the lifelong educator continued to demonstrate an unwavering commitment to public service.

Sources

Periodicals

New Orleans City Business, December 23, 2001, p. 23A.

Shreveport Times, October 31, 2014.

USA Today, December 27, 2014.

Online

Burnett, Lou, "Who Will Be Our Next Mayor?," The ForumNews.com, October 27, 2014, http://theforumnews.com/article-1145-who-will-be-our-next-mayor-.html (accessed June 29, 2015)

Longhini, Doug, "Mayoral Candidate Says She Fatally Shot Her Husband in 1968," CBS News, October 31, 2014, http://www.cbsnews.com/news/will-louisiana-mayoral-candidate-domestic-violence-case-affect-race/ (accessed June 29, 2015).

"Mayor Ollie S. Tyler," City of Shreveport, Louisiana, http://www.shreveportla.gov/index.aspx?NID=1217 (accessed June 29, 2015).

"Tyler Wins Shreveport Mayor's Seat," KTBS, December 6, 2014, http://www.ktbs.com/story/27566272/tyler-wins-shreveport-mayors-seat (accessed June 29, 2015).

—Stephen Meyer

Andrew Wiggins

1995—

Professional basketball player

Andrew Wiggins is an elite shooting guard in the National Basketball Association (NBA). Among the most athletic young guards in professional basketball, Wiggins combines natural quickness with a smooth shooting stroke and deft ball-handling abilities, making him a consistent scoring threat on the offensive end. Standing six feet, eight inches tall, with a wingspan of seven feet, Wiggins also brings exceptional size and length to his position, giving him a distinct advantage in defensive matchups against most NBA guards. Wiggins first rose to fame while playing for Huntington Prep School in West Virginia, where he emerged as one of the top high school players in the country. He later starred at the University of Kansas, earning second-team All-American honors as a freshman. Originally selected by the Cleveland Cavaliers with the first overall pick of the 2014 NBA draft, Wiggins was subsequently traded to the Minnesota Timberwolves as part of a multiplayer deal, becoming only the second number-one pick in league history never to play a game with the team that drafted him. Despite this perceived slight, Wiggins quickly embraced his role with the Timberwolves, outperforming all other first-year players to earn Rookie of the Year honors for the 2014–15 season.

Andrew Wiggins was born on February 23, 1995, in Toronto, Canada. He inherited his athletic ability from both of his parents. His father, Mitchell Wiggins, was a former NBA shooting guard who played for three teams over six seasons during the 1980s and early 1990s. Wiggins's mother, Marita Payne, was a track and field star who won two silver medals as a member of the Canadian relay team at the 1984 Summer Olympics in Los Angeles. A standout on the basketball court at a young age, Wiggins launched his high school career at Vaughan Secondary School in Vaughan, Ontario. He left after only one season, however, when it became clear that the overall lack of competition was not helping him improve his game. He eventually left home for West Virginia, where he attended Huntington Prep School. Playing primarily at the small forward position, Wiggins quickly established himself as one of the top talents in the region. As a junior, he scored 24.2 points per game while averaging 8.5 rebounds, 4.1 assists, and 2.7 blocks.

Soon Wiggins began to attract attention from both college and professional scouts. A turning point in his prep career came in April of 2012, when he participated in the Nike Hoop Summit as a member of the World Select Team. Competing against the top high school players in the world, Wiggins scored 20 points in his team's championship game victory over the United States while earning most valuable player honors for the tournament. Wiggins continued to impress that summer, when he competed for Canada at the International Basketball Federation Americas Under-18 Men's Championship tournament in São Sebastião do Paraíso, Brazil. In five games, Wiggins led the team with 15.2 points per contest while finishing second among his teammates in both rebounds (7.6) and assists (2.0).

At a Glance . . .

Born Andrew Christian Wiggins on February 23, 2015 in Toronto, Canada; son of Mitchell Wiggins (a professional basketball player) and Marita Payne-Wiggins (an Olympic track and field athlete). *Education:* Attended University of Kansas, 2013–14.

Career: Minnesota Timberwolves, shooting guard, 2014—.

Awards: McDonald's All-American Game selection, 2013; NBA First-Team All-Rookie, 2014–15; National Basketball Association (NBA) Rookie of the Year, 2015.

Addresses: *Office*—c/o Minnesota Timberwolves, 600 North 1st Ave., Minneapolis, MN 55403.

By the time he returned for his senior year at Huntington Prep, Wiggins was widely regarded as the number-one high school recruit in the country. In May of 2013, he announced his intention to play at the University of Kansas. In the eyes of many college basketball insiders, Wiggins had the potential to develop into a rare basketball talent. "This kid is even better than advertised when you see him in person," Dick Vitale, a longtime college basketball television broadcaster, told *USA Today.* "He fits into the category of LeBron James as a high school player we've never seen before because of his explosiveness." Wiggins continued his meteoric rise during his freshman campaign with the Jayhawks, averaging 17.1 points, 5.9 rebounds, and 1.5 points per game during the 2013–14 season. For the year, Wiggins finished fourth in the Big 12 Conference in points (597) and minutes played (1,148); he also finished ninth in the conference in field goal percentage (.448) and eighth in free throw percentage (.775).

Following his debut season at Kansas, Wiggins declared himself eligible for the 2014 NBA draft. In one of the most talent-heavy draft classes in years, Wiggins was taken by the Cleveland Cavaliers with the number-one overall pick. While Wiggins clearly had the ability to contribute at the NBA level as a rookie, however, his future in Cleveland was uncertain from the beginning. Soon after Wiggins was drafted, his name began to surface in trade rumors, as news emerged that the Cavaliers were trying to work a deal with the Minnesota Timberwolves to acquire All-Star center Kevin Love. In the face of rampant speculation, Cleveland repeatedly insisted that Wiggins would not be part of a deal for Love. The organization appeared to signal its long-term commitment to Wiggins on July 24, 2014, when it signed the rookie guard to a four-year deal worth nearly $25 million.

However, Wiggins's tenure in Cleveland proved short-lived. By August trade speculation once again surfaced in relation to the shooting guard. Ultimately, the Cavaliers decided they needed a big man under the basket to complement the playmaking abilities of guards LeBron James and Kyrie Irving. As trade talks between the two teams progressed, some NBA observers noted that Wiggins might have a better opportunity to thrive in Minnesota, where the Timberwolves were in the midst of a long-term rebuilding strategy, than by playing in the shadow of a superstar like James. At the same time, other writers wondered whether the experience of being traded so early in his career might undermine the young player's confidence. "Wiggins continues to be surrounded by hype and otherwordly expectations," Michael Lee wrote in the *Washington Post,* "but he now has much more to prove—to himself, to his new team and to the team that didn't have the patience to find out what he will become." On August 23, 2014, only one month after signing his first NBA contract, Wiggins was sent to Minnesota as part of a multiplayer, multiteam deal, with Cleveland receiving Love from the Timberwolves.

Wiggins quickly dispelled any doubts concerning his ability to perform at the NBA level. After a somewhat inconsistent beginning to his rookie season, Wiggins gradually began to show signs of his elite talent. A turning point came in December of 2014, when he faced the Cavaliers for the first time. Although the Timberwolves lost the game, Wiggins delivered an impressive performance, scoring 27 points with two rebounds, a steal, and a block. Later that season, Wiggins recalled receiving some timely motivation from his coaching staff. "One of the coaches was like, 'Any player can do it one night, but a great player does it every night,'" he told the *St. Paul Pioneer Press.* "That really stuck in my head." For the year, Wiggins averaged 16.9 points and 4.6 rebounds per game while appearing in all 82 games. By season's end, the Minnesota shooting guard had been named Rookie of the Year and earned comparisons to established stars such as Kevin Durant, Dwyane Wade, and Kobe Bryant. As he entered his second professional season, Wiggins had already built a promising foundation for his NBA future.

Sources

Periodicals

Ottawa Citizen, May 25, 2012, p. B5.
St. Paul (MN) Pioneer Press, August 22, 2014; November 23, 2014; January 20, 2015; April 30, 2015.
Toronto Star, March 19, 2015, p. S1.
Washington Post, May 15, 2013; August 19, 2014.

Online

"Andrew Wiggins," Basketball-Reference.com, http://www.basketball-reference.com/players/w/wiggian01.html (accessed June 26, 2015).

Gleeson, Scott, and Jim Halley, "Andrew Wiggins' Decision Weighs Heavily on College Hoops Landscape," USAToday.com, May 13, 2013, http://www.usatoday.com/story/sports/ncaab/2013/05/13/andrew-wiggins-decision-weighs-heavy-on-college-hoops-landscape/2155345/ (accessed June 26, 2015).

McPherson, Steve, "In Defense of Andrew Wiggins' Beautiful, Barely Begun Career," RollingStone.com, January 5, 2015, http://www.rollingstone.com/culture/features/in-defense-of-andrew-wiggins-beautiful-barely-begun-career-20150105 (accessed June 26, 2015).

—Stephen Meyer

Gerald Wiggins

1922–2008

Jazz pianist

Over the course of a distinguished career that spanned more than 70 years, pianist Gerald Wiggins collaborated with some of the biggest names in jazz, including trumpeter Louis Armstrong and vocalist Lena Horne. A dazzlingly proficient and versatile stylist, he worked for many years on Hollywood soundtracks and made a number of well-received recordings with his own trio. He is best remembered for his efforts as an accompanist for vocalists like Horne. His meticulous and understated approach to accompaniment was widely admired, not least by the vocalists themselves. "I play differently behind each one," he once said of his vocal partners, in a comment quoted by Steve Voce of the London *Independent,* "because each one sings different. I adapt my style to their way of singing."

Gerald Foster Wiggins, often known as "Gerry" or "Wig," was born on May 12, 1922, in New York City, where he was raised. The piano figured prominently in his life as early as age four, when he began lessons. By his own account, however, he was an indifferent student until he heard a recording by the great jazz pianist Art Tatum. Inspired by that discovery, he balanced his coursework at New York's famed High School of Music and Art with an intense but informal study of Tatum and other jazz stars, many of whom lived within walking distance of his home in Harlem.

By the late 1930s Tatum had recognized his talent, and in 1941, when the comedian Stepin Fetchit needed an accompanist, the older pianist recommended his protégé for the job. After several months in that position, Wiggins joined bandleader Les Hite, who took him to Los Angeles, and then had brief stints with Armstrong and bandleader Benny Carter before being inducted into the military for several years of wartime duty. Most of his time in uniform was spent in the Pacific Northwest, where he served in the 29th Special Service Band and moonlighted in local jazz clubs. Following his discharge in 1946 he returned to California, where he formed his own trio and began working extensively with singers like Horne, whom he joined for a successful international tour in the early 1950s. He went on to accompany many other prominent vocalists, including Nat King Cole, Joe Williams, and Eartha Kitt.

By the middle of the 1950s Wiggins was well established in Los Angeles, home to a relaxed—or "cool"—jazz sound that meshed well with his talents. In addition to his work as an accompanist he performed regularly with his own trio in clubs and recording studios around the city. Typical of his albums in this period was *Relax and Enjoy It!,* released on the Contemporary label in 1962. Completed with the help of bassist Joe Comfort and drummer Jackie Mills, it featured vivid renditions of familiar favorites such as "Frankie & Johnny" and "The Lady Is a Tramp" as well as one of his own compositions, "Blue Wig," which remained a prominent part of his repertoire for many years.

Time-consuming though it was, Wiggins's touring and recording work did not prevent him from building a lucrative side career in Hollywood, where he worked behind the scenes, typically on a freelance basis. His efforts there encompassed a wide range of tasks, from performing on soundtracks to coaching singers. At the

At a Glance . . .

Born Gerald Foster Wiggins on May 12, 1922, in New York, NY; died on July 13, 2008, in Los Angeles, CA; married Lynn; children: two children and three stepchildren. *Military service:* U.S. military, 1944–46.

Career: Jazz pianist, 1930s–2008.

Awards: Jazz Tribute Award, Los Angeles Jazz Society, 1988; "Gerald Wiggins Day," City of Los Angeles, September 11, 1988.

end of the 1950s, for example, he helped build screen icon Marilyn Monroe's vocal skills as she prepared for singing roles in *Some Like It Hot* (1959)—one of her most popular films—and *Let's Make Love* (1960). He also made a significant contribution to the soundtrack for *Lady Sings the Blues* (1972), providing much of the accompaniment for vocalist Diana Ross, the film's star.

By the late 1970s, as he marked the 40th anniversary of his professional debut, Wiggins was increasingly celebrated as one of the elder statesmen of jazz. His profile continued to rise over the course of the following decade; in 1988, for example, the members of the Los Angeles Jazz Society presented him with a Jazz Tribute Award. That honor, in turn, prompted Los Angeles mayor Tom Bradley to declare September 11, 1988, "Gerald Wiggins Day" throughout the city. He accepted these accolades with his characteristic modesty, telling Zan Stewart of the *Los Angeles Times* that the Jazz Society award, in particular, "floored" him. "There are so many deserving guys," he added. "I forget who I voted for, but it wasn't me."

In the wake of those honors came a burst of publicity and new opportunities. It was around this time, for example, that he began what proved to be a long and successful association with California-based Concord Records. In 1990 Concord brought him to Maybeck Recital Hall in Berkeley, California, for the completion of a live recording, the eighth in Concord's well-known Maybeck series. Released the following year as *Live at Maybeck Recital Hall: Volume Eight,* the album took full advantage of the venue's famous acoustics with a varied program that showcased Wiggins's range and sensitivity. Its highlights included "Berkeley Blues," one of his own compositions.

Active professionally well into his 80s, Wiggins served for years as an informal mentor to dozens of younger musicians, among them bassist Andy Simpkins and drummer Paul Humphrey, both of whom were long-time members of his trio. The easy camaraderie that characterized his relationship with those two under-rated figures can be heard particularly clearly on his album *Soulidarity,* recorded by Concord in 1995 and released the following year. Simpkins died soon there-after. Wiggins's health remained strong until the mid-2000s, when he was forced to curtail his schedule; after a long illness, he died in Los Angeles on July 13, 2008, at age 86. Joining his wife Lynn and five children in mourning were fans and fellow musicians around the world, many of whom recalled his engaging personality as well as his skills at the keyboard. Don Heckman, a longtime music critic for the *Los Angeles Times,* spoke for many of Wiggins's admirers, calling him "a musi-cian's musician and a singer's best friend."

Selected discography

The Loveliness of You..., Tampa, 1958.
Wiggin' Out, HiFi, 1960.
Relax and Enjoy It!, Contemporary, 1962.
Wig Is Here, Black and Blue, 1974.
Live at Maybeck Recital Hall: Volume Eight (includes "Berkeley Blues"), Concord, 1991.
Soulidarity, Concord, 1996.

Sources

Periodicals

Independent (London), September 1, 2008.
Los Angeles Times, June 11, 1989; July 15, 2008.

Online

Lyon, David, "Gerald Wiggins on Piano Jazz," National Public Radio, February 20, 2009, http://www.npr.org/2012/06/15/100923934/gerald-wiggins-on-piano-jazz (accessed July 4, 2015).

Ramsey, Doug, "Goodbye, Gerald Wiggins," ArtsJournal.com, July 13, 2008, http://www.artsjournal.com/rifftides/2008/07/goodbye_gerald_wiggins.html (accessed July 4, 2015).

Yanow, Scott, "Gerald Wiggins: Artist Biography," AllMusic.com, http://www.allmusic.com/artist/gerald-wiggins-mn0000653250/biography (accessed July 4, 2015).

—R. Anthony Kugler

Bernie Williams

1968—

Professional baseball player, recording artist

Williams, Bernie, photograph. lev radin/Shutterstock.com.

Bernie Williams is a former All-Star center fielder with the New York Yankees. In 16 major league seasons, Williams belted 287 home runs, the seventh-highest total in franchise history, while finishing with a career batting average of .297. In his prime Williams was a core player on a team that dominated the majors during the late 1990s, and he played a key role in helping New York win four World Series titles in a five-year span. Indeed, Williams was particularly successful during the postseason, and he holds a major league record with 80 runs batted in (RBIs) for his playoff career. At the same time, Williams was among the best defensive outfielders of his era, finishing in the top five in fielding percentage among center fielders nine times while claiming four Gold Glove Awards. Since leaving baseball after the 2006 season, Williams has also garnered acclaim as an accomplished classical and jazz guitarist, recording albums and performing concerts at venues throughout the Northeast.

Bernabe Figueroa Williams was born on September 13, 1968, in San Juan, Puerto Rico. His father, Bernabe Williams Sr., was a merchant marine, and his mother, Rufina Williams, was a schoolteacher. Williams discovered his passion for music as a child, after his father bought him a flamenco guitar during a trip to Spain. He later enrolled at the Escuela Libre de Musica, a performing arts school, where he studied classical guitar. At the same time, Williams also demonstrated exceptional athletic ability, excelling at both baseball and track. By the time he reached his teens, he had emerged as one of the most promising baseball prospects in Puerto Rico. In 1985, at age 17, he signed a minor league contract with the New York Yankees. A year later, he appeared in 62 games with the organization's Gulf Coast League squad, batting .270 with 33 stolen bases and 25 RBIs.

During the late 1980s, Williams made a steady climb through the Yankees minor league system. In 1988 he batted .335 with seven home runs and 45 RBIs with the Single-A Prince William Yankees of the Carolina League. Over the next two years, the center fielder divided his time between the franchise's Double-A and Triple-A affiliates, demonstrating both power at the plate and speed on the base paths. He made his big league debut on July 7, 1991, collecting a hit with two RBIs while starting in center field. For the year, Wil-

At a Glance . . .

Born Bernabe Figueroa Williams on September 13, 1968, in San Juan, Puerto Rico; son of Bernabe Sr. (a merchant marine) and Rufina (a teacher) Williams; married Waleska, 1990; children: Bernie Jr., Beatriz, Bianca.

Career: New York Yankees, center fielder, 1991–2006; recording artist, 2003—.

Awards: Most Valuable Player, American League Championship Series, 1996; Gold Glove Award, 1997–2000; Major League Baseball All-Star selection, 1997–2001; Silver Slugger Award, 2002.

Addresses: *Office*—c/o Fortch Unlimited, 2037 Fletcher Ave, Fort Lee, NJ 07024. *Web*—http://www.bernie51.com/. *Twitter*—@bw51official.

liams appeared in 85 games for the Yankees, batting .238 with three home runs and 34 RBIs. While he appeared poised for a breakout season in 1992, Williams still struggled to establish himself as the team's everyday center fielder. Shy and unassuming, Williams had trouble adjusting to the raucous, often aggressive atmosphere characteristic of major league clubhouses. He experienced particular difficulty with veteran out-fielder Mel Hall, who taunted the young player mercilessly during his first year with the team. "I think Mel Hall intimidated him," Yankees coach Clete Boyer told *Newsday* in 1993. "Bernie was scared to death of Mel." After Williams was sent back to Triple-A Columbus for much of the 1992 season, he began to wonder whether he had a future with the franchise.

By 1993, however, Hall had been released from the roster, and Williams finished spring training as the team's starting center fielder. The significance of the promotion was not lost on the young Puerto Rican star. "Think about it for a minute, playing center field for the Yankees. It's a position of a lot of pride and tradition the last 50 years," Williams told *Newsday*. "It's something to be very proud of. By the same token, it's a big responsibility." That year, Williams appeared in 139 games for the Yankees, batting .268 with 12 home runs and 58 RBIs. His offensive production improved steadily over the next two seasons, and by 1996 he had emerged as a vital factor in the team's resurgence as a playoff contender. "He adds a lot more credibility to our lineup," New York manager Joe Torre told *USA Today* in May of the year. "He has the ability to steal a base. He hits from both sides of the plate. No matter where I want to hit him, sixth or second, he protects the guy

in front of him because that guy's going to get good pitches to hit."

For the 1996 regular season, Williams hit .305 with 29 home runs and 102 RBIs, as the Yankees entered the postseason at the top of the American League East for the first time since 1981. Williams continued his stellar campaign during the team's playoff run. In the American League Divisional Series, the center fielder led the team in batting average (.467), home runs (3), and RBIs (5), as the Yankees defeated the Texas Rangers in four games. In the club's victory over the Baltimore Orioles in the American League Championship Series, Williams batted .474 with two home runs and six RBIs while also making several key defensive plays in the outfield. His performance earned him most valuable player honors for the series while helping propel New York to its first World Series bid in 15 years. While the center fielder's production stalled during the World Series matchup against the Atlanta Braves, his presence in the lineup and on the field remained critical to his team's success, as the Yankees won the championship in six games.

By 1997, Williams had garnered national recognition as one of the top hitters in the game. That season, he batted .328 with 21 home runs and 100 RBIs, while earning his first trip to the All-Star game. Indeed, between 1997 and 2001 Williams was named an American League All-Star five consecutive times and helped the Yankees win three more World Series titles. During that span, the center fielder hit .325, with 128 home runs and 527 RBIs. In 2002 Williams took home a Silver Slugger Award after batting .333 with 19 home runs and 102 RBIs. During these years, the star outfielder was also beginning to attract attention for his musical talent, releasing his first jazz guitar album, *The Journey Within,* in 2003.

Williams remained with the Yankees through the end of the 2006 season. When the organization declined to offer him a new major league contract, the center fielder decided to leave the game to devote himself full time to his music. He rejoined his former club in 2008, playing a guitar rendition of "Take Me Out to the Ball Game" during the team's final home game at the old Yankee Stadium. A year later, Williams released a second album, *Moving Forward* (2008), while continuing to perform live shows and concerts. Nine years after he left the game, Williams officially retired from the Yankees. On May 24, 2015, the club held "Bernie Williams Day," retiring the center fielder's number 51 jersey and installing a plaque in his honor in the club's celebrated Monument Park.

Selected works

Albums

The Journey Within, Grp Records, 2003.
Moving Forward, Reform Records, 2009.

Books

(With Dave Gluck and Bob Thompson) *Rhythms of the Game: The Link between Music and Athletic Performance,* Hal Leonard, 2011.

Sources

Periodicals

Atlanta Journal and Atlanta Constitution, October 26, 1996, p. E4.

Christian Science Monitor, October 18, 1996, p. 13.

Newsday, April 4, 1993, p. 13; September 22, 2009, p. B2.

New York Times, March 24, 1992, p. B11; September 21, 1995, p. B15; April 25, 2015.

USA Today, May 29, 1996, p. 4C; September 22, 2008, p. C6.

Wall Street Journal, March 14, 2011, p. A26; February 17, 2015; April 23, 2015.

Online

"Bernie Williams," Baseball-Reference.com, http://www.baseball-reference.com/players/w/willibe02.shtml (accessed July 2, 2015).

Bernie Williams, http://www.bernie51.com/ (accessed July 3, 2015).

—Stephen Meyer

Goodwill Zwelithini

1948—

Tribal and political leader

Goodwill Zwelithini is the eighth king of the Zulus, the largest indigenous tribe in the modern nation of South Africa. He is a direct descendent of Shaka kaSenzangakhona, better known as Shaka Zulu, who founded the modern Zulu empire in the early 19th century. Although Zwelithini has no direct influence on government policy in South Africa, he remains a revered figure within contemporary Zulu society, and his opinions on policy and other matters of state exert a profound influence on his followers. He is also among the most polarizing figures in South African politics, largely because of his controversial comments concerning immigrant workers and homosexuality, as well as what some perceive to be his extravagant standard of living. Indeed, the Zulu king and his extensive family inhabit a royal compound that comprises several palaces and a number of additional residences, all of which are maintained with public funds. Although he is a Christian, Zwelithini observes many of the rituals associated with the traditional indigenous religious practices of South Africa, including polygamy. As of 2015, Zwelithini had six wives, who collectively had borne him more than two dozen children.

Zwelithini, Goodwill, photograph. Stringer/AFP/Getty Images.

Gradually Asserted His Authority

Goodwill Zwelithini kaBhekuzulu was born on July 14, 1948, in Nongoma, Natal, South Africa. He is the son of Cyprian Bhekuzulu Nyangayezizwe kaSolomon, the seventh king of the Zulus, and his second wife, Queen Thomo Jezangani Ndwandwe. He received his early education at the Bhekezulu College of Chiefs and later studied under a private tutor at his father's royal palace. Throughout his childhood, Zwelithini also received combat training using knobkerrie sticks, the traditional weapon of Zulu warriors. His education came to an abrupt end in 1968, after his father's death from acute alcoholism put him in a position to inherit the Zulu throne. He initially ruled under the supervision of an uncle, who had been appointed regent over the kingdom. In 1969 Zwelithini married his first wife, Queen Sibongile Dlamini, with whom he would have five children. Two years later he was crowned eighth king of the Zulus. The official ceremony took place on December 3, 1971, with 20,000 Zulu citizens in attendance.

At a Glance . . .

Born Goodwill Zwelithini kaBhekuzulu on July 14, 1948, in Nongoma, Natal, South Africa; son of King Cyprian Bhekuzulu Nyangayezizwe kaSolomon and Queen Thomo Jezangani Ndwandwe; married Sibongile Winifred Dlamini, 1969; married Buthle MaMathe, 1974; married Mantfombi Dlamini, 1977; married Thandekile Ndlovu, 1988; married Nompumelelo Mchiza, 1992; married Zola Zelusiwe Mafu, 2014; children: 28.

Career: Eighth monarch of the Zulus, 1971—.

Addresses: *Home*—Nongoma, Natal, South Africa.

During the early part of his reign, Zwelithini had little involvement in the public affairs of KwaZulu, a semiautonomous territory that was given limited political rights by South Africa's apartheid government. Responsibility for governance over KwaZulu was traditionally granted to the prime minister, a position held by Zwelithini's uncle, Zulu chief Mangosuthu Buthelezi. Throughout the early 1970s, Zwelithini performed his ceremonial duties as the Zulu monarch while devoting most of his energies to farming the lands surrounding his palace. The Zulu king soon earned a reputation for raising exceptional livestock, becoming a specialist in the breeding of Nguni cattle. In 1974 Zwelithini married Buthle MaMathe, who would eventually give birth to eight children.

By the mid-1970s, the relationship between Zwelithini and Buthelezi had become strained, as the king attempted to exert greater influence over KwaZulu policy. In 1975, amid allegations that Zwelithini was overstepping his authority by interfering in political affairs, Buthelezi imposed more rigorous restrictions over his nephew's travel outside of Nongoma. That same year, as opposition to apartheid intensified throughout South Africa, Buthelezi launched the Inkatha National Cultural Liberation Movement, a political party dedicated to dismantling the country's racist regime; the movement subsequently became known as the Inkatha Freedom Party. As Buthelezi became increasingly involved in the national resistance movement, Zwelithini emerged as one of the prime minister's most outspoken critics, at one point contending that his uncle's administration was merely a puppet of the apartheid regime. In 1979

Buthelezi publicly accused Zwelithini of conspiring against his own government, asserting that the Zulu king was openly inciting violent unrest among the Zulu people and that he had even created his own political party, Inala, with the aim of unseating the prime minister. Although an ensuing investigation found no evidence of wrongdoing on the part of Zwelithini, the king's influence over the KwaZulu government was further curtailed, and he was prohibited from conducting interviews without the supervision of Buthelezi's justice minister.

Despite these animosities, Zwelithini and his uncle managed to mend their political rift during the early 1980s, as antigovernment conflict continued to spread throughout South Africa. As liberation groups such as the African National Congress (ANC) and the United Democratic Front assumed increasingly prominent roles in the fight against apartheid, Zwelithini strengthened his ties with the Inkatha Party, believing it was more closely aligned with KwaZulu interests than the other movements. By the end of the decade, Zwelithini had alienated ANC leaders with his inflammatory rhetoric, attracting particularly harsh criticism for his opposition to international economic sanctions against South Africa. During the early 1990s, as the fall of the apartheid regime appeared imminent, Zwelithini began to promote the cause of KwaZulu independence while suggesting that the ANC was a foreign influence with no legal right to political power in South Africa.

Formed a New Political Alliance

In 1994, as the country prepared to conduct its first free elections in decades, Zwelithini threatened to disrupt the democratic process if his demands for KwaZulu self-determination were not met. Zwelithini understood that with a total population of roughly 10 million, the Zulu people represented South Africa's single largest ethnic group, making its allegiance essential to a stable democratic government in the postapartheid era. In April of that year, on the eve of the historic election, ANC presidential candidate Nelson Mandela embarked on an extensive tour of Natal Province, openly praising Zwelithini's leadership in an effort to court the Zulu vote. During the campaign Mandela also promised to grant greater powers to the Zulu monarch, while also giving Zwelithini a direct voice in creating the new South African constitution. After Mandela won the presidency, Zwelithini strengthened his political alliance with the newly elected leader, causing a new rift in his relationship with his uncle. Buthelezi was ultimately appeased, however, after Mandela appointed him minister of home affairs in the new government.

Zwelithini continued to enjoy considerable political influence over South African affairs in the ensuing decades. After Zulu politician Jacob Zuma was elected as president in 2009, however, Zwelithini became increasingly vocal in his demands for greater autonomy for KwaZulu. He also became the subject of intense criticism for his incendiary public comments. In March of 2015, Zwelithini came under fire when he compared foreign workers to "head lice" in a speech. Waves of violence aimed at immigrant workers ensued after the address, and the Zulu king was compelled to clarify his

comments, insisting that his words had been misconstrued. Despite this attempt at conciliation, Zwelithini fanned the flames of dissent further at an April of 2015 demonstration in Durban, when he told a large crowd of Zulu followers that they would have reduced South Africa to "ashes" had he truly ordered them to wage war against immigrants. In the wake of these remarks, which elicited cheers from Zulu nationalists, some political observers began to speculate that King Zwelithini might be actively seeking to stoke civil unrest in an effort to seize greater power within the South African government. "This man is laying the basis for a serious contestation that South Africa is going to have," Nomboniso Gasa, a legal scholar at the University of Cape Town, told Ofeibea Quist-Arcton of National Public Radio. "He is pushing the boundaries. He has started with the most vulnerable—those who always suffer prejudice—but he's also saying to government and everybody else who is opposed to his absolute authority as a Zulu king: 'You watch it.'"

Sources

Periodicals

Cape Times (Cape Town, South Africa), September 25, 2012, p. 4.
Irish Times, April 21, 2015, p. 11.
Los Angeles Times, April 17, 1994, p. 4.
Times (London), July 13, 1993; April 10, 1994; September 21, 1994.

Online

Goweditswe, Kome, "Goodwill Zwelithini Cancels Visit," allAfrica.com, April 29, 2015, http://allafrica.com/stories/201504300326.html (accessed July 1, 2015).
"King Goodwill Zwelithini Commits Himself to Development," allAfrica.com, August 30, 2011, http://allafrica.com/stories/201108310112.html (accessed July 1, 2015).
"King Goodwill Zwelithini," South African History Online, http://www.sahistory.org.za/people/king-goodwill-zwelithini (accessed July 1, 2015).
Mdletshe, Canaan, "Gays Are Rotten, Says Zulu King," Times Live, January 23, 2012, http://www.timeslive.co.za/local/2012/01/23/gays-are-rotten-says-zulu-king (accessed July 1, 2015).
Oliphant, Nathi, "King Slams Officials over Palace Funding," IOL News, September 16, 2012, http://www.iol.co.za/news/south-africa/kwazulu-natal/king-slams-officials-over-palace-funding-1.1383960#.VZSQE_lViko (accessed July 1, 2015).
Paton, Callum, "King of the Zulus Goodwill Zwelithini Demands Compensation from British Royal Family," International Business Times, June 25, 2015, http://www.ibtimes.co.uk/south-africa-king-zulus-goodwill-zwelithini-demands-compensation-royal-family-1507776 (accessed July 1, 2015).
Quist-Arcton, Ofeibea, "South Africa's Xenophobic Attacks 'Vile,' Says Zulu King Accused of Inciting Them," National Public Radio, April 26, 2015, http://www.npr.org/2015/04/26/402400958/south-africas-xenophobic-attacks-vile-says-zulu-king-accused-of-inciting-them (accessed July 1, 2015).
"The Wives of a Zulu King," eNews Channel Africa, July 26, 2014, http://www.enca.com/wives-zulu-king (accessed July 2, 2015).
"Zulu Nationalism, Sparked by King, Confronts Modern South Africa," Voice of America, April 24, 2015, http://www.voanews.com/content/reu-zulu-nationalism-king-modern-south-africa/2733088.html (accessed July 1, 2015).

—Stephen Meyer

Cumulative Nationality Index

Volume numbers appear in **bold**

American

Aaliyah **30**
Aaron, Hank **5**
Aaron, Quinton **82**
Abbott, Robert Sengstacke **27**
Abdi, Barkhad **119**
Abdirahman, Abdi **126**
Abdul-Jabbar, Kareem **8**
Abdullah, Kazem **97**
Abdur-Rahim, Shareef **28**
Abele, Julian **55**
Abercrumbie, P. Eric **95**
Abernathy, Ralph David **1**
Aberra, Amsale **67**
Abraham, Kyle **116**
Abu-Jamal, Mumia **15**
Ace, Johnny **36**
Aces, The **117**
Ackerman, Arlene **108**
Acklin, Barbara Jean **107**
Adams, Alma **127**
Adams, Eula L. **39, 120**
Adams, Floyd, Jr. **12, 122**
Adams, Jenoyne **60**
Adams, Johnny **39**
Adams, Leslie **39**
Adams, Oleta **18**
Adams, Osceola Macarthy **31**
Adams, Sheila J. **25**
Adams, Yolanda **17, 67**
Adams-Campbell, Lucille L. **60**
Adams Earley, Charity **13, 34**
Adams-Ender, Clara **40**
Adderley, Julian "Cannonball" **30**
Adderley, Nat **29**
Adebimpe, Tunde **75**
Adegbile, Debo P. **119**
Adkins, Rod **41**
Adkins, Rutherford H. **21**
Adkins, Terry **122**
Adu, Freddy **67**
Aduba, Uzo **122**
Agyeman, Jaramogi Abebe **10, 63**
Ailey, Alvin **8**
Akil, Mara Brock **60, 82**
Akinmusire, Ambrose **103**
Akon **68**
Al-Amin, Jamil Abdullah **6**
Albert, Octavia V. R. **100**
Albright, Gerald **23**
Alcorn, George Edward, Jr. **59**
Aldridge, Ira **99**
Aldridge, LaMarcus **125**

Alert, Kool DJ Red **33**
Alexander, Archie Alphonso **14**
Alexander, Clifford **26**
Alexander, Elizabeth **75**
Alexander, Joseph L. **95**
Alexander, Joyce London **18**
Alexander, Khandi **43**
Alexander, Kwame **98**
Alexander, Margaret Walker **22**
Alexander, Michelle **98**
Alexander, Sadie Tanner Mossell **22**
Alexander, Shaun **58**
Ali, Hana Yasmeen **52**
Ali, Laila **27, 63**
Ali, Mahershala **122**
Ali, Muhammad **2, 16, 52**
Ali, Rashied **79**
Ali, Russlynn H. **92**
Ali, Tatyana **73**
Allain, Stephanie **49**
Allen, Betty **83**
Allen, Byron **3, 24, 97**
Allen, Claude **68**
Allen, Debbie **13, 42**
Allen, Dick **85**
Allen, Ethel D. **13**
Allen, Eugene **79**
Allen, Gori **92**
Allen, Larry **109**
Allen, Lucy **85**
Allen, Macon Bolling **104**
Allen, Marcus **20**
Allen, Ray **82**
Allen, Robert L. **38**
Allen, Samuel W. **38**
Allen, Tina **22, 75**
Allen, Will **74**
Allen-Buillard, Melba **55**
Allison, Luther **111**
Alonso, Laz **87**
Als, Hilton **105**
Alston, Charles **33**
Altidore, Jozy **109**
Amaker, Norman **63**
Amaker, Tommy **62**
Amaki, Amalia **76**
Amerie **52**
Ames, Wilmer **27**
Ammons, Albert **112**
Ammons, Gene **112**
Ammons, James H. **81**
Amos, Emma **63**
Amos, John **8, 62**

Amos, Wally **9**
Amy, Curtis **114**
Anderson, Anthony **51, 77**
Anderson, Carl **48**
Anderson, Charles Edward **37**
Anderson, Eddie "Rochester" **30**
Anderson, Elmer **25**
Anderson, Ezzrett **95**
Anderson, Fred **87**
Anderson, Ivie **126**
Anderson, Jamal **22**
Anderson, Lauren **72**
Anderson, Maceo **111**
Anderson, Marcia **115**
Anderson, Marian **2, 33**
Anderson, Michael P. **40**
Anderson, Mike **63**
Anderson, Norman B. **45**
Anderson, Reuben V. **81**
Anderson, T. J. **119**
Anderson, William G(ilchrist) **57**
Andrews, Benny **22, 59**
Andrews, Bert **13**
Andrews, Inez **108**
Andrews, Raymond **4**
Andrews, Tina **74**
Angelou, Maya **1, 15, 122**
Ansa, Tina McElroy **14**
Anthony, Carmelo **46, 94**
Anthony, La La **122**
Anthony, Wendell **25**
apl.de.ap **84**
Aplin-Brownlee, Vivian **96**
Appiah, Kwame Anthony **67, 101**
Archer, Dennis **7, 36**
Archer, Lee, Jr. **79**
Archibald, Tiny **90**
Archie-Hudson, Marguerite **44**
Ardoin, Alphonse **65**
Arenas, Gilbert **84**
Arkadie, Kevin **17**
Armstrong, Govind **81**
Armstrong, Henry **104**
Armstrong, Louis **2**
Armstrong, Robb **15**
Armstrong, Vanessa Bell **24**
Arnez J **53**
Arnold, Billy Boy **112**
Arnold, Kokomo **116**
Arnold, Tichina **63**
Arnwine, Barbara **28**
Arrington, Richard **24, 100**
Arroyo, Martina **30**
Artest, Ron **52**

Asante, Molefi Kete **3**
A$AP Rocky **109**
Ashanti **37, 96**
Ashe, Arthur **1, 18**
Ashford, Calvin, Jr. **74**
Ashford, Emmett **22**
Ashford, Evelyn **63**
Ashford, Nickolas **21, 97**
Ashley & JaQuavis **107**
Ashley-Ward, Amelia **23**
Ashong, Derrick **86**
Asim, Jabari **71**
Asomugha, Nnamdi **100**
Atkins, Cholly **40**
Atkins, Erica **34**
Atkins, Juan **50**
Atkins, Russell **45**
Atkins, Tina **34**
Atlantic Starr **122**
Attaway, William **102**
Aubert, Alvin **41**
Aubespin, Mervin **95**
Augusta, Alexander T. **111**
Auguste, Donna **29**
Austin, Bobby W. **95**
Austin, Gloria **63**
Austin, Jim **63**
Austin, Junius C. **44**
Austin, Lloyd **101**
Austin, Lovie **40**
Austin, Patti **24**
Austin, Wanda M. **94**
Autrey, Wesley **68**
Avant, Clarence **19, 86**
Avery, James **118**
Avant, Nicole A. **90**
Avery, Byllye Y. **66**
Ayers, Roy **16**
Ayler, Albert **104**
Babatunde, Obba **35**
Babyface **10, 31, 82**
Bacon-Bercey, June **38**
Badu, Erykah **22, 114**
Bahati, Wambui **60**
Bailey, Buster **38**
Bailey, Chauncey **68**
Bailey, Clyde **45**
Bailey, DeFord **33**
Bailey, Pearl **14**
Bailey, Philip **63**
Bailey, Radcliffe **19**
Bailey, Xenobia **11**
Baines, Harold **32**
Baiocchi, Regina Harris **41**

Baisden, Michael 25, 66
Baker, Anita 21, 48
Baker, Augusta 38
Baker, Delbert W. 110
Baker, Dusty 8, 43, 72, 110
Baker, Ella 5
Baker, Gwendolyn Calvert 9
Baker, Houston A., Jr. 6
Baker, Josephine 3
Baker, LaVern 26
Baker, Matt 76
Baker, Maxine B. 28
Baker, Mickey 95
Baker, Thurbert 22
Baker, Vernon Joseph 65, 87
Bakewell, Danny 99
Baldwin, Cynthia 74, 107
Baldwin, James 1
Ballance, Frank W. 41
Ballard, Allen Butler, Jr. 40
Ballard, Florence 112
Ballard, Hank 41
Ballard, John 95
Baltimore, Richard Lewis, III 71
Bambaataa, Afrika 34
Bambara, Toni Cade 10
Bandele, Asha 36
Banks, Azealia 107
Banks, Ernie 33, 126
Banks, Jeffrey 17
Banks, Lloyd 113
Banks, Michelle 59
Banks, Paula A. 68
Banks, Tyra 11, 50
Banks, William 11
Banneker, Benjamin 93
Banner, David 55
Bannister, Edward Mitchell 88
Baquet, Dean 63, 121
Baraka, Amiri 1, 38, 118
Baraka, Ras J. 121
Baraka, Sho 109
Barbee, Lloyd Augustus 71
Barber, Ronde 41
Barber, Tiki 57, 107
Barboza, Anthony 10
Barclay, Paris 37, 94
Barden, Donald H. 9, 20, 89
Bar-Kays, The 118
Barker, Danny 32
Barkley, Charles 5, 66
Barksdale, Don 103
Barlow, Roosevelt 49
Barnes, Ernie 16, 78
Barnes, Katreese 97
Barnes, Melody 75
Barnes, Roosevelt "Booba" 33
Barnes, Steven 54
Barnett, Amy Du Bois 46
Barnett, Etta Moten 56
Barnett, Herman 112
Barnett, Marguerite 46
Barney, Lem 26
Barnhill, David 30
Barrax, Gerald William 45
Barrett, Andrew C. 12
Barrett, Jacquelyn 28
Barrino, Fantasia 53, 94
Barron, Kenny 128
Barrow, Willie T. 85, 128
Barry, Marion, Jr. 7, 44, 125
Barthé, Earl 78
Barthe, Richmond 15

Basie, Count 23
Baskett, James 102
Basquiat, Jean-Michel 5
Bass, Charlotta Spears 40
Bass, Fontella 104, 109
Bass, Karen 70
Bassett, Angela 6, 23, 62
Bassey, Offiong 119
Baszile, Jennifer 79
Batch, Charlie 120
Bates, Daisy 13
Bates, Karen Grigsby 40
Bates, Peg Leg 14
Bath, Patricia E. 37
Batiste, Alvin 66
Batiste, Jonathan 108
Batiste, Lionel 105
Battle, Kathleen 70
Batts, Anthony 128
Baugh, David 23
Baylor, Don 6
Baylor, Elgin 93
Baylor, Helen 36
Beach, Michael 26, 120
Beal, Bernard B. 46
Beals, Jennifer 12
Beals, Melba Pattillo 15, 94
Beard, Matthew 120
Bearden, Romare 2, 50
Beasley, Jamar 29
Beasley, Phoebe 34
Beatty, Joyce 117
Beatty, Talley 35
Beaty, Zelmo 115
Beauvais, Garcelle 29, 95
Bechet, Sidney 18
Beckford, Tyson 11, 68
Beckham, Barry 41
Beckwith, Naomi 101
Becton, Julius W., Jr. 110
Belafonte, Harry 4, 65
Belgrave, Cynthia 75
Belgrave, Marcus 77
Bell, Carey 114
Bell, Carl C. 111
Bell, Darrin 77
Bell, Derrick 6, 98
Bell, James "Cool Papa" 36
Bell, James A. 50
Bell, James Madison 40
Bell, LeRoy 98
Bell, Michael 40
Bell, Robert Mack 22
Bell, Thom 112
Bell, W. Kamau 107
Bell, William A., Sr. 122
Bellamy, Bill 12
Bellamy, Terry 58
Bellamy, Walt 119
Belle, Albert 10
Belle, Regina 1, 51
Belton, Sharon Sayles 9, 16
Benberry, Cuesta 65
Benét, Eric 28, 77
Benham, Robert 78
Ben-Israel, Ben Ami 11
Benjamin, Andre 45
Benjamin, Regina 20, 75
Benjamin, Steve 98
Benjamin, Tritobia Hayes 53
Bennett, Estelle 77
Bennett, George Harold "Hal" 45
Bennett, Gwendolyn B. 59

Bennett, Lerone, Jr. 5, 84
Bennett, Richard 97
Benson, Angela 34
Benson, Obie 96
Bentley, Lamont 53
Benton, Brook 121
Berrien, Jacqueline A. 93
Berry, Edwin C. 81
Berry, Eric 125
Berry, Halle 4, 19, 57, 91
Berry, Bertice 8, 55
Berry, Chuck 29
Berry, Fred "Rerun" 48
Berry, Mary Frances 7
Berry, Moses 84
Berry, Theodore 31
Berrysmith, Don Reginald 49
Bethune, Mary McLeod 4
Betsch, MaVynee 28
Bettis, Jerome 64
Betts, Keter 85
Betts, R. Dwayne 86
Bevel, James L. 75
Beverly, Frankie 25
Bey, Yasiin 30, 96
Beyoncé 39, 70, 105
Bibb, Eric 49, 123
Bibb, Henry and Mary 54
Bickerstaff, Bernie 21
Big Daddy Kane 79
Big Freedia 128
Big L 120
Big Maybelle 117
Big Sean 96
Biggers, John 20, 33
Biggers, Sanford 62
Bilal 101
Billops, Camille 82
Billy Ward and the Dominoes 105
bin Wahad, Dhoruba 85
Bing, Dave 3, 59, 78
Bingham, Howard 96
Birch, Adolpho A., Jr. 85
Birch, Glynn R. 61
Birdman 110
Birdsong, Cindy 113
Bishop, Sanford D., Jr. 24, 111
Bishop, Stephen 95
Bivins, Michael 72
Blacc, Aloe 119
Black, Albert 51
Black, Barry C. 47
Black, Joe 75
Black, Keith Lanier 18, 84
Black Thought 63
Blackburn, Robert 28
Blackman, Toni 86
Blackmon, Brenda 58
Blackshear, Leonard 52
Blackwell, David 79
Blackwell, Gloria 127
Blackwell, Kenneth, Sr. 61
Blackwell, Otis 98
Blackwell, Robert D., Sr. 52
Blackwell, Unita 17
Blacque, Taurean 58
Blade, Brian 88
Blair, Jayson 50
Blair, Paul 36
Blake, Asha 26
Blake, Charles E. 82
Blake, Eubie 29
Blake, James 43

Blake, John, Jr. 123
Blakely, Delois N. 122
Blakely, Edward J. 88
Blakey, Art 37
Blanchard, Terence 43
Blanco, Mykki 106
Bland, Bobby 36, 113
Bland, Edward 111
Bland, Eleanor Taylor 39
Blanks, Billy 22
Blanks, Deborah K. 69
Blanton, Dain 29
Blanton, Jimmy 108
Blassingame, John Wesley 40
Blaylock, Ronald 86
Blayton, Jesse B., Sr. 55
Bleu, Corbin 65
Blige, Mary J. 20, 34, 60, 97
Blind Boys of Alabama, The 99
Blitz the Ambassador 115
Blockson, Charles L. 42
Bloomer, George 86
Blow, Charles M. 73
Blow, Kurtis 31, 122
Blue, Vida 122
Bluford, Guy 2, 35
Bluitt, Juliann S. 14
B.o.B. 91
Bobb, Robert C. 83
Bobo, Lawrence 60
Bogle, Donald 34
Bogues, Tyrone "Muggsy" 56
Bolden, Buddy 39
Bolden, Charles Frank, Jr. 7, 78
Bolden, Frank E. 44
Bolden, Tonya 32
Bolin, Jane 22, 59
Bolton, Terrell D. 25
Bolton-Holifield, Ruthie 28
Bond, Beverly 53
Bond, J. Max, Jr. 76
Bond, Julian 2, 35, 106
Bonds, Barry 6, 34, 63, 99
Bonds, Bobby 43
Bonds, Margaret 39
Bonet, Lisa 58
Bonner, Leroy 113
Bonney, Tabi 98
Bontemps, Arna 8
Booker, Cory Anthony 68
Booker, Simeon 23
Boozer, Bob 103
Borders, James 9
Borders, William Holmes 94
Boseman, Chadwick 111
Bosh, Chris 85
Bosley, Freeman, Jr. 7
Bostic, Earl 121
Bostic, Joe 95
Boston, Kelvin E. 25
Boston, Lloyd 24
Boulware, Harold R. 109
Bow Wow 35
Bowe, Riddick 6, 107
Bowen, John W. E., Sr. 89
Bowen, Ruth 83
Bowles, Cephas 127
Bowles, Todd 128
Bowman, Bertie 71
Bowser, Yvette Lee 17
Boyd, Edward 70
Boyd, Gerald M. 32, 59
Boyd, Gwendolyn 49

Boyd, John W., Jr. 20, 72
Boyd, Melba Joyce 86
Boyd, T. B., III 6
Boykin, Keith 14
Boykin, Otis 92
Boykin, Phillip 102
Boyz II Men 82
Bozella, Dewey 97
Bradford, Alex 121
Bradford, Mark 89
Bradley, Adam 101
Bradley, Charles 126
Bradley, David Henry, Jr. 39
Bradley, Ed 2, 59
Bradley, J. Robert 65
Bradley, Jennette B. 40
Bradley, Thomas 2, 20
Bradshaw, Tiny 102
Brady, St. Elmo 107
Brady, Wayne 32, 71
Brae, C. Michael 61
Braithwaite, William Stanley 52
Bramlett, Joseph 91
Branch, William Blackwell 39
Brand, Elton 31
Brandon, Barbara 3
Brandon, Terrell 16
Brandy 14, 34, 72
Branham, George, III 50
Branson, Herman 87
Brashear, Carl 29
Brashear, Donald 39
Braugher, Andre 13, 58, 91
Braun, Carol Moseley 4, 42
Brawley, Benjamin 44
Braxton, Anthony 128
Braxton, Brad 77
Braxton, Toni 15, 61, 91
Brazier, Arthur M. 115
Brazile, Donna 25, 70
Brewer, Rosalind 100
Brewster, W. Herbert 128
Bridges, Leon 126
Bridges, Ruby 77
Bridges, Sheila 36
Bridges, Todd 37
Bridgewater, Dee Dee 32, 92
Bridgforth, Glinda 36
Briggs, Curtis 84
Brim, John 117
Brimm, Charles E. 105
Brimmer, Andrew 2, 48, 106
Briscoe, Connie 15
Briscoe, Marlin 37
Britt, Donna 28
Broadbent, Hydeia 36
Brock, Lou 18
Brock, Roslyn McCallister 86
Bromery, Randolph Wilson 85
Broner, Adrien 109
Bronner, Nathaniel H., Sr. 32
Brooke, Edward W. 8, 88, 126
Brookins, Hamel Hartford 102
Brooks, Aaron 33
Brooks, Avery 9, 98
Brooks, Danielle 119
Brooks, Derrick 43, 119
Brooks, Golden 62
Brooks, Gwendolyn 1, 28
Brooks, Hadda 40
Brooks, Mehcad 62
Brooks, Roy 125
Brooks, Tyrone 59

Broonzy, Big Bill 82
Brower, William 49
Brown, Aja 115
Brown, Alvin 96
Brown, Angela M. 54
Brown, Anne 76
Brown, Anthony G. 72
Brown, Antron 85
Brown, Bobby 58, 124
Brown, Byrd 49
Brown, Byron W. 72
Brown, Cecil M. 46
Brown, Charles 23
Brown, Charlotte Hawkins 106
Brown, Chris 74, 109
Brown, Chuck 78, 102
Brown, Clarence Gatemouth 59
Brown, Claude 38
Brown, Clifford 86
Brown, Cora 33
Brown, Corrine 24, 90
Brown, Cupcake 63
Brown, Donald 19
Brown, Eddie C. 35
Brown, Elaine 8
Brown, Ernest 80
Brown, Erroll M. 23
Brown, Foxy 25
Brown, Frederick J. 102
Brown, George Leslie 62
Brown, Hallie Quinn 100
Brown, Homer S. 47
Brown, James 15, 60
Brown, James 22
Brown, Jamie Foster 91
Brown, Janice Rogers 43
Brown, Jason 125
Brown, Jerry 117
Brown, Jesse 6, 41
Brown, Jesse Leroy 31
Brown, Jim 11, 95
Brown, Joe 29
Brown, Joyce F. 25
Brown, Kwame R. 91
Brown, Lee P. 1, 24, 109
Brown, Les 5
Brown, Lloyd Louis 42
Brown, Marie Dutton 12
Brown, Mike 77, 107
Brown, Nappy 73
Brown, Oliver Leon 94
Brown, Oscar, Jr. 53
Brown, Patrick "Sleepy" 50
Brown, Raymond 102
Brown, Robert 65
Brown, Ron 5
Brown, Ronald K. 91
Brown, Ruth 90
Brown, Sterling Allen 10, 64
Brown, Tony 3
Brown, Uzee 42
Brown, Vivian 27
Brown, Warren 61
Brown, Wesley 23
Brown, Wesley A. 102
Brown, Willa 40
Brown, Willard 36
Brown, William Wells 99
Brown, Willie 7, 85
Brown, Zora Kramer 12
Browne, Roscoe Lee 66
Brownlee, Lawrence 88
Broyard, Anatole 68

Broyard, Bliss 68
Bruce, Blanche Kelso 33
Bruce, Bruce 56
Bruce, Isaac 26
Brunson, Dorothy 1, 87
Bryan, Ashley 41, 104
Bryant, Cullen 81
Bryant, Dez 116
Bryant, Jamal 128
Bryant, John 26
Bryant, John R. 45
Bryant, Kimberly 127
Bryant, Kobe 15, 31, 71, 110
Bryant, Paul 115
Bryant, Ray 95
Bryant, Wayne R. 6
Bryant, William Benson 61
Buchanan, Ray 32
Buckley, Gail Lumet 39
Buckley, Victoria 24
Buckner, Milt 110
Budden, Joe 108
Buery, Richard, Jr. 97
Bullard, Eugene 12
Bullard, Robert D. 121
Bullins, Ed 25, 121
Bullock, Steve 22
Bully-Cummings, Ella 48
Bumbry, Grace 5
Bun B 123
Bunch, Lonnie G., III 91
Bunche, Ralph J. 5
Bunkley, Anita Richmond 39
Burbridge, Kofi 120
Burbridge, Oteil 120
Buress, Hannibal 101
Burgess, John 46
Burgess, Marjorie L. 55
Burke, Clarence, Jr. 112
Burke, Glenn 122
Burke, Selma 16
Burke, Solomon 31, 86
Burke, Yvonne Brathwaite 42
Burkett, Ben 123
Burks, Juanita P. 95
Burks, Mary Fair 40
Burleigh, Henry Thacker 56
Burley, Dan 96
Burnett, Charles 16, 68
Burnim, Mickey L. 48
Burns, Anthony 102
Burns, Eddie 44
Burns, Ursula 60
Burnside, R. L. 56
Burrell, Tom 21, 51
Burris, Chuck 21
Burris, Roland W. 25, 75
Burroughs, Margaret Taylor 9
Burroughs, Nannie Helen 96
Burrows, Stephen 31
Burrus, William Henry "Bill" 45
Burt-Murray, Angela 59
Burton, Bill 96
Burton, LeVar 8
Burwell, Bryan 83
Busby, Jheryl 3, 74
Bush, Charles Vernon 125
Bush, Gordon 82
Bush, Reggie 59, 88
Butler, George, Jr. 70
Butler, Henry 121
Butler, Jerry 26
Butler, Leroy, III 17

Butler, Louis 70
Butler, Octavia 8, 43, 58
Butler, Paul D. 17
Butler, Selena Sloan 98
Butts, Calvin O., III 9, 90
Butts, Cassandra 78
Bynoe, Peter C. B. 40
Bynum, Juanita 31, 71
Byrd, Donald 10
Byrd, Donald 109
Byrd, Eugene 64
Byrd, Marlon 112
Byrd, Michelle 19
Byrd, Robert 11
Cabell, Enos 102
Cables, George 125
Cadillacs 107
Cadoria, Sherian Grace 14
Caesar, Shirley 19
Cage, Byron 53
Cain, Herman 15, 92
Cain, Lorenzo 128
Calabrese, Karyn 89
Caldwell, Benjamin 46
Caldwell, Earl 60
Caldwell, Jim 81
Caldwell, Kirbyjon 55
Calhoun, Lillian Scott 87
Callender, Clive O. 3
Callender, Eugene 119
Callier, Terry 106
Calloway, Blanche 100
Calloway, Cab 14
Cameo 120
Cameron, James 80
Camp, Kimberly 19
Campanella, Roy 25
Campbell, Bebe Moore 6, 24, 59
Campbell, Bill 9, 76
Campbell, Donald J. 66
Campbell, E. Simms 13
Campbell, Earl 104
Campbell, Lucie E. 118
Campbell, Mary Schmidt 43
Campbell, Milt 113
Campbell, Roy, Jr. 118
Campbell-Martin, Tisha 8, 42
Cam'ron 104
Canada, Geoffrey 23
Canady, Alexa 28
Cannon, Katie 10
Cannon, Nick 47, 73
Cannon, Patrick 120
Cannon, Reuben 50
Cara, Irene 77
Carney, William H. 104
Carr, James 117
Carr, Johnnie 69
Carr, Keela 74
Cardozo, Francis L. 33
Carew, Rod 20
Carey, Mariah 32, 53, 69
Cargill, Victoria A. 43
Carlos, John 97
Carmichael, Jerrod 124
Carolina Chocolate Drops 111
Carr, Kurt 56
Carr, Leroy 49
Carroll, Diahann 9
Carroll, L. Natalie 44
Carroll, Rocky 74
Carruthers, George R. 40
Carson, André 69

Carson, Ben 1, 35, 76, 128
Carson, Johnnie 85
Carson, Julia 23, 69
Carson, Lisa Nicole 21
Carter, Anson 24
Carter, Benny 46
Carter, Betty 19
Carter, Butch 27
Carter, Cris 21, 109
Carter, Edward A., Jr. 104
Carter, Herbert E. 108
Carter, Jill P. 110
Carter, Joe 30
Carter, Joye Maureen 41
Carter, Kenneth 53
Carter, Majora 77
Carter, Mandy 11
Carter, Nell 39
Carter, Pamela Lynn 67
Carter, Regina 23
Carter, Robert L. 51, 100
Carter, Ron 104
Carter, Rubin 26, 121
Carter, Stephen L. 4
Carter, Troy 98
Carter, Vince 26
Carter, Warrick L. 27
Cartey, Wilfred 47
Cartiér, Xam Wilson 41
Carver, George Washington 4
Cary, Lorene 3
Cary, Mary Ann Shadd 30
Cash, Rosalind 28
Cash, Swin 59
Cashin, Sheryll 63
CasSelle, Malcolm 11
Castor, Jimmy 100
Catchings, Tamika 43
Cathey, Reg E. 122
Catlett, Elizabeth 2, 120
Catto, Octavius V. 83
Cayton, Horace 26
Cedric the Entertainer 29, 60, 115
Celestin, Josaphat 101
Cenac, Wyatt 94
Chadiha, Jeffri 57
Chalmers, Mario 122
Chamberlain, Wilt 18, 47
Chambers, Julius 3
Chambers, Paul 121
Chambers Brothers, The 116
Chamillionaire 82
Chancler, Ndugu 115
Chandler, Gene 105
Chandler, Tyson 114
Chaney, Don 98
Chaney, John 67
Chantels, The 128
Chanticleer, Raven 91
Chapman, Nathan A., Jr. 21
Chapman, Susan E. 94
Chapman, Tracy 26
Chappell, Emma 18
Chappell, Roy M. 95
Chappelle, Dave 50, 115
Charles, Ezzard 95
Charles, Ray 16, 48
Charleston, Oscar 39
Chase, Debra Martin 49, 96
Chase, John Saunders, Jr. 99
Chase, Leah 57
Chase-Riboud, Barbara 20, 46
Chatard, Peter 44

Chavis, Benjamin 6
Che, Michael 123
Cheadle, Don 19, 52
Checker, Chubby 28
Cheeks, Maurice 47, 106
Chenault, John 40
Chenault, Kenneth 4, 36, 108
Cherry, Deron 40
Cherry, Don 119
Chesnutt, Charles 29
Chestnut, J. L., Jr. 73
Chestnut, Morris 31, 116
Chew, Robert F. 109
Chic 117
Chideya, Farai 14, 61
Chief Keef 112
Childers, Lulu Vere 95
Childress, Alice 15
Childress, Alvin 114
Chiles, Nick 98
Chineworth, Mary Alice 79
Chinn, May Edward 26
Chisholm, Daquan 93
Chisholm, Samuel 32
Chisholm, Shirley 2, 50
Christian, Barbara T. 44
Christian, Jodie 103
Christian, Spencer 15
Christian-Green, Donna M. 17
Christie, Angella 36
Christie, Ron 83
Chuck D 9
Churchwell, Robert, Sr. 76
Ciara 56, 115
Ciara, Barbara 69
Clack, Zoanne 73
Claiborne, Loretta 34
Clarence 13X 126
Clark, Carl 101
Clark, Celeste 15
Clark, Joe 1
Clark, Kenneth B. 5, 52
Clark, Mamie Phipps 79
Clark, Mattie Moss 61
Clark, Patrick 14
Clark, Ray 122
Clark, Septima 7
Clark, Sharón 105
Clark, Sonny 128
Clark, Wahida 107
Clark, Yvonne Young 95
Clark-Cole, Dorinda 66
Clarke, Anna Mac 95
Clarke, Cheryl 32
Clarke, Hope 14
Clarke, John Henrik 20
Clarke, Kenny 27
Clarke, Stanley 115
Clarke, Yvette 92
Clark-Sheard, Karen 22, 114
Clash, Kevin 14, 93
Clay, Bryan 57, 74
Clay, Otis 112
Clay, William Lacy 8
Clay, William Lacy, Jr. 95
Clayton, Constance 1
Clayton, Doctor 120
Clayton, Eva M. 20
Clayton, Gerald 111
Clayton, Mayme Agnew 62
Clayton, Merry 112
Clayton, Xernona 3, 45
Claytor, Helen 14, 52

Cleage, Pearl 17, 64
Cleaver, Eldridge 5
Cleaver, Emanuel 4, 45, 68, 107
Cleaver, Kathleen 29
Clemente, Rosa 74
Clement-Holmes, Linda 94
Clements, George 2
Clemmons, Reginal G. 41
Clemons, Clarence 41
Clemons, Michael "Pinball" 64
Clendenon, Donn 26, 56
Cleveland, James 19
Cliff, Michelle 42
Clifton, Lucille 14, 64, 91
Clifton, Nathaniel "Sweetwater" 47
Clinton, George 9, 93
Clovers, The 104
Clyburn, James E. 21, 71, 118
Clyburn, Mignon 78
C-Murder 99
Coachman, Alice 18, 123
Coasters, The 102
Coates, Dorothy Love 125
Coates, Ta-Nehisi 76
Cobb, Arnett 114
Cobb, Jewel Plummer 42
Cobb, Jimmy 119
Cobb, W. Montague 39
Cobb, William Jelani 59, 121
Cobbs, Bill 101
Cobbs, Price M. 9
Cobbs, Tasha 114
Cobham, Billy 123
Cochran, Johnnie 11, 39, 52
Cockrel, Kenneth V., Jr. 79
Cockrel, Kenneth Vern, Sr. 79
CoCo Brother 93
Cody, Radmilla 99
Cohen, Anthony 15
Cohen, Cathy J. 88
Colbert, Tom 115
Colbert, Virgis William 17
Cole, Cozy 123
Cole, Freddy 128
Cole, J. 97
Cole, Johnnetta B. 5, 43
Cole, Keyshia 63, 107
Cole, Lorraine 48
Cole, Maria 104
Cole, Nat "King" 17
Cole, Natalie 17, 60, 84
Cole, Rebecca 38
Cole, Teju 120
Coleman, Beatrice 120
Coleman, Bessie 9
Coleman, Chad L. 128
Coleman, Donald 24, 62
Coleman, Gary 35, 86
Coleman, George 106
Coleman, James E., Jr. 79
Coleman, Ken 57
Coleman, Leonard S., Jr. 12
Coleman, Mary 46
Coleman, Michael B. 28, 79
Coleman, Denardo 122
Coleman, Ornette 39, 69
Coleman, Ronald S. 110
Coleman, Steve 124
Coleman, Vince 128
Coleman, Wanda 48, 119
Coleman, William F., III 61
Coleman, William T. 76
Colemon, Johnnie 11

Coles, Alice 80
Coles, Honi 128
Colescott, Robert 69
Collette, Buddy 119
Collins, Albert 12
Collins, Barbara-Rose 7, 87
Collins, Bootsy 31
Collins, Cardiss 10, 80, 120
Collins, Janet 33, 64
Collins, Jason 111
Collins, Lyn 53
Collins, Marva 3, 71
Collins, Patricia Hill 67
Collins, Paul 61
Colston, Hal 72
Colter, Cyrus J. 36
Coltrane, Alice 70
Coltrane, John 19
Coltrane, Ravi 71
Combs, Sean 17, 43, 92
Comer, James P. 6
Common 31, 63, 98
Compton-Rock, Malaak 86
Cone, James H. 3, 82
Coney, PonJola 48
Connerly, Ward 14
Conrad, Barbara Smith 90
Conrad, Cecilia A. 94
Consolers, The 125
Contee, Cheryl 88
Contours, The 109
Conyers, John, Jr. 4, 45, 111
Conyers, Monica 85
Conyers, Nathan G. 24
Coogler, Ryan 114
Cook, Charles "Doc" 44
Cook, Junior 126
Cook, (Will) Mercer 40
Cook, Samuel DuBois 14
Cook, Suzan D. Johnson 22
Cook, Toni 23
Cook, Will Marion 40
Cooke, Marcia 60
Cooke, Marvel 31
Cooke, Sam 17
Cook-Parrish, Mary Virginia 95
Coolio 103
Cooper, Andrew W. 36
Cooper, Andy "Lefty" 63
Cooper, Anna Julia 20
Cooper, Barry 33
Cooper, Charles "Chuck" 47
Cooper, Chuck 75
Cooper, Edward S. 6
Cooper, Evern 40
Cooper, Helene 74
Cooper, J. California 12, 85, 125
Cooper, Lisa 73
Cooper, Margaret J. 46
Cooper, Michael 31
Cooper, Tarzan 96
Cooper Cafritz, Peggy 43
Cooper-Dyke, Cynthia 17, 89
Copeland, Johnny 110
Copeland, Michael 47
Copeland, Misty 125
Copeland, Shemekia 110
Coppola, Imani Francesca 82
Corbi, Lana 42
Corbin, Tyrone 126
Corley, Tony 62
Cornelius, Don 4, 100
Cornish, Sam 50

Cornwell, Edward E., III 70
Correia, De'Jaun 93
Cortez, Jayne 43, 109
Corthron, Kia 43
Cortor, Eldzier 42
Cosby, Bill 7, 26, 59, 125
Cosby, Camille 14, 80
Cose, Ellis 5, 50, 118
Cosey, Pete 103
Cotter, Joseph Seamon, Sr. 40
Cotton, James 123
Cottrell, Comer 11
Counce, Curtis 127
Council, LaVerne 94
Counter, S. Allen 74
Cousin, Ertharin 115
Cousins, DeMarcus 108
Covay, Don 127
Cowans, Adger W. 20
Cowboy Troy 54
Cox, Bryan 83
Cox, Donald Lee 93
Cox, Elbert Frank 111
Cox, Ida 42
Cox, Joseph Mason Andrew 51
Cox, Laverne 122
Cox, Renée 67
Cox, William E. 68
Craig, Carl 31, 71
Craig-Jones, Ellen Walker 44
Crawford, Carl 90
Crawford, Hank 77
Crawford, Randy 19
Cray, Robert 30
Creagh, Milton 27
Crennel, Romeo 54, 107
Crenshaw, Kimberlé Williams 88
Crew, Rudy 16, 113
Crew, Spencer R. 55
Crews, Terry 123
Crichlow, Ernest 75
Crisp, Coco 109
Criss, Sonny 128
Crite, Allan Rohan 29
Croal, N'Gai 76
Crocker, Frankie 29
Crockett, George W., Jr. 10, 64
Cromartie, Antonio 115
Croom, Sylvester 50
Cross, Dolores E. 23
Crosthwait, David 93
Crothers, Scatman 19
Crouch, Andraé 27, 115, 126
Crouch, Hubert 95
Crouch, Stanley 11, 87
Crowder, Henry 16
Crowdy, William Saunders 109
Crudup, Arthur 115
Crum, George 101
Crump, Steven 96
Crumpler, Rebecca Lee 89
Crusaders, The 116
Cruse, Harold 54
Crutchfield, James N. 55
Cruz, Victor 107
Cuffe, Paul 98
Cullen, Countee 8
Cullers, Vincent T. 49
Culp, Curley 110
Culpepper, Daunte 32, 85
Cummings, Elijah E. 24, 102
Cuney, William Waring 44
Cunningham, Evelyn 23, 85

Cunningham, Randall 23
Curren$y 114
Currie, Betty 21
Currie, Ulysses 73
Curry, Dell 126
Curry, George E. 23
Curry, Mark 17
Curry, Michael 85
Curry, Stephen 110
Curson, Ted 108
Curtis, Christopher Paul 26, 113
Curtis-Hall, Vondie 17
Da Don, Polow 86
Dabiri, John 93
DaCosta, YaYa 98
Daemyon, Jerald 64
Dailey, Ulysses Grant 87
Dale, Clamma 103
Daly, Marie Maynard 37
Dameron, Tadd 103
Dandridge, Dorothy 3
Dandridge, Ray 36
Dandridge, Raymond Garfield 45
D'Angelo 27, 123
Daniels, Billy 124
Daniels, Lee 36, 76
Daniels, Mel 106
Daniels-Carter, Valerie 23
Danner, Margaret Esse 49
Danquah, Meri Nana Ama 93
Danticat, Edwidge 15, 68, 128
Dantley, Adrian 72
Dara, Olu 35
Darden, Calvin 38
Darden, Christopher 13
Dash, Damon 31, 113
Dash, Darien 29
Dash, Julie 4
Dash, Leon 47
Datcher, Michael 60
Davenport, Cow Cow 115
David, Keith 27
Davidson, Jaye 5
Davidson, Tommy 21
Davis, Allison 12
Davis, Altovise 76
Davis, Angela 5, 114
Davis, Angela J. 88
Davis, Anthony 11
Davis, Anthony 120
Davis, Arthur Paul 41
Davis, Artur 41
Davis, Belva 61
Davis, Ben 115
Davis, Benjamin O., Jr. 2, 43
Davis, Benjamin O., Sr. 4
Davis, Bing 84
Davis, Carl 105
Davis, Charles T. 48
Davis, Chuck 33
Davis, Danny K. 24, 79
Davis, Doris A. 100
Davis, Ed 24
Davis, Eisa 68
Davis, Eric 116
Davis, Ernie 48
Davis, Erroll B., Jr. 57
Davis, Frank Marshall 47
Davis, Gary 41
Davis, George 36
Davis, Gordon J. 76
Davis, Guy 36
Davis, James E. 50

Davis, Mia Amber 94
Davis, Mike 41
Davis, Miles 4
Davis, Milt 74
Davis, Nolan 45
Davis, Ossie 5, 50
Davis, Piper 19
Davis, Ruth 37
Davis, Shani 58, 84
Davis, Terrell 20
Davis, Thulani 61
Davis, Tyrone 54
Davis, Viola 34, 76, 100
Davis, Wade, Jr. 103
Davis, Wild Bill 114
Davis Sisters, The 119
Dawes, Dominique 11, 126
Dawes, Kwame 126
Dawkins, Jimmy 111
Dawkins, Wayne 20
Dawn, Marpessa 75
Dawson, Andre 85
Dawson, Matel "Mat," Jr. 39
Dawson, Michael C. 63
Dawson, Rosario 72
Dawson, William Levi 39
Day, Leon 39
Days, Drew S., III 10
Dazz Band 116
De' Alexander, Quinton 57
De La Soul 119
de Lavallade, Carmen 78
de Passe, Suzanne 25
De Priest, Oscar Stanton 80
De Shields, André 72
De Veaux, Alexis 44
Dean, Fred 98
Dean, Mark E. 35
Dean, Phillip Hayes 122
Deas, Gerald 85
DeBaptiste, George 32
DeBarge, El 89
DeBerry, Lois M. 115
DeCarava, Roy 42, 81
Deconge-Watson, Lovenia 55
Dedeaux, Richard 119
Dee, Merri 55
Dee, Ruby 8, 50, 68, 122
Deezer D 53
DeFrantz, Anita 37
Deggans, Eric 71
DeJongh, John, Jr. 85
DeLaine, Joseph A. 110
Delaney, Beauford 19
Delaney, Joe 76
Delaney, Joseph 30
Delany, Bessie 12
Delany, Martin R. 27
Delany, Sadie 12
Delany, Samuel R., Jr. 9
Delco, Wilhelmina 33
DeLille, Henriette 30
Dells, The 109
Dellums, Ronald 2, 81
DeLoach, Nora 30
Delpit, Lisa 101
Delsarte, Louis 34
Demby, William 51
Dennard, Brazeal 37
Dennis, Gary C. 91
Dent, Richard 97
Dent, Thomas C. 50
DePreist, James 37, 109

DePrince, Michaela 104
DeRozan, DeMar 125
Derülo, Jason 93
DeSanto, Sugar Pie 122
Detroit Emeralds, The 121
DeVard, Jerri 61
DeVaughn, Raheem 91
Devers, Gail 7, 87
Devine, Loretta 24
DeVore-Mitchell, Ophelia 120
Dewitty, Thelma 114
Dial, Thornton 114
Diamond, Lydia R. 101
Dickens, Helen Octavia 14, 64
Dickenson, Vic 38
Dickerson, Debra J. 60
Dickerson, Eric 27, 108
Dickerson, Ernest R. 6, 17
Dickey, Eric Jerome 21, 56
Diddley, Bo 39, 72
Diesel, Vin 29
Diggs, Charles C. 21
Diggs, Taye 25, 63
Diggs-Taylor, Anna 20
Dillard, Godfrey J. 45
Dillon, Leo 103
Dinkins, David 4
Divine, Father 7
Dixie Cups, The 109
Dixon, Bill 87
Dixon, Dean 68
Dixon, Ivan 69
Dixon, Julian C. 24
Dixon, Margaret 14
Dixon, Sharon Pratt 1
Dixon, Sheila 68
Dixon, Willie 4
DJ Clue? 111
DJ Jazzy Jeff 32
DJ Lance Rock 94
DJ Rashad 121
DJ Screw 110
DMX 28, 64
Dobbs, John Wesley 89
Dobbs, Mattiwilda 34
Dobson, Tamara 111
Doby, Lawrence Eugene, Sr. 16, 41
Dodson, Howard, Jr. 7, 52
Dodson, Owen Vincent 38
Dogan, Matthew Winifred 91
Doggett, Bill 124
Dokes, Michael 105
Doley, Harold, Jr. 26
Dollar, Creflo 106
Domingo, Colman 94
Domino, Fats 20
Donald, Arnold 36, 126
Donaldson, Jeff 46
Donegan, Dorothy 19
Dorham, Kenny 113
Dorn, Michael 112
Dorrell, Karl 52
Dorsey, Lee 65
Dorsey, Thomas Andrew 15
Dorsey, Thomas J. 90
Dortch, Thomas W., Jr. 45
Dougherty, Mary Pearl 47
Douglas, Aaron 7
Douglas, Bob 96
Douglas, Buster 127
Douglas, Derek 88
Douglas, Donya 97
Douglas, Emory 89

Douglass, Frederick 87
Dourdan, Gary 37
Dove, Rita 6, 78, 101
Dove, Ulysses 5
Downing, George T. 91
Downing, Will 19
Dr. Dre 10, 14, 30, 116
Drake, Hamid 121
Drake, Michael V. 122
Dramatics, The 106
Draper, Sharon Mills 16, 43
Drew, Alvin, Jr. 67
Drew, Charles Richard 7
Drew, Kenny 123
Drexler, Clyde 4, 61
Drifters, The 121
Driskell, David C. 7
Driver, David E. 11
Driver, Donald 99
Drummond, William J. 40
Du Bois, David Graham 45
Du Bois, W. E. B. 3
du Cille, Michel 74
DuBois, Joshua 88
DuBois, Shirley Graham 21
Ducksworth, Marilyn 12
Dudley, Edward R. 58
Dudley, Sherman H. 117
Due, Patricia Stephens 100
Due, Tananarive 30
Duerson, Dave 93
Duggins, George 64
Duke, Bill 3, 96
Duke, George 21, 113
Dukes, Hazel Nell 56
Dumars, Joe 16, 65, 126
Dumas, Henry 41
Dumpson, James R. 108
Dunbar, Paul Laurence 8
Dunbar-Nelson, Alice Ruth Moore
    44
Duncan, Michael Clarke 26, 104
Duncan, Tim 20, 91
Duncan, Todd 76
Duncanson, Robert S. 127
Dungey, Merrin 62
Dungy, Camille 86
Dungy, Tony 17, 42, 59, 118
Dunham, Katherine 4, 59
Dunlap, Ericka 55
Dunn, Jerry 27
Dunn, Warrick 90
Dunner, Leslie B. 45
Dunnigan, Alice Allison 41
Dunston, Georgia Mae 48
Duplechan, Larry 55
DuPree, Johnny 96
Dupri, Jermaine 13, 46
Durant, Kevin 76, 107
Durham, Bobby 73
Durham, James 90
Duthiers, Vladimir 109
Dutton, Charles S. 4, 22
DuVernay, Ava 98, 126
Dworkin, Aaron P. 52
Dwight, Edward 65
Dye, Jermaine 58
Dyett, Walter 113
Dyson, Michael Eric 11, 40, 128
E-40 125
Eagleson, William Lewis 90
Early, Gerald 15
Early, Norman S., Jr. 124

Earthquake 55
Easley, Annie J. 61
Easton, Hosea 91
Ebanks, Michelle 60
Eberhardt, Jennifer 124
Eckstine, Billy 28
Edelin, Ramona Hoage 19
Edelman, Marian Wright 5, 42
Edison, Harry 114
Edley, Christopher 2, 48
Edley, Christopher F., Jr. 48
Edmonds, Terry 17
Edmonds, Tracey 16, 64
Edmunds, Gladys 48
Edwards, David 122
Edwards, Donna 77
Edwards, Esther Gordy 43
Edwards, Harry 2
Edwards, Herman 51
Edwards, Lena Frances 76
Edwards, Melvin 22
Edwards, Teddy 123
Edwards, Teresa 14, 95
Edwards, Willarda V. 59
Edwards, Willis 104
El Wilson, Barbara 35
Elder, Larry 25, 120
Elder, Lee 6
Elder, Lonne, III 38
Elders, Joycelyn 6
Eldridge, Roy 37
Elie, Lolis Eric 97
Elise, Kimberly 32, 101
Ellerbe, Brian 22
Ellington, Duke 5
Ellington, E. David 11
Ellington, Mercedes 34
Elliott, Missy 31, 90
Elliott, Sean 26
Ellis, Aunjanue 108
Ellis, Charles H., III 79
Ellis, Clarence A. 38
Ellis, Dock 78
Ellis, Jimmy 44, 127
Ellis, Larry R. 110
Ellis, Nelsan 105
Ellis, Trey 97
Ellis-Lamkins, Phaedra 88
Ellison, Keith 59
Ellison, Ralph 7
Elmore, Ronn 21
Elzy, Ruby 119
Emanuel, James A. 46
Emeagwali, Dale 31
Emotions, The 125
En Vogue 100
Ephriam, Mablean 29
Epperson, Sharon 54
Epps, Archie C., III 45
Epps, Mike 60
Epps, Omar 23, 59
Ericsson-Jackson, Aprille 28
Ervin, Anthony 66
Ervin, Booker 106
Ervin, Clark Kent 82
Erving, Julius 18, 47
Escobar, Damien 56
Escobar, Tourie 56
Esposito, Giancarlo 9
Espy, Mike 6
Estes, Rufus 29
Estes, Simon 28
Estes, Sleepy John 33

Eubanks, Kevin 15, 108
Eugene-Richard, Margie 63
Europe, James Reese 10
Evans, Darryl 22
Evans, Etu 55
Evans, Faith 22
Evans, Harry 25
Evans, Mari 26
Evans, Melvin H. 88
Evans, Warren C. 76
Eve 29
Everett, Carl 103
Everett, Francine 23
Everett, Percival 93
Evers, Medgar 3
Evers, Myrlie 8
Ewing, Patrick 17, 73
Fabio, Sarah Webster 48
Fabolous 93
Fabre, Shelton 71
Fagan, Garth 18, 98
Fair, Ronald L. 47
Fairbanks, Mabel 117
Faison, Donald 50
Faison, Frankie 55
Faison, George 16
Falana, Lola 42
Falconer, Etta Zuber 59
Falcons, The 128
Fales-Hill, Susan 88
Fargas, Antonio 50
Farley, Christopher John 54
Farley, James Conway 99
Farmer, Art 38
Farmer, Forest J. 1
Farmer, James 2, 64
Farmer-Paellmann, Deadria 43
Farr, Mel 24
Farrakhan, Louis 2, 15
Farrell, Herman D., Jr. 81
Farris, Isaac Newton, Jr. 63
Fattah, Chaka 11, 70, 112
Faulk, Marshall 35, 96
Fauntroy, Walter E. 11
Fauset, Crystal Dreda Bird 100
Fauset, Jessie 7
Favors, Steve 23
Fax, Elton 48
Feelings, Muriel 44
Feelings, Tom 11, 47
Felix, Allyson 48, 98
Felix, Larry R. 64
Felix Da Housecat 110
Feemster, Herbert 72
Fennoy, Ilene 72
Fenty, Adrian 60, 88
Ferbos, Lionel 95
Ferguson, Roger W., Jr. 25, 112
Ferguson, Ronald F. 75
Ferguson, Vernice D. 108
Ferrell, Rachelle 29
Fetchit, Stepin 32
Fiasco, Lupe 64
Fielder, Cecil 2, 112
Fielder, Prince Semien 68
Fields, C. Virginia 25
Fields, Cleo 13
Fields, Evelyn J. 27
Fields, Felicia P. 60
Fields, Julia 45
Fields, Kim 36
50 Cent 46, 83
Files, Lolita 35

Fils-Aimé, Reggie 74
Fine, Sam 60
Finley, Ron 110
Finner-Williams, Paris Michele 62
Fishbone 101
Fishburne, Laurence 4, 22, 70
Fisher, Ada Lois Sipuel 76
Fisher, Ada M. 76
Fisher, Antwone 40
Fisher, Derek 97
Fisher, Gail 85
Fisher, Miles Mark 91
Fisk Jubilee Singers 112
Fitzgerald, Ella 1, 18
Five Keys, The 104
Flack, Roberta 19
Flake, Floyd H. 18, 110
Flamingos, The 108
Flanagan, Tommy 69
Flavor Flav 67
Fleming, Erik R. 75
Fleming, Raymond 48
Fletcher, Arthur A. 63
Fletcher, Benjamin 90
Fletcher, Bill, Jr. 41
Fletcher, Buddy 16, 108
Fletcher, Geoffrey 85
Flo Rida 78
Flood, Curt 10, 93
Flowers, Sylester 50
Flowers, Vonetta 35
Floyd, Eddie 127
Floyd, Elson S. 41
Flying Lotus 124
Forbes, Calvin 46
Forbes, James A., Jr. 71
Ford, Barney 90
Ford, Cheryl 45
Ford, Clyde W. 40
Ford, Harold E(ugene) 42
Ford, Harold E(ugene), Jr. 16, 70
Ford, Jack 39
Ford, Johnny 70
Ford, Nick Aaron 44
Ford, T-Model 91, 113
Ford, Wallace 58
Forman, James 7, 51
Forman, James, Jr. 89
Forrest, Leon 44
Forrest, Vernon 40, 79
Forté, John 74
Forte, Linda Diane 54
Fortune, James 92
Foster, Andrew 79
Foster, Arian 114
Foster, Ezola 28
Foster, Frank 97
Foster, George "Pops" 40
Foster, Henry W., Jr. 26
Foster, Jylla Moore 45
Foster, Marie 48
Foster, William P. 88
Fowler, Reggie 51
Fox, Donal 114
Fox, John R. 105
Fox, Vivica A. 15, 53
Foxx, Anthony 81, 123
Foxx, Jamie 15, 48
Foxx, Redd 2
Foye, K'wan 97
Francis, Norman (C.) 60
Francis, Thais 93
Francois, Terry A. 106

Franklin, Aretha 11, 44, 115
Franklin, C. L. 68
Franklin, Hardy R. 9, 87
Franklin, J. E. 44
Franklin, John Hope 5, 77
Franklin, Kirk 15, 49, 97
Franklin, Shirley 34, 80
Franti, Michael 93
Fraser, Sarah Loguen 100
Frazer, Jendayi 68
Frazer, Victor O. 98
Frazier, E. Franklin 10
Frazier, Joe 19, 98
Frazier, Kenneth 97
Frazier, Kevin 58
Frazier, Oscar 58
Frazier, Ryan 89
Frazier, Walt 91
Frazier-Lyde, Jacqui 31
Freelon, Nnenna 32
Freeman, Aaron 52
Freeman, Al, Jr. 11, 105
Freeman, Charles 19
Freeman, Harold P. 23
Freeman, Leonard 27
Freeman, Marianna 23
Freeman, Morgan 2, 20, 62, 100
Freeman, Paul 39
Freeman, Von 104
Freeman, Yvette 27
Freestyle Fellowship 122
French, Albert 18
French, D. M. 94
Fresh, Doug E. 93
Friday, Jeff 24
Fryer, Roland G. 56
Fudge, Ann (Marie) 11, 55
Fudge, Marcia L. 76
Fuentes, Tito 123
Fulani, Lenora 11
Fuller, A. Oveta 43
Fuller, Arthur 27
Fuller, Blind Boy 86
Fuller, Charles 8
Fuller, Curtis 115
Fuller, Howard L. 37
Fuller, Hoyt 44
Fuller, Meta Vaux Warrick 27
Fuller, S. B. 13
Fuller, Solomon Carter, Jr. 15
Fuller, Thomas O. 90
Fuller, Vivian 33
Fulson, Lowell 118
Funches, Ron 121
Funderburg, I. Owen 38
Funnye, Capers C., Jr. 73
Fuqua, Antoine 35
Fuqua, Harvey 90
Futch, Eddie 33
Future 109
Gaines, Brenda 41
Gaines, Clarence E., Sr. 55
Gaines, Ernest J. 7
Gaines, Grady 38
Gaines, Lloyd 79
Gaines, Matthew 95
Gaines, Patrice 106
Gaiter, Dorothy J. 80
Gaither, Alonzo Smith (Jake) 14
Gaither, Israel L. 65
Gamble, Kenny 85
Gamble, Oscar 113
Gans, Joe 91

Gant, Richard 105
Gantt, Harvey 1
Gap Band, The 100
Gardere, Jeffrey 76
Gardner, Chris 65
Gardner, Edward G. 45
Garland, Red 115
Garner, Erroll 76
Garner, Tyron 99
Garnet, Henry Highland 100
Garnett, Kevin 14, 70, 118
Garrett, James F. 78
Garrett, Joyce Finley 59
Garrison, Zina 2
Garvin, Gerry 78
Gary, Willie E. 12, 117
Gaskins, Eric 64
Gaskins, Rudy 74
Gaspard, Patrick 84
Gaston, Arthur George 3, 38, 59
Gaston, Cito 71
Gaston, Marilyn Hughes 60
Gates, Henry Louis, Jr. 3, 38, 67
Gates, Sylvester James, Jr. 15
Gates, Theaster 118
Gates, William 97
Gatlin, Justin 123
Gay, Tyson 114
Gaye, Anna Gordy 121
Gaye, Marvin 2
Gaye, Nona 56
Gayle, Addison, Jr. 41
Gayle, Helene D. 3, 46
Gaynor, Gloria 36
Gentry, Alvin 23
George, Eddie 80
George, Nelson 12, 101
George, Paul 124
George, Zelma Watson 42
Gervin, George 80
Geto Boys 115
Ghostface Killah 90
Gibbons, Gary 107
Gibbs, Freddie 125
Gibbs, Marla 86
Gibbs, Mifflin W. 99
Gibson, Althea 8, 43
Gibson, Bob 33
Gibson, Donald Bernard 40
Gibson, John Trusty 87
Gibson, Johnnie Mae 23
Gibson, Josh 22
Gibson, Kenneth Allen 6
Gibson, Ted 66
Gibson, Truman K., Jr. 60
Gibson, Tyrese 27, 62
Gibson, William F. 6
Giddings, Paula 11
Gidron, Richard D. 68
Gilbert, Christopher 50
Gilbert, John Wesley 91
Giles, Roscoe C. 93
Gill, Gerald 69
Gill, Johnny 51
Gill, Turner 83
Gilles, Ralph 61
Gillespie, Dizzy 1
Gilliam, Frank 23
Gilliam, Jim 122
Gilliam, Joe 31
Gilliam, Sam 16
Gilliard, Steve 69
Gillum, Andrew 128

Gilmore, Artis 101
Gilmore, Marshall 46
Gilpin, Charles Sidney 81
Ginuwine 35
Giovanni, Nikki 9, 39, 85
Gist, Carole 1
Gittens, Charles L. 124
Givens, Adele 62
Givens, Robin 4, 25, 58
Givhan, Robin Deneen 72
Glanville, Douglas Metunwa 82
Glasper, Robert 101
Glass, Ron 111
Gloster, Hugh Morris, Sr. 90
Glover, Anwan 123
Glover, Cedric B. 103
Glover, Corey 34
Glover, Danny 1, 24, 103
Glover, Donald 85
Glover, Keith 79
Glover, Nathaniel, Jr. 12
Glover, Savion 14
Goapele 55
Goggins, Juanita 127
Goines, Donald 19
Goings, Russell 59
Goldberg, Whoopi 4, 33, 69
Golden, Marita 19, 99
Golden, Thelma 10, 55
Golden Gate Quartet 104
Goldsberry, Ronald 18
Golson, Benny 37
Golston, Allan C. 55
Gomes, Peter J. 15, 93
Gomez, Jewelle 30
Gomez-Preston, Cheryl 9
Gomillion, Charles 90
Good, Meagan 117
Goode, Mal 13
Goode, W. Wilson 4
Gooden, Dwight 20
Gooden, Linda 94
Gooding, Cuba, Jr. 16, 62
Goodlett, Carlton B. 91
Goodman, Al 87
Goodman, Kim C. 94
Goodnight, Paul 32
Gorden, W. C. 71
Gordon, Bruce S. 41, 53, 82
Gordon, Carl 87
Gordon, Dexter 25
Gordon, Ed 10, 53
Gordon, Josh 120
Gordone, Charles 15
Gordon-Reed, Annette 74
Gordy, Berry, Jr. 1
Gore, Frank 117
Goss, Carol A. 55
Goss, Tom 23
Gossett, Louis, Jr. 7
Gotti, Irv 39
Gourdin, Edward O. 93
Gourdine, Meredith 33
Gourdine, Simon 11
Grace, George H. 48
Graham, Katerina 99
Graham, Lawrence Otis 12
Graham, Lorenz 48
Graham, Stedman 13
Graham, Trevor 84
Graham Central Station 123
Granderson, Curtis 66
Granderson, LZ 103

Granger, Lester B. 75
Grant, Augustus O. 71
Grant, Bernie 57
Grant, Frank 100
Grant, Gwendolyn Goldsby 28
Grant, Micki 125
Granville, Evelyn Boyd 36
Gravely, Samuel L., Jr. 5, 49
Graves, Butch 77
Graves, Denyce Antoinette 19, 57
Graves, Earl G. 1, 35
Graves, Milford 126
Gray, Darius 69
Gray, Dobie 99
Gray, F. Gary 14, 49
Gray, Farrah 59
Gray, Fred 37
Gray, Ida 41
Gray, Macy 29
Gray, Vincent C. 88
Gray, Wardell 128
Gray, William H., III 3
Gray, Willie 46
Gray, Yeshimbra "Shimmy" 55
Greaves, R. B. 106
Greaves, William 38, 123
Greely, M. Gasby 27
Green, A. C. 32
Green, Al 13, 47, 74
Green, Al 118
Green, Cee Lo 70, 103
Green, Darrell 39, 74
Green, Dennis 5, 45
Green, Draymond 126
Green, Grant 56
Green, Isaac H. 79
Green, Jonathan 54
Green, Nancy 112
Greene, Frank S., Jr. 101
Greene, Jimmy 74
Greene, Joe 10
Greene, Maurice 27, 77
Greene, Petey 65
Greene, Richard Thaddeus, Sr. 67
Greenfield, Elizabeth Taylor 116
Greenfield, Eloise 9
Greenhouse, Bunnatine "Bunny" 57
Greenlee, Sam 48
Greenwood, L. C. 115
Greenwood, Monique 38
Greer, Hal 92
Greer, Sonny 127
Gregory, Ann 63
Gregory, Dick 1, 54
Gregory, Frederick 8, 51
Gregory, Wilton 37
Grier, Bobby 95
Grier, David Alan 28
Grier, Eliza Ann 90
Grier, Mike 43
Grier, Pam 9, 31, 86
Grier, Roosevelt 13
Griffey, Dick 89
Griffey, Ken, Jr. 12, 73
Griffin, Anthony 71
Griffin, Bessie Blout 43
Griffin, Blake 98
Griffin, Johnny 71
Griffin, LaShell 51
Griffin, Robert, III 107
Griffith, Emile 113
Griffith, Mark Winston 8
Griffith, Yolanda 25

Griffith-Joyner, Florence 28
Grillo, Evelio 95
Grimes, Henry 124
Grimké, Archibald H. 9
Griner, Brittney 128
Grist, Reri 84
Groff, Peter 96
Grooms, Henry R(andall) 50
Gryce, Gigi 124
Guillaume, Robert 3, 48
Guinier, Lani 7, 30
Guitar Slim 125
Gumbel, Bryant 14, 80
Gumbel, Greg 8
Gunn, Moses 10
Gurira, Danai 73
Guru 84
Guy, George "Buddy" 31
Guy, Jasmine 2
Guy, Rosa 5
Guyot, Lawrence 108
Guyse, Sheila 122
Guy-Sheftall, Beverly 13, 92
Guyton, Tyree 9, 94
Gwynn, Tony 18, 83, 122
Haddon, Dietrick 55
Hageman, Hans 36
Hageman, Ivan 36
Hagler, Marvelous Marvin 102
Hailey, JoJo 22
Hailey, K-Ci 22
Hairston, Jester 88
Hairston, Sam 88
Hale, Clara 16
Hale, Lorraine 8
Haley, Alex 4
Haley, George Williford Boyce 21
Hall, Aaron 57
Hall, Adelaide 126
Hall, Alvin D. 86
Hall, Arsenio 58
Hall, Arthur 39
Hall, Elliott S. 24
Hall, Juanita 62
Hall, Kevan 61
Hall, Lloyd A. 8
Hall, Tamron 96
Halliburton, Warren J. 49
Ham, Cynthia Parker 58
Hamblin, Ken 10
Hamburg, Beatrix 84
Hamburg, Margaret 78
Hamer, Fannie Lou 6
Hamilton, Anthony 61
Hamilton, Bernie 117
Hamilton, Chico 117
Hamilton, Lawrence 122
Hamilton, Leonard 100
Hamilton, Lisa Gay 71
Hamilton, Samuel C. 47
Hamilton, Vicki 95
Hamilton, Virginia 10
Hamlin, Larry Leon 49, 62
Hammon, Jupiter 124
Hammond, Fred 23
Hammond, Paula 119
Hammonds, Evelynn 69
Hammons, David 69
Hampton, Fred 18
Hampton, Henry 6
Hampton, Lionel 17, 41
Hancock, Herbie 20, 67
Hancock, Michael B. 123

Handy, W. C. 8
Haney, Lee 77
Hannah, Marc 10
Hansberry, Lorraine 6
Hansberry, Tony, II 93
Hansberry, William Leo 11
Hansen, Austin 88
Hardaway, Anfernee 13, 111
Hardaway, Tim 35
Harden, James 116
Harden, Monique 97
Hardin Armstrong, Lil 39
Harding, Vincent 67
Hardison, Bethann 12
Hardison, Kadeem 22
Hardwick, Omari 122
Hardy, Greg 118
Hare, Nathan 44
Harewood, Dorian 104
Harkless, Necia Desiree 19
Harmon, Clarence 26
Harold, Erika 54
Harold Melvin & the Blue Notes
    105
Harp, Toni 123
Harper, Ben 34, 62
Harper, Frances Ellen Watkins 11
Harper, Hill 32, 65, 97
Harper, Michael S. 34
Harper, Rachel M. 92
Harrell, Andre 9, 30
Harrington, Oliver W. 9
Harris, Alice 7
Harris, Barbara 12
Harris, Barry 68
Harris, Bernard A. 90
Harris, Bill 72
Harris, Carla A. 67
Harris, Corey 39, 73
Harris, Damon 110
Harris, E. Lynn 12, 33, 116
Harris, Eddy L. 18
Harris, Franco 97
Harris, Gary L. 87
Harris, James 79
Harris, Jay T. 19
Harris, Jessica B. 91
Harris, Kamala D. 64, 122
Harris, Kevin 120
Harris, Leslie 6
Harris, Lyle Ashton 83
Harris, Major 110
Harris, Marcelite Jordon 16
Harris, Mary Styles 31
Harris, Maya Lakshmi 88
Harris, Monica 18
Harris, Patricia Roberts 2
Harris, Rennie 120
Harris, Richard E. 61
Harris, Robin 7
Harris, Sylvia 70
Harris, Wesley L. 92
Harris, Wood 114
Harris, Wynonie 102
Harris-Lacewell, Melissa 81
Harrison, Alvin 28
Harrison, Calvin 28
Harrison, Charles 72
Harris-Stewart, Lusia 90
Harry, Jackée 111
Harsh, Vivian Gordon 14
Hart, Alvin Youngblood 61
Hart, Billy 126

Hart, Kevin 103
Hart, Thomas A., Sr. 113
Hartman, Johnny 109
Harvard, Beverly 11
Harvey, Steve 18, 58
Harvey, William R. 42
Harvin, Percy 123
Haskins, Clem 23
Haskins, James 36, 54
Hassell, Leroy Rountree, Sr. 41,
    116
Hastie, William H. 8
Hastings, Alcee 16, 119
Hatcher, Andrew T. 90
Hatcher, Richard G. 55
Hatchett, Glenda 32
Hathaway, Donny 18
Hathaway, Isaac Scott 33
Hathaway, Lalah 57, 88
Havens, Richie 111
Hawes, Hampton 121
Hawkins, Augustus F. 68
Hawkins, Coleman 9
Hawkins, Connie 91
Hawkins, Edwin 113
Hawkins, Erskine 14
Hawkins, La-Van 17, 54
Hawkins, Screamin' Jay 30
Hawkins, Steven 14
Hawkins, Tramaine 16
Hawkins, Walter 87
Hayden, Carla D. 47
Hayden, Lewis 105
Hayden, Palmer 13
Hayden, Robert 12
Hayes, Bob 77
Hayes, Cecil N. 46
Hayes, Dennis 54
Hayes, Elvin 93
Hayes, Isaac 20, 58, 73
Hayes, James C. 10
Hayes, Roland 4
Hayes, Teddy 40
Hayes, Terrance 124
Haygood, Wil 83
Haynes, Elizabeth Ross 102
Haynes, George Edmund 8
Haynes, Marques 22
Haynes, Roy 87
Haynes, Trudy 44
Haynie, Sharon 94
Haysbert, Dennis 42, 106
Haysbert, Raymond V., Sr. 87
Haywood, Gar Anthony 43
Haywood, Jimmy 58
Haywood, Margaret A. 24
Haywood, Spencer 99
Hazel, Darryl B. 50
Hazzard, Walt 98
Healy, James Augustine 30
Healy, Michael 90
Heard, Gar 25
Heard, Nathan C. 45
Hearns, Thomas 29
Heath, Percy 100
Heavy D 58, 98
Hector, Jamie 98
Hedgeman, Anna Arnold 22
Hegamin, Lucille 120
Height, Dorothy I. 2, 23, 78
Hemingway, Anthony 107
Hemphill, Essex 10
Hemphill, Jessie Mae 33, 59

Hemsley, Sherman 19, 104
Henderson, Angelo 122
Henderson, Cornelius Langston 26
Henderson, David 53
Henderson, Fletcher 32
Henderson, George Washington
    101
Henderson, Gordon 5
Henderson, Henry Fairfax, Jr. 89
Henderson, Jeff 72
Henderson, Joe 127
Henderson, Rickey 28, 78
Henderson, Stephen E. 45
Henderson, Thelton E. 68
Henderson, Wade J. 14
Henderson, Zelma 71
Hendrix, Jimi 10
Hendryx, Nona 56
Hendy, Francis 47
Henries, A. Doris Banks 44
Henry, Aaron 19
Henry, Clarence "Frogman" 46
Henry, Dwight 104
Henry, Joshua 94
Henry, Mark 116
Henry, Troy 85
Henson, Darrin 33
Henson, Josiah 90
Henson, Matthew 2
Henson, Taraji P. 58, 77, 127
Herbert, Bob 63, 96
Hercules, Frank 44
Herenton, Willie W. 24, 81
Herman, Alexis M. 15
Hernandez, Aileen Clarke 13
Herndon, Alonzo Franklin 89
Herndon, Angelo 90
Hernton, Calvin C. 51
Hickman, Fred 11
Higginbotham, A. Leon, Jr. 13, 25
Higginbotham, Jay C. 37
Higginbotham, Joan 124
Higginsen, Vy 65
Hightower, Dennis F. 13
Hill, Andrew 66
Hill, Anita 5, 65
Hill, Bonnie Guiton 20
Hill, Calvin 19
Hill, Donna 32
Hill, Dulé 29
Hill, Grant 13, 94
Hill, Hugh Morgan 83
Hill, Janet 19
Hill, Jemele 109
Hill, Jesse, Jr. 13
Hill, Lauryn 20, 53, 111
Hill, Leslie Pinckney 44
Hill, Marc Lamont 80, 128
Hill, Michael 95
Hill, Oliver W. 24, 63
Hill, Peter 92
Hill, Wyllstyne D. 94
Hillard, Terry 25
Hillary, Barbara 65
Hilliard, Asa Grant, III 66
Hilliard, David 7, 105
Hilliard, Earl F. 24
Hilliard, Wendy 53
Hilson, Keri 84
Himes, Chester 8
Hinderas, Natalie 5
Hine, Darlene Clark 24
Hines, Earl "Fatha" 39

Hines, Garrett 35
Hines, Gregory 1, 42
Hinton, Milt 30
Hinton, William Augustus 8
Hoagland, Everett H. 45
Hobson, Julius W. 44
Hobson, Mellody 40
Hodge, Aldis 124
Hodge, Derrick 114
Hogan, Beverly Wade 50
Holden, Kip 120
Holder, Eric, Jr. 9, 76, 104
Holder, Geoffrey 78, 124
Holder, Laurence 34
Holdsclaw, Chamique 24, 110
Holiday, Billie 1
Holiday, Jrue 115
Holland, Endesha Ida Mae 3, 57
Holland, Kimberly N. 62
Holland, Robert, Jr. 11
Holland-Dozier-Holland 36
Holloway, Brenda 65
Holloway, Loleatta 115
Hollowell, Donald L. 57
Holmes, Amy 69
Holmes, Clint 57
Holmes, Hamilton E. 82
Holmes, Larry 20, 68
Holmes, Santonio 87
Holmes, Shannon 70
Holmes, T. J. 98
Holsey, Lucius Henry 92
Holstein, Casper 89
Holt, Lester 66
Holt, Nora 38
Holt Baker, Arlene 73
Holton, Hugh, Jr. 39
Holyfield, Evander 6
Homesick James 124
Honeywood, Varnette P. 54, 88
Honoré, Russel L. 64
Hood, James Walker 91
Hooker, John Lee 30
hooks, bell 5, 90
Hooks, Benjamin L. 2, 85
Hooks, Robert 76
Hope, John 8
Hope, Lugenia Burns 89
Hopkins, Bernard 35, 69, 105
Hopkins, Donald R. 89
Hopkins, Lightnin' 83
Horn, Shirley 32, 56
Horne, Frank 44
Horne, Lena 5, 86
Horsford, Steven 88
Horton, Andre 33
Horton, Big Walter 115
Horton, George Moses 124
Horton, Gladys 92
Horton, James Oliver 58
Horton, Suki 33
Horton, Willie 104
Hoskins, Harold K. 103
Houghton, Israel 92
House, Son 8
Houston, Charles Hamilton 4
Houston, Cissy 20, 83
Houston, Whitney 7, 28, 83, 100
Howard, Ayanna 65
Howard, Desmond 16, 58
Howard, Dwight 113
Howard, Elston 125
Howard, Juwan 15

Howard, M. William, Jr. 26
Howard, Michelle 28, 125
Howard, Perry Wilbon, Jr. 112
Howard, Ryan 65, 113
Howard, Sherri 36
Howard, Terrence 59, 94
Howell, Ayinde 91
Howlin' Wolf 9
Howroyd, Janice Bryant 42
Hoyte, Lenon 50
Hrabowski, Freeman A., III 22
Hubbard, Arnette Rhinehart 38
Hubbard, Freddie 75
Hudlin, Reginald 9, 86
Hudlin, Warrington 9
Hudson, Cheryl 15
Hudson, Ernie 72
Hudson, Jennifer 63, 83
Hudson, Lou 121
Hudson, Wade 15
Huff, Leon 86
Huggins, Edie 71
Huggins, Larry 21
Huggins, Nathan Irvin 52
Hughes, Albert 7
Hughes, Allen 7
Hughes, Cathy 27
Hughes, Dora 88
Hughes, Ebony 57
Hughes, Langston 4
Hughley, D. L. 23, 76
Hull, Akasha Gloria 45
Humes, Helen 128
Humphrey, Bobbi 20
Humphrey, Claude 119
Humphries, Frederick 20
Hunt, Darnell 92
Hunt, Richard 6
Hunter, Alberta 42
Hunter, Billy 22, 109
Hunter, Clementine 45
Hunter, Ivory Joe 106
Hunter, Lindsey 110
Hunter, Torii 43, 109
Hunter-Gault, Charlayne 6, 31
Hurd, Sam 116
Hurston, Zora Neale 3
Hurt, Byron 61
Hurt, Mississippi John 84
Hurtt, Harold 46
Hutch, Willie 62
Hutcherson, Bobby 115
Hutcherson, Hilda Yvonne 54
Hutchinson, Earl Ofari 24
Hutson, Jean Blackwell 16
Hyde, Cowan F. "Bubba" 47
Hyman, Earle 25, 79
Hyman, Phyllis 19
Ibrahim, Fuad 109
Ice Cube 8, 30, 60
Iceberg Slim 11
Ice-T 6, 31, 96
Iman, Chanel 66
Imani Winds 113
Ifill, Gwen 28
Imes, Elmer Samuel 39
India.Arie 34
Ingram, James 84
Ingram, Rex 5
Ink Spots, The 102
Innis, Roy 5
Intruders, The 119
Irvin, Michael 64

Irvin, Monford Merrill 31
Irvin, Vernon 65
Irving, Barrington, Jr. 112
Irving, Kyrie 102
Irving, Larry, Jr. 12
Irvis, K. Leroy 67
Isaacs, Cheryl Boone 113
Isaacs, John 76
Isley, Marvin 87
Isley, Ronald 25, 56
Iverson, Allen 24, 46
Iverson, Johnathan Lee 22, 100
Ivey, Phil 72, 106
J Dilla 102
Ja Rule 35, 91
Jackson, Alexine Clement 22
Jackson, Alphonso R. 48
Jackson, Bobby 119
Jackson, Brenda 87
Jackson, Deborah 94
Jackson, DeSean 120
Jackson, Earl 31
Jackson, Edison O. 67
Jackson, Eric 127
Jackson, Frank G. 76
Jackson, Fred James 25
Jackson, George 14
Jackson, George 19
Jackson, Hal 41, 104
Jackson, Isaiah 3
Jackson, Jamea 64
Jackson, James A. 90
Jackson, Janet 6, 30, 68
Jackson, Jermaine 79
Jackson, Jesse 1, 27, 72
Jackson, Jesse, Jr. 14, 45, 81, 108
Jackson, Jimmie Lee 126
Jackson, Joe 78
Jackson, John 36
Jackson, Judith D. 57
Jackson, LaToya 95
Jackson, Lisa 77
Jackson, Mae 57
Jackson, Mahalia 5
Jackson, Mannie 14
Jackson, Mark 121
Jackson, Mary 73
Jackson, Maynard 2, 41
Jackson, Michael 19, 53, 76
Jackson, Millie 25
Jackson, Milt 26
Jackson, Phillip 115
Jackson, Rampage 83
Jackson, Randy 40
Jackson, Reggie 15
Jackson, Rickey 88
Jackson, Samuel L. 8, 19, 63, 102
Jackson, Sandi 108
Jackson, Sheneska 18
Jackson, Shirley Ann 12
Jackson, Stephen 118
Jackson, Tito 81
Jackson, Tom 70
Jackson, Vera 40
Jackson 5 103
Jackson Lee, Sheila 20
Jacob, John E. 2
Jacobs, George 118
Jacobs, Harriet 104
Jacobs, Regina 38
Jacquet, Illinois 49
Jagged Edge 117
Jaheim 58

Jakes, T. D. 17, 43, 116
Jamal, Ahmad 69
Jamerson, James 59
James, Charles H., III 62
James, Daniel, Jr. 16
James, Donna A. 51
James, Elmore 114
James, Etta 13, 52, 100
James, G. Larry 74
James, Juanita 13
James, LeBron 46, 78, 105
James, Leela 117
James, Nikki M. 94
James, Rick 19
James, Sharpe 23, 69
James, Skip 38
James, Sly 107
James Bracken and Vivian Bracken 107
Jamison, Judith 7, 67, 96
Jarreau, Al 21, 65, 105
Jarrett, Valerie 73
Jarrett, Vernon D. 42
Jarvis, Charlene Drew 21
Jarvis, Erich 67
Jarvis, Kristen 85
Jasper, John J. 91
Jasper, Kenji 39
Jay Electronica 125
Jay-Z 27, 69, 103
Jealous, Benjamin Todd 70, 113
Jefferson, Blind Lemon 81
Jefferson, Denise 87
Jefferson, Margo 108
Jefferson, Mildred Fay 89
Jefferson, William J. 25, 72
Jeffries, Hakeem 118
Jeffries, Herb 122
Jeffries, Leonard 8
Jemison, Mae C. 1, 35
Jemison, Major L. 48
Jemison, T. J. 119
Jenifer, Franklyn G. 2
Jenkins, Beverly 14
Jenkins, Ella 15
Jenkins, Kris 98
Jenkins, Ray 77
Jennings, Lyfe 56, 69
Jennings, Thomas L. 125
Jerkins, Rodney 31
Jeter, Claude 75
Jeter, Derek 27, 93, 124
Jimmy Jam 13
Joe, Yolanda 21
John, Daymond 23, 114
Johns, Vernon 38
Johnson, Al 119
Johnson, Andre 127
Johnson, Angela 52
Johnson, Anthony M. 92
Johnson, Avery 62
Johnson, Beverly 2, 102
Johnson, Buddy 36
Johnson, Bumpy 102
Johnson, Calvin 108
Johnson, Chad 108
Johnson, Charles 1, 82
Johnson, Charles S. 12
Johnson, Chris 92
Johnson, Clark 96
Johnson, Clifford "Connie" 52
Johnson, Conrad O. 97
Johnson, Dennis 89

Johnson, Eddie Bernice **8, 90**
Johnson, Edward Austin **107**
Johnson, Eunice W. **83**
Johnson, Fenton **91**
Johnson, George E. **29**
Johnson, Georgia Douglas **41**
Johnson, Gus **92**
Johnson, Hall **90**
Johnson, Hank, Jr. **80**
Johnson, Harry E. **57**
Johnson, Harvey, Jr. **24, 82**
Johnson, J. J. **37**
Johnson, J. Rosamond **121**
Johnson, Jack **8**
Johnson, James Weldon **5**
Johnson, Je'Caryous **63**
Johnson, Jeh **76, 125**
Johnson, Jeh Vincent **44**
Johnson, Joe **94**
Johnson, John H. **3, 54**
Johnson, John Henry **96**
Johnson, Johnnie **56**
Johnson, Judy **105**
Johnson, Katherine (Coleman Goble) **61**
Johnson, Kevin **70**
Johnson, Keyshawn **91**
Johnson, Larry **28**
Johnson, Le'Andria **108**
Johnson, Leroy R. **89**
Johnson, Levi **48**
Johnson, Lonnie **85**
Johnson, Lonnie G. **32, 93**
Johnson, Magic **3, 39, 101**
Johnson, Mamie "Peanut" **40**
Johnson, Mat **31, 105**
Johnson, Michael **13**
Johnson, Mordecai Wyatt **79**
Johnson, Norma H. **17, 97**
Johnson, R. M. **36**
Johnson, Rafer **33**
Johnson, Robert **2**
Johnson, Robert L. **3, 39, 121**
Johnson, Robert T. **17**
Johnson, Rodney Van **28**
Johnson, Sandra K. **94**
Johnson, Sheila Crump **48**
Johnson, Shoshana **47**
Johnson, Sterling, Jr. **124**
Johnson, Syl **97**
Johnson, Syleena **98**
Johnson, Tommy **106**
Johnson, Virginia **9**
Johnson, William **91**
Johnson, William Henry **3**
Johnson-George, Tamara **79**
Johnson-Powell, Gloria **107**
Joiner, Charlie **102**
Jolley, Willie **28**
Jones, Absalom **52**
Jones, Adam **103**
Jones, Adam **114**
Jones, Alex **64**
Jones, Andruw **98**
Jones, Bill T. **1, 46, 80**
Jones, Bobby **20, 94**
Jones, Bomani **121**
Jones, Booker T. **84**
Jones, Carl **7**
Jones, Caroline **29**
Jones, Clara Stanton **51**
Jones, Clarence B. **114**
Jones, Cobi N'Gai **18**

Jones, Cullen **73**
Jones, Deacon **92, 112**
Jones, Donell **29**
Jones, Doris W. **62**
Jones, Dwight C. **122**
Jones, E. Edward, Sr. **45**
Jones, Ed "Too Tall" **46**
Jones, Edith Mae Irby **65**
Jones, Edward P. **43, 67**
Jones, Elaine R. **7, 45**
Jones, Elvin **68**
Jones, Emil, Jr. **74**
Jones, Etta **35**
Jones, Eugene Kinckle **79**
Jones, Frederick McKinley **68**
Jones, Gayl **37**
Jones, Genevieve **101**
Jones, Hank **57, 86**
Jones, Ingrid Saunders **18**
Jones, Jacoby **117**
Jones, James Earl **3, 49, 79**
Jones, John **89**
Jones, Jon **121**
Jones, Jonah **39**
Jones, K. C. **83**
Jones, Lois Mailou **13**
Jones, Lou **64**
Jones, Marion **21, 66**
Jones, Merlakia **34**
Jones, Orlando **30**
Jones, Papa Jo **99**
Jones, Paul R. **76**
Jones, Philly Joe **121**
Jones, Quincy **8, 30**
Jones, Randy **35**
Jones, Rashida **101**
Jones, Robbie **113**
Jones, Robert Elijah **90**
Jones, Robert G. **81**
Jones, Sam **85**
Jones, Sarah **39**
Jones, Sharon **86**
Jones, Tayari **96**
Jones, Thad **68**
Jones, Theodore T., Jr. **108**
Jones, Thomas W. **41**
Jones, Van **70**
Jones, Walter **119**
Jones, Wayne **53**
Jones, William A., Jr. **61**
Jones-Drew, Maurice **113**
Joplin, Scott **6**
Jordan, Barbara **4, 78**
Jordan, Charles **122**
Jordan, Deloris **108**
Jordan, Eddie **82**
Jordan, Eddie **83**
Jordan, June **7, 35**
Jordan, Louis **104**
Jordan, Michael **6, 21**
Jordan, Michael B. **97**
Jordan, Montell **23**
Jordan, Vernon E. **3, 35**
Joseph, Jamal **101**
Joseph, Kathie-Ann **56**
Josey, E. J. **10**
Joyce, Dru **81**
Joyner, Marjorie Stewart **26**
Joyner, Matilda Sissieretta **15**
Joyner, Tom **19, 90**
Joyner-Kersee, Jackie **5**
Juicy J **116**
Julian, Hubert **90**

Julian, Percy Lavon **6**
July, William **27**
Just, Ernest Everett **3**
Justice, David **18**
Juvenile **96**
Kaigler, Denise **63**
Kaiser, Cecil **42**
Kandi **83**
Kani, Karl **10**
Karenga, Maulana **10, 71**
Karim, Benjamin **61**
Kaufman, Bob **105**
Kaufman, Monica **66**
Kay, Connie **114**
Kay, Ulysses **37**
KB **122**
Kearney, Beverly **109**
Kearney, Janis **54**
Kearse, Amalya Lyle **12**
Keb' Mo' **36, 124**
Keckley, Elizabeth **90**
Kee, John P. **43, 116**
Keene, John **73**
Keflezighi, Meb **49, 121**
Keith, Damon J. **16, 74**
Keith, Floyd A. **61**
Kelis **58, 122**
Kelley, Cliff **75**
Kelley, Elijah **65**
Kelley, Malcolm David **59**
Kellogg, Clark **64**
Kelly, Jim **113**
Kelly, Patrick **3**
Kelly, R. **18, 44, 71, 117**
Kelly, Robin **114**
Kelly, Wynton **121**
KEM **47, 127**
Kemp, Herb **94**
Kendrick, Erika **57**
Kendricks, Eddie **22**
Kennedy, Adrienne **11**
Kennedy, Cortez **104**
Kennedy, Florynce **12, 33**
Kennedy, Randall **40**
Kennedy-Overton, Jayne Harris **46**
Kenney, John A., Jr. **48**
Kenoly, Ron **45**
Kenyatta, Robin **54**
Kerry, Leon G. **46**
Key & Peele **107**
Keyes, Alan **11, 105**
Keys, Alicia **32, 68**
Khalifa, Wiz **96**
Khan, Chaka **12, 50**
Khanga, Yelena **6**
Kid Cudi **83**
Kidd, Jason **86**
Kidd, Mae Street **39**
Killens, John O. **54**
Killer Mike **117**
Killings, Debra **57**
Killingsworth, Cleve, Jr. **54**
Kilpatrick, Carolyn Cheeks **16**
Kilpatrick, Kwame **34, 71, 116**
Kimbro, Dennis **10**
Kimbro, Henry A. **25**
Kimbro, Warren **76**
Kincaid, Bernard **28**
Kincaid, Jamaica **4, 109**
King, Alonzo **38**
King, B. B. **7**
King, Barbara **22**
King, Ben E. **128**

King, Bernice **4, 81**
King, Chris Thomas **120**
King, Colbert I. **69**
King, Coretta Scott **3, 57**
King, Dexter **10**
King, Don **14, 128**
King, Freddie **92**
King, Gayle **19, 99**
King, Martin Luther, III **20**
King, Martin Luther, Jr. **1**
King, Martin Luther, Sr. **89**
King, Preston **28**
King, Reatha Clark **65**
King, Regina **22, 45**
King, Robert Arthur **58**
King, Robert Hillary **84**
King, Rodney **103**
King, Teresa **80**
King, Woodie, Jr. **27**
King, Yolanda **6**
King Curtis **92**
Kingston, Sean **94**
Kirby, George **14**
Kirk, Clara **95**
Kirk, Ron **11, 75, 111**
Kirkland, Eddie **99**
Kitt, Eartha **16, 75**
Kitt, Sandra **23**
Kittles, Rick **51**
Kitwana, Bakari **86**
Klugh, Earl **59**
Knight, Etheridge **37**
Knight, Gladys **16, 66**
Knight, Marie **80**
Knight, Suge **11, 30, 102**
Knowles, Mathew **96**
Knowles, Tina **61**
Knowling, Robert E., Jr. **38**
Knox, Simmie **49**
Knuckles, Frankie **42, 120**
Komunyakaa, Yusef **9**
Kong, B. Waine **50**
Kool Moe Dee **37**
Koontz, Elizabeth Duncan **101**
Kotto, Yaphet **7**
Kountz, Samuel L. **10**
Kravitz, Lenny **10, 34**
Krigger, Kevin **111**
KRS-One **34**
K-Swift **73**
Kunjufu, Jawanza **3, 50**
Kweli, Talib **93**
La Roca, Pete **107**
La Salle, Eriq **12**
LaBelle, Patti **13, 30**
LaChanze **93**
Lacks, Henrietta **101**
Lacy, Marc **111**
Lacy, Sam **30, 46**
Ladd, Ernie **64**
Ladner, Joyce A. **42**
Lafontant, Jewel Stradford **3, 51**
Lakeside **120**
Lamar, Jake **96**
Lamar, Kendrick **105**
Lampkin, Daisy **19**
Lampley, Oni Faida **43, 71**
Lancaster, Byard **105**
Lance, Major **111**
Land, Harold **125**
Lane, Charles **3**
Lane, Dick **92**
Lane, Lunsford **93**

Lane, Vincent 5
Lane, William Henry 90
Laneuville, Eric 123
Langford, Larry P. 74
Langhart Cohen, Janet 19, 60
Langston, John Mercer 101
Lanier, Bob 47
Lanier, Willie 33
Lankford, Ray 23
Larkin, Barry 24
Larrieux, Amel 63
Lars, Byron 32
Larsen, Nella 10
Laryea, Thomas Davies, III 67
LaSalle, Denise 111
Lashley, Bobby 63
Lassiter, Roy 24
Lateef, Yusef 91, 117
Lathan, Sanaa 27
Latimer, Lewis H. 4
Lattany, Kristin Hunter 88
Lattimore, Kenny 35, 128
LaVette, Bettye 85
Lavizzo-Mourey, Risa 48
Law, W. W. 121
Lawless, Theodore K. 8
Lawrence, Brenda 127
Lawrence, Donald 99
Lawrence, Jacob 4, 28
Lawrence, Margaret Morgan 100
Lawrence, Martin 6, 27
Lawrence, Robert H., Jr. 16
Lawrence-Lightfoot, Sara 10
Laws, Hubert 90
Lawson, James M., Jr. 90
Lawson, Jennifer 1, 50
Laymon, Kiese 113
Layton, William 87
Le1f 120
Lea, Babatunde 124
Leadbelly 82
Leakes, NeNe 107
Leary, Kathryn D. 10
Leavell, Dorothy R. 17
Lecrae 108
Ledisi 73
Lee, Annie Frances 22
Lee, Barbara 25, 102
Lee, Bertram M., Sr. 46
Lee, Canada 8
Lee, Consuela 84
Lee, Debra L. 62
Lee, Eric P. 79
Lee, Jarena 100
Lee, Joe A. 45
Lee, Joie 1
Lee, Leslie 85, 122
Lee, Malcolm D. 75
Lee, Raphael C. 87
Lee, Robert 112
Lee, Spike 5, 19, 86
Lee-Smith, Hughie 5, 22
Leevy, Carrol M. 42
Leffall, Lasalle, Jr. 3, 64
LeFlore, Lyah Beth 96
Legend, John 67, 116
Leggs, Kingsley 62
LeGrand, Eric 118
LeGrand, Naquasia 126
Leland, Mickey 2
Lemmons, Kasi 20
Lemon, Alton T. 112
Lemon, Don 94

Lennox, Betty 31
Lenoir, J. B. 117
LeNoire, Rosetta 37
Lenox, Adriane 59
Leon, Kenny 10, 98
Leonard, Buck 67
Leonard, Kawhi 122
Leonard, Sugar Ray 15
Leslie, Lisa 16, 73
Lester, Bill 42, 85
Lester, Julius 9, 115
Lesure, James 64
LeTang, Henry 66
Letson, Al 39
Levert, Eddie 70
Levert, Gerald 22, 59
Lewis, Ananda 28
Lewis, Aylwin B. 51, 88
Lewis, Butch 71, 99
Lewis, Byron E. 13
Lewis, Carl 4, 97
Lewis, David Levering 9
Lewis, Delano 7
Lewis, Edmonia 10
Lewis, Edward T. 21
Lewis, Emmanuel 36
Lewis, George 104
Lewis, Henry 38
Lewis, Jamal 115
Lewis, John 2, 46, 83
Lewis, Marvin 51, 87
Lewis, Norman 39
Lewis, Oliver 56
Lewis, Ramsey 35, 70
Lewis, Ray 33, 109
Lewis, Reginald F. 6
Lewis, Samella 25
Lewis, Shirley A. R. 14
Lewis, Terry 13
Lewis, Thomas 19
Lewis, William Henry 89
Lewis, William M., Jr. 40
Lewis-Hall, Freda 105
Lewis-Thornton, Rae 32
Ligging, Alfred, III 43
Lighty, Chris 105
Ligon, Glenn 82
Lil B 121
Lil Jon 124
Lil' Kim 28
Lil Mama 117
Lil Wayne 66, 84
Liles, Kevin 42, 99
Lillard, Damian 117
Lincoln, Abbey 3, 88
Lincoln, C. Eric 38
Lindsay, Peta 100
Lindsey, Tommie 51
Lipscomb, Mance 49
LisaRaye 27
Lister, Marquita 65
Lister, Tommy 127
Liston, Melba 118
Liston, Sonny 33
Little, Benilde 21
Little, Booker 105
Little, Cleavon 117
Little, Floyd 86
Little, Larry 90
Little, Robert L. 2
Little Anthony & the Imperials 107
Little Eva 128
Little Milton 36, 54

Little Richard 15
Little Walter 36
Littlepage, Craig 35
LL Cool J 16, 49, 94
Llewellyn, J. Bruce 13, 85
Lloyd 99
Lloyd, Earl 26, 127
Lloyd, John Henry "Pop" 30
Lloyd, Reginald 64
Locke, Alain 10
Locke, Attica 85
Locke, Eddie 44
Lockwood, Robert, Jr. 120
Lofton, James 42
Lofton, Kenny 12
Logan, Onnie Lee 14
Logan, Rayford W. 40
Loguen, J. W. 91
Lomax, Louis E. 90
Lomax, Michael L. 58
Long, Eddie L. 29, 89
Long, Huey 79
Long, Loretta 58
Long, Nia 17, 95
Long, Richard Alexander 65
Lopes, Davey 92
Lopes, Lisa "Left Eye" 36
Lord Infamous 117
Lord Jamar 126
Lorde, Audre 6
Lott, Ronnie 9
Loueke, Lionel 88
Louis, Errol T. 8
Louis, Joe 5
Louis, Willie 113
Loury, Glenn 36
Love, Darlene 23, 92
Love, Ed 58
Love, Laura 50
Love, Loni 113
Love, Mia 96, 125
Love, Nat 9
Love, Reggie 77
Lovell, Whitfield 74
Lover, Ed 10
Loving, Alvin, Jr. 35, 53
Loving, Mildred 69
Lowe, Herbert 57
Lowe, Rick 124
Lowe, Sidney 64
Lowery, Evelyn Gibson 115
Lowery, Joseph 2
Lowery, Myron 80
Lowry, A. Leon 60
Lucas, Bill 97
Lucas, John 7
Lucie, Lawrence 80
Lucien, Jon 66
Luckett, Letoya 61
Lucy, William 50
Lucy Foster, Autherine 35
Ludacris 37, 60
Luke, Derek 61
Lumbly, Carl 47
Lumet, Jenny 80
Lumumba, Chokwe 118
Luna, Donyale 88
Luper, Clara 94
Luter, Fred, Jr. 103
Lyle, Ron 125
Lyles, Lester Lawrence 31
Lymon, Frankie 22
Lynch, Loretta E. 103

Lynch, Marshawn 124
Lynch, Shola 61
Lynch, William, Jr. 115
Lynn, Barbara 126
Lynne, Gloria 115
Lyons, Henry 12, 118
Lyons, James E., Sr. 102
Lyttle, Hulda Margaret 14
Mabley, Moms 15
Mabon, Willie 119
Mabrey, Vicki 26
Mabry, Marcus 70
Mac, Bernie 29, 61, 72
Mac Daddy 111
Mack, Iris 105
Mack, Tony 104
Mack Maine 125
Mackey, Biz 82
Mackey, Nathaniel 75
Mackie, Anthony 102
Madame Sul-Te-Wan 95
Madhubuti, Haki 7, 85
Madison, Joseph E. 17
Madison, Paula 37, 99
Madison, Romell 45
Madlib 88
Magic Slim 110
Mahal, Taj 39
Mahorn, Rick 60
Maitreya, Sananda 85
Majette, Denise 41
Major, Clarence 9
Majors, Jeff 41
Malco, Romany 71
Mallett, Conrad, Jr. 16
Mallory, Mark 62
Mallory, William L., Sr. 119
Malone, Annie 13
Malone, Karl 18, 51, 90
Malone, Maurice 32
Malone, Moses 79
Malone Jones, Vivian 59
Malveaux, Floyd 54
Malveaux, Julianne 32, 70
Malveaux, Suzanne 88
Mandisa 119
Mane, Gucci 91
Manhattans, The 123
Manigault, Earl "The Goat" 15
Manley, Audrey Forbes 16
Manley, Dexter 116
Mann, Bob 126
Mann, Tamela 92
Manning, Frankie 78
Manuel, Jerry 94
Marable, Manning 10, 102
March, William Carrington 56
Marcille, Eva 97
Marian Anderson String Quartet 111
Mariner, Jonathan 41
Marino, Eugene Antonio 30
Mario 71
Markham, Pigmeat 106
Marks, John R., III 123
Marrow, Queen Esther 24
Marsalis, Branford 34, 103
Marsalis, Delfeayo 41
Marsalis, Ellis 90
Marsalis, Wynton 16, 90
Marsh, Henry, III 32
Marshall, Bella 22
Marshall, Brandon 116
Marshall, Kerry James 59

Marshall, Paule 7, 77
Marshall, Thurgood 1, 44
Marshall, William 107
Marte, Starling 117
Martin, Cuonzo 121
Martin, Curtis 104
Martin, Darnell 43, 78
Martin, Duane 108
Martin, Helen 31
Martin, Jesse L. 31
Martin, Jonathan 119
Martin, Louis E. 16
Martin, Michel 97
Martin, Roberta 58
Martin, Roland S. 49, 84
Martin, Ruby Grant 49
Martin, Sallie 120
Martin, Sara 38
Martin, Trayvon 105
Marvelettes, The 126
Mase 24
Masekela, Sal 106
Mason, Anthony 128
Mason, Biddy 89
Mason, Charles Harrison 107
Mason, Derek 120
Mason, Desmond 127
Mason, Felicia 31
Mason, Herman, Jr. 83
Mason, Judi Ann 112
Mason, Ronald 27
Massaquoi, Hans J. 30
Massenburg, Kedar 23, 110
Massey, Brandon 40
Massey, Walter E. 5, 45
Massie, Samuel Proctor, Jr. 29
Masta Ace 118
Master P 21, 115
Matejka, Adrian 87
Mathabane, Mark 5, 99
Mathis, Greg 26
Mathis, Johnny 20
Mathis, Robert 121
Matson, Ollie 93
Matthews, Ameena 105
Matthews, Benjamin 93
Matthews, Mark 59
Matthews Shatteen, Westina 51
Matzeliger, Jan 93
Maupin, John E., Jr. 92
Maxey, Randall 46
Maxis, Theresa 62
Maxwell 20, 81
May, Brother Joe 123
May, Derrick 41
May, Mark 117
Mayberry-Stewart, Melodie 94
Maye, Lee 111
Mayfield, Curtis 2, 43
Mayhew, Martin R. 76
Mayhew, Richard 39
Maynard, Nancy Hicks 73
Maynard, Robert C. 7
Maynor, Dorothy 19
Mayo, Whitman 32
Mays, Benjamin E. 7
Mays, Leslie A. 41
Mays, William G. 34
Mays, Willie 3
Mayweather, Floyd 57, 104
MC Breed 75
M.C. Hammer 20, 80
MC Lyte 34, 108

McAdoo, Bob 75
McAlpin, Harry 121
McAnulty, William E., Jr. 66
McBay, Henry C. 91
McBee, Cecil 123
McBride, Bryant 18
McBride, Chi 73
McBride, James 35, 87
McCabe, Jewell Jackson 10
McCain, Franklin 119
McCall, H. Carl 27
McCall, Nathan 8
McCann, Renetta 44
McCarthy, Sandy 64
McCarty, Osceola 16
McCauley, Gina 76
McClellan, George Marion 91
McClendon, Forrest 94
McClendon, Lisa 61
McClendon, Lloyd 123
McClinton, Marion Isaac 77
McClurkin, Donnie 25
McCoo, Marilyn 53
McCovey, Willie 103
McCoy, Elijah 8
McCoy, LeSean 123
McCoy, Van 123
McCracklin, Jimmy 108
McCraney, Tarell Alvin 116
McCrary, Darius 111
McCrary Anthony, Crystal 70
McCray, Nikki 18
McCullough, DeAndre 106
McCullough, Geraldine 58, 79
McCutchen, Andrew 116
McDaniel, Hattie 5
McDaniel, Randall Cornell 81
McDaniels, Ralph 79
McDonald, Audra 20, 62, 128
McDonald, Charles J. 120
McDonald, Erroll 1
McDonald, Gabrielle Kirk 20
McDougall, Gay J. 11, 43
McDuff, Jack 116
McDuffie, Dwayne 62
McEwen, Mark 5
McFadden, Bernice L. 39
McFarlan, Tyron 60
McFarland, Roland 49
McFerrin, Bobby 68
McFerrin, Robert, Sr. 94
McGee, Charles 10
McGee, James D. 74
McGee, James Madison 46
McGee, Vonetta 95
McGhee, Heather C. 106
McGhee, Howard 122
McGhee, Sharon K. 113
McGill, Anthony 76
McGlowan, Angela 64, 86
McGrady, Tracy 80
McGriff, Fred 24
McGriff, Jimmy 72
McGruder, Aaron 28, 56, 120
McGruder, Robert 22, 35
McGuire, Raymond J. 57
McHenry, Donald F. 83
McIntyre, Kalaparusha Maurice 117
McJunkin, George 93
McKay, Claude 6
McKay, Nellie Yvonne 17, 57
McKee, Lonette 12, 119
McKenzie, Vashti M. 29

McKinney, Cynthia 11, 52, 74
McKinney, Nina Mae 40
McKinney-Whetstone, Diane 27
McKinnon, Isaiah 9
McKissack, Leatrice 80
McKissick, Floyd B. 3
McKnight, Brian 18, 34
McLean, Jackie 78
McLendon, John B., Jr. 89
McLeod, Gus 27
McMillan, Rosalynn A. 36
McMillan, Terry 4, 17, 53
McMillan, Tracy 93
McMurray, Georgia L. 36
McNabb, Donovan 29, 119
McNair, Ronald 3, 58
McNair, Steve 22, 47, 79
McNeil, Lori 1
McPhail, Sharon 2, 119
McPherson, David 32
McPherson, James Alan 70
McQueen, Butterfly 6, 54
McRae, Carmen 77
McRae, Hal 84
McShann, Jay 110
McTell, Blind Willie 89
McWhorter, John 35, 119
McWorter, Free Frank 91
Meadows, Tim 30
Meek, Carrie 6, 36
Meek, Kendrick 41, 89
Meeks, Gregory W. 25, 117
Meeks, James T. 92
Mehretu, Julie 85
Mell, Patricia 49
Melton, Frank 81
Melton, Harold D. 79
Meminger, Dean 114
Memphis Minnie 33
Memphis Slim 105
Menard, John Willis 90
Mengestu, Dinaw 66, 114
Mercado-Valdes, Frank 43
Meredith, James H. 11
Merkerson, S. Epatha 47, 83
Merriweather, Big Maceo 109
Metcalfe, Ralph 26
Method Man 81
Mfume, Kweisi 6, 41
Michaux, Solomon Lightfoot 91
Micheaux, Oscar 7
Michele, Michael 31
Mickelbury, Penny 28
Mickens, Ronald Elbert 105
Middleton, Reggie 105
Midnight Star 110
Mighty Clouds of Joy 110
Migos 126
Miguel 98
Miles, Buddy 69
Miles, Tiya 116
Miles, William 112
Miley, Bubber 120
Millender-McDonald, Juanita 21, 61
Miller, Bebe 3
Miller, Cheryl 10, 74
Miller, Clyde 113
Miller, Dorie 29
Miller, Larry G. 72
Miller, Lorraine C. 119
Miller, Marcus 84
Miller, Omar Benson 93
Miller, Patina 94

Miller, Pepper 96
Miller, Reggie 33
Miller, Tangi 116
Miller, Warren F., Jr. 53
Miller, Wentworth 75
Miller-Travis, Vernice 64
Millinder, Lucky 101
Millines Dziko, Trish 28
Millner, Denene 76
Mills, Florence 22
Mills, Joseph C. 51
Mills, Sam 33
Mills, Stephanie 36
Mills, Steve 47
Mills Brothers, The 99
Milner, Ron 39
Milton, DeLisha 31
Minaj, Nicki 86, 124
Ming, Mel 106
Ming, William Robert, Jr. 125
Mingo, Frank 32
Mingus, Charles 15
Minkins, Shadrach 104
Minoso, Minnie 89, 127
Minor, DeWayne 32
Mississippi Sheiks 122
Mitchell, Arthur 2, 47
Mitchell, Arthur Wergs 91
Mitchell, Blue 126
Mitchell, Brian Stokes 21
Mitchell, Clarence M., Jr. 88
Mitchell, Corinne 8
Mitchell, Dwike 111
Mitchell, Elvis 67
Mitchell, Freddie 116
Mitchell, Juanita Jackson 128
Mitchell, Kel 66
Mitchell, Leona 42
Mitchell, Loften 31
Mitchell, Nicole 66
Mitchell, Parren J. 42, 66
Mitchell, Russ 21, 73
Mitchell, Sam 82
Mitchell, Shireen 89
Mitchell, Stephanie 36
Mitchell, Willie 114
Moffett, Charnett 127
Mohammed, Nazr 64
Mohammed, W. Deen 27
Mokae, Zakes 80
Monáe, Janelle 86
Monica 21
Mo'Nique 35, 84
Monk, Art 38, 73
Monk, Thelonious 1
Monroe, Bryan 71
Monroe, Earl 89
Monroe, Mary 35
Montgomery, Isaiah T. 91
Montgomery, Little Brother 117
Montgomery, Robbie 101
Montgomery, Tim 41
Montgomery, Wes 88
Moody, Anne 127
Moody, James 83
Moody-Adams, Michele 76
Moon, Warren 8, 66
Moondoc, Jemeel 119
Mooney, Paul 37, 120
Moonglows, The 108
Moore, Archie 120
Moore, Barbara C. 49
Moore, Chante 26

Moore, Davey 105
Moore, Dorothy Rudd 46
Moore, Gwendolynne S. 55
Moore, Harry T. 29
Moore, Jessica Care 30
Moore, Johnny B. 38
Moore, Juanita 83, 124
Moore, Kermit 116
Moore, LeRoi 72
Moore, Maya 94
Moore, Melba 21
Moore, Minyon 45
Moore, Shemar 21, 112
Moore, Tim 124
Moore, Undine Smith 28
Moore, Wes 86
Moorer, Michael 19
Moose, Charles 40
Moran, Jason 89
Moreland, Mantan 117
Morgan, Garrett 1
Morgan, Gertrude 63
Morgan, Irene 65
Morgan, Joe 9, 96
Morgan, Lee 102
Morgan, Rose 11
Morgan, Tracy 61, 102
Morial, Ernest "Dutch" 26
Morial, Marc H. 20, 51
Morón, Alonzo G. 91
Morris, Garrett 31
Morris, Greg 28
Morris, Melvin 120
Morris, Mercury 114
Morris, Raheem 77
Morrison, Sam 50
Morrison, Toni 2, 15, 86
Morrison, Vanessa 84
Morrow, E. Frederic 100
Morton, Azie Taylor 48
Morton, Ferdinand Q. 90
Morton, Frederick A., Jr. 93
Morton, Jelly Roll 29
Morton, Joe 18
Mosby, Marilyn 128
Moses, Edwin 8
Moses, Gilbert 12
Moses, Robert Parris 11
Mosley, Shane 32
Mosley, Walter 5, 25, 68
Moss, Carlton 17
Moss, J. 64
Moss, Otis, Jr. 72
Moss, Otis, III 72
Moss, Preacher 63
Moss, Randy 23, 90
Mossell, Gertrude Bustill 40
Mossell, Nathan Francis 91
Moten, Etta 18
Motley, Archibald, Jr. 30
Motley, Constance Baker 10, 55
Motley, Marion 26
Moton, Robert Russa 83
Mourning, Alonzo 17, 44
Moutoussamy-Ashe, Jeanne 7
Mowry, Jess 7
Mowry, Tamera 79
Mowry, Tia 78
Moyo, Karega Kofi 36
Moyo, Yvette Jackson 36
Muhammad, Ava 31
Muhammad, Elijah 4
Muhammad, Jabir Herbert 72

Muhammad, Khallid Abdul 10, 31
Mullen, Harryette 34
Mullen, Nicole C. 45
Muncie, Chuck 112
Murphy, Charles 95
Murphy, Eddie 4, 20, 61
Murphy, John H. 42
Murphy, Laura M. 43
Murphy, Matt 117
Murray, Albert L. 33
Murray, Cecil 12, 47
Murray, Eddie 12
Murray, Lenda 10
Murray, Pauli 38
Murray, Tai 47
Murrell, Sylvia Marilyn 49
Muse, Clarence Edouard 21
Musiq 37, 84
Mya 35
Myers, Lou 110
Myers, Walter Dean 8, 70, 123
Myles, Kim 69
Myles, Raymond Anthony 121
Nabrit, Samuel Milton 47
Nagin, Ray 42, 57, 88
Nail, John E. 92
Nance, Cynthia 71
Nanula, Richard D. 20
Napoleon, Benny N. 23
Nas 33, 111
Nash, Diane 72
Nash, Joe 55
Nash, Johnny 40
Nash, Niecy 66, 115
Nash, Shannon King 84
Nate Dogg 92
Naughton, Naturi 97
Naughty by Nature 124
Navarro, Fats 104
Naylor, Gloria 10, 42
Ndegeocello, Meshell 15, 83
Neal, Elise 29
Neal, Kenny 123
Neal, Larry 38
Neal, Mark Anthony 74
Neal, Raful 44, 121
Neals, Otto 73
Nell, William C. 128
Nelly 32, 90
Nelson, Jill 6, 54
Nelson, Kadir 115
Nelson, Oliver 113
Nelson, Sophia A. 93
Nelson, Stanley 92
Nelson Meigs, Andrea 48
Neville, Aaron 21
Neville, Arthel 53
New Birth 124
New Edition 101
Newborn, Phineas, Jr. 127
Newcombe, Don 24
Newkirk, Pamela 69
Newman, David 76
Newman, Lester C. 51
Newsome, Ozzie 26, 117
Newton, Cam 96
Newton, Huey 2
Ne-Yo 65
Ngaujah, Sahr 86
Nicholas, Denise 82
Nicholas, Fayard 20, 57
Nicholas, Harold 20
Nichols, Nichelle 11

Nighthawk, Robert 121
Nissel, Angela 42
Nix, Robert N. C., Jr. 51
Nixon, Edgar Daniel 100
Nixon, Otis 111
N'Namdi, George R. 17
Noble, Gil 76
Noble, Ronald 46
Noble Drew Ali 100
Norful, Smokie 127
Norman, Christina 47
Norman, Jessye 5
Norman, Maidie 20
Norman, Pat 10
Norris, Michele 83
Northup, Solomon 115
Norton, Eleanor Holmes 7, 93
Norton, Ken 101, 115
Norton, Meredith 72
Notorious B.I.G. 20
Nottage, Lynn 66
Nugent, Richard Bruce 39
Nunez, Elizabeth 62, 112
Nunn, Annetta 43
Nutter, Michael 69, 112
Obadele, Imari 84
Obama, Barack 49, 74, 91
Obama, Michelle 61, 90
O'Brien, Soledad 88
Ocean, Frank 100
Odetta 37, 74
Odom, Lamar 81
Ogden, Jonathan 110
Oglesby, Zena 12
Ogletree, Charles, Jr. 12, 47
O'Grady, Lorraine 73
Ojikutu, Bayo 66
Ojikutu, Bisola 65
Ol' Dirty Bastard 52
Olden, Georg(e) 44
O'Leary, Hazel 6
Oliver, Garrett 95
Oliver, Jerry 37
Oliver, Joe "King" 42
Oliver, John J., Jr. 48
Oliver, Kimberly 60
Oliver, Pam 54, 123
Oliver, Paul 115
Omarion 107
Omarosa 69, 110
O'Neal, Frederick 99
O'Neal, Patrice 99
O'Neal, Rodney 88
O'Neal, Ron 46
O'Neal, Shaquille 8, 30, 95
O'Neal, Stanley 38, 67
O'Neil, Buck 19, 59
Onyewu, Oguchi 60
Orange, James 74
Orioles, The 100
Orlandersmith, Dael 42
Orman, Roscoe 55
Ormes, Jackie 73
Orr, Kevyn 118
Ory, Kid 118
Osbey, Brenda Marie 102
Osborne, Jeffrey 26, 121
Osborne, Na'taki 54
Osman, Said 127
Otis, Clarence, Jr. 55
Otis, Clyde 67
Ouattara, Morou 74
Overton, Anthony 128

Owens, Brig 118
Owens, Helen 48
Owens, Jack 38
Owens, Jesse 2
Owens, Major 6, 117
Owens, Terrell 53, 106
Pace, Betty 59
Pace, Judy 119
Pace, Orlando 21
Packer, Daniel 56
Packer, Will 71
Packer, Z. Z. 64
Page, Alan 7
Page, Clarence 4
Page, Greg 78
Page, Inman 82
Page, Walter 117
Paige, Rod 29
Paige, Satchel 7
Painter, Nell Irvin 24, 88
Palmer, Keke 68, 120
Palmer, Rissi 65
Palmer, Violet 59
Parham, Marjorie B. 71
Parham, Truck 124
Parish, Robert 43
Parker, Barrington D. 92
Parker, Candace 74
Parker, Charlie 20
Parker, Jim 64
Parker, Junior 116
Parker, Kellis E. 30
Parker, Maceo 72
Parker, Nicole Ari 52
Parker, Pat 19
Parker, Ray, Jr. 85
Parker, Star 70
Parker, Vernon 97
Parks, Bernard C. 17
Parks, Gordon 1, 35, 58
Parks, Henry Green, Jr. 89
Parks, Rosa 1, 35, 56
Parks, Suzan-Lori 34, 85
Parlan, Horace 108
Parr, Russ 51
Parsons, James 14
Parsons, Richard 11, 33, 124
Paterson, Basil A. 69, 122
Paterson, David A. 59
Patrick, Deval 12, 61, 127
Patterson, Chuck 124
Patterson, Floyd 19, 58
Patterson, Frederick Douglass 12
Patterson, Gilbert Earl 41
Patterson, J. O., Jr. 80
Patterson, Louise 25
Patterson, Mary Jane 54
Patterson, Orlando 4, 127
Patton, Antwan 45
Patton, Charley 107
Patton, Paula 62
Patton, Venetria K. 125
Paul, Billy 127
Paul, Chris 84, 100
Paulk, Marcus T. 127
Payne, Allen 13
Payne, Donald M. 2, 57, 112
Payne, Ethel L. 28
Payne, Freda 58
Payne, Les 89
Payne, Ulice, Jr. 42
Payne, William D. 60
Payton, Benjamin F. 23

Payton, Gary 99
Payton, John 48, 124
Payton, Philip A., Jr. 88
Payton, Walter 11, 25
Pearson, Felicia 99
Peck, Carolyn 23
Peebles, Ann 114
Peete, Calvin 11
Peete, Holly Robinson 20
Peete, Rodney 60
Pena, Paul 58
Pendergrass, Teddy 22, 83
Penguins, The 107
Peoples, Dottie 22
Perez, Anna 1
Perkins, Carl 128
Perkins, Eddie 103
Perkins, Edward 5
Perkins, James, Jr. 55
Perkins, Marion 38
Perkins, Pinetop 70
Perkins, Tony 24
Perren, Freddie 60
Perrineau, Harold, Jr. 51
Perrot, Kim 23
Perry, Herman 89
Perry, James 83
Perry, Joe 95
Perry, Laval 64
Perry, Lowell 30
Perry, Matthew J., Jr. 96
Perry, Steve 98
Perry, Tyler 40, 54, 103
Perry, Warren 56
Person, Waverly 9, 51
Peters, Brock 96
Peters, Clarke 103
Peters, Jason 125
Peters, Margaret 43
Peters, Matilda 43
Petersen, Frank E. 31
Peterson, Adrian 109
Peterson, James 38
Peterson, James 81
Peterson, Jesse Lee 81
Peterson, Karen Carter 90
Peterson, Marvin "Hannibal" 27
Petioni, Muriel 99
Petry, Ann 19
Pettiford, Oscar 106
Pettigrew, Antonio 118
Pharcyde, The 127
Phifer, Mekhi 25, 103
Phillips, Brandon 116
Phillips, Carl 111
Phillips, Charles E., Jr. 57, 109
Phillips, Esther 107
Phillips, Helen L. 63
Phillips, Joseph C. 73
Phillips, Teresa L. 42
Phipps, Wintley 59
Pickens, James, Jr. 59
Pickett, Bill 11
Pickett, Cecil 39
Pierce, Elijah 84
Pierce, Harold 75
Pierce, Paul 71
Pierce, Wendell 90
Pierre, Percy Anthony 46
Pincham, R. Eugene, Sr. 69
Pinchback, P. B. S. 9
Pinckney, Bill 42
Pinckney, Sandra 56

Pindell, Howardena 55
Pinder, Jefferson 77
Pinderhughes, John 47
Pineda, Michael 121
Pinkett, Randal 61
Pinkett Smith, Jada 10, 41, 95
Pinkney, Arnold R. 122
Pinkney, Fayette 80
Pinkney, Jerry 15, 124
Pinkston, W. Randall 24
Pinn, Vivian Winona 49
Piper, Adrian 71
Pippen, Scottie 15, 89
Pippin, Horace 9
Pitts, Byron 71
Pitts, Derrick 77
Pitts, Leonard, Jr. 54, 85
Pitts, Robb 84
Pitts, Skip 103
Plaskett, Stacey 127
Platters, The 99
Player, Willa B. 43
Pleasant, Mary Ellen 9
Pleasure P 84
Plessy, Homer Adolph 31
Plinton, James O., Jr. 98
Plummer, Glenn 120
P.M. Dawn 54
Poindexter, Hildrus A. 87
Poitier, Sidney 11, 36
Poitier, Sydney Tamiia 65
Polite, Carlene Hatcher 82
Pollard, Fritz 53
Pollard, William L. 91
Pope.L, William 72
Porter, Billy 112
Porter, Bo 123
Porter, David 127
Porter, James A. 11
Porter, Terry 75
Potter, Myrtle 40
Pough, Terrell 58
Pounder, CCH 72
Poussaint, Alvin F. 5, 67
Poussaint, Renee 78
Powell, Adam Clayton, Jr. 3
Powell, Benny 87
Powell, Bud 24
Powell, Colin 1, 28, 75
Powell, Debra A. 23
Powell, Keith 101
Powell, Kevin 31, 74
Powell, Maxine 8, 115
Powell, Michael 32
Powell, Mike 7
Powell, Renee 34
Powell, William J. 82
Power, Will 83
Pratt, Awadagin 31
Pratt, Geronimo 18, 95
Pratt, Kyla 57
Preer, Evelyn 82
Premice, Josephine 41
Pressley, Condace L. 41
Preston, Billy 39, 59
Price, David 101
Price, Florence 37
Price, Frederick K. C. 21
Price, Glenda 22
Price, Hugh B. 9, 54
Price, Kelly 23
Price, Leontyne 1
Price, Lisa 97

Price, Lloyd 119
Price, Richard 51
Pride, Charley 26
Primas, Randy 106
Primus, Pearl 6, 125
Prince 18, 65
Prince, Richard E. 71
Prince, Ron 64
Prince, Tayshaun 68
Prince-Bythewood, Gina 31, 77
Pritchard, Robert Starling 21
Procope, Ernesta 23
Procope, John Levy 56
Proctor, Bernard Shaw 120
Professor Longhair 109
Proof 101
Prophet, Nancy Elizabeth 42
Prothrow-Stith, Deborah 10
Pruitt, Wendell O. 106
Pryce, Trevor 89
Pryor, Rain 65
Pryor, Richard 3, 24, 56
Pryor, Snooky 119
Prysock, Arthur 117
Puckett, Kirby 4, 58
Pugh, Charles 81
Purdie, Bernard 77
Purnell, Silas 59
Puryear, Martin 42, 101
Pusha T 123
Putney, Martha S. 75
Pyfrom, Estella 127
Quander, Nellie 102
Quarles, Benjamin Arthur 18
Quarles, Norma 25
Quarterman, Lloyd Albert 4
Queen Latifah 1, 16, 58, 119
?uestlove 74
Quigless, Helen G. 49
Quince, Peggy A. 69
Quivers, Robin 61
Rabb, Maurice F., Jr. 58
Radcliffe, Ted 74
Rae Sremmurd 126
Ragin, Derek Lee 84
Rahman, Aishah 37
Raines, Franklin 14, 107
Raines, Tim 107
Rainey, Ma 33
Ralph, Sheryl Lee 18, 108
Ramsey, Charles H. 21, 69
Rand, A. Barry 6
Randall, Alice 38
Randall, Dudley 8, 55
Randall, Vernellia R. 95
Randle, John 87
Randle, Theresa 16
Randolph, A. Philip 3
Randolph, Linda A. 52
Randolph, Willie 53
Rangel, Charles B. 3, 52, 85
Ransome, James E. 88
Raoul, Kwame 55
Rapier, James T. 82
Rare Essence 121
Rashad, Ahmad 18
Rashad, Phylicia 21
Raspberry, William 2
Ravens, The 103
Raven-Symoné 44, 113
Rawlings-Blake, Stephanie 93, 128
Rawlinson, Johnnie B. 79
Rawls, Lou 17, 57

Ray, Carline 113
Ray, Charlotte E. 60
Ray, Gene Anthony 47
Ray J 86
Razaf, Andy 19
Reagins, Tony 94
Reagon, Bernice Johnson 7
Reagon, Toshi 76
Reason, J. Paul 19
Reaves, Donald J. 102
Record, Eugene 60
Redd, Dana 93
Reddick, Lance 52, 128
Reddick, Lawrence Dunbar 20
Redding, Ann Holmes 77
Redding, J. Saunders 26
Redding, Louis L. 26
Redding, Otis 16
Redman 81
Redman, Joshua 30
Redmond, Eugene 23
Redwood, John Henry 78
Reece, Marcel 114
Reed, A. C. 36
Reed, Ishmael 8
Reed, Jimmy 38
Reed, Joe L. 110
Reed, Kasim 82
Reed, Natina 106
Reed, Willis, Jr. 86
Reed Hall, Alaina 83
Reedy, Jessica 101
Reems, Ernestine Cleveland 27
Rees, Dee 100
Reese, Della 6, 20, 96
Reese, Jerry 103
Reese, Milous J., Jr. 51
Reese, Pokey 28
Reese, Tracy 54
Reeves, Bass 100
Reeves, Dianne 32, 119
Reeves, Gregory 49
Reeves, Martha 85
Reeves, Rachel J. 23
Reeves, Triette Lipsey 27
Reid, Antonio "L.A." 28
Reid, Ira De A. 100
Reid, Irvin D. 20
Reid, Senghor 55
Reid, Tim 56
Reid, Vernon 34
Revels, Hiram Rhoades 98
Reverend Ike 79
Reynolds, Harold 77
Reynolds, Star Jones 10, 27, 61
Rhames, Ving 14, 50
Rhimes, Shonda Lynn 67
Rhoden, Dwight 40
Rhoden, William C. 67
Rhodes, Jewell Parker 84
Rhodes, Ray 14
Rhone, Sylvia 2
Rhymefest 97
Rhymes, Busta 31
Rhyne, Melvin 109
Ribbs, Willy T. 2
Ribeau, Sidney 70
Ribeiro, Alfonso 17
Rice, Condoleezza 3, 28, 72
Rice, Constance LaMay 60
Rice, Emmett J. 94
Rice, Jerry 5, 55, 89
Rice, Jim 75

Rice, Linda Johnson **9, 41**
Rice, Louise Allen **54**
Rice, Norm **8**
Rice, Ray **112**
Rice, Susan **74, 103**
Richard, Dawn **92**
Richard, J. R. **87**
Richards, Beah **30**
Richards, Hilda **49**
Richards-Ross, Sanya **66, 98**
Richardson, Desmond **39**
Richardson, Donna **39**
Richardson, Julieanna **81**
Richardson, LaTanya **71**
Richardson, Laura **81**
Richardson, Nolan **9**
Richardson, Rupert **67**
Richardson, Salli **68**
Richie, Leroy C. **18**
Richie, Lionel **27, 65, 114**
Richmond, Cedric **93**
Richmond, Mitch **19**
Rideau, Iris **46**
Ridley, John **69**
Riggins, Karriem **102**
Riggs, Marlon **5, 44**
Riles, Wilson C. **79**
Riley, Amber **97**
Riley, Boots **89**
Riley, Helen Caldwell Day **13**
Riley, Rochelle **50**
Riley, Teddy **116**
Rillieux, Norbert **92**
Ringgold, Faith **4, 81**
Riperton, Minnie **32**
Rivers, Doc **25, 81**
Rivers, Eugene F., III **81**
Rivers, Sam **95**
Roach, Max **21, 63**
Roaf, Andrée Layton **106**
Roaf, Willie **106**
Roberts, Darryl **70**
Roberts, Deborah **35**
Roberts, Joseph Jenkins **125**
Roberts, Kimberly Rivers **72**
Roberts, Lillian **83**
Roberts, Marcus **19, 113**
Roberts, Michele **123**
Roberts, Mike **57**
Roberts, Robin **16, 54, 113**
Roberts, Roy S. **14**
Robertson, Gil L., IV **85**
Robertson, Oscar **26**
Robeson, Eslanda Goode **13**
Robeson, Paul **2**
Robey, Don **115**
Robinson, Aminah **50**
Robinson, Bill "Bojangles" **11**
Robinson, Bishop L. **66**
Robinson, Cleo Parker **38**
Robinson, Craig **103**
Robinson, Craig **107**
Robinson, Dave **110**
Robinson, David **24, 90**
Robinson, Eddie G. **10**
Robinson, Eugene **77**
Robinson, Fatima **34**
Robinson, Fenton **38**
Robinson, Flynn **112**
Robinson, Frank **9, 87**
Robinson, Ida B. **106**
Robinson, Jackie **6**
Robinson, Joann Gibson **100**

Robinson, LaVaughn **69**
Robinson, Malcolm S. **44**
Robinson, Matt **69**
Robinson, Max **3**
Robinson, Patrick **19, 71**
Robinson, Rachel **16**
Robinson, Randall **7, 46**
Robinson, Reginald R. **53**
Robinson, Sharon **22**
Robinson, Shaun **36**
Robinson, Smokey **3, 49**
Robinson, Spottswood W., III **22**
Robinson, Sugar Ray **18**
Robinson, Sylvia **79**
Robinson, Will **51, 69**
Robinson-Berry, Joan **94**
Roble, Abdi **71**
Roby, Kimberla Lawson **86**
Roche, Joyce M. **17**
Rochon, Lela **16**
Rochon, Stephen W. **78**
Rock, Chris **3, 22, 66**
Rock, John S. **113**
Rock, Pete **121**
Rock, The **29, 66**
Rock, Tony **108**
Rodgers, Johnathan **6, 51**
Rodgers, Rod **36**
Rodman, Dennis **12, 44, 96, 118**
Rodriguez, Cheryl **64**
Rodriguez, Jimmy **47**
Rogers, Alan G. **72**
Rogers, Bobby **110**
Rogers, Desirée **88**
Rogers, Jimmy **38**
Rogers, Joe **27**
Rogers, Joel Augustus **30**
Rogers, John W., Jr. **5, 52**
Rogers, Rodney Ray **106**
Roker, Al **12, 49**
Roker, Roxie **68**
Rolle, Esther **13, 21**
Rolle, Janet **97**
Rolle, Myron **98**
Rollins, Charlemae Hill **27**
Rollins, Howard E., Jr. **16**
Rollins, Jimmy **70**
Rollins, Sonny **37, 94**
Romanthony **115**
Romeo **98**
Rondo, Rajon **111**
Roots, The **101**
Rose, Anika Noni **70**
Rose, Derrick **82**
Rose, Jalen **108**
Rose Royce **120**
Roseboro, John **123**
Ross, Charles **27**
Ross, Diana **8, 27**
Ross, Don **27**
Ross, Isaiah "Doc" **40**
Ross, Rick **79, 104**
Ross, Tracee Ellis **35**
Ross-Lee, Barbara **67**
Roundfield, Danny **109**
Roundtree, Dovey **80**
Roundtree, Richard **27**
Rouse, Cecilia **93**
Rowan, Carl T. **1, 30**
Rowe-Adams, Jackie **109**
Rowell, Victoria **13, 68**
Rowland, Kelly **100**
Roxanne Shante **33**

Roy, Brandon **98**
Roy, Kenny **51**
Rubin, Chanda **37**
Rucker, Darius **34, 74, 108**
Rudolph, Maya **46, 106**
Rudolph, Wilma **4**
Ruffin, Jimmy **125**
Ruffin, Josephine St. Pierre **75**
Ruffins, Kermit **85**
Ruggles, David **126**
Ruley, Ellis **38**
Run **31, 73, 75**
RuPaul **17, 91**
Rush, Bobby **26, 76**
Rush, Bobby **78**
Rush, Otis **38**
Rushen, Patrice **12**
Rushing, Jimmy **37**
Russell, Bill **8**
Russell, Brenda **52**
Russell, Herman Jerome **17**
Russell, Nipsey **66**
Russell-McCloud, Patricia A. **17**
Russwurm, John Brown **100**
Rust, Art, Jr. **83**
Rustin, Bayard **4**
RZA **80, 128**
Saadiq, Raphael **125**
Saar, Alison **16**
Saar, Betye **80**
Sabathia, CC **74**
St. Jacques, Raymond **8**
Saint James, Synthia **12**
St. John, Kristoff **25**
St. Julien, Marlon **29**
St. Louis, David **126**
St. Patrick, Mathew **48**
Saldana, Zoe **72, 118**
Sallee, Charles **38**
Salter, Nikkole **73**
Salters, Lisa **71**
Sam, Michael **121**
Sam and Dave **102**
Samara, Noah **15**
Sample, Joe **51, 123**
Sampson, Charles **13**
Samuelsson, Marcus **53, 120**
Sanchez, Sonia **17, 51**
Sanders, Angelia **86**
Sanders, Barry **1, 53**
Sanders, Bob **72**
Sanders, Deion **4, 31, 96**
Sanders, Joseph R., Jr. **11**
Sanders, Malika **48**
Sanders, Pharoah **64**
Sanders, Satch **77**
Sands, Diana **87**
Sanford, Isabel **53**
Sanneh, Kelefa **96**
Santamaria, Mongo **81**
Santana, Juelz **120**
Santiago-Hudson, Ruben **85**
Santigold **96**
Sapp, Marvin **74**
Sapp, Warren **38, 109**
Sapphire **14, 95**
Sasser, Sean **113**
Satcher, David **7, 57, 111**
Savage, Augusta **12**
Sawyer, Eugene **81**
Sayers, Gale **28**
Sayles Belton, Sharon **9, 16**
Sbraga, Kevin **88**

Scantlebury-White, Velma **64**
Schiavocampo, Mara **97**
Schmoke, Kurt **1, 48**
ScHoolboyQ **117**
Schuyler, George Samuel **40**
Schuyler, Philippa **50**
Scott, Byron **125**
Scott, C(ornelius) A(dolphus) **29**
Scott, David **41, 117**
Scott, Dread **106**
Scott, George **55**
Scott, George **113**
Scott, Harold Russell, Jr. **61**
Scott, Hazel **66**
Scott, Jill **29, 83**
Scott, Jimmy **48, 122**
Scott, John T. **65**
Scott, Milton **51**
Scott, Robert C. **23**
Scott, Stuart **34, 126**
Scott, Tim **87, 125**
Scott, Wendell Oliver, Sr. **19**
Scott-Heron, Gil **94**
Scott-Young, Mona **101**
Scurry, Briana **27**
Seals, Son **56**
Sealy, Lloyd G. **125**
Sealy, Malik **118**
Sears, Leah Ward **5, 79**
Sears, Stephanie **53**
Sebree, Charles **40**
Secada, Jon **97**
Seele, Pernessa **46**
Sengstacke, John **18**
Senna, Danzy **93**
Sermon, Erick **81**
Serrano, Andres **3**
Sessoms, Vivian **122**
Sewell, Terri **93**
Seymour, Richard **101**
Seymour, Teddy **110**
Seymour, William J. **106**
Shabazz, Attallah **6**
Shabazz, Betty **7, 26**
Shabazz, Ilyasah **36**
Shabazz Palaces **123**
Shadd, Abraham D. **81**
Shakur, Afeni **67**
Shakur, Assata **6**
Shakur, Tupac **14**
Shakur, Yusef **85**
Shange, Ntozake **8, 89**
Shanice **112**
Shank, Suzanne F. **77**
Shannon, Randy **82**
Sharpe, Shannon **97**
Sharper, Darren **32, 118**
Sharpton, Al **21, 97**
Shavers, Cheryl **31**
Shavers, Earnie **127**
Shaw, Bernard **2, 28**
Shaw, Brian **127**
Shaw, Marlena **105**
Shaw, William J. **30**
Sheard, Kierra **61, 114**
Sheffield, Gary **16, 108**
Shell, Art **1, 66**
Shelton, Paula Young **86**
Shelton, Trent **122**
Shepherd, Sherri **55**
Shepp, Archie **101**
Sherman, Richard **118**
Sherrod, Clayton **17**

Sherrod, Shirley 87
Shider, Garry 87
Shines, Johnny 116
Shinhoster, Earl 32
Shipp, E. R. 15
Shipp, Matthew 107
Shippen, John 43
Shirelles, The 111
Shirley, Aaron 126
Shirley, Donald 111
Shirley, George 33
Shmurda, Bobby 123
Shockley, Ann Allen 84
Shores, Arthur D. 99
Short, Bobby 52
Short, Columbus 79
Shorter, Wayne 75
Showers, Reggie 30
Shropshire, Thomas B. 49
Shuttlesworth, Fred 47, 98
Sidat-Singh, Wilmeth 116
Sidibe, Gabourey 84
Sidner, Sara 105
Sifford, Charlie 4, 49
Sigur, Wanda 44
Silas, Paul 24
Silver, Horace 26, 122
Siméus, Dumas M. 25, 110
Simkins, Modjeska Monteith 112
Simmons, Bob 29
Simmons, E. Denise 79
Simmons, Gary 58
Simmons, Henry 55
Simmons, Jamal 72
Simmons, Kimora Lee 51, 83
Simmons, Russell 1, 30
Simmons, Ruth J. 13, 38
Simms, Margaret 94
Simon, Joe 109
Simon, Lateefah 95
Simone, Nina 15, 41
Simpson, Carole 6, 30
Simpson, Lorna 4, 36
Simpson, Merton D. 110
Simpson, O. J. 15, 100
Simpson, Valerie 21, 97
Simpson-Hoffman, N'kenge 52
Sims, Danny 106
Sims, Howard "Sandman" 48
Sims, Lowery Stokes 27
Sims, Naomi 29, 79
Sinbad 1, 16
Singletary, Mike 4, 76
Singleton, John 2, 30, 122
Sinkford, Jeanne C. 13
Sir Mix-A-Lot 82
Sisqo 30
Sissle, Noble 29
Sister Souljah 11, 100
Sizemore, Barbara A. 26, 110
Sizemore, Grady 96
Skinner, Kiron K. 65
Sklarek, Norma Merrick 25, 101
Slater, Duke 125
Slater, Rodney E. 15, 125
Slaughter, John Brooks 53
Sledge, Percy 39, 128
Sleet, Gregory M. 109
Sleet, Moneta, Jr. 5
Slice, Kimbo 73
Slick Rick 93
Slim Harpo 120
Slim Thug 86

Slocumb, Jonathan 52
Slyde, Jimmy 70
Smalls, Robert 82
Smaltz, Audrey 12
Smiley, Rickey 59
Smiley, Tavis 20, 68
Smith, Amanda Berry 109
Smith, Anna Deavere 6, 44
Smith, B(arbara) 11
Smith, Barbara 28
Smith, Bessie 3
Smith, Bruce 80
Smith, Bruce W. 53
Smith, Bubba 96
Smith, Buster 116
Smith, Cecilia 102
Smith, Cladys "Jabbo" 32
Smith, Clarence 113
Smith, Clarence O. 21
Smith, Damu 54
Smith, Danyel 40
Smith, DeMaurice 92
Smith, Dr. Lonnie 49
Smith, Emmitt 7, 87
Smith, Gene 123
Smith, Geno 118
Smith, Greg 28
Smith, Hale 118
Smith, Hilton 29
Smith, Ian 62
Smith, Jaden 82
Smith, Jane E. 24
Smith, Jessie Carney 35
Smith, Jimmy 127
Smith, John L. 22
Smith, Joshua 10
Smith, Kemba 70
Smith, Kenny 114
Smith, LaQuan 113
Smith, Lee 101
Smith, Lonnie Liston 49
Smith, Lovie 66, 107
Smith, Malcolm A. 75
Smith, Mamie 32
Smith, Marie F. 70
Smith, Marvin 46
Smith, Mary Carter 26
Smith, Ming 100
Smith, Morgan 46
Smith, Myrna 92
Smith, Nate 49
Smith, Neil 109
Smith, Ozzie 77
Smith, Princella 86
Smith, Randy 81
Smith, Reggie 113
Smith, Rick 72
Smith, Roger Guenveur 12
Smith, Stephen A. 69
Smith, Steve 120
Smith, Stuff 37
Smith, Tasha 73
Smith, Tommie 102
Smith, Trixie 34
Smith, Tubby 18, 83
Smith, Vincent D. 48
Smith, Will 8, 18, 53
Smith, Willi 8
Smith, Willie 107
Smith, Willow 92
Smyre, Calvin 90
Smythe Haith, Mabel 61
Sneed, Paula A. 18

Snipes, Wesley 3, 24, 67
Snoop Dogg 35, 84
Snow, Samuel 71
Snowden, Frank M., Jr. 67
Snowden, Gail 108
Sohn, Sonja 100
Solange 97
Solomon, Jimmie Lee 38
Somi 85
Sommore 61
Songz, Trey 88
Soul Stirrers 127
Southern, Eileen 56
Southgate, Martha 58
Sowell, Thomas 2, 99
Spaniels, The 105
Spann, Otis 107
Sparks, Jordin 66
Spaulding, Charles Clinton 9
Spearman, Leonard H. O., Sr. 81
Spears, Warren 52
Spector, Ronnie 77
Speech 82
Spencer, Anne 27
Spencer, Michael G. 87
Spencer, Octavia 100
Spencer, Peter 128
Spencer, Vaino H. 99
Spigner, Archie 81
Spikes, Dolores 18
Spiller, Bill 64
Spivey, Victoria 119
Sprewell, Latrell 23
Spriggs, William 67
Springer, Ashton, Jr. 115
Stackhouse, Houston 122
Stackhouse, Jerry 30
Staley, Dawn 57
Stallings, George A., Jr. 6
Stallworth, John 102
Stampley, Micah 54
Stanford, John 20
Stanford, Olivia Lee Dilworth 49
Stanley, A. Knighton 117
Stanton, Alysa 78
Stanton, Robert 20
Staples, Brent 8
Staples, Cleotha 113
Staples, Mavis 50, 88
Staples, "Pops" 32
Stargell, Willie 29
Starr, Edwin 122
Staton, Candi 27
Staton, Dakota 62
Staupers, Mabel K. 7
Stearnes, Norman "Turkey" 31
Steave-Dickerson, Kia 57
Steele, Claude 13, 97
Steele, Lawrence 28
Steele, Michael 38, 73, 91
Steele, Sage 115
Steele, Shelby 13, 82
Steinberg, Martha Jean "The
    Queen" 28
Stephens, Charlotte Andrews 14
Stephens, Sloane 105
Stephenson, Lance 118
Stevenson, Bryan 128
Stew 69
Steward, David L. 36
Steward, Emanuel 18, 106
Stewart, Alison 13
Stewart, Billy 112

Stewart, Dave 117
Stewart, Ella 39
Stewart, James, Jr. 60, 98
Stewart, Kordell 21, 111
Stewart, Maria W. Miller 19
Stewart, Nzingha 89
Stewart, Paul Wilbur 12
Stewart, Slam 126
Stewart, Tonea Harris 78
Stewart, Tricky 98
Stickney, Phyllis Yvonne 108
Sticky Fingaz 86
Still, William Grant 37
Stingley, Darryl 69
Stinson, Denise L. 59
Stith, Charles R. 73
Stith, James H. 116
Stith, Tom 93
Stokes, Carl 10, 73
Stokes, Louis 3
Stone, Angie 31
Stone, Chuck 9, 120
Stone, Jesse 98
Stone, Sly 85
Stone, Toni 15
Stoney, Michael 50
Storyboard P 118
Stoudemire, Amar'e 59, 106
Stout, Juanita Kidd 24
Stout, Renee 63
Stoute, Steve 38
Stowers, Freddie 107
Stradford, J. B. 101
Strahan, Michael 35, 81
Strautmanis, Michael 87
Strawberry, Darryl 22
Strayhorn, Billy 31
Street, John F. 24
Street, Richard 110
Streeter, Sarah 45
Streeter, Sevyn 115
Stringer, C. Vivian 13, 66
Stringer, Korey 35
Stringer, Vickie 58
Strode, Woody 111
Strong, Barrett 89
Strong, Charlie 118
Studdard, Ruben 46
Sudarkasa, Niara 4
Sudduth, Jimmy Lee 65
Sugarhill Gang, The 79, 125
Suggs, Terrell 108
Sullivan, Jazmine 81
Sullivan, Leon H. 3, 30
Sullivan, Louis 8
Sullivan, Maxine 37
Sumlin, Hubert 101
Summer, Donna 25, 102
Sumner, Francis Cecil 112
Sun Ra 60
Sundiata, Sekou 66
Sunnyland Slim 118
Sutphen, Mona 77
Suttles, Mule 108
Sutton, Percy E. 42, 82
Swan Silvertones, The 110
Swann, Bettye 109
Swann, Lynn 28
Sweat, Keith 19
Sweatman, Wilbur 125
Sweatshirt, Earl 114
Sweatt, Heman Marion 114
Sweet, Ossian 68

Sweet Honey in the Rock 106
Swizz Beatz 108
Swoopes, Sheryl 12, 56
Swygert, H. Patrick 22
Sykes, Roosevelt 20
Sykes, Wanda 48, 81
Syler, Rene 53
Tacuma, Jamaaladeen 124
Tademy, Lalita 36
Tail Dragger 112
Tait, Michael 57
Take 6 112
Talbert, David E. 34, 93
Talbert, Mary B. 77
Talley, André Leon 56, 106
Tamar-kali 63
Tamia 24, 55
Tampa Red 63
Tancil, Gladys Quander 59
Tanksley, Ann 37
Tanner, Henry Ossawa 1
Tanner, Jack E. 100
Tapscott, Horace 126
Taste of Honey, A 115
Tate, Buddy 108
Tate, Eleanora E. 20, 55
Tate, Grady 106
Tate, John 107
Tate, Larenz 15
Tatum, Art 28
Tatum, Beverly Daniel 42, 84
Tatum, Elinor R. 78
Tatum, Jack 87
Tatum, Reece 104
Tatum, Wilbert 76
Taulbert, Clifton Lemoure 19
Tavares 115
Taylor, Billy 23, 92
Taylor, Bo 72
Taylor, Cecil 70
Taylor, Charles 20
Taylor, Eddie 116
Taylor, Ephren W., II 61
Taylor, Gardner C. 76
Taylor, Helen (Lavon Hollingshed) 30
Taylor, Hound Dog 120
Taylor, Jason 70
Taylor, Jermain 60
Taylor, Koko 40, 80
Taylor, Kristin Clark 8
Taylor, Lawrence 25
Taylor, Lonzie Odie 96
Taylor, Marshall Walter "Major" 62
Taylor, Meshach 4
Taylor, Mildred D. 26
Taylor, Natalie 47
Taylor, Recy 92
Taylor, Regina 9, 46, 97
Taylor, Robert Robinson 80
Taylor, Robert Rochon 104
Taylor, Ron 35
Taylor, Susan C. 62
Taylor, Susan L. 10, 86
Taylor, Susie King 13
T-Boz 108
Tchicai, John 102
Teague, Bob 111
Teasley, Lisa 92
Teer, Barbara Ann 81
Temple, Collis, Jr. 119
Temple, Ed 109
Temple, Lewis 102

Terrell, Dorothy A. 24
Terrell, Ernie 118
Terrell, Jean 116
Terrell, Mary Church 9
Terrell, Tammi 32
Terrell-Kearney, Kim 83
Terrence J 108
Terry, Bryant 128
Terry, Clark 39, 127
Terry, Sonny 88
Tex, Joe 116
Tharpe, Rosetta 65
The-Dream 74
Thigpen, Ed 110
Thigpen, Lynne 17, 41
Thomas, Alma 14
Thomas, Arthur Ray 52
Thomas, Carla 96
Thomas, Clarence 2, 39, 65
Thomas, Claudia Lynn 64
Thomas, Debi 26
Thomas, Derrick 25
Thomas, Emmitt 71
Thomas, Frank 12, 51
Thomas, Franklin A. 5, 49
Thomas, Irma 29
Thomas, Isiah 7, 26, 65
Thomas, Jefferson 88
Thomas, Michael 69
Thomas, Mickalene 61
Thomas, Rozonda 34, 78
Thomas, Rufus 20, 96
Thomas, Sean Patrick 35
Thomas, Tabby 119
Thomas, Thurman 75
Thomas, Trisha R. 65
Thomas, Vivien 9
Thomas-Graham, Pamela 29
Thomas-Greenfield, Linda 99
Thompson, Bennie 26, 119
Thompson, Cynthia Bramlett 50
Thompson, Don 56, 108
Thompson, John Douglas 81
Thompson, John W. 26
Thompson, Kenan 52
Thompson, Klay 126
Thompson, Larry D. 39
Thompson, Mychal 126
Thompson, Tazewell 13
Thompson, Tina 25, 75
Thompson, William C., Jr. 35, 114
Thoms, Tracie 61
Thornton, Big Mama 33
Thornton, Yvonne S. 69
Thrash, Dox 35
Threadgill, Henry 97
Thrower, Willie 35
Thurman, Howard 3
Thurman, Wallace 16
Thurmond, Nate 88
Thurston, Baratunde 79, 101
Thurston, Stephen J. 49
Tiant, Luis 102
Till, Emmett 7
Tillard, Conrad 47
Tillis, Frederick 40
Tillman, Deborah 98
Tillman, Dorothy 76
Tillman, George, Jr. 20
Timbaland 32
Tingling, Milton A. 110
Tinsley, Boyd 50
Tirico, Mike 68, 124

Tisdale, Wayman 50
Tobias, Channing H. 79
Tobin, Patricia 75
Todman, Terence A. 55
Tolbert, James L. 112
Tolbert, Mike 125
Tolbert, Terence 74
Toler, Burl 80
Tolliver, Mose 60
Tolliver, William 9
Tolson, Melvin 37
Tolton, Augustine 62
Tomlin, Mike 123
Tomlinson, LaDainian 65, 112
Tonex 54
Toney, James 89
Tony! Toni! Toné! 127
Tooks, Lance 62
Toomer, Jean 6
Toote, Gloria E. A. 64
Torres, Gina 52
Torry, Guy 31
Touré, Askia (Muhammad Abu Bakr el) 47
Touré, Faya Ora Rose 56
Toussaint, Allen 60
Towles, Nat 128
Towns, Edolphus 19, 75
Townsend, Robert 4, 23
T-Pain 73, 111
Trammps, The 108
Travis, Tracey T. 94
Treacherous Three 128
Tresvant, Ralph 57
Trethewey, Natasha 103
Tribbett, Tye 81
Tribble, Israel, Jr. 8
Trina 114
Trombone Shorty 97
Trotter, Donne E. 28
Trotter, Lloyd G. 56
Trotter, Monroe 9
Troupe, Quincy 83
Trouppe, Quincy Thomas, Sr. 84
True, Rachel 82
Trueheart, William E. 49
Tubbs Jones, Stephanie 24, 72
Tubman, Harriet 9
Tucker, C. Delores 12, 56
Tucker, Chris 13, 23, 62
Tucker, Cynthia 15, 61
Tucker, Rosina 14
Tucker, Tommy 127
Tuckson, Reed V. 71
Tuff, Antoinette 120
Tunie, Tamara 63
Tunnell, Emlen 54
Turman, Glynn 100
Turnbull, Charles Wesley 62
Turnbull, Walter 13, 60
Turner, Big Joe 92
Turner, Henry McNeal 5
Turner, Ike 68
Turner, Mark 126
Turner, Morrie 122
Turner, Tina 6, 27
Twiggs, Leo 127
Twilight, Alexander 125
2 Chainz 105
Tyga 117
Tyler, Aisha N. 36
Tyler, Ollie 128
Tyler, the Creator 100

Tyner, McCoy 92
Tyree, Omar Rashad 21
Tyson, Andre 40
Tyson, Asha 39
Tyson, Cicely 7, 51, 112
Tyson, Mike 28, 44, 93
Tyson, Neil deGrasse 15, 65
Uggams, Leslie 23, 114
Ulmer, James 79
Underwood, Blair 7, 27, 76
Union, Gabrielle 31, 92
Unseld, Wes 23
Upshaw, Gene 18, 47, 72
Upton, Justin 124
Upton, Melvin, Jr. 124
Urschel, John 126
Usher 23, 56, 95
Usry, James L. 23
Ussery, Terdema, II 29
Utendahl, John 23
Valentino, Bobby 62
Van Lierop, Robert 53
Van Peebles, Mario 2, 51
Van Peebles, Melvin 7, 95
Vance, Courtney B. 15, 60
Vance, Jim 110
VanDerZee, James 6
Vandross, Luther 13, 48, 59
Vanzant, Iyanla 17, 47, 108
Vaughan, Sarah 13
Vaughn, Countess 53
Vaughn, Gladys Gary 47
Vaughn, Jacque 127
Vaughn, Mo 16
Vaughn, Viola 70
Vaughns, Cleopatra 46
Vega, Marta Moreno 61
Velez-Rodriguez, Argelia 56
Verdelle, A. J. 26
Vereen, Ben 4
Verrett, Shirley 66, 91
Vesey, Denmark 100
Via, Dennis 108
Vick, Michael 39, 65, 94
Villarosa, Clara 85
Vincent, Marjorie Judith 2
Vincent, Troy 91
Vinnegar, Leroy 124
Vinson, Eddie 112
Von Lipsey, Roderick K. 11
Waddles, Charleszetta "Mother" 10, 49
Wade, Dwyane 61, 103
Wade, Ernestine 126
Wade-Gayles, Gloria Jean 41
Wagner, Albert 78
Wagner, Annice 22
Wainwright, Joscelyn 46
Waka Flocka Flame 110
Walcott, Dennis M. 112
Walcott, Jersey Joe 102
Waldon, Alton R., Jr. 98
Waldron, Mal 109
Wale 92
Walker, Albertina 10, 58, 89
Walker, A'lelia 14
Walker, Alice 1, 43
Walker, Arthur, II 87
Walker, Bernita Ruth 53
Walker, Cedric "Ricky" 19
Walker, Chet 106
Walker, Cora T. 68
Walker, Dianne 57

Walker, George 37
Walker, Herschel 1, 69
Walker, Hezekiah 34
Walker, Joe Louis 118
Walker, John T. 50
Walker, Joseph Edison 111
Walker, Kara 16, 80
Walker, LeRoy T. 106
Walker, Lucius, Jr. 88
Walker, Madame C. J. 7
Walker, Maggie Lena 17
Walker, Margaret 29
Walker, Ray 109
Walker, Rebecca 50
Walker, T. J. 7
Walker, T-Bone 111
Walker, Teshima 114
Walker, Tristan 98
Walker, Wyatt Tee 80
Wall, Orindatus S. B. 92
Wallace, Ben 54
Wallace, Joaquin 49
Wallace, Michele Faith 13
Wallace, Perry E. 47
Wallace, Phyllis A. 9
Wallace, Rasheed 56
Wallace, Sippie 1
Wallace, William 75
Waller, Fats 29
Wallis, Quvenzhané 109
Walters, Ronald 83
Walton, Cedar 114
Wanz 116
Ward, Andre 62
Ward, Anita 118
Ward, Benjamin 68
Ward, Douglas Turner 42
Ward, Hines 84
Ward, Lloyd 21, 46
Ward, Willa 105
Ward, William E. 107
Ware, Andre 37
Ware, Carl H. 30
Ware, David S. 106
Ware, DeMarcus 92
Warfield, Marsha 2
Warfield, William 94
Waring, Laura Wheeler 99
Warner, Malcolm-Jamal 22, 36, 110
Warren, Butch 116
Warren, Michael 27
Warwick, Dionne 18, 111
Washington, Alonzo 29
Washington, Booker T. 4
Washington, Denzel 1, 16, 93
Washington, Dinah 22
Washington, Ebonya 79
Washington, Elsie B. 78
Washington, Fredi 10
Washington, Gene 63
Washington, Grover, Jr. 17, 44
Washington, Harold 6
Washington, Harriet A. 69
Washington, Hayma 86
Washington, Isaiah 62
Washington, James, Jr. 38
Washington, James Melvin 50
Washington, Karen 117
Washington, Kenny 50
Washington, Kenny 107
Washington, Kerry 46, 107
Washington, Laura S. 18
Washington, MaliVai 8

Washington, Margaret Murray 119
Washington, Mary T. 57
Washington, Ora Mae 115
Washington, Patrice Clarke 12
Washington, Pauletta Pearson 86
Washington, Regynald G. 44
Washington, Ron 119
Washington, Val 12
Washington, Walter 45
Washington-Williams, Essie Mae
  118
Wasow, Omar 15
Waters, Benny 26
Waters, Ethel 7
Waters, Maxine 3, 67, 103
Waters, Muddy 34
Watkins, Craig 97
Watkins, Donald 35
Watkins, Joe 86
Watkins, Levi, Jr. 9
Watkins, Perry 12
Watkins, Shirley R. 17
Watkins, Ted 104
Watkins, Walter C. 24
Watley, Jody 54
Watson, Benjamin 126
Watson, Bob 25
Watson, Carlos 50
Watson, Diane 41
Watson, Johnny "Guitar" 18
Watson Coleman, Bonnie 127
Watt, Garland W. 113
Watt, Mel 26, 105
Wattleton, Faye 9
Watts, André 42, 101
Watts, J. C., Jr. 14, 38
Watts, Reggie 52, 102
Watts, Rolonda 9
Wayans, Damien 78
Wayans, Damon 8, 41
Wayans, Keenen Ivory 18
Wayans, Kim 80
Wayans, Marlon 29, 82
Wayans, Shawn 29
Weathers, Carl 10, 117
Weaver, Afaa Michael 37
Weaver, Mike 109
Weaver, Robert C. 8, 46
Webb, Chick 105
Webb, Veronica 10, 95
Webb, Wellington 3, 81
Webb-Christburg, Sheyann 110
Webber, Chris 15, 30, 59, 118
Webster, Katie 29
Wedgeworth, Robert W. 42
Weeks, Thomas, III 70
Weems, Carrie Mae 63, 116
Weems, Renita J. 44
Wein, Joyce 62
Welburn, Edward T. 50
Welch, Elisabeth 52
Welcome, Verda Freeman 112
Wellington, Valerie 118
Wells, Henrietta Bell 69
Wells, James Lesesne 10
Wells, Junior 102
Wells, Mary 28
Wells, Vernon 91
Wells, Willie 105
Wells-Barnett, Ida B. 8
Welsing, Frances Cress 5
Wesley, Dorothy Porter 19
Wesley, Richard 73

Wesley, Rutina 97
Wesley, Valerie Wilson 18
Wess, Frank 116
West, Allen 89
West, Cornel 5, 33, 80
West, Dorothy 12, 54
West, James E. 87
West, Kanye 52, 93
West, Togo D., Jr. 16
Westbrook, Kelvin 50
Westbrook, Peter 20
Westbrook, Russell 116
Westbrooks, Bobby 51
Whack, Rita Coburn 36
Whalum, Kirk 37, 64
Wharton, A. C., Jr. 110
Wharton, Clifton R., Jr. 7
Wharton, Clifton Reginald, Sr. 36
Wheat, Alan 14
Wheaton, James 103
Whispers, The 124
Whitaker, Forest 2, 49, 67
Whitaker, Mark 21, 47
Whitaker, Pernell 10, 89
White, Armond 80, 118
White, Augustus, III 100
White, Barry 13, 41
White, Bill 1, 48
White, Bukka 120
White, Charles 39
White, Dondi 34
White, Frank 95
White, Jesse 22, 75
White, Jessica 83
White, Jo Jo 112
White, John H. 27
White, Josh 86
White, Josh, Jr. 52
White, Lillias 120
White, Linda M. 45
White, Lois Jean 20
White, Maurice 29
White, Michael Jai 71, 117
White, Michael R. 5
White, Reggie 6, 50
White, Sylvain 96
White, Terri 82
White, Walter F. 4
White, Willye 67
White-Hammond, Gloria 61
Whitehead, Colson 77
Whiteside, Hassan 127
Whitfield, Fred 23
Whitfield, LeRoy 84
Whitfield, Lynn 18
Whitfield, Mal 60
Whitfield, Norman 73
Whitfield, Van 34
Whitlock, Jason 78
Whitmore, George 106
Whitney, Davey L. 110
Whitney, Marva 109
Wideman, John Edgar 5, 87
Widener, Warren 99
Wiggins, Andrew 128
Wiggins, Gerald 128
Wilbekin, Emil 63
Wilbon, Michael 68
Wilder, Deontay 121
Wilder, L. Douglas 3, 48
Wiley, Kehinde 62
Wiley, Ralph 8, 78
Wilfork, Vince 124

Wilkens, J. Ernest, Jr. 43
Wilkens, Lenny 11, 88
Wilkerson, Isabel 71
Wilkins, David 77
Wilkins, Dominique 74
Wilkins, Ray 47
Wilkins, Roger 2, 84
Wilkins, Roy 4
Wilkins, Thomas Alphonso 71
will.i.am 64
Williams, Ann Claire 82
Williams, Anthony 21
Williams, Armstrong 29
Williams, Bernie 128
Williams, Bert 18
Williams, Billy 86
Williams, Billy Dee 8, 105
Williams, Camilla 116
Williams, Clarence 33
Williams, Clarence 70
Williams, Clarence, III 26
Williams, Claude 80
Williams, Cootie 114
Williams, Daniel Hale 2
Williams, Darrent 116
Williams, David Rudyard 50
Williams, David W. 110
Williams, Deniece 36
Williams, Dennis P. 123
Williams, Deron 92
Williams, Doug 22, 112
Williams, Dudley 60
Williams, Eddie N. 44
Williams, Evelyn 10
Williams, Fannie Barrier 27
Williams, Frederick (B.) 63
Williams, George Washington 18
Williams, Gregory 11
Williams, Hosea 15, 31, 123
Williams, J. Mayo 83
Williams, Jody 113
Williams, Joe 5, 25
Williams, John A. 27
Williams, Juan 35, 80
Williams, Ken 68
Williams, Larry 118
Williams, Lauryn 58, 127
Williams, Lindsey 75
Williams, Maggie 7, 71
Williams, Malinda 57
Williams, Marco 53
Williams, Mary Lou 15
Williams, Michael Kenneth 97
Williams, Michael L. 86
Williams, Michelle 73
Williams, Montel 4, 57
Williams, Monty 125
Williams, Nat D. 91
Williams, Natalie 31
Williams, O. S. 13
Williams, Patricia 11, 54
Williams, Paul 112
Williams, Paul R. 9
Williams, Pharrell 47, 82, 119
Williams, Preston Warren, II 64
Williams, Rhonda Y. 86
Williams, Ricky 85
Williams, Robert F. 11
Williams, Ronald A. 57
Williams, Russell, II 70
Williams, Samm-Art 21
Williams, Saul 31
Williams, Serena 20, 41, 73

Williams, Sherley Anne 25
Williams, Spencer 126
Williams, Stanley "Tookie" 29, 57
Williams, Stevie 71
Williams, Ted 91
Williams, Terrie M. 35
Williams, Tony 67
Williams, Vanessa A. 32, 66
Williams, Vanessa L. 4, 17
Williams, Venus 17, 34, 62
Williams, Walter E. 4
Williams, Wendy 62
Williams, William T. 11
Williams, Willie L. 4
Williamson, Fred 67
Williamson, Mykelti 22
Williamson, Sonny Boy 84
Willie, Louis, Jr. 68
Willingham, Tyrone 43
Willis, Bill 68
Willis, Deborah 85
Willis, Dontrelle 55
Willis, Patrick 99
Williston, David Augustus 99
Wills, Harry 80
Wills, Maury 73
Wilmore, Larry 121
Wilson, Abram 104
Wilson, August 7, 33, 55
Wilson, Brian Courtney 94
Wilson, Cassandra 16
Wilson, Chandra 57
Wilson, Charlie 31, 77
Wilson, David 123
Wilson, Debra 38
Wilson, Demond 102
Wilson, Donald E. 88
Wilson, Dorien 55
Wilson, Ellis 39
Wilson, Flip 21
Wilson, Frank 106
Wilson, Frederica 92
Wilson, Gerald 49, 123
Wilson, Jackie 60
Wilson, Jimmy 45
Wilson, John 109
Wilson, Lionel 99
Wilson, Margaret Bush 79
Wilson, Mary 28
Wilson, Nancy 10, 98
Wilson, Natalie 38
Wilson, Phill 9, 104
Wilson, Reggie 116
Wilson, Russell 119
Wilson, Stephanie 72
Wilson, Sunnie 7, 55
Wilson, Tracey Scott 777
Wilson, William Julius 20
Winans, Angie 36
Winans, BeBe 14
Winans, CeCe 14, 43
Winans, David 77
Winans, Debbie 36
Winans, Marvin L. 17, 127
Winans, Ronald 54
Winans, Vickie 24
Winfield, Dave 5, 91
Winfield, Paul 2, 45
Winfrey, Oprah 2, 15, 61, 106
Winkfield, Jimmy 42
Winslow, Kellen 83
Wisdom, Kimberlydawn 57
Withers, Bill 61

Withers, Ernest C. 68, 88
Withers-Mendes, Elisabeth 64
Witherspoon, Jimmy 113
Witherspoon, John 38
Witt, Edwin T. 26
Wolfe, Ann 82
Wolfe, George C. 6, 43, 127
Womack, Bobby 60, 92, 123
Wonder, Stevie 11, 53, 121
Wood, Willie 111
Woodard, Alfre 9, 108
Woodard, Lynette 67
Woodruff, Hale 9
Woodruff, John 68
Woods, Abraham, Jr. 74
Woods, Belita 103
Woods, Cheyenne 103
Woods, Georgie 57
Woods, Granville T. 5
Woods, Jacqueline 52
Woods, Mattiebelle 63
Woods, Renn 110
Woods, Scott 55
Woods, Sylvia 34, 104
Woods, Teri 69
Woods, Tiger 14, 31, 81
Woodson, Ali Ollie 89
Woodson, Carter G. 2
Woodson, Jacqueline 125
Woodson, Mike 78
Woodson, Robert L. 10
Woodson, Rod 79
Woolard, Jamal 102
Worrill, Conrad 12
Worthy, James 49
Worthy, Kym 84
Wray, Noble 114
Wright, Antoinette 60
Wright, Beverly 97
Wright, Bruce McMarion 3, 52
Wright, Chalky 103
Wright, Charles H. 35
Wright, Deborah C. 25
Wright, Eugene 125
Wright, Jeffrey 54, 111
Wright, Jeremiah A., Jr. 45, 69, 103
Wright, Lewin 43
Wright, Louis Tompkins 4
Wright, Nathan, Jr. 56
Wright, O. V. 114
Wright, Rayfield 70
Wright, Richard 5
Wright, Richard Robert, Sr. 100
Wright, Sarah E. 95
Wright, Timothy 74
Wyatt, Addie L. 56
Wynn, Albert R. 25, 77
X, Malcolm 1
X, Marvin 45
Xuma, Madie Hall 59
Xzibit 78
Yancey, Jimmy 116
Yancy, Dorothy Cowser 42
Yarbrough, Camille 40
Yarbrough, Cedric 51
Yates, Jack 114
Yayo, Tony 113
Yearwood, Lennox, Jr. 112
Yerby, Frank 96
Yergan, Max 123
Yette, Samuel F. 63
YG 122
Ying Yang Twins 112

Yoba, Malik 11
York, Dwight D. 71
York, Vincent 40
Young, Al 82
Young, Andrew 3, 48, 110
Young, Charles 77
Young, Coleman 1, 20
Young, Darren 114
Young, Donald, Jr. 57
Young, Jean Childs 14
Young, Jimmy 54
Young, John 111
Young, Johnny 120
Young, Lee 72
Young, Lee Thompson 114
Young, Lester 37
Young, Perry H. 100
Young, Roger Arliner 29
Young, Whitney M., Jr. 4
Young Jeezy 63
Youngblood, Johnny Ray 8
Youngblood, Shay 32
Zane 71
Zollar, Alfred 40
Zollar, Jawole Willa Jo 28
Zook, Kristal Brent 62
Z-Ro 109

Angolan
Bonga, Kuenda 13
dos Santos, Isabel 114
dos Santos, José Eduardo 43, 114
Lopes, Leila 99
Neto, António Agostinho 43
Roberto, Holden 65
Savimbi, Jonas 2, 34

Antiguan
Kincaid, Jamaica 4, 109
McGuire, George Alexander 80
Spencer, Winston Baldwin 68
Williams, Denise 40

Aruban
Williams, David Rudyard 50

Australian
Freeman, Cathy 29
Irving, Kyrie 102
Mundine, Anthony 56
Rose, Lionel 56

Austrian
Kodjoe, Boris 34, 89

Bahamian
Christie, Perry Gladstone 53
Ferguson, Amos 81
Ingraham, Hubert A. 19
Munroe, Myles 125
Pindling, Lynden 81
Spence, Joseph 49
Thompson, Mychal 126

Barbadian
Adams, Grantley 82
Arthur, Owen 33
Brathwaite, Kamau 36
Clarke, Austin C. 32
Foster, Cecil 32
Fresh, Doug E. 93
Grandmaster Flash 33, 60
Kamau, Kwadwo Agymah 28
Lamming, George 35

Rihanna 65, 102

Belgian
Stromae 121

Belizean
Barrow, Dean 69
Jones, Marion 21, 66
Palacio, Andy 96
Shyne 101

Beninese
Gantin, Bernardin 70
Hounsou, Djimon 19, 45
Joachim, Paulin 34
Kerekou, Ahmed (Mathieu) 1
Kidjo, Angelique 50
Loueke, Lionel 88
Soglo, Nicéphore 15
Yayi, Boni T. 84

Bermudian
Cameron, Earl 44
Gordon, Pamela 17
Smith, Jennifer 21

Bissau-Guinean
Cabral, Amílcar 104
Sanhá Malam Bacai 84, 101
Vieira, João Bernardo 14, 84

Botswanan
Dow, Unity 104
Khama, Ian 95
Masire, Quett 5
Mogae, Festus Gontebanye 19, 79

Brazilian
Alves, Dani 121
Brown, Carlinhos 81
Caymmi, Dorival 72
da Silva, Benedita 5
dos Santos, Manuel Francisco 65
Gil, Gilberto 53
Jorge, Seu 73
Leônidas 96
Machado de Assis 74
Mello, Breno 73
Moura, Paulo 87
Nascimento, Abdias do 93
Nascimento, Milton 2, 64
Pelé 7
Pitta, Celso 17
Querino, Manuel Raimundo 84
Ronaldinho 69
Silva, Anderson 96
Silva, Marina 80

British
Abbott, Diane 9
Abrahams, Zaraah 127
Abudu, Mo 121
Adjaye, David 38, 78
Adoboli, Kweku 106
Akinnuoye-Agbaje, Adewale 56
Akomfrah, John 37
Amos, Valerie 41
Anderson, Ho Che 54
Anderson, Jacob 128
Anthony, Trey 63
Appiah, Kwame Anthony 67, 101
Armah, Esther 87
Armatrading, Joan 32
Bailey Rae, Corinne 83
Barnes, John 53

Bassey, Shirley 25
Berry, James 41
Blackwood, Maureen 37
Boateng, Ozwald 35, 113
Boateng, Paul Yaw 56
Breeze, Jean "Binta" 37
Brown, Melanie 73
Campbell, Naomi 1, 31, 120
Carby, Hazel 27
Charles, John 108
Christie, Linford 8
Cole, Ashley 106
Coleridge-Taylor, Samuel 75
Crooks, Garth 53
Cruz, Taio 104
D'Aguiar, Fred 50
Danjah, Terror 91
David, Craig 31, 53
Davidson, Jaye 5
DeGale, James 74
Edwards, Trevor 54
Ejiofor, Chiwetel 67, 116
Ejogo, Carmen 126
Elba, Idris 49, 89, 116
Emmanuel, Alphonsia 38
Equiano, Olaudah 78
Estelle 75
Evans, Diana 72
Farah, Mo 104
Fenton, Kevin 87
Ferdinand, Rio 82
FKA Twigs 123
Forna, Aminatta 95
Garrett, Sean 57
Gladwell, Malcolm 62
Griffin, Angela 80
Hall, Adelaide 126
Hall, Stuart 78
Hamilton, Lewis 66
Harewood, David 52
Harris, Naomie 55, 116
Haye, David 82
Henriques, Julian 37
Henry, Lenny 9, 52
Hill, Darryl 128
Holmes, Kelly 47
Ibrahim, Mo 67, 115
Ince, Paul 83
Jamelia 51
James, David 84
Jean-Baptiste, Marianne 17, 46
Johnson, Ken 106
Jordan, Ronny 26
Joseph, Paterson 126
Julien, Isaac 3
Kay, Jackie 37
Kinch, Soweto 108
King, Oona 27
Kiwanuka, Michael 126
Kwei-Armah, Kwame 84
Lester, Adrian 46
Lewis, Denise 33
Lewis, Lennox 27
Lewis, Leona 75
Lindo, Delroy 18, 45
Markham, E. A. 37
Mbatha-Raw, Gugu 89
McGrath, Pat 72
McKinney Hammond, Michelle 51
McQueen, Steve 84
Miller, Wentworth 75
Ming, Mel 106
Morris, William "Bill" 51

Muamba, Fabrice 104
Mvula, Laura 110
Newton, Thandie 26, 114
Ofili, Chris 124
Okonedo, Sophie 67
Oyelowo, David 82, 126
Pitt, David Thomas 10
Rascal, Dizzee 82
Regis, Cyrille 51
Sade 15, 92
Sandé, Emeli 113
Scantlebury, Janna 47
Seacole, Mary 54
Seal 14, 75
Selasi, Taiye 125
Sesay, Isha 107
Siji 56
Slash 75
Slick Rick 93
Smalling, Chris 118
Smith, Anjela Lauren 44
Smith, Richard 51
Smith, Zadie 51
Stoutt, H. Lavity 83
Stuart, Moira 82
Sturridge, Daniel 120
Taylor, John (David Beckett) 16
Thomason, Marsha 47
Tinie Tempah 115
Tricky 98
Walker, Eamonn 37
Williams, Roy 89

Burkinabé
Compaore, Blaise 87
Sankara, Thomas 17
Somé, Malidoma Patrice 10

Burundian
Bigirimana, Gael 115
Ndadaye, Melchior 7
Nkurunziza, Pierre 78
Ntaryamira, Cyprien 8

Cameroonian
Ahidjo, Ahmadou 81
Bebey, Francis 45
Beti, Mongo 36
Biya, Chantal 89
Biya, Paul 28, 114
Eto'o, Samuel 73
Fosso, Samuel 116
Kotto, Yaphet 7
Milla, Roger 2
Njawe, Pius 87
Nteff, Alain 127
Oyono, Ferdinand 38
Song, Alex 105

Canadian
Alexander, Lincoln 106
Auguste, Arnold A. 47
Augustine, Jean 53
Bannister, Edward Mitchell 88
Bell, Ralph S. 5
Best, Carrie 80
Boyd, Suzanne 52
Brand, Dionne 32
Brathwaite, Fred 35
Brown, Rosemary 62
Brown, Sean 52
Carnegie, Herbert 25
Chanté, Keshia 50
Chong, Rae Dawn 62

Clarke, Austin 32
Clarke, George 32
Cools, Anne 64
Cooper, Afua 53
Cox, Deborah 28
Croal, N'Gai 76
Curling, Alvin 34
Dixon, George 52
Doig, Jason 45
Drake 86
Edugyan, Esi 98
Elliot, Lorris 37
Fiona, Melanie 84
Foster, Cecil 32
Fox, Rick 27
Fuhr, Grant 1, 49
Grand-Pierre, Jean-Luc 46
Hammond, Lenn 34
Harris, Claire 34
Henry, Joshua 94
Iginla, Jarome 35
Isaac, Julius 34
James, Vanessa 84
Jean, Michaëlle; 70
Jenkins, Fergie 46
Johnson, Ben 1
Johnson, Clark 96
Kane, Evander 97
K'naan 76
Laraque, Georges 48
Lewis, Daurene 72
Mayers, Jamal 39
McKegney, Tony 3
Mollel, Tololwa 38
Neale, Haydain 52
O'Ree, Willie 5
Peterson, Oscar 52
Philip, Marlene Nourbese 32
Reuben, Gloria 15
Richards, Lloyd 2
Rodrigues, Percy 68
Sadlier, Rosemary 62
Salvador, Bryce 51
Scarlett, Millicent 49
Senior, Olive 37
Simmonds, Wayne 121
Sparks, Corinne Etta 53
Stiverne, Bermane 128
Subban, P. K. 121
Vanity 67
Verna, Gelsy 70
Weekes, Kevin 67
Williams, Denise 40

Cape Verdean
Antunes, Lúcio 109
Évora, Cesária 12, 99
Grace, Sweet Daddy 104
Pereira, Aristides 30, 97

Caymanian
Ebanks, Selita 67

Central African
Bozizé, François 96, 117
Djotodia, Michel 117

Chadian
Déby, Idriss 30, 125
Habré, Hissène 6, 104

Colombian
Pomare, Eleo 72

Congolese (Democratic Republic of the Congo)
Kabila, Joseph 30, 126
Kabila, Laurent 20
Kintaudi, Leon 62
Kolosoy, Wendo 73
Lubanga, Thomas 104
Mobutu Sese Seko 1, 56
Muamba, Fabrice 104
Mudimbe, V. Y. 61
Mutombo, Dikembe 7, 107
Nkunda, Laurent 75
Ntaganda, Bosco 111
Rochereau, Tabu Ley 117

Congolese (Republic of the Congo)
Lumumba, Patrice 33
Sassou-Nguesso, Denis 103

Costa Rican
McDonald, Erroll 1

Cuban
Dihigo, Martín 103
Ferrer, Ibrahim 41
Fuentes, Tito 123
Güines, Tata 69
Hernández, Orlando 96
León, Tania 13
Maceo, Antonio 82
Minoso, Minnie 89, 127
Portuondo, Omara 53
Puig, Yasiel 113
Quirot, Ana 13
Rodríguez, Arsenio 87
Santamaria, Mongo 81
Savón, Félix 105
Secada, Jon 97
Stevenson, Teófilo 103
Tiant, Luis 102
Valdés, Chucho 89
Velez-Rodriguez, Argelia 56

Curaçaoan
Jones, Andruw 98

Danish
Tchicai, John 102

Dominican (from Dominica)
Charles, Mary Eugenia 10, 55
Charles, Pierre 52
Skerrit, Roosevelt 72

Dominican (from Dominican Republic)
Cano, Robinson 97
Horford, Al 107
Martínez, Pedro 81, 126
Ortiz, David 52, 82
Perez, Pascual 108
Sosa, Sammy 21, 44
Uribe, Juan 122
Virgil, Ozzie 48

Dutch
Ali, Ayaan Hirsi 58, 92
Brigitha, Enith 126
Davids, Edgar 106
Liberia-Peters, Maria Philomena 12
Seedorf, Clarence 121

Ecuadoran
Benítez, Christian 113

Equatorial Guinean
Moussambani, Eric 105
Obiang, Teodoro 103

Eritrean
Afewerki, Isaias 98
Keflezighi, Meb 49, 121

Ethiopian
Aberra, Amsale 67
Abune Paulos 105
Afro, Teddy 78
Astatke, Mulatu 81
Bekele, Kenenisa 75
Birra, Ali 113
Desalegn, Hailemariam 105
Dibaba, Tirunesh 73, 109
Gabre-Medhin, Tsegaye 64
Gebrselassie, Haile 70
Gerima, Haile 38, 80
Haile Selassie 7
Ibrahim, Fuad 109
Kebede, Liya 59
Mengistu, Haile Mariam 65
Samuelsson, Marcus 53, 120
Yirga, Samuel 126
Zenawi, Meles 3, 99

Filipino
apl.de.ap 84

Finnish
Toivola, Jani 118

French
Anelka, Nicolas 118
Baker, Josephine 3
Baldwin, James 1
Baugé, Grégory 86
Bebey, Francis 45
Bonaly, Surya 7
Boulogne, Joseph, Chevalier de
    Saint-Georges 94
Chase-Riboud, Barbara 20, 46
Diaw, Boris 122
Dieudonné 67, 118
Evra, Patrice 102
Fanon, Frantz 44
Henry, Thierry 66, 127
James, Vanessa 84
Kanouté, Fred 68
Noah, Yannick 4, 60, 121
Parker, Tony 75
Song, Alex 105
Sy, Omar 109
Tanner, Henry Ossawa 1
Taubira, Christiane 117
Thiam, Tidjane 104
White, Sylvain 96

Gabonese
Bongo, Ali Ben 80
Bongo, Omar 1, 79

Gambian
Bensouda, Fatou 103
Jammeh, Yahya 23, 104
Peters, Lenrie 43
Sanneh, Kelefa 96

German
Ayim, May 126
Massaquoi, Hans J. 30

Ghanaian
Adoboli, Kweku 106
Adu, Freddy 67

Aidoo, Ama Ata 38
Ali, Mohammed Naseehu 60
Annan, Kofi Atta 15, 48
Appiah, Kwame Anthony 67, 101
Armah, Ayi Kwei 49
Atta Mills, John 75
Awoonor, Kofi 37, 115
Awuah, Patrick 111
Balotelli, Mario 104
Bartels, Peggielene 80
Blitz the Ambassador 115
Danquah, Meri Nana Ama 93
Dawuni, Rocky 94
DuBois, Shirley Graham 21
Gyan, Asamoah 87
Jawara, Dawda Kairaba 11
Kufuor, John Agyekum 54, 82
Lee, Robert 112
Mahama, John Dramani 103
Mensah, John 87
Mensah, Thomas 48
Nkrumah, Kwame 3
Pelé, Abedi 122
Rawlings, Jerry 9
Rawlings, Nana Konadu Agyeman
    13
Yeboah, Emmanuel Ofosu 53

Grenadian
Bishop, Maurice 39
Gairy, Eric Matthew 83
Isaac, Julius 34
Mitchell, Keith 82

Guinean
Camara, Moussa Dadis 76
Condé, Alpha 95
Conté, Lansana 7, 76
Diallo, Amadou 27
Diawara, Djeli Moussa 111
Niane, Katoucha 70
Touré, Sekou 6

Guyanese
Amos, Valerie 41
Beaton, Norman 14
Burnham, Forbes 66
Carter, Martin 49
Dabydeen, David 48
D'Aguiar, Fred 50
Damas, Léon-Gontran 46
Dathorne, O. R. 52
DoHarris, Brenda 116
Griffith, Patrick A. 64
Jagan, Cheddi 16
Lefel, Edith 41
van Sertima, Ivan 25

Haitian
Aristide, Jean-Bertrand 6, 45
Auguste, Rose-Anne 13
Beauvais, Garcelle 29, 95
Beauvoir, Max 74
Beken 111
Celestin, Josaphat 101
Charlemagne, Manno 11
Christophe, Henri 9
Danticat, Edwidge 15, 68, 128
Delice, Ronald 48
Delice, Rony 48
Duvalier, François 124
Duvalier, Jean-Claude 124
Hector, Jamie 98
Jean, Wyclef 20, 86

Jean-Juste, Gérard 78
Jean-Louis, Jimmy 76
Jeune, Vitolio 98
Laferriere, Dany 33
Lamothe, Laurent 122
Laraque, Paul 67
Laroche, Joseph Philippe Lemercier
    85
Magloire, Paul Eugène 68
Manigat, Mirlande 90
Martelly, Michel 90
Pape, Jean William 126
Pascal-Trouillot, Ertha 3
Peck, Raoul 32
Pierre, Andre 17
Pierre-Louis, Michèle 75
Préval, René 87
Siméus, Dumas M. 25, 110
Stiverne, Bermane 128
Verna, Gelsy 70
Villard-Appolon, Malya 106

Hungarian
Watts, André 42, 101

Irish
Adebari, Rotimi 83
Mumba, Samantha 29

Italian
Balotelli, Mario 104
Esposito, Giancarlo 9
Kyenge, Cécile 113

Ivorian
Bedie, Henri Konan 21
Blondy, Alpha 30
Dadié, Bernard 34
De Bankolé, Isaach 78
Drogba, Didier 78
Gbagbo, Laurent 43, 90
Guéï, Robert 66
Houphouët-Boigny, Félix 4, 64
Ouattara 43
Ouattara, Alassane 90
Ouattara, Morou 74
Thiam, Tidjane 104
Touré, Yaya 99

Jamaican
Ashley, Maurice 15, 47
Atkinson, Alia 126
Banton, Buju 93
Barnes, John 53
Barnes, Lloyd 77
Barrett, Lindsay 43
Beenie Man 32
Belafonte, Harry 4, 65
Bennett, Louise 69
Bennett, Richard 97
Berry, James 41
Big Youth 107
Bolt, Usain 73, 104
Brown, Dennis 99
Burning Spear 79
Campbell-Brown, Veronica 102
Channer, Colin 36
Chronixx 123
Cliff, Jimmy 28, 92
Cliff, Michelle 42
Coke, Christopher 108
Cooper, Afua 53
Cox, Renée 67
Curling, Alvin 34

Dawes, Kwame 126
Dekker, Desmond 104
Dodd, Coxsone 99
Dunbar, Sly 34
Ellis, Alton 74
Ellis, Hortense 97
Ewing, Patrick 17, 73
Fagan, Garth 18, 98
Fenton, Kevin 87
Figueroa, John J. 40
Ford, Vincent 75
Fraser-Pryce, Shelly-Ann 113
Garvey, Marcus 1
Golding, Bruce 78
Goodison, Lorna 71
Graham, Trevor 84
Griffiths, Marcia 29
Hamilton, Tanya 93
Hammond, Lenn 34
Hearne, John Edgar Caulwell 45
Heavy D 58, 98
Hibbert, Toots 103
Holness, Andrew 99
Irving, Barrington, Jr. 112
Isaacs, Gregory 89
James, Marlon 85, 124
Johnson, Ben 1
Johnson, Linton Kwesi 37
Joseph, Kathie-Ann 56
Kingston, Sean 94
Kong, B. Waine 50
Manley, Edna 26
Manley, Ruth 34
Marks, Audrey 99
Marley, Bob 5
Marley, Rita 32, 70
Marley, Stephen 100
Marley, Ziggy 41
McGregor, Stephen 99
McKay, Claude 6
McKenzie, Jaunel 73
Minott, Sugar 86
Moody, Ronald 30
Morrison, Keith 13
Mowatt, Judy 38
Palmer, Everard 37
Patterson, Orlando 4, 127
Patterson, P. J. 6, 20
Perry, Lee 19, 103
Perry, Ruth 19
Ranglin, Ernest 78
Reece, E. Albert 63
Rhoden, Wayne 70
Rhone, Trevor 80
Rogers, Joel Augustus 30
Russwurm, John Brown 100
Senior, Olive 37
Shaggy 31
Shakespeare, Robbie 34
Sharpe, Samuel 103
Shearer, Hugh 107
Simpson, Sherone 120
Simpson Miller, Portia 62, 100
Sinclair, Madge 78
Steely 80
Taylor, Karin 34
Tosh, Peter 9
White, Willard 53
Yabby You 83

Kenyan
Cheruiyot, Robert 69
Hayanga, Jeremiah 118

Jeptoo, Rita 121
Juma, Calestous 57
Kahora, Billy 125
Kariuki, J. M. 67
Kenyatta, Jomo 5
Kenyatta, Uhuru 110
Kibaki, Mwai 60
Kimetto, Dennis 125
Kipchoge, Eliud 124
Kipsang, Wilson 115
Kobia, Samuel 43
Loroupe, Tegla 59
Maathai, Wangari 43, 97
Mazrui, Ali 12, 124
Mboya, Tom 107
Moi, Daniel Arap 1, 35
Mutu, Wangechi 44
Mwangi, Meja 40
Ngilu, Charity 58
Ngugi wa Thiong'o 29, 61, 101
Nyong'o, Lupita 127
Odinga, Raila 67, 110
Osman, Said 127
Otunga, Maurice Michael 55
Rudisha, David 112
Tergat, Paul 59
Wambugu, Florence 42
Wanjiru, Sammy 94

Korean
Ward, Hines 84

Lesotho
Le Loka, Tsidii 116
Mofolo, Thomas 37
Mosisili, Pakalitha 96
Thabane, Thomas 123

Liberian
Conneh, Sekou Damate, Jr. 51
Cooper, Lisa 73
Doe, Samuel K. 100
Fuller, Solomon Carter, Jr. 15
Gbowee, Leymah 76
Keith, Rachel Boone 63
Perry, Ruth 15
Roberts, Joseph Jenkins 125
Sawyer, Amos 2, 123
Sirleaf, Ellen Johnson 71
Taylor, Charles 20
Tolbert, William R. 100
Tubman, William 99
Weah, George 58

Malawian
Banda, Hastings Kamuzu 6, 54
Banda, Joyce 101
Chikoti, Shadreck 125
Kayira, Legson 40
Malawi Mouse Boys 114
Muluzi, Bakili 14, 76

Malian
Amadou & Mariam 113
Diawara, Fatoumata 114
Keïta, Ibrahim Boubacar 113
Keita, Salif 83
Keïta, Seydou 124
Sangare, Oumou 18, 99
Sangho, Awa 127
Sidibé, Malick 124
Souleymane, Mahamane 78
Touré, Amadou Toumani 18

Traore, Dioncounda 103

Martinican
Césaire, Aimé 48, 69
Palcy, Euzhan 94

Mauritanian
Sissako, Abderrahmane 127

Mexican
Catlett, Elizabeth 2, 120
Nyong'o, Lupita 127

Mozambican
Chissano, Joaquim 7, 55, 67
Couto, Mia 45
Diogo, Luisa Dias 63
Eusebio 118
Guebuza, Armando 81
Machel, Graça 16, 102
Machel, Samora Moises 8
Mutola, Maria 12

Namibian
Mbuende, Kaire 12
Nujoma, Samuel 10
Pohamba, Hifikepunye 95

Nigerian
Abacha, Sani 11, 70
Abani, Chris 77
Abiola, Moshood 70
Abiola-Costello, Hafsat 108
Abubakar, Abdulsalami 66
Abudu, Mo 121
Achebe, Chinua 6, 99, 111
Ade, King Sunny 41
Adichie, Chimamanda Ngozi 64, 121
Aire, Chris 117
Ake, Claude 30
Akinola, Peter Jasper 65
Akpan, Uwem 70
Akunyili, Dora Nkem 58
Allen, Tony 117
Amadi, Elechi 40
Amata, Jeta 111
Arinze, Francis 19
Azikiwe, Nnamdi 13
Babangida, Ibrahim 4
Babatunde, Rotimi 104
Bandele, Biyi 68, 121
Buhari, Muhammadu 128
Clark-Bekedermo, J. P. 44
Cole, Teju 120
Dangote, Aliko 124
Darego, Agbani 52
D'banj 107
Ekwensi, Cyprian 37
Elumelu, Tony 116
Emeagwali, Philip 30
Emecheta, Buchi 30
Fela 1, 42
Jalade-Ekeinde, Omotola 118
Jonathan, Goodluck 83
Kuti, Femi 47, 110
Lawal, Kase L. 45
Muhammed, Murtala 119
Obasanjo, Olusegun 5, 22
Obasanjo, Stella 32, 56
Ogunlesi, Adebayo O. 37
Ojukwu, Odumegwu 99
Okara, Gabriel 37
Okigbo, Christopher 102
Okocha, Jay Jay 99

Okonjo-Iweala, Ngozi 101
Okosuns, Sonny 71
Olagundoye, Toks 113
Olajuwon, Hakeem 2, 72
Olatunji, Babatunde 36, 126
Olojede, Dele 59
Olopade, Olufunmilayo Falusi 58
Omolewa, Michael 119
Onwueme, Tess Osonye 23
Onwurah, Ngozi 38
Osotimehin, Babatunde 107
Prince Twins Seven-Seven 95
Rotimi, Ola 1
Sade 15, 92
Saro-Wiwa, Kenule 39
Siji 56
Sowande, Fela 39
Soyinka, Wole 4, 93
Tutuola, Amos 30
Ujiri, Masai 107
Ukpabio, Helen 86
Wiwa, Ken 67
Yar'Adua, Umaru 69, 89

Nigerien
Bombino 112
Issoufou, Mahamadou 102
Tandja, Mamadou 33, 78

Norwegian
Brown, Anne 76

Panamanian
Bailey, Preston 64
Cobham, Billy 123
Williams, Juan 35, 80

Peruvian
Baca, Susana 80

Polish
Bridgetower, George 78

Portuguese
Souza, Carmen 111

Puerto Rican
Cepeda, Orlando 98
Schomburg, Arthur Alfonso 9

Russian
Khanga, Yelena 6

Rwandan
Bizimungu, Pasteur 19
Habyarimana, Juvenal 8
Ilibagiza, Immaculée 66
Kabera, Eric 104
Kagame, Paul 54
Mbabazi, Esther 122
Mushikiwabo, Louise 88
Rusesabagina, Paul 60

St. Kitts and Nevis
Douglas, Bob 96
Douglas, Denzil Llewellyn 53

Saint Lucian
Compton, John 65

Saudi
Amoudi, Mohammed al- 88
Kalbani, Adil 77

Senegalese
Acogny, Germaine 55
Akon 68

Ba, Mariama 30
Boye, Madior 30
Diop, Birago 53
Diop, Cheikh Anta 4
Diouf, Abdou 3
Evra, Patrice 102
Maal, Baaba 66
Mbaye, Mariétou 31
Mboup, Souleymane 10
Ndiaye, Iba 74
N'Dour, Youssou 1, 53, 79
Paris, Adama 120
Sall, Macky 101
Sané, Pierre Gabriel 21
Sembène, Ousmane 13, 62
Senghor, Augustin Diamancoune 66
Senghor, Léopold Sédar 12, 66
Sy, Oumou 65
Wade, Abdoulaye 66

Sierra Leonean
Beah, Ishmael 69
Cheney-Coker, Syl 43
DePrince, Michaela 104
Jones, Monty 66
Kabbah, Ahmad Tejan 23
Koroma, Ernest Bai 84
Sankoh, Foday 74
Sesay, Isha 107
Yumkella, Kandeh 105

Somali
Abdirahman, Abdi 126
Ahmed, Sharif 80
Ali, Ayaan Hirsi 58, 92
Ali Mahdi Mohamed 5
Dirie, Waris 56
Farah, Mo 104
Farah, Nuruddin 27
Iman 4, 33, 87
K'naan 76
Mohamud, Hassan Sheikh 105
Omar, Samia Yusuf 107
Roble, Abdi 71

South African
Abrahams, Peter 39
Adams, Paul 50
Biko, Steven 4
Brutus, Dennis 38
Buthelezi, Mangosuthu Gatsha 9
Butler, Jonathan 28
Chaka Chaka, Yvonne 112
Chweneyagae, Presley 63
Cole, Ernest 123
Dandala, Mvume 77
Dlamini-Zuma, Nkosazana 34, 105
Dube, John Langalibalele 119
Dube, Lucky 77
Grae, Jean 51
Hani, Chris 6
Head, Bessie 28
Jansen, Jonathan 102
Jim, Songezo 111
Ka Dinizulu, Mcwayizeni 29
Kaka, Luthando 118
Kente, Gibson 52
Khumalo, Leleti 51
Khumalo, S'manga 119
Kuzwayo, Ellen 68
Ladysmith Black Mambazo 103
LaGuma, Alex 30
Lebo M 109
Luthuli, Albert 13

Mabuza, Lindiwe 18
Mabuza-Suttle, Felicia 43
Madikizela-Mandela, Winnie 2, 35, 112
Mahlasela, Vusi 65
Makeba, Miriam 2, 50, 74
Malema, Julius 98
Mandela, Nelson 1, 14, 77, 117
Maponya, Maishe 101
Maponya, Richard 101
Masekela, Barbara 18
Masekela, Hugh 1, 106
Mathabane, Mark 5, 99
Matshikiza, Pumeza 115
Mbeki, Govan A. 80
Mbeki, Thabo 14, 73
Meyiwa, Senzo 124
Mhlaba, Raymond 55
Mokae, Zakes 80
Motlanthe, Kgalema 74
Mphalele, Es'kia (Ezekiel) 40
Nakasa, Nat 123
Naki, Hamilton 63
Ngubane, Ben 33
Nkoli, Simon 60
Nkosi, Lewis 46
Noah, Trevor 128
Ntshona, Winston 52
Nyanda, Siphiwe 21
Nzo, Alfred 15
Petersen, Neal 96
Plaatje, Sol T. 80
Ramaphosa, Cyril 3, 117
Ramphele, Mamphela 29
Rapelang Rabana 112
Sisulu, Albertina 57, 95
Sisulu, Sheila Violet Makate 24
Sisulu, Walter 47
Sono, Jomo 86
Tau, Mpho Parks 124
Thugwane, Josia 21
Tutu, Desmond (Mpilo) 6, 44

Tutu, Nontombi Naomi 57
Uys, Ashley 125
Yende, Pretty 124
Zuma, Jacob 33, 75
Zwelithini, Goodwill 128

South Sudanese
Kiir, Salva Mayardit 85, 103
Machar, Riek 117
Wek, Alek 18, 63, 105

Spanish
Alves, Dani 121
Buika 120
Eto'o, Samuel 73

Sudanese
Bashir, Halima 73
Bashir, Omar al- 77
Bol, Manute 1
Cham, Adongo Agada Akway 77
Elbagir, Nima 121
Garang, John 105
Hussein, Lubna 80
Nour, Nawal M. 56
Salih, Al-Tayyib 37

Swazi
Mswati III 56

Swedish
Hendricks, Barbara 3, 67
Valdés, Bebo 75

Swiss
Sefolosha, Thabo 121

Tanzanian
Kikwete, Jakaya Mrisho 73
Mkapa, Benjamin W. 16, 77
Mollel, Tololwa 38
Mongella, Gertrude 11
Mwinyi, Ali Hassan 1, 77
Nyerere, Julius 5
Ongala, Remmy 9, 91

Rugambwa, Laurean 20
Thabeet, Hasheem 123

Togolese
Eyadéma, Gnassingbé 7, 52
Gnassingbé, Faure 67
Olympio, Sylvanus 126
Soglo, Nicéphore 15

Trinidadian
Anthony, Michael 29
Auguste, Arnold A. 47
Brand, Dionne 32
Carmichael, Stokely 5, 26
Cartey, Wilfred 47
Dymally, Mervyn 42
Francis, Thais 93
Guy, Rosa 5
Harris, Claire 34
Hendy, Francis 47
Hercules, Frank 44
Hill, Errol 40
Holder, Geoffrey 78, 124
Julian, Hubert 90
London, Theophilus 95
Lord Invader 117
Lord Kitchener 110
Lushington, Augustus Nathaniel 56
Nakhid, David 25
Nunez, Elizabeth 62, 112
Petioni, Muriel 99
Primus, Pearl 6, 125
Rudder, David 79
Shorty, Ras, I 47
Toussaint, Lorraine 32
Williams, Eric Eustace 65

Tunisian
Memmi, Albert 37

Ugandan
Amin, Idi 42
Arac de Nyeko, Monica 66
Atim, Julian 66

Atyam, Angelina 55
Kato, David 103
Kisekka, Samson 112
Kony, Joseph 101
Mugisha, Frank 119
Mupuya, Andrew 118
Museveni, Yoweri 4, 119
Mutebi, Ronald 25
Obote, Milton 63
Oboth, Isaac 117
Okaalet, Peter 58
Sentamu, John 58

West Indian
Césaire, Aimé 48, 69
Coombs, Orde M. 44
Innis, Roy 5
Knight, Gwendolyn 63
Pitt, David Thomas 10
Rojas, Don 33
Staupers, Mabel K. 7
Taylor, Susan L. 10, 86
Walcott, Derek 5, 94

Zambian
Chiluba, Frederick 56, 80
Chitalu, Godfrey 108
Kaunda, Kenneth 2
Moyo, Dambisa 76
Mwanawasa, Levy 72
Sata, Michael 102, 125
Zulu, Princess Kasune 54

Zimbabwean
Bulawayo, NoViolet 125
Chideya, Farai 14
Marechera, Dambudzo 39
Moyo, Lovemore 76
Mtukudzi, Oliver 109
Mugabe, Robert 10, 71
Mukoko, Jestina 75
Muzorewa, Abel 85
Nkomo, Joshua 4, 65
Tsvangirai, Morgan 26, 72
Vera, Yvonne 32

Cumulative Occupation Index

Volume numbers appear in **bold**

Art and design

Abele, Julian **55**
Aberra, Amsale **67**
Adjaye, David **38, 78**
Adkins, Terry **122**
Allen, Tina **22, 75**
Alston, Charles **33**
Amaki, Amalia **76**
Amos, Emma **63**
Anderson, Ho Che **54**
Andrews, Benny **22, 59**
Andrews, Bert **13**
Armstrong, Robb **15**
Ashford, Calvin, Jr. **74**
Bailey, Preston **64**
Bailey, Radcliffe **19**
Bailey, Xenobia **11**
Baker, Matt **76**
Bannister, Edward Mitchell **88**
Barboza, Anthony **10**
Barnes, Ernie **16, 78**
Barthé, Earl **78**
Barthe, Richmond **15**
Basquiat, Jean-Michel **5**
Bearden, Romare **2, 50**
Beasley, Phoebe **34**
Beckwith, Naomi **101**
Bell, Darrin **77**
Benberry, Cuesta **65**
Benjamin, Tritobia Hayes **53**
Biggers, John **20, 33**
Biggers, Sanford **62**
Billops, Camille **82**
Bingham, Howard **96**
Blackburn, Robert **28**
Bond, J. Max, Jr. **76**
Bradford, Mark **89**
Brandon, Barbara **3**
Bridges, Sheila **36**
Brown, Donald **19**
Brown, Frederick J. **102**
Brown, Robert **65**
Bryan, Ashley **41, 104**
Burke, Selma **16**
Burroughs, Margaret Taylor **9**
Camp, Kimberly **19**
Campbell, E. Simms **13**
Campbell, Mary Schmidt **43**
Catlett, Elizabeth **2, 120**
Chanticleer, Raven **91**
Chase, John Saunders, Jr. **99**
Chase-Riboud, Barbara **20, 46**
Cole, Ernest **123**

Colescott, Robert **69**
Collins, Paul **61**
Cortor, Eldzier **42**
Cowans, Adger W. **20**
Cox, Renée **67**
Crichlow, Ernest **75**
Crite, Allan Rohan **29**
Davis, Bing **84**
De Veaux, Alexis **44**
DeCarava, Roy **42, 81**
Delaney, Beauford **19**
Delaney, Joseph **30**
Delsarte, Louis **34**
Dial, Thornton **114**
Dillon, Leo **103**
Donaldson, Jeff **46**
Douglas, Aaron **7**
Douglas, Emory **89**
Driskell, David C. **7**
du Cille, Michel **74**
Duncanson, Robert S. **127**
Dwight, Edward **65**
Edwards, Melvin **22**
El Wilson, Barbara **35**
Ewing, Patrick **17, 73**
Farley, James Conway **99**
Fax, Elton **48**
Feelings, Tom **11, 47**
Ferguson, Amos **81**
Fine, Sam **60**
Fosso, Samuel **116**
Freeman, Leonard **27**
Fuller, Meta Vaux Warrick **27**
Gantt, Harvey **1**
Garvin, Gerry **78**
Gates, Theaster **118**
Gilles, Ralph **61**
Gilliam, Sam **16**
Golden, Thelma **10, 55**
Goodnight, Paul **32**
Green, Jonathan **54**
Guyton, Tyree **9, 94**
Hammons, David **69**
Hansen, Austin **88**
Harkless, Necia Desiree **19**
Harrington, Oliver W. **9**
Harris, Lyle Ashton **83**
Harrison, Charles **72**
Hathaway, Isaac Scott **33**
Hayden, Palmer **13**
Hayes, Cecil N. **46**
Holder, Geoffrey **78, 124**
Honeywood, Varnette P. **54, 88**
Hope, John **8**

Hudson, Cheryl **15**
Hudson, Wade **15**
Hunt, Richard **6**
Hunter, Clementine **45**
Hutson, Jean Blackwell **16**
Jackson, Earl **31**
Jackson, Mary **73**
Jackson, Vera **40**
Johnson, Jeh Vincent **44**
Johnson, William Henry **3**
Jones, Lois Mailou **13**
Jones, Paul R. **76**
Keïta, Seydou **124**
King, Robert Arthur **58**
Kitt, Sandra **23**
Knight, Gwendolyn **63**
Knox, Simmie **49**
Lawrence, Jacob **4, 28**
Lee, Annie Frances **22**
Lee-Smith, Hughie **5, 22**
Lewis, Edmonia **10**
Lewis, Norman **39**
Lewis, Samella **25**
Ligon, Glenn **82**
Lovell, Whitfield **74**
Loving, Alvin, Jr. **35, 53**
Lowe, Rick **124**
Manley, Edna **26**
Marshall, Kerry James **59**
Mason, Desmond **127**
Mayhew, Richard **39**
McCullough, Geraldine **58, 79**
McDuffie, Dwayne **62**
McGee, Charles **10**
McGruder, Aaron **28, 56, 120**
McQueen, Steve **84**
Mehretu, Julie **85**
Mitchell, Corinne **8**
Moody, Ronald **30**
Morrison, Keith **13**
Motley, Archibald, Jr. **30**
Moutoussamy-Ashe, Jeanne **7**
Mutu, Wangechi **44**
Myles, Kim **69**
Nascimento, Abdias do **93**
Nelson, Kadir **115**
Ndiaye, Iba **74**
Neals, Otto **73**
N'Namdi, George R. **17**
Nugent, Richard Bruce **39**
Ofili, Chris **124**
O'Grady, Lorraine **73**
Olden, Georg(e) **44**
Ormes, Jackie **73**

Ouattara **43**
Perkins, Marion **38**
Pierce, Elijah **84**
Pierre, Andre **17**
Pindell, Howardena **55**
Pinder, Jefferson **77**
Pinderhughes, John **47**
Pinkney, Jerry **15, 124**
Piper, Adrian **71**
Pippin, Horace **9**
Pope.L, William **72**
Porter, James A. **11**
Prince Twins Seven-Seven **95**
Prophet, Nancy Elizabeth **42**
Puryear, Martin **42, 101**
Querino, Manuel Raimundo **84**
Ransome, James E. **88**
Reid, Senghor **55**
Ringgold, Faith **4, 81**
Roble, Abdi **71**
Ruley, Ellis **38**
Saar, Alison **16**
Saar, Betye **80**
Saint James, Synthia **12**
Sallee, Charles **38**
Sanders, Joseph R., Jr. **11**
Savage, Augusta **12**
Scott, Dread **106**
Scott, John T. **65**
Sebree, Charles **40**
Serrano, Andres **3**
Shabazz, Attallah **6**
Shonibare, Yinka **58**
Sidibé, Malick **124**
Simmons, Gary **58**
Simpson, Lorna **4, 36**
Simpson, Merton D. **110**
Sims, Lowery Stokes **27**
Sklarek, Norma Merrick **25, 101**
Sleet, Moneta, Jr. **5**
Smith, Bruce W. **53**
Smith, Marvin **46**
Smith, Ming **100**
Smith, Morgan **46**
Smith, Vincent D. **48**
Steave-Dickerson, Kia **57**
Stout, Renee **63**
Sudduth, Jimmy Lee **65**
Tanksley, Ann **37**
Tanner, Henry Ossawa **1**
Taylor, Lonzie Odie **96**
Taylor, Robert Robinson **80**
Thomas, Alma **14**
Thrash, Dox **35**

Tolliver, Mose 60
Tolliver, William 9
Tooks, Lance 62
Turner, Morrie 122
Twiggs, Leo 127
VanDerZee, James 6
Verna, Gelsy 70
Wagner, Albert 78
Wainwright, Joscelyn 46
Walker, A'lelia 14
Walker, Kara 16, 80
Waring, Laura Wheeler 99
Washington, Alonzo 29
Washington, James, Jr. 38
Weems, Carrie Mae 63, 116
Wells, James Lesesne 10
White, Charles 39
White, Dondi 34
White, John H. 27
Wiley, Kehinde 62
Williams, Clarence 70
Williams, O. S. 13
Williams, Paul R. 9
Williams, William T. 11
Willis, Deborah 85
Williston, David Augustus 99
Wilson, Ellis 39
Wilson, John 109
Withers, Ernest C. 68, 88
Woodruff, Hale 9

Business

Abbott, Robert Sengstacke 27
Abiola, Moshood 70
Abudu, Mo 121
Adams, Eula L. 39, 120
Adams, Jenoyne 60
Adkins, Rod 41
Adoboli, Kweku 106
Aire, Chris 117
Akil, Mara Brock 60, 82
Alexander, Archie Alphonso 14
Allen-Buillard, Melba 55
Amos, Wally 9
Amoudi, Mohammed al- 88
Archer, Lee, Jr. 79
Armstrong, Govind 81
Auguste, Donna 29
Austin, Gloria 63
Austin, Jim 63
Austin, Wanda M. 94
Avant, Clarence 19, 86
Avant, Nicole A. 90
Baker, Ella 5
Baker, Maxine 28
Bakewell, Danny 99
Banks, Paula A. 68
Banks, William 11
Barden, Donald H. 9, 20, 89
Barrett, Andrew C. 12
Beal, Bernard B. 46
Beamon, Bob 30
Beasley, Phoebe 34
Bell, James A. 50
Bennett, Richard 97
Bing, Dave 3, 59, 78
Blackshear, Leonard 52
Blackwell, Robert D., Sr. 52
Blaylock, Ronald 86
Blayton, Jesse B., Sr. 55
Bolden, Frank E. 44
Boston, Kelvin E. 25
Boston, Lloyd 24

Bowen, Ruth 83
Bowles, Cephas 127
Boyd, Edward 70
Boyd, Gwendolyn 49
Boyd, John W., Jr. 20, 72
Boyd, T. B., III 6
Bradley, Jennette B. 40
Brae, C. Michael 61
Brewer, Rosalind 100
Bridgforth, Glinda 36
Briggs, Curtis 84
Brimmer, Andrew 2, 48, 106
Bronner, Nathaniel H., Sr. 32
Brown, Eddie C. 35
Brown, Jamie Foster 91
Brown, Les 5
Brown, Marie Dutton 12
Brunson, Dorothy 1, 87
Bryant, John 26
Bryant, Kimberly 127
Burgess, Marjorie L. 55
Burks, Juanita P. 95
Burns, Ursula 60
Burrell, Tom 21, 51
Burroughs, Margaret Taylor 9
Burrus, William Henry 45
Bush, Charles Vernon 125
Burt-Murray, Angela 59
Butler, George, Jr. 70
Cain, Herman 15, 92
Calabrese, Karyn 89
Caldwell, Earl 60
Cameron, James 80
Carter, Pamela Lynn 67
CasSelle, Malcolm 11
Chamberlain, Wilt 18, 47
Chapman, Nathan A., Jr. 21
Chapman, Susan E. 94
Chappell, Emma 18
Chase, Leah 57
Chenault, Kenneth 4, 36, 108
Cherry, Deron 40
Chisholm, Samuel J. 32
Clark, Celeste 15
Clark, Patrick 14
Clay, William Lacy 8
Clayton, Xernona 3, 45
Clement-Holmes, Linda 94
Clyburn, Mignon 78
Cobbs, Price M. 9
Coke, Christopher 108
Colbert, Virgis William 17
Coleman, Donald 24, 62
Coleman, Ken 57
Compton-Rock, Malaak 86
Conyers, Nathan G. 24
Cooper, Barry 33
Cooper, Evern 40
Corbi, Lana 42
Cornelius, Don 4, 100
Cottrell, Comer 11
Council, LaVerne 94
Cox, William E. 68
Creagh, Milton 27
Crum, George 101
Cuffe, Paul 98
Cullers, Vincent T. 49
Dangote, Aliko 124
Daniels-Carter, Valerie 23
Darden, Calvin 38
Dash, Darien 29
Davis, Belva 61
Davis, Ed 24

Davis, Erroll B., Jr. 57
Dawson, Matel, Jr. 39
de Passe, Suzanne 25
Dean, Mark 35
Dee, Merri 55
Delany, Bessie 12
Delany, Martin R. 27
Delany, Sadie 12
DeVard, Jerri 61
Diallo, Amadou 27
Doley, Harold, Jr. 26
Donald, Arnold 36, 126
Dorsey, Thomas J. 90
dos Santos, Isabel 114
Downing, George T. 91
Driver, David E. 11
Ducksworth, Marilyn 12
Duerson, Dave 93
Easley, Annie J. 61
Ebanks, Michelle 60
Edelin, Ramona Hoage 19
Edmonds, Tracey 16, 64
Edmunds, Gladys 48
Edwards, Trevor 54
El Wilson, Barbara 35
Ellington, E. David 11
Elumelu, Tony 116
Evans, Darryl 22
Farmer, Forest J. 1
Farr, Mel 24
Fauntroy, Walter E. 11
Ferguson, Roger W., Jr. 25, 112
Ferdinand, Rio 82
Fils-Aimé, Reggie 74
Fletcher, Buddy 16, 108
Flowers, Sylester 50
Ford, Barney 90
Ford, Harold E(ugene), Jr. 16, 70
Forte, Linda Diane 54
Foster, Jylla Moore 45
Fowler, Reggie 51
Franklin, Hardy R. 9
Frazier, Kenneth 97
Friday, Jeff 24
Fryer, Roland G. 56
Fudge, Ann 11, 55
Fuller, S. B. 13
Funderburg, I. Owen 38
Gaines, Brenda 41
Gardner, Chris 65
Gardner, Edward G. 45
Garrett, James F. 78
Gaskins, Rudy 74
Gaston, Arthur George 3, 38, 59
Gibbs, Mifflin W. 99
Gibson, John Trusty 87
Gibson, Kenneth Allen 6
Gibson, Ted 66
Gidron, Richard D. 68
Gilles, Ralph 61
Goings, Russell 59
Goldsberry, Ronald 18
Golston, Allan C. 55
Gooden, Linda 94
Goodman, Kim C. 94
Gordon, Bruce S. 41, 53, 82
Gordon, Pamela 17
Gordy, Berry, Jr. 1
Goss, Carol A. 55
Grace, George H. 48
Graham, Stedman 13
Graves, Butch 77
Graves, Earl G. 1, 35

Gray, Farrah 59
Greely, M. Gasby 27
Green, Isaac H. 79
Green, Nancy 112
Greene, Richard Thaddeus, Sr. 67
Greenwood, Monique 38
Griffith, Mark Winston 8
Grooms, Henry R(andall) 50
Hale, Lorraine 8
Hall, Alvin D. 86
Ham, Cynthia Parker 58
Hamilton, Samuel C. 47
Handy, W. C. 8
Hannah, Marc 10
Hardison, Bethann 12
Harrell, Andre 9, 30
Harris, Alice 7
Harris, Carla A. 67
Harris, Monica 18
Harris, Richard E. 61
Hart, Thomas A., Sr. 113
Harvey, Steve 18, 58
Harvey, William R. 42
Hawkins, La-Van 17, 54
Hayden, Carla D. 47
Haysbert, Raymond V., Sr. 87
Hazel, Darryl B. 50
Henderson, Gordon 5
Henderson, Henry Fairfax, Jr. 89
Henry, Dwight 104
Henry, Lenny 9, 52
Herndon, Alonzo Franklin 89
Hightower, Dennis F. 13
Hill, Bonnie Guiton 20
Hill, Calvin 19
Hill, Janet 19
Hill, Jesse, Jr. 13
Hill, Peter 92
Hobson, Mellody 40
Holland, Kimberly N. 62
Holland, Robert, Jr. 11
Holmes, Larry 20, 68
Holstein, Casper 89
Howell, Ayinde 91
Howroyd, Janice Bryant 42
Hudlin, Warrington 9
Hudson, Cheryl 15
Hudson, Wade 15
Huggins, Larry 21
Hughes, Cathy 27
Ibrahim, Mo 67, 115
Irvin, Vernon 65
Jackson, George 19
Jackson, Hal 41, 104
Jackson, Joe 78
Jackson, Mannie 14
Jackson, Michael 19, 53, 76
James, Charles H., III 62
James, Donna A. 51
James, Juanita 13
Jenkins, Ray 77
Jennings, Thomas L. 125
Johnson, Bumpy 102
Johnson, Eunice W. 83
Johnson, George E. 29
Johnson, John H. 3, 54
Johnson, Kevin 70
Johnson, Robert L. 3, 39, 121
Johnson, Sheila Crump 48
Johnson, William 91
Jolley, Willie 28
Jones, Carl 7

Jones, Caroline **29**
Jones, Ingrid Saunders **18**
Jones, John **89**
Jones, Thomas W. **41**
Jones, Wayne **53**
Jordan, Michael **6, 21**
Jordan, Montell **23**
Joyner, Marjorie Stewart **26**
Julian, Percy Lavon **6**
Kaigler, Denise **63**
Keith, Floyd A. **61**
Kemp, Herb **94**
Kendrick, Erika **57**
Kidd, Mae Street **39**
Killingsworth, Cleve, Jr. **54**
King, Dexter **10**
Knowles, Tina **61**
Knowling, Robert E., Jr. **38**
Lamothe, Laurent **122**
Lane, Vincent **5**
Langhart Cohen, Janet **19, 60**
Lanier, Willie **33**
Laryea, Thomas Davies, III **67**
Lawal, Kase L. **45**
Lawless, Theodore K. **8**
Lawson, Jennifer **1, 50**
Leary, Kathryn D. **10**
Leavell, Dorothy R. **17**
Lee, Annie Frances **22**
Lee, Bertram M., Sr. **46**
Lee, Debra L. **62**
Leonard, Sugar Ray **15**
Lewis, Aylwin B. **51, 88**
Lewis, Byron E. **13**
Lewis, Delano **7**
Lewis, Edward T. **21**
Lewis, Reginald F. **6**
Lewis, William M., Jr. **40**
Ligging, Alfred, III **43**
Llewellyn, J. Bruce **13, 85**
Long, Eddie L. **29, 89**
Louis, Errol T. **8**
Lucas, John **7**
Lucy, William **50**
Mack, Iris **105**
Malone, Annie **13**
Maponya, Richard **101**
March, William Carrington **56**
Marks, Audrey **99**
Matthews Shatteen, Westina **51**
Matzeliger, Jan **93**
Mayberry-Stewart, Melodie **94**
Maynard, Robert C. **7**
Mays, Leslie A. **41**
Mays, William G. **34**
McCabe, Jewell Jackson **10**
McCann, Renetta **44**
McCoy, Elijah **8**
McDonald, Erroll **1**
McGee, James Madison **46**
McGuire, Raymond J. **57**
McKissack, Leatrice **80**
McLeod, Gus **27**
McPherson, David **32**
McWorter, Free Frank **91**
Middleton, Reggie **105**
Miller, Larry G. **72**
Miller, Pepper **96**
Millines Dziko, Trish **28**
Mills, Steve **47**
Mingo, Frank **32**
Mitchell, Shireen **89**
Monk, Art **38, 73**

Monroe, Bryan **71**
Montgomery, Isaiah T. **91**
Montgomery, Robbie **101**
Moore, Wes **86**
Morgan, Garrett **1**
Morgan, Rose **11**
Morris, William **51**
Moyo, Karega Kofi **36**
Moyo, Yvette Jackson **36**
Muhammad, Jabir Herbert **72**
Mupuya, Andrew **118**
Nail, John E. **92**
Nanula, Richard D. **20**
Nash, Diane **72**
Nelson Meigs, Andrea **48**
Norman, Christina **47**
Ogunlesi, Adebayo O. **37**
Oliver, Garrett **95**
Olojede, Dele **59**
O'Neal, Rodney **88**
O'Neal, Stanley **38, 67**
Otis, Clarence, Jr. **55**
Ouattara, Morou **74**
Overton, Anthony **128**
Packer, Daniel **56**
Parham, Marjorie B. **71**
Parks, Henry Green, Jr. **89**
Parsons, Richard **11, 33, 124**
Payton, Philip A., Jr. **88**
Peck, Carolyn **23**
Perez, Anna **1**
Perkins, James, Jr. **55**
Perry, Laval **64**
Perry, Lowell **30**
Phillips, Charles E., Jr. **57, 109**
Pierce, Harold **75**
Pinckney, Bill **42**
Pinkett, Randal **61**
Pleasant, Mary Ellen **9**
Plinton, James O., Jr. **98**
Potter, Myrtle **40**
Price, Frederick K. C. **21**
Price, Hugh B. **9, 54**
Price, Lisa **97**
Procope, Ernesta **23**
Procope, John Levy **56**
Raines, Franklin **14, 107**
Rand, A. Barry **6**
Reeves, Rachel J. **23**
Reid, Antonio "L.A." **28**
Rhone, Sylvia **2**
Rice, Linda Johnson **9, 41**
Rice, Norm **8**
Richardson, Donna **39**
Richie, Leroy C. **18**
Rideau, Iris **46**
Roberts, Mike **57**
Roberts, Roy S. **14**
Robertson, Oscar **26**
Robinson, Randall **7, 46**
Roche, Joyce M. **17**
Rodgers, Johnathan **6, 51**
Rodriguez, Jimmy **47**
Rogers, Desirée **88**
Rogers, John W., Jr. **5, 52**
Rojas, Don **33**
Rolle, Janet **97**
Ross, Charles **27**
Ross, Diana **8, 27**
Russell, Bill **8**
Russell, Herman Jerome **17**
Russell-McCloud, Patricia **17**
Saint James, Synthia **12**

Samara, Noah **15**
Samuelsson, Marcus **53, 120**
Sanders, Angelia **86**
Sanders, Dori **8**
Sbraga, Kevin **88**
Scott, C. A. **29**
Scott, Milton **51**
Sengstacke, John **18**
Shakur, Afeni **67**
Shank, Suzanne F. **77**
Shropshire, Thomas B. **49**
Siméus, Dumas M. **25, 110**
Simmons, Kimora Lee **51, 83**
Simmons, Russell **1, 30**
Sims, Naomi **29, 79**
Smith, B(arbara) **11**
Smith, Clarence O. **21**
Smith, Jane E. **24**
Smith, Joshua **10**
Sneed, Paula A. **18**
Snowden, Gail **108**
Spaulding, Charles Clinton **9**
Staley, Dawn **57**
Stanford, Olivia Lee Dilworth **49**
Steinberg, Martha Jean "The
  Queen" **28**
Steward, David L. **36**
Stewart, Ella **39**
Stewart, Paul Wilbur **12**
Stinson, Denise L. **59**
Stradford, J. B. **101**
Stringer, Vickie **58**
Sullivan, Leon H. **3, 30**
Sutton, Percy E. **42, 82**
Taylor, Ephren W., II **61**
Taylor, Karin **34**
Taylor, Kristin Clark **8**
Taylor, Natalie **47**
Taylor, Robert Rochon **104**
Taylor, Susan L. **10, 86**
Temple, Lewis **102**
Terrell, Dorothy A. **24**
Thiam, Tidjane **104**
Thomas, Franklin A. **5, 49**
Thomas, Jefferson **88**
Thomas-Graham, Pamela **29**
Thompson, Cynthia Bramlett **50**
Thompson, Don **56, 108**
Thompson, John W. **26**
Tobin, Patricia **75**
Travis, Tracey T. **94**
Tribble, Israel, Jr. **8**
Trotter, Lloyd G. **56**
Trotter, Monroe **9**
Tuckson, Reed V. **71**
Tyson, Asha **39**
Ussery, Terdema, II **29**
Utendahl, John **23**
Uys, Ashley **125**
VanDerZee, James **6**
Vaughn, Gladys Gary **47**
Vaughns, Cleopatra **46**
Villarosa, Clara **85**
Walker, A'lelia **14**
Walker, Cedric **19**
Walker, Joseph Edison **111**
Walker, Madame C. J. **7**
Walker, Maggie Lena **17**
Walker, Ray **109**
Walker, T. J. **7**
Walker, Tristan **98**
Ward, Lloyd **21, 46**
Ware, Carl H. **30**

Washington, Alonzo **29**
Washington, Mary T. **57**
Washington, Regynald G. **44**
Washington, Val **12**
Wasow, Omar **15**
Watkins, Donald **35**
Watkins, Walter C., Jr. **24**
Wein, Joyce **62**
Welburn, Edward T. **50**
Wells-Barnett, Ida B. **8**
Westbrook, Kelvin **50**
White, Linda M. **45**
White, Walter F. **4**
Wilkins, Ray **47**
Williams, Armstrong **29**
Williams, Lindsey **75**
Williams, O. S. **13**
Williams, Paul R. **9**
Williams, Ronald A. **57**
Williams, Terrie **35**
Williams, Walter E. **4**
Williams, Wendy **62**
Willie, Louis, Jr. **68**
Wilson, Sunnie **7, 55**
Woods, Jacqueline **52**
Woods, Sylvia **34, 104**
Woodson, Robert L. **10**
Wright, Antoinette **60**
Wright, Charles H. **35**
Wright, Deborah C. **25**
Wright, Rayfield **70**
Wright, Richard Robert, Sr. **100**
Yoba, Malik **11**
Young, Perry H. **100**
Zollar, Alfred **40**

Dance
Abraham, Kyle **116**
Acogny, Germaine **55**
Adams, Jenoyne **60**
Ailey, Alvin **8**
Allen, Debbie **13, 42**
Anderson, Lauren **72**
Anderson, Maceo**111**
Atkins, Cholly **40**
Babatunde, Obba **35**
Baker, Josephine **3**
Bates, Peg Leg **14**
Beatty, Talley **35**
Brown, Ernest **80**
Brown, Ronald K. **91**
Byrd, Donald **10**
Chanticleer, Raven **91**
Clarke, Hope **14**
Coles, Honi **128**
Collins, Janet **33, 64**
Copeland, Misty **125**
Davis, Chuck **33**
de Lavallade, Carmen **78**
DePrince, Michaela **104**
Dove, Ulysses **5**
Dunham, Katherine **4, 59**
Ellington, Mercedes **34**
Fagan, Garth **18, 98**
Falana, Lola **42**
Glover, Savion **14**
Hall, Arthur **39**
Harris, Rennie **120**
Henson, Darrin **33**
Hines, Gregory **1, 42**
Jamison, Judith **7, 67, 96**
Jefferson, Denise **87**
Jeune, Vitolio **98**

Johnson, Ken 106
Johnson, Virginia 9
Jones, Bill T. 1, 46, 80
Jones, Doris W. 62
King, Alonzo 38
Lane, William Henry 90
LeTang, Henry 66
Manning, Frankie 78
Miller, Bebe 3
Mills, Florence 22
Mitchell, Arthur 2, 47
Moten, Etta 18
Muse, Clarence Edouard 21
Nash, Joe 55
Nicholas, Fayard 20, 57
Nicholas, Harold 20
Nichols, Nichelle 11
Polite, Carlene Hatcher 82
Pomare, Eleo 72
Premice, Josephine 41
Primus, Pearl 6, 125
Ray, Gene Anthony 47
Rhoden, Dwight 40
Ribeiro, Alfonso 17
Richardson, Desmond 39
Robinson, Bill "Bojangles" 11
Robinson, Cleo Parker 38
Robinson, Fatima 34
Robinson, LaVaughn 69
Rodgers, Rod 36
Sims, Howard "Sandman" 48
Slyde, Jimmy 70
Spears, Warren 52
Storyboard P 118
Tyson, Andre 40
Vereen, Ben 4
Walker, Dianne 57
Washington, Fredi 10
Williams, Dudley 60
Wilson, Reggie 116
Zollar, Jawole Willa Jo 28

Education

Abani, Chris 77
Abercrumbie, P. Eric 95
Ackerman, Arlene 108
Adams, Alma 127
Adams, Leslie 39
Adams-Ender, Clara 40
Adkins, Rutherford H. 21
Aidoo, Ama Ata 38
Ake, Claude 30
Albert, Octavia V. R. 100
Alexander, Margaret Walker 22
Alexander, Michelle 98
Allen, Robert L. 38
Allen, Samuel W. 38
Allen-Buillard, Melba 55
Alston, Charles 33
Amadi, Elechi 40
Ammons, James H. 81
Anderson, Charles Edward 37
Appiah, Kwame Anthony 67, 101
Archie-Hudson, Marguerite 44
Asante, Molefi Kete 3
Aubert, Alvin 41
Austin, Bobby W. 95
Awuah, Patrick 111
Bacon-Bercey, June 38
Bahati, Wambui 60
Baiocchi, Regina Harris 41
Baker, Augusta 38
Baker, Delbert W. 110

Baker, Gwendolyn Calvert 9
Baker, Houston A., Jr. 6
Baldwin, Cynthia 74, 107
Ballard, Allen Butler, Jr. 40
Barbee, Lloyd Augustus 71
Barboza, Anthony 10
Barnett, Marguerite 46
Barthé, Earl 78
Bath, Patricia E. 37
Batiste, Alvin 66
Beals, Melba Pattillo 15, 94
Beckham, Barry 41
Belgrave, Marcus 77
Bell, Derrick 6, 98
Benberry, Cuesta 65
Benjamin, Tritobia Hayes 53
Berry, Bertice 8, 55
Berry, Mary Frances 7
Bethune, Mary McLeod 4
Biggers, John 20, 33
Black, Albert 51
Blackwell, David 79
Blackwell, Gloria 127
Blakely, Edward J. 88
Blassingame, John Wesley 40
Blockson, Charles L. 42
Bluitt, Juliann S. 14
Bobo, Lawrence 60
Bogle, Donald 34
Bolden, Tonya 32
Bosley, Freeman, Jr. 7
Boyd, Melba Joyce 86
Boyd, T. B., III 6
Bradley, Adam 101
Bradley, David Henry, Jr. 39
Branch, William Blackwell 39
Brathwaite, Kamau 36
Braun, Carol Moseley 4, 42
Braxton, Anthony 128
Briscoe, Marlin 37
Bromery, Randolph Wilson 85
Brown, Claude 38
Brown, Hallie Quinn 100
Brown, Joyce F. 25
Brown, Sterling Allen 10, 64
Brown, Uzee 42
Brown, Wesley 23
Brown, Willa 40
Bruce, Blanche Kelso 33
Brutus, Dennis 38
Bunch, Lonnie G., III 91
Burke, Selma 16
Burks, Mary Fair 40
Burnim, Mickey L. 48
Burroughs, Margaret Taylor 9
Burroughs, Nannie Helen 96
Butler, Paul D. 17
Butler, Selena Sloan 98
Butts, Calvin O., III 9, 90
Callender, Clive O. 3
Campbell, Mary Schmidt 43
Cannon, Katie 10
Carby, Hazel 27
Cardozo, Francis L. 33
Carnegie, Herbert 25
Carruthers, George R. 40
Carter, Herbert E. 108
Carter, Joye Maureen 41
Carter, Kenneth 53
Carter, Warrick L. 27
Cartey, Wilfred 47
Carver, George Washington 4
Cary, Lorene 3

Cary, Mary Ann Shadd 30
Cayton, Horace 26
Chaney, John 67
Cheney-Coker, Syl 43
Childers, Lulu Vere 95
Clark, Joe 1
Clark, Kenneth B. 5, 52
Clark, Septima 7
Clark, Yvonne Young 95
Clarke, Cheryl 32
Clarke, George 32
Clarke, John Henrik 20
Clayton, Constance 1
Cleaver, Kathleen Neal 29
Clements, George 2
Clemmons, Reginal G. 41
Cobb, Jewel Plummer 42
Cobb, W. Montague 39
Cobb, William Jelani 59, 121
Cobbs, Price M. 9
Cohen, Anthony 15
Cohen, Cathy J. 88
Cole, Johnnetta B. 5, 43
Coleman, Beatrice 120
Coleman, Steve 124
Coleman, William F., III 61
Colescott, Robert 69
Collette, Buddy 119
Collins, Janet 33, 64
Collins, Marva 3, 71
Collins, Patricia Hill 67
Comer, James P. 6
Coney, PonJola 48
Conrad, Cecilia A. 94
Cook, Mercer 40
Cook, Samuel DuBois 14
Cook, Toni 23
Cooper, Afua 53
Cooper, Anna Julia 20
Cooper, Edward S. 6
Cooper Cafritz, Peggy 43
Copeland, Michael 47
Cotter, Joseph Seamon, Sr. 40
Cottrell, Comer 11
Counter, S. Allen 74
Cox, Elbert Frank 111
Cox, Joseph Mason Andrew 51
Cox, William E. 68
Creagh, Milton 27
Crenshaw, Kimberlé Williams 88
Crew, Rudy 16, 113
Crew, Spencer R. 55
Cross, Dolores E. 23
Crouch, Hubert 95
Cruse, Harold 54
Cullen, Countee 8
Daly, Marie Maynard 37
Dathorne, O. R. 52
Davis, Allison 12
Davis, Angela J. 88
Davis, Arthur P. 41
Davis, Charles T. 48
Davis, Erroll B., Jr. 57
Davis, George 36
Davis, Milt 74
Dawson, William Levi 39
Days, Drew S., III 10
Deconge-Watson, Lovenia 55
Delany, Sadie 12
Delany, Samuel R., Jr. 9
Delco, Wilhelmina R. 33
Delpit, Lisa 101
Delsarte, Louis 34

Dennard, Brazeal 37
Dewitty, Thelma 114
Dickens, Helen Octavia 14, 64
Dixon, Margaret 14
Dodson, Howard, Jr. 7, 52
Dodson, Owen Vincent 38
Dogan, Matthew Winifred 91
Donaldson, Jeff 46
Dove, Ulysses 5
Drake, Michael V. 122
Draper, Sharon Mills 16, 43
Drummond, William J. 40
Du Bois, David Graham 45
Dube, John Langalibalele 119
Dumas, Henry 41
Dunbar-Nelson, Alice Ruth Moore 44
Dunnigan, Alice Allison 41
Dunston, Georgia Mae 48
Dymally, Mervyn 42
Dyson, Michael Eric 11, 40, 128
Early, Gerald 15
Edelin, Ramona Hoage 19
Edelman, Marian Wright 5, 42
Edley, Christopher 2, 48
Edley, Christopher F., Jr. 48
Edwards, Harry 2
Elders, Joycelyn 6
Elliot, Lorris 37
Ellis, Clarence A. 38
Ellison, Ralph 7
Epps, Archie C., III 45
Evans, Mari 26
Everett, Percival 93
Falconer, Etta Zuber 59
Fauset, Jessie 7
Favors, Steve 23
Feelings, Muriel 44
Ferguson, Ronald F. 75
Figueroa, John J. 40
Fleming, Raymond 48
Fletcher, Bill, Jr. 41
Floyd, Elson S. 41
Ford, Jack 39
Forman, James, Jr. 89
Foster, Ezola 28
Foster, Henry W., Jr. 26
Foster, William P. 88
Francis, Norman (C.) 60
Franklin, Hardy R. 9, 87
Franklin, John Hope 5, 77
Franklin, Robert M. 13
Frazier, E. Franklin 10
Fryer, Roland G. 56
Fuller, A. Oveta 43
Fuller, Arthur 27
Fuller, Howard L. 37
Fuller, Solomon Carter, Jr. 15
Futrell, Mary Hatwood 33
Gaines, Ernest J. 7
Gates, Henry Louis, Jr. 3, 38, 67
Gates, Sylvester James, Jr. 15
Gayle, Addison, Jr. 41
George, Zelma Watson 42
Gerima, Haile 38, 80
Gibson, Donald Bernard 40
Giddings, Paula 11
Gilbert, John Wesley 91
Gill, Gerald 69
Gloster, Hugh Morris, Sr. 90
Gomes, Peter J. 15, 93
Gomez, Jewelle 30
Gomillion, Charles 90

Goodison, Lorna 71
Granville, Evelyn Boyd 36
Graves, Milford 126
Greenfield, Eloise 9
Groff, Peter 96
Guinier, Lani 7, 30
Guy-Sheftall, Beverly 13, 92
Hageman, Hans and Ivan 36
Hale, Lorraine 8
Hall, Stuart 78
Halliburton, Warren J. 49
Hamburg, Beatrix 84
Hammonds, Evelynn 69
Handy, W. C. 8
Hansberry, William Leo 11
Harding, Vincent 67
Harkless, Necia Desiree 19
Harper, Michael S. 34
Harris, Alice 7
Harris, Barry 68
Harris, Bill 72
Harris, Gary L. 87
Harris, Jay T. 19
Harris, Jessica B. 91
Harris, Kevin 120
Harris, Patricia Roberts 2
Harris-Lacewell, Melissa 81
Harsh, Vivian Gordon 14
Harvey, William R. 42
Haskins, James 36, 54
Hathaway, Isaac Scott 33
Hayden, Carla D. 47
Hayden, Robert 12
Haynes, George Edmund 8
Henderson, George Washington
   101
Henderson, Stephen E. 45
Henries, A. Doris Banks 44
Herenton, Willie W. 24, 81
Hill, Andrew 66
Hill, Anita 5, 65
Hill, Bonnie Guiton 20
Hill, Errol 40
Hill, Leslie Pinckney 44
Hill, Marc Lamont 80, 128
Hilliard, Asa Grant, III 66
Hine, Darlene Clark 24
Hinton, William Augustus 8
Hoagland, Everett H. 45
Hogan, Beverly Wade 50
Holland, Endesha Ida Mae 3, 57
Holt, Nora 38
Hope, John 8
Horton, James Oliver 58
Houston, Charles Hamilton 4
Hoyte, Lenon 50
Hrabowski, Freeman A., III 22
Huggins, Nathan Irvin 52
Hughes, Ebony 57
Hull, Akasha Gloria 45
Humphries, Frederick 20
Hunt, Darnell 92
Hunt, Richard 6
Hutcherson, Hilda Yvonne 54
Hutson, Jean Blackwell 16
Imes, Elmer Samuel 39
Jackson, Edison O. 67
Jackson, Fred James 25
Jackson, Vera 40
Jansen, Jonathan 102
Jarrett, Vernon D. 42
Jarvis, Charlene Drew 21
Jarvis, Erich 67

Jefferson, Denise 87
Jefferson, Margo 108
Jeffries, Leonard 8
Jenifer, Franklyn G. 2
Jenkins, Ella 15
Johns, Vernon 38
Johnson, Anthony M. 92
Johnson, Conrad O. 97
Johnson, Hazel 22
Johnson, James Weldon 5
Johnson, Katherine 61
Johnson, Mordecai Wyatt 79
Jones, Clara Stanton 51
Jones, Edward P. 43, 67
Jones, Gayl 37
Jones, Ingrid Saunders 18
Jones, Lois Mailou 13
Joplin, Scott 6
Jordan, June 7, 35
Joseph, Jamal 101
Josey, E. J. 10
Just, Ernest Everett 3
Karenga, Maulana 10, 71
Kay, Ulysses 37
Keith, Damon J. 16, 74
Kennedy, Florynce 12, 33
Kennedy, Randall 40
Kimbro, Dennis 10
King, Preston 28
King, Reatha Clark 65
Kittles, Rick 51
Komunyakaa, Yusef 9
Koontz, Elizabeth Duncan 101
Kunjufu, Jawanza 3, 50
Ladner, Joyce A. 42
Lawrence, Jacob 4, 28
Lawrence-Lightfoot, Sara 10
Lee, Annie Frances 22
Lee, Joe A. 45
Leevy, Carrol M. 42
Leffall, Lasalle 3, 64
Lewis, David Levering 9
Lewis, Norman 39
Lewis, Samella 25
Lewis, Shirley A. R. 14
Lewis, Thomas 19
Liberia-Peters, Maria Philomena 12
Lincoln, C. Eric 38
Lindsey, Tommie 51
Locke, Alain 10
Logan, Rayford W. 40
Lomax, Michael L. 58
Long, Loretta 58
Long, Richard Alexander 65
Lorde, Audre 6
Loury, Glenn 36
Loving, Alvin, Jr. 35, 53
Lowry, A. Leon 60
Lucy Foster, Autherine 35
Luper, Clara 94
Lyons, James E., Sr. 102
Lyttle, Hulda Margaret 14
Mackey, Nathaniel 75
Major, Clarence 9
Malveaux, Floyd 54
Manley, Audrey Forbes 16
Marable, Manning 10, 102
Markham, E. A. 37
Marsalis, Ellis 90
Marshall, Paule 7, 77
Masekela, Barbara 18
Mason, Herman, Jr. 83
Mason, Ronald 27

Massey, Walter E. 5, 45
Massie, Samuel P., Jr. 29
Matejka, Adrian 87
Maupin, John E., Jr. 92
Mayhew, Richard 39
Maynard, Robert C. 7
Maynor, Dorothy 19
Mayo, Whitman 32
Mays, Benjamin E. 7
Mazrui, Ali 12, 124
McBay, Henry C. 91
McCarty, Osceola 16
McCullough, Geraldine 58, 79
McDaniel, Randall Cornell 81
McKay, Nellie Yvonne 17, 57
McLendon, John B., Jr. 89
McMurray, Georgia L. 36
McPherson, James Alan 70
McWhorter, John 35, 119
Mell, Patricia 49
Memmi, Albert 37
Meredith, James H. 11
Millender-McDonald, Juanita 21, 61
Ming, William Robert, Jr. 125
Mitchell, Corinne 8
Mitchell, Nicole 66
Mitchell, Sharon 36
Mofolo, Thomas Mokopu 37
Mollel, Tololwa 38
Mongella, Gertrude 11
Moody-Adams, Michele 76
Moore, Barbara C. 49
Moore, Harry T. 29
Morón, Alonzo G. 91
Morrison, Keith 13
Morrison, Sam 50
Morrison, Toni 2, 15, 86
Moses, Robert Parris 11
Moton, Robert Russa 83
Mphalele, Es'kia (Ezekiel) 40
Mudimbe, V. Y. 61
Mullen, Harryette 34
Murray, Pauli 38
Nabrit, Samuel Milton 47
Nance, Cynthia 71
Naylor, Gloria 10, 42
Neal, Larry 38
Neal, Mark Anthony 74
Newkirk, Pamela 69
Newman, Lester C. 51
N'Namdi, George R. 17
Norman, Maidie 20
Nour, Nawal M. 56
Obadele, Imari 84
Ogletree, Charles, Jr. 12, 47
Ojikutu, Bisola 65
Oliver, Kimberly 60
Omolewa, Michael 119
Onwueme, Tess Osonye 23
Onwurah, Ngozi 38
Owens, Helen 48
Page, Alan 7
Page, Inman 82
Paige, Rod 29
Painter, Nell Irvin 24, 88
Palmer, Everard 37
Parker, Kellis E. 30
Patterson, Frederick Douglass 12
Patterson, Mary Jane 54
Patterson, Orlando 4, 127
Patton, Venetria K. 125
Payton, Benjamin F. 23
Perry, Steve 98

Perry, Warren 56
Peters, Margaret 43
Peters, Matilda 43
Peterson, James 81
Pickett, Cecil 39
Pinckney, Bill 42
Pindell, Howardena 55
Piper, Adrian 71
Player, Willa B. 43
Pollard, William L. 91
Porter, James A. 11
Poussaint, Alvin F. 5, 67
Powell, Benny 87
Price, Florence 37
Price, Glenda 22
Price, Richard 51
Proctor, Bernard Shaw 120
Prophet, Nancy Elizabeth 42
Purnell, Silas 59
Putney, Martha S. 75
Pyfrom, Estella 127
Quarles, Benjamin Arthur 18
Querino, Manuel Raimundo 84
Quigless, Helen G. 49
Rahman, Aishah 37
Ramphele, Mamphela 29
Randall, Vernellia R. 95
Reaves, Donald J. 102
Reddick, Lawrence Dunbar 20
Redding, J. Saunders 26
Redmond, Eugene 23
Reid, Ira De A. 100
Reid, Irvin D. 20
Rhodes, Jewell Parker 84
Ribeau, Sidney 70
Rice, Condoleezza 3, 28, 72
Rice, Louise Allen 54
Richards, Hilda 49
Riles, Wilson C. 79
Robinson, Joann Gibson 100
Robinson, Sharon 22
Robinson, Spottswood W., III 22
Rodriguez, Cheryl 64
Rogers, Joel Augustus 30
Rollins, Charlemae Hill 27
Ross-Lee, Barbara 67
Rouse, Cecilia 93
Russell-McCloud, Patricia 17
Russwurm, John Brown 100
Salih, Al-Tayyib 37
Sallee, Charles Louis, Jr. 38
Schomburg, Arthur Alfonso 9
Sears, Stephanie 53
Senior, Olive 37
Shabazz, Betty 7, 26
Shange, Ntozake 8, 89
Shelton, Paula Young 86
Shipp, E. R. 15
Shirley, George 33
Shockley, Ann Allen 84
Simkins, Modjeska Monteith 112
Simmons, Ruth J. 13, 38
Sinkford, Jeanne C. 13
Sisulu, Sheila Violet Makate 24
Sizemore, Barbara A. 26, 110
Smith, Anna Deavere 6
Smith, Barbara 28
Smith, Gene 123
Smith, Jessie Carney 35
Smith, John L. 22
Smith, Mary Carter 26
Smith, Tubby 18, 83
Snowden, Frank M., Jr. 67

Southern, Eileen 56
Sowande, Fela 39
Spearman, Leonard H. O., Sr. 81
Spears, Warren 52
Spikes, Dolores 18
Spriggs, William 67
Stanford, John 20
Steele, Claude 13, 97
Steele, Shelby 13, 82
Stephens, Charlotte Andrews 14
Stewart, Maria W. Miller 19
Stewart, Tonea Harris 78
Stone, Chuck 9, 120
Sudarkasa, Niara 4
Sullivan, Louis 8
Swygert, H. Patrick 22
Talbert, Mary B. 77
Tancil, Gladys Quander 59
Tanksley, Ann 37
Tatum, Beverly Daniel 42, 84
Taylor, Helen (Lavon Hollingshed) 30
Taylor, Susie King 13
Terrell, Mary Church 9
Thomas, Alma 14
Thomas, Michael 69
Thurman, Howard 3
Tillis, Frederick 40
Tillman, Deborah 98
Tobias, Channing H. 79
Toler, Burl 80
Tolson, Melvin 37
Tribble, Israel, Jr. 8
Trueheart, William E. 49
Tucker, Rosina 14
Tuff, Antoinette 120
Turnbull, Charles Wesley 62
Turnbull, Walter 13, 60
Tutu, Nontombi Naomi 57
Tutuola, Amos 30
Twilight, Alexander 125
Tyler, Ollie 128
Tyson, Andre 40
Tyson, Asha 39
Tyson, Neil deGrasse 15, 65
Usry, James L. 23
van Sertima, Ivan 25
Vaughn, Viola 70
Vega, Marta Moreno 61
Velez-Rodriguez, Argelia 56
Verna, Gelsy 70
Wade-Gayles, Gloria Jean 41
Walcott, Dennis M. 112
Walcott, Derek 5, 94
Walker, George 37
Wallace, Michele Faith 13
Wallace, Perry E. 47
Wallace, Phyllis A. 9
Walters, Ronald 83
Washington, Booker T. 4
Washington, Margaret Murray 119
Watkins, Shirley R. 17
Wattleton, Faye 9
Weaver, Afaa Michael 37
Wedgeworth, Robert W. 42
Wells, Henrietta Bell 69
Wells, James Lesesne 10
Wells-Barnett, Ida B. 8
Welsing, Frances Cress 5
Wesley, Dorothy Porter 19
Wesley, Richard 73
West, Cornel 5, 33, 80
Wharton, Clifton R., Jr. 7

White, Charles 39
White, Lois Jean 20
Wilkens, J. Ernest, Jr. 43
Wilkins, Roger 2, 84
Williams, David Rudyard 50
Williams, Fannie Barrier 27
Williams, Gregory 11
Williams, Patricia 11, 54
Williams, Rhonda Y. 86
Williams, Sherley Anne 25
Williams, Walter E. 4
Wilson, Donald E. 88
Wilson, William Julius 22
Woodruff, Hale 9
Woodson, Carter G. 2
Worrill, Conrad 12
Wright, Antoinette 60
Wright, Richard Robert, Sr. 100
Xuma, Madie Hall 59
Yancy, Dorothy Cowser 42
Young, Jean Childs 14
Zook, Kristal Brent 62

Fashion
Aberra, Amsale 67
Banks, Jeffrey 17
Banks, Tyra 11, 50
Barboza, Anthony 10
Beals, Jennifer 12
Beauvais, Garcelle 29, 95
Beckford, Tyson 11, 68
Boateng, Ozwald 35, 113
Bond, Beverly 53
Bonney, Tabi 98
Boyd, Suzanne 52
Brown, Joyce F. 25
Burrows, Stephen 31
Campbell, Naomi 1, 31, 120
Chanticleer, Raven 91
DaCosta, YaYa 98
Darego, Agbani 52
Davidson, Jaye 5
Davis, Mia Amber 94
De' Alexander, Quinton 57
Delice, Ronald 48
Delice, Rony 48
DeVore-Mitchell, Ophelia 120
Dirie, Waris 56
Dobson, Tamara 111
Ebanks, Selita 67
Evans, Etu 55
Finley, Ron 110
Gaskins, Eric 64
Gibson, Ted 66
Givhan, Robin Deneen 72
Hall, Kevan 61
Harold, Erika 54
Henderson, Gordon 5
Hendy, Francis 47
Iman 4, 33, 87
Iman, Chanel 66
John, Daymond 23, 114
Johnson, Beverly 2, 102
Johnson, Eunice W. 83
Jones, Carl 7
Jones, Genevieve 101
Kani, Karl 10
Kebede, Liya 59
Keckley, Elizabeth 90
Kelly, Patrick 3
Kodjoe, Boris 34, 89
Lars, Byron 32
Lopes, Leila 99

Luna, Donyale 88
Malone, Maurice 32
Marcille, Eva 97
McGrath, Pat 72
McKenzie, Jaunel 73
Michele, Michael 31
Niane, Katoucha 70
Onwurah, Ngozi 38
Paris, Adama 120
Powell, Maxine 8, 115
Reese, Tracy 54
Rhymes, Busta 31
Robinson, Patrick 19, 71
Rochon, Lela 16
Rowell, Victoria 13, 68
Simmons, Kimora Lee 51, 83
Sims, Naomi 29, 79
Smaltz, Audrey 12
Smith, B(arbara) 11
Smith, LaQuan 113
Smith, Willi 8
Smythe Haith, Mabel 61
Steele, Lawrence 28
Stoney, Michael 50
Sy, Oumou 65
Talley, André Leon 56, 106
Taylor, Karin 34
Walker, T. J. 7
Webb, Veronica 10, 95
Wek, Alek 18, 63, 105
White, Jessica 83
Williams, Serena 20, 41, 73

Film
Aaliyah 30
Aaron, Quinton 82
Abrahams, Zaraah 127
Adebimpe, Tunde 75
Abdi, Barkhad 119
Akinnuoye-Agbaje, Adewale 56
Akomfrah, John 37
Ali, Tatyana 73
Allain, Stephanie 49
Allen, Debbie 13, 42
Alonso, Laz 87
Amata, Jeta 111
Amos, John 8, 62
Anderson, Anthony 51, 77
Anderson, Eddie "Rochester" 30
Anderson, Jacob 128
Andrews, Tina 74
Anthony, La La 122
Armah, Esther 87
Babatunde, Obba 35
Babyface 10, 31, 82
Baker, Josephine 3
Banks, Michelle 59
Banks, Tyra 11, 50
Barclay, Paris 37, 94
Barnett, Etta Moten 56
Baskett, James 102
Bassett, Angela 6, 23, 62
Beach, Michael 26, 120
Beals, Jennifer 12
Beard, Matthew 120
Beckford, Tyson 11, 68
Belafonte, Harry 4, 65
Bellamy, Bill 12
Bennett, Louise 69
Bentley, Lamont 53
Berry, Fred "Rerun" 48
Berry, Halle 4, 19, 57, 91
Bey, Yasiin 30, 96

Billops, Camille 82
Bivins, Michael 72
Blackwood, Maureen 37
Bleu, Corbin 65
Bogle, Donald 34
Boseman, Chadwick 111
Brady, Wayne 32, 71
Brandy 14, 34, 72
Breeze, Jean "Binta" 37
Brooks, Golden 62
Brooks, Hadda 40
Brown, Jim 11, 95
Brown, Tony 3
Browne, Roscoe Lee 66
Burnett, Charles 16, 68
Byrd, Michelle 19
Byrd, Robert 11
Calloway, Cab 14
Campbell-Martin, Tisha 8, 42
Cannon, Nick 47, 73
Cannon, Reuben 50
Cara, Irene 77
Carmichael, Jerrod 124
Carroll, Diahann 9
Carroll, Rocky 74
Carson, Lisa Nicole 21
Cash, Rosalind 28
Cathey, Reg E. 122
Cedric the Entertainer 29, 60, 115
Chase, Debra Martin 49, 96
Cheadle, Don 19, 52
Chestnut, Morris 31, 116
Chong, Rae Dawn 62
Chweneyagae, Presley 63
Cobbs, Bill 101
Common 31, 63, 98
Coogler, Ryan 114
Crump, Steven 96
Curtis-Hall, Vondie 17
DaCosta, YaYa 98
Dandridge, Dorothy 3
Daniels, Lee 36, 76
Dash, Julie 4
David, Keith 27
Davidson, Jaye 5
Davidson, Tommy 21
Davis, Eisa 68
Davis, Guy 36
Davis, Ossie 5, 50
Davis, Sammy, Jr. 18
Davis, Viola 34, 76, 100
Dawn, Marpessa 75
Dawson, Rosario 72
De Bankolé, Isaach 78
de Passe, Suzanne 25
De Shields, André 72
Dee, Ruby 8, 50, 68, 122
Devine, Loretta 24
Dickerson, Ernest 6, 17
Diesel, Vin 29
Dieudonné 67, 118
Diggs, Taye 25, 63
Dixon, Ivan 69
DMX 28, 64
Dobson, Tamara 111
Domingo, Colman 94
Duke, Bill 3, 96
Duncan, Michael Clarke 26, 104
Dutton, Charles S. 4, 22
DuVernay, Ava 98, 126
Ejiofor, Chiwetel 67, 116
Ejogo, Carmen 126
Elba, Idris 49, 89, 116

Elder, Lonne, III 38
Elie, Lolis Eric 97
Elise, Kimberly 32, 101
Ellis, Aunjanue 108
Ellis, Nelsan 105
Ellis, Trey 97
Elzy, Ruby 119
Emmanuel, Alphonsia 38
Epps, Omar 23, 59
Esposito, Giancarlo 9
Evans, Darryl 22
Everett, Francine 23
Faison, Donald 50
Faison, Frankie 55
Fetchit, Stepin 32
Fishburne, Laurence 4, 22, 70
Fisher, Antwone 40
Fisher, Gail 85
Fletcher, Geoffrey 85
Fox, Rick 27
Fox, Vivica A. 15, 53
Foxx, Jamie 15, 48
Franklin, Carl 11
Freeman, Al, Jr. 11, 105
Freeman, Morgan 2, 20, 62, 100
Freeman, Yvette 27
Friday, Jeff 24
Fuller, Charles 8
Fuqua, Antoine 35
Gant, Richard 105
Gaye, Nona 56
Gerima, Haile 38, 80
Gibbs, Marla 86
Gibson, Tyrese 27, 62
Givens, Adele 62
Glover, Danny 1, 24, 103
Glover, Donald 85
Glover, Savion 14
Goldberg, Whoopi 4, 33, 69
Good, Meagan 117
Gooding, Cuba, Jr. 16, 62
Gordon, Dexter 25
Gossett, Louis, Jr. 7
Gray, F. Gary 14, 49
Greaves, William 38, 123
Grier, David Alan 28
Grier, Pam 9, 31, 86
Gunn, Moses 10
Gurira, Danai 73
Guyse, Sheila 122
Hairston, Jester 88
Hall, Juanita 62
Hamilton, Bernie 117
Hamilton, Lisa Gay 71
Hamilton, Tanya 93
Hampton, Henry 6
Hardwick, Omari 122
Harewood, David 52
Harewood, Dorian 104
Harper, Hill 32, 65, 97
Harris, Leslie 6
Harris, Naomie 55, 116
Harris, Robin 7
Hart, Kevin 103
Hayes, Teddy 40
Hector, Jamie 98
Henriques, Julian 37
Henry, Dwight 104
Henry, Lenny 9, 52
Henson, Darrin 33
Henson, Taraji P. 58, 77, 127
Hill, Darryl 128
Hines, Gregory 1, 42

Hodge, Aldis 124
Hooks, Robert 76
Horne, Lena 5, 86
Hounsou, Djimon 19, 45
Howard, Sherri 36
Howard, Terrence 59, 94
Howell, Ayinde 91
Hudlin, Reginald 9, 86
Hudlin, Warrington 9
Hudson, Ernie 72
Hudson, Jennifer 63, 83
Hughes, Albert 7
Hughes, Allen 7
Hurt, Byron 61
Ice Cube 8, 30, 60
Ice-T 6, 31, 96
Ingram, Rex 5
Isaacs, Cheryl Boone 113
Jackson, George 19
Jackson, Janet 6, 30, 68
Jackson, Rampage 83
Jackson, Samuel L. 8, 19, 63, 102
Jalade-Ekeinde, Omotola 118
Jean, Michaëlle; 70
Jean-Baptiste, Marianne 17, 46
Jean-Louis, Jimmy 76
Jeffries, Herb 122
Johnson, Clark 96
Jones, James Earl 3, 49, 79
Jones, Orlando 30
Jones, Quincy 8, 30
Jones, Rashida 101
Jones, Robbie 113
Jordan, Michael B. 97
Jorge, Seu 73
Joseph, Paterson 126
Julian, Hubert 90
Julien, Isaac 3
Kabera, Eric 104
Kelley, Elijah 65
Kelly, Jim 113
Keys, Alicia 32, 68
Khumalo, Leleti 51
King, Regina 22, 45
King, Woodie, Jr. 27
Kirby, George 14
Kitt, Eartha 16, 75
Kodjoe, Boris 34, 89
Kool Moe Dee 37
Kotto, Yaphet 7
Kunjufu, Jawanza 3, 50
Lane, Charles 3
Laneuville, Eric 123
Lathan, Sanaa 27
Lawrence, Martin 6, 27, 60
Lebo M 109
Lee, Joie 1
Lee, Malcolm D. 75
Lee, Spike 5, 19, 86
Lemmons, Kasi 20
LeNoire, Rosetta 37
Lester, Adrian 46
Lewis, Samella 25
Lil' Kim 28
Lincoln, Abbey 3, 88
Lindo, Delroy 18, 45
LisaRaye 27
Lister, Tommy 127
Little, Cleavon 117
LL Cool J 16, 49, 94
Long, Nia 17, 95
Love, Loni 113
Lover, Ed 10

Luke, Derek 61
Lumet, Jenny 80
Luna, Donyale 88
Lynch, Shola 61
Mac, Bernie 29, 61, 72
Mackie, Anthony 102
Madame Sul-Te-Wan 95
Malco, Romany 71
Mann, Tamela 92
Marcille, Eva 97
Marshall, William 107
Martin, Darnell 43, 78
Martin, Duane 108
Martin, Helen 31
Mason, Judi Ann 112
Mbatha-Raw, Gugu 89
McBride, Chi 73
McDaniel, Hattie 5
McGee, Vonetta 95
McKee, Lonette 12, 119
McKinney, Nina Mae 40
McQueen, Butterfly 6, 54
McQueen, Steve 84
Meadows, Tim 30
Mello, Breno 73
Micheaux, Oscar 7
Miles, William 112
Miller, Omar Benson 93
Miller, Tangi 116
Miller, Wentworth 75
Mitchell, Kel 66
Mokae, Zakes 80
Mo'Nique 35, 84
Moore, Chante 26
Moore, Juanita 83, 124
Moore, Melba 21
Moore, Tim 124
Moreland, Mantan 117
Morris, Garrett 31
Morrison, Vanessa 84
Morton, Joe 18
Moses, Gilbert 12
Moss, Carlton 17
Murphy, Charles 95
Murphy, Eddie 4, 20, 61
Murphy, Matt 117
Muse, Clarence Edouard 21
Nash, Johnny 40
Naughton, Naturi 97
Neal, Elise 29
Nelson, Stanley 92
Newton, Thandie 26, 114
Nicholas, Fayard 20, 57
Nicholas, Harold 20
Nichols, Nichelle 11
Norman, Maidie 20
Nyong'o, Lupita 127
Oboth, Isaac 117
Okonedo, Sophie 67
O'Neal, Ron 46
O'Neal, Shaquille 8, 30, 95
Onwurah, Ngozi 38
Oyelowo, David 82, 126
Pace, Judy 119
Packer, Will 71
Palcy, Euzhan 94
Palmer, Keke 68, 120
Parker, Nicole Ari 52
Parks, Gordon 1, 35, 58
Patterson, Chuck 124
Patton, Paula 62
Paulk, Marcus T. 127
Payne, Allen 13

Peck, Raoul 32
Perrineau, Harold, Jr. 51
Perry, Tyler 40, 54, 103
Peters, Brock 96
Peters, Clarke 103
Pierce, Wendell 90
Pinkett Smith, Jada 10, 41, 95
Plummer, Glenn 120
Poitier, Sidney 11, 36
Poitier, Sydney Tamiia 65
Pounder, CCH 72
Pratt, Kyla 57
Preer, Evelyn 82
Prince-Bythewood, Gina 31, 77
Pryor, Richard 3, 24, 56
Queen Latifah 1, 16, 58, 119
Ralph, Sheryl Lee 18, 108
Randle, Theresa 16
Reddick, Lance 52, 128
Reed, Natina 106
Rees, Dee 100
Reuben, Gloria 15
Rhames, Ving 14, 50
Rhimes, Shonda Lynn 67
Rhymes, Busta 31
Richards, Beah 30
Richardson, LaTanya 71
Richardson, Salli 68
Ridley, John 69
Riggs, Marlon 5, 44
Riley, Amber 97
Roberts, Darryl 70
Roberts, Kimberly Rivers 72
Robinson, Craig 103
Robinson, Matt 69
Robinson, Shaun 36
Rochon, Lela 16
Rock, Chris 3, 22, 66
Rock, The 29, 66
Rodrigues, Percy 68
Rolle, Esther 13, 21
Rollins, Howard E., Jr. 16
Rose, Anika Noni 70
Ross, Diana 8, 27
Roundtree, Richard 27
Rowell, Victoria 13, 68
Rudolph, Maya 46, 106
St. Jacques, Raymond 8
St. John, Kristoff 25
Saldana, Zoe 72, 118
Salter, Nikkole 73
Sands, Diana 87
Schultz, Michael A. 6
Scott, Hazel 66
Scott, Jill 29, 83
Sembène, Ousmane 13, 62
Shakur, Tupac 14
Shepherd, Sherri 55
Short, Columbus 79
Sidibe, Gabourey 84
Sinbad 1, 16
Sinclair, Madge 78
Singleton, John 2, 30, 122
Sisqo 30
Sissako, Abderrahmane 127
Smith, Anjela Lauren 44
Smith, Anna Deavere 6, 44
Smith, Bubba 96
Smith, Jaden 82
Smith, Roger Guenveur 12
Smith, Tasha 73
Smith, Will 8, 18, 53
Smith, Willow 92

Snipes, Wesley 3, 24, 67
Solange 97
Souleymane, Mahamane 78
Spencer, Octavia 100
Strode, Woody 111
Sullivan, Maxine 37
Sy, Omar 109
Sykes, Wanda 48, 81
Tate, Larenz 15
Taylor, Meshach 4
Taylor, Regina 9, 46, 97
Terrence J 108
Thigpen, Lynne 17, 41
Thomas, Sean Patrick 35
Thompson, Kenan 52
Thurman, Wallace 16
Tillman, George, Jr. 20
Torres, Gina 52
Torry, Guy 31
Toussaint, Lorraine 32
Townsend, Robert 4, 23
True, Rachel 82
Tucker, Chris 13, 23, 62
Tunie, Tamara 63
Turman, Glynn 100
Turner, Tina 6, 27
Tyler, Aisha N. 36
Tyson, Cicely 7, 51, 112
Underwood, Blair 7, 27, 76
Union, Gabrielle 31, 92
Usher 23, 56, 95
Van Lierop, Robert 53
Van Peebles, Mario 2, 51
Van Peebles, Melvin 7, 95
Vance, Courtney B. 15, 60
Vanity 67
Vereen, Ben 4
Walker, Eamonn 37
Wallace, William 75
Wallis, Quvenzhané 109
Ward, Douglas Turner 42
Washington, Denzel 1, 16, 93
Washington, Fredi 10
Washington, Kerry 46, 107
Waters, Ethel 7
Wayans, Damien 78
Wayans, Damon 8, 41
Wayans, Keenen Ivory 18
Wayans, Kim 80
Wayans, Marlon 29, 82
Wayans, Shawn 29
Weathers, Carl 10, 117
Wesley, Richard 73
Wesley, Rutina 97
Wheaton, James 103
Whitaker, Forest 2, 49, 67
White, Armond 80, 118
White, Lillias 120
White, Michael Jai 71, 117
White, Sylvain 96
Whitfield, Lynn 18
Williams, Billy Dee 8, 105
Williams, Clarence, III 26
Williams, Marco 53
Williams, Michael Kenneth 97
Williams, Russell, II 70
Williams, Samm-Art 21
Williams, Saul 31
Williams, Spencer 126
Williams, Vanessa A. 32, 66
Williams, Vanessa L. 4, 17
Williamson, Fred 67
Williamson, Mykelti 22

Wilson, Debra 38
Wilson, Dorien 55
Winfield, Paul 2, 45
Witherspoon, John 38
Woodard, Alfre 9, 108
Woolard, Jamal 102
Wright, Jeffrey 54, 111
Yarbrough, Cedric 51
Yoba, Malik 11

**Government and politics--
international**
Abacha, Sani 11, 70
Abbott, Diane 9
Abiola, Moshood 70
Abubakar, Abdulsalami 66
Adebari, Rotimi 83
Afewerki, Isaias 98
Ahidjo, Ahmadou 81
Akunyili, Dora Nkem 58
Alexander, Lincoln 106
Ali Mahdi Mohamed 5
Amadi, Elechi 40
Amin, Idi 42
Amos, Valerie 41
Annan, Kofi Atta 15, 48
Aristide, Jean-Bertrand 6, 45
Arthur, Owen 33
Atta Mills, John 75
Augustine, Jean 53
Avant, Nicole A. 90
Azikiwe, Nnamdi 13
Babangida, Ibrahim 4
Baker, Gwendolyn Calvert 9
Banda, Hastings Kamuzu 6, 54
Banda, Joyce 101
Barnes, Melody 75
Barrow, Dean 69
Bartels, Peggielene 80
Bashir, Omar al- 77
Bedie, Henri Konan 21
Berry, Mary Frances 7
Biko, Steven 4
Bishop, Maurice 39
Biya, Chantal 89
Biya, Paul 28, 114
Bizimungu, Pasteur 19
Boateng, Paul Yaw 56
Bongo, Ali Ben 80
Bongo, Omar 1, 79
Boye, Madior 30
Bozizé, François 96, 117
Brown, Rosemary 62
Buhari, Muhammadu 128
Bunche, Ralph J. 5
Burnham, Forbes 66
Buthelezi, Mangosuthu Gatsha 9
Cabral, Amílcar 104
Camara, Moussa Dadis 76
Césaire, Aimé 48, 69
Cham, Adongo Agada Akway 77
Charlemagne, Manno 11
Charles, Mary Eugenia 10, 55
Charles, Pierre 52
Chiluba, Frederick 56, 80
Chissano, Joaquim 7, 55, 67
Christie, Perry Gladstone 53
Christophe, Henri 9
Compaore, Blaise 87
Compton, John 65
Condé, Alpha 95
Conneh, Sekou Damate, Jr. 51
Conté, Lansana 7, 76

Cools, Anne 64
Cousin, Ertharin 115
Curling, Alvin 34
da Silva, Benedita 5
Dadié, Bernard 34
Dandala, Mvume 77
Davis, Ruth 37
Déby, Idriss 30, 125
Desalegn, Hailemariam 105
Diogo, Luisa Dias 63
Diouf, Abdou 3
Djotodia, Michel 117
Dlamini-Zuma, Nkosazana 34, 105
Doe, Samuel K. 100
dos Santos, José Eduardo 43, 114
Douglas, Denzil Llewellyn 53
Dube, John Langalibalele 119
Duvalier, François 124
Duvalier, Jean-Claude 124
Ekwensi, Cyprian 37
Eyadéma, Gnassingbé 7, 52
Fela 1, 42
Gairy, Eric Matthew 83
Garang, John 105
Gbagbo, Laurent 43, 90
Gnassingbé, Faure 67
Golding, Bruce 78
Gordon, Pamela 17
Grant, Bernie 57
Guebuza, Armando 81
Habré, Hissène 6, 104
Habyarimana, Juvenal 8
Haile Selassie 7
Haley, George Williford Boyce 21
Hani, Chris 6
Holness, Andrew 99
Houphouët-Boigny, Félix 4, 64
Hussein, Lubna 80
Ifill, Gwen 28
Ingraham, Hubert A. 19
Isaac, Julius 34
Issoufou, Mahamadou 102
Jagan, Cheddi 16
Jammeh, Yahya 23, 104
Jawara, Dawda Kairaba 11
Jean, Michaëlle; 70
Jean, Wyclef 20, 86
Jonathan, Goodluck 83
Ka Dinizulu, Mcwayizeni 29
Kabbah, Ahmad Tejan 23
Kabila, Joseph 30, 126
Kabila, Laurent 20
Kabunda, Kenneth 2
Kagame, Paul 54
Kariuki, J. M. 67
Keïta, Ibrahim Boubacar 113
Kenyatta, Jomo 5
Kenyatta, Uhuru 110
Kerekou, Ahmed (Mathieu) 1
Khama, Ian 95
Kibaki, Mwai 60
Kiir, Salva Mayardit 85, 103
Kikwete, Jakaya Mrisho 73
King, Oona 27
Kisekka, Samson 112
Kony, Joseph 101
Koroma, Ernest Bai 84
Kufuor, John Agyekum 54, 82
Kyenge, Cécile 113
Laraque, Paul 67
Lewis, Daurene 72
Liberia-Peters, Maria Philomena 12
Lubanga, Thomas 104

Lumumba, Patrice 33
Luthuli, Albert 13
Maathai, Wangari 43, 97
Mabuza, Lindiwe 18
Machar, Riek 117
Machel, Graça 16, 102
Machel, Samora Moises 8
Magloire, Paul Eugène 68
Mahama, John Dramani 103
Malema, Julius 98
Mandela, Nelson 1, 14, 77, 117
Mandela, Winnie 2, 35, 112
Manigat, Mirlande 90
Marks, Audrey 99
Martelly, Michel 90
Masekela, Barbara 18
Masire, Quett 5
Mbeki, Govan A. 80
Mbeki, Thabo 14, 73
Mboya, Tom 107
Mbuende, Kaire 12
Mengistu, Haile Mariam 65
Mhlaba, Raymond 55
Mitchell, Keith 82
Mkapa, Benjamin W. 16, 77
Mobutu Sese Seko 1, 56
Mogae, Festus Gontebanye 19, 79
Mohamud, Hassan Sheikh 105
Moi, Daniel Arap 1, 35
Mongella, Gertrude 11
Mosisili, Pakalitha 96
Motlanthe, Kgalema 74
Moyo, Dambisa 76
Moyo, Lovemore 76
Mswati III 56
Mugabe, Robert 10, 71
Muhammed, Murtala 119
Mukoko, Jestina 75
Muluzi, Bakili 14, 76
Museveni, Yoweri 4, 119
Mushikiwabo, Louise 88
Mutebi, Ronald 25
Muzorewa, Abel 85
Mwanawasa, Levy 72
Mwinyi, Ali Hassan 1, 77
Nascimento, Abdias do 93
Ndadaye, Melchior 7
Nelson, Sophia A. 93
Neto, António Agostinho 43
Ngilu, Charity 58
Ngubane, Ben 33
Nkoli, Simon 60
Nkomo, Joshua 4, 65
Nkrumah, Kwame 3
Nkurunziza, Pierre 78
Ntaryamira, Cyprien 8
Nujoma, Samuel 10
Nyanda, Siphiwe 21
Nyerere, Julius 5
Nzo, Alfred 15
Obasanjo, Olusegun 5, 22
Obasanjo, Stella 32, 56
Obiang, Teodoro 103
Obote, Milton 63
Odinga, Raila 67, 110
Okara, Gabriel 37
Okonjo-Iweala, Ngozi 101
Olympio, Sylvanus 126
Ouattara, Alassane 90
Oyono, Ferdinand 38
Pascal-Trouillot, Ertha 3
Patterson, P. J. 6, 20
Pereira, Aristides 30, 97

Perkins, Edward 5
Perry, Ruth 15
Pierre-Louis, Michèle 75
Pindling, Lynden 81
Pitt, David Thomas 10
Pitta, Celso 17
Pohamba, Hifikepunye 95
Préval, René 87
Ramaphosa, Cyril 3, 117
Rawlings, Jerry 9
Rawlings, Nana Konadu Agyeman 13
Roberto, Holden 65
Roberts, Joseph Jenkins 125
Robinson, Randall 7, 46
Rochereau, Tabu Ley 117
Russwurm, John Brown 100
Sall, Macky 101
Sampson, Edith S. 4
Sanhá Malam Bacai 84, 101
Sankara, Thomas 17
Sankoh, Foday 74
Sassou-Nguesso, Denis 103
Sata, Michael 102, 125
Savimbi, Jonas 2, 34
Sawyer, Amos 2, 123
Senghor, Augustin Diamacoune 66
Senghor, Léopold Sédar 12, 66
Shearer, Hugh 107
Silva, Marina 80
Simpson Miller, Portia 62, 100
Sirleaf, Ellen Johnson 71
Sisulu, Walter 47
Skerrit, Roosevelt 72
Skinner, Kiron K. 65
Smith, Jennifer 21
Soglo, Nicephore 15
Spencer, Winston Baldwin 68
Tandja, Mamadou 33, 78
Tau, Mpho Parks 124
Taubira, Christiane 117
Taylor, Charles 20
Taylor, John (David Beckett) 16
Thabane, Thomas 123
Thiam, Tidjane 104
Todman, Terence A. 55
Toivola, Jani 118
Tolbert, William R. 100
Touré, Amadou Toumani 18
Touré, Sekou 6
Traore, Dioncounda 103
Tsvangirai, Morgan 26, 72
Tubman, William 99
Tutu, Desmond 6, 44
Van Lierop, Robert 53
Vieira, João Bernardo 14, 84
Wade, Abdoulaye 66
Weah, George 58
Wharton, Clifton R., Jr. 7
Wharton, Clifton Reginald, Sr. 36
Williams, Eric Eustace 65
Wiwa, Ken 67
Yar'Adua, Umaru 69, 89
Yayi, Boni T. 84
Yumkella, Kandeh 105
Zenawi, Meles 3, 99
Zuma, Jacob G. 33, 75
Zwelithini, Goodwill 128

Government and politics--U.S.
Adams, Alma 127
Adams, Floyd, Jr. 12, 122
Adams, Grantley 82

Adegbile, Debo P. 119
Ahmed, Sharif 80
Alexander, Archie Alphonso 14
Alexander, Clifford 26
Allen, Claude 68
Allen, Ethel D. 13
Allen, Eugene 79
Archer, Dennis 7, 36
Arrington, Richard 24, 100
Avant, Clarence 19, 86
Baker, Thurbert 22
Ballance, Frank W. 41
Baltimore, Richard Lewis, III 71
Baraka, Ras J. 121
Barbee, Lloyd Augustus 71
Barrett, Andrew C. 12
Barrett, Jacqueline 28
Barry, Marion, Jr. 7, 44, 125
Bass, Karen 70
Beatty, Joyce 117
Becton, Julius W., Jr. 110
Bell, Michael 40
Bell, William A., Sr. 122
Bellamy, Terry 58
Belton, Sharon Sayles 9, 16
Benjamin, Steve 98
Berrien, Jacqueline A. 93
Berry, Edwin C. 81
Berry, Mary Frances 7
Berry, Theodore M. 31
Bethune, Mary McLeod 4
Bing, Dave 3, 59, 78
Bishop, Sanford D., Jr. 24, 111
Blackwell, Kenneth, Sr. 61
Blackwell, Unita 17
Bobb, Robert C. 83
Bond, Julian 2, 35, 106
Booker, Cory Anthony 68
Bosley, Freeman, Jr. 7
Bowman, Bertie 71
Boykin, Keith 14
Bradley, Jennette B. 40
Bradley, Thomas 2
Braun, Carol Moseley 4, 42
Brazile, Donna 25, 70
Brimmer, Andrew 2, 48, 106
Brooke, Edward W. 8, 88, 126
Brookins, Hamel Hartford 102
Brooks, Tyrone 59
Brown, Aja 115
Brown, Alvin 96
Brown, Anthony G. 72
Brown, Byrd 49
Brown, Byron W. 72
Brown, Cora 33
Brown, Corrine 24, 90
Brown, Elaine 8
Brown, George Leslie 62
Brown, Jesse 6, 41
Brown, Kwame R. 91
Brown, Les 5
Brown, Ron 5
Brown, Willie 7, 85
Bruce, Blanche K. 33
Bryant, Wayne R. 6
Buckley, Victoria (Vicki) 24
Bunche, Ralph J. 5
Burke, Yvonne Brathwaite 42
Burris, Chuck 21
Burris, Roland W. 25, 75
Burton, Bill 96
Bush, Gordon 82
Butler, Jerry 26

Butts, Cassandra 78
Caesar, Shirley 19
Campbell, Bill 9, 76
Cannon, Patrick 120
Cardozo, Francis L. 33
Carson, André 69
Carson, Ben 1, 35, 76, 128
Carson, Johnnie 85
Carson, Julia 23, 69
Carter, Jill P. 110
Carter, Pamela Lynn 67
Celestin, Josaphat 101
Chavis, Benjamin 6
Chisholm, Shirley 2, 50
Christian-Green, Donna M. 17
Christie, Ron 83
Clarke, Yvette 92
Clay, William Lacy 8
Clay, William Lacy, Jr. 95
Clayton, Eva M. 20
Cleaver, Eldridge 5
Cleaver, Emanuel 4, 45, 68, 107
Clemente, Rosa 74
Clyburn, James E. 21, 71, 118
Clyburn, Mignon 78
Cockrel, Kenneth V., Jr. 79
Cockrel, Kenneth Vern, Sr. 79
Coleman, Mary 46
Coleman, Michael B. 28, 79
Coleman, William T. 76
Collins, Barbara-Rose 7, 87
Collins, Cardiss 10, 80, 120
Colter, Cyrus J. 36
Connerly, Ward 14
Conyers, John, Jr. 4, 45, 111
Conyers, Monica 85
Cook, Mercer 40
Craig-Jones, Ellen Walker 44
Crockett, George W., Jr. 10, 64
Cummings, Elijah E. 24, 102
Cunningham, Evelyn 23, 85
Currie, Betty 21
Currie, Ulysses 73
Davis, Artur 41
Davis, Benjamin O., Jr. 2, 43
Davis, Benjamin O., Sr. 4
Davis, Danny K. 24, 79
Davis, Doris A. 100
Davis, Gordon J. 76
Davis, James E. 50
Days, Drew S., III 10
De Priest, Oscar Stanton 80
DeBerry, Lois M. 115
DeJongh, John, Jr. 85
Delany, Martin R. 27
Delco, Wilhelmina R. 33
Dellums, Ronald 2, 81
Diggs, Charles R. 21
Dinkins, David 4
Dixon, Julian C. 24
Dixon, Sharon Pratt 1
Dixon, Sheila 68
Dougherty, Mary Pearl 47
Douglas, Derek 88
Du Bois, W. E. B. 3
Dudley, Edward R. 58
Dukes, Hazel Nell 56
Dunbar-Nelson, Alice Ruth Moore 44
DuPree, Johnny 96
Dymally, Mervyn 42
Easley, Annie J. 61
Edmonds, Terry 17

Edwards, Donna 77
Edwards, Willis 104
Ellison, Keith 59
Ervin, Clark Kent 82
Espy, Mike 6
Evans, Melvin H. 88
Farmer, James 2, 64
Farrakhan, Louis 2
Farrell, Herman D., Jr. 81
Fattah, Chaka 11, 70, 112
Fauntroy, Walter E. 11
Fauset, Crystal Dreda Bird 100
Felix, Larry R. 64
Fenty, Adrian 60, 88
Fields, C. Virginia 25
Fields, Cleo 13
Fisher, Ada M. 76
Flake, Floyd H. 18, 110
Fleming, Erik R. 75
Fletcher, Arthur A. 63
Flipper, Henry O. 3
Ford, Harold E(ugene) 42
Ford, Harold E(ugene), Jr. 16, 70
Ford, Jack 39
Ford, Johnny 70
Fortune, T. Thomas 6
Foster, Ezola 28
Foxx, Anthony 81, 123
Francois, Terry A. 106
Franklin, Shirley 34, 80
Franks, Gary 2
Frazer, Jendayi 68
Frazer, Victor O. 98
Frazier, Ryan 89
Fudge, Marcia L. 76
Fulani, Lenora 11
Fuller, Thomas O. 90
Gaines, Matthew 95
Gantt, Harvey 1
Garrett, Joyce Finley 59
Garvey, Marcus 1
Gaspard, Patrick 84
Gibbs, Mifflin W. 99
Gibson, Johnnie Mae 23
Gibson, Kenneth Allen 6
Gibson, William F. 6
Gillum, Andrew 128
Glover, Cedric B. 103
Goggins, Juanita 127
Goode, W. Wilson 4
Gravely, Samuel L., Jr. 5, 49
Gray, Vincent C. 88
Gray, William H., III 3
Green, Al 118
Grillo, Evelio 95
Grimké, Archibald H. 9
Groff, Peter 96
Guinier, Lani 7, 30
Haley, George Williford Boyce 21
Hamer, Fannie Lou 6
Hancock, Michael B. 123
Harmon, Clarence 26
Harp, Toni 123
Harris, Alice 7
Harris, Kamala D. 64, 122
Harris, Patricia Roberts 2
Harvard, Beverly 11
Hastie, William H. 8
Hastings, Alcee 16, 119
Hatcher, Andrew T. 90
Hatcher, Richard G. 55
Hawkins, Augustus F. 68
Hayes, James C. 10

Henderson, Thelton E. 68
Henry, Aaron 19
Herenton, Willie W. 24, 81
Herman, Alexis M. 15
Hernandez, Aileen Clarke 13
Hill, Bonnie Guiton 20
Hilliard, Earl F. 24
Hobson, Julius W. 44
Holden, Kip 120
Holder, Eric H., Jr. 9, 76, 104
Holmes, Amy 69
Holt Baker, Arlene 73
Horsford, Steven 88
Howard, Perry Wilbon, Jr. 112
Hughes, Dora 88
Ifill, Gwen 28
Irving, Larry, Jr. 12
Irvis, K. Leroy 67
Jackson, Alphonso R. 48
Jackson, Eric 127
Jackson, Frank G. 76
Jackson, George 14
Jackson, Jesse 1, 27, 72
Jackson, Jesse, Jr. 14, 45, 81, 108
Jackson, Lisa 77
Jackson, Mae 57
Jackson, Maynard 2, 41
Jackson, Sandi 108
Jackson, Shirley Ann 12
Jackson Lee, Sheila 20
Jacob, John E. 2
James, Sharpe 23, 69
James, Sly 107
Jarrett, Valerie 73
Jarvis, Charlene Drew 21
Jarvis, Kristen 85
Jefferson, William J. 25, 72
Jeffries, Hakeem 118
Johnson, Eddie Bernice 8, 90
Johnson, Edward Austin 107
Johnson, Hank, Jr. 80
Johnson, Harvey, Jr. 24, 82
Johnson, James Weldon 5
Johnson, Jeh 76, 125
Johnson, Katherine (Coleman
    Goble) 61
Johnson, Kevin 70
Johnson, Leroy R. 89
Johnson, Norma H. 17, 97
Johnson, Robert T. 17
Jones, Dwight C. 122
Jones, Elaine R. 7, 45
Jones, Emil, Jr. 74
Jones, John 89
Jordan, Barbara 4, 78
Jordan, Charles 122
Jordan, Vernon 3, 35
Kelley, Cliff 75
Kelly, Robin 114
Kennard, William Earl 18
Keyes, Alan 11, 105
Kidd, Mae Street 39
Kilpatrick, Carolyn Cheeks 16
Kilpatrick, Kwame 34, 71, 116
Kincaid, Bernard 28
King, Martin Luther, III 20
Kirk, Ron 11, 75, 111
Lafontant, Jewel Stradford 3, 51
Lamothe, Laurent 122
Langford, Larry P. 74
Langston, John Mercer 101
Lawrence, Brenda 127
Layton, William 87

Lee, Barbara 25, 102
Leland, Mickey 2
Lewis, Delano 7
Lewis, John 2, 46, 83
Lewis, William Henry 89
Lindsay, Peta 100
Love, Mia 96, 125
Love, Reggie 77
Lowery, Myron 80
Lumumba, Chokwe 118
Lynch, William, Jr. 115
Mack, Tony 104
Majette, Denise 41
Mallett, Conrad, Jr. 16
Mallory, Mark 62
Mallory, William L., Sr. 119
Marks, John R., III 123
Marsh, Henry, III 32
Marshall, Bella 22
Marshall, Thurgood 1, 44
Martin, Louis E. 16
Martin, Ruby Grant 49
McCall, H. Carl 27
McGee, James D. 74
McGee, James Madison 46
McGlowan, Angela 64, 86
McHenry, Donald F. 83
McKinney, Cynthia 11, 52, 74
McKissick, Floyd B. 3
McPhail, Sharon 2, 119
Meek, Carrie 6, 36
Meek, Kendrick 41, 89
Meeks, Gregory T. 25, 117
Meeks, James T. 92
Melton, Frank 81
Menard, John Willis 90
Meredith, James H. 11
Metcalfe, Ralph 26
Mfume, Kweisi 6, 41
Millender-McDonald, Juanita 21, 61
Miller, Lorraine C. 119
Mitchell, Arthur Wergs 91
Mitchell, Parren J. 42, 66
Moore, Gwendolynne S. 55
Moore, Minyon 45
Morial, Ernest "Dutch" 26
Morial, Marc H. 20, 51
Morrow, E. Frederic 100
Morton, Azie Taylor 48
Morton, Ferdinand Q. 90
Mosby, Marilyn 128
Moses, Robert Parris 11
Murrell, Sylvia Marilyn 49
Nagin, Ray 42, 57, 88
Nix, Robert N. C., Jr. 51
Norton, Eleanor Holmes 7, 93
Nutter, Michael 69, 112
Obama, Barack 49, 74, 91
Obama, Michelle 61, 90
O'Leary, Hazel 6
Owens, Major 6, 117
Page, Alan 7
Paige, Rod 29
Parker, Vernon 97
Paterson, Basil A. 69, 122
Paterson, David A. 59
Patrick, Deval 12, 61, 127
Patterson, J. O., Jr. 80
Patterson, Louise 25
Payne, Donald M. 2, 57, 112
Payne, William D. 60
Perez, Anna 1
Perkins, Edward 5

Perkins, James, Jr. 55
Perry, James 83
Perry, Lowell 30
Peterson, Karen Carter 90
Pinchback, P. B. S. 9
Pinkney, Arnold R. 122
Pitts, Robb 84
Plaskett, Stacey 127
Powell, Adam Clayton, Jr. 3
Powell, Colin 1, 28, 75
Powell, Debra A. 23
Powell, Michael 32
Primas, Randy 106
Pugh, Charles 81
Randolph, A. Philip 3
Rangel, Charles B. 3, 52, 85
Raoul, Kwame 55
Rapier, James T. 82
Rawlings-Blake, Stephanie 93, 128
Redd, Dana 93
Reed, Joe L. 110
Reed, Kasim 82
Reeves, Gregory 49
Reeves, Martha 85
Reeves, Triette Lipsey 27
Revels, Hiram Rhoades 98
Rice, Condoleezza 3, 28, 72
Rice, Emmett J. 94
Rice, Norm 8
Rice, Susan 74, 103
Richardson, Laura 81
Richardson, Rupert 67
Richmond, Cedric 93
Riles, Wilson C. 79
Roberts, Lillian 83
Robinson, Bishop L. 66
Robinson, Randall 7, 46
Rochon, Stephen W. 78
Rogers, Desirée 88
Rogers, Joe 27
Ross, Don 27
Rouse, Cecilia 93
Rush, Bobby 26, 76
Rustin, Bayard 4
Sampson, Edith S. 4
Sanders, Malika 48
Sawyer, Eugene 81
Sayles Belton, Sharon 9
Schmoke, Kurt 1, 48
Scott, David 41, 117
Scott, Robert C. 23
Scott, Tim 87, 125
Sewell, Terri 93
Shakur, Assata 6
Shavers, Cheryl 31
Shelton, Paula Young 86
Sherrod, Shirley 87
Simmons, E. Denise 79
Simmons, Jamal 72
Simpson, Carole 6, 30
Sisulu, Sheila Violet Makate 24
Slater, Rodney E. 15, 125
Smith, Malcolm A. 75
Smith, Nate 49
Smith, Princella 86
Smyre, Calvin 90
Smythe Haith, Mabel 61
Spearman, Leonard H. O., Sr. 81
Spencer, Vaino H. 99
Spigner, Archie 81
Stanton, Robert 20
Staupers, Mabel K. 7
Steele, Michael 38, 73, 91

Stewart, Nzingha 89
Stokes, Carl 10, 73
Stokes, Louis 3
Stoutt, H. Lavity 83
Strautmanis, Michael 87
Street, John F. 24
Sullivan, Louis 8
Sutphen, Mona 77
Sutton, Percy E. 42, 82
Taylor, Robert Rochon 104
Thomas, Clarence 2, 39, 65
Thomas-Greenfield, Linda 99
Thompson, Bennie 26, 119
Thompson, Larry D. 39
Thompson, William C., Jr. 35, 114
Tillman, Dorothy 76
Todman, Terence A. 55
Tolbert, Terence 74
Toote, Gloria E. A. 64
Towns, Edolphus 19, 75
Tribble, Israel, Jr. 8
Trotter, Donne E. 28
Tubbs Jones, Stephanie 24, 72
Tucker, C. Delores 12, 56
Turnbull, Charles Wesley 62
Turner, Henry McNeal 5
Twilight, Alexander 125
Tyler, Ollie 128
Usry, James L. 23
Vaughn, Gladys Gary 47
Von Lipsey, Roderick K. 11
Waldon, Alton R., Jr. 98
Wallace, Phyllis A. 9
Washington, Harold 6
Washington, Val 12
Washington, Walter 45
Waters, Maxine 3, 67, 103
Watkins, Craig 97
Watkins, Joe 86
Watkins, Shirley R. 17
Watson, Diane 41
Watson Coleman, Bonnie 127
Watt, Mel 26, 105
Watts, J. C., Jr. 14, 38
Weaver, Robert C. 8, 46
Webb, Wellington 3, 81
Welcome, Verda Freeman 112
West, Allen 89
Wharton, A. C., Jr. 110
Wharton, Clifton R., Jr. 7
Wharton, Clifton Reginald, Sr. 36
Wheat, Alan 14
White, Jesse 22, 75
White, Michael R. 5
Widener, Warren 99
Wilder, L. Douglas 3, 48
Williams, Anthony 21
Williams, Dennis P. 123
Williams, Eddie N. 44
Williams, George Washington 18
Williams, Hosea 15, 31, 123
Williams, Maggie 7, 71
Williams, Michael L. 86
Wilson, Frederica 92
Wilson, Lionel 99
Wilson, Margaret Bush 79
Woods, Abraham, Jr. 74
Wynn, Albert 25, 77
Young, Andrew 3, 48, 110

Law

Adegbile, Debo P. 119
Alexander, Clifford 26

Alexander, Joyce London 18
Alexander, Michelle 98
Alexander, Sadie Tanner Mossell 22
Ali, Russlynn H. 92
Allen, Macon Bolling 104
Allen, Samuel W. 38
Amaker, Norman 63
Anderson, Reuben V. 81
Archer, Dennis 7, 36
Arnwine, Barbara 28
Bailey, Clyde 45
Baldwin, Cynthia 74, 107
Banks, William 11
Barbee, Lloyd Augustus 71
Barrett, Andrew C. 12
Barrett, Jacqueline 28
Batts, Anthony 128
Baugh, David 23
Benham, Robert 78
Benjamin, Steve 98
Bensouda, Fatou 103
Berrien, Jacqueline A. 93
Berry, Theodore M. 31
Birch, Adolpho A., Jr. 85
Bolin, Jane 22, 59
Bolton, Terrell D. 25
Booker, Cory Anthony 68
Bosley, Freeman, Jr. 7
Boulware, Harold R. 109
Boykin, Keith 14
Bradley, Thomas 2
Brown, Byrd 49
Brown, Cora 33
Brown, Cupcake 63
Brown, Homer S. 47
Brown, Janice Rogers 43
Brown, Joe 29
Brown, Lee P. 1, 24, 109
Brown, Ron 5
Bryant, Wayne R. 6
Bryant, William Benson 61
Buery, Richard, Jr. 97
Bully-Cummings, Ella 48
Burris, Roland W. 25, 75
Butler, Louis 70
Butler, Paul D. 17
Bynoe, Peter C. B. 40
Campbell, Bill 9, 76
Carter, Pamela Lynn 67
Carter, Robert L. 51, 100
Carter, Stephen L. 4
Cashin, Sheryll 63
Chambers, Julius 3
Chestnut, J. L., Jr. 73
Clark, Ray 122
Cleaver, Kathleen Neal 29
Clendenon, Donn 26, 56
Cochran, Johnnie 11, 39, 52
Colbert, Tom 115
Coleman, James E., Jr. 79
Coleman, William T. 76
Colter, Cyrus J. 36
Crenshaw, Kimberlé Williams 88
Darden, Christopher 13
Davis, Angela J. 88
Davis, Artur 41
Davis, Gordon J. 76
Days, Drew S., III 10
DeFrantz, Anita 37
Dillard, Godfrey J. 45
Dow, Unity 104
Early, Norman S., Jr. 124

Edley, Christopher 2, 48
Edley, Christopher F., Jr. 48
Ellington, E. David 11
Ephriam, Mablean 29
Ervin, Clark Kent 82
Espy, Mike 6
Evans, Warren C. 76
Farmer-Paellmann, Deadria 43
Feemster, Herbert 72
Fenty, Adrian 60, 88
Fields, Cleo 13
Finner-Williams, Paris Michele 62
Fisher, Ada Lois Sipuel 76
Ford, Wallace 58
Forman, James, Jr. 89
Foxx, Anthony 81, 123
Frazer, Victor O. 98
Freeman, Charles 19
Gaines, Lloyd 79
Gary, Willie E. 12, 117
Gibson, Johnnie Mae 23
Gittens, Charles L. 124
Glover, Nathaniel, Jr. 12
Gomez-Preston, Cheryl 9
Gordon-Reed, Annette 74
Gourdin, Edward O. 93
Graham, Lawrence Otis 12
Gray, Fred 37
Gray, Willie 46
Greenhouse, Bunnatine 57
Grimké, Archibald H. 9
Guinier, Lani 7, 30
Haley, George Williford Boyce 21
Hall, Elliott S. 24
Harden, Monique 97
Harris, Kamala D. 64, 122
Harris, Maya Lakshmi 88
Harris, Patricia Roberts 2
Harvard, Beverly 11
Hassell, Leroy Rountree, Sr. 41, 116
Hastie, William H. 8
Hatcher, Richard G. 55
Hatchett, Glenda 32
Hawkins, Augustus F. 68
Hawkins, Steven 14
Hayes, Dennis 54
Haywood, Margaret A. 24
Henderson, Thelton E. 68
Higginbotham, A. Leon, Jr. 13, 25
Hill, Anita 5, 65
Hillard, Terry 25
Hills, Oliver W. 24
Holder, Eric H., Jr. 9, 76, 104
Hollowell, Donald L. 57
Holton, Hugh, Jr. 39
Hooks, Benjamin L. 2, 85
Houston, Charles Hamilton 4
Howard, Perry Wilbon, Jr. 112
Hubbard, Arnette Rhinehart 38
Hurtt, Harold 46
Isaac, Julius 34
Jackson, Maynard 2, 41
Jackson Lee, Sheila 20
Johnson, Edward Austin 107
Johnson, Harry E. 57
Johnson, James Weldon 5
Johnson, Leroy R. 89
Johnson, Norma H. 17, 97
Johnson, Sterling, Jr. 124
Jones, Clarence B. 114
Jones, Elaine R. 7, 45
Jones, Theodore T., Jr. 108

Jones, Van 70
Jordan, Eddie 82
Jordan, Vernon E. 3, 35
Kearse, Amalya Lyle 12
Keith, Damon J. 16, 74
Kennard, William Earl 18
Kennedy, Florynce 12, 33
Kennedy, Randall 40
Kibaki, Mwai 60
La Roca, Pete 107
Lafontant, Jewel Stradford 3, 51
Lewis, Delano 7
Lewis, William Henry 89
Lloyd, Reginald 64
Lynch, Loretta E. 103
Majette, Denise 41
Mallett, Conrad, Jr. 16
Marks, John R., III 123
Marsh, Henry, III 32
Marshall, Thurgood 1, 44
Mathis, Greg 26
McAnulty, William E., Jr. 66
McCrary Anthony, Crystal 70
McDonald, Gabrielle Kirk 20
McDougall, Gay J. 11, 43
McGhee, Heather C. 106
McKinnon, Isaiah 9
McPhail, Sharon 2, 119
Melton, Harold D. 79
Ming, William Robert, Jr. 125
Mitchell, Arthur Wergs 91
Mitchell, Clarence M., Jr. 88
Mitchell, Juanita Jackson 128
Moose, Charles 40
Morial, Ernest "Dutch" 26
Morton, Ferdinand Q. 90
Morton, Frederick A., Jr. 93
Mosby, Marilyn 128
Motley, Constance Baker 10, 55
Muhammad, Ava 31
Murray, Pauli 38
Nance, Cynthia 71
Napoleon, Benny N. 23
Nash, Shannon King 84
Nelson, Sophia A. 93
Nix, Robert N. C., Jr. 51
Noble, Ronald 46
Nunn, Annetta 43
Obama, Michelle 61, 90
Ogletree, Charles, Jr. 12, 47
Ogunlesi, Adebayo O. 37
Oliver, Jerry 37
Orr, Kevyn 118
Page, Alan 7
Parker, Barrington D. 92
Parker, Kellis E. 30
Parks, Bernard C. 17
Parsons, James 14
Pascal-Trouillot, Ertha 3
Paterson, Basil A. 69, 122
Patrick, Deval 12
Payne, Ulice, Jr. 42
Payton, John 48, 124
Perry, Lowell 30
Perry, Matthew J., Jr. 96
Philip, Marlene Nourbese 32
Pincham, R. Eugene, Sr. 69
Powell, Michael 32
Quince, Peggy A. 69
Ramsey, Charles H. 21, 69
Raoul, Kwame 55
Rawlinson, Johnnie B. 79
Ray, Charlotte E. 60

Redding, Louis L. 26
Reed, Kasim 82
Reeves, Bass 100
Reynolds, Star Jones 10, 27, 61
Rice, Constance LaMay 60
Richie, Leroy C. 18
Roaf, Andrée Layton 106
Roberts, Michele 123
Robinson, Bishop L. 66
Robinson, Malcolm S. 44
Robinson, Randall 7, 46
Rock, John S. 113
Roundtree, Dovey 80
Russell-McCloud, Patricia 17
Sampson, Edith S. 4
Schmoke, Kurt 1, 48
Sealy, Lloyd G. 125
Sears, Leah Ward 5, 79
Shores, Arthur D. 99
Slater, Duke 125
Sleet, Gregory M. 109
Smith, DeMaurice 92
Solomon, Jimmie Lee 38
Sparks, Corinne Etta 53
Stevenson, Bryan 128
Stokes, Louis 3
Stout, Juanita Kidd 24
Strautmanis, Michael 87
Sutton, Percy E. 42, 82
Tanner, Jack E. 100
Taylor, John (David Beckett) 16
Thomas, Arthur Ray 52
Thomas, Clarence 2, 39, 65
Thomas, Franklin A. 5, 49
Thompson, Larry D. 39
Tingling, Milton A. 110
Tolbert, James L. 112
Touré, Faya Ora Rose 56
Tubbs Jones, Stephanie 24, 72
Van Lierop, Robert 53
Wagner, Annice 22
Wainwright, Joscelyn 46
Waldon, Alton R., Jr. 98
Walker, Cora T. 68
Wallace, Perry E. 47
Ward, Benjamin 68
Washington, Harold 6
Watkins, Craig 97
Watkins, Donald 35
Watt, Garland W. 113
Watt, Melvin 26
Wharton, Clifton Reginald, Sr. 36
Widener, Warren 99
Wilder, L. Douglas 3, 48
Wilkins, David 77
Williams, Ann Claire 82
Williams, David W. 110
Williams, Evelyn 10
Williams, Gregory 11
Williams, Patricia 11, 54
Williams, Willie L. 4
Wilson, Jimmy 45
Worthy, Kym 84
Wray, Noble 114
Wright, Bruce McMarion 3, 52
Wynn, Albert 25, 77

Military
Abacha, Sani 11, 70
Adams Early, Charity 13, 34
Adams-Ender, Clara 40
Alexander, Margaret Walker 22
Amin, Idi 42

Anderson, Marcia 115
Archer, Lee, Jr. 79
Austin, Lloyd 101
Babangida, Ibrahim 4
Baker, Vernon Joseph 65, 87
Bashir, Omar al- 77
Becton, Julius W., Jr. 110
Bennett, Richard 97
Black, Barry C. 47
Bolden, Charles Frank, Jr. 7, 78
Brashear, Carl 29
Brown, Anthony G. 72
Brown, Erroll M. 23
Brown, Jesse 6, 41
Brown, Jesse Leroy 31
Brown, Wesley A. 102
Brown, Willa 40
Bullard, Eugene 12
Bush, Charles Vernon 125
Cadoria, Sherian Grace 14
Carney, William H. 104
Carter, Edward A., Jr. 104
Chappell, Roy M. 95
Chissano, Joaquim 7, 55, 67
Christophe, Henri 9
Clark, Carl 101
Clarke, Anna Mac 95
Clemmons, Reginal G. 41
Coleman, Ronald S. 110
Compaore, Blaise 87
Conté, Lansana 7, 76
Cooke, Marcia 60
Davis, Benjamin O., Jr. 2, 43
Davis, Benjamin O., Sr. 4
Drew, Alvin, Jr. 67
Duggins, George 64
Ellis, Larry R. 110
Europe, James Reese 10
Eyadéma, Gnassingbé 7, 52
Fields, Evelyn J. 27
Flipper, Henry O. 3
Fox, John R. 105
Gravely, Samuel L., Jr. 5, 49
Gregory, Frederick 8, 51
Guéï, Robert 66
Habré, Hissène 6, 104
Habyarimana, Juvenal 8
Harris, Marcelite Jordan 16
Healy, Michael 90
Honoré, Russel L. 64
Hoskins, Harold K. 103
Howard, Michelle 28, 125
Jackson, Fred James 25
James, Daniel, Jr. 16
Johnson, Hazel 22
Johnson, Shoshana 47
Julian, Hubert 90
Kagame, Paul 54
Kerekou, Ahmed (Mathieu) 1
Khama, Ian 95
King, Teresa 80
Kony, Joseph 101
Laraque, Paul 67
Lawrence, Robert H., Jr. 16
Lubanga, Thomas 104
Lyles, Lester 31
Maceo, Antonio 82
Magloire, Paul Eugène 68
Matthews, Mark 59
Miller, Dorie 29
Morris, Melvin 120
Muhammed, Murtala 119
Nkunda, Laurent 75

Ntaganda, Bosco 111
Nyanda, Siphiwe 21
Obasanjo, Olusegun 5, 22
Ojukwu, Odumegwu 99
Perry, Herman 89
Petersen, Frank E. 31
Plinton, James O., Jr. 98
Powell, Colin 1, 28, 75
Pruitt, Wendell O. 106
Rawlings, Jerry 9
Reason, J. Paul 19
Rochon, Stephen W. 78
Rogers, Alan G. 72
Scantlebury, Janna 47
Smalls, Robert 82
Snow, Samuel 71
Stanford, John 20
Staupers, Mabel K. 7
Stokes, Louis 3
Stowers, Freddie 107
Touré, Amadou Toumani 18
Via, Dennis 108
Von Lipsey, Roderick K. 11
Ward, William E. 107
Watkins, Perry 12
West, Togo D., Jr. 16
Wilson, Jimmy 45
Wright, Lewin 43
Young, Charles 77

Music

Aaliyah 30
Abdullah, Kazem 97
Ace, Johnny 36
Aces, The 117
Acklin, Barbara Jean 107
Adams, Johnny 39
Adams, Leslie 39
Adams, Oleta 18
Adams, Yolanda 17, 67
Adderley, Julian "Cannonball" 30
Adderley, Nat 29
Ade, King Sunny 41
Adebimpe, Tunde 75
Afro, Teddy 78
Akinmusire, Ambrose 103
Akon 68
Albright, Gerald 23
Alert, Kool DJ 33
Ali, Rashied 79
Allen, Betty 83
Allen, Geri 92
Allen, Tony 117
Allison, Luther 111
Amadou & Mariam 113
Amerie 52
Ammons, Albert 112
Ammons, Gene 112
Amy, Curtis 114
Anderson, Carl 48
Anderson, Fred 87
Anderson, Ivie 126
Anderson, Jacob 128
Anderson, Marian 2, 33
Anderson, T. J. 119
Andrews, Inez 108
apl.de.ap 84
Ardoin, Alphonse 65
Armatrading, Joan 32
Armstrong, Louis 2
Armstrong, Vanessa Bell 24
Arnold, Billy Boy 112
Arnold, Kokomo 116

Arroyo, Marina 30
A$AP Rocky 109
Ashanti 37, 96
Ashford, Nickolas 21, 97
Ashong, Derrick 86
Astatke, Mulatu 81
Atkins, Juan 50
Atlantic Starr 122
Attaway, William 102
Austin, Lovie 40
Austin, Patti 24
Avant, Clarence 19, 86
Avant, Nicole A. 90
Ayers, Roy 16
Ayler, Albert 104
Babyface 10, 31, 82
Baca, Susana 80
Badu, Erykah 22, 114
Bailey, Buster 38
Bailey, DeFord 33
Bailey, Pearl 14
Bailey, Philip 63
Bailey Rae, Corinne 83
Baiocchi, Regina Harris 41
Baker, Anita 21, 48
Baker, Josephine 3
Baker, LaVern 26
Baker, Mickey 95
Ballard, Florence 112
Ballard, Hank 41
Bambaataa, Afrika 34
Banks, Azealia 107
Banks, Lloyd 113
Banner, David 55
Banton, Buju 93
Baraka, Sho 109
Bar-Kays, The 118
Barker, Danny 32
Barnes, Katreese 97
Barnes, Lloyd 77
Barnes, Roosevelt "Booba" 33
Barrino, Fantasia 53, 94
Barron, Kenny 128
Basie, Count 23
Bass, Fontella 104, 109
Bassey, Offiong 119
Bassey, Shirley 25
Batiste, Alvin 66
Batiste, Jonathan 108
Batiste, Lionel 105
Battle, Kathleen 70
Baylor, Helen 36
Bebey, Francis 45
Bechet, Sidney 18
Beenie Man 32
Beken 111
Belafonte, Harry 4, 65
Belgrave, Marcus 77
Bell, Carey 114
Bell, LeRoy 98
Bell, Thom 112
Belle, Regina 1, 51
Benét, Eric 28, 77
Benjamin, Andre 45
Bennett, Estelle 77
Benson, Obie 96
Bentley, Lamont 53
Benton, Brook 121
Berry, Chuck 29
Betts, Keter 85
Beverly, Frankie 25
Bey, Yasiin 30, 96
Beyoncé 39, 70, 105

Bibb, Eric 49, 123
Big Daddy Kane 79
Big Freedia 128
Big L 120
Big Maybelle 117
Big Sean 96
Big Youth 107
Bilal 101
Billy Ward and the Dominoes 105
Birdman 110
Birdsong, Cindy 113
Birra, Ali 113
Bivins, Michael 72
Blacc, Aloe 119
Black Thought 63
Blackman, Toni 86
Blackwell, Otis 98
Blade, Brian 88
Blake, Eubie 29
Blake, John, Jr. 123
Blakey, Art 37
Blanchard, Terence 43
Blanco, Mykki 106
Bland, Bobby 36, 113
Bland, Edward 111
Blanton, Jimmy 108
Bleu, Corbin 65
Blige, Mary J. 20, 34, 60, 97
Blind Boys of Alabama, The 99
Blitz the Ambassador 115
Blondy, Alpha 30
Blow, Kurtis 31, 122
B.o.B. 91
Bolden, Buddy 39
Bombino 112
Bond, Beverly 53
Bonds, Margaret 39
Bonga, Kuenda 13
Bonner, Leroy 113
Bonney, Tabi 98
Bostic, Earl 121
Boulogne, Joseph, Chevalier de
  Saint-Georges 94
Bow Wow 35
Boykin, Phillip 102
Boyz II Men 82
Bradford, Alex 121
Bradley, Charles 126
Bradley, J. Robert 65
Bradshaw, Tiny 102
Brae, C. Michael 61
Brandy 14, 34, 72
Braxton, Anthony 128
Braxton, Toni 15, 61, 91
Brewster, W. Herbert 128
Bridges, Leon 126
Bridgetower, George 78
Bridgewater, Dee Dee 32, 92
Brim, John 117
Brooks, Hadda 40
Brooks, Roy 125
Broonzy, Big Bill 82
Brown, Angela M. 54
Brown, Anne 76
Brown, Bobby 58, 124
Brown, Carlinhos 81
Brown, Charles 23
Brown, Chris 74, 109
Brown, Chuck 78, 102
Brown, Clarence Gatemouth 59
Brown, Clifford 86
Brown, Dennis 99
Brown, Foxy 25

Brown, James 15, 60
Brown, Melanie 73
Brown, Nappy 73
Brown, Oscar, Jr. 53
Brown, Patrick "Sleepy" 50
Brown, Ruth 90
Brown, Uzee 42
Brownlee, Lawrence 88
Bryant, Paul 115
Bryant, Ray 95
Buckner, Milt 110
Budden, Joe 108
Buika 120
Bumbry, Grace 5
Bun B 123
Burbridge, Kofi 120
Burbridge, Oteil 120
Burke, Clarence, Jr. 112
Burke, Solomon 31, 86
Burleigh, Henry Thacker 56
Burley, Dan 96
Burning Spear 79
Burns, Eddie 44
Burnside, R. L. 56
Busby, Jheryl 3, 74
Butler, George, Jr. 70
Butler, Henry 121
Butler, Jerry 26
Butler, Jonathan 28
Byrd, Donald 109
Cables, George 125
Cadillacs 107
Caesar, Shirley 19
Cage, Byron 53
Callier, Terry 106
Calloway, Blanche 100
Calloway, Cab 1
Cameo 120
Campbell, Lucie E. 118
Campbell, Roy, Jr. 118
Campbell-Martin, Tisha 8, 42
Cam'ron 104
Cannon, Nick 47, 73
Carey, Mariah 32, 53, 69
Carolina Chocolate Drops 111
Carr, James 117
Carr, Kurt 56
Carr, Leroy 49
Carter, Benny 46
Carter, Betty 19
Carter, Nell 39
Carter, Regina 23
Carter, Ron 104
Carter, Troy 98
Carter, Warrick L. 27
Cartiér, Xam Wilson 41
Castor, Jimmy 100
Caymmi, Dorival 72
Chaka Chaka, Yvonne 112
Chambers, Paul 121
Chambers Brothers, The 116
Chamillionaire 82
Chancler, Ndugu 115
Chandler, Gene 105
Chanté, Keshia 50
Chantels, The 128
Chapman, Tracy 26
Charlemagne, Manno 11
Charles, Ray 16, 48
Cheatham, Doc 17
Checker, Chubby 28
Chenault, John 40
Cherry, Don 119

Chic 117
Chief Keef 112
Childers, Lulu Vere 95
Chi-Lites 106
Christian, Jodie 103
Christie, Angella 36
Chronixx 123
Chuck D 9
Ciara 56, 115
Clark, Mattie Moss 61
Clark, Sharón 105
Clark, Sonny 128
Clark-Cole, Dorinda 66
Clarke, Kenny 27
Clarke, Stanley 115
Clark-Sheard, Karen 22, 114
Clay, Otis 112
Clayton, Doctor 120
Clayton, Gerald 111
Clayton, Merry 112
Clemons, Clarence 41
Cleveland, James 19
Cliff, Jimmy 28, 92
Clinton, George 9, 93
Clovers, The 104
C-Murder 99
Coasters, The 102
Coates, Dorothy Love 125
Cobb, Arnett 114
Cobb, Jimmy 119
Cobbs, Tasha 114
Cobham, Billy 123
Cody, Radmilla 99
Cole, Cozy 123
Cole, Freddy 128
Cole, J. 97
Cole, Keyshia 63, 107
Cole, Marla 104
Cole, Nat "King" 17
Cole, Natalie 17, 60, 84
Coleman, Denardo 122
Coleman, George 106
Coleman, Ornette 39, 69
Coleman, Steve 124
Coleridge-Taylor, Samuel 75
Collette, Buddy 119
Collins, Albert 12
Collins, Bootsy 31
Collins, Lyn 53
Coltrane, Alice 70
Coltrane, John 19
Coltrane, Ravi 71
Combs, Sean 17, 43, 92
Commodores, The 118
Common 31, 63, 98
Conrad, Barbara Smith 90
Consolers, The 125
Contours, The 109
Cook, Charles "Doc" 44
Cook, Junior 126
Cook, Will Marion 40
Cooke, Sam 17
Coolio 103
Copeland, Johnny 110
Copeland, Shemekia 110
Coppola, Imani Francesca 82
Cosey, Pete 103
Cotton, James 123
Counce, Curtis 127
Count Basie 23
Covay, Don 127
Cowboy Troy 54
Cox, Deborah 28

Cox, Ida 42
Craig, Carl 31, 71
Crawford, Hank 77
Crawford, Randy 19
Cray, Robert 30
Creagh, Milton 27
Criss, Sonny 128
Crocker, Frankie 29
Crothers, Scatman 19
Crouch, Andraé 27, 115, 126
Crowder, Henry 16
Crudup, Arthur 115
Crusaders, The 116
Cruz, Taio 104
Curren$y 114
Curson, Ted 108
Da Don, Polow 86
Daemyon, Jerald 64
Dale, Clamma 103
Dameron, Tadd 103
D'Angelo 27, 123
Daniels, Billy 124
Danjah, Terror 91
Dara, Olu 35
Dash, Damon 31, 113
Dash, Darien 29
Davenport, Cow Cow 115
David, Craig 31, 53
Davis, Anthony 11
Davis, Carl 105
Davis, Gary 41
Davis, Guy 36
Davis, Miles 4
Davis, Sammy, Jr. 18
Davis, Tyrone 54
Davis, Wild Bill 114
Davis Sisters, The 119
Dawkins, Jimmy 111
Dawson, William Levi 39
Dawuni, Rocky 94
Dazz Band 116
D'banj 107
De La Soul 119
de Passe, Suzanne 25
DeBarge, El 89
Dedeaux, Richard 119
Deezer D 53
Dekker, Desmond 104
Dells, The 109
Dennard, Brazeal 37
DePreist, James 37, 109
Derülo, Jason 93
DeSanto, Sugar Pie 122
Detroit Emeralds, The 121
DeVaughn, Raheem 91
Diawara, Djeli Moussa 111
Diawara, Fatoumata 114
Dickenson, Vic 38
Diddley, Bo 39, 72
Dixie Cups, The 109
Dixon, Bill 87
Dixon, Dean 68
Dixon, Willie 4
DJ Clue? 111
DJ Jazzy Jeff 32
DJ Lance Rock 94
DJ Rashad 121
DJ Screw 110
DMX 28, 64
Dobbs, Mattiwilda 34
Dodd, Coxsone 99
Doggett, Bill 124
Domino, Fats 20

Donegan, Dorothy 19
Dorham, Kenny 113
Dorsey, Lee 65
Dorsey, Thomas 15
Downing, Will 19
Dr. Dre 10, 14, 30, 116
Drake 86
Drake, Hamid 121
Dramatics, The 106
Drew, Kenny 123
Drifters, The 121
Dube, Lucky 77
Duke, George 21, 113
Dumas, Henry 41
Duncan, Todd 76
Dunner, Leslie B. 45
Duplechan, Larry 55
Dupri, Jermaine 13, 46
Durham, Bobby 73
Dworkin, Aaron P. 52
Dyett, Walter 113
E-40 125
Earth, Wind & Fire 98
Earthquake 55
Eckstine, Billy 28
Edison, Harry 114
Edmonds, Tracey 16, 64
Edwards, David 122
Edwards, Esther Gordy 43
Edwards, Teddy 123
Eldridge, Roy 37
Ellington, Duke 5
Elliott, Missy 31, 90
Ellis, Alton 74
Ellis, Hortense 97
Elzy, Ruby 119
Emotions, The 125
En Vogue 100
Ervin, Booker 106
Escobar, Damien 56
Escobar, Tourie 56
Estelle 75
Estes, Simon 28
Estes, Sleepy John 33
Eubanks, Kevin 15, 108
Europe, James Reese 10
Evans, Faith 22
Eve 29
Évora, Cesária 12, 99
Fabolous 93
Falana, Lola 42
Falcons, The 128
Farmer, Art 38
Fat Boys 92
Feemster, Herbert 72
Fela 1, 42
Felix Da Housecat 110
Ferbos, Lionel 95
Ferrell, Rachelle 29
Ferrer, Ibrahim 41
Fiasco, Lupe 64
50 Cent 46, 83
Fiona, Melanie 84
Fishbone 101
Fisk Jubilee Singers 112
Fitzgerald, Ella 8, 18
Five Keys, The 104
FKA Twigs 123
Flack, Roberta 19
Flamingos, The 108
Flanagan, Tommy 69
Flavor Flav 67
Flo Rida 78

Floyd, Eddie 127
Flying Lotus 124
Ford, T-Model 91, 113
Ford, Vincent 75
Forté, John 74
Fortune, James 92
Foster, Frank 97
Foster, George "Pops" 40
Foster, William P. 88
Fox, Donal 114
Franklin, Aretha 11, 44, 115
Franklin, Kirk 15, 49, 97
Franti, Michael 93
Freelon, Nnenna 32
Freeman, Paul 39
Freeman, Von 104
Freeman, Yvette 27
Freestyle Fellowship 122
Fresh, Doug E. 93
Fuller, Blind Boy 86
Fuller, Curtis 115
Fulson, Lowell 118
Fuqua, Antoine 35
Fuqua, Harvey 90
Future 109
Gaines, Grady 38
Gamble, Kenny 85
Gap Band, The 100
Garland, Red 115
Garner, Erroll 76
Garrett, Sean 57
Gaye, Anna Gordy 121
Gaye, Marvin 2
Gaye, Nona 56
Gaynor, Gloria 36
George, Zelma Watson 42
Geto Boys 115
Ghostface Killah 90
Gibbs, Freddie 125
Gibson, Althea 8, 43
Gibson, Tyrese 27, 62
Gil, Gilberto 53
Gill, Johnny 51
Gillespie, Dizzy 1
Ginuwine 35
Glasper, Robert 101
Glover, Corey 34
Goapele 55
Golden Gate Quartet 104
Golson, Benny 37
Goodman, Al 87
Gordon, Dexter 25
Gordy, Berry, Jr. 1
Gotti, Irv 39
Grae, Jean 51
Graham, Katerina 99
Graham Central Station 123
Grandmaster Flash 33, 60
Grant, Micki 125
Graves, Denyce Antoinette 19, 57
Graves, Milford 126
Gray, Dobie 99
Gray, F. Gary 14, 49
Gray, Macy 29
Gray, Wardell 128
Greaves, R. B. 106
Greely, M. Gasby 27
Green, Al 13, 47, 74
Green, Cee Lo 70, 103
Green, Grant 56
Greene, Jimmy 74
Greenfield, Elizabeth Taylor 116
Greer, Sonny 127

Griffey, Dick 89
Griffin, Johnny 71
Griffin, LaShell 51
Griffiths, Marcia 29
Grimes, Henry 124
Grist, Reri 84
Gryce, Gigi 124
Güines, Tata 69
Guitar Slim 125
Guru 84
Guy, Buddy 31
Guyse, Sheila 122
Haddon, Dietrick 55
Hailey, JoJo 22
Hailey, K-Ci 22
Hairston, Jester 88
Hall, Aaron 57
Hall, Adelaide 126
Hall, Juanita 62
Hamilton, Anthony 61
Hamilton, Chico 117
Hammond, Fred 23
Hammond, Lenn 34
Hampton, Lionel 17, 41
Hancock, Herbie 20, 67
Handy, W. C. 8
Hardin Armstrong, Lil 39
Harold Melvin & the Blue Notes
   105
Harper, Ben 34, 62
Harrell, Andre 9, 30
Harris, Barry 68
Harris, Corey 39, 73
Harris, Damon 110
Harris, Kevin 120
Harris, Major 110
Harris, Wynonie 102
Hart, Alvin Youngblood 61
Hart, Billy 126
Hartman, Johnny 109
Hathaway, Donny 18
Hathaway, Lalah 57, 88
Havens, Richie 111
Hawes, Hampton 121
Hawkins, Coleman 9
Hawkins, Edwin 113
Hawkins, Erskine 14
Hawkins, Screamin' Jay 30
Hawkins, Tramaine 16
Hawkins, Walter 87
Hayes, Isaac 20, 58, 73
Hayes, Roland 4
Hayes, Teddy 40
Haynes, Roy 87
Heath, Percy 100
Heavy D 58, 98
Hegamin, Lucille 120
Hemphill, Jessie Mae 33, 59
Henderson, Fletcher 32
Henderson, Joe 127
Hendricks, Barbara 3, 67
Hendrix, Jimi 10
Hendryx, Nona 56
Henry, Clarence "Frogman" 46
Hibbert, Toots 103
Higginbotham, J. C. 37
Higginsen, Vy 65
Hill, Andrew 66
Hill, Darryl 128
Hill, Lauryn 20, 53, 111
Hilson, Keri 84
Hinderas, Natalie 5
Hines, Earl "Fatha" 39

Hinton, Milt 30
Hodge, Derrick 114
Holiday, Billie 1
Holland-Dozier-Holland 36
Holloway, Brenda 65
Holloway, Loleatta 115
Holmes, Clint 57
Holt, Nora 38
Homesick James 124
Hooker, John Lee 30
Hopkins, Lightnin' 83
Horn, Shirley 32, 56
Horne, Lena 5, 86
Horton, Big Walter 115
Horton, Gladys 92
Houghton, Israel 92
House, Son 8
Houston, Cissy 20, 83
Houston, Whitney 7, 28, 83, 100
Howell, Ayinde 91
Howlin' Wolf 9
Hubbard, Freddie 75
Hudson, Jennifer 63, 83
Huff, Leon 86
Humes, Helen 128
Humphrey, Bobbi 20
Hunter, Alberta 42
Hunter, Ivory Joe 106
Hurt, Mississippi John 84
Hutch, Willie 62
Hutcherson, Bobby 115
Hyman, Phyllis 19
Ice Cube 8, 30, 60
Ice-T 6, 31, 96
Imani Winds 113
India.Arie 34
Ingram, James 84
Ink Spots, The 102
Intruders, The 119
Isaacs, Gregory 89
Isley, Marvin 87
Isley, Ronald 25, 56
J Dilla 102
Ja Rule 35, 91
Jackson, Bobby 119
Jackson, Fred James 25
Jackson, George 19
Jackson, Hal 41, 104
Jackson, Isaiah 3
Jackson, Janet 6, 30, 68
Jackson, Jermaine 79
Jackson, John 36
Jackson, LaToya 95
Jackson, Mahalia 5
Jackson, Michael 19, 53, 76
Jackson, Millie 25
Jackson, Milt 26
Jackson, Randy 40
Jackson, Tito 81
Jackson 5 103
Jacquet, Illinois 49
Jagged Edge 117
Jaheim 58
Jamal, Ahmad 69
Jamelia 51
Jamerson, James 59
James, Elmore 114
James, Etta 13, 52, 100
James, Leela 117
James, Rick 17
James, Skip 38
James Bracken and Vivian Bracken
   107

Jarreau, Al 21, 65, 105
Jay Electronica 125
Jay-Z 27, 69, 103
Jean, Wyclef 20, 86
Jefferson, Blind Lemon 81
Jeffries, Herb 122
Jenkins, Ella 15
Jennings, Lyfe 56, 69
Jerkins, Rodney 31
Jeter, Claude 75
Jimmy Jam 13
Johnson, Al 119
Johnson, Buddy 36
Johnson, Conrad O. 97
Johnson, Hall 90
Johnson, J. J. 37
Johnson, J. Rosamond 121
Johnson, James Weldon 5
Johnson, Johnnie 56
Johnson, Ken 106
Johnson, Le'Andria 108
Johnson, Lonnie 85
Johnson, Robert 2
Johnson, Syl 97
Johnson, Syleena 98
Johnson, Tommy 106
Johnson-George, Tamara 79
Jones, Bobby 20, 94
Jones, Booker T. 84
Jones, Donell 29
Jones, Elvin 14, 68
Jones, Etta 35
Jones, Hank 57, 86
Jones, Jonah 39
Jones, Papa Jo 99
Jones, Philly Joe 121
Jones, Quincy 8, 30
Jones, Robert G. 81
Jones, Sharon 86
Jones, Thad 68
Joplin, Scott 6
Jordan, Louis 104
Jordan, Montell 23
Jordan, Ronny 26
Jorge, Seu 73
Joyner, Matilda Sissieretta 15
Juicy J 116
Juvenile 96
Kandi 83
Kay, Connie 114
Kay, Ulysses 37
KB 122
Keb'Mo' 36, 124
Kee, John P. 43, 116
Keita, Salif 83
Kelis 58, 122
Kelley, Elijah 65
Kelly, R. 18, 44, 71, 117
Kelly, Wynton 121
KEM 47, 127
Kendricks, Eddie 22
Kenoly, Ron 45
Kenyatta, Robin 54
Keys, Alicia 32, 68
Khalifa, Wiz 96
Khan, Chaka 12, 50
Kid Cudi 83
Kidjo, Angelique 50
Killer Mike 117
Killings, Debra 57
Kinch, Soweto 108
King, B. B. 7
King, Ben E. 128

King, Chris Thomas 120
King, Freddie 92
King Curtis 92
Kingston, Sean 94
Kirkland, Eddie 99
Kitt, Eartha 16, 75
Kiwanuka, Michael 126
Klugh, Earl 59
K'naan 76
Knight, Gladys 16, 66
Knight, Marie 80
Knight, Suge 11, 30, 102
Knowles, Mathew 96
Knowles, Tina 61
Knuckles, Frankie 42, 120
Kolosoy, Wendo 73
Kool Moe Dee 37
Kravitz, Lenny 10, 34
KRS-One 34
K-Swift 73
Kuti, Femi 47, 110
Kweli, Talib 93
La Roca, Pete 107
LaBelle, Patti 13, 30
Ladysmith Black Mambazo 103
Lakeside 120
Lamar, Kendrick 105
Lancaster, Byard 105
Lance, Major 111
Land, Harold 125
Larrieux, Amel 63
LaSalle, Denise 111
Lateef, Yusef 91, 117
Lattimore, Kenny 35, 128
LaVette, Bettye 85
Lawrence, Donald 99
Laws, Hubert 90
Le Loka, Tsidii 116
Le1f 120
Lea, Babatunde 124
Leadbelly 82
Lebo M 109
Lecrae 108
Ledisi 73
Lee, Consuela 84
Lefel, Edith 41
Legend, John 67, 116
Lenoir, J. B. 117
León, Tania 13
Levert, Eddie 70
Levert, Gerald 22, 59
Lewis, Ananda 28
Lewis, Butch 71, 99
Lewis, George 104
Lewis, Henry 38
Lewis, Leona 75
Lewis, Ramsey 35, 70
Lewis, Terry 13
Lighty, Chris 105
Lil B 121
Lil Jon 124
Lil' Kim 28
Lil Mama 117
Lil Wayne 66, 84
Liles, Kevin 42, 99
Lincoln, Abbey 3, 88
Lipscomb, Mance 49
Lister, Marquita 65
Liston, Melba 118
Little, Booker 105
Little Anthony & the Imperials 107
Little Eva 128
Little Milton 36, 54

Little Richard 15
Little Walter 36
LL Cool J 16, 49, 94
Lloyd 99
Locke, Eddie 44
Lockwood, Robert, Jr. 120
London, Theophilus 95
Long, Huey 79
Lopes, Lisa "Left Eye" 36
Lord Infamous 117
Lord Invader 117
Lord Jamar 126
Lord Kitchener 110
Loueke, Lionel 88
Love, Darlene 23, 92
Love, Ed 58
Love, Laura 50
Lover, Ed 10
Lucie, Lawrence 80
Lucien, Jon 66
Luckett, Letoya 61
Ludacris 37, 60
Lymon, Frankie 22
Lynn, Barbara 126
Lynne, Gloria 115
Maal, Baaba 66
Mabon, Willie 119
Mac Daddy 111
Mack Maine 125
Madlib 88
Magic Slim 110
Mahal, Taj 39
Mahlasela, Vusi 65
Maitreya, Sananda 85
Majors, Jeff 41
Makeba, Miriam 2, 50, 74
Malawi Mouse Boys 114
Mandisa 119
Mane, Gucci 91
Manhattans, The 123
Mann, Tamela 92
Marian Anderson String Quartet 111
Mario 71
Marley, Bob 5
Marley, Rita 32, 70
Marley, Stephen 100
Marley, Ziggy 41
Marrow, Queen Esther 24
Marsalis, Branford 34, 103
Marsalis, Delfeayo 41
Marsalis, Ellis 90
Marsalis, Wynton 16, 90
Martelly, Michel 90
Martin, Roberta 58
Martin, Sallie 120
Martin, Sara 38
Marvelettes, The 126
Mary Mary 34, 92
Mase 24
Masekela, Hugh 1, 106
Massenburg, Kedar 23, 110
Masta Ace 118
Master P 21, 115
Mathis, Johnny 20
Matshikiza, Pumeza 115
Matthews, Benjamin 93
Maxwell 20, 81
May, Brother Joe 123
May, Derrick 41
Maye, Lee 111
Mayfield, Curtis 2, 43
Maynor, Dorothy 19
MC Breed 75

M.C. Hammer 20, 80
MC Lyte 34, 108
McBee, Cecil 123
McClendon, Lisa 61
McClurkin, Donnie 25
McCoo, Marilyn 53
McCoy, Van 123
McCracklin, Jimmy 108
McDaniel, Hattie 5
McDuff, Jack 116
McFerrin, Bobby 68
McFerrin, Robert, Sr. 94
McGhee, Howard 122
McGill, Anthony 76
McGregor, Stephen 99
McGriff, Jimmy 72
McIntyre, Kalaparusha Maurice 117
McKinney, Nina Mae 40
McKnight, Brian 18, 34
McLean, Jackie 78
McPherson, David 32
McRae, Carmen 77
McShann, Jay 110
McTell, Blind Willie 89
Memphis Minnie 33
Memphis Slim 105
Merriweather, Big Maceo 109
Meters, The 118
Method Man 81
Midnight Star 110
Mighty Clouds of Joy 110
Migos 126
Miguel 98
Miles, Buddy 69
Miley, Bubber 120
Miller, Marcus 84
Millinder, Lucky 101
Mills, Stephanie 36
Mills Brothers, The 99
Minaj, Nicki 86, 124
Mingus, Charles 15
Minott, Sugar 86
Mississippi Sheiks 122
Mitchell, Blue 126
Mitchell, Dwike 111
Mitchell, Leona 42
Mitchell, Nicole 66
Mitchell, Willie 114
Moffett, Charnett 127
Monáe, Janelle 86
Monica 21
Monk, Thelonious 1
Montgomery, Little Brother 117
Montgomery, Robbie 101
Montgomery, Wes 88
Moody, James 83
Moondoc, Jemeel 119
Moonglows, The 108
Moore, Chante 26
Moore, Dorothy Rudd 46
Moore, Johnny B. 38
Moore, Kermit 116
Moore, LeRoi 72
Moore, Melba 21
Moore, Undine Smith 28
Moran, Jason 89
Morgan, Lee 102
Morton, Jelly Roll 29
Moses, Gilbert 12
Moss, J 64
Moten, Etta 18
Moura, Paulo 87
Mowatt, Judy 38

Mtukudzi, Oliver 109
Mullen, Nicole C. 45
Mumba, Samantha 29
Murphy, Eddie 4, 20, 61
Murphy, Matt 117
Murray, Tai 47
Muse, Clarence Edouard 21
Musiq 37, 84
Mvula, Laura 110
Mya 35
Myles, Raymond Anthony 121
Nas 33, 111
Nascimento, Milton 2, 64
Nash, Johnny 40
Nate Dogg 92
Naughton, Naturi 97
Naughty by Nature 124
Navarro, Fats 104
Ndegeocello, Meshell 15, 83
N'Dour, Youssou 1, 53, 79
Neal, Kenny 123
Neal, Raful 44, 121
Neale, Haydain 52
Nelly 32, 90
Nelson, Oliver 113
Neville, Aaron 21
New Birth 124
New Edition 101
Newborn, Phineas, Jr. 127
Newman, David 76
Ne-Yo 65
Nicholas, Fayard 20, 57
Nicholas, Harold 20
Nighthawk, Robert 121
Noah, Yannick 4, 60, 121
Norful, Smokie 127
Norman, Jessye 5
Notorious B.I.G. 20
Ocean, Frank 100
Odetta 37, 74
O'Jays, The 98
Okosuns, Sonny 71
Ol' Dirty Bastard 52
Olatunji, Babatunde 36, 126
Oliver, Joe "King" 42
Omarion 37
O'Neal, Shaquille 8, 30, 95
Ongala, Remmy 9, 91
Orioles, The 100
Ory, Kid 118
Osborne, Jeffrey 26, 121
Otis, Clyde 67
OutKast 35
Owens, Jack 38
Page, Walter 117
Palacio, Andy 96
Palmer, Keke 68, 120
Palmer, Rissi 65
Parham, Truck 124
Parker, Charlie 20
Parker, Junior 116
Parker, Maceo 72
Parker, Ray, Jr. 85
Parks, Gordon 1, 35, 58
Parlan, Horace 108
Patton, Antwan 45
Patton, Charley 107
Paul, Billy 127
Payne, Freda 58
Peebles, Ann 114
Pena, Paul 58
Pendergrass, Teddy 22, 83
Penguins, The 107

Peoples, Dottie 22
Perkins, Carl 128
Perkins, Pinetop 70
Perren, Freddie 60
Perry, Lee 19, 103
Perry, Ruth 19
Peterson, James 38
Peterson, Marvin "Hannibal" 27
Peterson, Oscar 52
Pettiford, Oscar 106
Pharcyde, The 127
Phillips, Esther 107
Phillips, Helen L. 63
Phipps, Wintley 59
Pinkney, Fayette 80
Pitts, Skip 103
Platters, The 99
Pleasure P 84
P.M. Dawn 54
Porter, David 127
Portuondo, Omara 53
Powell, Benny 87
Powell, Bud 24
Pratt, Awadagin 31
Premice, Josephine 41
Preston, Billy 39, 59
Price, Florence 37
Price, Kelly 23
Price, Leontyne 1
Price, Lloyd 119
Pride, Charley 26
Prince 18, 65
Pritchard, Robert Starling 21
Professor Longhair 109
Proof 101
Pryce, Trevor 89
Pryor, Rain 65
Pryor, Snooky 119
Prysock, Arthur 117
Public Enemy 98
Purdie, Bernard 77
Pusha T 123
Queen Latifah 1, 16, 58, 119
?uestlove 74
Rae Sremmurd 126
Ragin, Derek Lee 84
Rainey, Ma 33
Randall, Alice 38
Ranglin, Ernest 78
Rare Essence 121
Rascal, Dizzee 82
Ravens, The 103
Ray, Carline 113
Ray J 86
Razaf, Andy 19
Reagon, Bernice Johnson 7
Reagon, Toshi 76
Record, Eugene 60
Redman 81
Redman, Joshua 30
Reed, A. C. 36
Reed, Jimmy 38
Reed, Natina 106
Reedy, Jessica 101
Reese, Della 6, 20, 96
Reeves, Dianne 32, 119
Reeves, Martha 85
Reid, Antonio "L.A." 28
Reid, Vernon 34
Rhoden, Wayne 70
Rhone, Sylvia 2
Rhymefest 97
Rhymes, Busta 31

Rhyne, Melvin 109
Richard, Dawn 92
Richie, Lionel 27, 65, 114
Riggins, Karriem 102
Rihanna 65, 102
Riley, Boots 89
Riley, Teddy 116
Riperton, Minnie 32
Rivers, Sam 95
Roach, Max 21, 63
Roberts, Kimberly Rivers 72
Roberts, Marcus 19, 113
Robeson, Paul 2
Robey, Don 115
Robinson, Fenton 38
Robinson, Reginald R. 53
Robinson, Smokey 3, 49
Robinson, Sylvia 79
Rochereau, Tabu Ley 117
Rock, Pete 121
Rodríguez, Arsenio 87
Rogers, Bobby 110
Rogers, Jimmy 38
Rollins, Sonny 37, 94
Romanthony 115
Romeo 98
Roots, The 101
Rose Royce 120
Ross, Diana 8, 27
Ross, Isaiah "Doc" 40
Ross, Rick 79, 104
Rowland, Kelly 100
Roxanne Shante 33
Rucker, Darius 34, 74, 108
Rudder, David 79
Ruffin, Jimmy 125
Ruffins, Kermit 85
Run 31, 73
Run-DMC 31, 75
RuPaul 17, 91
Rush, Bobby 78
Rush, Otis 38
Rushen, Patrice 12
Rushing, Jimmy 37
Russell, Brenda 52
RZA 80, 128
Saadiq, Raphael 125
Sade 15, 92
Sam and Dave 102
Sample, Joe 51, 123
Sandé, Emeli 113
Sanders, Angelia 86
Sanders, Pharoah 64
Sangare, Oumou 18, 99
Sangho, Awa 127
Santamaria, Mongo 81
Santana, Juelz 120
Santigold 96
Sapp, Marvin 74
Scarlett, Millicent 49
ScHoolboyQ 117
Schuyler, Philippa 50
Scott, George 55
Scott, Hazel 66
Scott, Jill 29, 83
Scott, Jimmy 48, 122
Scott-Heron, Gil 94
Scott-Young, Mona 101
Seal 14, 75
Seals, Son 56
Secada, Jon 97
Sermon, Erick 81
Sessoms, Vivian 122

Shabazz Palaces 123
Shaggy 31
Shakur, Afeni 67
Shakur, Tupac 14
Shanice 112
Shaw, Marlena 105
Sheard, Kierra 61, 114
Shepp, Archie 101
Shider, Garry 87
Shines, Johnny 116
Shipp, Matthew 107
Shirelles, The 111
Shirley, Donald 111
Shirley, George 33
Shmurda, Bobby 123
Short, Bobby 52
Shorter, Wayne 75
Shorty, Ras, I 47
Shyne 101
Siji 56
Silver, Horace 26, 122
Simmons, Russell 1, 30
Simon, Joe 109
Simone, Nina 15, 41
Simpson, Valerie 21, 97
Simpson-Hoffman, N'kenge 52
Sims, Danny 106
Sir Mix-A-Lot 82
Sisqo 30
Sissle, Noble 29
Sister Souljah 11, 100
Slash 75
Sledge, Percy 39, 128
Slick Rick 93
Slim Harpo 120
Slim Thug 86
Sly & Robbie 34
Smith, Bessie 3
Smith, Buster 116
Smith, Cecilia 102
Smith, Cladys "Jabbo" 32
Smith, Clarence 113
Smith, Dr. Lonnie 49
Smith, Hale 118
Smith, Jimmy 127
Smith, Lonnie Liston 49
Smith, Mamie 32
Smith, Myrna 92
Smith, Stuff 37
Smith, Trixie 34
Smith, Will 8, 18, 53
Smith, Willie 107
Smith, Willow 92
Snoop Dogg 35, 84
Solange 97
Somi 85
Songz, Trey 88
Soul Stirrers 127
Southern, Eileen 56
Souza, Carmen 111
Sowande, Fela 39
Spaniels, The 105
Spann, Otis 107
Sparks, Jordin 66
Spector, Ronnie 77
Speech 82
Spence, Joseph 49
Spivey, Victoria 119
Stackhouse, Houston 122
Stampley, Micah 54
Stanford, Olivia Lee Dilworth 49
Staples, Cleotha 113
Staples, Mavis 50, 88

Staples, "Pops" 32
Starr, Edwin 122
Staton, Candi 27
Staton, Dakota 62
Steely 80
Steinberg, Martha Jean "The
    Queen" 28
Stew 69
Stewart, Billy 112
Stewart, Slam 126
Stewart, Tricky 98
Sticky Fingaz 86
Still, William Grant 37
Stone, Angie 31
Stone, Jesse 98
Stone, Sly 85
Stoute, Steve 38
Strayhorn, Billy 31
Street, Richard 110
Streeter, Sarah 45
Streeter, Sevyn 115
Stromae 121
Strong, Barrett 89
Studdard, Ruben 46
Sugarhill Gang, The 79, 125
Sullivan, Jazmine 81
Sullivan, Maxine 37
Sumlin, Hubert 101
Summer, Donna 25, 102
Sun Ra 60
Sundiata, Sekou 66
Sunnyland Slim 118
Supremes, The 33
Swan Silvertones, The 110
Swann, Bettye 109
Sweat, Keith 19
Sweatman, Wilbur 125
Sweatshirt, Earl 114
Sweet Honey in the Rock 106
Swizz Beatz 108
Sykes, Roosevelt 20
Tacuma, Jamaaladeen 124
Tail Dragger 112
Tait, Michael 57
Take 6 112
Tamar-kali 63
Tamia 24, 55
Tampa Red 63
Tapscott, Horace 126
Taste of Honey, A 115
Tate, Buddy 108
Tate, Grady 106
Tatum, Art 28
Tavares 115
Taylor, Billy 23, 92
Taylor, Cecil 70
Taylor, Eddie 116
Taylor, Hound Dog 120
Taylor, Koko 40, 80
T-Boz 108
Tchicai, John 102
Tempations, The 33
Terrell, Jean 116
Terrell, Tammi 32
Terry, Clark 39, 127
Terry, Sonny 88
Tex, Joe 116
Tharpe, Rosetta 65
The-Dream 74
Thigpen, Ed 110
Thomas, Carla 96
Thomas, Irma 29
Thomas, Rozonda 34, 78

Thomas, Rufus **20, 96**
Thomas, Tabby **119**
Thornton, Big Mama **33**
Threadgill, Henry **97**
Three Mo' Tenors **35**
Thurston, Stephen J. **49**
Tillis, Frederick **40**
Timbaland **32**
Tinie Tempah **115**
Tinsley, Boyd **50**
Tisdale, Wayman **50**
TLC **34**
Tonex **54**
Tony! Toni! Toné! **127**
Tosh, Peter **9**
Toussaint, Allen **60**
Towles, Nat **128**
T-Pain **73, 111**
Trammps, The **108**
Treacherous Three **128**
Tresvant, Ralph **57**
Tribbett, Tye **81**
Tricky **98**
Trina **114**
Trombone Shorty **97**
Tucker, Tommy **127**
Turnbull, Walter **13, 60**
Turner, Big Joe **92**
Turner, Ike **68**
Turner, Tina **6, 27**
2 Chainz **105**
Tyga **117**
Tyler, the Creator **100**
Tyner, McCoy **92**
Uggams, Leslie **23, 114**
Ulmer, James **79**
Usher **23, 56, 95**
Valdés, Bebo **75**
Valdés, Chucho **89**
Valentino, Bobby **62**
Vandross, Luther **13, 48, 59**
Vanity **67**
Vaughan, Sarah **13**
Vereen, Ben **4**
Verrett, Shirley **66, 91**
Vinnegar, Leroy **124**
Vinson, Eddie **112**
Waka Flocka Flame **110**
Waldron, Mal **109**
Wale **92**
Walker, Albertina **10, 58, 89**
Walker, Cedric **19**
Walker, George **37**
Walker, Hezekiah **34**
Walker, Joe Louis **118**
Walker, T-Bone **111**
Wallace, Sippie **1**
Waller, Fats **29**
Walton, Cedar **114**
Wanz **116**
Ward, Anita **118**
Ward, Willa **105**
Ware, David S. **106**
Warfield, William **94**
Warren, Butch **116**
Warwick, Dionne **18, 111**
Washington, Dinah **22**
Washington, Grover, Jr. **17, 44**
Washington, Kenny **107**
Waters, Benny **26**
Waters, Ethel **7**
Waters, Muddy **34**
Watley, Jody **54**

Watson, Johnny "Guitar" **18**
Watts, André **42, 101**
Watts, Reggie **52, 102**
Webb, Chick **105**
Webster, Katie **29**
Wein, Joyce **62**
Welch, Elisabeth **52**
Wellington, Valerie **118**
Wells, Junior **102**
Wells, Mary **28**
Wess, Frank **116**
West, Kanye **52, 93**
Whalum, Kirk **37, 64**
Whispers, The **124**
White, Barry **13, 41**
White, Bukka **120**
White, Josh **86**
White, Josh, Jr. **52**
White, Maurice **29**
White, Willard **53**
Whitfield, Norman **73**
Whitney, Marva **109**
Wiggins, Gerald **128**
Wilkins, Thomas Alphonso **71**
will.i.am **64**
Williams, Bert **18**
Williams, Camilla **116**
Williams, Clarence **33**
Williams, Claude **80**
Williams, Cootie **114**
Williams, Deniece **36**
Williams, Denise **40**
Williams, J. Mayo **83**
Williams, Jody **113**
Williams, Joe **5, 25**
Williams, Larry **118**
Williams, Mary Lou **15**
Williams, Michelle **73**
Williams, Nat D. **91**
Williams, Paul **112**
Williams, Pharrell **47, 82, 119**
Williams, Saul **31**
Williams, Tony **67**
Williams, Vanessa L. **4, 17**
Williamson, Sonny Boy **84**
Wilson, Abram **104**
Wilson, Brian Courtney **94**
Wilson, Cassandra **16**
Wilson, Charlie **31, 77**
Wilson, Frank **106**
Wilson, Gerald **49, 123**
Wilson, Jackie **60**
Wilson, Mary **28**
Wilson, Nancy **10, 98**
Wilson, Natalie **38**
Winans, Angie **36**
Winans, BeBe **14**
Winans, CeCe **14, 43**
Winans, David **77**
Winans, Debbie **36**
Winans, Marvin L. **17, 127**
Winans, Ronald **54**
Winans, Vickie **24**
Withers, Bill **61**
Withers-Mendes, Elisabeth **64**
Witherspoon, Jimmy **113**
Womack, Bobby **60, 92, 123**
Wonder, Stevie **11, 53, 121**
Woods, Belita **103**
Woods, Georgie **57**
Woods, Scott **55**
Woodson, Ali Ollie **89**
Woolard, Jamal **102**

Wright, Eugene **125**
Wright, O. V. **114**
Wright, Timothy **74**
Xzibit **78**
Yabby You **83**
Yancey, Jimmy **116**
Yarbrough, Camille **40**
Yayo, Tony **113**
Yende, Pretty **124**
YG **122**
Ying Yang Twins **112**
Yoba, Malik **11**
York, Vincent **40**
Young, Johnny **120**
Young, Lee **72**
Young, Lester **37**
Young Jeezy **63**
Z-Ro **109**

Religion

Abernathy, Ralph David **1**
Abune Paulos **105**
Adams, Yolanda **17, 67**
Agyeman, Jaramogi Abebe **10, 63**
Akinola, Peter Jasper **65**
Akpan, Uwem **70**
Al-Amin, Jamil Abdullah **6**
Anthony, Wendell **25**
Arinze, Francis **19**
Aristide, Jean-Bertrand **6, 45**
Armstrong, Vanessa Bell **24**
Austin, Junius C. **44**
Baker, Delbert W. **110**
Banks, William **11**
Barrow, Willie T. **85, 128**
Baylor, Helen **36**
Beauvoir, Max **74**
Bell, Ralph S. **5**
Ben-Israel, Ben Ami **11**
Berry, Moses **84**
Black, Barry C. **47**
Blake, Charles E. **82**
Blanks, Deborah K. **69**
Bloomer, George **86**
Blow, Kurtis **31, 122**
Borders, William Holmes **94**
Bowen, John W. E., Sr. **89**
Boyd, T. B., III **6**
Braxton, Brad **77**
Brazier, Arthur M. **115**
Brewster, W. Herbert **128**
Brookins, Hamel Hartford **102**
Bryant, Jamal **128**
Bryant, John R. **45**
Burgess, John **46**
Butts, Calvin O., III **9, 90**
Bynum, Juanita **31, 71**
Caesar, Shirley **19**
Cage, Byron **53**
Caldwell, Kirbyjon **55**
Callender, Eugene **119**
Cannon, Katie **10**
Cardozo, Francis L. **33**
Carr, Kurt **56**
Chavis, Benjamin **6**
Chineworth, Mary Alice **79**
Clarence 13X **126**
Cleaver, Emanuel **4, 45, 68, 107**
Clements, George **2**
Cleveland, James **19**
Colemon, Johnnie **11**
Collins, Janet **33, 64**
Coltrane, Alice **70**

Cone, James H. **3, 82**
Cook, Suzan D. Johnson **22**
Crouch, Andraé **27, 115, 126**
Crowdy, William Saunders **109**
Dandala, Mvume **77**
DeLille, Henriette **30**
Divine, Father **7**
Dollar, Creflo **106**
DuBois, Joshua **88**
Easton, Hosea **91**
Ellis, Charles H., III **79**
Elmore, Ronn **21**
Fabre, Shelton **71**
Farrakhan, Louis **2, 15**
Fauntroy, Walter E. **11**
Fisher, Miles Mark **91**
Flake, Floyd H. **18, 110**
Forbes, James A., Jr. **71**
Franklin, C. L. **68**
Franklin, Robert M. **13**
Fuller, Thomas O. **90**
Funnye, Capers C., Jr. **73**
Gaither, Israel L. **65**
Gantin, Bernardin **70**
Gilmore, Marshall **46**
Gomes, Peter J. **15, 93**
Grace, Sweet Daddy **104**
Gray, Darius **69**
Gray, William H., III **3**
Green, Al **13, 47, 74**
Gregory, Wilton **37**
Grier, Roosevelt **13**
Haddon, Dietrick **55**
Harding, Vincent **67**
Harris, Barbara **12**
Hawkins, Tramaine **16**
Hawkins, Walter **87**
Hayes, James C. **10**
Healy, James Augustine **30**
Holsey, Lucius Henry **92**
Hood, James Walker **91**
Hooks, Benjamin L. **2, 85**
Howard, M. William, Jr. **26**
Jackson, Jesse **1, 27, 72**
Jakes, T. D. **17, 43, 116**
Jasper, John J. **91**
Jean-Juste, Gérard **78**
Jemison, Major L. **48**
Jemison, T. J. **119**
Johns, Vernon **38**
Jones, Absalom **52**
Jones, Alex **64**
Jones, Dwight C. **122**
Jones, E. Edward, Sr. **45**
Jones, Robert Elijah **90**
Jones, William A., Jr. **61**
Kalbani, Adil **77**
Karim, Benjamin **61**
Kelly, Leontine **33**
King, Barbara **22**
King, Bernice **4, 81**
King, Martin Luther, Jr. **1**
King, Martin Luther, Sr. **89**
Kobia, Samuel **43**
Lawson, James M., Jr. **90**
Lee, Eric P. **79**
Lee, Jarena **100**
Lewis-Thornton, Rae **32**
Lincoln, C. Eric **38**
Little Richard **15**
Loguen, J. W. **91**
Long, Eddie L. **29, 89**
Lowery, Joseph **2**

Lowry, A. Leon 60
Luter, Fred, Jr. 103
Lyons, Henry 12, 118
Majors, Jeff 41
Marino, Eugene Antonio 30
Mason, Charles Harrison 107
Maxis, Theresa 62
Mays, Benjamin E. 7
McClellan, George Marion 91
McClurkin, Donnie 25
McGuire, George Alexander 80
McKenzie, Vashti M. 29
Meeks, James T. 92
Michaux, Solomon Lightfoot 91
Miller, Clyde 113
Morgan, Gertrude 63
Moss, J 64
Moss, Otis, Jr. 72
Moss, Otis, III 72
Muhammad, Ava 31
Muhammad, Elijah 4
Muhammad, Jabir Herbert 72
Muhammad, Khallid Abdul 10, 31
Muhammed, W. Deen 27
Munroe, Myles 125
Murray, Cecil 12, 47
Muzorewa, Abel 85
Noble Drew Ali 100
Norful, Smokie 127
Okaalet, Peter 58
Otunga, Maurice Michael 55
Patterson, Gilbert Earl 41
Patterson, J. O., Jr. 80
Peterson, Jesse Lee 81
Phipps, Wintley 59
Pierre, Andre 17
Powell, Adam Clayton, Jr. 3
Price, Frederick K. C. 21
Redding, Ann Holmes 77
Reems, Ernestine Cleveland 27
Reese, Della 6, 20, 96
Reverend Ike 79
Riley, Helen Caldwell Day 13
Rivers, Eugene F., III 81
Robinson, Ida B. 106
Rogers, Alan G. 72
Roundtree, Dovey 80
Sapp, Marvin 74
Scott, George 55
Senghor, Augustin Diamancoune 66
Sentamu, John 58
Seymour, William J. 106
Shabazz, Betty 7, 26
Sharpe, Samuel 103
Sharpton, Al 21, 97
Shaw, William J. 30
Shelton, Trent 122
Shuttlesworth, Fred 47, 98
Slocumb, Jonathan 52
Smith, Amanda Berry 109
Spencer, Peter 128
Stallings, George A., Jr. 6
Stampley, Micah 54
Stanley, A. Knighton 117
Stanton, Alysa 78
Steinberg, Martha Jean "The Queen" 28
Stith, Charles R. 73
Sullivan, Leon H. 3, 30
Taylor, Gardner C. 76
Taylor, Lonzie Odie 96
Thurman, Howard 3

Tillard, Conrad 47
Tolton, Augustine 62
Tonex 54
Tribbett, Tye 81
Turner, Henry McNeal 5
Tutu, Desmond 6, 44
Ukpabio, Helen 86
Vanity 67
Vanzant, Iyanla 17, 47, 108
Waddles, Charleszetta "Mother" 10, 49
Walker, Hezekiah 34
Walker, John T. 50
Walker, Lucius, Jr. 88
Walker, Wyatt Tee 80
Washington, James Melvin 50
Waters, Ethel 7
Watkins, Joe 86
Weeks, Thomas, III 70
Weems, Renita J. 44
White, Reggie 6, 50
White-Hammond, Gloria 61
Williams, Frederick (B.) 63
Williams, Preston Warren, II 64
Wilson, Frank 106
Wilson, Natalie 38
Winans, BeBe 14
Winans, CeCe 14, 43
Winans, Marvin L. 17, 127
Winans, Ronald 54
Woods, Abraham, Jr. 74
Wright, Jeremiah A., Jr. 45, 69, 103
Wright, Nathan, Jr. 56
Wright, Timothy 74
Wyatt, Addie L. 56
X, Malcolm 1
Yates, Jack 114
Yearwood, Lennox, Jr. 112
York, Dwight D. 71
Youngblood, Johnny Ray 8

Science and technology
Adams-Campbell, Lucille L. 60
Adkins, Rod 41
Adkins, Rutherford H. 21
Alcorn, George Edward, Jr. 59
Alexander, Archie Alphonso 14
Alexander, Joseph L. 95
Allen, Ethel D. 13
Allen, Will 74
Anderson, Charles Edward 37
Anderson, Michael P. 40
Anderson, Norman B. 45
Anderson, William G(ilchrist) 57
Atim, Julian 66
Augusta, Alexander T. 111
Auguste, Donna 29
Auguste, Rose-Anne 13
Austin, Wanda M. 94
Bacon-Bercey, June 38
Banda, Hastings Kamuzu 6, 54
Banneker, Benjamin 93
Barnett, Herman 112
Bashir, Halima 73
Bath, Patricia E. 37
Bell, Carl C. 111
Benjamin, Regina 20, 75
Benson, Angela 34
Bishop, Stephen 95
Black, Keith Lanier 18, 84
Blackwell, David 79
Bluford, Guy 2, 35
Bluitt, Juliann S. 14

Bolden, Charles Frank, Jr. 7, 78
Boykin, Otis 92
Brady, St. Elmo 107
Branson, Herman 87
Brimm, Charles E. 105
Brown, Vivian 27
Brown, Willa 40
Bullard, Eugene 12
Bullard, Robert D. 121
Callender, Clive O. 3
Campbell, Donald J. 66
Canady, Alexa 28
Cargill, Victoria A. 43
Carroll, L. Natalie 44
Carruthers, George R. 40
Carson, Ben 1, 35, 76, 128
Carter, Joye Maureen 41
Carter, Majora 77
Carver, George Washington 4
CasSelle, Malcolm 11
Chatard, Peter 44
Chinn, May Edward 26
Christian, Spencer 15
Clack, Zoanne 73
Clark, Mamie Phipps 79
Clark, Yvonne Young 95
Cobb, W. Montague 39
Cobbs, Price M. 9
Cole, Rebecca 38
Coleman, Bessie 9
Coleman, Ken 57
Comer, James P. 6
Coney, PonJola 48
Cooper, Edward S. 6
Cooper, Lisa 73
Cornwell, Edward E., III 70
Counter, S. Allen 74
Crosthwait, David 93
Crouch, Hubert 95
Crumpler, Rebecca Lee 89
Dabiri, John 93
Dailey, Ulysses Grant 87
Daly, Marie Maynard 37
Davis, Allison 12
Dean, Mark 35
Deas, Gerald 85
Deconge-Watson, Lovenia 55
Delany, Bessie 12
Delany, Martin R. 27
Dennis, Gary C. 91
Dickens, Helen Octavia 14, 64
Douglas, Donya 97
Drake, Michael V. 122
Drew, Alvin, Jr. 67
Drew, Charles Richard 7
Dunham, Katherine 4, 59
Dunston, Georgia Mae 48
Durham, James 90
Eberhardt, Jennifer 124
Edwards, Lena Frances 76
Edwards, Willarda V. 59
Elders, Joycelyn 6
Ellington, E. David 11
Ellis, Clarence A. 38
Emeagwali, Dale 31
Emeagwali, Philip 30
Ericsson-Jackson, Aprille 28
Fennoy, Ilene 72
Fenton, Kevin 87
Ferguson, Vernice D. 108
Fields, Evelyn J. 27
Fisher, Ada M. 76
Fisher, Rudolph 17

Flipper, Henry O. 3
Flowers, Sylester 50
Foster, Henry W., Jr. 26
Fraser, Sarah Loguen 100
Freeman, Harold P. 23
French, D. M. 94
Fulani, Lenora 11
Fuller, A. Oveta 43
Fuller, Arthur 27
Fuller, Solomon Carter, Jr. 15
Gardere, Jeffrey 76
Gaston, Marilyn Hughes 60
Gates, Sylvester James, Jr. 15
Gayle, Helene D. 3, 46
Gibbons, Gary 107
Gibson, Kenneth Allen 6
Gibson, William F. 6
Giles, Roscoe C. 93
Gilliard, Steve 69
Goodlett, Carlton B. 91
Gourdine, Meredith 33
Grant, Augustus O. 71
Granville, Evelyn Boyd 36
Gray, Ida 41
Greene, Frank S., Jr. 101
Gregory, Frederick 8, 51
Grier, Eliza Ann 90
Griffin, Anthony 71
Griffin, Bessie Blout 43
Griffith, Patrick A. 64
Hall, Lloyd A. 8
Hamburg, Margaret 78
Hamilton, Vicki 95
Hammond, Paula 119
Hammonds, Evelynn 69
Hannah, Marc 10
Hansberry, Tony, II 93
Harris, Bernard A. 90
Harris, Gary L. 87
Harris, Mary Styles 31
Harris, Wesley L. 92
Hayanga, Jeremiah 118
Haynie, Sharon 94
Haywood, Jimmy 58
Henderson, Cornelius Langston 26
Henderson, Henry Fairfax, Jr. 89
Henson, Matthew 2
Higginbotham, Joan 124
Hill, Wyllstyne D. 94
Hillary, Barbara 65
Hinton, William Augustus 8
Holmes, Hamilton E. 82
Hopkins, Donald R. 89
Hughes, Dora 88
Howard, Ayanna 65
Hutcherson, Hilda Yvonne 54
Imes, Elmer Samuel 39
Irving, Barrington, Jr. 112
Irving, Larry, Jr. 12
Jackson, Deborah 94
Jackson, Lisa 77
Jackson, Shirley Ann 12
Jarvis, Erich 67
Jawara, Dawda Kairaba 11
Jefferson, Mildred Fay 89
Jemison, Mae C. 1, 35
Jenifer, Franklyn G. 2
Johnson, Anthony M. 92
Johnson, Lonnie G. 32, 93
Johnson, Sandra K. 94
Johnson-Powell, Gloria 107
Jones, Edith Mae Irby 65
Jones, Frederick McKinley 68

Jones, Monty 66
Jones, Randy 35
Jones, Wayne 53
Joseph, Kathie-Ann 56
Julian, Hubert 90
Julian, Percy Lavon 6
Juma, Calestous 57
Just, Ernest Everett 3
Keith, Rachel Boone 63
Kenney, John A., Jr. 48
King, Reatha Clark 65
Kintaudi, Leon 62
Kittles, Rick 51
Knowling, Robert E., Jr. 38
Kong, B. Waine 50
Kountz, Samuel L. 10
Kyenge, Cécile 113
Lacks, Henrietta 101
Laroche, Joseph Philippe Lemercier 85
Laryea, Thomas Davies, III 67
Latimer, Lewis H. 4
Lavizzo-Mourey, Risa 48
Lawless, Theodore K. 8
Lawrence, Margaret Morgan 100
Lawrence, Robert H., Jr. 16
Lee, Raphael C. 87
Lee, Robert 112
Leevy, Carrol M. 42
Leffall, Lasalle 3, 64
Lewis, Daurene 72
Lewis, Delano 7
Lewis-Hall, Freda 105
Logan, Onnie Lee 14
Lushington, Augustus Nathaniel 56
Lyttle, Hulda Margaret 14
Madison, Romell 45
Malveaux, Floyd 54
Manley, Audrey Forbes 16
Massey, Walter E. 5, 45
Massie, Samuel P., Jr. 29
Maupin, John E., Jr. 92
Maxey, Randall 46
Mays, William G. 34
Mbabazi, Esther 122
Mboup, Souleymane 10
McBay, Henry C. 91
McCain, Franklin 119
McCoy, Elijah 8
McDonald, Charles J. 120
McJunkin, George 93
McNair, Ronald 3, 58
Mensah, Thomas 48
Mickens, Ronald Elbert 105
Miller, Warren F., Jr. 53
Millines Dziko, Trish 28
Mills, Joseph C. 51
Morgan, Garrett 1
Mossell, Nathan Francis 91
Murray, Pauli 38
Nabrit, Samuel Milton 47
Naki, Hamilton 63
Neto, António Agostinho 43
Nour, Nawal M. 56
Nteff, Alain 127
Ojikutu, Bisola 65
Olopade, Olufunmilayo Falusi 58
Osborne, Na'taki 54
Osman, Said 127
Pace, Betty 59
Pape, Jean William 126
Perry, Warren 56
Person, Waverly 9, 51

Peters, Lenrie 43
Petioni, Muriel 99
Pickett, Cecil 39
Pierre, Percy Anthony 46
Pinn, Vivian Winona 49
Pitt, David Thomas 10
Pitts, Derrick 77
Poindexter, Hildrus A. 87
Poussaint, Alvin F. 5, 67
Price, Richard 51
Prothrow-Stith, Deborah 10
Quarterman, Lloyd Albert 4
Rabb, Maurice F., Jr. 58
Randolph, Linda A. 52
Rapelang Rabana 112
Reece, E. Albert 63
Reese, Milous J., Jr. 51
Riley, Helen Caldwell Day 13
Rillieux, Norbert 92
Robinson-Berry, Joan 94
Roker, Al 12, 49
Ross-Lee, Barbara 67
Samara, Noah 15
Satcher, David 7, 57, 111
Schiavocampo, Mara 97
Seacole, Mary 54
Shabazz, Betty 7, 26
Shavers, Cheryl 31
Shirley, Aaron 126
Sigur, Wanda 44
Sinkford, Jeanne C. 13
Slaughter, John Brooks 53
Smith, Ian 62
Smith, Richard 51
Spencer, Michael G. 87
Staples, Brent 8
Staupers, Mabel K. 7
Stewart, Ella 39
Stith, James H. 116
Sullivan, Louis 8
Sumner, Francis Cecil 112
Sweet, Ossian 68
Taylor, Susan C. 62
Terrell, Dorothy A. 24
Thomas, Vivien 9
Thornton, Yvonne S. 69
Tuckson, Reed V. 71
Tyson, Neil deGrasse 15, 65
Uys, Ashley 125
Walker, Arthur, II 87
Walker, Joseph Edison 111
Walker, Tristan 98
Wambugu, Florence 42
Washington, Patrice Clarke 12
Watkins, Levi, Jr. 9
Wein, Joyce 62
Welsing, Frances Cress 5
West, James E. 87
Westbrooks, Bobby 51
White, Augustus, III 100
White-Hammond, Gloria 61
Wilkens, J. Ernest, Jr. 43
Williams, Daniel Hale 2
Williams, David Rudyard 50
Williams, O. S. 13
Wilson, Donald E. 88
Wilson, Stephanie 72
Wisdom, Kimberlydawn 57
Witt, Edwin T. 26
Woods, Granville T. 5
Wright, Louis Tompkins 4

Young, Roger Arliner 29

Social issues

Abbott, Diane 9
Abbott, Robert Sengstacke 27
Abernathy, Ralph David 1
Abiola-Costello, Hafsat 108
Abu-Jamal, Mumia 15
Adams, Sheila J. 25
Agyeman, Jaramogi Abebe 10, 63
Ake, Claude 30
Al-Amin, Jamil Abdullah 6
Alexander, Clifford 26
Alexander, Sadie Tanner Mossell 22
Allen, Lucy 85
Allen, Will 74
Ali, Muhammad 2, 16, 52
Allen, Ethel D. 13
Amaker, Norman 63
Andrews, Benny 22, 59
Annan, Kofi Atta 15, 48
Anthony, Wendell 25
Appiah, Kwame Anthony 67, 101
Arac de Nyeko, Monica 66
Aristide, Jean-Bertrand 6, 45
Arnwine, Barbara 28
Asante, Molefi Kete 3
Ashe, Arthur 1, 18
Atyam, Angelina 55
Auguste, Rose-Anne 13
Austin, Bobby W. 95
Autrey, Wesley 68
Avery, Byllye Y. 66
Ayim, May 126
Azikiwe, Nnamdi 13
Ba, Mariama 30
Baisden, Michael 25, 66
Baker, Ella 5
Baker, Gwendolyn Calvert 9
Baker, Houston A., Jr. 6
Baker, Josephine 3
Baker, Thurbert 22
Baldwin, James 1
Ballard, John 95
Banks, Paula A. 68
Barbee, Lloyd Augustus 71
Barlow, Roosevelt 49
Barnett, Etta Moten 56
Barrow, Willie T. 85, 128
Bass, Charlotta Spears 40
Bates, Daisy 13
Bell, Derrick 6, 98
Bell, Ralph S. 5
Berry, Bertice 8, 55
Berry, Edwin C. 81
Berry, Mary Frances 7
Berrysmith, Don Reginald 49
Bethune, Mary McLeod 4
Betsch, MaVynee 28
Betts, R. Dwayne 86
Bevel, James L. 75
Bibb, Henry and Mary 54
Biko, Steven 4
bin Wahad, Dhoruba 85
Birch, Glynn R. 61
Black, Albert 51
Blackwell, Gloria 127
Blackwell, Unita 17
Blakely, Delois N. 122
Blakely, Edward J. 88
Bobo, Lawrence 60
Bolin, Jane 22, 59

Bond, Julian 2, 35, 106
Bonga, Kuenda 13
Booker, Cory Anthony 68
Bosley, Freeman, Jr. 7
Boyd, Gwendolyn 49
Boyd, John W., Jr. 20, 72
Boyd, T. B., III 6
Boykin, Keith 14
Bozella, Dewey 97
Bradley, David Henry, Jr. 39
Braun, Carol Moseley 4, 42
Brazier, Arthur M. 115
Bridges, Ruby 77
Broadbent, Hydeia 36
Brock, Roslyn McCallister 86
Brown, Byrd 49
Brown, Charlotte Hawkins 106
Brown, Cora 33
Brown, Eddie C. 35
Brown, Elaine 8
Brown, Homer S. 47
Brown, Jesse 6, 41
Brown, Jim 11, 95
Brown, Les 5
Brown, Lloyd Louis 10 42
Brown, Oliver Leon 94
Brown, Oscar, Jr. 53
Brown, Tony 3
Brown, Willa 40
Brown, Zora Kramer 12
Brutus, Dennis 38
Bryant, Jamal 128
Bryant, Wayne R. 6
Buery, Richard, Jr. 97
Bullard, Robert D. 121
Bullock, Steve 22
Bunch, Lonnie G., III 91
Bunche, Ralph J. 5
Burkett, Ben 123
Burks, Mary Fair 40
Burns, Anthony 102
Burroughs, Margaret Taylor 9
Burroughs, Nannie Helen 96
Butler, Paul D. 17
Butler, Selena Sloan 98
Butts, Calvin O., III 9, 90
Callender, Eugene 119
Cameron, James 80
Campbell, Bebe Moore 6, 24, 59
Canada, Geoffrey 23
Carby, Hazel 27
Carlos, John 97
Carmichael, Stokely 5, 26
Carr, Johnnie 69
Carr, Keela 74
Carter, Majora 77
Carter, Mandy 11
Carter, Rubin 26, 121
Carter, Stephen L. 4
Cary, Lorene 3
Cary, Mary Ann Shadd 30
Catto, Octavius V. 83
Cayton, Horace 26
Chavis, Benjamin 6
Chestnut, J. L., Jr. 73
Chideya, Farai 14, 61
Childress, Alice 15
Chisholm, Daquan 93
Chissano, Joaquim 7, 55, 67
Christophe, Henri 9
Clark, Joe 1
Clark, Kenneth B. 5, 52
Clark, Septima 7

Clay, William Lacy 8
Clayton, Mayme Agnew 62
Claytor, Helen 14, 52
Cleaver, Eldridge 5
Cleaver, Kathleen Neal 29
Clements, George 2
Cobbs, Price M. 9
Cole, Johnnetta B. 5, 43
Cole, Lorraine 48
Coles, Alice 80
Collins, Patricia Hill 67
Colston, Hal 72
Comer, James P. 6
Compton-Rock, Malaak 86
Connerly, Ward 14
Cook, Toni 23
Cooke, Marvel 31
Cook-Parrish, Mary Virginia 95
Cooper, Anna Julia 20
Cooper, Edward S. 6
Cooper, Margaret J. 46
Correia, De'Jaun 93
Cosby, Camille 14, 80
Cox, Donald Lee 93
Creagh, Milton 27
Crew, Spencer R. 55
Cruse, Harold 54
Cuffe, Paul 98
da Silva, Benedita 5
Davis, Angela 5, 114
Davis, Artur 41
Davis, Danny K. 24
Dawson, Matel, Jr. 39
Dawson, Michael C. 63
DeBaptiste, George 32
DeLaine, Joseph A. 110
Delany, Martin R. 27
Dellums, Ronald 2, 81
Dent, Thomas C. 50
Diallo, Amadou 27
Dickerson, Ernest 6
Diop, Cheikh Anta 4
Dirie, Waris 56
Divine, Father 7
Dixon, Margaret 14
Dobbs, John Wesley 89
Dodson, Howard, Jr. 7, 52
Dortch, Thomas W., Jr. 45
Douglas, Derek 88
Douglass, Frederick 87
Drew, Charles Richard 7
Du Bois, W. E. B. 3
DuBois, Shirley Graham 21
Due, Patricia Stephens 100
Duggins, George 64
Dukes, Hazel Nell 56
Dumas, Henry 41
Dumpson, James R. 108
Dunham, Katherine 4, 59
Dyson, Michael Eric 11, 40, 128
Eagleson, William Lewis 90
Early, Gerald 15
Easton, Hosea 91
Eberhardt, Jennifer 124
Edelman, Marian Wright 5, 42
Edley, Christopher 2, 48
Edwards, Harry 2
Edwards, Lena Frances 76
Elder, Larry 25, 120
Ellis-Lamkins, Phaedra 88
Ellison, Ralph 7
Esposito, Giancarlo 9
Espy, Mike 6

Eugene-Richard, Margie 63
Europe, James Reese 10
Evers, Medgar 3
Evers, Myrlie 8
Farmer, James 2, 64
Farrakhan, Louis 15
Farris, Isaac Newton, Jr. 63
Fauntroy, Walter E. 11
Fauset, Jessie 7
Fela 1, 42
Fields, C. Virginia 25
Finley, Ron 110
Finner-Williams, Paris Michele 62
Fletcher, Benjamin 90
Fletcher, Bill, Jr. 41
Forbes, James A., Jr. 71
Forman, James 7, 51
Fortune, T. Thomas 6
Foster, Marie 48
Franklin, Hardy R. 9
Franklin, John Hope 5, 77
Franklin, Robert M. 13
Frazier, E. Franklin 10
French, D. M. 94
Fulani, Lenora 11
Fuller, Arthur 27
Fuller, Charles 8
Gaines, Ernest J. 7
Gamble, Kenny 85
Gardner, Chris 65
Garner, Tyron 99
Garnet, Henry Highland 100
Garvey, Marcus 1
Gates, Henry Louis, Jr. 3, 38, 67
Gayle, Helene D. 3
Gbowee, Leymah 76
George, Nelson 12, 101
George, Zelma Watson 42
Gibson, Kenneth Allen 6
Gibson, William F. 6
Gilbert, Christopher 50
Gist, Carole 1
Golston, Allan C. 55
Gomez, Jewelle 30
Gomez-Preston, Cheryl 9
Gomillion, Charles 90
Goss, Carol A. 55
Gossett, Louis, Jr. 7
Graham, Lawrence Otis 12
Granger, Lester B. 75
Gray, Fred 37
Greene, Petey 65
Gregory, Dick 1, 54
Gregory, Wilton 37
Grier, Roosevelt 13
Griffith, Mark Winston 8
Grimké, Archibald H. 9
Guy, Rosa 5
Guyot, Lawrence 108
Hale, Lorraine 8
Haley, Alex 4
Hall, Elliott S. 24
Hall, Stuart 78
Hamblin, Ken 10
Hamer, Fannie Lou 6
Hampton, Fred 18
Hampton, Henry 6
Hani, Chris 6
Hansberry, William Leo 11
Harden, Monique 97
Harding, Vincent 67
Harper, Frances Ellen Watkins 11
Harrington, Oliver W. 9

Harris, Alice 7
Harris, Leslie 6
Harris, Marcelite Jordan 16
Harris, Patricia Roberts 2
Hawkins, Augustus F. 68
Hawkins, Steven 14
Hayden, Lewis 105
Hayes, Dennis 54
Haynes, Elizabeth Ross 102
Haynes, George Edmund 8
Hedgeman, Anna Arnold 22
Height, Dorothy I. 2, 23, 78
Henderson, Thelton E. 68
Henderson, Wade J. 14
Henderson, Zelma 71
Henry, Aaron Edd 19
Henry, Lenny 9, 52
Henson, Josiah 90
Hernandez, Aileen Clarke 13
Herndon, Angelo 90
Hernton, Calvin C. 51
Hill, Anita 5, 65
Hill, Jesse, Jr. 13
Hill, Oliver W. 24, 63
Hilliard, Asa Grant, III 66
Hilliard, David 7, 105
Holland, Endesha Ida Mae 3, 57
Holt Baker, Arlene 73
Hood, James Walker 91
Hooks, Benjamin L. 2, 85
Hope, Lugenia Burns 89
Houston, Charles Hamilton 4
Howard, M. William, Jr. 26
Hoyte, Lenon 50
Hubbard, Arnette Rhinehart 38
Huggins, Nathan Irvin 52
Hughes, Albert 7
Hughes, Allen 7
Hughes, Langston 4
Hunt, Darnell 92
Hunter-Gault, Charlayne 6, 31
Hutchinson, Earl Ofari 24
Hutson, Jean Blackwell 16
Ingram, Rex 5
Innis, Roy 5
Irvis, K. Leroy 67
Jackson, Edison O. 67
Jackson, Fred James 25
Jackson, George 14
Jackson, Jesse 1, 27, 72
Jackson, Jimmie Lee 126
Jackson, Judith D. 57
Jackson, Phillip 115
Jacob, John E. 2
Jagan, Cheddi 16
James, Daniel, Jr. 16
Jansen, Jonathan 102
Jealous, Benjamin Todd 70, 113
Jean, Wyclef 20, 86
Jeffries, Leonard 8
Jemison, T. J. 119
Jenkins, Ray 77
Johnson, Charles S. 12
Johnson, James Weldon 5
Johnson, Kevin 70
Jolley, Willie 28
Jones, Clarence B. 114
Jones, Cullen 73
Jones, Elaine R. 7, 45
Jones, Eugene Kinckle 79
Jones, John 89
Jones, Van 70
Jones, William A., Jr. 61

Jordan, June 7, 35
Jordan, Vernon E. 3, 35
Joseph, Kathie-Ann 56
Josey, E. J. 10
Joyner, Marjorie Stewart 26
Joyner, Tom 19, 90
Julian, Percy Lavon 6
Karim, Benjamin 61
Kato, David 103
Kaunda, Kenneth 2
Keita, Salif 83
Kelley, Cliff 75
Kennedy, Florynce 12, 33
Khanga, Yelena 6
Kidd, Mae Street 39
Kimbro, Warren 76
King, Bernice 4, 81
King, Coretta Scott 3, 57
King, Dexter 10
King, Martin Luther, III 20
King, Martin Luther, Jr. 1
King, Martin Luther, Sr. 89
King, Preston 28
King, Robert Hillary 84
King, Rodney 103
King, Yolanda 6
Kirk, Clara 95
Kitwana, Bakari 86
Koontz, Elizabeth Duncan 101
Kuzwayo, Ellen 68
Ladner, Joyce A. 42
LaGuma, Alex 30
Lampkin, Daisy 19
Lane, Charles 3
Lane, Vincent 5
Langston, John Mercer 101
Laraque, Paul 67
Law, W. W. 121
Lawson, James M., Jr. 90
Lee, Canada 8
Lee, Eric P. 79
LeGrand, Naquasia 126
Leland, Mickey 2
Lemon, Alton T. 112
Lewis, Ananda 28
Lewis, Delano 7
Lewis, Thomas 19
Lewis-Thornton, Rae 32
Little, Robert L. 2
Logan, Rayford W. 40
Loguen, J. W. 91
Louis, Errol T. 8
Louis, Willie 113
Loving, Mildred 69
Lowe, Rick 124
Lowery, Evelyn Gibson 115
Lowery, Joseph 2
Lowry, A. Leon 60
Lucas, John 7
Lucy, William 50
Lucy Foster, Autherine 35
Luper, Clara 94
Maathai, Wangari 43, 97
Mabuza-Suttle, Felicia 43
Madison, Joseph E. 17
Makeba, Miriam 2, 50, 74
Malone Jones, Vivian 59
Malveaux, Julianne 32, 70
Mandela, Nelson 1, 14, 77, 117
Mandela, Winnie 2, 35, 112
Manley, Audrey Forbes 16
Maponya, Maishe 101
Marable, Manning 10, 102

Marshall, Paule **7, 77**
Marshall, Thurgood **1, 44**
Martin, Louis E. **16**
Martin, Trayvon **105**
Masekela, Barbara **18**
Mason, Biddy **89**
Mason, Ronald **27**
Matthews, Ameena **105**
Maynard, Robert C. **7**
Mays, Benjamin E. **7**
Mbeki, Thabo **14, 73**
McCabe, Jewell Jackson **10**
McCain, Franklin **119**
McCarty, Osceola **16**
McDougall, Gay J. **11, 43**
McKay, Claude **6**
McKenzie, Vashti M. **29**
McKinney Hammond, Michelle **51**
McKissick, Floyd B. **3**
McMurray, Georgia L. **36**
McQueen, Butterfly **6, 54**
McWhorter, John **35, 119**
McWorter, Free Frank **91**
Meredith, James H. **11**
Mfume, Kweisi **6, 41**
Mhlaba, Raymond **55**
Micheaux, Oscar **7**
Millender-McDonald, Juanita **21, 61**
Miller, Clyde **113**
Miller-Travis, Vernice **64**
Millines Dziko, Trish **28**
Minkins, Shadrach **104**
Mitchell, Clarence M., Jr. **88**
Mitchell, Juanita Jackson **128**
Mkapa, Benjamin W. **16, 77**
Mongella, Gertrude **11**
Moody, Anne **127**
Moore, Gwendolynne S. **55**
Moore, Harry T. **29**
Morgan, Irene **65**
Morial, Ernest "Dutch" **26**
Moses, Robert Parris **11**
Moss, Otis, Jr. **72**
Mossell, Gertrude Bustill **40**
Motley, Constance Baker **10, 55**
Moton, Robert Russa **83**
Moutoussamy-Ashe, Jeanne **7**
Mowry, Jess **7**
Mugisha, Frank **119**
Muhammad, Elijah **4**
Muhammad, Khallid Abdul **10, 31**
Mukoko, Jestina **75**
Murphy, Laura M. **43**
Murray, Pauli **38**
Nash, Diane **72**
Ndadaye, Melchior **7**
Nell, William C. **128**
Nelson, Jill **6, 54**
Newton, Huey **2**
Niane, Katoucha **70**
Nixon, Edgar Daniel **100**
Nkoli, Simon **60**
Nkrumah, Kwame **3**
Noble, Gil **76**
Norman, Pat **10**
Nour, Nawal M. **56**
Nzo, Alfred **15**
Obasanjo, Olusegun **5**
Oglesby, Zena **12**
Ojikutu, Bisola **65**
O'Neal, Frederick **99**
Orange, James **74**
Ormes, Jackie **73**

Osborne, Na'taki **54**
Osotimehin, Babatunde **107**
Page, Alan **7**
Page, Clarence **4**
Parker, Kellis E. **30**
Parker, Pat **19**
Parks, Rosa **1, 35, 56**
Parr, Russ **51**
Patterson, Frederick Douglass **12**
Patterson, Louise **25**
Patterson, P. J. **6, 20**
Perkins, Edward **5**
Perry, James **83**
Perry, Matthew J., Jr. **96**
Peterson, Jesse Lee **81**
Pitt, David Thomas **10**
Pleasant, Mary Ellen **9**
Plessy, Homer Adolph **31**
Pough, Terrell **58**
Poussaint, Alvin F. **5, 67**
Powell, Adam Clayton, Jr. **3**
Powell, Kevin **31, 74**
Pratt, Geronimo **18, 95**
Pressley, Condace L. **41**
Price, Hugh B. **9, 54**
Pritchard, Robert Starling **21**
Prothrow-Stith, Deborah **10**
Pyfrom, Estella **127**
Quander, Nellie **102**
Quarles, Benjamin Arthur **18**
Quigless, Helen G. **49**
Ramphele, Mamphela **29**
Ramsey, Charles H. **21, 69**
Rand, A. Barry **6**
Randolph, A. Philip **3**
Randolph, Linda A. **52**
Rawlings, Nana Konadu Agyeman **13**
Reed, Ishmael **8**
Reid, Ira De A. **100**
Rice, Louise Allen **54**
Rice, Norm **8**
Richards, Hilda **49**
Richardson, Julieanna **81**
Richardson, Rupert **67**
Riley, Boots **89**
Riley, Helen Caldwell Day **13**
Rivers, Eugene F., III **81**
Roberts, Lillian **83**
Robeson, Eslanda Goode **13**
Robeson, Paul **2**
Robinson, Jackie **6**
Robinson, Rachel **16**
Robinson, Randall **7, 46**
Robinson, Sharon **22**
Robinson, Spottswood W., III **22**
Roble, Abdi **71**
Rock, John S. **113**
Rodriguez, Cheryl **64**
Rolle, Myron **98**
Rowan, Carl T. **1, 30**
Rowe-Adams, Jackie **109**
Rowell, Victoria **13, 68**
Ruffin, Josephine St. Pierre **75**
Ruggles, David **126**
Rusesabagina, Paul **60**
Russwurm, John Brown **100**
Rustin, Bayard **4**
Sampson, Edith S. **4**
Sanders, Malika **48**
Sané, Pierre Gabriel **21**
Sapphire **14, 95**
Saro-Wiwa, Kenule **39**

Sasser, Sean **113**
Savimbi, Jonas **2, 34**
Sayles Belton, Sharon **9, 16**
Scantlebury-White, Velma **64**
Seacole, Mary **54**
Seale, Bobby **3**
Sears, Stephanie **53**
Seele, Pernessa **46**
Senghor, Léopold Sédar **12**
Shabazz, Attallah **6**
Shabazz, Betty **7, 26**
Shadd, Abraham D. **81**
Shakur, Afeni **67**
Shakur, Assata **6**
Shakur, Yusef **85**
Sharpe, Samuel **103**
Sharpton, Al **21, 97**
Sherrod, Shirley **87**
Shinhoster, Earl **32**
Shuttlesworth, Fred **47, 98**
Sifford, Charlie **4, 49**
Simkins, Modjeska Monteith **112**
Simms, Margaret **94**
Simon, Lateefah **95**
Sisulu, Albertina **57, 95**
Sisulu, Sheila Violet Makate **24**
Sleet, Moneta, Jr. **5**
Smith, Anna Deavere **6**
Smith, Barbara **28**
Smith, Damu **54**
Smith, Greg **28**
Smith, Kemba **70**
Smith, Marie F. **70**
Smith, Nate **49**
Smith, Tommie **102**
Snowden, Frank M., Jr. **67**
Sohn, Sonja **100**
Spriggs, William **67**
Stallings, George A., Jr. **6**
Staupers, Mabel K. **7**
Steele, Claude **13, 97**
Steele, Shelby **13, 82**
Stevenson, Bryan **128**
Stewart, Alison **13**
Stewart, Ella **39**
Stewart, Maria W. Miller **19**
Sullivan, Leon H. **3, 30**
Sweatt, Heman Marion **114**
Sweet, Ossian **68**
Talbert, Mary B. **77**
Tate, Eleanora E. **20, 55**
Tatum, Wilbert **76**
Taulbert, Clifton Lemoure **19**
Taylor, Bo **72**
Taylor, Mildred D. **26**
Taylor, Recy **92**
Taylor, Robert Rochon **104**
Terrell, Mary Church **9**
Thomas, Arthur Ray **52**
Thomas, Franklin A. **5, 49**
Thomas, Jefferson **88**
Thompson, Cynthia Bramlett **50**
Thurman, Howard **3**
Thurman, Wallace **16**
Till, Emmett **7**
Tobias, Channing H. **79**
Toomer, Jean **6**
Tosh, Peter **9**
Touré, Askia (Muhammad Abu Bakr el) **47**
Touré, Faya Ora Rose **56**
Tribble, Israel, Jr. **8**
Trotter, Donne E. **28**

Trotter, Monroe **9**
Tsvangirai, Morgan **26, 72**
Tubman, Harriet **9**
Tucker, C. Delores **12, 56**
Tucker, Cynthia **15, 61**
Tucker, Rosina **14**
Tutu, Desmond **6, 44**
Tyree, Omar Rashad **21**
Vaughn, Viola **70**
Vega, Marta Moreno **61**
Velez-Rodriguez, Argelia **56**
Vesey, Denmark **100**
Villard-Appolon, Malya **106**
Vincent, Marjorie Judith **2**
Waddles, Charleszetta "Mother" **10, 49**
Walcott, Derek **5, 94**
Walker, A'lelia **14**
Walker, Alice **1, 43**
Walker, Bernita Ruth **53**
Walker, Lucius, Jr. **88**
Wall, Orindatus S. B. **92**
Wallace, Joaquin **49**
Wallace, Michele Faith **13**
Wallace, Phyllis A. **9**
Wallace, William **75**
Washington, Booker T. **4**
Washington, Ebonya **79**
Washington, Fredi **10**
Washington, Harold **6**
Washington, Karen **117**
Washington, Pauletta Pearson **86**
Watkins, Ted **104**
Wattleton, Faye **9**
Webb-Christburg, Sheyann **110**
Wells, Henrietta Bell **69**
Wells, James Lesesne **10**
Wells-Barnett, Ida B. **8**
Welsing, Frances Cress **5**
West, Cornel **5, 33, 80**
White, Michael R. **5**
White, Reggie **6, 50**
White, Walter F. **4**
White, Willye **67**
White-Hammond, Gloria **61**
Whitmore, George **106**
Wilkins, Roy **4**
Williams, Armstrong **29**
Williams, Evelyn **10**
Williams, Fannie Barrier **27**
Williams, George Washington **18**
Williams, Hosea **15, 31, 123**
Williams, Maggie **7, 71**
Williams, Montel **4, 57**
Williams, Patricia **11, 54**
Williams, Robert F. **11**
Williams, Stanley "Tookie" **29, 57**
Williams, Walter E. **4**
Williams, Willie L. **4**
Wilson, August **7, 33, 55**
Wilson, Margaret Bush **79**
Wilson, Phill **9, 104**
Wilson, Sunnie **7, 55**
Wilson, William Julius **22**
Withers, Ernest C. **68, 88**
Wiwa, Ken **67**
Woodson, Robert L. **10**
Worrill, Conrad **12**
Wright, Beverly **97**
Wright, Charles H. **35**
Wright, Louis Tompkins **4**
Wright, Nathan, Jr. **56**
Wright, Richard **5**

Wyatt, Addie L. 56
X, Malcolm 1
Xuma, Madie Hall 59
Yancy, Dorothy Cowser 42
Yarbrough, Camille 40
Yearwood, Lennox, Jr. 112
Yeboah, Emmanuel Ofosu 53
Yergan, Max 123
Yoba, Malik 11
Young, Jean Childs 14
Young, Whitney M., Jr. 4
Youngblood, Johnny Ray 8
Yumkella, Kandeh 105
Zulu, Princess Kasune 54

Sports
Aaron, Hank 5
Abdirahman, Abdi 126
Abdul-Jabbar, Kareem 8
Abdur-Rahim, Shareef 28
Adams, Paul 50
Adu, Freddy 67
Aldridge, LaMarcus 125
Alexander, Shaun 58
Ali, Laila 27, 63
Ali, Muhammad 2, 16, 52
Allen, Dick 85
Allen, Larry 109
Allen, Marcus 20
Allen, Ray 82
Altidore, Jozy 109
Alves, Dani 121
Amaker, Tommy 62
Amos, John 8, 62
Anderson, Elmer 25
Anderson, Ezzrett 95
Anderson, Jamal 22
Anderson, Mike 63
Anderson, Viv 58
Anelka, Nicolas 118
Anthony, Carmelo 46, 94
Antunes, Lúcio 109
Archibald, Tiny 90
Arenas, Gilbert 84
Armstrong, Henry 104
Artest, Ron 52
Ashe, Arthur 1, 18
Ashford, Emmett 22
Ashford, Evelyn 63
Ashley, Maurice 15, 47
Asomugha, Nnamdi 100
Atkinson, Alia 126
Baines, Harold 32
Baker, Dusty 8, 43, 72, 110
Balotelli, Mario 104
Banks, Ernie 33, 126
Barber, Ronde 41
Barber, Tiki 57, 107
Barkley, Charles 5, 66
Barksdale, Don 103
Barnes, Ernie 16, 78
Barnes, John 53
Barnes, Steven 54
Barney, Lem 26
Barnhill, David 30
Batch, Charlie 120
Baugé, Grégory 86
Baylor, Don 6
Baylor, Elgin 93
Beamon, Bob 30
Beasley, Jamar 29
Beaty, Zelmo 115
Bekele, Kenenisa 75

Bell, James "Cool Papa" 36
Bellamy, Walt 119
Belle, Albert 10
Benítez, Christian 113
Berry, Eric 125
Bettis, Jerome 64
Bickerstaff, Bernie 21
Bing, Dave 3, 59, 78
Bigirimana, Gael 115
Bivins, Michael 72
Black, Joe 75
Blair, Paul 36
Blake, James 43
Blanks, Billy 22
Blanton, Dain 29
Blue, Vida 122
Bogues, Tyrone "Muggsy" 56
Bol, Manute 1
Bolt, Usain 73, 104
Bolton-Holifield, Ruthie 28
Bonaly, Surya 7
Bonds, Barry 6, 34, 63, 99
Bonds, Bobby 43
Bonheur, Yannick 84
Boozer, Bob 103
Bosh, Chris 85
Bostic, Joe 95
Bowe, Riddick 6, 107
Bowles, Todd 128
Bozella, Dewey 97
Bramlett, Joseph 91
Brand, Elton 31
Brandon, Terrell 16
Branham, George, III 50
Brashear, Donald 39
Brathwaite, Fred 35
Brigitha, Enith 126
Briscoe, Marlin 37
Brock, Lou 18
Broner, Adrien 109
Brooks, Aaron 33
Brooks, Derrick 43, 119
Brown, Antron 85
Brown, James 22
Brown, Jason 125
Brown, Jerry 117
Brown, Jim 11, 95
Brown, Mike 77, 107
Brown, Raymond 102
Brown, Sean 52
Brown, Willard 36
Bruce, Isaac 26
Bryant, Cullen 81
Bryant, Dez 116
Bryant, Kobe 15, 31, 71, 110
Buchanan, Ray 32
Burke, Glenn 122
Bush, Reggie 59, 88
Butler, Leroy, III 17
Bynoe, Peter C. B. 40
Byrd, Marlon 112
Cabell, Enos 102
Cain, Lorenzo 128
Caldwell, Jim 81
Campanella, Roy 25
Campbell, Earl 104
Campbell, Milt 113
Campbell-Brown, Veronica 102
Cano, Robinson 97
Carew, Rod 20
Carlos, John 97
Carnegie, Herbert 25
Carter, Anson 24

Carter, Butch 27
Carter, Cris 21, 109
Carter, Joe 30
Carter, Kenneth 53
Carter, Rubin 26, 121
Carter, Vince 26
Cash, Swin 59
Catchings, Tamika 43
Cepeda, Orlando 98
Chalmers, Mario 122
Chamberlain, Wilt 18, 47
Chandler, Tyson 114
Chaney, Don 98
Chaney, John 67
Charles, Ezzard 95
Charles, John 108
Charleston, Oscar 39
Cheeks, Maurice 47, 106
Cherry, Deron 40
Cheruiyot, Robert 69
Chitalu, Godfrey 108
Christie, Linford 8
Claiborne, Loretta 34
Clay, Bryan 57, 74
Clemons, Michael "Pinball" 64
Clendenon, Donn 26, 56
Clifton, Nathaniel "Sweetwater" 47
Coachman, Alice 18, 123
Cole, Ashley 106
Coleman, Leonard S., Jr. 12
Coleman, Vince 128
Collins, Jason 111
Cooper, Andy "Lefty" 63
Cooper, Charles "Chuck" 47
Cooper, Michael 31
Cooper, Tarzan 96
Cooper-Dyke, Cynthia 17, 89
Copeland, Michael 47
Corbin, Tyrone 126
Corley, Tony 62
Cottrell, Comer 11
Cousins, DeMarcus 108
Cox, Bryan 83
Crawford, Carl 90
Crennel, Romeo 54, 107
Crisp, Coco 109
Cromartie, Antonio 115
Crooks, Garth 53
Croom, Sylvester 50
Cruz, Victor 107
Culp, Curley 110
Culpepper, Daunte 32, 85
Cunningham, Randall 23
Curry, Dell 126
Curry, Michael 85
Curry, Stephen 110
Dandridge, Ray 36
Daniels, Mel 106
Dantley, Adrian 72
Davids, Edgar 106
Davis, Anthony 120
Davis, Ben 115
Davis, Eric 116
Davis, Ernie 48
Davis, Mike 41
Davis, Milt 74
Davis, Piper 19
Davis, Shani 58, 84
Davis, Terrell 20
Davis, Wade, Jr. 103
Dawes, Dominique 11, 126
Dawson, Andre 85
Day, Leon 39

Dean, Fred 98
DeFrantz, Anita 37
DeGale, James 74
Delaney, Joe 76
Dent, Richard 97
DeRozan, DeMar 125
Devers, Gail 7, 87
Diaw, Boris 122
Dibaba, Tirunesh 73, 109
Dickerson, Eric 27, 108
Dihigo, Martín 103
Dixon, George 52
Doby, Lawrence Eugene, Sr. 16, 41
Doig, Jason 45
Dokes, Michael 105
Dorrell, Karl 52
dos Santos, Manuel Francisco 65
Douglas, Bob 96
Douglas, Buster 127
Drew, Charles Richard 7
Drexler, Clyde 4, 61
Driver, Donald 99
Drogba, Didier 78
Duerson, Dave 93
Dumars, Joe 16, 65, 126
Duncan, Tim 20, 91
Dungy, Tony 17, 42, 59, 118
Dunn, Jerry 27
Dunn, Warrick 90
Durant, Kevin 76, 107
Dye, Jermaine 58
Edwards, Harry 2
Edwards, Herman 51
Edwards, Teresa 14, 95
Elder, Lee 6
Ellerbe, Brian 22
Elliott, Sean 26
Ellis, Dock 78
Ellis, Jimmy 44, 127
Ervin, Anthony 66
Erving, Julius 18, 47
Eto'o, Samuel 73
Eusebio 118
Everett, Carl 103
Evra, Patrice 102
Ewing, Patrick 17, 73
Fairbanks, Mabel 117
Farah, Mo 104
Farr, Mel 24
Faulk, Marshall 35, 96
Felix, Allyson 48, 98
Ferdinand, Rio 82
Fielder, Cecil 2, 112
Fielder, Prince 68
Fisher, Derek 97
Flood, Curt 10, 93
Flowers, Vonetta 35
Ford, Cheryl 45
Foreman, George 1, 15
Forrest, Vernon 40, 79
Foster, Andrew 79
Foster, Arian 114
Fowler, Reggie 51
Fox, Rick 27
Fraser-Pryce, Shelly-Ann 113
Frazier, Joe 19, 98
Frazier, Walt 91
Frazier-Lyde, Jacqui 31
Freeman, Cathy 29
Freeman, Marianna 23
Fuentes, Tito 123
Fuhr, Grant 1, 49
Fuller, Vivian 33

Futch, Eddie **33**
Gaines, Clarence E., Sr. **55**
Gaither, Alonzo Smith (Jake) **14**
Gamble, Oscar **113**
Gans, Joe **91**
Garnett, Kevin **14, 70, 118**
Garrison, Zina **2**
Gaston, Cito **71**
Gates, William **97**
Gatlin, Justin **123**
Gay, Tyson **114**
Gebrselassie, Haile **70**
Gentry, Alvin **23**
George, Eddie **80**
George, Paul **124**
Gervin, George **80**
Gibson, Althea **8, 43**
Gibson, Bob **33**
Gibson, Josh **22**
Gibson, Truman K., Jr. **60**
Gill, Turner **83**
Gilliam, Frank **23**
Gilliam, Jim **122**
Gilliam, Joe **31**
Gilmore, Artis **101**
Glanville, Douglas Metunwa **82**
Gooden, Dwight **20**
Gorden, W. C. **71**
Gordon, Josh **120**
Gore, Frank **117**
Goss, Tom **23**
Gourdine, Meredith **33**
Gourdine, Simon **11**
Graham, Trevor **84**
Granderson, Curtis **66**
Grand-Pierre, Jean-Luc **46**
Grant, Frank **100**
Gray, Yeshimbra "Shimmy" **55**
Green, A. C. **32**
Green, Darrell **39, 74**
Green, Dennis **5, 45**
Green, Draymond **126**
Greene, Joe **10**
Greene, Maurice **27, 77**
Greenwood, L. C. **115**
Greer, Hal **92**
Gregg, Eric **16**
Gregory, Ann **63**
Grier, Bobby **95**
Grier, Mike **43**
Grier, Roosevelt **1**
Griffey, Ken, Jr. **12, 73**
Griffin, Blake **98**
Griffin, Robert, III **107**
Griffith, Emile **113**
Griffith, Yolanda **25**
Griffith-Joyner, Florence **28**
Griner, Brittney **128**
Gumbel, Greg **8**
Gwynn, Tony **18, 83, 122**
Gyan, Asamoah **87**
Hagler, Marvelous Marvin **102**
Hairston, Sam **88**
Hamilton, Leonard **100**
Hamilton, Lewis **66**
Haney, Lee **77**
Hardaway, Anfernee **13, 111**
Hardaway, Tim **35**
Harden, James **116**
Hardy, Greg **118**
Harris, Franco **97**
Harris, James **79**
Harris, Sylvia **70**

Harrison, Alvin **28**
Harrison, Calvin **28**
Harris-Stewart, Lusia **90**
Hart, Thomas A., Sr. **113**
Harvin, Percy **123**
Haskins, Clem **23**
Hawkins, Connie **91**
Haye, David **82**
Hayes, Bob **77**
Hayes, Elvin **93**
Haywood, Spencer **99**
Hazzard, Walt **98**
Heard, Gar **25**
Hearns, Thomas **29**
Henderson, Rickey **28, 78**
Henry, Mark **116**
Henry, Thierry **66, 127**
Hernández, Orlando **96**
Hickman, Fred **11**
Hill, Calvin **19**
Hill, Grant **13, 94**
Hill, Michael **95**
Hillary, Barbara **65**
Hilliard, Wendy **53**
Hines, Garrett **35**
Holdsclaw, Chamique **24, 110**
Holiday, Jrue **115**
Holland, Kimberly N. **62**
Holmes, Kelly **47**
Holmes, Larry **20, 68**
Holmes, Santonio **87**
Holyfield, Evander **6**
Hopkins, Bernard **35, 69, 105**
Horford, Al **107**
Horton, Andre **33**
Horton, Suki **33**
Horton, Willie **104**
Howard, Desmond **16, 58**
Howard, Dwight **113**
Howard, Elston **125**
Howard, Juwan **15**
Howard, Ryan **65, 113**
Howard, Sherri **36**
Hudson, Lou **121**
Humphrey, Claude **119**
Hunter, Billy **22, 109**
Hunter, Lindsey **110**
Hunter, Torii **43, 109**
Hurd, Sam **116**
Hyde, Cowan F. "Bubba" **47**
Ibrahim, Fuad **109**
Iginla, Jarome **35**
Ince, Paul **83**
Irvin, Michael **64**
Irvin, Monte **31**
Irving, Kyrie **102**
Isaacs, John **76**
Iverson, Allen **24, 46**
Ivey, Phil **72, 106**
Jackson, DeSean **120**
Jackson, Jamea **64**
Jackson, Mannie **14**
Jackson, Mark **121**
Jackson, Rampage **83**
Jackson, Reggie **15**
Jackson, Rickey **88**
Jackson, Stephen **118**
Jackson, Tom **70**
Jacobs, Regina **38**
James, David **84**
James, G. Larry **74**
James, LeBron **46, 78, 105**
James, Vanessa **84**

Jenkins, Fergie **46**
Jenkins, Kris **98**
Jeptoo, Rita **121**
Jeter, Derek **27, 93, 124**
Jim, Songezo **111**
Johnson, Andre **127**
Johnson, Avery **62**
Johnson, Ben **1**
Johnson, Calvin **108**
Johnson, Chad **108**
Johnson, Chris **92**
Johnson, Clifford "Connie" **52**
Johnson, Dennis **89**
Johnson, Gus **92**
Johnson, Jack **8**
Johnson, Joe **94**
Johnson, John Henry **96**
Johnson, Judy **105**
Johnson, Kevin **70**
Johnson, Keyshawn **91**
Johnson, Larry **28**
Johnson, Levi **48**
Johnson, Magic **3, 39, 101**
Johnson, Mamie "Peanut" **40**
Johnson, Michael **13**
Johnson, Rafer **33**
Johnson, Rodney Van **28**
Joiner, Charlie **102**
Jones, Adam **103**
Jones, Adam **114**
Jones, Andruw **98**
Jones, Cobi N'Gai **18**
Jones, Cullen **73**
Jones, Deacon **92, 112**
Jones, Ed "Too Tall" **46**
Jones, Jacoby **117**
Jones, Jon **121**
Jones, K. C. **83**
Jones, Lou **64**
Jones, Marion **21, 66**
Jones, Merlakia **34**
Jones, Randy **35**
Jones, Robbie **113**
Jones, Roy, Jr. **22**
Jones, Sam **85**
Jones, Walter **119**
Jones Drew, Maurice **113**
Jordan, Eddie **83**
Jordan, Michael **6, 21**
Joyce, Dru **81**
Joyner-Kersee, Jackie **5**
Justice, David **18**
Kaiser, Cecil **42**
Kaka, Luthando **118**
Kane, Evander **97**
Kanouté, Fred **68**
Kearney, Beverly **109**
Keflezighi, Meb **49, 121**
Keith, Floyd A. **61**
Kellogg, Clark **64**
Kelly, Jim **113**
Kennedy, Cortez **104**
Kennedy-Overton, Jayne Harris **46**
Kerry, Leon G. **46**
Khumalo, S'manga **119**
Kidd, Jason **86**
Kimbro, Henry A. **25**
Kimetto, Dennis **125**
King, Don **14, 128**
Kipchoge, Eliud **124**
Kipsang, Wilson **115**
Krigger, Kevin **111**
Lacy, Sam **30, 46**

Ladd, Ernie **64**
Lane, Dick **92**
Lanier, Bob **47**
Lanier, Willie **33**
Lankford, Ray **23**
Laraque, Georges **48**
Larkin, Barry **24**
Lashley, Bobby **63**
Lassiter, Roy **24**
Lee, Canada **8**
LeGrand, Eric **118**
Lennox, Betty **31**
Leonard, Buck **67**
Leonard, Kawhi **122**
Leonard, Sugar Ray **15**
Leônidas **96**
Leslie, Lisa **16, 73**
Lester, Bill **42, 85**
Lewis, Butch **71, 99**
Lewis, Carl **4, 97**
Lewis, Denise **33**
Lewis, Jamal **115**
Lewis, Lennox **27**
Lewis, Marvin **51, 87**
Lewis, Oliver **56**
Lewis, Ray **33, 109**
Lillard, Damian **117**
Lister, Tommy **127**
Liston, Sonny **33**
Little, Floyd **86**
Little, Larry **90**
Littlepage, Craig **35**
Lloyd, Earl **26, 127**
Lloyd, John Henry "Pop" **30**
Lofton, James **42**
Lofton, Kenny **12**
Lopes, Davey **92**
Loroupe, Tegla **59**
Lott, Ronnie **9**
Louis, Joe **5**
Love, Nat **9**
Love, Reggie **77**
Lowe, Sidney **64**
Lucas, Bill **97**
Lucas, John **7**
Lyle, Ron **125**
Lynch, Marshawn **124**
Mackey, Biz **82**
Madison, Paula **37, 99**
Mahorn, Rick **60**
Malone, Karl **18, 51, 90**
Malone, Moses **79**
Manigault, Earl "The Goat" **15**
Manley, Dexter **116**
Mann, Bob **126**
Manuel, Jerry **94**
Mariner, Jonathan **41**
Marshall, Brandon **116**
Marte, Starling **117**
Martin, Cuonzo **121**
Martin, Curtis **104**
Martin, Jonathan **119**
Martínez, Pedro **81, 126**
Masekela, Sal **106**
Mason, Anthony **128**
Mason, Derek **120**
Mason, Desmond **127**
Mathis, Robert **121**
Matson, Ollie **93**
May, Mark **117**
Maye, Lee **111**
Mayers, Jamal **39**
Mayhew, Martin R. **76**

Tergat, Paul 59
Terrell, Ernie 118
Terrell-Kearney, Kim 83
Thabeet, Hasheem 123
Thomas, Debi 26
Thomas, Derrick 25
Thomas, Emmitt 71
Thomas, Frank 12, 51
Thomas, Isiah 7, 26, 65
Thomas, Thurman 75
Thompson, Klay 126
Thompson, Mychal 126
Thompson, Tina 25, 75
Thrower, Willie 35
Thugwane, Josia 21
Thurmond, Nate 88
Tiant, Luis 102
Tirico, Mike 68, 124
Tisdale, Wayman 50
Tolbert, Mike 125
Toler, Burl 80
Tomlin, Mike 123
Tomlinson, LaDainian 65, 112
Toney, James 89
Touré, Yaya 99
Trouppe, Quincy Thomas, Sr. 84
Tunnell, Emlen 54
Turman, Glynn 100
Turner, Mark 126
Tyson, Mike 28, 44, 93
Ujiri, Masai 107
Unseld, Wes 23
Upshaw, Gene 18, 47, 72
Upton, Justin 124
Upton, Melvin, Jr. 124
Uribe, Juan 122
Urschel, John 126
Ussery, Terdema, II 29
Vanessa James and Yannick Bonheur 84
Vaughn, Jacque 127
Vick, Michael 39, 65, 94
Vincent, Troy 91
Virgil, Ozzie 48
Wade, Dwyane 61, 103
Walcott, Jersey Joe 102
Walker, Chet 106
Walker, Herschel 1, 69
Walker, LeRoy T. 106
Wallace, Ben 54
Wallace, Perry E. 47
Wallace, Rasheed 56
Wanjiru, Sammy 94
Ward, Andre 62
Ward, Hines 84
Ware, Andre 37
Ware, DeMarcus 92
Washington, Gene 63
Washington, Kenny 50
Washington, MaliVai 8
Washington, Ora Mae 115
Washington, Ron 119
Watson, Benjamin 126
Watson, Bob 25
Watts, J. C., Jr. 14, 38
Weah, George 58
Weaver, Mike 109
Webber, Chris 15, 30, 59, 118
Weekes, Kevin 67
Wells, Vernon 91
Wells, Willie 105
Westbrook, Peter 20
Westbrook, Russell 116

Whitaker, Pernell 10, 89
White, Bill 1, 48
White, Frank 95
White, Jesse 22, 75
White, Jo Jo 112
White, Reggie 6, 50
White, Willye 67
Whiteside, Hassan 127
Whitfield, Fred 23
Whitfield, Mal 60
Whitney, Davey L. 110
Wiggins, Andrew 128
Wilbon, Michael 68
Wilder, Deontay 121
Wilfork, Vince 124
Wilkens, Lenny 11, 88
Wilkins, Dominique 74
Williams, Bernie 128
Williams, Billy 86
Williams, Darrent 116
Williams, Deron 92
Williams, Doug 22, 112
Williams, J. Mayo 83
Williams, Ken 68
Williams, Lauryn 58, 127
Williams, Monty 125
Williams, Natalie 31
Williams, Ricky 85
Williams, Serena 20, 41, 73
Williams, Stevie 71
Williams, Venus 17, 34, 62
Williamson, Fred 67
Willingham, Tyrone 43
Willis, Bill 68
Willis, Dontrelle 55
Willis, Patrick 99
Wills, Harry 80
Wills, Maury 73
Wilson, David 123
Wilson, Russell 119
Winfield, Dave 5, 91
Winkfield, Jimmy 42
Winslow, Kellen 83
Wolfe, Ann 82
Wood, Willie 111
Woodard, Lynette 67
Woodruff, John 68
Woods, Cheyenne 103
Woods, Tiger 14, 31, 81
Woodson, Mike 78
Woodson, Rod 79
Worthy, James 49
Wright, Chalky 103
Wright, Rayfield 70
Yeboah, Emmanuel Ofosu 53
Yirga, Samuel 126
Young, Darren 114
Young, Donald, Jr. 57
Young, Jimmy 54
Young, John 111

Television

Abrahams, Zaraah 127
Abudu, Mo 121
Aduba, Uzo 122
Akil, Mara Brock 60, 82
Akinnuoye-Agbaje, Adewale 56
Alexander, Khandi 43
Ali, Mahershala 122
Ali, Tatyana 73
Allen, Byron 3, 24, 97
Allen, Debbie 13, 42
Allen, Marcus 20

Alonso, Laz 87
Amos, John 8, 62
Anderson, Anthony 51, 77
Anderson, Eddie "Rochester" 30
Anderson, Jacob 128
Andrews, Tina 74
Anthony, La La 122
Arkadie, Kevin 17
Arnez J 53
Arnold, Tichina 63
Avery, James 118
Babatunde, Obba 35
Banks, Michelle 59
Banks, William 11
Barclay, Paris 37, 94
Bassett, Angela 6, 23, 62
Beach, Michael 26, 120
Beard, Matthew 120
Beaton, Norman 14
Beauvais, Garcelle 29, 95
Bell, LeRoy 98
Bell, W. Kamau 107
Bellamy, Bill 12
Bennett, Louise 69
Bentley, Lamont 53
Berry, Bertice 8, 55
Berry, Fred "Rerun" 48
Bey, Yasiin 30, 96
Big Freedia 128
Blackmon, Brenda 58
Blackwood, Maureen 37
Blacque, Taurean 58
Blake, Asha 26
Bleu, Corbin 65
Bonet, Lisa 58
Boseman, Chadwick 111
Boston, Kelvin E. 25
Bowser, Yvette Lee 17
Bradley, Ed 2, 59
Brady, Wayne 32, 71
Brandy 14, 34, 72
Braugher, Andre 13, 58, 91
Bridges, Todd 37
Brooks, Avery 9, 98
Brooks, Danielle 119
Brooks, Golden 62
Brooks, Hadda 40
Brooks, Mehcad 62
Brown, James 22
Brown, Joe 29
Brown, Les 5
Brown, Tony 3
Brown, Vivian 27
Brown, Warren 61
Browne, Roscoe Lee 66
Bruce, Bruce 56
Buress, Hannibal 101
Burnett, Charles 16, 68
Burton, LeVar 8
Byrd, Eugene 64
Byrd, Robert 11
Caldwell, Benjamin 46
Cameron, Earl 44
Campbell, Naomi 1, 31, 120
Campbell-Martin, Tisha 8, 42
Cannon, Nick 47, 73
Cannon, Reuben 50
Cara, Irene 77
Carmichael, Jerrod 124
Carroll, Rocky 74
Carroll, Diahann 9
Carson, Lisa Nicole 21
Carter, Nell 39

Cash, Rosalind 28
Cathey, Reg E. 122
Cedric the Entertainer 29, 60, 115
Cenac, Wyatt 94
Chappelle, Dave 50, 115
Chase, Debra Martin 49, 96
Che, Michael 123
Cheadle, Don 19, 52
Chestnut, Morris 31, 116
Chew, Robert F. 109
Chideya, Farai 14, 61
Childress, Alvin 114
Christian, Spencer 15
Ciara, Barbara 69
Clack, Zoanne 73
Clash, Kevin 14, 93
Clayton, Xernona 3, 45
Cobbs, Bill 101
CoCo Brother 93
Cole, Keyshia 63, 107
Cole, Nat "King" 17
Coleman, Chad L. 128
Coleman, Gary 35, 86
Common 31, 63, 98
Coolio 103
Corbi, Lana 42
Cornelius, Don 4, 100
Cosby, Bill 7, 26, 59, 125
Cox, Laverne 122
Crews, Terry 123
Crothers, Scatman 19
Crump, Steven 96
Curry, Dell 126
Curry, Mark 17
Curtis-Hall, Vondie 17
DaCosta, YaYa 98
Daniels, Billy 124
Davidson, Tommy 21
Davis, Eisa 68
Davis, Mia Amber 94
Davis, Ossie 5, 50
Davis, Viola 34, 76, 100
de Passe, Suzanne 25
De Shields, André 72
Dee, Ruby 8, 50, 68, 122
Deezer D 53
Devine, Loretta 24
Dickerson, Ernest 6
Diggs, Taye 25, 63
Dixon, Ivan 69
DJ Lance Rock 94
Dorn, Michael 112
Dourdan, Gary 37
Drake 86
Duke, Bill 3, 96
Dungey, Merrin 62
Duthiers, Vladimir 109
Dutton, Charles S. 4, 22
Earthquake 55
Ejogo, Carmen 126
Elba, Idris 49, 89, 116
Elbagir, Nima 121
Elder, Larry 25, 120
Elie, Lolis Eric 97
Elise, Kimberly 32, 101
Ellis, Aunjanue 108
Ellis, Trey 97
Emmanuel, Alphonsia 38
Ephriam, Mablean 29
Epperson, Sharon 54
Erving, Julius 18, 47
Esposito, Giancarlo 9
Eubanks, Kevin 15, 108

Evans, Harry 25
Faison, Donald 50
Faison, Frankie 55
Falana, Lola 42
Fales-Hill, Susan 88
Fargas, Antonio 50
Fields, Kim 36
Fishburne, Laurence 4, 22, 70
Fisher, Gail 85
Fox, Rick 27
Foxx, Jamie 15, 48
Foxx, Redd 2
Frazier, Kevin 58
Freeman, Aaron 52
Freeman, Morgan 2, 20, 62, 100
Freeman, Yvette 27
Funches, Ron 121
Gaines, Ernest J. 7
Gant, Richard 105
Gardere, Jeffrey 76
Garvin, Gerry 78
Gibbs, Marla 86
Gibson, Tyrese 27, 62
Givens, Adele 62
Givens, Robin 4, 25, 58
Glass, Ron 111
Glover, Anwan 123
Glover, Danny 1, 24, 103
Glover, Donald 85
Glover, Savion 14
Goldberg, Whoopi 4, 33, 69
Good, Meagan 117
Goode, Mal 13
Gooding, Cuba, Jr. 16, 62
Gordon, Carl 87
Gordon, Ed 10, 53
Gossett, Louis, Jr. 7
Graham, Katerina 99
Gray, Darius 69
Greely, M. Gasby 27
Greene, Petey 65
Grier, David Alan 28
Grier, Pam 9, 31, 86
Griffin, Angela 80
Guillaume, Robert 3, 48
Gumbel, Bryant 14, 80
Gumbel, Greg 8
Gunn, Moses 10
Gurira, Danai 73
Guy, Jasmine 2
Hairston, Jester 88
Haley, Alex 4
Hall, Arsenio 58
Hall, Tamron 96
Hamilton, Bernie 117
Hamilton, Lisa Gay 71
Hampton, Henry 6
Hardison, Kadeem 22
Hardwick, Omari 122
Harewood, David 52
Harewood, Dorian 104
Harper, Hill 32, 65, 97
Harrell, Andre 9, 30
Harris, Naomie 55, 116
Harris, Robin 7
Harris, Wood 114
Harry, Jackée 111
Hart, Kevin 103
Harvey, Steve 18, 58
Hatchett, Glenda 32
Hayes, Isaac 20, 58, 73
Haynes, Trudy 44
Haysbert, Dennis 42, 106

Hector, Jamie 98
Hemingway, Anthony 107
Hemsley, Sherman 19, 104
Henderson, Jeff 72
Henriques, Julian 37
Henry, Lenny 9, 52
Henson, Darrin 33
Henson, Taraji P. 58, 77, 127
Hickman, Fred 11
Hill, Darryl 128
Hill, Dulé 29
Hinderas, Natalie 5
Hines, Gregory 1, 42
Hodge, Aldis 124
Holmes, Amy 69
Holmes, T. J. 98
Holt, Lester 66
Hooks, Robert 76
Hounsou, Djimon 19, 45
Howard, Sherri 36
Howard, Terrence 59, 94
Hudson, Ernie 72
Huggins, Edie 71
Hughley, D. L. 23, 76
Hunter-Gault, Charlayne 6, 31
Hyman, Earle 25, 79
Ice-T 6, 31, 96
Ifill, Gwen 28
Ingram, Rex 5
Jackson, George 19
Jackson, Janet 6, 30, 68
Jackson, Randy 40
Jackson, Tom 70
Jarrett, Vernon D. 42
Jenkins, Kris 98
Joe, Yolanda 21
Johnson, Clark 96
Johnson, Linton Kwesi 37
Johnson, Robert L. 3, 39
Johnson, Rodney Van 28
Jones, Bomani 121
Jones, James Earl 3, 49, 79
Jones, Orlando 30
Jones, Quincy 8, 30
Jones, Rashida 101
Jones, Robbie 113
Jordan, Michael B. 97
Joseph, Paterson 126
Kandi 83
Kaufman, Monica 66
Kelley, Malcolm David 59
Kennedy-Overton, Jayne Harris 46
Key & Peele 107
Keys, Alicia 32, 68
Kid Cudi 83
King, Gayle 19, 99
King, Regina 22, 45
King, Woodie, Jr. 27
Kirby, George 14
Kitt, Eartha 16, 75
Knight, Gladys 16, 66
Kodjoe, Boris 34, 89
Kotto, Yaphet 7
Kwei-Armah, Kwame 84
La Salle, Eriq 12
LaBelle, Patti 13, 30
Laneuville, Eric 123
Langhart Cohen, Janet 19, 60
Lathan, Sanaa 27
Lawrence, Martin 6, 27, 60
Lawson, Jennifer 1, 50
Leakes, NeNe 107
LeFlore, Lyah Beth 96

Lemmons, Kasi 20
Lemon, Don 94
Lesure, James 64
Lewis, Ananda 28
Lewis, Byron E. 13
Lewis, Emmanuel 36
Lil' Kim 28
Lindo, Delroy 18, 45
LisaRaye 27
Little, Cleavon 117
LL Cool J 16, 49, 94
Lofton, James 42
Long, Loretta 58
Long, Nia 17, 95
Love, Loni 113
Lover, Ed 10
Luke, Derek 61
Lumbly, Carl 47
Mabrey, Vicki 26
Mabuza-Suttle, Felicia 43
Mac, Bernie 29, 61, 72
Madison, Paula 37, 99
Malco, Romany 71
Malveaux, Suzanne 88
Mann, Tamela 92
Marcille, Eva 97
Marshall, William 107
Markham, Pigmeat 106
Martin, Duane 108
Martin, Helen 31
Martin, Jesse L. 31
Martin, Michel 97
Masekela, Sal 106
Mason, Judi Ann 112
Mathis, Greg 26
Mayo, Whitman 32
Mbatha-Raw, Gugu 89
McBride, Chi 73
McCrary, Darius 111
McCrary Anthony, Crystal 70
McCullough, DeAndre 106
McDaniel, Hattie 5
McDaniels, Ralph 79
McDonald, Audra 20, 62, 128
McEwen, Mark 5
McFarland, Roland 49
McGee, Vonetta 95
McGlowan, Angela 64, 86
McKee, Lonette 12, 119
McKenzie, Vashti M. 29
McKinney, Nina Mae 40
McQueen, Butterfly 6, 54
Meadows, Tim 30
Mello, Breno 73
Melton, Frank 81
Mercado-Valdes, Frank 43
Merkerson, S. Epatha 47, 83
Michele, Michael 31
Mickelbury, Penny 28
Miles, William 112
Miller, Omar Benson 93
Miller, Tangi 116
Miller, Wentworth 75
Ming, Mel 106
Mitchell, Brian Stokes 21
Mitchell, Kel 66
Mitchell, Russ 21, 73
Mokae, Zakes 80
Mo'Nique 35, 84
Montgomery, Robbie 101
Mooney, Paul 37, 120
Moore, Chante 26
Moore, Melba 21

Moore, Shemar 21, 112
Moore, Tim 124
Morgan, Tracy 61, 102
Morris, Garrett 31
Morris, Greg 28
Morton, Frederick A., Jr. 93
Morton, Joe 18
Moses, Gilbert 12
Moss, Carlton 17
Mowry, Tamera 79
Mowry, Tia 78
Murphy, Charles 95
Murphy, Eddie 4, 20, 61
Muse, Clarence Edouard 21
Myers, Lou 110
Myles, Kim 69
Nash, Johnny 40
Nash, Niecy 66, 115
Naughton, Naturi 97
Neal, Elise 29
Nicholas, Denise 82
Nichols, Nichelle 11
Nissel, Angela 42
Neville, Arthel 53
Noah, Trevor 128
Noble, Gil 76
Norman, Christina 47
Norman, Maidie 20
O'Brien, Soledad 88
Okonedo, Sophie 67
Olagundoye, Toks 113
Oliver, Pam 54, 123
Omarosa 69, 110
O'Neal, Patrice 99
Onwurah, Ngozi 38
Orman, Roscoe 55
Pace, Judy 119
Palcy, Euzhan 94
Palmer, Keke 68, 120
Parker, Nicole Ari 52
Parr, Russ 51
Patterson, Chuck 124
Paulk, Marcus T. 127
Payne, Allen 13
Pearson, Felicia 99
Peete, Holly Robinson 20
Peete, Rodney 60
Perkins, Tony 24
Perrineau, Harold, Jr. 51
Perry, Lowell 30
Perry, Tyler 40, 54, 103
Peters, Brock 96
Peters, Clarke 103
Phifer, Mekhi 25, 103
Phillips, Joseph C. 73
Pickens, James, Jr. 59
Pierce, Wendell 90
Pinckney, Sandra 56
Pinkett Smith, Jada 10, 41, 95
Pinkston, W. Randall 24
Pitts, Byron 71
Plummer, Glenn 120
Poitier, Sydney Tamiia 65
Pounder, CCH 72
Poussaint, Renee 78
Powell, Keith 101
Price, Frederick K. C. 21
Price, Hugh B. 9, 54
Prince-Bythewood, Gina 31, 77
Pugh, Charles 81
Quarles, Norma 25
Queen Latifah 1, 16, 58, 119
Quivers, Robin 61

Ralph, Sheryl Lee 18, 108
Randle, Theresa 16
Rashad, Ahmad 18
Rashad, Phylicia 21
Raven-Symoné 44, 113
Ray, Gene Anthony 47
Ray J 86
Reddick, Lance 52, 128
Reed Hall, Alaina 83
Reese, Della 6, 20, 96
Reid, Tim 56
Reuben, Gloria 15
Reynolds, Star Jones 10, 27, 61
Rhimes, Shonda Lynn 67
Ribeiro, Alfonso 17
Richards, Beah 30
Richardson, Donna 39
Richardson, LaTanya 71
Richardson, Salli 68
Ridley, John 69
Riley, Amber 97
Roberts, Deborah 35
Roberts, Robin 16, 54, 113
Robinson, Craig 103
Robinson, Matt 69
Robinson, Max 3
Robinson, Shaun 36
Rochon, Lela 16
Rock, Chris 3, 22, 66
Rock, Tony 108
Rodgers, Johnathan 6, 51
Rodrigues, Percy 68
Roker, Al 12, 49
Roker, Roxie 68
Rolle, Esther 13, 21
Rollins, Howard E., Jr. 16
Romeo 98
Roots, The 101
Rose, Jalen 108
Ross, Tracee Ellis 35
Roundtree, Richard 27
Rowell, Victoria 13, 68
Rowland, Kelly 100
Rudolph, Maya 46, 106
Run 31, 73
RuPaul 17, 91
Russell, Bill 8
Russell, Nipsey 66
Rust, Art, Jr. 83
St. Jacques, Raymond 8
St. John, Kristoff 25
St. Patrick, Mathew 48
Salters, Lisa 71
Sands, Diana 87
Sanford, Isabel 53
Santiago-Hudson, Ruben 85
Sasser, Sean 113
Schiavocampo, Mara 97
Schultz, Michael A. 6
Scott, Hazel 66
Scott, Jill 29, 83
Scott, Stuart 34, 126
Scott-Young, Mona 101
Shaw, Bernard 2, 28
Sesay, Isha 107
Shepherd, Sherri 55
Sidner, Sara 105
Simmons, Henry 55
Simmons, Jamal 72
Simmons, Kimora Lee 51, 83
Simpson, Carole 6, 30
Sinbad 1, 16
Sinclair, Madge 78

Smiley, Tavis 20, 68
Smith, Anjela Lauren 44
Smith, B(arbara) 11
Smith, Ian 62
Smith, Roger Guenveur 12
Smith, Tasha 73
Smith, Will 8, 18, 53
Sohn, Sonja 100
Spencer, Octavia 100
Stewart, Alison 13
Stewart, Nzingha 89
Stickney, Phyllis Yvonne 108
Stokes, Carl 10, 73
Strahan, Michael 35, 81
Stuart, Moira 82
Sykes, Wanda 48, 81
Syler, Rene 53
Swann, Lynn 28
Tate, Larenz 15
Taylor, Jason 70
Taylor, Karin 34
Taylor, Meshach 4
Taylor, Regina 9, 46, 97
Teague, Bob 111
Terrence J 108
Thigpen, Lynne 17, 41
Thomas-Graham, Pamela 29
Thomason, Marsha 47
Thompson, Kenan 52
Thoms, Tracie 61
Thurston, Baratunde 79, 101
Tillman, Deborah 98
Tirico, Mike 68, 124
Torres, Gina 52
Torry, Guy 31
Toussaint, Lorraine 32
Townsend, Robert 4, 23
True, Rachel 82
Tucker, Chris 13, 23, 62
Tunie, Tamara 63
Turman, Glynn 100
Tyler, Aisha N. 36
Tyson, Cicely 7, 51, 112
Uggams, Leslie 23, 114
Underwood, Blair 7, 27, 76
Union, Gabrielle 31, 92
Usher 23, 56, 95
Van Peebles, Mario 2, 51
Vance, Jim 110
Vaughn, Countess 53
Vereen, Ben 4
Wade, Ernestine 126
Walker, Chet 106
Walker, Eamonn 37
Ware, Andre 37
Warfield, Marsha 2
Warner, Malcolm-Jamal 22, 36, 110
Warren, Michael 27
Washington, Denzel 1, 16, 93
Washington, Hayma 86
Washington, Isaiah 62
Washington, Kerry 46, 107
Watson, Carlos 50
Watts, Rolonda 9
Wayans, Damien 78
Wayans, Damon 8, 41
Wayans, Kim 80
Wayans, Keenen Ivory 18
Wayans, Marlon 29, 82
Wayans, Shawn 29
Weathers, Carl 10, 117
Wesley, Richard 73
Wesley, Rutina 97

Whack, Rita Coburn 36
Wheaton, James 103
White, Lillias 120
White, Michael Jai 71, 117
Whitfield, Lynn 1, 18
Wilbon, Michael 68
Williams, Armstrong 29
Williams, Clarence, III 26
Williams, Juan 35, 80
Williams, Malinda 57
Williams, Michael Kenneth 97
Williams, Montel 4, 57
Williams, Russell, II 70
Williams, Samm-Art 21
Williams, Spencer 126
Williams, Vanessa A. 32, 66
Williams, Vanessa L. 4, 17
Williams, Wendy 62
Williamson, Mykelti 22
Wills, Maury 73
Wilmore, Larry 121
Wilson, Chandra 57
Wilson, Debra 38
Wilson, Demond 102
Wilson, Dorien 55
Wilson, Flip 21
Winfield, Paul 2, 45
Winfrey, Oprah 2, 15, 61, 106
Witherspoon, John 38
Woodard, Alfre 9, 108
Wright, Jeffrey 54, 111
Yarbrough, Cedric 51
Yoba, Malik 11
Young, Lee Thompson 114

Theater
Adams, Osceola Macarthy 31
Aldridge, Ira 99
Allen, Debbie 13, 42
Anderson, Carl 48
Andrews, Bert 13
Anthony, Trey 63
Arkadie, Kevin 17
Armstrong, Vanessa Bell 24
Arnez J 53
Babatunde, Obba 35
Babatunde, Rotimi 104
Bandele, Biyi 68, 121
Barclay, Paris 37, 94
Barnett, Etta Moten 56
Barrett, Lindsay 43
Baskett, James 102
Beach, Michael 26, 120
Beaton, Norman 14
Belgrave, Cynthia 75
Bennett, Louise 69
Blanco, Mykki 106
Borders, James 9
Boseman, Chadwick 111
Boykin, Phillip 102
Branch, William Blackwell 39
Braugher, Andre 13, 58, 91
Brooks, Avery 9, 98
Brown, Oscar, Jr. 53
Brown, Ruth 90
Bruce, Bruce 56
Caldwell, Benjamin 46
Calloway, Cab 14
Cameron, Earl 44
Cara, Irene 77
Carroll, Rocky 74
Carroll, Vinnette 29
Carter, Nell 39

Cash, Rosalind 28
Cheadle, Don 19, 52
Chenault, John 40
Childress, Alice 15
Clarke, Hope 14
Cleage, Pearl 17, 64
Cook, Will Marion 40
Cooper, Chuck 75
Corthron, Kia 43
Curtis-Hall, Vondie 17
Dadié, Bernard 34
David, Keith 27
Davis, Altovise 76
Davis, Eisa 68
Davis, Ossie 5, 50
Davis, Sammy, Jr. 18
Davis, Viola 34, 76, 100
Dawn, Marpessa 75
De Shields, André 72
Dean, Phillip Hayes 122
Dee, Ruby 8, 50, 68, 122
Devine, Loretta 24
Diamond, Lydia R. 101
Dieudonné 67, 118
Diggs, Taye 25, 63
Dixon, Ivan 69
Dodson, Owen Vincent 38
Domingo, Colman 94
Dudley, Sherman H. 117
Dunham, Katherine 4, 59
Dutton, Charles S. 4, 22
Ejiofor, Chiwetel 67, 116
Elder, Lonne, III 38
Ellis, Nelsan 105
Elzy, Ruby 119
Emmanuel, Alphonsia 38
Epps, Mike 60
Esposito, Giancarlo 9
Europe, James Reese 10
Faison, Frankie 55
Falana, Lola 42
Fargas, Antonio 50
Fields, Felicia P. 60
Fishburne, Laurence 4, 22, 70
Francis, Thais 93
Franklin, J. E. 44
Freeman, Aaron 52
Freeman, Al, Jr. 11, 105
Freeman, Yvette 27
Fuller, Charles 8
Gibson, John Trusty 87
Gilpin, Charles Sidney 81
Givens, Adele 62
Glover, Danny 1, 24, 103
Glover, Keith 79
Glover, Savion 14
Goldberg, Whoopi 4, 33, 69
Gordone, Charles 15
Gossett, Louis, Jr. 7
Graves, Denyce Antoinette 19, 57
Guillaume, Robert 3, 48
Gunn, Moses 10
Gurira, Danai 73
Guyse, Sheila 122
Hall, Juanita 62
Hamilton, Lawrence 122
Hamilton, Lisa Gay 71
Hamlin, Larry Leon 49, 62
Hansberry, Lorraine 6
Harewood, David 52
Harris, Bill 72
Harris, Robin 7
Hayes, Teddy 40

Henry, Joshua **94**
Higginsen, Vy **65**
Hill, Errol **40**
Hill, Hugh Morgan **83**
Hines, Gregory **1, 42**
Holder, Geoffrey **78, 124**
Holder, Laurence **34**
Holland, Endesha Ida Mae **3, 57**
Hooks, Robert **76**
Hyman, Earle **25, 79**
Hyman, Phyllis **19**
Ingram, Rex **5**
Iverson, Johnathan Lee **22, 100**
Jackson, Millie **25**
James, Nikki M. **94**
Jamison, Judith **7, 67, 96**
Jean-Baptiste, Marianne **17, 46**
Johnson, Je'Caryous **63**
Jones, James Earl **3, 49, 79**
Jones, Sarah **39**
Joseph, Paterson **126**
Joyner, Matilda Sissieretta **15**
Kente, Gibson **52**
Khumalo, Leleti **51**
King, Woodie, Jr. **27**
Kitt, Eartha **16, 75**
Kotto, Yaphet **7**
Kwei-Armah, Kwame **84**
La Salle, Eriq **12**
LaChanze **93**
Lacy, Marc **111**
Lampley, Oni Faida **43, 71**
Lathan, Sanaa **27**
Le Loka, Tsidii **116**
Lee, Canada **8**
Lee, Leslie **85, 122**
Leggs, Kingsley **62**
Lemmons, Kasi **20**
LeNoire, Rosetta **37**
Lenox, Adriane **59**
Leon, Kenny **10, 98**
Lester, Adrian **46**
Letson, Al **39**
Lindo, Delroy **18, 45**
Lister, Marquita **65**
Little, Cleavon **117**
Mackie, Anthony **102**
Mann, Tamela **92**
Maponya, Maishe **101**
Marrow, Queen Esther **24**
Martin, Helen **31**
Martin, Jesse L. **31**
Mason, Judi Ann **112**
Mbatha-Raw, Gugu **89**
McClendon, Forrest **94**
McClinton, Marion Isaac **77**
McCraney, Tarell Alvin **116**
McDaniel, Hattie **5**
McDonald, Audra **20, 62, 128**
McFarlan, Tyron **60**
McQueen, Butterfly **6, 54**
Merkerson, S. Epatha **47, 83**
Mickelbury, Penny **28**
Miller, Patina **94**
Mills, Florence **22**
Milner, Ron **39**
Mitchell, Brian Stokes **21**
Mokae, Zakes **80**
Mollel, Tololwa **38**
Moore, Melba **21**
Moore, Tim **124**
Moses, Gilbert **12**
Moss, Carlton **17**

Moss, Preacher **63**
Moten, Etta **18**
Muse, Clarence Edouard **21**
Nascimento, Abdias do **93**
Ngaujah, Sahr **86**
Nicholas, Fayard **20, 57**
Nicholas, Harold **20**
Norman, Maidie **20**
Nottage, Lynn **66**
Ntshona, Winston **52**
Okonedo, Sophie **67**
O'Neal, Frederick **99**
Orlandersmith, Dael **42**
Patterson, Chuck **124**
Payne, Allen **13**
Perrineau, Harold, Jr. **51**
Perry, Tyler **40, 54, 103**
Peters, Brock **96**
Peters, Clarke **103**
Pierce, Wendell **90**
Porter, Billy **112**
Pounder, CCH **72**
Powell, Keith **101**
Power, Will **83**
Preer, Evelyn **82**
Premice, Josephine **41**
Pryor, Rain **65**
Randle, Theresa **16**
Rashad, Phylicia **21**
Redwood, John Henry **78**
Richards, Beah **30**
Richards, Lloyd **2**
Richardson, Desmond **39**
Richardson, LaTanya **71**
Robeson, Paul **2**
Rolle, Esther **13, 21**
Rollins, Howard E., Jr. **16**
Rose, Anika Noni **70**
Rotimi, Ola **1**
St. Jacques, Raymond **8**
St. Louis, David **126**
Salter, Nikkole **73**
Sands, Diana **87**
Sanford, Isabel **53**
Santiago-Hudson, Ruben **85**
Schultz, Michael A. **6**
Scott, Harold Russell, Jr. **61**
Shabazz, Attallah **6**
Slocumb, Jonathan **52**
Smiley, Rickey **59**
Smith, Anjela Lauren **44**
Smith, Anna Deavere **6, 44**
Smith, Roger Guenveur **12**
Snipes, Wesley **3, 24, 67**
Sommore **61**
Soyinka, Wole **4, 93**
Springer, Ashton, Jr. **115**
Stew **69**
Stewart, Tonea Harris **78**
Sundiata, Sekou **66**
Talbert, David E. **34, 93**
Taylor, Meshach **4**
Taylor, Regina **9, 46, 97**
Taylor, Ron **35**
Teer, Barbara Ann **81**
Thigpen, Lynne **17, 41**
Thompson, John Douglas **81**
Thompson, Tazewell **13**
Thurman, Wallace **16**
Torres, Gina **52**
Toussaint, Lorraine **32**
Townsend, Robert **4, 23**
Turman, Glynn **100**

Uggams, Leslie **23, 114**
Underwood, Blair **7, 27, 76**
Vance, Courtney B. **15, 60**
Vereen, Ben **4**
Walcott, Derek **5, 94**
Walker, Eamonn **37**
Ward, Douglas Turner **42**
Warfield, William **94**
Washington, Fredi **10**
Waters, Ethel **7**
Wesley, Rutina **97**
Wheaton, James **103**
Whitaker, Forest **2, 49, 67**
White, Lillias **120**
White, Terri **82**
White, Willard **53**
Whitfield, Lynn **18**
Williams, Bert **18**
Williams, Clarence, III **26**
Williams, Michelle **73**
Williams, Samm-Art **21**
Williamson, Mykelti **22**
Wilson, August **7, 33, 55**
Wilson, Dorien **55**
Wilson, Tracey Scott **777**
Winfield, Paul **2, 45**
Withers-Mendes, Elisabeth **64**
Wolfe, George C. **6, 43, 127**
Woods, Renn **110**
Wright, Jeffrey **54, 111**
Yarbrough, Cedric **51**

Writing

Abani, Chris **77**
Abrahams, Peter **39**
Abu-Jamal, Mumia **15**
Achebe, Chinua **6, 99, 111**
Adams, Jenoyne **60**
Adichie, Chimamanda Ngozi **64, 121**
Aidoo, Ama Ata **38**
Akpan, Uwem **70**
Alexander, Elizabeth **75**
Alexander, Kwame **98**
Alexander, Margaret Walker **22**
Ali, Ayaan Hirsi **58, 92**
Ali, Hana Yasmeen **52**
Ali, Mohammed Naseehu **60**
Als, Hilton **105**
Amadi, Elechi **40**
Ames, Wilmer **27**
Anderson, Ho Che **54**
Andrews, Raymond **4**
Andrews, Tina **74**
Angelou, Maya **1, 15, 122**
Ansa, Tina McElroy **14**
Anthony, Michael **29**
Aplin-Brownlee, Vivian **96**
Arac de Nyeko, Monica **66**
Aristide, Jean-Bertrand **6, 45**
Arkadie, Kevin **17**
Armah, Ayi Kwei **49**
Armah, Esther **87**
Asante, Molefi Kete **3**
Ashley & JaQuavis **107**
Ashley-Ward, Amelia **23**
Asim, Jabari **71**
Atkins, Cholly **40**
Atkins, Russell **45**
Attaway, William **102**
Aubert, Alvin **41**
Aubespin, Mervin **95**
Auguste, Arnold A. **47**

Awoonor, Kofi **37, 115**
Ayim, May **126**
Azikiwe, Nnamdi **13**
Ba, Mariama **30**
Babatunde, Rotimi **104**
Bahati, Wambui **60**
Bailey, Chauncey **68**
Baiocchi, Regina Harris **41**
Baisden, Michael **25, 66**
Baker, Augusta **38**
Baker, Houston A., Jr. **6**
Baldwin, James **1**
Ballard, Allen Butler, Jr. **40**
Bambara, Toni Cade **10**
Bandele, Asha **36**
Bandele, Biyi **68, 121**
Baquet, Dean **63, 121**
Baraka, Amiri **1, 38, 118**
Barnes, Steven **54**
Barnett, Amy Du Bois **46**
Barrax, Gerald William **45**
Barrett, Lindsay **43**
Bashir, Halima **73**
Bass, Charlotta Spears **40**
Baszile, Jennifer **79**
Bates, Karen Grigsby **40**
Beah, Ishmael **69**
Beals, Melba Pattillo **15, 94**
Bebey, Francis **45**
Beckham, Barry **41**
Bell, James Madison **40**
Benberry, Cuesta **65**
Bennett, George Harold **45**
Bennett, Gwendolyn B. **59**
Bennett, Lerone, Jr. **5, 84**
Bennett, Louise **69**
Benson, Angela **34**
Berry, James **41**
Berry, Mary Frances **7**
Best, Carrie **80**
Beti, Mongo **36**
Betts, R. Dwayne **86**
Bishop, Maurice **39**
Blackman, Toni **86**
Blair, Jayson **50**
Bland, Eleanor Taylor **39**
Blassingame, John Wesley **40**
Blockson, Charles L. **42**
Blow, Charles M. **73**
Bluitt, Juliann S. **14**
Bolden, Tonya **32**
Bontemps, Arna **8**
Booker, Simeon **23**
Bostic, Joe **95**
Boston, Lloyd **24**
Boyd, Gerald M. **32, 59**
Boyd, Melba Joyce **86**
Boyd, Suzanne **92**
Bradley, Adam **101**
Bradley, David Henry, Jr. **39**
Braithwaite, William Stanley **52**
Branch, William Blackwell **39**
Brand, Dionne **32**
Brathwaite, Kamau **36**
Brawley, Benjamin **44**
Breeze, Jean "Binta" **37**
Briscoe, Connie **15**
Britt, Donna **28**
Brooks, Gwendolyn **1, 28**
Brower, William **49**
Brown, Cecil M. **46**
Brown, Claude **38**
Brown, Elaine **8**

Brown, Lloyd Louis 10, 42
Brown, Marie Dutton 12
Brown, Sterling Allen 10, 64
Brown, Tony 3
Brown, Wesley 23
Brown, William Wells 99
Broyard, Anatole 68
Broyard, Bliss 68
Brutus, Dennis 38
Bryan, Ashley 41, 104
Buckley, Gail Lumet 39
Bulawayo, NoViolet 125
Bullins, Ed 25, 121
Bunche, Ralph J. 5
Bunkley, Anita Richmond 39
Burgess, Marjorie L. 55
Burley, Dan 96
Burroughs, Margaret Taylor 9
Burwell, Bryan 83
Butler, Octavia 8, 43, 58
Bynum, Juanita 31, 71
Caldwell, Earl 60
Calhoun, Lillian Scott 87
Campbell, Bebe Moore 6, 24, 59
Carby, Hazel 27
Carmichael, Stokely 5, 26
Carter, Joye Maureen 41
Carter, Martin 49
Carter, Stephen L. 4
Cartey, Wilfred 47
Cartiér, Xam Wilson 41
Cary, Lorene 3
Cary, Mary Ann Shadd 30
Cayton, Horace 26
Cenac, Wyatt 94
Césaire, Aimé 48, 69
Chadiha, Jeffri 57
Channer, Colin 36
Chase-Riboud, Barbara 20, 46
Chenault, John 40
Cheney-Coker, Syl 43
Chesnutt, Charles 29
Chideya, Farai 14, 61
Chikoti, Shadreck 125
Childress, Alice 15
Chiles, Nick 98
Christian, Barbara T. 44
Churchwell, Robert, Sr. 76
Clack, Zoanne 73
Clark, Kenneth B. 5, 52
Clark, Septima 7
Clark, Wahida 107
Clark-Bekederemo, J. P. 44
Clarke, Austin C. 32
Clarke, Cheryl 32
Clarke, George 32
Cleage, Pearl 17, 64
Cleaver, Eldridge 5
Cliff, Michelle 42
Clifton, Lucille 14, 64, 91
Coates, Ta-Nehisi 76
Cobb, William Jelani 59, 121
Cobbs, Price M. 9
Cohen, Anthony 15
Cole, Johnnetta B. 5, 43
Cole, Teju 120
Coleman, Wanda 48, 119
Collins, Patricia Hill 67
Colter, Cyrus J. 36
Comer, James P. 6
Contee, Cheryl 88
Cook, Suzan D. Johnson 22
Cooke, Marvel 31

Cook-Parrish, Mary Virginia 95
Coombs, Orde M. 44
Cooper, Afua 53
Cooper, Andrew W. 36
Cooper, Anna Julia 20
Cooper, Helene 74
Cooper, J. California 12, 85, 125
Cornish, Sam 50
Cortez, Jayne 43, 109
Cose, Ellis 5, 50, 118
Cotter, Joseph Seamon, Sr. 40
Couto, Mia 45
Cox, Joseph Mason Andrew 51
Creagh, Milton 27
Croal, N'Gai 76
Crouch, Stanley 11, 87
Cruse, Harold 54
Crutchfield, James N. 55
Cullen, Countee 8
Cuney, William Waring 44
Cunningham, Evelyn 23, 85
Curry, George E. 23
Curtis, Christopher Paul 26, 113
Dabydeen, David 48
Dadié, Bernard 34
D'Aguiar, Fred 50
Damas, Léon-Gontran 46
Dandridge, Raymond Garfield 45
Danner, Margaret Esse 49
Danquah, Meri Nana Ama 93
Danticat, Edwidge 15, 68, 128
Dash, Leon 47
Datcher, Michael 60
Dathorne, O. R. 52
Davis, Allison 12
Davis, Charles T. 48
Davis, Eisa 68
Davis, Frank Marshall 47
Davis, George 36
Davis, Nolan 45
Davis, Thulani 61
Dawes, Kwame 126
Dawkins, Wayne 20
de Passe, Suzanne 25
De Veaux, Alexis 44
Dedeaux, Richard 119
Deggans, Eric 71
Delany, Martin R. 27
Delany, Samuel R., Jr. 9
DeLoach, Nora 30
Demby, William 51
Dent, Thomas C. 50
Dickerson, Debra J. 60
Dickey, Eric Jerome 21, 56
Diop, Birago 53
Diop, Cheikh Anta 4
Dodson, Howard, Jr. 7, 52
Dodson, Owen Vincent 38
DoHarris, Brenda 116
Douglass, Frederick 87
Dove, Rita 6, 78, 101
Draper, Sharon Mills 16, 43
Driver, David E. 11
Drummond, William J. 40
Du Bois, David Graham 45
Du Bois, W. E. B. 3
DuBois, Shirley Graham 21
Due, Tananarive 30
Dumas, Henry 41
Dunbar, Paul Laurence 8
Dunbar-Nelson, Alice Ruth Moore 44
Dungy, Camille 86

Dunnigan, Alice Allison 41
Duplechan, Larry 55
Dyson, Michael Eric 11, 40, 128
Eagleson, William Lewis 90
Edmonds, Terry 17
Edugyan, Esi 98
Ekwensi, Cyprian 37
Elder, Larry 25, 120
Elder, Lonne, III 38
Elie, Lolis Eric 97
Elliot, Lorris 37
Ellis, Trey 97
Ellison, Ralph 7
Elmore, Ronn 21
Emanuel, James A. 46
Emecheta, Buchi 30
Equiano, Olaudah 78
Estes, Rufus 29
Evans, Diana 72
Evans, Mari 26
Everett, Percival 93
Fabio, Sarah Webster 48
Fair, Ronald L. 47
Fales-Hill, Susan 88
Fanon, Frantz 44
Farah, Nuruddin 27
Farley, Christopher John 54
Fauset, Jessie 7
Feelings, Muriel 44
Feelings, Tom 11, 47
Fields, Julia 45
Figueroa, John J. 40
Files, Lolita 35
Finner-Williams, Paris Michele 62
Fisher, Antwone 40
Fisher, Rudolph 17
Fleming, Raymond 48
Fletcher, Bill, Jr. 41
Fletcher, Geoffrey 85
Forbes, Calvin 46
Ford, Clyde W. 40
Ford, Nick Aaron 44
Ford, Wallace 58
Forman, James 7, 51
Forna, Aminatta 95
Forrest, Leon 44
Fortune, T. Thomas 6
Foster, Cecil 32
Foster, Jylla Moore 45
Foye, K'wan 97
Franklin, John Hope 5, 77
Franklin, Robert M. 13
Frazier, E. Franklin 10
Frazier, Oscar 58
French, Albert 18
Fuller, Charles 8
Fuller, Hoyt 44
Gabre-Medhin, Tsegaye 64
Gaines, Ernest J. 7
Gaines, Patrice 106
Gaiter, Dorothy J. 80
Gardner, Chris 65
Gaston, Marilyn Hughes 60
Gates, Henry Louis, Jr. 3, 38, 67
Gayle, Addison, Jr. 41
George, Nelson 12, 101
Gibson, Donald Bernard 40
Giddings, Paula 11
Gilbert, Christopher 50
Gilliard, Steve 69
Giovanni, Nikki 9, 39, 85
Givhan, Robin Deneen 72
Gladwell, Malcolm 62

Gloster, Hugh Morris, Sr. 90
Glover, Donald 85
Goines, Donald 19
Golden, Marita 19, 99
Gomez, Jewelle 30
Goodison, Lorna 71
Goodlett, Carlton B. 91
Gordon-Reed, Annette 74
Graham, Lawrence Otis 12
Graham, Lorenz 48
Granderson, LZ 103
Grant, Gwendolyn Goldsby 28
Gray, Darius 69
Greenfield, Eloise 9
Greenlee, Sam 48
Greenwood, Monique 38
Griffith, Mark Winston 8
Grimké, Archibald H. 9
Guy, Rosa 5
Guy-Sheftall, Beverly 13, 92
Haley, Alex 4
Halliburton, Warren J. 49
Hamblin, Ken 10
Hamilton, Virginia 10
Hammon, Jupiter 124
Hansberry, Lorraine 6
Harding, Vincent 67
Hare, Nathan 44
Harkless, Necia Desiree 19
Harper, Frances Ellen Watkins 11
Harper, Hill 32, 65, 97
Harper, Michael S. 34
Harper, Rachel M. 92
Harrington, Oliver W. 9
Harris, Bill 72
Harris, Claire 34
Harris, E. Lynn 12, 33, 116
Harris, Eddy L. 18
Harris, Jay 19
Harris, Jessica B. 91
Harris, Leslie 6
Harris, Monica 18
Harrison, Alvin 28
Harrison, Calvin 28
Haskins, James 36, 54
Hayden, Robert 12
Hayes, Teddy 40
Hayes, Terrance 124
Haygood, Wil 83
Haywood, Gar Anthony 43
Head, Bessie 28
Heard, Nathan C. 45
Hearne, John Edgar Caulwell 45
Hemphill, Essex 10
Henderson, Angelo 122
Henderson, David 53
Henderson, Stephen E. 45
Henries, A. Doris Banks 44
Henriques, Julian 37
Henry, Lenny 9, 52
Henson, Josiah 90
Henson, Matthew 2
Herbert, Bob 63, 96
Hercules, Frank 44
Herndon, Angelo 90
Hernton, Calvin C. 51
Hill, Donna 32
Hill, Errol 40
Hill, Jemele 109
Hill, Leslie Pinckney 44
Hill, Marc Lamont 80, 128
Hilliard, David 7, 105
Hoagland, Everett H. 45

Hobson, Julius W. 44
Holland, Endesha Ida Mae 3, 57
Holmes, Shannon 70
Holt, Nora 38
Holton, Hugh, Jr. 39
hooks, bell 5, 90
Horne, Frank 44
Horton, George Moses 124
Hrabowski, Freeman A., III 22
Hudlin, Reginald 9, 86
Hudson, Cheryl 15
Hudson, Wade 15
Hughes, Langston 4
Hull, Akasha Gloria 45
Hunter-Gault, Charlayne 6, 31
Hurston, Zora Neale 3
Iceberg Slim 11
Ifill, Gwen 28
Ilibagiza, Immaculée 66
Jackson, Brenda 87
Jackson, Fred James 25
Jackson, George 14
Jackson, James A. 90
Jackson, Sheneska 18
Jacobs, George 118
Jacobs, Harriet 104
James, Marlon 85, 124
Jarrett, Vernon D. 42
Jasper, Kenji 39
Jefferson, Margo 108
Jenkins, Beverly 14
Joachim, Paulin 34
Joe, Yolanda 21
Johnson, Angela 52
Johnson, Charles 1, 82
Johnson, Charles S. 12
Johnson, Fenton 91
Johnson, Georgia Douglas 41
Johnson, James Weldon 5
Johnson, John H. 3, 54
Johnson, Linton Kwesi 37
Johnson, Mat 31, 105
Johnson, R. M. 36
Johnson, Sandra K. 94
Johnson, William 91
Jolley, Willie 28
Jones, Bomani 121
Jones, Edward P. 43, 67
Jones, Gayl 37
Jones, Orlando 30
Jones, Sarah 39
Jones, Tayari 96
Jordan, Deloris 108
Jordan, June 7, 35
Joseph, Jamal 101
Josey, E. J. 10
July, William 27
Just, Ernest Everett 3
Kahora, Billy 125
Kamau, Kwadwo Agymah 28
Karenga, Maulana 10, 71
Kariuki, J. M. 67
Kaufman, Bob 105
Kay, Jackie 37
Kayira, Legson 40
Kearney, Janis 54
Keckley, Elizabeth 90
Keene, John 73
Kendrick, Erika 57
Kennedy, Adrienne 11
Kennedy, Florynce 12, 33
Kennedy, Randall 40
Khanga, Yelena 6

Killens, John O. 54
Kimbro, Dennis 10
Kincaid, Jamaica 4, 109
King, Colbert I. 69
King, Coretta Scott 3, 57
King, Preston 28
King, Woodie, Jr. 27
Kitt, Sandra 23
Kitwana, Bakari 86
Knight, Etheridge 37
Kobia, Samuel 43
Komunyakaa, Yusef 9
Kunjufu, Jawanza 3, 50
Lacy, Marc 111
Lacy, Sam 30, 46
Ladner, Joyce A. 42
Laferriere, Dany 33
LaGuma, Alex 30
Lamar, Jake 96
Lamming, George 35
Lampley, Oni Faida 43, 71
Lane, Lunsford 93
Larsen, Nella 10
Lattany, Kristin Hunter 88
Lawrence, Martin 6, 27, 60
Lawrence-Lightfoot, Sara 10
Laymon, Kiese 113
Lee, Jarena 100
LeFlore, Lyah Beth 96
Lemon, Don 94
Lester, Julius 9, 115
Letson, Al 39
Lewis, David Levering 9
Lewis, Samella 25
Lincoln, C. Eric 38
Little, Benilde 21
Locke, Alain 10
Locke, Attica 85
Lomax, Louis E. 90
Lorde, Audre 6
Louis, Errol T. 8
Loury, Glenn 36
Lowe, Herbert 57
Mabry, Marcus 70
Mabuza-Suttle, Felicia 43
Machado de Assis 74
Mackey, Nathaniel 75
Madhubuti, Haki 7, 85
Major, Clarence 9
Makeba, Miriam 2, 50, 74
Malveaux, Julianne 32, 70
Manley, Ruth 34
Marechera, Dambudzo 39
Markham, E. A. 37
Marshall, Paule 7, 77
Martin, Michel 97
Martin, Roland S. 49, 84
Mason, Felicia 31
Mason, Herman, Jr. 83
Massaquoi, Hans J. 30
Matejka, Adrian 87
Mathabane, Mark 5, 99
Maynard, Nancy Hicks 73
Maynard, Robert C. 7
Mays, Benjamin E. 7
Mazrui, Ali 12, 124
Mbaye, Mariétou 31
McAlpin, Harry 121
McBride, James 35, 87
McCall, Nathan 8
McCauley, Gina 76
McClellan, George Marion 91
McCrary Anthony, Crystal 70

McDuffie, Dwayne 62
McFadden, Bernice L. 39
McGhee, Sharon K. 113
McGruder, Aaron 28, 56, 120
McGruder, Robert 22, 35
McKay, Claude 6
McKinney Hammond, Michelle 51
McKinney-Whetstone, Diane 27
McMillan, Rosalynn A. 36
McMillan, Terry 4, 17, 53
McMillan, Tracy 93
McPherson, James Alan 70
McWhorter, John 35, 119
Memmi, Albert 37
Menard, John Willis 90
Mengestu, Dinaw 66, 114
Meredith, James H. 11
Mickelbury, Penny 28
Miles, Tiya 116
Miller, Pepper 96
Millner, Denene 76
Milner, Ron 39
Mitchell, Elvis 67
Mitchell, Loften 31
Mitchell, Russ 21, 73
Mitchell, Sharon 36
Mofolo, Thomas Mokopu 37
Mollel, Tololwa 38
Monroe, Bryan 71
Monroe, Mary 35
Moore, Jessica Care 30
Moore, Wes 86
Morrison, Toni 2, 15, 86
Mosley, Walter 5, 25, 68
Moss, Carlton 17
Mossell, Gertrude Bustill 40
Moutoussamy-Ashe, Jeanne 7
Mowry, Jess 7
Mphalele, Es'kia 40
Mudimbe, V. Y. 61
Mugo, Micere Githae 32
Mullen, Harryette 34
Murphy, John H. 42
Murray, Albert L. 33
Murray, Pauli 38
Mwangi, Meja 40
Myers, Walter Dean 8, 70, 123
Nakasa, Nat 123
Nash, Shannon King 84
Naylor, Gloria 10, 42
Neal, Larry 38
Neal, Mark Anthony 74
Nell, William C. 128
Nelson, Jill 6, 54
Nelson, Kadir 115
Neto, António Agostinho 43
Newkirk, Pamela 69
Newton, Huey 2
Ngugi wa Thiong'o 29, 61, 101
Nissel, Angela 42
Njawe, Pius 87
Nkosi, Lewis 46
Norris, Michele 83
Northup, Solomon 115
Norton, Meredith 72
Nugent, Richard Bruce 39
Nunez, Elizabeth 62, 112
Ojikutu, Bayo 66
Okara, Gabriel 37
Okigbo, Christopher 102
Oliver, John J., Jr. 48
Onwueme, Tess Osonye 23
Orlandersmith, Dael 42

Osbey, Brenda Marie 102
Oyono, Ferdinand 38
Packer, Z. Z. 64
Page, Clarence 4
Painter, Nell Irvin 24, 88
Palmer, Everard 37
Parker, Pat 19
Parker, Star 70
Parks, Suzan-Lori 34, 85
Patton, Venetria K. 125
Payne, Ethel L. 28
Payne, Les 89
Pearson, Felicia 99
Peters, Lenrie 43
Petersen, Neal 96
Petry, Ann 19
Philip, Marlene Nourbese 32
Phillips, Carl 111
Phillips, Joseph C. 73
Piper, Adrian 71
Pitts, Leonard, Jr. 54, 85
Plaatje, Sol T. 80
Polite, Carlene Hatcher 82
Poussaint, Alvin F. 5, 67
Poussaint, Renee 78
Powell, Kevin 31, 74
Power, Will 83
Pressley, Condace L. 41
Prince, Richard E. 71
Pryce, Trevor 89
Quarles, Benjamin Arthur 18
Rahman, Aishah 37
Randall, Alice 38
Randall, Dudley 8, 55
Rapier, James T. 82
Raspberry, William 2
Reddick, Lawrence Dunbar 20
Redding, J. Saunders 26
Redmond, Eugene 23
Reed, Ishmael 8
Reid, Ira De A. 100
Rhimes, Shonda Lynn 67
Rhoden, William C. 67
Rhodes, Jewell Parker 84
Rhone, Trevor 80
Richards, Beah 30
Ridley, John 69
Riley, Rochelle 50
Ringgold, Faith 4, 81
Robertson, Gil L., IV 85
Robeson, Eslanda Goode 13
Robinson, Aminah 50
Robinson, Eugene 77
Robinson, Matt 69
Roby, Kimberla Lawson 86
Rogers, Joel Augustus 30
Rollins, Charlamae Hill 27
Rotimi, Ola 1
Rowan, Carl T. 1, 30
Ruffin, Josephine St. Pierre 75
Run 31, 73
Russwurm, John Brown 100
Rust, Art, Jr. 83
Sadlier, Rosemary 62
Saint James, Synthia 12
St. John, Kristoff 25
Salih, Al-Tayyib 37
Sanchez, Sonia 17, 51
Sanders, Dori 8
Sanneh, Kelefa 96
Sapphire 14, 95
Saro-Wiwa, Kenule 39
Shelton, Paula Young 86

Schomburg, Arthur Alfonso 9
Schuyler, George Samuel 40
Scott-Heron, Gil 94
Seale, Bobby 3
Selasi, Taiye 125
Sembène, Ousmane 13, 62
Senghor, Léopold Sédar 12, 66
Sengstacke, John 18
Senior, Olive 37
Senna, Danzy 93
Shabazz, Attallah 6
Shabazz, Ilyasah 36
Shakur, Assata 6
Shakur, Yusef 85
Shange, Ntozake 8, 89
Shaw, Bernard 2, 28
Shipp, E. R. 15
Shockley, Ann Allen 84
Simone, Nina 15, 41
Simpson, Carole 6, 30
Singletary, Mike 4, 76
Sister Souljah 11, 100
Skinner, Kiron K. 65
Smiley, Tavis 20, 68
Smith, Anna Deavere 6
Smith, B(arbara) 11
Smith, Barbara 28
Smith, Bruce W. 53
Smith, Danyel 40
Smith, Jessie Carney 35
Smith, Mary Carter 26
Smith, Stephen A. 69
Smith, Zadie 51
Snowden, Frank M., Jr. 67
Somé, Malidoma Patrice 10
Southgate, Martha 58
Sowell, Thomas 2, 99
Soyinka, Wole 4, 93
Spencer, Anne 27

Spriggs, William 67
Staples, Brent 8
Stewart, Alison 13
Stone, Chuck 9, 120
Stringer, Vickie 58
Sundiata, Sekou 66
Tademy, Lalita 36
Talbert, David E. 34, 93
Tate, Eleanora E. 20, 55
Tatum, Beverly Daniel 42, 84
Tatum, Elinor R. 78
Tatum, Wilbert 76
Taulbert, Clifton Lemoure 19
Taylor, Kristin Clark 8
Taylor, Mildred D. 26
Taylor, Susan C. 62
Taylor, Susan L. 10, 86
Teasley, Lisa 92
Terry, Bryant 128
Thomas, Michael 69
Thomas, Trisha R. 65
Thomas-Graham, Pamela 29
Thornton, Yvonne S. 69
Thurman, Howard 3
Thurston, Baratunde 79, 101
Tillis, Frederick 40
Tolson, Melvin 37
Toomer, Jean 6
Touré, Askia 47
Townsend, Robert 4
Trethewey, Natasha 103
Trotter, Monroe 9
Troupe, Quincy 83
Tucker, Cynthia 15, 61
Turner, Henry McNeal 5
Tutuola, Amos 30
Tyree, Omar Rashad 21
Tyson, Asha 39
van Sertima, Ivan 25

Vanzant, Iyanla 17, 47, 108
Vega, Marta Moreno 61
Vera, Yvonne 32
Verdelle, A. J. 26
Wade-Gayles, Gloria Jean 41
Walcott, Derek 5, 94
Walker, Alice 1, 43
Walker, Margaret 29
Walker, Rebecca 50
Walker, Teshima 114
Wallace, Michele Faith 13
Wallace, Phyllis A. 9
Walters, Ronald 83
Ward, Douglas Turner 42
Washington, Booker T. 4
Washington, Elsie B. 78
Washington, Harriet A. 69
Washington, James, Jr. 38
Washington, Laura S. 18
Washington-Williams, Essie Mae 118
Weaver, Afaa Michael 37
Weems, Renita J. 44
Wells-Barnett, Ida B. 8
Wesley, Dorothy Porter 19
Wesley, Richard 73
Wesley, Valerie Wilson 18
West, Cornel 5, 33, 80
West, Dorothy 12, 54
Whack, Rita Coburn 36
Wharton, Clifton R., Jr. 7
Whitaker, Mark 21, 47
White, Walter F. 4
Whitehead, Colson 77
Whitfield, LeRoy 84
Whitfield, Van 34
Whitlock, Jason 78
Wideman, John Edgar 5, 87
Wilbekin, Emil 63

Wiley, Ralph 8, 78
Wilkerson, Isabel 71
Wilkins, Roger 2, 84
Wilkins, Roy 4
Williams, Armstrong 29
Williams, George Washington 18
Williams, John A. 27
Williams, Juan 35, 80
Williams, Patricia 11, 54
Williams, Robert F. 11
Williams, Roy 89
Williams, Saul 31
Williams, Sherley Anne 25
Williams, Wendy 62
Wilmore, Larry 121
Wilson, August 7, 33, 55
Wilson, Mary 28
Wilson, William Julius 22
Wiwa, Ken 67
Woods, Mattiebelle 63
Woods, Scott 55
Woods, Teri 69
Woodson, Carter G. 2
Woodson, Jacqueline 125
Worrill, Conrad 12
Wright, Bruce McMarion 3, 52
Wright, Richard 5
Wright, Sarah E. 95
X, Marvin 45
Yarbrough, Camille 40
Yerby, Frank 96
Yette, Samuel F. 63
Young, Al 82
Young, Whitney M., Jr. 4
Youngblood, Shay 32
Zane 71
Zook, Kristal Brent 62

Cumulative Subject Index

Volume numbers appear in **bold**

A cappella
Cooke, Sam **17**
Fisk Jubilee Singers **112**
Ladysmith Black Mambazo **103**
Reagon, Bernice Johnson **7**
Swan Silvertones, The **110**
Sweet Honey in the Rock **106**
Take 6 **112**

AA
See Alcoholics Anonymous

AAAS
See American Association for the
Advancement of Science

AARP
Dixon, Margaret **14**
Smith, Marie F. **70**

ABC
See American Broadcasting Company

Abstract expressionism
Alston, Charles **33**
Bearden, Romare **2, 50**
Delaney, Beauford **19**
Lewis, Norman **39**
Simpson, Merton D. **110**
Thomas, Alma **14**
Woodruff, Hale **9**

Academy awards
Berry, Halle **4, 19, 57, 91**
Cara, Irene **77**
Fletcher, Geoffrey **85**
Foxx, Jamie **15, 48**
Freeman, Morgan **2, 20, 62, 100**
Goldberg, Whoopi **4, 33, 69**
Gooding, Cuba, Jr. **16, 62**
Gossett, Louis, Jr. **7**
Hancock, Herbie **20, 67**
Hayes, Isaac **20, 58, 73**
Hudson, Jennifer **63, 83**
McDaniel, Hattie **5**
Mo'Nique **35, 84**
Nyong'o, Lupita **127**
Poitier, Sidney **11, 36**
Prince **18, 65**
Richie, Lionel **27, 65, 114**
Spencer, Octavia **100**
Washington, Denzel **1, 16, 93**
Whitaker, Forest **2, 49, 67**
Williams, Russell, II **70**

Wonder, Stevie **11, 53, 121**

ACLU
See American Civil Liberties Union

**Acquired immune deficiency
syndrome (AIDS)**
Ashe, Arthur **1, 18**
Atim, Julian **66**
Broadbent, Hydeia **36**
Cargill, Victoria A. **43**
Fenton, Kevin **87**
Gayle, Helene D. **3, 46**
Hale, Lorraine **8**
Lewis-Thornton, Rae **32**
Mboup, Souleymane **10**
Moutoussamy-Ashe, Jeanne **7**
Norman, Pat **10**
Ojikutu, Bisola **65**
Okaalet, Peter **58**
Pickett, Cecil **39**
Sasser, Sean **113**
Seele, Pernessa **46**
Whitfield, LeRoy **84**
Wilson, Phill **9, 104**
Zulu, Princess Kasune **54**

Acting
Aaliyah **30**
Aaron, Quinton **82**
Abdi, Barkhad **119**
Abrahams, Zaraah **127**
Adams, Osceola Macarthy **31**
Adebimpe, Tunde **75**
Aduba, Uzo **122**
Akinnuoye-Agbaje, Adewale **56**
Aldridge, Ira **99**
Alexander, Khandi **43**
Ali, Mahershala **122**
Ali, Tatyana **73**
Allen, Debbie **13, 42**
Alonso, Laz **87**
Amos, John **8, 62**
Anderson, Anthony **51, 77**
Anderson, Carl **48**
Anderson, Eddie "Rochester" **30**
Anderson, Jacob **128**
Andrews, Tina **74**
Anthony, La La **122**
Armstrong, Vanessa Bell **24**
Ashanti **37, 96**
Avery, James **118**
Babatunde, Obba **35**
Bahati, Wambui **60**
Bailey, Pearl **14**

Baker, Josephine **3**
Banks, Michelle **59**
Barnett, Etta Moten **56**
Baskett, James **102**
Bassett, Angela **6, 23, 62**
Beach, Michael **26, 120**
Beals, Jennifer **12**
Beard, Matthew **120**
Beaton, Norman **14**
Beauvais, Garcelle **29, 95**
Belgrave, Cynthia **75**
Bennett, Louise **69**
Bentley, Lamont **53**
Berry, Fred "Rerun" **48**
Berry, Halle **4, 19, 57, 91**
Bey, Yasiin **30, 96**
Bivins, Michael **72**
Blacque, Taurean **58**
Blanks, Billy **22**
Bonet, Lisa **58**
Borders, James **9**
Boseman, Chadwick **111**
Bow Wow **35**
Boykin, Phillip **102**
Brady, Wayne **32, 71**
Branch, William Blackwell **39**
Braugher, Andre **13, 58, 91**
Bridges, Todd **37**
Brooks, Avery **9, 98**
Brooks, Danielle **119**
Brooks, Golden **62**
Brooks, Mehcad **62**
Brown, Jim **11, 95**
Browne, Roscoe Lee **66**
Byrd, Eugene **64**
Caesar, Shirley **19**
Calloway, Cab **14**
Cameron, Earl **44**
Campbell-Martin, Tisha **8, 42**
Cannon, Nick **47, 73**
Cara, Irene **77**
Carroll, Diahann **9**
Carroll, Rocky **74**
Carson, Lisa Nicole **21**
Carey, Mariah **32, 53, 69**
Cash, Rosalind **28**
Cathey, Reg E. **122**
Cedric the Entertainer **29, 60, 115**
Cheadle, Don **19, 52**
Chestnut, Morris **31, 116**
Chew, Robert F. **109**
Childress, Alice **15**
Childress, Alvin **114**
Chong, Rae Dawn **62**

Chweneyagae, Presley **63**
Clarke, Hope **14**
Cobbs, Bill **101**
Coleman, Chad L. **128**
Coleman, Gary **35, 86**
Combs, Sean **17, 43, 92**
Common **31, 63, 98**
Cooper, Chuck **75**
Cox, Laverne **122**
Crews, Terry **123**
Crothers, Scatman **19**
Curry, Mark **17**
Curtis-Hall, Vondie **17**
DaCosta, YaYa **98**
Dandridge, Dorothy **3**
Daniels, Billy **124**
David, Keith **27**
Davidson, Jaye **5**
Davis, Altovise **76**
Davis, Eisa **68**
Davis, Guy **36**
Davis, Ossie **5, 50**
Davis, Sammy, Jr. **18**
Davis, Viola **34, 76, 100**
Dawn, Marpessa **75**
Dawson, Rosario **72**
De Bankolé, Isaach **78**
De Shields, André **72**
Dee, Ruby **8, 50, 68, 122**
Devine, Loretta **24**
Diesel, Vin **29**
Diggs, Taye **25, 63**
Dixon, Ivan **69**
DMX **28, 64**
Dobson, Tamara **111**
Domingo, Colman **94**
Dorn, Michael **112**
Dourdan, Gary **37**
Duke, Bill **3, 96**
Duncan, Michael Clarke **26, 104**
Dungey, Merrin **62**
Dutton, Charles S. **4, 22**
Ejiofor, Chiwetel **67, 116**
Ejogo, Carmen **126**
Elba, Idris **49, 89, 116**
Elise, Kimberly **32, 101**
Ellis, Aunjanue **108**
Ellis, Nelsan **105**
Emmanuel, Alphonsia **38**
Epps, Mike **60**
Epps, Omar **23, 59**
Esposito, Giancarlo **9**
Everett, Francine **23**
Faison, Donald **50**

Faison, Frankie 55
Fargas, Antonio 50
Fetchit, Stepin 32
Fields, Felicia P. 60
Fields, Kim 36
Fishburne, Laurence 4, 22, 70
Fisher, Gail 85
Fox, Rick 27
Fox, Vivica A. 15, 53
Foxx, Jamie 15, 48
Foxx, Redd 2
Francis, Thais 93
Freeman, Al, Jr. 11, 105
Freeman, Morgan 2, 20, 62, 100
Freeman, Yvette 27
Gant, Richard 105
Gaye, Nona 56
Gibbs, Marla 86
Gibson, Tyrese 27, 62
Gilpin, Charles Sidney 81
Ginuwine 35
Givens, Adele 62
Givens, Robin 4, 25, 58
Glass, Ron 111
Glover, Anwan 123
Glover, Danny 1, 24, 103
Glover, Donald 85
Goldberg, Whoopi 4, 33, 69
Good, Meagan 117
Gooding, Cuba, Jr. 16, 62
Gordon, Dexter 25
Gossett, Louis, Jr. 7
Graham, Katerina 99
Grant, Micki 125
Grier, David Alan 28
Grier, Pam 9, 31, 86
Griffin, Angela 80
Guillaume, Robert 3, 48
Gunn, Moses 10
Gurira, Danai 73
Guy, Jasmine 2
Guyse, Sheila 122
Hairston, Jester 88
Hamilton, Bernie 117
Hamilton, Lawrence 122
Hamilton, Lisa Gay 71
Hamlin, Larry Leon 49, 62
Hammond, Fred 23
Hardison, Kadeem 22
Hardwick, Omari 122
Harewood, David 52
Harewood, Dorian 104
Harper, Hill 32, 65, 97
Harris, Naomie 55, 116
Harris, Robin 7
Harris, Wood 114
Harry, Jackée 111
Harvey, Steve 18, 58
Hawkins, Screamin' Jay 30
Hayes, Isaac 20, 58, 73
Haysbert, Dennis 42, 106
Hector, Jamie 98
Hemsley, Sherman 19, 104
Henry, Dwight 104
Henry, Joshua 94
Henry, Lenny 9, 52
Henson, Taraji P. 58, 77, 127
Hill, Darryl 128
Hill, Dulé 29
Hines, Gregory 1, 42
Hodge, Aldis 124
Holder, Geoffrey 78, 124
Hooks, Robert 76

Horne, Lena 5, 86
Hounsou, Djimon 19, 45
Houston, Whitney 7, 28, 83, 100
Howard, Sherri 36
Howard, Terrence 59, 94
Howell, Ayinde 91
Hudson, Ernie 72
Hudson, Jennifer 63, 83
Hughley, D. L. 23, 76
Hyman, Earle 25, 79
Ice Cube 8, 30, 60
Ice-T 6, 31, 96
Ingram, Rex 5
Jackson, Millie 25
Jackson, Samuel L. 8, 19, 63, 102
Jalade-Ekeinde, Omotola 118
James, Nikki M. 94
Jean-Baptiste, Marianne 17, 46
Jean-Louis, Jimmy 76
Jeffries, Herb 122
Johnson, Clark 96
Johnson, Rodney Van 28
Jones, James Earl 3, 49, 79
Jones, Orlando 30
Jones, Rashida 101
Jones, Robbie 113
Jordan, Michael B. 97
Jorge, Seu 73
Joseph, Paterson 126
Kelley, Elijah 65
Kelley, Malcolm David 59
Kelly, Jim 113
Kennedy-Overton, Jayne Harris 46
Khumalo, Leleti 51
Kid Cudi 83
King, Regina 22, 45
King, Woodie, Jr. 27
Kirby, George 14
Kitt, Eartha 16, 75
Knight, Gladys 16, 66
Kodjoe, Boris 34, 89
Kotto, Yaphet 7
La Salle, Eriq 12
LaBelle, Patti 13, 30
LaChanze 93
Lampley, Oni Faida 43, 71
Lane, Charles 3
Laneuville, Eric 123
Lassiter, Roy 24
Lathan, Sanaa 27
Lawrence, Martin 6, 27, 60
Le Loka, Tsidii 116
Leakes, NeNe 107
Lee, Canada 8
Lee, Joie 1
Leggs, Kingsley 62
Lemmons, Kasi 20
LeNoire, Rosetta 37
Lenox, Adriane 59
Lester, Adrian 46
Lesure, James 64
Lewis, Emmanuel 36
Lincoln, Abbey 3, 88
Lindo, Delroy 18, 45
LisaRaye 27
Lister, Tommy 127
Little, Cleavon 117
LL Cool J 16, 49, 94
Long, Nia 17, 95
Luke, Derek 61
Lumbly, Carl 47
Mabley, Jackie "Moms" 15
Mac, Bernie 29, 61, 72

Mackie, Anthony 102
Madame Sul-Te-Wan 95
Malco, Romany 71
Mann, Tamela 92
Maponya, Maishe 101
Marcille, Eva 97
Mario 71
Marrow, Queen Esther 24
Marshall, William 107
Martin, Duane 108
Martin, Helen 31
Martin, Jesse L. 31
Mayo, Whitman 32
Mbatha-Raw, Gugu 89
M.C. Hammer 20, 80
McBride, Chi 73
McClendon, Forrest 94
McClinton, Marion Isaac 77
McCrary, Darius 111
McCullough, DeAndre 106
McDaniel, Hattie 5
McDonald, Audra 20, 62, 128
McGee, Vonetta 95
McKee, Lonette 12, 119
McKinney, Nina Mae 40
McQueen, Butterfly 6, 54
Meadows, Tim 30
Mello, Breno 73
Merkerson, S. Epatha 47, 83
Michele, Michael 31
Miller, Omar Benson 93
Miller, Patina 94
Miller, Tangi 116
Miller, Wentworth 75
Mitchell, Brian Stokes 21
Mitchell, Kel 66
Mokae, Zakes 80
Mo'Nique 35, 84
Moore, Chante 26
Moore, Juanita 83, 124
Moore, Shemar 21, 112
Moreland, Mantan 117
Morgan, Tracy 61, 102
Morris, Garrett 31
Morris, Greg 28
Morton, Joe 18
Moten, Etta 18
Mowry, Tamera 79
Mowry, Tia 78
Murphy, Charles 95
Murphy, Eddie 4, 20, 61
Muse, Clarence Edouard 21
Myers, Lou 110
Nash, Johnny 40
Nash, Niecy 66, 115
Naughton, Naturi 97
Neal, Elise 29
Newton, Thandie 26, 114
Ngaujah, Sahr 86
Nicholas, Denise 82
Nicholas, Fayard 20, 57
Nicholas, Harold 20
Nichols, Nichelle 11
Norman, Maidie 20
Notorious B.I.G. 20
Ntshona, Winston 52
Nyong'o, Lupita 127
Okonedo, Sophie 67
Olagundoye, Toks 113
O'Neal, Frederick 99
O'Neal, Ron 46
O'Neal, Shaquille 8, 30, 95
Orlandersmith, Dael 42

Orman, Roscoe 55
Oyelowo, David 82, 126
Pace, Judy 119
Palmer, Keke 68, 120
Parker, Nicole Ari 52
Patterson, Chuck 124
Patton, Paula 62
Paulk, Marcus T. 127
Payne, Allen 13
Payne, Freda 58
Pearson, Felicia 99
Peete, Holly Robinson 20
Perrineau, Harold, Jr. 51
Peters, Brock 96
Peters, Clarke 103
Phifer, Mekhi 25, 103
Phillips, Joseph C. 73
Pickens, James, Jr. 59
Pierce, Wendell 90
Pinkett Smith, Jada 10, 41, 95
Plummer, Glenn 120
Poitier, Sidney 11, 36
Poitier, Sydney Tamiia 65
Porter, Billy 112
Pounder, CCH 72
Pratt, Kyla 57
Preer, Evelyn 82
Premice, Josephine 41
Pryor, Rain 65
Pryor, Richard 3, 24, 56
Queen Latifah 1, 16, 58, 119
Ralph, Sheryl Lee 18, 108
Randle, Theresa 16
Rashad, Phylicia 21
Raven-Symoné 44, 113
Ray, Gene Anthony 47
Reddick, Lance 52, 128
Reed, Natina 106
Reed Hall, Alaina 83
Reese, Della 6, 20, 96
Reid, Tim 56
Reuben, Gloria 15
Rhames, Ving 14, 50
Rhymes, Busta 31
Ribeiro, Alfonso 17
Richards, Beah 30
Richards, Lloyd 2
Richardson, LaTanya 71
Richardson, Salli 68
Riley, Amber 97
Robeson, Paul 2
Robinson, Craig 103
Robinson, Shaun 36
Rock, Chris 3, 22, 66
Rock, The 29 66
Rodgers, Rod 36
Rodrigues, Percy 68
Roker, Roxie 68
Rolle, Esther 13, 21
Rollins, Howard E., Jr. 17
Romeo 98
Rose, Anika Noni 70
Ross, Diana 8, 27
Ross, Tracee Ellis 35
Roundtree, Richard 27
Rowell, Victoria 13, 68
Rowland, Kelly 100
Rudolph, Maya 46, 106
RZA 80, 128
St. Jacques, Raymond 8
St. John, Kristoff 25
St. Louis, David 126
St. Patrick, Mathew 48

Saldana, Zoe 72, 118
Salter, Nikkole 73
Sands, Diana 87
Sanford, Isabel 53
Santiago-Hudson, Ruben 85
Scott, Hazel 66
Scott, Jill 29, 83
Shakur, Tupac 14
Short, Columbus 79
Sidibe, Gabourey 84
Simmons, Henry 55
Sinbad 1, 16
Sinclair, Madge 78
Sisqo 30
Smith, Anjela Lauren 44
Smith, Anna Deavere 6, 44
Smith, B(arbara) 11
Smith, Bubba 96
Smith, Jaden 82
Smith, Roger Guenveur 12
Smith, Tasha 73
Smith, Will 8, 18, 53
Smith, Willow 92
Snipes, Wesley 3, 24, 67
Snoop Dogg 35, 84
Sohn, Sonja 100
Sommore 61
Spencer, Octavia 100
Stewart, Tonea Harris 78
Sticky Fingaz 86
Strode, Woody 111
Sy, Omar 109
Sykes, Wanda 48, 81
Tamia 24, 55
Tate, Larenz 15
Taylor, Meshach 4
Taylor, Regina 9, 46, 97
Taylor, Ron 35
Terrence J 108
Thigpen, Lynne 17, 41
Thomas, Sean Patrick 35
Thomason, Marsha 47
Thompson, John Douglas 81
Thompson, Kenan 52
Thompson, Tazewell 13
Thoms, Tracie 61
Toivola, Jani 118
Torres, Gina 52
Torry, Guy 31
Toussaint, Lorraine 32
Townsend, Robert 4, 23
True, Rachel 82
Tucker, Chris 13, 23, 62
Tunie, Tamara 63
Turman, Glynn 100
Turner, Tina 6, 27
Tyler, Aisha N. 36
Tyson, Cicely 7, 51, 112
Uggams, Leslie 23, 114
Underwood, Blair 7, 27, 76
Union, Gabrielle 31, 92
Usher 23, 56, 95
Van Peebles, Mario 2, 51
Van Peebles, Melvin 7, 95
Vance, Courtney B. 15, 60
Vanity 67
Vereen, Ben 4
Wade, Ernestine 126
Walker, Eamonn 37
Wallis, Quvenzhané 109
Ward, Douglas Turner 42
Warfield, Marsha 2
Warfield, William 94

Warner, Malcolm-Jamal 22, 36, 110
Warren, Michael 27
Washington, Denzel 1, 16, 93
Washington, Fredi 10
Washington, Isaiah 62
Washington, Kerry 46, 107
Waters, Ethel 7
Wayans, Damon 8, 41
Wayans, Keenen Ivory 18
Wayans, Kim 80
Wayans, Marlon 29, 82
Wayans, Shawn 29
Weathers, Carl 10
Wesley, Rutina 97
Wheaton, James 103
Whitaker, Forest 2, 49, 67
White, Lillias 120
White, Michael Jai 71, 117
White, Terri 82
Whitfield, Lynn 18
Williams, Bert 18
Williams, Billy Dee 8, 105
Williams, Clarence, III 26
Williams, Joe 5, 25
Williams, Malinda 57
Williams, Michael Kenneth 97
Williams, Samm-Art 21
Williams, Saul 31
Williams, Spencer 126
Williams, Vanessa A. 32, 66
Williams, Vanessa L. 4, 17
Williamson, Fred 67
Williamson, Mykelti 22
Wilson, Chandra 57
Wilson, Debra 38
Wilson, Demond 102
Wilson, Dorien 55
Wilson, Flip 21
Winfield, Paul 2, 45
Winfrey, Oprah 2, 15, 61, 106
Withers-Mendes, Elisabeth 64
Witherspoon, John 38
Woodard, Alfre 9, 108
Woods, Renn 110
Woodson, Ali Ollie 89
Wright, Jeffrey 54, 111
Yarbrough, Cedric 51
Yoba, Malik 11
Young, Lee Thompson 114

Adoption and foster care
Clements, George 2
Hale, Clara 16
Hale, Lorraine 8
Oglesby, Zena 12
Rowell, Victoria 13, 68

Advertising
Barboza, Anthony 10
Boyd, Edward 70
Burrell, Tom 21, 51
Campbell, E. Simms 13
Chisholm, Samuel J. 32
Coleman, Donald 24, 62
Cullers, Vincent T. 49
Gaskins, Rudy 74
Green, Nancy 112
Jones, Caroline R. 29
Jordan, Montell 23
Kemp, Herb 94
Lewis, Byron E. 13
McKinney Hammond, Michelle 51
Mingo, Frank 32

Olden, Georg(e) 44
Pinderhughes, John 47
Roche, Joyce M. 17

Affirmative action
Arnwine, Barbara 28
Coleman, William T. 76
Edley, Christopher F., Jr. 48
Higginbotham, A. Leon, Jr. 13, 25
Maynard, Robert C. 7

AFL-CIO
See American Federation of Labor and Congress of Industrial Organizations

African American art
Jones, Paul R. 76
Twiggs, Leo 127
Wainwright, Joscelyn 46

African American folklore
Bailey, Xenobia 11
Brown, Sterling Allen 10, 64
Dial, Thornton 114
Driskell, David C. 7
Ellison, Ralph 7
Gaines, Ernest J. 7
Hamilton, Virginia 10
Hurston, Zora Neale 3
Lester, Julius 9, 115
Tillman, George, Jr. 20
Williams, Bert 18
Yarbrough, Camille 40

African American history
Benberry, Cuesta 65
Bennett, Lerone, Jr. 5, 84
Berry, Mary Frances 7
Blackshear, Leonard 52
Blockson, Charles L. 42
Burroughs, Margaret Taylor 9
Camp, Kimberly 19
Chase-Riboud, Barbara 20, 46
Clarke, John Henrik 20
Clayton, Mayme Agnew 62
Cobb, William Jelani 59, 121
Coombs, Orde M. 44
Cooper, Anna Julia 20
Dodson, Howard, Jr. 7, 52
Douglas, Aaron 7
DuBois, Shirley Graham 21
Dyson, Michael Eric 11, 40, 128
Feelings, Tom 11, 47
Franklin, John Hope 5, 77
Gaines, Ernest J. 7
George, Nelson 12, 101
Gill, Gerald 69
Gordon-Reed, Annette 74
Haley, Alex 4
Halliburton, Warren J. 49
Harkless, Necia Desiree 19
Harris, Richard E. 61
Hine, Darlene Clark 24
Lewis, David Levering 9
Marable, Manning 10, 102
Mason, Herman, Jr. 83
Miles, Tiya 116
Nell, William C. 128
Painter, Nell Irvin 24, 88
Pritchard, Robert Starling 21
Putney, Martha S. 75
Quarles, Benjamin Arthur 18
Richardson, Julieanna 81

Schomburg, Arthur Alfonso 9
Shadd, Abraham D. 81
Southern, Eileen 56
Tancil, Gladys Quander 59
Woodson, Carter G. 2
Yarbrough, Camille 40

African American literature
Andrews, Raymond 4
Angelou, Maya 1, 15, 122
Baisden, Michael 25, 66
Baker, Houston A., Jr. 6
Baldwin, James 1
Bambara, Toni Cade 1
Bennett, George Harold "Hal" 45
Bontemps, Arna 8
Briscoe, Connie 15
Brooks, Gwendolyn 1, 28
Brown, Claude 38
Brown, Wesley 23
Brown, William Wells 99
Burroughs, Margaret Taylor 9
Campbell, Bebe Moore 6, 24, 59
Cary, Lorene 3
Childress, Alice 15
Cleage, Pearl 17, 64
Cullen, Countee 8
Davis, Arthur P. 41
Davis, Nolan 45
Dickey, Eric Jerome 21, 56
Du Bois, W. E. B. 3
Dunbar, Paul Laurence 8
Ellison, Ralph 7
Evans, Mari 26
Fair, Ronald L. 47
Fauset, Jessie 7
Feelings, Tom 11, 47
Fisher, Rudolph 17
Ford, Nick Aaron 44
Fuller, Charles 8
Gaines, Ernest J. 7
Gates, Henry Louis, Jr. 3, 38, 67
Gayle, Addison, Jr. 41
Gibson, Donald Bernard 40
Giddings, Paula 11
Giovanni, Nikki 9, 39, 85
Goines, Donald 19
Golden, Marita 19, 99
Guy, Rosa 5
Haley, Alex 4
Hansberry, Lorraine 6
Harper, Frances Ellen Watkins 11
Heard, Nathan C. 45
Himes, Chester 8
Holland, Endesha Ida Mae 3, 57
Holmes, Shannon 70
Hughes, Langston 4
Hull, Akasha Gloria 45
Hurston, Zora Neale 3
Iceberg Slim 11
Joe, Yolanda 21
Johnson, Charles 1, 82
Johnson, James Weldon 5
Jones, Gayl 37
Jordan, June 7, 35
July, William 27
Kitt, Sandra 23
Larsen, Nella 10
Little, Benilde 21
Lorde, Audre 6
Madhubuti, Haki 7, 85
Major, Clarence 9
Marshall, Paule 7, 77

McKay, Claude 6
McKay, Nellie Yvonne 17, 57
McKinney-Whetstone, Diane 27
McMillan, Terry 4, 17, 53
McPherson, James Alan 70
Morrison, Toni 2, 15, 86
Mowry, Jess 7
Naylor, Gloria 10, 42
Patton, Venetria K. 125
Petry, Ann 19
Rahman, Aishah 37
Randall, Dudley 8, 55
Redding, J. Saunders 26
Redmond, Eugene 23
Reed, Ishmael 8
Ringgold, Faith 4, 81
Sanchez, Sonia 17, 51
Schomburg, Arthur Alfonso 9
Schuyler, George Samuel 40
Shange, Ntozake 8, 89
Smith, Mary Carter 26
Taylor, Mildred D. 26
Thomas, Trisha R. 65
Thurman, Wallace 16
Toomer, Jean 6
Tyree, Omar Rashad 21
Verdelle, A. J. 26
Villarosa, Clara 85
Walker, Alice 1, 43
Wesley, Valerie Wilson 18
Wideman, John Edgar 5, 87
Williams, John A. 27
Williams, Sherley Anne 25
Wilson, August 7, 33, 55
Wright, Richard 5
Wright, Sarah E. 95
Yarbrough, Camille 40

African American studies
Alexander, Elizabeth 75
Baszile, Jennifer 79
Brawley, Benjamin 44
Carby, Hazel 27
Christian, Barbara T. 44
De Veaux, Alexis 44
Ford, Nick Aaron 44
Hare, Nathan 44
Harris-Lacewell, Melissa 81
Henderson, Stephen E. 45
Huggins, Nathan Irvin 52
Long, Richard Alexander 65
Neal, Mark Anthony 74
Peterson, James 81
West, Cornel 5, 33, 80

African art
Simpson, Merton D. 110

African Canadian literature
Elliott, Lorris 37
Foster, Cecil 32
Senior, Olive 37

African dance
Acogny, Germaine 55
Adams, Jenoyne 60
Ailey, Alvin 8
Davis, Chuck 33
Primus, Pearl 6, 125

African history
Chase-Riboud, Barbara 20, 46
Clarke, John Henrik 20
Counter, S. Allen 74

Diop, Cheikh Anta 4
Dodson, Howard, Jr. 7, 52
DuBois, Shirley Graham 21
Feelings, Muriel 44
Halliburton, Warren J. 49
Hansberry, William Leo 11
Harkless, Necia Desiree 19
Henries, A. Doris Banks 44
Hilliard, Asa Grant, III 66
Jawara, Dawda Kairaba 11
Marshall, Paule 7, 77
van Sertima, Ivan 25

African literature
Abrahams, Peter 39
Achebe, Chinua 6, 99, 111
Aidoo, Ama Ata 38
Akpan, Uwem 70
Amadi, Elechi 40
Arac de Nyeko, Monica 66
Armah, Ayi Kwei 49
Awoonor, Kofi 37, 115
Babatunde, Rotimi 104
Bandele, Biyi 68, 121
Barrett, Lindsay 43
Beti, Mongo 36
Brutus, Dennis 38
Cartey, Wilfred 47
Cheney-Coker, Syl 43
Chikoti, Shadreck 125
Couto, Mia 45
Dadié, Bernard 34
Dathorne, O. R. 52
Ekwensi, Cyprian 37
Farah, Nuruddin 27
Gabre-Medhin, Tsegaye 64
Head, Bessie 28
Kahora, Billy 125
Kayira, Legson 40
Mazrui, Ali 12, 124
Memmi, Albert 37
Mofolo, Thomas 37
Mphalele, Es'kia 40
Mwangi, Meja 40
Ngugi wa Thiong'o 29, 61, 101
Okigbo, Christopher 102
Onwueme, Tess Osonye 23
Oyono, Ferdinand 38
Peters, Lenrie 43
Rotimi, Ola 1
Salih, Al-Tayyib 37
Saro-Wiwa, Kenule 39
Selasi, Taiye 125
Soyinka, Wole 4, 93

African Methodist Episcopal Church (AME)
Blanks, Deborah K. 69
Blow, Kurtis 31, 122
Brookins, Hamel Hartford 102
Bryant, Jamal 128
Bryant, John R. 45
Flake, Floyd H. 18, 110
Lee, Jarena 100
Loguen, J. W. 91
McKenzie, Vashti M. 29
Mudimbe, V. Y. 61
Murray, Cecil 12, 47
Roundtree, Dovey 80
Turner, Henry McNeal 5
Youngblood, Johnny Ray 8

African music
Ade, King Sunny 41
Afro, Teddy 78
Allen, Tony 117
Amadou & Mariam 113
Ashong, Derrick 86
Bassey, Offiong 119
Birra, Ali 113
Bombino 112
Chaka Chaka, Yvonne 112
Diawara, Djeli Moussa 111
Diawara, Fatoumata 114
Fela 1, 42
Keita, Salif 83
Kidjo, Angelique 50
Kolosoy, Wendo 73
Kuti, Femi 47, 110
Maal, Baaba 66
Mahlasela, Vusi 65
Makeba, Miriam 2, 50, 74
Malawi Mouse Boys 114
Nascimento, Milton 2 64
Olatunji, Babatunde 36, 126
Rochereau, Tabu Ley 117
Sangare, Oumou 18, 99
Sangho, Awa 127
Somi 85

African National Congress (ANC)
Dlamini-Zuma, Nkosazana 34, 105
Dube, John Langalibalele 119
Hani, Chris 6
Ka Dinizulu, Mcwayizeni 29
Kaunda, Kenneth 2
Kuzwayo, Ellen 68
Luthuli, Albert 13
Madikizela-Mandela, Winnie 2, 35, 112
Malema, Julius 98
Mandela, Nelson 1, 14, 77, 117
Masekela, Barbara 18
Mbeki, Govan A. 80
Mbeki, Thabo 14, 73
Mhlaba, Raymond 55
Motlanthe, Kgalema 74
Nkomo, Joshua 4, 65
Nyanda, Siphiwe 21
Nzo, Alfred 15
Ramaphosa, Cyril 3, 117
Sisulu, Albertina 57, 95
Sisulu, Walter 47
Tutu, Desmond Mpilo 6, 44
Weems, Renita J. 44
Xuma, Madie Hall 59
Zuma, Jacob 33, 75

African Union
Dlamini-Zuma, Nkosazana 34, 105
Haile Selassie 7
Kaunda, Kenneth 2
Kenyatta, Jomo 5
Nkrumah, Kwame 3
Nujoma, Samuel 10
Nyerere, Julius 5
Sassou-Nguesso, Denis 103
Touré, Sekou 6

Afro-Brazilian music
Brown, Carlinhos 81
Caymmi, Dorival 72
Gil, Gilberto 53
Jorge, Seu 73

Moura, Paulo 87

Afrocentricity
Asante, Molefi Kete 3
Biggers, John 20, 33
Diop, Cheikh Anta 4
Hansberry, William Leo 11
Sanchez, Sonia 17, 51
Turner, Henry McNeal 5

Afro-Cuban music
Lefel, Edith 41
Rodríguez, Arsenio 87
Santamaria, Mongo 81
Secada, Jon 97

Afro-Peruvian music
Baca, Susana 80

Agriculture
Allen, Will 74
Boyd, John W., Jr. 20, 72
Brown, Jason 125
Burkett, Ben 123
Carver, George Washington 4
Finley, Ron 110
Hall, Lloyd A. 8
Jones, Monty 66
Sanders, Dori 8
Wambugu, Florence 42
Washington, Karen 117

AHA
See American Heart Association

AIDS
See Acquired immune deficiency syndrome

Akron Beacon Journal
Crutchfield, James N. 55

ALA
See American Library Association

Alabama state government
Davis, Artur 41
Ford, Johnny 70
Gray, Fred 37
Rapier, James T. 82

Alcoholics Anonymous (AA)
Lucas, John 7

All Afrikan People's Revolutionary Party
Carmichael, Stokely 5, 26
Moses, Robert Parris 11

Alpha & Omega Ministry
White, Reggie 6, 50

Alpha Kappa Alpha Sorority
Quander, Nellie 102
White, Linda M. 45

Alternative music
Santigold 96

Alvin Ailey American Dance Theater
Ailey, Alvin 8
Clarke, Hope 14
Dove, Ulysses 5
Faison, George 16
Jamison, Judith 7, 67, 96
Jefferson, Denise 87

Rhoden, Dwight **40**
Richardson, Desmond **39**
Spears, Warren **52**
Tyson, Andre **40**
Williams, Dudley **60**

Ambassadors
Avant, Nicole A. **90**
Awoonor, Kofi **37, 115**
Braun, Carol Moseley **4, 42**
Carson, Johnnie **85**
Cook, Mercer **40**
Davis, Ruth **37**
Dudley, Edward R. **58**
Dymally, Mervyn **42**
Frazer, Jendayi **68**
Mbuende, Kaire **12**
Perkins, Edward **5**
Smythe Haith, Mabel **61**
Spearman, Leonard H. O., Sr. **81**
Stith, Charles R. **73**
Todman, Terence A. **55**
Watson, Diane **41**
Wharton, Clifton Reginald, Sr. **36**
Whitfield, Mal **60**

AME
See African Methodist Episcopal
Church

**American Association for the
Advancement of Science
(AAAS)**
Cobb, W. Montague **39**
Massey, Walter E. **5, 45**
Pickett, Cecil **39**

American Ballet Theatre
Copeland, Misty **125**
Dove, Ulysses **5**
Richardson, Desmond **39**

American Bar Association
Archer, Dennis **7, 36**
Pincham, R. Eugene, Sr. **69**
Thompson, Larry D. **39**
Walker, Cora T. **68**

American Book Award
Baraka, Amiri **1, 38, 118**
Bates, Daisy **13**
Bradley, David Henry, Jr. **39**
Clark, Septima **7**
Danticat, Edwidge **15, 68, 128**
Dyson, Michael Eric **11, 40, 128**
Ellis, Trey **97**
Gates, Henry Louis, Jr. **3, 38, 67**
Lorde, Audre **6**
Loury, Glenn **36**
Marshall, Paule **7, 77**
Sanchez, Sonia **17, 51**
Troupe, Quincy **83**
Walker, Alice **1, 43**

American Broadcasting Company (ABC)
Christian, Spencer **15**
Goode, Mal **13**
Martin, Michel **97**
Mickebury, Penny **28**
Reynolds, Star Jones **10, 27, 61**
Roberts, Robin **16, 54, 113**
Robinson, Max **3**

Simpson, Carole **6, 30**

**American Civil Liberties
Union (ACLU)**
Baugh, David **23**
Harris, Maya Lakshmi **88**
Murphy, Laura M. **43**
Murray, Pauli **38**
Pincham, R. Eugene, Sr. **69**

American Civil War
Augusta, Alexander T. **111**
Carney, William H. **104**

American Enterprise Institute
Woodson, Robert L. **10**

American Express Company
Adams, Eula L. **39, 120**
Chapman, Susan E. **94**
Chenault, Kenneth **4, 36, 108**
Goodman, Kim C. **94**

**American Federation of Labor
and Congress of Industrial
Organizations (AFL-CIO)**
Fletcher, Bill, Jr. **41**
Holt Baker, Arlene **73**
O'Neal, Frederick **99**
Randolph, A. Philip **3**

**American Heart Association
(AHA)**
Cooper, Edward S. **6**
Grant, Augustus O. **71**
Richardson, Donna **39**

American Idol
Barrino, Fantasia **53, 94**
Hudson, Jennifer **63, 83**
Jackson, Randy **40**

**American Library Association
(ALA)**
Franklin, Hardy R. **9, 87**
Hayden, Carla D. **47**
Jones, Clara Stanton **51**
Josey, E. J. **10**
McFadden, Bernice L. **39**
Rollins, Charlamae Hill **27**
Wedgeworth, Robert W. **42**

American Negro Theater
Martin, Helen **31**
O'Neal, Frederick **99**

American Psychological Association (APA)
Anderson, Norman B. **45**

American Red Cross
Bullock, Steve **22**
Drew, Charles Richard **7**

**American Society of Magazine
Editors**
Curry, George E. **23**

American Tennis Association
Gibson, Althea **8, 43**
Peters, Margaret and Matilda **43**

American Writers Association
Schuyler, George Samuel **40**

Amsterdam News
Bostic, Joe **95**
Burley, Dan **96**

Cooper, Andrew W. **36**
Holt, Nora **38**
Tatum, Elinor R. **78**
Tatum, Wilbert **76**

ANA
See American Nurses Association

ANC
See African National Congress

Anglican Church
Akinola, Peter Jasper **65**
Tutu, Desmond Mpilo **6, 44**

Angola government
dos Santos, José Eduardo **43, 114**
Neto, António Agostinho **43**

Anheuser-Busch distribution
Cherry, Deron **40**

Anthropology
Asante, Molefi Kete **3**
Cole, Johnnetta B. **5, 43**
Davis, Allison **12**
Diop, Cheikh Anta **4**
Dunham, Katherine **4, 59**
Hansberry, William Leo **11**
Primus, Pearl **6, 125**
Robeson, Eslanda Goode **13**
Rodriguez, Cheryl **64**

Antoinette Perry awards
See Tony awards

APA
See American Psychological Association

Apartheid
Abrahams, Peter **39**
Ashe, Arthur **18**
Biko, Steven **4**
Brutus, Dennis **38**
Butler, Jonathan **28**
Cole, Ernest **123**
Howard, M. William, Jr. **26**
Jansen, Jonathan **102**
Ka Dinizulu, Mcwayizeni **29**
Kuzwayo, Ellen **68**
LaGuma, Alex **30**
Luthuli, Albert **13**
Madikizela-Mandela, Winnie **2, 35, 112**
Mahlasela, Vusi **65**
Makeba, Miriam **2, 50, 74**
Mandela, Nelson **1, 14, 77, 117**
Maponya, Maishe **101**
Masekela, Hugh **1, 106**
Mbeki, Thabo **14, 73**
McDougall, Gay J. **11, 43**
Mhlaba, Raymond **55**
Mphalele, Es'kia **40**
Nkoli, Simon **60**
Ntshona, Winston **52**
Nyanda, Siphiwe **21**
Nzo, Alfred **15**
Plaatje, Sol T. **80**
Ramaphosa, Cyril **3, 117**
Ramphele, Mamphela **29**
Robinson, Randall **7, 46**
Sisulu, Albertina **57, 95**
Sisulu, Walter **47**
Sullivan, Leon H. **13, 30**
Tau, Mpho Parks **124**

Tutu, Desmond Mpilo **6, 44**

Apollo
Williams, O. S. **13**

Apollo Theater
Sims, Howard **48**
Sutton, Percy E. **42, 82**

Archaeology
Gilbert, John Wesley **91**
McJunkin, George **93**
Perry, Warren **56**

Architecture
Abele, Julian **55**
Adjaye, David **38, 78**
Bond, J. Max, Jr. **76**
Chase, John Saunders, Jr. **99**
Gantt, Harvey **1**
Johnson, Jeh Vincent **44**
King, Robert Arthur **58**
Lowe, Rick **124**
McKissack, Leatrice **80**
Sklarek, Norma Merrick **25, 101**
Taylor, Robert Robinson **80**
Williams, Paul R. **9**

Argonne National Laboratory
Massey, Walter E. **5, 45**
Quarterman, Lloyd Albert **4**

Ariel Capital Management
Hobson, Mellody **40**
Rogers, John W., Jr. **5, 52**

Arista Records
Reid, Antonio "L.A." **28**

Arkansas government
Elders, Joycelyn **6**

Arkansas Supreme Court
Roaf, Andrée Layton **106**

Art history
Amaki, Amalia **76**
Benjamin, Tritobia Hayes **53**
Campbell, Mary Schmidt **43**

Astronauts
Anderson, Michael P. **40**
Bluford, Guy **2, 35**
Bolden, Charles Frank, Jr. **7, 78**
Gregory, Frederick **8, 51**
Harris, Bernard A. **90**
Jemison, Mae C. **1, 35**
Lawrence, Robert H., Jr. **16**
McNair, Ronald **3, 58**
Wilson, Stephanie **72**

Astronomy
Banneker, Benjamin **93**
Pitts, Derrick **77**

Astrophysics
Alcorn, George Edward, Jr. **59**
Carruthers, George R. **40**
Walker, Arthur, II **87**

Atlanta Baptist College
See Morehouse College

Atlanta Board of Education
Mays, Benjamin E. **7**

Atlanta Braves baseball team
Aaron, Hank **5**
Jones, Andruw **98**

Justice, David 18
Lucas, Bill 97
McGriff, Fred 24

Atlanta city government
Campbell, Bill 9, 76
Franklin, Shirley 34, 80
Jackson, Maynard 2, 41
Pitts, Robb 84
Reed, Kasim 82
Williams, Hosea 15, 31, 123
Young, Andrew 3, 48, 110

Atlanta Police Department
Harvard, Beverly 11

Authors Guild
Schuyler, George Samuel 40

Authors League of America
Abrahams, Peter 39
Cotter, Joseph Seamon, Sr. 40

Automobile dealership
Farr, Mel 24
Gidron, Richard D. 68
Parker, Jim 64

Aviation
Brown, Jesse Leroy 31
Brown, Willa 40
Bullard, Eugene 12
Coleman, Bessie 9
Irving, Barrington, Jr. 112
Julian, Hubert 90
Mbabazi, Esther 122
McLeod, Gus 27
Petersen, Frank E. 31
Plinton, James O., Jr. 98
Roy, Kenny 51
Turner, Henry McNeal 5
Young, Perry H. 100

Bahamas government
Christie, Perry Gladstone 53
Pindling, Lynden 81

Ballet
Ailey, Alvin 8
Allen, Debbie 13, 42
Anderson, Lauren 72
Collins, Janet 33, 64
DePrince, Michaela 104
Dove, Ulysses 5
Faison, George 16
Jamison, Judith 7, 67, 96
Johnson, Virginia 9
Jones, Doris W. 62
Mitchell, Arthur 2, 47
Nichols, Nichelle 11
Parks, Gordon 1, 35, 58
Rhoden, Dwight 40
Richardson, Desmond 39
Rowell, Victoria 13, 68
Tyson, Andre 40

Baltimore city government
Dixon, Sheila 68
Rawlings-Blake, Stephanie 93, 128
Robinson, Bishop L. 66
Schmoke, Kurt 1, 48

Baltimore Orioles baseball team
Baylor, Don 6
Blair, Paul 36

Carter, Joe 30
Jackson, Reggie 15
Robinson, Frank 9, 87

Banking
Blaylock, Ronald 86
Boyd, T. B., III 6
Bradley, Jennette B. 40
Bridgforth, Glinda 36
Bryant, John 26
Chapman, Nathan A., Jr. 21
Chappell, Emma 18
Elumelu, Tony 116
Forte, Linda Diane 54
Funderburg, I. Owen 38
Greene, Richard Thaddeus, Sr. 67
Griffith, Mark Winston 8
Harris, Carla A. 67
Lawless, Theodore K. 8
Louis, Errol T. 8
March, William Carrington 56
McGuire, Raymond J. 57
Morgan, Rose 11
Overton, Anthony 128
Snowden, Gail 108
Taylor, Robert Rochon 104
Utendahl, John 23
Walker, Maggie Lena 17
Watkins, Donald 35
Watkins, Walter C. 24
Willie, Louis, Jr. 68
Wright, Deborah C. 25
Wright, Richard Robert, Sr. 100

Baptist
Austin, Junius C. 44
Borders, William Holmes 94
Bradley, J. Robert 65
Braxton, Brad 77
Brewster, W. Herbert 128
Butts, Calvin O., III 9, 90
Davis, Gary 41
Forbes, James A., Jr. 71
Franklin, C. L. 68
Fuller, Thomas O. 90
Gomes, Peter J. 15, 93
Hooks, Benjamin L. 2, 85
Jasper, John J. 91
Jemison, Major L. 48
Jones, Dwight C. 122
Jones, E. Edward, Sr. 45
King, Martin Luther, Sr. 89
Long, Eddie L. 29, 89
Luter, Fred, Jr. 103
Meeks, James T. 92
Moss, Otis, Jr. 72
Rogers, Alan G. 72
Sharpe, Samuel 103
Sharpton, Al 21, 97
Shuttlesworth, Fred 47, 98
Taylor, Gardner C. 76
Taylor, Lonzie Odie 96
Thurston, Stephen J. 49
Walker, Lucius, Jr. 88
Walker, Wyatt Tee 80
Yates, Jack 114
Yergan, Max 123

Barbados government
Adams, Grantley 82
Arthur, Owen 33

Baseball
Aaron, Hank 5
Allen, Dick 85

Anderson, Elmer 25
Ashford, Emmett 22
Baines, Harold 32
Baker, Dusty 8, 43, 72, 110
Banks, Ernie 33, 126
Barnhill, David 30
Baylor, Don 6
Bell, James "Cool Papa" 36
Belle, Albert 10
Black, Joe 75
Blair, Paul 36
Blue, Vida 122
Bonds, Barry 6, 34, 63, 99
Bonds, Bobby 43
Brock, Lou 18
Brown, Raymond 102
Brown, Willard 36
Burke, Glenn 122
Byrd, Marlon 112
Cabell, Enos 102
Cain, Lorenzo 128
Campanella, Roy 25
Cano, Robinson 97
Carew, Rod 20
Carter, Joe 30
Cepeda, Orlando 98
Charleston, Oscar 39
Clendenon, Donn 26, 56
Coleman, Leonard S., Jr. 12
Coleman, Vince 128
Cooper, Andy "Lefty" 63
Cottrell, Comer 11
Crawford, Carl 90
Crisp, Coco 109
Dandridge, Ray 36
Davis, Eric 116
Davis, Piper 19
Dawson, Andre 85
Day, Leon 39
Dihigo, Martín 103
Doby, Lawrence Eugene, Sr. 16
Dye, Jermaine 58
Ellis, Dock 78
Everett, Carl 103
Fielder, Cecil 2, 112
Fielder, Prince 68
Flood, Curt 10, 93
Foster, Andrew 79
Fuentes, Tito 123
Gamble, Oscar 113
Gaston, Cito 71
Gibson, Bob 33
Gibson, Josh 22
Gilliam, Jim 122
Glanville, Douglas Metunwa 82
Gooden, Dwight 20
Granderson, Curtis 66
Grant, Frank 100
Gregg, Eric 16
Griffey, Ken, Jr. 12, 73
Gwynn, Tony 18, 83, 122
Hairston, Sam 88
Henderson, Rickey 28, 78
Hernández, Orlando 96
Horton, Willie 104
Howard, Elston 125
Howard, Ryan 65, 113
Hunter, Torii 43, 109
Hyde, Cowan F. "Bubba" 47
Irvin, Monte 31
Jackson, Reggie 15
Jenkins, Fergie 46
Jeter, Derek 27, 93, 124

Johnson, Clifford "Connie" 52
Johnson, Judy 105
Johnson, Mamie "Peanut" 40
Jones, Adam 114
Jones, Andruw 98
Justice, David 18
Kaiser, Cecil 42
Kimbro, Henry A. 25
Lacy, Sam 30, 46
Lankford, Ray 23
Larkin, Barry 24
Lloyd, John Henry "Pop" 30
Lofton, Kenny 12
Lopes, Davey 92
Lucas, Bill 97
Mackey, Biz 82
Manuel, Jerry 94
Mariner, Jonathan 41
Marte, Starling 117
Martínez, Pedro 81, 126
Maye, Lee 111
Mays, Willie 3
McClendon, Lloyd 123
McCovey, Willie 103
McCutchen, Andrew 116
McGriff, Fred 24
McRae, Hal 84
Minoso, Minnie 89, 127
Morgan, Joe 9, 96
Murray, Eddie 12
Newcombe, Don 24
Nixon, Otis 111
O'Neil, Buck 19, 59
Ortiz, David 52, 82
Paige, Satchel 7
Perez, Pascual 108
Phillips, Brandon 116
Pineda, Michael 121
Porter, Bo 123
Price, David 101
Pride, Charley 26
Puckett, Kirby 4, 58
Puig, Yasiel 113
Radcliffe, Ted 74
Raines, Tim 107
Randolph, Willie 53
Reagins, Tony 94
Reese, Pokey 28
Reynolds, Harold 77
Rice, Jim 75
Richard, J. R. 87
Robinson, Frank 9, 87
Robinson, Jackie 6
Robinson, Sharon 22
Rollins, Jimmy 70
Roseboro, John 123
Sabathia, CC 74
Sanders, Deion 4, 31, 96
Scott, George 113
Sheffield, Gary 16, 108
Sizemore, Grady 96
Smith, Hilton 29
Smith, Lee 101
Smith, Ozzie 77
Smith, Reggie 113
Sosa, Sammy 21, 44
Stargell, Willie 29
Stearnes, Norman "Turkey" 31
Stewart, Dave 117
Stone, Toni 15
Strawberry, Darryl 22
Suttles, Mule 108
Thomas, Frank 12, 51

Tiant, Luis 102
Trouppe, Quincy Thomas, Sr. 84
Upton, Justin 124
Upton, Melvin, Jr. 124
Uribe, Juan 122
Vaughn, Mo 16
Virgil, Ozzie 48
Washington, Ron 119
Watson, Bob 25
Wells, Vernon 91
Wells, Willie 105
White, Bill 1, 48
White, Frank 95
Whitney, Davey L. 110
Williams, Bernie 128
Williams, Billy 86
Williams, Ken 68
Willis, Dontrelle 55
Wills, Maury 73
Winfield, Dave 5, 91

Baseball Hall of Fame
Banks, Ernie 33, 126
Bell, James "Cool Papa" 36
Brown, Raymond 102
Brown, Willard 36
Campanella, Roy 25
Cepeda, Orlando 98
Charleston, Oscar 39
Dandridge, Ray 36
Dawson, Andre 85
Day, Leon 39
Dihigo, Martín 103
Doby, Lawrence Eugene, Sr. 16, 41
Foster, Andrew 79
Gibson, Josh 22
Gwynn, Tony 18, 83, 122
Henderson, Rickey 28, 78
Irvin, Monte 31
Johnson, Judy 105
Leonard, Buck 67
Lloyd, John Henry "Pop" 30
Mackey, Biz 82
Martínez, Pedro 81, 126
McCovey, Willie 103
Morgan, Joe 9, 96
Paige, Satchel 7
Rice, Jim 75
Robinson, Frank 9, 87
Robinson, Jackie 6
Smith, Hilton 29
Smith, Ozzie 77
Stearnes, Norman "Turkey" 31
Wells, Willie 105
Williams, Billy 86
Winfield, Dave 5, 91

Basket making
Jackson, Mary 73

Basketball
Abdul-Jabbar, Kareem 8
Abdur-Rahim, Shareef 28
Aldridge, LaMarcus 125
Allen, Ray 82
Amaker, Tommy 62
Anderson, Mike 63
Anthony, Carmelo 46, 94
Archibald, Tiny 90
Arenas, Gilbert 84
Artest, Ron 52
Barkley, Charles 5, 66
Barksdale, Don 103
Baylor, Elgin 93

Beaty, Zelmo 115
Bellamy, Walt 119
Bing, Dave 3, 59, 78
Bogues, Tyrone "Muggsy" 56
Bol, Manute 1
Bolton-Holifield, Ruthie 28
Bosh, Chris 85
Brand, Elton 31
Brandon, Terrell 16
Brown, Mike 77, 107
Bryant, Kobe 15, 31, 71, 110
Bynoe, Peter C. B. 40
Carter, Butch 27
Carter, Kenneth 53
Carter, Vince 26
Catchings, Tamika 43
Chalmers, Mario 122
Chamberlain, Wilt 18, 47
Chandler, Tyson 114
Chaney, Don 98
Chaney, John 67
Cheeks, Maurice 47, 106
Clifton, Nathaniel "Sweetwater" 47
Collins, Jason 111
Cooper, Charles "Chuck" 47
Cooper, Michael 31
Cooper, Tarzan 96
Cooper-Dyke, Cynthia 17, 89
Corbin, Tyrone 126
Cousins, DeMarcus 108
Curry, Dell 126
Curry, Michael 85
Curry, Stephen 110
Daniels, Mel 106
Dantley, Adrian 72
Davis, Anthony 120
Davis, Mike 41
DeRozan, DeMar 125
Diaw, Boris 122
Douglas, Bob 96
Drexler, Clyde 4, 61
Dumars, Joe 16, 65, 126
Duncan, Tim 20, 91
Dunn, Jerry 27
Durant, Kevin 76, 107
Edwards, Teresa 14, 95
Ellerbe, Brian 22
Elliott, Sean 26
Erving, Julius 18, 47
Ewing, Patrick 17, 73
Fisher, Derek 97
Fox, Rick 27
Frazier, Walt 91
Freeman, Marianna 23
Gaines, Clarence E., Sr. 55
Garnett, Kevin 14, 70, 118
Gates, William 97
Gentry, Alvin 23
George, Paul 124
Gilmore, Artis 101
Gourdine, Simon 11
Gray, Yeshimbra "Shimmy" 55
Green, A. C. 32
Green, Draymond 126
Greer, Hal 92
Griffin, Blake 98
Griffith, Yolanda 25
Griner, Brittney 128
Hamilton, Leonard 100
Hardaway, Anfernee 13, 111
Hardaway, Tim 35
Harden, James 116
Harris-Stewart, Lusia 90

Haskins, Clem 23
Hawkins, Connie 91
Hayes, Elvin 93
Haynes, Marques 22
Haywood, Spencer 99
Hazzard, Walt 98
Heard, Gar 25
Hill, Grant 13, 94
Holdsclaw, Chamique 24, 110
Holiday, Jrue 115
Horford, Al 107
Howard, Dwight 113
Howard, Juwan 15
Hudson, Lou 121
Hunter, Billy 22, 109
Hunter, Lindsey 110
Irving, Kyrie 102
Isaacs, John 76
Iverson, Allen 24, 46
Jackson, Mark 121
Jackson, Stephen 118
James, LeBron 46, 78, 105
Johnson, Avery 62
Johnson, Dennis 89
Johnson, Gus 92
Johnson, Joe 94
Johnson, Kevin 70
Johnson, Larry 28
Johnson, Magic 3, 39, 101
Jones, K. C. 83
Jones, Merlakia 34
Jones, Robbie 113
Jones, Roy, Jr. 22
Jones, Sam 85
Jordan, Eddie 83
Jordan, Michael 6, 21
Joyce, Dru 81
Justice, David 18
Kellogg, Clark 64
Kidd, Jason 86
Lanier, Bob 47
Lennox, Betty 31
Leonard, Kawhi 122
Leslie, Lisa 16, 73
Lillard, Damian 117
Lloyd, Earl 26, 127
Lowe, Sidney 64
Lucas, John 7
Mahorn, Rick 60
Malone, Karl 18, 51, 90
Malone, Moses 79
Manigault, Earl "The Goat" 15
Martin, Cuonzo 121
Mason, Anthony 128
Mason, Desmond 127
McAdoo, Bob 75
McGrady, Tracy 80
McLendon, John B., Jr. 89
Meminger, Dean 114
Miller, Cheryl 10, 74
Milton, DeLisha 31
Mitchell, Sam 82
Mohammed, Nazr 64
Monroe, Earl 89
Mourning, Alonzo 17, 44
Mutombo, Dikembe 7, 107
Odom, Lamar 81
Olajuwon, Hakeem 2, 72
O'Neal, Shaquille 8, 30, 95
Palmer, Violet 59
Parish, Robert 43
Parker, Candace 74
Parker, Tony 75

Paul, Chris 84, 100
Payton, Gary 99
Peck, Carolyn 23
Phillips, Teresa L. 42
Pierce, Paul 71
Pippen, Scottie 15, 89
Porter, Terry 75
Prince, Tayshaun 68
Reed, Willis, Jr. 86
Richardson, Nolan 9
Richmond, Mitch 19
Rivers, Doc 25, 81
Robertson, Oscar 26
Robinson, Craig 107
Robinson, David 24, 90
Robinson, Flynn 112
Robinson, Will 51, 69
Rodman, Dennis 12, 44, 96, 118
Rogers, Rodney Ray 106
Rondo, Rajon 111
Rose, Derrick 82
Rose, Jalen 108
Roundfield, Danny 109
Roy, Brandon 98
Russell, Bill 8
Sanders, Satch 77
Scott, Byron 125
Sealy, Malik 118
Sefolosha, Thabo 121
Shaw, Brian 127
Sidat-Singh, Wilmeth 116
Silas, Paul 24
Smith, Kenny 114
Smith, Randy 81
Smith, Stephen A. 69
Smith, Tubby 18, 83
Sprewell, Latrell 23
Stackhouse, Jerry 30
Staley, Dawn 57
Stephenson, Lance 118
Stith, Tom 93
Stoudemire, Amar'e 59, 106
Stringer, C. Vivian 13, 66
Swoopes, Sheryl 12, 56
Tatum, Reec'e 104
Temple, Collis, Jr. 119
Thabeet, Hasheem 123
Thomas, Isiah 7, 26, 65
Thompson, Klay 126
Thompson, Mychal 126
Thompson, Tina 25, 75
Thurmond, Nate 88
Tisdale, Wayman 50
Ujiri, Masai 107
Unseld, Wes 23
Ussery, Terdema, II 29
Vaughn, Jacque 127
Wade, Dwyane 61, 103
Walker, Chet 106
Wallace, Ben 54
Wallace, Perry E. 47
Wallace, Rasheed 56
Washington, Ora Mae 115
Webber, Chris 15, 30, 59, 118
Westbrook, Russell 116
White, Jo Jo 112
Whiteside, Hassan 127
Whitney, Davey L. 110
Wiggins, Andrew 128
Wilkens, Lenny 11, 88
Williams, Deron 92
Williams, Monty 125
Williams, Natalie 31

Woodard, Lynette 67
Woodson, Mike 78
Worthy, James 49

Basketball Hall of Fame
Abdul-Jabbar, Kareem 8
Archibald, Tiny 90
Barkley, Charles 5, 66
Barksdale, Don 103
Baylor, Elgin 93
Bellamy, Walt 119
Bing, Dave 3, 59, 78
Boozer, Bob 103
Chamberlain, Wilt 18, 47
Chaney, John 67
Cooper, Tarzan 96
Cooper-Dyke, Cynthia 17, 89
Daniels, Mel 106
Dantley, Adrian 72
Douglas, Bob 96
Drexler, Clyde 4, 61
Dumars, Joe 16, 65, 126
Edwards, Teresa 14, 95
Ewing, Patrick 17, 73
Frazier, Walt 91
Gaines, Clarence E., Sr. 55
Gates, William 97
Gervin, George 80
Gilmore, Artis 101
Greer, Hal 92
Harris-Stewart, Lusia 90
Hawkins, Connie 91
Hayes, Elvin 93
Haynes, Marques 22
Johnson, Dennis 89
Johnson, Gus 92
Johnson, Magic 3, 39, 101
Jones, K. C. 83
Jones, Sam 85
Lanier, Bob 47
Lloyd, Earl 26, 127
Malone, Karl 18, 51, 90
Malone, Moses 79
McAdoo, Bob 75
McLendon, John B., Jr. 89
Miller, Cheryl 10, 74
Monroe, Earl 89
Olajuwon, Hakeem 2, 72
Parish, Robert 43
Pippen, Scottie 15, 89
Reed, Willis, Jr. 86
Robertson, Oscar 26
Robinson, David 24, 90
Rodman, Dennis 12, 44, 96, 118
Russell, Bill 8
Sanders, Satch 77
Thomas, Isiah 7, 26, 65
Thurmond, Nate 88
Unseld, Wes 23
Walker, Chet 106
Wilkens, Lenny 11, 88
Wilkins, Dominique 74
Woodard, Lynette 67
Worthy, James 49

Bass
Blanton, Jimmy 108
Burbridge, Oteil 120
Carter, Ron 104
Chambers, Paul 121
Clarke, Stanley 115
Counce, Curtis 127
Foster, George "Pops" 40

Grimes, Henry 124
Isley, Marvin 87
Jamerson, James 59
McBee, Cecil 123
Moffett, Charnett 127
Page, Walter 117
Parham, Truck 124
Pettiford, Oscar 106
Stewart, Slam 126
Tacuma, Jamaaladeen 124
Towles, Nat 128
Vinnegar, Leroy 124
Warren, Butch 116
Wright, Eugene 125

BBC
See British Broadcasting Company

Beatrice International
See TLC Beatrice International
   Holdings, Inc.

Beauty salons and products
Cottrell, Comer 11
Fine, Sam 60
Fuller, S. B. 13
Gardner, Edward G. 45
Gibson, Ted 66
Johnson, George E. 29
Johnson, William 91
Joyner, Marjorie Stewart 26
Malone, Annie 13
Price, Lisa 97
Roche, Joyce M. 17
Stanford, Olivia Lee Dilworth 49
Walker, Madame C. J. 7

Bebop
Carter, Betty 19
Clarke, Kenny 27
Coltrane, John 19
Dameron, Tadd 103
Davis, Miles 4
Eckstine, Billy 28
Fitzgerald, Ella 8, 18
Freeman, Von 104
Gillespie, Dizzy 1
Gordon, Dexter 25
Hancock, Herbie 20, 67
Harris, Barry 68
Hawkins, Coleman 9
Jackson, Milt 26
McGhee, Howard 122
Navarro, Fats 104
Parker, Charlie 20
Powell, Bud 24
Roach, Max 21, 63
Vaughan, Sarah 13

Ben & Jerry's Homemade Ice Cream, Inc.
Holland, Robert, Jr. 11

Benin government
Kerekou, Ahmed 1
Soglo, Nicéphore 15
Yayi, Boni T. 84

Bermuda government
Gordon, Pamela 17

BET
See Black Entertainment Television

Bethune-Cookman College
Bethune, Mary McLeod 4

Big Easy Award
Adams, Johnny 39

Bill and Melinda Gates Foundation
Golston, Allan C. 55

Biology
Cobb, Jewel Plummer 42
Crouch, Hubert 95
Emeagwali, Dale 31
Jarvis, Erich 67
Malveaux, Floyd 54
Pickett, Cecil 39

Biotechnology
Dabiri, John 93
Donald, Arnold 36, 126
Haynie, Sharon 94
Juma, Calestous 57
Uys, Ashley 125
Wambugu, Florence 42

Birmingham (AL) city government
Arrington, Richard 24, 100
Bell, William A., Sr. 122
Kincaid, Bernard 28
Langford, Larry P. 74
Nunn, Annetta 43

Birmingham (AL) Police Department
Nunn, Annetta 43
Woods, Abraham, Jr. 74

Bishop College
Cottrell, Comer 11

Black Alliance for Educational Options
Fuller, Howard L. 37

Black American West Museum
Stewart, Paul Wilbur 12

Black arts movement
Baraka, Amiri 1, 38, 118
Barrett, Lindsay 43
Caldwell, Benjamin 46
Cornish, Sam 50
Cortez, Jayne 43, 109
Cortor, Eldzier 42
Cruse, Harold 54
Dent, Thomas C. 50
Donaldson, Jeff 46
Dumas, Henry 41
Gayle, Addison, Jr. 41
Giovanni, Nikki 9, 39, 85
Henderson, David 53
Hoagland, Everett H. 45
Neal, Larry 38
Pomare, Eleo 72
Sebree, Charles 40
Smith, Vincent D. 48
Touré, Askia 47
X, Marvin 45

Black Coaches Association (BCA)
Freeman, Marianna 23
Keith, Floyd A. 61

Black Consciousness movement
Biko, Steven 4
Fanon, Frantz 44

Fuller, Hoyt 44
Muhammad, Elijah 4
Ramphele, Mamphela 29

***Black Enterprise* magazine**
Graves, Butch 77
Graves, Earl G. 1, 35
Wallace, Phyllis A. 9

Black Entertainment Television (BET)
Gordon, Ed 10, 53
Greely, M. Gasby 27
Holmes, T. J. 98
Johnson, Robert L. 3, 39, 121
Johnson, Sheila Crump 48
Jones, Bobby 20, 94
Lee, Debra L. 62
McCrary Anthony, Crystal 70
Rolle, Janet 97
Smiley, Tavis 20, 68

Black Filmmakers Hall of Fame
Barnett, Etta Moten 18, 56
Blake, Eubie 29
Browne, Roscoe Lee 66
Carroll, Diahann 9
Carter, Benny 46
Cash, Rosalind 28
Crothers, Scatman 19
Davis, Sammy, Jr. 18
de Passe, Suzanne 25
Dee, Ruby 8, 50, 68, 122
Dixon, Ivan 69
Dunham, Katherine 4, 59
Fetchit, Stepin 32
Glover, Danny 1, 24, 103
Greaves, William 38, 123
Johnson, Hall 90
Lincoln, Abbey 3, 88
Madame Sul-Te-Wan 95
McDaniel, Hattie 5
McKinney, Nina Mae 40
McQueen, Butterfly 6, 54
Micheaux, Oscar 7
Miles, William 112
Muse, Clarence Edouard 21
Nicholas, Fayard 20, 57, 61
Nicholas, Harold 20
Norman, Maidie 20
Parks, Gordon 1, 35, 58
Peters, Brock 96
Poitier, Sidney 11, 36
Robeson, Paul 2
Schultz, Michael A. 6
Tyson, Cicely 7, 51, 112
Van Peebles, Melvin 7, 95
Washington, Fredi 10
Williams, Billy Dee 8, 105
Wilson, August 7, 33, 55

Black History Month
Woodson, Carter G. 2

Black nationalism
Caldwell, Benjamin 46
Carmichael, Stokely 5, 26
Cuffe, Paul 98
Donaldson, Jeff 46
Farrakhan, Louis 2
Forman, James 7, 51
Garvey, Marcus 1
Heard, Nathan C. 45

Innis, Roy **5**
Muhammad, Elijah **4**
Obadele, Imari **84**
Turner, Henry McNeal **5**
X, Malcolm **1**
York, Dwight D. **71**

Black Panther Party (BPP)
Abu-Jamal, Mumia **15**
Al-Amin, Jamil Abdullah **6**
bin Wahad, Dhoruba **85**
Brown, Elaine **8**
Carmichael, Stokely **5**
Cleaver, Eldridge **5**
Cleaver, Kathleen Neal **29**
Coates, Ta-Nehisi **76**
Cox, Donald Lee **93**
Davis, Angela **5, 114**
Douglas, Emory **89**
Forman, James **7, 51**
Hampton, Fred **18**
Hilliard, David **7, 105**
Jackson, George Lester **14**
Joseph, Jamal **101**
Kimbro, Warren **76**
Neal, Larry **38**
Newton, Huey **2**
Pratt, Geronimo **18, 95**
Rush, Bobby **26, 76**
Seale, Bobby **3**
Shakur, Afeni **67**
Shakur, Assata **6**

Black Power movement
Al-Amin, Jamil Abdullah **6**
Brown, Elaine **8**
Carmichael, Stokely **5, 26**
Dodson, Howard, Jr. **7, 52**
Donaldson, Jeff **46**
Dumas, Henry **41**
Hare, Nathan **44**
McKissick, Floyd B. **3**

Black Think Tank
Hare, Nathan **44**

Blackvoices.com
Cooper, Barry **33**

Black World magazine
See *Negro Digest* magazine

Blogging
Contee, Cheryl **88**

Blues
Ace, Johnny **36**
Aces, The **117**
Allison, Luther **111**
Amy, Curtis **114**
Arnold, Billy Boy **112**
Arnold, Kokomo **116**
Austin, Lovie **40**
Barnes, Roosevelt "Booba" **33**
Bell, Carey **114**
Bibb, Eric **49, 123**
Big Maybelle **117**
Bland, Bobby **36, 113**
Bombino **112**
Brim, John **117**
Broonzy, Big Bill **82**
Brown, Charles **23**
Brown, Nappy **73**
Burbridge, Kofi **120**
Burns, Eddie **44**

Burnside, R. L. **56**
Carr, Leroy **49**
Chambers Brothers, The **116**
Clark, Sharón **105**
Clarke, Kenny **27**
Clayton, Doctor **120**
Collins, Albert **12**
Copeland, Johnny **110**
Copeland, Shemekia **110**
Cotton, James **123**
Cox, Ida **42**
Cray, Robert **30**
Crudup, Arthur **115**
Davis, Gary **41**
Davis, Guy **36**
Davis, Tyrone **54**
Dawkins, Jimmy **111**
Dixon, Willie **4**
Dorsey, Thomas **15**
Edwards, David **122**
Estes, Sleepy John **33**
Évora, Cesária **12, 99**
Ford, T-Model **91, 113**
Freeman, Yvette **27**
Fuller, Blind Boy **86**
Fulson, Lowell **118**
Gaines, Grady **38**
Guitar Slim **125**
Guy, Buddy **31**
Handy, W. C. **8**
Harris, Corey **39, 73**
Harris, Wynonie **102**
Hegamin, Lucille **120**
Hemphill, Jessie Mae **33, 59**
Holiday, Billie **1**
Homesick James **124**
Hooker, John Lee **30**
Hopkins, Lightnin' **83**
House, Son **8**
Howlin' Wolf **9**
Humes, Helen **128**
Hunter, Alberta **42**
Hurt, Mississippi John **84**
Jackson, John **36**
James, Elmore **114**
James, Skip **38**
Jefferson, Blind Lemon **81**
Johnson, Buddy **36**
Johnson, Lonnie **85**
Johnson, Syl **97**
Johnson, Tommy **106**
Keb' Mo' **36, 124**
King, B. B. **7**
King, Chris Thomas **120**
King, Freddie **92**
Kirkland, Eddie **99**
LaVette, Bettye **85**
Leadbelly **82**
Lenoir, J. B. **117**
Lipscomb, Mance **49**
Little Milton **36**
Little Walter **36**
Lockwood, Robert, Jr. **120**
Magic Slim **110**
Mahal, Taj **39**
Martin, Sara **38**
McCracklin, Jimmy **108**
McGriff, Jimmy **72**
McShann, Jay **110**
McTell, Blind Willie **89**
Memphis Slim **105**
Merriweather, Big Maceo **109**
Mississippi Sheiks **122**

Montgomery, Little Brother **117**
Moore, Johnny B. **38**
Murphy, Matt **117**
Muse, Clarence Edouard **21**
Neal, Kenny **123**
Neal, Raful **44, 121**
Nighthawk, Robert **121**
Odetta **37, 74**
Owens, Jack **38**
Parker, Charlie **20**
Parker, Junior **116**
Patton, Charley **107**
Peebles, Ann **114**
Pena, Paul **58**
Perkins, Pinetop **70**
Peterson, James **38**
Professor Longhair **109**
Pryor, Snooky **119**
Rawls, Lou **17, 57**
Reed, A. C. **36**
Reed, Jimmy **38**
Robinson, Fenton **38**
Rogers, Jimmy **38**
Ross, Isaiah "Doc" **40**
Rush, Bobby **78**
Rush, Otis **38**
Seals, Son **56**
Shines, Johnny **116**
Slim Harpo **120**
Smith, Bessie **3**
Smith, Clarence **113**
Smith, Mamie **32**
Smith, Trixie **34**
Spann, Otis **107**
Spivey, Victoria **119**
Stackhouse, Houston **122**
Streeter, Sarah **45**
Sumlin, Hubert **101**
Sunnyland Slim **118**
Sykes, Roosevelt **20**
Tail Dragger **112**
Tampa Red **63**
Taylor, Eddie **116**
Taylor, Hound Dog **120**
Taylor, Koko **40, 80**
Terry, Sonny **88**
Thomas, Tabby **119**
Tucker, Tommy **127**
Turner, Big Joe **92**
Turner, Ike **68**
Walker, Joe Louis **118**
Walker, T-Bone **111**
Wallace, Sippie **1**
Washington, Dinah **22**
Waters, Ethel **7**
Waters, Muddy **34**
Watson, Johnny "Guitar" **18**
Webster, Katie **29**
Wellington, Valerie **118**
Wells, Junior **102**
White, Bukka **120**
White, Josh, Jr. **52**
Williams, Jody **113**
Williams, Joe **5, 25**
Williamson, Sonny Boy **84**
Witherspoon, Jimmy **113**
Young, Johnny **120**

Blues Hall of Fame
Allison, Luther **111**
Bland, Bobby **36, 113**
Broonzy, Big Bill **82**
Cotton, James **123**

Crudup, Arthur **115**
Edwards, David **122**
Fulson, Lowell **118**
Guitar Slim **125**
Hopkins, Lightnin' **83**
Hunter, Alberta **42**
Hurt, Mississippi John **84**
Lenoir, J. B. **117**
Little Milton **36**
Lockwood, Robert, Jr. **120**
Nighthawk, Robert **121**
Parker, Junior **116**
Shines, Johnny **116**
Slim Harpo **120**
Sunnyland Slim **118**
Taylor, Eddie **116**
Taylor, Hound Dog **120**
Walker, Joe Louis **118**
White, Bukka **120**
Williamson, Sonny Boy **84**

Bobsledding
Flowers, Vonetta **35**
Hines, Garrett **35**
Jones, Randy **35**
Moses, Edwin **8**
Williams, Lauryn **58, 127**

Bodybuilding
Haney, Lee **77**
Murray, Lenda **10**

Boeing Company, The
Bell, James A. **50**
Grooms, Henry R(andall) **50**
Mills, Joseph C. **51**
Robinson-Berry, Joan **94**

Boogie-woogie music
Brooks, Hadda **40**
Smith, Clarence **113**

Boston Celtics basketball team
Allen, Ray **82**
Chaney, Don **98**
Cooper, Charles "Chuck" **47**
Fox, Rick **27**
Parish, Robert **43**
Pierce, Paul **71**
Rivers, Doc **25, 81**
Russell, Bill **8**
Sanders, Satch **77**
Silas, Paul **24**
White, Jo Jo **112**

Boston Red Sox baseball team
Baylor, Don **6**
Martínez, Pedro **81, 126**
Ortiz, David **52, 82**
Rice, Jim **75**
Tiant, Luis **102**
Vaughn, Mo **16**

Botswana government
Khama, Ian **95**
Masire, Quett **5**
Mogae, Festus Gontebanye **19, 79**

Bowling
Branham, George, III **50**
Terrell-Kearney, Kim **83**

Boxing
Ali, Laila **27, 63**
Ali, Muhammad **2, 16, 52**

Armstrong, Henry 104
Bowe, Riddick 6, 107
Bozella, Dewey 97
Broner, Adrien 109
Carter, Rubin 26, 121
Charles, Ezzard 95
DeGale, James 74
Dixon, George 52
Dokes, Michael 105
Douglas, Buster 127
Ellis, Jimmy 44, 127
Foreman, George 1, 15
Forrest, Vernon 40, 79
Frazier, Joe 19, 98
Frazier-Lyde, Jacqui 31
Futch, Eddie 33
Gans, Joe 91
Gibson, Truman K., Jr. 60
Griffith, Emile 113
Hagler, Marvelous Marvin 102
Haye, David 82
Hearns, Thomas 29
Holmes, Larry 20, 68
Holyfield, Evander 6
Hopkins, Bernard 35, 69, 105
Johnson, Jack 8
Jones, Roy, Jr. 22
King, Don 14, 128
Lee, Canada 8
Leonard, Sugar Ray 15
Lewis, Butch 71, 99
Lewis, Lennox 27
Louis, Joe 5
Lyle, Ron 125
Mayweather, Floyd 57, 104
Moore, Archie 120
Moore, Davey 105
Moorer, Michael 19
Mosley, Shane 32
Muhammad, Jabir Herbert 72
Mundine, Anthony 56
Norton, Ken 101, 115
Page, Greg 78
Patterson, Floyd 19, 58
Perkins, Eddie 103
Robinson, Sugar Ray 18
Rose, Lionel 56
Savón, Félix 105
Shavers, Earnie 127
Stevenson, Teófilo 103
Steward, Emanuel 18, 106
Stiverne, Bermane 128
Tate, John 107
Taylor, Jermain 60
Terrell, Ernie 118
Toney, James 89
Tyson, Mike 28, 44, 93
Walcott, Jersey Joe 102
Ward, Andre 62
Weaver, Mike 109
Whitaker, Pernell 10, 89
Wilder, Deontay 121
Wills, Harry 80
Wolfe, Ann 82
Wright, Chalky 103
Young, Jimmy 54

Boys Choir of Harlem
Turnbull, Walter 13, 60

BPP
See Black Panther Party

Brazil government
da Silva, Benedita 5
Nascimento, Abdias do 93
Silva, Marina 80

Breast cancer awareness
Brown, Zora Kramer 12
Norton, Meredith 72
Riperton, Minnie 32

British Broadcasting Company (BBC)
Armah, Esther 87
Figueroa, John J. 40
Stuart, Moira 82

British Film Institute
Akomfrah, John 37

British government
Abbott, Diane 9
Amos, Valerie 41
Boateng, Paul Yaw 56
Grant, Bernie 57
King, Oona 27
Pitt, David Thomas 10

British Virgin Islands government
Stoutt, H. Lavity 83

Broadcasting
Abudu, Mo 121
Allen, Byron 3, 24, 97
Ashley, Maurice 15, 47
Bettis, Jerome 64
Blackmon, Brenda 58
Bostic, Joe 95
Bradley, Ed 2, 59
Branch, William Blackwell 39
Brown, Les 5
Brown, Tony 3
Brown, Vivian 27
Brunson, Dorothy 1, 87
Clayton, Xernona 3, 45
Cornelius, Don 4, 100
Crump, Steven 96
Curry, Dell 126
Dee, Merri 55
Evans, Harry 25
Figueroa, John J. 40
Freeman, Aaron 52
Fuentes, Tito 123
Goode, Mal 13
Gumbel, Bryant 14, 80
Gumbel, Greg 8
Hall, Tamron 96
Hamblin, Ken 10
Hickman, Fred 11
Holt, Lester 66
Hunter-Gault, Charlayne 6, 31
Jackson, Hal 41, 104
Jackson, Mark 121
Johnson, Rafer 33
Joyner, Tom 19, 90
Kellogg, Clark 64
Kennedy-Overton, Jayne Harris 46
King, Gayle 19, 99
Langhart Cohen, Janet 19, 60
Lawson, Jennifer 1, 50
Lemon, Don 94
Lewis, Delano 7
Lomax, Louis E. 90
Mabrey, Vicki 26

Madison, Joseph E. 17
McEwen, Mark 5
McFarland, Roland 49
Melton, Frank 81
Mickelbury, Penny 28
Miller, Cheryl 10, 74
Ming, Mel 106
Mitchell, Russ 21, 73
Morgan, Joe 9, 96
Morton, Frederick A., Jr. 93
Neville, Arthel 53
Peete, Rodney 60
Pinckney, Sandra 56
Pinkston, W. Randall 24
Quarles, Norma 25
Reynolds, Star Jones 10, 27, 61
Roberts, Deborah 35
Roberts, Robin 16, 54, 113
Rodgers, Johnathan 6, 51
Rose, Jalen 108
Russell, Bill 8
Sanders, Deion 4, 31, 96
Shaw, Bernard 2, 28
Simmons, Jamal 72
Simpson, Carole 6, 30
Smiley, Tavis 20, 68
Steele, Sage 115
Stewart, Alison 13
Swann, Lynn 28
Syler, Rene 53
Thompson, Mychal 126
Watts, Rolonda 9
White, Bill 1, 48
Williams, Armstrong 29
Williams, Juan 35, 80
Williams, Montel 4, 57
Winfrey, Oprah 2, 15, 61, 106

Broadside Press
Hoagland, Everett H. 45
Randall, Dudley 8, 55

Brookings Institute
Ladner, Joyce A. 42

Brooklyn Dodgers baseball team
Black, Joe 75
Campanella, Roy 25
Gilliam, Jim 122
Newcombe, Don 24
Robinson, Jackie 6

Brotherhood of Sleeping Car Porters
Randolph, A. Philip 3
Tucker, Rosina 14

Brown University
Beckham, Barry 41
Simmons, Ruth 13, 38

Brown v. Board of Education of Topeka
Boulware, Harold R. 109
Brown, Oliver Leon 94
Carter, Robert L. 51, 100
Clark, Kenneth B. 5, 52
Franklin, John Hope 5, 77
Henderson, Zelma 71
Hill, Oliver W. 24, 63
Houston, Charles Hamilton 4
Malone Jones, Vivian 59
Marshall, Thurgood 1, 44
Motley, Constance Baker 10, 55

Redding, Louis L. 26
Robinson, Spottswood W., III 22
Simkins, Modjeska Monteith 112

Buffalo Bills football team
Simpson, O. J. 15, 100
Smith, Bruce 80
Thomas, Thurman 75

Bull-riding
Sampson, Charles 13

Burundi government
Ndadaye, Melchior 7
Nkurunziza, Pierre 78
Ntaryamira, Cyprien 8

Busing (anti-busing legislation)
Bosley, Freeman, Jr. 7

Cabinet
See U.S. Cabinet

Cable News Network (CNN)
Chideya, Farai 14, 61
Hickman, Fred 11
Malveaux, Suzanne 88
O'Brien, Soledad 88
Quarles, Norma 25
Rolle, Janet 97
Shaw, Bernard 2, 28
Sidner, Sara 105
Watson, Carlos 50

Caldecott medal
Dillon, Leo 103
Pinkney, Jerry 15, 124

California Angels baseball team
See Los Angeles Angels baseball team

California state government
Bass, Karen 70
Brown, Janice Rogers 43
Brown, Willie 7, 85
Dixon, Julian C. 24
Dymally, Mervyn 42
Harris, Kamala D. 64, 122
Hawkins, Augustus F. 68
Lee, Barbara 25, 102
Millender-McDonald, Juanita 21, 61
Richardson, Laura 81
Riles, Wilson C. 79
Waters, Maxine 3, 67, 103
Watson, Diane 41

California State University
Cobb, Jewel Plummer 42
Karenga, Maulana 10, 71

California Supreme Court
Brown, Janice Rogers 43

Calypso
Belafonte, Harry 4, 65
Lord Invader 117
Lord Kitchener 110
Premice, Josephine 41
Rhoden, Wayne 70
Rudder, David 79

Cameroon government
Ahidjo, Ahmadou 81
Biya, Paul 28, 114

Oyono, Ferdinand 38

Canadian Football League (CFL)
Anderson, Ezzrett 95
Clemons, Michael "Pinball" 64
Gilliam, Frank 23
Moon, Warren 8, 66
Thrower, Willie 35
Weathers, Carl 10

Canada government
Alexander, Lincoln 106
Augustine, Jean 53
Brown, Rosemary 62
Cools, Anne 64
Jean, Michaëlle; 70
Lewis, Daurene 72
Sparks, Corinne Etta 53

Cancer research
Adams-Campbell, Lucille L. 60
Chinn, May Edward 26
Clark, Celeste 15
Daly, Marie Maynard 37
Dunston, Georgia Mae 48
Freeman, Harold P. 23
Leffall, Lasalle 3, 64
Olopade, Olufunmilayo Falusi 58

Capital punishment
Correia, De'Jaun 93
Hawkins, Steven 14
Stevenson, Bryan 128

Caribbean dance
Ailey, Alvin 8
Dunham, Katherine 4, 59
Fagan, Garth 18, 98
Nichols, Nichelle 11

Caribbean literature/West Indian literature
Beken 111
Breeze, Jean "Binta" 37
Carter, Martin 49
Cartey, Wilfred 47
Channer, Colin 36
Coombs, Orde M. 44
Dabydeen, David 48
Guy, Rosa 5
Hearne, John Edgar Caulwell 45
Markham, E. A. 37
Marshall, Paule 7, 77
McKay, Claude 6
Nunez, Elizabeth 62, 112
Walcott, Derek 5, 94

Caribbean music
Ellis, Alton 74
Ellis, Hortense 97
Lefel, Edith 41
Ranglin, Ernest 78

Casting
Cannon, Reuben 50

Carolina Panthers
Smith, Steve 120

Cartoonists
Armstrong, Robb 15
Bell, Darrin 77
Brandon, Barbara 3
Brown, Robert 65
Campbell, E. Simms 13

Fax, Elton 48
Harrington, Oliver W. 9
McDuffie, Dwayne 62
McGruder, Aaron 28, 56, 120
Ormes, Jackie 73
Smith, Bruce W. 53
Turner, Morrie 122

Catering
See Restaurants/Catering/Cooking

Catholicism
See Roman Catholic Church

CBS
See Columbia Broadcasting System

CDC
See Centers for Disease Control and Prevention

CDF
See Children's Defense Fund

Celebrities for a Drug-Free America
Vereen, Ben 4

Censorship
Butts, Calvin O., III 9, 90

Centers for Disease Control and Prevention (CDC)
Fenton, Kevin 87
Gayle, Helene D. 3
Satcher, David 7, 57, 111
Wisdom, Kimberlydawn 57

Central African Republic government
Bozizé, François 96, 117
Djotodia, Michel 117

Central Intercollegiate Athletic Association (CIAA)
Kerry, Leon G. 46
Yancy, Dorothy Cowser 42

Certified public accountant
Jones, Thomas W. 41
Washington, Mary T. 57

CFL
See Canadian Football League

Chad government
Déby, Idriss 30, 125
Habré, Hissène 6, 104

Chama Cha Mapinduzi (Tanzania; Revolutionary Party)
Kikwete, Jakaya Mrisho 73
Mkapa, Benjamin W. 16, 77
Mongella, Gertrude 11
Mwinyi, Ali Hassan 1, 77
Nyerere, Julius 5

Chemistry
Brady, St. Elmo 107
Daly, Marie Maynard 37
Hall, Lloyd A. 8
Hammond, Paula 119
Haynie, Sharon 94
Humphries, Frederick 20
Julian, Percy Lavon 6
King, Reatha Clark 65
Massie, Samuel Proctor, Jr. 29

Mays, William G. 34
McBay, Henry C. 91
McCain, Franklin 119
Mensah, Thomas 48
Quarterman, Lloyd Albert 4

Chess
Ashley, Maurice 15, 47

Chicago Bears football team
Dent, Richard 97
Page, Alan 7
Payton, Walter 11, 25
Sayers, Gale 28
Singletary, Mike 4, 76
Thrower, Willie 35

Chicago Bulls basketball team
Brand, Elton 31
Jordan, Michael 6, 21

Chicago city government
Berry, Edwin C. 81
De Priest, Oscar Stanton 80
Jackson, Sandi 108
Jones, Emil, Jr. 74
Jones, John 89
Kelley, Cliff 75
Lane, Vincent 5
Metcalfe, Ralph 26
Sawyer, Eugene 81
Taylor, Robert Rochon 104
Tillman, Dorothy 76
Washington, Harold 6

Chicago Cubs baseball team
Banks, Ernie 33, 126
Carter, Joe 30
Sosa, Sammy 21, 44
Williams, Billy 86

Chicago Defender
Abbott, Robert Sengstacke 27
Burley, Dan 96
Holt, Nora 38
Martin, Roland S. 49, 84
Ormes, Jackie 73
Payne, Ethel L. 28

Chicago Eight
Seale, Bobby 3

Chicago Negro Chamber of Commerce
Fuller, S. B. 13

Chicago Police Department
Hillard, Terry 25
Holton, Hugh, Jr. 39

Chicago Reporter
Calhoun, Lillian Scott 87
Washington, Laura S. 18

Chicago Tribune
Page, Clarence 4

Chicago White Sox baseball team
Baines, Harold 32
Doby, Lawrence Eugene, Sr. 16, 41
Johnson, Clifford "Connie" 52
Minoso, Minnie 89, 127
Thomas, Frank 12, 51

Williams, Ken 68

Child care
Tillman, Deborah 98

Children's Defense Fund (CDF)
Edelman, Marian Wright 5, 42
Williams, Maggie 7, 71

Children's literature
Asim, Jabari 71
Berry, James 41
Bryan, Ashley 41, 104
Curtis, Christopher Paul 26, 113
De Veaux, Alexis 44
Feelings, Muriel 44
Graham, Lorenz 48
Greenfield, Eloise 9
Haskins, James 36, 54
Johnson, Angela 52
Jordan, Deloris 108
Lester, Julius 9, 115
Mollel, Tololwa 38
Myers, Walter Dean 8, 20, 123
Nelson, Kadir 115
Okara, Gabriel 37
Palmer, Everard 37
Pinkney, Jerry 15, 124
Shelton, Paula Young 86
Woodson, Jacqueline 125
Yarbrough, Camille 40

Chi-Lites
Record, Eugene 60

Chiropractics
Ford, Clyde W. 40
Reese, Milous J., Jr. 51
Westbrooks, Bobby 51

Choreography
Abraham, Kyle 116
Acogny, Germaine 55
Ailey, Alvin 8
Alexander, Khandi 43
Allen, Debbie 13, 42
Atkins, Cholly 40
Babatunde, Obba 35
Beatty, Talley 35
Brown, Ronald K. 91
Byrd, Donald 10
Collins, Janet 33, 64
Davis, Chuck 33
de Lavallade, Carmen 78
de Passe, Suzanne 25
De Shields, André 72
Dove, Ulysses 5
Dunham, Katherine 4, 59
Ellington, Mercedes 34
Fagan, Garth 18, 98
Faison, George 16
Glover, Savion 14
Hall, Arthur 39
Harris, Rennie 120
Henson, Darrin 33
Jamison, Judith 7, 67, 96
Jeune, Vitolio 98
Johnson, Virginia 9
Jones, Bill T. 1, 46, 80
King, Alonzo 38
LeTang, Henry 66
Manning, Frankie 78
Miller, Bebe 3
Mitchell, Arthur 2, 47

Nicholas, Fayard 20, 57
Nicholas, Harold 20
Pomare, Eleo 72
Primus, Pearl 6, 125
Rhoden, Dwight 40
Richardson, Desmond 39
Robinson, Cleo Parker 38
Robinson, Fatima 34
Rodgers, Rod 36
Spears, Warren 52
Storyboard P 118
Tyson, Andre 40
Wilson, Reggie 116
Zollar, Jawole 28

Chrysler Corporation
Colbert, Virgis William 17
Farmer, Forest 1
Gilles, Ralph 61
Richie, Leroy C. 18

Church of God in Christ
Blake, Charles E. 82
Franklin, Robert M. 13
Hayes, James C. 10
Kee, John P. 43, 116
Patterson, Gilbert Earl 41
Yearwood, Lennox, Jr. 112

CIAA
See Central Intercollegiate Athletic
Association

Cincinnati city government
Berry, Theodore M. 31
Mallory, Mark 62

Cincinnati Reds baseball team
Blair, Paul 36
Davis, Eric 116
Larkin, Barry 24
Morgan, Joe 9, 96
Phillips, Brandon 116
Reese, Pokey 28
Robinson, Frank 9, 87

Cinematography
Dickerson, Ernest 6, 17

Circus
Iverson, Johnathan Lee 22, 100
McFarlan, Tyron 60
Walker, Cedric "Ricky" 19

Citigroup
Gaines, Brenda 41
Jones, Thomas W. 41
McGuire, Raymond J. 57
Parsons, Richard 11, 33, 124

City government--U.S.
Adams, Floyd, Jr. 12, 122
Bell, Michael 40
Bellamy, Terry 58
Benjamin, Steve 98
Bobb, Robert C. 83
Bradley, Jennette B. 40
Brown, Aja 115
Brown, Alvin 96
Brown, Willie 7, 85
Burris, Chuck 21
Bush, Gordon 82
Caesar, Shirley 19
Cannon, Patrick 120
Celestin, Josaphat 101
Clayton, Constance 1

Cleaver, Emanuel 4, 45, 68, 107
Coleman, Michael 28, 79
Craig-Jones, Ellen Walker 44
Davis, Doris A. 100
Dellums, Ronald 2, 81
DuPree, Johnny 96
Ford, Jack 39
Ford, Johnny 70
Foxx, Anthony 81, 123
Francois, Terry A. 106
Gibbs, Mifflin W. 99
Gillum, Andrew 128
Glover, Cedric B. 103
Harp, Toni 123
Hatcher, Richard G. 55
Hayes, James C. 10
Herenton, Willie W. 24, 81
Holden, Kip 120
Jackson, Eric 127
James, Sly 107
Johnson, Harvey, Jr. 24, 82
Jones, Dwight C. 122
Jordan, Charles 122
Love, Mia 96, 125
Lowery, Myron 80
Lumumba, Chokwe 118
Mack, Tony 104
Mallett, Conrad, Jr. 16
Marks, John R., III 123
Marsh, Henry 32
Melton, Frank 81
Morial, Ernest "Dutch" 26
Morial, Marc H. 20, 51
Murrell, Sylvia Marilyn 49
Parker, Vernon 97
Patterson, J. O., Jr. 80
Perkins, James, Jr. 55
Powell, Adam Clayton, Jr. 3
Powell, Debra A. 23
Primas, Randy 106
Redd, Dana 93
Tyler, Ollie 128
Usry, James L. 23
Wharton, A. C., Jr. 110
Widener, Warren 99
Williams, Dennis P. 123
Wilson, Lionel 99

City government--international
Tau, Mpho Parks 124

Civil rights
Abbott, Diane 9
Abernathy, Ralph 1
Agyeman, Jaramogi Abebe 10, 63
Al-Amin, Jamil Abdullah 6
Alexander, Clifford 26
Alexander, Michelle 98
Amaker, Norman 63
Anthony, Wendell 25
Aristide, Jean-Bertrand 6, 45
Arnwine, Barbara 28
Baker, Ella 5
Baker, Josephine 3
Ballance, Frank W. 41
Ballard, John 95
Barbee, Lloyd Augustus 71
Barrow, Willie T. 85, 128
Bashir, Halima 73
Bass, Charlotta Spears 40
Bates, Daisy 13
Baugh, David 23
Beals, Melba Pattillo 15, 94

Bell, James Madison 40
Berry, Theodore M. 31
Bevel, James L. 75
Biko, Steven 4
Blackwell, Gloria 127
Bond, Julian 2, 35, 106
Booker, Simeon 23
Borders, William Holmes 94
Boyd, John W., Jr. 20, 72
Bradle, David Henry, Jr. 39
Bridges, Ruby 77
Brock, Roslyn McCallister 86
Brooks, Tyrone 59
Brown, Byrd 49
Brown, Charlotte Hawkins 106
Brown, Elaine 8
Brown, Homer S. 47
Brown, Tony 3
Brown, Wesley 23
Brown, Willa 40
Burks, Mary Fair 40
Caldwell, Earl 60
Cameron, James 80
Carmichael, Stokely 5, 26
Carr, Johnnie 69
Carter, Mandy 11
Carter, Rubin 26, 121
Cary, Mary Ann Shadd 30
Catto, Octavius V. 83
Cayton, Horace 26
Chambers, Julius 3
Chavis, Benjamin 6
Chestnut, J. L., Jr. 73
Clark, Septima 7
Clay, William Lacy 8
Cleaver, Eldridge 5
Cleaver, Kathleen Neal 29
Cobb, W. Montague 39
Cobbs, Price M. 9
Coleman, James E., Jr. 79
Cooper, Anna Julia 20
Cunningham, Evelyn 23, 85
Davis, Angela 5, 114
Davis, Artur 41
Davis, James E. 50
Dent, Thomas C. 50
Diallo, Amadou 27
Diggs, Charles C. 21
Divine, Father 7
Dobbs, John Wesley 89
Dodson, Howard, Jr. 7, 52
Douglass, Frederick 87
Du Bois, W. E. B. 3
Dudley, Edward R. 58
Due, Patricia Stephens 100
Dukes, Hazel Nell 56
Dumas, Henry 41
Eagleson, William Lewis 90
Edwards, Willis 104
Ellison, Ralph 7
Evers, Medgar 3
Evers, Myrlie 8
Farmer, James 2, 64
Farmer-Paellmann, Deadria 43
Fisher, Ada Lois Sipuel 76
Forman, James 7, 51
Fortune, T. Thomas 6
Foster, Marie 48
Franklin, C. L. 68
French, D. M. 94
Gaines, Ernest J. 7
Gaines, Lloyd 79
Gibson, William F. 6

Gomillion, Charles 90
Granger, Lester B. 75
Gray, Fred 37
Gregory, Dick 1, 54
Grillo, Evelio 95
Grimké, Archibald H. 9
Guinier, Lani 7, 30
Guyot, Lawrence 108
Haley, George Williford Boyce 21
Hall, Elliott S. 24
Hamer, Fannie Lou 6
Hampton, Fred 18
Hampton, Henry 6
Harding, Vincent 67
Harper, Frances Ellen Watkins 11
Hastie, William H. 8
Hatcher, Richard G. 55
Hawkins, Augustus F. 68
Hawkins, Steven 14
Hayes, Dennis 54
Hedgeman, Anna Arnold 22
Height, Dorothy I. 2, 23, 78
Henderson, Thelton E. 68
Henry, Aaron 19
Higginbotham, A. Leon, Jr. 13, 25
Hill, Jesse, Jr. 13
Hill, Oliver W. 24, 63
Hilliard, David 7, 105
Hobson, Julius W. 44
Holland, Endesha Ida Mae 3, 57
Hollowell, Donald L. 57
Hooks, Benjamin L. 2, 85
Hope, Lugenia Burns 89
Houston, Charles Hamilton 4
Howard, M. William, Jr. 26
Irvis, K. Leroy 67
Jackson, Alexine Clement 22
Jackson, Jesse 1, 27, 72
Jackson, Jimmie Lee 126
James, Daniel, Jr. 16
Jarrett, Vernon D. 42
Jemison, T. J. 119
Jenkins, Ray 77
Johns, Vernon 38
Johnson, Georgia Douglas 41
Johnson, James Weldon 5
Johnson, Norma H. 17, 97
Jones, Clarence B. 114
Jones, Elaine R. 7, 45
Jones, John 89
Jones, William A., Jr. 61
Jordan, Barbara 4, 78
Jordan, June 7, 35
Jordan, Vernon E. 3, 35
Julian, Percy Lavon 6
Karim, Benjamin 61
Kennedy, Florynce 12, 33
Kenyatta, Jomo 5
Kidd, Mae Street 39
King, Bernice 4, 81
King, Coretta Scott 3, 57
King, Martin Luther, III 20
King, Martin Luther, Jr. 1
King, Martin Luther, Sr. 89
King, Preston 28
King, Robert Hillary 84
King, Rodney 103
King, Yolanda 6
Ladner, Joyce A. 42
Lampkin, Daisy 19
Lawson, James M., Jr. 90
Lewis, William Henry 89
Logan, Rayford W. 40

Louis, Willie 113
Loving, Mildred 69
Lowery, Evelyn Gibson 115
Lowery, Joseph 2
Lowry, A. Leon 60
Lucy Foster, Autherine 35
Luper, Clara 94
Madikizela-Mandela, Winnie 2, 35, 112
Makeba, Miriam 2, 50, 74
Malone Jones, Vivian 59
Mandela, Nelson 1, 14, 77, 117
Martin, Louis E. 16
Martin, Ruby Grant 49
Mays, Benjamin E. 7
Mbeki, Thabo 14, 73
McCain, Franklin 119
McDonald, Gabrielle Kirk 20
McDougall, Gay J. 11, 43
McKissick, Floyd B. 3
Meredith, James H. 11
Metcalfe, Ralph 26
Miller, Clyde 113
Mitchell, Clarence M., Jr. 88
Mitchell, Juanita Jackson 128
Morgan, Irene 65
Moody, Anne 127
Moore, Barbara C. 49
Moore, Harry T. 29
Morial, Ernest "Dutch" 26
Moses, Robert Parris 11
Moss, Otis, Jr. 72
Motley, Constance Baker 10, 55
Mowry, Jess 7
Murphy, Laura M. 43
Murray, Pauli 38
Nash, Diane 72
Ndadaye, Melchior 7
Nelson, Jill 6, 54
Newton, Huey 2
Nixon, Edgar Daniel 100
Nkoli, Simon 60
Nkomo, Joshua 4, 65
Noble, Gil 76
Nunn, Annetta 43
Nzo, Alfred 15
Orange, James 74
Parker, Kellis E. 30
Parks, Rosa 1, 35, 56
Patterson, Louise 25
Perry, Matthew J., Jr. 96
Pincham, R. Eugene, Sr. 69
Pinchback, P. B. S. 9
Player, Willa B. 43
Pleasant, Mary Ellen 9
Plessy, Homer Adolph 31
Poitier, Sidney 11, 36
Powell, Adam Clayton, Jr. 3
Price, Hugh B. 9, 54
Randolph, A. Philip 3
Redding, Louis L. 26
Rivers, Eugene F., III 81
Robeson, Paul 2
Robinson, Jackie 6
Robinson, Joann Gibson 100
Robinson, Rachel 16
Robinson, Randall 7, 46
Robinson, Sharon 22
Robinson, Spottswood W., III 22
Roundtree, Dovey 80
Rush, Bobby 26, 76
Rustin, Bayard 4
Sadlier, Rosemary 62

Sanders, Malika 48
Sané, Pierre Gabriel 21
Saro-Wiwa, Kenule 39
Seale, Bobby 3
Shabazz, Attallah 6
Shabazz, Betty 7, 26
Shakur, Assata 6
Sharpton, Al 21, 97
Shelton, Paula Young 86
Shinhoster, Earl 32
Shores, Arthur D. 99
Shuttlesworth, Fred 47, 98
Simkins, Modjeska Monteith 112
Simon, Lateefah 95
Simone, Nina 15, 41
Sisulu, Albertina 57, 95
Sisulu, Sheila Violet Makate 24
Sleet, Moneta, Jr. 5
Smith, Barbara 28
Staupers, Mabel K. 7
Sullivan, Leon H. 3, 30
Sutton, Percy E. 42, 82
Sweet, Ossian 68
Taylor, Recy 92
Taylor, Robert Rochon 104
Thurman, Howard 3
Till, Emmett 7
Tillman, Dorothy 76
Tolson, Melvin B. 37
Touré, Faya Ora Rose 56
Trotter, Monroe 9
Tsvangirai, Morgan 26, 72
Turner, Henry McNeal 5
Walker, Rebecca 50
Washington, Booker T. 4
Washington, Fredi 10
Webb-Christburg, Sheyann 110
Wells, James Lesesne 10
Wells-Barnett, Ida B. 8
White, Walter F. 4
Whitmore, George 106
Wilkins, Roy 4
Williams, Evelyn 10
Williams, Fannie Barrier 27
Williams, Hosea 15, 31, 123
Williams, Robert F. 11
Williams, Walter E. 4
Wilson, William Julius 22
Woods, Abraham, Jr. 74
Woodson, Robert L. 10
Wright, Nathan, Jr. 56
X, Malcolm 1
Yoba, Malik 11
Young, Jean Childs 14
Young, Whitney M., Jr. 4

Clarinet
Bechet, Sidney 18
McGill, Anthony 76
Sweatman, Wilbur 125

Classical music
Abdullah, Kazem 97
Adams, Leslie 39
Baiocchi, Regina Harris 41
Bonds, Margaret 39
Brown, Uzee 42
Burleigh, Henry Thacker 56
Coleridge-Taylor, Samuel 75
Cook, Will Marion 40
Dawson, William Levi 39
DePreist, James 37, 109
Dixon, Dean 68

Dunner, Leslie B. 45
Fox, Donal 114
Freeman, Paul 39
Imani Winds 113
Kay, Ulysses 37
Lewis, Henry 38
Marian Anderson String Quartet 111
McFerrin, Bobby 68
McGill, Anthony 76
Moore, Dorothy Rudd 46
Moore, Kermit 116
Murray, Tai 47
Pratt, Awadagin 31
Price, Florence 37
Schuyler, Philippa 50
Smith, Hale 118
Sowande, Fela 39
Still, William Grant 37
Tillis, Frederick 40
Walker, George 37
Wilkins, Thomas Alphonso 71
Williams, Denise 40

Classical singers
Anderson, Marian 2, 33
Battle, Kathleen 70
Bumbry, Grace 5
Burleigh, Henry Thacker 56
Hayes, Roland 4
Hendricks, Barbara 3, 67
Lister, Marquita 65
Norman, Jessye 5
Price, Leontyne 1
Three Mo' Tenors 35
Williams, Denise 40

Clergy
Abune Paulos 105
Agyeman, Jaramogi Abebe 10, 63
Anthony, Wendell 25
Baker, Delbert W. 110
Bell, Ralph S. 5
Ben-Israel, Ben Ami 11
Berry, Moses 84
Black, Barry C. 47
Bloomer, George 86
Bowen, John W. E., Sr. 89
Burgess, John 46
Bynum, Juanita 31, 71
Caesar, Shirley 19
Caldwell, Kirbyjon 55
Clarence 13X 126
Cleveland, James 19
Cook, Suzan D. Johnson 22
Crowdy, William Saunders 109
Dollar, Creflo 106
Easton, Hosea 91
Ellis, Charles H., III 79
Falana, Lola 42
Gilmore, Marshall 46
Grace, Sweet Daddy 104
Gregory, Wilton 37
Henson, Josiah 90
Holsey, Lucius Henry 92
Hood, James Walker 91
Howard, M. William, Jr. 26
Jakes, T. D. 17, 43, 116
James, Skip 38
Jemison, Major L. 48
Johns, Vernon 38
Jones, Absalom 52
Jones, Alex 64
Jones, Robert Elijah 90

Jones, William A., Jr. 61
Karim, Benjamin 61
Kelly, Leontine 33
King, Barbara 22
King, Bernice 4, 81
Kobia, Samuel 43
Lee, Eric P. 79
Lincoln, C. Eric 38
Maxis, Theresa 62
McClurkin, Donnie 25
McGuire, George Alexander 80
McKenzie, Vashti M. 29
Michaux, Solomon Lightfoot 91
Morgan, Gertrude 63
Noble Drew Ali 100
Norful, Smokie 127
Okaalet, Peter 58
Otunga, Maurice Michael 55
Peterson, Jesse Lee 81
Phipps, Wintley 59
Reems, Ernestine Cleveland 27
Reese, Della 6, 20, 96
Reverend Ike 79
Robinson, Ida B. 106
Sentamu, John 58
Smith, Amanda Berry 109
Spencer, Peter 128
Taylor, Gardner C. 76
Thurman, Howard 3
Thurston, Stephen J. 49
Tillard, Conrad 47
Tolton, Augustine 62
Twilight, Alexander 125
Ukpabio, Helen 86
Walker, John T. 50
Washington, James Melvin 50
Watkins, Joe 86
Weeks, Thomas, III 70
Weems, Renita J. 44
White-Hammond, Gloria 61
Williams, David Rudyard 50
Williams, Frederick (B.) 63
Williams, Preston Warren, II 64
Wright, Nathan, Jr. 56

Cleveland Browns football team
Brown, Jim 11, 95
Hill, Calvin 19
Motley, Marion 26
Newsome, Ozzie 26, 117
Willis, Bill 68

Cleveland city government
Jackson, Frank G. 76
Stokes, Carl 10, 73
White, Michael R. 5

Cleveland Indians baseball team
Belle, Albert 10
Carter, Joe 30
Doby, Lawrence Eugene, Sr. 16, 41
Justice, David 18
Lofton, Kenny 12
Murray, Eddie 12
Paige, Satchel 7
Robinson, Frank 9, 87
Sabathia, CC 74
Sizemore, Grady 96

CLIO Awards
Lewis, Emmanuel 36

Clothing design

Aberra, Amsale 67
Bailey, Xenobia 11
Bonney, Tabi 98
Burrows, Stephen 31
DeVore-Mitchell, Ophelia 120
Gaskins, Eric 64
Henderson, Gordon 5
Jones, Carl 7
Kani, Karl 10
Kelly, Patrick 3
Lars, Byron 32
Malone, Maurice 32
Paris, Adama 120
Robinson, Patrick 19, 71
Smith, Willi 8
Walker, T. J. 7
Williams, Serena 20, 41, 73

CNBC

Epperson, Sharon 54
Thomas-Graham, Pamela 29

CNN

See Cable News Network

Coaching/Managing, Sports

Amaker, Tommy 62
Anderson, Mike 63
Ashley, Maurice 15, 47
Baker, Dusty 8, 43, 72, 110
Baylor, Don 6
Bickerstaff, Bernie 21
Bonds, Bobby 43
Bowles, Todd 128
Brown, Mike 77, 107
Caldwell, Jim 81
Campanella, Roy 25
Carter, Butch 27
Carter, Kenneth 53
Chaney, Don 98
Chaney, John 67
Cheeks, Maurice 47, 106
Cooper, Michael 31
Cox, Bryan 83
Crennel, Romeo 54, 107
Curry, Michael 85
Davis, Mike 41
Dorrell, Karl 52
Dungy, Tony 17, 42, 59, 118
Dunn, Jerry 27
Edwards, Herman 51
Ellerbe, Brian 22
Freeman, Marianna 23
Gaines, Clarence E., Sr. 55
Gaither, Alonzo Smith (Jake) 14
Gaston, Cito 71
Gates, William 97
Gentry, Alvin 23
Gibson, Bob 33
Gill, Turner 83
Gilliam, Jim 122
Gorden, W. C. 71
Graham, Trevor 84
Gray, Yeshimbra "Shimmy" 55
Green, Dennis 5, 45
Greene, Joe 10
Hamilton, Leonard 100
Hart, Thomas A., Sr. 113
Haskins, Clem 23
Hazzard, Walt 98
Heard, Gar 25
Johnson, Avery 62

Jordan, Eddie 83
Joyce, Dru 81
Kearney, Beverly 109
Keith, Floyd A. 61
Lewis, Marvin 51, 87
Lloyd, Earl 26, 127
Lofton, James 42
Manuel, Jerry 94
Martin, Cuonzo 121
Mason, Derek 120
McClendon, Lloyd 123
Miller, Cheryl 10, 74
Mitchell, Sam 82
Morris, Raheem 77
O'Neil, Buck 19, 59
Parish, Robert 43
Phillips, Teresa L. 42
Porter, Bo 123
Rhodes, Ray 14
Richardson, Nolan 9
Rivers, Doc 25, 81
Robinson, Craig 107
Robinson, Eddie G. 10, 61
Robinson, Frank 9, 87
Robinson, Will 51, 69
Russell, Bill 8
Sanders, Satch 77
Scott, Byron 125
Shannon, Randy 82
Shaw, Brian 127
Shell, Art 1, 66
Silas, Paul 24
Simmons, Bob 29
Singletary, Mike 4, 76
Smith, Lovie 66, 107
Smith, Tubby 18, 83
Stringer, C. Vivian 13, 66
Thomas, Emmitt 71
Tomlin, Mike 123
Tunnell, Emlen 54
Vaughn, Jacque 127
Washington, Ron 119
White, Frank 95
White, Jesse 22, 75
Whitney, Davey L. 110
Williams, Doug 22, 112
Williams, Monty 125
Willingham, Tyrone 43
Wills, Maury 73

Coca-Cola Company

Llewellyn, J. Bruce 13, 85
Ware, Carl T. 30

Coca-Cola Foundation

Jones, Ingrid Saunders 18

Collage

Andrews, Benny 22, 59
Bearden, Romare 2, 50
Bradford, Mark 89
Driskell, David C. 7
Pindell, Howardena 55
Pinder, Jefferson 77
Robinson, Aminah 50
Saar, Betye 80
Thomas, Mickalene 61
Verna, Gelsy 70

College and university administration

Abercrumbie, P. Eric 95
Ammons, James H. 81
Archie-Hudson, Marguerite 44

Austin, Bobby W. 95
Awuah, Patrick 111
Baker, Delbert W. 110
Ballard, Allen Butler, Jr. 40
Barnett, Marguerite 46
Becton, Julius W., Jr. 110
Bromery, Randolph Wilson 85
Burnim, Mickey L. 48
Christian, Barbara T. 44
Cole, Johnnetta B. 5, 43
Cook, Samuel DuBois 14
Crew, Rudy 16, 113
Cross, Dolores E. 23
Davis, Erroll B., Jr. 57
Dogan, Matthew Winifred 91
Drake, Michael V. 122
Favors, Steve 23
Floyd, Elson S. 41
Ford, Nick Aaron 44
Francis, Norman (C.) 60
Gilbert, John Wesley 91
Harvey, William R. 42
Hill, Leslie Pinckney 44
Hogan, Beverly Wade 50
Horne, Frank 44
Jackson, Edison O. 67
King, Reatha Clark 65
Lee, Joe A. 45
Lewis, Shirley A. R. 14
Lomax, Michael L. 58
Lyons, James E., Sr. 102
Mason, Ronald 27
Massey, Walter E. 5, 45
Maupin, John E., Jr. 92
Mell, Patricia 49
Moody-Adams, Michele 76
Morón, Alonzo G. 91
Nance, Cynthia 71
Newman, Lester C. 51
Page, Inman 82
Pollard, William L. 91
Proctor, Bernard Shaw 120
Reaves, Donald J. 102
Ribeau, Sidney 70
Sizemore, Barbara A. 26, 110
Smith, Gene 123
Trueheart, William E. 49

Colorado Rockies baseball team

Baylor, Don 6

Colorado state government

Brown, George Leslie 62
Buckley, Victoria (Vikki) 24
Groff, Peter 96
Rogers, Joe 27

Columbia Broadcasting System (CBS)

Bradley, Ed 2, 59
Kellogg, Clark 64
Mabrey, Vicki 26
McEwen, Mark 5
Mitchell, Russ 21, 73
Olden, Georg(e) 44
Pinkston, W. Randall 24
Pitts, Byron 71
Rodgers, Johnathan 6, 51
Ware, Andre 37

Columbia Records

Jackson, Randy 40
Knowles, Tina 61

Columbia University

Huggins, Nathan Irvin 52
Joseph, Jamal 101
Marable, Manning 10, 102
Moody-Adams, Michele 76
Steele, Claude 13, 97

Comedy

Allen, Byron 3, 24, 97
Amos, John 8, 62
Anderson, Anthony 51, 77
Anderson, Eddie "Rochester" 30
Anthony, Trey 63
Arnez J 53
Beaton, Norman 14
Bell, W. Kamau 107
Bellamy, Bill 12
Berry, Bertice 8, 55
Brady, Wayne 32, 71
Bruce, Bruce 56
Buress, Hannibal 101
Cannon, Nick 47, 73
Carmichael, Jerrod 124
Cedric the Entertainer 29, 60, 115
Cenac, Wyatt 94
Chappelle, Dave 50, 115
Che, Michael 123
Cosby, Bill 7, 26, 59, 125
Curry, Mark 17
Davidson, Tommy 21
Davis, Sammy, Jr. 18
Dieudonné 67, 118
Earthquake 55
Epps, Mike 60
Foxx, Jamie 15, 48
Foxx, Redd 2
Freeman, Aaron 52
Funches, Ron 121
Givens, Adele 62
Glover, Donald 85
Goldberg, Whoopi 4, 33, 69
Harris, Robin 7
Hart, Kevin 103
Harvey, Steve 18, 58
Henry, Lenny 9, 52
Hughley, D. L. 23, 76
Key & Peele 107
Kirby, George 14
Lawrence, Martin 6, 27, 60
Love, Loni 113
Mabley, Jackie "Moms" 15
Mac, Bernie 29, 61, 72
Markham, Pigmeat 106
Mayo, Whitman 32
McEwen, Mark 5
Meadows, Tim 30
Mooney, Paul 37, 120
Moore, Tim 124
Morgan, Tracy 61, 102
Morris, Garrett 31
Moss, Preacher 63
Murphy, Charles 95
Murphy, Eddie 4, 20, 61
Nash, Niecy 66, 115
Noah, Trevor 128
O'Neal, Patrice 99
Powell, Keith 101
Pryor, Richard 3, 24, 56
Robinson, Craig 103
Rock, Chris 3, 22, 66
Rock, Tony 108
Russell, Nipsey 66
Schultz, Michael A. 6

Slocumb, Jonathan 52
Smiley, Rickey 59
Sommore 61
Stickney, Phyllis Yvonne 108
Sykes, Wanda 48, 81
Thompson, Kenan 52
Thurston, Baratunde 79, 101
Torry, Guy 31
Townsend, Robert 4, 23
Tucker, Chris 13, 23, 62
Tyler, Aisha N. 36
Watts, Reggie 52, 102
Wayans, Damon 8, 41
Wayans, Keenen Ivory 18
Wayans, Kim 80
Wayans, Marlon 29, 82
Wayans, Shawn 29
Wilson, Debra 38
Wilson, Flip 21
Witherspoon, John 38
Yarbrough, Cedric 51

Comerica Bank
Forte, Linda Diane 54

Commercial art
Freeman, Leonard 27

Communist Party
Brown, Lloyd Louis 42
Davis, Angela 5, 114
Herndon, Angelo 90
Patterson, Louise 25
Wright, Richard 5

Community activism
Blakely, Delois N. 122
Brazier, Arthur M. 115
Bryant, Jamal 128
Buery, Richard, Jr. 97
Harden, Monique 97
Kimbro, Warren 76
LeGrand, Naquasia 126
Matthews, Ameena 105
Rowe-Adams, Jackie 109
Shakur, Yusef 85
Simon, Lateefah 95
Tapscott, Horace 126
Washington, Karen 117
Watkins, Ted 104
Yearwood, Lennox, Jr. 112

Computer science
Adkins, Rod 41
Auguste, Donna 29
Bryant, Kimberly 127
Coleman, Ken 57
Dean, Mark 35
Easley, Annie J. 61
Ellis, Clarence 38
Emeagwali, Philip 30
Hannah, Marc 10
Irvin, Vernon 65
Laryea, Thomas Davies, III 67
Mensah, Thomas 48
Millines Dziko, Trish 28
Pyfrom, Estella 127
Zollar, Alfred 40

Conceptual art
Allen, Tina 22, 75
Bailey, Xenobia 11
Blanco, Mykki 106
Cortez, Jayne 43, 109
Gates, Theaster 118

Harris, Lyle Ashton 83
London, Theophilus 95
O'Grady, Lorraine 73
Piper, Adrian 71
Pope.L, William 72
Robinson, Aminah 50
Scott, Dread 106
Shonibare, Yinka 58
Simpson, Lorna 4, 36

Conductors
Abdullah, Kazem 97
Calloway, Blanche 100
Calloway, Cab 14
Cook, Will Marion 40
Dawson, William Levi 39
DePreist, James 37, 109
Dixon, Dean 68
Dunner, Leslie B. 45
Foster, William P. 88
Freeman, Paul 39
Hairston, Jester 88
Jackson, Isaiah 3
León, Tania 13
Lewis, Henry 38

Congo, Democratic Republic of the, government
Kabila, Joseph 30, 126
Kabila, Laurent 20
Mobutu Sese Seko 1, 56
Rochereau, Tabu Ley 117

Congo, Republic of the, government
Lumumba, Patrice 33
Sassou-Nguesso, Denis 103

Congress of Racial Equality (CORE)
Farmer, James 2, 64
Hobson, Julius W. 44
Innis, Roy 5
Jackson, Jesse 1, 27, 72
McKissick, Floyd B. 3
Rustin, Bayard 4

Construction industry
Bennett, Richard 97
Russell, Herman Jerome 17

Contemporary Christian music
Baraka, Sho 109
Griffin, LaShell 51
KB 122
Lecrae 108
Tait, Michael 57

Continental Basketball Association (CBA)
Davis, Mike 41
Thomas, Isiah 7, 26, 65
Ussery, Terdema, II 29

Cooking
See Restaurants/Catering/Cooking

CORE
See Congress of Racial Equality

Coretta Scott King Awards
Bryan, Ashley 41, 104
Clifton, Lucille 14, 64, 91
Curtis, Christopher Paul 26, 113
Dillon, Leo 103

Draper, Sharon Mills 16, 43
Fax, Elton 48
Greenfield, Eloise 9
Hamilton, Virginia 10
Haskins, James 36, 54
Johnson, Angela 52
Lester, Julius 9, 115
Myers, Walter Dean 8, 20, 123
Morrison, Toni 2, 15, 86
Nelson, Kadir 115
Rollins, Charlemae Hill 27
Taylor, Mildred D. 26
Woodson, Jacqueline 125

Coronet
Oliver, Joe "King" 42

Corporate executive
Brewer, Rosalind 100
Coleman, Ken 57
Cottrell, Comer 11
Donald, Arnold 36, 126
Dortch, Thomas W., Jr. 45
Frazier, Kenneth 97
Hannah, Marc 10
Hill, Wyllstyne D. 94
Jackson, Mannie 14
James, Donna A. 51
Johnson, George E. 29
Knowling, Robert 38
Lawal, Kase L. 45
Lewis, William M., Jr. 40
Lewis-Hall, Freda 105
Mays, Leslie A. 41
Ogunlesi, Adebayo 37
Phillips, Charles E., Jr. 57, 109
Rand, A. Barry 6
Scott, Milton 51
Siméus, Dumas M. 25, 110
Smith, Joshua 10
Thompson, Cynthia Bramlett 50
Walker, Joseph Edison 111
Westbrook, Kelvin 50

Corporation for Public Broadcasting (CPB)
Brown, Tony 3

Cosmetology
Cottrell, Comer 11
Fuller, S. B. 13
McGrath, Pat 72
Morgan, Rose 11
Powell, Maxine 8, 115
Roche, Joyce M. 17
Walker, A'lelia 14
Walker, Madame C. J. 7

Council on Legal Education Opportunities (CLEO)
Henderson, Wade J. 14
Henry, Aaron 19

Count Basie Orchestra
Count Basie 23
Dickenson, Vic 38
Eldridge, Roy 37
Foster, Frank 97
Jacquet, Illinois 49
Johnson, J. J. 37
Jones, Papa Jo 99
Jones, Thad 68
Powell, Benny 87
Rushing, Jimmy 37
Terry, Clark 39, 127

Williams, Joe 5, 25
Young, Lester 37

Country music
Bailey, DeFord 33
Carolina Chocolate Drops 111
Cowboy Troy 54
Gray, Dobie 99
Palmer, Rissi 65
Pride, Charley 26
Randall, Alice 38
Rucker, Darius 34, 74, 108

Cowboys
Jeffries, Herb 122
Love, Nat 9
Pickett, Bill 11

CPB
See Corporation for Public Broadcasting

Craftwork
Hill, Peter 92

Creative Artists Agency
Nelson Meigs, Andrea 48

Creole music
Ardoin, Alphonse 65

Cricket
Adams, Paul 50

Critical race theory
Crenshaw, Kimberlé Williams 88
Williams, Patricia 11, 54

Crusader
Williams, Robert F. 11

Cuban League
Charleston, Oscar 39
Day, Leon 39

Cuban military
Maceo, Antonio 82

Cuban music
Ferrer, Ibrahim 41
Portuondo, Omara 53
Valdés, Bebo 75
Valdés, Chucho 89

Cubism
Bearden, Romare 2, 50
Green, Jonathan 54

Culinary arts
Allen, Eugene 79
Brown, Warren 61
Calabrese, Karyn 89
Chase, Leah 57
Clark, Patrick 14
Estes, Rufus 29
Evans, Darryl 22
Garvin, Gerry 78
Henderson, Jeff 72
Ouattara, Morou 74
Samuelsson, Marcus 53, 120
Sasser, Sean 113

Cultural pluralism
Locke, Alain 10
Vega, Marta Moreno 61

Curator/exhibition designer
Amaki, Amalia 76
Beckwith, Naomi 101

Camp, Kimberly 19
Campbell, Mary Schmidt 43
Golden, Thelma 10, 55
Hoyte, Lenon 50
Hutson, Jean Blackwell 16
Pindell, Howardena 55
Sanders, Joseph R., Jr. 11
Sims, Lowery Stokes 27
Stewart, Paul Wilbur 12

Cy Young Award
Blue, Vida 122
Gibson, Bob 33
Gooden, Dwight 20
Jenkins, Fergie 46
Martínez, Pedro 81, 126
Newcombe, Don 24
Price, David 101
Sabathia, CC 74

Cycling
Baugé, Grégory 86
Jim, Songezo 111
Kaka, Luthando 118
Taylor, Marshall Walter "Major" 62
Yeboah, Emmanuel Ofosu 53

Dallas city government
Kirk, Ron 11, 75, 111

Dallas Cowboys football team
Allen, Larry 109
Hayes, Bob 77
Hill, Calvin 19
Irvin, Michael 64
Jones, Ed "Too Tall" 46
Smith, Emmitt 7, 87
Wright, Rayfield 70

Dallas Police Department
Bolton, Terrell D. 25

Dance Theatre of Harlem
DePrince, Michaela 104
Johnson, Virginia 9
King, Alonzo 38
Mitchell, Arthur 2, 47
Nicholas, Fayard 20, 57
Nicholas, Harold 20
Peters, Brock 96

DAV
See Disabled American Veterans

Daytona Institute
See Bethune-Cookman College

D.C. sniper
Moose, Charles 40

Def Jam Records
Jay-Z 27, 69, 103
Liles, Kevin 42, 99
LL Cool J 16, 49, 94
Simmons, Russell 1, 30

Defense Communications Agency
Gravely, Samuel L., Jr. 5, 49

Delaware state government
Williams, Dennis P. 123

Delta Sigma Theta Sorority
Rice, Louise Allen 54

Dentistry
Bluitt, Juliann S. 14
Delany, Bessie 12

Gray, Ida 41
Lee, Robert 112
Madison, Romell 45
Maupin, John E., Jr. 92
Rock, John S. 113
Sinkford, Jeanne C. 13

Denver Broncos football team
Barnes, Ernie 16, 78
Briscoe, Marlin 37
Davis, Terrell 20
Jackson, Tom 70
Little, Floyd 86
Sharpe, Shannon 97

Denver city government
Early, Norman S., Jr. 124
Hancock, Michael B. 123
Webb, Wellington 3, 81

Denver Nuggets basketball team
Bickerstaff, Bernie 21
Bynoe, Peter C. B. 40
Hardaway, Tim 35
Lee, Bertram M., Sr. 46

Depression/The Great Depression
Hampton, Henry 6

Dermatology
McDonald, Charles J. 120
Taylor, Susan C. 62

Destiny's Child
Beyoncé 39, 70, 105
Luckett, Letoya 61
Rowland, Kelly 100
Williams, Michelle 73

Detective fiction
See Mystery/detective fiction

Detroit city government
Archer, Dennis 7, 36
Bing, Dave 3, 59, 78
Cockrel, Kenneth V., Jr. 79
Cockrel, Kenneth Vern, Sr. 79
Collins, Barbara-Rose 7, 87
Conyers, Monica 85
Crockett, George W., Jr. 10, 64
Evans, Warren C. 76
Garrett, Joyce Finley 59
Kilpatrick, Kwame 34, 71, 116
Marshall, Bella 22
McPhail, Sharon 2, 119
Orr, Kevyn 118
Pugh, Charles 81
Reeves, Martha 85
Young, Coleman 1, 20

Detroit Lions football team
Barney, Lem 26
Farr, Mel 24
Johnson, Levi 48
Mayhew, Martin R. 76
Sanders, Barry 1, 53
Ware, Andre 37

Detroit Pistons basketball team
Bing, Dave 3, 59, 78
Dumars, Joe 16, 65, 126
Gentry, Alvin 23
Hill, Grant 13, 94

Hunter, Lindsey 110
Lanier, Bob 47
Lloyd, Earl 26, 127
Lowe, Sidney 64
Mahorn, Rick 60
Mohammed, Nazr 64
Prince, Tayshaun 68
Robinson, Will 51, 69
Rodman, Dennis 12, 44, 96, 118
Stackhouse, Jerry 30
Thomas, Isiah 7, 26, 65
Wallace, Ben 54

Detroit Police Department
Bully-Cummings, Ella 48
Gomez-Preston, Cheryl 9
McKinnon, Isaiah 9
Napoleon, Benny N. 23

Detroit Tigers baseball team
Fielder, Cecil 2, 112
Horton, Willie 104
Virgil, Ozzie 48

Diabetes
Fennoy, Ilene 72
Wisdom, Kimberlydawn 57

Dictators
Abacha, Sani 11, 70
Afewerki, Isaias 98
Ahidjo, Ahmadou 81
Amin, Idi 42
Bashir, Omar al- 77
Biya, Paul 28, 114
Compaore, Blaise 87
Conté, Lansana 7, 76
Eyadéma, Gnassingbé 7, 52
Gbagbo, Laurent 43, 90
Habré, Hissène 6, 104
Kabila, Laurent 20
Mengistu, Haile Mariam 65
Moi, Daniel Arap 1, 35
Mswati III 56
Mugabe, Robert 10, 71
Obiang, Teodoro 103
Sassou-Nguesso, Denis 103
Traore, Dioncounda 103
Touré, Sekou 6
Zenawi, Meles 3, 99

Diner's Club
Gaines, Brenda 41

Diplomatic Corps
See U.S. Department of State

Disabled American Veterans (DAV)
Brown, Jesse 6, 41

Disco
Chic 117
Gaynor, Gloria 36
Holloway, Loleatta 115
Payne, Freda 58
Perren, Freddie 60
Rose Royce 120
Shaw, Marlena 105
Staton, Candi 27
Summer, Donna 25, 102
Tavares 115
Trammps, The 108

Ward, Anita 118

Distance running
Abdirahman, Abdi 126
Cheruiyot, Robert 69
Jeptoo, Rita 121
Keflezighi, Meb 49, 121
Kimetto, Dennis 125
Kipchoge, Eliud 124
Kipsang, Wilson 115
Loroupe, Tegla 59
Tergat, Paul 59
Wanjiru, Sammy 94

Diving
Brashear, Carl 29

DJ
Alert, Kool DJ Red 32
Atkins, Juan 50
Bond, Beverly 53
DJ Clue? 111
DJ Jazzy Jeff 32
DJ Lance Rock 94
DJ Screw 110
Felix Da Housecat 110
Grandmaster Flash 33, 60
Knuckles, Frankie 42, 120
Love, Ed 58

Documentary film
Billops, Camille 82
Blackwood, Maureen 37
Branch, William Blackwell 39
Byrd, Robert 11
Crump, Steven 96
Dash, Julie 4
DuVernay, Ava 98, 126
Elie, Lolis Eric 97
Gray, Darius 69
Greaves, William 38, 123
Hampton, Henry 6
Henry, Lenny 9, 52
Hudlin, Reginald 9, 86
Hudlin, Warrington 9
Hurt, Byron 61
Jean, Michaëlle; 70
Julien, Isaac 3
Kabera, Eric 104
Lynch, Shola 61
Miles, William 112
Nelson, Stanley 92
Peck, Raoul 32
Rees, Dee 100
Riggs, Marlon 5, 44
Roberts, Kimberly Rivers 72
Whack, Rita Coburn 36
Williams, Marco 53

Dollmaking
El Wilson, Barbara 35

Dominica government
Charles, Mary Eugenia 10, 55
Charles, Pierre 52
Skerrit, Roosevelt 72

Drama Desk Awards
Carter, Nell 39
Coles, Honi 128
Holder, Geoffrey 78, 124
McDonald, Audra 20, 62, 128
Taylor, Ron 35
Wesley, Richard 73

Wolfe, George C. **6, 43, 127**

Drug abuse prevention
Clements, George **2**
Creagh, Milton **27**
Hale, Lorraine **8**
Harris, Alice **7**
Lucas, John **7**

Drums
Ali, Rashied **79**
Allen, Tony **117**
Batiste, Lionel **105**
Blade, Brian **88**
Blakey, Art **37**
Brooks, Roy **125**
Brown, Carlinhos **81**
Chancler, Ndugu **115**
Cobb, Jimmy **119**
Cobham, Billy **123**
Cole, Cozy **123**
Coleman, Denardo **122**
Drake, Hamid **121**
Durham, Bobby **73**
Graves, Milford **126**
Greer, Sonny **127**
Güines, Tata **69**
Haynes, Roy **87**
Hamilton, Chico **117**
Hart, Billy **126**
Jones, Elvin **14, 68**
Jones, Philly Joe **121**
Kay, Connie **114**
La Roca, Pete **107**
Lea, Babatunde **124**
Locke, Eddie **44**
Miles, Buddy **69**
Purdie, Bernard **77**
Rodríguez, Arsenio **87**
Tate, Grady **106**
Thigpen, Ed **110**
Washington, Kenny **107**
Webb, Chick **105**
Williams, Tony **67**
Young, Lee **72**

Dunham Dance Company
Dunham, Katherine **4, 59**

DuSable Museum of African American History
Burroughs, Margaret Taylor **9**
Wright, Antoinette **60**

E Street Band
Clemons, Clarence **41**

East Harlem School at Exodus House
Hageman, Hans **36**
Hageman, Ivan **36**

Ebonics
Cook, Toni **23**

***Ebony* magazine**
Bennett, Lerone, Jr. **5, 84**
Branch, William Blackwell **39**
Cullers, Vincent T. **49**
Fuller, Hoyt **44**
Johnson, Eunice W. **83**
Johnson, John H. **3, 54**
Massaquoi, Hans J. **30**
Rice, Linda Johnson **9, 41**

Sleet, Moneta, Jr. **5**

Ebony Museum of African American History
See DuSable Museum of African American History

Economics
Ake, Claude **30**
Arthur, Owen **33**
Boyd, T. B., III **6**
Brimmer, Andrew **2, 48, 106**
Brown, Tony **3**
Conrad, Cecilia A. **94**
Fryer, Roland G. **56**
Gibson, William F. **6**
Hampton, Henry **6**
Juma, Calestous **57**
Malveaux, Julianne **32, 70**
Moyo, Dambisa **76**
Okonjo-Iweala, Ngozi **101**
Pitta, Celso **17**
Raines, Franklin **14, 107**
Robinson, Randall **7, 46**
Simms, Margaret **94**
Sowell, Thomas **2, 99**
Spriggs, William **67**
Sullivan, Leon H. **3, 30**
Wallace, Phyllis A. **9**
Washington, Ebonya **79**
Wharton, Clifton R., Jr. **7**
White, Michael R. **5**
Williams, Walter E. **4**
Woodson, Robert L. **10**

Editing
Abani, Chris **77**
Aubert, Alvin **41**
Bass, Charlotta Spears **40**
Brown, Lloyd Louis **42**
Curry, George E. **23**
Delany, Martin R. **27**
Dumas, Henry **41**
Murphy, John H. **42**
Schuyler, George Samuel **40**

Edmonton Oilers hockey team
Fuhr, Grant **1, 49**
Grier, Mike **43**
Laraque, Georges **48**

EEOC
See Equal Employment Opportunity Commission

Electronic music
Atkins, Juan **50**
Craig, Carl **31, 71**
DJ Rashad **121**
Felix Da Housecat **110**
May, Derrick **41**
Romanthony **115**

Emmy Awards
Aduba, Uzo **122**
Allen, Debbie **13, 42**
Amos, John **8, 62**
Ashe, Arthur **1, 18**
Barclay, Paris **37, 94**
Barnes, Katreese **97**
Belafonte, Harry **4, 65**
Bradley, Ed **2, 59**
Branch, William Blackwell **39**
Brown, James **22**
Brown, Les **5**

Browne, Roscoe Lee **66**
Carter, Nell **39**
Clayton, Xernona **3, 45**
Coleman, Wanda **48, 119**
Cosby, Bill **7, 26, 59, 125**
Curtis-Hall, Vondie **17**
Dawes, Kwame **126**
De Shields, André **72**
Dee, Ruby **8, 50, 68, 122**
Fisher, Gail **85**
Foxx, Redd **2**
Freeman, Al, Jr. **11, 105**
Goldberg, Whoopi **4, 33, 69**
Gossett, Louis, Jr. **7**
Guillaume, Robert **3, 48**
Gumbel, Greg **8**
Hunter-Gault, Charlayne **6, 31**
Jones, James Earl **3, 49, 79**
Kitt, Eartha **16, 75**
La Salle, Eriq **12**
Mabrey, Vicki **26**
Martin, Michel **97**
McQueen, Butterfly **6, 54**
Moore, Shemar **21, 112**
Parks, Gordon **1, 35, 58**
Pinkston, W. Randall **24**
Quarles, Norma **25**
Richards, Beah **30**
Robinson, Max **3**
Rock, Chris **3, 22, 66**
Rolle, Esther **13, 21**
St. John, Kristoff **25**
Schiavocampo, Mara **97**
Taylor, Billy **23, 92**
Thigpen, Lynne **17, 41**
Tyson, Cicely **7, 51, 112**
Uggams, Leslie **23, 114**
Washington, Hayma **86**
Wayans, Damon **8, 41**
Whack, Rita Coburn **36**
Whitfield, Lynn **18**
Williams, Montel **4, 57**
Williams, Russell, II **70**
Williams, Sherley Anne **25**
Wilmore, Larry **121**
Winfrey, Oprah **2, 15, 61, 106**
Woodard, Alfre **9, 108**

Endocrinology
Fennoy, Ilene **72**

Engineering
Alexander, Archie Alphonso **14**
Anderson, Charles Edward **37**
Auguste, Donna **29**
Austin, Wanda M. **94**
Benson, Angela **34**
Boyd, Gwendolyn **49**
Boykin, Otis **92**
Burns, Ursula **60**
Clark, Yvonne Young **95**
Crosthwait, David **93**
Dabiri, John **93**
Douglas, Donya **97**
Emeagwali, Philip **30**
Ericsson-Jackson, Aprille **28**
Gibson, Kenneth Allen **6**
Gourdine, Meredith **33**
Greene, Frank S., Jr. **101**
Grooms, Henry R(andall) **50**
Hammond, Paula **119**
Harris, Gary L. **87**
Harris, Wesley L. **92**

Henderson, Cornelius Langston **26**
Henderson, Henry Fairfax, Jr. **89**
Howard, Ayanna **65**
Johnson, Anthony M. **92**
Johnson, Sandra K. **94**
Jones, Wayne **53**
Laroche, Joseph Philippe Lemercier **85**
Laryea, Thomas Davies, III **67**
McCoy, Elijah **8**
Miller, Warren F., Jr. **53**
Mills, Joseph C. **51**
Nteff, Alain **127**
O'Neal, Rodney **88**
Pierre, Percy Anthony **46**
Price, Richard **51**
Rillieux, Norbert **92**
Robinson-Berry, Joan **94**
Sigur, Wanda **44**
Slaughter, John Brooks **53**
Spencer, Michael G. **87**
Trotter, Lloyd G. **56**
West, James E. **87**
Wilkens, J. Ernest, Jr. **43**
Williams, O. S. **13**

Entertainment promotion
Bowen, Ruth **83**
Carter, Troy **98**
Isaacs, Cheryl Boone **113**
Lewis, Butch **71, 99**

Entrepreneur
Aire, Chris **117**
Bakewell, Danny **99**
Barden, Donald H. **9, 20, 89**
Burks, Juanita P. **95**
Dangote, Aliko **124**
Dash, Damon **31, 113**
Dash, Darien **29**
Downing, George T. **91**
Fletcher, Buddy **16, 108**
Fudge, Ann (Marie) **11, 55**
Gardner, Edward G. **45**
Gaston, Arthur George **3, 38, 59**
Gordy, Berry, Jr. **1**
Graves, Earl G. **1, 35**
Henderson, Henry Fairfax, Jr. **89**
Herndon, Alonzo Franklin **89**
Jennings, Thomas L. **125**
John, Daymond **23, 114**
Johnson, John H. **3, 54**
Jones, Carl **7**
Lamothe, Laurent **122**
Lewis, Reginald F. **6**
Maponya, Richard **101**
McCann, Renetta **44**
Middleton, Reggie **105**
Mupuya, Andrew **118**
Nteff, Alain **127**
Oboth, Isaac **117**
Otis, Clarence, Jr. **55**
Overton, Anthony **128**
Parks, Henry Green, Jr. **89**
Payton, Philip A., Jr. **88**
Perry, Tyler **40, 54, 103**
Rapelang Rabana **112**
Roberts, Mike **57**
Spaulding, Charles Clinton **9**
Steward, David L. **36**
Uys, Ashley **125**
Walker, Madame C. J. **7**
Walker, Maggie Lena **17**

Walker, T. J. 7
Winfrey, Oprah 2, 15, 61, 106
Woods, Granville T. 5

Environmental issues
Betsch, MaVynee 28
Bullard, Robert D. 121
Carter, Majora 77
Ellis-Lamkins, Phaedra 88
Eugene-Richard, Margie 63
Harden, Monique 97
Hill, Bonnie Guiton 20
Jackson, Lisa 77
Jones, Van 70
Jordan, Charles 122
Maathai, Wangari 43, 97
Miller-Travis, Vernice 64
Osborne, Na'taki 54
Saro-Wiwa, Kenule 39
Wright, Beverly 97

Epidemiology
Fenton, Kevin 87
Gayle, Helene D. 3
Poindexter, Hildrus A. 87

Episcopalian
Burgess, John 46
Harris, Barbara 12
Jones, Absalom 52
Redding, Ann Holmes 77
Walker, John T. 50
Williams, Frederick (B.) 63

Equal Employment Opportunity Commission (EEOC)
Alexander, Clifford 26
Berrien, Jacqueline A. 93
Hill, Anita 5, 65
Lewis, Delano 7
Norton, Eleanor Holmes 7, 93
Thomas, Clarence 2, 39, 65
Wallace, Phyllis A. 9

Equatorial Guinea government
Obiang, Teodoro 103

Eritrea government
Afewerki, Isaias 98

ESPN
Jackson, Tom 70
Lewis, Ray 33, 109
Masekela, Sal 106
Roberts, Robin 16, 54, 113
Salters, Lisa 71
Scott, Stuart 34, 126
Smith, Stephen A. 69
Tirico, Mike 68, 124
Wilbon, Michael 68

Essence magazine
Bandele, Asha 36
Burt-Murray, Angela 59
De Veaux, Alexis 44
Ebanks, Michelle 60
Grant, Gwendolyn Goldsby 28
Greenwood, Monique 38
Lewis, Edward T. 21
Parks, Gordon 1, 35, 58
Smith, Clarence O. 21
Taylor, Susan L. 10, 86

Wesley, Valerie Wilson 18

Essence Award
Broadbent, Hydeia 36
McMurray, Georgia L. 36

Ethiopia government
Desalegn, Hailemariam 105
Haile Selassie 7
Mengistu, Haile Mariam 65
Zenawi, Meles 3, 99

Etiquette
Bates, Karen Grigsby 40

Event planning
Bailey, Preston 64
Williams, Lindsey 75

Exiled heads of state
Amin, Idi 42
Aristide, Jean-Bertrand 6, 45
Mengistu, Haile Mariam 65
Mobutu Sese Seko 1, 56

Exploration
Bishop, Stephen 95
Henson, Matthew 2

Famine relief
See World hunger

Fannie Mae
Jackson, Maynard 2, 41
Raines, Franklin 14, 107

Fashion
Biya, Chantal 89
Boateng, Ozwald 35, 113
Boyd, Suzanne 52
Chanticleer, Raven 91
DaCosta, YaYa 98
Delice, Ronald 48
Delice, Rony 48
Evans, Etu 55
Fine, Sam 60
Finley, Ron 110
Givhan, Robin Deneen 72
Hall, Kevan 61
Hendy, Francis 47
Jones, Genevieve 101
Keckley, Elizabeth 90
Knowles, Tina 61
Luna, Donyale 88
McGrath, Pat 72
Reese, Tracy 54
Simmons, Kimora Lee 51, 83
Smaltz, Audrey 12
Smith, LaQuan 113
Steele, Lawrence 28
Stoney, Michael 50
Sy, Oumou 65
Talley, André Leon 56, 106
White, Jessica 83

Fashion Institute of Technology (FIT)
Brown, Joyce F. 25

FCC
See Federal Communications Commission

Federal Bureau of Investigation (FBI)
Gibson, Johnnie Mae 23
Harvard, Beverly 11

Federal Communications Commission (FCC)
Barrett, Andrew C. 12
Clyburn, Mignon 78
Hughes, Cathy 27
Kennard, William Earl 18
Powell, Michael 32
Russell-McCloud, Patricia A. 17

Federal Court of Canada
Isaac, Julius 34

Federal Emergency Management Agency
Becton, Julius W., Jr. 110

Federal Reserve Bank
Brimmer, Andrew 2, 48, 106
Ferguson, Roger W., Jr. 25, 112
Layton, William 87
Rice, Emmett J. 94

Fencing
Boulogne, Joseph, Chevalier de Saint-Georges 94
Westbrook, Peter 20

Fiction
Adams, Jenoyne 60
Adichie, Chimamanda Ngozi 64, 121
Alexander, Margaret Walker 22
Ali, Mohammed Naseehu 60
Amadi, Elechi 40
Anthony, Michael 29
Ansa, Tina McElroy 14
Armah, Ayi Kwei 49
Ashley & JaQuavis 107
Attaway, William 102
Ba, Mariama 30
Baiocchi, Regina Harris 41
Baisden, Michael 25, 66
Beckham, Barry 41
Benson, Angela 34
Berry, James 41
Bolden, Tonya 32
Bradley, David Henry, Jr. 39
Brand, Dionne 32
Briscoe, Connie 15
Brown, Cecil M. 46
Brown, Lloyd Louis 42
Bulawayo, NoViolet 125
Bunkley, Anita Richmond 39
Butler, Octavia 8, 43, 58
Campbell, Bebe Moore 6, 24, 59
Cartiér, Xam Wilson 41
Chase-Riboud, Barbara 20, 46
Cheney-Coker, Syl 43
Chesnutt, Charles 29
Clark, Wahida 107
Clarke, Austin 32
Cleage, Pearl 17, 64
Cliff, Michelle 42
Cole, Teju 120
Colter, Cyrus J. 36
Cooper, J. California 12, 85, 125
Creagh, Milton 27
Danticat, Edwidge 15, 68, 128
Dathorne, O. R. 52
Demby, William 51
Diop, Birago 53
DoHarris, Brenda 116
Draper, Sharon Mills 16, 43
Due, Tananarive 30

Dumas, Henry 41
Dunbar-Nelson, Alice Ruth Moore 44
Duplechan, Larry 55
Edugyan, Esi 98
Ellis, Trey 97
Emecheta, Buchi 30
Evans, Diana 72
Everett, Percival 93
Fair, Ronald L. 47
Fales-Hill, Susan 88
Farah, Nuruddin 27
Farley, Christopher John 54
Files, Lolita 35
Ford, Nick Aaron 44
Ford, Wallace 58
Forna, Aminatta 95
Forrest, Leon 44
Foye, K'wan 97
Gomez, Jewelle 30
Gray, Darius 69
Greenlee, Sam 48
Harper, Rachel M. 92
Harris, E. Lynn 12, 33, 116
Haywood, Gar Anthony 43
Hercules, Frank 44
Hill, Donna 32
Holton, Hugh, Jr. 39
Horne, Frank 44
Jackson, Sheneska 18
Jakes, T. D. 17, 43, 116
James, Marlon 85, 124
Jasper, Kenji 39
Jenkins, Beverly 14
Johnson, Georgia Douglas 41
Jones, Edward P. 43, 67
Jones, Gayl 37
Jones, Tayari 96
Kamau, Kwadwo Agymah 28
Kay, Jackie 37
Kayira, Legson 40
Keene, John 73
Kendrick, Erika 57
Killens, John O. 54
Kincaid, Jamaica 4, 109
Laferriere, Dany 33
LaGuma, Alex 30
Lamar, Jake 96
Lamming, George 35
Lattany, Kristin Hunter 88
Laymon, Kiese 113
LeFlore, Lyah Beth 96
Locke, Attica 85
Machado de Assis 74
Marechera, Dambudzo 39
Markham, E. A. 37
Mason, Felicia 31
Mathabane, Mark 5, 99
Mbaye, Mariétou 31
McCrary Anthony, Crystal 70
McFadden, Bernice L. 39
McKinney-Whetstone, Diane 27
McMillan, Rosalynn A. 36
McMillan, Terry 4, 17, 53
Memmi, Albert 37
Mengestu, Dinaw 66, 114
Mitchell, Sharon 36
Monroe, Mary 35
Mosley, Walter 5, 25, 68
Mossell, Gertrude Bustill 40
Mphalele, Es'kia 40
Mwangi, Meja 40
Naylor, Gloria 10, 42

Nkosi, Lewis 46
Nugent, Richard Bruce 39
Okara, Gabriel 37
Ojikutu, Bayo 66
Packer, Z. Z. 64
Peters, Lenrie 43
Philip, Marlene Nourbese 32
Polite, Carlene Hatcher 82
Randall, Alice 38
Ridley, John 69
Roby, Kimberla Lawson 86
Sapphire 14, 95
Schuyler, George Samuel 40
Senior, Olive 37
Senna, Danzy 93
Smith, Danyel 40
Smith, Zadie 51
Southgate, Martha 58
Tate, Eleanora E. 20, 55
Taylor, Mildred D. 26
Teasley, Lisa 92
Thomas, Michael 69
Thomas-Graham, Pamela 29
Tutuola, Amos 30
Vera, Yvonne 32
Verdelle, A. J. 26
Walker, Margaret 29
Weaver, Afaa Michael 37
Whitehead, Colson 77
Whitfield, Van 34
Williams, Sherley Anne 25
Williams, Stanley "Tookie" 29, 57
Woods, Teri 69
Yarbrough, Camille 40
Yerby, Frank 96
Young, Al 82
Youngblood, Shay 32
Zane 71

Figure skating
Bonaly, Surya 7
Bonheur, Yannick 84
Fairbanks, Mabel 117
James, Vanessa 84
Thomas, Debi 26
Vanessa James and Yannick Bonheur 84

Film criticism
Mitchell, Elvis 67
White, Armond 80, 118

Film direction/video direction
Akomfrah, John 37
Allain, Stephanie 49
Barclay, Paris 37, 94
Blackwood, Maureen 37
Bonney, Tabi 98
Burnett, Charles 16, 68
Byrd, Robert 11
Coogler, Ryan 114
Daniels, Lee 36, 76
Dash, Julie 4
Dickerson, Ernest 6, 17
Duke, Bill 3, 96
DuVernay, Ava 98, 126
Franklin, Carl 11
Fuqua, Antoine 35
Gerima, Haile 38, 80
Gray, Darius 69
Gray, F. Gary 14, 49
Hamilton, Tanya 93
Harris, Leslie 6
Hayes, Teddy 40

Henriques, Julian 37
Hudlin, Reginald 9, 86
Hudlin, Warrington 9
Hughes, Albert 7
Hughes, Allen 7
Hurt, Byron 61
Jackson, George 19
Johnson, Clark 96
Julien, Isaac 3
Lane, Charles 3
Lee, Malcolm D. 75
Lee, Spike 5, 19, 86
Lemmons, Kasi 20
Lewis, Samella 25
Martin, Darnell 43, 78
McQueen, Steve 84
Micheaux, Oscar 7
Morton, Joe 18
Moses, Gilbert 12
Moss, Carlton 17
Mwangi, Meja 40
Onwurah, Ngozi 38
Palcy, Euzhan 94
Peck, Raoul 32
Perry, Tyler 40, 54, 103
Prince-Bythewood, Gina 31, 77
Rees, Dee 100
Riggs, Marlon 5, 44
Roberts, Darryl 70
RZA 80, 128
St. Jacques, Raymond 8
Schultz, Michael A. 6
Sembène, Ousmane 13, 62
Singleton, John 2, 30, 122
Sissako, Abderrahmane 127
Smith, Roger Guenveur 12
Souleymane, Mahamane 78
Tillman, George, Jr. 20
Townsend, Robert 4, 23
Tyler, Aisha N. 36
Underwood, Blair 7, 27, 76
Van Peebles, Mario 2, 51
Van Peebles, Melvin 7, 95
Wallace, William 75
Ward, Douglas Turner 42
Wayans, Damon 8, 41
Wayans, Keenen Ivory 18
White, Sylvain 96
Whitaker, Forest 2, 49, 67
Williams, Spencer 126

Film production
Allain, Stephanie 49
Amata, Jeta 111
Chase, Debra Martin 49, 96
Daniels, Lee 36, 76
Gerima, Haile 38, 80
Isaacs, Cheryl Boone 113
Julian, Hubert 90
McKee, Lonette 12, 119
Morrison, Vanessa 84
Onwurah, Ngozi 38
Packer, Will 71
Patton, Paula 62
Robinson, Matt 69
Stewart, Nzingha 89
Tyler, Aisha N. 36
Van Lierop, Robert 53
Walker, Chet 106
Ward, Douglas Turner 42
Wayans, Damien 78
Whitaker, Forest 2, 49, 67
Williams, Marco 53

Williams, Russell, II 70
Williamson, Fred 67

Film scores
Blanchard, Terence 43
Crouch, Andraé 27, 115, 126
Hancock, Herbie 20, 67
Jones, Quincy 8, 30
Lebo M 109
Prince 18, 65
RZA 80, 128

Finance
Adoboli, Kweku 106
Banks, Jeffrey 17
Bell, James A. 50
Boston, Kelvin E. 25
Brown, Eddie C. 35
Bryant, John 26
Chapman, Nathan A., Jr. 21
Chapman, Susan E. 94
Doley, Harold, Jr. 26
Epperson, Sharon 54
Ferguson, Roger W., Jr. 25, 112
Fletcher, Buddy 16, 108
Funderburg, I. Owen 38
Gaines, Brenda 41
Griffith, Mark Winston 8
Hall, Alvin D. 86
Harris, Carla A. 67
Hobson, Mellody 40
Jones, Thomas W. 41
Lawless, Theodore K. 8
Lewis, William M., Jr. 40
Louis, Errol T. 8
Mack, Iris 105
Marshall, Bella 22
Moyo, Dambisa 76
Nash, Shannon King 84
O'Neal, Stanley 38, 67
Rogers, John W., Jr. 5, 52
Ross, Charles 27
Shank, Suzanne F. 77
Taylor, Ephren W., II 61
Travis, Tracey T. 94

Finland government
Toivola, Jani 118

Firefighters
Barlow, Roosevelt 49
Bell, Michael 40

Fisk University
Imes, Elmer Samuel 39
Johnson, Charles S. 12
Phillips, Teresa L. 42
Smith, John L. 22

Fitness
Richardson, Donna 39
Smith, Ian 62

Florida A & M University
Ammons, James H. 81
Foster, William P. 88
Gaither, Alonzo Smith (Jake) 14
Humphries, Frederick 20

Florida Marlins baseball team
Hill, Michael 95
Mariner, Jonathan 41

Florida state government
Brown, Corrine 24, 90
Meek, Carrie 6, 36

Meek, Kendrick 41, 89
Menard, John Willis 90
Tribble, Israel, Jr. 8
Wilson, Frederica 92

Florida Supreme Court
Quince, Peggy A. 69

Flute
Collette, Buddy 119
Laws, Hubert 90
Wess, Frank 116

Folk music
Bailey, DeFord 33
Beken 111
Broonzy, Big Bill 82
Callier, Terry 106
Carolina Chocolate Drops 111
Chambers Brothers, The 116
Chapman, Tracy 26
Charlemagne, Manno 11
Cody, Radmilla 99
Cuney, William Waring 44
Davis, Gary 41
Dawson, William Levi 39
Handy, W. C. 8
Harper, Ben 34, 62
Havens, Richie 111
House, Son 8
Jenkins, Ella 15
King, Chris Thomas 120
Love, Laura 50
Nascimento, Milton 2, 64
Odetta 37, 74
Reagon, Toshi 76
Southern, Eileen 56
Spence, Joseph 49
White, Josh 86
Williams, Denise 40

Food products
Amos, Wally 9
Briggs, Curtis 84
Oliver, Garrett 95
Parks, Henry Green, Jr. 89
Siméus, Dumas M. 25, 110

Football
Buchanan, Ray 32
Clemons, Michael "Pinball" 64
Davis, Ernie 48
Dorrell, Karl 52
Gaither, Alonzo Smith 14
Gill, Turner 83
Gorden, W. C. 71
Grier, Bobby 95
Grier, Roosevelt 13
Jones, Ed "Too Tall" 46
Keith, Floyd A. 61
Lanier, Willie 33
Lewis, Marvin 51, 87
Lewis, William Henry 89
Mason, Derek 120
Perry, Lowell 30
Pollard, Fritz 53
Prince, Ron 64
Robinson, Eddie G. 10, 61
Shannon, Randy 82
Simmons, Bob 29
Smith, Lovie 66, 107
Strong, Charlie 118
Watts, J. C., Jr. 14, 38
Williams, Doug 22, 112

Willingham, Tyrone 43
Willis, Bill 68
Woodson, Rod 79

Football Hall of Fame, professional
Allen, Larry 109
Allen, Marcus 20
Barney, Lem 26
Briscoe, Marlin 37
Brooks, Derrick 43, 119
Brown, Jim 11, 95
Campbell, Earl 104
Carter, Cris 21, 109
Culp, Curley 110
Dean, Fred 98
Dent, Richard 97
Dickerson, Eric 27, 108
Faulk, Marshall 35, 96
Green, Darrell 39, 74
Greene, Joe 10
Harris, Franco 97
Hayes, Bob 77
Humphrey, Claude 119
Irvin, Michael 64
Jackson, Rickey 88
Johnson, John Henry 96
Joiner, Charlie 102
Jones, Deacon 92, 112
Jones, Walter 119
Kennedy, Cortez 104
Lane, Dick 92
Lanier, Willie 33
Little, Floyd 86
Little, Larry 90
Lofton, James 42
Lott, Ronnie 9
Martin, Curtis 104
Matson, Ollie 93
McDaniel, Randall Cornell 81
Monk, Art 38, 73
Moon, Warren 8, 66
Motley, Marion 26
Newsome, Ozzie 26, 117
Ogden, Jonathan 110
Page, Alan (Cedric) 7
Parker, Jim 64
Payton, Walter (Jerry) 11, 25
Perry, Joe 95
Pollard, Fritz 53
Randle, John 87
Rice, Jerry 5, 55, 89
Roaf, Willie 106
Robinson, Dave 110
Sanders, Barry 1, 53
Sanders, Deion 4, 31, 96
Sapp, Warren 38, 109
Sayers, Gale 28
Sharpe, Shannon 97
Shell, Art 1, 66
Simpson, O. J. 15, 100
Singletary, Mike 4, 76
Smith, Bruce 80
Smith, Emmitt 7, 87
Stallworth, John 102
Swann, Lynn 28
Taylor, Lawrence 25
Thomas, Derrick 25
Thomas, Emmitt 71
Thomas, Thurman 75
Tunnell, Emlen 54
Upshaw, Gene 18, 47, 72
White, Reggie 6, 50

Willis, Bill 68
Winslow, Kellen 83
Wood, Willie 111
Woodson, Rod 79
Wright, Rayfield 70

Ford Foundation
Franklin, Robert M. 13
Thomas, Franklin A. 5, 49

Ford Motor Company
Cherry, Deron 40
Dawson, Matel, Jr. 39
Goldsberry, Ronald 18
Hazel, Darryl B. 50
McMillan, Rosalynn A. 36

Foreign investment
Amoudi, Mohammed al- 88
dos Santos, Isabel 114

Forensic science
Griffin, Bessie Blout 43

Foster care
Hale, Clara 16
Hale, Lorraine 8

Fox Broadcasting Company
Corbi, Lana 42
McFarland, Roland 49
Oliver, Pam 54, 123
Strahan, Michael 35, 81

Fraternities/sororities
Thomas, Arthur Ray 52

Freddie Mac
Baker, Maxine 28

French Guiyana government
Taubira, Christiane 117

Funeral homes
March, William Carrington 56

Funk music
Ayers, Roy 16
Bar-Kays, The 118
Bonner, Leroy 113
Brown, James 15, 60
Cameo 120
Castor, Jimmy 100
Clinton, George 9, 93
Collins, Bootsy 31
Collins, Lyn 53
Gap Band, The 100
Johnson, Conrad O. 97
Love, Laura 50
Midnight Star 110
Monáe, Janelle 86
New Birth 124
Parker, Maceo 72
Parker, Ray, Jr. 85
Purdie, Bernard 77
Shider, Garry 87
Stone, Sly 85
Watson, Johnny "Guitar" 18
Woods, Belita 103

Fusion
Davis, Miles 4
Jones, Quincy 8, 30
Williams, Tony 67

Gabon government
Bongo, Ali Ben 80
Bongo, Omar 1, 79

Gambian government
Jammeh, Yahya 23, 104
Jawara, Dawda Kairaba 11

Gambling
Ivey, Phil 72, 106

Gangs
Coke, Christopher 108
Matthews, Ameena 105
Shakur, Yusef 85
Taylor, Bo 72
Williams, Stanley "Tookie" 29, 57

Garifuna music
Palacio, Andy 96

Gay and lesbian issues
Boykin, Keith 14
Carter, Mandy 11
Clarke, Cheryl 32
Collins, Jason 111
Davis, Wade, Jr. 103
De Veaux, Alexis 44
Garner, Tyron 99
Griner, Brittney 128
Hemphill, Essex 10
Julien, Isaac 3
Kato, David 103
Mugisha, Frank 119
Norman, Pat 10
Riggs, Marlon 5, 44
Wilson, Phill 9, 104

Genealogy
Allen, Lucy 85
Blockson, Charles L. 42
Haley, Alex 4

General Hospital TV series
Cash, Rosalind 28

General Motors Corporation
O'Neal, Stanley 38, 67
Roberts, Roy S. 14
Welburn, Edward T. 50

Genetics
Dunston, Georgia Mae 48
Harris, Mary Styles 31
Kittles, Rick 51
Olopade, Olufunmilayo Falusi 58

Geometric symbolism
Douglas, Aaron 7

Geophysics
Person, Waverly 9, 51

George Foster Peabody Awards
Bradley, Ed 2, 59
Hunter-Gault, Charlayne 6, 31
Mac, Bernie 29, 61, 72
Shaw, Bernard 2
Wilmore, Larry 121

Georgia state government
Baker, Thurbert 22
Bishop, Sanford D., Jr. 24, 111
Bond, Julian 2, 35, 106
Brooks, Tyrone 59
Johnson, Hank, Jr. 80

Johnson, Leroy R. 89
Majette, Denise 41
McKinney, Cynthia 11, 52, 74
Reed, Kasim 82
Scott, David 41, 117
Smyre, Calvin 90
Williams, Hosea 15, 31, 123

Georgia Supreme Court
Benham, Robert 78
Melton, Harold D. 79
Sears, Leah Ward 5, 79

Ghana government
Atta Mills, John 75
Bartels, Peggielene 80
Kufuor, John Agyekum 54, 82
Lee, Robert 112
Mahama, John Dramani 103
Nkrumah, Kwame 3
Rawlings, Jerry 9

Girl Scouts of the USA
Thompson, Cynthia Bramlett 50

Goddard Space Flight Center
Douglas, Donya 97
Ericsson-Jackson, Aprille 28

Golden Globe awards
Allen, Debbie 13, 42
Bassett, Angela 6, 23, 62
Cara, Irene 77
Carroll, Diahann 9
Cosby, Bill 7, 26, 59, 125
Fisher, Gail 85
Freeman, Morgan 2, 20, 62, 100
Ross, Diana 8, 27
Spencer, Octavia 100
Taylor, Regina 9, 46, 97

Golf
Bramlett, Joseph 91
Davis, Ben 115
Elder, Lee 6
Gibson, Althea 8, 43
Gregory, Ann 63
Jackson, Fred James 25
Peete, Calvin 11
Powell, Renee 34
Powell, William J. 82
Richmond, Mitch 19
Shippen, John 43
Sifford, Charlie 4, 49
Spiller, Bill 64
Woods, Cheyenne 103
Woods, Tiger 14, 31, 81

Gospel music
Adams, Oleta 18
Adams, Yolanda 17, 67
Andrews, Inez 108
Armstrong, Vanessa Bell 24
Bass, Fontella 104, 109
Baylor, Helen 36
Blind Boys of Alabama, The 99
Bonds, Margaret 39
Bradford, Alex 121
Bradley, J. Robert 65
Brewster, W. Herbert 128
Caesar, Shirley 19
Cage, Byron 53
Campbell, Lucie E. 118
Clark, Mattie Moss 61
Clark-Cole, Dorinda 66

Clark-Sheard, Karen 22, 114
Clayton, Merry 112
Cleveland, James 19
Christie, Angella 36
Coates, Dorothy Love 125
Cobbs, Tasha 114
Consolers, The 125
Cooke, Sam 17
Crouch, Andraé 27, 115, 126
Davis, Gary 41
Davis Sisters, The 119
Dorsey, Thomas 15
Fortune, James 92
Franklin, Aretha 11, 44, 115
Franklin, Kirk 15, 49, 97
Gaynor, Gloria 36
Golden Gate Quartet 104
Green, Al 13, 47, 74
Haddon, Dietrick 55
Hammond, Fred 23
Hawkins, Edwin 113
Hawkins, Tramaine 16
Hawkins, Walter 87
Higginsen, Vy 65
Holloway, Loleatta 115
Houghton, Israel 92
Houston, Cissy 20, 83
Jackson, Mahalia 5
Jeter, Claude 75
Johnson, Le'Andria 108
Jones, Bobby 20, 94
Kee, John P. 43, 116
Kenoly, Ron 45
Killings, Debra 57
Knight, Gladys 16, 66
Knight, Marie 80
Lassiter, Roy 24
Lawrence, Donald 99
Little Richard 15
Majors, Jeff 41
Mandisa 119
Mann, Tamela 92
Marrow, Queen Esther 24
Martin, Roberta 58
Martin, Sallie 120
Mary Mary 34, 92
May, Brother Joe 123
Mayfield, Curtis 2, 43
McClendon, Lisa 61
McClurkin, Donnie 25
Mighty Clouds of Joy 110
Mills, Stephanie 36
Monica 21
Moss, J 64
Mullen, Nicole C. 45
Myles, Raymond Anthony 121
Norful, Smokie 127
Peoples, Dottie 22
Phipps, Wintley 59
Preston, Billy 39, 59
Reagon, Bernice Johnson 7
Reedy, Jessica 101
Reese, Della 6, 20, 96
Sapp, Marvin 74
Scott, George 55
Sheard, Kierra 61, 114
Soul Stirrers 127
Stampley, Micah 54
Staples, Cleotha 113
Staples, Mavis 50, 88
Staples, "Pops" 32
Staton, Candi 27

Steinberg, Martha Jean "The
  Queen" 28
Swan Silvertones, The 110
Sweet Honey in the Rock 106
Take 6 112
Tharpe, Rosetta 65
Tonex 54
Tribbett, Tye 81
Walker, Albertina 10, 58, 89
Walker, Hezekiah 34
Ward, Willa 105
Washington, Dinah 22
Whalum, Kirk 37, 64
Williams, Deniece 36
Williams, Michelle 73
Wilson, Brian Courtney 94
Wilson, Natalie 38
Winans, Angie 36
Winans, BeBe 14
Winans, CeCe 14, 43
Winans, David 77
Winans, Debbie 36
Winans, Marvin L. 17, 127
Winans, Ronald 54
Winans, Vickie 24
Wright, O. V. 114
Wright, Timothy 74

Graffiti art
Scott, Dread 106
White, Dondi 34

Grammy Awards
Adams, Oleta 18
Adderley, Nat 29
Babyface 10, 31, 82
Badu, Erykah 22, 114
Battle, Kathleen 70
Belafonte, Harry 4, 65
Beyoncé 39, 70, 105
Blade, Brian 88
Blige, Mary J. 20, 34, 60, 97
Blind Boys of Alabama, The 99
Brandy 14, 34, 72
Caesar, Shirley 19
Cara, Irene 77
Carolina Chocolate Drops 111
Carter, Ron 104
Chapman, Tracy 26
Cleveland, James 19
Cole, Natalie 17, 60, 84
Combs, Sean 17, 43, 92
Coolio 103
Cosby, Bill 7, 26, 59, 125
Cotton, James 123
Cray, Robert 30
Crouch, Andraé 27, 115, 126
D'Angelo 27, 123
Davis, Miles 4
Dee, Ruby 8, 50, 68, 122
Duke, George 21, 113
Earth, Wind & Fire 98
Edwards, David 122
Ellington, Duke 5
Estelle 75
Évora, Cesária 12, 99
Ferrer, Ibrahim 41
Fitzgerald, Ella 8
Forté, John 74
Franklin, Aretha 11, 44, 115
Gamble, Kenny 85
Gaye, Marvin 2
Gaynor, Gloria 36

Gibson, Tyrese 27, 62
Glover, Corey 34
Goldberg, Whoopi 4, 33, 69
Gray, Macy 29
Green, Cee Lo 70, 103
Guy, Buddy 31
Harris, Damon 110
Hathaway, Donny 18
Hawkins, Tramaine 16
Hawkins, Walter 87
Hayes, Isaac 20, 58, 73
Hill, Lauryn 20, 53, 111
Holland-Dozier-Holland 36
Hooker, John Lee 30
Houston, Cissy 20, 83
Houston, Whitney 7, 28, 83, 100
Hubbard, Freddie 75
Isley, Ronald 25, 56
Jackson, Janet 6, 30, 68
Jackson, Michael 19, 53, 76
James, Etta 13, 52, 100
Jarreau, Al 21, 65, 105
Jay-Z 27, 69, 103
Jean, Wyclef 20, 86
Jimmy Jam 13
Johnson, Le'Andria 108
Jones, Bobby 20, 94
Jones, Quincy 8, 30
Keb' Mo' 36, 124
Kelly, R. 18, 44, 71, 117
Keys, Alicia 32, 68
Knight, Gladys 16, 66
Knuckles, Frankie 42, 120
LaBelle, Patti 13, 30
Lecrae 108
Lawrence, Donald 99
Lebo M 109
Legend, John 67, 116
Lewis, Terry 13
Lopes, Lisa 36
Mahal, Taj 39
Maitreya, Sananda 85
Makeba, Miriam 2, 50, 74
Marley, Ziggy 41
Marsalis, Branford 34, 103
M.C. Hammer 20, 80
McBee, Cecil 123
McCoy, Van 123
McDonald, Audra 20, 62, 128
Method Man 81
Mighty Clouds of Joy 110
Mills, Stephanie 36
Moore, LeRoi 72
Murphy, Eddie 4, 20, 61
Naughty by Nature 124
Norful, Smokie 127
Norman, Jessye 5
Obama, Barack 49, 74, 91
Olatunji, Babatunde 36, 126
Paul, Billy 127
Perkins, Pinetop 70
Poitier, Sidney 11, 36
Price, Leontyne 1
Pride, Charley 26
Prince 18, 65
Queen Latifah 1, 16, 58, 119
?uestlove 74
Redding, Otis 16
Reeves, Dianne 32, 119
Reid, Vernon 34
Rhymefest 97
Richie, Lionel 27, 65, 114
Rihanna 65, 102

Robinson, Smokey 3, 49
Rollins, Sonny 37, 94
Roots, The 101
Ross, Isaiah "Doc" 40
Rucker, Darius 34, 74, 108
Sade 15, 92
Scott, Jill 29, 83
Seal 14, 75
Shaggy 31
Shorter, Wayne 75
Simon, Joe 109
Slash 75
Smith, Will 8, 18
Stewart, Tricky 98
Street, Richard 110
Summer, Donna 25, 102
Swizz Beatz 108
Temptations, The 33
Trammps, The 108
Turner, Tina 6, 27
Walker, Hezekiah 34
Warwick, Dionne 18, 111
West, Kanye 52, 93
White, Barry 13, 41
White, Maurice 29
Whitfield, Norman 73
Williams, Deniece 36
Williams, Joe 5, 25
Williams, Michelle 73
Williams, Paul 112
Williams, Pharrell 47, 82, 119
Wilson, Nancy 10, 98
Winans, CeCe 14, 43
Winans, Marvin L. 17, 127
Wonder, Stevie 11, 53, 121

Grand Ole Opry
Bailey, DeFord 33

Graphic novels
Anderson, Ho Che 54
Johnson, Mat 31, 105
Jones, Rashida 101
McDuffie, Dwayne 62
Tooks, Lance 62

**Green Bay Packers football
team**
Brooks, Aaron 33
Butler, Leroy, III 17
Driver, Donald 99
Howard, Desmond 16, 58
Mann, Bob 126
Sharper, Darren 32, 118
White, Reggie 6, 50
Wood, Willie 111

Green Party
Clemente, Rosa 74
McKinney, Cynthia 11, 52, 74

Grenada government
Bishop, Maurice 39
Gairy, Eric Matthew 83
Mitchell, Keith 82

Guardian
Trotter, Monroe 9

Guggenheim fellowship
Anderson, T. J. 119
Braxton, Anthony 128
Bullins, Ed 25, 121
Coleman, Wanda 48, 119
Holder, Geoffrey 78, 124

Miles, William 112
Pope.L, William 72
Rollins, Sonny 37, 94
Taylor, Cecil 70
Wilson, Ellis 39

Guinea government
Camara, Moussa Dadis 76
Condé, Alpha 95
Conté, Lansana 7, 76
Touré, Sekou 6

Guinea-Bissau government
Cabral, Amílcar 104
Sanhá Malam Bacai 84, 101
Vieira, João 14, 84

Guitar
Ade, King Sunny 41
Arnold, Kokomo 116
Baker, Mickey 95
Barker, Danny 32
Barnes, Roosevelt "Booba" 33
Bibb, Eric 49, 123
Brim, John 117
Brown, Clarence Gatemouth 59
Butler, Jonathan 28
Burns, Eddie 44
Burnside, R. L. 56
Caymmi, Dorival 72
Collins, Bootsy 31
Copeland, Johnny 110
Cosey, Pete 103
Cray, Robert 30
Davis, Gary 41
Dawkins, Jimmy 111
Diddley, Bo 39, 72
Estes, Sleepy John 33
Fuller, Blind Boy 86
Fulson, Lowell 118
Green, Grant 56
Guitar Slim 125
Guy, Buddy 31
Harris, Corey 39, 73
Hemphill, Jessie Mae 33, 59
Hendrix, Jimi 10
Homesick James 124
House, Son 8
Hooker, John Lee 30
Hopkins, Lightnin' 83
Howlin' Wolf 9
James, Elmore 114
Johnson, Robert 2
Johnson, Syl 97
Johnson, Tommy 106
Jordan, Ronny 26
Killings, Debra 57
King, B. B. 7
King, Freddie 92
Klugh, Earl 59
Kolosoy, Wendo 73
Kravitz, Lenny 10, 34
Leadbelly 82
Lenoir, J. B. 117
Lipscomb, Mance 49
Long, Huey 79
Loueke, Lionel 88
Lynn, Barbara 126
Magic Slim 110
Marley, Bob 5
Mayfield, Curtis 2, 43
McTell, Blind Willie 89
Montgomery, Wes 88
Murphy, Matt 117

Ndegeocello, Meshell 15, 83
Nighthawk, Robert 121
Ongala, Remmy 9, 91
Parker, Ray, Jr. 85
Patton, Charley 107
Pena, Paul 58
Pitts, Skip 103
Ranglin, Ernest 78
Rodríguez, Arsenio 87
Rush, Bobby 78
Seals, Son 56
Shider, Garry 87
Shines, Johnny 116
Slash 75
Spence, Joseph 49
Sumlin, Hubert 101
Taylor, Eddie 116
Taylor, Hound Dog 120
Ulmer, James 79
Walker, Joe Louis 118
Walker, T-Bone 111
Watson, Johnny "Guitar" 18
White, Bukka 120
White, Josh 86
Williams, Jody 113

Guyana government
Burnham, Forbes 66
Jagan, Cheddi 16

Gymnastics
Dawes, Dominique 11, 126
Hilliard, Wendy 53
White, Jesse 22, 75

Hair care
See Beauty salons and products

Haiti government
Aristide, Jean-Bertrand 6, 45
Duvalier, François 124
Duvalier, Jean-Claude 124
Lamothe, Laurent 122
Manigat, Mirlande 90
Martelly, Michel 90
Pascal-Trouillot, Ertha 3
Pierre-Louis, Michèle 75
Préval, René 87

Hale House
Hale, Clara 16
Hale, Lorraine 8

Harlem Globetrotters
Chamberlain, Wilt 18, 47
Gates, William 97
Haynes, Marques 22
Jackson, Mannie 14
Tatum, Reece 104
Woodard, Lynette 67

Harlem Renaissance
Alexander, Margaret Walker 22
Bennett, Gwendolyn B. 59
Christian, Barbara T. 44
Crichlow, Ernest 75
Cullen, Countee 8
Cuney, William Waring 44
Dandridge, Raymond Garfield 45
Davis, Arthur P. 41
Delaney, Beauford 19
Ellington, Duke 5
Fauset, Jessie 7
Fisher, Rudolph 17
Frazier, E. Franklin 10

Horne, Frank 44
Hughes, Langston 4
Hurston, Zora Neale 3
Imes, Elmer Samuel 39
Johnson, Georgia Douglas 41
Johnson, James Weldon 5
Johnson, William Henry 3
Larsen, Nella 10
Locke, Alain 10
McKay, Claude 6
Mills, Florence 22
Morton, Ferdinand Q. 90
Nail, John E. 92
Nugent, Richard Bruce 39
Patterson, Louise 25
Payton, Philip A., Jr. 88
Petry, Ann 19
Thurman, Wallace 16
Toomer, Jean 6
VanDerZee, James 6
Waring, Laura Wheeler 99
West, Dorothy 12, 54
Wilson, Ellis 39

Harlem Writers Guild
Guy, Rosa 5
Killens, John O. 54
Wesley, Valerie Wilson 18

Harmonica
Arnold, Billy Boy 112
Bailey, DeFord 33
Barnes, Roosevelt "Booba" 33
Bell, Carey 114
Burns, Eddie 44
Cotton, James 123
Horton, Big Walter 115
Howlin' Wolf 9
Neal, Raful 44, 121
Parker, Junior 116
Pryor, Snooky 119
Ross, Isaiah "Doc" 40
Slim Harpo 120
Terry, Sonny 88

Harp
Coltrane, Alice 70
Majors, Jeff 41

Harvard Law School
Bell, Derrick 6, 98
Dickerson, Debra J. 60
Ogletree, Charles, Jr. 12, 47
Wilkins, David 77

Harvard University
Amaker, Tommy 62
Epps, Archie C., III 45
Ferguson, Ronald F. 75
Gomes, Peter J. 15, 93
Hammonds, Evelynn 69
Huggins, Nathan Irvin 52
Loury, Glenn 36
Poindexter, Hildrus A. 87

Head Start
Edelman, Marian Wright 5, 42
Taylor, Helen 30

Health care reform
Adams-Campbell, Lucille L. 60
Berrysmith, Don Reginald 49
Brown, Jesse 6, 41
Carroll, L. Natalie 44
Cole, Lorraine 48

Cooper, Edward S. 6
Dirie, Waris 56
Gibson, Kenneth A. 6
Hughes, Dora 88
Hughes, Ebony 57
Kintaudi, Leon 62
Lavizzo-Mourey, Risa 48
Potter, Myrtle 40
Randall, Vernellia R. 95
Richardson, Rupert 67
Tuckson, Reed V. 71
Vaughn, Viola 70
Williams, Daniel Hale 2
Williams, David Rudyard 50

Heart disease
Cooper, Edward S. 6
Grant, Augustus O. 71
Watkins, Levi, Jr. 9

Heisman Trophy
Allen, Marcus 20
Bush, Reggie 59, 88
Campbell, Earl 104
Davis, Ernie 48
George, Eddie 80
Griffin, Robert, III 107
Howard, Desmond 16, 58
Newton, Cam 96
Sanders, Barry 1, 53
Simpson, O. J. 15, 100
Walker, Herschel 1, 69
Ware, Andre 37
Williams, Ricky 85

Heroism
Autrey, Wesley 68
Delaney, Joe 76

HEW
See U.S. Department of Health,
  Education, and Welfare

HHS
See U.S. Department of Health and
  Human Services

Hip-hop music
Akon 68
apl.de.ap 84
Ashanti 37, 96
Banks, Azealia 107
Baraka, Sho 109
Benjamin, Andre 45
Big Freedia 128
Blacc, Aloe 119
Blackman, Toni 86
Blige, Mary J. 20, 34, 60, 97
Blitz the Ambassador 115
B.o.B. 91
Bradley, Adam 101
Budden, Joe 108
Cole, J. 97
Combs, Sean 17, 43, 92
D'banj 107
De La Soul 119
DJ Clue? 111
Elliott, Missy 31, 90
Estelle 75
Fabolous 93
Fat Boys 92
Fiasco, Lupe 64
FKA Twigs 123
Flying Lotus 124
Forté, John 74

Franti, Michael **93**
Fresh, Doug E. **93**
Garrett, Sean **57**
Ghostface Killah **90**
Glasper, Robert **101**
Guru **84**
Hill, Lauryn **20, 53, 111**
Hodge, Derrick **114**
Jean, Wyclef **20, 86**
Jennings, Lyfe **56, 69**
Kid Cudi **83**
Kitwana, Bakari **86**
K-Swift **73**
Kweli, Talib **93**
Lighty, Chris **105**
Lil Jon **124**
Lil Mama **117**
Lil Wayne **66, 84**
Madlib **88**
Mane, Gucci **91**
Masta Ace **118**
Method Man **81**
Miguel **98**
Minaj, Nicki **86, 124**
Nelly **32, 90**
Nate Dogg **92**
Patton, Antwan **45**
Peterson, James **81**
Pharcyde, The **127**
Public Enemy **98**
?uestlove **74**
Rae Sremmurd **126**
Rascal, Dizzee **82**
Redman **81**
Riggins, Karriem **102**
Rock, Pete **121**
Roots, The **101**
Run **31, 73**
Santana, Juelz **120**
Scott-Young, Mona **101**
Sermon, Erick **81**
Shabazz Palaces **123**
Slick Rick **93**
Smith, Danyel **40**
Swizz Beatz **108**
Tricky **98**
2 Chainz **105**
Wale **92**
West, Kanye **52, 93**
will.i.am **64**
Williams, Pharrell **47, 82, 119**

Hip-hop theater
Power, Will **83**

Historians
Blassingame, John Wesley **40**
Bogle, Donald **34**
Cooper, Afua **53**
Crew, Spencer R. **55**
Cruse, Harold **54**
Fisher, Miles Mark **91**
Franklin, John Hope **5, 77**
Gates, Henry Louis, Jr. **3, 38, 67**
Giddings, Paula **11**
Hammonds, Evelynn **69**
Harris, Jessica B. **91**
Harris, Rennie **120**
Horton, James Oliver **58**
Huggins, Nathan Irvin **52**
Logan, Rayford W. **40**
Nash, Joe **55**
Moore, Wes **86**

Patterson, Orlando **4, 127**
Querino, Manuel Raimundo **84**
Reddick, Lawrence Dunbar **20**
Rogers, Joel Augustus **30**
Sadlier, Rosemary **62**
Skinner, Kiron K. **65**
Snowden, Frank M., Jr. **67**
Washington, James Melvin **50**
Williams, George Washington **18**
Williams, Rhonda Y. **86**

Hockey
Carnegie, Herbert **25**
Doig, Jason **45**
Grand-Pierre, Jean-Luc **46**

Horse racing
Harris, Sylvia **70**
Khumalo, S'manga **119**
Krigger, Kevin **111**
Minor, DeWayne **32**
St. Julien, Marlon **29**
Winkfield, Jimmy **42**

House of Representatives
See U.S. House of Representatives

Houston Astros baseball team
Richard, J. R. **87**
Watson, Bob **25**

Houston Rockets basketball team
Lucas, John **7**
Olajuwon, Hakeem **2, 72**
Smith, Kenny **114**

Howard University
Adams-Campbell, Lucille L. **60**
Benjamin, Tritobia Hayes **53**
Branson, Herman **87**
Cardozo, Francis L. **33**
Childers, Lulu Vere **95**
Cobb, W. Montague **39**
Davis, Arthur P. **41**
Dodson, Owen **38**
Gerima, Haile **38, 80**
Harris, Gary L. **87**
Jenifer, Franklyn G. **2**
Johnson, Mordecai Wyatt **79**
Ladner, Joyce A. **42**
Langston, John Mercer **101**
Locke, Alain **10**
Logan, Rayford W. **40**
Malveaux, Floyd **54**
Neal, Larry **38**
Payton, Benjamin F. **23**
Porter, James A. **11**
Reid, Irvin D. **20**
Ribeau, Sidney **70**
Robinson, Spottswood W., III **22**
Snowden, Frank M., Jr. **67**
Sowande, Fela **39**
Spriggs, William **67**
Swygert, H. Patrick **22**
Wells, James Lesesne **10**
Wesley, Dorothy Porter **19**
White, Charles **39**
Young, Roger Arliner **29**

HUD
See U.S. Department of Housing
　and Urban Development

Hugo awards
Butler, Octavia **8, 43, 58**
Delany, Samuel R., Jr. **9**

Human resources
Howroyd, Janice Bryant **42**

Human rights
Abiola-Costello, Hafsat **108**
Atyam, Angelina **55**
Carter, Mandy **11**
Dow, Unity **104**
Harden, Monique **97**
Kato, David **103**
Maathai, Wangari **43, 97**
McDougall, Gay J. **11, 43**
Mugisha, Frank **119**
Mukoko, Jestina **75**
Stevenson, Bryan **128**

Hunter College
DeCarava, Roy **42, 81**
Mayhew, Richard **39**
Thomas, Michael **69**

IBM
Adkins, Rod **41**
Blackwell, Robert D., Sr. **52**
Dean, Mark **35**
Foster, Jylla Moore **45**
Thompson, John W. **26**
Zollar, Alfred **40**

Ice skating
See Figure skating

Illinois state government
Braun, Carol Moseley **4, 42**
Burris, Roland W. **25, 75**
Colter, Cyrus J. **36**
Jones, Emil, Jr. **74**
Kelly, Robin **114**
Meeks, James T. **92**
Obama, Barack **49, 74, 91**
Raoul, Kwame **55**
Trotter, Donne E. **28**
Washington, Harold **6**
White, Jesse **22, 75**

Illustrations
Anderson, Ho Che **54**
Baker, Matt **76**
Biggers, John **20, 33**
Bryan, Ashley **41, 104**
Crichlow, Ernest **75**
Dillon, Leo **103**
Fax, Elton **48**
Honeywood, Varnette P. **54, 88**
Hudson, Cheryl **15**
Kitt, Sandra **23**
Nelson, Kadir **115**
Pinkney, Jerry **15, 124**
Ransome, James E. **88**
Saint James, Synthia **12**
Simmons, Gary **58**

IMF
See International Monetary Fund

Indiana state government
Carson, Julia **23, 69**
Carter, Pamela Lynn **67**

Indianapolis Colts football team
Caldwell, Jim **81**
Sanders, Bob **72**

Indianapolis 500
Ribbs, Willy T. **2**

Industrial design
Harrison, Charles **72**

Information technology
Blackwell, Robert D., Sr. **52**
Coleman, Ken **57**
Council, LaVerne **94**
Gooden, Linda **94**
Hamilton, Vicki **95**
Hill, Wyllstyne D. **94**
Mayberry-Stewart, Melodie **94**
Pinkett, Randal **61**
Smith, Joshua **10**
Steward, David L. **36**
Walker, Tristan **98**
Woods, Jacqueline **52**
Zollar, Alfred **40**

Insurance
Gaston, Arthur George **3, 38, 59**
Herndon, Alonzo Franklin **89**
Hill, Jesse, Jr. **13**
Holstein, Casper **89**
James, Donna A. **51**
Kidd, Mae Street **39**
Killingsworth, Cleve, Jr. **54**
Overton, Anthony **128**
Procope, Ernesta **23**
Procope, John Levy **56**
Spaulding, Charles Clinton **9**
Thiam, Tidjane **104**
Vaughns, Cleopatra **46**
Williams, Ronald A. **57**
Willie, Louis, Jr. **68**

Interior design
Ashford, Calvin, Jr. **74**
Bridges, Sheila **36**
De' Alexander, Quinton **57**
Ham, Cynthia Parker **58**
Hayes, Cecil N. **46**
King, Robert Arthur **58**
Myles, Kim **69**
Steave-Dickerson, Kia **57**
Taylor, Karin **34**

International Monetary Fund (IMF)
Babangida, Ibrahim **4**
Chissano, Joaquim **7, 55, 67**
Patterson, P. J. **6, 20**

Internet
CasSelle, Malcolm **11**
Cooper, Barry **33**
Ellington, E. David **11**
Gilliard, Steve **69**
Knowling, Robert **38**
Mitchell, Shireen **89**
Thomas-Graham, Pamela **29**
Thompson, John W. **26**
Walker, Tristan **98**

Interpol
Noble, Ronald **46**

Inventions
Chisholm, Daquan **93**
Johnson, Lonnie G. **32, 93**
Jones, Frederick McKinley **68**
Julian, Percy Lavon **6**
Latimer, Lewis H. **4**

Matzeliger, Jan 93
McCoy, Elijah 8
Morgan, Garrett 1
Temple, Lewis 102
West, James E. 87
Woods, Granville T. 5

Investment banking
Jones, Clarence B. 114
McGuire, Raymond J. 57

Investment management
Beal, Bernard B. 46
Bryant, John 26
Ford, Wallace 58
Gardner, Chris 65
Goings, Russell 59
Green, Isaac H. 79
Harris, Carla A. 67
Middleton, Reggie 105
Procope, Ernesta 23
Rogers, John W., Jr. 5, 52
Utendahl, John 23

Islam
Ali, Ayaan Hirsi 58, 92
Kalbani, Adil 77
Muhammed, W. Deen 27
Noble Drew Ali 100
Redding, Ann Holmes 77

Italy government
Kyenge, Cécile 113

Ivory Coast government
Bedie, Henri Konan 21
Gbagbo, Laurent 43, 90
Guéï, Robert 66
Houphouët-Boigny, Félix 4, 64
Ouattara, Alassane 90
Thiam, Tidjane 104

Jackson State University
Mason, Ronald 27

Jamaica government
Golding, Bruce 78
Holness, Andrew 99
Marks, Audrey 99
Patterson, P. J. 6, 20
Shearer, Hugh 107
Simpson Miller, Portia 62, 100

Jazz
Adderley, Julian "Cannonball" 30
Adderley, Nat 29
Akinmusire, Ambrose 103
Albright, Gerald 23
Ali, Rashied 79
Allen, Geri 92
Allen, Tony 117
Ammons, Albert 112
Ammons, Gene 112
Amy, Curtis 114
Anderson, Carl 48
Anderson, Fred 87
Anderson, Ivie 126
Armstrong, Louis 2
Astatke, Mulatu 81
Austin, Lovie 40
Austin, Patti 24
Ayers, Roy 16
Ayler, Albert 104
Bailey, Buster 38
Bailey, Philip 63

Barker, Danny 32
Barron, Kenny 128
Bassey, Offiong 119
Batiste, Alvin 66
Batiste, Jonathan 108
Batiste, Lionel 105
Bechet, Sidney 18
Belgrave, Marcus 77
Belle, Regina 1, 51
Betts, Keter 85
Blade, Brian 88
Blake, John, Jr. 123
Blakey, Art 37
Blanchard, Terence 43
Bland, Edward 111
Blanton, Jimmy 108
Bolden, Buddy 39
Bostic, Earl 121
Braxton, Anthony 128
Bridgewater, Dee Dee 32, 92
Brooks, Roy 125
Brown, Clifford 86
Bryant, Ray 95
Buckner, Milt 110
Buika 120
Burbridge, Kofi 120
Burley, Dan 96
Butler, Henry 121
Butler, Jonathan 28
Byrd, Donald 109
Cables, George 125
Callier, Terry 106
Calloway, Blanche 100
Calloway, Cab 14
Campbell, Roy, Jr. 118
Carter, Benny 46
Carter, Regina 23
Carter, Ron 104
Carter, Warrick L. 27
Cartiér, Xam Wilson 41
Chambers, Paul 121
Charles, Ray 16, 48
Cheatham, Doc 17
Cherry, Don 119
Christian, Jodie 103
Clark, Sharón 105
Clark, Sonny 128
Clarke, Kenny 27
Clayton, Gerald 111
Cobb, Arnett 114
Cobb, Jimmy 119
Cobham, Billy 123
Cole, Cozy 123
Cole, Freddy 128
Cole, Maria 104
Cole, Nat "King" 17
Cole, Natalie 17, 60, 84
Coleman, Denardo 122
Coleman, George 106
Coleman, Ornette 39, 69
Coleman, Steve 124
Collette, Buddy 119
Coltrane, Alice 70
Coltrane, John 19
Coltrane, Ravi 71
Cook, Charles "Doc" 44
Cook, Junior 126
Cosey, Pete 103
Counce, Curtis 127
Count Basie 23
Crawford, Hank 77
Crawford, Randy 19
Criss, Sonny 128

Crothers, Scatman 19
Crouch, Stanley 11, 87
Crowder, Henry 16
Crusaders, The 116
Curson, Ted 108
Daemyon, Jerald 64
Daniels, Billy 124
Dara, Olu 35
Davis, Anthony 11
Davis, Frank Marshall 47
Davis, Miles 4
Davis, Wild Bill 114
Dickenson, Vic 38
Dixon, Bill 87
Doggett, Bill 124
Donegan, Dorothy 19
Dorham, Kenny 113
Downing, Will 19
Drake, Hamid 121
Drew, Kenny 123
Duke, George 21, 113
Dumas, Henry 41
Durham, Bobby 73
Dyett, Walter 113
Eckstine, Billy 28
Edison, Harry 114
Edwards, Teddy 123
Eldridge, Roy 37
Ellington, Duke 5
Ellison, Ralph 7
Ervin, Booker 106
Eubanks, Kevin 15, 108
Farmer, Art 38
Ferbos, Lionel 95
Ferbos, Lionel 95
Ferrell, Rachelle 29
Fitzgerald, Ella 8, 18
Flanagan, Tommy 69
Foster, Frank 97
Foster, George "Pops" 40
Fox, Donal 114
Freelon, Nnenna 32
Freeman, Von 104
Freeman, Yvette 27
Fuller, Arthur 27
Garner, Erroll 76
Gillespie, Dizzy 1
Glasper, Robert 101
Golson, Benny 37
Gordon, Dexter 25
Graves, Milford 126
Gray, Wardell 128
Green, Grant 56
Greene, Jimmy 74
Greer, Sonny 127
Griffin, Johnny 71
Grimes, Henry 124
Gryce, Gigi 124
Güines, Tata 69
Hall, Adelaide 126
Hamilton, Chico 117
Hampton, Lionel 17, 41
Hancock, Herbie 20, 67
Hardin Armstrong, Lil 39
Harris, Barry 68
Harris, Kevin 120
Hart, Billy 126
Hartman, Johnny 109
Hawes, Hampton 121
Hawkins, Coleman 9
Haynes, Roy 87
Heath, Percy 100
Henderson, Fletcher 32

Henderson, Joe 127
Higginbotham, J. C. 37
Hill, Andrew 66
Hines, Earl "Fatha" 39
Hinton, Milt 30
Hodge, Derrick 114
Holiday, Billie 1
Horn, Shirley 32, 56
Hubbard, Freddie 75
Humes, Helen 128
Hyman, Phyllis 19
Jackson, Bobby 119
Jackson, Milt 26
Jacquet, Illinois 49
Jamal, Ahmad 69
James, Etta 13, 52, 100
Jarreau, Al 21, 65, 105
Jeffries, Herb 122
Johnson, Buddy 36
Johnson, J. J. 37
Johnson, Ken 106
Johnson, Lonnie 85
Jones, Elvin 14, 68
Jones, Etta 35
Jones, Hank 57, 86
Jones, Jonah 39
Jones, Papa Jo 99
Jones, Philly Joe 121
Jones, Quincy 8, 30
Jones, Thad 68
Jordan, Louis 104
Jordan, Ronny 26
Kay, Connie 114
Kelly, Wynton 121
Kenyatta, Robin 54
Klugh, Earl 59
La Roca, Pete 107
Lancaster, Byard 105
Land, Harold 125
Lateef, Yusef 91, 117
Laws, Hubert 90
Lea, Babatunde 124
Ledisi 73
Lee, Consuela 84
Lewis, George 104
Lewis, Ramsey 35, 70
Lincoln, Abbey 3, 88
Liston, Melba 118
Little, Booker 105
Locke, Eddie 44
Long, Huey 79
Loueke, Lionel 88
Lucie, Lawrence 80
Lucien, Jon 66
Lynne, Gloria 115
Marsalis, Branford 34, 103
Marsalis, Delfeayo 41
Marsalis, Ellis 90
Marsalis, Wynton 16, 90
McBee, Cecil 123
McBride, James 35, 87
McDuff, Jack 116
McGhee, Howard 122
McGriff, Jimmy 72
McIntyre, Kalaparusha Maurice 117
McLean, Jackie 78
McRae, Carmen 77
Miley, Bubber 120
Miller, Marcus 84
Millinder, Lucky 101
Mills, Florence 22
Mingus, Charles 15
Mitchell, Blue 126

Mitchell, Dwike 111
Mitchell, Nicole 66
Moffett, Charnett 127
Monk, Thelonious 1
Montgomery, Little Brother 117
Montgomery, Wes 88
Moody, James 83
Moondoc, Jemeel 119
Moore, Melba 21
Moran, Jason 89
Morgan, Lee 102
Morton, Jelly Roll 29
Muse, Clarence Edouard 21
Nascimento, Milton 2, 64
Navarro, Fats 104
Nelson, Oliver 113
Newborn, Phineas, Jr. 127
Newman, David 76
Oliver, Joe "King" 42
Ory, Kid 118
Page, Walter 117
Parham, Truck 124
Parker, Charlie 20
Parker, Maceo 72
Parlan, Horace 108
Payne, Freda 58
Perkins, Carl 128
Peterson, Marvin "Hannibal" 27
Peterson, Oscar 52
Pettiford, Oscar 106
Powell, Benny 87
Powell, Bud 24
Prysock, Arthur 117
Purdie, Bernard 77
Ray, Carline 113
Redman, Joshua 30
Reeves, Dianne 32, 119
Rhyne, Melvin 109
Riggins, Karriem 102
Rivers, Sam 95
Roach, Max 21, 63
Roberts, Marcus 19, 113
Rollins, Sonny 37, 94
Ruffins, Kermit 85
Rushing, Jimmy 37
Sample, Joe 51, 123
Santamaria, Mongo 81
Scarlett, Millicent 49
Scott, Hazel 66
Scott, Jimmy 48, 122
Sessoms, Vivian 122
Shaw, Marlena 105
Shepp, Archie 101
Shipp, Matthew 107
Shirley, Donald 111
Shorter, Wayne 75
Silver, Horace 26, 122
Simpson-Hoffman, N'kenge 52
Sissle, Noble 29
Smith, Bessie 3
Smith, Buster 116
Smith, Cecilia 102
Smith, Cladys "Jabbo" 32
Smith, Dr. Lonnie 49
Smith, Jimmy 127
Smith, Lonnie Liston 49
Smith, Stuff 37
Smith, Willie 107
Somi 85
Souza, Carmen 111
Staton, Dakota 62
Stewart, Slam 126
Strayhorn, Billy 31

Sullivan, Maxine 37
Sun Ra 60
Swann, Lynn 28
Sweatman, Wilbur 125
Tacuma, Jamaaladeen 124
Take 6 112
Tampa Red 63
Tapscott, Horace 126
Tate, Buddy 108
Tate, Grady 106
Taylor, Billy 23, 92
Taylor, Cecil 70
Tchicai, John 102
Terry, Clark 39, 127
Thigpen, Ed 110
Threadgill, Henry 97
Tisdale, Wayman 50
Towles, Nat 128
Trombone Shorty 97
Turner, Mark 126
Tyner, McCoy 92
Ulmer, James 79
Valdés, Bebo 75
Valdés, Chucho 89
Vaughan, Sarah 13
Vinnegar, Leroy 124
Vinson, Eddie 112
Waldron, Mal 109
Waller, Fats 29
Walton, Cedar 114
Ware, David S. 106
Warren, Butch 116
Washington, Dinah 22
Washington, Grover, Jr. 17, 44
Washington, Kenny 107
Waters, Benny 26
Watson, Johnny "Guitar" 18
Watts, Reggie 52, 102
Webb, Chick 105
Webster, Katie 29
Wein, Joyce 62
Wess, Frank 116
Whalum, Kirk 37, 64
White, Maurice 29
Wiggins, Gerald 128
Williams, Claude 80
Williams, Cootie 114
Williams, Joe 5, 25
Williams, Mary Lou 15
Williams, Tony 67
Wilson, Abram 104
Wilson, Cassandra 16
Wilson, Gerald 49, 123
Wilson, Nancy 10, 98
Wright, Eugene 125
York, Vincent 40
Young, Lee 72
Young, Lester 37

Jet magazine
Johnson, John H. 3, 54
Massaquoi, Hans J. 30
Sleet, Moneta, Jr. 5

Jewelry
Aire, Chris 117

Jockeys
Harris, Sylvia 70
Lewis, Oliver 56
Winkfield, Jimmy 42

Johnson C. Smith University
Yancy, Dorothy Cowser 42

Johnson Products
Johnson, George E. 29

Johnson Publishing Company, Inc.
Booker, Simeon 23
Johnson, Eunice W. 83
Johnson, John H. 3, 54
Monroe, Bryan 71
Rice, Linda Johnson 9, 41
Rogers, Desirée 88
Sleet, Moneta, Jr. 5

Joint Center for Political and Economic Studies
Williams, Eddie N. 44

Joint Chiefs of Staff
See U.S. Joint Chiefs of Staff

Journalism
Abbott, Robert Sengstacke 27
Abrahams, Peter 39
Abu-Jamal, Mumia 15
Als, Hilton 105
Ansa, Tina McElroy 14
Aplin-Brownlee, Vivian 96
Ashley-Ward, Amelia 23
Asim, Jabari 71
Aubespin, Mervin 95
Auguste, Arnold A. 47
Azikiwe, Nnamdi 13
Bailey, Chauncey 68
Baquet, Dean 63, 121
Barnett, Amy Du Bois 46
Barrett, Lindsay 43
Bass, Charlotta Spears 40
Bates, Karen Grigsby 40
Bennett, Gwendolyn B. 59
Bennett, Lerone, Jr. 5, 84
Best, Carrie 80
Blair, Jayson 50
Blake, Asha 26
Blow, Charles M. 73
Bolden, Frank E. 44
Booker, Simeon 23
Borders, James 9
Boyd, Gerald M. 32, 59
Boyd, Suzanne 52
Bradley, Ed 2, 59
Britt, Donna 28
Brower, William 49
Brown, George Leslie 62
Brown, Lloyd Louis 42
Brown, Tony 3
Buckley, Gail Lumet 39
Burt-Murray, Angela 59
Burwell, Bryan 83
Caldwell, Earl 60
Campbell, Bebe Moore 6, 24, 59
Cary, Mary Ann Shadd 30
Cayton, Horace 26
Chadiha, Jeffri 57
Chideya, Farai 14, 61
Chiles, Nick 98
Churchwell, Robert, Sr. 76
Ciara, Barbara 69
Cooke, Marvel 31
Cook-Parrish, Mary Virginia 95
Cooper, Andrew W. 36
Cooper, Barry 33
Cooper, Helene 74
Cose, Ellis 5, 50
Croal, N'Gai 76

Crouch, Stanley 11, 87
Crump, Steven 96
Crutchfield, James N. 55
Cullen, Countee 8
Cunningham, Evelyn 23, 85
Dash, Leon 47
Datcher, Michael 60
Davis, Belva 61
Davis, Frank Marshall 47
Davis, Thulani 61
Dawkins, Wayne 20
Deggans, Eric 71
Douglass, Frederick 87
Drummond, William J. 40
Due, Tananarive 30
Dunnigan, Alice Allison 41
Duthiers, Vladimir 109
Eagleson, William Lewis 90
Edmonds, Terry 17
Elbagir, Nima 121
Elder, Larry 25, 120
Elie, Lolis Eric 97
Epperson, Sharon 54
Farley, Christopher John 54
Forman, James 7, 51
Fortune, T. Thomas 6
Fuller, Hoyt 44
Gaiter, Dorothy J. 80
Giddings, Paula 11
Gilliard, Steve 69
Givhan, Robin Deneen 72
Goode, Mal 13
Gordon, Ed 10, 53
Granderson, LZ 103
Grimké, Archibald H. 9
Gumbel, Bryant 14, 80
Gumbel, Greg 8
Hall, Tamron 96
Hare, Nathan 44
Harris, Claire 34
Harris, Jay 19
Harris, Richard E. 61
Hatcher, Andrew T. 90
Haygood, Wil 83
Haynes, Trudy 44
Henderson, Angelo 122
Henriques, Julian 37
Herbert, Bob 63, 96
Hickman, Fred 11
Hill, Jemele 109
Holmes, T. J. 98
Holt, Lester 66
Huggins, Edie 71
Hunter-Gault, Charlayne 6, 31
Ifill, Gwen 28
Jackson, James A. 90
Jarrett, Vernon D. 42
Jasper, Kenji 39
Jealous, Benjamin Todd 70, 113
Joachim, Paulin 34
Johnson, Georgia Douglas 41
Jones, Bomani 121
Kaufman, Monica 66
Kearney, Janis 54
Khanga, Yelena 6
Killens, John O. 54
King, Colbert I. 69
King, Gayle 19, 99
Kitwana, Bakari 86
Knight, Etheridge 37
LaGuma, Alex 30
Lacy, Sam 30, 46
Lamar, Jake 96

Lampkin, Daisy 19
Leavell, Dorothy R. 17
Lemon, Don 94
Lewis, Edward T. 21
Lomax, Louis E. 90
Lowe, Herbert 57
Mabrey, Vicki 26
Mabry, Marcus 70
Mabuza-Suttle, Felicia 43
Malveaux, Suzanne 88
Martin, Louis E. 16
Martin, Michel 97
Mason, Felicia 31
Maynard, Nancy Hicks 73
Maynard, Robert C. 7
Mbeki, Govan A. 80
McAlpin, Harry 121
McBride, James 35, 87
McCall, Nathan 8
McGruder, Robert 22, 35
McKay, Claude 6
Mickelbury, Penny 28
Mitchell, Elvis 67
Mitchell, Russ 21, 73
Mkapa, Benjamin W. 16, 77
Monroe, Bryan 71
Mossell, Gertrude Bustill 40
Mukoko, Jestina 75
Murphy, John H. 42
Murray, Pauli 38
Nakasa, Nat 123
Nelson, Jill 6, 54
Neville, Arthel 53
Newkirk, Pamela 69
Njawe, Pius 87
Nkosi, Lewis 46
Noble, Gil 76
Norris, Michele 83
O'Brien, Soledad 88
Oliver, Pam 54, 123
Olojede, Dele 59
Page, Clarence 4
Palmer, Everard 37
Parham, Marjorie B. 71
Parker, Star 70
Parks, Gordon 1, 35, 58
Payne, Ethel L. 28
Payne, Les 89
Perez, Anna 1
Perkins, Tony 24
Phillips, Joseph C. 73
Pinkston, W. Randall 24
Pitts, Byron 71
Pitts, Leonard, Jr. 54, 85
Plaatje, Sol T. 80
Poussaint, Renee 78
Pressley, Condace L. 41
Price, Hugh B. 9, 54
Prince, Richard E. 71
Pugh, Charles 81
Quarles, Norma 25
Rapier, James T. 82
Raspberry, William 2
Reed, Ishmael 8
Reeves, Rachel J. 23
Rhoden, William C. 67
Riley, Rochelle 50
Robertson, Gil L., IV 85
Robinson, Eugene 77
Robinson, Max 3
Rodgers, Johnathan 6, 51
Ross, Don 27
Rowan, Carl T. 1, 30

Russwurm, John Brown 100
Rust, Art, Jr. 83
Salih, Al-Tayyib 37
Salters, Lisa 71
Sanders, Pharoah 64
Sanneh, Kelefa 96
Schiavocampo, Mara 97
Schuyler, George Samuel 40
Schuyler, Philippa 50
Senior, Olive 37
Sesay, Isha 107
Shaw, Bernard 2, 28
Shipp, E. R. 15
Sidner, Sara 105
Simpson, Carole 6, 30
Smith, Clarence O. 21
Smith, Danyel 40
Smith, Stephen A. 69
Sowell, Thomas 2, 99
Staples, Brent 8
Stewart, Alison 13
Stokes, Carl 10, 73
Stone, Chuck 9, 120
Syler, Rene 53
Tate, Eleanora E. 20, 55
Tatum, Elinor R. 78
Tatum, Wilbert 76
Taylor, Kristin Clark 8
Teague, Bob 111
Thurman, Wallace 16
Tolson, Melvin B. 37
Trotter, Monroe 9
Tucker, Cynthia 15, 61
Walker, Teshima 114
Wallace, Michele Faith 13
Washington, Elsie B. 78
Washington, Harriet A. 69
Watson, Carlos 50
Watts, Rolonda 9
Wells-Barnett, Ida B. 8
Wesley, Valerie Wilson 18
Whitaker, Mark 21, 47
Whitfield, LeRoy 84
Whitlock, Jason 78
Wilbekin, Emil 63
Wilbon, Michael 68
Wiley, Ralph 8, 78
Wilkerson, Isabel 71
Wilkins, Roger 2, 84
Williams, Armstrong 29
Williams, Clarence 70
Williams, Juan 35, 80
Wiwa, Ken 67
Woods, Mattiebelle 63
Yette, Samuel F. 63
Zook, Kristal Brent 62

Judaism
Funnye, Capers C., Jr. 73
Stanton, Alysa 78

Judiciary
Allen, Macon Bolling 104
Gibbs, Mifflin W. 99
Hatchett, Glenda 32
Hubbard, Arnette 38
Sampson, Edith S. 4
Slater, Duke 125
Spencer, Vaino H. 99

Watt, Garland W. 113

Kansas City Chiefs football team
Allen, Marcus 20
Cherry, Deron 40
Delaney, Joe 76
Smith, Neil 109
Thomas, Derrick 25
Thomas, Emmitt 71

Kansas City Royals baseball team
White, Frank 95

Kansas State University
Prince, Ron 64

Kappa Alpha Psi
Hamilton, Samuel C. 47

Kentucky Derby
Krigger, Kevin 111
Winkfield, Jimmy 42

Kentucky Negro Educational Association
Cotter, Joseph Seamon, Sr. 40

Kentucky state government
Kidd, Mae Street 39

Kenya government
Kariuki, J. M. 67
Kenyatta, Jomo 5
Kenyatta, Uhuru 110
Kibaki, Mwai 60
Maathai, Wangari 43, 97
Mboya, Tom 107
Moi, Daniel Arap 1, 35
Ngilu, Charity 58
Odinga, Raila 67, 110

King Center
See Martin Luther King Jr. Center for Nonviolent Social Change

King Oliver's Creole Band
Armstrong, Louis 2
Hardin Armstrong, Lil 39
Oliver, Joe "King" 42

King's Troop of the Royal Horse Artillery
Scantlebury, Janna 47

Kraft General Foods
Fudge, Ann (Marie) 11, 55
Sneed, Paula A. 18

Kwanzaa
Karenga, Maulana 10, 71

Labour Party
Amos, Valerie 41

LaFace Records
Babyface 10, 31, 82
Benjamin, Andre 45
OutKast 35
Patton, Antwan 45
Reid, Antonio "L.A." 28

Landscape architecture
Williston, David Augustus 99

LAPD
See Los Angeles Police Department

Latin baseball leagues
Kaiser, Cecil 42

Law education
Alexander, Michelle 98
Bell, Derrick 6, 98
Carter, Stephen L. 4
Forman, James, Jr. 89
Guinier, Lani 7, 30
Johnson, Edward Austin 107
Langston, John Mercer 101
Williams, Patricia 11, 54

Law enforcement
Alexander, Joyce London 18
Barrett, Jacquelyn 28
Batts, Anthony 128
Bolton, Terrell D. 25
Bradley, Thomas 2, 20
Brown, Lee P. 1, 24, 109
Bully-Cummings, Ella 48
Evans, Warren C. 76
Feemster, Herbert 72
Freeman, Charles 19
Gibson, Johnnie Mae 23
Gittens, Charles L. 124
Glover, Nathaniel, Jr. 12
Gomez-Preston, Cheryl 9
Harvard, Beverly 11
Hillard, Terry 25
Holton, Hugh, Jr. 39
Hurtt, Harold 46
Johnson, Norma H. 17, 97
Johnson, Robert T. 17
Johnson, Sterling, Jr. 124
Jordan, Eddie 82
McKinnon, Isaiah 9
Moose, Charles 40
Napoleon, Benny N. 23
Noble, Ronald 46
Oliver, Jerry 37
Parks, Bernard C. 17
Ramsey, Charles H. 21, 69
Reeves, Bass 100
Robinson, Bishop L. 66
Schmoke, Kurt 1, 48
Sealy, Lloyd G. 125
Smith, Richard 51
Thomas, Franklin A. 5, 49
Wainwright, Joscelyn 46
Ward, Benjamin 68
Watkins, Craig 97
Williams, Dennis P. 123
Williams, Willie L. 4
Wilson, Jimmy 45
Wray, Noble 114

LDF
See NAACP Legal Defense and Educational Fund

League of Nations
Haile Selassie 7

Legal Defense Fund
See NAACP Legal Defense and Educational Fund

Lesotho government
Mosisili, Pakalitha 96
Thabane, Thomas 123

Lexicography
Major, Clarence 9

Liberia government
Doe, Samuel K. 100
Henries, A. Doris Banks 44
Roberts, Joseph Jenkins 125
Russwurm, John Brown 100
Sawyer, Amos 2, 123
Sirleaf, Ellen Johnson 71
Tolbert, William R. 100
Tubman, William 99
Weah, George 58

Library science
Bontemps, Arna 8
Franklin, Hardy R. 9, 87
Harsh, Vivian Gordon 14
Hutson, Jean Blackwell 16
Jones, Clara Stanton 51
Josey, E. J. 10
Kitt, Sandra 23
Larsen, Nella 10
Morrison, Sam 50
Rollins, Charlemae Hill 27
Shockley, Ann Allen 84
Smith, Jessie Carney 35
Spencer, Anne 27
Wedgeworth, Robert W. 42
Wesley, Dorothy Porter 19

Librettos
Chenault, John 40

Lincoln University (MO)
Page, Inman 82
Randall, Dudley 8, 55

Lincoln University (PA)
Cuney, William Waring 44
Sudarkasa, Niara 4

Linguistics
McWhorter, John 35, 119

Literacy
Amos, Wally 9
Omolewa, Michael 119

Literary criticism
Braithwaite, William Stanley 52
Brown, Sterling Allen 10, 64
Broyard, Anatole 68
Cartey, Wilfred 47
Christian, Barbara T. 44
Cook, Mercer 40
De Veaux, Alexis 44
Emanuel, James A. 46
Fleming, Raymond 48
Ford, Nick Aaron 44
Joachim, Paulin 34
Mackey, Nathaniel 75
Mugo, Micere Githae 32
Ngugi wa Thiong'o 29, 61, 101
Redding, J. Saunders 26
Reed, Ishmael 8
Smith, Barbara 28
Wesley, Valerie Wilson 18
West, Cornel 5, 33, 80

Litigation
Adegbile, Debo P. 119
Allen, Lucy 85
Baldwin, Cynthia 74, 107
Clark, Ray 122

Cochran, Johnnie 11, 39, 52
Gary, Willie E. 12, 117
Ming, William Robert, Jr. 125
Mitchell, Juanita Jackson 128
Patrick, Deval 12, 61, 127
Payne, Ulice, Jr. 42
Payton, John 48, 124
Plaskett, Stacey 127
Roberts, Michele 123
Rock, John S. 113
Slater, Rodney E. 15, 125
Sweatt, Heman Marion 114
Tolbert, James L. 112
Watt, Garland W. 113
Worthy, Kym 84

"Little Rock Nine"
Bates, Daisy 13
Beals, Melba Pattillo 15, 94
Thomas, Jefferson 88

Lobbying
Boyd, John W., Jr. 20, 72
Brown, Elaine 8
Brown, Jesse 6, 41
Christie, Ron 83
Hart, Thomas A., Sr. 113
Lee, Canada 8
Mallett, Conrad, Jr. 16
Reeves, Gregory 49
Robinson, Randall 7, 46
Wynn, Albert R. 25, 77

Los Angeles Angels baseball team
Baylor, Don 6
Reagins, Tony 94

Los Angeles city government
Bradley, Thomas 2, 20
Brookins, Hamel Hartford 102
Edwards, Willis 104
Evers, Myrlie 8

Los Angeles Clippers basketball team
Baylor, Elgin 93
Brand, Elton 31
Griffin, Blake 98
Parsons, Richard 11, 33, 124

Los Angeles Dodgers baseball team
Gilliam, Jim 122
Newcombe, Don 24
Roseboro, John 123
Strawberry, Darryl 22
Wills, Maury 73

Los Angeles Lakers basketball team
Abdul-Jabbar, Kareem 8
Baylor, Elgin 93
Chamberlain, Wilt 18, 47
Fisher, Derek 97
Fox, Rick 27
Green, A. C. 32
Hazzard, Walt 98
Johnson, Magic 3, 39, 101
Odom, Lamar 81
O'Neal, Shaquille 8, 30, 95
Thompson, Mychal 126

Worthy, James 49

Los Angeles Philharmonic
Lewis, Henry 38

Los Angeles Police Department (LAPD)
Parks, Bernard C. 17
Smith, Richard 51
Williams, Willie L. 4

Lost-Found Nation of Islam
Ali, Muhammad 2, 16, 52
Ellison, Keith 59
Farrakhan, Louis 2, 15
Heard, Nathan C. 45
Karim, Benjamin 61
Muhammad, Ava 31
Muhammad, Elijah 4
Muhammad, Jabir Herbert 72
Muhammad, Khallid Abdul 10, 31
Muhammed, W. Deen 27
Sutton, Percy E. 42, 82
Tillard, Conrad 47
X, Malcolm 1
X, Marvin 45

Louisiana state government
Fields, Cleo 13
Francis, Norman (C.) 60
Glover, Cedric B. 103
Jefferson, William J. 25, 72
Morial, Ernest "Dutch" 26
Peterson, Karen Carter 90
Pinchback, P. B. S. 9
Richardson, Rupert 67
Richmond, Cedric 93

Lynching (anti-lynching legislation)
Moore, Harry T. 29
Till, Emmett 7

MacArthur Foundation Fellowship
Abraham, Kyle 116
Allen, Will 74
Benjamin, Regina 20, 75
Braxton, Anthony 128
Butler, Octavia 8, 43, 58
Carter, Majora 77
Carter, Regina 23
Coleman, Steve 124
Cooper, Lisa 73
Dabiri, John 93
Danticat, Edwidge 15, 68, 128
Eberhardt, Jennifer 124
Gordon-Reed, Annette 74
Hammons, David 69
Harris, Corey 39, 73
Hayes, Terrance 124
Jackson, Mary 73
Johnson, Angela 52
Johnson, Charles 1, 82
Jones, Edward P. 43, 67
Lee, Raphael C. 87
Lindsey, Tommie 51
Lovell, Whitfield 74
Lowe, Rick 124
McCraney, Tarell Alvin 116
Mehretu, Julie 85
Moran, Jason 89
Nelson, Stanley 92
Olopade, Olufunmilayo Falusi 58
Parks, Suzan-Lori 34, 85

Robinson, Aminah 50
Shirley, Aaron 126
Stevenson, Bryan 128
Taylor, Cecil 70
Walcott, Derek 5, 94
Whitehead, Colson 77
Williams, Patricia 11, 54

MacNeil/Lehrer NewsHour
Hunter-Gault, Charlayne 6, 31

Mad TV
Jones, Orlando 30
Wilson, Debra 38

Madame C. J. Walker Manufacturing Company
Joyner, Marjorie Stewart 26
Walker, A'lelia 14
Walker, Madame C. J. 7

Major League Baseball administration
Hill, Michael 95
Lucas, Bill 97
Mariner, Jonathan 41
Solomon, Jimmie Lee 38
Young, John 111

Malawi government
Banda, Hastings Kamuzu 6, 54
Banda, Joyce 101
Muluzi, Bakili 14, 76

Mali government
Keïta, Ibrahim Boubacar 113
Touré, Amadou Toumani 18
Traore, Dioncounda 103

Managing, Sports
See Coaching/Managing, Sports

Manhattan Project
Quarterman, Lloyd Albert 4
Wilkens, J. Ernest, Jr. 43

March on Washington/Freedom March
Baker, Josephine 3
Belafonte, Harry 4, 65
Bunche, Ralph J. 5
Davis, Ossie 5, 50
Fauntroy, Walter E. 11
Forman, James 7, 51
Franklin, John Hope 5, 77
Hedgeman, Anna Arnold 22
Jackson, Mahalia 5
Jones, Clarence B. 114
King, Coretta Scott 3, 57
King, Martin Luther, Jr. 1
Lewis, John 2, 46, 83
Meredith, James H. 11
Randolph, A. Philip 3
Rustin, Bayard 4
Sleet, Moneta, Jr. 5
Wilkins, Roy 4
Woods, Abraham, Jr. 74
Young, Whitney M., Jr. 4

Marketing
DeVard, Jerri 61
Edwards, Trevor 54
Fils-Aimé, Reggie 74
Gaskins, Rudy 74
Jackson, James A. 90
Kaigler, Denise 63

Kendrick, Erika 57
Leary, Kathryn D. 10
Miller, Pepper 96
Moyo, Karega Kofi 36
Moyo, Yvette Jackson 36
Rolle, Janet 97

Martial arts
Barnes, Steven 54
Copeland, Michael 47
Kelly, Jim 113
Slice, Kimbo 73
White, Michael Jai 71, 117

Martin Luther King Jr. Center for Nonviolent Social Change
Dodson, Howard, Jr. 7, 52
Farris, Isaac Newton, Jr. 63
King, Bernice 4, 81
King, Coretta Scott 3, 57
King, Dexter 10
King, Martin Luther, Jr. 1
King, Yolanda 6

Martin Luther King Jr. National Memorial Project
Johnson, Harry E. 57

Marxism
Bishop, Maurice 39
Jagan, Cheddi 16
Machel, Samora Moises 8
Nkrumah, Kwame 3
Sankara, Thomas 17

Maryland state government
Brown, Anthony G. 72
Carter, Jill P. 110
Currie, Ulysses 73
Lyons, James E., Sr. 102
Steele, Michael 38, 73, 91
Welcome, Verda Freeman 112

Massachusetts state government
Brooke, Edward W. 8, 88, 126
Gourdin, Edward O. 93
Hayden, Lewis 105
Lewis, William Henry 89
Patrick, Deval 12, 61, 127

Masters Golf Tournament
Elder, Lee 6
Woods, Tiger 14, 31, 81

Mathematics
Alcorn, George Edward, Jr. 59
Banneker, Benjamin 93
Blackwell, David 79
Cox, Elbert Frank 111
Deconge-Watson, Lovenia 55
Emeagwali, Philip 30
Falconer, Etta Zuber 59
Gates, Sylvester James, Jr. 15
Granville, Evelyn Boyd 36
Johnson, Katherine 61
Price, Richard 51
Urschel, John 126
Wilkens, J. Ernest, Jr. 43

Maxwell House Coffee Company
Fudge, Ann (Marie) 11, 55

McDonald's Corporation
Thompson, Don 56, 108

McGill University (Canada)
Elliott, Lorris 37

MCP
See Malawi Congress Party

Medical examiners
Carter, Joye Maureen 41

Medicine
Adams-Campbell, Lucille L. 60
Anderson, William G(ilchrist) 57
Atim, Julian 66
Augusta, Alexander T. 111
Banda, Hastings Kamuzu 6, 54
Barnett, Herman 112
Bashir, Halima 73
Benjamin, Regina 20, 75
Black, Keith Lanier 18, 84
Brimm, Charles E. 105
Callender, Clive O. 3
Carroll, L. Natalie 44
Carter, Joye Maureen 41
Chatard, Peter 44
Chinn, May Edward 26
Christian-Green, Donna M. 17
Cobb, W. Montague 39
Cole, Rebecca 38
Comer, James P. 6
Coney, PonJola 48
Cooper, Edward S. 6
Cooper, Lisa 73
Cornwell, Edward E., III 70
Counter, S. Allen 74
Crumpler, Rebecca Lee 89
Dailey, Ulysses Grant 87
Deas, Gerald 85
Dickens, Helen Octavia 14, 64
Drake, Michael V. 122
Drew, Charles Richard 7
Durham, James 90
Edwards, Lena Frances 76
Edwards, Willarda V. 59
Fennoy, Ilene 72
Fisher, Ada M. 76
Fisher, Rudolph 17
Flowers, Sylester 50
Foster, Henry W., Jr. 26
Fraser, Sarah Loguen 100
Freeman, Harold P. 23
French, D. M. 94
Fuller, Solomon Carter, Jr. 15
Gayle, Helene D. 3
Gibbons, Gary 107
Gibson, William F. 6
Giles, Roscoe C. 93
Goodlett, Carlton B. 91
Grant, Augustus O. 71
Grier, Eliza Ann 90
Griffin, Anthony 71
Griffith, Patrick A. 64
Hamburg, Margaret 78
Hansberry, Tony, II 93
Harris, Bernard A. 90
Hinton, William Augustus 8
Holmes, Hamilton E. 82
Hopkins, Donald R. 89
Hutcherson, Hilda Yvonne 54
Jefferson, Mildred Fay 89
Jemison, Mae C. 1, 35
Johnson, R. M. 36
Jones, Edith Mae Irby 65
Joseph, Kathie-Ann 56

Keith, Rachel Boone 63
Kenney, John A., Jr. 48
Kintaudi, Leon 62
Kong, B. Waine 50
Kountz, Samuel L. 10
Kyenge, Cécile 113
Lacks, Henrietta 101
Lavizzo-Mourey, Risa 48
Lawless, Theodore K. 8
Lee, Raphael C. 87
Leevy, Carrol M. 42
Leffall, Lasalle 3, 64
Logan, Onnie Lee 14
Malveaux, Floyd 54
Maxey, Randall 46
Mossell, Nathan Francis 91
Naki, Hamilton 63
Nour, Nawal M. 56
Okaalet, Peter 58
Olopade, Olufunmilayo Falusi 58
Osman, Said 127
Pace, Betty 59
Pape, Jean William 126
Petioni, Muriel 99
Pinn, Vivian Winona 49
Pitt, David Thomas 10
Rabb, Maurice F., Jr. 58
Randolph, Linda A. 52
Reece, E. Albert 63
Ross-Lee, Barbara 67
Scantlebury-White, Velma 64
Smith, Ian 62
Stewart, Ella 39
Sweet, Ossian 68
Taylor, Susan C. 62
Thomas, Claudia Lynn 64
Thomas, Vivien 9
Thornton, Yvonne S. 69
Tuckson, Reed V. 71
Walker, Joseph Edison 111
Washington, Harriet A. 69
Watkins, Levi, Jr. 9
Welsing, Frances Cress 5
White, Augustus, III 100
White-Hammond, Gloria 61
Williams, Daniel Hale 2
Wilson, Donald E. 88
Witt, Edwin T. 26
Wright, Charles H. 35
Wright, Louis Tompkins 4

Meharry Medical College
Coney, PonJola 48
Foster, Henry W., Jr. 26
Griffith, Patrick A. 64
Lyttle, Hulda Margaret 14

Men's movement
Somé, Malidoma Patrice 10

Merrill Lynch & Co., Inc.
Ford, Harold E(ugene), Jr. 16, 70
Matthews Shatteen, Westina 51
O'Neal, Stanley 38, 67

Meteorology
Anderson, Charles Edward 37
Bacon-Bercey, June 38

Mexican baseball league
Bell, James "Cool Papa" 36
Dandridge, Ray 36

Miami Dolphins football team
Cox, Bryan 83
Greene, Joe 10

Little, Larry 90
Morris, Mercury 114
Williams, Ricky 85

Michigan state government
Brown, Cora 33
Collins, Barbara-Rose 7, 87
Kilpatrick, Carolyn Cheeks 16
Reeves, Triette Lipsey 27
Wisdom, Kimberlydawn 57

Michigan Supreme Court
Archer, Dennis 7, 36
Mallett, Conrad, Jr. 16

Michigan State University
Wharton, Clifton R., Jr. 7

Midwifery
Logan, Onnie Lee 14
Mason, Biddy 89
Robinson, Sharon 22

Military police
Cadoria, Sherian Grace 14

Militia
Kony, Joseph 101
Lubanga, Thomas 104
Nkunda, Laurent 75
Ojukwu, Odumegwu 99

Miller Brewing Company
Colbert, Virgis William 17
Shropshire, Thomas B. 49

Millinery
Bailey, Xenobia 11

Million Man March
Farrakhan, Louis 2, 15
Hawkins, La-Van 17, 54
Worrill, Conrad 12

Milwaukee Brewers baseball team
Aaron, Hank 5
Baylor, Don 6

Milwaukee Bucks basketball team
Abdul-Jabbar, Kareem 8
Robertson, Oscar 26

Minneapolis city government
Belton, Sharon Sayles 9, 16

Minnesota Supreme Court
Page, Alan 7

Minnesota Timberwolves basketball team
Garnett, Kevin 14, 70, 118

Minnesota Twins baseball team
Baylor, Don 6
Carew, Rod 20
Puckett, Kirby 4, 58

Minnesota Vikings football team
Carter, Cris 21, 109
Culpepper, Daunte 32, 85
Cunningham, Randall 23
Fowler, Reggie 51
Gilliam, Frank 23
Green, Dennis 5, 45

McDaniel, Randall Cornell 81
Moon, Warren 8, 66
Moss, Randy 23, 90
Page, Alan 7
Peterson, Adrian 109
Randle, John 87
Rashad, Ahmad 18
Stringer, Korey 35

**Minority Business Enterprise
Legal Defense and Education
Fund**
Mitchell, Parren J. 42, 66

Minstrel shows
Lane, William Henry 90
McDaniel, Hattie 5

Miss America
Dunlap, Ericka 55
Harold, Erika 54
Vincent, Marjorie Judith 2
Williams, Vanessa L. 4, 17

Miss Universe
Lopes, Leila 99

Miss USA
Gist, Carole 1

Miss World
Darego, Agbani 52

Mississippi state government
Anderson, Reuben V. 81
Fleming, Erik R. 75

Missouri state government
Wilson, Margaret Bush 79

Mixed martial arts
Jackson, Rampage 83
Jones, Jon 121
Silva, Anderson 96

Modeling
Allen-Buillard, Melba 55
Banks, Tyra 11, 50
Beauvais, Garcelle 29, 95
Beckford, Tyson 11, 68
Berry, Halle 4, 19, 57, 91
Campbell, Naomi 1, 31, 120
Darego, Agbani 52
Davis, Mia Amber 94
Dirie, Waris 56
Dobson, Tamara 111
Ebanks, Selita 67
Gibson, Tyrese 27, 62
Hardison, Bethann 12
Hounsou, Djimon 19, 45
Iman 4, 33, 87
Iman, Chanel 66
Johnson, Beverly 2, 102
Kebede, Liya 59
Kodjoe, Boris 34, 89
Langhart Cohen, Janet 19, 60
Leslie, Lisa 16, 73
LisaRaye 27
Lopes, Leila 99
Marcille, Eva 97
McKenzie, Jaunel 73
Michele, Michael 31
Niane, Katoucha 70
Onwurah, Ngozi 38
Rochon, Lela 16
RuPaul 17, 91

Simmons, Kimora Lee 51, 83
Sims, Naomi 29, 79
Smith, B(arbara) 11
Tamia 24, 55
Taylor, Karin 34
Watley, Jody 54
Webb, Veronica 10, 95
Wek, Alek 18, 63, 105

Modern dance
Ailey, Alvin 8
Allen, Debbie 13, 42
Brown, Ronald K. 91
Byrd, Donald 10
Collins, Janet 33, 64
Davis, Chuck 33
Diggs, Taye 25, 63
Dove, Ulysses 5
Fagan, Garth 18, 98
Faison, George 16
Henson, Darrin 33
Jeune, Vitolio 98
Jones, Bill T. 1, 46, 80
King, Alonzo 38
Kitt, Eartha 16, 75
Miller, Bebe 3
Pomare, Eleo 72
Spears, Warren 52
Vereen, Ben 4
Williams, Dudley 60

Montgomery bus boycott
Abernathy, Ralph David 1
Baker, Ella 5
Burks, Mary Fair 40
Carr, Johnnie 69
Jackson, Mahalia 5
Killens, John O. 54
King, Martin Luther, Jr. 1
Nixon, Edgar Daniel 100
Parks, Rosa 1, 35, 56
Robinson, Joann Gibson 100
Rustin, Bayard 4

**Montgomery County (MD) Po-
lice Department**
Moose, Charles 40

Montreal Expos baseball team
Dawson, Andre 85
Doby, Lawrence Eugene, Sr. 16, 41

Morehouse College
Brown, Uzee 42
Gloster, Hugh Morris, Sr. 90
Hill, Marc Lamont 80, 128
Hope, John 8
Mays, Benjamin E. 7
Satcher, David 7, 57, 111

Motivational speaking
Bahati, Wambui 60
Baisden, Michael 66
Bozella, Dewey 97
Brown, Les 5
Bunkley, Anita Richmond 39
Creagh, Milton 27
Gardner, Chris 65
Grant, Gwendolyn Goldsby 28
Gray, Farrah 59
Jolley, Willie 28
July, William 27
Kimbro, Dennis 10
LeGrand, Eric 118
Munroe, Myles 125

Russell-McCloud, Patricia 17
Shabazz, Ilyasah 36
Shelton, Trent 122
Tuff, Antoinette 120
Tyson, Asha 39

Motorcycle racing
Brown, Antron 85
Showers, Reggie 30
Stewart, James, Jr. 60, 98

Motown Records
Atkins, Cholly 40
Avant, Clarence 19, 86
Ballard, Florence 112
Birdsong, Cindy 113
Bizimungu, Pasteur 19
Busby, Jheryl 3, 74
de Passe, Suzanne 25
Edwards, Esther Gordy 43
Gaye, Anna Gordy 121
Gaye, Marvin 2
Gordy, Berry, Jr. 1
Harrell, Andre 9, 30
Holland-Dozier-Holland 36
Holloway, Brenda 65
Hutch, Willie 62
Jackson, George 19
Jamerson, James 59
Jones, Robert G. 81
Kendricks, Eddie 22
Knight, Gladys 16, 66
Massenburg, Kedar 23, 110
Powell, Maxine 8, 115
Richie, Lionel 27, 65, 114
Robinson, Smokey 3, 49
Ross, Diana 8, 27
Sanders, Angelia 86
Supremes, The 33
Terrell, Jean 116
Terrell, Tammi 32
Wells, Mary 28
Whitfield, Norman 73
Wilson, Frank 106
Wilson, Mary 28
Wonder, Stevie 11, 53, 121

Mount Holyoke College
Tatum, Beverly Daniel 42, 84

**Movement for Democratic
Change (MDC)**
Moyo, Lovemore 76
Tsvangirai, Morgan 26, 72

Mozambique government
Chissano, Joaquim 7, 55, 67
Diogo, Luisa Dias 63
Guebuza, Armando 81
Machel, Graça 16, 102
Machel, Samora Moises 8

Multimedia art
Adkins, Terry 122
Amaki, Amalia 76
Bailey, Xenobia 11
Lovell, Whitfield 74
Pinder, Jefferson 77
Robinson, Aminah 50
Simpson, Lorna 4, 36

Muppets, The
Clash, Kevin 14, 93

Murals
Alston, Charles 33
Biggers, John 20, 33

Douglas, Aaron 7
Lee-Smith, Hughie 5
Walker, Kara 16, 80

Museum of Modern Art
Pindell, Howardena 55
Smith, Ming 100

Music Critics Circle
Holt, Nora 38

Music publishing
Avant, Nicole A. 90
Edmonds, Tracey 16, 64
Griffey, Dick 89
Gryce, Gigi 124
Handy, W. C. 8
Holland-Dozier-Holland 36
Humphrey, Bobbi 20
Jackson, George 19
James, Rick 17
Martin, Sallie 120
Mayfield, Curtis 2, 43
Otis, Clyde 67
Pryce, Trevor 89
Redding, Otis 16
Riley, Boots 89
Shakur, Afeni 67
Shorty, Ras, I 47
Strong, Barrett 89

Music Television (MTV)
Bellamy, Bill 12
Chideya, Farai 14, 61
Morton, Frederick A., Jr. 93
Norman, Christina 47
Powell, Kevin 31, 74
Run 31, 73

Musical composition
Anderson, T. J. 119
Armatrading, Joan 32
Ashford, Nickolas 21, 97
Ashford and Simpson 21, 97
Attaway, William 102
Baiocchi, Regina Harris 41
Ballard, Hank 41
Bebey, Francis 45
Bell, LeRoy 98
Benson, Obie 96
Bland, Edward 111
Blige, Mary J. 20, 34, 60, 97
Bonds, Margaret 39
Bonga, Kuenda 13
Boulogne, Joseph, Chevalier de
　Saint-Georges 94
Braxton, Anthony 128
Bridgetower, George 78
Brown, Dennis 99
Brown, Patrick "Sleepy" 50
Brown, Uzee 42
Burke, Solomon 31, 86
Burleigh, Henry Thacker 56
Caesar, Shirley 19
Campbell, Lucie E. 118
Carter, Ron 104
Carter, Warrick L. 27
Castor, Jimmy 100
Chapman, Tracy 26
Charlemagne, Manno 11
Charles, Ray 16, 48
Cleveland, James 19
Cole, J. 97
Cole, Natalie 17, 60, 84

Coleman, Ornette 39, 69
Coleman, Steve 124
Collins, Bootsy 31
Davis, Anthony 11
Davis, Miles 4
Davis, Sammy, Jr. 18
Dawson, William Levi 39
Diddley, Bo 39, 72
Domino, Fats 20
Ellington, Duke 5
Europe, James Reese 10
Evans, Faith 22
Freeman, Paul 39
Fuller, Arthur 27
Gamble, Kenny 85
Garrett, Sean 57
Gaynor, Gloria 36
Gillespie, Dizzy 1
Golson, Benny 37
Grant, Micki 125
Greaves, R. B. 106
Green, Al 13, 47, 74
Gryce, Gigi 124
Hailey, JoJo 22
Hailey, K-Ci 22
Handy, W. C. 8
Harris, Corey 39, 73
Hathaway, Donny 18
Hayes, Isaac 20, 58, 73
Hayes, Teddy 40
Hibbert, Toots 103
Holland-Dozier-Holland 36
Holmes, Clint 57
Holt, Nora 38
Humphrey, Bobbi 20
Hutch, Willie 62
Isley, Ronald 25, 56
Jackson, Fred James 25
Jackson, Michael 19, 53, 76
Jackson, Randy 40
James, Rick 17
Jerkins, Rodney 31
Johnson, Buddy 36
Johnson, Georgia Douglas 41
Johnson, J. Rosamond 121
Jones, Jonah 39
Jones, Quincy 8, 30
Jones, Thad 68
Joplin, Scott 6
Jordan, Montell 23
Jordan, Ronny 26
Kay, Ulysses 37
Kelly, R. 18, 44, 71, 117
Keys, Alicia 32, 68
Kidjo, Angelique 50
Killings, Debra 57
King, B. B. 7
Lebo M 109
León, Tania 13
Lewis, George 104
Little Milton 36, 54
Little Walter 36
Mahlasela, Vusi 65
Majors, Jeff 41
Martin, Roberta 58
Maxwell 20, 81
Mayfield, Curtis 2, 43
M.C. Hammer 20, 80
McClurkin, Donnie 25
McFerrin, Bobby 68
Mills, Stephanie 36
Mitchell, Brian Stokes 21
Monica 21

Moore, Chante 26
Moore, Dorothy Rudd 46
Moore, Undine Smith 28
Muse, Clarence Edouard 21
Nash, Johnny 40
Ndegeocello, Meshell 15, 83
Nelson, Oliver 113
Osborne, Jeffrey 26, 121
Otis, Clyde 67
Parker, Ray, Jr. 85
Pratt, Awadagin 31
Price, Florence 37
Prince 18, 65
Pritchard, Robert Starling 21
Redding, Otis 16
Reed, A. C. 36
Reid, Antonio "L.A." 28
Roach, Max 21, 63
Robinson, Reginald R. 53
Run-DMC 31, 75
Russell, Brenda 52
Santigold 96
Scott-Heron, Gil 94
Seal 14, 75
Shirley, Donald 111
Shorty, Ras, I 47
Simone, Nina 15, 41
Simpson, Valerie 21, 97
Smith, Hale 118
Somi 85
Sowande, Fela 39
Stewart, Tricky 98
Still, William Grant 37
Strayhorn, Billy 31
Sundiata, Sekou 66
Sweat, Keith 19
Threadgill, Henry 97
Tillis, Frederick 40
Trombone Shorty 97
Usher 23, 56, 95
Van Peebles, Melvin 7, 95
Walker, George 37
Washington, Grover, Jr. 17, 44
Williams, Deniece 36
Williams, Tony 67
Wilson, Abram 104
Wilson, Frank 106
Winans, Angie 36
Winans, Debbie 36
Withers, Bill 61

Musical direction
Barnes, Katreese 97
Bonds, Margaret 39
Johnson, Ken 106
Rushen, Patrice 12

Musicology
George, Zelma Watson 42

Mystery/detective fiction
Bates, Karen Grigsby 40
Bland, Eleanor Taylor 39
Creagh, Milton 27
DeLoach, Nora 30
Hayes, Teddy 40
Haywood, Gar Anthony 43
Himes, Chester 8
Holton, Hugh, Jr. 39
Mickelbury, Penny 28
Mosley, Walter 5, 25, 68
Thomas-Graham, Pamela 29

Wesley, Valerie Wilson 18

Mystic Seaport Museum
Pinckney, Bill 42

NAACP
See National Association for the
Advancement of Colored People

NAACP Image Awards
Alexander, Michelle 98
Brandy 14, 34, 72
Cosby, Bill 7, 26, 59, 125
Dyson, Michael Eric 11, 40, 128
Ejogo, Carmen 126
Fields, Kim 36
Freeman, Morgan 2, 20, 62, 100
Glover, Danny 1, 24, 103
Henson, Taraji P. 58, 77, 127
Lattimore, Kenny 35, 128
Lawrence, Martin 6, 27, 60
Mac, Bernie 29, 61, 72
McRae, Carmen 77
Moore, Shemar 21, 112
Nelson, Kadir 115
Nyong'o, Lupita 127
Okonedo, Sophie 67
Prince-Bythewood, Gina 31, 77
Rhimes, Shonda Lynn 67
Spencer, Octavia 100
Taylor, Regina 9, 46, 97
Tony! Toni! Toné! 127
Warner, Malcolm-Jamal 22, 36, 110
Washington, Kerry 46, 107
Wesley, Richard 73

**NAACP Legal Defense and
Educational Fund (LDF)**
Berrien, Jacqueline A. 93
Chambers, Julius 3
Coleman, James E., Jr. 79
Coleman, William T. 76
Days, Drew S., III 10
Edelman, Marian Wright 5, 42
Fisher, Ada Lois Sipuel 76
Guinier, Lani 7, 30
Jones, Elaine R. 7, 45
Marshall, Thurgood 1, 44
Motley, Constance Baker 10, 55
Payton, John 48, 124
Rice, Constance LaMay 60
Smith, Kemba 70
Smythe Haith, Mabel 61

NABJ
See National Association of Black
Journalists

NACW
See National Association of Colored Women

Namibia government
Mbuende, Kaire 12
Nujoma, Samuel 10
Pohamba, Hifikepunye 95

NASA
See National Aeronautics and
Space Administration

NASCAR
See National Association for Stock
Car Auto Racing

Nation of Islam
See Lost-Found Nation of Islam

**National Aeronautics and
Space Administration (NASA)**
Anderson, Michael P. 40
Bluford, Guy 2, 35
Bolden, Charles Frank, Jr. 7, 78
Campbell, Donald J. 66
Carruthers, George R. 40
Douglas, Donya 97
Drew, Alvin, Jr. 67
Easley, Annie J. 61
Ericsson-Jackson, Aprille 28
Gregory, Frederick 8, 51
Harris, Bernard A. 90
Higginbotham, Joan 124
Jemison, Mae C. 1, 35
Johnson, Katherine (Coleman
Goble) 61
Johnson, Lonnie G. 32, 93
McNair, Ronald 3, 58
Mills, Joseph C. 51
Nichols, Nichelle 11
Sigur, Wanda 44
Wilson, Stephanie 72

**National Association for the
Advancement of Colored
People (NAACP)**
Anderson, Reuben V. 81
Anderson, William G(ilchrist) 57
Anthony, Wendell 25
Austin, Junius C. 44
Ballance, Frank W. 41
Brock, Roslyn McCallister 86
Brown, Homer S. 47
Chambers, Julius 3
Chavis, Benjamin 6
Cobb, W. Montague 39
Coleman, Beatrice 120
Du Bois, W. E. B. 3
DuBois, Shirley Graham 21
Dukes, Hazel Nell 56
Farmer, James 2, 64
Fuller, S. B. 13
Grimké, Archibald H. 9
Hampton, Fred 18
Hayes, Dennis 54
Henderson, Wade 14
Hollowell, Donald L. 57
Hooks, Benjamin L. 2, 85
Houston, Charles Hamilton 4
Jealous, Benjamin Todd 70, 113
Kidd, Mae Street 39
Lampkin, Daisy 19
Law, W. W. 121
Madison, Joseph E. 17
Marshall, Thurgood 1, 44
McKissick, Floyd B. 3
Meredith, James H. 11
Mfume, Kweisi 6, 41
Miller, Lorraine C. 119
Mitchell, Clarence M., Jr. 88
Moore, Harry T. 29
Morgan, Irene 65
Moses, Robert Parris 11
Motley, Constance Baker 10, 55
Moyo, Yvette Jackson 36
Richardson, Rupert 67
Rustin, Bayard 4
Simkins, Modjeska Monteith 112
Sutton, Percy E. 42, 82

Talbert, Mary B. **77**
Terrell, Mary Church **9**
Tobias, Channing H. **79**
Tucker, C. Delores **12, 56**
Van Lierop, Robert **53**
White, Walter F. **4**
Wilkins, Roy **4**
Wilson, Margaret Bush **79**
Wright, Louis Tompkins **4**

National Association of Black Journalists (NABJ)
Curry, George E. **23**
Dawkins, Wayne **20**
Harris, Jay T. **19**
Jarrett, Vernon D. **42**
Lowe, Herbert **57**
Payne, Les **89**
Pressley, Condace L. **41**
Rice, Linda Johnson **9, 41**
Shipp, E. R. **15**
Stone, Chuck **9, 120**
Washington, Laura S. **18**

National Association of Broadcasters Hall of Fame
Harvey, Steve **18, 58**
Jackson, Hal **41, 104**
Joyner, Tom **19, 90**

National Association of Colored Women (NACW)
Bethune, Mary McLeod **4**
Butler, Selena Sloan **98**
Cook-Parrish, Mary Virginia **95**
Cooper, Margaret J. **46**
Harper, Frances Ellen Watkins **11**
Lampkin, Daisy **19**
Ruffin, Josephine St. Pierre **75**
Stewart, Ella **39**
Talbert, Mary B. **77**
Terrell, Mary Church **9**
Washington, Margaret Murray **119**

National Association of Social Workers
Jackson, Judith D. **57**
McMurray, Georgia L. **36**

National Association for Stock Car Auto Racing (NASCAR)
Lester, Bill **42, 85**

National Baptist Convention USA
Bradley, J. Robert **65**
Jemison, T. J. **119**
Jones, E. Edward, Sr. **45**
Lyons, Henry **12, 118**
Shaw, William J. **30**
Thurston, Stephen J. **49**

National Bar Association
Alexander, Joyce London **18**
Alexander, Sadie Tanner Mossell **22**
Archer, Dennis **7, 36**
Bailey, Clyde **45**
Hubbard, Arnette **38**
Pincham, R. Eugene, Sr. **69**
Quince, Peggy A. **69**
Ray, Charlotte E. **60**
Robinson, Malcolm S. **44**
Thompson, Larry D. **39**

Walker, Cora T. **68**

National Basketball Players Association
Erving, Julius **18, 47**
Ewing, Patrick **17, 73**
Fisher, Derek **97**
Gourdine, Simon **11**
Hunter, Billy **22, 109**
Roberts, Michele **123**

National Black Farmers Association (NBFA)
Boyd, John W., Jr. **20, 72**

National Book Award
Ellison, Ralph **7**
Haley, Alex **4**
Hayes, Terrance **124**
Johnson, Charles **1, 82**
Mackey, Nathaniel **75**
Patterson, Orlando **4, 127**
Woodson, Jacqueline **125**

National Broadcasting Company (NBC)
Gumbel, Bryant **14, 80**
Hinderas, Natalie **5**
Holt, Lester **66**
Johnson, Rodney Van **28**
Madison, Paula **37, 99**
Reynolds, Star Jones **10, 27, 61**
Roker, Al **12, 49**
Schiavocampo, Mara **97**
Simpson, Carole **6, 30**
Thomas-Graham, Pamela **29**
Williams, Montel **4, 57**

National Coalition of 100 Black Women (NCBW)
Mays, Leslie A. **41**
McCabe, Jewell Jackson **10**

National Council of Negro Women (NCNW)
Bethune, Mary McLeod **4**
Blackwell, Unita **17**
Cole, Johnnetta B. **5, 43**
Height, Dorothy I. **2, 23, 78**
Lampkin, Daisy **19**
Smith, Jane E. **24**

National Cowboys of Color Museum and Hall of Fame
Austin, Gloria **63**
Austin, Jim **63**
Pickett, Bill **11**
Pride, Charley **26**
Sampson, Charles **13**

National Education Association (NEA)
Futrell, Mary Hatwood **33**
Koontz, Elizabeth Duncan **101**

National Endowment for the Arts (NEA)
Barthé, Earl **78**
Bradley, David Henry, Jr. **39**
Brown, Chuck **78, 102**
Bullins, Ed **25, 121**
Coleman, Wanda **48, 119**
Edwards, David **122**
Hall, Arthur **39**
Hemphill, Essex **10**

Pope.L, William **72**
Serrano, Andres **3**
Williams, John A. **27**
Williams, William T. **11**

National Football League (NFL)
Alexander, Shaun **58**
Allen, Larry **109**
Allen, Marcus **20**
Anderson, Jamal **22**
Asomugha, Nnamdi **100**
Barber, Ronde **41**
Barber, Tiki **57, 107**
Barney, Lem **26**
Batch, Charlie **120**
Berry, Eric **125**
Bettis, Jerome **64**
Bowles, Todd **128**
Briscoe, Marlin **37**
Brooks, Aaron **33**
Brooks, Derrick **43, 119**
Brown, Jason **125**
Brown, Jerry **117**
Brown, Jim **11, 95**
Bruce, Isaac **26**
Bryant, Cullen **81**
Bryant, Dez **116**
Bush, Reggie **59, 88**
Butler, Leroy, III **17**
Caldwell, Jim **81**
Campbell, Earl **104**
Carter, Cris **21, 109**
Cherry, Deron **40**
Cox, Bryan **83**
Crennel, Romeo **54, 107**
Cromartie, Antonio **115**
Croom, Sylvester **50**
Cruz, Victor **107**
Culp, Curley **110**
Culpepper, Daunte **32, 85**
Cunningham, Randall **23**
Davis, Milt **74**
Davis, Terrell **20**
Davis, Wade, Jr. **103**
Dean, Fred **98**
Delaney, Joe **76**
Dent, Richard **97**
Dickerson, Eric **27, 108**
Driver, Donald **99**
Duerson, Dave **93**
Dungy, Tony **17, 42, 59, 118**
Dunn, Warrick **90**
Edwards, Herman **51**
Farr, Mel **24**
Faulk, Marshall **35, 96**
Foster, Arian **114**
Fowler, Reggie **51**
George, Eddie **80**
Gilliam, Frank **23**
Gilliam, Joe **31**
Gordon, Josh **120**
Gore, Frank **117**
Green, Darrell **39, 74**
Green, Dennis **5, 45**
Greene, Joe **10**
Greenwood, L. C. **115**
Griffin, Robert, III **107**
Hardy, Greg **118**
Harris, Franco **97**
Harris, James **79**
Harvin, Percy **123**
Hill, Calvin **19**

Holmes, Santonio **87**
Howard, Desmond **16, 58**
Humphrey, Claude **119**
Hurd, Sam **116**
Irvin, Michael **64**
Jackson, DeSean **120**
Jackson, Rickey **88**
Jackson, Tom **70**
Jenkins, Kris **98**
Johnson, Andre **127**
Johnson, Calvin **108**
Johnson, Chad **108**
Johnson, Chris **92**
Johnson, John Henry **96**
Johnson, Keyshawn **91**
Johnson, Levi **48**
Joiner, Charlie **102**
Jones, Adam **103**
Jones, Deacon **92, 112**
Jones, Jacoby **117**
Jones, Walter **119**
Jones-Drew, Maurice **113**
Kennedy, Cortez **104**
Ladd, Ernie **64**
Lane, Dick **92**
Lewis, Jamal **115**
Lewis, Ray **33, 109**
Little, Floyd **86**
Little, Larry **90**
Lofton, James **42**
Lott, Ronnie **9**
Lynch, Marshawn **124**
Manley, Dexter **116**
Mann, Bob **126**
Marshall, Brandon **116**
Martin, Curtis **104**
Martin, Jonathan **119**
Mathis, Robert **121**
Matson, Ollie **93**
May, Mark **117**
Mayhew, Martin R. **76**
McCoy, LeSean **123**
McDaniel, Randall Cornell **81**
McNabb, Donovan **29, 119**
McNair, Steve **22, 47, 79**
Mitchell, Freddie **116**
Monk, Art **38, 73**
Moon, Warren **8, 66**
Morris, Mercury **114**
Moss, Randy **23, 90**
Motley, Marion **26**
Muncie, Chuck **112**
Newsome, Ozzie **26, 117**
Newton, Cam **96**
Ogden, Jonathan **110**
Oliver, Paul **115**
Owens, Brig **118**
Owens, Terrell **53, 106**
Pace, Orlando **21**
Page, Alan **7**
Parker, Jim **64**
Payton, Walter **11, 25**
Peete, Rodney **60**
Perry, Joe **95**
Peters, Jason **125**
Peterson, Adrian **109**
Pryce, Trevor **89**
Randle, John **87**
Rashad, Ahmad **18**
Reece, Marcel **114**
Reese, Jerry **103**
Rhodes, Ray **14**
Rice, Jerry **5, 55, 89**

Rice, Ray 112
Roaf, Willie 106
Robinson, Dave 110
Rolle, Myron 98
Sam, Michael 121
Sanders, Barry 1, 53
Sanders, Bob 72
Sanders, Deion 4, 31, 96
Sapp, Warren 38, 109
Sayers, Gale 28
Seymour, Richard 101
Sharpe, Shannon 97
Sharper, Darren 32, 118
Shell, Art 1, 66
Shelton, Trent 122
Sherman, Richard 118
Simpson, O. J. 15, 100
Singletary, Mike 4, 76
Slater, Duke 125
Smith, Bubba 96
Smith, Bruce 80
Smith, DeMaurice 92
Smith, Emmitt 7, 87
Smith, Geno 118
Smith, Neil 109
Smith, Rick 72
Smith, Steve 120
Stallworth, John 102
Stewart, Kordell 21, 111
Stingley, Darryl 69
Strahan, Michael 35, 81
Stringer, Korey 35
Strode, Woody 111
Suggs, Terrell 108
Swann, Lynn 28
Tatum, Jack 87
Taylor, Jason 70
Taylor, Lawrence 25
Thomas, Derrick 25
Thomas, Emmitt 71
Thomas, Thurman 75
Thrower, Willie 35
Tolbert, Mike 125
Toler, Burl 80
Tomlin, Mike 123
Tomlinson, LaDainian 65, 112
Tunnell, Emlen 54
Upshaw, Gene 18, 47, 72
Urschel, John 126
Vick, Michael 39, 65, 94
Vincent, Troy 91
Walker, Herschel 1, 69
Ward, Hines 84
Ware, Andre 37
Ware, DeMarcus 92
Washington, Kenny 50
Watson, Benjamin 126
White, Reggie 6, 50
Wilfork, Vince 124
Williams, Darrent 116
Williams, Doug 22, 112
Williams, J. Mayo 83
Williams, Ricky 85
Williamson, Fred 67
Willis, Patrick 99
Wilson, David 123
Wilson, Russell 119
Winslow, Kellen 83
Wood, Willie 111
Wright, Rayfield 70

National Hockey League (NHL)
Brashear, Donald 39
Brathwaite, Fred 35
Brown, Sean 52
Doig, Jason 45
Fuhr, Grant 1, 49
Grand-Pierre, Jean-Luc 46
Grier, Mike 43
Iginla, Jarome 35
Kane, Evander 97
Laraque, Georges 48
Mayers, Jamal 39
McBride, Bryant 18
McCarthy, Sandy 64
McKegney, Tony 3
O'Ree, Willie 5
Salvador, Bryce 51
Simmonds, Wayne 121
Subban, P. K. 121
Weekes, Kevin 67

National Institutes of Health (NIH)
Anderson, Norman B. 45
Cargill, Victoria A. 43
Dunston, Georgia Mae 48
Gibbons, Gary 107
Pinn, Vivian Winona 49

National Inventors Hall of Fame
Carruthers, George R. 40

National Medical Association
Cole, Lorraine 48
Giles, Roscoe C. 93
Maxey, Randall 46
Ojikutu, Bisola 65

National Newspaper Publishers Association
Cooper, Andrew W. 36
Jealous, Benjamin Todd 70, 113
Oliver, John J., Jr. 48

National Oceanic and Atmospheric Administration
Bacon-Bercey, June 38
Fields, Evelyn J. 27

National Organization for Women (NOW)
Hernandez, Aileen Clarke 13
Kennedy, Florynce 12, 33
Murray, Pauli 38

National Parent Teacher Association
Butler, Selena Sloan 98

National Public Radio (NPR)
Abu-Jamal, Mumia 15
Bates, Karen Grigsby 40
Bowles, Cephas 127
Drummond, William J. 40
Early, Gerald 15
Jackson, Bobby 119
Lewis, Delano 7
Martin, Michel 97
Mitchell, Elvis 67
Norris, Michele 83
Smiley, Tavis 20, 68
Walker, Teshima 114
Williams, Juan 35, 80

Zook, Kristal Brent 62

National Rifle Association (NRA)
Williams, Robert F. 11

National Science Foundation (NSF)
Jackson, Deborah 94
Massey, Walter E. 5, 45

National Security Council
Frazer, Jendayi 68
Powell, Colin 1, 28, 75
Rice, Condoleezza 3, 28, 72
Rice, Susan 74, 103
Sutphen, Mona 77

National Union for the Total Independence of Angola (UNITA)
Roberto, Holden 65
Savimbi, Jonas 2, 34

National Urban League
Barrow, Willie T. 85, 128
Berry, Edwin C. 81
Gordon, Bruce S. 41, 53, 82
Granger, Lester B. 75
Greely, M. Gasby 27
Haynes, George Edmund 8
Jacob, John E. 2
Jones, Eugene Kinckle 79
Jordan, Vernon E. 3, 35
Price, Hugh B. 9, 54
Spriggs, William 67
Young, Whitney M., Jr. 4

National Wildlife Federation
Osborne, Na'taki 54

National Women's Hall of Fame
Cary, Mary Ann Shadd 30
Kelly, Leontine 33
Talbert, Mary B. 77

NBC
See National Broadcasting Company

NCBW
See National Coalition of 100 Black Women

NCNW
See National Council of Negro Women

NEA
See National Education Association; National Endowment for the Arts

Nebula awards
Butler, Octavia 8, 43, 58
Delany, Samuel R., Jr. 9

Négritude
Césaire, Aimé 48, 69
Damas, Léon-Gontran 46
Ndiaye, Iba 74

Negro Ensemble Company
Cash, Rosalind 28
Gordon, Carl 87
Hooks, Robert 76
Rolle, Esther 13, 21

Schultz, Michael A. 6
Ward, Douglas Turner 42

Negro Leagues
Barnhill, David 30
Bell, James "Cool Papa" 36
Black, Joe 75
Brown, Raymond 102
Brown, Willard 36
Campanella, Roy 25
Charleston, Oscar 39
Dandridge, Ray 36
Davis, Piper 19
Day, Leon 39
Dihigo, Martín 103
Foster, Andrew 79
Gibson, Josh 22
Gilliam, Jim 122
Grant, Frank 100
Hairston, Sam 88
Hyde, Cowan F. "Bubba" 47
Irvin, Monte 31
Johnson, Clifford "Connie" 52
Johnson, Judy 105
Johnson, Mamie "Peanut" 40
Kaiser, Cecil 42
Kimbro, Henry A. 25
Leonard, Buck 67
Lloyd, John Henry "Pop" 30
Mackey, Biz 82
Morton, Ferdinand Q. 90
O'Neil, Buck 19, 59
Paige, Satchel 7
Pride, Charley 26
Radcliffe, Ted 74
Smith, Hilton 29
Stearnes, Norman "Turkey" 31
Stone, Toni 15
Suttles, Mule 108
Wells, Willie 105
Whitney, Davey L. 110

Netherlands Antilles government
Liberia-Peters, Maria Philomena 12

Neurosurgery
Black, Keith Lanier 18, 84
Canady, Alexa 28
Carson, Ben 1, 35, 76, 128
Dennis, Gary C. 91

Nevada state government
Horsford, Steven 88

New Jersey state government
Bryant, Wayne R. 6
Payne, William D. 60
Watson Coleman, Bonnie 127

New Negro movement
See Harlem Renaissance

New Orleans city government
Henry, Troy 85
Mason, Ronald 27
Nagin, Ray 42, 57, 88
Perry, James 83

New Orleans Saints football team
Brooks, Aaron 33
Mills, Sam 33

New York City government
Campbell, Mary Schmidt 43
Davis, Gordon J. 76

Dinkins, David 4
Farrell, Herman D., Jr. 81
Fields, C. Virginia 25
Ford, Wallace 58
Hageman, Hans 36
Paterson, Basil A. 69, 122
Spigner, Archie 81
Sutton, Percy E. 42
Thompson, William, Jr. 35, 114
Tolbert, Terence 74
Walcott, Dennis M. 112

New York Giants football team
Barber, Tiki 57, 107
Reese, Jerry 103
Strahan, Michael 35, 81
Taylor, Lawrence 25

New York Jets football team
Jenkins, Kris 98
Martin, Curtis 104
Smith, Geno 118

New York Knicks basketball team
Ewing, Patrick 17, 73
Johnson, Larry 28
Meminger, Dean 114
Reed, Willis, Jr. 86
Stith, Tom 93

New York Mets baseball team
Clendenon, Donn 26, 56
Manuel, Jerry 94

New York Public Library
Baker, Augusta 38
Dodson, Howard, Jr. 7, 52

New York Shakespeare Festival
Browne, Roscoe Lee 66
Gunn, Moses 10
Wolfe, George C. 6, 43, 127

New York state government
Brown, Byron W. 72
Farrell, Herman D., Jr. 81
Jeffries, Hakeem 118
Johnson, Edward Austin 107
McCall, H. Carl 27
Meeks, Gregory T. 25, 117
Motley, Constance Baker 10, 55
Owens, Major 6, 117
Paterson, Basil A. 69, 122
Paterson, David A. 59
Smith, Malcolm A. 75
Waldon, Alton R., Jr. 98

New York State Supreme Court
Dudley, Edward R. 58
Jones, Theodore T., Jr. 108
Tingling, Milton A. 110
Wright, Bruce McMarion 3, 52

New York Stock Exchange
Doley, Harold, Jr. 26

New York Times
Blair, Jayson 50
Blow, Charles M. 73
Boyd, Gerald M. 32, 59
Broyard, Anatole 68
Caldwell, Earl 60
Cooper, Helene 74

Herbert, Bob 63, 96
Hunter-Gault, Charlayne 6, 31
Mabry, Marcus 70
Price, Hugh B. 9, 54
Rhoden, William C. 67
Wilkins, Roger 2, 84

New York University
Campbell, Mary Schmidt 43
Newkirk, Pamela 69

New York Yankees baseball team
Baylor, Don 6
Cano, Robinson 97
Howard, Elston 125
Jackson, Reggie 15
Jeter, Derek 27, 93, 124
Sabathia, CC 74
Strawberry, Darryl 22
Watson, Bob 25
Williams, Bernie 128
Winfield, Dave 5, 91

Newark (NJ) city government
Baraka, Ras J. 121
Booker, Cory Anthony 68
Gibson, Kenneth Allen 6
James, Sharpe 23, 69

Newbery medal
Alexander, Kwame 98
Curtis, Christopher Paul 26, 113
Hamilton, Virginia 10

NFL
See National Football League

NHL
See National Hockey League

Niagara movement
Du Bois, W. E. B. 3
Hope, John 8
Talbert, Mary B. 77
Trotter, Monroe 9

Nickelodeon
DJ Lance Rock 94
Thompson, Kenan 52

Niger government
Issoufou, Mahamadou 102
Tandja, Mamadou 33, 78

Nigeria government
Abiola, Moshood 70
Abubakar, Abdulsalami 66
Akunyili, Dora Nkem 58
Buhari, Muhammadu 128
Jonathan, Goodluck 83
Muhammed, Murtala 119
Obasanjo, Olusegun 5
Okonjo-Iweala, Ngozi 101
Yar'Adua, Umaru 69, 89

Nigerian military
Abacha, Sani 11, 70
Abiola, Moshood 70
Babangida, Ibrahim 4
Buhari, Muhammadu 128
Muhammed, Murtala 119
Obasanjo, Olusegun 5, 22

Ojukwu, Odumegwu 99

NIH
See National Institutes of Health

Nike, Inc.
Edwards, Trevor 54
Miller, Larry G. 72

Nobel Peace Prize
Annan, Kofi Atta 15, 48
Bunche, Ralph J. 5
King, Martin Luther, Jr. 1
Luthuli, Albert 13
Maathai, Wangari 43, 97
Obama, Barack 49, 74, 91
Tutu, Desmond Mpilo 6, 44

Nobel Prize in Literature
Morrison, Toni 2, 15, 86
Soyinka, Wole 4, 93
Walcott, Derek 5, 94

Nonfiction
Abrahams, Peter 39
Adams-Ender, Clara 40
Ali, Hana Yasmeen 52
Allen, Debbie 13, 42
Allen, Robert L. 38
Andrews, Tina 74
Atkins, Cholly 40
Baisden, Michael 66
Bashir, Halima 73
Beah, Ishmael 69
Blassingame, John Wesley 40
Blockson, Charles L. 42
Bogle, Donald 34
Brown, Cecil M. 46
Brown, Lloyd Louis 42
Broyard, Bliss 68
Buckley, Gail Lumet 39
Carby, Hazel 27
Carter, Stephen L. 4
Cashin, Sheryll 63
Chiles, Nick 98
Cole, Johnnetta B. 5, 43
Cook, Mercer 40
Cox, Joseph Mason Andrew 51
Cruse, Harold 54
Danquah, Meri Nana Ama 93
Datcher, Michael 60
Davis, Angela J. 88
Davis, Arthur P. 41
Davis, George 36
Davis, Thulani 61
Dickerson, Debra J. 60
Dube, John Langalibalele 119
Dunnigan, Alice Allison 41
Elder, Larry 25, 120
Elliott, Lorris 37
Fine, Sam 60
Finner-Williams, Paris Michele 62
Fisher, Antwone 40
Forna, Aminatta 95
Foster, Cecil 32
Gayle, Addison, Jr. 41
Gladwell, Malcolm 62
Golden, Marita 19, 99
Greenwood, Monique 38
Harrison, Alvin 28
Harrison, Calvin 28
Henderson, David 53
Henries, A. Doris Banks 44
Henriques, Julian 37

Hercules, Frank 44
Hernton, Calvin C. 51
Hill, Errol 40
Horne, Frank 44
Ilibagiza, Immaculée 66
Jacobs, George 118
Jefferson, Margo 108
Johnson, Sandra K. 94
Johnson, William 91
Jolley, Willie 28
Jordan, Vernon E. 7, 35
Kayira, Legson 40
Kearney, Janis 54
Kennedy, Randall 40
Kincaid, Jamaica 4, 109
Knight, Etheridge 37
Ladner, Joyce A. 42
Lampley, Oni Faida 43, 71
Lane, Lunsford 93
Laymon, Kiese 113
Lee, Jarena 100
Lincoln, C. Eric 38
Mabuza-Suttle, Felicia 43
Malveaux, Julianne 32, 70
Manley, Ruth 34
Mathabane, Mark 5, 99
Matthews Shatteen, Westina 51
McKenzie, Vashti M. 29
McKinney Hammond, Michelle 51
Miller, Pepper 96
Mossell, Gertrude Bustill 40
Murray, Pauli 38
Naylor, Gloria 10, 42
Neal, Mark Anthony 74
Newkirk, Pamela 69
Nissel, Angela 42
Norton, Meredith 72
Parks, Rosa 1, 35, 56
Pearson, Felicia 99
Petersen, Neal 96
Pitts, Leonard, Jr. 54, 85
Reid, Ira De A. 100
Run 31, 73
Rusesabagina, Paul 60
Sadlier, Rosemary 62
Shakur, Yusef 85
Smith, Jessie Carney 35
Steele, Shelby 13, 82
Thornton, Yvonne S. 69
Wade-Gayles, Gloria Jean 41
Walker, Rebecca 50
Wambugu, Florence 42
Washington-Williams, Essie Mae 118
Williams, Terrie 35
Williams, Wendy 62
Wiwa, Ken 67
Wright, Nathan, Jr. 56
Zook, Kristal Brent 62

North Carolina state government
Adams, Alma 127
Ballance, Frank W. 41
Fuller, Thomas O. 90
Watt, Mel 26, 105

North Carolina State University
Lowe, Sidney 64

North Pole
Counter, S. Allen 74
Delany, Martin R. 27

Henson, Matthew 2
Hillary, Barbara 65
McLeod, Gus 27

NOW
See National Organization for
Women

NPR
See National Public Radio

NRA
See National Rifle Association

NSF
See National Science Foundation

Nuclear energy
O'Leary, Hazel 6
Packer, Daniel 56
Quarterman, Lloyd Albert 4

Nuclear Regulatory Commission
Jackson, Shirley Ann 12

Nursing
Adams-Ender, Clara 40
Auguste, Rose-Anne 13
Ferguson, Vernice D. 108
Hillary, Barbara 65
Hughes, Ebony 57
Hunter, Alberta 42
Johnson, Hazel 22
Johnson, Mamie "Peanut" 40
Larsen, Nella 10
Lewis, Daurene 72
Lyttle, Hulda Margaret 14
Richards, Hilda 49
Riley, Helen Caldwell Day 13
Robinson, Rachel 16
Robinson, Sharon 22
Seacole, Mary 54
Shabazz, Betty 7, 26
Staupers, Mabel K. 7
Taylor, Susie King 13

Nutrition
Clark, Celeste 15
Gregory, Dick 1, 54
Smith, Ian 62
Watkins, Shirley R. 17

Oakland Athletics baseball team
Baylor, Don 6
Blue, Vida 122
Henderson, Rickey 28, 78
Jackson, Reggie 15

Oakland Tribune
Bailey, Chauncey 68
Maynard, Nancy Hicks 73
Maynard, Robert C. 7

OAU
See African Union

Obie Awards
Browne, Roscoe Lee 66
Bullins, Ed 25, 121
Carter, Nell 39
Cathey, Reg E. 122
De Shields, André 72
Freeman, Morgan 2, 20, 62, 100
Freeman, Yvette 27
Orlandersmith, Dael 42

Sands, Diana 87
Thigpen, Lynne 17, 41
White, Lillias 120
Wolfe, George C. 6, 43, 127

Office of Civil Rights
See U.S. Department of Education

Ohio state government
Beatty, Joyce 117
Brown, Les 5
Ford, Jack 39
Mallory, William L., Sr. 119
Stokes, Carl 10, 73
White, Michael R. 5
Williams, George Washington 18

Oklahoma state government
Ross, Don 27

Oklahoma Supreme Court
Colbert, Tom 115

Olympics
Abdirahman, Abdi 126
Ali, Muhammad 2, 16, 52
Atkinson, Alia 126
Barksdale, Don 103
Beamon, Bob 30
Bekele, Kenenisa 75
Bolt, Usain 73, 104
Bonaly, Surya 7
Bonheur, Yannick 84
Boozer, Bob 103
Bowe, Riddick 6, 107
Brigitha, Enith 126
Campbell, Milt 113
Campbell-Brown, Veronica 102
Carlos, John 97
Christie, Linford 8
Clay, Bryan 57, 74
Coachman, Alice 18, 123
Davis, Anthony 120
Davis, Shani 58, 84
Dawes, Dominique 11, 126
DeFrantz, Anita 37
DeGale, James 74
Devers, Gail 7, 87
Dibaba, Tirunesh 73, 109
Edwards, Teresa 14, 95
Ervin, Anthony 66
Eto'o, Samuel 73
Farah, Mo 104
Felix, Allyson 48, 98
Flowers, Vonetta 35
Fraser-Pryce, Shelly-Ann 113
Frazier, Joe 19, 98
Freeman, Cathy 29
Garrison, Zina 2
Gatlin, Justin 123
Gay, Tyson 114
Gebrselassie, Haile 70
Gourdin, Edward O. 93
Gourdine, Meredith 33
Greene, Maurice 27, 77
Griffith, Yolanda 25
Griffith-Joyner, Florence 28
Harrison, Alvin 28
Harrison, Calvin 28
Harris-Stewart, Lusia 90
Hayes, Bob 77
Hazzard, Walt 98
Hernández, Orlando 96
Hines, Garrett 35

Holmes, Kelly 47
Holyfield, Evander 6
Howard, Sherri 36
Iginla, Jarome 35
James, G. Larry 74
James, Vanessa 84
Jeptoo, Rita 121
Johnson, Ben 1
Johnson, Michael 13
Johnson, Rafer 33
Jones, Cullen 73
Jones, Lou 64
Jones, Randy 35
Joyner-Kersee, Jackie 5
Keflezighi, Meb 49, 121
Kidd, Jason 86
Kipchoge, Eliud 124
Kipsang, Wilson 115
Lewis, Carl 4, 97
Malone, Karl 18, 51, 90
Matson, Ollie 93
Metcalfe, Ralph 26
Miller, Cheryl 10, 74
Montgomery, Tim 41
Moses, Edwin 8
Moussambani, Eric 105
Mutola, Maria 12
Omar, Samia Yusuf 107
Owens, Jesse 2
Pettigrew, Antonio 118
Powell, Mike 7
Quirot, Ana 13
Richards-Ross, Sanya 66, 98
Rudolph, Wilma 4
Savón, Félix 105
Scurry, Briana 27
Simpson, Sherone 120
Smith, Tommie 102
Stevenson, Teófilo 103
Temple, Ed 109
Thomas, Debi 26
Thugwane, Josia 21
Vanessa James and Yannick Bonheur 84
Wade, Dwyane 61, 103
Walker, LeRoy T. 106
Wanjiru, Sammy 94
Ward, Andre 62
Ward, Lloyd 21, 46
Westbrook, Peter 20
Whitaker, Pernell 10, 89
White, Willye 67
Whitfield, Mal 60
Wilder, Deontay 121
Williams, Lauryn 58, 127
Woodruff, John 68

100 Black Men of America
Dortch, Thomas W., Jr. 45
Llewellyn, J. Bruce 13, 85

Ontario Legislature
Curling, Alvin 34

Opera
Adams, Leslie 39
Allen, Betty 83
Anderson, Marian 2, 33
Arroyo, Martina 30
Battle, Kathleen 70
Brown, Angela M. 54
Brown, Anne 76
Brown, Uzee 42
Brownlee, Lawrence 88

Bumbry, Grace 5
Collins, Janet 33, 64
Conrad, Barbara Smith 90
Dale, Clamma 103
Davis, Anthony 11
Dobbs, Mattiwilda 34
Duncan, Todd 76
Elzy, Ruby 119
Estes, Simon 28
Freeman, Paul 39
Graves, Denyce Antoinette 19, 57
Greely, M. Gasby 27
Greenfield, Elizabeth Taylor 116
Grist, Reri 84
Hendricks, Barbara 3, 67
Joplin, Scott 6
Joyner, Matilda Sissieretta 15
Lister, Marquita 65
Matshikiza, Pumeza 115
Matthews, Benjamin 93
Maynor, Dorothy 19
McFerrin, Robert, Sr. 94
Mitchell, Leona 42
Norman, Jessye 5
Phillips, Helen L. 63
Price, Leontyne 1
Ragin, Derek Lee 84
Simpson-Hoffman, N'kenge 52
Still, William Grant 37
Three Mo' Tenors 35
Verrett, Shirley 66, 91
Warfield, William 94
White, Willard 53
Williams, Camilla 116
Yende, Pretty 124

Ophthalmology
Bath, Patricia E. 37

Oracle Corporation
Phillips, Charles E., Jr. 57, 109
Woods, Jacqueline 52

Organ
Bryant, Paul 115
Buckner, Milt 110
Davis, Wild Bill 114
Doggett, Bill 124
McDuff, Jack 116
McGriff, Jimmy 72
Rhyne, Melvin 109
Smith, Jimmy 127

Organization executive
Baker, Maxine 28
Edelin, Ramona Hoage 19
Gayle, Helene D. 3, 46
Jackson, Phillip 115
McGhee, Heather C. 106

Organization of African Unity
See African Union

Organized crime
Coke, Christopher 108
Holstein, Casper 89
Johnson, Bumpy 102

Osteopathy
Allen, Ethel D. 13
Anderson, William G(ilchrist) 57
Ross-Lee, Barbara 67

Painting
Alston, Charles 33
Amos, Emma 63

Andrews, Benny 22, 59
Bailey, Radcliffe 19
Bannister, Edward Mitchell 88
Barnes, Ernie 16, 78
Barthe, Richmond 15
Basquiat, Jean-Michel 5
Bearden, Romare 2, 50
Beasley, Phoebe 34
Biggers, John 20, 33
Bradford, Mark 89
Brown, Frederick J. 102
Colescott, Robert 69
Collins, Paul 61
Cortor, Eldzier 42
Cowans, Adger W. 20
Crichlow, Ernest 75
Crite, Allan Rohan 29
Davis, Bing 84
Delaney, Beauford 19
Delaney, Joseph 30
Delsarte, Louis 34
Douglas, Aaron 7
Driskell, David C. 7
Duncanson, Robert S. 127
Ferguson, Amos 81
Freeman, Leonard 27
Gilliam, Sam 16
Goodnight, Paul 32
Green, Jonathan 54
Guyton, Tyree 9, 94
Harkless, Necia Desiree 19
Hayden, Palmer 13
Honeywood, Varnette P. 54, 88
Hunter, Clementine 45
Jackson, Earl 31
Johnson, William Henry 3
Jones, Lois Mailou 13
Knight, Gwendolyn 63
Knox, Simmie 49
Lawrence, Jacob 4, 28
Lee, Annie Frances 22
Lee-Smith, Hughie 5, 22
Lewis, Norman 39
Lewis, Samella 25
Ligon, Glenn 82
Loving, Alvin, Jr. 35, 53
Major, Clarence 9
Marshall, Kerry James 59
Mason, Desmond 127
Mayhew, Richard 39
McGee, Charles 10
Mehretu, Julie 85
Mitchell, Corinne 8
Motley, Archibald, Jr. 30
Mutu, Wangechi 44
Nascimento, Abdias do 93
Ndiaye, Iba 74
Neals, Otto 73
Nugent, Richard Bruce 39
Ofili, Chris 124
Ouattara 43
Pierre, Andre 17
Pindell, Howardena 55
Pippin, Horace 9
Porter, James A. 11
Prince Twins Seven-Seven 95
Ransome, James E. 88
Reid, Senghor 55
Ringgold, Faith 4, 81
Ruley, Ellis 38
Sallee, Charles 38
Sebree, Charles 40
Simpson, Merton D. 110

Smith, Vincent D. 48
Sudduth, Jimmy Lee 65
Tanksley, Ann 37
Tanner, Henry Ossawa 1
Thomas, Alma 14
Thomas, Mickalene 61
Tolliver, Mose 60
Tolliver, William 9
Verna, Gelsy 70
Wagner, Albert 78
Waring, Laura Wheeler 99
Washington, James, Jr. 38
Wells, James Lesesne 10
White, Charles 39
Wiley, Kehinde 62
Williams, William T. 11
Wilson, Ellis 39
Wilson, John 109
Woodruff, Hale 9

Pan-Africanism
Carmichael, Stokely 5, 26
Clarke, John Henrik 20
Cuffe, Paul 98
Du Bois, David Graham 45
Garvey, Marcus 1
Haile Selassie 7
Kenyatta, Jomo 5
Lee, Robert 112
Logan, Rayford W. 40
Madhubuti, Haki 7, 85
Marshall, Paule 7, 77
Nkrumah, Kwame 3
Nyerere, Julius 5
Touré, Sekou 6
Turner, Henry McNeal 5

Patents
Jennings, Thomas L. 125

PBS
See Public Broadcasting Service

Peace Corps
See U.S. Peace Corps

Pediatrics
Carson, Ben 1, 35, 76, 128
Elders, Joycelyn 6
Fennoy, Ilene 72
Lawrence, Margaret Morgan 100
Shirley, Aaron 126
Witt, Edwin T. 26

PEN/Faulkner award
Bradley, David Henry, Jr. 39
Mayhew, Richard 39
Wideman, John Edgar 5, 87

Pennsylvania state government
Allen, Ethel D. 13
Brown, Homer S. 47
Fattah, Chaka 11, 70, 112
Fauset, Crystal Dreda Bird 100
Irvis, K. Leroy 67
Nix, Robert N. C., Jr. 51

Pennsylvania Supreme Court
Baldwin, Cynthia 74, 107

Pentecostal church
Brazier, Arthur M. 115
DuBois, Joshua 88
Mason, Charles Harrison 107

Munroe, Myles 125
Patterson, Gilbert Earl 41
Patterson, J. O., Jr. 80
Rivers, Eugene F., III 81
Sapp, Marvin 74
Seymour, William J. 106
Winans, Marvin L. 17, 127
Wright, Timothy 74

People United to Serve Humanity (PUSH)
Barrow, Willie T. 85, 128
Jackson, Jesse 1, 27, 72
Jackson, Jesse, Jr. 14, 45, 81, 108

PepsiCo Inc.
Banks, Paula A. 68
Boyd, Edward 70

Pharmaceuticals
Flowers, Sylester 50
Frazier, Kenneth 97
Lewis-Hall, Freda 105
Potter, Myrtle 40

Pharmacist
Akunyili, Dora Nkem 58
Flowers, Sylester 50
Pickett, Cecil 39
Stewart, Ella 39

Philadelphia city government
Allen, Ethel D. 13
Goode, W. Wilson 4
Nutter, Michael 69, 112
Street, John F. 24

Philadelphia Eagles football team
Cunningham, Randall 23
McNabb, Donovan 29, 119
Mitchell, Freddie 116
Rhodes, Ray 14
White, Reggie 6, 50

Philadelphia Flyers hockey team
Brashear, Donald 39
Charleston, Oscar 39

Philadelphia Phillies baseball team
Howard, Ryan 65, 113
Rollins, Jimmy 70

Philadelphia 76ers basketball team
Barkley, Charles 5, 66
Bol, Manute 1
Chamberlain, Wilt 18, 47
Erving, Julius 18, 47
Iverson, Allen 24, 46
Stackhouse, Jerry 30

Philanthropy
Banks, Paula A. 68
Brown, Eddie C. 35
Bryant, Kimberly 127
Cole, Maria 104
Cooper, Evern 40
Cosby, Camille 14, 80
Dawson, Matel, Jr. 39
Edley, Christopher 2, 48
Gardner, Chris 65
Gray, Willie 46
Ibrahim, Mo 67, 115

Johnson, Kevin 70
Johnson, Sheila Crump 48
Jones, Paul R. 76
Lavizzo-Mourey, Risa 48
Malone, Annie 13
McCarty, Osceola 16
Millines Dziko, Trish 28
Pleasant, Mary Ellen 9
Pyfrom, Estella 127
Reeves, Rachel J. 23
Rolle, Myron 98
Thomas, Franklin A. 5, 49
Waddles, Charleszetta "Mother" 10, 49
Walker, Madame C. J. 7
Washington, Pauletta Pearson 86
Wein, Joyce 62
White, Reggie 6, 50
Williams, Fannie Barrier 27

Philosophy
Appiah, Kwame Anthony 67, 101
Hall, Stuart 78
Piper, Adrian 71
Toomer, Jean 6
West, Cornel 5, 33, 80

Photography
Andrews, Bert 13
Barboza, Anthony 10
Bingham, Howard 96
Cowans, Adger W. 20
Cox, Renée 67
DeCarava, Roy 42, 81
Farley, James Conway 99
Fosso, Samuel 116
Hansen, Austin 88
Harris, Lyle Ashton 83
Hinton, Milt 30
Keïta, Seydou 124
Moutoussamy-Ashe, Jeanne 7
Parks, Gordon 1, 35, 58
Pinderhughes, John 47
Robeson, Eslanda Goode 13
Roble, Abdi 71
Serrano, Andres 3
Sidibé, Malick 124
Simpson, Lorna 4, 36
Sleet, Moneta, Jr. 5
Smith, Marvin 46
Smith, Ming 100
Smith, Morgan 46
Tanner, Henry Ossawa 1
Thomas, Mickalene 61
Taylor, Lonzie Odie 96
VanDerZee, James 6
Weems, Carrie Mae 63, 116
White, John H. 27
Williams, Clarence 70
Willis, Deborah 85

Photojournalism
Ashley-Ward, Amelia 23
Cole, Ernest 123
du Cille, Michel 74
Jackson, Vera 40
Moutoussamy-Ashe, Jeanne 7
Parks, Gordon 1, 35, 58
Sleet, Moneta, Jr. 5
Van Lierop, Robert 53
Wallace, William 75
White, John H. 27
Williams, Clarence 70
Withers, Ernest C. 68, 88

Yette, Samuel F. 63

Physical therapy
Griffin, Bessie Blout 43

Physics
Adkins, Rutherford H. 21
Branson, Herman 87
Gates, Sylvester James, Jr. 15
Gourdine, Meredith 33
Imes, Elmer Samuel 39
Jackson, Deborah 94
Jackson, Shirley Ann 12
Johnson, Anthony M. 92
Massey, Walter E. 5, 45
Mickens, Ronald Elbert 105
Stith, James H. 116
Tyson, Neil deGrasse 15, 65

Piano
Adams, Leslie 39
Allen, Geri 92
Ammons, Albert 112
Austin, Lovie 40
Barron, Kenny 128
Batiste, Jonathan 108
Bonds, Margaret 39
Brooks, Hadda 40
Bryant, Ray 95
Buckner, Milt 110
Butler, Henry 121
Cables, George 125
Cartiér, Xam Wilson 41
Christian, Jodie 103
Clark, Sonny 128
Clayton, Gerald 111
Cole, Nat "King" 17
Coltrane, Alice 70
Cook, Charles "Doc" 44
Count Basie 23
Dameron, Tadd 103
Davenport, Cow Cow 115
Davis, Wild Bill 114
Doggett, Bill 124
Domino, Fats 20
Donegan, Dorothy 19
Drew, Kenny 123
Duke, George 21, 113
Ellington, Duke 5
Flanagan, Tommy 69
Fox, Donal 114
Garland, Red 115
Garner, Erroll 76
Hancock, Herbie 20, 67
Hardin Armstrong, Lil 39
Harris, Barry 68
Harris, Kevin 120
Hawes, Hampton 121
Hayes, Isaac 20, 58, 73
Hinderas, Natalie 5
Hines, Earl "Fatha" 39
Horn, Shirley 32, 56
Jamal, Ahmad 69
Johnson, Johnnie 56
Jones, Hank 57, 86
Joplin, Scott 6
Kelly, Wynton 121
Keys, Alicia 32, 68
Lee, Consuela 84
Mabon, Willie 119
Marsalis, Ellis 90
McRae, Carmen 77
McShann, Jay 110
Merriweather, Big Maceo 109

Mitchell, Dwike 111
Monk, Thelonious 1
Montgomery, Little Brother 117
Moran, Jason 89
Newborn, Phineas, Jr. 127
Parlan, Horace 108
Perkins, Carl 128
Perkins, Pinetop 70
Peterson, Oscar 52
Powell, Bud 24
Pratt, Awadagin 31
Preston, Billy 39, 59
Price, Florence 37
Pritchard, Robert Starling 21
Professor Longhair 109
Roberts, Marcus 19, 113
Robinson, Reginald R. 53
Sample, Joe 51, 123
Schuyler, Philippa 50
Scott, Hazel 66
Shipp, Matthew 107
Shirley, Donald 111
Silver, Horace 26, 122
Simone, Nina 15, 41
Smith, Willie 107
Sun Ra 60
Swann, Lynn 28
Southern, Eileen 56
Spann, Otis 107
Spivey, Victoria 119
Sunnyland Slim 118
Sykes, Roosevelt 20
Tapscott, Horace 126
Taylor, Billy 23, 92
Taylor, Cecil 70
Tucker, Tommy 127
Turner, Ike 68
Tyner, McCoy 92
Valdés, Bebo 75
Valdés, Chucho 89
Vaughan, Sarah 13
Waldron, Mal 109
Walker, George 37
Waller, Fats 29
Walton, Cedar 114
Watts, André 42, 101
Webster, Katie 29
Wiggins, Gerald 128
Williams, Mary Lou 15
Yancey, Jimmy 116
Yirga, Samuel 126

Pittsburgh Pirates baseball team
Bonds, Barry 6, 34, 63, 99
Clendenon, Donn 26, 56
Ellis, Dock 78
Stargell, Willie 29

Pittsburgh Steelers football team
Batch, Charlie 120
Gilliam, Joe 31
Greene, Joe 10
Greenwood, L. C. 115
Harris, Franco 97
Perry, Lowell 30
Stallworth, John 102
Stewart, Kordell 21, 111
Swann, Lynn 28
Ward, Hines 84

Woodson, Rod 79

Planned Parenthood Federation of America Inc.
Wattleton, Faye 9

Playboy
Brown, Robert 65
Taylor, Karin 34

Playwright
Anthony, Trey 63
Arkadie, Kevin 17
Armah, Esther 87
Babatunde, Rotimi 104
Baldwin, James 1
Bandele, Biyi 68, 121
Baraka, Amiri 1, 38, 118
Barrett, Lindsay 43
Beckham, Barry 41
Branch, William Blackwell 39
Brown, Cecil M. 46
Brown, Oscar, Jr. 53
Bullins, Ed 25, 121
Caldwell, Benjamin 46
Carroll, Vinnette 29
Césaire, Aimé 48, 69
Chenault, John 40
Childress, Alice 15
Clark-Bekedermo, J. P. 44
Clarke, George 32
Cleage, Pearl 17, 64
Corthron, Kia 43
Cotter, Joseph Seamon, Sr. 40
Cox, Joseph Mason Andrew 51
Dadié, Bernard 34
Davis, Eisa 68
De Veaux, Alexis 44
Dean, Phillip Hayes 122
Dent, Thomas C. 50
Diamond, Lydia R. 101
Dodson, Owen 38
Domingo, Colman 94
Elder, Lonne, III 38
Evans, Mari 26
Farah, Nuruddin 27
Franklin, J. E. 44
Glover, Keith 79
Gordone, Charles 15
Grant, Micki 125
Gurira, Danai 73
Hansberry, Lorraine 6
Harris, Bill 72
Hayes, Teddy 40
Hill, Errol 40
Hill, Leslie Pinckney 44
Holder, Laurence 34
Hughes, Langston 4
Johnson, Georgia Douglas 41
Johnson, Je'Caryous 63
Jones, Sarah 39
Kennedy, Adrienne 11
Kente, Gibson 52
King, Woodie, Jr. 27
Kwei-Armah, Kwame 84
Lampley, Oni Faida 43, 71
Lee, Leslie 85, 122
Long, Richard Alexander 65
Maponya, Maishe 101
Marechera, Dambudzo 39
Mason, Judi Ann 112
McClinton, Marion Isaac 77
McCraney, Tarell Alvin 116
McGhee, Sharon K. 113

Milner, Ron 39
Mitchell, Loften 31
Moss, Carlton 17
Mugo, Micere Githae 32
Ngugi wa Thiong'o 29, 61, 101
Nottage, Lynn 66
Onwueme, Tess Osonye 23
Orlandersmith, Dael 42
Parks, Suzan-Lori 34, 85
Perry, Tyler 40, 54, 103
Rahman, Aishah 37
Redwood, John Henry 78
Rhone, Trevor 80
Salter, Nikkole 73
Sanchez, Sonia 17, 51
Santiago-Hudson, Ruben 85
Schuyler, George Samuel 40
Sebree, Charles 40
Smith, Anna Deavere 6, 44
Talbert, David E. 34, 93
Taylor, Regina 9, 46, 97
Teer, Barbara Ann 81
Thurman, Wallace 17
Tolson, Melvin B. 37
Walcott, Derek 5, 94
Ward, Douglas Turner 42
Wesley, Richard 73
Williams, Roy 89
Williams, Samm-Art 21
Wilson, August 7, 33, 55
Wilson, Tracey Scott 777
Wolfe, George C. 6, 43, 127
Youngblood, Shay 32

Poet laureate (U.S.)
Dove, Rita 6, 78, 101
Trethewey, Natasha 103

Poetry
Abani, Chris 77
Adams, Jenoyne 60
Alexander, Elizabeth 75
Alexander, Kwame 98
Alexander, Margaret Walker 22
Allen, Samuel L. 38
Angelou, Maya 1, 15, 122
Atkins, Russell 45
Aubert, Alvin 41
Ayim, May 126
Baiocchi, Regina Harris 41
Bandele, Asha 36
Baraka, Amiri 1, 38, 118
Barrax, Gerald William 45
Barrett, Lindsay 43
Bell, James Madison 40
Bennett, Gwendolyn B. 59
Bennett, Louise 69
Berry, James 41
Blanco, Mykki 106
Bontemps, Arna 8
Boyd, Melba Joyce 86
Braithwaite, William Stanley 52
Brand, Dionne 32
Brathwaite, Kamau 36
Breeze, Jean "Binta" 37
Brooks, Gwendolyn 1, 28
Brown, Cecil M. 46
Brutus, Dennis 38
Burgess, Marjorie L. 55
Carter, Martin 49
Cartey, Wilfred 47
Césaire, Aimé 48, 69
Chenault, John 40

Cheney-Coker, Syl 43
Clark-Bekedermo, J. P. 44
Clarke, Cheryl 32
Clarke, George 32
Cleage, Pearl 17, 64
Cliff, Michelle 42
Clifton, Lucille 14, 64, 91
Coleman, Wanda 48, 119
Cooper, Afua 53
Cornish, Sam 50
Cortez, Jayne 43, 109
Cotter, Joseph Seamon, Sr. 40
Cox, Joseph Mason Andrew 51
Cuney, William Waring 44
Dabydeen, David 48
Dadié, Bernard 34
D'Aguiar, Fred 50
Damas, Léon-Gontran 46
Dandridge, Raymond Garfield 45
Danner, Margaret Esse 49
Datcher, Michael 60
Davis, Charles T. 48
Davis, Frank Marshall 47
Dawes, Kwame 126
De Veaux, Alexis 44
Dedeaux, Richard 119
Dent, Thomas C. 50
Dodson, Owen 38
Dove, Rita 6, 78, 101
Draper, Sharon Mills 16, 43
Dumas, Henry 41
Dunbar, Paul Laurence 8
Dunbar-Nelson, Alice Ruth Moore 44
Dungy, Camille 86
Emanuel, James A. 46
Evans, Mari 26
Fabio, Sarah Webster 48
Fair, Ronald L. 47
Figueroa, John J. 40
Fisher, Antwone 40
Fleming, Raymond 48
Forbes, Calvin 46
Ford, Nick Aaron 44
Frazier, Oscar 58
Gabre-Medhin, Tsegaye 64
Gilbert, Christopher 50
Goings, Russell 59
Goodison, Lorna 71
Hammon, Jupiter 124
Harkless, Necia Desiree 19
Harper, Frances Ellen Watkins 11
Harper, Michael S. 34
Harris, Bill 72
Harris, Claire 34
Hayden, Robert 12
Hayes, Terrance 124
Henderson, David 53
Hernton, Calvin C. 51
Hill, Leslie Pinckney 44
Hoagland, Everett H. 45
Horne, Frank 44
Horton, George Moses 124
Hughes, Langston 7
Jackson, Fred James 25
Joachim, Paulin 34
Johnson, Fenton 91
Johnson, Georgia Douglas 41
Johnson, Linton Kwesi 37
Jones, Sarah 39
Kaufman, Bob 105
Kay, Jackie 37
Keene, John 73

Knight, Etheridge 37
Lacy, Marc 111
Laraque, Paul 67
Letson, Al 39
Lorde, Audre 6
Mackey, Nathaniel 75
Manley, Ruth 34
Marechera, Dambudzo 39
Matejka, Adrian 87
McClellan, George Marion 91
Moore, Jessica Care 30
Mugo, Micere Githae 32
Mullen, Harryette 34
Naylor, Gloria 10, 42
Neto, António Agostinho 43
Nugent, Richard Bruce 39
Okara, Gabriel 37
Okigbo, Christopher 102
Osbey, Brenda Marie 102
Parker, Pat 19
Peters, Lenrie 43
Philip, Marlene Nourbese 32
Phillips, Carl 111
Powell, Kevin 31, 74
Quigless, Helen G. 49
Randall, Dudley 8, 55
Redmond, Eugene 23
Richards, Beah 30
Sanchez, Sonia 17, 51
Sapphire 14, 95
Scott-Heron, Gil 94
Senghor, Léopold Sédar 12
Senior, Olive 37
Smith, Mary Carter 26
Spencer, Anne 27
Sundiata, Sekou 66
Tolson, Melvin B. 37
Touré, Askia (Muhammad Abu Bakr el) 47
Trethewey, Natasha 103
Troupe, Quincy 83
van Sertima, Ivan 25
Walker, Margaret 29
Washington, James, Jr. 38
Weaver, Afaa Michael 37
Williams, Saul 31
Williams, Sherley Anne 25
Woods, Scott 55
Young, Al 82

Poetry Slam, Inc.
Woods, Scott 55

Political science
Ake, Claude 30
Cohen, Cathy J. 88
Dawson, Michael C. 63
Harris-Lacewell, Melissa 81
Skinner, Kiron K. 65
Walters, Ronald 83
Watson, Carlos 50

Politics
Adebari, Rotimi 83
Alexander, Archie Alphonso 14
Ali, Ayaan Hirsi 58, 92
Allen, Claude 68
Austin, Junius C. 44
Avant, Clarence 19, 86
Barnes, Melody 75
Barrow, Dean 69
Blackwell, Unita 17
Boye, Madior 30
Brazile, Donna 25, 70

Brown, Oscar, Jr. 53
Burris, Roland W. 25, 75
Burton, Bill 96
Buthelezi, Mangosuthu Gatsha 9
Butler, Jerry 26
Cain, Herman 15, 92
Carson, Ben 1, 35, 76, 128
Césaire, Aimé 48, 69
Chideya, Farai 14, 61
Coleman, Mary 46
Compton, John 65
Conneh, Sekou Damate, Jr. 51
Connerly, Ward 14
Davis, James E. 50
Edmonds, Terry 17
Fields, Julia 45
Foster, Ezola 28
Frazier, Ryan 89
Greenlee, Sam 48
Hatcher, Andrew T. 90
Henry, Aaron 19
Holmes, Amy 69
Ingraham, Hubert A. 19
Jackson, Mae 57
Jarrett, Valerie 73
Kelley, Cliff 75
Keyes, Alan 11, 105
Lindsay, Peta 100
Lynch, William, Jr. 115
Magloire, Paul Eugène 68
McGlowan, Angela 64, 86
Moore, Minyon 45
Morton, Ferdinand Q. 90
Nelson, Sophia A. 93
Obasanjo, Stella 32
Pereira, Aristides 30, 97
Perry, Ruth 15
Pinkney, Arnold R. 122
Pitta, Celso 17
Reed, Joe L. 110
Sankoh, Foday 74
Simmons, E. Denise 79
Simmons, Jamal 72
Sisulu, Sheila Violet Makate 24
Smith, Jennifer 21
Smith, Princella 86
Spencer, Winston Baldwin 68
Watkins, Joe 86
Williams, Eddie N. 44
Williams, Eric Eustace 65
Williams, Maggie 7, 71

Pop music
Ashford, Nickolas 21, 97
Ashford and Simpson 21, 97
Babyface 10, 31, 82
Bailey, Pearl 14
Bailey Rae, Corinne 83
Bassey, Shirley 25
Benson, Obie 96
Birdsong, Cindy 113
Bleu, Corbin 65
Brown, Bobby 58, 124
Brown, Melanie 73
Butler, Jonathan 28
Cameo 120
Cannon, Nick 47, 73
Carey, Mariah 32, 53, 69
Chanté, Keshia 50
Checker, Chubby 28
Clayton, Merry 112
Coasters, The 102
Cole, Nat "King" 17

Commodores, The 118
Coppola, Imani Francesca 82
Cox, Deborah 28
Cruz, Taio 104
David, Craig 31, 53
Derülo, Jason 93
Dixie Cups, The 109
Ferrell, Rachelle 29
Graham, Katerina 99
Gray, Macy 29
Hailey, JoJo 22
Hailey, K-Ci 22
Harris, Damon 110
Harris, Major 110
Hawkins, Screamin' Jay 30
Hayes, Isaac 20, 58, 73
Holmes, Clint 57
Horton, Gladys 92
Houston, Whitney 7, 28, 83, 100
Hudson, Jennifer 63, 83
Humphrey, Bobbi 20
Ink Spots, The 102
Isley, Ronald 25, 56
Jackson, Janet 6, 30, 68
Jackson, Jermaine 79
Jackson, LaToya 95
Jackson, Michael 19, 53, 76
Jackson 5 103
James, Rick 17
Jones, Booker T. 84
Jones, Quincy 8, 30
Jordan, Montell 23
Kelis 58, 122
Kendricks, Eddie 22
Keys, Alicia 32, 68
Khan, Chaka 12, 50
Kingston, Sean 94
Knowles, Mathew 96
LaBelle, Patti 13, 30
Lewis, Leona 75
Little Eva 128
Luckett, Letoya 61
Martelly, Michel 90
Mathis, Johnny 20
McFerrin, Bobby 68
Mills Brothers, The 99
Monica 21
Moore, Chante 26
Mtukudzi, Oliver 109
Mumba, Samantha 29
Mvula, Laura 110
Mya 35
Naughton, Naturi 97
Neville, Aaron 21
New Edition 101
Ne-Yo 65
Noah, Yannick 4, 60, 121
Osborne, Jeffrey 26, 121
Otis, Clyde 67
Palmer, Keke 68, 120
P.M. Dawn 54
Preston, Billy 39, 59
Prince 18, 65
Raven-Symoné 44, 113
Reid, Antonio "L.A." 28
Reid, Vernon 34
Richie, Lionel 27, 65, 114
Rihanna 65, 102
Robinson, Smokey 3, 49
Rogers, Bobby 110
Rowland, Kelly 100
Rucker, Darius 34, 74, 108
Sandé, Emeli 113

Seal 14, 75
Secada, Jon 97
Sessoms, Vivian 122
Shirelles, The 111
Short, Bobby 52
Simpson, Valerie 21, 97
Sisqo 30
Smith, Myrna 92
Smith, Willow 92
Solange 97
Staton, Candi 27
Street, Richard 110
Streeter, Sevyn 115
Stromae 121
Summer, Donna 25, 102
Supremes, The 33
Sweat, Keith 19
Temptations, The 33
Terrell, Jean 116
The-Dream 74
Thomas, Irma 29
Turner, Tina 6, 27
Usher 23, 56, 95
Vanity 67
Warwick, Dionne 18, 111
Washington, Dinah 22
Washington, Grover, Jr. 17, 44
Washington, Val 12
Welch, Elisabeth 52
White, Barry 13, 41
White, Josh, Jr. 52
will.i.am 64
Williams, Paul 112
Wilson, Jackie 60
Wilson, Mary 28
Withers-Mendes, Elisabeth 64
Wonder, Stevie 11, 53, 121

Portland (OR) Police Department
Moose, Charles 40

Portland Trail Blazers basketball team
Aldridge, LaMarcus 125
Drexler, Clyde 4, 61
Miller, Larry G. 72
Porter, Terry 75
Roy, Brandon 98

Pratt Institute
Mayhew, Richard 39

Presbyterianism
Callender, Eugene 119
Cannon, Katie 10

Princeton University
Appiah, Kwame Anthony 67, 101
Blanks, Deborah K. 69
Harris-Lacewell, Melissa 81
Rouse, Cecilia 93
Simmons, Ruth 13, 38

Printmaking
Blackburn, Robert 28
Crichlow, Ernest 75
Neals, Otto 73
Tanksley, Ann 37
Thrash, Dox 35
Wells, James Lesesne 10
Wilson, John 109

Prison ministry
Bell, Ralph S. 5

Prison reform
Betts, R. Dwayne 86

Procter & Gamble
Clement-Holmes, Linda 94

Professional Women's Club of Chicago
Gray, Ida 41

Proposition 209
Connerly, Ward 14

Prosecution
Bensouda, Fatou 103
Darden, Christopher 13
Mosby, Marilyn 128
Worthy, Kym 84

Provincial Freeman
Cary, Mary Ann Shadd 30

Psychiatry
Bell, Carl C. 111
Cobbs, Price M. 9
Comer, James P. 6
Eberhardt, Jennifer 124
Fanon, Frantz 44
Fuller, Solomon Carter, Jr. 15
Hamburg, Beatrix 84
Johnson-Powell, Gloria 107
Lawrence, Margaret Morgan 100
Poussaint, Alvin F. 5, 67
Welsing, Frances Cress 5

Psychology
Anderson, Norman B. 45
Brown, Joyce F. 25
Clark, Kenneth B. 5, 52
Clark, Mamie Phipps 79
Edwards, Harry 2
Finner-Williams, Paris Michele 62
Fulani, Lenora 11
Gardere, Jeffrey 76
Gilbert, Christopher 50
Hale, Lorraine 8
Hare, Nathan 44
Hilliard, Asa Grant, III 66
Staples, Brent 8
Steele, Claude 13, 97
Sumner, Francis Cecil 112
Tatum, Beverly Daniel 42, 84

Psychotheraphy
Berrysmith, Don Reginald 49
Ford, Clyde W. 40

Public Broadcasting Service (PBS)
Brown, Les 5
Brown, Tony 3
Creagh, Milton 27
Hampton, Henry 6
Hunter-Gault, Charlayne 6, 31
Ifill, Gwen 28
Lawson, Jennifer 1, 50
Long, Loretta 58
Lynch, Shola 61
Roker, Al 12, 49

Public housing
Lane, Vincent 5
Perry, James 83

Reems, Ernestine Cleveland 27

Public policy
Douglas, Derek 88

Public relations
Barrett, Andrew C. 12
Calhoun, Lillian Scott 87
Compton-Rock, Malaak 86
Edmonds, Terry 17
Graham, Stedman 13
Jones, Robert G. 81
McCabe, Jewell Jackson 10
Perez, Anna 1
Pritchard, Robert Starling 21
Rowan, Carl T. 1, 30
Taylor, Kristin Clark 8
Tobin, Patricia 75

Public schools
Ackerman, Arlene 108
Baker, Gwendolyn Calvert 9
Clayton, Constance 1
Coleman, William F., III 61
Collins, Marva 3, 71
Crew, Rudy 16, 113
Dewitty, Thelma 114
Lemon, Alton T. 112
Tyler, Ollie 128

Public speaking
Bell, James Madison 40
Brown, Hallie Quinn 100
Douglass, Frederick 87
Kennedy, Randall 40

Publishing
Abbott, Robert Sengstacke 27
Alexander, Kwame 98
Ames, Wilmer 27
Ashley-Ward, Amelia 23
Aubert, Alvin 41
Auguste, Arnold A. 47
Baisden, Michael 25, 66
Bakewell, Danny 99
Boston, Lloyd 24
Boyd, T. B., III 6
Brown, Jamie Foster 91
Brown, Marie Dutton 12
Cary, Mary Ann Shadd 30
Coombs, Orde M. 44
Cox, William E. 68
Dawkins, Wayne 20
Driver, David E. 11
Ducksworth, Marilyn 12
Dumas, Henry 41
Fuller, Hoyt 44
Giddings, Paula 11
Goodlett, Carlton B. 91
Harris, Jay 19
Harris, Monica 18
Hill, Bonnie Guiton 20
Hudson, Cheryl 15
Hudson, Wade 15
James, Juanita 13
Jones, Quincy 8, 30
Kunjufu, Jawanza 3, 50
Lawson, Jennifer 1, 50
Leavell, Dorothy R. 17
Lewis, Edward T. 21
Lorde, Audre 6
Madhubuti, Haki 7, 85
Maynard, Nancy Hicks 73
Maynard, Robert C. 7

McDonald, Erroll 1
Moore, Jessica Care 30
Morgan, Garrett 1
Murphy, John H. 42
Overton, Anthony 128
Parks, Gordon 1, 35, 58
Perez, Anna 1
Randall, Dudley 8, 55
Scott, C. A. 29
Sengstacke, John 18
Smith, Clarence O. 21
Stinson, Denise L. 59
Stringer, Vickie 58
Tyree, Omar Rashad 21
Vanzant, Iyanla 17, 47, 108
Walker, Alice 1, 43
Washington, Alonzo 29
Washington, Laura S. 18
Wells-Barnett, Ida B. 8
Williams, Armstrong 29
Woods, Teri 69

Pulitzer Prize
Baquet, Dean 63, 121
Brooks, Gwendolyn 1, 28
Dash, Leon 47
Dove, Rita 6, 78, 101
du Cille, Michel 74
Fuller, Charles 8
Givhan, Robin Deneen 72
Gordone, Charles 15
Haley, Alex 4
Henderson, Angelo 122
Jefferson, Margo 108
Jones, Edward P. 43, 67
King, Colbert I. 69
Komunyakaa, Yusef 9
Lewis, David Levering 9
Marable, Manning 10, 102
McPherson, James Alan 70
Morrison, Toni 2, 15, 86
Newkirk, Pamela 69
Page, Clarence 4
Parks, Suzan-Lori 34, 85
Payne, Les 89
Pitts, Leonard, Jr. 54, 85
Raspberry, William 2
Robinson, Eugene 77
Shipp, E. R. 15
Sleet, Moneta, Jr. 5
Tucker, Cynthia 15, 61
Walker, Alice 1, 43
Walker, George 37
White, John H. 27
Wilkerson, Isabel 71
Wilkins, Roger 2, 84
Williams, Clarence 70
Wilson, August 7, 33, 55

Puppetry
Clash, Kevin 14, 93

PUSH
See People United to Serve Humanity

Quiltmaking
Benberry, Cuesta 65
Ringgold, Faith 4, 81

Qwest Records
Jones, Quincy 8, 30

Race car driving
Brown, Antron 85
Hamilton, Lewis 66

Lester, Bill **42, 85**
Ribbs, Willy T. **2**
Scott, Wendell Oliver, Sr. **19**

Race relations
Abbott, Diane **9**
Alexander, Clifford **26**
Anthony, Wendell **25**
Asante, Molefi Kete **3**
Ayim, May **126**
Baldwin, James **1**
Bethune, Mary McLeod **4**
Bobo, Lawrence **60**
Booker, Simeon **23**
Bosley, Freeman, Jr. **7**
Boyd, T. B., III **6**
Bradley, David Henry, Jr. **39**
Branch, William Blackwell **39**
Brown, Elaine **8**
Butler, Paul D. **17**
Cary, Lorene **3**
Cashin, Sheryll **63**
Cayton, Horace **26**
Chavis, Benjamin **6**
Clark, Kenneth B. **5, 52**
Clark, Septima **7**
Cobbs, Price M. **9**
Cochran, Johnnie **11, 39, 52**
Cole, Johnnetta B. **5, 43**
Comer, James P. **6**
Cone, James H. **3, 82**
Cook, Suzan D. Johnson **22**
Cook, Toni **23**
Davis, Angela **5, 114**
Davis, Benjamin O., Jr. **2, 43**
Davis, Benjamin O., Sr. **4**
Delany, Martin R. **27**
Diallo, Amadou **27**
Dickerson, Debra J. **60**
Divine, Father **7**
DuBois, Shirley Graham **21**
Dunbar-Nelson, Alice Ruth Moore **44**
Dyson, Michael Eric **11, 40, 128**
Edelman, Marian Wright **5, 42**
Ellison, Ralph **7**
Farmer, James **2, 64**
Farmer-Paellmann, Deadria **43**
Farrakhan, Louis **2**
Fauset, Jessie **7**
Franklin, John Hope **5, 77**
Fuller, Charles **8**
Gibson, William F. **6**
Goode, W. Wilson **4**
Graham, Lawrence Otis **12**
Gregory, Dick **1, 54**
Grimké, Archibald H. **9**
Hall, Elliott S. **24**
Hampton, Henry **6**
Harris, Alice **7**
Hastie, William H. **8**
Haynes, George Edmund **8**
Henry, Aaron **19**
Henry, Lenny **9, 52**
Hill, Oliver W. **24, 63**
Hope, John **8**
Howard, M. William, Jr. **26**
Hunt, Darnell **92**
Ingram, Rex **5**
Jeffries, Leonard **8**
Jones, Elaine R. **7, 45**
Khanga, Yelena **6**
King, Bernice **4, 81**

King, Coretta Scott **3, 57**
King, Martin Luther, Jr. **1**
King, Yolanda **6**
Lane, Charles **3**
Lee-Smith, Hughie **5, 22**
Lorde, Audre **6**
Mabuza-Suttle, Felicia **43**
Martin, Louis E. **16**
Martin, Trayvon **105**
Maynard, Robert C. **7**
McDougall, Gay J. **11, 43**
McKay, Claude **6**
McWhorter, John **35, 119**
Meredith, James H. **11**
Micheaux, Oscar **7**
Moore, Harry T. **29**
Mosley, Walter **5, 25, 68**
Muhammad, Khallid Abdul **10, 31**
Page, Clarence **4**
Pitt, David Thomas **10**
Poussaint, Alvin F. **5, 67**
Price, Frederick K. C. **21**
Price, Hugh B. **9, 54**
Reid, Ira De A. **100**
Robeson, Paul **2**
Robinson, Spottswood W., III **22**
Shabazz, Attallah **6**
Sifford, Charlie **4, 49**
Simpson, Carole **6, 30**
Sister Souljah **11, 100**
Sisulu, Sheila Violet Makate **24**
Smith, Anna Deavere **6, 44**
Sowell, Thomas **2, 99**
Spaulding, Charles Clinton **9**
Staples, Brent **8**
Steele, Shelby **13, 82**
Stradford, J. B. **101**
Taulbert, Clifton Lemoure **19**
Till, Emmett **7**
Tutu, Desmond Mpilo **6, 44**
Tutu, Nontombi Naomi **57**
Tyree, Omar Rashad **21**
Walcott, Derek **5, 94**
Walker, Maggie **17**
Washington, Booker T. **4**
Washington, Harold **6**
Wells-Barnett, Ida B. **8**
Welsing, Frances Cress **5**
Wiley, Ralph **8, 78**
Wilkins, Roy **4**
Williams, Gregory **11**
Williams, Walter E. **4**
Wilson, Sunnie **7, 55**
Wright, Richard **5**
Young, Whitney M., Jr. **4**

Radio
Abrahams, Peter **39**
Abu-Jamal, Mumia **15**
Alert, Kool DJ Red **33**
Anderson, Eddie "Rochester" **30**
Ashong, Derrick **86**
Banks, William **11**
Baskett, James **102**
Bates, Karen Grigsby **40**
Beasley, Phoebe **34**
Blayton, Jesse B., Sr. **55**
Booker, Simeon **23**
Branch, William Blackwell **39**
Brewster, W. Herbert **128**
CoCo Brother **93**
Crocker, Frankie **29**
Elder, Larry **25, 120**

Fuller, Charles **8**
Gibson, Truman K., Jr. **60**
Goode, Mal **13**
Greene, Petey **65**
Gumbel, Greg **8**
Hamblin, Ken **10**
Haynes, Trudy **44**
Holt, Nora **38**
Hughes, Cathy **27**
Jackson, Hal **41, 104**
Jarrett, Vernon D. **42**
Joe, Yolanda **21**
Joyner, Tom **19, 90**
Kelley, Cliff **75**
Lewis, Delano **7**
Lewis, Ramsey **35, 70**
Ligging, Alfred, III **43**
Love, Ed **58**
Lover, Ed **10**
Ludacris **37, 60**
Luper, Clara **94**
Madison, Joseph E. **17**
Majors, Jeff **41**
McGhee, Sharon K. **113**
Michaux, Solomon Lightfoot **91**
Mickelbury, Penny **28**
Moss, Carlton **17**
Parr, Russ **51**
Pressley, Condace L. **41**
Pugh, Charles **81**
Quivers, Robin **61**
Samara, Noah **15**
Smiley, Rickey **59**
Smiley, Tavis **20, 68**
Smith, Greg **28**
Steinberg, Martha Jean "The Queen" **28**
Stuart, Moira **82**
Thomas, Rufus **20, 96**
Tirico, Mike **68, 124**
Wade, Ernestine **126**
Whack, Rita Coburn **36**
Williams, Armstrong **29**
Williams, Nat D. **91**
Williams, Ted **91**
Williams, Wendy **62**
Woods, Georgie **57**
Yarbrough, Camille **40**

Radio Hall of Fame
Jackson, Hal **41, 104**
Joyner, Tom **19, 90**
Williams, Wendy **62**

Ragtime
Blake, Eubie **29**
Europe, James Reese **10**
Joplin, Scott **6**
Robinson, Reginald R. **53**
Sissle, Noble **29**

Rap music
Alert, Kool DJ Red **33**
A$AP Rocky **109**
Bambaataa, Afrika **34**
Banks, Lloyd **113**
Banner, David **55**
Benjamin, Andre **45**
Bey, Yasiin **30, 96**
Big Daddy Kane **79**
Big L **120**
Big Sean **96**
Birdman **110**
Black Thought **63**

Blackman, Toni **86**
Blow, Kurtis **31, 122**
B.o.B. **91**
Bonney, Tabi **98**
Bow Wow **35**
Bradley, Adam **101**
Brown, Foxy **25**
Bun B **123**
Cam'ron **104**
Chamillionaire **82**
Chief Keef **112**
Chuck D. **9**
C-Murder **99**
Combs, Sean **17, 43, 92**
Common **31, 63, 98**
Coolio **103**
Curren$y **114**
Da Don, Polow **86**
De La Soul **119**
Deezer D **53**
DJ Jazzy Jeff **32**
DJ Screw **110**
DMX **28, 64**
Dr. Dre **10, 14, 30, 116**
Drake **86**
Dupri, Jermaine **13, 46**
E-40 **125**
Elliott, Missy **31, 90**
Eve **29**
Fabolous **93**
Fat Boys **92**
50 Cent **46, 83**
Flavor Flav **67**
Flo Rida **78**
Freestyle Fellowship **122**
Future **109**
Geto Boys **115**
Ghostface Killah **90**
Gibbs, Freddie **125**
Gotti, Irv **39**
Grae, Jean **51**
Grandmaster Flash **33, 60**
Gray, F. Gary **14, 49**
Harrell, Andre **9, 30**
Heavy D **58, 98**
Ice Cube **8, 30, 60**
Ice-T **6, 31, 96**
J Dilla **102**
Ja Rule **35, 91**
Jay Electronica **125**
Jay-Z **27, 69, 103**
Jones, Quincy **8, 30**
Juicy J **116**
Juvenile **96**
KB **122**
Khalifa, Wiz **96**
Kid Cudi **83**
Killer Mike **117**
K'naan **76**
Knight, Suge **11, 30, 102**
KRS-One **34**
Kweli, Talib **93**
Lamar, Kendrick **105**
Le1f **120**
Lighty, Chris **105**
Lil B **121**
Lil Jon **124**
Lil' Kim **28**
Lil Wayne **66, 84**
LL Cool J **16, 49, 94**
London, Theophilus **95**
Lopes, Lisa **36**
Lord Infamous **117**

Lord Jamar 126
Lover, Ed 10
Ludacris 37, 60
Mac Daddy 111
Mack Maine 125
Madlib 88
Mane, Gucci 91
Mase 24
Masta Ace 118
Master P 21, 115
MC Breed 75
M.C. Hammer 20, 80
MC Lyte 34, 108
McDaniels, Ralph 79
Method Man 81
Migos 126
Nas 33, 111
Nate Dogg 92
Naughty by Nature 124
Nelly 32, 90
Notorious B.I.G. 20
Ol' Dirty Bastard 52
O'Neal, Shaquille 8, 30, 95
OutKast 35
Peterson, James 81
Proof 101
Public Enemy 98
Pusha T 123
Queen Latifah 1, 16, 58, 119
?uestlove 74
Ray J 86
Redman 81
Rhymefest 97
Rhymes, Busta 31
Riley, Boots 89
Roberts, Kimberly Rivers 72
Rock, Pete 121
Romeo 98
Ross, Rick 79, 104
Run-DMC 31, 75
RZA 80, 128
Santana, Juelz 120
ScHoolboyQ 117
Sermon, Erick 81
Shakur, Afeni 67
Shakur, Tupac 14
Shmurda, Bobby 123
Shyne 101
Simmons, Russell 1, 30
Sir Mix-A-Lot 82
Sister Souljah 11, 100
Slick Rick 93
Slim Thug 86
Smith, Will 8, 18, 53
Snoop Dogg 35, 84
Speech 82
Sticky Fingaz 86
Sugarhill Gang, The 79, 125
Sweatshirt, Earl 114
Timbaland 32
Tinie Tempah 115
T-Pain 73, 111
Treacherous Three 128
Trina 114
2 Chainz 105
Tyga 117
Tyler, the Creator 100
Waka Flocka Flame 110
Wale 92
Wanz 116
Woolard, Jamal 102
Xzibit 78
Yarbrough, Camille 40

Yayo, Tony 113
YG 122
Ying Yang Twins 112
Young Jeezy 63
Z-Ro 109

Rastafarianism
Burning Spear 79
Dube, Lucky 77
Haile Selassie 7
Marley, Bob 5
Marley, Rita 32, 70
Tosh, Peter 9

Reader's Choice Award
Holton, Hugh, Jr. 39

Reading Is Fundamental
Trueheart, William E. 49

Real estate development
Amoudi, Mohammed al- 88
Bakewell, Danny 99
Burks, Juanita P. 95
Chapman, Susan E. 94
Lane, Vincent 5
Maponya, Richard 101
Marshall, Bella 22
Nail, John E. 92
Payton, Philip A., Jr. 88
Russell, Herman Jerome 17
Toote, Gloria E. A. 64

Record producer
Albright, Gerald 23
Ayers, Roy 16
Babyface 10, 31, 82
Bambaataa, Afrika 34
Barnes, Lloyd 77
Bivins, Michael 72
Butler, George, Jr. 70
Carter, Troy 98
Cole, J. 97
Coleman, Ornette 39, 69
Da Don, Polow 86
Danjah, Terror 91
Davis, Carl 105
de Passe, Suzanne 25
DJ Jazzy Jeff 32
Dodd, Coxsone 99
Dr. Dre 10, 14, 30, 116
Duke, George 21, 113
Dupri, Jermaine 13, 46
Elliott, Missy 31, 90
Felix Da Housecat 110
Flying Lotus 124
Fuqua, Harvey 90
Gotti, Irv 39
Hailey, JoJo 22
Hailey, K-Ci 22
Hammond, Fred 23
Hawkins, Walter 87
Huff, Leon 86
Ice Cube 8, 30, 60
Ja Rule 35, 91
Jackson, George 19
Jackson, Joe 78
Jackson, Michael 19, 53, 76
Jackson, Randy 40
Jean, Wyclef 20, 86
Jerkins, Rodney 31
Jimmy Jam 13
Jones, Quincy 8, 30
Kelly, R. 18, 44, 71, 117

Knowles, Mathew 96
Lewis, Terry 13
Marley, Rita 32, 70
Marley, Stephen 100
Mayfield, Curtis 2, 43
McGregor, Stephen 99
Minott, Sugar 86
Mitchell, Willie 114
Osborne, Jeffrey 26, 121
Prince 18, 65
Reid, Antonio "L.A." 28
Robinson, Sylvia 79
Sermon, Erick 81
Sims, Danny 106
Stewart, Tricky 98
Sweat, Keith 19
Timbaland 32
Turner, Ike 68
Tyler, the Creator 100
Vandross, Luther 13, 48, 59
White, Barry 13, 41
Whitfield, Norman 73
Williams, J. Mayo 83
Williams, Pharrell 47, 82, 119
Yabby You 83
Young, Lee 72

Recording executive
Birdman 110
Brae, C. Michael 61
Busby, Jheryl 3, 74
Butler, George, Jr. 70
Dash, Damon 31, 113
de Passe, Suzanne 25
Dupri, Jermaine 13, 46
Gaye, Anna Gordy 121
Gordy, Berry, Jr. 1
Gotti, Irv 39
Harrell, Andre 9, 30
Jackson, George 19
Jackson, Randy 40
James Bracken and Vivian Bracken 107
Jimmy Jam 13
Jones, Quincy 8, 30
Knight, Suge 11, 30, 102
Lewis, Terry 13
Liles, Kevin 42, 99
Mack Maine 125
Massenburg, Kedar 23, 110
Master P 21, 115
Mayfield, Curtis 2, 43
McPherson, David 32
Reid, Antonio "L.A." 28
Rhone, Sylvia 2
Robey, Don 115
Sanders, Angelia 86
Simmons, Russell 1, 30
Spivey, Victoria 119
Stoute, Steve 38
Thomas, Tabby 119
Williams, J. Mayo 83

Reggae
Afro, Teddy 78
Banton, Buju 93
Barnes, Lloyd 77
Beenie Man 32
Big Youth 107
Blondy, Alpha 30
Brown, Dennis 99
Burning Spear 79
Chronixx 123

Cliff, Jimmy 28, 92
Dawuni, Rocky 94
Dekker, Desmond 104
Dodd, Coxsone 99
Dube, Lucky 77
Ellis, Alton 74
Ellis, Hortense 97
Ford, Vincent 75
Griffiths, Marcia 29
Hammond, Lenn 34
Hibbert, Toots 103
Isaacs, Gregory 89
Johnson, Linton Kwesi 37
Marley, Bob 5
Marley, Rita 32, 70
Marley, Stephen 100
Marley, Ziggy 41
McGregor, Stephen 99
Minott, Sugar 86
Mowatt, Judy 38
Perry, Lee 19, 103
Perry, Ruth 19
Rhoden, Wayne 70
Shaggy 31
Sly & Robbie 34
Steely 80
Tosh, Peter 9
Yabby You 83

Republican Party
Allen, Ethel D. 13
Fisher, Ada M. 76
Howard, Perry Wilbon, Jr. 112
Scott, Tim 87, 125
Steele, Michael 38, 73, 91
Toote, Gloria E. A. 64

Restaurants/Catering/Cooking
Armstrong, Govind 81
Cain, Herman 15, 92
Calabrese, Karyn 89
Crum, George 101
Daniels-Carter, Valerie 23
Dorsey, Thomas J. 90
Downing, George T. 91
Ford, Barney 90
Garvin, Gerry 78
Hawkins, La-Van 17, 54
Henry, Dwight 104
Howell, Ayinde 94
James, Charles H., III 62
Lewis, Aylwin B. 51, 88
Montgomery, Robbie 101
Otis, Clarence, Jr. 55
Ouattara, Morou 74
Pierce, Harold 75
Rodriguez, Jimmy 47
Samuelsson, Marcus 53, 120
Sbraga, Kevin 88
Smith, B(arbara) 11
Terry, Bryant 128
Washington, Regynald G. 44
Williams, Lindsey 75
Woods, Sylvia 34, 104

Rhode Island School of Design
Bannister, Edward Mitchell 88
Prophet, Nancy Elizabeth 42

Rhodes scholar
Booker, Cory Anthony 68
Braxton, Brad 77
Kennedy, Randall 40

Locke, Alain 10
Pinkett, Randal 61
Rice, Susan 74, 103
Rolle, Myron 98
Wideman, John Edgar 5, 87

Rhythm and blues/soul music
Aaliyah 30
Ace, Johnny 36
Acklin, Barbara Jean 107
Adams, Johnny 39
Adams, Oleta 18
Akon 68
Amerie 52
Anderson, Jacob 128
Ashanti 37, 96
Ashford, Nickolas 21, 97
Ashford and Simpson 21, 97
Atlantic Starr 122
Austin, Patti 24
Ayers, Roy 16
Babyface 10, 31, 82
Badu, Erykah 22, 114
Bailey, Philip 63
Baker, Anita 21, 48
Baker, LaVern 26
Baker, Mickey 95
Ballard, Florence 112
Ballard, Hank 41
Bar-Kays, The 118
Barrino, Fantasia 53, 94
Bass, Fontella 104, 109
Belgrave, Marcus 77
Bell, LeRoy 98
Bell, Thom 112
Belle, Regina 1, 51
Benét, Eric 28, 77
Benton, Brook 121
Berry, Chuck 29
Beverly, Frankie 25
Beyoncé 39, 70, 105
Big Maybelle 117
Bilal 101
Billy Ward and the Dominoes 105
Bivins, Michael 72
Blacc, Aloe 119
Blige, Mary J. 20, 34, 60, 97
Bostic, Earl 121
Boyz II Men 82
Bradley, Charles 126
Bradshaw, Tiny 102
Brandy 14, 34, 72
Braxton, Toni 15, 61, 91
Bridges, Leon 126
Brooks, Hadda 40
Brown, Bobby 58, 124
Brown, Charles 23
Brown, Chris 74, 109
Brown, Chuck 78, 102
Brown, Clarence Gatemouth 59
Brown, James 15, 60
Brown, Nappy 73
Brown, Oscar, Jr. 53
Brown, Ruth 90
Burke, Clarence, Jr. 112
Burke, Solomon 31, 86
Busby, Jheryl 3, 74
Butler, Jerry 26
Cadillacs 107
Cameo 120
Carey, Mariah 32, 53, 69
Carr, James 117
Castor, Jimmy 100

Chandler, Gene 105
Chantels, The 128
Charles, Ray 16, 48
Chi-Lites 106
Ciara 56, 115
Clay, Otis 112
Clinton, George 9, 93
Clovers, The 104
Cole, Keyshia 63, 107
Cole, Natalie 17, 60, 84
Commodores, The 118
Contours, The 109
Cooke, Sam 17
Covay, Don 127
Cox, Deborah 28
Crawford, Hank 77
Crusaders, The 116
D'Angelo 27, 123
David, Craig 31, 53
Davis, Tyrone 54
Dazz Band 116
DeBarge, El 89
Dells, The 109
Derülo, Jason 93
DeSanto, Sugar Pie 122
Detroit Emeralds, The 121
DeVaughn, Raheem 91
Diddley, Bo 39, 72
Doggett, Bill 124
Domino, Fats 20
Dorsey, Lee 65
Downing, Will 19
Dramatics, The 106
Drifters, The 121
Dupri, Jermaine 13, 46
Earth, Wind & Fire 98
Emotions, The 125
En Vogue 100
Escobar, Damien 56
Escobar, Tourie 56
Evans, Faith 22
Falcons, The 128
Feemster, Herbert 72
Fiona, Melanie 84
Five Keys, The 104
FKA Twigs 123
Flamingos, The 108
Floyd, Eddie 127
Franklin, Aretha 11, 44, 115
Fuqua, Harvey 90
Gamble, Kenny 85
Gap Band, The 100
Garrett, Sean 57
Gaye, Marvin 2
Gaynor, Gloria 36
Gibson, Tyrese 27, 62
Gill, Johnny 51
Ginuwine 35
Goapele 55
Goodman, Al 87
Gotti, Irv 39
Graham Central Station 123
Gray, Dobie 99
Gray, Macy 29
Greaves, R. B. 106
Green, Al 13, 47, 74
Green, Cee Lo 70, 103
Hailey, JoJo 22
Hailey, K-Ci 22
Hall, Aaron 57
Hamilton, Anthony 61
Harold Melvin & the Blue Notes
    105

Harris, Corey 39, 73
Harris, Damon 110
Harris, Major 110
Hart, Alvin Youngblood 61
Hathaway, Donny 18
Hathaway, Lalah 57, 88
Hayes, Isaac 20, 58, 73
Hendryx, Nona 56
Henry, Clarence "Frogman" 46
Hill, Darryl 128
Hill, Lauryn 20, 53, 111
Hilson, Keri 84
Holloway, Brenda 65
Houston, Cissy 20, 83
Houston, Whitney 7, 28, 83, 100
Huff, Leon 86
Humes, Helen 128
Hunter, Ivory Joe 106
Hyman, Phyllis 19
India.Arie 34
Ingram, James 84
Intruders, The 119
Isley, Marvin 87
Isley, Ronald 25, 56
Jackson, Janet 6, 30, 68
Jackson, Michael 19, 53, 76
Jackson, Millie 25
Jackson, Tito 81
Jagged Edge 117
Jaheim 58
Jamelia 51
James, Etta 13, 52, 100
James, Leela 117
James, Rick 17
Jennings, Lyfe 56, 69
Johnson, Al 119
Johnson, Robert 2
Johnson, Syl 97
Johnson, Syleena 98
Johnson-George, Tamara 79
Jones, Booker T. 84
Jones, Donell 29
Jones, Quincy 8, 30
Jones, Sharon 86
Jordan, Louis 104
Jordan, Montell 23
Kandi 83
Kay, Connie 114
Kelly, R. 18, 44, 71, 117
KEM 47, 127
Kendricks, Eddie 22
Keys, Alicia 32, 68
King, Ben E. 128
King Curtis 92
Kiwanuka, Michael 126
Knight, Gladys 16, 66
Knight, Marie 80
LaBelle, Patti 13, 30
Lakeside 120
Lance, Major 111
Larrieux, Amel 63
LaSalle, Denise 111
Lattimore, Kenny 35, 128
LaVette, Bettye 85
Ledisi 73
Legend, John 67, 116
Levert, Eddie 70
Levert, Gerald 22, 59
Little Anthony & the Imperials 107
Little Eva 128
Little Richard 15
Lloyd 99
Lopes, Lisa 36

Love, Darlene 23, 92
Luckett, Letoya 61
Lynn, Barbara 126
Mabon, Willie 119
Maitreya, Sananda 85
Manhattans, The 123
Mario 71
Marvelettes, The 126
Maxwell 20, 81
Maye, Lee 111
Mayfield, Curtis 2, 43
McCoo, Marilyn 53
McCoy, Van 123
McKnight, Brian 18, 34
Meters, The 118
Midnight Star 110
Miguel 98
Miles, Buddy 69
Millinder, Lucky 101
Mitchell, Willie 114
Monáe, Janelle 86
Monica 21
Montgomery, Robbie 101
Moonglows, The 108
Moore, Chante 26
Moore, Melba 21
Musiq 37, 84
Mvula, Laura 110
Mya 35
Nash, Johnny 40
Ndegeocello, Meshell 15, 83
Neale, Haydain 52
Neville, Aaron 21
New Birth 124
New Edition 101
Ne-Yo 65
Notorious B.I.G. 20
Ocean, Frank 100
O'Jays, The 98
Omarion 107
Orioles, The 100
Otis, Clyde 67
Parker, Maceo 72
Parker, Ray, Jr. 85
Paul, Billy 127
Peebles, Ann 114
Pendergrass, Teddy 22, 83
Penguins, The 107
Phillips, Esther 107
Pinkney, Fayette 80
Pitts, Skip 103
Platters, The 99
Pleasure P 84
Porter, David 127
Preston, Billy 39, 59
Price, Kelly 23
Price, Lloyd 119
Prince 18, 65
Prysock, Arthur 117
Rare Essence 121
Ravens, The 103
Reagon, Toshi 76
Record, Eugene 60
Redding, Otis 16
Reed, A. C. 36
Reed, Natina 106
Reeves, Martha 85
Richard, Dawn 92
Riley, Teddy 116
Riperton, Minnie 32
Robinson, Smokey 3, 49
Rogers, Bobby 110
Rose Royce 120

Ross, Diana 8, 27
Ruffin, Jimmy 125
Russell, Brenda 52
Saadiq, Raphael 125
Sade 15, 92
Sam and Dave 102
Scott, Jill 29, 83
Scott, Jimmy 48, 122
Scott-Heron, Gil 94
Shanice 112
Shaw, Marlena 105
Siji 56
Simon, Joe 109
Simpson, Valerie 21, 97
Sisqo 30
Sledge, Percy 39, 128
Songz, Trey 88
Spaniels, The 105
Sparks, Jordin 66
Starr, Edwin 122
Staton, Candi 27
Steinberg, Martha Jean "The
  Queen" 28
Stewart, Billy 112
Stone, Angie 31
Stone, Jesse 98
Street, Richard 110
Streeter, Sevyn 115
Strong, Barrett 89
Studdard, Ruben 46
Sullivan, Jazmine 81
Supremes, The 33
Swann, Bettye 109
Sweat, Keith 19
Tamia 24, 55
Taste of Honey, A 115
Tavares 115
T-Boz 108
Temptations, The 33
Terrell, Tammi 32
Tex, Joe 116
The-Dream 74
Thomas, Carla 96
Thomas, Irma 29
Thomas, Rozonda 34, 78
Thomas, Rufus 20, 96
TLC 34
Tony! Toni! Toné! 127
Tresvant, Ralph 57
Tucker, Tommy 127
Turner, Ike 68
Turner, Tina 6, 27
Ulmer, James 79
Usher 23, 56, 95
Valentino, Bobby 62
Vandross, Luther 13, 48, 59
Ward, Anita 118
Warwick, Dionne 18, 111
Watley, Jody 54
Wellington, Valerie 118
Wells, Mary 28
West, Kanye 52, 93
Whispers, The 124
White, Barry 13, 41
Whitney, Marva 109
Williams, Larry 118
Williams, Michelle 73
Williams, Paul 112
Wilson, Cassandra 16
Wilson, Charlie 31, 77
Wilson, Mary 28
Wilson, Nancy 10, 98
Withers, Bill 61

Witherspoon, Jimmy 113
Womack, Bobby 60, 92, 123
Wonder, Stevie 11, 53, 121
Woods, Belita 103
Woodson, Ali Ollie 89
Wright, O. V. 114

**Robert C. Maynard Institute
for Journalism Education**
Harris, Jay T. 19
Maynard, Nancy Hicks 73
Maynard, Robert C. 7

Rock and Roll Hall of Fame
Ballard, Florence 112
Ballard, Hank 41
Bennett, Estelle 77
Berry, Chuck 29
Bland, Bobby 36, 113
Brown, Charles 23
Burke, Solomon 31, 86
Clinton, George 9, 93
Cole, Nat "King" 17
Davis, Miles 4
Diddley, Bo 39, 72
Drifters, The 121
Franklin, Aretha 11, 44, 115
Gamble, Kenny 85
Grandmaster Flash 33, 60
Green, Al 13, 47, 74
Guy, Buddy 31
Harris, Damon 110
Hayes, Isaac 20, 58, 73
Holiday, Billie 1
Holland-Dozier-Holland 36
Hooker, John Lee 30
Isley, Marvin 87
Isley, Ronald 25, 56
Jackson, Mahalia 5
Jackson, Michael 19, 53, 76
Jackson, Tito 81
Jackson 5 103
Jamerson, James 59
James, Etta 13, 52, 100
Johnson, Johnnie 56
Jones, Booker T. 84
Jones, Quincy 8, 30
King, Ben E. 128
Knight, Gladys 16, 66
Love, Darlene 23, 92
Mayfield, Curtis 2, 43
Morton, Jelly Roll 29
Orioles, The 100
Price, Lloyd 119
Prince 18, 65
Public Enemy 98
Reeves, Martha 85
Ross, Diana 8, 27
Run-DMC 31, 75
Sam and Dave 102
Shider, Garry 87
Sledge, Percy 39, 128
Soul Stirrers 127
Spector, Ronnie 77
Steinberg, Martha Jean "The
  Queen" 28
Stone, Jesse 98
Stone, Sly 85
Summer, Donna 25, 102
Supremes, The 33
Toussaint, Allen 60
Turner, Big Joe 92
Turner, Ike 68

Turner, Tina 6, 27
Walker, T-Bone 111
Wilson, Jackie 60
Wilson, Mary 28
Womack, Bobby 60, 92, 123
Wonder, Stevie 11, 53, 121
Yancey, Jimmy 116

Rock music
Adebimpe, Tunde 75
Ballard, Hank 41
Bennett, Estelle 77
Berry, Chuck 29
Blackwell, Otis 98
Burbridge, Kofi 120
Burbridge, Oteil 120
Clemons, Clarence 41
Diddley, Bo 39, 72
Domino, Fats 20
Edwards, Esther Gordy 43
Fishbone 101
Glover, Corey 34
Hendrix, Jimi 10
Johnson, Johnnie 56
King, Chris Thomas 120
King Curtis 92
Kravitz, Lenny 10, 34
Little Richard 15
Lymon, Frankie 22
Mayfield, Curtis 2, 43
Miles, Buddy 69
Moore, LeRoi 72
Preston, Billy 39, 59
Prince 18, 65
Reagon, Toshi 76
Reid, Vernon 34
Run-DMC 31, 75
Slash 75
Spector, Ronnie 77
Stew 69
Stone, Jesse 98
Stone, Sly 85
Tait, Michael 57
Tamar-kali 63
Tinsley, Boyd 50
Toussaint, Allen 60
Turner, Ike 68
Turner, Big Joe 92
Turner, Tina 6, 27
will.i.am 64
Williams, Larry 118
Wilson, Jackie 60

Rockefeller Foundation
Price, Hugh B. 9, 54

Rockets
Williams, O. S. 13

Rodeo
Nash, Johnny 40
Pickett, Bill 11
Sampson, Charles 13
Turman, Glynn 100
Whitfield, Fred 23

Roman Catholic Church
Akpan, Uwem 70
Arinze, Francis 19
Aristide, Jean-Bertrand 6, 45
Chineworth, Mary Alice 79
Clements, George 2
DeLille, Henriette 30
Fabre, Shelton 71

Gantin, Bernardin 70
Gregory, Wilton D. 37
Guy, Rosa 5
Healy, James Augustine 30
Jean-Juste, Gérard 78
Jones, Alex 64
Marino, Eugene Antonio 30
Otunga, Maurice Michael 55
Rugambwa, Laurean 20
Senghor, Augustin Diamacoune 66
Stallings, George A., Jr. 6

Romance fiction
Bunkley, Anita Richmond 39
Hill, Donna 32
Jackson, Brenda 87
Washington, Elsie B. 78

Royalty
Christophe, Henri 9
Ka Dinizulu, Mcwayizeni 29
Mswati III 56
Mutebi, Ronald 25

Rugby
Mundine, Anthony 56

Rutgers University
Gibson, Donald Bernard 40

Rwanda government
Habyarimana, Juvenal 8
Kagame, Paul 54
Mushikiwabo, Louise 88

Sailing
Petersen, Neal 96
Pinckney, Bill 42
Seymour, Teddy 110

**St. Kitts and Nevis govern-
ment**
Douglas, Denzil Llewellyn 53

St. Louis Blues hockey team
Brathwaite, Fred 35
Mayers, Jamal 39

**St. Louis Cardinals baseball
team**
Baylor, Don 6
Brock, Lou 18
Coleman, Vince 128
Flood, Curt 10, 93
Gibson, Bob 33
Lankford, Ray 23
Smith, Ozzie 77

St. Louis city government
Bosley, Freeman, Jr. 7
Harmon, Clarence 26

Salvation Army
Gaither, Israel L. 65

**San Antonio Spurs basketball
team**
Duncan, Tim 20, 91
Elliott, Sean 26
Gervin, George 80
Mohammed, Nazr 64
Parker, Tony 75
Robinson, David 24, 90

**San Diego Chargers football
team**
Barnes, Ernie 16, 78
Joiner, Charlie 102

Oliver, Paul 115
Tomlinson, LaDainian 65, 112
Winslow, Kellen 83

San Diego Padres baseball team
Carter, Joe 30
Gwynn, Tony 18, 83, 122
McGriff, Fred 24
Smith, Ozzie 77
Winfield, Dave 5, 91

San Francisco 49ers football team
Gore, Frank 117
Green, Dennis 5, 45
Hayes, Bob 77
Lott, Ronnie 9
Perry, Joe 95
Rice, Jerry 5, 55, 89
Singletary, Mike 4, 76
Washington, Gene 63
Willis, Patrick 99

San Francisco Giants baseball team
Bonds, Barry 6, 34, 63, 99
Bonds, Bobby 43
Carter, Joe 30
Fuentes, Tito 123
Mays, Willie 3
McCovey, Willie 103
Strawberry, Darryl 22

Saturday Night Live
Barnes, Katreese 97
Che, Michael 123
Meadows, Tim 30
Morgan, Tracy 61, 102
Morris, Garrett 31
Murphy, Eddie 4, 20, 61
Rock, Chris 3, 22, 66
Rudolph, Maya 46, 106
Thompson, Kenan 52

Saxophone
Adderley, Julian "Cannonball" 30
Adkins, Terry 122
Albright, Gerald 23
Ammons, Gene 112
Amy, Curtis 114
Anderson, Fred 87
Ayler, Albert 104
Bechet, Sidney 18
Bostic, Earl 121
Braxton, Anthony 128
Clemons, Clarence 41
Cobb, Arnett 114
Coleman, George 106
Coleman, Steve 124
Coltrane, John 19
Coltrane, Ravi 71
Cook, Junior 126
Crawford, Hank 77
Criss, Sonny 128
Edwards, Teddy 123
Ervin, Booker 106
Foster, Frank 97
Freeman, Von 104
Golson, Benny 37
Gordon, Dexter 25
Gray, Wardell 128
Greene, Jimmy 74
Griffin, Johnny 71

Hawkins, Coleman 9
Henderson, Joe 127
Jacquet, Illinois 49
Kay, Ulyssess 37
Kenyatta, Robin 54
Kinch, Soweto 108
King Curtis 92
Land, Harold 125
McIntyre, Kalaparusha Maurice 117
McLean, Jackie 78
Moody, James 83
Moondoc, Jemeel 119
Moore, LeRoi 72
Moura, Paulo 87
Nelson, Oliver 113
Newman, David 76
Parker, Charlie 20
Parker, Maceo 72
Redman, Joshua 30
Rivers, Sam 95
Rollins, Sonny 37, 94
Sanders, Pharoah 64
Shepp, Archie 101
Shider, Garry 87
Shorter, Wayne 75
Smith, Buster 116
Tate, Buddy 108
Tchicai, John 102
Turner, Mark 126
Vinson, Eddie 112
Ware, David S. 106
Washington, Grover, Jr. 17, 44
Waters, Benny 26
Wess, Frank 116
Whalum, Kirk 37, 64
York, Vincent 40
Young, Lester 37

Schomburg Center for Research in Black Culture
Andrews, Bert 13
Dodson, Howard, Jr. 7, 52
Hutson, Jean Blackwell 16
Morrison, Sam 50
Reddick, Lawrence Dunbar 20
Schomburg, Arthur Alfonso 9

School desegregation
Boulware, Harold R. 109
Bridges, Ruby 77
Brown, Oliver Leon 94
Chestnut, J. L., Jr. 73
DeLaine, Joseph A. 110
Fortune, T. Thomas 6
Hobson, Julius W. 44
Holmes, Hamilton E. 82
Nell, William C. 128
Sweatt, Heman Marion 114

Science fiction
Barnes, Steven 54
Butler, Octavia 8, 43, 58
Delany, Samuel R., Jr. 9

SCLC
See Southern Christian Leadership Conference

Scotland Yard
Griffin, Bessie Blout 43

Screenplay writing
Akil, Mara Brock 60, 82
Brown, Cecil M. 46
Clack, Zoanne 73

Davis, Thulani 61
Elder, Lonne, III 38
Ellis, Trey 97
Fisher, Antwone 40
Fletcher, Geoffrey 85
Jones, Orlando 30
Lancaster, Byard 105
Lumet, Jenny 80
Mason, Judi Ann 112
McMillan, Tracy 93
Nissel, Angela 42
Prince-Bythewood, Gina 31, 77
Pryce, Trevor 89
Rhimes, Shonda Lynn 67
Rhone, Trevor 80
Ridley, John 69
Robinson, Matt 69
RZA 80, 128
Singleton, John 2, 30, 122
Talbert, David E. 34, 93
Van Peebles, Melvin 7, 95
Wesley, Richard 73
Wilmore, Larry 121

Sculpture
Allen, Tina 22, 75
Amos, Emma 63
Bailey, Radcliffe 19
Barthe, Richmond 15
Biggers, John 20, 33
Biggers, Sanford 62
Billops, Camille 82
Brown, Donald 19
Burke, Selma 16
Catlett, Elizabeth 2, 120
Chanticleer, Raven 91
Chase-Riboud, Barbara 20, 46
Cortor, Eldzier 42
Dwight, Edward 65
Edwards, Melvin 22
Fuller, Meta Vaux Warrick 27
Guyton, Tyree 9, 94
Hammons, David 69
Hathaway, Isaac Scott 33
Hunt, Richard 6
Lewis, Edmonia 10
Lewis, Samella 25
Manley, Edna 26
Marshall, Kerry James 59
McCullough, Geraldine 58, 79
McGee, Charles 10
Moody, Ronald 30
Neals, Otto 73
Perkins, Marion 38
Pierce, Elijah 84
Prophet, Nancy Elizabeth 42
Puryear, Martin 42, 101
Saar, Alison 16
Saar, Betye 80
Savage, Augusta 12
Scott, John T. 65
Shabazz, Attallah 6
Simmons, Gary 58
Stout, Renee 63
Washington, James, Jr. 38
Wilson, John 109

Seattle city government
Rice, Norm 8

Seattle Mariners baseball team
Griffey, Ken, Jr. 12, 73
Reynolds, Harold 77

Seattle Supersonics basketball team
Bickerstaff, Bernie 21
Payton, Gary 99
Silas, Paul 24

Security and defense services
Garrett, James F. 78

Senegal government
Diouf, Abdou 3
Sall, Macky 101
Senghor, Léopold Sédar 66
Wade, Abdoulaye 66

Sesame Street
Byrd, Eugene 64
Clash, Kevin 14, 93
Glover, Savion 14
Long, Loretta 58
Orman, Roscoe 55
Reed Hall, Alaina 83
Robinson, Matt 69

Sexual harassment
Gomez-Preston, Cheryl 9
Hill, Anita 5, 65
McCauley, Gina 76
Thomas, Clarence 2, 39, 65
Auguste, Arnold A. 47

Ship captain
Cuffe, Paul 98

Sickle cell anemia
Edwards, Willarda V. 59
Pace, Betty 59

Sierra Leone government
Kabbah, Ahmad Tejan 23
Koroma, Ernest Bai 84

Skateboarding
Williams, Stevie 71

Skiing
Horton, Andre 33
Horton, Suki 33

Skillman Foundation
Goss, Carol A. 55

Slavery
Albert, Octavia V. R. 100
Allen, Richard 14
Asante, Molefi Kete 3
Bibb, Henry and Mary 54
Blackshear, Leonard 52
Blassingame, John Wesley 40
Brown, William Wells 99
Burns, Anthony 102
Chase-Riboud, Barbara 20, 46
Cooper, Anna Julia 20
Douglas, Aaron 7
Du Bois, W. E. B. 3
Dunbar, Paul Laurence 8
Durham, James 90
Easton, Hosea 91
Equiano, Olaudah 78
Farmer-Paellmann, Deadria 43
Gaines, Ernest J. 7
Garnet, Henry Highland 100
Gordon-Reed, Annette 74
Haley, Alex 4
Harper, Frances Ellen Watkins 11
Hayden, Lewis 105

Henson, Josiah 90
Horton, George Moses 124
Huggins, Nathan Irvin 52
Jacobs, Harriet 104
Johnson, Charles 1, 82
Keckley, Elizabeth 90
Lane, Lunsford 93
Langston, John Mercer 101
Mason, Biddy 89
McWorter, Free Frank 91
Miles, Tiya 116
Minkins, Shadrach 104
Montgomery, Isaiah T. 91
Muhammad, Elijah 4
Nell, William C. 128
Northup, Solomon 115
Pleasant, Mary Ellen 9
Reeves, Bass 100
Ruggles, David 126
Russwurm, John Brown 100
Sharpe, Samuel 103
Stephens, Charlotte Andrews 14
Stewart, Maria W. Miller 19
Tancil, Gladys Quander 59
Taylor, Susie King 13
Tubman, Harriet 9
Vesey, Denmark 100
Wall, Orindatus S. B. 92
Yates, Jack 114

Smithsonian Institution
Bunch, Lonnie G., III 91

Smith College
Mayhew, Richard 39
Simmons, Ruth 13, 38

SNCC
See Student Nonviolent Coordinating Committee

Soccer
Adu, Freddy 67
Altidore, Jozy 109
Alves, Dani 121
Anderson, Viv 58
Anelka, Nicolas 118
Antunes, Lúcio 109
Balotelli, Mario 104
Barnes, John 53
Beasley, Jamar 29
Benítez, Christian 113
Bigirimana, Gael 115
Charles, John 108
Chitalu, Godfrey 108
Cole, Ashley 106
Crooks, Garth 53
Davids, Edgar 106
dos Santos, Manuel Francisco 65
Drogba, Didier 78
Eto'o, Samuel 73
Eusebio 118
Evra, Patrice 102
Ferdinand, Rio 82
Gyan, Asamoah 87
Henry, Thierry 66, 127
Ibrahim, Fuad 109
Ince, Paul 83
James, David 84
Jones, Cobi N'Gai 18
Kanouté, Fred 68
Leônidas 96
Mello, Breno 73
Mensah, John 87

Meyiwa, Senzo 124
Milla, Roger 2
Muamba, Fabrice 104
Nakhid, David 25
Okocha, Jay Jay 99
Onyewu, Oguchi 60
Pelé 7
Pelé, Abedi 122
Regis, Cyrille 51
Ronaldinho 69
Scurry, Briana 27
Seedorf, Clarence 121
Smalling, Chris 118
Song, Alex 105
Sono, Jomo 86
Sturridge, Daniel 120
Touré, Yaya 99
Weah, George 58

Social science/social criticism
Austin, Bobby W. 95
Berry, Mary Frances 7
Black, Albert 51
Bobo, Lawrence 60
Cayton, Horace 26
Clark, Kenneth B. 5, 52
Cobbs, Price M. 9
Collins, Patricia Hill 67
Edwards, Harry 2
Frazier, E. Franklin 10
George, Zelma Watson 42
Hall, Stuart 78
Hare, Nathan 44
Harris, Eddy L. 18
Haynes, George Edmund 8
hooks, bell 5, 90
Hunt, Darnell 92
Ladner, Joyce A. 42
Lawrence-Lightfoot, Sara 10
Marable, Manning 10, 102
Reid, Ira De A. 100
Williams, David Rudyard 50
Woodson, Robert L. 10

Social work
Auguste, Rose-Anne 13
Berry, Bertice 8, 55
Berrysmith, Don Reginald 49
Blakely, Delois N. 122
Brown, Cora 33
Canada, Geoffrey 23
Coles, Alice 80
Colston, Hal 72
Compton-Rock, Malaak 86
Dumpson, James R. 108
Dunham, Katherine 4, 59
Fields, C. Virginia 25
Finner-Williams, Paris Michele 62
Gbowee, Leymah 76
Granger, Lester B. 75
Grillo, Evelio 95
Hale, Clara 16
Hale, Lorraine 8
Harris, Alice 7
Haynes, George Edmund 8
Jackson, Judith D. 57
Jackson, Mae 57
King, Barbara 22
Kirk, Clara 95
Lewis, Thomas 19
Little, Robert L. 2
Quander, Nellie 102
Robinson, Rachel 16

Sears, Stephanie 53
Smith, Damu 54
Vaughn, Viola 70
Waddles, Charleszetta "Mother" 10, 49
Walker, Bernita Ruth 53
Wallace, Joaquin 49
Wells, Henrietta Bell 69
White-Hammond, Gloria 61
Thrower, Willie 35
Young, Whitney M., Jr. 4

Soledad Brothers
Jackson, George Lester 14

Somalia government
Ahmed, Sharif 80
Mohamud, Hassan Sheikh 105

Sororities
See Fraternities/sororities

Soul food
Terry, Bryant 128
Williams, Lindsey 75
Woods, Sylvia 34, 104

Soul Train
Cornelius, Don 4, 100
D'Angelo 27, 123
Winans, CeCe 14, 43

South African Communist Party
Hani, Chris 6
Mhlaba, Raymond 55

South Africa government
Dandala, Mvume 77
Dlamini-Zuma, Nkosazana 34, 105
Mhlaba, Raymond 55
Motlanthe, Kgalema 74
Sisulu, Walter 47
Zuma, Jacob 33, 75
Zwelithini, Goodwill 128

South Carolina state government
Cardozo, Francis L. 33
Goggins, Juanita 127
Scott, Tim 87, 125

South Sudan government
Kiir, Salva Mayardit 85, 103
Machar, Riek 117

Southeastern University
Jarvis, Charlene Drew 21

Southern Christian Leadership Conference (SCLC)
Abernathy, Ralph 1
Barrow, Willie T. 85, 128
Brooks, Tyrone 59
Chavis, Benjamin 6
Hooks, Benjamin L. 2, 85
Jackson, Jesse 1, 27, 72
Jones, William A., Jr. 61
King, Bernice 4, 81
King, Martin Luther, Jr. 1
King, Martin Luther, III 20
Lawson, James M., Jr. 90
Lee, Eric P. 79
Lowery, Joseph 2
Moses, Robert Parris 11
Moss, Otis, Jr. 72

Nash, Diane 72
Orange, James 74
Rustin, Bayard 4
Shuttlesworth, Fred 47, 98
Walker, Wyatt Tee 80
Williams, Hosea 15, 31, 123

Space shuttle
Gregory, Frederick 8, 51
Jemison, Mae C. 1, 35
McNair, Ronald 3, 58
Wilson, Stephanie 72

Special Olympics
Clairborne, Loretta 34

Speedskating
Davis, Shani 58, 84

Spelman College
Cole, Johnnetta B. 5, 43
Falconer, Etta Zuber 59
Price, Glenda 22
Simmons, Ruth 13, 38
Tatum, Beverly Daniel 42, 84
Wade-Gayles, Gloria Jean 41

Sphinx Organization
Dworkin, Aaron P. 52

Spingarn medal
Aaron, Hank 5
Ailey, Alvin 8
Anderson, Marian 2, 33
Angelou, Maya 1, 15, 122
Bates, Daisy 13
Belafonte, Harry 4, 65
Bethune, Mary McLeod 4
Bond, Julian 2, 35, 106
Bradley, Thomas 2, 20
Braithwaite, William Stanley 52
Brooke, Edward W. 8, 88, 126
Bunche, Ralph J. 5
Burleigh, Henry Thacker 56
Carson, Ben 1, 35, 76, 128
Carter, Robert L. 51, 100
Carver, George Washington 4
Chesnutt, Charles 29
Clark, Kenneth B. 5, 52
Conyers, John, Jr. 4, 45, 111
Cosby, Bill 7, 26, 59, 125
Davis, Sammy, Jr. 18
Dee, Ruby 8, 50, 68, 122
Drew, Charles Richard 7
Du Bois, W. E. B. 3
Ellington, Duke 5
Evers, Medgar 3
Evers, Myrlie 8
Franklin, John Hope 5, 77
Gilpin, Charles Sidney 81
Graves, Earl G. 1, 35
Grimké, Archibald H. 9
Haley, Alex 4
Hastie, William H. 8
Hayes, Roland 4
Height, Dorothy I. 2, 23, 78
Higginbotham, A. Leon, Jr. 13, 25
Hill, Oliver W. 24, 63
Hinton, William Augustus 8
Hooks, Benjamin L. 2, 85
Hope, John 8
Horne, Lena 5, 86
Houston, Charles Hamilton 4
Hughes, Langston 4
Jackson, Jesse 1, 27, 72

Johnson, James Weldon 5
Johnson, John H. 3, 54
Johnson, Mordecai Wyatt 79
Jordan, Barbara 4, 78
Jordan, Vernon E. 3, 35
Julian, Percy Lavon 6
Just, Ernest Everett 3
Keith, Damon J. 16, 74
King, Martin Luther, Jr. 1
Lawless, Theodore K. 8
Lawrence, Jacob 4
Lewis, John 2, 46, 83
Logan, Rayford 40
Marshall, Thurgood 1, 44
Mays, Benjamin E. 7
Mitchell, Clarence M., Jr. 88
Moore, Harry T. 29
Motley, Constance Baker 10, 55
Moton, Robert Russa 83
Overton, Anthony 128
Parks, Gordon 1, 35, 58
Parks, Rosa 1, 35, 56
Patterson, Frederick Douglass 12
Powell, Colin 1, 28, 75
Price, Leontyne 1
Randolph, A. Philip 3
Riles, Wilson C. 79
Robeson, Paul 2
Robinson, Jackie 6
Rowan, Carl T. 1, 30
Staupers, Mabel K. 7
Sullivan, Leon H. 3, 30
Sutton, Percy E. 42, 82
Talbert, Mary B. 77
Tobias, Channing H. 79
Tyson, Cicely 7, 51, 112
Weaver, Robert C. 8, 46
White, Walter F. 4
Wilder, L. Douglas 3, 48
Wilkins, Roy 4
Williams, Paul R. 9
Winfrey, Oprah 2, 15, 61, 106
Woodson, Carter G. 2
Wright, Louis Tompkins 4
Wright, Richard 5
Young, Andrew 3, 48, 110
Young, Charles 77
Young, Coleman 1, 20

Spirituals
Anderson, Marian 2, 33
Carr, Kurt 56
Fisher, Miles Mark 91
Hairston, Jester 88
Hayes, Roland 4
Jackson, Mahalia 5
Johnson, Hall 90
Joyner, Matilda Sissieretta 15
Norman, Jessye 5
Reese, Della 6, 20, 96
Williams, Denise 40

Sports administration
Dumars, Joe 16, 65, 126
Fuller, Vivian 33
Goss, Tom 23
Kerry, Leon G. 46
Lee, Bertram M., Sr. 46
Littlepage, Craig 35
Mills, Steve 47
Newsome, Ozzie 26, 117
Payne, Ulice, Jr. 42
Phillips, Teresa L. 42

Randolph, Willie 53
Smith, Gene 123
Ujiri, Masai 107
Ussery, Terdema, II 29

Sports agent
Holland, Kimberly N. 62
Owens, Brig 118
Stewart, Dave 117

Stanford University
Bobo, Lawrence 60
Rice, Condoleezza 3, 28, 72
Steele, Claude 13, 97
Walker, Arthur, II 87
Washington, Gene 63

State University of New York
Butts, Calvin O., III 9, 90
Clemente, Rosa 74
Wharton, Clifton R., Jr. 7

Stellar Awards
Baylor, Helen 36
Hawkins, Walter 87
Lawrence, Donald 99
Norful, Smokie 127
Sapp, Marvin 74
Tribbett, Tye 81
Walker, Hezekiah 34

Storytelling
Baker, Augusta 38
Bennett, Louise 69
Hill, Hugh Morgan 83

Student Nonviolent Coordinating Committee (SNCC)
Al-Amin, Jamil Abdullah 6
Anderson, William G(ilchrist) 57
Blackwell, Unita 17
Carmichael, Stokely 5, 26
Clark, Septima 7
Forman, James 7, 51
Hamer, Fannie Lou 6
Holland, Endesha Ida Mae 3, 57
Moses, Robert Parris 11
Nash, Diane 72
Touré, Askia (Muhammad Abu Bakr el) 47

Sudan government
Bashir, Omar al- 77
Cham, Adongo Agada Akway 77
Garang, John 105

Sun Microsystems
Tademy, Lalita 36

Sundance Film Festival
Coogler, Ryan 114
DuVernay, Ava 98, 126
Harris, Leslie 6
Nelson, Stanley 92

Supreme Court
See U.S. Supreme Court

Surfing
Corley, Tony 62

Surrealism
Ellison, Ralph 7
Lee-Smith, Hughie 5, 22

Swaziland government
Mswati III 56

Swimming
Atkinson, Alia 126
Brigitha, Enith 126
Ervin, Anthony 66
Jones, Cullen 73
Moussambani, Eric 105

Tampa Bay Buccaneers football team
Barber, Ronde 41
Brooks, Derrick 43, 119
McDaniel, Randall Cornell 81
Morris, Raheem 77
Sapp, Warren 38, 109

Tanganyikan African National Union (TANU)
Kikwete, Jakaya Mrisho 73
Nyerere, Julius 5

TANU
See Tanganyikan African National Union

Tanzanian African National Union (TANU)
See Tanganyikan African National Union

Tap dancing
Anderson, Maceo 111
Atkins, Cholly 40
Bates, Peg Leg 14
Brown, Ernest 80
Coles, Honi 128
Glover, Savion 14
Hines, Gregory 1, 42
Lane, William Henry 90
Robinson, LaVaughn 69
Sims, Howard "Sandman" 48
Slyde, Jimmy 70
Walker, Dianne 57

Teaching
Abani, Chris 77
Adams-Ender, Clara 40
Alexander, Margaret Walker 22
Amadi, Elechi 40
Archie-Hudson, Marguerite 44
Aubert, Alvin 41
Baiocchi, Regina Harris 41
Ballard, Allen Butler, Jr. 40
Beals, Melba Pattillo 15, 94
Belgrave, Marcus 77
Bibb, Henry and Mary 54
Blackwell, Gloria 127
Blassingame, John Wesley 40
Branch, William Blackwell 39
Brawley, Benjamin 44
Brown, Charlotte Hawkins 106
Burroughs, Nannie Helen 96
Campbell, Mary Schmidt 43
Cardozo, Francis L. 33
Carter, Joye Maureen 41
Chenault, John 40
Cheney-Coker, Syl 43
Clarke, John Henrik 20
Clemmons, Reginal G. 41
Cobb, Jewel Plummer 42
Cobb, W. Montague 39
Cole, Johnnetta B. 5, 43
Coleman, Beatrice 120
Colescott, Robert 69
Collins, Patricia Hill 67
Cook, Mercer 40

Cooper Cafritz, Peggy 43
Cortor, Eldzier 42
Cotter, Joseph Seamon, Sr. 40
Crouch, Hubert 95
Dailey, Ulysses Grant 87
Davis, Arthur P. 41
Davis, Gary 41
Davis, George 36
Davis, Milt 74
De Veaux, Alexis 44
Delpit, Lisa 101
Dennard, Brazeal 37
Draper, Sharon Mills 16, 43
Drummond, William J. 40
Dumas, Henry 41
Dunnigan, Alice Allison 41
Dyett, Walter 113
Dymally, Mervyn 42
Early, Gerald 15
Everett, Percival 93
Falconer, Etta Zuber 59
Feelings, Muriel 44
Ferguson, Ronald F. 75
Figueroa, John J. 40
Ford, Nick Aaron 44
Forrest, Leon 44
Fuller, A. Oveta 43
Fuller, Arthur 27
Fuller, Howard L. 37
Gates, Sylvester James, Jr. 15
Gayle, Addison, Jr. 41
Gill, Gerald 69
Granville, Evelyn Boyd 36
Graves, Milford 126
Hall, Arthur 39
Hamburg, Beatrix 84
Hammonds, Evelynn 69
Harding, Vincent 67
Hare, Nathan 44
Harris, Barry 68
Haskins, James 36, 54
Henries, A. Doris Banks 44
Hill, Errol 40
Hill, Leslie Pinckney 44
Horne, Frank 44
Humphries, Frederick 20
Imes, Elmer Samuel 39
Jackson, Fred James 25
Jansen, Jonathan 102
Jarrett, Vernon D. 42
Jarvis, Erich 67
Kennedy, Randall 40
Ladner, Joyce A. 42
Leevy, Carrol M. 42
Lewis, Norman 39
Lindsey, Tommie 51
Luper, Clara 94
Logan, Rayford W. 40
McCullough, Geraldine 58, 79
Mickens, Ronald Elbert 105
Ming, William Robert, Jr. 125
Mitchell, Parren J. 42, 66
Moore, Harry T. 29
Mphalele, Es'kia 40
Naylor, Gloria 10, 42
Norman, Maidie 20
Oliver, Kimberly 60
Owens, Helen 48
Palmer, Everard 37
Patterson, Mary Jane 54
Perry, Steve 98
Peters, Margaret and Matilda 43
Player, Willa B. 43

Prophet, Nancy Elizabeth **42**
Putney, Martha S. **75**
Querino, Manuel Raimundo **84**
Ray, Charlotte E. **60**
Redmond, Eugene **23**
Reid, Senghor **55**
Rhodes, Jewell Parker **84**
Ross-Lee, Barbara **67**
Shockley, Ann Allen **84**
Simpson-Hoffman, N'kenge **52**
Smith, Anna Deavere **6, 44**
Smith, John L. **22**
Spencer, Peter **128**
Toler, Burl **80**
Tutu, Nontombi Naomi **57**
Twilight, Alexander **125**
Wambugu, Florence **42**
Watson, Diane **41**
Wells, Henrietta Bell **69**
Wesley, Richard **73**
Wilkens, J. Ernest, Jr. **43**
Yancy, Dorothy Cowser **42**
Yarbrough, Camille **40**
York, Vincent **40**

Teatro Experimental do Negro
Nascimento, Abdias do **93**

Telecommunications
Clyburn, Mignon **78**
Gordon, Bruce S. **41, 53, 82**
Ibrahim, Mo **67, 115**
Irvin, Vernon **65**
Rapelang Rabana **112**
Wilkins, Ray **47**

Television
Akil, Mara Brock **60, 82**
Allen, Byron **3, 24, 97**
Arkadie, Kevin **17**
Arnold, Tichina **63**
Banks, Tyra **11, 50**
Big Freedia **128**
Blake, Asha **26**
Bowser, Yvette Lee **17**
Brady, Wayne **32, 71**
Brown, James **22**
Brown, Joe **29**
Brown, Vivian **27**
Burnett, Charles **16, 68**
Carter, Nell **39**
Chase, Debra Martin **49, 96**
Clack, Zoanne **73**
CoCo Brother **93**
Corbi, Lana **42**
Creagh, Milton **27**
de Passe, Suzanne **25**
Deezer D **53**
Earthquake **55**
Ephriam, Mablean **29**
Evans, Harry **25**
Fales-Hill, Susan **88**
Frazier, Kevin **58**
Gardere, Jeffrey **76**
George, Nelson **12, 101**
Gray, Willie **46**
Greely, M. Gasby **27**
Greene, Petey **65**
Hall, Arsenio **58**
Hatchett, Glenda **32**
Haynes, Trudy **44**
Henriques, Julian **37**
Hill, Marc Lamont **80, 128**

Jackson, George **19**
Jackson, Randy **40**
Jackson, Tom **70**
Jarrett, Vernon D. **42**
Joe, Yolanda **21**
Kandi **83**
LeFlore, Lyah Beth **96**
Long, Loretta **58**
Lomax, Louis E. **90**
Mabuza-Suttle, Felicia **43**
Mathis, Greg **26**
McCrary Anthony, Crystal **70**
McFarland, Roland **49**
McGlowan, Angela **64, 86**
McKenzie, Vashti M. **29**
Mercado-Valdes, Frank **43**
Mitchell, Russ **21, 73**
Moss, Carlton **16**
Neville, Arthel **53**
Nissel, Angela **42**
Norman, Christina **47**
Omarosa **69, 110**
Perry, Tyler **40, 54, 103**
Pitts, Byron **71**
Poussaint, Renee **78**
Price, Frederick K. C. **21**
Prince-Bythewood, Gina **31, 77**
Quarles, Norma **25**
Reynolds, Star Jones **10, 27, 61**
Rhimes, Shonda Lynn **67**
Ridley, John **69**
Roberts, Deborah **35**
Roker, Al **12, 49**
Russell, Nipsey **66**
Salters, Lisa **71**
Shepherd, Sherri **55**
Simmons, Kimora Lee **51, 83**
Smiley, Tavis **20, 68**
Stewart, Nzingha **89**
Stuart, Moira **82**
Taylor, Jason **70**
Taylor, Karin **34**
Tillman, Deborah **98**
Vance, Jim **110**
Vaughn, Countess **53**
Wainwright, Joscelyn **46**
Washington, Hayma **86**
Watson, Carlos **50**
Wayans, Damien **78**
Wayans, Damon **8, 41**
Wayans, Marlon **29, 82**
Wayans, Shawn **29**
Williams, Armstrong **29**
Williams, Wendy **62**
Wilmore, Larry **121**

Television direction
Barclay, Paris **37, 94**
Duke, Bill **3, 96**
Hemingway, Anthony **107**
Johnson, Clark **96**
Laneuville, Eric **123**
Warner, Malcolm-Jamal **22, 36, 110**
Whack, Rita Coburn **36**

Tennessee state government
DeBerry, Lois M. **115**
Ford, Harold E. **42**

Tennessee State University
Clark, Yvonne Young **95**
Phillips, Teresa L. **42**

Tennessee Supreme Court
Birch, Adolpho A., Jr. **85**

Tennessee Titans football team
George, Eddie **80**
McNair, Steve **22, 47, 79**
Rolle, Myron **98**

Tennis
Ashe, Arthur **1, 18**
Blake, James **43**
Garrison, Zina **2**
Gibson, Althea **8, 43**
Jackson, Jamea **64**
McNeil, Lori **1**
Noah, Yannick **4, 60, 121**
Peters, Margaret and Matilda **43**
Rubin, Chanda **37**
Stephens, Sloane **105**
Washington, MaliVai **8**
Washington, Ora Mae **115**
Williams, Samm-Art **21**
Williams, Serena **20, 41, 73**
Williams, Venus **17, 34, 62**
Young, Donald, Jr. **57**

Texas Rangers baseball team
Cottrell, Comer **11**

Texas state government
Delco, Wilhelmina **33**
Gaines, Matthew **95**
Johnson, Eddie Bernice **8, 90**
Jordan, Barbara **4, 78**

Theater administration/ownership
Austin, Lovie **40**
Banks, Michelle **59**
Borders, James **9**
Cox, Ida **42**
Dudley, Sherman H. **117**
Gibson, John Trusty **87**
Hamlin, Larry Leon **49, 62**
Leggs, Kingsley **62**
LeNoire, Rosetta **37**
Leon, Kenny **10, 98**
Marsalis, Delfeayo **41**
Spears, Warren **52**

Theatrical direction/production
Belgrave, Cynthia **75**
Glover, Keith **79**
Hall, Juanita **62**
Hayes, Teddy **40**
Leon, Kenny **10, 98**
McClinton, Marion Isaac **77**
Milner, Ron **39**
Perry, Tyler **40, 54, 103**
Scott, Harold Russell, Jr. **61**
Springer, Ashton, Jr. **115**
Taylor, Regina **9, 46, 97**
Teer, Barbara Ann **81**
Thompson, Tazewell **13**
Wolfe, George C. **6, 43, 127**

Theology
Cone, James H. **3, 82**
Franklin, Robert M. **13**
Harding, Vincent **67**

Henderson, George Washington **101**

Time Warner Inc.
Parsons, Richard **11, 33, 124**

TLC Beatrice International Holdings, Inc.
Lewis, Reginald F. **6**

Togo government
Eyadéma, Gnassingbé **7, 52**
Gnassingbé, Faure **67**
Olympio, Sylvanus **126**

The Tonight Show
Eubanks, Kevin **15, 108**

Tony Awards
Allen, Debbie **13, 42**
Bailey, Pearl **14**
Belafonte, Harry **4, 65**
Carroll, Diahann **9**
Carter, Nell **39**
Clarke, Hope **14**
Coles, Honi **128**
Cooper, Chuck **75**
Davis, Viola **34, 76, 100**
Faison, George **16**
Falana, Lola **42**
Fishburne, Laurence **4, 22, 70**
Glover, Savion **14**
Goldberg, Whoopi **4, 33, 69**
Hall, Juanita **62**
Hines, Gregory **1, 42**
Holder, Geoffrey **78, 124**
Horne, Lena **5, 86**
Hyman, Phyllis **19**
James, Nikki M. **94**
Jones, Bill T. **1, 46, 80**
Jones, James Earl **3, 49, 79**
Jones, Sarah **39**
LaChanze **93**
Lenox, Adriane **59**
McDonald, Audra **20, 62, 128**
Mitchell, Brian Stokes **21**
Mokae, Zakes **80**
Moore, Melba **21**
Porter, Billy **112**
Premice, Josephine **41**
Rashad, Phylicia **21**
Richards, Lloyd **2**
Rose, Anika Noni **70**
Santiago-Hudson, Ruben **85**
Thigpen, Lynne **17, 41**
Tyson, Cicely **7, 51, 112**
Uggams, Leslie **23, 114**
Vereen, Ben **4**
Washington, Denzel **1, 16, 93**
White, Lillias **120**
Wilson, August **7, 33, 55**
Wolfe, George C. **6, 43, 127**
Wright, Jeffrey **54, 111**

Toronto Blue Jays baseball team
Carter, Joe **30**
Gaston, Cito **71**
McGriff, Fred **24**

Toronto Raptors basketball team
Carter, Butch **27**
Carter, Vince **26**
Olajuwon, Hakeem **2, 72**

Thomas, Isiah **7, 26, 65**

Tourism
Edmunds, Gladys **48**

Track and field
Ashford, Evelyn **63**
Beamon, Bob **30**
Bekele, Kenenisa **75**
Bolt, Usain **73, 104**
Campbell, Milt **113**
Campbell-Brown, Veronica **102**
Carlos, John **97**
Christie, Linford **8**
Clay, Bryan **57, 74**
Coachman, Alice **18, 123**
Devers, Gail **7, 87**
Dibaba, Tirunesh **73, 109**
Farah, Mo **104**
Felix, Allyson **48, 98**
Fraser-Pryce, Shelly-Ann **113**
Freeman, Cathy **29**
Gatlin, Justin **123**
Gay, Tyson **114**
Gebrselassie, Haile **70**
Graham, Trevor **84**
Greene, Maurice **27, 77**
Griffith-Joyner, Florence **28**
Harrison, Alvin **28**
Harrison, Calvin **28**
Hayes, Bob **77**
Holmes, Kelly **47**
Jacobs, Regina **38**
James, G. Larry **74**
Johnson, Michael **13**
Johnson, Rodney Van **28**
Jones, Lou **64**
Jones, Marion **21, 66**
Joyner-Kersee, Jackie **5**
Kearney, Beverly **109**
Kipchoge, Eliud **124**
Lewis, Carl **4, 97**
Matson, Ollie **93**
Metcalfe, Ralph **26**
Montgomery, Tim **41**
Moses, Edwin **8**
Mutola, Maria **12**
Omar, Samia Yusuf **107**
Owens, Jesse **2**
Pettigrew, Antonio **118**
Pollard, Fritz **53**
Powell, Mike **7**
Quirot, Ana **13**
Richards-Ross, Sanya **66, 98**
Rudisha, David **112**
Rudolph, Wilma **4**
Simpson, Sherone **120**
Smith, Tommie **102**
Temple, Ed **109**
Thugwane, Josia **21**
Walker, LeRoy T. **106**
White, Willye **67**
Whitfield, Mal **60**
Williams, Lauryn **58, 127**
Wilson, David **123**
Woodruff, John **68**

Transplant surgery
Alexander, Joseph L. **95**
Callender, Clive O. **3**
Hayanga, Jeremiah **118**

Kountz, Samuel L. **10**

Trombone
Fuller, Curtis **115**
Lewis, George **104**
Liston, Melba **118**
Marsalis, Delfeayo **41**
Ory, Kid **118**
Powell, Benny **87**
Trombone Shorty **97**

Trumpet
Adderley, Nat **29**
Akinmusire, Ambrose **103**
Armstrong, Louis **2**
Belgrave, Marcus **77**
Blanchard, Terence **43**
Brown, Clifford **86**
Byrd, Donald **109**
Campbell, Roy, Jr. **118**
Cherry, Don **119**
Curson, Ted **108**
Dara, Olu **35**
Davis, Miles **4**
Dixon, Bill **87**
Dorham, Kenny **113**
Edison, Harry **114**
Eldridge, Roy **37**
Ellison, Ralph **7**
Farmer, Art **38**
Ferbos, Lionel **95**
Gillespie, Dizzy **1**
Hubbard, Freddie **75**
Jones, Jonah **39**
Jones, Thad **68**
Little, Booker **105**
Marsalis, Wynton **16, 90**
Masekela, Hugh **1, 106**
McGhee, Howard **122**
Miley, Bubber **120**
Mitchell, Blue **126**
Morgan, Lee **102**
Navarro, Fats **104**
Smith, Cladys "Jabbo" **32**
Terry, Clark **39, 127**
Williams, Cootie **114**
Wilson, Abram **104**
Wilson, Gerald **49, 123**

Tuskegee Airmen
Archer, Lee, Jr. **79**
Bromery, Randolph Wilson **85**
Brown, Willa **40**
Carter, Herbert E. **108**
Chappell, Roy M. **95**
Davis, Benjamin O., Jr. **2, 43**
Haysbert, Raymond V., Sr. **87**
Hoskins, Harold K. **103**
James, Daniel, Jr. **16**
Plinton, James O., Jr. **98**
Proctor, Bernard Shaw **120**
Pruitt, Wendell O. **106**
Stone, Chuck **9, 120**
Young, Perry H. **100**

Tuskegee University
Carver, George Washington **4**
Dawson, William Levi **39**
Gomillion, Charles **90**
Moton, Robert Russa **83**
Patterson, Frederick Douglass **12**
Payton, Benjamin F. **23**
Taylor, Robert Robinson **80**
Washington, Margaret Murray **119**

Williston, David Augustus **99**

UCC
See United Church of Christ

Uganda government
Amin, Idi **42**
Kisekka, Samson **112**
Museveni, Yoweri **4, 119**
Obote, Milton **63**

UN
See United Nations

UNCF
See United Negro College Fund

Underground Railroad
Blockson, Charles L. **42**
Cohen, Anthony **15**
Crew, Spencer R. **55**
DeBaptiste, George **32**
Ruggles, David **126**
Shadd, Abraham D. **81**
Spencer, Peter **128**

UNIA
See Universal Negro Improvement Association

Unions
Brown, Lloyd Louis **42**
Burrus, William Henry "Bill" **45**
Clay, William Lacy **8**
Ellis-Lamkins, Phaedra **88**
Europe, James Reese **10**
Farmer, James **2, 64**
Fletcher, Benjamin **90**
Fletcher, Bill, Jr. **41**
Holt Baker, Arlene **73**
LeGrand, Naquasia **126**
Lucy, William **50**
McGee, James Madison **46**
Morris, William "Bill" **51**
Ramaphosa, Cyril **3, 117**
Randolph, A. Philip **3**
Roberts, Lillian **83**
Smith, Nate **49**
Tucker, Rosina **14**
Wyatt, Addie L. **56**

UNIP
See United National Independence Party

UNITA
See National Union for the Total Independence of Angola

United Church of Christ (UCC)
Chavis, Benjamin **6**
Forbes, James A., Jr. **71**
Miller, Clyde **113**
Moss, Otis, III **72**
Stanley, A. Knighton **117**
Wright, Jeremiah A., Jr. **45, 69, 103**

United Democratic Front (UDF; Malawi)
Muluzi, Bakili **14, 76**

United Methodist Church
Caldwell, Kirbyjon **55**
Cleaver, Emanuel **4, 45, 68, 107**
Lawson, James M., Jr. **90**
Lewis, Shirley A. R. **14**
Muzorewa, Abel **85**

Stith, Charles R. **73**

United Nations (UN)
Annan, Kofi Atta **15, 48**
Bunche, Ralph J. **5**
Cousin, Ertharin **115**
Frazier, E. Franklin **10**
Juma, Calestous **57**
Lafontant, Jewel Stradford **3, 51**
McDonald, Gabrielle Kirk **20**
McHenry, Donald F. **83**
Mongella, Gertrude **11**
Omolewa, Michael **119**
Osotimehin, Babatunde **107**
Perkins, Edward **5**
Rice, Susan **74, 103**
Smythe Haith, Mabel **61**
Young, Andrew **3, 48, 110**
Yumkella, Kandeh **105**

United Negro College Fund (UNCF)
Boyd, T. B., III **6**
Bunkley, Anita Richmond **39**
Creagh, Milton **27**
Dawson, Matel, Jr. **39**
Edley, Christopher **2, 48**
Lomax, Michael L. **58**
Patterson, Frederick Douglass **12**

United Parcel Service
Cooper, Evern **40**
Darden, Calvin **38**
Washington, Patrice Clarke **12**

United Somali Congress
Ali Mahdi Mohamed **5**

United States Football League (USFL)
White, Reggie **6, 50**
Williams, Doug **22, 112**

Universal Negro Improvement Association (UNIA)
Austin, Junius C. **44**
Garvey, Marcus **1**
McGuire, George Alexander **80**

University administration
See College and university administration

University of Alabama
Davis, Mike **41**
Lucy Foster, Autherine **35**

University of Californi-a—Berkeley
Blackwell, David **79**
Drummond, William J. **40**
Edley, Christopher F., Jr. **48**

University of Chicago Hospitals
Lee, Raphael C. **87**

University of Michigan
Amaker, Tommy **62**
Dillard, Godfrey J. **45**
Fuller, A. Oveta **43**
Goss, Tom **23**
Gray, Ida **41**
Imes, Elmer Samuel **39**

Hill, Errol 40

Upscale magazine
Bronner, Nathaniel H., Sr. 32

Urban League (regional)
Adams, Sheila J. 25
Clayton, Xernona 3, 45
Jacob, John E. 2
Layton, William 87
Walcott, Dennis M. 112
Young, Whitney M., Jr. 4

Urban planning/renewal
Blakely, Edward J. 88
Bosley, Freeman, Jr. 7
Brown, Aja 115
Carter, Majora 77
Gates, Theaster 118
Harris, Alice 7
Lane, Vincent 5
Lowe, Rick 124

U.S. Air Force
Anderson, Michael P. 40
Bush, Charles Vernon 125
Davis, Benjamin O., Jr. 2, 43
Drew, Alvin, Jr. 67
Dwight, Edward 65
Gregory, Frederick 8, 51
Harris, Marcelite Jordan 16
James, Daniel, Jr. 16
Johnson, Lonnie G. 32, 93
Jones, Wayne 53
Lyles, Lester 31

U.S. Army
Adams-Ender, Clara 40
Anderson, Marcia 115
Augusta, Alexander T.111
Austin, Lloyd 101
Baker, Vernon Joseph 65, 87
Becton, Julius W., Jr. 110
Brown, Anthony G. 72
Cadoria, Sherian Grace 14
Carter, Edward A., Jr. 104
Clarke, Anna Mac 95
Clemmons, Reginal G. 41
Davis, Benjamin O., Sr. 4
Delany, Martin R. 27
Ellis, Larry R. 110
Flipper, Henry O. 3
Fox, John R. 105
Greenhouse, Bunnatine "Bunny" 57
Honoré, Russel L. 64
Jackson, Fred James 25
Johnson, Hazel 22
Johnson, Shoshana 47
King, Teresa 80
Matthews, Mark 59
Morris, Melvin 120
Perry, Herman 89
Poindexter, Hildrus A. 87
Powell, Colin 1, 28, 75
Rogers, Alan G. 72
Sidat-Singh, Wilmeth 116
Snow, Samuel 71
Stanford, John 20
Stowers, Freddie 107
Via, Dennis 108
Ward, William E. 107
Watkins, Perry 12
West, Allen 89
West, Togo D., Jr. 16

Young, Charles 77

U.S. Army Air Corps
Anderson, Charles Edward 37

U.S. Atomic Energy Commission
Nabrit, Samuel Milton 47

U.S. Attorney's Office
Johnson, Sterling, Jr. 124
Jordan, Eddie 82
Lafontant, Jewel Stradford 3, 51
Lynch, Loretta E. 103

U.S. Bureau of Engraving and Printing
Felix, Larry R. 64

U.S. Cabinet
Kirk, Ron 11, 75, 111

U.S. Coast Guard
Brown, Erroll M. 23
Healy, Michael 90
Rochon, Stephen W. 78

U.S. Commission on Civil Rights
Berry, Mary Frances 7
Edley, Christopher 2, 48
Fletcher, Arthur A. 63

U.S. Conference of Catholic Bishops
Gregory, Wilton D. 37

U.S. Court of Appeals
Hastie, William H. 8
Higginbotham, A. Leon, Jr. 13, 25
Kearse, Amalya Lyle 12
Keith, Damon J. 16, 74
Rawlinson, Johnnie B. 79
Williams, Ann Claire 82

U.S. Department of Agriculture (USDA)
Espy, Mike 6
Layton, William 87
Sherrod, Shirley 87
Vaughn, Gladys Gary 47
Watkins, Shirley R. 17

U.S. Department of Commerce
Brown, Ron 5
Irving, Larry, Jr. 12
Morrow, E. Frederic 100
Shavers, Cheryl 31

U.S. Department of Defense
Greenhouse, Bunnatine "Bunny" 57
Johnson, Jeh 76, 125
Tribble, Israel, Jr. 8

U.S. Department of Education
Ali, Russlynn H. 92
Groff, Peter 96
Hill, Anita 5, 65
Hill, Bonnie Guiton 20
Paige, Rod 29
Purnell, Silas 59
Thomas, Clarence 2, 39, 65
Tribble, Israel, Jr. 8
Velez-Rodriguez, Argelia 56

U.S. Department of Energy
O'Leary, Hazel 6

U.S. Department of Health and Human Services (HHS)
See also U.S. Department of Health, Education, and Welfare
Gaston, Marilyn Hughes 60
Hamburg, Margaret 78
Hughes, Dora 88

U.S. Department of Health, Education, and Welfare (HEW)
Harris, Patricia Roberts 2
Randolph, Linda A. 52
Spearman, Leonard H. O., Sr. 81
Sullivan, Louis 8

U.S. Department of Homeland Security
Johnson, Jeh 76, 125

U.S. Department of Housing and Urban Development (HUD)
Blackwell, J. Kenneth, Sr. 61
Gaines, Brenda 41
Harris, Patricia Roberts 2
Jackson, Alphonso R. 48
Weaver, Robert C. 8, 46

U.S. Department of Justice
Campbell, Bill 9, 76
Days, Drew S., III 10
Guinier, Lani 7, 30
Harris, Maya Lakshmi 88
Holder, Eric, Jr. 9, 76, 104
Lafontant, Jewel Stradford 3, 51
Lewis, Delano 7
Patrick, Deval 12, 61, 127
Thompson, Larry D. 39
Williams, Michael L. 86

U.S. Department of Labor
Crockett, George W., Jr. 10, 64
Fletcher, Arthur A. 63
Herman, Alexis M. 15

U.S. Department of State
Baltimore, Richard Lewis, III 71
Bethune, Mary McLeod 4
Bunche, Ralph J. 5
Davis, Ruth 37
Dougherty, Mary Pearl 47
Frazer, Jendayi 68
Ervin, Clark Kent 82
Garrett, Joyce Finley 59
Grimké, Archibald H. 9
Haley, George Williford Boyce 21
Harris, Patricia Roberts 2
Lafontant, Jewel Stradford 3, 51
McGee, James D. 74
Powell, Colin 1, 28, 75
Rice, Condoleezza 3, 28, 72
Rice, Susan 74, 103
Stokes, Carl 10, 73
Sutphen, Mona 77
Thomas-Greenfield, Linda 99
Van Lierop, Robert 53
Wharton, Clifton R., Jr. 7
Wharton, Clifton Reginald, Sr. 36

U.S. Department of the Treasury
Morton, Azie Taylor 48

U.S. Department of Transportation
Coleman, William T. 76
Davis, Benjamin O., Jr. 2, 43
Foxx, Anthony 81, 123
Slater, Rodney E. 15, 125

U.S. Department of Veterans Affairs
Brown, Jesse 6, 41

U.S. Diplomatic Corps
See U.S. Department of State

U.S. District Attorney
Harris, Kamala D. 64, 122
Lloyd, Reginald 64

U.S. District Court judge
Bryant, William Benson 61
Carter, Robert L. 51, 100
Cooke, Marcia 60
Diggs-Taylor, Anna 20
Henderson, Thelton E. 68
Johnson, Norma H. 17, 97
Johnson, Sterling, Jr. 124
Keith, Damon J. 16, 74
Parker, Barrington D. 92
Parsons, James 14
Perry, Matthew J., Jr. 96
Sleet, Gregory M. 109
Tanner, Jack E. 100
Williams, Ann Claire 82
Williams, David W. 110

U.S. Dream Academy
Phipps, Wintley 59

U.S. Environmental Protection Agency
Jackson, Lisa 77

U.S. Foreign Service
See U.S. Department of State

U.S. Geological Survey
Bromery, Randolph Wilson 85
Person, Waverly 9, 51

U.S. House of Representatives
Adams, Alma 127
Archie-Hudson, Marguerite 44
Ballance, Frank W. 41
Beatty, Joyce 117
Bishop, Sanford D., Jr. 24, 111
Brown, Corrine 24, 90
Burke, Yvonne Brathwaite 42
Carson, André 69
Carson, Julia 23, 69
Chisholm, Shirley 2, 50
Clarke, Yvette 92
Clay, William Lacy 8
Clay, William Lacy, Jr. 95
Clayton, Eva M. 20
Cleaver, Emanuel 4, 45, 68, 107
Clyburn, James E. 21, 71, 118
Collins, Barbara-Rose 7, 87
Collins, Cardiss 10, 80, 120
Conyers, John, Jr. 4, 45, 111
Crockett, George W., Jr. 10, 64
Cummings, Elijah E. 24, 102
Davis, Artur 41
Davis, Danny K. 24, 79
De Priest, Oscar Stanton 80

Dellums, Ronald 2, 81
Diggs, Charles C. 21
Dixon, Julian C. 24
Dymally, Mervyn 42
Edwards, Donna 77
Ellison, Keith 59
Espy, Mike 6
Fattah, Chaka 11, 70, 112
Fauntroy, Walter E. 11
Fields, Cleo 13
Flake, Floyd H. 18, 110
Ford, Harold E(ugene) 42
Ford, Harold E(ugene), Jr. 16, 70
Franks, Gary 2
Frazer, Victor O. 98
Fudge, Marcia L. 76
Gray, William H., III 3
Green, Al 118
Hastings, Alcee 16, 119
Hawkins, Augustus F. 68
Hilliard, Earl F. 24
Jackson, Jesse, Jr. 14, 45, 81, 108
Jackson Lee, Sheila 20
Jefferson, William J. 25, 72
Jeffries, Hakeem 118
Johnson, Eddie Bernice 8, 90
Johnson, Hank, Jr. 80
Jordan, Barbara 4, 78
Kelly, Robin 114
Kilpatrick, Carolyn Cheeks 16
Langston, John Mercer 101
Lawrence, Brenda 127
Lee, Barbara 25, 102
Leland, Mickey 2
Lewis, John 2, 46, 83
Love, Mia 96, 125
Majette, Denise 41
McKinney, Cynthia 11, 52, 74
Meek, Carrie 6, 36
Meek, Kendrick 41, 89
Meeks, Gregory T. 25, 117
Menard, John Willis 90
Metcalfe, Ralph 26
Mfume, Kweisi 6, 41
Millender-McDonald, Juanita 21, 61
Miller, Lorraine C. 119
Mitchell, Arthur Wergs 91
Mitchell, Parren J. 42, 66
Moore, Gwendolynne S. 55
Norton, Eleanor Holmes 7, 93
Owens, Major 6, 117
Payne, Donald M. 2, 57, 112
Pinchback, P. B. S. 9
Plaskett, Stacey 127
Powell, Adam Clayton, Jr. 3
Rangel, Charles B. 3, 52, 85
Rapier, James T. 82
Richardson, Laura 81
Richmond, Cedric 93
Rush, Bobby 26, 76
Scott, David 41, 117
Scott, Robert C. 23
Scott, Tim 87, 125
Sewell, Terri 93
Smalls, Robert 82
Stokes, Louis 3
Thompson, Bennie 26, 119
Towns, Edolphus 19, 75
Tubbs Jones, Stephanie 24, 72
Waldon, Alton R., Jr. 98
Washington, Harold 6
Waters, Maxine 3, 67, 103
Watson, Diane 41

Watson Coleman, Bonnie 127
Watt, Mel 26, 105
Watts, J. C., Jr. 14, 38
West, Allen 89
Wheat, Alan 14
Wilson, Frederica 92
Wynn, Albert R. 25, 77
Young, Andrew 3, 48, 110

U.S. Information Agency
Allen, Samuel 38

U.S. Marines
Bennett, Richard 97
Bolden, Charles Frank, Jr. 7, 78
Brown, Jesse 6, 41
Coleman, Ronald S. 110
Petersen, Franke E. 31
Von Lipsey, Roderick K. 11

U.S. Navy
Black, Barry C. 47
Brashear, Carl 29
Brown, Jesse Leroy 31
Brown, Wesley A. 102
Clark, Carl 101
Doby, Lawrence Eugene, Sr. 16, 41
Fields, Evelyn J. 27
Gravely, Samuel L., Jr. 5, 49
Howard, Michelle 28, 125
Miller, Dorie 29
Pinckney, Bill 42
Pruitt, Wendell O. 106
Reason, J. Paul 19
Wright, Lewin 43

U.S. Peace Corps
Days, Drew S., III 10
Johnson, Rafer 33
Lewis, Delano 7

U.S. presidency
Obama, Barack 49, 74, 91

U.S. Register of the Treasury
Bruce, Blanche Kelso 33

U.S. Senate
Black, Barry C. 47
Bowman, Bertie 71
Braun, Carol Moseley 4, 42
Brooke, Edward W. 8, 88, 126
Bruce, Blanche Kelso 33
Burris, Roland W. 25, 75
Obama, Barack 49, 74, 91
Pinchback, P. B. S. 9
Revels, Hiram Rhoades 98
Scott, Tim 87, 125

U.S. State Department
See U.S. Department of State

U.S. Supreme Court
Marshall, Thurgood 1, 44
Thomas, Clarence 2, 39, 65

U.S. surgeon general
Benjamin, Regina 20, 75
Elders, Joycelyn 6
Satcher, David 7, 57, 111

U.S. Virgin Islands government
Christian-Green, Donna M. 17
DeJongh, John, Jr. 85
Evans, Melvin H. 88

Frazer, Victor O. 98
Hastie, William H. 8
Turnbull, Charles Wesley 62

USDA
See U.S. Department of Agriculture

USFL
See United States Football League

Vancouver Grizzlies basketball team
Abdur-Rahim, Shareef 28

Vaudeville
Anderson, Eddie "Rochester" 30
Austin, Lovie 40
Bates, Peg Leg 14
Cox, Ida 42
Davis, Sammy, Jr. 18
Dudley, Sherman H. 117
Gilpin, Charles Sidney 81
Johnson, J. Rosamond 121
Johnson, Jack 8
Martin, Sara 38
McDaniel, Hattie 5
Mills, Florence 22
Moore, Tim 124
Robinson, Bill "Bojangles" 11
Waters, Ethel 7

Vermont state government
Twilight, Alexander 125

Veterans's issues
Carr, Keela 74

Veterinary science
Jawara, Dawda Kairaba 11
Lushington, Augustus Nathaniel 56
Thomas, Vivien 9

Vibe
Jones, Quincy 8, 30
Smith, Danyel 40
Wilbekin, Emil 63

Vibraphone
Hampton, Lionel 17, 41
Hutcherson, Bobby 115
Smith, Cecilia 102

Victim's Bill of Rights
Dee, Merri 55

Video gaming
Croal, N'Gai 76
Fils-Aimé, Reggie 74

Vietnam Veterans of America
Duggins, George 64

Village Voice
Cooper, Andrew W. 36
Crouch, Stanley 11

Violin
Blake, John, Jr. 123
Boulogne, Joseph, Chevalier de Saint-Georges 94
Bridgetower, George 78
Daemyon, Jerald 64
Dworkin, Aaron P. 52
Escobar, Damien 56
Escobar, Tourie 56
Murray, Tai 47
Smith, Stuff 37

Tinsley, Boyd 50
Williams, Claude 80

Virginia state government
Jones, Dwight C. 122
Marsh, Henry 32
Martin, Ruby Grant 49
Wilder, L. Douglas 3, 48

Virginia Supreme Court
Hassell, Leroy Rountree, Sr. 41, 116

Virology
Fuller, A. Oveta 43

Vogue magazine
Talley, André Leon 56, 106

Volleyball
Blanton, Dain 29

Voodoo
Beauvoir, Max 74
Dunham, Katherine 4, 59
Guy, Rosa 5
Hurston, Zora Neale 3
Pierre, Andre 17

Voting rights
Cary, Mary Ann Shadd 30
Chestnut, J. L., Jr. 73
Clark, Septima 7
Forman, James 7, 51
Hamer, Fannie Lou 6
Harper, Frances Ellen Watkins 11
Hill, Jesse, Jr. 13
Lampkin, Daisy 19
Moore, Harry T. 29
Moses, Robert Parris 11
Terrell, Mary Church 9
Touré, Faya Ora Rose 56
Trotter, Monroe 9
Tubman, Harriet 9
Wells-Barnett, Ida B. 8

WAAC (Women's Auxiliary Army Corps)
See Women's Army Corps

WAC
See Women's Army Corps

War criminals
Lubanga, Thomas 104
Ntaganda, Bosco 111
Sankoh, Foday 74

Washington, D.C., city government
Barry, Marion, Jr. 7, 44, 125
Brown, Kwame R. 91
Cooper Cafritz, Peggy 43
Dixon, Sharon Pratt 1
Fenty, Adrian 60, 88
Gray, Vincent C. 88
Hobson, Julius W. 44
Jarvis, Charlene Drew 21
Neal, Larry 38
Norton, Eleanor Holmes 7, 93
Washington, Walter 45
Williams, Anthony 21

Washington Post
Aplin-Brownlee, Vivian 96
Britt, Donna 28
Gaines, Patrice 106

Givhan, Robin Deneen 72
Haygood, Wil 83
King, Colbert I. 69
Maynard, Robert C. 7
McCall, Nathan 8
Nelson, Jill 6, 54
Raspberry, William 2

Washington Redskins football team
Green, Darrell 39, 74
Manley, Dexter 116
May, Mark 117
Monk, Art 38, 73
Owens, Brig 118

Washington Wizards basketball team
Bickerstaff, Bernie 21
Heard, Gar 25
Howard, Juwan 15
Unseld, Wes 23

Weather
Brown, Vivian 27
Christian, Spencer 15
McEwen, Mark 5
Roker, Al 12, 49

Welfare reform
Bryant, Wayne R. 6
Carson, Julia 23, 69
Parker, Star 70
Wallace, Joaquin 49
Williams, Walter E. 4

West Indian folk songs
Rhoden, Wayne 70

West Indian literature
See Caribbean literature/West Indian literature

West Point
Davis, Benjamin O., Jr. 2, 43
Flipper, Henry O. 3
Young, Charles 77

White House
Allen, Eugene 79
Burton, Bill 96
Butts, Cassandra 78
Christie, Ron 83
Currie, Betty 21
Gaspard, Patrick 84
Hatcher, Andrew T. 90
Jarvis, Kristen 85
Keckley, Elizabeth 90
Love, Reggie 77
McAlpin, Harry 121
Obama, Michelle 61, 90
Rochon, Stephen W. 78
Rogers, Desirée 88
Rouse, Cecilia 93
Strautmanis, Michael 87

Wine/winemaking
Allen-Buillard, Melba 55
Rideau, Iris 46
Walker, Ray 109

Wisconsin Supreme Court
Butler, Louis 70

Women Helping Offenders
Holland, Endesha Ida Mae 3, 57

Women's Army Corps (WAC)
Adams Earley, Charity 13, 34
Cadoria, Sherian Grace 14
Clarke, Anna Mac 95

Women's Auxiliary Army Corps
See Women's Army Corps

Women's issues
Abiola-Costello, Hafsat 108
Allen, Ethel D. 13
Avery, Byllye Y. 66
Ba, Mariama 30
Bashir, Halima 73
Brown, Elaine 8
Burroughs, Nannie Helen 96
Campbell, Bebe Moore 6, 24, 59
Cannon, Katie 10
Carby, Hazel 27
Cary, Mary Ann Shadd 30
Charles, Mary Eugenia 10, 55
Chinn, May Edward 26
Christian, Barbara T. 44
Christian-Green, Donna M. 17
Clark, Septima 7
Cook-Parrish, Mary Virginia 95
Cooper, Anna Julia 20
De Veaux, Alexis 44
Edwards, Lena Frances 76
Evans, Diana 72
Fauset, Jessie 7
Giddings, Paula 11
Gomez, Jewelle 30
Grimké, Archibald H. 9
Guy-Sheftall, Beverly 13, 92
Hale, Clara 16
Hale, Lorraine 8
Hamer, Fannie Lou 6
Harper, Frances Ellen Watkins 11
Harris, Leslie 6
Haynes, Elizabeth Ross 102
Height, Dorothy I. 2, 23, 78
Hernandez, Aileen Clarke 13
Hill, Anita 5, 65
Hine, Darlene Clark 24
Holland, Endesha Ida Mae 3, 57
hooks, bell 5, 90
Hughes, Ebony 57
Hull, Akasha Gloria 45
Hussein, Lubna 80
Jackson, Alexine Clement 22
Joe, Yolanda 21
Jordan, June 7, 35
Koontz, Elizabeth Duncan 101
Lampkin, Daisy 19
Larsen, Nella 10
Lorde, Audre 6
Marshall, Paule 7, 77
Mbaye, Mariétou 31
McCabe, Jewell Jackson 10
McCauley, Gina 76
McKenzie, Vashti M. 29
McMillan, Terry 4, 17, 53
Millender-McDonald, Juanita 21, 61
Millner, Denene 76
Mongella, Gertrude 11
Mossell, Gertrude Bustill 40
Naylor, Gloria 10, 42
Nelson, Jill 6, 54
Niane, Katoucha 70
Nichols, Nichelle 11
Parker, Pat 19

Rawlings, Nana Konadu Agyeman 13
Ruffin, Josephine St. Pierre 75
Shange, Ntozake 8, 89
Sherrod, Shirley 87
Simpson, Carole 6, 30
Smith, Barbara 28
Smith, Jane E. 24
Talbert, Mary B. 77
Terrell, Mary Church 9
Tubman, Harriet 9
Vanzant, Iyanla 17, 47, 108
Villard-Appolon, Malya 106
Walker, Alice 1, 43
Walker, Rebecca 50
Wallace, Michele Faith 13
Williams, Fannie Barrier 27
Xuma, Madie Hall 59

Women's Leadership Forum
Shabazz, Ilyasah 36

Women's National Basketball Association
Bolton-Holifield, Ruthie 28
Cash, Swin 59
Catchings, Tamika 43
Cooper, Cynthia 17
Edwards, Teresa 14, 95
Ford, Cheryl 45
Griffith, Yolanda 25
Griner, Brittney 128
Holdsclaw, Chamique 24, 110
Jones, Merlakia 34
Lennox, Betty 31
Leslie, Lisa 16, 73
Madison, Paula 37, 99
McCray, Nikki 18
Miller, Cheryl 10, 74
Milton, DeLisha 31
Moore, Maya 94
Palmer, Violet 59
Parker, Candace 74
Peck, Carolyn 23
Perrot, Kim 23
Staley, Dawn 57
Swoopes, Sheryl 12, 56
Thompson, Tina 25, 75
Williams, Natalie 31
Woodard, Lynette 67

Workplace equity
Clark, Septima 7
Hill, Anita 5, 65
Nelson, Jill 6, 54
Simpson, Carole 6, 30

Works Progress (Projects) Administration (WPA)
Alexander, Margaret Walker 22
Blackburn, Robert 28
DeCarava, Roy 42, 81
Douglas, Aaron 7
Dunham, Katherine 4, 59
Fauset, Crystal Dreda Bird 100
Hall, Juanita 62
Lawrence, Jacob 4, 28
Lee-Smith, Hughie 5, 22
Murray, Pauli 38
Sallee, Charles 38
Sebree, Charles 40
Winkfield, Jimmy 42

Wright, Richard 5

World Bank
Okonjo-Iweala, Ngozi 101
Soglo, Nicéphore 15

World beat
Fela 1, 42
Maal, Baaba 66
N'Dour, Youssou 1, 53, 79
Okosuns, Sonny 71
Ongala, Remmy 9, 91

World Cup
dos Santos, Manuel Francisco 65
Eusebio 118
Gyan, Asamoah 87
Mensah, John 87
Milla, Roger 2
Pelé 7
Scurry, Briana 27
Sturridge, Daniel 120

World hunger
Iman 4, 33, 87
Leland, Mickey 2

WPA
See Works Progress (Projects) Administration

Wrestling
Henry, Mark 116
Ladd, Ernie 64
Lashley, Bobby 63
Lister, Tommy 127
Rock, The 29, 66
Young, Darren 114

Xerox Corp.
Burns, Ursula 60
Rand, A. Barry 6

Yale Repertory Theater
Dutton, Charles S. 4, 22
Richards, Lloyd 2

Yale University
Blassingame, John Wesley 40
Carby, Hazel 27
Davis, Charles T. 48
Hill, Errol 40
Neal, Larry 38

YMCA
See Young Men's Christian Association

Yoruban folklore
Soyinka, Wole 4, 93

Young adult literature
Anderson, Ho Che 54
Bolden, Tonya 32
Ekwensi, Cyprian 37
Johnson, Angela 52
Millner, Denene 76
Myers, Walter Dean 8, 20, 123

Young Men's Christian Association (YMCA)
Goode, Mal 13
Hope, John 8
Tobias, Channing H. 79

Cumulative Name Index

Volume numbers appear in **bold**

Aaliyah 1979–2001 **30**

Aaron, Hank 1934— **5**

Aaron, Henry Louis *See Aaron, Hank*

Aaron, Quinton 1984— **82**

Abacha, Sani 1943–1998 **11, 70**

Abani, Chris 1966— **77**

Abbott, Diane 1953— **9**

Abbott, Robert Sengstacke 1868–1940 **27**

Abdi, Barkhad 1985— **119**

Abdirahman, Abdi 1977— **126**

Abdirahman, Abdihakem *See Abdirahman, Abdi*

Abdul-Jabbar, Kareem 1947— **8**

Abdullah, Imaam Isa *See York, Dwight D.*

Abdullah, Kazem 1979(?)— **97**

Abdulmajid, Iman Mohamed *See Iman*

Abdul-Rahman, Mahdi *See Hazzard, Walt*

Abdur-Rahim, Shareef 1976— **28**

Abele, Julian 1881–1950 **55**

Abercrumbie, P. Eric 1948— **95**

Abernathy, Ralph David 1926–1990 **1**

Aberra, Amsale 1954— **67**

Abiola, Moshood 1937–1998 **70**

Abiola-Costello, Hafsat 1974— **108**

Abraham, Kyle 1977— **116**

Abrahams, Peter 1919— **39**

Abrahams, Zaraah 1987— **127**

Abubakar, Abdulsalami 1942— **66**

Abudu, Mo 1964— **121**

Abudu, Mosunmola *See Abudu, Mo*

Abu-Jamal, Mumia 1954— **15**

Abune Paulos 1935–2012 **105**

Ace, Johnny 1929–1954 **36**

Aces, The **117**

Aceyalone *See Freestyle Fellowship*

Achebe, Albert Chinualumogu *See Achebe, Chinua*

Achebe, Chinua 1930–2013 **6, 99, 111**

Ackerman, Arlene 1947–2013 **108**

Acklin, Barbara Jean 1943–1998 **107**

Acogny, Germaine 1944— **55**

Adam, Mariam *See Imani Winds*

Adams, Alma 1946— **127**

Adams, Eula L. 1950— **39, 120**

Adams, Floyd, Jr. 1945–2014 **12, 122**

Adams, Grantley 1898–1971 **82**

Adams, H. Leslie *See Adams, Leslie*

Adams, Jenoyne (?)— **60**

Adams, Johnny 1932–1998 **39**

Adams, Leslie 1932— **39**

Adams, Oleta 19(?)(?)— **18**

Adams, Osceola Macarthy 1890–1983 **31**

Adams, Paul 1977— **50**

Adams, Sheila J. 1943— **25**

Adams, Yolanda 1961— **17, 67**

Adams-Campbell, Lucille L. 1953— **60**

Adams Earley, Charity (Edna) 1918— **13, 34**

Adams-Ender, Clara 1939— **40**

Adderley, Julian "Cannonball" 1928–1975 **30**

Adderley, Nat 1931–2000 **29**

Adderley, Nathaniel *See Adderley, Nat*

Ade, Sunny King 1946— **41**

Adebari, Rotimi 1963(?)— **83**

Adebimpe, Tunde 1975— **75**

Adegbile, Debo P. 1966— **119**

Adeniyi, Sunday *See Ade, Sunny King*

Adichie, Chimamanda Ngozi 1977— **64, 121**

Adjaye, David 1966— **38, 78**

Adkins, Rod 1958— **41**

Adkins, Rutherford H. 1924–1998 **21**

Adkins, Terry 1953–2014 **122**

Adoboli, Kweku 1980— **106**

Adu, Freddy 1989— **67**

Adu, Fredua Koranteng *See Adu, Freddy*

Adu, Helen Folasade *See Sade*

Aduba, Uzo 1981(?)— **122**

Aduba, Uzoamaka *See Aduba, Uzo*

Afewerki, Isaias 1946— **98**

Afro, Teddy 1976— **78**

Agyeman, Jaramogi Abebe 1911–2000 **10, 63**

Agyeman Rawlings, Nana Konadu 1948— **13**

Ahidjo, Ahmadou 1924–1989 **81**

Ahmed, Sharif 1964— **80**

Aidoo, Ama Ata 1942— **38**

Aiken, Loretta Mary *See Mabley, Jackie "Moms"*

Ailey, Alvin 1931–1989 **8**

Ainsworth, Leonard Victor *See Gray, Dobie*

Aire, Chris 1965(?)— **117**

Ake, Claude 1939–1996 **30**

Akil, Mara Brock 1970— **60, 82**

Akinmusire, Ambrose 1982— **103**

Akinnuoye-Agbaje, Adewale 1967— **56**

Akinola, Peter Jasper 1944— **65**

Akintimehin, Olubowale Victor *See Wale*

Akomfrah, John 1957— **37**

Akon 1973(?)— **68**

Akpan, Uwem 1971— **70**

Akunyili, Dora Nkem 1954— **58**

Al-Amin, Jamil Abdullah 1943— **6**

Albert, Octavia V. R. 1853–1890(?) **100**

Albright, Gerald 1947— **23**

Alcindor, Ferdinand Lewis *See Abdul-Jabbar, Kareem*

Alcorn, George Edward, Jr. 1940— **59**

Aldridge, Ira 1807–1867 **99**

Aldridge, LaMarcus 1985— **125**

Alert, Kool DJ Red 19(?)(?)— **33**

Alexander, Archie Alphonso 1888–1958 **14**

Alexander, Clifford 1933— **26**

Alexander, Elizabeth 1962— **75**

Alexander, James *See Bar-Kays, The*

Alexander, John Marshall *See Ace, Johnny*

Alexander, Joseph L. 1930–2002 **95**

Alexander, Joyce London 1949— **18**

Alexander, Khandi 1957— **43**

Alexander, Kwame 1969(?)— **98**

Alexander, Lincoln 1922–2012 **106**

Alexander, Margaret Walker 1915–1998 **22**

Alexander, Michelle 1967— **98**

Alexander, Sadie Tanner Mossell 1898–1989 **22**

Alexander, Shaun 1977— **58**

Ali, Ayaan Hirsi 1969— **58, 92**

Ali, Hana Yasmeen 1976— **52**

Ali, Laila 1977— **27, 63**

Ali, Mahershala 1974— **122**

Ali, Mohammed Naseehu 1971— **60**

Ali, Muhammad 1942— **2, 16, 52**

Ali, Rashied 1935–2009 **79**

Ali, Russlynn H. 1971(?)— **92**

Ali, Tatyana 1979— **73**

Ali Mahdi Mohamed 1940— **5**

Allain, Stephanie 1959— **49**

Allen, Betty 1927–2009 **83**

Allen, Byron 1961— **3, 24, 97**

Allen, Claude 1960— **68**

Allen, Debbie 1950— **13, 42**

Allen, Dick 1942— **85**

Allen, Ethel D. 1929–1981 **13**

Allen, Eugene 1919— **79**

Allen, Fulton *See Fuller, Blind Boy*

Allen, Geri 1957— **92**

Allen, Larry 1971— **109**

Allen, Lucy 1932— **85**

Allen, Macon Bolling 1816–1894 **104**

Allen, Marcus 1960— **20**

Allen, Ora Denise *See LaSalle, Denise*

Allen, Ray 1975— **82**

Allen, Richard 1760–1831 **14**

Allen, Robert L. 1942— **38**

Allen, Samuel W. 1917— **38**

Allen, Tina 1949–2008 **22, 75**

Allen, Tony 1940— **117**

Allen, Will 1949— **74**

Allen-Buillard, Melba 1960— **55**

Allison, Luther 1939–1997 **111**

Allison, Verne *See Dells, The*

Almoctar, Goumour *See Bombino*

Alonso, Laz 1974— **87**

Als, Hilton 1961— **105**

Alston, Charles Henry 1907–1977 **33**

Alston, Gerald *See Manhattans, The*

Altidore, Josmer *See Altidore, Jozy*

Altidore, Jozy 1989— **109**

Alves, Dani 1983— **121**

Amadi, Elechi 1934— **40**

Amadou & Mariam **113**

Amaker, Harold Tommy, Jr. *See Amaker, Tommy*

Amaker, Norman 1935–2000 **63**

Amaker, Tommy 1965— **62**

Amaki, Amalia 1949— **76**

Amata, Jeta 1975— **111**

Amerie 1980— **52**

Ames, Wilmer 1950–1993 **27**

Amin, Idi 1925–2003 **42**

Ammons, Albert 1907–1949 **112**

Ammons, Gene 1925–1974 **112**

Ammons, James H. 1952(?)— 81

Amos, Emma 1938— 63

Amos, John 1941— 8, 62

Amos, Valerie 1954— 41

Amos, Wally 1937— 9

Amy, Curtis 1927–2002 114

Amoudi, Mohammed al- 1946— 88

Anderson, Alfa See Chic

Anderson, Anthony 1970— 51, 77

Anderson, Carl 1945–2004 48

Anderson, Charles Edward 1919–1994 37

Anderson, Eddie "Rochester" 1905–1977 30

Anderson, Elmer 1941— 25

Anderson, Ezzrett 1920— 95

Anderson, Fred 1929–2010 87

Anderson, Ho Che 1969— 54

Anderson, Ivie 1905(?)–1949 126

Anderson, Jacob 1990— 128

Anderson, Jamal 1972— 22

Anderson, Katherine See Marvelettes, The

Anderson, Kisean See Kingston, Sean

Anderson, Lauren 1965— 72

Anderson, Maceo 1910–2001 111

Anderson, Marcia 1958(?)— 115

Anderson, Marian 1902— 2, 33

Anderson, Michael P. 1959–2003 40

Anderson, Mike 1959— 63

Anderson, Norman B. 1955— 45

Anderson, Reuben V. 1942— 81

Anderson, Sean Michael Leonard See Big Sean

Anderson, Sugarfoot See Anderson, Ezzrett

Anderson, T. J. 1928— 119

Anderson, Thomas Jefferson See Anderson, T. J.

Anderson, Viv 1956— 58

Anderson, William See Drifters, The

Anderson, William G(ilchrist) 1927— 57

Andler, Sylvia Brigitte Gertrud See Ayim, May

Andre 3000 See Benjamin, Andre

Andrews, Benny 1930–2006 22, 59

Andrews, Bert 1929–1993 13

Andrews, Inez 1929–2012 108

Andrews, Mark See Sisqo

Andrews, Raymond 1934–1991 4

Andrews, Tina 1951— 74

Andrews, Troy See Trombone Shorty

Anelka, Nicolas 1979— 118

Angelou, Maya 1928–2014 1, 15, 122

Anna Marie See Lincoln, Abbey

Annan, Kofi Atta 1938— 15, 48

Ansa, Tina McElroy 1949— 14

Anthony, Alani See Anthony, La La

Anthony, Carmelo 1984— 46, 94

Anthony, Crystal See McCrary Anthony, Crystal

Anthony, La La 1979— 122

Anthony, Michael 1930(?)— 29

Anthony, Trey 1974— 63

Anthony, Wendell 1950— 25

Antunes, Lúcio 1966— 109

apl.de.ap 1974— 84

Aplin-Brownlee, Vivian 1946–2007 96

Appiah, Kwame Anthony 1954— 67, 101

Arac de Nyeko, Monica 1979— 66

Arach, Monica See Arac de Nyeko, Monica

Archer, Clifford See Atlantic Starr

Archer, Dennis (Wayne) 1942— 7, 36

Archer, Lee, Jr. 1919— 79

Archer, Michael Eugene See D'Angelo

Archer, Osceola See Adams, Osceola Macarthy

Archibald, Nathaniel See Archibald, Tiny

Archibald, Tiny 1948— 90

Archie-Hudson, Marguerite 1937— 44

Ardoin, Alphonse 1915–2007 65

Arenas, Gilbert 1982— 84

Arinze, Francis 1932— 19

Aristide, Jean-Bertrand 1953— 6, 45

Arkadie, Kevin 1957— 17

Armah, Ayi Kwei 1939— 49

Armah, Esther 1963— 87

Armatrading, Joan 1950— 32

Armstrong, Govind 1968— 81

Armstrong, Henry 1912–1988 104

Armstrong, Louis 1900–1971 2

Armstrong, Robb 1962— 15

Armstrong, Vanessa Bell 1953— 24

Arnez J, 1966(?)— 53

Arnold, Billy Boy 1935— 112

Arnold, James See Arnold, Kokomo

Arnold, Kokomo 1901–1968 116

Arnold, Monica See Monica

Arnold, Tichina 1971— 63

Arnold, William See Arnold, Billy Boy

Arnwine, Barbara 1951(?)— 28

Arrington, Joseph, Jr. See Tex, Joe

Arrington, Richard 1934— 24, 100

Arroyo, Martina 1936— 30

Artest, Ron 1979— 52

Arthur, Owen 1949— 33

Artist, The See Prince

Asante, Molefi Kete 1942— 3

A$AP Rocky 1988— 109

Ashanti 1980— 37, 96

Ashe, Arthur Robert, Jr. 1943–1993 1, 18

Ashford, Calvin, Jr. 1935(?)–2008 74

Ashford, Emmett 1914–1980 22

Ashford, Evelyn 1957— 63

Ashford, Nickolas 1941–2011 21, 97

Ashford and Simpson 21, 97

Ashley, Maurice 1966— 15, 47

Ashley & JaQuavis 107

Ashley-Ward, Amelia 1957— 23

Ashong, Derrick 1975— 86

Asim, Jabari 1962— 71

Asomugha, Nnamdi 1981— 100

Astatke, Mulatu 1942(?)— 81

Atim, Julian 1980(?)— 66

Atkins, Cholly 1930–2003 40

Atkins, David See Sinbad

Atkins, Erica 1972— See Mary Mary

Atkins, Jeffrey See Ja Rule

Atkins, Juan 1962— 50

Atkins, Russell 1926— 45

Atkins, Tina 1974— See Mary Mary

Atkinson, Alia 1988— 126

Atlantic Starr 122

Atta Mills, John 1944— 75

Attaway, William 1911–1986 102

Atyam, Angelina 1946— 55

Aubert, Alvin 1930— 41

Aubespin, Mervin 1937— 95

Augusta, Alexander T. 1825–1890 111

Auguste, Arnold A. 1946— 47

Auguste, Donna 1958— 29

Auguste, (Marie Carmele) Rose-Anne 1963— 13

Augustine, Jean 1937— 53

Austin, Bobby W. 1944— 95

Austin, Gloria 1956— 63

Austin, Jim 1951— 63

Austin, Junius C. 1887–1968 44

Austin, Lloyd 1953— 101

Austin, Lovie 1887–1972 40

Austin, Patti 1948— 24

Austin, Wanda M. 1953(?)— 94

Autrey, Wesley 1956— 68

Avant, Clarence 1931— 19, 86

Avant, Nicole A. 1968— 90

Avery, Byllye Y. 1937— 66

Avery, James 1945(?)–2013 118

Awoonor, Kofi 1935–2013 37, 115

Awoonor-Williams, George See Awoonor, Kofi

Awoyinka, Adesiji See Siji

Awuah, Patrick 1965— 111

Ayers, Roy 1940— 16

Ayew, Abedi See Pelé, Abedi

Ayim, May 1960–1996 126

Ayler, Albert 1936–1970 104

Azikiwe, Nnamdi 1904–1996 13

Ba, Mariama 1929–1981 30

Babangida, Ibrahim (Badamasi) 1941— 4

Babatunde, Obba 19(?)(?)— 35

Babatunde, Rotimi 19(?)(?)— 104

Babyface 1959— 10, 31, 82

Baca, Susana 1954— 80

Bacon-Bercey, June 1942— 38

Badu, Erykah 1971— 22, 114

Bagayoko, Amadou See Amadou & Mariam

Bahati, Wambui 1950(?)— 60

Bailey, Buddy See Clovers, The

Bailey, Buster 1902–1967 38

Bailey, Chauncey 1949–2007 68

Bailey, Clyde 1946— 45

Bailey, DeFord 1899–1982 33

Bailey, Jimmy See Cadillacs

Bailey, Pearl Mae 1918–1990 14

Bailey, Philip 1951— 63

Bailey, Preston 1948(?)— 64

Bailey, Radcliffe 1968— 19

Bailey, William C. See Bailey, Buster

Bailey, Xenobia 1955(?)— 11

Bailey Rae, Corinne 1979— 83

Baines, Harold 1959— 32

Baiocchi, Regina Harris 1956— 41

Baisden, Michael 1963— 25, 66

Baker, Anita 1957— 21, 48

Baker, Arlene Holt See Holt Baker, Arlene

Baker, Augusta 1911–1998 38

Baker, Constance See Motley, Constance Baker

Baker, Delbert W. 1953— 110

Baker, Dusty 1949— 8, 43, 72, 110

Baker, Ella 1903–1986 5

Baker, George See Divine, Father

Baker, Gwendolyn Calvert 1931— 9

Baker, Houston A(lfred), Jr. 1943— 6

Baker, James See New Birth

Baker, Johnnie B., Jr. See Baker, Dusty

Baker, Josephine 1906–1975 3

Baker, LaVern 1929–1997 26

Baker, Matt 1921–1959 76

Baker, Maxine 1952— 28

Baker, Mickey 1925— 95

Baker, Thurbert 1952— 22

Baker, Vernon Joseph 1919–2010 65, 87

Bakewell, Danny 1946— 99

Balance, Frank W. 1942— 41

Baldwin, Cynthia 1945— 74, 107

Baldwin, David See Drifters, The

Baldwin, James 1924–1987 1

Balentino, Umberto Alejandro See Jeffries, Herb

Balinton, Umpeylia Marsema See DeSanto, Sugar Pie

Ball, Kirshnik See Migos

Ballard, Allen Butler, Jr. 1930— 40

Ballard, Florence 1943–1976 112

See also Supremes, The

Ballard, Hank 1927–2003 41

Ballard, John 1830–1905 95

Balotelli, Mario 1990— 104

Baltimore, Richard Lewis, III 1946— 71

Bambaataa, Afrika 1958— 34

Bambara, Toni Cade 1939— 10

Banda, Hastings Kamuzu 1898(?)–1997 6, 54

Banda, Joyce 1950— 101

Bandele, Asha 1970(?)— 36

Bandele, Biyi 1967— 68, 121

Bandele-Thomas, Biyi See Bandele, Biyi

Banks, A. Doris See Henries, A. Doris Banks

Banks, Azealia 1991— 107

Banks, Ernie 1931–2015 33, 126

Banks, Jeffrey 1953— 17

Banks, Lloyd 1982— 113

Banks, Michelle 1968(?)— 59

Banks, Patryce See Graham Central Station

Banks, Paula A. 1950— 68

Banks, Ron See Dramatics, The

Banks, Tyra 1973— 11, 50

Banks, William (Venoid) 1903–1985 11

Banneker, Benjamin 1731–1806 93

Banner, David 1975(?)— 55

Bannister, Edward Mitchell 1828–1901 88

Banton, Buju 1973— 93

Baquet, Dean 1956— 63, 121

Baraka, Amiri 1934–2014 1, 38, 118

Baraka, Ras J. 1970— 121

Baraka, Sho 19(?)(?)— 109

Barbee, Lloyd Augustus 1925–2002 71

Barber, Atiim Kiambu Hakeem-Ah
See Barber, Tiki
Barber, Ronde 1975— 41
Barber, Tiki 1975— 57, 107
Barboza, Anthony 1944— 10
Barclay, Paris 1956— 37, 94
Barden, Donald H. 1943— 9, 20,
89
Bar-Kays, The 118
Barker, Danny 1909–1994 32
Barkley, Charles 1963— 5, 66
Barksdale, Chuck See Dells, The
Barksdale, Don 1923–1993 103
Barlow, Roosevelt 1917–2003 49
Barnes, Ernie 1938–2009 16, 78
Barnes, John 1963— 53
Barnes, Katreese 196(?)— 97
Barnes, Lloyd 1944— 77
Barnes, Melody 1964— 75
Barnes, Prentiss See Moonglows,
The
Barnes, Roosevelt "Booba"
1936–1996 33
Barnes, Steven 1952— 54
Barnett, Amy Du Bois 1969— 46
Barnett, Etta Moten 1901–2004 18,
56
Barnett, Herman 1926–1973 112
Barnett, Marguerite 1942–1992 46
Barnett, Tahliah Debrett See FKA
Twigs
Barney, Lem 1945— 26
Barnhill, David 1914–1983 30
Barnwell, Ysaye See Sweet Honey
in the Rock
Barrax, Gerald William 1933— 45
Barrett, Andrew C. 1942(?)— 12
Barrett, Jacqueline 1950— 28
Barrett, Lindsay 1941— 43
Barrett, Mario Dewar See Mario
Barrino, Fantasia 1984— 53, 94
Barron, Kenny 1943— 128
Barrow, Dean 1951— 69
Barrow, Jamal See Shyne
Barrow, Joseph Louis See Louis,
Joe
Barrow, Willie T. 1924–2015 85,
128
Barry, Marion, Jr. 1936–2014 7, 44,
125
Bartels, Peggielene 1953(?)— 80
Barthé, Earl 19(?)(?)— 78
Barthe, Richmond 1901–1989 15
Barwuah, Mario See Balotelli, Mario
Bashir, Halima 1979— 73
Bashir, Omar al- 1944— 77
Basie, William James See Count
Basie
Baskett, James 1904–1948 102
Basquiat, Jean-Michel 1960–1988 5
Bass, Charlotta Amanda Spears
1874–1969 40
Bass, Fontella 1940–2012 104, 109
Bass, Karen 1953— 70
Bassett, Angela 1958— 6, 23, 62
Bassey, Offiong 1985— 119
Bassey, Shirley 1937— 25
Baszile, Jennifer 1969(?)— 79
Batch, Charlie 1974— 120
Bates, Clayton See Bates, Peg Leg
Bates, Daisy (Lee Gatson)
1914(?)— 13
Bates, Elias See Diddley, Bo

Bates, Karen Grigsby 19(?)(?)— 40
Bates, Peg Leg 1907— 14
Bath, Patricia E. 1942— 37
Batiste, Alvin 1932–2007 66
Batiste, Jonathan 1986— 108
Batiste, Lionel 1932(?)–2012 105
Batiste, Russell See Meters, The
Battle, Kathleen 1948— 70
Batts, Anthony 1960— 128
Baugé, Grégory 1985— 86
Baugh, David 1947— 23
Baughn, David See Drifters, The
Baylor, Don(ald Edward) 1949— 6
Baylor, Elgin 1934— 93
Baylor, Helen 1953— 36
Bazawule, Samuel See Blitz the
Ambassador
Beach, Michael 1963— 26, 120
Beah, Ishmael 1980— 69
Beal, Bernard B. 1954(?)— 46
Beals, Jennifer 1963— 12
Beals, Melba Pattillo 1941— 15, 94
Beamon, Bob 1946— 30
Beard, Matthew 1925–1981 120
Bearden, Romare 1912–1988 2, 50
Beasley, Jamar 1979— 29
Beasley, Myrlie See Evers, Myrlie
Beasley, Phoebe 1943— 34
Beaton, Norman Lugard 1934–1994
14
Beatty, Joyce 1950— 117
Beatty, Talley 1923(?)–1995 35
Beaty, Zelmo 1939–2013 115
Beauvais, Garcelle 1966— 29, 95
Beauvoir, Max 1936(?)— 74
Bebey, Francis 1929–2001 45
Bechet, Sidney 1897–1959 18
Beck, Robert See Iceberg Slim
Beckford, Tyson 1970— 11, 68
Beckham, Barry 1944— 41
Beckwith, Naomi 1976— 101
Becton, Julius W., Jr. 1926— 110
Bedie, Henri Konan 1934— 21
Beenie Man 1973— 32
Bekele, Kenenisa 1982— 75
Beken 1956(?)— 111
Belafonte, Harold George, Jr. See
Belafonte, Harry
Belafonte, Harry 1927— 4, 65
Belgrave, Cynthia 1920–1997 75
Belgrave, Marcus 1936— 77
Bell, Carey 1936–2007 114
Bell, Carl C. 1947— 111
Bell, Cool Papa See Bell, James
"Cool Papa"
Bell, Darrin 1975— 77
Bell, Derrick 1930–2011 6, 98
Bell, James "Cool Papa"
1901–1991 36
Bell, James A. 1948— 50
Bell, James Madison 1826–1902 40
Bell, LeRoy 1951— 98
Bell, Michael 1955— 40
Bell, Ralph S. 1934— 5
Bell, Ricky See New Edition
Bell, Robert Mack 1943— 22
Bell, Thom 1943— 112
Bell, Thomas Randolph See Bell,
Thom
Bell, W. Kamau 19(?)(?)— 107
Bell, Walter Kamau See Bell, W.
Kamau
Bell, William A., Sr. 1949— 122

Bellamy, Bill 1967— 12
Bellamy, Terry 1972— 58
Bellamy, Walt 1939–2013 119
Belle, Albert (Jojuan) 1966— 10
Belle, Regina 1963— 1, 51
Below, Fred See Aces, The
Belton, Sharon Sayles 1951— 9,
16
Benberry, Cuesta 1923–2007 65
Benét, Eric 1966— 28, 77
Benham, Robert 1946— 78
Ben-Israel, Ben Ami 1940(?)— 11
Benítez, Christian 1986–2013 113
Benjamin, Andre (3000) 1975— 45
See also OutKast
Benjamin, Regina 1956— 20, 75
Benjamin, Steve 1969— 98
Benjamin, Tritobia Hayes 1944—
53
Bennett, Estelle 1941–2009 77
Bennett, George Harold "Hal"
1930— 45
Bennett, Gwendolyn B. 1902–1981
59
Bennett, Lerone, Jr. 1928— 5, 84
Bennett, Louise 1919–2006 69
Bennett, Richard 1980(?)— 97
Benson, Angela 19(?)(?)— 34
Benson, Obie 1936–2005 96
Benson, Renaldo See Benson,
Obie
Benson, Ricci See Rose Royce
Bensouda, Fatou 1961— 103
Bentley, Lamont 1973–2005 53
Benton, Brook 1931–1988 121
Bernard, Marvin See Yayo, Tony
Berrien, Jacqueline A. 1961— 93
Berry, Bertice 1960— 8, 55
Berry, Bill See Berry, Edwin C.
Berry, Charles Edward Anderson
See Berry, Chuck
Berry, Chuck 1926— 29
Berry, Edwin C. 1910–1987 81
Berry, Eric 1988— 125
Berry, Fred "Rerun" 1951–2003 48
Berry, Halle 1966— 4, 19, 57, 91
Berry, James 1925— 41
Berry, James Eric See Berry, Eric
Berry, Mary Frances 1938— 7
Berry, Moses 1950(?)— 84
Berry, Theodore M. 1905–2000 31
Berrysmith, Don Reginald 1936—
49
Best, Carrie 1903–2001 80
Betha, Mason Durrell 1977(?)— 24
Bethune, Mary (Jane) McLeod
1875–1955 4
Beti, Mongo 1932–2001 36
Betsch, MaVynee 1935— 28
Bettis, Jerome 1972— 64
Betts, Keter 1928–2005 85
Betts, R. Dwayne 1979(?)— 86
Bevel, James L. 1936–2008 75
Beverly, Frankie 1946— 25
Bey, Yasiin 1973— 30, 96
Beyoncé 1981— 39, 70, 105
Bibb, Eric 1951— 49, 123
Bibb, Henry 1815–1854 54
Bibb, Mary 1820–1877 54
Bickerstaff, Bernard Tyrone 1944—
21
Big Bank Hank See Sugarhill Gang,
The

Big Boi See Patton, Antwan
Big Daddy Kane 1968— 79
Big Freedia 1981(?)— 128
Big G See Glover, Anwan
Big L 1974–1999 120
Big Maybelle 1924–1972 117
Big Sean 1977— 96
Big Youth 1949— 107
Biggers, John 1924–2001 20, 33
Biggers, Sanford 1970— 62
Bigirimana, Gael 1993— 115
Biko, Stephen See Biko, Steven
(Bantu)
Biko, Steven (Bantu) 1946–1977 4
Bilal 1979— 101
Billingslea, Joe See Contours, The
Billong, Alexandre Dimitri Song See
Song, Alex
Billops, Camille 1933— 82
Billy Ward and the Dominoes 105
bin Wahad, Dhoruba 1943— 85
Bing, Dave 1943— 3, 59, 78
Bingham, Howard 1939— 96
Birch, Adolpho A., Jr. 1932— 85
Birch, Glynn R. 195(?)— 61
Birdman 1969— 110
Birdsong, Cindy 1939— 113
Birra, Ali 1948— 113
Bishop, Eric See Foxx, Jamie
Bishop, Maurice 1944–1983 39
Bishop, Sanford D., Jr. 1947— 24,
111
Bishop, Stephen 1820–1857 95
Bivins, Edward See Manhattans,
The
Bivins, Michael 1968— 72 See also
New Edition
Biya, Chantal 1970— 89
Biya, Paul 1933— 28, 114
Biyidi-Awala, Alexandre See Beti,
Mongo
Bizimungu, Pasteur 1951— 19
Blacc, Aloe 1979— 119
Black, Albert 1940— 51
Black, Barry C. 1948— 47
Black, Joe 1924–2002 75
Black, Keith Lanier 1957— 18, 84
Black Kold Madina See Roberts,
Kimberly Rivers
Black Thought 1972— 63
Blackburn, Robert 1920— 28
Blackman, Toni 1968— 86
Blackmon, Brenda 1952— 58
Blackmon, Larry See Cameo
Blackmore, Amos Wells See Wells,
Junior
Blackshear, Leonard 1943— 52
Blackwell, David 1919— 79
Blackwell, Gloria 1927–2010 127
Blackwell, Kenneth, Sr. 1948— 61
Blackwell, Otis 1932–2002 98
Blackwell, Robert D., Sr. 1937— 52
Blackwell, Unita 1933— 17
Blackwood, Maureen 1960— 37
Blacque, Taurean 1941— 58
Blade, Brian 1970— 88
Blair, Jayson 1976— 50
Blair, Maxine See Powell, Maxine
Blair, Paul 1944— 36
Blake, Asha 1961(?)— 26
Blake, Charles E. 1940— 82
Blake, Eubie 1883–1983 29
Blake, James 1979— 43

Blake, James Hubert *See Blake, Eubie*

Blake, John, Jr. 1947–2014 123

Blakely, Delois N. 1942(?)— 122

Blakely, Edward J. 1938— 88

Blakely, Queen Mother Dr. Delois *See Blakely, Delois N.*

Blakey, Art(hur) 1919–1990 37

Blanchard, Terence 1962— 43

Blanco, Mykki 1986(?)— 106

Bland, Bobby 1930–2013 36, 113

Bland, Bobby "Blue" *See Bland, Bobby*

Bland, Edward 1926–2013 111

Bland, Eleanor Taylor 1944–2010 39

Blanks, Billy 1955(?)— 22

Blanks, Deborah K. 1958— 69

Blanton, Dain 1971— 29

Blanton, Jimmy 1918–1942 108

Blassingame, John Wesley 1940–2000 40

Blaylock, Ronald 1960(?)— 86

Blayton, Jesse B., Sr. 1897–1977 55

Bleu, Corbin 1989— 65

Blige, Mary J. 1971— 20, 34, 60, 97

Blind Boys of Alabama, The 99

Blitz the Ambassador 1982— 115

Blockson, Charles L. 1933— 42

Blondy, Alpha 1953— 30

Bloomer, George 1963— 86

Blow, Charles M. 1968(?)— 73

Blow, Kurtis 1959— 31, 122

Blue, Vida 1949— 122

Bluford, Guion Stewart, Jr. *See Bluford, Guy*

Bluford, Guy 1942— 2, 35

Bluitt, Juliann Stephanie 1938— 14

Boateng, Ozwald 1968(?)— 35, 113

Boateng, Paul Yaw 1951— 56

B.o.B. 1988— 91

Bobb, Robert C. 1945— 83

Bobo, Lawrence 1958— 60

Bogan, Ann *See New Birth*

Bogle, Donald 19(?)(?)— 34

Bogues, Tyrone "Muggsy" 1965— 56

Bol, Manute 1963— 1

Bolden, Buddy 1877–1931 39

Bolden, Charles Frank, Jr. 1946— 7, 78

Bolden, Charles Joseph *See Bolden, Buddy*

Bolden, Frank E. 1913–2003 44

Bolden, Tonya 1959— 32

Bolin, Jane 1908–2007 22, 59

Bolling, Allen Macon *See Allen, Macon Bolling*

Bolt, Usain 1986— 73, 104

Bolton, Terrell D. 1959(?)— 25

Bolton-Holifield, Ruthie 1967— 28

Bombino 1980— 112

Bonaly, Surya 1973— 7

Bond, Beverly 1970— 53

Bond, J. Max, Jr. 1935— 76

Bond, Julian 1940— 2, 35, 106

Bonds, Barry 1964— 6, 34, 63, 99

Bonds, Bobby 1946— 43

Bonds, Margaret 1913–1972 39

Bonet, Lisa 1967— 58

Boney, Lisa Michelle *See Bonet, Lisa*

Bonga, Kuenda 1942— 13

Bongo, Albert-Bernard *See Bongo, Omar*

Bongo, Ali Ben 1959— 80

Bongo, Omar 1935–2009 1, 79

Bonheur, Yannick 1982— 84

Bonner, Leroy 1943–2013 113

Bonney, Tabi 1978(?)— 98

Bontemps, Arna(ud Wendell) 1902–1973 8

Booker, Cory Anthony 1969— 68

Booker, Simeon 1918— 23

Bootie Brown *See Pharcyde, The*

Boozer, Bob 1937–2012 103

Borders, James (Buchanan, IV) 1949— 9

Borders, William Holmes 1905–1993 94

Boseman, Chadwick 1982— 111

Bosh, Chris 1984— 85

Bosley, Freeman (Robertson), Jr. 1954— 7

Bossard, Henry K. *See Swan Silvertones, The*

Bostic, Earl 1913–1965 121

Bostic, Eugene Earl *See Bostic, Earl*

Bostic, Joe 1909–1988 95

Boston, Kelvin E. 1955(?)— 25

Boston, Lloyd 1970(?)— 24

Boulogne, Joseph, Chevalier de Saint-Georges 1745(?)–1799 94

Boulware, Harold R. 1913–1983 109

Bow Wow 1987— 35

Bowe, Riddick 1967— 6, 107

Bowen, John W. E., Sr. 1855–1933 89

Bowen, Ruth 1924–2009 83

Bowles, Cephas 1952–2015 127

Bowles, Todd 1963— 128

Bowman, Bertie 1931— 71

Bowman, Herbert *See Bowman, Bertie*

Bowser, Yvette Lee 1965(?)— 17

Boyd, Edward 1914–2007 70

Boyd, Eva Narcissus *See Little Eva*

Boyd, Gerald M. 1950–2006 32, 59

Boyd, Gwendolyn 1955— 49

Boyd, John W., Jr. 1965— 20, 72

Boyd, Melba Joyce 1950— 86

Boyd, Steven *See Dramatics, The*

Boyd, Suzanne 1963— 52

Boyd, T(heophilus) B(artholomew), III 1947— 6

Boye, Madior 1940— 30

Boykin, Keith 1965— 14

Boykin, Otis 1920–1982 92

Boykin, Phillip 1968— 102

Boyz II Men 82

Bozella, Dewey 1959— 97

Bozizé, François 1946— 96, 117

Bracken, James 1909–1972 107

Bracken, Vivian 1921–1989 107

Bradford, Alex 1927–1978 121

Bradford, Mark 1961— 89

Bradley, Adam 1974— 101

Bradley, Alton *See Golden Gate Quartet*

Bradley, Charles 1948— 126

Bradley, David Henry, Jr. 1950— 39

Bradley, Ed 1941–2006 2, 59

Bradley, J. Robert 1919–2007 65

Bradley, Jennette B. 1952— 40

Bradley, Thomas 1917— 2, 20

Bradshaw, Myron C. *See Bradshaw, Tiny*

Bradshaw, Tiny 1907–1958 102

Brady, St. Elmo 1884–1966 107

Brady, Wayne 1972— 32, 71

Brae, C. Michael 1963(?)— 61

Braithwaite, William Stanley 1878–1962 52

Bramlett, Joseph 1988— 91

Branch, William Blackwell 1927— 39

Brand, Dionne 1953— 32

Brand, Elton 1979— 31

Brandon, Barbara 1960(?)— 3

Brandon, Thomas Terrell 1970— 16

Brandy 1979— 14, 34, 72

Branham, George, III 1962— 50

Branson, Herman 1914–1995 87

Brashear, Carl Maxie 1931— 29

Brashear, Donald 1972— 39

Brathwaite, Fred 1972— 35

Brathwaite, Kamau 1930— 36

Brathwaite, Lawson Edward *See Kamau Brathwaite*

Braugher, Andre 1962— 13, 58, 91

Braun, Carol Moseley 1947— 4, 42

Brawley, Benjamin 1882–1939 44

Braxton, Anthony 1945— 128

Braxton, Brad 1969(?)— 77

Braxton, Gene *See Herndon, Angelo*

Braxton, Toni 1967— 15, 61, 91

Brazier, Arthur M. 1921–2010 115

Brazile, Donna 1959— 25, 70

Breaux, Christopher *See Ocean, Frank*

Breed, Eric T. *See MC Breed*

Breed, MC *See MC Breed*

Breedlove, Sarah *See Walker, Madame C. J.*

Breeze, Jean "Binta" 1956— 37

Brembly, Paul *See Golden Gate Quartet*

Brewer, Rosalind 1962— 100

Brewster, T. L. *See Soul Stirrers*

Brewster, W. Herbert 1897(?)–1987 128

Brewster, William Herbert *See Brewster, W. Herbert*

Bridges, Christopher *See Ludacris*

Bridges, Leon 1990(?)— 126

Bridges, Ruby 1954— 77

Bridges, Sheila 1964— 36

Bridges, Todd 1965— 37

Bridgetower, George 1780(?)–1860 78

Bridgewater, Dee Dee 1950— 32, 92

Bridgforth, Glinda 1952— 36

Briggs, Curtis 1952(?)— 84

Brigitha, Enith 1955— 126

Brim, John 1922–2003 117

Brimm, Charles E. 1924–2010 105

Brimmer, Andrew 1926–2012 2, 48, 106

Briscoe, Connie 1952— 15

Briscoe, Marlin 1946(?)— 37

Britt, Donna 1954(?)— 28

Broadbent, Hydeia 1984— 36

Brock, Lou 1939— 18

Brock, Michael *See Dramatics, The*

Brock, Roslyn McCallister 1965— 86

Brodie, Roosevelt *See Harold Melvin & the Blue Notes*

Bromery, Randolph Wilson 1926— 85

Broner, Adrien 1989— 109

Bronner, Nathaniel H., Sr. 1914–1993 32

Brooke, Edward W. 1919–2015 8, 88, 126

Brookins, Hamel Hartford 1925–2012 102

Brooks, Aaron 1976— 33

Brooks, Avery 1948— 9, 98

Brooks, Danielle 1989— 119

Brooks, Derrick 1973— 43, 119

Brooks, Golden 1970— 62

Brooks, Gwendolyn 1917–2000 1, 28

Brooks, Hadda 1916–2002 40

Brooks, Mehcad 1980— 62

Brooks, Orville *See Golden Gate Quartet*

Brooks, Robert Calvin *See Bland, Bobby*

Brooks, Roy 1938–2005 125

Brooks, Tyrone 1945— 59

Broonzy, Big Bill 1893–1958 82

Brother Blue *See Hill, Hugh Morgan*

Brower, William 1916–2004 49

Brown, Aaquil *See Rae Sremmurd*

Brown, Aja 1982— 115

Brown, Alvin 1963— 96

Brown, Angela M. 1964(?)— 54

Brown, Anne 1912–2009 76

Brown, Anthony G. 1961— 72

Brown, Antron 1976— 85

Brown, Beverly *See Dixie Cups, The*

Brown, Bill *See Billy Ward and the Dominoes*

Brown, Bobby 1969— 58, 124 *See also New Edition*

Brown, Buck *See Brown, Robert*

Brown, Byrd 1930–2001 49

Brown, Byron W. 1958— 72

Brown, Carlinhos 1962— 81

Brown, Cecil M. 1943— 46

Brown, Charles 1922–1999 23

Brown, Charlotte Hawkins 1883–1961 106

Brown, Chris 1989— 74, 109

Brown, Chuck 1936–2012 78, 102

Brown, Clarence Gatemouth 1924–2005 59

Brown, Claude 1937–2002 38

Brown, Clifford 1930–1956 86

Brown, Cora 1914–1972 33

Brown, Corrine 1946— 24, 90

Brown, Cupcake 1964— 63

Brown, Dennis 1957–1999 99

Brown, Donald 1963— 19

Brown, Eddie C. 1940— 35

Brown, Elaine 1943— 8

Brown, Ernest 1916–2009 80

Brown, Erroll M. 1950(?)— 23

Brown, Foxy 1979— 25

Brown, Frederick J. 1945–2012 102

Brown, George Leslie 1926–2006 62

Brown, H. Rap *See Al-Amin, Jamil Abdullah*

Brown, Hallie Quinn 1850(?)–1949 **100**

Brown, Harley *See Dramatics, The*

Brown, Homer S. 1896–1977 **47**

Brown, Hubert Gerold *See Al-Amin, Jamil Abdullah*

Brown, James 1933–2006 **15, 60**

Brown, James 1951— **22**

Brown, James Mack *See Dramatics, The*

Brown, James Nathaniel *See Brown, Jim*

Brown, James Willie, Jr. *See Komunyakaa, Yusef*

Brown, Jamie Foster 19(?)(?)— **91**

Brown, Janice Rogers 1949— **43**

Brown, Jason 1983— **125**

Brown, Jerry 1987–2012 **117**

Brown, Jesse 1944–2003 **6, 41**

Brown, Jesse Leroy 1926–1950 **31**

Brown, Jim 1936— **11, 95**

Brown, Joe 19(?)(?)— **29**

Brown, Joyce F. 1946— **25**

Brown, Kenji *See Rose Royce*

Brown, Khalif *See Rae Sremmurd*

Brown, Kwame R. 1970— **91**

Brown, Lawrence Darrow *See Gray, Dobie*

Brown, Lee P. 1937— **1, 24, 109**

Brown, Les(lie Calvin) 1945— **5**

Brown, Lloyd Louis 1913–2003 **42**

Brown, Melanie 1975— **73**

Brown, Mike 1970— **77, 107**

Brown, Nappy 1929–2008 **73**

Brown, Oliver Leon 1918–1961 **94**

Brown, Oscar, Jr. 1926–2005 **53**

Brown, Patrick "Sleepy" 1970— **50**

Brown, Raymond 1908–1965 **102**

Brown, Robert 1936–2007 **65**

Brown, Ron(ald Harmon) 1941–1996 **5**

Brown, Ronald K. 1966— **91**

Brown, Rosemary 1930–2003 **62**

Brown, Ruth 1928–2006 **90**

Brown, Sam *See Intruders, The*

Brown, Sean 1976— **52**

Brown, Sterling Allen 1901–1989 **10, 64**

Brown, Tony 1933— **3**

Brown, Uzee 1950— **42**

Brown, Vincent *See Naughty by Nature*

Brown, Vivian 1964— **27**

Brown, Warren 1971(?)— **61**

Brown, Wesley 1945— **23**

Brown, Wesley A. 1927–2012 **102**

Brown, Willa Beatrice 1906–1992 **40**

Brown, Willard 1911(?)–1996 **36**

Brown, William Anthony *See Brown, Tony*

Brown, William Wells 1814(?)–1884 **99**

Brown, Willie 1934— **7, 85**

Brown, Zora Kramer 1949— **12**

Brown Bomber, The *See Louis, Joe*

Browne, Roscoe Lee 1925–2007 **66**

Brownlee, Lawrence 1972(?)— **88**

Broyard, Anatole 1920–1990 **68**

Broyard, Bliss 1966— **68**

Bruce, Blanche Kelso 1849–1898 **33**

Bruce, Bruce 19(?)(?)— **56**

Bruce, Isaac 1972— **26**

Brunson, Dorothy 1938— **1, 87**

Brutus, Dennis 1924— **38**

Bryan, Ashley 1923— **41, 104**

Bryant, Cullen 1951–2009 **81**

Bryant, Desmond *See Bryant, Dez*

Bryant, Dez 1988— **116**

Bryant, Jamal 1971— **128**

Bryant, John 1966— **26**

Bryant, John R. 1943— **45**

Bryant, Kimberly 1967— **127**

Bryant, Kobe 1978— **15, 31, 71, 110**

Bryant, Paul 1933–2010 **115**

Bryant, Ray 1931–2011 **95**

Bryant, Sharon *See Atlantic Starr*

Bryant, Wayne R(ichard) 1947— **6**

Bryant, William Benson 1911–2005 **61**

Bryant, William Cullen *See Bryant, Cullen*

Buchanan, Manley Augustus *See Big Youth*

Buchanan, Ray 1971— **32**

Buckley, Gail Lumet 1937— **39**

Buckley, Victoria (Vikki) 1947–1999 **24**

Buckner, Milt 1915–1977 **110**

Budden, Joe 1980— **108**

Budden, Joseph Anthony, II *See Budden, Joe*

Buery, Richard, Jr. 1972— **97**

Buff Love *See Fat Boys*

Buhari, Muhammadu 1942— **128**

Bulka 1972— **120**

Bulawayo, NoViolet 1981— **125**

Bullard, Eugene Jacques 1894–1961 **12**

Bullard, Robert D. 1946— **121**

Bullins, Ed 1935— **25, 121**

Bullock, Anna Mae *See Turner, Tina*

Bullock, Steve 1936— **22**

Bully Cummings, Ella 1957(?)— **48**

Bumbry, Grace (Ann) 1937— **5**

Bun B 1973— **123**

Bunch, Lonnie G., III 1952— **91**

Bunche, Ralph J(ohnson) 1904–1971 **5**

Bunkley, Anita Richmond 19(?)(?)— **39**

Burbridge, Kofi 1961— **120**

Burbridge, Oteil 1964— **120**

Buress, Hannibal 1983— **101**

Burgess, John 1909–2003 **46**

Burgess, Kevin Elijah *See KB*

Burgess, Marjorie L. 1929— **55**

Burgess, Marlina *See Shaw, Marlena*

Burke, Clarence, Jr. 1949–2013 **112**

Burke, Glenn 1952–1995 **122**

Burke, Selma Hortense 1900–1995 **16**

Burke, Solomon 1940— **31, 86**

Burke, Yvonne Brathwaite 1932— **42**

Burkett, Ben 1951— **123**

Burks, Juanita P. 1920— **95**

Burks, Mary Fair 1920–1991 **40**

Burleigh, Henry Thacker 1866–1949 **56**

Burley, Dan 1907–1962 **96**

Burley, Mary Lou *See Williams, Mary Lou*

Burnett, Charles 1944— **16, 68**

Burnett, Chester Arthur *See Howlin' Wolf*

Burnett, Dorothy 1905–1995 **19**

Burnham, Forbes 1923–1985 **66**

Burnim, Mickey L. 1949— **48**

Burning Spear 194(?)— **79**

Burns, Anthony 1834–1862 **102**

Burns, Eddie 1928— **44**

Burns, Jesse Louis *See Jackson, Jesse*

Burns, Ursula 1958— **60**

Burnside, R. L. 1926–2005 **56**

Burrell, Orville Richard *See Shaggy*

Burrell, Stanley Kirk *See M.C. Hammer*

Burrell, Tom 1939— **21, 51**

Burris, Chuck 1951— **21**

Burris, Roland W. 1937— **25, 75**

Burroughs, Margaret Taylor 1917— **9**

Burroughs, Nannie Helen 1879(?)–1961 **96**

Burrows, Stephen 1943— **31**

Burrus, William Henry "Bill" 1936— **45**

Burruss, Kandi *See Kandi*

Burt-Murray, Angela 1970— **59**

Burton, Bill 1977— **96**

Burton, LeVar 1957— **8**

Burwell, Bryan 1955— **83**

Busby, Jheryl 1949–2008 **3, 74**

Bush, Charles Vernon 1939–2012 **125**

Bush, Gordon 1942— **82**

Bush, Reggie 1985— **59, 88**

Bushwick Bill *See Geto Boys*

Buthelezi, Mangosuthu Gatsha 1928— **9**

Butler, George, Jr. 1931–2008 **70**

Butler, Henry 1949— **121**

Butler, Ishmael *See Shabazz Palaces*

Butler, Jorry 1939— **26**

Butler, Jonathan 1961— **28**

Butler, Leroy, III 1968— **17**

Butler, Louis 1952— **70**

Butler, Octavia 1947–2006 **8, 43, 58**

Butler, Paul D. 1961— **17**

Butler, Selena Sloan 1872(?)–1964 **98**

Butts, Calvin O., III 1949— **9, 90**

Butts, Cassandra 1965— **78**

Bwino, Ndiwa *See Malawi Mouse Boys*

Bynoe, Peter C. B. 1951— **40**

Bynum, Juanita 1959— **31, 71**

Byrd, Donald 1932–2013 **109**

Byrd, Donald 1949— **10**

Byrd, Eugene 1975— **64**

Byrd, Henry Roeland *See Professor Longhair*

Byrd, Marlon 1977— **112**

Byrd, Michelle 1965— **19**

Byrd, Robert (Oliver Daniel, III) 1952— **11**

Byron, JoAnne Deborah *See Shakur, Assata*

Cabell, Enos 1949— **102**

Cables, George 1944— **125**

Cabral, Amílcar 1924–1973 **104**

Cade, Toni *See Bambara, Toni Cade*

Cadillacs **107**

Cadoria, Sherian Grace 1940— **14**

Caesar, Shirley 1938— **19**

Cage, Byron 1965(?)— **53**

Cain, Herman 1945— **15, 92**

Cain, Lorenzo 1986— **128**

Calabrese, Karyn 1947— **89**

Caldwell, Benjamin 1937— **46**

Caldwell, Earl 1941(?)— **60**

Caldwell, Jim 1955— **81**

Caldwell, Kirbyjon 1953(?)— **55**

Caldwell, Nicholas *See Whispers, The*

Caldwell, Ronnie *See Bar-Kays, The*

Calhoun, Cora *See Austin, Lovie*

Calhoun, Lillian Scott 1923–2006 **87**

Callaway, Thomas DeCarlo *See Green, Cee Lo*

Callender, Clive O(rville) 1936— **3**

Callender, Eugene 1926–2013 **119**

Callier, Terry 1945–2012 **106**

Calloway, Blanche 1902–1978 **100**

Calloway, Cab 1907–1994 **14**

Calloway, Reggie *See Midnight Star*

Calloway, Vincent *See Midnight Star*

Camara, Moussa Dadis 1964— **76**

Cameo **120**

Cameron, Earl 1917— **44**

Cameron, James 1914–2006 **80**

Camp, Georgia Blanche Douglas *See Johnson, Georgia Douglas*

Camp, Kimberly 1956— **19**

Campanella, Roy 1921–1993 **25**

Campbell, Bebe Moore 1950–2006 **6, 24, 59**

Campbell, Bill 1954— **9, 76**

Campbell, Charleszetta Lena *See Waddles, Charleszetta (Mother)*

Campbell, Donald J. 1935— **66**

Campbell, E(lmer) Simms 1906–1971 **13**

Campbell, Earl 1955— **104**

Campbell, Lucie E. 1885–1963 **118**

Campbell, Mary Schmidt 1947— **43**

Campbell, Michael Che *See Che, Michael*

Campbell, Milt 1933–2012 **113**

Campbell, Milton *See Little Milton*

Campbell, Naomi 1970— **1, 31, 120**

Campbell, Roy, Jr. 1952–2014 **118**

Campbell, Tisha *See Campbell-Martin, Tisha*

Campbell-Brown, Veronica 1982— **102**

Campbell-Martin, Tisha 1969— **8, 42**

Campbell-Williams, Lucie E. *See Campbell, Lucie E.*

Cam'ron 1976— **104**

Canada, Geoffrey 1954— **23**

Canady, Alexa 1950— **28**

Canegata, Leonard Lionel Cornelius *See Lee, Canada*

Cannon, Katie 1950— **10**

Cannon, Nick 1980— **47, 73**

Cannon, Patrick 1966— **120**

Cannon, Reuben 1946— **50**

Cano, Robinson 1982— 97
Canó Mercedes, Robinson José
  See Cano, Robinson
Cara, Irene 1959— 77
Carby, Hazel 1948— 27
Cardozo, Francis L. 1837–1903 33
Carew, Rod 1945— 20
Carey, Jake See Flamingos, The
Carey, Mariah 1970— 32, 53, 69
Carey, Zeke See Flamingos, The
Cargill, Victoria A. 19(?)(?)— 43
Carlos, John 1945— 97
Carmichael, Jerrod 1988(?)— 124
Carmichael, Stokely 1941–1998 5,
  26
Carnegie, Herbert 1919— 25
Carney, William H. 1840–1908 104
Carolina Chocolate Drops 111
Carr, James 1942–2001 117
Carr, Johnnie 1911–2008 69
Carr, Keela 1973— 74
Carr, Kurt 196(?)— 56
Carr, Leroy 1905–1935 49
Carroll, Diahann 1935— 9
Carroll, Earl See Cadillacs
Carroll, L. Natalie 1950— 44
Carroll, Porter, Jr. See Atlantic Starr
Carroll, Rocky 1963— 74
Carroll, Vinnette 1922— 29
Carruthers, George R. 1939— 40
Carson, André 1974— 69
Carson, Ben 1951— 1, 35, 76, 128
Carson, Johnnie 1943— 85
Carson, Josephine See Baker, Jo-
  sephine
Carson, Julia 1938–2007 23, 69
Carson, Lisa Nicole 1969— 21
Carter, Anson 1974— 24
Carter, Ben See Ben-Israel, Ben
  Ami
Carter, Benny 1907–2003 46
Carter, Betty 1930— 19
Carter, Bo See Mississippi Sheiks
Carter, Butch 1958— 27
Carter, Cris 1965— 21, 109
Carter, Dwayne Michael, Jr. See Lil
  Wayne
Carter, Edward A., Jr. 1916–1963
  104
Carter, Herbert E. 1919–2012 108
Carter, Hurricane See Carter, Rubin
Carter, Jill P. 1964— 110
Carter, Joe 1960— 30
Carter, Johnny See Dells, The; Fla-
  mingos, The
Carter, Joye Maureen 1957— 41
Carter, Kenneth 1959(?)— 53
Carter, Majora 1966— 77
Carter, Mandy 1946— 11
Carter, Martin 1927–1997 49
Carter, Nell 1948–2003 39
Carter, Pamela Lynn 1949— 67
Carter, Regina 1966(?)— 23
Carter, Rob See Dramatics, The
Carter, Robert L. 1917–2012 51,
  100
Carter, Ron 1937— 104
Carter, Rubin 1937–2014 26, 121
Carter, Shawn Corey See Jay-Z
Carter, Stephen L(isle) 1954— 4
Carter, Troy 1973(?)— 98
Carter, Vince 1977— 26
Carter, Warrick L. 1942— 27

Cartey, Wilfred 1931–1992 47
Cartiér, Xam Wilson 1949— 41
Carver, George Washington
  1861(?)–1943 4
Cary, Lorene 1956— 3
Cary, Mary Ann Shadd 1823–1893
  30
Casel, Nitanju Bolade See Sweet
  Honey in the Rock
Casey, Brandon See Jagged Edge
Casey, Brian See Jagged Edge
Cash, Nayvadius See Future
Cash, Rosalind 1938–1995 28
Cash, Swin 1979— 59
Cashin, Sheryll 1962— 63
CasSelle, Malcolm 1970— 11
Castor, Jimmy 1940–2012 100
Catchings, Tamika 1979— 43
Cathey, Reg E. 1958— 122
Catlett, Elizabeth 1915–2012 2, 120
Catto, Octavius V. 1839–1871 83
Cauley, Ben See Bar-Kays, The
Caymmi, Dorival 1914–2008 72
Cayton, Horace 1903–1970 26
Cedric the Entertainer 1964— 29,
  60, 115
Cee Lo See Green, Cee Lo
Celestin, Joe See Celestin,
  Josaphat
Celestin, Josaphat 1956— 101
Cenac, Wyatt 1976— 94
Cepeda, Orlando 1937— 98
Cephus, Kiari See Migos
Césaire, Aimé 1913–2008 48, 69
Chadiha, Jeffri 1970— 57
Chaka Chaka, Yvonne 1965— 112
Chalmers, Almario See Chalmers,
  Mario
Chalmers, Mario 1986— 122
Cham, Adongo Agada Akway
  1954(?)— 77
Chamberlain, Wilt 1936–1999 18,
  47
Chambers, George See Chambers
  Brothers, The
Chambers, James See Cliff, Jimmy
Chambers, Joe See Chambers
  Brothers, The
Chambers, Julius (LeVonne)
  1936— 3
Chambers, Lester See Chambers
  Brothers, The
Chambers, Paul 1935–1969 121
Chambers, Willie See Chambers
  Brothers, The
Chambers Brothers, The 116
Chamillionaire 1979— 82
Champion, Betty Jean See Swann,
  Bettye
Chandler, Gene 1937— 105
Chandler, Tyson 1982— 114
Chaney, Don 1946— 98
Chaney, John 1932— 67
Channer, Colin 1963— 36
Chanté, Keshia 1988— 50
Chantels, The 128
Chanticleer, Raven 1928–2002 91
Chapman, Nathan A., Jr. 1957— 21
Chapman, Susan E. 1968— 94
Chapman, Tracy 1964— 26
Chappell, Emma C. 1941— 18
Chappell, Roy M. 1921–2002 95
Chappelle, Dave 1973— 50, 115

Charlemagne, Emmanuel See
  Charlemagne, Manno
Charlemagne, Manno 1948— 11
Charles, Ezzard 1921–1975 95
Charles, John 1944–2002 108
Charles, Mary Eugenia 1919–2005
  10, 55
Charles, Pierre 1954–2004 52
Charles, Ray 1930–2004 16, 48
Charleston, Oscar 1896–1954 39
Chase, Debra Martin 1956— 49, 96
Chase, John Saunders, Jr. 1925—
  99
Chase, Leah 1923— 57
Chase-Riboud, Barbara 1939— 20,
  46
Chatard, Peter 1936— 44
Chatman, John Len See Memphis
  Slim
Chatmon, Bo See Mississippi
  Sheiks
Chatmon, Lonnie See Mississippi
  Sheiks
Chatmon, Sam See Mississippi
  Sheiks
Chavis, Benjamin (Franklin, Jr.)
  1948— 6
Che, Michael 1983— 123
Chea, Alvin See Take 6
Cheadle, Don 1964— 19, 52
Cheatham, Doc 1905–1997 17
Checker, Chubby 1941— 28
Cheeks, Maurice 1956— 47, 106
Chenault, John 1952— 40
Chenault, Kenneth 1951— 4, 36,
  108
Cheney-Coker, Syl 1945— 43
Cheruiyot, Robert 1978— 69
Cherry, Deron 1959— 40
Cherry, Don 1936–1995 119
Cherry, Nicole See Marian Ander-
  son String Quartet
Chesimard, JoAnne (Deborah) See
  Shakur, Assata
Chesnutt, Charles 1858–1932 29
Chester, Brenda See DoHarris,
  Brenda
Chestnut, J. L., Jr. 1930–2008 73
Chestnut, Morris 1969— 31, 116
Chew, Robert F. 1960–2013 109
Chic 117
Chideya, Farai 1969— 14, 61
Chief Black Thunderbird Eagle See
  York, Dwight D.
Chief Keef 1995— 112
Chikoti, Shadreck 1979— 125
Childers, Lulu Vere 1870–1946 95
Childress, Alice 1920–1994 15
Childress, Alvin 1907–1986 114
Chiles, Nick 1965— 98
Chi-Lites 106
Chiluba, Frederick 1943— 56, 80
Chineworth, Mary Alice 1917— 79
Chinn, May Edward 1896–1980 26
Chisholm, Daquan 1993— 93
Chisholm, Samuel J. 1942— 32
Chisholm, Shirley 1924–2005 2, 50
Chissano, Joaquim 1939— 7, 55,
  67
Chitalu, Godfrey 1947–1993 108
Chong, Rae Dawn 1961— 62
Christian, Barbara T. 1946–2000 44
Christian, Jodie 1932-2012 103
Christian, Spencer 1947— 15

Christian-Green, Donna M. 1945—
  17
Christie, Angella 36
Christie, Linford 1960— 8
Christie, Perry Gladstone 1944—
  53
Christie, Ron 1969(?)— 83
Christophe, Henri 1767–1820 9
Chronixx 1992— 123
Chuck D 1960— 9 See also Public
  Enemy
Church, Bruce See Bruce, Bruce
Churchill, Tony See New Birth
Churchwell, Robert, Sr. 1917–2009
  76
Chweneyagae, Presley 1984— 63
Ciara 1985— 56, 115
Ciara, Barbara 195(?)— 69
Cissé, Souleymane See Souley-
  mane, Mahamane
Clack, Zoanne 1968(?)— 73
Claiborne, Loretta 1953— 34
Chancler, Leon See Chancler,
  Ndugu
Chancler, Ndugu 1952— 115
Clarence 13X 1928–1969 126
Clark, Carl 1916— 101
Clark, Celeste (Clesteen) Abraham
  1953— 15
Clark, Conrad Yeatis See Clark,
  Sonny
Clark, Joe 1939— 1
Clark, John Pepper See Clark-
  Bekedermo, J. P.
Clark, Kenneth B. 1914–2005 5, 52
Clark, Kristin See Taylor, Kristin
  Clark
Clark, Mamie Phipps 1917–1983 79
Clark, Mattie Moss 1925–1994 61
Clark, Patrick 1955— 14
Clark, Ray 1931–2014 122
Clark, Septima (Poinsette)
  1898–1987 7
Clark, Sharón 1961— 105
Clark, Sonny 1931–1963 128
Clark, Wahida 19(?)(?)— 107
Clark, Yvonne Young 1929— 95
Clark-Bekedermo, J. P. 1935— 44
Clark-Cole, Dorinda 1957— 66
Clarke, Anna Mac 1919–1944 95
Clarke, Austin C. 1934— 32
Clarke, Cheryl 1947— 32
Clarke, George Elliott 1960— 32
Clarke, Hope 1943(?)— 14
Clarke, John Henrik 1915–1998 20
Clarke, Kenny 1914–1985 27
Clarke, Patrice Francise See Wash-
  ington, Patrice Clarke
Clarke, Peter See Peters, Clarke
Clarke, Stanley 1951— 115
Clarke, Yvette 1964— 92
Clark-Sheard, Karen 1960— 22,
  114
Clash, Kevin 1960— 14, 93
Clay, Bryan 1980— 57, 74
Clay, Cassius Marcellus, Jr. See
  Ali, Muhammad
Clay, Otis 1942— 112
Clay, William Lacy 1931— 8
Clay, William Lacy, Jr. 1956— 95
Clayton, Constance 1937— 1
Clayton, Doctor 1898–1947 120
Clayton, Eva M. 1934— 20
Clayton, Gerald 1984— 111

Clayton, Mayme Agnew 1923–2006 **62**

Clayton, Merry 1948— **112**

Clayton, Peter Joe *See Clayton, Doctor*

Clayton, Xernona 1930— **3, 45**

Claytor, Helen 1907–2005 **14, 52**

Cleage, Albert B., Jr. *See Agyeman, Jaramogi Abebe*

Cleage, Pearl 1948— **17, 64**

Clear, Duval *See Masta Ace*

Cleaver, Eldridge 1935— **5**

Cleaver, Emanuel, II 1944— **4, 45, 68, 107**

Cleaver, Kathleen Neal 1945— **29**

Cleighton, Peter Joe *See Clayton, Doctor*

Clemente, Rosa 1972— **74**

Clement-Holmes, Linda 1962— **94**

Clements, George (Harold) 1932— **2**

Clemmons, Reginal G. 19(?)(?)— **41**

Clemons, Clarence 1942— **41**

Clemons, Michael "Pinball" 1965— **64**

Clendenon, Donn 1935–2005 **26, 56**

Cleveland, James 1932(?)–1991 **19**

Cliff, Jimmy 1948— **28, 92**

Cliff, Michelle 1946— **42**

Clifton, Lucille 1936–2010 **14, 64, 91**

Clifton, Nathaniel "Sweetwater" 1922(?)–1990 **47**

Clinkscale, Aja Lena *See Brown, Aja*

Clinton, George 1941— **9, 93**

Clovers, The **104**

Clyburn, James E. 1940— **21, 71, 118**

Clyburn, Mignon 1962— **78**

C-Murder 1971— **99**

Coachman, Alice 1923–2014 **18, 123**

Coasters, The **102**

Coates, Dorothy Love 1928–2002 **125**

Coates, Ta-Nehisi 1975— **76**

Cobb, Arnett 1918–1989 **114**

Cobb, Jewel Plummer 1924— **42**

Cobb, Jimmy 1929— **119**

Cobb, Monty *See Cobb, W. Montague*

Cobb, W. Montague 1904–1990 **39**

Cobb, William Anthony *See Cobb, William Jelani*

Cobb, William Jelani 1969— **59, 121**

Cobbs, Bill 1934— **101**

Cobbs, Natasha *See Cobbs, Tasha*

Cobbs, Price M(ashaw) 1928— **9**

Cobbs, Tasha 1981— **114**

Cobham, Billy 1944— **123**

Cobham, William Emanuel, Jr. *See Cobham, Billy*

Cochran, Johnnie 1937–2005 **11, 39, 52**

Cockrel, Kenneth V., Jr. 1965— **79**

Cockrel, Kenneth Vern, Sr. 1938–1989 **79**

CoCo Brother 19(?)(?)— **93**

Cody, Radmilla 1975— **99**

Coggins, Danny *See Moonglows, The*

Cohen, Anthony 1963— **15**

Cohen, Cathy J. 1962— **88**

Coke, Christopher 1969— **108**

Colbert, Thomas *See Colbert, Tom*

Colbert, Tom 1949— **115**

Colbert, Virgis William 1939— **17**

Cole, Ashley 1980— **106**

Cole, Cozy 1909–1981 **123**

Cole, Ernest 1940–1990 **123**

Cole, Freddy 1931— **128**

Cole, J. 1985— **97**

Cole, Johnnetta B(etsch) 1936— **5, 43**

Cole, Keyshia 1981— **63, 107**

Cole, Lionel Frederick *See Cole, Freddy*

Cole, Lorraine 195(?)— **48**

Cole, Maria 1922–2012 **104**

Cole, Nat "King" 1919–1965 **17**

Cole, Natalie 1950— **17, 60, 84**

Cole, Rebecca 1846–1922 **38**

Cole, Teju 1975— **120**

Cole, William Randolph *See Cole, Cozy*

Coleman, Ashley Antoinette Snell *See Ashley & JaQuavis*

Coleman, Beatrice 1904–2014 **120**

Coleman, Bessie 1892–1926 **9**

Coleman, Bonnie Watson *See Watson Coleman, Bonnie*

Coleman, Chad L. 196(?)— **128**

Coleman, Denardo 1956— **122**

Coleman, Donald 1952— **24, 62**

Coleman, Gary 1968–2010 **35, 86**

Coleman, George 1935— **106**

Coleman, James E., Jr. 1948(?)— **79**

Coleman, JaQuavis Javon *See Ashley & JaQuavis*

Coleman, Ken 1942— **57**

Coleman, Lamont *See Big L*

Coleman, Leonard S., Jr. 1949— **12**

Coleman, Mary 1946— **46**

Coleman, Michael B. 1954— **28, 79**

Coleman, Ornette 1930— **39, 69**

Coleman, Ornette Denardo *See Coleman, Denardo*

Coleman, Ronald S. 1948— **110**

Coleman, Steve 1956— **124**

Coleman, Troy *See Cowboy Troy*

Coleman, Valerie *See Imani Winds*

Coleman, Vince 1961— **128**

Coleman, Wanda 1946–2013 **48, 119**

Coleman, William F., III 1955(?)— **61**

Coleman, William T. 1920— **76**

Colemon, Johnnie 1921(?)— **11**

Coleridge-Taylor, Samuel 1875–1912 **75**

Coles, Alice 1951(?)— **80**

Coles, Charles *See Coles, Honi*

Coles, Dennis *See Ghostface Killah*

Coles, Honi 1911–1992 **128**

Colescott, Robert 1925— **69**

Collette, Buddy 1921–2010 **119**

Collette, William Marcel *See Collette, Buddy*

Collins, Albert 1932–1993 **12**

Collins, Barbara-Rose 1939— **7, 87**

Collins, Bootsy 1951— **31**

Collins, Cardiss 1931–2013 **10, 80, 120**

Collins, Clarence *See Little Anthony & the Imperials*

Collins, Janet 1917–2003 **33, 64**

Collins, Jason 1978— **111**

Collins, Lyn 1948–2005 **53**

Collins, Marva 1936— **3, 71**

Collins, Patricia Hill 1948— **67**

Collins, Paul 1936— **61**

Collins, William *See Collins, Bootsy*

Colston, Hal 1953(?)— **72**

Colter, Cyrus J. 1910–2002 **36**

Coltrane, Alice 1937–2007 **70**

Coltrane, John William 1926–1967 **19**

Coltrane, Ravi 1965— **71**

Combs, Sean 1969— **17, 43, 92**

Comer, James P(ierpont) 1934— **6**

Commodores, The **118**

Common 1972— **31, 63, 98**

Compaore, Blaise 1951— **87**

Compton, John 1925–2007 **65**

Compton-Rock, Malaak 1969— **86**

Concha Buika *See Buika*

Condé, Alpha 1938— **95**

Condrey, Cory *See CoCo Brother*

Cone, James H. 1938— **3, 82**

Coney, PonJola 1951— **48**

Conley, Nellie *See Madame Sul-Te-Wan*

Conneh, Sekou Damate, Jr. 1960— **51**

Connerly, Ward 1939— **14**

Connor, William *See Swan Silvertones, The*

Conrad, Barbara Smith 1940(?)— **90**

Conrad, Cecilia A. 1955— **94**

Consolers, The **125**

Conté, Lansana 1934(?)–2008 **7, 76**

Contee, Cheryl 1971— **88**

Contours, The **109**

Conyers, John, Jr. 1929— **4, 45, 111**

Conyers, Monica 1964— **85**

Conyers, Nathan G. 1932— **24**

Coogler, Ryan 1986— **114**

Cook, Charles "Doc" 1891–1958 **44**

Cook, Herman *See Cook, Junior*

Cook, Junior 1934–1992 **126**

Cook, (Will) Mercer 1903–1987 **40**

Cook, Samuel DuBois 1928— **14**

Cook, Suzan D. Johnson 1957— **22**

Cook, Toni 1944— **23**

Cook, Victor Trent *See Three Mo' Tenors*

Cook, Wesley *See Abu-Jamal, Mumia*

Cook, Will Marion 1869–1944 **40**

Cooke, Charles L. *See Cook, Charles "Doc"*

Cooke, Marcia 1954— **60**

Cooke, Marvel 1901(?)–2000 **31**

Cooke, Sam 1931–1964 **17** *See also Soul Stirrers*

Cook-Parrish, Mary Virginia 1862(?)–1945 **95**

Cooks, Patricia 1944–1989 **19**

Coolio 1963— **103**

Cools, Anne 1943— **64**

Coombs, Orde M. 1939–1984 **44**

Cooper, Afua 1957— **53**

Cooper, Andrew Lewis *See Cooper, Andy "Lefty"*

Cooper, Andrew W. 1928–2002 **36**

Cooper, Andy "Lefty" 1898–1941 **63**

Cooper, Anna Julia 1858–1964 **20**

Cooper, Barry 1956— **33**

Cooper, Charles "Chuck" 1926–1984 **47**

Cooper, Charles Theodore *See Cooper, Tarzan*

Cooper, Chuck 1954— **75**

Cooper, Cynthia *See Cooper-Dyke, Cynthia*

Cooper, Edward S(awyer) 1926— **6**

Cooper, Evern 19(?)(?)— **40**

Cooper, Helene 1966— **74**

Cooper, J. California 1931–2014 **12, 85, 125**

Cooper, Jeffrey *See Midnight Star*

Cooper, Joan *See Cooper, J. California*

Cooper, Lisa 1963— **73**

Cooper, Marcus *See Pleasure P*

Cooper, Margaret J. 194(?)— **46**

Cooper, Michael 1956— **31**

Cooper, Tarzan 1907–1980 **96**

Cooper Cafritz, Peggy 1947— **43**

Cooper-Dyke, Cynthia 1963— **17, 89**

Copeland, Johnny 1937–1997 **110**

Copeland, Kenny *See Rose Royce*

Copeland, Michael 1954— **47**

Copeland, Misty 1982— **125**

Copeland, Shemekia 1979— **110**

Coppola, Imani Francesca 1978— **82**

Corbi, Lana 1955— **42**

Corbin, Tyrone 1962— **126**

Corley, Tony 1949— **62**

Cornelius, Don 1936–2012 **4, 100**

Cornish, Sam 1935— **50**

Cornwell, Edward E., III 1956— **70**

Correia, Antoné De'Jaun *See Correia, De'Jaun*

Correia, De'Jaun 1994— **93**

Cortez, Jayne 1934–2012 **43, 109**

Corthron, Kia 1961— **43**

Cortor, Eldzier 1916— **42**

Cosby, Bill 1937— **7, 26, 59, 125**

Cosby, Camille 1945— **14, 80**

Cosby, William Henry, Jr. *See Cosby, Bill*

Cose, Ellis 1951— **5, 50, 118**

Cosey, Pete 1943–2012 **103**

Cosey, Peter Palus *See Cosey, Pete*

Cotter, Joseph Seamon, Sr. 1861–1949 **40**

Cotton, James 1935— **123**

Cottrell, Comer 1931— **11**

Counce, Curtis 1926–1963 **127**

Council, LaVerne 1961(?)— **94**

Count Basie 1904–1984 **23**

Counter, S. Allen 1944— **74**

Courtney, Opal, Jr. *See Spaniels, The*

Cousin, Ertharin 1957— **115**

Cousins, DeMarcus 1990— **108**

Couto, Mia 1955— **45**

Covay, Don 1936–2015 **127**

Coverley, Louise Bennett See Bennett, Louise
Cowans, Adger W. 1936— 20
Cowboy Troy, 1970— 54
Cox, Bryan 1968— 83
Cox, Deborah 1974(?)— 28
Cox, Donald Lee 1936–2011 93
Cox, Elbert Frank 1895–1969 111
Cox, Ida 1896–1967 42
Cox, Joseph Mason Andrew 1930— 51
Cox, Laverne 198(?)— 122
Cox, Renée 1960— 67
Cox, Roderick Leverne See Cox, Laverne
Cox, William E. 1942— 68
Cozart, Keith See Chief Keef
Craig, Carl 1969— 31, 71
Craig-Jones, Ellen Walker 1906–2000 44
Crain, S. R. See Soul Stirrers
Crawford, Carl 1981— 90
Crawford, Hank 1934–2009 77
Crawford, Randy 1952— 19
Crawford, Veronica See Crawford, Randy
Cray, Robert 1953— 30
Creagh, Milton 1957— 27
Cream, Arnold Raymond See Walcott, Jersey Joe
Crennel, Romeo 1947— 54, 107
Crenshaw, Kimberlé Williams 1959— 88
Crenshaw, Robert See Swan Silvertones, The
Crew, Rudolph F. See Crew, Rudy
Crew, Rudy 1950— 16, 113
Crew, Spencer R. 1949— 55
Crews, Terrence Alan See Crews, Terry
Crews, Terry 1968— 123
Crichlow, Ernest 1914–2005 75
Crisp, Coco 1979— 109
Crisp, Covelli Loyce See Crisp, Coco
Criss, Anthony See Naughty by Nature
Criss, Sonny 1927–1977 128
Criss, William See Criss, Sonny
Crite, Allan Rohan 1910–2007 29
Croal, N'Gai 1972— 76
Crocker, Frankie 1937–2000 29
Crockett, George W., Jr. 1909–1997 10, 64
Cromartie, Antonio 1984— 115
Crooks, Garth 1958— 53
Croom, Sylvester 1954— 50
Cross, Dolores E. 1938— 23
Crosthwait, David 1892–1976 93
Crothers, Benjamin Sherman See Crothers, Scatman
Crothers, Scatman 1910–1986 19
Crouch, Andraé 1942–2015 27, 115, 126
Crouch, Hubert 1906–1980 95
Crouch, Stanley 1945— 11, 87
Crowder, Henry 1895–1954(?) 16
Crowdy, William Saunders 1847–1908 109
Crudup, Arthur 1905–1974 115
Crudup, Big Boy See Crudup, Arthur
Crum, George 1822–1914 101
Crume, Arthur See Soul Stirrers

Crump, Lavell See Banner, David
Crump, Steven 1957— 96
Crumpler, Rebecca Lee 1831–1895 89
Crusaders, The 116
Cruse, Harold 1916–2005 54
Crutchfield, James N. 1947— 55
Cruz, Taio 1983— 104
Cruz, Victor 1986— 107
Cuffe, Paul 1759–1817 98
Cullen, Countee 1903–1946 8
Cullers, Vincent T. 1924(?)–2003 49
Culp, Curley 1946— 110
Culp, Napoleon Brown Goodson See Brown, Nappy
Culpepper, Daunte 1977— 32, 85
Cummings, Elijah E. 1951— 24, 102
Cuney, William Waring 1906–1976 44
Cunningham, Carl See Bar-Kays, The
Cunningham, Evelyn 1916–2010 23, 85
Cunningham, Randall 1963— 23
Cunningham, Roy See Bar-Kays, The
Curling, Alvin 1939— 34
Curren$y 1981— 114
Currie, Betty 1939(?)— 21
Currie, Ulysses 1937— 73
Curry, Dell 1964— 126
Curry, George E. 1947— 23
Curry, Mark 1964— 17
Curry, Michael 1968— 85
Curry, Stephen 1988— 110
Curson, Ted 1935–2012 108
Curtis, Christopher Paul 1953— 26, 113
Curtis-Hall, Vondie 1956— 17
Da Don, Polow 1978— 86
da Silva, Benedita 1942— 5
da Silva, Jorge Mário See Jorge, Seu
da Silva, Leônidas See Leônidas
da Silva Ferreira, Eusebio See Eusebio
Dabiri, John 1980(?)— 93
Dabydeen, David 1956— 48
DaCosta, YaYa 1982— 98
Dacres, Desmond Adolphus See Dekker, Desmond
Dadié, Bernard 1916— 34
Daemyon, Jerald 1970(?)— 64
D'Aguiar, Fred 1960— 50
Dailey, Ulysses Grant 1885–1961 87
Dale, Clamma 1948— 103
Daly, Marie Maynard 1921— 37
Damas, Léon-Gontran 1912–1978 46
Dameron, Tadd 1917–1965 103
Dance, Kelvin See Kitwana, Bakari
Dandala, Mvume 1951— 77
Dandridge, Dorothy 1922–1965 3
Dandridge, Ray 1913–1994 36
Dandridge, Raymond Garfield 1882–1930 45
D'Angelo 1974— 27, 123
Dangote, Aliko 1957— 124
Daniels, Billy 1915–1988 124
Daniels, Gertrude See Haynes, Trudy
Daniels, Jerry See Ink Spots, The

Daniels, Lee 1959— 36, 76
Daniels, Mel 1944— 106
Daniels, William Boone See Daniels, Billy
Daniels-Carter, Valerie 19(?)(?)— 23
Danjah, Terror 1977— 91
Danner, Margaret Esse 1915–1986 49
Danquah, Meri Nana Ama 1967— 93
Danticat, Edwidge 1969— 15, 68, 128
Dantley, Adrian 1956— 72
Dara, Olu 1941— 335
D'Arby, Terence Trent See Maitreya, Sananda
Darden, Calvin 1950— 38
Darden, Christopher 1957— 13
Darego, Agbani 1982— 52
Dash, Damon 1971— 31, 113
Dash, Darien 1972(?)— 29
Dash, Julie 1952— 4
Dash, Leon 1944— 47
Datcher, Michael 1967— 60
Dathorne, O. R. 1934— 52
Daughtry, Eugene See Intruders, The
Davenport, Arthur See Fattah, Chaka
Davenport, Charles Edward See Davenport, Cow Cow
Davenport, Cow Cow 1894–1955 115
David, Craig 1981— 31, 53
David, Keith 1954— 27
Davids, Edgar 1973— 106
Davidson, Jaye 1967(?)— 5
Davidson, Quentin See Rare Essence
Davidson, Tommy 1963(?)— 21
Davis, Alfreda See Davis Sisters, The
Davis, Allison 1902–1983 12
Davis, Altovise 1943–2009 76
Davis, Angela 1944— 5, 114
Davis, Angela J. 1956— 88
Davis, Anthony 1951— 11
Davis, Anthony 1993— 120
Davis, Anthony Moses See Beenie Man
Davis, Arthur P. 1904–1996 41
Davis, Artur 1967— 41
Davis, Audrey See Davis Sisters, The
Davis, Belva 1932— 61
Davis, Ben 1912–2013 115
Davis, Benjamin O(liver), Jr. 1912–2002 2, 43
Davis, Benjamin O(liver), Sr. 1877–1970 4
Davis, Bing 1937— 84
Davis, Carl 1934–2012 105
Davis, Charles T. 1918–1981 48
Davis, Chuck 1937— 33
Davis, Danny K. 1941— 24, 79
Davis, Doris A. 1936(?)— 100
Davis, Douglas E. See Fresh, Doug E.
Davis, Ed 1911–1999 24
Davis, Eisa 1971— 68
Davis, Erellon Benjamin See Davis, Ben
Davis, Eric 1962— 116

Davis, Ernie 1939–1963 48
Davis, Erroll B., Jr. 1944— 57
Davis, Frank Marshall 1905–1987 47
Davis, Gary 1896–1972 41
Davis, George 1939— 36
Davis, Gordon J. 1941— 76
Davis, Guy 1952— 36
Davis, Jamelia Niela See Jamelia
Davis, James E. 1962–2003 50
Davis, Lorenzo "Piper" 1917–1997 19
Davis, Mia Amber 1974–2011 94
Davis, Mike 1960— 41
Davis, Miles (Dewey, III) 1926–1991 4
Davis, Milt 1929–2008 74
Davis, Mtulazaji See Freestyle Fellowship
Davis, Nolan 1942— 45
Davis, Ossie 1917–2005 5, 50
Davis, Peylia See DeSanto, Sugar Pie
Davis, Rob See Dramatics, The
Davis, Robert Earl, Jr. See DJ Screw
Davis, Ruth See Davis Sisters, The
Davis, Ruth 1943— 37
Davis, Sammy, Jr. 1925–1990 18
Davis, Shani 1982— 58, 84
Davis, Terrell 1972— 20
Davis, Thelma See Davis Sisters, The
Davis, Theresa See Emotions, The
Davis, Thulani 1948— 61
Davis, Tyrone 1938–2005 54
Davis, Viola 1965— 34, 76, 100
Davis, Wade, Jr. 1977— 103
Davis, Wild Bill 1918–1995 114
Davis, William Strethen See Davis, Wild Bill
Davis Sisters, The 119
Dawes, Dominique 1976— 11, 126
Dawes, Kwame 1962— 126
Dawkins, Egbert Nathaniel, III See Blacc, Aloe
Dawkins, James Henry See Dawkins, Jimmy
Dawkins, Jimmy 1936–2013 111
Dawkins, Wayne 1955— 20
Dawn, Marpessa 1934–2008 75
Dawn, Sandra See Chantels, The
Dawson, Andre 1954— 85
Dawson, Matel "Mat," Jr. 1921–2002 39
Dawson, Michael C. 1951— 63
Dawson, Rosario 1979— 72
Dawson, William Levi 1899–1990 39
Dawuni, Rocky 1969— 94
Day, Leon 1916–1995 39
Days, Drew S(aunders, III) 1941— 10
Dazz Band 116
D'banj 1980— 107
De' Alexander, Quinton 19??— 57
de Assís Moreira, Ronaldo See Ronaldinho
De Bankolé, Isaach 1957— 78
de Carvalho, Barcelo See Bonga, Kuenda
De La Soul 119
de Lavallade, Carmen 1931— 78

de Passe, Suzanne 1948(?)— 25
De Priest, Oscar Stanton 1871–1951 80
De Shields, André 1946— 72
De Veaux, Alexis 1948— 44
"Deadwood Dick" See Love, Nat
Dean, Charles See Commodores, The
Dean, Fred 1952— 98
Dean, Kasseem David See Swizz Beatz
Dean, Mark E. 1957— 35
Dean, Phillip Hayes 1931–2014 122
Deas, Gerald 1931— 85
Deauphin, Jean-Prosper See Beken
DeBaptiste, George 1814(?)–1875 32
DeBarge, El 1961— 89
DeBerry, Lois M. 1945–2013 115
Déby, Idriss 1952— 30, 125
DeCarava, Roy 1919–2009 42, 81
DeChalus, Lorenzo See Lord Jamar
Deconge-Watson, Lovenia 1933— 55
Dedeaux, Richard 1940–2013 119
Dee, Merri 1936— 55
Dee, Ruby 1924–2014 8, 50, 68, 122
Deezer D 1965— 53
DeFrantz, Anita 1952— 37
DeGale, James 1986— 74
Deggans, Eric 1965— 71
Degree, Leaveil See Whispers, The
DeJongh, John, Jr. 1957— 85
Dekker, Desmond 1941–2006 104
DeLaine, Joseph A. 1898–1974 110
Delaney, Beauford 1901–1979 19
Delaney, Joe 1958–1983 76
Delaney, Joseph 1904–1991 30
Delany, Annie Elizabeth 1891–1995 12
Delany, Martin R. 1812–1885 27
Delany, Samuel R(ay), Jr. 1942— 9
Delany, Sarah (Sadie) 1889— 12
Delco, Wilhelmina R. 1929— 33
Delice, Ronald 1966— 48
Delice, Rony 1966— 48
DeLille, Henriette 1813–1862 30
Dells, The 109
Dellums, Ronald 1935— 2, 81
DeLoach, Nora 1940–2001 30
Delpit, Lisa 1952— 101
Delsarte, Louis 1944— 34
Demby, William 1922— 51
Demps, Larry See Dramatics, The
DeMudd, Pierre See Dazz Band
Dennard, Brazeal 1929— 37
Dennis, Gary C. 1950— 91
Dent, Cedric See Take 6
Dent, Richard 1960— 97
Dent, Thomas C. 1932–1998 50
Dent, Tom See Dent, Thomas C.
Dentley, Khristian See Take 6
DePreist, James 1936–2013 37, 109
DePrince, Michaela 1995— 104
Derham, James See Durham, James
DeRozan, DeMar 1989— 125
Derülo, Jason 1989— 93

Desalegn, Hailemariam 1965— 105
DeSanto, Sugar Pie 1935— 122
Desrouleaux, Jason See Derülo, Jason
Detroit Emeralds, The 121
DeVard, Jerri 1957(?)— 61
DeVaughn, Raheem 1975— 91
Devers, Gail 1966— 7, 87
Devine, Loretta 1953— 24
Devine, Major J. See Divine, Father
DeVoe, Ronnie See New Edition
DeVore-Mitchell, Ophelia 1922–2014 120
Dewese, Mohandas See Kool Moe Dee
Dewitty, Thelma 1912–1977 114
Di Genius See McGregor, Stephen
Dial, Thornton 1928— 114
Diallo, Amadou 1976–1999 27
Diamond, Lydia R. 1969— 101
Diaw, Boris 1982— 122
Diawara, Djeli Moussa 1962— 111
Diawara, Fatoumata 1982— 114
Dibaba, Tirunesh 1985— 73, 109
Dickens, Helen Octavia 1909–2001 14, 64
Dickenson, Vic 1906–1984 38
Dickerson, Debra J. 1959— 60
Dickerson, Eric 1960— 27, 108
Dickerson, Ernest 1952(?)— 6, 17
Dickerson, Isaac See Fisk Jubilee Singers
Dickey, Eric Jerome 1961— 21, 56
Dickey, Gwen See Rose Royce
Diddley, Bo 1928–2008 39, 72
Diesel, Vin 1967(?)— 29
Dieudonné 1966— 67, 118
Difda, Kalaparusha Ahrah See McIntyre, Kalaparusha Maurice
Diggs, Charles C. 1922–1998 21
Diggs, Robert Fitzgerald See RZA
Diggs, Scott See Diggs, Taye
Diggs, Taye 1972— 25, 63
Diggs-Taylor, Anna 1932— 20
Dihigo, Martín 1905(?)–1971 103
Dilla, J See J Dilla
Dillard, Godfrey J. 1948— 45
Dillard, Tramar See Flo Rida
Dillon, Leo 1933–2012 103
Dinkins, David 1927— 4
Diogo, Luisa Dias 1958— 63
Diop, Birago 1906–1989 53
Diop, Cheikh Anta 1923–1986 4
Diouf, Abdou 1935— 3
Diouf, Khalif See Le1f
Dirie, Waris 1965(?)— 56
Divine, Father 1877(?)–1965 7
Dixie Cups, The 109
Dixon, Bill 1925–2010 87
Dixon, Dean 1915–1976 68
Dixon, George 1870–1909 52
Dixon, Ivan 1931–2008 69
Dixon, Julian C. 1934— 24
Dixon, Margaret 192(?)— 14
Dixon, Rodrick See Three Mo' Tenors
Dixon, Sharon Pratt 1944— 1
Dixon, Sheila 1953— 68
Dixon, Willie (James) 1915–1992 4
DJ Clue? 1975— 111
DJ Easy Lee See Treacherous Three
DJ Jazzy Jeff 1965— 32

DJ Lance Rock 1965— 94
DJ Rashad 1979–2014 121
DJ Ready Red See Geto Boys
DJ Red Alert See Alert, Kool DJ Red
DJ Screw 1971–2000 110
Djotodia, Michel 1949— 117
Dlamini-Zuma, Nkosazana 1949— 34, 105
DMC See Run-DMC
DMX 1970— 28, 64
do Nascimento, Edson Arantes See Pelé
Dobbs, John Wesley 1882–1961 89
Dobbs, Mattiwilda 1925— 34
Dobson, Tamara 1947–2006 111
Doby, Larry See Doby, Lawrence Eugene, Sr.
Doby, Lawrence Eugene, Sr. 1924–2003 16, 41
Dodd, Clement Seymour See Dodd, Coxsone
Dodd, Coxsone 1932–2004 99
Dodson, Howard, Jr. 1939— 7, 52
Dodson, Larry See Bar-Kays, The
Dodson, Owen 1914–1983 38
Doe, Samuel K. 1951–1990 100
Dogan, Matthew Winifred 1863–1947 91
Doggett, Bill 1916–1996 124
Doggett, William Ballard See Doggett, Bill
DoHarris, Brenda 1946— 116
Doig, Jason 1977— 45
Dokes, Michael 1958— 105
Doley, Harold, Jr. 1947— 26
Dollar, Creflo 1962— 106
Domingo, Colman 1969— 94
Domini, Rey See Lorde, Audre (Geraldine)
Domino, Fats 1928— 20
Donald, Arnold 1954— 36, 126
Donaldson, Jeff 1932–2004 46
Donegan, Dorothy 1922–1998 19
Donovan, Kevin See Bambaataa, Afrika
Dorham, Kenny 1924–1972 113
Dorham, McKinley Howard See Dorham, Kenny
Dorhan, Carlita See Taste of Honey, A
Dorn, Michael 1952— 112
Dorrell, Karl 1963— 52
Dorsey, Lee 1926–1986 65
Dorsey, Thomas Andrew 1899–1993 15
Dorsey, Thomas J. 1812(?)–1875 90
Dortch, Thomas W., Jr. 1950— 45
dos Santos, Isabel 1973— 114
dos Santos, José Eduardo 1942— 43, 114
dos Santos, Manuel Francisco 1933 65
Dougherty, Mary Pearl 1915–2003 47
Douglas, Aaron 1899–1979 7
Douglas, Ashanti Shequoiya See Ashanti
Douglas, Bob 1882–1979 96
Douglas, Buster 1960— 127
Douglas, Denzil Llewellyn 1953— 53
Douglas, Derek 1971— 88

Douglas, Donya 1970(?)— 97
Douglas, Emory 1943— 89
Douglas, James See Douglas, Buster
Douglas, Lizzie See Memphis Minnie
Douglass, Frederick 1817(?)–1895 87
Doumbia, Mariam See Amadou & Mariam
Dourdan, Gary 1966— 37
Dove, Rita 1952— 6, 78, 101
Dove, Ulysses 1947— 5
Dow, Unity 1959— 104
Downing, George T. 1819–1903 91
Downing, Will 19(?)(?)— 19
Downs, Bobby See New Birth
Dozier, Lamont See Holland-Dozier-Holland
Dr. Dre 1965— 10, 14, 30, 116
Dr. J See Erving, Julius
Drake 1986— 86
Drake, Hamid 1955— 121
Drake, Lavern See Cadillacs
Drake, Michael V. 1950(?)— 122
Dramatics, The 106
Draper, Sharon Mills 1952— 16, 43
Drayton, William Jonathan, Jr. See Flavor Flav
Dream, The See The-Dream
Drew, Alvin, Jr. 1962— 67
Drew, Charles Richard 1904–1950 7
Drew, Kenneth Sidney, Sr. See Drew, Kenny
Drew, Kenny 1928–1993 123
Drew, Maurice See Jones-Drew, Maurice
Drew, Timothy See Noble Drew Ali
Drew Ali See Noble Drew Ali
Drexler, Clyde 1962— 4, 61
Drifters, The 121
Driskell, David C(lyde) 1931— 7
Driver, David E. 1955— 11
Driver, Donald 1975— 99
D-Roc See Ying Yang Twins
Drogba, Didier 1978— 78
Drummond, William J. 1944— 40
Du Bois, David Graham 1925— 45
Du Bois, W(illiam) E(dward) B(urghardt) 1868–1963 3
du Cille, Michel 1955(?)— 74
Dube, John Langalibalele 1871–1946 119
Dube, Lucky 1964–2007 77
DuBois, Joshua 1982— 88
DuBois, Shirley Graham 1907–1977 21
Duchemin, Alamaine See Maxis, Theresa
Duchemin, Marie See Maxis, Theresa
Duchemin, Theresa Maxis See Maxis, Theresa
Ducksworth, Marilyn 1957— 12
Duckworth, Kendrick Lamar See Lamar, Kendrick
Dudley, Edward R. 1911–2005 58
Dudley, Sherman H. 1870(?)–1940 117
Dudus See Coke, Christopher
Due, Patricia Stephens 1939–2012 100
Due, Tananarive 1966— 30

Duerson, Dave 1960–2011 **93**
Duggins, George 1943–2005 **64**
Duke, Bill 1943— **3, 96**
Duke, George 1946–2013 **21, 113**
Dukes, Hazel Nell 1932— **56**
Dumars, Joe 1963— **16, 65, 126**
Dumars, Joseph, III See Dumars, Joe
Dumas, Henry 1934–1968 **41**
Dumpson, James R. 1909–2012 **108**
Dunbar, Alice See Dunbar-Nelson, Alice Ruth Moore
Dunbar, Paul Laurence 1872–1906 **8**
Dunbar, Sly 1952— See Sly & Robbie
Dunbar-Nelson, Alice Ruth Moore 1875–1935 **44**
Duncan, Cleveland See Penguins, The
Duncan, Michael Clarke 1957–2012 **26, 104**
Duncan, Tim 1976— **20, 91**
Duncan, Todd 1903–1998 **76**
Duncanson, Robert S. 1821(?)–1872 **127**
Dungey, Merrin 1971— **62**
Dungy, Camille 1972— **86**
Dungy, Tony 1955— **17, 42, 59, 118**
Dunham, Katherine 1910–2006 **4, 59**
Dunigan, Ricky See Lord Infamous
Dunlap, Ericka 1982(?)— **55**
Dunn, Freddie See Rose Royce
Dunn, Jerry 1953— **27**
Dunn, Warrick 1975— **90**
Dunner, Leslie B. 1956— **45**
Dunnigan, Alice Allison 1906–1983 **41**
Dunston, Georgia Mae 1944— **48**
Duplechan, Larry 1956— **55**
DuPree, Johnny 1953— **96**
Dupri, Jermaine 1972— **13, 46**
Durant, Kevin 1988— **76, 107**
Durham, Bobby 1937–2008 **73**
Durham, James 1762–1834(?) **90**
Durham, Robert Joseph See Durham, Bobby
Duthiers, Vladimir 1969— **109**
Dutton, Charles S. 1951— **4, 22**
Dutton, Marie Elizabeth 1940— **12**
Duvalier, Baby Doc See Duvalier, Jean-Claude
Duvalier, François 1907–1971 **124**
Duvalier, Jean-Claude 1951–2014 **124**
Duvalier, Papa Doc See Duvalier, François
DuVernay, Ava 1972— **98, 126**
Dwight, Edward 1933— **65**
Dworkin, Aaron P. 1970— **52**
Dye, Jermaine 1974— **58**
Dyett, Walter 1901–1969 **113**
Dymally, Mervyn 1926— **42**
Dyson, Michael Eric 1958— **11, 40, 128**
E-40 1967— **125**
Eagleson, William Lewis 1835–1899 **90**
Early, Deloreese Patricia See Reese, Della
Early, Gerald (Lyn) 1952— **15**

Early, Norman S., Jr. 1945— **124**
Earth, Wind & Fire **98**
Earthquake, 1963— **55**
Easley, Annie J. 1933— **61**
Easton, Hosea 1798–1837 **91**
Ebanks, Michelle 1962— **60**
Ebanks, Selita 1983— **67**
Eberhardt, Jennifer 1965— **124**
Eckstein, William Clarence See Eckstine, Billy
Eckstine, Billy 1914–1993 **28**
Edelin, Ramona Hoage 1945— **19**
Edelman, Marian Wright 1939— **5, 42**
Edgerton, Khia Danielle See K-Swift
Edison, Harry 1915(?)–1999 **114**
Edison, Harry "Sweets" See Edison, Harry
Edley, Christopher 1928–2003 **2, 48**
Edley, Christopher F., Jr. 1953— **48**
Edmonds, Kenneth See Babyface
Edmonds, Terry 1950(?)— **17**
Edmonds, Tracey 1967— **16, 64**
Edmunds, Gladys 1951(?)— **48**
Edugyan, Esi 1978— **98**
Edwards, Bernard See Chic
Edwards, David 1915–2011 **122**
Edwards, Dennis See Contours, The
Edwards, Donna 1958— **77**
Edwards, Eli See McKay, Claude
Edwards, Esther Gordy 1920(?)— **43**
Edwards, Harry 1942— **2**
Edwards, Herman 1954— **51**
Edwards, Honeyboy See Edwards, David
Edwards, Lena Frances 1900–1986 **76**
Edwards, Melvin 1937— **22**
Edwards, Robert See Intruders, The
Edwards, Teddy 1924–2003 **123**
Edwards, Teresa 1964— **14, 95**
Edwards, Theodore Marcus, Sr. See Edwards, Teddy
Edwards, Trevor 1962— **54**
Edwards, Willarda V. 1951— **59**
Edwards, Willis 1946–2012 **104**
Eikerenkoetter, Frederick J., II See Reverend Ike
Ejiofor, Chiwetel 1977— **67, 116**
Ejogo, Carmen 1974— **126**
Ekwensi, Cyprian 1921— **37**
El Wilson, Barbara 1959— **35**
Elam, Keith See Guru
Elba, Idris 1971— **49, 89, 116**
Elbagir, Nima 1978— **121**
Elder, Larry 1952— **25, 120**
Elder, (Robert) Lee 1934— **6**
Elder, Lonne, III 1931–1996 **38**
Elders, Joycelyn (Minnie) 1933— **6**
Eldridge, Roy 1911–1989 **37**
El-Hajj Malik El-Shabazz See X, Malcolm
Elie, Lolis Eric 1985— **97**
Elise, Kimberly 1967— **32, 101**
Ellerbe, Brian 1963— **22**
Ellington, Duke 1899–1974 **5**
Ellington, E. David 1960— **11**

Ellington, Edward Kennedy See Ellington, Duke
Ellington, Mercedes 1939— **34**
Ellington, Robert See Dramatics, The
Elliott, Lorris 1931–1999 **37**
Elliott, Missy 1971— **31, 90**
Elliott, Sean 1968— **26**
Ellis, Alton 1938–2008 **74**
Ellis, Aunjanue 1969— **108**
Ellis, Charles H., III 1958(?)— **79**
Ellis, Clarence A. 1943— **38**
Ellis, Dock 1945–2008 **78**
Ellis, Hortense 1941–2000 **97**
Ellis, Jimmy 1940–2014 **44, 127**
Ellis, Jimmy, II See Trammps, The
Ellis, Larry R. 1946— **110**
Ellis, Monica See Imani Winds
Ellis, Nelsan 1981— **105**
Ellis, Trey 1962— **97**
Ellis-Lamkins, Phaedra 1976— **88**
Ellison, Keith 1963— **59**
Ellison, Ralph (Waldo) 1914–1994 **7**
Ellison, Steven See Flying Lotus
Elmore, Ronn 1957— **21**
El-Shabazz, El-Hajj Malik See X, Malcolm
Elumelu, Tony 1963— **116**
Elzy, Ruby 1908–1943 **119**
Emanuel, James A. 1921— **46**
Emeagwali, Dale 1954— **31**
Emeagwali, Philip 1954— **30**
Emecheta, Buchi 1944— **30**
Emmanuel, Alphonsia 1956— **38**
Emotions, The **125**
En Vogue **100**
English, Alvin See Contours, The
Ensley, Carol Denise See Nash, Niecy
Ephriam, Mablean 1949(?)— **29**
Epperson, Sharon 1969(?)— **54**
Epps, Archie C., III 1937–2003 **45**
Epps, Mike 1970— **60**
Epps, Omar 1973— **23, 59**
Epps, Tauheed See 2 Chainz
Equiano, Olaudah 1745(?)–1797 **78**
Ericsson-Jackson, Aprille 19(?)(?)— **28**
Ervin, Anthony 1981— **66**
Ervin, Booker 1930–1970 **106**
Ervin, Clark Kent 1959— **82**
Erving, Julius 1950— **18, 47**
Escobar, Damien 1987— **56**
Escobar, Tourie 1985— **56**
Esposito, Giancarlo (Giusseppi Alessandro) 1958— **9**
Espy, Alphonso Michael See Espy, Mike
Espy, Mike 1953— **6**
Estelle 1980— **75**
Esters, Monica Ann See Conyers, Monica
Estes, Rufus 1857–19(?)(?) **29**
Estes, Simon 1938— **28**
Estes, Sleepy John 1899–1977 **33**
Eto'o, Samuel 1981— **73**
Eubanks, Kevin 1957— **15, 108**
Eugene-Richard, Margie 1941— **63**
Europe, (William) James Reese 1880–1919 **10**
Eusebio 1942–2014 **118**
Evans, Darryl 1961— **22**

Evans, Diana 1972(?)— **72**
Evans, Ernest See Checker, Chubby
Evans, Etu 1969— **55**
Evans, Faith 1973(?)— **22**
Evans, Greene See Fisk Jubilee Singers
Evans, Harry 1956(?)— **25**
Evans, Mari 1923— **26**
Evans, Melvin H. 1917–1984 **88**
Evans, Warren C. 1948— **76**
Eve 1979— **29**
Everett, Carl 1971— **103**
Everett, Francine 1917–1999 **23**
Everett, Percival 1956— **93**
Everett, Ronald McKinley See Karenga, Maulana
Evers, Medgar (Riley) 1925–1963 **3**
Evers, Myrlie 1933— **8**
Évora, Cesária 1941–2011 **12, 99**
Evra, Patrice 1981— **102**
Ewing, Patrick 1962— **17, 73**
Eyadéma, Gnassingbé 1937–2005 **7, 52**
Fabio, Sarah Webster 1928–1979 **48**
Fabolous 1977— **93**
Fabre, Shelton 1963— **71**
Fagan, Garth 1940— **18, 98**
Fair, Leroy See Contours, The
Fair, Ronald L. 1932— **47**
Fair, Yvonne See Chantels, The
Fairbanks, Mabel 1915(?)–2001 **117**
Faison, Donald 1974— **50**
Faison, Frankie 1949— **55**
Faison, George William 1946— **16**
Falana, Lola 1942— **42**
Falconer, Etta Zuber 1933–2002 **59**
Falcons, The **128**
Fales-Hill, Susan 1962— **88**
Fanon, Frantz 1925–1961 **44**
Fantasia See Barrino, Fantasia
Farah, Mo 1983— **104**
Farah, Nuruddin 1945— **27**
Fargas, Antonio 1946(?)— **50**
Farley, Christopher John 1966— **54**
Farley, J. J. See Soul Stirrers
Farley, James Conway 1854–1910(?) **99**
Farmer, Art(hur Stewart) 1928–1999 **38**
Farmer, Forest J(ackson) 1941— **1**
Farmer, James 1920–1999 **2, 64**
Farmer-Paellmann, Deadria 1966— **43**
Farr, Mel 1944— **24**
Farrakhan, Louis 1933— **2, 15**
Farrell, Herman D., Jr. 1932— **81**
Farris, Isaac Newton, Jr. 1962— **63**
Fat Boys **92**
Father Goose See Rhoden, Wayne
Fatlip See Pharcyde, The
Fattah, Chaka 1956— **11, 70, 112**
Faulk, Marshall 1973— **35, 96**
Fauntroy, Walter E(dward) 1933— **11**
Fauset, Crystal Dreda Bird 1893–1965 **100**
Fauset, Jessie (Redmon) 1882–1961 **7**
Favors, Steve 1948— **23**
Fax, Elton 1909–1993 **48**

Fearman, Eric *See Dazz Band*

Feaster, Robert Franklin *See Sundiata, Sekou*

Feelings, Muriel 1938— **44**

Feelings, Tom 1933–2003 **11, 47**

Feemster, Herbert 1942— **72**

Fela 1938–1997 **1, 42**

Felder, Wilton *See Crusaders, The*

Felix, Allyson 1985— **48, 98**

Felix, Larry R. (?)— **64**

Felix Da Housecat 1971— **110**

Fennoy, Ilene 1947— **72**

Fenton, Kevin 1966(?)— **87**

Fenty, Adrian 1970— **60, 88**

Fenty, Robyn Rihanna *See Rihanna*

Ferbee, Willie *See Drifters, The*

Ferbos, Lionel 1911— **95**

Ferdinand, Rio 1978— **82**

Ferguson, Amos 1920–2009 **81**

Ferguson, Kevin *See Slice, Kimbo*

Ferguson, Roger W., Jr. 1951— **25, 112**

Ferguson, Ronald F. 1950(?)— **75**

Ferguson, Vernice D. 1928–2012 **108**

Ferrell, Rachelle 1961— **29**

Ferrer, Ibrahim 1927— **41**

Fetchit, Stepin 1892–1985 **32**

Fiasco, Lupe 1982— **64**

Fielder, Cecil 1963— **2, 112**

Fielder, Prince 1984— **68**

Fields, C. Virginia 1946— **25**

Fields, Cleo 1962— **13**

Fields, Evelyn J. 1949— **27**

Fields, Felicia P. (?)— **60**

Fields, Julia 1938— **45**

Fields, Kim 1969— **36**

50 Cent 1976— **46, 83**

Figueroa, John J. 1920–1999 **40**

Files, Lolita 1964(?)— **35**

Fils-Aimé, Reggie 1961— **74**

Fine, Sam 1969— **60**

Finley, Ron 1978(?)— **110**

Finner-Williams, Paris Michele 1951— **62**

Finnie, Lance *See Falcons, The*

Fiona, Melanie 1983— **84**

Fishbone **101**

Fishburne, Larry *See Fishburne, Laurence*

Fishburne, Laurence 1961— **4, 22, 70**

Fisher, Ada Lois Sipuel 1924–1995 **76**

Fisher, Ada M. 1947— **76**

Fisher, Antwone Quenton 1959— **40**

Fisher, Derek 1974— **97**

Fisher, Gail 1935–2000 **85**

Fisher, George *See Peters, Brock*

Fisher, Miles Mark 1899–1970 **91**

Fisher, Rudolph John Chauncey 1897–1934 **17**

Fisher, Thelma *See Dewitty, Thelma*

Fisk Jubilee Singers **112**

Fitzgerald, Ella 1918–1996 **8, 18**

Five Blind Boys of Alabama, The *See Blind Boys of Alabama, The*

Five Keys, The **104**

FKA Twigs 1988— **123**

Flack, Roberta 1940— **19**

Flake, Floyd H. 1945— **18, 110**

Flamingos, The **108**

Flanagan, Tommy 1930–2001 **69**

Flash, Grandmaster *See Grandmaster Flash*

Flavor Flav 1959— **67** *See also Public Enemy*

Fleming, Erik R. 1965— **75**

Fleming, Raymond 1945— **48**

Flemons, Dom *See Carolina Chocolate Drops*

Flemons, Wade *See Earth, Wind & Fire*

Fletcher, Alphonse, Jr. *See Fletcher, Buddy*

Fletcher, Arthur A. 1924–2005 **63**

Fletcher, Benjamin 1890–1949 **90**

Fletcher, Bill, Jr. 1954— **41**

Fletcher, Buddy 1965— **16, 108**

Fletcher, Geoffrey 1970— **85**

Flipper, Henry O(ssian) 1856–1940 **3**

Flo Rida 1979— **78**

Flood, Curt 1938–1997 **10, 93**

Florence, Kenneth Howard *See Norton, Ken*

Flowers, Sylester 1935— **50**

Flowers, Vonetta 1973— **35**

Floyd, Eddie 1937— **127**

Floyd, Elson S. 1956— **41**

Flying Lotus 1983— **124**

Folks, Byron *See Allen, Byron*

Forbes, Audrey Manley 1934— **16**

Forbes, Calvin 1945— **46**

Forbes, James A., Jr. 1935— **71**

Ford, Barney 1822–1902 **90**

Ford, Cheryl 1981— **45**

Ford, Clyde W. 1951— **40**

Ford, Harold E(ugene) 1945— **42**

Ford, Harold E(ugene), Jr. 1970— **16, 70**

Ford, Jack 1947— **39**

Ford, James Lewis Carter *See Ford, T-Model*

Ford, Johnny 1942— **70**

Ford, Nick Aaron 1904–1982 **44**

Ford, T-Model 1920(?)–2013 **91, 113**

Ford, Vincent 1940(?)–2008 **75**

Ford, Wallace 1950— **58**

Ford, Willie *See Dramatics, The*

Foreman, George 1948— **1, 15**

Forman, James 1928–2005 **7, 51**

Forman, James, Jr. 1967— **89**

Forna, Aminatta 1964— **95**

Forrest, Leon 1937–1997 **44**

Forrest, Vernon 1971–2009 **40, 79**

Forté, John 1975— **74**

Forte, Linda Diane 1952— **54**

Fortune, James 1977(?)— **92**

Fortune, T(imothy) Thomas 1856–1928 **6**

Fosso, Samuel 1962— **116**

Foster, Andrew 1879–1930 **79**

Foster, Arian 1986— **114**

Foster, Cecil (A.) 1954— **32**

Foster, Ezola 1938— **28**

Foster, Frank 1928–2011 **97**

Foster, George "Pops" 1892–1969 **40**

Foster, Henry W., Jr. 1933— **26**

Foster, Jylla Moore 1954— **45**

Foster, Marie 1917–2003 **48**

Foster, Rube *See Foster, Andrew*

Foster, William P. 1919–2010 **88**

Four Tops, The *See Benson, Obie*

Fowler, Reggie 1959— **51**

Fowles, Gloria *See Gaynor, Gloria*

Fox, Donal 1952— **114**

Fox, John R. 1917–1944 **105**

Fox, Rick 1969— **27**

Fox, Ulrich Alexander *See Fox, Rick*

Fox, Vivica A. 15, 53

Foxx, Anthony 1971— **81, 123**

Foxx, Jamie 1967— **15, 48**

Foxx, Redd 1922–1991 **2**

Foye, K'wan 19(?)(?)— **97**

Francis, Norman (C.) 1931— **60**

Francis, Thais 1980— **93**

Francois, Terry A. 1940–1989 **106**

Franklin, Aretha 1942— **11, 44, 115**

Franklin, C. L. 1915–1984 **68**

Franklin, Carl 1949— **11**

Franklin, Elmo *See Mighty Clouds of Joy*

Franklin, Hardy R. 1929–2004 **9, 87**

Franklin, J. E. 1937— **44**

Franklin, John Hope 1915–2009 **5, 77**

Franklin, Kirk 1970— **15, 49, 97**

Franklin, Robert M(ichael) 1954— **13**

Franklin, Shante Anthony *See Curren$y*

Franklin, Shirley 1945— **34, 80**

Franks, Gary 1954(?)— **2**

Franti, Michael 1966— **93**

Fraser, Sarah Loguen 1850–1933 **100**

Fraser, Shelly-Ann *See Fraser-Pryce, Shelly-Ann*

Fraser-Pryce, Shelly-Ann 1986— **113**

Frazer, Jendayi 196(?)— **68**

Frazer, Victor O. 1943— **98**

Frazier, Edward Franklin 1894–1962 **10**

Frazier, Joe 1944–2011 **19, 98**

Frazier, Kenneth 1954— **97**

Frazier, Kevin 1964— **58**

Frazier, Oscar 1956–2005 **58**

Frazier, Ryan 1977— **89**

Frazier, Walt 1945— **91**

Frazier-Lyde, Jacqui 1961— **31**

Fredericks, Henry Saint Claire *See Mahal, Taj*

Freelon, Nnenna 1954— **32**

Freeman, Aaron 1956— **52**

Freeman, Al, Jr. 1934–2012 **11, 105**

Freeman, Albert Cornelius, Jr. *See Freeman, Al, Jr.*

Freeman, Bernard *See Bun B*

Freeman, Cathy 1973— **29**

Freeman, Charles Eldridge 1933— **19**

Freeman, Harold P. 1933— **23**

Freeman, Leonard 1950— **27**

Freeman, Marianna 1957— **23**

Freeman, Morgan 1937— **2, 20, 62, 100**

Freeman, Paul 1936— **39**

Freeman, Von 1923–2012 **104**

Freeman, Yvette **27**

Freestyle Fellowship **122**

French, Albert 1943— **18**

French, D. M. 1924–2011 **94**

Fresh, Doug E. 1966— **93**

Fresh Prince, The *See Smith, Will*

Frey, Alan *See New Birth*

Friday, Jeff 1964(?)— **24**

Fryer, Roland G. 1977— **56**

Fudge, Ann (Marie) 1951— **11, 55**

Fudge, Marcia L. 1952— **76**

Fuentes, Rigoberto *See Fuentes, Tito*

Fuentes, Tito 1944— **123**

Fuhr, Grant 1962— **1, 49**

Fulani, Lenora (Branch) 1950— **11**

Fuller, A. Oveta 1955— **43**

Fuller, Arthur 1972— **27**

Fuller, Blind Boy 1907(?)–1941 **86**

Fuller, Charles (Henry) 1939— **8**

Fuller, Curtis 1934— **115**

Fuller, Howard L. 1941— **37**

Fuller, Hoyt 1923–1981 **44**

Fuller, Meta Vaux Warrick 1877–1968 **27**

Fuller, S. B. 1895–1988 **13**

Fuller, Solomon Carter, Jr. 1872–1953 **15**

Fuller, Thomas O. 1867–1942 **90**

Fuller, Vivian 1954— **33**

Fulson, Lowell 1921–1999 **118**

Funches, Johnny *See Dells, The*

Funches, Ron 1983— **121**

Funderburg, I. Owen 1924–2002 **38**

Funnye, Capers C., Jr. 1952(?)— **73**

Fuqua, Antoine 1966— **35**

Fuqua, Charlie *See Ink Spots, The*

Fuqua, Harvey 1927–2010 **90** *See also Moonglows, The*

Futch, Eddie 1911–2001 **33**

Future 1983— **109**

Gabre-Medhin, Tsegaye 1936–2006 **64**

Gabriel, Athelgra Neville *See Dixie Cups, The*

Gaines, Brenda 19(?)(?)— **41**

Gaines, Clarence E., Sr. 1923–2005 **55**

Gaines, Ernest J(ames) 1933— **7**

Gaines, Grady 1934— **38**

Gaines, LaDonna Andrea *See Summer, Donna*

Gaines, Lloyd 1911–19(?)(?) **79**

Gaines, Matthew 1840–1900 **95**

Gaines, Patrice 1950— **106**

Gairy, Eric Matthew 1922–1997 **83**

Gaiter, Dorothy J. 1950(?)— **80**

Gaither, Israel L. 1944— **65**

Gaither, Jake 1903–1994 **14**

Gamble, Kenny 1943— **85**

Gamble, Oscar 1949— **113**

Gans, Joe 1874–1910 **91**

Gant, Kenneth *See Midnight Star*

Gant, Richard 1944— **105**

Gantin, Bernardin 1922–2008 **70**

Gantt, Harvey (Bernard) 1943— **1**

Gap Band, The **100**

Garang, John 1945–2005 **105**

Gardere, Jeffrey 1956— **76**

Gardner, Carl *See Coasters, The*

Gardner, Chris 1954— **65**

Gardner, Edward G. 1925— **45**

Garland, Red 1923–1984 **115**

Garland, William M. *See Garland, Red*

Garner, Erroll 1921–1977 **76**

Garner, Henry See Rose Royce
Garner, Tyron 1967–2006 99
Garnet, Henry Highland 1815–1882 100
Garnett, Kevin 1976— 14, 70, 118
Garrett, James F. 1942— 78
Garrett, Joyce Finley 1931–1997 59
Garrett, Sean 1979— 57
Garrincha See dos Santos, Manuel Francisco
Garrison, Zina 1963— 2
Gartin, Lydia See Diamond, Lydia R.
Garvey, Marcus 1887–1940 1
Garvin, Gerry 1967(?)— 78
Gary, Willie E. 1947— 12, 117
Gaskins, Eric 1958— 64
Gaskins, Rudy 1960(?)— 74
Gaspard, Patrick 1967— 84
Gaston, Arthur George 1892–1996 3, 38, 59
Gaston, Cito 1944— 71
Gaston, Clarence Edwin See Gaston, Cito
Gaston, Marilyn Hughes 1939— 60
Gates, Henry Louis, Jr. 1950— 3, 38, 67
Gates, Pop See Gates, William
Gates, Rosalind See Brewer, Rosalind
Gates, Sylvester James, Jr. 1950— 15
Gates, Theaster 1973— 118
Gates, William 1917–1999 97
Gatlin, Justin 1982— 123
Gay, Council See Contours, The
Gay, Marvin Pentz, Jr. See Gaye, Marvin
Gay, Tyson 1982— 114
Gaye, Anna Gordy 1922–2014 121
Gaye, Marvin 1939–1984 2
Gaye, Nona 1974— 56
Gayle, Addison, Jr. 1932–1991 41
Gayle, Helene D. 1955— 3, 46
Gaynor, Gloria 1947— 36
Gbagbo, Laurent 1945— 43, 90
Gbowee, Leymah 1971(?)— 76
Gebrselassie, Haile 1973— 70
Gee, Kay See Naughty by Nature
Gentry, Alvin 1954— 23
Gentry, Melvin See Midnight Star
George, Eddie 1973— 80
George, Nelson 1957— 12, 101
George, Paul 1990— 124
George, Zelma Watson 1903–1994 42
Gerima, Haile 1946— 38, 80
Gervin, George 1952— 80
Geto Boys 115
Ghostface Killah 1970— 90
Gibbons, Gary 1956— 107
Gibbs, Freddie 1982— 125
Gibbs, Marla 1931— 86
Gibbs, Mifflin W. 1823–1915 99
Gibson, Althea 1927–2003 8, 43
Gibson, Bob 1935— 33
Gibson, Donald Bernard 1933— 40
Gibson, John Trusty 1878–1937 87
Gibson, Johnnie Mae 1949— 23
Gibson, Josh 1911–1947 22
Gibson, Kenneth Allen 1932— 6
Gibson, Ted 1965— 66

Gibson, Truman K., Jr. 1912–2005 60
Gibson, Tyrese 1978— 27, 62
Gibson, William F(rank) 1933— 6
Giddens, Rhiannon See Carolina Chocolate Drops
Giddings, Paula (Jane) 1947— 11
Gidron, Richard D. 1939–2007 68
Gil, Gilberto 1942— 53
Gilbert, Christopher 1949— 50
Gilbert, John Wesley 1864–1923 91
Giles, Cameron See Cam'ron
Giles, Roscoe C. 1890–1970 93
Gill, Gerald 1948–2007 69
Gill, Johnny 1966— 51 See also New Edition
Gill, Turner 1962— 83
Gilles, Ralph 1970— 61
Gillespie, Dizzy 1917–1993 1
Gillespie, John Birks See Gillespie, Dizzy
Gilliam, Frank 1934(?)— 23
Gilliam, Jim 1928–1978 122
Gilliam, Joe, Jr. 1950–2000 31
Gilliam, Junior See Gilliam, Jim
Gilliam, Sam 1933— 16
Gilliard, Steve 1964–2007 69
Gillis, Jesse, Jr. See Harold Melvin & the Blue Notes
Gillum, Andrew 1979— 128
Gilmore, Artis 1949— 101
Gilmore, Mahershalalhashbaz See Ali, Mahershala
Gilmore, Marshall 1931— 46
Gilpin, Charles Sidney 1878–1930 81
Ginuwine 1975(?)— 35
Ginyard, Caleb J. C. See Golden Gate Quartet
Giovanni, Nikki 1943— 9, 39, 85
Gist, Carole 1970(?)— 1
Gist, Keir See Naughty by Nature
Gittens, Charles L. 1928–2011 124
Givens, Adele 19(?)(?)— 62
Givens, Cliff See Billy Ward and the Dominoes; Golden Gate Quartet
Givens, Robin 1964— 4, 25, 58
Givhan, Robin Deneen 1964— 72
Gladney, Paul See Mooney, Paul
Gladwell, Malcolm 1963— 62
Glanville, Douglas Metunwa 1970— 82
Glasper, Robert 1978— 101
Glass, Ron 1945— 111
Glenn, Ornette See Freestyle Fellowship
Gloster, Hugh Morris, Sr. 1911–2002 90
Glover, Anwan 1973— 123
Glover, Cedric B. 1965— 103
Glover, Corey 1964— 34
Glover, Danny 1948— 1, 24, 103
Glover, Donald 1983— 85
Glover, Keith 1966— 79
Glover, Nathaniel, Jr. 1943— 12
Glover, Ralph Anwan See Glover, Anwan
Glover, Savion 1974— 14
Gnassingbé, Faure 1966— 67
Goapele 1977— 55
"The Goat" See Manigault, Earl "The Goat"

Godbolt, James Titus See Slyde, Jimmy
Goff, Houston See Stackhouse, Houston
Goggins, Juanita 1934–2010 127
Goines, Donald 1937(?)–1974 19
Goings, Russell 1932(?)— 59
Goldberg, Whoopi 1955— 4, 33, 69
Golden, Marita 1950— 19, 99
Golden, Thelma 1965— 10, 55
Golden Gate Quartet 104
Golding, Bruce 1947— 78
Goldsberry, Ronald 1942— 18
Golson, Benny 1929— 37
Golston, Allan C. 1967(?)— 55
Gomes, Peter J. 1942–2011 15, 93
Gomez, Jewelle 1948— 30
Gomez-Preston, Cheryl 1954— 9
Gomillion, Charles 1900–1995 90
Good, Meagan 1981— 117
Goode, Mal(vin Russell) 1908–1995 13
Goode, W(oodrow) Wilson 1938— 4
Gooden, Dwight 1964— 20
Gooden, Linda 1953(?)— 94
Gooden, Lolita See Roxanne Shante
Gooding, Cuba, Jr. 1968— 16, 62
Goodison, Lorna 1947— 71
Goodlett, Carlton B. 1914–1997 91
Goodman, Al 1943–2010 87
Goodman, Kim C. 1966— 94
Goodnight, Paul 1946— 32
Gorden, W. C. 1930— 71
Gorden, William C. See Gorden, W. C.
Gordon, Billy See Contours, The
Gordon, Bruce S. 1946— 41, 53, 82
Gordon, Carl 1932–2010 87
Gordon, Dexter 1923–1990 25
Gordon, Ed 1960— 10, 53
Gordon, Josh 1991— 120
Gordon, Pamela 1955— 17
Gordon, Ronnie See Bar-Kays, The
Gordone, Charles 1925–1995 15
Gordon-Reed, Annette 1958— 74
Gordy, Anna See Gaye, Anna Gordy
Gordy, Berry, Jr. 1929— 1
Gore, Frank 1983— 117
Goreed, Joseph See Williams, Joe
Goring, Sonia See Chantels, The
Goss, Carol A. 1947— 55
Goss, Tom 1946— 23
Gossett, Louis, Jr. 1936— 7
Gotti, Irv 1971— 39
Gourdin, Edward O. 1897–1966 93
Gourdine, Anthony See Little Anthony & the Imperials
Gourdine, Meredith 1929–1998 33
Gourdine, Simon (Peter) 1940— 11
Graca, Marcelino Manuel da See Grace, Sweet Daddy
Grace, Charles Manuel See Grace, Sweet Daddy
Grace, George H. 1948— 48
Grace, Sweet Daddy 1881–1960 104
Grae, Jean 1976— 51
Graham, Aubrey Drake See Drake
Graham, Katerina 1989— 99

Graham, Larry See Graham Central Station
Graham, Lawrence Otis 1962— 12
Graham, Lorenz 1902–1989 48
Graham, Stedman 1951(?)— 13
Graham, Trevor 1962(?)— 84
Graham Central Station 123
Grandberry, Omari Ishmael See Omarion
Granderson, Curtis 1981— 66
Granderson, LZ 1972— 103
Grandmaster Flash 1958— 33, 60
Grand-Pierre, Jean-Luc 1977— 46
Granger, Lester B. 1896–1976 75
Grant, Augustus O. 1946(?)— 71
Grant, Bernie 1944–2000 57
Grant, Frank 1865–1937 100
Grant, Gwendolyn Goldsby 19(?)(?)— 28
Grant, Micki 1941(?)— 125
Grant, Rupert Westmore See Lord Invader
Granville, Evelyn Boyd 1924— 36
Gravely, Samuel L., Jr. 1922–2004 5, 49
Graves, Alexander See Moonglows, The
Graves, Butch 1962— 77
Graves, Denyce Antoinette 1964— 19, 57
Graves, Earl G(ilbert) 1935— 1, 35
Graves, Earl Gilbert, Jr. See Graves, Butch
Graves, Milford 1941— 126
Gray, Carl Wardell See Gray, Wardell
Gray, Darius 1945— 69
Gray, Dobie 1940(?)–2011 99
Gray, F. Gary 1969— 14, 49
Gray, Farrah 1984— 59
Gray, Fred Sr. 1930— 37
Gray, Frizzell See Mfume, Kweisi
Gray (Nelson Rollins), Ida 1867–1953 41
Gray, Macy 1970— 29
Gray, Terius See Juvenile
Gray, Vincent C. 1942— 88
Gray, Wardell 1921–1955 128
Gray, William H., III 1941— 3
Gray, Willie 1947— 46
Gray, Yeshimbra "Shimmy" 1972— 55
Greaves, R. B. 1943–2012 106
Greaves, William 1926–2014 38, 123
Greely, M. Gasby 1946— 27
Greely, Margaret Gasby See Greely, M. Gasby
Green, A. C. 1963— 32
Green, Al 1946— 13, 47, 74
Green, Al 1947— 118
Green, Cee Lo 1974— 70, 103
Green, Darrell 1960— 39, 74
Green, Dennis 1949— 5, 45
Green, Draymond 1990— 126
Green, Grant 1935–1979 56
Green, Isaac H. 1959— 79
Green, Jerry See Contours, The
Green, Jonathan 1955— 54
Green, Nancy 1834–1923 112
Greene, Frank S., Jr. 1938–2009 101
Greene, Imogene See Davis Sisters, The

Greene, Jimmy 1975— **74**
Greene, Joe 1946— **10**
Greene, Maurice 1974— **27, 77**
Greene, Petey 1931–1984 **65**
Greene, Ralph Waldo *See Greene, Petey*
Greene, Richard Thaddeus, Sr. 1913–2006 **67**
Greene, Talib Kweli *See Kweli, Talib*
Greenfield, Elizabeth Taylor 1819(?)–1876 **116**
Greenfield, Eloise 1929— **9**
Greenfield, Ronnie Spector *See Spector, Ronnie*
Greenhouse, Bunnatine "Bunny" 1944— **57**
Greenlee, Sam 1930— **48**
Greenwood, L. C. 1946–2013 **115**
Greenwood, Monique 1959— **38**
Greer, Hal 1936— **92**
Greer, Sonny 1903(?)–1982 **127**
Greer, William Alexander *See Greer, Sonny*
Gregg, Eric 1951— **16**
Gregory, Ann 1912–1990 **63**
Gregory, Dick 1932— **1, 54**
Gregory, Frederick 1941— **8, 51**
Gregory, Gerald *See Spaniels, The*
Gregory, Wilton 1947— **37**
Grice, George *See Gryce, Gigi*
Grier, Bobby 1933— **95**
Grier, David Alan 1955— **28**
Grier, Eliza Ann 1863(?)–1902 **90**
Grier, Mike 1975— **43**
Grier, Pam 1949— **9, 31, 86**
Grier, Roosevelt (Rosey) 1932— **13**
Griffey, Dick 1938–2010 **89**
Griffey, Ken, Jr. 1969— **12, 73**
Griffin, Angela 1976— **80**
Griffin, Anthony 1960— **71**
Griffin, Bessie Blout 1914— **43**
Griffin, Blake 1989— **98**
Griffin, John Arnold, III *See Griffin, Johnny*
Griffin, Johnny 1928–2008 **71**
Griffin, LaShell 1967— **51**
Griffin, Robert, III 1990— **107**
Griffith, Emile 1938–2013 **113**
Griffith, Mark Winston 1963— **8**
Griffith, Patrick A. 1944— **64**
Griffith, Yolanda 1970— **25**
Griffith-Joyner, Florence 1959–1998 **28**
Griffiths, Marcia 1948(?)— **29**
Grillo, Evelio 1919–2008 **95**
Grimes, Henry 1935— **124**
Grimké, Archibald H(enry) 1849–1930 **9**
Griner, Brittney 1990— **128**
Grist, Reri 1932— **84**
Groff, Peter 1963— **96**
Grooms, Henry R(andall) 1944— **50**
Gryce, George *See Gryce, Gigi*
Gryce, Gigi 1925–1983 **124**
Guarionex *See Schomburg, Arthur Alfonso*
Guebuza, Armando 1943— **81**
Guéï, Robert 1941–2002 **66**
Guillaume, Robert 1927— **3, 48**
Güines, Tata 1930–2008 **69**
Guinier, (Carol) Lani 1950— **7, 30**

Guitar Slim 1926(?)–1959 **125**
Gumbel, Bryant 1948— **14, 80**
Gumbel, Greg 1946— **8**
Gunn, Moses 1929–1993 **10**
Gurira, Danai 1978(?)— **73**
Guru 1961–2010 **84**
Guy, Billy *See Coasters, The*
Guy, (George) Buddy 1936— **31**
Guy, Jasmine 1964(?)— **2**
Guy, Rosa 1925(?)— **5**
Guyot, Lawrence 1939–2012 **108**
Guyse, Etta Drucille *See Guyse, Sheila*
Guyse, Sheila 1925–2013 **122**
Guy-Sheftall, Beverly 1946— **13, 92**
Guyton, Tyree 1955— **9, 94**
Gwynn, Tony 1960–2014 **18, 83, 122**
Gyan, Asamoah 1985— **87**
Habré, Hissène 1942— **6, 104**
Habyarimana, Juvenal 1937–1994 **8**
Haddon, Dietrick 1973(?)— **55**
Hageman, Hans 19(?)(?)— **36**
Hageman, Ivan 19(?)(?)— **36**
Hagler, Marvelous Marvin 1954— **102**
Haile Selassie 1892–1975 **7**
Hailey, JoJo 1971— **22**
Hailey, K-Ci 1969— **22**
Hairston, Jester 1901–2000 **88**
Hairston, Sam 1920–1997 **88**
Haju, Gerard *See Malawi Mouse Boys*
Hale, Clara 1902–1992 **16**
Hale, Lorraine 1926(?)— **8**
Hale, Nathaniel Dawayne *See Nate Dogg*
Haley, Alex (Palmer) 1921–1992 **4**
Haley, George Williford Boyce 1925— **21**
Hall, Aaron 1963— **57**
Hall, Adelaide 1901–1993 **126**
Hall, Alvin D. 1952— **86**
Hall, Arsenio 1955— **58**
Hall, Arthur 1943–2000 **39**
Hall, Elliott S. 1938(?)— **24**
Hall, Juanita 1901–1968 **62**
Hall, Kevan 19(?)(?)— **61**
Hall, Lloyd A(ugustus) 1894–1971 **8**
Hall, Syren *See Fiona, Melanie*
Hall, Stuart 1932— **78**
Hall, Tamron 1970— **96**
Hall, Valerie Eileen *See Wellington, Valerie*
Hall, Willie *See Bar-Kays, The*
Halliburton, Warren J. 1924— **49**
Hallim, Melanie Fiona *See Fiona, Melanie*
Ham, Cynthia Parker 1970(?)— **58**
Hamblin, Ken 1940— **10**
Hamburg, Beatrix 1923— **84**
Hamburg, Margaret 1955— **78**
Hamer, Fannie Lou 1917–1977 **6**
Hamilton, Anthony 1971— **61**
Hamilton, Bernie 1928–2008 **117**
Hamilton, Chico 1921–2013 **117**
Hamilton, Foreststorn *See Hamilton, Chico*
Hamilton, Lawrence 1954–2014 **122**
Hamilton, Leonard 1948— **100**

Hamilton, Lewis 1985— **66**
Hamilton, Lisa Gay 1964— **71**
Hamilton, Samuel C. 19(?)(?)— **47**
Hamilton, Tanya 1968— **93**
Hamilton, Vicki 1964(?)— **95**
Hamilton, Virginia 1936— **10**
Hamlin, Larry Leon 1948–2007 **49, 62**
Hammer, M. C. *See M.C. Hammer*
Hammon, Jupiter 1711–1806(?) **124**
Hammond, Fred 1960— **23**
Hammond, Lenn 1970(?)— **34**
Hammond, Paula 1963— **119**
Hammonds, Evelynn 1953— **69**
Hammons, David 1943— **69**
Hampton, Fred 1948–1969 **18**
Hampton, Henry (Eugene, Jr.) 1940— **6**
Hampton, Lionel 1908(?)–2002 **17, 41**
Hancock, Herbie 1940— **20, 67**
Hancock, Michael B. 1969— **123**
Handy, W(illiam) C(hristopher) 1873–1937 **8**
Haney, Lee 1959— **77**
Hani, Chris 1942–1993 **6**
Hani, Martin Thembisile *See Hani, Chris*
Hanley, Quincy Matthew *See ScHoolboy Q*
Hannah, Marc (Regis) 1956— **10**
Hansberry, Lorraine (Vivian) 1930–1965 **6**
Hansberry, Tony, II 1994— **93**
Hansberry, William Leo 1894–1965 **11**
Hansen, Austin 1910–1996 **88**
Happy Land Jubilee Singers *See Blind Boys of Alabama, The*
Hardaway, Anfernee 1971— **13, 111**
Hardaway, Penny *See Hardaway, Anfernee*
Hardaway, Tim 1966— **35**
Harden, James 1989— **116**
Harden, Monique 1968— **97**
Harden, Rashad Hanif *See DJ Rashad*
Hardin Armstrong, Lil 1898–1971 **39**
Hardin, Lillian Beatrice *See Hardin Armstrong, Lil*
Harding, Vincent 1931— **67**
Hardison, Bethann 19(?)(?)— **12**
Hardison, Kadeem 1966— **22**
Hardson, Tre *See Pharcyde, The*
Hardwick, Omari 1974— **122**
Hardy, Antonio *See Big Daddy Kane*
Hardy, Greg 1988— **118**
Hardy, Nell *See Carter, Nell*
Hare, Nathan 1934— **44**
Harewood, David 1965— **52**
Harewood, Dorian 1950— **104**
Harkless, Necia Desiree 1920— **19**
Harmon, Clarence 1940(?)— **26**
Harmon, Gordy *See Whispers, The*
Harold, Erika 1980(?)— **54**
Harold Melvin & the Blue Notes **105**
Harp, Toni 1949— **123**
Harper, Ben 1969— **34, 62**

Harper, Frances E(llen) W(atkins) 1825–1911 **11**
Harper, Frank *See Harper, Hill*
Harper, Hill 1966— **32, 65, 97**
Harper, Michael S. 1938— **34**
Harper, Rachel M. 1972— **92**
Harrell, Andre (O'Neal) 1962(?)— **9, 30**
Harrington, Carey Bell *See Bell, Carey*
Harrington, Oliver W(endell) 1912— **9**
Harris, Addie *See Shirelles, The*
Harris, Alice 1934— **7**
Harris, Barbara 1930— **12**
Harris, Barry 1929— **68**
Harris, Bernard A. 1956— **90**
Harris, Bill *See Clovers, The*
Harris, Bill 1941— **72**
Harris, Bobby *See Dazz Band*
Harris, Carla A. 1962— **67**
Harris, Ciara Princess *See Ciara*
Harris, Claire 1937— **34**
Harris, Corey 1969— **39, 73**
Harris, Damon 1950–2013 **110**
Harris, E. Lynn 1955–2009 **12, 33, 116**
Harris, Eddy L. 1956— **18**
Harris, Franco 1950— **97**
Harris, Gary L. 1953— **87**
Harris, James 1947— **79**
Harris, James, III *See Jimmy Jam*
Harris, Jay **19**
Harris, Jessica B. 1948— **91**
Harris, Kamala D. 1964— **64, 122**
Harris, Kevin 1975— **120**
Harris, Leslie 1961— **6**
Harris, Lois *See Chantels, The*
Harris, Lorenzo *See Harris, Rennie*
Harris, Lyle Ashton 1965— **83**
Harris, Major 1947–2012 **110**
Harris, Marcelite Jordon 1943— **16**
Harris, Mary Styles 1949— **31**
Harris, Maya Lakshmi 1966— **88**
Harris, Monica 1968— **18**
Harris, Naomie 1976— **55, 116**
Harris, Otis Robert, Jr. *See Harris, Damon*
Harris, Patricia Roberts 1924–1985 **2**
Harris, R. H. *See Soul Stirrers*
Harris, Rennie 1964— **120**
Harris, Richard E. 1912(?)— **61**
Harris, Rhonda *See Vanzant, Iyanla*
Harris, Robin 1953–1990 **7**
Harris, Shack *See Harris, James*
Harris, Sherwin David *See Harris, Wood*
Harris, "Sweet" Alice *See Harris, Alice*
Harris, Sylvia 1967(?)— **70**
Harris, Wesley L. 1941— **92**
Harris, William Anthony *See Harris, Bill*
Harris, Wood 1969— **114**
Harris, Wynonie 1915(?)–1969 **102**
Harris-Lacewell, Melissa 1973— **81**
Harrison, Alvin 1974— **28**
Harrison, Calvin 1974— **28**
Harrison, Charles 1931— **72**
Harrison, Mya *See Mya*
Harris-Stewart, Lusia 1955— **90**
Harry, Jackée 1956— **111**

Harsh, Vivian Gordon 1890–1960 **14**

Hart, Alvin Youngblood 1963— **61**

Hart, Billy 1940— **126**

Hart, Gregory Edward *See Hart, Alvin Youngblood*

Hart, Kevin 1980— **103**

Hart, Thomas A., Sr. 1919–2013 **113**

Hartman, Johnny 1923–1983 **109**

Harvard, Beverly (Joyce Bailey) 1950— **11**

Harvey, Steve 1956— **18, 58**

Harvey, William R. 1941— **42**

Harvin, Percy 1988— **123**

Harvin, William Percival, III *See Harvin, Percy*

Haskins, Clem 1943— **23**

Haskins, James 1941–2005 **36, 54**

Hassell, Leroy Rountree, Sr. 1955–2011 **41, 116**

Hastie, William H(enry) 1904–1976 **8**

Hastings, Alcee 1936— **16, 119**

Hatcher, Andrew T. 1923–1990 **90**

Hatcher, Charles Edwin *See Starr, Edwin*

Hatcher, Richard G. 1933— **55**

Hatchett, Glenda 1951(?)— **32**

Hathaway, Donny 1945–1979 **18**

Hathaway, Isaac Scott 1874–1967 **33**

Hathaway, Lalah 1968— **57, 88**

Haughton, Aaliyah *See Aaliyah*

Havens, Richard Pierce *See Havens, Richie*

Havens, Richie 1941–2013 **111**

Hawes, Hampton 1928–1977 **121**

Hawkins, Adrienne Lita *See Kennedy, Adrienne*

Hawkins, Augustus F. 1907–2007 **68**

Hawkins, Barbara Ann *See Dixie Cups, The*

Hawkins, Coleman 1904–1969 **9**

Hawkins, Connie 1942— **91**

Hawkins, Edwin 1943— **113**

Hawkins, Erskine Ramsey 1914–1993 **14**

Hawkins, Jamesetta *See James, Etta*

Hawkins, La-Van 1960— **17, 54**

Hawkins, Rosa Lee *See Dixie Cups, The*

Hawkins, "Screamin'" Jay 1929–2000 **30**

Hawkins, Steven Wayne 1962— **14**

Hawkins, Tramaine Aunzola 1951— **16**

Hawkins, Walter 1949–2010 **87**

Hayanga, Awori *See Hayanga, Jeremiah*

Hayanga, Jeremiah 1974(?)— **118**

Hayden, Carla D. 1952— **47**

Hayden, Lewis 1811–1889 **105**

Hayden, Palmer 1890–1973 **13**

Hayden, Robert Earl 1913–1980 **12**

Haye, David 1980— **82**

Hayes, Bob 1942–2002 **77**

Hayes, Cecil N. 1945— **46**

Hayes, Dennis 1951— **54**

Hayes, Edwin *See Freestyle Fellowship*

Hayes, Elvin 1945— **93**

Hayes, Isaac 1942–2008 **20, 58, 73**

Hayes, James C. 1946— **10**

Hayes, Robert Lee *See Hayes, Bob*

Hayes, Roland 1887–1977 **4**

Hayes, Teddy 1951— **40**

Hayes, Terrance 1971— **124**

Haygood, Wil 1954— **83**

Haynes, Cornell, Jr. *See Nelly*

Haynes, Elizabeth Ross 1883–1953 **102**

Haynes, George Edmund 1880–1960 **8**

Haynes, Marques 1926— **22**

Haynes, Roy 1925— **87**

Haynes, Trudy 1926— **44**

Haynie, Sharon 1955— **94**

Haysbert, Dennis 1954— **42, 106**

Haysbert, Raymond V., Sr. 1920–2010 **87**

Haywood, Gar Anthony 1954— **43**

Haywood, Jimmy 1993(?)— **58**

Haywood, Margaret A. 1912— **24**

Haywood, Spencer 1949— **99**

Hazel, Darryl B. 1949— **50**

Hazzard, Walt 1942–2011 **98**

Hazziez, Joseph *See Tex, Joe*

Hazziez, Jusef *See Tex, Joe*

Hazziez, Yusef *See Tex, Joe*

Head, Bessie 1937–1986 **28**

Healy, James Augustine 1830–1900 **30**

Healy, Michael 1839–1904 **90**

Heard, Gar 1948— **25**

Heard, Nathan C. 1936–2004 **45**

Hearne, John Edgar Caulwell 1926–1994 **45**

Hearns, Thomas 1958— **29**

Heath, Percy 1923–2005 **100**

Heavy D 1967–2011 **58, 98**

Hector, Jamie 1975— **98**

Hedgeman, Anna Arnold 1899–1990 **22**

Hedgeman, Peyton Cole *See Hayden, Palmer*

Hegamin, Lucille 1894–1970 **120**

Height, Dorothy I. 1912— **2, 23, 78**

Hemingway, Anthony 1977— **107**

Hemphill, Essex 1957— **10**

Hemphill, Jessie Mae 1923–2006 **33, 59**

Hemsley, Sherman 1938–2012 **19, 104**

Henderson, Angelo 1962–2014 **122**

Henderson, Cornelius Langston 1888(?)–1976 **26**

Henderson, David 1942— **53**

Henderson, Fletcher 1897–1952 **32**

Henderson, George Washington 1850–1936 **101**

Henderson, Gordon 1957— **5**

Henderson, Harvey *See Bar-Kays, The*

Henderson, Henry Fairfax, Jr. 1928— **89**

Henderson, Jeff 1964— **72**

Henderson, Joe 1937–2001 **127**

Henderson, John William *See Homesick James*

Henderson, Natalie Leota *See Hinderas, Natalie*

Henderson, Rickey 1958— **28, 78**

Henderson, Stephen E. 1925–1997 **45**

Henderson, Thelton E. 1933— **68**

Henderson, Wade 1944(?)— **14**

Henderson, Wayne *See Crusaders, The*

Henderson, Zelma 1920–2008 **71**

Hendricks, Barbara 1948— **3, 67**

Hendrix, James Marshall *See Hendrix, Jimi*

Hendrix, Jimi 1942–1970 **10**

Hendrix, Johnny Allen *See Hendrix, Jimi*

Hendryx, Nona 1944— **56**

Hendy, Francis 195(?)— **47**

Henries, A. Doris Banks 1913–1981 **44**

Henriques, Julian 1955(?)— **37**

Henry, Aaron Edd 1922–1997 **19**

Henry, Clarence "Frogman" 1937— **46**

Henry, Dwight 1963— **104**

Henry, Joshua 1994— **94**

Henry, Lenny 1958— **9, 52**

Henry, Marianne *See Marian Anderson String Quartet*

Henry, Mark 1971— **116**

Henry, Richard Bullock *See Obadele, Imari*

Henry, Thierry 1977— **66, 127**

Henry, Troy 1960(?)— **85**

Henson, Darrin 1970(?)— **33**

Henson, Josiah 1789–1883 **90**

Henson, Matthew (Alexander) 1866–1955 **2**

Henson, Taraji P. 1970— **58, 77, 127**

Herbert, Bob 1945— **63, 96**

Hercules, Frank 1911–1996 **44**

Herenton, Willie W. 1940— **24, 81**

Herman, Alexis Margaret 1947— **15**

Hernandez, Aileen Clarke 1926— **13**

Hernández, Orlando 1965— **96**

Herndon, Alonzo Franklin 1858–1927 **89**

Herndon, Angelo 1913–1997 **90**

Herndon, Charlie *See New Birth*

Hernton, Calvin C. 1932–2001 **51**

Hibbert, Frederick Nathaniel *See Hibbert, Toots*

Hibbert, Toots 1946— **103**

Hickman, Fred(erick Douglass) 1951— **11**

Hicks, Ulysses *See Five Keys, The*

Hicks Maynard, Nancy *See Maynard, Nancy Hicks*

Higginbotham, A. Leon, Jr. 1928–1998 **13, 25**

Higginbotham, Jack *See Higginbotham, Jay C.*

Higginbotham, Jay C. 1906–1973 **37**

Higginbotham, Joan 1963— **124**

Higginbotham, Robert *See Tucker, Tommy*

Higginsen, Vy 1945(?)— **65**

Hightower, Dennis F(owler) 1941— **13**

Hill, Andrew 1931–2007 **66**

Hill, Anita 1956— **5, 65**

Hill, Beatrice *See Moore, Melba*

Hill, Bonnie Guiton 1941— **20**

Hill, Calvin 1947— **19**

Hill, Darryl 1990— **128**

Hill, Donna 1955— **32**

Hill, Dulé 1975(?)— **29**

Hill, Errol 1921— **40**

Hill, Grant 1972— **13, 94**

Hill, Hugh Morgan 1921–2009 **83**

Hill, Janet 1947— **19**

Hill, Jemele 1975— **109**

Hill, Jesse, Jr. 1927— **13**

Hill, Lamar *See Treacherous Three*

Hill, Lauryn 1975— **20, 53, 111**

Hill, Leslie Pinckney 1880–1960 **44**

Hill, Marc Lamont 1978— **80, 128**

Hill, Michael 1971— **95**

Hill, Oliver W. 1907–2007 **24, 63**

Hill, Peter 1767–1829 **92**

Hill, Tamia *See Tamia*

Hill, Wyllstyne D. 1949(?)— **94**

Hillard, Terry 1954— **25**

Hillary, Barbara 1923(?)— **65**

Hilliard, Asa Grant, III 1933–2007 **66**

Hilliard, David 1942— **7, 105**

Hilliard, Earl F. 1942— **24**

Hilliard, Wendy 196(?)— **53**

Hilson, Keri 1982— **84**

Himes, Chester 1909–1984 **8**

Hinderas, Natalie 1927–1987 **5**

Hine, Darlene Clark 1947— **24**

Hines, Earl "Fatha" 1905–1983 **39**

Hines, Garrett 1969— **35**

Hines, Gregory (Oliver) 1946–2003 **1, 42**

Hinton, Milt 1910–2000 **30**

Hinton, William Augustus 1883–1959 **8**

Hoagland, Everett H. 1942— **45**

Hoagland, Jaheim *See Jaheim*

Hobson, Julius W. 1919–1977 **44**

Hobson, Mellody 1969— **40**

Hodge, Aldis 1986— **124**

Hodge, Derrick 1979— **114**

Hogan, Beverly Wade 1951— **50**

Hoggs, Billy *See Contours, The*

Holden, Kip 1952— **120**

Holden, Melvin *See Holden, Kip*

Holder, Eric, Jr. 1951— **9, 76, 104**

Holder, Geoffrey 1930–2014 **78, 124**

Holder, Laurence 1939— **34**

Holdsclaw, Chamique 1977— **24, 110**

Holiday, Billie 1915–1959 **1**

Holiday, Jrue 1990— **115**

Holland, Brian *See Holland-Dozier-Holland*

Holland, Eddie *See Holland-Dozier-Holland*

Holland, Endesha Ida Mae 1944–2006 **3, 57**

Holland, Kimberly N. 19(?)(?)— **62**

Holland, Robert, Jr. 1940— **11**

Holland-Dozier-Holland **36**

Holloway, Brenda 1946— **65**

Holloway, Loleatta 1946–2011 **115**

Hollowell, Donald L. 1917–2004 **57**

Holmes, Amy 1973— **69**

Holmes, Benjamin *See Fisk Jubilee Singers*

Holmes, Clint 1946— **57**

Holmes, De'Angelo *See Ying Yang Twins*

Holmes, Hamilton E. 1941–1995 **82**

Holmes, Kelly 1970— **47**

Holmes, Larry 1949— **20, 68**

Holmes, Loutelious Ann, Jr. See Holmes, T. J.
Holmes, Santonio 1984— 87
Holmes, Shannon 1973(?)— 70
Holmes, T. J. 1977— 98
Holness, Andrew 1972— 99
Holsey, Lucius Henry 1842–1920 92
Holstein, Casper 1876–1944 89
Holt, Lester 1959— 66
Holt, Morris See Magic Slim
Holt, Nora 1885(?)–1974 38
Holt Baker, Arlene 1951— 73
Holte, Patricia Louise See LaBelle, Patti
Holton, DeShaun Dupree See Proof
Holton, Hugh, Jr. 1947–2001 39
Holyfield, Evander 1962— 6
Homesick James 1910(?)–2006 124
Honeywood, Varnette P. 1950–2010 54, 88
Honoré, Russel L. 1947— 64
Hood, James Walker 1831–1918 91
Hooker, John Lee 1917–2000 30
hooks, bell 1952— 5, 90
Hooks, Benjamin L. 1925–2010 2, 85
Hooks, Robert 1937— 76
Hooper, Stix See Crusaders, The
Hope, John 1868–1936 8
Hope, Lugenia Burns 1871–1947 89
Hopgood, Hadda See Brooks, Hadda
Hopkins, Bernard 1965— 35, 69, 105
Hopkins, Donald R. 1941— 89
Hopkins, Lightnin' 1912–1982 83
Hopkins, Sam See Hopkins, Lightnin'
Horford, Al 1988— 107
Horford Reynoso, Alfred Joel See Horford, Al
Horn, Shirley 1934–2005 32, 56
Horne, Frank 1899–1974 44
Horne, Lena 1917–2010 5, 86
Horsford, Steven 1973— 88
Horton, Andre 1979— 33
Horton, Big Walter 1918(?)–1981 115
Horton, George Moses 1798(?)–1883(?) 124
Horton, Gladys 1945–2011 92 See also Marvelettes, The
Horton, James Oliver 1943— 58
Horton, (Andreana) Suki 1982— 33
Horton, Walter See Horton, Big Walter
Horton, Willie 1942— 104
Hoskins, Harold K. 1927–2012 103
Houghton, Israel 1971— 92
Hounsou, Djimon 1964— 19, 45
Houphouët, Dia See Houphouët-Boigny, Félix
Houphouët-Boigny, Félix 1905–1993 4, 64
House, Eddie James, Jr. See House, Son
House, Eugene See House, Son
House, Son 1902–1988 8
Houston, Charles Hamilton 1895–1950 4
Houston, Cissy 1933— 20, 83

Houston, Jordan Michael See Juicy J
Houston, Whitney 1963–2012 7, 28, 83, 100
Howard, Ayanna 1972— 65
Howard, Corinne See Mitchell, Corinne
Howard, Desmond 1970— 16, 58
Howard, Dwight 1985— 113
Howard, Elston 1929–1980 125
Howard, Juwan Antonio 1973— 15
Howard, M. William, Jr. 1946— 26
Howard, Michelle 1960— 28, 125
Howard, Perry Wilbon, Jr. 1877–1961 112
Howard, Ryan 1979— 65, 113
Howard, Sherri 1962— 36
Howard, Terrence 1969— 59, 94
Howard, William See Dramatics, The
Howell, Ayinde 1978— 91
Howlin' Wolf 1910–1976 9
Howroyd, Janice Bryant 1953— 42
Hoyte, Lenon 1905–1999 50
Hrabowski, Freeman A., III 1950— 22
Hubbard, Arnette 19(?)(?)— 38
Hubbard, Freddie 1948–2008 75
Hubbard, Frederick DeWayne See Hubbard, Freddie
Huddleston, William Emanuel See Lateef, Yusef
Hudlin, Reginald 1961— 9, 86
Hudlin, Warrington, Jr. 1953(?)— 9
Hudson, Cheryl 19(?)(?)— 15
Hudson, Ernie 1945— 72
Hudson, James See Spaniels, The
Hudson, Jennifer 1981— 63, 83
Hudson, Lou 1944–2014 121
Hudson, Louis Clyde See Hudson, Lou
Hudson, Saul See Slash
Hudson, Wade 1946— 15
Huff, Leon 1942— 86
Huggins, Edie 1935–2008 71
Huggins, Larry 1950— 21
Huggins, Nathan Irvin 1927–1989 52
Hughes, Albert 1972— 7
Hughes, Allen 1972— 7
Hughes, Cathy 1947(?)— 27
Hughes, Dora 1970(?)— 88
Hughes, Ebony 1948— 57
Hughes, (James Mercer) Langston 1902–1967 4
Hughes, Leon See Coasters, The
Hughley, D. L. 1963— 23, 76
Hughley, Darryl Lynn See Hughley, D. L.
Hull, Akasha Gloria 1944— 45
Humes, Helen 1913–1981 128
Humphrey, Bobbi 1950— 20
Humphrey, Claude 1944— 119
Humphries, Frederick 1935— 20
Hundley, Mandisa Lynn See Mandisa
Hunt, Darnell 1962— 92
Hunt, Richard (Howard) 1935— 6
Hunter, Alberta 1895–1984 42
Hunter, Billy 1942— 22, 109
Hunter, Charlayne See Hunter-Gault, Charlayne
Hunter, Clementine 1887–1988 45

Hunter, George William See Hunter, Billy
Hunter, Ivory Joe 1914–1974 106
Hunter, Lindsey 1970— 110
Hunter, Torii 1975— 43, 109
Hunter-Gault, Charlayne 1942— 6, 31
Hurd, Sam 1985— 116
Hurston, Zora Neale 1891–1960 3
Hurt, Byron 1970— 61
Hurt, Mississippi John 1892(?)–1966 84
Hurtt, Harold 1947(?)— 46
Hussein, Lubna 1970(?)— 80
Hutch, Willie 1944–2005 62
Hutcherson, Bobby 1941— 115
Hutcherson, Hilda Yvonne 1955— 54
Hutchinson, Earl Ofari 1945— 24
Hutchinson, Jeanette See Emotions, The
Hutchinson, Pamela See Emotions, The
Hutchinson, Sheila See Emotions, The
Hutchinson, Wanda See Emotions, The
Hutson, Jean Blackwell 1914— 16
Hutson, Marcus See Whispers, The
Hyde, Cowan F. "Bubba" 1908–2003 47
Hyman, Earle 1926— 25, 79
Hyman, Phyllis 1949(?)–1995 19
Ibrahim, Fuad 1991— 109
Ibrahim, Ibee See Ibrahim, Fuad
Ibrahim, Mo 1946— 67, 115
Ice Cube 1969— 8, 30, 60
Iceberg Slim 1918–1992 11
Ice-T 1958— 6, 31, 96
Ifill, Gwen 1955— 28
Iginla, Jarome 1977— 35
Ilibagiza, Immaculée 1972(?)— 66
Iluobe, Christopher Airemiokhai See Aire, Chris
Iman 1955— 4, 33, 87
Iman, Chanel 1989— 66
Imani See Pharcyde, The
Imani Winds 113
Imes, Elmer Samuel 1883–1941 39
Ince, Paul 1967— 83
India.Arie 1975— 34
Ingraham, Hubert A. 1947— 19
Ingram, James 1952— 84
Ingram, Raphael See Five Keys, The
Ingram, Rex 1895–1969 5
Ingram, Ripley See Five Keys, The
Ink Spots, The 102
Innis, Roy (Emile Alfredo) 1934— 5
Intruders, The 119
Irvin, Michael 1966— 64
Irvin, (Monford Merrill) Monte 1919— 31
Irvin, Vernon 1961— 65
Irving, Barrington, Jr. 1983— 112
Irving, Clarence (Larry) 1955— 12
Irving, Kyrie 1992— 102
Irvis, K. Leroy 1917(?)–2006 67
Isaac, Julius 1928— 34
Isaacs, Cheryl Boone 1949— 113
Isaacs, Gregory 1951–2010 89
Isaacs, John 1915–2009 76
Isles, Bill See O'Jays, The

Isley, Marvin 1953–2010 87
Isley, Ronald 1941— 25, 56
Issoufou, Mahamadou 1952— 102
Iverson, Allen 1975— 24, 46
Iverson, Johnathan Lee 1976— 22, 100
Ivey, Artis, Jr. See Coolio
Ivey, Phil 1976— 72, 106
J Dilla 1974–2006 102
Ja Rule 1976— 35, 91
Jackée See Harry, Jackée
Jackson, Alexine Clement 1936— 22
Jackson, Alphonso R. 1946— 48
Jackson, Bobby 1956–2013 119
Jackson, Brenda 1953— 87
Jackson, Deborah 1952— 94
Jackson, DeSean 1986— 120
Jackson, Earl 1948— 31
Jackson, Edison O. 1943(?)— 67
Jackson, Eric 1959— 127
Jackson, Eric, Jr. See Ying Yang Twins
Jackson, Frank G. 1946— 76
Jackson, Fred James 1950— 25
Jackson, George 1960(?)— 19
Jackson, George Lester 1941–1971 14
Jackson, Hal 1915–2012 41, 104
Jackson, Henry Melody, Jr. See Armstrong, Henry
Jackson, Isaiah (Allen) 1945— 3
Jackson, Jackie See Jackson 5
Jackson, Jamea 1986— 64
Jackson, James A. 1878–1960 90
Jackson, James Curtis, III See 50 Cent
Jackson, Janet 1966— 6, 30, 68
Jackson, Jennie See Fisk Jubilee Singers
Jackson, Jermaine 1954— 79 See also Jackson 5
Jackson, Jesse 1941— 1, 27, 72
Jackson, Jesse, Jr. 1965— 14, 45, 81, 108
Jackson, Jimmie Lee 1938–1965 126
Jackson, Joe 1929— 78
Jackson, John 1924–2002 36
Jackson, John David See Fabolous
Jackson, Judith D. 1950— 57
Jackson, Keenon Daequan Ray See YG
Jackson, LaToya 1956— 95
Jackson, Lisa 1962— 77
Jackson, Mae 1941–2005 57
Jackson, Mahalia 1911–1972 5
Jackson, Mannie 1939— 14
Jackson, Mark 1965— 121
Jackson, Marlon See Jackson 5
Jackson, Mary 1945— 73
Jackson, Maynard 1938–2003 2, 41
Jackson, Michael 1958–2009 19, 53, 76 See also Jackson 5
Jackson, Millie 1944— 25
Jackson, Milt 1923–1999 26
Jackson, O'Shea See Ice Cube
Jackson, Otis, Jr. See Madlib
Jackson, Phillip 1950— 115
Jackson, Quinton See Jackson, Rampage
Jackson, Rampage 1978— 83
Jackson, Randy 1956— 40

Jackson, Reginald Martinez 1946—
15

Jackson, Rickey 1958— 88

Jackson, Robert See New Birth

Jackson, Samuel L. 1948— 8, 19, 63, 102

Jackson, Sandi 1963— 108

Jackson, Sheneska 1970(?)— 18

Jackson, Shirley Ann 1946— 12

Jackson, Stephen 1978— 118

Jackson, Tito 1953— 81 See also Jackson 5

Jackson, Tom 1951— 70

Jackson, Vera 1912— 40

Jackson, Vivian See Yabby You

Jackson, Willie See Spaniels, The

Jackson, Zelda Mavin See Ormes, Jackie

Jackson 5 103

Jackson Lee, Sheila 1950— 20

Jaco, Wasalu Muhammad See Fiasco, Lupe

Jacob, John E(dward) 1934— 2

Jacobs, George 1927–2013 118

Jacobs, Harriet 1813–1897 104

Jacobs, Marion Walter See Little Walter

Jacobs, Regina 1963— 38

Jacquet, Illinois 1922(?)–2004 49

Jagan, Cheddi 1918–1997 16

Jagged Edge 117

Jaheim 1978— 58

Jakes, T. D. 1957— 17, 43, 116

Jakes, Thomas Dexter See Jakes, T. D.

Jalade-Ekeinde, Omotola 1978— 118

Jam, Jimmy See Jimmy Jam

Jam Master Jay See Run-DMC

Jamal, Ahmad 1930— 69

Jamelia 1981— 51

Jamerson, James 1936–1983 59

James, Charles H., III 1959(?)— 62

James, Daniel "Chappie," Jr. 1920–1978 16

James, David 1970— 84

James, Donna A. 1957— 51

James, Elmo See James, Elmore

James, Elmore 1918–1963 114

James, Etta 1938–2012 13, 52, 100

James, G. Larry 1947–2008 74

James, Juanita (Therese) 1952— 13

James, LaRon Louis See Santana, Juelz

James, LeBron 1984— 46, 78, 105

James, Leela 1983— 117

James, Marlon 1970— 85, 124

James, Nikki M. 1981— 94

James, Sharpe 1936— 23, 69

James, Skip 1902–1969 38

James, Sly 1951— 107

James, Sylvester, Jr. See James, Sly

James, Vanessa 1987— 84

James Bracken and Vivian Bracken 107

Jamison, Judith 1943— 7, 67, 96

Jammeh, Yahya 1965— 23, 104

Jansen, Jonathan 1956— 102

Jarreau, Al 1940— 21, 65, 105

Jarreau, Alwyn Lopez See Jarreau, Al

Jarrett, Valerie 1956— 73

Jarrett, Vernon D. 1921— 42

Jarvis, Charlene Drew 1941— 21

Jarvis, Erich 1965— 67

Jarvis, Kristen 1981(?)— 85

Jasper, John J. 1812–1901 91

Jasper, Kenji 1976(?)— 39

Jawara, Dawda Kairaba 1924— 11

Jawara, Jali Musa See Diawara, Djeli Moussa

Jay Electronica 1976— 125

Jay-Z 1969— 27, 69, 103

Jazz Crusaders, The See Crusaders, The

Jealous, Benjamin Todd 1973— 70, 113

Jean, Michaëlle 1957— 70

Jean, Wyclef 1970— 20, 86

Jean-Baptiste, Marianne 1967— 17, 46

Jean-Juste, Gérard 1946–2009 78

Jean-Louis, Jimmy 1968— 76

Jeffers, Eve Jihan See Eve

Jefferson, Blind Lemon 1893(?)–1929 81

Jefferson, Denise 1944–2010 87

Jefferson, Margo 1947— 108

Jefferson, Mildred Fay 1927–2010 89

Jefferson, William J. 1947— 25, 72

Jeffrey, Herbert See Jeffries, Herb

Jeffries, Hakeem 1970— 118

Jeffries, Herb 1913(?)–2014 122

Jeffries, Leonard 1937— 8

Jemison, Mae C. 1957— 1, 35

Jemison, Major L. 1955(?)— 48

Jemison, T. J. 1918–2013 119

Jemison, Theodore Judson See Jemison, T. J.

Jenifer, Franklyn G(reen) 1939— 2

Jenkins, Beverly 1951— 14

Jenkins, Ella (Louise) 1924— 15

Jenkins, Fergie 1943— 46

Jenkins, Hubby See Carolina Chocolate Drops

Jenkins, Jay See Young Jeezy

Jenkins, Kris 1979— 98

Jenkins, Ray 1920–2009 77

Jenkins, Terrence See Terrence J

Jenkins, Tomi See Cameo

Jennings, Chester See Jennings, Lyfe

Jennings, Lyfe 1973— 56, 69

Jennings, Thomas L. 1791–1859 125

Jeptoo, Rita 1981— 121

Jerkins, Rodney 1978(?)— 31

Jesu, Kunjoya Mwa See Malawi Mouse Boys

Jeter, Claude 1914–2009 75 See also Swan Silvertones

Jeter, Derek 1974— 27, 93, 124

Jeune, Vitolio 1982— 98

Jim, Songezo 1990— 111

Jimmy Jam 1959— 13

Joachim, Paulin 1931— 34

Jobe, Duke See Rose Royce

Jobe, Lequeint See Rose Royce

Joe, Yolanda 19(?)(?)— 21

John, Daymond 1969— 23, 114

Johns, Vernon 1892–1965 38

Johnson, Al 1948–2013 119

Johnson, Alfred Orlando, Jr. See Johnson, Al

Johnson, Andre See Rare Essence

Johnson, Andre 1981— 127

Johnson, Angela 1961— 52

Johnson, Anthony M. 1954— 92

Johnson, Arnez See Arnez J

Johnson, Avery 1965— 62

Johnson, Ben 1961— 1

Johnson, Beverly 1952— 2, 102

Johnson, Buddy 1915–1977 36

Johnson, Bumpy 1905(?)–1968 102

Johnson, Calvin 1985— 108

Johnson, Camará DaCosta See DaCosta, YaYa

Johnson, Carol Diann See Carroll, Diahann

Johnson, Caryn E. See Goldberg, Whoopi

Johnson, Chad 1978— 108

Johnson, Charles 1948— 1, 82

Johnson, Charles Arthur See St. Jacques, Raymond

Johnson, Charles Spurgeon 1893–1956 12

Johnson, Chris 1985— 92

Johnson, Clarence See Chi-Lites

Johnson, Clark 1954— 96

Johnson, Clifford "Connie" 1922–2004 52

Johnson, Conrad O. 1915–2008 97

Johnson, Dennis 1954–2007 89

Johnson, Donald Ray See Taste of Honey, A

Johnson, Dwayne See Rock, The

Johnson, Earvin See Johnson, Magic

Johnson, Eddie Bernice 1935— 8, 90

Johnson, Edward Austin 1860–1944 107

Johnson, Ellsworth Raymond See Johnson, Bumpy

Johnson, Eunice W. 1916–2010 83

Johnson, Fenton 1888–1958 91

Johnson, George E. 1927— 29

Johnson, Georgia Douglas 1880–1966 41

Johnson, Gus 1938–1987 92

Johnson, Hall 1888–1970 90

Johnson, Hank, Jr. 1954— 80

Johnson, Harry E. 1954— 57

Johnson, Harvey, Jr. 1947(?)— 24, 82

Johnson, Hazel 1927— 22

Johnson, Hubert See Contours, The

Johnson, J. J. 1924–2001 37

Johnson, J. Rosamond 1873–1954 121

Johnson, Jack 1878–1946 8

Johnson, James See Drifters, The

Johnson, James Louis See Johnson, J. J.

Johnson, James Weldon 1871–1938 5

Johnson, James William See Johnson, James Weldon

Johnson, Janice Marie See Taste of Honey, A

Johnson, Je'Caryous 1977— 63

Johnson, Jeh 1957— 76, 125

Johnson, Jeh Vincent 1931— 44

Johnson, Joan Marie See Dixie Cups, The

Johnson, Joe See Golden Gate Quartet

Johnson, Joe 1981— 94

Johnson, John Arthur See Johnson, Jack

Johnson, John H. 1918–2005 3, 54

Johnson, John Henry 1929–2011 96

Johnson, John Rosamond See Johnson, J. Rosamond

Johnson, Johnnie 1924–2005 56

Johnson, Judy 1899–1989 105

Johnson, Katherine (Coleman Goble) 1918— 61

Johnson, Ken 1914–1941 106

Johnson, Kevin 1966— 70

Johnson, Keyshawn 1972— 91

Johnson, Larry 1969— 28

Johnson, Le'Andria 1983— 108

Johnson, Leroy R. 1928— 89

Johnson, Levi 1950— 48

Johnson, Linton Kwesi 1952— 37

Johnson, Lonnie 1899(?)–1970 85

Johnson, Lonnie G. 1949— 32, 93

Johnson, Louis See Swan Silvertones, The

Johnson, Magic 1959— 3, 39, 101

Johnson, Mamie "Peanut" 1932— 40

Johnson, Marguerite See Angelou, Maya

Johnson, Mat 1970— 31, 105

Johnson, Michael (Duane) 1967— 13

Johnson, Michelle See Ndegeocello, Meshell

Johnson, Mordecai Wyatt 1890–1976 79

Johnson, Norma H. 1932–2011 17, 97

Johnson, R. M. 1968— 36

Johnson, Rafer 1934— 33

Johnson, Robert 1911–1938 2

Johnson, Robert L. 1946— 3, 39, 121

Johnson, Robert T. 1948— 17

Johnson, Rodney Van 19(?)(?)— 28

Johnson, Sandra K. 1960(?)— 94

Johnson, Sheila Crump 1949(?)— 48

Johnson, Shoshana 1973— 47

Johnson, Sterling, Jr. 1934— 124

Johnson, Syl 1938— 97

Johnson, Syleena 1977— 98

Johnson, Taalib See Musiq

Johnson, Tommy 1896–1956 106

Johnson, Virginia (Alma Fairfax) 1950— 9

Johnson, William 1809–1851 91

Johnson, William Henry 1901–1970 3

Johnson, William Julius See Johnson, Judy

Johnson, Willie See Golden Gate Quartet

Johnson, Woodrow Wilson See Johnson, Buddy

Johnson, Wycliffe See Steely

Johnson-Brown, Hazel W. See Johnson, Hazel

Johnson-George, Tamara 1971— 79

Johnson-Powell, Gloria 1937— 107

Joiner, Alvin Nathaniel See Xzibit

Joiner, Charlie 1947— 102

Jolicoeur, David Jude See De La Soul

Jolley, Willie 1956— 28

Jonathan, Goodluck 1957— 83

Jones, Absalom 1746–1818 52

Jones, Adam 1983— 103

Jones, Adam 1985— 114

Jones, Alex 1941— 64

Jones, Andruw 1977— 98

Jones, Anthony See Jones, Van

Jones, Bill T. 1952— 1, 46, 80

Jones, Bob See Jones, Robert G.

Jones, Bobby 1938— 20, 94

Jones, Bomani 1980— 121

Jones, Booker T. 1944— 84

Jones, Carl 1955(?)— 7

Jones, Caroline R. 1942— 29

Jones, Clara Stanton 1913–2012 51

Jones, Clarence B. 1931— 114

Jones, Cobi N'Gai 1970— 18

Jones, Creadel See Chi-Lites

Jones, Cullen 1984— 73

Jones, Daron See 112

Jones, David D. See Jones, Deacon

Jones, Deacon 1938–2013 92, 112

Jones, Donell 1973— 29

Jones, Doris W. 1914(?)–2006 62

Jones, Dwight C. 1948— 122

Jones, E. Edward, Sr. 1931— 45

Jones, Ed "Too Tall" 1951— 46

Jones, Eddie Lee See Guitar Slim

Jones, Edith Mae Irby 1927— 65

Jones, Edward P. 1950— 43, 67

Jones, Elaine R. 1944— 7, 45

Jones, Elvin 1927–2004 14, 68

Jones, Emil, Jr. 1935— 74

Jones, Etta 1928–2001 35

Jones, Eugene Kinckle 1885–1954 79

Jones, Frederick McKinley 1893–1961 68

Jones, Frederick Russell See Jamal, Ahmad

Jones, Gayl 1949— 37

Jones, Genevieve 1975(?)— 101

Jones, Hank 1918–2010 57, 86

Jones, Ingrid Saunders 1945— 18

Jones, Jacoby 1984— 117

Jones, James Earl 1931— 3, 49, 79

Jones, James Yancy See Tail Dragger

Jones, Jo See Jones, Papa Jo

Jones, John See Rare Essence

Jones, John 1816–1879 89

Jones, Jon 1987— 121

Jones, Jonah 1909–2000 39

Jones, Jonathan David Samuel See Jones, Papa Jo

Jones, Joseph Rudolph See Jones, Philly Joe

Jones, K. C. 1932— 83

Jones, Kelis See Kelis

Jones, Kimberly Denise See Lil' Kim

Jones, Kirk See Sticky Fingaz

Jones, LeRoi See Baraka, Amiri

Jones, Lillie Mae See Carter, Betty

Jones, Lois Mailou 1905— 13

Jones, Lou 1932–2006 64

Jones, Marion 1975— 21, 66

Jones, Merlakia 1973— 34

Jones, Monty 1951(?)— 66

Jones, Nasir bin Olu Dara See Nas

Jones, Ollie See Ravens, The

Jones, Orlando 1968— 30

Jones, Orville See Ink Spots, The

Jones, Papa Jo 1911–1985 99

Jones, Paul R. 1928— 76

Jones, Phalon See Bar-Kays, The

Jones, Philly Joe 1923–1985 121

Jones, Quincy 1933— 8, 30

Jones, Randy 1969— 35

Jones, Rashida 1976— 101

Jones, Robert Elijah 1872–1960 90

Jones, Robert Elliott See Jones, Jonah

Jones, Robert G. 1936–2008 81

Jones, Robbie 1977— 113

Jones, Roy Jr. 1969— 22

Jones, Russell See Ol' Dirty Bastard

Jones, Ruth Lee See Washington, Dinah

Jones, Sam 1933— 85

Jones, Sarah 1974— 39

Jones, Sharon 1955(?)— 86

Jones, Sissieretta See Joyner, Matilda Sissieretta

Jones, Star See Reynolds, Star Jones

Jones, Tayari 1970— 96

Jones, Thad 1923–1986 68

Jones, Theodore T., Jr. 1944–2012 108

Jones, Thomas W. 1949— 41

Jones, Van 1968— 70

Jones, Walter 1974— 119

Jones, Wayne 1952— 53

Jones, William A., Jr. 1934–2006 61

Jones-Drew, Maurice 1985— 113

Joplin, Scott 1868–1917 6

Jordan, Barbara 1936–1996 4, 78

Jordan, Charles 1937–2014 122

Jordan, Deloris 1941— 108

Jordan, Eddie 1952— 82

Jordan, Eddie 1955— 83

Jordan, Eric Benét See Benét, Eric

Jordan, June 1936— 7, 35

Jordan, Louis 1908–1975 104

Jordan, Michael 1963— 6, 21

Jordan, Michael B. 1987— 97

Jordan, Montell 1968(?)— 23

Jordan, Ronny 1962— 26

Jordan, Vernon E(ulion, Jr.) 1935— 3, 35

Jorge, Seu 1970— 73

Joseph, Edward See Joseph, Jamal

Joseph, Jamal 1953— 101

Joseph, Kathie-Ann 1970(?)— 56

Joseph, Paterson 1964— 126

Josey, E. J. 1924— 10

Joyce, Dru 1955— 81

Joyner, Jacqueline See Joyner-Kersee, Jackie

Joyner, Marjorie Stewart 1896–1994 26

Joyner, Matilda Sissieretta 1869(?)–1933 15

Joyner, Tom 1949(?)— 19, 90

Joyner-Kersee, Jackie 1962— 5

J-Swift See Pharcyde, The

Juicy J 1975— 116

Julian, Hubert 1897–1983 90

Julian, Percy Lavon 1899–1975 6

Julien, Isaac 1960— 3

July, William, II 19(?)(?)— 27

Juma, Calestous 1953— 57

Junior, Marvin See Dells, The

Just, Ernest Everett 1883–1941 3

Justice, David Christopher 1966— 18

Juvenile 1975— 96

Ka Dinizulu, Israel See Ka Dinizulu, Mcwayizeni

Ka Dinizulu, Mcwayizeni 1932–1999 29

Kabbah, Ahmad Tejan 1932— 23

Kabera, Eric 1970— 104

Kabila, Joseph 1971— 30, 126

Kabila, Laurent 1939— 20

Kachinwe, Zondiwe See Malawi Mouse Boys

Kagame, Paul 1957— 54

Kahlil, Aisha See Sweet Honey in the Rock

Kahora, Billy 197(?)— 125

Kaigler, Denise 1962— 63

Kaine See Ying Yang Twins

Kaiser, Cecil 1916–2011 42

Kaka, Luthando 1986— 118

Kalbani, Adil 1959(?)— 77

Kamau, Johnstone See Kenyatta, Jomo

Kamau, Kwadwo Agymah 1960(?)— 28

Kandi 1976— 83

Kane, Evander 1991— 97

Kani, Karl 1968(?)— 10

Kanouté, Fred 1977— 68

Karenga, Maulana 1941— 10, 71

Karim, Benjamin 1932–2005 61

Karim-Ali, Mahershalalhashbaz See Ali, Mahershala

Kariuki, J. M. 1929–1975 67

Kassahun, Tewodros See Afro, Teddy

Kato, David 1964–2011 103

Katoucha See Niane, Katoucha

Kaufman, Bob 1925–1986 105

Kaufman, Monica 1948(?)— 66

Kaufman, Robert Garnell See Kaufman, Bob

Kaunda, Kenneth (David) 1924— 2

Kay, Connie 1927–1994 114

Kay, Jackie 1961— 37

Kay, Ulysses 1917–1995 37

Kayira, Legson 1942— 40

KB 1988— 122

Kearney, Beverly 1958— 109

Kearney, Janis 1953— 54

Kearse, Amalya Lyle 1937— 12

Keaton, Kevin See Treacherous Three

Keb' Mo', 1951— 36, 124

Kebede, Liya 1978— 59

Keckley, Elizabeth 1818–1907 90

Kee, John P. 1962— 43, 116+

Keenan, Brian See Chambers Brothers, The

Keene, John 1965— 73

Keflezighi, Meb 1975— 49, 121

Keïta, Ibrahim Boubacar 1945— 113

Keita, Salif 1949— 83

Keïta, Seydou 1921(?)–2001 124

Keith, Damon J. 1922— 16, 74

Keith, Floyd A. 1948— 61

Keith, Michael See 112

Keith, Rachel Boone 1924–2007 63

Kelis 1979— 58, 122

Kelley, Cliff 1941— 75

Kelley, Elijah 1986— 65

Kelley, Kenny See Manhattans, The

Kelley, Malcolm David 1992— 59

Kellogg, Clark 1961— 64

Kelly, Chris See Mac Daddy

Kelly, Jim 1946–2013 113

Kelly, Leontine 1920— 33

Kelly, Patrick 1954(?)–1990 3

Kelly, R. 1967— 18, 44, 71, 117

Kelly, Robert See Kelly, R.

Kelly, Robin 1956— 114

Kelly, Sharon Pratt See Dixon, Sharon Pratt

Kelly, Winzell See Dramatics, The

Kelly, Wynton 1931–1971 121

KEM 1969— 47, 127

Kemp, Herb 1941–2011 94

Kendrick, Erika 1975— 57

Kendricks, Eddie 1939–1992 22

Kennard, William Earl 1957— 18

Kennedy, Adrienne 1931— 11

Kennedy, Cortez 1968— 104

Kennedy, Florynce Rae 1916–2000 12, 33

Kennedy, Hershall See Graham Central Station

Kennedy, Lelia McWilliams Robinson 1885–1931 14

Kennedy, Randall 1954— 40

Kennedy-Overton, Jayne Harris 1951— 46

Kenner-Jackson, Doris See Shirelles, The

Kenney, John A., Jr. 1914–2003 48

Kenoly, Ron 1944— 45

Kente, Gibson 1932–2004 52

Kenyatta, Jomo 1891(?)–1978 5

Kenyatta, Robin 1942–2004 54

Kenyatta, Uhuru 1961— 110

Kerekou, Ahmed (Mathieu) 1933— 1

Kerry, Leon G. 1949(?)— 46

Key, Keegan-Michael See Key & Peele

Key & Peele 107

Keyes, Alan 1950— 11, 105

Keys, Alicia 1981— 32, 68

Kgositsile, Thebe Neruda See Sweatshirt, Earl

Khalifa, Wiz 1987— 96

Khama, Ian 1953— 95

Khan, Chaka 1953— 12, 50

Khanga, Yelena 1962— 6

Khumalo, Leleti 1970— 51

Khumalo, S'manga 1985— 119

Kibaki, Mwai 1931— 60

Kibble, Joey See Take 6

Kibble, Mark See Take 6

Kid Cudi 1984— 83

Kidd, Jason 1973— 86

Kidd, Mae Street 1904–1995 39

Kidjo, Angelique 1960— **50**

Kiir, Salva Mayardit 1951— **85, 103**

Kikwete, Jakaya Mrisho 1950— **73**

Killens, John O. 1967–1987 **54**

Killer Mike 1975— **117**

Killings, Debra 196(?)— **57**

Killingsworth, Cleve, Jr. 1952— **54**

Kilpatrick, Carolyn Cheeks 1945— **16**

Kilpatrick, Kwame 1970— **34, 71, 116**

Kimble, Perry *See Taste of Honey, A*

Kimbro, Dennis (Paul) 1950— **10**

Kimbro, Henry A. 1912–1999 **25**

Kimbro, Warren 1934–2009 **76**

Kimetto, Dennis 1984— **125**

Kincaid, Bernard 1945— **28**

Kincaid, Jamaica 1949— **4, 109**

Kinch, Soweto 1978— **108**

King, Alonzo 19(?)(?)— **38**

King, B. B. 1925— **7**

King, Barbara 19(?)(?)— **22**

King, Ben E. 1938–2015 **128** See also Drifters, The

King, Bernice 1963— **4, 81**

King, Chris Thomas 1964— **120**

King, Colbert I. 1939— **69**

King, Coretta Scott 1927–2006 **3, 57**

King, Dexter (Scott) 1961— **10**

King, Don 1931— **14, 128**

King, Freddie 1934–1976 **92**

King, Gayle 1954— **19, 99**

King, Jimmie *See Bar-Kays, The*

King, Martin Luther, III 1957— **20**

King, Martin Luther, Jr. 1929–1968 **1**

King, Martin Luther, Sr. 1899–1984 **89**

King, Oona 1967— **27**

King, Preston 1936— **28**

King, Reatha Clark 1938— **65**

King, Regina 1971— **22, 45**

King, Riley B. *See King, B. B.*

King, Robert Arthur 1945— **58**

King, Robert Hillary 1942— **84**

King, Rodney 1965–2012 **103**

King, Teresa 1961— **80**

King, William *See Commodores, The*

King, Woodie Jr. 1937— **27**

King, Yolanda (Denise) 1955— **6**

King Curtis 1934–1971 **92**

Kingston, Sean 1990— **94**

Kinsman Dazz *See Dazz Band*

Kintaudi, Leon 1949(?)— **62**

Kintaudi, Ngoma Miezi *See Kintaudi, Leon*

Kipchoge, Eliud 1984— **124**

Kiprotich, Wilson Kipsang *See Kipsang, Wilson*

Kipsang, Wilson 1982— **115**

Kirby, George 1924–1995 **14**

Kirk, Clara 1941— **95**

Kirk, Ron 1954— **11, 75, 111**

Kirkland, Eddie 1923–2011 **99**

Kirkland, Niatia Jessica *See Lil Mama*

Kirnan, Conrad Henry *See Kay, Connie*

Kisekka, Samson 1912–1999 **112**

Kisule, David Kato *See Kato, David*

Kitt, Eartha 1927–2008 **16, 75**

Kitt, Sandra 1947— **23**

Kittles, Rick 1976(?)— **51**

Kitwana, Bakari 19(?)(?)— **86**

Kiwanuka, Michael 1987— **126**

Klugh, Earl 1953— **59**

K'naan 1978— **76**

Knight, Etheridge 1931–1991 **37**

Knight, Gladys 1944— **16, 66**

Knight, Gwendolyn 1913–2005 **63**

Knight, Marie 1925(?)–2009 **80**

Knight, Marion Hugh, Jr. *See Knight, Suge*

Knight, Suge 1965— **11, 30, 102**

Knowles, Beyoncé *See Beyoncé*

Knowles, Mathew 1952— **96**

Knowles, Solange *See Solange*

Knowles, Tina 1954(?)— **61**

Knowling, Robert Jr. 1955(?)— **38**

Knox, Simmie 1935— **49**

Knuckles, Frankie 1955–2014 **42, 120** *See also Roots, The*

Kobia, Samuel 1947— **43**

Kodjoe, Boris 1973— **34, 89**

Kole, Ernest Levi Tsoloane *See Cole, Ernest*

Kolosoy, Wendo 1925–2008 **73**

Komunyakaa, Yusef 1941— **9**

Kone, Seydou *See Blondy, Alpha*

Kong, B. Waine 1943— **50**

Kony, Joseph 1961(?)— **101**

Kool DJ Red Alert *See Alert, Kool DJ Red*

Kool Moe Dee 1963— **37**

Kool Rock Ski *See Fat Boys*

Koontz, Elizabeth Duncan 1919–1989 **101**

Koroma, Ernest Bai 1953— **84**

Kotto, Yaphet (Fredrick) 1944— **7**

Kountz, Samuel L(ee) 1930–1981 **10**

Kravitz, Lenny 1964— **10, 34**

Kravitz, Leonard *See Kravitz, Lenny*

Krigger, Kevin 1983— **111**

KRS-One 1965— **34**

Krute, Fred *See Alert, Kool DJ Red*

K-Swift 1978–2008 **73**

Kufuor, John Agyekum 1938— **54, 82**

Kunjufu, Jawanza 1953— **3, 50**

Kuti, Fela Anikulapo *See Fela*

Kuti, Femi 1962— **47, 110**

Kuzwayo, Ellen 1914–2006 **68**

Kwei-Armah, Kwame 1967— **84**

Kweli, Talib 1975— **93**

Kyenge, Cécile 1964— **113**

Kyles, Cedric Antonio *See Cedric the Entertainer*

La Beaux, W. L. *See Soul Stirrers*

La Menthe, Ferdinand Joseph *See Morton, Jelly Roll*

La Roca, Pete 1938–2012 **107**

La Salle, Eriq 1962— **12**

L.A. Sunshine *See Treacherous Three*

LaBelle, Patti 1944— **13, 30**

LaChanze 1961— **93**

Lacks, Henrietta 1921–1951 **101**

Lacy, Marc 1969— **111**

Lacy, Sam 1903–2003 **30, 46**

Lacy, Walter Marcellus *See Lacy, Marc*

Ladd, Ernie 1938–2007 **64**

Ladner, Joyce A. 1943— **42**

Ladysmith Black Mambazo **103**

Laferriere, Dany 1953— **33**

Lafontant, Jewel Stradford 1922–1997 **3, 51**

Lafontant-MANkarious, Jewel Stradford *See Lafontant, Jewel Stradford*

LaGuma, Alex 1925–1985 **30**

Lakeside **120**

Lamar, Jake 1961— **96**

Lamar, Kendrick 1987— **105**

Lamming, George 1927— **35**

Lamont, William Joseph *See Billy Ward and the Dominoes*

Lamothe, Laurent 1972— **122**

Lampkin, Daisy 1883(?)–1965 **19**

Lampley, Oni Faida 1959–2008 **43, 71**

Lampley, Vera *See Lampley, Oni Faida*

Lancaster, Byard 1942–2012 **105**

Lance, Major 1939–1994 **111**

Land, Harold 1928–2001 **125**

Lander, Austin *See New Birth*

Landry, Jackie *See Chantels, The*

Lane, Charles 1953— **3**

Lane, Dick 1927–2002 **92**

Lane, Lunsford 1803–18(?)(?) **93**

Lane, Vincent 1942— **5**

Lane, William Henry 1825(?)–1852(?) **90**

Laneuville, Eric 1952— **123**

Langford, Larry P. 1948— **74**

Langford, William *See Golden Gate Quartet*

Langhart Cohen, Janet 1941— **19, 60**

Langston, John Mercer 1829–1897 **101**

Lanier, Bob 1948— **47**

Lanier, Willie 1945— **33**

Lankford, Raymond Lewis 1967— **23**

LaPread, Ronald *See Commodores, The*

Laraque, Georges 1976— **48**

Laraque, Paul 1920–2007 **67**

Larkin, Barry 1964— **24**

Laroche, Joseph Philippe Lemercier 1889–1912 **85**

Larrieux, Amel 1973(?)— **63**

Lars, Byron 1965— **32**

Larsen, Nella 1891–1964 **10**

Laryea, Thomas Davies, III 1979— **67**

LaSalle, Denise 1939— **111**

Lashley, Bobby 1976— **63**

Lashley, Franklin Roberto *See Lashley, Bobby*

Lassiter, Roy 1969— **24**

Lateef, Yusef 1920–2013 **91, 117**

Lathan, Sanaa 1971— **27**

Latimer, Lewis H(oward) 1848–1928 **4**

Lattany, Kristin Hunter 1931–2008 **88**

Lattimore, Kenny 1970— **35, 128**

LaVette, Bettye 1946— **85**

Lavizzo-Mourey, Risa 1954— **48**

Law, W. W. 1923–2002 **121**

Law, Westley Wallace *See Law, W. W.*

Lawal, Kase L. 19(?)(?)— **45**

Lawless, Theodore K(enneth) 1892–1971 **8**

Lawrence, Brenda 1954— **127**

Lawrence, Diedra *See Marian Anderson String Quartet*

Lawrence, Donald 1958— **99**

Lawrence, Jacob (Armstead) 1917–2000 **4, 28**

Lawrence, Margaret Morgan 1914— **100**

Lawrence, Martin 1965— **6, 27, 60**

Lawrence, Robert Henry, Jr. 1935–1967 **16**

Lawrence-Lightfoot, Sara 1944— **10**

Laws, Hubert 1939— **90**

Lawson, James M., Jr. 1928— **90**

Lawson, Jennifer 1946— **1, 50**

Laymon, Kiese 197(?)— **113**

Layton, William 1915–2007 **87**

Lazare, Palaceer *See Shabazz Palaces*

Le Loka, Tsidii 1968(?)— **116**

Le1f 1989— **120**

Lea, Babatunde 1948(?)— **124**

Lea, Michael *See Lea, Babatunde*

Leadbelly 1885–1949 **82**

Leakes, NeNe 1967— **107**

Leary, Kathryn D. 1952— **10**

Leavell, Dorothy R. 1944— **17**

Lebo M 1964— **109**

Lecrae 1979— **108**

Ledbetter, Hudson William *See Leadbelly*

Ledisi 197(?)— **73**

Lee, Annie Frances 1935— **22**

Lee, Barbara 1946— **25, 102**

Lee, Bertram M., Sr. 1939–2003 **46**

Lee, Beverly *See Shirelles, The*

Lee, Canada 1907–1952 **8**

Lee, Consuela 1926–2009 **84**

Lee, Debra L. 1954— **62**

Lee, Don Luther *See Madhubuti, Haki R.*

Lee, Eric P. 1958— **79**

Lee, Gabby *See Lincoln, Abbey*

Lee, Jarena 1783–1855(?) **100**

Lee, Joe A. 1946(?)— **45**

Lee, Joie 1962(?)— **1**

Lee, Leslie 1930–2014 **85, 122**

Lee, Malcolm D. 1970— **75**

Lee, Raphael C. 1949— **87**

Lee, Robert 1920–2010 **112**

Lee, Shelton Jackson *See Lee, Spike*

Lee, Spike 1957— **5, 19, 86**

Lee-Smith, Hughie 1915— **5, 22**

Leevy, Carrol M. 1920— **42**

Lefel, Edith 1963–2003 **41**

Leffall, Lasalle, Jr. 1930— **3, 64**

LeFlore, Lyah Beth 1970— **96**

Leftenant, Nathan *See Cameo*

Legend, John 1978— **67, 116**

Legendary Oricles, The *See Orioles, The*

Leggs, Kingsley 196(?)— **62**

LeGrand, Eric 1990— **118**

LeGrand, Naquasia 1991— **126**

Leibowitz, Helen *See Chantels, The*

Leland, George Thomas *See Leland, Mickey*

Leland, Mickey 1944–1989 **2**

Lemmons, Kasi 1961— **20**
Lemon, Alton T. 1928–2013 **112**
Lemon, Don 1966— **94**
Lennox, Betty 1976— **31**
Lenoir, J. B. 1929–1967 **117**
LeNoire, Rosetta 1911–2002 **37**
Lenox, Adriane 1956— **59**
Leon, Kenny 1956— **10, 98**
León, Tania 1943— **13**
Leonard, Buck 1907— **67**
Leonard, Kawhi 1991— **122**
Leonard, Sugar Ray 1956— **15**
Leonard, Walter Fenner See Leonard, Buck
Leônidas 1913–2004 **96**
Leslie, Lisa 1972— **16, 73**
Lester, Adrian 1968— **46**
Lester, Bill 1961— **42, 85**
Lester, Bobby See Moonglows, The
Lester, Julius 1939— **9, 115**
Lester, Robert See Chi-Lites
Lesure, James 1975— **64**
LeTang, Henry 1915–2007 **66**
Letson, Al 1972— **39**
Levert, Eddie 1942— **70** See also O'Jays, The
Levert, Gerald 1966–2006 **22, 59**
Levi, Moses See Shyne
Lewis, Amisho Baraka See Baraka, Sho
Lewis, Aylwin B. 1954— **51, 88**
Lewis, Butch 1946–2011 **71, 99**
Lewis, Byron E(ugene) 1931— **13**
Lewis, Carl 1961— **4, 97**
Lewis, Daurene 194(?)— **72**
Lewis, David See Atlantic Starr
Lewis, David Levering 1936— **9**
Lewis, Delano (Eugene) 1938— **7**
Lewis, Denise 1972— **33**
Lewis, Earl See Flamingos, The
Lewis, (Mary) Edmonia 1845(?)–1911(?) **10**
Lewis, Edward T. 1940— **21**
Lewis, Emmanuel 1971— **36**
Lewis, Frederick Carlton See Lewis, Carl
Lewis, George 1952— **104**
Lewis, Henry 1932–1996 **38**
Lewis, Jamal 1979— **115**
Lewis, John 1940— **2, 46, 83**
Lewis, Jonathan See Atlantic Starr
Lewis, Lennox 1965— **27**
Lewis, Leona 1985— **75**
Lewis, Marvin 1958— **51, 87**
Lewis, Norman 1909–1979 **39**
Lewis, Oliver 1856–1924 **56**
Lewis, Ramsey 1935— **35, 70**
Lewis, Ray 1975— **33, 109**
Lewis, Reginald F. 1942–1993 **6**
Lewis, Ronald See Lewis, Butch
Lewis, Samella 1924— **25**
Lewis, Shirley Ann Redd 1937— **14**
Lewis, Terry 1956— **13**
Lewis, Thomas 1939— **19**
Lewis, Wayne See Atlantic Starr
Lewis, William Henry 1868–1949 **89**
Lewis, William M., Jr. 1956— **40**
Lewis-Hall, Freda 1955(?)— **105**
Lewis-Thornton, Rae 1962— **32**
Ligging, Alfred, III 1965— **43**
Lighty, Chris 1968–2012 **105**

Lighty, Darrell Steven See Lighty, Chris
Ligon, Glenn 1960— **82**
Ligon, Joe See Mighty Clouds of Joy
Lil B 1989— **121**
Lil' Bow Wow See Bow Wow
Lil Jon 1971— **124**
Lil' Kim 1975— **28**
Lil Mama 1989— **117**
Lil' Romeo See Romeo
Lil Wayne 1982— **66, 84**
Lilakoi Moon See Bonet, Lisa
Liles, Kevin 1968— **42, 99**
Lillard, Damian 1990— **117**
Lincoln, Abbey 1930–2010 **3, 88**
Lincoln, C(harles) Eric 1924–2000 **38**
Lindo, Allen Pineda See apl.de.ap
Lindo, Delroy 1952— **18, 45**
Lindsay, Peta 1984— **100**
Lindsey, Tommie 1951— **51**
Lipscomb, Belinda See Midnight Star
Lipscomb, Mance 1895–1976 **49**
LisaRaye 1967— **27**
Lister, Marquita 1965(?) **65**
Lister, Tiny See Lister, Tommy
Lister, Tommy 1958— **127**
Liston, Melba 1926–1999 **118**
Liston, Sonny 1928(?)–1970 **33**
Little, Benilde 1958— **21**
Little, Booker 1938–1961 **105**
Little, Cleavon 1939–1992 **117**
Little, Floyd 1942— **86**
Little, Larry 1945— **90**
Little, Malcolm See X, Malcolm
Little, Robert L(angdon) 1938— **2**
Little Anthony See Little Anthony & the Imperials
Little Anthony & the Imperials **107**
Little Chronicle See Chronixx
Little Eva 1943–2003 **128**
Little Milton 1934–2005 **36, 54**
Little Richard 1932— **15**
Little Walter 1930–1968 **36** See also Aces, The
Little Warrior See Barrow, Willie T.
Littlepage, Craig 1951— **35**
LL Cool J 1968— **16, 49, 94**
Llewellyn, J. Bruce 1927–2010 **13, 85**
Lloyd 1986— **99**
Lloyd, Christopher See Banks, Lloyd
Lloyd, Earl 1928–2015 **26, 127**
Lloyd, John Henry "Pop" 1884–1965 **30**
Lloyd, Reginald 1967— **64**
Locke, Alain 1886–1954 **10**
Locke, Attica 1974— **85**
Locke, Eddie 1930— **44**
Lockwood, Robert, Jr. 1915–2006 **120**
Lofton, James 1956— **42**
Lofton, Kenneth 1967— **12**
Lofton, Ramona See Sapphire
Logan, Onnie Lee 1910(?)–1995 **14**
Logan, Rayford W. 1897–1982 **40**
Loguen, J. W. 1813–1872 **91**
Lomax, Louis E. 1922–1970 **90**
Lomax, Michael L. 1947— **58**
London, Theophilus 1987— **95**

Long, Eddie L. 1953— **29, 89**
Long, Huey 1904–2009 **79**
Long, Loretta 1940— **58**
Long, Nia 1970— **17, 95**
Long, Richard Alexander 1927— **65**
Loper, Ramon See Five Keys, The
Lopes, Davey 1945— **92**
Lopes, Leila 1986— **99**
Lopes, Lisa 1971–2002 **36** See also TLC
Lord, Tracy See Little Anthony & the Imperials
Lord Infamous 1973–2013 **117**
Lord Invader 1914–1961 **117**
Lord Jamar 1968— **126**
Lord Kitchener 1922–2000 **110**
Lord Pitt of Hampstead See Pitt, David Thomas
Lorde, Audre (Geraldine) 1934–1992 **6**
Lorenzo, Irving See Gotti, Irv
Loroupe, Tegla 1973— **59**
Lott, Ronnie 1959— **9**
Loueke, Lionel 1973(?)— **88**
Louis, Errol T. 1962— **8**
Louis, Joe 1914–1981 **5**
Louis, Willie 1937–2013 **113**
Loury, Glenn 1948— **36**
Love, Darlene 1941— **23, 92**
Love, Ed 1932(?)— **58**
Love, Laura 1960— **50**
Love, Loni 1971— **113**
Love, Ludmya Bourdeau See Love, Mia
Love, Mia 1975— **96, 125**
Love, Nat 1854–1921 **9**
Love, Reggie 1982— **77**
Lovelace, Bobby See Midnight Star
Lovell, Whitfield 1959— **74**
Lover, Ed **10**
Lovett, Winfred See Manhattans, The
Loving, Alvin, Jr., 1935–2005 **35, 53**
Loving, Mildred 1939–2008 **69**
Lowe, Herbert 1962— **57**
Lowe, Rick 1961— **124**
Lowe, Sidney 1960— **64**
Lowery, Evelyn Gibson 1925–2013 **115**
Lowery, Joseph E. 1924— **2**
Lowery, Myron 1946(?)— **80**
Lowry, A. Leon 1913–2005 **60**
Luandrew, Albert See Sunnyland Slim
Lubanga, Thomas 1960— **104**
Lucas, Bill 1936–1979 **97**
Lucas, Harold See Clovers, The
Lucas, John 1953— **7**
Lucas, William DeVaughn See Lucas, Bill
Lucie, Lawrence 1907–2009 **80**
Lucien, Jon 1942–2007 **66**
Luckett, Letoya 1981— **61**
Lucy, William 1933— **50**
Lucy Foster, Autherine 1929— **35**
Ludacris, 1978— **37, 60**
Lufeyo, Jameson See Malawi Mouse Boys
Luke, Derek 1974— **61**
Lumbly, Carl 1952— **47**
Lumet, Jenny 1967— **80**
Lumpkin, Elgin Baylor See Ginuwine

Lumumba, Chokwe 1947–2014 **118**
Lumumba, Patrice 1925–1961 **33**
Luna, Donyale 1946–1979 **88**
Luper, Clara 1923–2011 **94**
Lushington, Augustus Nathaniel 1869–1939 **56**
Luter, Fred, Jr. 1956— **103**
Luthuli, Albert (John Mvumbi) 1898(?)–1967 **13**
Lyfe See Jennings, Lyfe
Lyle, Marcenia See Stone, Toni
Lyle, Ron 1941–2011 **125**
Lyles, Lester Lawrence 1946— **31**
Lymon, Frankie 1942–1968 **22**
Lynch, Bill See Lynch, William, Jr
Lynch, Loretta E. 1959— **103**
Lynch, Marshawn 1986— **124**
Lynch, Shola 1969— **61**
Lynch, William, Jr. 1941–2013 **115**
Lynn, Barbara 1942— **126**
Lynn, Lonnie Rashid, Jr. See Common
Lynne, Gloria 1929(?)–2013 **115**
Lyons, Henry 1942— **12, 118**
Lyons, James E., Sr. 1944(?)— **102**
Lyttle, Hulda Margaret 1889–1983 **14**
Maal, Baaba 1953— **66**
Maathai, Wangari 1940–2011 **43, 97**
Mabior, John Garang de See Garang, John
Mabley, Jackie "Moms" 1897(?)–1975 **15**
Mabon, Willie 1925–1985 **119**
Mabrey, Vicki 1957(?)— **26**
Mabry, Marcus 1967— **70**
Mabuza, Lindiwe 1938— **18**
Mabuza-Suttle, Felicia 1950— **43**
Mac, Bernie 1957–2008 **29, 61, 72**
Mac Daddy 1978–2013 **111**
Maceo, Antonio 1845–1896 **82**
Machado de Assis 1839–1908 **74**
Machaka, Yvonne See Chaka Chaka, Yvonne
Machar, Riek 1952— **117**
Machel, Graça 1945— **16, 102**
Machel, Samora Moises 1933–1986 **8**
Mack, Iris 1955(?)— **105**
Mack, Tony 1966— **104**
Mack Maine 1982— **125**
Mackey, Biz 1897–1965 **82**
Mackey, Nathaniel 1947— **75**
Mackie, Anthony 1979— **102**
Madame Sul-Te-Wan 1873–1959 **95**
Madhubuti, Haki R. 1942— **7, 85**
Madikizela-Mandela, Winnie 1934— **2, 35, 112**
Madison, Joseph E. 1949— **17**
Madison, Paula 1952— **37, 99**
Madison, Romell 1952— **45**
Madlib 1973— **88**
Magan, Ayaan Hirsi See Ali, Ayaan Hirsi
Magic Slim 1937–2013 **110**
Magloire, Paul Eugène 1907–2001 **68**
Mahal, Taj 1942— **39**
Mahama, John Dramani 1958— **103**
Mahlasela, Vusi 1965— **65**
Mahorn, Rick 1958— **60**

Maillard, Carol See Sweet Honey in the Rock

Mainor, Dorothy Leigh 1910(?)–1996 19

Maitreya, Sananda 1962— 85

Majette, Denise 1955— 41

Major, Clarence 1936— 9

Majors, Jeff 1960(?)— 41

Makeba, Miriam 1932–2008 2, 50, 74

Malawi Mouse Boys 114

Malco, Romany 1968— 71

Malcolm X See X, Malcolm

Malema, Julius 1981— 98

Mallett, Conrad, Jr. 1953— 16

Mallory, Mark 1962— 62

Mallory, William L., Sr. 1931–2013 119

Malone, Annie (Minerva Turnbo Pope) 1869–1957 13

Malone, Karl 1963— 18, 51, 90

Malone, Maurice 1965— 32

Malone, Moses 1955— 79

Malone Jones, Vivian 1942–2005 59

Malonga, Eric Moussambani See Moussambani, Eric

Malphurs, Juaquin James See Waka Flocka Flame

Malveaux, Floyd 1940— 54

Malveaux, Julianne 1953— 32, 70

Malveaux, Suzanne 1966— 88

Manardo, Bob See Falcons, The

Mandela, Nelson 1918–2013 1, 14, 77, 117

Mandela, Winnie See Madikizela-Mandela, Winnie

Mandisa 1976— 119

Mane, Gucci 1980— 91

Manhattans, The 123

Manigat, Mirlande 1940— 90

Manigault, Earl "The Goat" 1943— 15

Manigault, Omarosa See Omarosa

Manigault-Stallworth, Omarosa See Omarosa

Manka, Hashim Thabit See Thabeet, Hasheem

Manley, Audrey Forbes 1934— 16

Manley, Dexter 1959— 116

Manley, Edna 1900–1987 26

Manley, Ruth 1947— 34

Mann, Bob 1924–2006 126

Mann, Robert See Mann, Bob

Mann, Tamela 1966— 92

Manning, Frankie 1914–2009 78

Manning, Marva Ann See Whitney, Marva

Manson, John See Swan Silvertones, The

Manuel, Jerry 1953— 94

Maponya, Maishe 1951— 101

Maponya, Richard 1926— 101

Marable, Manning 1950–2011 10, 102

Maraire, Tendai See Shabazz Palaces

Maraj, Onika Tanya indexref See Minaj, Nicki

March, William Carrington 1923–2002 56

Marchand, Inga See Foxy Brown

Marcille, Eva 1984— 97

Marechera, Charles William See Marechera, Dambudzo

Marechera, Dambudzo 1952–1987 39

Marechera, Tambudzai See Marechera, Dambudzo

Marian Anderson String Quartet 111

Mariner, Jonathan 1954(?)— 41

Marino, Eugene Antonio 1934–2000 30

Mario 1986— 71

Markham, Dewey See Markham, Pigmeat

Markham, E(dward) A(rchibald) 1939— 37

Markham, Pigmeat 1904–1981 106

Marks, Audrey 19(?)(?)— 99

Marks, John R., III 1947(?)— 123

Marle, Milton See Billy Ward and the Dominoes

Marley, Bob 1945–1981 5

Marley, David See Marley, Ziggy

Marley, Rita 1947— 32, 70

Marley, Robert Nesta See Marley, Bob

Marley, Stephen 1972— 100

Marley, Ziggy 1968— 41

Marrow, Queen Esther 1943(?)— 24

Marrow, Tracy See Ice-T

Marsalis, Branford 1960— 34, 103

Marsalis, Delfeayo 1965— 41

Marsalis, Ellis 1934— 90

Marsalis, Wynton 1961— 16, 90

Marsh, Henry L., III 1934(?)— 32

Marshall, Bella 1950— 22

Marshall, Brandon 1984— 116

Marshall, Gloria See Sudarkasa, Niara

Marshall, Kerry James 1955— 59

Marshall, Paule 1929— 7, 77

Marshall, Quavious See Migos

Marshall, Thurgood 1908–1993 1, 44

Marshall, Valenza Pauline Burke See Marshall, Paule

Marshall, William 1924–2003 107

Marte, Starling 1988— 117

Martelly, Michel 1961— 90

Martha Jean "The Queen" See Steinberg, Martha Jean

Martin, Cuonzo 1971— 121

Martin, Curtis 1973— 104

Martin, Darnell 1964— 43, 78

Martin, Duane 1965— 108

Martin, Helen 1909–2000 31

Martin, Jesse L. 19(?)(?)— 31

Martin, Johnny See Mighty Clouds of Joy

Martin, Jonathan 1989— 119

Martin, Louis Emanuel 1912–1997 16

Martin, Luci See Chic

Martin, Michel 19(?)(?)— 97

Martin, Porscha See Atlantic Starr

Martin, Roberta 1907–1969 58

Martin, Roland S. 1968— 49, 84

Martin, Ruby Grant 1933–2003 49

Martin, Sallie 1895(?)–1988 120

Martin, Sara 1884–1955 38

Martin, Skip, III See Dazz Band

Martin, Trayvon 1995–2012 105

Martinez, Juan See Pharcyde, The

Martínez, Pedro 1971— 81, 126

Marvelettes, The 126

Marvin X See X, Marvin

Mary Mary 34, 92

Mase 1977(?)— 24

Masekela, Barbara 1941— 18

Masekela, Hugh 1939— 1, 106

Masekela, Sal 1971— 106

Masire, Quett (Ketumile Joni) 1925— 5

Mason, Anthony 1966–2015 128

Mason, Biddy 1818–1891 89

Mason, Charles Harrison 1866–1961 107

Mason, Derek 1970— 120

Mason, Desmond 1977— 127

Mason, Felicia 1963(?)— 31

Mason, Herman, Jr. 1962— 83

Mason, Judi Ann 1955–2009 112

Mason, Ronald 1949— 27

Mason, Vincent See De La Soul

Massaquoi, Hans J. 1926— 30

Massenburg, Kedar 1963(?)— 23, 110

Massey, Bobby See O'Jays, The

Massey, Brandon 1973— 40

Massey, Walter E(ugene) 1938— 5, 45

Massie, Samuel Proctor, Jr. 1919— 29

Masta Ace 1966— 118

Master Gee See Sugarhill Gang, The

Master P 1970— 21, 115

Matejka, Adrian 1971(?)— 87

Mathabane, Johannes See Mathabane, Mark

Mathabane, Mark 1960— 5, 99

Mathis, Greg 1960— 26

Mathis, Johnny 1935— 20

Mathis, Robert 1981— 121

Matshikiza, Pumeza 1979(?)— 115

Matson, Ollie 1930–2011 93

Matta, Adam See Carolina Chocolate Drops

Matthews, Ameena 19(?)(?)— 105

Matthews, Benjamin 1932–2006 93

Matthews, Denise See Vanity

Matthews, Mark 1894–2005 59

Matthews, Shatteen, Westina 1948— 51

Matzeliger, Jan 1852–1889 93

Mauldin, Jermaine Dupri See Dupri, Jermaine

Maupin, John E., Jr. 1946— 92

Maxey, Randall 1941— 46

Maxis, Theresa 1810–1892 62

Maxwell 1973— 20, 81

May, Brother Joe 1912–1972 123

May, Derrick 1963— 41

May, Joseph W. See May, Brother Joe

May, Mark 1959— 117

Mayberry-Stewart, Melodie 1948— 94

Maye, Arthur Lee See Maye, Lee

Maye, Lee 1934–2002 111

Mayers, Jamal 1974— 39

Mayers, Rakim See A$AP Rocky

Mayes, Lenny See Dramatics, The

Mayfield, Curtis 1942–1999 2, 43

Mayhew, Martin R. 1965— 76

Mayhew, Richard 1924— 39

Maynard, Nancy Hicks 1946–2008 73

Maynard, Robert C(lyve) 1937–1993 7

Maynor, Dorothy 1910–1996 19

Mayo, Whitman 1930–2001 32

Mays, Benjamin E(lijah) 1894–1984 7

Mays, Leslie A. 19(?)(?)— 41

Mays, William G. 1946— 34

Mays, William Howard, Jr. See Mays, Willie

Mays, Willie 1931— 3

Mayweather, Floyd 1977— 57, 104

Mazrui, Ali 1933–2014 12, 124

M'bala M'bala, Dieudonné See Dieudonné

Mbabazi, Esther 1988(?)— 122

Mbatha-Raw, Gugu 1983— 89

Mbaye, Mariétou 1948— 31

Mbeki, Govan A. 1910–2001 80

Mbeki, Thabo 1942— 14, 73

Mboup, Souleymane 1951— 10

Mboya, Thomas Joseph Odhiambo See Mboya, Tom

Mboya, Tom 1930–1969 107

Mbuende, Kaire Munionganda 1953— 12

MC Breed 1971–2008 75

M.C. Hammer 1963— 20, 80

MC Lyte 1971— 34, 108

McAdoo, Bob 1951— 75

McAlpin, Harry 1906–1985 121

McAnulty, William E., Jr. 1947–2007 66

McBay, Henry C. 1914–1995 91

McBee, Cecil 1935— 123

McBride, Bryant Scott 1965— 18

McBride, Chi 1961— 73

McBride, James 1957— 35, 87

McCabe, Jewell Jackson 1945— 10

McCain, Franklin 1941–2014 119

McCall, H. Carl 1938(?)— 27

McCall, Nathan 1955— 8

McCalla, Leyla See Carolina Chocolate Drops

McCann, Renetta 1957(?)— 44

McCarthy, Sandy 1972— 64

McCartney, Brandon See Lil B

McCarty, Osceola 1908— 16

McCary, Michael S. See Boyz II Men

McCauley, Gina 1976(?)— 76

McClary, Thomas See Commodores, The

McClellan, George Marion 1860–1934 91

McClendon, Forrest 1965— 94

McClendon, Lisa 1975(?)— 61

McClendon, Lloyd 1959— 123

McClinton, Marion Isaac 1954— 77

McClurkin, Donnie 1961— 25

McCollum, Robert Lee See Nighthawk, Robert

McCoo, Marilyn 1943— 53

McCovey, Willie 1938— 103

McCowin, Michael See Mighty Clouds of Joy

McCoy, Elijah 1844–1929 8

McCoy, LeSean 1988— 123

McCoy, Robert Lee See Nighthawk, Robert

McCoy, Van 1940–1979 123

McCracklin, Jimmy 1921–2012 108

McCraney, Tarell Alvin 1980— **116**

McCrary, Crystal *See McCrary Anthony, Crystal*

McCrary, Darius 1976— **111**

McCrary Anthony, Crystal 1969— **70**

McCray, Nikki 1972— **18**

McCullough, Bernard Jeffrey *See Mac, Bernie*

McCullough, DeAndre 1977–2012 **106**

McCullough, Geraldine 1917–2008 **58, 79**

McCullum, Robert Lee *See Nighthawk, Robert*

McCutchen, Andrew 1986— **116**

McDaniel, Hattie 1895–1952 **5**

McDaniel, Prudence *See Marian Anderson String Quartet*

McDaniel, Randall Cornell 1964— **81**

McDaniel, Rudy *See Tacuma, Jamaaladeen*

McDaniels, Darryl *See DMC*

McDaniels, Ralph 19(?)(?)— **79**

McDonald, Audra 1970— **20, 62, 128**

McDonald, Butch *See New Birth*

McDonald, Charles J. 1931— **120**

McDonald, Erroll 1954(?)— **1**

McDonald, Gabrielle Kirk 1942— **20**

McDougall, Gay J. 1947— **11, 43**

McDuff, Jack 1926–2001 **116**

McDuffie, Dwayne 1962— **62**

McDuffy, Eugene *See McDuff, Jack*

McElroy, Sollie *See Flamingos, The*

McEwen, Mark 1954— **5**

McFadden, Bernice L. 1966— **39**

McFarlan, Tyron 1971(?)— **60**

McFarland, Roland 1940— **49**

McFerrin, Bobby 1950— **68**

McFerrin, Robert, Jr. *See McFerrin, Bobby*

McFerrin, Robert, Sr. 1921–2006 **94**

McGee, Charles 1924— **10**

McGee, James D. 1949— **74**

McGee, James Madison 1940— **46**

McGee, Vonetta 1945–2010 **95**

McGhee, Heather C. 1981— **106**

McGhee, Howard 1918–1987 **122**

McGhee, Maggie *See McGhee, Howard*

McGhee, Sharon K. 1957–2012 **113**

McGill, Anthony 1979— **76**

McGill, Lucius *See Dells, The*

McGill, Mickey *See Dells, The*

McGlowan, Angela 1970— **64, 86**

McGrady, Tracy 1979— **80**

McGrath, Pat 1970— **72**

McGregor, Stephen 1990— **99**

McGriff, Dorothy *See Coates, Dorothy Love*

McGriff, Fred 1963— **24**

McGriff, James Harrell *See McGriff, Jimmy*

McGriff, Jimmy 1936–2008 **72**

McGruder, Aaron 1974— **28, 56, 120**

McGruder, Robert 1942— **22, 35**

McGuire, George Alexander 1866–1934 **80**

McGuire, Raymond J. 1957(?)(—) **57**

McHenry, Donald F. 1936— **83**

McIntosh, Winston Hubert *See Tosh, Peter*

McIntyre, Kalaparusha Maurice 1936–2013 **117**

McIntyre, Maurice Benford *See McIntyre, Kalaparusha Maurice*

McIntyre, Natalie *See Gray, Macy*

McJunkin, George 1851–1922 **93**

McKay, Claude 1889–1948 **6**

McKay, Festus Claudius *See McKay, Claude*

McKay, Nellie Yvonne 19(?)(?)–2006 **17, 57**

McKee, Lonette 1954— **12, 119**

McKegney, Tony 1958— **3**

McKenzie, Jaunel 1986— **73**

McKenzie, Vashti M. 1947— **29**

McKinney, Cynthia 1955— **11, 52, 74**

McKinney, Nina Mae 1912–1967 **40**

McKinney Hammond, Michelle 1957— **51**

McKinney-Whetstone, Diane 1954(?)— **27**

McKinnon, Ike *See McKinnon, Isaiah*

McKinnon, Isaiah 1943— **9**

McKissack, Leatrice 1930— **80**

McKissick, Floyd B(ixler) 1922–1981 **3**

McKnight, Brian 1969— **18, 34**

McKnight, Claude V., III *See Take 6*

McLean, Jackie 1931–2006 **78**

McLendon, John B., Jr. 1915–1999 **89**

McLeod, Gus 1955(?)— **27**

McMillan, Rosalynn A. 1953— **36**

McMillan, Terry 1951— **4, 17, 53**

McMillan, Tracy 1964— **93**

McMurray, Georgia L. 1934–1992 **36**

McNabb, Donovan 1976— **29, 119**

McNair, Ronald 1950–1986 **3, 58**

McNair, Stevo 1973–2009 **22, 47, 79**

McNaughton, Jamar Rolando *See Chronixx*

McNeil, David *See Billy Ward and the Dominoes*

McNeil, Lori 1964(?)— **1**

McPhail, Sharon 1948— **2, 119**

McPhatter, Clyde *See Billy Ward and the Dominoes; Drifters, The*

McPherson, David 1968— **32**

McPherson, James Alan 1943— **70**

McQuater, Matthew *See Clovers, The*

McQueen, Butterfly 1911–1995 **6, 54**

McQueen, Steve 1969— **84**

McRae, Carmen 1920–1994 **77**

McRae, Hal 1945— **84**

McShann, Jay 1916–2006 **110**

McTell, Blind Willie 1901–1959 **89**

McVey, Joseph Wayne *See Z-Ro*

McWhorter, John 1965— **35, 119**

McWorter, Free Frank 1777–1854 **91**

Meadows, Tim 1961— **30**

Meek, Carrie (Pittman) 1926— **6, 36**

Meek, Kendrick 1966— **41, 89**

Meeks, Gregory W. 1953— **25, 117**

Meeks, James T. 1956— **92**

Mehretu, Julie 1970— **85**

Meles Zenawi *See Zenawi, Meles*

Mell, Patricia 1953— **49**

Mello, Breno 1931–2008 **73**

Melton, Frank 1949–2009 **81**

Melton, Harold D. 1966— **79**

Melvin, Harold *See Harold Melvin & the Blue Notes*

Meminger, Dean 1948–2013 **114**

Memmi, Albert 1920— **37**

Memphis Minnie 1897–1973 **33**

Memphis Slim 1915–1988 **105**

Menard, John Willis 1838–1893 **90**

Mengestu, Dinaw 1978— **66, 114**

Mengistu, Haile Mariam 1937— **65**

Mensah, John 1982— **87**

Mensah, Thomas 1950— **48**

Mercado-Valdes, Frank 1962— **43**

Mercer, Kelvin *See De La Soul*

Meredith, James H(oward) 1933— **11**

Merkerson, S. Epatha 1952— **47, 83**

Merriweather, Big Maceo 1905–1953 **109**

Merriweather, Major *See Merriweather, Big Maceo*

Mescudi, Scott Ramon Seguro *See Kid Cudi*

Messenger, The *See Divine, Father*

Metcalfe, Ralph 1910–1978 **26**

Meters, The **118**

Method Man 1971— **81**

Meyer, June *See Jordan, June*

Meyiwa, Senzo 1984–2014 **124**

Mfume, Kweisi 1948— **6, 41**

Mhinga, Yvonne *See Chaka Chaka, Yvonne*

Mhlaba, Raymond 1920–2005 **55**

Michaux, Solomon Lightfoot 1884–1968 **91**

Micheaux, Oscar (Devereaux) 1884–1951 **7**

Michele, Michael 1966— **31**

Mickelbury, Penny 1948— **28**

Mickens, Ronald Elbert 1943— **105**

Mickle, Dale *See Dixie Cups, The*

Middleton, Reggie 1967— **105**

Midnight Star **110**

Mighty Clouds of Joy **110**

Migos **126**

Miguel 1986(?)— **98**

Miles, Buddy 1947–2008 **69**

Miles, George Allen, Jr. *See Miles, Buddy*

Miles, Tiya 1970— **116**

Miles, William 1931–2013 **112**

Miley, Bubber 1903–1932 **120**

Miley, James Wesley *See Miley, Bubber*

Milla, Roger 1952— **2**

Millender-McDonald, Juanita 1938–2007 **21, 61**

Miller, Bebe 1950— **3**

Miller, Cheryl 1964— **10, 74**

Miller, Clyde 1927–2011 **113**

Miller, Corey *See C-Murder*

Miller, Dorie 1919–1943 **29**

Miller, Doris *See Miller, Dorie*

Miller, Larry G. 1950(?)— **72**

Miller, Lorraine C. 1948— **119**

Miller, Marcus 1959— **84**

Miller, Maria 1803–1879 **19**

Miller, Omar Benson 1978— **93**

Miller, Patina 1984— **94**

Miller, Pepper 1953— **96**

Miller, Percy *See Master P*

Miller, Percy Romeo, Jr. *See Romeo*

Miller, Portia Simpson *See Simpson Miller, Portia*

Miller, Reggie 1965— **33**

Miller, Rice *See Williamson, Sonny Boy*

Miller, Romeo *See Romeo*

Miller, Tangi 1975— **116**

Miller, Warren F., Jr. 1943— **53**

Miller, Wentworth 1972— **75**

Miller-Travis, Vernice 1959— **64**

Millinder, Lucius Venable *See Millinder, Lucky*

Millinder, Lucky 1900–1966 **101**

Millines Dziko, Trish 1957— **28**

Millner, Denene 1969(?)— **76**

Mills, Dylan Kwabena *See Rascal, Dizzee*

Mills, Florence 1896–1927 **22**

Mills, Joseph C. 1946— **51**

Mills, Sam 1959— **33**

Mills, Stephanie 1957— **36**

Mills, Steve 1960(?)— **47**

Mills Brothers, The **99**

Milner, Ron 1938— **39**

Milton, DeLisha 1974— **31**

Minaj, Nicki 1984— **86, 124**

Ming, Bob *See Ming, William Robert, Jr.*

Ming, Mel 1944— **106**

Ming, William Robert, Jr. 1911–1973 **125**

Mingo, Frank L. 1939–1989 **32**

Mingus, Charles Jr. 1922–1979 **15**

Minkins, Shadrach 1814(?)–1875 **104**

Minor, DeWayne 1956— **32**

Minoso, Minnie 1925–2015 **89, 127**

Minott, Sugar 1956–2010 **86**

Minus, Rene *See Chantels, The*

Mississippi Sheiks **122**

Mitchell, Arthur 1934— **2, 47**

Mitchell, Arthur Wergs 1883–1968 **91**

Mitchell, Blue 1930–1979 **126**

Mitchell, Brian Stokes 1957— **21**

Mitchell, Clarence M., Jr. 1911–1984 **88**

Mitchell, Corinne 1914–1993 **8**

Mitchell, Dwike 1930–2013 **111**

Mitchell, Elvis 1958— **67**

Mitchell, Freddie 1978— **116**

Mitchell, Ivory, Jr. *See Mitchell, Dwike*

Mitchell, James *See Detroit Emeralds, The*

Mitchell, Juanita Jackson 1913–1992 **128**

Mitchell, Keith 1946— **82**

Mitchell, Kel 1978— **66**

Mitchell, Leona 1949— **42**

Mitchell, Loften 1919–2001 **31**

Mitchell, Nicole 1967(?)— **66**

Mitchell, Parren J. 1922–2007 **42, 66**

Mitchell, Richard Allen *See Mitchell, Blue*
Mitchell, Russ 1960— **21, 73**
Mitchell, Sam 1963— **82**
Mitchell, Sharon 1962— **36**
Mitchell, Shireen 1970— **89**
Mitchell, Willie 1928–2010 **114**
Mizell, Jason *See Run-DMC*
Mkapa, Benjamin W. 1938— **16, 77**
Mo', Keb' *See Keb' Mo'*
Mobutu Sese Seko 1930–1997 **1, 56**
Moctar, Omara *See Bombino*
Modeliste, Joseph *See Meters, The*
Moffett, Charnett 1967— **127**
Mofolo, Thomas (Mokopu) 1876–1948 **37**
Mogae, Festus Gontebanye 1939— **19, 79**
Mohamed, Ali Mahdi *See Ali Mahdi Mohamed*
Mohammed, Nazr 1977— **64**
Mohammed, W. Deen 1933— **27**
Mohammed, Warith Deen *See Mohammed, W. Deen*
Mohamud, Hassan Sheikh 1955— **105**
Mohlabane, Goapele *See Goapele*
Moi, Daniel Arap 1924— **1, 35**
Mokae, Zakes 1934–2009 **80**
Mollel, Tololwa 1952— **38**
Monáe, Janelle 1985— **86**
Mongella, Gertrude 1945— **11**
Monica 1980— **21**
Mo'Nique 1967— **35, 84**
Monk, Art 1957— **38, 73**
Monk, Thelonious 1917–1982 **1**
Monroe, Bryan 1965— **71**
Monroe, Earl 1944— **89**
Monroe, Mary 19(?)(?)— **35**
Monteith, Mary Modjeska *See Simkins, Modjeska Monteith*
Montgomery, Eurreal Wilford *See Montgomery, Little Brother*
Montgomery, Isaiah T. 1847–1924 **91**
Montgomery, Little Brother 1906–1985 **117**
Montgomery, Robbie 1940— **101**
Montgomery, Tim 1975— **41**
Montgomery, Wes 1923–1968 **88**
Moody, Anne 1940–2015 **127**
Moody, James 1925— **83**
Moody, Ronald 1900–1984 **30**
Moody-Adams, Michele 1956— **76**
Moon, Warren 1956— **8, 66**
Moondoc, Jemeel 1951— **119**
Mooney, Paul 1941— **37, 120**
Moonglows, The **108**
Moore, Alice Ruth *See Dunbar-Nelson, Alice Ruth Moore*
Moore, Anthony *See Romanthony*
Moore, Archie 1916(?)–1998 **120**
Moore, Barbara C. 1949— **49**
Moore, Bobby *See Rashad, Ahmad*
Moore, Chante 1970(?)— **26**
Moore, Davey 1933–1963 **105**
Moore, David Schultz *See Moore, Davey*
Moore, Dorothy Rudd 1940— **46**
Moore, Gwendolynne S. 1951— **55**
Moore, Harry Roscoe *See Moore, Tim*

Moore, Harry T. 1905–1951 **29**
Moore, James Isaac *See Slim Harpo*
Moore, Jessica Care 1971— **30**
Moore, Johnny *See Drifters, The*
Moore, Johnny B. 1950— **38**
Moore, Juanita 1922– 2014 **83, 124**
Moore, Kermit 1929–2013 **116**
Moore, Kevin *See Mo', Keb'*
Moore, Lecrae *See Lecrae*
Moore, LeRoi 1961–2008 **72**
Moore, Maya 1989— **94**
Moore, Melba 1945— **21**
Moore, Michael *See Rose Royce*
Moore, Minyon 19(?)(?)— **45**
Moore, Richard *See bin Wahad, Dhoruba*
Moore, Sam *See Sam and Dave*
Moore, Shemar 1970— **21, 112**
Moore, Tim 1887–1958 **124**
Moore, Undine Smith 1904–1989 **28**
Moore, Wes 1978— **86**
Moorer, Lana *See MC Lyte*
Moorer, Michael 1967— **19**
Moose, Charles 1953— **40**
Morake, Lebohang *See Lebo M*
Morales, Mark 1960— *See Fat Boys*
Moran, Jason 1975— **89**
Moreland, Mantan 1902–1973 **117**
Morgan, Garrett (Augustus) 1877–1963 **1**
Morgan, Gertrude 1900–1986 **63**
Morgan, Irene 1917–2007 **65**
Morgan, Joe 1943— **9, 96**
Morgan, Lee 1938–1972 **102**
Morgan, Rose (Meta) 1912(?)— **11**
Morgan, Tracy 1968— **61, 102**
Morgan Lawrence, Margaret *See Lawrence, Margaret Morgan*
Morganfield, McKinley *See Muddy Waters*
Morial, Ernest "Dutch" 1929–1989 **26**
Morial, Marc H. 1958— **20, 51**
Morón, Alonzo G. 1909–1971 **91**
Morris, Eugene Edward *See Morris, Mercury*
Morris, Garrett 1937— **31**
Morris, Greg 1934–1996 **28**
Morris, Melvin 1942— **120**
Morris, Mercury 1947— **114**
Morris, Nathan *See Boyz II Men*
Morris, Raheem 1976— **77**
Morris, Wanya *See Boyz II Men*
Morris, William "Bill" 1938— **51**
Morris, Stevland Judkins *See Wonder, Stevie*
Morrison, Keith 1942— **13**
Morrison, Mary Thelma *See Washington, Mary T.*
Morrison, Sam 1936— **50**
Morrison, Toni 1931— **2, 15, 86**
Morrison, Vanessa 1969(?)— **84**
Morrow, E. Frederic 1909–1994 **100**
Morton, Azie Taylor 1936–2003 **48**
Morton, Ferdinand Q. 1881–1949 **90**
Morton, Frederick A., Jr. 1967(?)— **93**
Morton, Jelly Roll 1885(?)–1941 **29**

Morton, Joe 1947— **18**
Mos Def *See Bey, Yasiin*
Mosby, Marilyn 1980— **128**
Moseley-Braun, Carol *See Braun, Carol Moseley*
Moses, Edwin 1955— **8**
Moses, Gilbert, III 1942–1995 **12**
Moses, Robert Parris 1935— **11**
Mosisili, Pakalitha 1945— **96**
Mosley, "Sugar" Shane 1971— **32**
Mosley, Tim *See Timbaland*
Mosley, Walter 1952— **5, 25, 68**
Moss, Bryant *See Moss, Preacher*
Moss, Carlton 1909–1997 **17**
Moss, J. (?)— **64**
Moss, Otis, Jr. 1935— **72**
Moss, Otis, III 1971(?)— **72**
Moss, Preacher 1967— **63**
Moss, Randy 1977— **23, 90**
Moss, Shad Gregory *See Lil' Bow Wow*
Mossell, Gertrude Bustill 1855–1948 **40**
Mossell, Nathan Francis 1856–1946 **91**
Moten, Etta *See Barnett, Etta Moten*
Motlanthe, Kgalema 1949— **74**
Motley, Archibald, Jr. 1891–1981 **30**
Motley, Constance Baker 1921–2005 **10, 55**
Motley, Marion 1920–1999 **26**
Moton, Robert Russa 1867–1940 **83**
Moura, Paulo 1932–2010 **87**
Mourning, Alonzo 1970— **17, 44**
Moussambani, Eric 1978— **105**
Moutoussamy-Ashe, Jeanne 1951— **7**
Mowatt, Judy 1952(?)— **38**
Mowry, Jess 1960— **7**
Mowry, Tamera 1978— **79**
Mowry, Tia 1978— **78**
Moy'e, Theodore *See Treacherous Three*
Moyo, Dambisa 1970(?)— **76**
Moyo, Karega Kofi 19(?)(?)— **36**
Moyo, Lovemore 1965— **76**
Moyo, Yvette Jackson 1953— **36**
Mphalele, Es'kia (Ezekiel) 1919— **40**
Mswati III 1968— **56**
Mtukudzi, Oliver 1952— **109**
Muamba, Fabrice 1988— **104**
Mudimbe, V. Y. 1941— **61**
Mugabe, Robert 1924— **10, 71**
Mugisha, Frank 1979— **119**
Mugo, Madeleine *See Mugo, Micere Githae*
Mugo, Micere Githae 1942— **32**
Muhajir, El *See X, Marvin*
Muhammad, Ava 1951— **31**
Muhammad, Elijah 1897–1975 **4**
Muhammad, Jabir Herbert 1929–2008 **72**
Muhammad, Khallid Abdul 1951(?)— **10, 31**
Muhammad, Murtala 1938–1976 **119**
Mukoko, Jestina 1957(?)— **75**
Mullen, Harryette 1953— **34**
Mullen, Nicole C. 1967— **45**
Muluzi, Bakili 1943— **14, 76**
Mumba, Samantha 1983— **29**

Mumford, Eugene *See Billy Ward and the Dominoes; Golden Gate Quartet*
Muncie, Chuck 1953–2013 **112**
Muncie, Harry Vance *See Muncie, Chuck*
Mundine, Anthony 1975— **56**
Munroe, Myles 1954–2014 **125**
Munsey, Harry Vance *See Muncie, Chuck*
Mupuya, Andrew 1992— **118**
Murphy, Charles 1959— **95**
Murphy, Charlie *See Murphy, Charles*
Murphy, Eddie 1961— **4, 20, 61**
Murphy, Edward Regan *See Murphy, Eddie*
Murphy, John H. 1916— **42**
Murphy, Laura M. 1955— **43**
Murphy, Matt 1929(?)— **117**
Murphy, Matt "Guitar" *See Murphy, Matt*
Murphy McKenzie, Vashti *See McKenzie, Vashti M.*
Murray, Albert L. 1916— **33**
Murray, Cecil 1929— **12, 47**
Murray, Eddie 1956— **12**
Murray, Lenda 1962— **10**
Murray, Margaret James *See Washington, Margaret Murray*
Murray, Pauli 1910–1985 **38**
Murray, Tai 1982— **47**
Murrell, Sylvia Marilyn 1947— **49**
Musa, Ali, Mohammed *See Birra, Ali*
Muse, Clarence Edouard 1889–1979 **21**
Museveni, Yoweri 1944— **4, 119**
Mushikiwabo, Louise 1961— **88**
Musiq 1977— **37, 84**
Muslim, Saalim *See Storyboard P*
Mutebi, Ronald 1956— **25**
Mutola, Maria de Lurdes 1972— **12**
Mutombo, Dikembe 1966— **7, 107**
Mutu, Wangechi 19(?)(?)— **44**
Muzorewa, Abel 1925–2010 **85**
Mvula, Laura 1987— **110**
Mwanawasa, Levy 1948–2008 **72**
Mwangi, Meja 1948— **40**
Mwinyi, Ali Hassan 1925— **1, 77**
Mya 1979— **35**
Myers, Dave *See Aces, The*
Myers, Dwight *See Heavy D*
Myers, Lewis Eddy *See Myers, Lou*
Myers, Lou 1935(?)–2013 **110**
Myers, Louis *See Aces, The*
Myers, Walter Dean 1937–2014 **8, 70, 123**
Myka 9 *See Freestyle Fellowship*
Myles, John H. *See Swan Silvertones, The*
Myles, Kim 1974— **69**
Myles, Raymond Anthony 1958(?)–1998 **121**
Myrie, Mark Anthony *See Banton, Buju*
Nabrit, Samuel Milton 1905–2003 **47**
Nagin, Ray 1956— **42, 57, 88**
Nail, John E. 1883–1947 **92**
Najm, Faheem Rasheed *See T-Pain*
Nakasa, Nat 1937–1965 **123**

Nakasa, Ndazana Nathaniel *See Nakasa, Nat*

Nakhid, David 1964— **25**

Naki, Hamilton 1926–2005 **63**

Nance, Cynthia 1958— **71**

Nanula, Richard D. 1960— **20**

Napoleon, Benny N. 1956(?)— **23**

Nas 1973— **33, 111**

Nascimento, Abdias do 1914–2011 **93**

Nascimento, Milton 1942— **2, 64**

Nash, Diane 1938— **72**

Nash, Joe 1919–2005 **55**

Nash, Johnny 1940— **40**

Nash, Michael *See Rose Royce*

Nash, Niecy 1970— **66, 115**

Nash, Shannon King 1971— **84**

Nash, Terius Youngdell *See The-Dream*

Nate Dogg 1969–2011 **92**

Naughton, Naturi 1984— **97**

Naughty by Nature **124**

Navarro, Fats 1923–1950 **104**

Navarro, Theodore, Jr. *See Navarro, Fats*

Naylor, Gloria 1950— **10, 42**

Nazario, Zoe Yadira Zaldaña *See Saldana, Zoe*

Ndadaye, Melchior 1953–1993 **7**

Ndegeocello, Meshell 1968— **15, 83**

Ndiaye, Adama Amanda *See Paris, Adama*

Ndiaye, Iba 1928–2008 **74**

N'Dour, Youssou 1959— **1, 53, 79**

Ndungane, Winston Njongonkulu 1941— **16**

Neal, Elise 1970— **29**

Neal, Kenny 1957— **123**

Neal, Larry 1937–1981 **38**

Neal, Mark Anthony 1965(?)— **74**

Neal, Michael *See Rare Essence*

Neal, Raful 1936–2014 **44, 121**

Neale, Haydain 1970— **52**

Neals, Otto 1930— **73**

Nell, William C. 1816–1874 **128**

Nelly 1974— **32, 90**

Nelson, Benjamin Earl *See King, Ben E.*

Nelson, Jill 1952— **6, 54**

Nelson, Kadir 1974— **115**

Nelson, Lucille *See Hegamin, Lucille*

Nelson, Oliver 1932–1975 **113**

Nelson, Prince Rogers *See Prince*

Nelson, Sophia A. 1967— **93**

Nelson, Stanley 1951— **92**

Nelson Meigs, Andrea 1968— **48**

Neto, António Agostinho 1922— **43**

Nettles, Marva Deloise *See Collins, Marva*

Neverson, Tremaine Aldon *See Songz, Trey*

Neville, Aaron 1941— **21**

Neville, Art *See Meters, The*

Neville, Arthel 1962— **53**

Neville, Cyril *See Meters, The*

Neville, Ian *See Meters, The*

New Birth **124**

New Edition **101**

Newborn, Phineas, Jr. 1931–1989 **127**

Newcombe, Don 1926— **24**

Newkirk, Pamela 1957— **69**

Newman, David 1933–2009 **76**

Newman, Lester C. 1952— **51**

Newsome, Ozzie 1956— **26, 117**

Newton, Cam 1989— **96**

Newton, Huey (Percy) 1942–1989 **2**

Newton, Thandie 1972— **26, 114**

Newton, Thandiwe *See Newton, Thandie*

Ne-Yo 1982— **65**

Ngaujah, Sahr 1976— **86**

Ngengi, Kamau wa *See Kenyatta, Jomo*

Ngilu, Charity 1952— **58**

Ngubane, (Baldwin Sipho) Ben 1941— **33**

Nguema Mbasogo, Teodoro Obiang *See Obiang, Teodoro*

Ngugi, James T. *See Ngugi wa Thiong'o*

Ngugi wa Thiong'o 1938— **29, 61, 101**

Nguyen-Stevenson, Michael Ray *See Tyga*

Niane, Katoucha 1960–2008 **70**

Nicholas, Denise 1944— **82**

Nicholas, Fayard 1914–2006 **20, 57, 61**

Nicholas, Harold 1921— **20**

Nicholas, J. D. *See Commodores, The*

Nicholls, Frankie Warren, Jr. *See Knuckles, Frankie*

Nichols, Grace *See Nichols, Nichelle*

Nichols, James Thomas *See Bell, James "Cool Papa"*

Nichols, Nichelle 1933(?)— **11**

Nighthawk, Robert 1909–1967 **121**

Nissel, Angela 1974— **42**

Nix, Robert N. C., Jr. 1928–2003 **51**

Nix, Victor *See Rose Royce*

Nixon, Edgar Daniel 1899–1987 **100**

Nixon, Otis 1959— **111**

Njawe, Pius 1957–2010 **87**

Njongonkulu, Winston Ndungane 1941— **16**

Nkoli, Simon 1957–1998 **60**

Nkomo, Joshua 1917–1999 **4, 65**

Nkosi, Lewis 1936— **46**

Nkrumah, Kwame 1909–1972 **3**

Nkunda, Laurent 1967— **75**

Nkurunziza, Pierre 1963— **78**

N'Namdi, George R. 1946— **17**

Noah, Trevor 1984— **128**

Noah, Yannick 1960— **4, 60, 121**

Noble, Gil 1932— **76**

Noble, Reginald *See Redman*

Noble, Ronald 1957— **46**

Noble Drew Ali 1886–1929 **100**

Nocentelli, Leo *See Meters, The*

Norful, Smokie 1975— **127**

Norful, Willie Ray, Jr. *See Norful, Smokie*

Norman, Christina 1960(?)— **47**

Norman, Jessye 1945— **5**

Norman, Kyle *See Jagged Edge*

Norman, Maidie 1912–1998 **20**

Norman, Pat 1939— **10**

Norris, Michele 1961— **83**

Northup, Solomon 1808–1863(?) **115**

Norton, Eleanor Holmes 1937— **7, 93**

Norton, Ken 1943–2013 **101, 115**

Norton, Meredith 1970(?)— **72**

Norwood, Brandy *See Brandy*

Norwood, William Raymond, Jr. *See Ray J*

Notorious B.I.G. 1972–1997 **20**

Nottage, Cynthia DeLores *See Tucker, C. DeLores*

Nottage, Lynn 1964— **66**

Nour, Nawal M. 1965(?)— **56**

Ntaganda, Bosco 1972— **111**

Ntaryamira, Cyprien 1955–1994 **8**

Nteff, Alain 1992— **127**

Ntshona, Winston 1941— **52**

Nugent, Richard Bruce 1906–1987 **39**

Nujoma, Samuel 1929— **10**

Nunez, Elizabeth 1944— **62, 112**

Nunez-Harrell, Elizabeth *See Nunez, Elizabeth*

Nunn, Annetta 1959— **43**

Nunn, Bobby *See Coasters, The*

Nutter, Michael 1957— **69, 112**

Nuttin' but Stringz *See Escobar, Tourie, and Escobar, Damien*

Nyanda, Siphiwe 1950— **21**

Nyerere, Julius (Kambarage) 1922— **5**

Nyong'o, Lupita 1983— **127**

Nzo, Alfred (Baphethuxolo) 1925— **15**

Obadele, Imari 1930–2010 **84**

Obama, Barack 1961— **49, 74, 91**

Obama, Michelle 1964— **61, 90**

Obasanjo, Olusegun 1937— **5, 22**

Obasanjo, Stella 1945–2005 **32, 56**

Obiang, Teodoro 1942— **103**

Obote, Milton 1925–2005 **63**

Oboth, Isaac 1990(?)— **117**

O'Brien, Soledad 1966— **88**

Ocean, Frank 1987— **100**

Ochocinco, Chad *See Johnson, Chad*

ODB *See Ol' Dirty Bastard*

Odetta 1930— **37, 74**

Odinga, Raila 1945— **67, 110**

Odom, Lamar 1979— **81**

Odumegwu-Ojukwu, Chukwuemeka *See Ojukwu, Odumegwu*

Offset *See Migos*

Ofili, Chris 1968— **124**

Ogden, Jonathan 1974— **110**

Oglesby, Zena 1947— **12**

Ogletree, Charles, Jr. 1952— **12, 47**

O'Grady, Lorraine 1934— **73**

Ogunlesi, Adebayo O. 19(?)(?)— **37**

O'Jays, The **98**

Ojikutu, Bayo 1971— **66**

Ojikutu, Bisola 1974— **65**

Ojukwu, Emeka *See Ojukwu, Odumegwu*

Ojukwu, Odumegwu 1933–2011 **99**

Okaalet, Peter 1953— **58**

Okara, Gabriel 1921— **37**

Okigbo, Christopher 1932–1967 **102**

Okogwu, Patrick Chukwuemeka *See Tinie Tempah*

Okonedo, Sophie 1969— **67**

Okonjo-Iweala, Ngozi 1954— **101**

Okonma, Tyler *See Tyler, the Creator*

Okosuns, Sonny 1947–2008 **71**

Okocha, Augustine Azuka *See Okocha, Jay Jay*

Okocha, Jay Jay 1973— **99**

Ol' Dirty Bastard 1968–2004 **52**

Olagundoye, Olatokunbo Susan Olasobunmi Abeke *See Olagundoye, Toks*

Olagundoye, Toks 1975— **113**

Olajuwon, Akeem *See Olajuwon, Hakeem*

Olajuwon, Hakeem 1963— **2, 72**

Olatunji, Babatunde 1927–2003 **36, 126**

Olden, Georg(e) 1920–1975 **44**

O'Leary, Hazel (Rollins) 1937— **6**

Oliver, Bilal Sayeed *See Bilal*

Oliver, Garrett 1962— **95**

Oliver, Jerry 1947— **37**

Oliver, Joe "King" 1885–1938 **42**

Oliver, John J., Jr. 1945— **48**

Oliver, Kimberly 1976— **60**

Oliver, Pam 1961— **54, 123**

Oliver, Paul 1984–2013 **115**

Oliver, Rachel *See Atlantic Starr*

Olojede, Dele 1961— **59**

Olopade, Olufunmilayo Falusi 1957(?)— **58**

Olympio, Sylvanus 1902–1963 **126**

Omar, Samia Yusuf 1991–2012 **107**

Omarion 1984— **107**

Omarosa 1974— **69, 110**

Omolewa, Michael 194(?)— **119**

Omotola *See Jalade-Ekeinde, Omotola*

O'Neal, Frederick 1905–1992 **99**

O'Neal, Patrice 1969–2011 **99**

O'Neal, Rodney 1954— **88**

O'Neal, Ron 1937–2004 **46**

O'Neal, Shaquille 1972— **8, 30, 95**

O'Neal, Stanley 1951— **38, 67**

O'Neil, Buck 1911–2006 **19, 59**

O'Neil, John Jordan *See O'Neil, Buck*

Ongala, Ramadhani Mtoro *See Ongala, Remmy*

Ongala, Remmy 1947–2010 **9, 91**

Onile-Ere, Adetayo Ayowale *See Cruz, Taio*

Onwueme, Tess Osonye 1955— **23**

Onwurah, Ngozi 1966(?)— **38**

Onyewu, Oguchi 1982— **60**

Opitz, May *See Ayim, May*

Orange, James 1942–2008 **74**

Orange, Walter *See Commodores, The*

O'Ree, William Eldon *See O'Ree, Willie*

O'Ree, Willie 1935— **5**

Orioles, The **100**

Orlandersmith, Dael 1959— **42**

Orman, Roscoe 1944— **55**

Ormes, Jackie 1911–1985 **73**

Orr, Kevyn 1958— **118**

Ortiz, Ami *See Chantels, The*

Ortiz, David 1975— **52, 82**

Ory, Edward *See Ory, Kid*

Ory, Kid 1886–1973 **118**
Osbey, Brenda Marie 1957— **102**
Osborne, Jeffrey 1948— **26, 121**
Osborne, Na'taki 1974— **54**
Osman, Said 1952(?)— **127**
Osotimehin, Babatunde 1949— **107**
Otis, Clarence, Jr. 1956— **55**
Otis, Clyde 1924— **67**
Otunga, Maurice Michael
    1923–2003 **55**
Ouattara 1957— **43**
Ouattara, Alassane 1942— **90**
Ouattara, Morou 1966— **74**
Ousley, Curtis See King Curtis
Ousmane, Sembène See Sem-
    bène, Ousmane
OutKast **35**
Outler, Jimmy See Soul Stirrers
Overton, Anthony 1865–1946 **128**
Owens, Brig 1943— **118**
Owens, Brigman See Owens, Brig
Owens, Dana See Queen Latifah
Owens, Helen 1937— **48**
Owens, Henry See Golden Gate
    Quartet
Owens, J. C. See Owens, Jesse
Owens, Jack 1904–1997 **38**
Owens, James Cleveland See Ow-
    ens, Jesse
Owens, Jesse 1913–1980 **2**
Owens, Kim Lamont See KEM
Owens, Major 1936–2013 **6, 117**
Owens, Paul See Swan Silver-
    tones, The
Owens, Terrell 1973— **53, 106**
Oyebanjo, Dapo Daniel See D'banj
Oyelowo, David 1976— **82, 126**
Oyewale, Taiwo Bamidele Olaniyi
    See Prince Twins Seven-Seven
Oyono, Ferdinand 1929— **38**
Ozen, Barbara Lynn See Lynn, Bar-
    bara
P. Diddy See Combs, Sean
Pace, Betty 1954— **59**
Pace, Judy 1942— **119**
Pace, Orlando 1975— **21**
Packer, Daniel 1947— **56**
Packer, Will 1974(?)— **71**
Packer, Z. Z. 1973— **64**
Page, Alan (Cedric) 1945— **7**
Page, Clarence 1947— **4**
Page, Greg 1958–2009 **78**
Page, Inman 1853–1935 **82**
Page, Walter 1900–1957 **117**
Paige, Leroy Robert See Paige,
    Satchel
Paige, Rod 1933— **29**
Paige, Satchel 1906–1982 **7**
Painter, Nell Irvin 1942— **24, 88**
Palacio, Andy 1960–2008 **96**
Palcy, Euzhan 1958— **94**
Palmer, Everard 1930— **37**
Palmer, Keke 1993— **68, 120**
Palmer, Lauren Keyana See
    Palmer, Keke
Palmer, Rissi 1981— **65**
Palmer, Violet 1964— **59**
Papa Wendo See Kolosoy, Wendo
Pape, Jean William 1946— **126**
Parham, Charles Valdez See Par-
    ham, Truck
Parham, Marjorie B. 1918— **71**
Parham, Truck 1911–2002 **124**

Paris, Adama 1976— **120**
Parish, Robert 1953— **43**
Parker, Barrington D. 1915–1993
    92
Parker, Candace 1986— **74**
Parker, Charlie 1920–1955 **20**
Parker, Herman, Jr. See Parker,
    Junior
Parker, Jim 1934–2005 **64**
Parker, Junior 1932–1971 **116**
Parker, Kellis E. 1942–2000 **30**
Parker, (Lawrence) Kris(hna) See
    KRS-One
Parker, LarStella Irby See Parker,
    Star
Parker, Maceo 1943— **72**
Parker, Nicole Ari 1970— **52**
Parker, Q See 112
Parker, Quinnes See 112
Parker, Ray, Jr. 1954— **85**
Parker, Star 1956— **70**
Parker, Tony 1982— **75**
Parker, Vernon 1959— **97**
Parks, Bernard C. 1943— **17**
Parks, Gordon 1912–2006 **1, 35,
    58**
Parks, Henry Green, Jr. 1916–1989
    89
Parks, Rosa 1913–2005 **1, 35, 56**
Parks, Suzan-Lori 1963— **34, 85**
Parlan, Horace 1931— **108**
Parr, Russ 196(?)— **51**
Parsons, James Benton 1911–1993
    14
Parsons, Richard 1948— **11, 33,
    124**
Pascal-Trouillot, Ertha 1943— **3**
Paterson, Basil A. 1926–2014 **69,
    122**
Paterson, David A. 1954— **59**
Patillo, Melba Joy 1941— **15**
Patrick, Deval 1956— **12, 61, 127**
Patterson, Chuck 1945–2013 **124**
Patterson, Floyd 1935–2006 **19, 58**
Patterson, Frederick Douglass
    1901–1988 **12**
Patterson, Gilbert Earl 1939— **41**
Patterson, J. O., Jr. 1935— **80**
Patterson, Louise 1901–1999 **25**
Patterson, Mary Jane 1840–1894
    54
Patterson, Orlando 1940— **4, 127**
Patterson, P(ercival) J(ames)
    1936(?)— **6, 20**
Patterson, Robert, Jr. See Ali,
    Rashied
Patton, Antwan 1975— **45** See also
    OutKast
Patton, Charley 1891(?)–1934 **107**
Patton, Paula 1975— **62**
Patton, Venetria K. 1968— **125**
Paul, Billy 1934(?)— **127**
Paul, Chris 1985— **84, 100**
Paulk, Marcus T. 1986— **127**
Payne, Allen 1962(?)— **13**
Payne, Donald M. 1934–2012 **2,
    57, 112**
Payne, Ethel L. 1911–1991 **28**
Payne, Freda 1942— **58**
Payne, Hazel See Taste of Honey,
    A
Payne, Les 1941— **89**
Payne, Ulice, Jr. 1955— **42**
Payne, William D. 1932— **60**

Payton, Benjamin F. 1932— **23**
Payton, Gary 1968— **99**
Payton, John 1946–2012 **48, 124**
Payton, Philip A., Jr. 1876–1917 **88**
Payton, Walter 1954–1999 **11, 25**
P.E.A.C.E. See Freestyle Fellow-
    ship
Peake, Tadley Ewing See Dam-
    eron, Tadd
Peaker, Franklin See Harold Melvin
    & the Blue Notes
Pearman, Raven-Symoné Christina
    See Raven-Symoné
Pearson, Felicia 1980— **99**
Peck, Carolyn 1966(?)— **23**
Peck, Raoul 1953— **32**
Peebles, Ann 1947— **114**
Peebles, Annie Murray See
    Peebles, Ann
Peele, Jordan See Key & Peele
Peete, Calvin 1943— **11**
Peete, Holly Robinson 1965— **20**
Peete, Rodney 1966— **60**
Pelé 1940— **7**
Pelé, Abedi 1964— **122**
Pena, Paul 1950–2005 **58**
Pendergrass, Teddy 1950–2010 **22,
    83**
Penguins, The **107**
Penniman, Richard Wayne See
    Little Richard
Peoples, Dottie 19(?)(?)— **22**
Pereira, Aristides 1923–2011 **30, 97**
Perez, Anna 1951— **1**
Perez, Pascual 1957–2012 **108**
Perkins, Anthony 1959(?)— **24**
Perkins, Carl 1928–1958 **128**
Perkins, Eddie 1937–2012 **103**
Perkins, Edward (Joseph) 1928— **5**
Perkins, James, Jr. 1953(?)— **55**
Perkins, Joe Willie See Perkins,
    Pinetop
Perkins, Marion 1908–1961 **38**
Perkins, Minnie See Grant, Micki
Perkins, Pinetop 1913— **70**
Perren, Freddie 1943–2004 **60**
Perrineau, Harold, Jr. 1968— **51**
Perrot, Kim 1967–1999 **23**
Perry, Emmitt, Jr. See Perry, Tyler
Perry, Herman 1922–1945 **89**
Perry, James 1975— **83**
Perry, Joe 1927–2011 **95**
Perry, Laval 195(?)— **64**
Perry, Lee 1936— **19, 103**
Perry, Lincoln See Fetchit, Stepin
Perry, Lowell 1931–2001 **30**
Perry, Matthew J., Jr. 1921–2011
    96
Perry, Rainford Hugh See Perry,
    Lee
Perry, Ruth 1936— **19**
Perry, Ruth Sando 1939— **15**
Perry, Scratch See Perry, Lee
Perry, Steve 1970— **98**
Perry, Tyler 1969— **40, 54, 103**
Perry, Warren 1942(?)— **56**
Person, Waverly 1927— **9, 51**
Peters, Brock 1927–2005 **96**
Peters, Clarke 1952— **103**
Peters, Jason 1982— **125**
Peters, Lenrie 1932— **43**
Peters, Margaret 1915— **43**
Peters, Maria Philomena 1941— **12**

Peters, Matilda 1917— **43**
Petersen, Frank E. 1932— **31**
Petersen, Neal 1967— **96**
Peterson, Adrian 1985— **109**
Peterson, Hannibal See Peterson,
    Marvin
Peterson, James 19(?)(?)— **81**
Peterson, James 1937— **38**
Peterson, Jesse Lee 1949— **81**
Peterson, Karen Carter 1969— **90**
Peterson, Marvin 1948— **27**
Peterson, Oscar 1925— **52**
Petioni, Muriel 1914 –2011 **99**
Petry, Ann 1909–1997 **19**
Pettiford, Oscar 1922–1960 **106**
Pettigrew, Antonio 1967–2010 **118**
Pettus, Kenny See Dazz Band
Pharcyde, The **127**
Phifer, Mekhi 1974— **25, 103**
Philip, M. Nourbese See Philip,
    Marlene Nourbese
Philip, Marlene Nourbese 1947—
    32
Phillips, Arthur See Dramatics, The
Phillips, Bobby See Cadillacs
Phillips, Brandon 1981— **116**
Phillips, Carl 1959— **111**
Phillips, Charles E., Jr. 1959— **57,
    109**
Phillips, Esther 1935–1984 **107**
Phillips, Helen L. 1919–2005 **63**
Phillips, Joseph See Atlantic Starr
Phillips, Joseph C. 1962— **73**
Phillips, Peter See Rock, Pete
Phillips, Teresa L. 1958— **42**
Phipps, Wintley 1955— **59**
Pickens, James, Jr. 1954— **59**
Pickett, Bill 1870–1932 **11**
Pickett, Cecil 1945— **39**
Pickett, Wilson See Falcons, The
Pierce, Elijah 1892–1984 **84**
Pierce, Harold 1917-1988 **75**
Pierce, Maryland See Five Keys,
    The
Pierce, Paul 1977— **71**
Pierce, Wendell 1962— **90**
Pierre, Andre 1915— **17**
Pierre, Percy Anthony 1939— **46**
Pierre-Louis, Michèle 1947— **75**
Pigford, Eva See Marcille, Eva
Pimentel, Miguel Jontel See Miguel
Pincham, R. Eugene, Sr.
    1925–2008 **69**
Pinchback, P(inckney) B(enton)
    S(tewart) 1837–1921 **9**
Pinckney, Bill 1935— **42**
Pinckney, Sandra 194(?)— **56**
Pindell, Howardena 1943— **55**
Pinder, Jefferson 1970— **77**
Pinderhughes, John 1946— **47**
Pindling, Lynden 1930–2000 **81**
Pineda, Michael 1989— **121**
Pinkett, Jada See Pinkett Smith,
    Jada
Pinkett, Randal 1971— **61**
Pinkett Smith, Jada 1971— **10, 41,
    95**
Pinkney, Arnold R. 1931–2014 **122**
Pinkney, Bill See Drifters, The
Pinkney, Fayette 1948–2009 **80**
Pinkney, Jerry 1939— **15, 124**
Pinkston, W. Randall 1950— **24**
Pinn, Vivian Winona 1941— **49**

Piper, Adrian 1948— **71**
Pippen, Scottie 1965— **15, 89**
Pippin, Horace 1888–1946 **9**
Pitt, David Thomas 1913–1994 **10**
Pitta (do Nascimento), Celso (Roberto) 19(?)(?)— **17**
Pitts, Byron 1960— **71**
Pitts, Charles See Pitts, Skip
Pitts, Derrick 1956(?)— **77**
Pitts, Leonard, Jr. 1957— **54, 85**
Pitts, Robb 1941— **84**
Pitts, Robert Lee See Pitts, Robb
Pitts, Skip 1947–2012 **103**
Plaatje, Sol T. 1876–1932 **80**
Plaskett, Stacey 1966— **127**
Platters, The **99**
Player, Willa B. 1909–2003 **43**
Pleasant, Loretta See Lacks, Henrietta
Pleasant, Mary Ellen 1814–1904 **9**
Pleasure P 1984— **84**
Plessy, Homer Adolph 1862–1925 **31**
Plinton, James O., Jr. 1914–1996 **98**
Plummer, Glenn 1961— **120**
P.M. Dawn **54**
Pohamba, Hifikepunye 1935— **95**
Poindexter, Hildrus A. 1901–1987 **87**
Poitier, Sidney 1927— **11, 36**
Poitier, Sydney Tamiia 1973— **65**
Polite, Carlene Hatcher 1932–2009 **82**
Polite, Lloyd, Jr. See Lloyd
Pollard, Ackquille Jean See Shmurda, Bobby
Pollard, Fritz 1894–1986 **53**
Pollard, William L. 1945(?)— **91**
Pomare, Eleo 1937–2008 **72**
Poole, Elijah See Muhammad, Elijah
Pope.L, William 1955— **72**
Porter, Billy 1969— **112**
Porter, Bo 1972— **123**
Porter, Countee Leroy See Cullin, Countee
Porter, David 1941— **127**
Porter, Dorothy See Wesley, Dorothy Porter
Porter, George, Jr. See Meters, The
Porter, James A(mos) 1905–1970 **11**
Porter, Maggie See Fisk Jubilee Singers
Porter, Marquis Donnell See Porter, Bo
Porter, Terry 1963— **75**
Portuondo, Omara 1930— **53**
Potter, Myrtle 1958— **40**
Potts, Sylvester See Contours, The
Pough, Terrell 1987(?)–2005 **58**
Pounder, Carol Christine Hilaria See Pounder, CCH
Pounder, CCH 1952— **72**
Poussaint, Alvin F. 1934— **5, 67**
Poussaint, Renee 1944— **78**
Powell, Adam Clayton, Jr. 1908–1972 **3**
Powell, Benny 1930–2010 **87**
Powell, Bud 1924–1966 **24**
Powell, Colin 1937— **1, 28, 75**
Powell, Debra A. 1964— **23**

Powell, Keith 1979(?)— **101**
Powell, Kevin 1966— **31, 74**
Powell, Maxine 1915–2013 **8, 115**
Powell, Michael Anthony See Powell, Mike
Powell, Michael K. 1963— **32**
Powell, Mike 1963— **7**
Powell, Renee 1946— **34**
Powell, William See O'Jays, The
Powell, William J. 1916–2009 **82**
Power, Will 1970— **83**
Prater, Dave See Sam and Dave
Pratt, Awadagin 1966— **31**
Pratt, Elmer See Pratt, Geronimo
Pratt, Geronimo 1947–2011 **18, 95**
Pratt, Kyla 1986— **57**
Pratt Dixon, Sharon See Dixon, Sharon Pratt
Pree, Dawn See New Birth
Preer, Evelyn 1896–1932 **82**
Premice, Josephine 1926–2001 **41**
Pressley, Condace L. 1964— **41**
Preston, Billy 1946–2006 **39, 59**
Preston, William Everett See Preston, Billy
Préval, René 1943— **87**
Preyan, Jermaine See Mack Maine
Price, David 1985— **101**
Price, Florence 1887–1953 **37**
Price, Frederick K. C. 1932— **21**
Price, Glenda 1939— **22**
Price, Hugh B. 1941— **9, 54**
Price, Kelly 1973(?)— **23**
Price, Leontyne 1927— **1**
Price, Lisa 1962— **97**
Price, Lloyd 1933— **119**
Price, Richard 1930(?)— **51**
Pride, Charley 1938(?)— **26**
Primas, Randy 1949–2012 **106**
Primus, Pearl 1919–1994 **6, 125**
Prince 1958— **18, 65**
Prince, Richard E. 1947— **71**
Prince, Ron 1969— **64**
Prince, Tayshaun 1980— **68**
Prince Johnny C See Geto Boys
Prince Markie Dee See Fat Boys
Prince Twins Seven-Seven 1944–2011 **95**
Prince-Bythewood, Gina 1969— **31, 77**
Pritchard, Robert Starling 1927— **21**
Procope, Ernesta 19(?)(?)— **23**
Procope, John Levy 1925–2005 **56**
Proctor, Bernard Shaw 1921–2013 **120**
Professor Griff See Public Enemy
Professor Longhair 1918–1980 **109**
Proof 1973–2006 **101**
Prophet, Nancy Elizabeth 1890–1960 **42**
Prothrow, Deborah Boutin See Prothrow-Stith, Deborah
Prothrow-Stith, Deborah 1954— **10**
Pruitt, Wendell O. 1920–1945 **106**
Pryce, Trevor 1975— **89**
Pryor, James Edward See Pryor, Snooky
Pryor, Rain 1969— **65**
Pryor, Richard 1940–2005 **3, 24, 56**
Pryor, Snooky 1921–2006 **119**
Prysock, Arthur 1929–1997 **117**
Public Enemy **98**

Puckett, Kirby 1960–2006 **4, 58**
Puff Daddy See Combs, Sean
Pugh, Charles 1971— **81**
Pugh, Iola Lewis See Consolers, The
Pugh, Sullivan See Consolers, The
Puig, Yasiel 1990— **113**
Purdie, Bernard 1939— **77**
Purnell, Silas 1923–2003 **59**
Puryear, Martin 1941— **42, 101**
Pusha T 1977— **123**
Putney, Martha S. 1916–2008 **75**
Puzey, Leonard See Ravens, The
Pyfrom, Estella 1936— **127**
Quander, Nellie 1880–1961 **102**
Quarles, Benjamin Arthur 1904–1996 **18**
Quarles, Norma 1936— **25**
Quarterman, Lloyd Albert 1918–1982 **4**
Quattlebaum, Michael David, Jr. See Blanco, Mykki
Quavno See Migos
Queen Latifah 1970— **1, 16, 58, 119**
Querino, Manuel Raimundo 1851–1923 **84**
?uestlove 1971— **74** See Roots, The
Quigless, Helen G. 1944–2004 **49**
Quince, Peggy A. 1948— **69**
Quirot, Ana 1963— **13**
Quisim, Basheer See Gryce, Gigi
Quivers, Robin 1952— **61**
Qusim, Basheer See Gryce, Gigi
Rabb, Maurice F., Jr. 1932–2005 **58**
Rabia, Aliyah See Staton, Dakota
Rackley, Gloria See Blackwell, Gloria
Radcliffe, Ted 1902–2005 **74**
Radcliffe, Theodore Roosevelt See Radcliffe, Ted
Rae Sremmurd **126**
Ragin, Derek Lee 1958— **84**
Rahman, Aishah 1936— **37**
Raines, Franklin 1949— **14, 107**
Raines, Rock See Raines, Tim
Raines, Tim 1959— **107**
Rainey, Ma 1886–1939 **33**
Raleigh Ritchie See Anderson, Jacob
Ralph, Sheryl Lee 1956— **18, 108**
Ramaphosa, Cyril 1952— **3, 117**
Rambough, Lori Ann See Sommore
Ramphele, Mamphela 1947— **29**
Ramsey, Charles H. 1948— **21, 69**
Rand, A(ddison) Barry 1944— **6**
Randall, Alice 1959— **38**
Randall, Dudley 1914–2000 **8, 55**
Randall, Vernellia R. 1948— **95**
Randle, John 1967— **87**
Randle, Theresa 1967— **16**
Randolph, A(sa) Philip 1889–1979 **3**
Randolph, Donald James See Covay, Don
Randolph, Linda A. 1941— **52**
Randolph, Willie 1954— **53**
Rangel, Charles B. 1930— **3, 52, 85**
Ranglin, Ernest 1932— **78**
Rankin Don See Rhoden, Wayne
Ransome, James E. 1961— **88**

Raoul, Kwame 1964— **55**
Rapelang Rabana 198(?)— **112**
Rapier, James T. 1837–1883 **82**
Rare Essence **121**
Ras Tafari See Haile Selassie
Rascal, Dizzee 1985— **82**
Rashad, Ahmad 1949— **18**
Rashad, Phylicia 1948— **21**
Raspberry, William 1935— **2**
Raven See Raven-Symoné
Ravens, The **103**
Raven-Symoné 1985— **44, 113**
Rawlings, Jerry (John) 1947— **9**
Rawlings-Blake, Stephanie 1970— **93, 128**
Rawlinson, Johnnie B. 1952— **79**
Rawls, Lou 1936–2006 **17, 57**
Ray, Carline 1925–2013 **113**
Ray, Charlotte E. 1850–1911 **60**
Ray, Gene Anthony 1962–2003 **47**
Ray J 1981— **86**
Raymond, Usher See Usher
Razaf, Andy 1895–1973 **19**
Razafkeriefo, Andreamentania Paul See Razaf, Andy
Ready, Stephanie 1975— **33**
Reagins, Tony 1967— **94**
Reagon, Bernice Johnson 1942— **7**
Reagon, Toshi 1964— **76**
Reason, Joseph Paul 1943— **19**
Reaves, Donald J. 1946— **102**
Record, Eugene 1940–2005 **60** See also Chi-Lites
Redd, Dana 1968— **93**
Reddick, Lance 1962— **52, 128**
Reddick, Lawrence Dunbar 1910–1995 **20**
Redding, Ann Holmes 1951— **77**
Redding, J. Saunders 1906–1988 **26**
Redding, Louis L. 1901–1998 **26**
Redding, Otis, Jr. 1941— **16**
Redman 1970— **81**
Redman, Joshua 1969— **30**
Redmond, Eugene 1937— **23**
Redwood, John Henry 1942–2003 **78**
Reece, E. Albert 1950— **63**
Reece, Marcel 1985— **114**
Reed, A. C. 1926— **36**
Reed, Alaina See Reed Hall, Alaina
Reed, Ishmael 1938— **8**
Reed, Jimmy 1925–1976 **38**
Reed, Joe L. 1939(?)— **110**
Reed, Kasim 1969— **82**
Reed, Larry See Dramatics, The
Reed, Natina 1979–2012 **106**
Reed, Willie See Louis, Willie
Reed, Willis, Jr. 1942— **86**
Reed Amini, Alaina See Reed Hall, Alaina
Reed Hall, Alaina 1946–2009 **83**
Reeder, Joyce See Beatty, Joyce
Reedy, Jessica 1988— **101**
Reems, Ernestine Cleveland 1932—? **?**
Rees, Dee 197(?)— **100**
Reese, Calvin See Reese, Pokey
Reese, Della 1931— **6, 20, 96**
Reese, Jerry 1963— **103**
Reese, Milous J., Jr. 1904— **51**
Reese, Pokey 1973— **28**
Reese, Tracy 1964— **54**

Reeves, Bass 1838–1910 **100**
Reeves, Dianne 1956— **32, 119**
Reeves, Gregory 1952— **49**
Reeves, Martha 1941— **85**
Reeves, Rachel J. 1950(?)— **23**
Reeves, Shirley Alston *See Shirelles, The*
Reeves, Triette Lipsey 1963— **27**
Regis, Cyrille 1958— **51**
Reid, Antonio "L.A." 1958(?)— **28**
Reid, Ira De A. 1901–1968 **100**
Reid, Irvin D. 1941— **20**
Reid, L.A. *See Reid, Antonio "L.A."*
Reid, Senghor 1976— **55**
Reid, Tim 1944— **56**
Reid, Vernon 1958— **34**
Reivers, Corbin Bleu *See Corbin Bleu*
Render, Michael *See Killer Mike*
Reuben, Gloria 19(?)(?)— **15**
Rev Run *See Run; Run-DMC*
Revels, Hiram Rhoades 1827–1901 **98**
Reverend Ike 1935–2009 **79**
Reynolds, Harold 1960— **77**
Reynolds, L. J. *See Dramatics, The*
Reynolds, Star Jones 1962(?)— **10, 27, 61**
Rhames, Ving 1959— **14, 50**
Rhimes, Shonda Lynn 1970— **67**
Rhoden, Dwight 1962— **40**
Rhoden, Wayne 1966— **70**
Rhoden, William C. 1950(?)— **67**
Rhodes, Jewell Parker 1954— **84**
Rhodes, Ray 1950— **14**
Rhone, Sylvia 1952— **2**
Rhone, Trevor 1940–2009 **80**
Rhymefest 1977— **97**
Rhymes, Busta 1972— **31**
Rhyne, Melvin 1936–2013 **109**
Ribbs, William Theodore, Jr. *See Ribbs, Willy T.*
Ribbs, Willy T. 1956— **2**
Ribeau, Sidney 1947(?)— **70**
Ribeiro, Alfonso 1971— **17**
Rice, Condoleezza 1954— **3, 28, 72**
Rice, Constance LaMay 1956— **60**
Rice, Emmett J. 1920–2011 **94**
Rice, Jerry 1962— **5, 55, 89**
Rice, Jim 1953— **75**
Rice, Linda Johnson 1958— **9, 41**
Rice, Louise Allen 1941— **54**
Rice, Mack *See Falcons, The*
Rice, Norm(an Blann) 1943— **8**
Rice, Ray 1987— **112**
Rice, Susan 1964— **74, 103**
Richard, Dawn 1983— **92**
Richard, J. R. 1950— **87**
Richards, Beah 1926–2000 **30**
Richards, Hilda 1936— **49**
Richards, Lloyd 1923(?)— **2**
Richards, Sanya *See Richards-Ross, Sanya*
Richardson, Desmond 1969— **39**
Richardson, Donna 1962— **39**
Richardson, Elaine Potter *See Kincaid, Jamaica*
Richardson, Julieanna 1954— **81**
Richardson, LaTanya 1949— **71**
Richardson, Laura 1962— **81**
Richardson, Nolan 1941— **9**
Richardson, Pat *See Norman, Pat*

Richardson, Rupert 1930–2008 **67**
Richardson, Salli 1967— **68**
Richards-Ross, Sanya 1985— **66, 98**
Richie, Leroy C. 1941— **18**
Richie, Lionel 1949— **27, 65, 114**
See also Commodores, The
Richmond, Cedric 1973— **93**
Richmond, Mitchell James 1965— **19**
Ricks, Jimmy *See Ravens, The*
Riddick, Clyde *See Golden Gate Quartet*
Rideau, Iris 1940(?)— **46**
Ridenhour, Carlton *See Chuck D.*
Ridley, John 1965— **69**
Riggins, Karriem 1975— **102**
Riggs, Marlon 1957–1994 **5, 44**
Rihanna 1988— **65, 102**
Riles, Wilson C. 1917–1999 **79**
Riley, Amber 1986— **97**
Riley, Boots 1971— **89**
Riley, Helen Caldwell Day 1926— **13**
Riley, Rochelle 1959(?)— **50**
Riley, Teddy 1967— **116**
Riley, Timothy Christian *See Tony! Toni! Toné!*
Rillieux, Norbert 1806–1894 **92**
Ringgold, Faith 1930— **4, 81**
Riperton, Minnie 1947–1979 **32**
Rivers, Doc 1961— **25, 81**
Rivers, Eugene F., III 1950— **81**
Rivers, Glenn *See Rivers, Doc*
Rivers, Kim *See Roberts, Kimberly Rivers*
Rivers, Sam 1923— **95**
Roach, Max 1924–2007 **21, 63**
Roaf, Andrée Layton 1941–2009 **106**
Roaf, William Layton *See Roaf, Willie*
Roaf, Willie 1970— **106**
Roberto, Holden 1923–2007 **65**
Roberts, Aldwyn *See Lord Kitchener*
Roberts, Darryl 1962(?)— **70**
Roberts, Deborah 1960— **35**
Roberts, Ian *See Kwei-Armah, Kwame*
Roberts, James *See Lover, Ed*
Roberts, Joseph Jenkins 1809–1876 **125**
Roberts, Kimberly Rivers 1981(?)— **72**
Roberts, Kristina LaFerne *See Zane*
Roberts, Lillian 1928— **83**
Roberts, Marcus 1963— **19, 113**
Roberts, Marthaniel *See Roberts, Marcus*
Roberts, Michele 1956— **123**
Roberts, Mike 1948— **57**
Roberts, Robin 1960— **16, 54, 113**
Roberts, Roy S. 1939(?)— **14**
Roberts, William Leonard, II *See Ross, Rick*
Robertson, Cardiss Hortense *See Collins, Cardiss*
Robertson, Gil L., IV 1964— **85**
Robertson, Lance *See DJ Lance Rock*
Robertson, Oscar 1938— **26**

Robeson, Eslanda Goode 1896–1965 **13**
Robeson, Paul (Leroy Bustill) 1898–1976 **2**
Robey, Don 1903–1975 **115**
Robinson, Aminah 1940— **50**
Robinson, Arnett *See Falcons, The*
Robinson, Bill "Bojangles" 1878–1949 **11**
Robinson, Bishop L. 1927— **66**
Robinson, Cleo Parker 1948(?)— **38**
Robinson, Craig 1962— **107**
Robinson, Craig 1971— **103**
Robinson, Darren 1967–1995 *See Fat Boys*
Robinson, Dave 1941— **110**
Robinson, David 1965— **24, 90**
Robinson, Eddie G. 1919–2007 **10, 61**
Robinson, Eugene 1955— **77**
Robinson, Fatima 19(?)(?)— **34**
Robinson, Fenton 1935–1997 **38**
Robinson, Flynn 1941–2013 **112**
Robinson, Frank 1935— **9, 87**
Robinson, Ida B. 1891–1946 **106**
Robinson, Jack Roosevelt *See Robinson, Jackie*
Robinson, Jackie 1919–1972 **6**
Robinson, Joann Gibson 1912–1992 **100**
Robinson, Justin *See Carolina Chocolate Drops*
Robinson, LaVaughn 1927–2008 **69**
Robinson, Louise *See Sweet Honey in the Rock*
Robinson, Luther *See Robinson, Bill "Bojangles"*
Robinson, Malcolm S. 1948— **44**
Robinson, Matt 1937–2002 **69**
Robinson, Matthew, Jr. *See Robinson, Matt*
Robinson, Max 1939–1988 **3**
Robinson, Patrick 1966— **19, 71**
Robinson, Rachel 1922— **16**
Robinson, Randall 1941— **7, 46**
Robinson, Reginald R. 1972— **53**
Robinson, Romye *See Pharcyde, The*
Robinson, Sharon 1950— **22**
Robinson, Shaun 19(?)(?)— **36**
Robinson, Smokey 1940— **3, 49**
Robinson, Spottswood W., III 1916–1998 **22**
Robinson, Sugar Ray 1921— **18**
Robinson, Sylvia 1936— **79**
Robinson, Will 1911–2008 **51, 69**
Robinson, William, Jr. *See Robinson, Smokey*
Robinson-Berry, Joan 19(?)(?)— **94**
Roble, Abdi 1964— **71**
Roby, Kimberla Lawson 1965— **86**
Roche, Joyce M. 1947— **17**
Rochereau, Tabu Ley 1937(?)–2013 **117**
Rochester *See Anderson, Eddie "Rochester"*
Rochon, Lela 1965(?)— **16**
Rochon, Stephen W. 1950(?)— **78**
Rock, Chris 1967(?)— **3, 22, 66**
Rock, John S. 1825–1866 **113**
Rock, John Sweat *See Rock, John S.*

Rock, John Swett *See Rock, John S.*
Rock, Pete 1970— **121**
Rock, The 1972— **29, 66**
Rock, Tony 1974— **108**
Rock, Vin *See Naughty by Nature*
Rodgers, Johnathan 1946— **6, 51**
Rodgers, Nile *See Chic*
Rodgers, Rod 1937–2002 **36**
Rodman, Dennis 1961— **12, 44, 96, 118**
Rodney, Winston *See Burning Spear*
Rodrigues, Percy 1918–2007 **68**
Rodríguez, Arsenio 1911–1970 **87**
Rodriguez, Cheryl 1952— **64**
Rodriguez, Jimmy 1963(?)— **47**
Rogers, Alan G. 1967–2008 **72**
Rogers, Bobby 1940–2013 **110**
Rogers, Desirée 1959— **88**
Rogers, Jimmy 1924–1997 **38**
Rogers, Joe 1964— **27**
Rogers, Joel Augustus 1883(?)–1996 **30**
Rogers, John W., Jr. 1958— **5, 52**
Rogers, Kelis *See Kelis*
Rogers, Nat *See Little Anthony & the Imperials*
Rogers, Rodney Ray 1971— **106**
Rogers, Willie *See Soul Stirrers*
Rojas, Don 1949— **33**
Roker, Al 1954— **12, 49**
Roker, Roxie 1929–1995 **68**
Rolle, Esther 1920–1998 **13, 21**
Rolle, Janet 1961— **97**
Rolle, Myron 1986— **98**
Rollins, Billy *See Contours, The*
Rollins, Charlemae Hill 1897–1979 **27**
Rollins, Howard E., Jr. 1950–1996 **16**
Rollins, Ida Gray Nelson *See Gray (Nelson Rollins), Ida*
Rollins, James Calvin, III *See Rollins, Jimmy*
Rollins, Jimmy 1978— **70**
Rollins, Sonny 1930— **37, 94**
Rollins, Theodore Walter *See Rollins, Sonny*
Romanthony 1967–2013 **115**
Romeo 1989— **98**
Ronaldinho 1980— **69**
Rondo, Rajon 1986— **111**
Rooakhptah, Amunnubi *See York, Dwight D.*
Roots, The **101**
Rose, Anika Noni 1972— **70**
Rose, Derrick 1988— **82**
Rose, Jalen 1973— **108**
Rose, Lionel 1948— **56**
Rose Royce **120**
Roseboro, John 1933–2002 **123**
Ross, Araminta *See Tubman, Harriet*
Ross, Charles 1957— **27**
Ross, Diana 1944— **8, 27**
Ross, Don 1941— **27**
Ross, Freddie *See Big Freedia*
Ross, Isaiah "Doc" 1925–1993 **40**
Ross, Rick 1976— **79, 104**
Ross, Tracee Ellis 1972— **35**
Rosser, Frederick Douglas, III *See Young, Darren*

Ross-Lee, Barbara 1942— 67

Rotimi, (Emmanuel Gladstone) Ola-(wale) 1938— 1

Roundfield, Danny 1953–2012 109

Roundtree, Dovey 1914— 80

Roundtree, Richard 1942— 27

Rouse, Cecilia 1963— 93

Rowan, Carl T(homas) 1925— 1, 30

Rowe-Adams, Jackie 194(?)— 109

Rowell, Victoria 1960— 13, 68

Rowland, Kelly 1981— 100

Roxanne Shante 1969— 33

Roy, Brandon 1984— 98

Roy, Kenny 1990(?)— 51

Rubin, Chanda 1976— 37

Rucker, Darius 1966— 34, 74, 108

Rudder, David 1953— 79

Rudisha, David 1988— 112

Rudolph, Maya 1972— 46, 106

Rudolph, Wilma (Glodean) 1940— 4

Ruffin, Jimmy 1936–2014 125

Ruffin, Joseph Lee See Shakur, Yusef

Ruffin, Josephine St. Pierre 1842–1924 75

Ruffins, Kermit 1964— 85

Rugambwa, Laurean 1912–1997 20

Ruggles, David 1810–1849 126

Ruley, Ellis 1882–1959 38

Run 1964— 31, 73, 75

Run-DMC 31, 75

RuPaul 1960— 17, 91

Rusesabagina, Paul 1954— 60

Rush, Bobby 1940— 78

Rush, Bobby 1946— 26, 76

Rush, Otis 1934— 38

Rushen, Patrice 1954— 12

Rushing, Jimmy 1903–1972 37

Russell, Bill 1934— 8

Russell, Brenda 1944(?)— 52

Russell, Herman Jerome 1931(?)— 17

Russell, Nipsey 1924–2005 66

Russell, Robin See New Birth

Russell, William Felton See Russell, Bill

Russell-McCloud, Patricia 1946— 17

Russwurm, John Brown 1799–1851 100

Rust, Art, Jr. 1927–2010 83

Rustin, Bayard 1910–1987 4

Rutling, Thomas See Fisk Jubilee Singers

RZA 1969— 80, 128

Saadiq, Raphael 1966— 125 See also See Tony! Toni! Toné!

Saar, Alison 1956— 16

Saar, Betye 1926— 80

Sabathia, Carsten Charles, Jr. See Sabathia, CC

Sabathia, CC 1980— 74

Sade 1959— 15, 92

Sadler, Joseph See Grandmaster Flash

Sadlier, Rosemary 19(?)(?)— 62

St. Jacques, Raymond 1930–1990 8

Saint James, Synthia 1949— 12

St. John, Kristoff 1966— 25

St. Julien, Marlon 1972— 29

St. Louis, David 1974(?)— 126

St. Patrick, Mathew 1969— 48

Saint-Georges, Chevalier de See Boulogne, Joseph, Chevalier de Saint-Georges

Saint-Georges, Joseph Boulogne See Boulogne, Joseph, Chevalier de Saint-Georges

Saldana, Zoe 1978— 72, 118

Salih, Al-Tayyib 1929— 37

Sall, Macky 1961— 101

Sallee, Charles 1911— 38

Salley, Sam See Harold Melvin & the Blue Notes

Salter, Nikkole 1979(?)— 73

Salters, Alisia See Salters, Lisa

Salters, Lisa 1966(?)— 71

Salvador, Bryce 1976— 51

Sam, Michael 1990— 121

Sam, Robert See Graham Central Station

Sam and Dave 102

Samara, Noah 1956— 15

SAMO See Basquiat, Jean-Michel

Sample, Joe 1939–2014 51, 123

See also Crusaders, The

Sampson, Charles 1957— 13

Sampson, Edith S(purlock) 1901–1979 4

Samuel, Sealhenry Olumide See Seal

Samuelsson, Marcus 1970— 53, 120

Sanchez, Sonia 1934— 17, 51

Sandé, Emeli 1987— 113

Sanders, Angelia 1961(?)— 86

Sanders, Barry 1968— 1, 53

Sanders, Bob 1981— 72

Sanders, Deion 1967— 4, 31, 96

Sanders, Demond See Sanders, Bob

Sanders, Dori(nda) 1935— 8

Sanders, Joseph R(ichard, Jr.) 1954— 11

Sanders, Malika 1973— 48

Sanders, Pharoah 1940— 64

Sanders, Rose M. See Touré, Faya Ora Rose

Sanders, Satch 1938— 77

Sanders, Thomas Ernest See Sanders, Satch

Sands, Diana 1934–1973 87

Sané, Pierre Gabriel 1948–1998 21

Sanford, Isabel 1917–2004 53

Sanford, John Elroy See Foxx, Redd

Sangare, Oumou 1968— 18, 99

Sangho, Awa 1972— 127

Sanhá Malam Bacai 1947–2012 84, 101

Sankara, Thomas 1949–1987 17

Sankoh, Foday 1937–2003 74

Sanneh, Kelefa 1975— 96

Santamaria, Mongo 1917–2003 81

Santana, Juelz 1982— 120

Santiago-Hudson, Ruben 1956— 85

Santiel, Terral See Rose Royce

Santiel, Terry See Rose Royce

Santigold 1976— 96

Santogold See Santigold

Santos de Freitas, Antonio Carlos See Brown, Carlinhos

Sapp, Marvin 1966(?)— 74

Sapp, Rhonda LaChanze See LaChanze

Sapp, Warren 1972— 38, 109

Sapphire 1950— 14, 95

Saro-Wiwa, Kenule 1941–1995 39

Sasser, Sean 1968–2013 113

Sassou-Nguesso, Denis 1943— 103

Sata, Michael 1937–2014 102, 125

Satcher, David 1941— 7, 57, 111

Satchmo See Armstrong, (Daniel) Louis

Saunders, Mahalia See Ellis, Hortense

Savage, Augusta Christine 1892(?)–1962 12

Savimbi, Jonas (Malheiro) 1934–2002 2, 34

Savón, Félix 1967— 105

Sawyer, Amos 1945— 2, 123

Sawyer, Eugene 1934–2008 81

Saxton, Shirley Childress See Sweet Honey in the Rock

Sayers, Gale 1943— 28

Sayles Belton, Sharon See Belton, Sharon Sayles

Sbraga, Kevin 1979(?)— 88

Scandrick, Marvin See 112

Scandrick, Slim See 112

Scantlebury, Janna 1984(?)— 47

Scantlebury-White, Velma 1955— 64

Scarface See Geto Boys

Scarlett, Millicent 1971— 49

Schiavocampo, Mara 1979— 97

Schmoke, Kurt 1949— 1, 48

Schofield, Willie See Falcons, The

Schomburg, Arthur Alfonso 1874–1938 9

Schomburg, Arturo Alfonso See Schomburg, Arthur Alfonso

ScHoolboy Q 1986— 117

Schultz, Michael A. 1938— 6

Schuyler, George Samuel 1895–1977 40

Schuyler, Philippa 1931–1967 50

Scott, Byron 1961— 125

Scott, C. A. 1908–2000 29

Scott, Coretta See King, Coretta Scott

Scott, Cornelius Adolphus See Scott, C. A.

Scott, David 1946— 41, 117

Scott, Dread 1965— 106

Scott, George 1929–2005 55 See also Blind Boys of Alabama, The

Scott, George 1944–2013 113

Scott, Harold Russell, Jr. 1935–2006 61

Scott, Hazel 1920–1981 66

Scott, Jeff See Imani Winds

Scott, Jill 1972— 29, 83

Scott, Jimmy 1925–2014 48, 122

Scott, John T. 1940–2007 65

Scott, "Little" Jimmy See Scott, Jimmy

Scott, Milton 1956— 51

Scott, Robert C. 1947— 23

Scott, Stuart 1965— 34, 126

Scott, Tim 1965–2015 87, 125

Scott, Wallace See Whispers, The

Scott, Walter See Whispers, The

Scott, Wendell Oliver, Sr. 1921–1990 19

Scott-Heron, Gil 1949–2011 94

Scott-Young, Mona 1967(?)— 101

Scruggs, Mary Elfrieda See Williams, Mary Lou

Scurry, Briana 1971— 27

Seacole, Mary 1805–1881 54

Seal 14, 75

Seale, Bobby 1936— 3

Seale, Robert George See Seale, Bobby

Seals, Frank See Seals, Son

Seals, Son 1942–2004 56

Sealy, Lloyd G. 1917–1985 125

Sealy, Malik 1970–2000 118

Sears, Leah Ward 1955— 5, 79

Sears, Stephanie 1964— 53

Sears-Collins, Leah J(eanette) See Sears, Leah Ward

Sebree, Charles 1914–1985 40

Secada, Jon 1962— 97

Secada, Juan Francisco See Secada, Jon

Seedorf, Clarence 1976— 121

Seele, Pernessa 1954— 46

Sefolosha, Thabo 1984— 121

Selasi, Taiye 1979— 125

Selassie, Haile See Haile Selassie

Self Jupiter See Freestyle Fellowship

Sembène, Ousmane 1923–2007 13, 62

Senghor, Augustin Diamacoune 1928–2007 66

Senghor, Léopold Sédar 1906–2001 12, 66

Sengstacke, John Herman Henry 1912–1997 18

Senior, Olive 1941— 37

Senna, Danzy 1970— 93

Sentamu, John 1949— 58

Sermon, Erick 1968— 81

Serrano, Andres 1951(?)— 3

Sesay, Isha 1976— 107

Sessoms, Vivian 198(?)— 122

Seven-Seven, Prince Twins See Prince Twins Seven-Seven

Sewell, Terri 1965— 93

Seymour, Richard 1979— 101

Seymour, Teddy 1941(?)— 110

Seymour, William J. 1879–1922 106

Shabazz, Attallah 1958— 6

Shabazz, Betty 1936–1997 7, 26

Shabazz, Ilyasah 1962— 36

Shabazz Palaces 123

Shadd, Abraham D. 1801–1882 81

Shaggy 1968— 31

Shakespeare, Robbie 1953— See Sly & Robbie

Shakur, Afeni 1947— 67

Shakur, Assata 1947— 6

Shakur, Meshell Suihailia Bashir See Ndegeocello, Meshell

Shakur, Tupac Amaru 1971–1996 14

Shakur, Yusef 1973— 85

Shange, Ntozake 1948— 8, 89

Shanice 1973— 112

Shank, Suzanne F. 1962(?)— 77

Shannon, Randy 1966— 82

Sharpe, Samuel 1801(?)–1832 103

Sharpe, Shannon 1968— 97

Sharper, Darren 1975— 32, 118

Sharpton, Al 1954— **21, 97**

Shaver, Earnie Dee *See Shavers, Earnie*

Shavers, Cheryl 19(?)(?)— **31**

Shavers, Earnie 1944— **127**

Shaw, Bernard 1940— **2, 28**

Shaw, Brian 1966— **127**

Shaw, Ernesto D., Jr. *See DJ Clue?*

Shaw, Marlena 1942— **105**

Shaw, William J. 1934— **30**

Sheard, Kierra 1987— **61, 114**

Sheard, Kiki *See Sheard, Kierra*

Shearer, Hugh 1923–2004 **107**

Sheffey, Asa Bundy *See Hayden, Robert Earl*

Sheffield, Gary 1968— **16, 108**

Shelby, Thomas *See Lakeside*

Shell, Art 1946— **1, 66**

Shelton, Billy *See Clovers, The*

Shelton, Paula Young 1961— **86**

Shelton, Trent 1984— **122**

Shepherd, Sherri 1970— **55**

Shepp, Archie 1937— **101**

Sheppard, Ella *See Fisk Jubilee Singers*

Sherman, Richard 1988— **118**

Sherrod, Clayton 1944— **17**

Sherrod, Shirley 1948— **87**

Shetler, Tom *See Falcons, The*

Shider, Garry 1953–2010 **87**

Shines, John Ned *See Shines, Johnny*

Shines, Johnny 1915–1992 **116**

Shinhoster, Earl 1950(?)–2000 **32**

Shipp, E. R. 1955— **15**

Shipp, Matthew 1960— **107**

Shippen, John 1879–1968 **43**

Shirelles, The **111**

Shirley, Aaron 1933–2014 **126**

Shirley, Donald 1927–2013 **111**

Shirley, George I. 1934— **33**

Shmurda, Bobby 1994— **123**

Shocklee, Hank *See Public Enemy*

Shockley, Ann Allen 1927— **84**

Shockley, Stephen *See Lakeside*

Shonibare, Yinka 1962— **58**

Shores, Arthur D. 1904–1996 **99**

Short, Bobby 1924–2005 **52**

Short, Columbus 1982— **79**

Shorter, Wayne 1933— **75**

Shorty, Ras, I 1941–2000 **47**

Showers, Reggie 1964— **30**

Shropshire, Thomas B. 1925–2003 **49**

Shuttlesworth, Fred 1922–2011 **47, 98**

Shyne 1978— **101**

Sidat-Singh, Wilmeth 1918–1943 **116**

Sidibe, Gabourey 1983— **84**

Sidibé, Malick 1936(?)— **124**

Sidner, Sara 1972— **105**

Sifford, Charlie 1922— **4, 49**

Sigur, Wanda 1958— **44**

Siji 1971(?)— **56**

Silas, Paul 1943— **24**

Silva, Anderson 1975— **96**

Silva, Marina 1958— **80**

Silver, Horace 1928–2014 **26, 122**

Siméus, Dumas M. 1939— **25, 110**

Simkins, Modjeska Monteith 1899–1992 **112**

Simmonds, Wayne 1988— **121**

Simmons, Bill *See Midnight Star*

Simmons, Bob 1948— **29**

Simmons, E. Denise 19(?)(?)— **79**

Simmons, Gary 1964— **58**

Simmons, Henry 1970— **55**

Simmons, Jamal 1971— **72**

Simmons, Joseph *See Run; Run-DMC*

Simmons, Kimora Lee 1975— **51, 83**

Simmons, Russell 1957(?)— **1, 30**

Simmons, Ruth J. 1945— **13, 38**

Simms, Margaret 1946— **94**

Simon, Joe 1943— **109**

Simon, Lateefah 1977— **95**

Simone, Nina 1933–2003 **15, 41**

Simpson, Carole 1940— **6, 30**

Simpson, Lorna 1960— **4, 36**

Simpson, Merton D. 1928–2013 **110**

Simpson, O. J. 1947— **15, 100**

Simpson, Sherone 1984— **120**

Simpson, Valerie 1946— **21, 97**

Simpson-Hoffman, N'kenge 1975(?)— **52**

Simpson Miller, Portia 1945— **62, 100**

Sims, Danny 1936–2012 **106**

Sims, Howard "Sandman" 1917–2003 **48**

Sims, Lowery Stokes 1949— **27**

Sims, Naomi 1948–2009 **29, 79**

Sims, Peter *See La Roca, Pete*

Sinbad 1957(?)— **1, 16**

Sinclair, Floyd *See Mayweather, Floyd*

Sinclair, Madge 1938–1995 **78**

Singletary, Mike 1958— **4, 76**

Singleton, John 1968— **2, 30, 122**

Sinkford, Jeanne C. 1933— **13**

Sir Mix-A-Lot 1963— **82**

Sirleaf, Ellen Johnson 1938— **71**

Sisqo 1976— **30**

Sissako, Abderrahmane 1961— **127**

Sissle, Noble 1889–1975 **29**

Sister Souljah 1964— **11, 100**

Sisulu, Albertina 1918–2011 **57, 95**

Sisulu, Sheila Violet Makate 1948(?)— **24**

Sisulu, Walter 1912–2003 **47**

Sizemore, Barbara A. 1927–2004 **26, 110**

Sizemore, Grady 1982— **96**

Skerrit, Roosevelt 1972— **72**

Skinner, Kiron K. 1962(?) **65**

Sklarek, Norma Merrick 1926–2012 **25, 101**

Slash 1975— **75**

Slater, Duke 1898–1966 **125**

Slater, Frederick Wayman *See Slater, Duke*

Slater, Rodney E. 1955— **15, 125**

Slaughter, John Brooks 1934— **53**

Sledge, Percy 1940–2015 **39, 128**

Sleet, Gregory M. 1951— **109**

Sleet, Moneta (J.), Jr. 1926— **5**

Slice, Kimbo 1974— **73**

Slick Rick 1965— **93**

Slim *See 112*

Slim Harpo 1924–1970 **120**

Slim Jimmy *See Rae Sremmurd*

Slim Jxmmi *See Rae Sremmurd*

Slim Jukebox, The *See Geto Boys*

Slim Thug 1980— **86**

Slimkid3 *See Pharcyde, The*

Slocumb, Jonathan 19(?)(?)— **52**

Sly & Robbie **34**

Slyde, Jimmy 1927–2008 **70**

Smalling, Chris 1989— **118**

Smalls, Robert 1839–1915 **82**

Smaltz, Audrey 1937(?)— **12**

Smiley, Rickey 1968— **59**

Smiley, Tavis 1964— **20, 68**

Smith, Amanda Berry 1837–1915 **109**

Smith, Anjela Lauren 1973— **44**

Smith, Anna Deavere 1950— **6, 44**

Smith, Annette *See Chantels, The*

Smith, Arlene *See Chantels, The*

Smith, Arthur Lee, *See Asante, Molefi Kete*

Smith, B. *See Smith, B(arbara)*

Smith, B(arbara) 1949(?)— **11**

Smith, Barbara 1946— **28**

Smith, Bessie 1894–1937 **3**

Smith, Bruce 1984— **80**

Smith, Bruce W. 19(?)(?)— **53**

Smith, Bubba 1945–2011 **96**

Smith, Buster 1904–1991 **116**

Smith, Carl Reginald *See Smith, Reggie*

Smith, Cecilia 1960(?)— **102**

Smith, Charles Aaron *See Smith, Bubba*

Smith, Che *See Rhymefest*

Smith, Cladys "Jabbo" 1908–1991 **32**

Smith, Clarence 1904–1929 **113**

Smith, Clarence Edward *See Clarence 13X*

Smith, Clarence O. 1933— **21**

Smith, Clifford *See Method Man*

Smith, Damu 1951— **54**

Smith, Dante Terrell *See Bey, Yasiin*

Smith, Danyel 1966(?)— **40**

Smith, DeMaurice 1964— **92**

Smith, Dickie *See Five Keys, The*

Smith, Dr. Lonnie 1942— **49**

Smith, Emmitt 1969— **7, 87**

Smith, Eugene *See Smith, Gene*

Smith, Eugene Cyril, III *See Smith, Geno*

Smith, Gene 1955— **123**

Smith, Geno 1990— **118**

Smith, George *See Manhattans, The*

Smith, Greg 1964— **28**

Smith, Hale 1925–2009 **118**

Smith, Henry *See Smith, Buster*

Smith, Hezekiah Leroy Gordon *See Smith, Stuff*

Smith, Hilton 1912–1983 **29**

Smith, Ian 1970(?)— **62**

Smith, Jabbo *See Smith, Cladys "Jabbo"*

Smith, Jaden 1998— **82**

Smith, James Oscar *See Smith, Jimmy*

Smith, James Todd *See LL Cool J*

Smith, Jane E. 1946— **24**

Smith, Jennifer 1947— **21**

Smith, Jessie Carney 1930— **35**

Smith, Jimmy 1928–2005 **127**

Smith, John L. 1938— **22**

Smith, Jonathan Mortimer *See Lil Jon*

Smith, Joshua (Isaac) 1941— **10**

Smith, Kemba 1971— **70**

Smith, Kenneth *See Smith, Kenny*

Smith, Kenny 1965— **114**

Smith, LaQuan 1988— **113**

Smith, Lee 1957— **101**

Smith, Lenithia Bonita *See Leakes, NeNe*

Smith, Lonnie Liston 1940— **49**

Smith, Lovie 1958— **66, 107**

Smith, Mabel Louise *See Big Maybelle*

Smith, Malcolm A. 1956— **75**

Smith, Mamie 1883–1946 **32**

Smith, Marie F. 1939— **70**

Smith, Marvin 1910–2003 **46**

Smith, Mary Carter 1919— **26**

Smith, Ming 19(?)(?)— **100**

Smith, Morgan 1910–1993 **46**

Smith, Myrna 1941–2010 **92**

Smith, Nate 1929— **49**

Smith, Neil 1966— **109**

Smith, Orlando *See Smith, Tubby*

Smith, Ozzie 1954— **77**

Smith, Pinetop *See Smith, Clarence*

Smith, Princella 1983— **86**

Smith, Randy 1948–2009 **81**

Smith, Reggie 1945— **113**

Smith, Richard 1957— **51**

Smith, Rick 1969— **72**

Smith, Roger Guenveur 1960— **12**

Smith, Shaffer Chimere *See Ne-Yo*

Smith, Stephen A. 1967— **69**

Smith, Steve 1979— **120**

Smith, Stuff 1909–1967 **37**

Smith, Tasha 1971— **73**

Smith, Tommie 1944— **102**

Smith, Trevor, Jr. *See Rhymes, Busta*

Smith, Trixie 1895–1943 **34**

Smith, Tubby 1951— **18, 83**

Smith, Vincent D. 1929–2003 **48**

Smith, Walker, Jr. *See Robinson, Sugar Ray*

Smith, Will 1968— **8, 18, 53**

Smith, Willi (Donnell) 1948–1987 **8**

Smith, Willie 1897(?)–1973 **107**

Smith, Willow 2000— **92**

Smith, Zadie 1975— **51**

Smyre, Calvin 1947— **90**

Smythe Haith, Mabel 1918–2006 **61**

Sneed, Paula A. 1947— **18**

Snipes, Wesley 1962— **3, 24, 67**

Snoop Dogg 1971— **35, 84**

Snow, Samuel 1923–2008 **71**

Snowden, Frank M., Jr. 1911–2007 **67**

Snowden, Gail 1945— **108**

Soglo, Nicéphore 1935— **15**

Sohn, Sonja 1964— **100**

Solange 1986— **97**

Solomon, Jimmie Lee 1947(?)— **38**

Somé, Malidoma Patrice 1956— **10**

Somi 1979— **85**

Sommore, 1966— **61**

Song, Alex 1987— **105**

Songz, Trey 1984— **88**

Sono, Jomo 1955— **86**

Sosa, Sammy 1968— **21, 44**

Soto Alejo, Federico Arístides *See Güines, Tata*

Soul Stirrers **127**

Soulchild, Musiq *See Musiq*

Souleymane, Mahamane 1940— **78**

Southern, Eileen 1920–2002 **56**

Southgate, Martha 1960(?)— **58**

Souza, Carmen 1981— **111**

Sowande, Fela 1905–1987 **39**

Sowande, Olufela Obafunmilayo *See Sowande, Fela*

Sowell, Thomas 1930— **2, 99**

Soyinka, Wole 1934— **4, 93**

Spaniels, The **105**

Spann, Otis 1930(?)–1970 **107**

Sparks, Corinne Etta 1953— **53**

Sparks, Jordin 1989— **66**

Sparks, Willie *See Graham Central Station*

Spaulding, Charles Clinton 1874–1952 **9**

Spearman, Leonard H. O., Sr. 1929–2008 **81**

Spearman, Ollie *See Tyler, Ollie*

Spears, Warren 1954–2005 **52**

Special K *See Treacherous Three*

Speck, George *See Crum, George*

Spector, Ronnie 1943— **77**

Speech 1968— **82**

Spellman-Diaz, Toyin *See Imani Winds*

Spence, Joseph 1910–1984 **49**

Spencer, Anne 1882–1975 **27**

Spencer, Michael G. 1952— **87**

Spencer, Octavia 1972— **100**

Spencer, Peter 1782(?)–1843 **128**

Spencer, Vaino H. 1920— **99**

Spencer, Winston Baldwin 1948— **68**

Spigner, Archie 1928— **81**

Spikes, Dolores Margaret Richard 1936— **18**

Spiller, Bill 1913–1988 **64**

Spivey, Victoria 1906–1976 **119**

Sprewell, Latrell 1970— **23**

Spriggs, William 195(?)— **67**

Springer, Ashton, Jr. 1930–2013 **115**

Stackhouse, Houston 1910–1980 **122**

Stackhouse, Jerry 1974— **30**

Staley, Dawn 1970— **57**

Stallings, Felix, Jr. *See Felix Da Housecat*

Stallings, George A(ugustus), Jr. 1948— **6**

Stallworth, John 1952— **102**

Stampley, Micah 1971— **54**

Stanford, John 1938— **20**

Stanford, Olivia Lee Dilworth 1914–2004 **49**

Stanley, A. Knighton 1937–2013 **117**

Stanley, Knighton *See Stanley, A. Knighton*

Stanley, Tony *See Stanley, A. Knighton*

Stanton, Alysa 1963— **78**

Stanton, Robert 1940— **20**

Staples, Brent 1951— **8**

Staples, Cleotha 1934–2013 **113**

Staples, Mavis 1939(?)— **50, 88**

Staples, "Pops" 1915–2000 **32**

Staples, Roebuck *See Staples, "Pops"*

Staples, Ron *See Mighty Clouds of Joy*

Stargell, Willie 1940(?)–2001 **29**

Starr, Bobby *See Intruders, The*

Starr, Edwin 1942–2003 **122**

Staton, Candi 1940(?)— **27**

Staton, Dakota 1930(?)–2007 **62**

Staupers, Mabel K(eaton) 1890–1989 **7**

Stearnes, Norman "Turkey" 1901–1979 **31**

Steave-Dickerson, Kia 1970— **57**

Steele, Claude 1946— **13, 97**

Steele, Lawrence 1963— **28**

Steele, Michael 1958— **38, 73, 91**

Steele, Sage 1972— **115**

Steele, Shelby 1946— **13, 82**

Steely 1962–2009 **80**

Steinberg, Martha Jean 1930(?)–2000 **28**

Stephens, Charlotte Andrews 1854–1951 **14**

Stephens, John *See Legend, John*

Stephens, Myrtle *See Potter, Myrtle*

Stephens, Sloane 1993— **105**

Stephenson, Lance 1990— **118**

Stevens, Earl *See E-40*

Stevens, Yvette *See Khan, Chaka*

Stevenson, Bryan 1959— **128**

Stevenson, Teófilo 1952–2012 **103**

Stew 1961— **69**

Steward, David L. 19(?)(?)— **36**

Steward, Emanuel 1944–2012 **18, 106**

Stewart, Alison 1966(?)— **13**

Stewart, Billy 1937–1970 **112**

Stewart, Bubba *See Stewart, James, Jr.*

Stewart, Christopher Alan *See Stewart, Tricky*

Stewart, Dave 1957— **117**

Stewart, Derrick *See Pharcyde, The*

Stewart, Ella 1893–1987 **39**

Stewart, James, Jr. 1985— **60, 98**

Stewart, Kordell 1972— **21, 111**

Stewart, Leroy *See Stewart, Slam*

Stewart, Mark *See Stew*

Stewart, Nzingha 1974— **89**

Stewart, Paul Wilbur 1925— **12**

Stewart, Slam 1914–1987 **126**

Stewart, Sylvester *See Stone, Sly*

Stewart, Tonea Harris 1947— **78**

Stewart, Tricky 1974— **98**

Stickney, Phyllis Yvonne 19(?)(?)— **108**

Sticky Fingaz 1970— **86**

Still, William Grant 1895–1978 **37**

Stingley, Darryl 1951–2007 **69**

Stinson, Denise L. 1954— **59**

Stith, Charles R. 1949— **73**

Stith, James H. 1941— **116**

Stith, Tom 1939–2010 **93**

Stiverne, Bermane 1978— **128**

Stockman, Shawn *See Boyz II Men*

Stokes, Carl 1927–1996 **10, 73**

Stokes, Louis 1925— **3**

Stokes, Otis *See Lakeside*

Stoltz, Brian *See Meters, The*

Stone, Angie 1965(?)— **31**

Stone, Charles Sumner, Jr. *See Stone, Chuck*

Stone, Chuck 1924–2014 **9, 120**

Stone, Jesse 1901–1999 **98** *See also Drifters, The*

Stone, Sly 1943— **85**

Stone, Toni 1921–1996 **15**

Stoney, Michael 1969— **50**

Storyboard P 1990(?)— **118**

Stott, Dorothy M. *See Stout, Renee*

Stott, Dot *See Stout, Renee*

Stoudemire, Amar'e 1982— **59, 106**

Stout, Juanita Kidd 1919–1998 **24**

Stout, Renee 1958— **63**

Stoute, Steve 1971(?)— **38**

Stoutt, H. Lavity 1929–1995 **83**

Stowers, Freddie 1896–1918 **107**

Stradford, J. B. 1861–1935 **101**

Strahan, Michael 1971— **35, 81**

Strain, Sammy *See Little Anthony & the Imperials*

Strautmanis, Michael 1969— **87**

Strawberry, Darryl 1962— **22**

Strayhorn, Billy 1915–1967 **31**

Street, John F. 1943(?)— **24**

Street, Richard 1942–2013 **110**

Streeter, Amber Denise *See Streeter, Sevyn*

Streeter, Sarah 1953— **45**

Streeter, Sevyn 1986— **115**

Stringer, C. Vivian 1948— **13, 66**

Stringer, Korey 1974–2001 **35**

Stringer, Vickie 196(?)— **58**

Strode, Woodrow Wilson Woolwine *See Strode, Woody*

Strode, Woody 1914–1994 **111**

Stromae 1985— **121**

Stroman, Nathaniel *See Earthquake*

Strong, Barrett 1941— **89**

Strong, Charlie 1960— **118**

Stuart, Moira 1949— **82**

Stubbs, Joe *See Contours, The*

Studdard, Ruben 1978— **46**

Sturridge, Daniel 1989— **120**

Subban, P. K. 1989— **121**

Subban, Pernell Karl *See Subban, P. K*

Sudarkasa, Niara 1938— **4**

Sudduth, Jimmy Lee 1910–2007 **65**

Sugarhill Gang, The **79, 125**

Suggs, Terrell 1982— **108**

Sullivan, Jazmine 1987— **81**

Sullivan, Leon H(oward) 1922— **3, 30**

Sullivan, Louis (Wade) 1933— **8**

Sullivan, Maxine 1911–1987 **37**

Sul-Te-Wan, Madame *See Madame Sul-Te-Wan*

Sumlin, Hubert 1931–2011 **101**

Summer, Donna 1948–2012 **25, 102**

Sumner, Francis Cecil 1926–1973 **112**

Sun Ra, 1914–1993 **60**

Sundiata, Sekou 1948–2007 **66**

Sunnyland Slim 1907(?)–1995 **118**

Supremes, The **33**

Sutphen, Mona 1967— **77**

Suttles, George *See Suttles, Mule*

Suttles, Mule 1900–1966 **108**

Suttles, Warren *See Ravens, The*

Sutton, Percy E. 1920–2009 **42, 82**

Swae Lee *See Rae Sremmurd*

Swan Silvertones, The **110**

Swann, Bettye 1944— **109**

Swann, Lynn 1952— **28**

Swaray, Fanta Estelle *See Estelle*

Sweat, Keith 1961(?)— **19**

Sweatman, Wilbur 1882–1961 **125**

Sweatshirt, Earl 1994— **114**

Sweatt, Heman Marion 1912–1982 **114**

Sweet, Ossian 1895–1960 **68**

Sweet Honey in the Rock **106**

Swizz Beatz 1978— **108**

Swoopes, Sheryl 1971— **12, 56**

Swygert, H. Patrick 1943— **22**

Sy, Omar 1978— **109**

Sy, Oumou 1952— **65**

Sykes, Roosevelt 1906–1984 **20**

Sykes, Wanda 1964— **48, 81**

Syler, Rene 1963— **53**

Tabu Ley *See Rochereau, Tabu Ley*

Tacuma, Jamaaladeen 1956— **124**

Tademy, Lalita 1948— **36**

Tafari Makonnen *See Haile Selassie*

Tail Dragger 1940— **112**

Tait, Michael 1966— **57**

Take 6 **112**

Takeoff *See Migos*

Talbert, David E. 1966(?)— **34, 93**

Talbert, Mary B. 1866–1923 **77**

Taliaferro, Edwin *See Lumumba, Chokwe*

Talley, André Leon 1949— **56, 106**

Tamar-kali 1973(?)— **63**

Tamia 1975— **24, 55**

Tampa Red 1904(?)–1980 **63**

Tancil, Gladys Quander 1921–2002 **59**

Tandja, Mamadou 1938— **33, 78**

Tanksley, Ann (Graves) 1934— **37**

Tanner, Henry Ossawa 1859–1937 **1**

Tanner, Jack E. 1919–2006 **100**

Tapscott, Horace 1934–1999 **126**

Taste of Honey, A **115**

Tate, Bruce *See Penguins, The*

Tate, Buddy 1913–2001 **108**

Tate, Eleanora E. 1948— **20, 55**

Tate, George Holmes *See Tate, Buddy*

Tate, Grady 1932— **106**

Tate, John 1955–1998 **107**

Tate, Larenz 1975— **15**

Tate, Minnie *See Fisk Jubilee Singers*

Tatum, Art 1909–1956 **28**

Tatum, Beverly Daniel 1954— **42, 84**

Tatum, Elinor R. 197(?)— **78**

Tatum, Jack 1948— **87**

Tatum, Reece 1921–1967 **104**

Tatum, Wilbert 1933–2009 **76**

Tau, Mpho Parks 1970— **124**

Taubira, Christiane 1952— **117**

Taulbert, Clifton Lemoure 1945— **19**

Tavares **115**

Tavares, Butch *See Tavares*

Tavares, Chubby *See Tavares*

Tavares, Pooch *See Tavares*

Tavares, Ralph *See Tavares*

Tavares, Tiny *See Tavares*

Taylor, Bennie See Dramatics, The
Taylor, Billy 1921–2010 23, 92
Taylor, Bo 1966–2008 72
Taylor, Cecil 1929— 70
Taylor, Charles 1948— 20
Taylor, Darren See Taylor, Bo
Taylor, Eddie 1923–1985 116
Taylor, Ephren W., II 1982— 61
Taylor, Gardner C. 1918— 76
Taylor, Helen (Lavon Hollingshed) 1942–2000 30
Taylor, Hound Dog 1917(?)–1975 120
Taylor, Jason 1974— 70
Taylor, Jermain 1978— 60
Taylor, John (David Beckett) 1952— 16
Taylor, Johnnie See Soul Stirrers
Taylor, Karin 1971— 34
Taylor, Katrina Laverne See Trina
Taylor, Koko 1928–2009 40, 80
Taylor, Kristin Clark 1959— 8
Taylor, Lawrence 1959— 25
Taylor, Leroy See New Birth
Taylor, Lonzie Odie 1899–1977 96
Taylor, Marshall Walter "Major" 1878–1932 62
Taylor, Meshach 1947(?)— 4
Taylor, Mildred D. 1943— 26
Taylor, Natalie 1959— 47
Taylor, Recy 1919— 92
Taylor, Regina 1960— 9, 46, 97
Taylor, Richard See Manhattans, The
Taylor, Robert Robinson 1868–1942 80
Taylor, Robert Rochon 1899–1957 104
Taylor, Ron 1952–2002 35
Taylor, Susan C. 1957— 62
Taylor, Susan L. 1946— 10, 86
Taylor, Susie King 1848–1912 13
Taylor, Theodore Roosevelt See Taylor, Hound Dog
T-Boz 1970— 108 See also TLC
Tchicai, John 1936— 102
Teague, Bob 1929–2013 111
Teasley, Lisa 1962— 92
Teer, Barbara Ann 1937–2008 81
Temple, Collis, Jr. 1952— 119
Temple, Ed 1927— 109
Temple, Lewis 1800–1854 102
Temptations, The 33
Tergat, Paul 1969— 59
Terminator X See Public Enemy
Terrell, Dorothy A. 1945— 24
Terrell, Ernie 1939— 118
Terrell, Jean 1944— 116
Terrell, Mary (Elizabeth) Church 1863–1954 9
Terrell, Tammi 1945–1970 32
Terrell, Velma Jean See Terrell, Jean
Terrell-Kearney, Kim 1965— 83
Terrence J 1982— 108
Terrill, Saunders See Terry, Sonny
Terry, Bryant 1976— 128
Terry, Clark 1920–2015 39, 127
Terry, Phil See Intruders, The
Terry, Sonny 1911–1986 88
Tex, Joe 1933(?)–1982 116
Thabane, Motsoahae Thomas See Thabane, Thomas

Thabane, Thomas 1939— 123
Thabeet, Hasheem 1987— 123
Tharpe, Rosetta 1915–1973 65
Thaws, Adrian Nicholas Matthews See Tricky
The Artist See Prince
Thedford, Timothy Elpadaro See Jay Electronica
The-Dream 1982— 74
Thiam, Aliaune Akon See Akon
Thiam, Tidjane 1962— 104
Thigpen, Ed 1930–2010 110
Thigpen, Lynne 1948–2003 17, 41
Thomas, Alma Woodsey 1891–1978 14
Thomas, Arthur Ray 1951— 52
Thomas, Carla 1942— 96
Thomas, Chris See King, Chris Thomas
Thomas, Clarence 1948— 2, 39, 65
Thomas, Claudia Lynn 1950— 64
Thomas, David See Take 6
Thomas, Debi 1967— 26
Thomas, Derrick 1967–2000 25
Thomas, Emmitt 1943— 71
Thomas, Ernest Joseph See Thomas, Tabby
Thomas, Frank 1968— 12, 51
Thomas, Franklin A. 1934— 5, 49
Thomas, Irma 1941— 29
Thomas, Isiah 1961— 7, 26, 65
Thomas, Jefferson 1942–2010 88
Thomas, Michael 1967— 69
Thomas, Mickalene 1971— 61
Thomas, Rozonda 1971— 78 See also TLC
Thomas, Rufus 1917–2001 20, 96
Thomas, Sean Patrick 1970— 35
Thomas, Stayve Jerome See Slim Thug
Thomas, Tabby 1929–2014 119
Thomas, Thurman 1966— 75
Thomas, Todd See Speech
Thomas, Trisha R. 1964— 65
Thomas, Vivien (T.) 1910–1985 9
Thomas-Graham, Pamela 1963(?)— 29
Thomas-Greenfield, Linda 1952— 99
Thomason, Marsha 1976— 47
Thomaz, Cameron Jibril See Khalifa, Wiz
Thompson, Ahmir See ?uestlove
Thompson, Bennie 1948— 26, 119
Thompson, Cynthia Bramlett 1949— 50
Thompson, Dearon See Deezer D
Thompson, Don 1963— 56, 108
Thompson, John Douglas 1964— 81
Thompson, John W. 1949— 26
Thompson, Kenan 1978— 52
Thompson, Klay 1990— 126
Thompson, Larry D. 1945— 39
Thompson, Marshall See Chi-Lites
Thompson, Mychal 1955— 126
Thompson, Sylvester See Johnson, Syl
Thompson, Tazewell (Alfred, Jr.) 1954— 13
Thompson, Tina 1975— 25, 75
Thompson, Tony See Chic

Thompson, William C., Jr. 1953— 35, 114
Thoms, Tracie 1975— 61
Thornton, Big Mama 1926–1984 33
Thornton, Terrence See Pusha T
Thornton, Yvonne S. 1947— 69
Thrash, Dox 1893–1965 35
Thrasher, Andrew See Drifters, The
Thrasher, Gerhart See Drifters, The
Threadgill, Henry 1944— 97
Three Mo' Tenors 35
Thrower, Willie 1930–2002 35
Thugwane, Josia 1971— 21
Thurman, Howard 1900–1981 3
Thurman, Wallace Henry 1902–1934 16
Thurmond, Nate 1941— 88
Thurston, Baratunde 1977— 79, 101
Thurston, Stephen J. 1952— 49
Tiant, Luis 1940— 102
Till, Emmett (Louis) 1941–1955 7
Tillard, Conrad 1964— 47
Tillis, Frederick 1930— 40
Tillman, Deborah 1962(?)— 98
Tillman, Dorothy 1947— 76
Tillman, George, Jr. 1968— 20
Tillman, Georgeanna See Marvelettes, The
Tilmon, Abe See Detroit Emeralds, The
Tilmon, Cleofas See Detroit Emeralds, The
Tilmon, Ivory See Detroit Emeralds, The
Tilmon, Raymond See Detroit Emeralds, The
Timbaland 1971— 32
Tingling, Milton A. 1953— 110
Tinie Tempah 1988— 115
Tinsley, Boyd 1964— 50
Tipton, Fredrick See Gibbs, Freddie
Tirico, Michael See Tirico, Mike
Tirico, Mike 1966— 68, 124
Tisby, Dexter See Penguins, The
Tisdale, Wayman 1964— 50
TLC 34
Tobias, Channing H. 1882–1961 79
Tobin, Patricia 1943–2008 75
Todd, Franck See Golden Gate Quartet
Todman, Terence A. 1926— 55
Tolbert, James L. 1926–2013 112
Tolbert, Mike 1985— 125
Tolbert, Terence 1964— 74
Tolbert, William Michael See Tolbert, Mike
Tolbert, William R. 1913–1980 100
Toler, Burl 1928–2009 80
Toles, Michael See Bar-Kays, The
Toivola, Jani 1977— 118
Tolliver, Mose 1915(?)–2006 60
Tolliver, William (Mack) 1951— 9
Tolson, Melvin B(eaunorus) 1898–1966 37
Tolton, Augustine 1854–1897 62
Tomlin, Michael Pettaway See Tomlin, Mike
Tomlin, Mike 1972— 123
Tomlinson, LaDainian 1979— 65, 112
Tonex, 1978(?)— 54
Toney, James 1968— 89

Tony! Toni! Toné! 127
Tooks, Lance 1962— 62
Toomer, Jean 1894–1967 6
Toomer, Nathan Pinchback See Toomer, Jean
Toote, Gloria E. A. 1931— 64
Toots and the Maytals See Hibbert, Toots
Torres, Gina 1969— 52
Torry, Guy 19(?)(?)— 31
Tosh, Peter 1944–1987 9
Touré, Amadou Toumani 1948(?)— 18
Touré, Askia (Muhammad Abu Bakr el) 1938— 47
Touré, Faya Ora Rose 1945— 56
Touré, Sekou 1922–1984 6
Touré, Yaya 1983— 99
Toussaint, Allen 1938— 60
Toussaint, Lorraine 1960— 32
Towles, Nat 1905–1963 128
Townes, Jeffrey Allan See DJ Jazzy Jeff
Towns, Edolphus 1934— 19, 75
Townsend, Robert 1957— 4, 23
T-Pain 1985— 73, 111
Trammell, Kimberly N. See Holland, Kimberly N.
Trammps, The 108
Traore, Dioncounda 1942— 103
Travis, Tracey T. 1962— 94
Treach See Naughty by Nature
Treacherous Three 128
Tresvant, Ralph 1968— 57 See also New Edition
Trethewey, Natasha 1966— 103
Tribbett, Tye 1977— 81
Tribble, Israel, Jr. 1940— 8
Tricky 1967— 98
Trina 1974— 114
Trombone Shorty 1986— 97
Trotter, Donne E. 1950— 28
Trotter, Lloyd G. 1945(?)— 56
Trotter, (William) Monroe 1872–1934 9
Trotter, Tariq Luqmaan See Black Thought; Roots, The
Trouillot, Ertha Pascal See Pascal-Trouillot, Ertha
Troupe, Quincy 1943— 83
Trouppe, Quincy Thomas, Sr. 1912–1993 84
Troy, Michael See Freestyle Fellowship
True, Rachel 1966— 82
Trueheart, William E. 1942— 49
Tshele, Elizabeth Zandile See Bulawayo, NoViolet
Tsvangirai, Morgan 1952— 26, 72
Tuakli-Wosornu, Taiye See Selasi, Taiye
Tubbs Jones, Stephanie 1949–2008 24, 72
Tubman, Harriet 1820(?)–1913 9
Tubman, William 1895–1971 99
Tucker, C. Delores 1927–2005 12, 56
Tucker, Chris 1972— 13, 23, 62
Tucker, Cynthia 1955— 15, 61
Tucker, Rosina Budd Harvey Corrothers 1881–1987 14
Tucker, Tommy 1933–1982 127
Tuckson, Reed V. 1951(?)— 71
Tuff, Antoinette 1966— 120

Tuku *See Mtukudzi, Oliver*
Tunie, Tamara 1959— **63**
Tunnell, Emlen 1925–1975 **54**
Ture, Kwame *See Carmichael, Stokely*
Turman, Glynn 1947— **100**
Turnbull, Charles Wesley 1935— **62**
Turnbull, Walter 1944— **13, 60**
Turner, Big Joe 1911–1985 **92**
Turner, Henry McNeal 1834–1915 **5**
Turner, Ike 1931–2007 **68**
Turner, Izear *See Turner, Ike*
Turner, Mark 1965— **126**
Turner, Morrie 1923–2014 **122**
Turner, Morris Nolten *See Turner, Morrie*
Turner, Tina 1939— **6, 27**
Tutu, Desmond (Mpilo) 1931— **6, 44**
Tutu, Nontombi Naomi 1960— **57**
Tutuola, Amos 1920–1997 **30**
Twiggs, Leo 1934— **127**
Twilight, Alexander 1795–1857 **125**
2 Chainz 1976— **105**
Tyga 1989— **117**
Tyler, Aisha N. 1970— **36**
Tyler, Ollie 1945— **128**
Tyler, the Creator 1991— **100**
Tyner, McCoy 1938— **92**
Tyree, Omar Rashad 1969— **21**
Tyrese *See Gibson, Tyrese*
Tyson, Andre 1960— **40**
Tyson, Asha 1970— **39**
Tyson, Cicely 1924(?)— **7, 51, 112**
Tyson, Mike 1966— **28, 44, 93**
Tyson, Neil deGrasse 1958— **15, 65**
Uggams, Leslie 1943— **23, 114**
Ujiri, Masai 1970— **107**
Ukpabio, Helen 1969— **86**
Ulmer, James 1942— **79**
Underwood, Blair 1964— **7, 27, 76**
Union, Gabrielle 1972— **31, 92**
Unseld, Wes 1946— **23**
Upshaw, Gene 1945–2008 **18, 47, 72**
Upton, B. J. *See Upton, Melvin, Jr.*
Upton, Justin 1987— **124**
Upton, Melvin, Jr. 1984— **124**
Uribe, Juan 1979— **122**
Urschel, John 1991— **126**
Usher 1977— **23, 56, 95**
Usry, James L. 1922— **23**
Ussery, Terdema Lamar, II 1958— **29**
Utendahl, John 1956— **23**
Uys, Ashley 1983— **125**
Valdés, Bebo 1918— **75**
Valdés, Chucho 1941— **89**
Valdés, Dionisio Ramón Emilio *See Valdés, Bebo*
Valentine, Johnny *See Mighty Clouds of Joy*
Valentino, Bobby 1980— **62**
Van Haver, Paul *See Stromae*
Van Lierop, Robert 1939— **53**
Van Loan, James *See Billy Ward and the Dominoes*
Van Peebles, Mario 1957— **2, 51**
Van Peebles, Melvin 1932— **7, 95**
van Sertima, Ivan 1935— **25**
Vance, Courtney B. 1960— **15, 60**

Vance, Jim 1942— **110**
VanDerZee, James (Augustus Joseph) 1886–1983 **6**
Vandross, Luther 1951–2005 **13, 48, 59**
Vanessa James and Yannick Bonheur **84**
Vanity 1959— **67**
Vann, Harold Moore *See Muhammad, Khallid Abdul*
Vanzant, Iyanla 1953— **17, 47, 108**
Vaughan, Sarah (Lois) 1924–1990 **13**
Vaughn, Countess 1978— **53**
Vaughn, Gladys Gary 1942(?)— **47**
Vaughn, Jacque 1975— **127**
Vaughn, Mo 1967— **16**
Vaughn, Viola 1947— **70**
Vaughns, Cleopatra 1940— **46**
Vega, David *See Graham Central Station*
Vega, Marta Moreno 1942(?)— **61**
Velez-Rodriguez, Argelia 1936— **56**
Vera, Yvonne 1964— **32**
Verdell, Jackie *See Davis Sisters, The*
Verdelle, A. J. 1960— **26**
Vereen, Ben(jamin Augustus) 1946— **4**
Verna, Gelsy 1961–2008 **70**
Verrett, Shirley 1931–2010 **66, 91**
Vesey, Denmark 1767(?)–1822 **100**
Via, Dennis 1958(?)— **108**
Vibra-Naires, The *See Orioles, The*
Vick, Michael 1980— **39, 65, 94**
Vieira, João Bernardo 1939–2009 **14, 84**
Villard-Appolon, Malya 1959(?)— **106**
Villarosa, Clara 1930(?)— **85**
Vincent, Marjorie Judith 1965(?)— **2**
Vincent, Mark *See Diesel, Vin*
Vincent, Troy 1971— **91**
Vinnegar, Leroy 1928–1999 **124**
Vinson, Cleanhead *See Vinson, Eddie*
Vinson, Eddie 1917–1988 **112**
Vinson, Walter *See Mississippi Sheiks*
Virgil, Ozzie 1933— **48**
Vogue, En *See En Vogue*
Von Lipsey, Roderick 1959— **11**
wa Ngengi, Kamau *See Kenyatta, Jomo*
Waddles, Charleszetta 1912–2001 **10, 49**
Waddles, Mother *See Waddles, Charleszetta*
Wade, Abdoulaye 1926— **66**
Wade, Dwyane 1982— **61, 103**
Wade, Ernestine 1906–1983 **126**
Wade, Harold *See Trammps, The*
Wade, Stanley *See Trammps, The*
Wade-Gayles, Gloria Jean 1937(?)— **41**
Wagner, Albert 1924–2006 **78**
Wagner, Annice 1937— **22**
Wainwright, Joscelyn 1941— **46**
Waka Flocka Flame 1986— **110**
Walcott, Dennis M. 1951— **112**
Walcott, Derek 1930— **5, 94**
Walcott, Jersey Joe 1914–1994 **102**
Waldon, Alton R., Jr. 1936— **98**

Waldron, Mal 1925–2002 **109**
Wale 1984— **92**
Walker, Aaron Thibeaux *See Walker, T-Bone*
Walker, Albertina 1929–2010 **10, 58, 89**
Walker, Alice 1944— **1, 43**
Walker, Arthur, II 1936–2001 **87**
Walker, Bernita Ruth 1946— **53**
Walker, Cedric "Ricky" 1953— **19**
Walker, Chet 1940— **106**
Walker, Cora T. 1922–2006 **68**
Walker, Dianne 1951— **57**
Walker, Eamonn 1961(?)— **37**
Walker, Eliza *See Fisk Jubilee Singers*
Walker, George 1922— **37**
Walker, Greg *See Taste of Honey, A*
Walker, Herschel 1962— **1, 69**
Walker, Hezekiah 1962— **34**
Walker, Joe Louis 1949— **118**
Walker, John T. 1925–1989 **50**
Walker, Joseph Edison 1880–1958 **111**
Walker, Kara 1969— **16, 80**
Walker, Kurtis *See Blow, Kurtis*
Walker, LeRoy T. 1918–2012 **106**
Walker, Lucius, Jr. 1930–2010 **88**
Walker, Madame C. J. 1867–1919 **7**
Walker, Maggie Lena 1867(?)–1934 **17**
Walker, Margaret 1915–1998 **29**
Walker, Nellie Marian *See Larsen, Nella*
Walker, Ray 1981— **109**
Walker, Rebecca 1969— **50**
Walker, T. J. 1961(?)— **7**
Walker, T-Bone 1910–1975 **111**
Walker, Teshima 1968–2013 **114**
Walker, Thomas *See Walker, T. J.*
Walker, Tristan 1984— **98**
Walker, Wyatt Tee 1929— **80**
Wall, Orindatus S. B. 1825–1891 **92**
Wallace, Ben 1974— **54**
Wallace, Joaquin 1965— **49**
Wallace, Michele Faith 1952— **13**
Wallace, Perry E. 1948— **47**
Wallace, Phyllis A(nn) 1920(?)–1993 **9**
Wallace, Rasheed 1974— **56**
Wallace, Richard *See Mighty Clouds of Joy*
Wallace, Ruby Ann *See Dee, Ruby*
Wallace, Sippie 1898–1986 **1**
Wallace, William 1939–2008 **75**
Waller, Fats 1904–1943 **29**
Waller, Thomas Wright *See Waller, Fats*
Wallis, Quvenzhané 2003— **109**
Walters, Richard *See Slick Rick*
Walters, Ronald 1938— **83**
Walton, Alex *See Moonglows, The*
Walton, Cedar 1934–2013 **114**
Walton, Cora *See Taylor, Koko*
Wambugu, Florence 1953— **42**
Wamutombo, Dikembe Mutombo Mpolondo Mukamba Jean Jacque *See Mutombo, Dikembe*
Wanjiru, Sammy 1986–2011 **94**
Wansley, Michael *See Wanz*

Wanz 1961— **116**
Ward, Andre 1984— **62**
Ward, Anita 1957(?)— **118**
Ward, Benjamin 1926–2002 **68**
Ward, Billy *See Billy Ward and the Dominoes*
Ward, Douglas Turner 1930— **42**
Ward, Eugene *See Commodores, The*
Ward, Hines 1976— **84**
Ward, Lloyd 1949— **21, 46**
Ward, Willa 1920–2012 **105**
Ward, William E. 1949— **107**
Ware, Andre 1968— **37**
Ware, Carl H. 1943— **30**
Ware, David S. 1949–2012 **106**
Ware, DeMarcus 1982— **92**
Warfield, Marsha 1955— **2**
Warfield, William 1920–2002 **94**
Waring, Laura Wheeler 1887–1948 **99**
Warner, Malcolm-Jamal 1970— **22, 36, 110**
Warren, Butch 1939–2013 **116**
Warren, Edward Rudolph, Jr. *See Warren, Butch*
Warren, Ernest *See Spaniels, The*
Warren, Mervyn *See Take 6*
Warren, Michael 1946— **27**
Warrick, Marie Dionne *See Warwick, Dionne*
Warsame, Keinan Abdi *See K'naan*
Warwick, Dionne 1940— **18, 111**
Washington, Alonzo 1967— **29**
Washington, Booker T(aliaferro) 1856–1915 **4**
Washington, Denzel 1954— **1, 16, 93**
Washington, Dinah 1924–1963 **22**
Washington, Ebonya 1973(?)— **79**
Washington, Elsie B. 1942–2009 **78**
Washington, Essie Mae *See Washington-Williams, Essie Mae*
Washington, Fred(er)i(cka Carolyn) 1903–1994 **10**
Washington, Gene 1947— **63**
Washington, Grover, Jr. 1943–1999 **17, 44**
Washington, Harold 1922–1987 **6**
Washington, Harriet A. 1951— **69**
Washington, Hayma 19(?)(?)— **86**
Washington, Isaiah 1963— **62**
Washington, James, Jr. 1909(?)–2000 **38**
Washington, James Melvin 1948–1997 **50**
Washington, Karen 1958(?)— **117**
Washington, Kenny 1918–1971 **50**
Washington, Kenny 1958— **107**
Washington, Kerry 1977— **46, 107**
Washington, Laura S. 1956(?)— **18**
Washington, MaliVai 1969— **8**
Washington, Margaret Murray 1865–1925 **119**
Washington, Mary T. 1906–2005 **57**
Washington, Ora Mae 1899(?)–1971 **115**
Washington, Patrice Clarke 1961— **12**
Washington, Pauletta Pearson 1950— **86**
Washington, Regynald G. 1954(?)— **44**
Washington, Ron 1952— **119**

Washington, Tamia Reneé *See Ta-mia*

Washington, Valores James 1903–1995 **12**

Washington, Walter 1915–2003 **45**

Washington-Williams, Essie Mae 1925–2013 **118**

Wasow, Omar 1970— **15**

Waters, Benny 1902–1998 **26**

Waters, Ethel 1895–1977 **7**

Waters, Maxine 1938— **3, 67, 103**

Waters, Muddy 1915–1983 **34**

Watkins, Craig 1967— **97**

Watkins, Donald 1948— **35**

Watkins, Frances Ellen *See Harper, Frances Ellen Watkins*

Watkins, Gloria Jean *See hooks, bell*

Watkins, Joe 1953— **86**

Watkins, Levi, Jr. 1945— **9**

Watkins, Perry James Henry 1948–1996 **12**

Watkins, Shirley R. 1938— **17**

Watkins, Ted 1923(?)–1993 **104**

Watkins, Tionne *See T-Boz; TLC*

Watkins, Walter C. 1946— **24**

Watley, Jody 1959— **54**

Watson, Benjamin 1980— **126**

Watson, Bo *See Midnight Star*

Watson, Bob 1946— **25**

Watson, Carlos 1970— **50**

Watson, Diane 1933— **41**

Watson, Ivory *See Ink Spots, The*

Watson, Johnny "Guitar" 1935–1996 **18**

Watson Coleman, Bonnie 1945— **127**

Watt, Garland W. 1932–2013 **113**

Watt, Mel 1945— **26, 105**

Wattleton, (Alyce) Faye 1943— **9**

Watts, André 1946— **42, 101**

Watts, J(ulius) C(aesar), Jr. 1957— **14, 38**

Watts, Reggie 1972— **52, 102**

Watts, Rolonda 1959— **9**

Wayans, Damien 198(?)— **78**

Wayans, Damon 1961— **8, 41**

Wayans, Keenen Ivory 1958— **18**

Wayans, Kim 1961— **80**

Wayans, Marlon 1972— **29, 82**

Wayans, Shawn 1971— **29**

Waymon, Eunice Kathleen *See Si-mone, Nina*

Weah, George 1966— **58**

Weathers, Barbara *See Atlantic Starr*

Weathers, Carl 1948— **10, 117**

Weaver, Afaa Michael 1951— **37**

Weaver, Michael S. *See Weaver, Afaa Michael*

Weaver, Mike 1951— **109**

Weaver, Robert C. 1907–1997 **8, 46**

Webb, Chick 1909–1939 **105**

Webb, Sheyann *See Webb-Christburg, Sheyann*

Webb, Veronica 1965— **10, 95**

Webb, Wellington 1941— **3, 81**

Webb, William Henry *See Webb, Chick*

Webb, Wilmeth *See Sidat-Singh, Wilmeth*

Webb-Christburg, Sheyann 1956— **110**

Webber, Chris 1973— **15, 30, 59, 118**

Webber, Mayce Edward Christo-pher, III *See Webber, Chris*

Webster, Katie 1936–1999 **29**

Wedgeworth, Robert W. 1937— **42**

Weekes, Kevin 1975— **67**

Weeks, Thomas, III 1967— **70**

Weems, Carrie Mae 1953— **63, 116**

Weems, Renita J. 1954— **44**

Wein, Joyce 1928–2005 **62**

Wek, Alek 1977— **18, 63, 105**

Welburn, Edward T. 1950— **50**

Welch, Elisabeth 1908–2003 **52**

Welcome, Verda Freeman 1907–1990 **112**

Welles, Rosalind *See Washington, Elsie B.*

Wellington, Valerie 1959–1993 **118**

Wells, Henrietta Bell 1912–2008 **69**

Wells, James Lesesne 1902–1993 **10**

Wells, Junior 1934–1998 **102** *See also Aces, The*

Wells, Mary 1943–1992 **28**

Wells, Vernon 1978— **91**

Wells, Willie 1906–1989 **105**

Wells-Barnett, Ida B(ell) 1862–1931 **8**

Welsing, Frances (Luella) Cress 1935— **5**

Wendo *See Kolosoy, Wendo*

Wesley, Dorothy Porter 1905–1995 **19**

Wesley, Richard 1945— **73**

Wesley, Rutina 1979— **97**

Wesley, Valerie Wilson 194(?)— **18**

Wess, Frank 1922–2013 **116**

West, Allen 1961— **89**

West, Bernie *See Five Keys, The*

West, Cornel 1953— **5, 33, 80**

West, Dorothy 1907–1998 **12, 54**

West, James E. 1931— **87**

West, Kanye 1977— **52, 93**

West, Rudy *See Five Keys, The*

West, Togo Dennis, Jr. 1942— **16**

Westbrook, Kelvin 1955— **50**

Westbrook, Peter 1952— **20**

Westbrook, Russell 1988— **116**

Westbrooks, Bobby 1930(?)–1995 **51**

Whack, Rita Coburn 1958— **36**

Whalum, Kirk 1958— **37, 64**

Wharton, A. C., Jr. 1944— **110**

Wharton, Clifton R(eginald), Jr. 1926— **7**

Wharton, Clifton Reginald, Sr. 1899–1990 **36**

Wheat, Alan Dupree 1951— **14**

Wheaton, James 1924–2002 **103**

Whispers, The **124**

Whitaker, Forest 1961— **2, 49, 67**

Whitaker, Mark 1957— **21, 47**

Whitaker, Pernell 1964— **10, 89**

Whitaker, "Sweet Pea" *See Whita-ker, Pernell*

White, Armond 1953— **80, 118**

White, Augustus, III 1936— **100**

White, Barry 1944–2003 **13, 41**

White, Bill 1933(?)— **1, 48**

White, Booker T. Washington *See White, Bukka*

White, Bukka 1906(?)–1977 **120**

White, Charles 1918–1979 **39**

White, Charlie *See Billy Ward and the Dominoes*

White, (Donald) Dondi 1961–1998 **34**

White, Frank 1950— **95**

White, Jesse 1934— **22, 75**

White, Jessica 1984— **83**

White, Jo Jo 1946— **112**

White, John H. 1945— **27**

White, Joseph Henry *See White, Jo Jo*

White, Josh 1914(?)–1969 **86**

White, Josh, Jr. 1940— **52**

White, Lillias 1951— **120**

White, Linda M. 1942— **45**

White, Lois Jean 1938— **20**

White, Maurice 1941— **29** *See also Earth, Wind & Fire*

White, Michael Jai 1967— **71, 117**

White, Michael R(eed) 1951— **5**

White, Reggie 1961–2004 **6, 50**

White, Reginald Howard *See White, Reggie*

White, Santi *See Santigold*

White, Sylvain 1971— **96**

White, Terri 1948— **82**

White, Walter F(rancis) 1893–1955 **4**

White, Willard 1946— **53**

White, William DeKova *See White, Bill*

White, Willye 1939— **67**

White-Hammond, Gloria 1951(?)— **61**

Whitehead, Colson 1969— **77**

Whitehead, Don *See Earth, Wind & Fire*

Whiteside, Hassan 1989— **127**

Whitfield, Fred 1967— **23**

Whitfield, LeRoy 1969–2005 **84**

Whitfield, Lynn 1954— **18**

Whitfield, Mal 1924— **60**

Whitfield, Norman 1940–2008 **73**

Whitfield, Van 1960(?)— **34**

Whitlock, Jason 1967— **78**

Whitmore, George 1944–2012 **106**

Whitney, Davey L. 1930— **110**

Whitney, Marva 1944–2012 **109**

Whittaker, Hudson *See Tampa Red*

Wideman, John Edgar 1941— **5, 87**

Widener, Warren 1938— **99**

Wiggins, Andrew 1995— **128**

Wiggins, Charles Ray *See Saadiq, Raphael; Tony! Toni! Toné!*

Wiggins, D'Wayne *See Tony! Toni! Toné!*

Wiggins, Gerald 1922–2008 **128**

Wiggins, Londee *See New Birth*

Wiggins, Raphael *See Saadiq, Ra-phael; Tony! Toni! Toné!*

Wilbekin, Emil 1968— **63**

Wilbon, Michael 1958— **68**

Wilburn, Nayvadius *See Future*

Wilcox, Emandu *See Pharcyde, The*

Wilder, Deontay 1985— **121**

Wilder, L. Douglas 1931— **3, 48**

Wiley, Isaac *See Dazz Band*

Wiley, Kehinde 1977— **62**

Wiley, Michael *See Dazz Band*

Wiley, Ralph 1952–2004 **8, 78**

Wilfork, Vince 1981— **124**

Wilkens, J. Ernest, Jr. 1923— **43**

Wilkens, Lenny 1937— **11, 88**

Wilkens, Leonard Randolph *See Wilkens, Lenny*

Wilkerson, Isabel 1961— **71**

Wilkerson, Robert King *See King, Robert Hillary*

Wilkins, David 1956— **77**

Wilkins, Dominique 1960— **74**

Wilkins, Elbert *See Dramatics, The*

Wilkins, Ray 1951— **47**

Wilkins, Roger 1932— **2, 84**

Wilkins, Roy 1901–1981 **4**

Wilkins, Thomas Alphonso 1956— **71**

will.i.am 1975— **64**

Williams, Alice Faye *See Shakur, Afeni*

Williams, Ann Claire 1949— **82**

Williams, Anthony 1951— **21**

Williams, Anthony Charles *See Tonex*

Williams, Armstrong 1959— **29**

Williams, Bernard *See Harold Mel-vin & the Blue Notes*

Williams, Bernie 1968— **128**

Williams, Bert 1874–1922 **18**

Williams, Billy 1938— **86**

Williams, Billy Dee 1937— **8, 105**

Williams, Bryan *See Birdman*

Williams, Calvin *See Golden Gate Quartet*

Williams, Camilla 1919–2012 **116**

Williams, Carl *See Kani, Karl*

Williams, Charles Melvin *See Wil-liams, Cootie*

Williams, Clarence 1893(?)–1965 **33**

Williams, Clarence 1967— **70**

Williams, Clarence, III 1939— **26**

Williams, Claude 1908–2004 **80**

Williams, Cootie 1908(?)–1985 **114**

Williams, Curtis *See Penguins, The*

Williams, Daniel Hale (III) 1856–1931 **2**

Williams, Darrent 1982–2007 **116**

Williams, David Rudyard 1954— **50**

Williams, David W. 1910–2000 **110**

Williams, Deniece 1951— **36**

Williams, Denise 1958— **40**

Williams, Dennis P. 1953— **123**

Williams, Deron 1984— **92**

Williams, Doug 1955— **22, 112**

Williams, Dudley 1938— **60**

Williams, Eddie N. 1932— **44**

Williams, Eric Eustace 1911–1981 **65**

Williams, Evelyn 1922(?)— **10**

Williams, Fannie Barrier 1855–1944 **27**

Williams, Frederick (B.) 1939–2006 **63**

Williams, George Washington 1849–1891 **18**

Williams, Gertrude *See Morgan, Gertrude*

Williams, Gregory (Howard) 1943— **11**

Williams, Hosea 1926–2000 **15, 31, 123**

Williams, J. Mayo 1894–1980 **83**

Williams, Jody 1935— **113**

Williams, Joe 1918–1999 **5, 25**

Williams, John A. 1925— **27**

Williams, Joseph Leon *See Williams, Jody*

Williams, Juan 1954— **35, 80**

Williams, Ken 1964— **68**

Williams, Larry 1935–1980 **118**

Williams, Lauryn 1983— **58, 127**

Williams, Lindsey 1966— **75**

Williams, Maggie 1954— **7, 71**

Williams, Malinda 1975— **57**

Williams, Marco 1956— **53**

Williams, Margaret Ann *See Williams, Maggie*

Williams, Mary Lou 1910–1981 **15**

Williams, Michael Kenneth 1966— **97**

Williams, Michael L. 1953— **86**

Williams, Michelle 1980— **73**

Williams, Milan *See Commodores, The*

Williams, Montel 1956— **4, 57**

Williams, Monty 1971— **125**

Williams, Nat D. 1907–1983 **91**

Williams, Natalie 1970— **31**

Williams, O(swald) S. 1921— **13**

Williams, Patricia 1951— **11, 54**

Williams, Paul *See Paul, Billy*

Williams, Paul 1939–1971 **112** *See also Temptations, The*

Williams, Paul R(evere) 1894–1980 **9**

Williams, Paulette Linda *See Shange, Ntozake*

Williams, Pharrell 1973— **47, 82, 119**

Williams, Preston Warren, II 1939(?)— **64**

Williams, Rhonda Y. 1967(?)— **86**

Williams, Ricky 1977— **85**

Williams, Robert F(ranklin) 1925— **11**

Williams, Robert Peter *See Guillaume, Robert*

Williams, Ronald A. 1949— **57**

Williams, Roy 1968— **89**

Williams, Russell, II 1952— **70**

Williams, Samuel Arthur 1946— **21**

Williams, Saul 1972— **31**

Williams, Serena 1981— **20, 41, 73**

Williams, Sherley Anne 1944–1999 **25**

Williams, Spencer 1893–1969 **126**

Williams, Stanley "Tookie" 1953–2005 **29, 57**

Williams, Stevie 1979— **71**

Williams, Taiye *See Selasi, Taiye*

Williams, Ted 1957— **91**

Williams, Terrie N. 1954— **35**

Williams, Tony 1945–1997 **67**

Williams, Vanessa A. 1963— **32, 66**

Williams, Vanessa L. 1963— **4, 17**

Williams, Venus 1980— **17, 34, 62**

Williams, Walter *See O'Jays, The*

Williams, Walter E(dward) 1936— **4**

Williams, Wendy 1964— **62**

Williams, Wilbert *See Mighty Clouds of Joy*

Williams, William December *See Williams, Billy Dee*

Williams, William T(homas) 1942— **11**

Williams, Willie L(awrence) 1943— **4**

Williamson, Fred 1938— **67**

Williamson, Homesick James *See Homesick James*

Williamson, James *See Homesick James*

Williamson, Lisa *See Sister Souljah*

Williamson, Mykelti 1957— **22**

Williamson, Sonny Boy 1899(?)–1965 **84**

Willie, Louis, Jr. 1923–2007 **68**

Willie D *See Geto Boys*

Willingham, Tyrone 1953— **43**

Willis, Bill 1921–2007 **68**

Willis, Cheryl *See Hudson, Cheryl*

Willis, Deborah 1948— **85**

Willis, Dontrelle 1982— **55**

Willis, Patrick 1985— **99**

Willis, William Karnet *See Willis, Bill*

Williston, David Augustus 1868–1962 **99**

Wills, Harry 1889(?)–1958 **80**

Wills, Maury 1932— **73**

Wilmore, Larry 1961— **121**

Wilson, Abram 1973–2012 **104**

Wilson, August 1945–2005 **7, 33, 55**

Wilson, Brian Courtney 19(?)(?)— **94**

Wilson, Cassandra 1955— **16**

Wilson, Chandra 1969— **57**

Wilson, Charlie 1953— **31, 77** *See also Gap Band, The*

Wilson, David 1991— **123**

Wilson, Debra 1970(?)— **38**

Wilson, Demond 1946— **102**

Wilson, Donald E. 1936(?)— **88**

Wilson, Dorien 1962(?)— **55**

Wilson, Ellis 1899–1977 **39**

Wilson, Frank 1940–2012 **106**

Wilson, Frederica 1942— **92**

Wilson, Flip 1933–1998 **21**

Wilson, Gerald 1918–2014 **49, 123**

Wilson, Gloria Mai *See Lynne, Gloria*

Wilson, Grady Demond *See Wilson, Demond*

Wilson, Jackie 1934–1984 **60** *See also Billy Ward and the Dominoes*

Wilson, Jimmy 1946— **45**

Wilson, John 1922— **109**

Wilson, Leslie *See New Birth*

Wilson, Lionel 1915–1998 **99**

Wilson, Margaret Bush 1919–2009 **79**

Wilson, Mary 1944 **28**

Wilson, Melvin *See New Birth*

Wilson, Nancy 1937— **10, 98**

Wilson, Natalie 1972(?)— **38**

Wilson, Orlandus *See Golden Gate Quartet*

Wilson, Paul *See Flamingos, The*

Wilson, Phill 1956— **9, 104**

Wilson, Reggie 1967— **116**

Wilson, Robert *See Gap Band, The*

Wilson, Ronnie *See Gap Band, The*

Wilson, Russell 1988— **119**

Wilson, Shanice Lorraine *See Shanice*

Wilson, Stephanie 1966— **72**

Wilson, Sunnie 1908–1999 **7, 55**

Wilson, Tracey Scott 1967(?)— **77**

Wilson, William Julius 1935— **22**

Wilson, William Nathaniel *See Wilson, Sunnie*

Wimbley, Damon 1966— *See Fat Boys*

Winans, Angie 1968— **36**

Winans, Benjamin 1962— **14**

Winans, CeCe 1964— **14, 43**

Winans, David 1934–2009 **77**

Winans, Debbie 1972— **36**

Winans, Marvin L. 1958— **17, 127**

Winans, Ronald 1956–2005 **54**

Winans, Vickie 1953(?)— **24**

Winfield, Dave 1951— **5, 91**

Winfield, David Mark *See Winfield, Dave*

Winfield, Paul (Edward) 1941–2004 **2, 45**

Winfrey, Oprah 1954— **2, 15, 61, 106**

Wingo, Richard *See Jagged Edge*

Winkfield, Jimmy 1882–1974 **42**

Winley, Harold *See Clovers, The*

Winslow, Kellen 1957— **83**

Wisdom, Kimberlydawn 1956— **57**

Withers, Bill 1938— **61**

Withers, Ernest C. 1922–2007 **68, 88**

Withers-Mendes, Elisabeth 1973(?)— **64**

Witherspoon, Jimmy 1920(?)–1997 **113**

Witherspoon, John 1942— **38**

Witt, Edwin T. 1920— **26**

Wiwa, Ken 1968— **67**

Wiz Khalifa *See Khalifa, Wiz*

Wofford, Chloe Anthony *See Morrison, Toni*

Wolde Yohannes, Gebre Medhin *See Abune Paulos*

Wolfe, Ann 1971— **82**

Wolfe, George C. 1954— **6, 43, 127**

Womack, Bobby 1944–2014 **60, 92, 123**

Womack, Solomon *See Swan Silvertones, The*

Wonder, Stevie 1950— **11, 53, 121**

Wonder Mike *See Sugarhill Gang, The*

Wood, Mark Adam, Jr. *See Lakeside*

Wood, William Vernell *See Wood, Willie*

Wood, Willie 1936— **111**

Woodard, Alfre 1953— **9, 108**

Woodard, Lynette 1959— **67**

Woodbridge, Hudson *See Tampa Red*

Woodruff, Hale (Aspacio) 1900–1980 **9**

Woodruff, John 1915–2007 **68**

Woods, Abraham, Jr. 1928–2008 **74**

Woods, Belita 1948–2012 **103**

Woods, Cheyenne 1990— **103**

Woods, Eldrick *See Woods, Tiger*

Woods, Georgie 1927–2005 **57**

Woods, Granville T. 1856–1910 **5**

Woods, Jacqueline 1962— **52**

Woods, Mattiebelle 1902–2005 **63**

Woods, Renn 1958— **110**

Woods, Scott 1971— **55**

Woods, Sylvia 1926–2012 **34, 104**

Woods, Teri 1968— **69**

Woods, Thomas *See Clovers, The*

Woods, Tiger 1975— **14, 31, 81**

Woodson, Ali Ollie 1951–2010 **89**

Woodson, Carter G(odwin) 1875–1950 **2**

Woodson, Jacqueline 1963— **125**

Woodson, Mike 1958— **78**

Woodson, Robert L. 1937— **10**

Woodson, Rod 1965— **79**

Woolard, Jamal 1975— **102**

Wooldridge, Anna Marie *See Lincoln, Abbey*

Worrill, Conrad 1941— **12**

Worthy, James 1961— **49**

Worthy, Kym 1956— **84**

Wosornu, Taiye *See Selasi, Taiye*

Wray, Noble 1960— **114**

Wright, Albert *See Wright, Chalky*

Wright, Antoinette 195(?)— **60**

Wright, Archibald Lee *See Moore, Archie*

Wright, Beverly 1947— **97**

Wright, Bruce McMarion 1918–2005 **3, 52**

Wright, Chalky 1912–1957 **103**

Wright, Charles H. 1918–2002 **35**

Wright, Clyde *See Golden Gate Quartet*

Wright, Deborah C. 1958— **25**

Wright, Erica *See Badu, Erykah*

Wright, Ernest, Jr. *See Little Anthony & the Imperials*

Wright, Eugene 1923— **125**

Wright, Jeffrey 1965— **54, 111**

Wright, Jeremiah A., Jr. 1941— **45, 69, 103**

Wright, Lewin 1962— **43**

Wright, Louis Tompkins 1891–1952 **4**

Wright, Nathan, Jr. 1923–2005 **56**

Wright, Norma Jean *See Chic*

Wright, O. V. 1939–1980 **114**

Wright, Overton Vertis *See Wright, O. V.*

Wright, Rayfield 1945— **70**

Wright, Richard 1908–1960 **5**

Wright, Richard Robert, Sr. 1855–1947 **100**

Wright, Sarah E. 1928–2009 **95**

Wright, Timothy 1947— **74**

Wyatt, Addie L. 1924— **56**

Wylie, Mary T. Washington *See Washington, Mary T.*

Wynn, Albert R. 1951— **25, 77**

X, Malcolm 1925–1965 **1**

X, Marvin 1944— **45**

Xuma, Madie Hall 1894–1982 **59**

Xzibit 1974— **78**

Yabby You 1946–2010 **83**

Yancey, James DeWitt *See J Dilla*

Yancey, Jimmy 1898(?)–1951 **116**

Yancy, Dorothy Cowser 1944— **42**

Yar'Adua, Umaru 1951–2010 **69, 89**

Yarbrough, Camille 1938— **40**

Yarbrough, Cedric 1971— **51**

Yasiin *See Bey, Yasiin*

Yates, Jack 1828–1897 **114**

Yates, John Henry *See Yates, Jack*

Yayi, Boni T. 1952— **84**

Yayo, Tony 1978— **113**

Yearwood, Lennox, Jr. 1969— **112**

Yeboah, Emmanuel Ofosu 1977— **53**

Yende, Pretty 1985— **124**

Yerby, Frank 1916–1991 **96**

Yergan, Max 1892–1975 **123**

Yette, Samuel F. 1929— **63**

YG 1990— **122**

Ying Yang Twins **112**

Yirga, Samuel 1985(?) **126**

Yoba, (Abdul-)Malik (Kashie) 1967— **11**

York, Dwight D. 1945— **71**

York, Malachi Z. *See York, Dwight D.*

York, Vincent 1952— **40**

Young, Al 1939— **82**

Young, Andre Romelle *See Dr. Dre*

Young, Andrew 1932— **3, 48, 110**

Young, Charles 1864–1922 **77**

Young, Coleman 1918–1997 **1, 20**

Young, Darren 1979— **114**

Young, Dewey *See Swan Silvertones, The*

Young, Donald, Jr. 1989— **57**

Young, Earl *See Trammps, The*

Young, Jean Childs 1933–1994 **14**

Young, Jimmy 1948–2005 **54**

Young, John 1949— **111**

Young, Johnny 1917(?)–1974 **120**

Young, Ledisi Anibade *See Ledisi*

Young, Lee 1914–2008 **72**

Young, Lee Thompson 1984–2013 **114**

Young, Leonidas Raymond *See Young, Lee*

Young, Perry H. 1919–1998 **100**

Young, Roger Arliner 1899–1964 **29**

Young, Thomas *See Three Mo' Tenors*

Young, Wanda *See Marvelettes, The*

Young, Whitney M(oore), Jr. 1921–1971 **4**

Young Jeezy 1977— **63**

Youngblood, Johnny Ray 1948— **8**

Youngblood, Shay 1959— **32**

Yumkella, Kandeh 1959— **105**

Zane 1967(?)— **71**

Zenawi, Meles 1955)— **3, 99**

Zollar, Alfred 1955(?)— **40**

Zollar, Jawole Willa Jo 1950— **28**

Zook, Kristal Brent 1966(?)— **62**

Z-Ro 1977— **109**

Zulu, Princess Kasune 1977— **54**

Zuma, Jacob 1942— **33, 75**

Zuma, Nkosazana Dlamini *See Dlamini-Zuma, Nkosazana*

Zwelithini, Goodwill 1948— **128**